World of Tennis 2001

With a spectacular Olympic Games in sunny Sydney, plus another vintage Grand Slam season, a dramatic Davis Cup final in Spain, and a sensational end to the new men's Champions Race, the year 2000 was packed with action and thrills – all of them covered fully within these pages.

It all began with Agassi the assassin, alongside Davenport the destroyer, bringing home the titles in Melbourne. In Paris it was Pierce who peaked, while the brave Brazilian, 'Guga' Kuerten won for a second time. At Wimbledon there were wondrous performances from seven-time Sampras and first-time Williams – Venus was rising, and so was sister Serena who teamed with her to win the doubles at the All England Club. In New York Venus soared into the stratosphere to win a second Grand Slam, while a brilliant young Russian won a first. Marat Safin was his name and the world watched open-mouthed as he swooped from cloud nine on the unsuspecting Sampras and swamped him.

Russia were also triumphant at the Olympics with Kafelnikov taking the men's gold and teenage tigress Dementieva winning silver. Meanwhile the Williams bandwagon rolled on – it was gold in singles for Venus, gold in doubles for the super sisters.

Without the sisters in Las Vegas for the Fed Cup final, the USA gambled on Davenport and Seles, Capriati and Raymond against Spain. It had always looked a safe bet and the Americans duly brought home the trophy for the 17th time.

But it was bedlam in Barcelona as Spain downed the holders Australia 3–1 to become the 10th nation to win the Davis Cup.

World No.1 Hingis regained the season-ending Chase Championships to salvage her self respect at the end of a Slamless year. Finally, in the last game of the last match of the last tournament of the year, the inaugural Masters Cup in Lisbon, Kuerten won the new ATP Tour Champions Race and made himself world No.1. You could not have scripted it better!

For the 33rd time *World of Tennis* comprehensively covers the complexities of another tennis year. Within its 544 pages there are features and articles by some of the world's leading tennis writers, the full draws of all the major Championships, full results of the Davis Cup and the Fed Cup competitions, tournament results from the men's and women's professional Tours, plus details of the principal junior, veteran and wheelchair competitions – all beautifully illustrated with pictures from our two contributing photographers, Paul Zimmer and Stephen Wake. Once again Christine Forrest has supplied biographies of the leading men and women with full career details for the top ten.

A feature by American columnist Chris Clarey examines the outstanding career of Pete Sampras and assesses his place in tennis history; French writer Alain Deflassieux remembers fondly his departed friend, leading administrator Philippe Chatrier, the former President of the French Federation and of the ITF; and Wendy Kewley reviews the remarkable growth of wheelchair tennis.

The first of the two colour sections looks at the Olympic Games; the second captures the mood of the four Grand Slams before looking at the prominent men, women and juniors who have shaped the year's events.

Once again there is something for everyone.

The capture of an Olympic Gold medal was the highlight of an otherwise average year for Russia's Yevgeny Kafelnikov who nevertheless earned prize money of £3.75 million from the 32 tournaments he contested. (Stephen Wake)

World of Tennis

2001

Celebrating the Millennium Olympics

Edited by John Barrett
Compiled by Joanne Sirman
Biographies by Christine Forrest

Collins Willow

An Imprint of HarperCollins*Publishers*

This edition published in 2001 by
CollinsWillow
an imprint of HarperCollins*Publishers*
London

© John Barrett 2001

A CIP catalogue record for this book is available
from the British Library

ISBN 0 00 711129 0

Printed and bound in Great Britain by The Bath Press

Please note: Country Abbreviations used in this book
can be found on page 541

Cover photographs: Front (clockwise from top): *Pete Sampras, Lleyton Hewitt,
Venus Williams, Yevgeny Kafelnikov.* Back: *Mary Pierce.*
(Paul Zimmer and Stephen Wake)

Contents

Preface

The optimism which was apparent this time last year seems to have been fully justified. All four Grand Slams have improved their facilities; another successful Olympic Games and an equally triumphant Paralympic Games have enhanced the position of tennis in the world's two largest sporting assemblies; the success of Spain in the Davis Cup has produced a worthy new champion nation; the ATP Tour's new Champions Race brought a sharper focus to the men's game and produced a final twist in the plot at the Masters Cup that even Agatha Christie could not have bettered, while the emphatic arrival of Venus Williams among the world leaders as a double Grand Slam champion and Olympic gold medallist has added a new dimension to the Sanex WTA Tour where record attendances last year must have delighted the new sponsors.

Early in 2000 the ITF launched an initiative on Marketing the Game throughout the world. Activities associated with that project are reported upon elsewhere in these pages. There has been a continuation of the growth in junior tennis, essential if our sport is to compete successfully against the claims of rival sports and leisure pursuits. Growth has never been a problem for the veterans. Their insatiable appetite for competition continues, a fact which must say something about the health benefits of our wonderful game.

Thanks to the efforts of some very dedicated individuals this 33rd edition of *World of Tennis* contains commentary on all the principal events of another busy year, together with all the facts and figures. I am indebted to them all. Without naming them individually, I would like to thank all those colleagues among the tennis writers who have contributed some outstanding features and articles. What is more, without exception all have met their deadlines. It never used to be like this!

Despite a heavier workload than ever this year, the indefatigable Joanne Sirman and her team at the ITF have produced the mass of material that fills these pages, cheerfully accepting the need to work unsocial hours. What is more they have produced it all on time – well, almost – and always with a smile.

John Treleven is another whose contribution is greatly valued. Without his statisticians and their databases we could not possibly survive. My thanks to them all.

One who should have been thanked last year is Andrew Hunt who must have spent many painstaking hours searching through the statistics. He was kind enough to pass on all the errors he found and we were most grateful to include the corrections in last year's edition.

Another who has been most helpful is Cuthbert James. Mr James is one of those tennis fanatics who delve into the dustiest corners in search of obscure facts. Some that he has passed on to us this year have been very useful and I thank him for his interest.

At the ATP Tour...oops...sorry, the ATP now, of course (we'll never get used to it), all the communications managers do a tremendous job week by week while, in Ponte Vedra, Greg Sharko has again been unfailingly helpful in arranging to send us all the information on rankings, prize money, award winners, board members and so on.

For the WTA Tour Jim Hill has turned up trumps again, producing all those lovely lists even before I had asked for them. On the road Vani Vosburgh always seems to know which buttons to press whenever we need one of those obscure facts she has buried somewhere inside her computer.

The computer of our gifted designer, Roger Walker, has been purring long into the night these past few weeks so that we can produce copies in time for distribution at the Australian Open. It has meant another crazy Christmas and New Year for Roger and his patient wife Brenda who have once again adopted me as an extra member of the family. To them a special thank you.

Another who deserves special thanks is Christine Forrest who, for many years now, has been prepared to forego her Christmas shopping so that she can produce the biographies of the leading players, such a popular section of the book, with her usual attention to detail.

At Collins Willow Chris Stone has slotted into the system with the ease of a good professional. Nothing seems to phase him – which is just as well because, inevitably in a project of this sort, there are crises along the way, both mini and major.

Finally I would like to pay a long overdue tribute to my wife, Angela, who for the past 33 years has generously allowed me the time to indulge my passion for the history of the game. Only a former champion could have understood how totally consuming such an interest can become.

Now, though, it is time to call a halt, time to give up my selfish pursuits. In saying farewell may I thank the many readers who have written to me over the years with constructive criticisms and helpful suggestions. If this latest volume brings you as much pleasure as previous ones seem to have done, then our combined efforts will all have been worthwhile.

JOHN BARRETT
January 2001

Foreword

In its 33rd edition, *World of Tennis* is a highly respected source of information and a comprehensive guide to the sport of tennis. This volume of *World of Tennis,* covering the 2000 year, includes full reports on the very successful Olympic Tennis Event in Sydney and the new Tennis Masters Cup, co-owned by the ATP, the Grand Slams and the ITF.

As President of the ITF, one of the great privileges of my position is the opportunity to see some wonderful tennis – from the juniors through the best of professional tennis to the vets. From my vantage point, I have been able to witness the transition that has begun to take place this year from the old guard players like Pete Sampras and Andre Agassi to the new, young personalities like Juan Carlos Ferrero, Lleyton Hewitt, Elena Dementieva and Jelena Dokic. Some of yesterday's youngsters – Gustavo Kuerten, Marat Safin, Venus and Serena Williams – are, at their still tender ages, now fully fledged stars of the game with a whole generation of talent coming up behind them.

One of the highlights of 2000 was the Olympic Tennis Event in Sydney. To quote IOC President Juan Antonio Samaranch, the Sydney Olympics were the 'best ever' and that includes Olympic Tennis. The fields were the strongest ever for both men and women and we were pleased to be able to offer the men ranking points for the first time in history, thanks to an agreement between the ITF and the ATP with the full co-operation of the International Olympic Committee. Russia's Yevgeny Kafelnikov, who won the gold medal in men's singles, has rarely looked happier than he did after defeating Tommy Haas of Germany in the final match while the exuberant Williams sisters celebrated Venus's singles gold medal and the pair's doubles gold medal. Although they lost in the final to Canada's Sebastien Lareau and Daniel Nestor, we had a chance to say a proper goodbye to Australia's magnificent Woodies who added a silver medal to the gold they won in Atlanta. To my mind, they are without question the greatest doubles team of all time and it was wonderful to see them finish their careers at the top of the game.

Davis Cup by NEC has also had a successful year with a dream final between Spain and Australia. The atmosphere in Barcelona was electric as the Spanish staged a home Davis Cup Final for the first time in history. Our congratulations go to the hosts for their impressive 3–1 victory. Of the top 20 men, only Nicolas Kiefer declined to participate in Davis Cup in 2000 and he has indicated that he will represent Germany in the 2001 competition.

The 2000 Fed Cup Final, played in Las Vegas, was won again by the United States. The semifinals and final featured teams from Spain, Belgium and Czech Republic as well as defending champions USA and such stars as Lindsay Davenport, Monica Seles, Arantxa Sanchez-Vicario and Kim Clijsters.

This year has been marked by a new spirit of co-operation in tennis. I have noted above that the ATP Tour and the ITF were able to come to an agreement over points for the Olympic Games and that the ITF and the Grand Slams have joined with the Tour as co-owners of the Tennis Masters Cup. Our relationship with the Sanex WTA Tour also continues to expand and we look forward to working closely together for the future of the game.

Finally, in November 2000, the ITF hosted and organised what we feel is one of the most important initiatives for the future prosperity of tennis. The ITF invited representatives from the Grand Slams, the Tours, National Associations, the tennis industry and player management organisations to meet in the first Marketing the Game Summit. This very successful event, the first of its kind, generated ideas and proposals on which we intend to act to ensure the future of the game.

Finally, I would like to recognise the work of editor John Barrett and the staff from Collins Willow who work so diligently on this publication. I would also like to thank Joanne Sirman of the Communications Department who capably manages this project for the ITF and John Treleven from the ITF's Professional Tennis Department whose research contribution to the book is very important.

Francesco Ricci Bitti
President of the International Tennis Federation

Despite frustrating injuries, Pete Sampras had an outstanding year in which he won for the seventh time at Wimbledon, a success that gave him a record 13th Grand Slam title.
(Paul Zimmer)

The Year in Review

Ronald Atkin

Perhaps it was the new broom element provided by the millennium, but the year 2000 saw the men's game embark on important changes, sweeping as well as cosmetic. The ATP Tour, in what was billed as an effort to make the rankings more understandable to the general public, introduced the Champions Race. All the contestants were lined up with zero points on 1 January and a winner was pronounced in December. Though this produced the anomaly of Fabrice Santoro, champion of Doha, as the early race leader, the ATP Tour managed to come up with the perfect finish as Gustavo Kuerten won the Masters Cup in Lisbon to edge past Marat Safin and take the title in the very last match of the season.

The Masters Cup was the new brand name for the competition which emerged from the amalgamation of those conflicting events, the ATP World Championship and the ITF's Compaq Grand Slam Cup. It remained a round-robin affair involving the eight leading players in the points race, in many ways no different from the old World Championship, or indeed the even-older Masters, after which it was affectionately named. Those whose role it is to study such things had responded to comments of media and public that the name 'Masters' was sorely missed, both as a marketing vehicle and a recognition symbol; and they acted accordingly, with the former Super Nine series of tournaments also being relaunched as the Masters Series.

The old year-round rolling rankings also had to be retained, under the name Entry System, in order to provide a sane way of assessing tournament entries and the seedings for Grand Slam and other events – otherwise Santoro would have been top seed for the Australian Open. In the end the existence of two ranking lists served only to confuse where clarity had been the intention. But whichever list you looked at the year provided marvellous tennis, wonderful achievements and, perhaps most vital of all, new names.

Having won Roland Garros in 1997 and being 24 years old, Kuerten hardly qualified as a new name, but his breakthrough to the very top was just what the ATP had been hoping for – a lively and attractive personality, excellent player (on surfaces other than clay, at last) and someone to usurp the USA's domination of the number one spot stretching back nine years.

The surge of youth thoroughly justified the ATP poster campaign New Balls Please, despite its cringe-making appellation which caused Pete Sampras to come out with the stiff upper lip comment, 'Not my cup of tea.' Most of those pictured on the list of up-and-comers duly upped and came, just as predicted. Safin's was the most sensational breakthrough of the year, with the highlight his astonishing destruction of Sampras in the US Open final. Other youngsters had a fine year, too – Lleyton Hewitt, Juan Carlos Ferrero (Spain's Davis Cup hero), Nicolas Lapentti and Roger Federer among them.

The move of the former World Championship from Hanover to Lisbon was an unqualified success. The Atlantic Pavilion site was first-rate, the arrangements were excellent and the tennis was unforgettable. Safin had marched into Portugal with what looked like an unassailable lead of 115 points in the Champions Race but, in the way these things are structured, Sampras, Safin and Kuerten all had a chance to end the year at number one by some mathematical quirk or other. In the end, Kuerten ended all arguments by bouncing back from an opening day round-robin loss to Andre Agassi to sweep to a popular victory, eliminating former world number ones, Sampras and Agassi, in succession to pip an astonished Safin by 15 points. Kuerten was the first player from South America to end the year as number one, though Guillermo Vilas and Marcelo Rios have got to number one previously. Furthermore it was Kuerten's first tournament victory on a surface other than clay, and it could not have happened to a nicer guy.

Safin's turn will come. He ended a year which had opened disastrously by winning seven titles, including that first Grand Slam, and did so in fascinating fashion by taking the advice of a series of different coaches for different surfaces and situations. As John McEnroe observed of the 6ft 4in Russian, 'He's the real deal.'

Hewitt, too, enjoyed an outstanding year, marred only by a mystery virus which affected his stamina from August onwards, while Ferrero's glory in the Davis Cup final enchanted all in Spain and many in other parts of the globe.

That Davis Cup final, the last great contest of a memorable season, brought Spain their first-ever success in the competition, following defeats in the finals of 1965 and 1967 by the same nation, Australia, they faced in the Palau Sant Jordi in Barcelona. It was an occasion of swirling banners and tumultuous noise as Spain deservedly triumphed 3–1 with Ferrero's four-set victory over Hewitt proving the clinching rubber. The matches were intensely fought in front of a 14,000 crowd so raucous that Australia's captain John Newcombe was moved to complain about lack of sportsmanship, both among the crowd and on the Spanish team bench.

Newcombe, retiring along with team coach and pal Tony Roche after seven years in the job, termed the crowd's attitude 'disgraceful' and, after the crucial doubles went to Spain, said, 'I've never been in a match like today's where every time our boys hit a winner 14,000 people booed. They might feel proud of themselves but the whole world has been watching this.'

Newcombe went on to suggest that ticket sales for future finals should be split evenly between the two competing nations, since Australia's contingent of some 1,5000 were comprehensively outshouted. It was one of several interesting comments from distinguished voices about possible changes to the game's oldest team competition. Sampras, whose absence, along with Agassi's, from the semi-final against Spain in Santander, resulted in a 5–0 humiliation for the United States, is proposing that the Davis Cup be held every other year, while McEnroe, who resigned as American captain after just 14 months following that loss to Spain, wants to see the whole event staged in one location or country, like the Olympics or World Cup football. McEnroe's rapid departure, after having lobbied so vigorously for the job, was a setback for the USTA, who responded by awarding the captaincy to his younger brother Patrick.

At the Sydney Olympics the singles gold medals went to Yevgeny Kafelnikov and Venus Williams, with the defending champions, Agassi and Lindsay Davenport, pulling out of the competition, one for family reasons the other due to injury. Kafelnikov's three and a half hour, five-set win over Tommy Haas was his first tournament success in what had, until then, been a disappointing year. It also marked Russia's first golden success in tennis.

The victory of Venus was just another milestone, albeit a mightily prestigious one, in an incredible six-month spell and an unforgettable year. To be strictly accurate, one should say two milestones, since she teamed with her sister Serena to take the doubles gold, too. Yet Venus had been sidelined until the spring with tendinitis in both wrists and there was much speculation about her future, including one explosive comment from her father Richard that he had advised her to retire. Then, on her return to the clay court segment of the season, there had been little to show what was about to happen as she lost to Jelena Dokic in Rome and to Arantxa Sanchez-Vicario in the quarter-finals of the French Open.

Venus did not suffer another singles defeat until late October, when her 35-match streak was terminated by Davenport in the Linz final, the longest run of success in the women's game for three years. It was belated revenge for Davenport, beaten by Venus in both the Wimbledon and US Open finals.

The 20-year-old Williams was the only player, man or woman, to lift more than one Grand Slam Championship in 2000. Davenport, who opened her season in irresistible fashion, took the Australian Open and, to much acclaim and some surprise, Mary Pierce finally got her act together to win her 'home' title at Roland Garros, just as the French fans were beginning to despair of 'Marie.' Among the men Agassi continued his wonderful 1999 run by sweeping to success in the Australian Open, which turned out to be the only title of a downbeat, injury-riddled and disappointing year – if one excludes his ongoing friendship with Steffi Graf.

Kuerten claimed his second French title and then Sampras annexed his seventh Wimbledon, beating Patrick Rafter in near-darkness after a rain-delayed final to overtake Roy Emerson as the men's winner of most Grand Slams with 13. He had fond hopes of making that 14 when he marched into the US Open final, only for Safin to shock Sampras, himself and the world with a stunning straight-sets success.

Sampras was clearly continuing his wind-down after that record effort of six straight years at number one. Wimbledon apart, he won only one other final, the Masters Series of Miami, and after the US Open took a long break to marry Bridgette Wilson and enjoy a spell of wedded bliss until coming back for the Masters Cup in Lisbon.

The Wimbledon success of Venus was hailed with warmth, and typical reserve, by the British audience but the uninhibited Richard Williams celebrated with an impromptu jig on the roof of a commentary box just beneath the VIP area where he had been seated for the singles final.

The joy of victory for two Americans in the singles Championship provided a fine climax for the All England Club, whose perennial dignity had been undermined on the eve of the 2000

Championships when three Spaniards – Ferrero, Alex Corretja and Albert Costa – all members of that Davis Cup-winning side, incidentally – pulled out at the last minute in protest at not being seeded in accordance with their world ranking. Ferrero, who belatedly produced a sickness note via his agents as the reason for not playing, would have been making an eagerly anticipated debut.

The All England Club's seeding committee clearly felt that clay court specialists such as the Spanish trio should give way to those with greater skills and a better record on grass but in a diplomatically-worded statement which acknowledged that feathers had been ruffled, Wimbledon and the ATP Tour agreed to work closely together to prevent a repetition of this embarrassing episode.

While no fewer than eight men led the Champions Race at one time or another during the year, the women's tussle for number one (on their rolling ranking system) was between two familiar opponents, Davenport and Martina Hingis. It was the American six-footer who tended to dominate early on, thanks to a spectacular start to the year but Hingis proved the better long-distance operator by winning the Chase Championships – the last time it was held in Madison Square Garden before moving this year to Munich – and ending as number one for the third time in four years. And the lady is still only 20!

The Fed Cup continues to be dominated by the United States. Using a format similar to that suggested for the Davis Cup, the four semi-final nations met up in Las Vegas, where the Americans shrugged off the absence of the Williams sisters (away at school doing their fashion design courses) to edge past Belgium 2–1 and then rout Spain 5–0 to capture the trophy for the 17th time in 38 years. The smile on the face of the US captain Billie Jean King said it all.

King was happy, too, at the news from Melbourne that this year the Australian Open will pay equal prize money to the women, a cause which has been dear to her for a long time. But the megabucks news was saved until the very end of December, when Reebok announced it had signed a five-year endorsement deal with Venus Williams worth $40 million, the most ever paid to a female athlete.

The year saw an innovation or two, such as the early experiment with a shorter set format, larger tennis balls and purple coloured clay courts designed to make tennis easier on the eye for spectators and TV viewers. Inevitably, too there was the arrival of the cyber age when the Atlanta men's event had galleryfurniture.com as its main sponsor.

The year was marked by some notable retirements. Jim Courier, winner of four Grand Slams and 17 other titles and a former number one, called it a day after a dozen years on the tour which brought him 506 wins. Dominique Van Roost quit the women's game at the age of 27 following the death of her mother in the spring and the record-shattering Australian doubles pair, the Woodies, were split when Mark Woodforde decided to close his career at the age of 35 with his appearance in the Davis Cup final in Barcelona. Woodforde and Todd Woodbridge won a record 61 titles together, leaving in their wake the previous joint holders on 57, McEnroe/Peter Fleming and Bob Hewitt/Frew McMillan. The Woodies won six Wimbledons, another record, and it was a pity Woodforde should exit on a losing note in Barcelona, especially a sour note when he said the crowd had made him feel 'like a caged animal.' Woodbridge will continue on the circuit in partnership with Jonas Bjorkman.

Finally, there was the retirement of Petr Korda. Having served a year's suspension for drug offences, Korda made his comeback in a Challenger event in his home city, Prague, lost in the first round and promptly announced he was giving up.

The tennis world lost three distinguished names in 2000. Philippe Chatrier, guiding light of the ITF and the French Federation, died at the age of 74 following long illness after a career in which he proved himself the most able and influential administrator in the sport's history. Tennis also mourned the passing, at 84, of Don Budge, the first man to win the Grand Slam of tennis in 1938. Included in that achievement was a crushing victory in the Wimbledon final over Henry 'Bunny' Austin, who also sadly died, aged 94, in August, soon after taking part in Wimbledon's parade of former champions on the middle Saturday of this year's Championships.

Russia's Marat Safin, the new US Open champion was pipped at the post in Lisbon. (Stephen Wake)

Below: Lindsay Davenport, Australian Open champion was hit by injury at the Olympic Games. (Stephen Wake)

Above: Brazil's French Open champion, Gustavo Kuerten, winner of the first Champions Race. (Paul Zimmer)

Right: Wimbledon champion and US Open finalist Pete Sampras. (Paul Zimmer)

Below: A French title at last for French No.1, Mary Pierce who ended the year ranked No. 4. (Paul Zimmer)

Above: Dual Grand Slam winner and Olympic champion Venus Williams. (Stephen Wake)

Left: World No.1 Martina Hingis, headed the earnings table with $3,457,049. (Stephen Wake)

Players of the Year

John Barrett

GUSTAVO KUERTEN

To look at him, a tall gangling figure with a mop of unruly curls atop a lean, bewhiskered face, you would never suppose that he was a great athlete. Yet, despite the friendly smile, this 24-year-old Brazilian from the seaside town of Florianopolis has proved himself to be a ruthless killer-of-the-courts, his backhand a shot of immense authority. With tournament wins in Santiago, the Masters Series, Hamburg and the French Open (his second title there), plus final round appearances in two more Master Series events in Miami and Rome, Gustavo Kuerten, 'Guga' to his friends, lifted himself to the top of the ATP Champions Race in June. Displaced for a while by Pete Sampras after the American's seventh Wimbledon win, Guga regained the lead and held it altogether for 17 weeks, longer than anyone else.

When the new US Open champion Marat Safin won the St. Petersburg title on 12th November the young Russian overtook him and seemed certain to win the race in the home straight. But that was to reckon without Guga's burning ambition to prove himself the best. Symbolically, Guga had cut his hair short. It made him look meaner and more businesslike, an appearance reflected in the clinically efficient tennis he played.

Coming into Lisbon for the last tournament of the year, the inaugural Tennis Masters Cup, there were a lot of 'ifs' to consider. The position was as follows. Safin had a lead of 75 points over Guga. If he reached the final no-one could catch the young Russian. But if Kuerten reached the final and Safin lost every round robin match, then Kuerten would be the year-end No.1. If Safin won two of his round robin matches and lost in the semi-finals, Kuerten would still have to win the tournament to overtake him. At the start of the week that scenario seemed most unlikely.

Kuerten's first match ended with a defeat at the hands of Andre Agassi after he had squandered a winning lead. Strained hamstrings and a painful back, both conditions treated on court by trainer Bill Norris, contributed to the loss. It seemed doubtful whether the Brazilian beanpole would last the course. But, as Magnus Norman had discovered in the French final, beneath that casual happy-go-lucky exterior there is a core as hard as toughened steel.

With an astonishing burst of energy Guga swept aside a bewildered Norman and a despondent Kafelnikov to reach the semi-finals. There he beat Sampras 6–7 6–3-6–4 with an exhibition of power serving that was remarkable. 'I couldn't get my racket on the ball enough times' a frustrated Sampras admitted. Safin, meanwhile, had won two of his round robin matches but had lost his semi-final to a red hot Agassi. Accordingly everything was on the line in the title match. A win would make Kuerten the No.1, a loss would give that honour to Safin.

The final was proof that miracles do happen. In front of his mother, his grandmother, his elder brother Rafael, and his ever-loyal coach, Larri Passos, Guga out-Agassied Agassi. Responding to the urgings of an ecstatic crowd he hit the 1990 winner off the court in just over two hours of furious driving that had to be seen to be believed. It was an inspired performance by a man who seemed to know that his time had come. By the end Kuerten was walking with destiny, sublimely unaware of the risks that he was taking. He simply went for outrageous winners knowing that they would come off. And they did. Agassi was reduced to the role of spectator.

With these performances Gustavo Kuerten made himself THE player of the year.

MARAT SAFIN

There used to be a Jekyll and Hyde quality about Marat Safin. The Jekyll in him could produce power tennis of a sublime quality, of the sort that electrified us at Roland Garros in 1998. That year, aged 18, Marat had come through from the qualifying to beat Andre Agassi and the defending champion Gustavo Kuerten. It was the first time in open history that the title holder had lost to a qualifier in a Grand Slam Championship. Cedric Pioline had been mightily relieved to repel the Russian invader in five fierce sets.

The Hyde in Safin would make him a monster on court, likely to break half a dozen rackets during a match when things were going wrong. By his own admission there were more than 50 shattered frames scattered around the world in 1999.

All that changed in 2000. Arriving in Barcelona with a miserable record of six first round losses and a few more broken frames in his first nine tournaments, Marat asked Andrei Chesnokov to help him. The former Soviet No.1 could identify with Safin's problem. He told Marat to try on every point – a simple enough remedy but one which had never occurred to the young giant.

The transformation was astonishing, a complete transmogrification in fact. The sullen monster suddenly became a fully focused executioner. With back-to-back wins in Barcelona and Mallorca, Marat had tasted the heady wine of success. Intoxicated by its effect he sought more gratification. After some near misses in Hamburg and Paris he found it again in Toronto. By the time of the US Open Marat was ready for the ultimate intoxication, a Grand Slam title. His unfortunate victim in an amazing final was none other than Pete Sampras, himself the surprise winner in 1990 when he was a gangling 19-year-old. With ruthless precision Safin hit the four-time former champion off the court. Sampras might just as well have tried to halt a whirlwind. His game was blown apart and scattered to the elements. It was the performance of a lifetime.

Further tournament wins in Tashkent, St. Petersburg and Paris brought Marat to the last hurdle with the No.1 ranking within his grasp. He was supported now by his former coach Rafael Mensua to whose school in Valencia Marat had been sent by his parents at the age of 14. Needing only to beat Sampras again to be sure of attaining an unassailable lead in the ATP Tour Champions Race, Safin faltered. Against the proud defending champion he never found his range and frittered the match away. As the Hyde in him surfaced for a few moments Marat even broke another racket, something that had become a rarity.

In dismay, Safin flew straight home for a much needed rest, not even waiting to see whether he would become the world's No.1. It had been a long and hard year, but a rewarding one.

PETE SAMPRAS

Pete Sampras has always set his heart on being the best. The best thing he did in 2000 was to give his heart to another. When his fiancee, Bridgette Wilson, became Mrs. Sampras on 30th September, Pete was embarking upon a new chapter in his life.

In Bridgette's eyes Pete was THE man of the year. By winning at Wimbledon for the seventh time in eight years, the 28-year-old American made himself THE tennis player of the 20th century. This win (itself a record because five of William Renshaw's seven titles in the 1880s depended on winning only one match in the Challenge Round), brought Sampras a 13th Grand Slam title. He thus overtook Australia's Roy Emerson with whom, for one year, he had shared the record.

The year 2000 had started promisingly enough. At the Australian Open, despite a hip-flexor injury that would keep him off court for a month afterwards, Sampras participated in one of the year's great matches – a five set semi-final against Andre Agassi that sparkled with skill and courage. Both men excelled themselves.

On returning to action at Indian Wells, Pete went through to the quarter-finals and two weeks later in Miami he scored his first tournament win of the year. The final there against Gustavo Kuerten provided another throbbing finish in which Guga saved six match points.

This was Pete's 62nd career title. There followed a Davis Cup outing for the United States and Pete made amends for a loss to Jiri Novak on the opening day by scoring the winning point against Slava Dosedel. He would play no more Davis Cup tennis in 2000.

A leg injury kept Pete away from the European clay court season and his first round loss to Mark Philippoussis at the French Open was not altogether unexpected. You had the feeling that the great man was already focusing on London, SW19 and that Grand Slam record.

A loss to Lleyton Hewitt in the Queen's Club final was just the jolt he needed going into Wimbledon. The story of that dramatic campaign is graphically told elsewhere in these pages. Suffice it to say that history was made in the most spectacular fashion with the wounded hero fighting for his life in the gathering darkness against an inspired Pat Rafter whose own semi-final win over Agassi had been the match of the tournament.

Despite only two warm up outings in Cincinnati and Toronto, Sampras swept into the final at the US Open with impressive wins over Krajicek and Hewitt. He seemed to have run into form at exactly the right moment. Unfortunately for him, so had Marat Safin. The young Russian produced the performance of a lifetime, hitting a stream of unreturnable serves and blazing back court winners. Sampras was helpless. If he was despondent, Pete didn't show it.

There were more important things on his mind. Marriage and a honeymoon left no time for competition between the US Open and the season-ending Masters Cup. He arrived in Lisbon full of hope and left a semi-final loser, beaten by an inspired Kuerten.

As Pete approaches 30 there is little to suggest that his powers are failing. The serve is still as lethal, the volleys as crisp, the ground strokes just as penetrating as they always were. Perhaps he has lost the edge of his speed about the court. Perhaps there is the suspicion that, having eclipsed Emerson's Grand Slam record, Pete is no longer quite as hungry for success.

Yet it would be a mistake to underestimate the greatest player of modern times. No-one has more experience in planning his Grand Slam campaigns. Obviously this is where his priorities will lie in the years ahead, alongside his new responsibilities as a husband. Let us be thankful that the game has enjoyed Pete's undivided attention for the past ten years and be grateful for all that he has contributed to its success. Let us also wish Pete and Bridgette the best of good fortune in whatever dreams they build together. Perhaps we shall be lucky enough to share in some of them.

VENUS WILLIAMS

In many ways it was a case of Venus Williams first, the rest nowhere. I know the computer thinks otherwise, and computers never lie, do they? But how was the computer to know that Venus was going to be injured at the end of 1999? Or that she would miss the first four months of 2000 until the tendinitis in both wrists had been cured?

Her return to action in May was uneventful. After two warm-up tournaments it was back to serious business at the French Open. There Arantxa Sanchez-Vicario proved too good for Venus in the quarter-finals.

But for the next four months Venus was far too good for everybody else. With tournament wins at Wimbledon, in Stanford, San Diego, New Haven, the US Open and the Olympic Games (where she teamed with sister Serena to add Olympic gold to their Wimbledon title), she put together a winning streak of 35 matches that stamped her as one of the greatest athletes ever to pick up a racket.

Her speed about the court, her powerful serving, her ability to hit blazing winners on the run, her sensible use of the volley – and even the drop shot – all these qualities came together in that brilliant spell to make Venus utterly unstoppable. There was a feeling that she had lifted the game to a new power level. The world was in awe of her intensity, her confident assumption that she would win no matter what the odds. In truth, so compelling was her all-round game, so athletic her movement, that the odds were usually in her favour.

Then suddenly she was gone. A loss to Davenport in the final at Linz in October was the last we heard of her. Anaemia, we were told, was responsible. For half a year Venus had shone so brightly that everyone had been dazzled. When she departed it was as if the sun had set prematurely.

What of the future? Venus Williams has proved that when she puts her mind to it she is unquestionably the best player in the world. But how can we judge her properly against the giants of the past – or even today's leaders – until she puts her reputation on the line on a regular basis.

Sensibly Venus did not add her voice to her father's assertion that his two daughters ought to receive a larger slice of the tennis pie because, he claims, they are the biggest draw cards in women's tennis. That argument has been raised before by others who, at the time, have been equally as dominant. They discovered, as Richard Williams will, that no player is bigger than the game. Hard as it is for Richard to believe, there will come a day when tennis fans will say, 'Venus and Serena who'?

LINDSAY DAVENPORT

As with her fellow American, Andre Agassi, the year had started well for Lindsay Davenport. A third Grand Slam title in Australia, her second victory over Martina Hingis in a major final, gave promise of a change at the top of the world rankings. Yet something always went wrong.

Three times her body let her down. In Rome, Montreal and at the Olympics, where she was the title-holder, Lindsay failed to finish the course. The problem in Paris was Dominique van Roost. Playing the match of her life the experienced Belgian got to so many of Lindsay's powerful drives that the No.2 seed started to overhit. It was the errors which eventually caused her downfall but the credit for that must go to van Roost.

In defence of her title at Wimbledon Lindsay looked to be in good form when she swept into the final with convincing wins over Jennifer Capriati, Monica Seles and Jelena Dokic. She was unlucky to find Venus Williams in such devastating form in the title match. No-one would have lived with her fellow American that day.

It was the same story at Flushing Meadows. Having dropped only one set on the way to the final – that against another Belgian, the very promising Kim Clijsters – Lindsay looked as if she might revenge herself against Venus in the final. It was not to be. At this stage Venus was in the middle of a brilliant streak of form and won the battle of the big hitters in straight sets.

Unquestionably the biggest disappointment for Lindsay was her forced withdrawal from the Olympic Games in Sydney. Four years earlier in Atlanta she had described the capture of the gold medal as being the most exciting and important event in her life. But it was already apparent during her first round win against Paola Suarez that she was not able to run properly. Accordingly, it was no surprise when she defaulted with a leg injury. It was the same complaint that had dogged her for much of the year and a reminder that in matters physical all athletes need a little luck as well as good advice.

A member of the successful US Fed Cup team Lindsay remains one of the most popular players on the Tour and will be hoping for an injury free year in 2001.

MARY PIERCE
You could feel the agony of expectation even before last year's French Open final had begun. Mary Pierce, darling of the Paris crowd and finalist in 1994, was here to claim her inheritance at last. Yet there was the sneaking feeling that the whole situation might be too much for her.

Against her, the former Wimbledon champion from Spain, Conchita Martinez, a lady who has made a habit of shattering cherished dreams. Ask Martina Navratilova, her victim in that 1994 Wimbledon final when the American left-hander was going for a record 10th title.

All the telltale signs were there, the exaggerated poses between points, the anguished heavenward gazes, the excessive fluttering of the eyelids. It was all so familiar...and quite understandable. Here was a player who had already proved in Australia five years ago that she is a worthy champion. Yet in Paris all they could remember was the failure in 1994 against another Spanish woman – Arantxa Sanchez-Vicario. Was that an evil omen?

To her immense credit Mary put all doubts behind her. On the day of her life she played the tennis of her life. Martinez was swept aside imperiously (Mary would make a good Empress), her attempts to upset Pierce's groundstroke rhythm with moonballs and heavy topspin were countered with patience and sensible counter-attacks. There was only the mildest of flutters when Martinez threatened a recovery in the second set.

To see the relief in Mary's eyes when her victory was complete was to know just how much this win on home soil meant to her. Yet even in victory there was anguish. A shoulder that had been troubling her for some time threatened to prevent her appearing at Wimbledon. In the end she did play but lost in the second round to Magui Serna. Thereafter she did not compete until the US Open where the tendinitis flared up again and caused her to retire in the middle of her fourth round match against Anke Huber. She did not play again.

It was a sad end to what had been a year of significant advance on the court and one of personal happiness of it. Mary's engagement to Roberto Alomar of the Cleveland Indians was greeted with enthusiasm by her many fans around the world.

MARTINA HINGIS
For so long has she dominated women's tennis, it is hard to believe that Martina Hingis is still only 20. When she exploded on the world scene as a super-confident 16-year-old in 1997, winning three Grand Slam titles and losing narrowly in the final of the fourth in Paris, it seemed that the tennis world was at her twinkling feet.

It did not quite work out that way. The suspicion that Martina's skilful but lightweight game could no longer cope with the power games of the big-hitters like the Williams sisters and Davenport, evident already in 1999, was confirmed a year later.

Devastated by Davenport in Melbourne, pummelled by Pierce in Paris and walloped by Williams at Wimbledon – and again in New York – the world No.1 ended the year with her ego battered and bruised. For the first time in four years her Grand Slam cupboard was bare.

Yet in many ways it was a mighty successful year. With nine tournament wins, including the season-ending Chase Championships, Martina did better than anyone else and increased her lead on the WTA ranking list. Yet what matters most to her, and to every player, is success at the majors. That is what eventually decides a player's place in history.

Major ITF Events

The Olympic Games • The ITF Year • Davis Cup by NEC •
Fed Cup • Hyundai Hopman Cup • ITF Sunshine Cup
ITF Connolly Continental Cup • NEC World Youth Cup
Cesky Telecom World Junior Tennis

Tommy Haas of Germany played with tremendous conviction in Sydney but had to be content with a silver medal after a long but unsuccessful fight against Kafelnikov in the final.
(Stephen Wake)

At the end of a busy Olympic campaign Venus Williams proved she was outstandingly the best player by walking off with two gold medals. Serena Williams could not get a singles place in Sydney but made up for that disappointment by winning a gold medal in doubles with her sister. (Stephen Wake)

The Olympic Games

John Barrett

In most respects the tennis event at the Games of the XXVII Olympiad was an outstanding success. Capacity crowds thronged the spacious and beautifully designed New South Wales Tennis Centre, Yevgeny Kafelnikov and Venus Williams were worthy singles champions, the tennis was of the highest order in all four events, and even the weather was pleasant and warm, if at times a little windy.

Only 35 of the top men eligible on the post-Wimbledon ranking list were present but, as with the women, 7 of the top ten did participate. Only 6 men actually chose not to play. Obviously they had not been swayed by the Olympic message, so assiduously transmitted by the ITF to all players through their highly structured promotional strategy. Apparently not everyone is yet convinced that Olympic honour ranks higher than any other. Even the award of ATP ranking points, itself a significant breakthrough in co-operation between the men's Tour and the ITF, failed to convince the doubters.

Five men would have played but were injured, while defending champion Andre Agassi and the new French Open champion Mary Pierce had good reason to be absent. Agassi has pressing family problems, Pierce was injured. Both had signalled their intention to take part. Others, like Pete Sampras and Martina Hingis believed that they could not fit the Olympic Games into their schedules but, in any case, Hingis was ineligible. Nathalie Tauziat wanted to be there but was not selected because of derogatory remarks made about other French players in her book.

Yet those who did make the quick dash Down Under from the US Open were amply rewarded. Sydney wore the friendliest of faces and the 40,000 ever-helpful volunteers made everyone feel welcome. The organising team of local officials, led by the experienced Mike Daws, and the ITF's group headed by Debbie Jevans did a wonderful job. In fact the Games in general were a triumph both for the harbour city and the entire Australian nation. Even the transport arrangements, predicted to be a recipe for chaos, were outstandingly successful. A fleet of water buses augmented the frequent rail and road services that whisked happy commuters from city to site and back again with impressive speed and in relative comfort.

The players who were present in Sydney felt that they were taking part in the greatest show on earth. To see India's flag-bearer Leander Paes marching proudly past at the Opening Ceremony, to watch the smiling Jelena Dokic among the large Australian contingent waving to the massed bank of cheering spectators, to see Gustavo Kuerten, smartly attired in gold jacket and white hat among the team of happy Brazilians, all of them beaming and waving, was to know what they felt about the importance of Olympic sport.

Britain's Tim Henman summed up the general feeling when he said, 'Success at the Olympics ranks with winning Wimbledon or any of the Grand Slams. It is the absentees who are missing out.' Commenting on his missing colleagues Henman added, 'It only happens once every four years so it's going to take time for the event to become established in the minds of the players'.

That was a shrewd observation. With tennis out of the Games as a full medal sport between 1924 and 1988 there has been no Olympic tradition among tennis players. None of the great post-war champions like Maureen Connolly, Billie Jean King, and Margaret Court, or Ken Rosewall, Rod Laver, John Newcombe, Jimmy Connors, Bjorn Borg and John McEnroe ever had the chance to compete for an Olympic medal. It will take time to build that tradition.

Favourite to set a new tradition for Russia, who had never won an Olympic medal for tennis, was the new US Open champion and top seed Marat Safin. Yet as soon as the draw had been made there were doubts about his chances. The 20-year-old's first round opponent was the unorthodox Frenchman Fabrice Santoro, a man who had won all four of their previous meetings. If he survived, Safin could look forward to stern tests against the French Open semi-finalist Franco Squillari (10) and then either Tim Henman (7) or Michael Chang (16).

At the foot of the draw second seeded Kuerten had an easier first match against wild card Christophe Pognon of Benin but ahead in his quarter lay Todd Martin and the No.15 seed Albert Costa. Further danger lurked in the form of either Kafelnikov (5) or Mark Philippoussis (11) in the quarter-finals.

Whatever the reason – perhaps the timing of the Olympic tournament so soon after a Grand Slam, or maybe the Olympic spirit burning brightly in the minds of the lower ranked men, or perhaps even the contrast between autumn in the Northern hemisphere and spring in Australia – whatever was responsible – there was a catastrophic collapse of form in the men's singles.

No fewer than nine of the seeds went out in the first round – seven of them in the top half. Among them was Safin, once again driven mad by the wiles of Santoro who beat the favourite 1–6 6–1–6 4. The only seeded survivor in the top half was Alex Corretja (8) but even the experienced Spaniard was cut down in the third round by Germany's Tommy Haas, one of the eager young men who seized the moment.

Two others who surged spectacularly in Sydney were Arnaud Di Pasquale of France and the Swiss teenager Roger Federer. Both reached the semi-finals. Di Pasquale's victims were Germany's No. 9 seed Nicolas Kiefer who went down 6–3 6–4, Wimbledon semi-finalist Vladimir Voltchkov, beaten 6–2 6–2, Sweden's French Open finalist Magnus Norman (3) who lost a superb scrap 7–6 7–6, and yet another seed, Juan Carlos Ferrero (8) of Spain, who was outhit 6–2 6–1. Quite a collection of scalps for a man ranked 62 in the world.

Reacting slightly after this superb run, the Frenchman, starting now to make a few costly errors which up to that moment he had stubbornly refused to do, was beaten 6–4 6–4 by Kafelnikov in the semi-finals. Nevertheless it had been a wonderful performance from the ITF's world junior champion of 1997.

Federer's progress to the last four, built on the merits of a lethal forehand, electrifying pace about the court and an increasing use of the volley, was equally impressive. The young Swiss beat in succession David Prinosil of Germany, Karol Kucera (who had upset British No.1 Tim Henman (7) in the first round), Mikael Tillstrom of Sweden and the Moroccan, Karim Alami, all in straight sets. It had been a rich haul for a young man whose growing confidence at the net spells trouble for all his opponents in 2001.

In the bronze medal play-off Di Pasquale won a spirited encounter against Federer 7–6 6–7 6–3, his lower error percentage being largely responsible.

To the home fans the biggest disappointment was the early losses of Australian seeds Lleyton Hewitt (4) and Pat Rafter (13). Both had looked tremendous in practice. Both harboured dreams of a gold medal. Yet both lost tamely. Hewitt, playing on the same court where he had won the Adidas Open in January, was a first round casualty, beaten in straight sets by the tall Belarusian, Max Mirnyi. Rafter went through to the second round at the expense of Vince Spadea but then fell 7–5 7–6 to the doubles specialist Daniel Nestor. This was a career-best win for the left-handed Canadian who reacted in the next round and lost to Ferrero.

Inspired by his performance in the singles, Nestor wet on to claim gold in the doubles with fellow countryman Sebastien Lareau, a pairing that had come together only the previous September. This first-ever tennis medal for Canada was another blow for Australia whose best hope of gold had seemed to be through their world No.1 doubles pair, Todd Woodbridge and Mark Woodforde. Playing together for the last time, the defending champions had swept through to the final in impressive fashion at the expense of Bhupathi and Paes of India, the Slovaks Hrbaty and Kucera, plus Corretja and Costa. The Spaniards were destined to become bronze medalists by beating the South Africans, David Adams and John Laffnie de Jager, in the play-offs.

Against the Canadians, however, the Woodies appeared inhibited. Even in winning a close first set they were not playing with their normal freedom. Nestor in particular was returning serve so well that every Australian service game seemed threatened. Furthermore, both Canadians were serving well so breaking back was always a problem .

Although understandably disappointed about their 5–7 6–3 6–4 7–6 defeat, Woodbridge was philosophical about the loss. 'It's silver today' he said. 'But I think our whole partnership has been gold.' Everyone who has witnessed the great contribution this outstanding pair has made to the world game over the last decade would echo that thought.

The best Australian performance came from Mark Philippoussis who did at least reach the third round. There, however, he ran into a red hot Kafelnikov, the glint of gold already apparent in his eyes. The Russian then accounted for Kuerten with equal skill and then ended the challenge of Di Pasquale to reach the final without losing a set.

His opponent there was Tommy Haas who had opened his campaign impressively by beating a seeded player in his opening match. After dismissing Wayne Ferreira (14), the talented young German rode his wave of inspiration past Andreas Vinciguerra, Alex Corretja (8), Mirnyi and Federer to move into his second final of the year.

Maintaining a steely resolve, he pushed Kafelnikov to the limit during a series of punishing rallies that tested the concentration and fitness of both men. Not until the closing stages did Haas begin to wilt, his more frequent errors giving his opponent a few cheap points which were gratefully accepted. 'I am so proud of myself' said the elated winner. 'I'm proud of my country, too' he added. Then, mindful of Elena Dementieva's silver medal, won the previous day, he said with a broad grin 'Russia is taking over in tennis'. Everyone smiled with him.

Smiles in the American camp were even wider. With Venus Williams taking gold in the singles and her sister Serena joining her to win the doubles, the United States scored a rare double, last achieved by Helen Wills in Paris 76 years earlier.

As she had done ever since winning a first Grand Slam title at Wimbledon, Venus completely dominated the opposition. Seeded two, she raced through the first three rounds without allowing Henrieta Nagyova, Tamarine Tanasugarn or Jana Kandarr a single set between them. In the quarter-finals Arantxa Sanchez-Vicario (5), a silver medallist in Atlanta, drew on her experience to take one set. Monica Seles did the same in the semi-finals. It was the closest anyone got. Seles, though, did have the consolation of winning a bronze medal, her greater experience overcoming the youthful enthusiasm of Australia's Dokic 6–3 6–4 in the play-off.

Because the WTA Tour had not agreed to award ranking points like the men it meant that a maximum of three players from any country could be accepted in the women's draw. Thus Serena Williams and two other Americans did not merit a place; nor did two of the highly ranked French women.

Accordingly form among the women ran more true than it had done in the men's singles. Only six of the sixteen seeds lost before reaching their appointed places in the third round. Ai Sugiyama (14) was brought down at the first hurdle by Dokic who, to the delight of the home crowd, carried her challenge right through to the semi-finals at the expense of seventh seeded Amanda Coetzer of South Africa.

The two others who failed to win a round were Amelie Mauresmo (9), a loser in three sets to Fabiola Zuluaga of Columbia, and Russia's Elena Likhovtseva (15) who was Kandarr's first victim.

The saddest departure was that of the Atlanta gold medallist and top seed, Lindsay Davenport. Still unable to rely upon the left ankle she had damaged in Canada just before the US Open, the American limped through her opening round against Paola Suarez but was not fit enough to start against the wild card from Paraguay, Rossana de los Rios. 'Ever since Atlanta I've looked forward to coming to Sydney. I'm just sad and disappointed not to be able to continue' she said.

The two other second round losers were Conchita Martinez (4), beaten in a close third set by Karina Habsudova of the Slovak Republic, and Silvija Talaja (13) who fell to Italy's Silvia Farina-Elia in another close three-setter.

Until she ran into Seles, Dominique van Roost of Belgium, seeded eight, had played impressively in her last year on the Tour. The same was true of Barbara Schett (12) whose progress was halted in the quarter-finals by Dementieva. The Russian teenager, who had played so impressively at the US Open to reach the semi-finals there, went one better in Sydney. Her 2–6 6–4 6–4 battle with Dokic was the match of the tournament, in doubt until the last rally of the last game. The crowd, noisy but fair, gave these two tearaway teenagers a standing ovation after witnessing some truly remarkable shot-making on the run from both of them. If this was the future of women's tennis it will be a bright one indeed.

The present, though, belongs firmly to Venus Williams. Once Davenport had departed it was clear that no-one left in the draw had the game to beat her. Hard as Dementieva tried in the final there was never any doubt about the outcome. Nevertheless, the young Russian was overjoyed to become the first from her country to win a medal of any sort for tennis.

Venus was equally delighted with her gold medal. 'This is the one moment in time for me, for my country, for my family, for the team' she said. Serena echoed the same thoughts after their 6–1 6–1 doubles victory over the Belgians, Kristie Boogert and Miriam Oremans. 'This takes the cake' she said. 'You only have one moment in time and I wanted to capitalise on it.'

The ITF will want to capitalise on this enthusiasm by persuading those who were not in Sydney to reconsider their positions for Athens in 2004. Perhaps they should also consult with all constituent parties to see if a team formula would be more appropriate for tennis at the Olympics than the present formula. A five match format that included a men's singles, a women's singles, a men's doubles, a women's doubles and a mixed might prove very attractive both to the players and spectators. This would add the extra dimension of team participation that has proved overwhelmingly successful in the Davis Cup and Fed Cup competitions.

OLYMPIC RESULTS: SYDNEY 2000

WOMENS' SINGLES – 1st Round: L. Davenport (USA) (1) d. P. Suarez (ARG) 6–2 6–2; R. De Los Rios (PAR) (WC) d. K. Hrdlickova (CZE) 6–3 6–0; R. Grande (ITA) d. S. Plischke (AUT) 6–2 6–2; J. Dokic (AUS) d. A. Sugiyama (JPN) (14) 6–0 7–6(1); S. Appelmans (BEL) (16) d. S. Jeyaseelan (CAN) 7–5 6–2; M. Alejandra Vento (VEN) (WC) d. A. Hopmans (NED) 6–4 6–3; A. Kremer (LUX) d. I. Majoli (CRO) (WC) 6–2 6–4; A. Coetzer (RSA) (7) d. R. Kuti Kis (HUN) 6–1 6–1; C. Martinez (ESP) (4) d. P. Mandula (HUN) (WC) 6–1 6–0; K. Habsudova (SVK) d. K. Srebotnik (SLO) (WC) 6–3 7–6(7); K. Boogert (NED) d. I. Tulyaganova (UZB) (WC) 6–2 6–2; E. Dementieva (RUS) (10) d. M. Vavrinec (SUI) (WC) 6–1 6–1; B. Schett (AUT) (12) d. A. Molik (AUS) (WC) 7–6(7) 6–2; M. Salerni (ARG) (WC) d. N. Zvereva (BLR) 6–3 4–6 6–2; D. Bedanova (CZE) (Alt) d. J. Yi (CHN) 6–2 6–7(3) 6–3; J. Halard-Decugis (FRA) (Alt) d. T. Garbin (ITA) 6–4 6–2; D. Van Roost (BEL) (8) d. A. Gersi (CZE) 6–1 6–1; A. Myskina (RUS) d. E. Danilidou (GRE) (WC) 6–1 7–5; S. Farina-Elia (ITA) d. C. Black (ZIM) 6–2 3–6 6–3; S. Talaja (CRO) (13) d. E. Neyssa (HAI) (WC) 6–1 6–0; N. Dechy (FRA) (11) d. M. Serna (ESP) 6–1 6–2; N. Pratt (AUS) d. R. Dragomir (ROM) 6–3 6–3; M. Oremans (NED) (Alt) d. F. Labat (ARG) 6–2 6–4; M. Seles (USA) (3) d. K. Marosi-Aracama (HUN) (WC) 6–0 6–1; A. Sanchez-Vicario (ESP) (5) d. N. Li (CHN) (WC) 6–1 7–5; P. Wartusch (AUT) d. O. Barabanschikova (BLR) 6–4 6–2; E. Callens (BEL) (Alt) d. S. Asagoe (JPN) (WC) 6–0 6–4; F. Zuluaga (COL) d. A. Mauresmo (FRA) (9) 6–3 3–6 6–2; J. Kandarr (GER) d. E. Likhovtseva (RUS) (15) 6–4 6–4; E. Gagliardi (SUI) d. W. Prakusya (INA) (WC) 6–4 7–6(2); T. Tanasugarn (THA) d. T. Pisnik (SLO) 6–4 6–3; V. Williams (USA) (2) d. H. Nagyova (SVK) 6–2 6–2.

2nd Round: De Los Rios (WC) d. Davenport (1) w/o; Dokic d. Grande 5–7 6–3 6–3; Appelmans (16) d. Vento (WC) 6–2 6–2; Coetzer (7) d. Kremer 4–6 6–3 6–4; Habsudova d. C. Martinez (4) 1–6 6–0 6–4; Dementieva (10) d. Boogert 6–2 4–6 7–5; Schett (12) d. Salerni (WC) 7–6(5) 6–4; Halard-Decugis (Alt) d. Bedanova (Alt) 6–3 6–4; Van Roost (8) d. Myskina 6–2 6–3; Farina-Elia d. Talaja (13) 3–6 6–4 6–4; Dechy (11) d. Pratt 6–3 6–1; Seles (3) d. Oremans (Alt) 6–1 6–1; Sanchez-Vicario (5) d. Wartusch 6–2 6–4; Zuluaga d. Callens (Alt) 6–3 6–2; Kandarr d. Gagliardi 7–5 6–4; V. Williams (2) d. Tanasugarn 6–2 6–3.

3rd round: Dokic d. De Los Rios (WC) 7–6(5) 7–5; Coetzer (7) d. Appelmans (16) 6–3 6–1; Dementieva (10) d. Habsudova 6–2 6–1; Schett (12) d. Halard-Decugis (Alt) 2–6 6–2 6–1; Van Roost (8) d. Farina-Elia 6–1 7–5; Seles (3) d. Dechy (11) 6–3 6–2; Sanchez-Vicario (5) d. Zuluaga 6–2 6–0; V. Williams (2) d. Kandarr 6–2 6–2.

Quarter-finals: Dokic d. Coetzer (7) 6–1 1–6 6–1; Dementieva (10) d. Schett (12) 2–6 6–2 6–1; Seles (3) d. Van Roost (8) 6–0 6–2; V. Williams (2) d. Sanchez-Vicario (5) 3–6 6–2 6–4.

Semi-finals: Dementieva (10) d. Dokic 2–6 6–4 6–4; V. Williams (2) d. Seles (3) 6–1 4–6 6–3.

Final (Gold/Silver): V. Williams (2) d. Dementieva (10) 6–2 6–4.

Play-off (Bronze): Seles (3) d. Dokic 6–1 6–4.

WOMEN'S DOUBLES – Semi-finals: S. Williams/V. Williams d. Callens/Van Roost (5) 6–4 6–1; Boogert/Oremans d. Barabanschikova/Zvereva 6–3 6–2.

Final (Gold/Silver): S. Williams/V. Williams d. Boogert/Oremans 6–1 6–1.

Play-off (Bronze): Callens/Van Roost (5) d. Barabanschikova/Zvereva 4–6 6–4 6–1.

MEN'S SINGLES – 1st Round: F. Santoro (FRA) d. M. Safin (RUS) (1) 1–6 6–1 6–4; F. Vicente (ESP) d. A. Ilie (AUS) 6–3 6–3; G. Pozzi (ITA) d. J. Novak (CZE) 6–1 6–2; K. Alami (MAR) d. F. Squillari (ARG) (10) 6–4 7–6(5); S. Lareau (CAN) (WC) d. M. Chang (USA) (16) 7–6(6) 6–3; M. Tillstrom (SWE) (Alt) d. L. Paes (IND) (WC) 6–2 6–4; R. Federer (SUI) d. D. Prinosil (GER) 6–2 6–2; K. Kucera (SVK) d. T. Henman (GBR) (7) 6–3 6–2; M. Mirnyi (BLR) d. L. Hewitt (AUS) (4) 6–3 6–3; J. Vanek (CZE) d. W. Black (ZIM) (Alt) 5–7 6–1 6–1; J. Tarango (USA) d. D. Camacho (BOL) (WC) 6–0 6–1; M. Zabaleta (ARG) d. M. Rios (CHI) (12) 6–7(8) 6–4 7–5; T. Haas (GER) d. W. Ferreira (RSA) (14) 7–5 6–2; A. Vinciguerra (SWE) d. C. Ruud (NOR) 6–2 6–4; A. Clement (FRA) d. G. Rusedski (GBR) 6–2 6–3; A. Corretja (ESP) (6) d. G. Ivanisevic (CRO) 7–6(3) 7–6(2); J. Ferrero (ESP) (8) d. H. Lee (KOR) (Alt) 6–7(5) 7–6(6) 7–5; N. Massu (CHI) d. S. Dosedel (CZE) 6–2 7–6(5); D. Nestor (CAN) (Alt) d. B. Cowan (GBR) (Alt) 5–7 6–1 6–4; P. Rafter (AUS) (13) d. V. Spadea (USA) 6–4 6–3; A. Di Pasquale (FRA) d. N. Kiefer (GER) (9) 6–4 6–3; V. Voltchkov (BLR) d. G. Gaudio (ARG) 7–6(4) 4–6 6–1; P. Srichaphan (THA) (WC) d. A. Savolt (HUN) (WC) 6–2 4–6 7–5; M. Norman (SWE) (3) d. A. Pavel (ROM) 6–7(1) 6–3 10–8; Y. Kafelnikov (RUS) (5) d. J. Marin (CRC) (WC) 6–0 6–1; J. Chela (ARG) d. N. Escude (FRA) 6–7(5) 7–5 6–1; K. Pless (DEN) (WC) d. S. Sargsian (ARM) 6–3 6–4; M. Philippoussis (AUS) (11) d. T. Johansson (SWE) 7–6(6) 6–4; K. Ullyett (ZIM) (Alt) d. A. Costa (ESP) (15) 6–3 3–6 11–9; I. Ljubicic (CRO) d. D. Hrbaty (SVK) 6–1 1–6 6–3; R. Schuttler (GER) d. T. Martin (USA) 6–2 6–0; G. Kuerten (BRA) (2) d. C. Pognon (BEN) (WC) 6–1 6–1.

2nd Round: Santoro d. Vicente 6–1 6–7(2) 7–5; Alami d. Pozzi 6–2 4–6 8–6; Tillstrom (Alt) d. Lareau (WC) 6–1 3–6 6–3; Federer d. Kucera 6–4 7–6(5); Mirnyi d. Vanek 6–7(4) 6–4 11–9; Zabaleta d. Tarango 6–2 6–3; Haas d. Vinciguerra 4–6 6–4 6–2; Corretja (6) d. Clement 6–7(5) 6–4 6–4; Ferrero (8) d. Massu 6–4 7–6(6); Nestor (Alt) d. Rafter (13) 7–5 7–6(4); Di Pasquale d. Voltchkov 6–2 6–2; Norman (3) d. Srichaphan (WC) 7–5 6–2; Kafelnikov (5) d. Chela 7–6(4) 6–4; Philippoussis (11) d. Pless (WC) 6–4 6–4; Ljubicic d. Ullyett (Alt) 6–2 4–6 6–4; Kuerten (2) d. Schuttler 6–4 6–4.

3rd round: Alami d. Santoro 6–2 5–7 6–4; Federer d. Tillstrom (Alt) 6–1 6–2; Mirnyi d. Zabaleta 7–6(4) 6–2; Haas d. Corretja (6) 7–6(7) 6–3; Ferrero (8) d. Nestor (Alt) 7–6(4) 6–3; Di Pasquale d. Norman (3) 7–6(4) 7–6(2); Kafelnikov (5) d. Philippoussis (11) 7–6(4) 6–3; Kuerten (2) d. Ljubicic 7–6(2) 6–3.

Quarter-finals: Federer d. Alami 7–6(2) 6–1; Haas d. Mirnyi 4–6 7–5 6–3; Di Pasquale d. Ferrero (8) 6–2 6–1; Kafelnikov (5) d. Kuerten (2) 6–4 7–5.

Semi-finals: Haas d. Federer 6–3 6–2; Kafelnikov (5) d. Di Pasquale 6–4 6–4.
Final (Gold/Silver): Kafelnikov (5) d. Haas 7–6(4) 3–6 6–2 4–6 6–3.
Play-off (Bronze): Di Pasquale d. Federer 7–6(5) 6–7(7) 6–3.

MEN'S DOUBLES – Semi-finals: Woodbridge/Woodforde (1) d. Corretja/Costa 6–3 7–6(5); Lareau/Nestor (4) d. Adams/De Jager (5) 6–1 6–2.
Final (Gold/Silver): Lareau/Nestor (4) d. Woodbridge/Woodforde (1) d. 5–7 6–3 6–4 7–6(2).
Play-off (Bronze): Corretja/Costa d. Adams/De Jager (5) 2–6 6–4 6–3.

The Paralympic Games, 20–28 October

Wendy Kewley

Attracting record crowds, the fourth Paralympic Tennis Event, held at the New South Wales tennis centre, Sydney, crowned two new champions with David Hall and Esther Vergeer capturing gold in the men's and women's singles events.

Sydney 2000 unfolded into a sporting extravaganza of epic proportions, with the Paralympic tennis universally considered the best event of its kind ever. With 18 of the top 20 men and 16 of the top women competing, it was no surprise that the tennis competition produced so many thrilling moments on court. With David Hall, Laurent Giammartini, Ricky Molier, Kai Schrameyer, Randy Snow and Stephen Welch competing, all six men's ITF World Champions were also present.

The drama peaked in the men's final when Hall became the first tennis player to win a gold in singles before a home crowd. His gutsy 6–7(3) 6–4 6–2 victory over USA's Stephen Welch brought the 10,000-strong crowd to their feet in celebration.

'It's hard to believe,' Hall said after proudly parading his medal to the crowd, his shoulders draped in the Australian flag that a fan had handed to him moments before. 'There were a few tears – I expected it to be very emotional. I've been thinking about this ever since Sydney was awarded the Olympics… For me it was a mental battle – a few points here and there and he (Welch) could have been the winner.'

Held on Saturday, the men's final produced one of the most riveting duels of the entire competition. With little to separate both performers – Welch was world No. 1 last year while Hall's victory at the preceding US Open had earned him pole position – the gold medallist was going to be the one who dared most. In the end the homegrown 'cool as a cat' Aussie dared most. After Welch made the better start, Hall remained calm, capitalising on the rare chances that came his way until victory was secured.

A silver medallist at Atlanta, Welch was particularly disappointed to miss out on gold once again. But the American praised Hall's greater mental strength and said, 'I was definitely focused on gold when I came here… but I'm happy that I put up a really good fight and today David was stronger… when his back's against the wall he still comes back fighting.'

Partnering Scott Douglas in the men's doubles, Welch added a bronze to his Paralympic medal collection. Seeded third, the Americans outplayed British pairing Simon Hall and Jayant Mistry, seeded fourth.

On Friday, Hall and David Johnson had taken silver in the men's doubles. The 'Wheelchair Woodies' lost 7–5 1–6 6–3 to Dutch partnership Robin Ammerlaan and Ricky Molier in an epic contest that fused skill and courage, producing just over two hours of nail-biting tennis. Molier was particularly pleased to win the gold after having his medal chances dashed by Austria's Martin Legner in the men's singles. Legner had dismantled Molier's power play to beat the defending Paralympic champion in the quarter-finals producing the biggest shock of the tournament.

While the host nation took two medals in the men's event, it was the Netherlands which topped the tennis medalware table, enjoying its most successful Paralympic Tennis Event ever. The Dutch won five medals which included a clean sweep of the women's singles medals. Competing in her first Paralympics, world No. 1 and top seed Esther Vergeer took gold in both singles and doubles.

GOLD

Esther Vergeer of Holland completed the golden double at the Paralympic Tennis Event in Sydney, which followed the Olympic Games at the same site. (Gordon Gillespie)

In the women's final, Vergeer lived up to her top seed status, outhitting compatriot Sharon Walraven 6–0 6–4 to add her first Paralympic gold singles medal to her ever increasing title haul. She has already won two US Open trophies and two NEC Wheelchair Tennis Masters titles. In truth, the match was Vergeer's from the start. Dominating a nervous Walraven, she wrapped up the first set within 22 minutes. After losing her concentration early in the second set, Vergeer regrouped and upped the pressure with penetrating drives. A vicious cross court forehand brought her matchpoint which she snatched with an equally emphatic forehand down the line.

Vergeer then teamed with Smit to defeat Daniela Di Toro and Branka Pupovac of Australia 7–6(5) 6–2 for the doubles gold medal. After losing to Walraven in the quarter-finals of the women's singles, the second seeded Di Toro was delighted to claim Australia's third Paralympic medal. Pupovac said, 'We did our very best and it was close. But I'm at the Paralympics… This is history in the making. Wheelchair tennis has never had so many people attend and it's just sensational.'

For her part, a delighted Vergeer spoke of her incredible achievement. 'It's unreal. My goal was to win gold in the singles and doubles – but my dream came true.' The 19-year-old added, 'It's a special tournament because all kinds of sport are playing together – normally you just win a title but here you have a title and a medal and everybody knows who you are and everybody knows about wheelchair tennis now.'

Atlanta gold medallist Maaike Smit earned bronze after beating Great Britain's Kimberly Dell to give the Dutch their second consecutive clean sweep in the Paralympic women's event. Four years ago, all three medals in the women's singles at Atlanta were won by Dutch players with Smit winning gold while Monique Kalkman and Chantal Vandierendonck took silver and bronze respectively.

Germany also won a brace of medals, claiming bronze in the men's singles and the women's doubles. Kai Schrameyer struggled against a virus all week but managed to beat Austria's Martin Legner to earn this third Paralympic medal. His compatriots Christine Otterbach and Petra Sax-Scharl found themselves embroiled in a dramatic evening encounter with Canada's Yuka Chokyu and Helene Simard. The Germany partnership finally secured a bronze medal, winning 5–7 6–4 6–4 after a marathon two hours, 53 minutes.

With 72 people from 24 countries taking part in the Paralympic Tennis Event, Sydney also provided a welcome spotlight for the up and coming wheelchair tennis nations. Competing in the women's Paralympic tennis competition for the first time, Thai girls Narumol Chinprahus and Sakhorn Khanthasit both defeated higher ranked German players in their opening matches – Petra Sax-Scharl and Christine Otterbach respectively. Korea's Myun-Hee Hwang came back from a set down against the favoured Arlette Racineux of France in the opening round, to give her country its first ever win at a Paralympic women's tennis event.

In the men's competition Oscar Diaz also celebrated his country's first appearance in the men's Paralympic Tennis Event with a comfortable win over the higher ranked Bob Dockerill of Great Britain. A delighted Diaz said afterwards, 'I was very tense as I have not played on the tour but I am very proud to be the first Argentinian to play in the Paralympics.'

The ITF Wheelchair Tennis Committee also held three workshops during the competition to discuss eligibility as well as the marketing and development of the game. All issues were thoroughly examined producing much positive feedback.

After such an amazing Paralympics, the future looks rosy for wheelchair tennis. But as Ellen de Lange says, 'Our task now is to channel the amazing energy created by the Paralympics so that wheelchair tennis can benefit from the incredible success of Sydney.'

It was an eventful year for Arantxa Sanchez-Vicario who got married in July, won a first mixed doubles title at the US Open and returned to the top ten. (Paul Zimmer)

The ITF Year

Jenny Cooke

The past year has seen great success for tennis on the international sporting stage with record crowds witnessing the best Olympic and Paralympic Tennis Events in history and a record number of nations participating in the ITF's premier team competitions Fed Cup and Davis Cup by NEC.

Fittingly for the beginning of the new millennium, 2000 was a year of firsts for the ITF with a number of key initiatives being implemented throughout the course of the year.

One major initiative was the announcement of a series of events planned for 2000 focusing on increasing tennis participation across the globe and linked under the banner of 'Marketing the Game: Drive for Growth.' The first event, a Seminar on the Future of the Game, was held in London in March and involved a number of key partners such as National and Regional Associations and Tennis Industry representatives.

Building on the Marketing the Game initiative, the 2000 AGM, held in Antalya in Turkey, followed the theme 'Tennis beyond 2000: Drive for Growth'. In his opening address, ITF President Francesco Ricci Bitti acknowledged the challenges that the future would bring to the ITF. 'This is the single most important challenge that we face now and in the years ahead. We need to be sure that the positive messages about our sport are reaching the appropriate audiences. This needs to be our number one priority if we as a sport are to prosper.'

The AGM agreed a number of new initiatives including the creation of an Athletes Commission to advise and make recommendations to the Board of Directors on all questions of concern to athletes. Boris Becker (GER), Arantxa Sanchez-Vicario (ESP), Mary Joe Fernandez (USA) and Mark Woodforde (AUS) have agreed to serve on this commission.

The AGM also reaffirmed the ITF's role as the caretaker of the Rules of Tennis and took several important decisions with regard to these rules including:

- To include No Ad System of Scoring as an optional method of scoring in the Rules of Tennis. This came after the completion of a successful two-year experiment.
- To come into line with the professional game by approving for all levels of tennis an amendment to the Rule on Continuous Play and Rest Periods. The Rule states that after the first game of each set and during a tie-break, play shall be continuous and players shall change ends without a rest period. At the conclusion of each set, there shall be a set break of a maximum of 120 seconds.
- To begin experimentation of three alternative scoring systems – Short Sets, Deciding Tie-Break Game and Deciding Sudden Death. These experiments came into effect on 1 July 2000 and will continue until 31 December 2001. The Short Sets scoring system uses a best of five sets format, the first player/team to win four games winning the set given there is a margin of two games over the opponent(s). Tie-breaks are played at four-all. The Short Sets system is designed to increase the number of exciting moments and points during a match, shortening each set in order to progress more quickly to its most exciting part, and playing more sets, providing more opportunities for fresh starts and momentum changes. The Deciding Tie-Break Game scoring method allows for 'best of two' format where matches comprise two sets with a tie break only if the match is at one set all. The Australian Open 2001 has adopted this scoring system for use in the Mixed Doubles event and will encourage its use at national level.

One of the highlights of the AGM was the unveiling of the new ITF merchandise line, the 'Davis Cup Collection'. The collection includes clothing and related merchandise and is designed to produce another revenue stream for both the ITF and its National Associations while reinforcing the power of Davis Cup as a brand. The collection was launched to the public in July and was featured at the Davis Cup Final in Barcelona in December.

The second major event in the Marketing the Game Programme, the inaugural ITF Tennis Participation Coaches Workshop – 'More Tennis; More Often; More Fun' – was held in Bath,

UK, in June. The week-long workshop was directed primarily at educating coaches involved in grass roots tennis programmes worldwide and attracted more than 280 participants from over 80 countries.

This event was followed by the ITF's 1st International Congress on Tennis Science and Technology, held at the University of Surrey in Roehampton, UK, in August. A total of 160 delegates from 23 nations attended the event hosted by Jan Franke, Chairman ITF Technical Commission, Andrew Coe, ITF Head of Technical and Product Development, and Dr Steve Haake, ITF Research Consultant. An exhibition demonstrating cutting edge developments in tennis equipment, facilities, sports science and coaching was held in conjunction with the Congress.

The ITF's Technical Department also continued its trial of the larger Type 3 ball and this ball has now been endorsed as the official ball of the ATP Seniors Tour. The ball was also used at Davis Cup Group III and IV ties, ITF Men's Satellite and Futures events and in 2001 will be used for the first time in women's events such as Fed Cup Qualifying Group II events.

A second 'Future of the Game' Seminar for the ITF Foundation was held in New York during the US Open in September and the final event on the Marketing the Game Programme for the year – a Marketing the Game Summit – was held in Windsor, UK, in November. The Summit identified a number of key issues widely considered to be fundamental to the future health and growth of tennis and from 2001 priority will be given to issues such as a generic advertising campaign aimed at participation, an international ratings/handicap conversion chart, global strategies to facilitate cross-promotion of events, a National or team tennis apparel strategy and developing an international internet project aimed at schools.

Building on the progress made in 1999 the relationship between the ITF and the ATP Tour continued to strengthen in 2000. Significant agreements were reached on the allocation of ranking points for the Men's Singles event at the Olympics, calendar dates for the Davis Cup by NEC competition until 2004, and the inaugural Tennis Masters Cup – the end-of-year men's tournament co-owned by the ITF, Grand Slams and ATP Tour and replacing the Grand Slam Cup and the ATP Tour World Championship. The first Tennis Masters Cup was a great success with the top eight players in the world competing for the title. For the first time the World No. 1 position hung on the last match of the year and in a dramatic final Brazil's Gustavo Kuerten defeated Andre Agassi in Lisbon, Portugal, to clinch both the championship and the No. 1 spot.

The Olympic and Paralympic Tennis Events in Sydney, Australia were two of the major highlights of 2000. Both events were the most successful ever held with record elite player participation levels and record crowds attending. Congratulations go to gold medallists Yevgeny Kafelnikov (RUS), Venus Williams (USA), Sebastien Lareau and Daniel Nestor (CAN), Venus and Serena Williams (USA), David Hall (AUS), Esther Vergeer (NED), David Hall and David Johnson (AUS) and Esther Vergeer and Maaike Smit (NED) and all the tennis medallists. In January 2000, the ITF launched its successful Olympic magazine 02k to encourage the top players to compete at Sydney and to help players get the most out of their Olympic/Paralympic experience. The ITF's Olympic Promotional Programme also included running Olympic stories in *This Week*, the ITF's weekly news bulletin with special daily reports during the Olympic Tennis Event. For the first time ever the ITF also ran dedicated Olympic and Paralympic Tennis weblets.

Olympic and Paralympic tennis was also the theme of the World Champions Dinner in Paris in June when medallists were honoured with a special gold and silver pin. Special guests at the dinner included IOC President His Excellency Juan Antonio Samaranch and Robert Steadward, President of the International Paralympic Committee. Mr Samaranch was awarded the ITF's highest honour, the Philippe Chatrier award for services to tennis. Philippe Chatrier, a former President of the ITF, sadly passed away on 23 June, 2000, aged 72.

In addition to the success of the Paralympic Tennis Event, wheelchair tennis in general continued to grow in 2000. With 116 international tournaments on the NEC Wheelchair Tennis Tour, the sport is prospering at the start of the new millennium. A total of 32 teams competed for the World Team Cup and a further 12 played in the qualifying events. A doubles event was also introduced at the 2000 NEC Tennis Masters and 1999 singles champions Esther Vergeer (NED) and Robin Ammerlaan (NED) made history by successfully defending their singles titles. In 2001 the ITF is proud to be celebrating 25 years of Wheelchair Tennis.

Several other notable firsts were also achieved during ITF events in 2000. At the Australian Open in January 1999, ITF World Champion Andre Agassi (USA) became the first man to reach four consecutive Grand Slam Finals since Rod Laver in 1969. At Wimbledon in July, Pete Sampras (USA) made history by winning his seventh Wimbledon singles trophy and in doing so surpassed Roy Emerson's record of 12 Grand Slam titles. Wimbledon 2000 was also history-making for the Australian doubles team of Todd Woodbridge and Mark Woodforde as they captured their sixth Wimbledon doubles title – a record 60th career title and 11th Grand Slam win.

The ITF's premier team competitions Davis Cup by NEC and Fed Cup also provided many memorable moments in 2000. In Davis Cup, Spain won the prestigious trophy for the first time with a thrilling victory over the defending champion Australia in Barcelona in December. In the Fed Cup World Finals in Las Vegas the United States extended their record number of Fed Cup titles to 17 with victory over Spain. The ITF, in partnership with ISL, has agreed a new format for the 2001 Fed Cup competition comprising a 16 nation World Group and a three-week schedule.

A record level of tournaments and prize money was offered on the ITF Women's Circuit Events in 2001 with 309 events offering a total of $5.89 million in prizemoney. Tournaments were played in 52 countries worldwide. The ITF Men's Circuit in 2000 provided 39 Satellite Circuits for men in 21 countries and 249 Futures tournaments in 55 countries.

The ITF Junior Circuit went from strength to strength in 2000 and in a major step forward launched a dedicated website www.itfjuniors.com for all players, media, officials and followers of the ITF Junior Circuit. Visitors to the site can access current ITF World Junior Rankings, player biographies, news from the circuit, calendars, tournament drawsheets, historical records and tournament rules and regulations.

Vets Tennis enjoyed another successful year with an impressive 423 entrants, including a number of former Davis Cup and Fed Cup players, contesting the 2000 ITF Vets World Championships in Buenos Aires.

In the coming year the ITF, as the world governing body of the sport of tennis, will continue to play a leadership role in facilitating even greater understanding and co-operation among all members of the tennis industry in an effort to find new ways to lift the profile of tennis internationally.

ITF WORLD CHAMPIONS

SINGLES

	Men	Women		Men	Women
1978	Bjorn Borg	Chris Evert	1990	Ivan Lendl	Steffi Graf
1979	Bjorn Borg	Martina Navratilova	1991	Stefan Edberg	Monica Seles
1980	Bjorn Borg	Chris Evert	1992	Jim Courier	Monica Seles
1981	John McEnroe	Chris Evert	1993	Pete Sampras	Steffi Graf
1982	Jimmy Connors	Martina Navratilova	1994	Pete Sampras	Arantxa Sanchez-Vicario
1983	John McEnroe	Martina Navratilova	1995	Pete Sampras	Steffi Graf
1984	John McEnroe	Martina Navratilova	1996	Pete Sampras	Steffi Graf
1985	Ivan Lendl	Martina Navratilova	1997	Pete Sampras	Martina Hingis
1986	Ivan Lendl	Martina Navratilova	1998	Pete Sampras	Lindsay Davenport
1987	Ivan Lendl	Steffi Graf	1999	Andre Agassi	Martina Hingis
1988	Mats Wilander	Steffi Graf	2000	Gustavo Kuerten	Martina Hingis
1989	Boris Becker	Steffi Graf			

DOUBLES

	Men	Women
1996	Todd Woodbridge/Mark Woodforde	Lindsay Davenport/Mary Joe Fernandez
1997	Todd Woodbridge/Mark Woodforde	Lindsay Davenport/Jana Novotna
1998	Jacco Eltingh/Paul Haarhuis	Lindsay Davenport/Natasha Zvereva
1999	Mahesh Bhupathi/Leander Paes	Martina Hingis/Anna Kournikova
2000	Todd Woodbridge/Mark Woodforde	Julie Halard-Decugis/Ai Sugiyama

ITF JUNIOR WORLD CHAMPIONS

	Boys' singles	Girls' singles
1978	Ivan Lendl (TCH)	Hana Mandlikova (TCH)
1979	Raul Viver (ECU)	Mary-Lou Piatek (USA)
1980	Thierry Tulasne (FRA)	Susan Mascarin (USA)
1981	Pat Cash (AUS)	Zina Garrison (USA)
1982	Guy Forget (FRA)	Gretchen Rush (USA)
1983	Stefan Edberg (SWE)	Pascale Paradis (FRA)

Boys' doubles	**Girls' doubles**
1984 Mark Kratzmann (AUS)	Gabriela Sabatini (ARG)
1985 Claudio Pistolesi (ITA)	Laura Garrone (USA)
1986 Javier Sanchez (ESP)	Patricia Tarabini (ARG)
1987 Jason Stoltenberg (AUS)	Natalia Zvereva (URS)
1988 Nicolas Pereira (VEN)	Cristina Tessi (ARG)
1989 Nicklas Kulti (SWE)	Florencia Labat (ARG)
1990 Andrea Gaudenzi (ITA)	Karina Habsudova (TCH)
1991 Thomas Enqvist (SWE)	Zdenka Malkova (TCH)
1992 Brian Dunn (USA)	Rossana De Los Rios (PAR)
1993 Marcelo Rios (CHI)	Nino Louarssabichvilli (GEO)
1994 Federico Browne (ARG)	Martina Hingis (SUI)
1995 Marian Zabaleta (ARG)	Anna Kournikova (RUS)
1996 Sebastien Grosjean (FRA)	Amelie Mauresmo (FRA)
1997 Arnaud di Pasquale (FRA)	Cara Black (ZIM)
1998 Roger Federer (SUI)	Jelena Dokic (AUS)
1999 Kristian Pless (DEN)	Lina Krasnoroutskaia (RUS)
2000 Andy Roddick (USA)	Maria Emilia Salerni (ARG)
1982 Fernando Perez (MEX)	Beth Herr (USA)
1983 Mark Kratzman (AUS)	Larissa Savchenko (URS)
1984 Augustin Moreno (MEX)	Mercedes Paz (ARG)
1985 Petr Korda (TCH)/ Cyril Suk (TCH)	Mariana Perez-Roldan (ARG)/Patricia Tarabini (ARG)
1986 Tomas Carbonell (ESP)	Leila Meskhi (URS)
1987 Jason Stoltenberg (AUS)	Natalia Medvedeva (URS)
1988 David Rikl (TCH)/Tomas Zdrazila (TCH)	Jo-Anne Faull (AUS)
1989 Wayne Ferreira (RSA)	Andrea Strnadova (TCH)
1990 Marten Renstroem (SWE)	Karina Habsudova (TCH)
1991 Karim Alami (MAR)	Eva Martincova (TCH)
1992 Enrique Abaroa (MEX)	Nancy Feber (BEL)/Laurence Courtois (BEL)
1993 Steven Downs (NZL)	Cristina Moros (USA)
1994 Benjamin Ellwood (AUS)	Martina Nedelkova (SLK)
1995 Kepler Orellana (VEN)	Ludmilla Varmuzova (CZE)
1996 Sebastien Grosjean (FRA)	Michaela Pastikova (CZE)/Jitka Schonfeldova (CZE)
1997 Nicolas Massu (CHI)	Cara Black (ZIM)/Irina Selyutina (KAZ)
1998 Jose De Armas (VEN)	Eva Dyrberg (DEN)
1999 Julien Benneteau (FRA)/Nicolas Mahut (FRA)	Daniela Bedanova (CZE)
2000 Lee Childs (GBR)/James Nelson (GBR)	Maria Emilia Salerni (ARG)

ITF WHEELCHAIR TENNIS WORLD CHAMPIONS

Men	**Women**
1991 Randy Snow (USA)	Chantal Vandierendonck (NED)
1992 Laurent Giammartini (FRA)	Monique Kalkman (NED)
1993 Kai Schrameyer (GER)	Monique Kalkman (NED)
1994 Laurent Giammartini (FRA)	Monique Kalkman (NED)
1995 David Hall (AUS)	Monique Kalkman (NED)
1996 Ricky Molier (NED)	Chantal Vandierendonck (NED)
1997 Ricky Molier (NED)	Chantal Vandierendonck (NED)
1998 David Hall (AUS)	Daniela Di Toro (AUS)
1999 Stephen Welch (USA)	Daniela Di Toro (AUS)
2000 David Hall (AUS)	Esther Vergeer (NED)

Davis Cup by NEC

Nick Imison

After all the excitement generated by its Centenary celebrations, the 2000 Davis Cup by NEC had a lot to live up to. A record 136 nations took part in the event, but from the moment the draw had been made, it was Spain's possible date with destiny that dominated the competition. And the team didn't disappoint, defeating Australia 3–1 in front of a fanatical home crowd in Barcelona to become only the 10th nation to capture the Davis Cup crown.

Spain first entered the competition in 1921 and had reached the Final on two previous occasions, losing both times to Australia away on grass courts. Although Australia were to be their opponents in the Final again in 2000, crucially this time the contest was to be played at home on the nation's favourite surface of clay.

The tie had been billed as the biggest sporting event in Spain since the 1992 Barcelona Olympics and was fittingly held at a former Olympic venue, the Palau Sant Jordi. With King Juan Carlos and Queen Sofia in attendance, it was as if the whole of Spain, not just the majority of the 14,500 spectators, was getting behind their team.

With three singles players on the Spanish team, there was much speculation as to who would be chosen to play singles on the opening day. However, it was still a shock when Albert Costa and Juan Carlos Ferrero were nominated, leaving their number one Alex Corretja to partner Juan Balcells in Saturday's doubles.

The plan looked to have backfired when 19-year-old Lleyton Hewitt came back from two-sets-to-one down to defeat Costa 3–6 6–1 2–6 6–4 6–4 in a titanic struggle lasting four hours and 10 minutes. The pressure was then on Final debutante Ferrero, who was leading Patrick Rafter 6–7 7–6 6–2 3–1, when the Australian was forced to retire with cramp. Rafter, who started to have treatment at the end of the third set, was at a loss for an explanation, though his captain John Newcombe later put it down to the tension of sitting in the locker room.

The Australians were hopeful of victory in doubles, but Balcells and Corretja combined

The winning Spanish team: (l to r) Javier Duarte (capt.), Albert Costa, Juan Balcells, Juan Carlos Ferrero, Alex Corretja, who played magnificently to keep their date with destiny. (Ron Angle)

Australia's team that failed to retain the trophy (l to r: John Newcombe (Capt.), Lleyton Hewitt, Pat Rafter, Sandon Stolle and Mark Woodforde) had to endure over-enthusiastic support from crowd and team bench that Capt. Newcombe considered at times to be unsporting. (Ron Angle)

superbly to defeat Sandon Stolle and Mark Woodforde 6–4 6–4 6–4, a disappointing end to Woodforde's 16-year career. Wisely concentrating their firepower on Stolle, the Spaniards fought off a 2–4 second set deficit for their third win in four outings this year.

Spanish captain Javier Duarte substituted Corretja for Costa in Sunday's reverse singles for a possible championship decider against Rafter. However, the final match never took place, after 20-year-old Ferrero emerged as the hero of the weekend with his 6–2 7–6 4–6 6–4 victory over Hewitt. In another epic encounter lasting three hours and 36 minutes, Ferrero clinched the crucial second set from 1–3 down, before breaking his opponent in the final game for victory.

Amidst wild celebrations on court afterwards, Duarte said: 'I think today, this title, is the summary of everything. It's the best ever generation of Spanish players, not only these four, but everybody. I also want to underline that they are very young.'

Newcombe, retiring from the captaincy after seven years, responded: 'We tried our best, but in the end they were just too good. Lleyton's two singles matches were what sport's all about: two guys just going at one another. Today was something special because we saw two of the future people of the world of tennis playing in that sort of match.'

Spain had a surprisingly easy route to the Final, although the fact that they never left home soil played its part. In the opening round they defeated Italy 4–1 in Murcia, building up a winning 3–0 lead for the loss of a single set. Costa and Corretja enjoyed easy singles victories, before Corretja partnered Balcells to a rare Spanish doubles win.

Spain faced a potentially tough quarter-final with Russia in Malaga, but were again convincing 4–1 winners. Yevgeny Kafelnikov and Marat Safin won a hard fought doubles rubber, but offered little resistance in singles. Kafelnikov, struggling to find form and motivation, suffered straight set defeats to both Ferrero and Costa, after Safin had lost the opening rubber in four sets to Corretja.

Spain's semi-final opponents, the United States, had already made a couple of inspired comebacks under their new captain John McEnroe. Their first round opponents Zimbabwe built up a 2–1 lead in Harare, before Andre Agassi levelled the match with a straight sets victory over Byron Black. Davis Cup first-timer Chris Woodruff, outplayed by Byron on the opening day, then played the match of his life to defeat his brother Wayne in four sets to seal the US triumph. Against the Czech Republic in the quarter-finals in Los Angeles, the USA again trailed 1–2, after a shock defeat for Pete Sampras by Jiri Novak on day one. Straight sets victories for Andre Agassi and Sampras in Sunday's reverse singles spared US embarrassment.

However, there was to be no fairy tale comeback in the semi-final where, without Agassi or Sampras, the USA were whitewashed 5–0 by Spain in Santander. Costa outplayed Todd Martin in straight sets, before Corretja recovered from a first set drubbing to see off Jan-Michael Gambill in four. Balcells and Corretja wrapped up the tie with victory over Martin and Woodruff, although the Americans did extend the match to five sets.

Santander was also the venue for John McEnroe's last match as US captain. McEnroe went on to announce his retirement from the position at the end of the year. Brother Patrick will fill his shoes in 2001.

Australia meanwhile enjoyed a bumpier route into the Final, having been fortunate to defeat Switzerland 3–2 in their first round encounter in Zurich. The host nation took a 2–1 lead after teenager Roger Federer defeated Mark Philippoussis and then partnered Lorenzo Manta to a doubles victory. Hewitt restored equality in a four–set victory over Federer, before Philippoussis defeated George Bastl in a five-set thriller.

Australia went on to defeat Germany 3–2 in the quarter-finals in Adelaide, although they had to win two five set marathons in building up a winning 3–0 lead. Wayne Arthurs defeated David Prinosil 11–9 in the fifth set, before Rafter and Woodforde overcame Marc-Kevin Goellner and Prinosil 10–8 in the final set of the doubles to seal Australia's victory.

Gustavo Kuerten had inspired Brazil to only their second Davis Cup semi-final with a 4–1 victory over 1999 finalists France in the opening round, then a 3–2 triumph over the Slovak Republic. Both wins had been achieved at home on clay, where the atmosphere is always intimidating for away teams. Grass courts proved a different prospect, and Australia had few problems defeating Brazil 5–0 in Brisbane to secure their place in the Final. Rafter and Hewitt scored straight sets victories over Kuerten and Fernando Meligeni respectively, but the doubles pairing of Stolle and Woodforde needed five sets to see off the challenge of Kuerten and Jaime Oncins.

The World Group Qualifying Round saw Ecuador and Morocco qualify for the World Group for the first time. Giovanni Lapentti, the 17-year-old brother of Nicolas, was the hero as Ecuador defeated Great Britain 3–2 at Wimbledon. Italy meanwhile was relegated from the World Group for the first time after being beaten 4–1 at home by Belgium, for whom the Rochus brothers, Christophe and Olivier, made a vital contribution.

2000 DAVIS CUP BY NEC

WORLD GROUP

FIRST ROUND: 4–6 February – USA d. Zimbabwe 3–2, Harare ZIM; Hard (I): Andre Agassi (USA) d. Wayne Black (ZIM) 7–5 6–3 7–5; Byron Black (ZIM) d. Chris Woodruff (USA) 7–6(2) 6–3 6–2; Wayne Black/Kevin Ullyett (ZIM) d. Rick Leach/Alex O'Brien (USA) 7–6(4) 5–7 0–6 7–5 7–5; Andre Agassi (USA) d. Byron Black (ZIM) 6–2 6–3 7–6(4); Chris Woodruff (USA) d. Wayne Black (ZIM) 6–3 6–7(2) 6–2 6–4. **Czech Republic d. Great Britain 4–1, Ostrava CZE; Clay (I):** Tim Henman (GBR) d. Slava Dosedel (CZE) 6–7(4) 5–7 6–1 7–5 6–3; Jiri Novak (CZE) d. Jamie Delgado (GBR) 6–4 7–6(4) 6–3; Jiri Novak/David Rikl (CZE) d. Neil Broad/Tim Henman (GBR) 7–6(4) 6–4 6–7(4) 6–2; Jiri Novak (CZE) d. Tim Henman (GBR) 6–4 6–2 6–2; Bohdan Ulihrach (CZE) d. Jamie Delgado (GBR) 5–7 7–5 6–4. **Spain d. Italy 4–1, Murcia ESP; Clay (O):** Albert Costa (ESP) d. Davide Sanguinetti (ITA) 6–4 6–4 6–2; Alex Corretja (ESP) d. Andrea Gaudenzi (ITA) 4–6 6–1 6–1 6–1; Juan Balcells/Alex Corretja (ESP) d. Andrea Gaudenzi/Diego Nargiso (ITA) 6–3 6–4 6–1; Andrea Gaudenzi (ITA) d. Albert Costa (ESP) 5–7 7–5 6–4; Francisco Clavet (ESP) d. Vincenzo Santopadre (ITA) 6–7(5) 6–1 6–3. **Russia d. Belgium 4–1, Moscow RUS; Carpet (I):** Yevgeny Kafelnikov (RUS) d. Filip Dewulf (BEL) 6–7(3) 6–4 7–5 6–2; Marat Safin (RUS) d. Christophe Rochus (BEL) 7–5 3–6 6–2 6–4; Andrei Cherkasov/Marat Safin (RUS) d. Christophe Rochus/Olivier Rochus (BEL) 4–6 7–6(2) 1–6 6–1 6–3; Mikhail Youzhny (RUS) d. Olivier Rochus (BEL) 7–6(6) 6–2; Filip Dewulf (BEL) d. Andrei Cherkasov (RUS) 6–0 4–6 6–1. **Slovak Republic d. Austria 3–2, Bratislava SVK; Carpet (I):** Karol Kucera (SVK) d. Markus Hipfl (AUT) 6–2 6–3 6–3; Dominik Hrbaty (SVK) d. Stefan Koubek (AUT) 6–4 6–4 6–4; Dominik Hrbaty/Karol Kucera (SVK) d. Julian Knowle/Alexander Peya (AUT) 6–4 6–3 6–4; Stefan Koubek (AUT) d. Jan Kroslak (SVK) 6–3 6–2; Markus Hipfl (AUT) d. Ladislav Svarc (SVK) 6–2 6–4. **Brazil d. France 4–1, Florianopolis BRA; Clay (O):** Fernando Meligeni (BRA) d. Cedric Pioline (FRA) 7–5 5–7 4–6 6–1 6–4; Gustavo Kuerten (BRA) d. Jerome Golmard (FRA) 6–3 3–6 6–3 6–2; Gustavo Kuerten/Jaime Oncins (BRA) d. Nicolas Escude/Cedric Pioline (FRA) 6–4 6–4 6–4; Nicolas Escude (FRA) d. Gustavo Kuerten (BRA) 6–2 7–6(3); Francisco Costa (BRA) d. Arnaud Clement (FRA) 7–6(5) 5–7 6–2. **Germany d. Netherlands 4–1, Leipzig GER; Carpet (I):** Tommy Haas (GER) d. John Van Lottum (NED) 4–6 7–6(4) 6–3 6–2; Sjeng Schalken (NED) d. Rainer Schuttler (GER) 3–6 7–6(2) 6–1 6–0; Marc-Kevin Goellner/David Prinosil (GER) d. Paul Haarhuis/Jan Siemerink (NED) 4–6 6–3 7–6(3) 6–3, Tommy Haas (GER) d. Sjeng Schalken (NED) 6–2 6–2 6–3; David Prinosil (GER) d. John Van Lottum (NED) 6–3 6–3.

Australia d. Switzerland 3–2, Zurich SUI; Hard (I): Lleyton Hewitt (AUS) d. George Bastl (SUI) 4–6 6–3 6–2 6–4; Roger Federer (SUI) d. Mark Philippoussis (AUS) 6–4 7–6(3) 4–6 6–4; Roger Federer/Lorenzo Manta (SUI) d. Wayne Arthurs/Sandon Stolle (AUS) 3–6 6–3 6–4 7–6(4); Lleyton Hewitt (AUS) d. Roger Federer (SUI) 6–2 3–6 7–6(2) 6–1; Mark Philippoussis (AUS) d. George Bastl (SUI) 6–7(3) 6–4 3–6 6–3 6–4.

SECOND ROUND: 7–9 April – USA d. Czech Republic 3–2, Inglewood, CA, USA; Carpet (I): Jiri Novak (CZE) d. Pete Sampras (USA) 7–6(1) 6–3 6–2; Andre Agassi (USA) d. Slava Dosedel (CZE) 6–3 6–3 6–3; Jiri Novak/David Rikl (CZE) d. Alex O'Brien/Jared Palmer (USA) 7–5 6–4 6–4; Andre Agassi (USA) d. Jiri Novak (CZE) 6–3 6–3 6–1; Pete Sampras (USA) d. Slava Dosedel (CZE) 6–4 6–4 7–6(2). **Spain d. Russia 4–1, Malaga ESP; Clay (O):** Alex Corretja (ESP) d. Marat Safin (RUS) 6–4 6–3 5–7 6–1; Juan Carlos Ferrero (ESP) d. Yevgeny Kafelnikov (RUS) 6–2 6–2 6–2; Yevgeny Kafelnikov/Marat Safin (RUS) d. Juan Balcells/Alex Corretja (ESP) 7–6(4) 2–6 7–6(3) 6–4; Albert Costa (ESP) d. Yevgeny Kafelnikov (RUS) 6–0 6–3 6–0; Juan Carlos Ferrero (ESP) d. Marat Safin (RUS) 6–0 6–3. **Brazil d. Slovak Republic 3–2, Rio de Janeiro BRA; Clay (O):** Dominik Hrbaty (SVK) d. Fernando Meligeni (BRA) 6–1 7–5 6–2; Gustavo Kuerten (BRA) d. Karol Kucera (SVK) 2–6 6–3 4–6 7–5 6–1; Gustavo Kuerten/Jaime Oncins (BRA) d. Dominik Hrbaty/Karol Kucera (SVK) 6–3 2–6 6–2 6–3; Dominik Hrbaty (SVK) d. Gustavo Kuerten (BRA) 7–5 6–4 7–6(5); Fernando Meligeni (BRA) d. Karol Kucera (SVK) 5–7 7–6(6) 6–2 6–4. **Australia d. Germany 3–2, Adelaide AUS; Grass (O):** Lleyton Hewitt (AUS) d. Michael Kohlmann (GER) 6–1 6–1 6–2; Wayne Arthurs (AUS) d. David Prinosil (GER) 7–6(4) 3–6 7–6(3) 6–7(7) 11–9; Patrick Rafter/Mark Woodforde (AUS) d. Marc-Kevin Goellner/David Prinosil (GER) 6–3 6–2 2–6 6–7(4) 10–8; Rainer Schuttler (GER) d. Lleyton Hewitt (AUS) 2–6 6–3 6–4; Michael Kohlmann (GER) d. Wayne Arthurs (AUS) 7–5 7–6(5).

SEMI-FINALS: 14–16 July – Australia d. Brazil 5–0, Brisbane AUS; Grass (O): Patrick Rafter (AUS) d. Gustavo Kuerten (BRA) 6–3 6–2 6–3; Lleyton Hewitt (AUS) d. Fernando Meligeni (BRA) 6–4 6–2 6–3; Sandon Stolle/Mark Woodforde (AUS) d. Gustavo Kuerten/Jaime Oncins (BRA) 6–7(3) 6–4 3–6 6–3 6–4; Lleyton Hewitt (AUS) d. Andre Sa (BRA) 6–4 6–1; Patrick Rafter (AUS) d. Fernando Meligeni (BRA) 6–3 6–4. **21–23 July Spain d. USA 5–0, Santander ESP; Clay (O):** Albert Costa (ESP) d. Todd Martin (USA) 6–4 6–4 6–4; Alex Corretja (ESP) d. Jan Michael Gambill (USA) 1–6 6–3 6–4 6–4; Juan Balcells/Alex Corretja (ESP) d. Todd Martin/Chris Woodruff (USA) 7–6(6) 2–6 6–3 6–7(5) 6–3; Juan Carlos Ferrero (ESP) d. Vince Spadea (USA) 4–6 6–1 6–4; Juan Balcells (ESP) d. Jan Michael Gambill (USA) 1–6 7–6(2) 6–4.

FINAL: 8–10 December – Spain d. Australia 3–1, Barcelona ESP; Clay (I): Lleyton Hewitt (AUS) d. Albert Costa (ESP) 3–6 6–1 2–6 6–4 6–4; Juan Carlos Ferrero (ESP) d. Patrick Rafter (AUS) 6–7(4) 7–6(2) 6–2 3–1 ret; Juan Balcells/Alex Corretja (ESP) d. Sandon Stolle/Mark Woodforde (AUS) 6–4 6–4 6–4; Juan Carlos Ferrero (ESP) d. Lleyton Hewitt (AUS) 6–2 7–6(5) 4–6 6–4; Alex Corretja (ESP) v Patrick Rafter (AUS) – not played.

QUALIFYING ROUND FOR THE WORLD GROUP: 14–16 July – Ecuador d. Great Britain 3–2, London GBR; Grass (O): Nicolas Lapentti (ECU) d. Greg Rusedski (GBR) 6–3 6–7(3) 7–5 4–6 7–5; Tim Henman (GBR) d. Luis Morejon (ECU) 6–2 6–1 6–4; Giovanni Lapentti/Nicolas Lapentti (ECU) d. Tim Henman/Arvind Parmar (GBR) 6–3 7–5 6–3; Tim Henman (GBR) d. Nicolas Lapentti (ECU) 6–1 6–4 6–4; Giovanni Lapentti (ECU) d. Arvind Parmar (GBR) 4–6 3–6 6–1 6–3 6–3. **Romania d. Zimbabwe 3–2, Harare ZIM; Hard (I):** Byron Black (ZIM) d. Razvan Sabau (ROM) 6–2 4–6 7–5 6–2; Andrei Pavel (ROM) d. Kevin Ullyett (ZIM) 6–4 7–6(2) 6–2; Andrei Pavel/Gabriel Trifu (ROM) d. Wayne Black/Kevin Ullyett (ZIM) 7–5 6–2 7–6(2); Andrei Pavel (ROM) d. Byron Black (ZIM) 6–2 6–4 6–1; Wayne Black (ZIM) d. Razvan Sabau (ROM) 6–3 7–6(2). **Netherlands d. Uzbekistan 4–1, Tashkent UZB; Clay (O):** Richard Krajicek (NED) d. Oleg Ogorodov (UZB) 6–4 6–3 6–4; Sjeng Schalken (NED) d. Vadim Kutsenko (UZB) 6–2 6–1 6–4; Paul Haarhuis/Sjeng Schalken (NED) d. Oleg Ogorodov/Dmitri Tomashevich (UZB) 6–3 6–1 7–6(0); Paul Haarhuis (NED) d. Vadim Kutsenko (UZB) 6–1 6–2; Oleg Ogorodov (UZB) d. Sjeng Schalken (NED) 6–4 6–3. **21–23 July – France d. Austria 5–0, Rennes FRA; Carpet (I):** Nicolas Escude (FRA) d. Jurgen Melzer (AUT) 6–2 6–4 6–2; Sebastien Grosjean (FRA) d. Stefan Koubek (AUT) 6–3 6–2 6–3; Olivier Delaitre/Nicolas Escude (FRA) d. Julian Knowle/Thomas Strengberger (AUT) 6–4 6–3 6–3; Jerome Golmard (FRA) d. Stefan Koubek (AUT) 6–4 6–4; Sebastien Grosjean (FRA) d. Jurgen Melzer (AUT) 3–6 6–3 7–5. **Sweden d. India 5–0, Bastad SWE; Clay (O):** Andreas Vinciguerra (SWE) d. Harsh Mankad (IND) 6–3 6–1 6–1; Mikael Tillstrom (SWE) d. Prahlad Srinath (IND) 6–2 6–0 6–1; Nicklas Kulti/Mikael Tillstrom (SWE) d. Mahesh Bhupathi/Fazaluddin Syed (IND) 6–3 3–6 4–6 6–3 6–3; Andreas Vinciguerra (SWE) d. Prahlad Srinath (IND) 6–2 6–1; Mikael Tillstrom (SWE) d. Harsh Mankad (IND) 6–3 6–0. **Belgium d. Italy 4–1, Mestre Venezia ITA; Clay (O):** Olivier Rochus (BEL) d. Andrea Gaudenzi (ITA) 6–2 7–5 6–3; Davide Sanguinetti (ITA) d. Filip Dewulf (BEL) 1–6 7–6(5) 7–5 6–0; Christophe Rochus/Tom Van Houdt (BEL) d. Andrea Gaudenzi/Diego Nargiso (ITA) 6–4 6–4 6–4; Christophe Rochus (BEL) d. Davide Sanguinetti (ITA) 6–2 7–6 6–7(6) 1–6 7–5; Filip Dewulf (BEL) d. Renzo Furlan (ITA) 7–5 6–2. **Switzerland d. Belarus 5–0, St Gallen SUI; Hard (I):** George Bastl (SUI) d. Max Mirnyi (BLR) 6–4 7–6(4) 6–2; Roger Federer (SUI) d. Vladimir Voltchkov (BLR) 4–6 7–5 7–6(1) 5–7 6–2; Roger Federer/Lorenzo Manta (SUI) d. Max Mirnyi/Vladimir Voltchkov (BLR) 2–6 7–6(5) 7–5 7–6(4); Michel Kratochvil (SUI) d. Alexander Shvec (BLR) 6–0 6–0; Lorenzo Manta (SUI) d. Vassili Kajera (BLR) 7–6(0) 6–1.

The winners of these seven ties, along with Morocco, qualified for the World Group in 2001.
The losers remained in, or were relegated to, their respective Group I Zones in 2001.

GROUP I
EURO/AFRICAN ZONE

FIRST ROUND: 4–6 February – *Ukraine d. Portugal 4–1, Kiev UKR; Carpet (I):* Andrey Dernovskiy (UKR) d. Joao Cunha-Silva (POR) 7–6(6) 6–4 3–6 3–6 6–4; Andrei Medvedev (UKR) d. Bernardo Mota (POR) 6–1 6–3 4–6 6–2; Andrei Medvedev/Andrei Rybalko (UKR) d. Emanuel Couto/Joao Cunha-Silva (POR) 7–5 6–4 6–4; Orest Tereshchuk (UKR) d. Joao Cunha-Silva (POR) 6–3 6–4; Bernardo Mota (POR) d. Andrey Dernovskiy (UKR) 7–5 3–6 7–6(5).

SECOND ROUND: 7–9 April – *Sweden d. Finland 3–2, Helsinki FIN; Hard (I):* Magnus Norman (SWE) d. Ville Liukko (FIN) 6–3 4–6 6–1 7–6(7); Tuomas Ketola (FIN) d. Mikael Tillstrom (SWE) 6–3 3–6 4–6 6–4 6–3; Nicklas Kulti/Mikael Tillstrom (SWE) d. Tuomas Ketola/Ville Liukko (FIN) 6–1 6–1 6–4; Magnus Norman (SWE) d. Tuomas Ketola (FIN) 6–2 6–4 6–1; Jarkko Nieminen (FIN) d. Mikael Tillstrom (SWE) 6–1 6–4. *Romania d. Hungary 3–2, Bucharest HUN; Hard (I):* Andrei Pavel (ROM) d. Gergely Kisgyorgy (HUN) 6–2 7–6(5) 5–7 6–7(8) 6–2; Attila Savolt (HUN) d. Razvan Sabau (ROM) 6–4 6–3 6–2; Gabor Koves/Attila Savolt (HUN) d. Dinu Pescariu/Gabriel Trifu (ROM) 6–1 5–7 6–3 3–6 7–5; Andrei Pavel (ROM) d. Attila Savolt (HUN) 6–4 1–6 6–4 6–2; Dinu Pescariu (ROM) d. Gergely Kisgyorgy (HUN) 6–3 7–5 6–7(3) 6–4. *Belarus d. South Africa 4–1, Belarus BLR; Carpet (I):* Vladimir Voltchkov (BLR) d. Neville Godwin (RSA) 6–2 7–6(2) 7–5; Max Mirnyi (BLR) d. Jeff Coetzee (RSA) 6–3 6–2 6–4; David Adams/John-Laffnie De Jager (RSA) d. Sergei Samoseiko/Alexander Shvec (BLR) 7–6(2) 6–1 6–3; Max Mirnyi (BLR) d. Neville Godwin (RSA) 6–4 6–3 6–4; Vladimir Voltchkov (BLR) d. Jeff Coetzee (RSA) 6–1 6–2. *Morocco d. Ukraine 3–2, Casablanca MAR; Clay (O):* Andrei Medvedev (UKR) d. Hicham Arazi (MAR) 6–4 1–6 6–2 3–6 7–5; Younes El Aynaoui (MAR) d. Andrey Dernovskiy (UKR) 6–2 6–2 6–3; Karim Alami/Hicham Arazi (MAR) d. Andrei Medvedev/Andrei Rybalko (UKR) 3–6 6–1 7–5 6–3; Andrei Medvedev (UKR) d. Younes El Aynaoui (MAR) 7–5 7–5 6–2; Hicham Arazi (MAR) d. Orest Tereshchuk (UKR) 6–4 6–0 6–1.

Sweden, Romania, Belarus and Morocco qualified for World Group Qualifying Round.

3RD ROUND/PLAYOFF: 6–8 October – *Finland d. Hungary 4–1, Helsinki FIN; Carpet (I):* Ville Liukko (FIN) d. Gergely Kisgyorgy (HUN) 6–1 6–3 6–3; Jarkko Nieminen (FIN) d. Attila Savolt (HUN) 6–2 1–6 7–6(5) 6–0; Gabor Koves/Attila Savolt (HUN) d. Tuomas Ketola/Ville Liukko (FIN) 4–6 7–6(5) 6–4 7–5; Ville Liukko (FIN) d. Attila Savolt (HUN) 2–6 5–7 6–4 6–4 6–4; Jarkko Nieminen (FIN) d. Gergely Kisgyorgy (HUN) 6–3 6–2. *Portugal d. South Africa 3–2, Maia POR; Clay (O):* Bernardo Mota (POR) d. Justin Bower (RSA) 6–4 6–1 7–5; Wayne Ferreira (RSA) d. Emanuel Couto (POR) 6–1 6–4 6–4; Emanuel Couto/Nuno Marques (POR) d. John-Laffnie De Jager/Piet Norval (RSA) 4–6 7–6(7) 6–3 3–6 8–6; Wayne Ferreira (RSA) d. Bernardo Mota (POR) 6–3 6–2 4–6 6–3; Emanuel Couto (POR) d. Justin Bower (RSA) 7–6(4) 4–6 4–6 7–6(6) 6–4.

Hungary and South Africa relegated to Euro/African Zone Group II in 2001.

AMERICAN ZONE

FIRST ROUND: 4–6 February – *Chile d. Canada 4–1, Vina Del Mar CHI; Clay (O):* Fernando Gonzalez (CHI) d. Sebastien Lareau (CAN) 2–6 6–3 1–6 6–2 6–1; Nicolas Massu (CHI) d. Simon Larose (CAN) 6–0 6–7(2) 3–1 ret; Fernando Gonzalez/Nicolas Massu (CHI) d. Sebastien Lareau/Jocelyn Robichaud (CAN) 6–4 6–4 2–6 6–2; Frederic Niemeyer (CAN) d. Adrian Garcia (CHI) 4–6 6–1 7–6(6); Hermes Gamonal (CHI) d. Simon Larose (CAN) 6–2 7–5. *Ecuador d. Colombia 5–0, Bogota COL; Clay (O):* Luis Morejon (ECU) d. Eduardo Rincon (COL) 2–6 7–5 7–5 2–6 6–0; Nicolas Lapentti (ECU) d. Pablo Gonzalez (COL) 4–6 6–4 7–6(12) 7–6(3); Andres Gomez/Nicolas Lapentti (ECU) d. Pablo Gonzalez/Ruben Torres (COL) 6–2 6–4 6–0; Giovanni Lapentti (ECU) d. Ruben Torres (COL) 7–6(2) 6–1; Luis Morejon (ECU) d. Pablo Gonzalez (COL) 6–7(7) 6–4 7–6(4). *Peru d. Bahamas 4–1, Lima PER; Clay (O):* Americo Venero (PER) d. Mark Knowles (BAH) 6–4 6–4 3–6 3–1 ret; Luis Horna (PER) d. Mark Merklein (BAH) 6–4 6–4 6–4; Mark Knowles/Mark Merklein (BAH) d. Luis Horna/Americo Venero (PER) 6–3 6–2 4–2 ret; Luis Horna (PER) d. Mark Knowles (BAH) 6–2 2–6 6–4 3–1 ret; Ivan Miranda (PER) d. Dentry Mortimer (BAH) 6–1 6–0.

SECOND ROUND: 7–9 April – *Chile d. Argentina 5–0, Santiago CHI; Hard (I):* Marcelo Rios (CHI) d. Hernan Gumy (ARG) 6–4 6–3 4–6 6–1; Mariano Zabaleta (ARG) led Nicolas Massu (CHI) 7–5 2–6 7–6(1) 3–1 – match suspended. Argentina subsequently withdrew and the tie was awarded to Chile. *Ecuador d. Peru 3–2, Lima PER; Clay (O):* Luis Horna (PER) d. Giovanni Lapentti (ECU) 2–6 6–3 6–4 6–1; Nicolas Lapentti (ECU) d. Ivan Miranda (PER) 6–1 6–2 6–2; Luis Horna/Americo Venero (PER) d. Andres Gomez/Nicolas Lapentti (ECU) 6–2 6–2 2–6 7–6(3) 7–5; Nicolas Lapentti (ECU) d. Luis Horna (PER) 4–6 2–6 7–5 6–7(2) 6–3; Luis Morejon (ECU) d. Americo Venero (PER) 6–3 3–6 6–2 6–1.

Chile and Ecuador qualified for World Group Qualifying Round.

SECOND ROUND/PLAYOFF: 21–23 July – *Canada d. Argentina 4–1, Montreal, Hard (O):* Daniel Nestor (CAN) d. Juan Ignacio Chela (ARG) 6–3 7–6(3) 6–3; Agustin Calleri (ARG) d. Sebastien Lareau (CAN) 6–3 6–2 6–3; Sebastien Lareau/Daniel Nestor (CAN) d. Martin Garcia/Martin Rodriguez (ARG) 6–2 6–1 6–3; Sebastien Lareau (CAN) d. Juan Ignacio Chela (ARG) 6–3 6–4 4–6 2–6 6–4; Daniel Nestor (CAN) d. Agustin Calleri (ARG) 6 3 6 2. *Bahamas d. Colombia 3–2, Nassau BAH; Hard (O):* Carlos Drada (COL) d. Mark Knowles (BAH) 6–7(5) 5–7 2–2 (30-30) ret; Mark Merklein (BAH) d. Eduardo Rincon (COL) 6 4 6 4 6 4; Mark Knowles/Mark

Merklein (BAH) d. Carlos Drada/Pablo Gonzalez (COL) 6–1 6–4 6–2; Eduardo Rincon (COL) d. Roger Smith (BAH) 7–6(1) 4–6 1–6 6–1 6–1; Mark Merklein (BAH) d. Pablo Gonzalez (COL) 7–5 7–6(4) 6–3.

3RD ROUND/PLAYOFF: 6–8 October – *Argentina d. Colombia 4–1, Bogota COL; Clay (O):* Franco Squillari (ARG) d. Eduardo Rincon (COL) 6–4 6–2 6–2; Mariano Puerta (ARG) d. Pablo Gonzalez (COL) 6–0 6–2 3–6 6–0; Martin Garcia/Mariano Puerta (ARG) d. Michael Quintero/Pablo Gonzalez (COL) 6–4 7–5 6–2; Agustin Calleri (ARG) d. Pablo Gonzalez (COL) 6–3 6–1; Michael Quintero (COL) d. Martin Garcia (ARG) 7–5 2–6 6–3.

Colombia relegated to American Zone Group II in 2001.

ASIA/OCEANIA ZONE

FIRST ROUND: 28–30 January – *Uzbekistan d. China PR 3–0, Kun Ming CHN; Hard (O):* Vadim Kutsenko (UZB) d. Ben-Qiang Zhu (CHN) 6–4 6–7(5) 6–3 6–7(2) 6–3; Oleg Ogorodov (UZB) d. Yu Zhang (CHN) 7–6(5) 6–3 6–4; Oleg Ogorodov/Dmitri Tomashevich (UZB) d. Ran Xu/Jing-Zhu Yang (CHN) 7–6(1) 7–6(1) 6–3; reverse singles not played – bad weather. **4–6 February – *New Zealand d. Thailand 4–1, Timaru NZL; Hard (O):*** Mark Nielsen (NZL) d. Danai Udomchoke (THA) 6–1 6–1 6–3; Alistair Hunt (NZL) d. Paradorn Srichaphan (THA) 7–6(6) 7–6(7) 3–6 6–1; James Greenhalgh/Alistair Hunt (NZL) d. Ekkarin Pisuth-Arnonth/Wittaya Samrej (THA) 6–1 6–0 6–2; Mark Nielsen (NZL) d. Ekkarin Pisuth-Arnonth (THA) 6–2 7–5; Danai Udomchoke (THA) d. James Shortall (NZL) 6–7(4) 7–6(4) 6–1. **India d. Lebanon 3–2, Lucknow IND; Grass (O):** Leander Paes (IND) d. Ali Hamadeh (LIB) 6–4 7–5 7–6(3); Fazalludin Syed (IND) d. Jisham Zaatini (LIB) 6–4 3–6 7–5 7–6(3); Ali Hamadeh/Jisham Zaatini (LIB) d. Leander Paes/Fazalludin Syed (IND) 6–7(2) 7–6(3) 4–6 6–3 6–4; Leander Paes (IND) d. Jisham Zaatini (LIB) 6–3 6–1 6–4; Ali Hamadeh (LIB) d. Fazalludin Syed (IND) 2–6 7–5 6–1. **Korea d. Japan 3–2, Kashima JPN; Carpet (I):** Hyung-Taik Lee (KOR) d. Yaoki Ishii (JPN) 4–6 4–6 6–2 6–1 1–08; Gouichi Motomura (JPN) d. Yong-Il Yoon (KOR) 6–3 4–6 6–4 2–6 6–3; Hyung-Taik Lee/Yong-Il Yoon (KOR) d. Satoshi Iwabuchi/Thomas Shimada (JPN) 7–6(4) 6–4 3–6 6–2; Hyung-Taik Lee (KOR) d. Gouichi Motomura (JPN) 7–5 6–4 7–5; Yaoki Ishii (JPN) d. Hee-Sung Chung (KOR) 6–4 6–4.

SECOND ROUND: 7–9 April – *Uzbekistan d. New Zealand 4–1, Tashkent UZB; Hard (I):* Vadim Kutsenko (UZB) d. Mark Nielsen (NZL) 7–6(3) 6–3 6–2; Oleg Ogorodov (UZB) d. Alistair Hunt (NZL) 7–6(2) 6–2 6–7(4) 7–5; Oleg Ogorodov/Dmitri Tomashevich (UZB) d. James Greenhalgh/Alistair Hunt (NZL) 7–5 7–6(5) 6–4; Mark Nielsen (NZL) d. Oleg Ogorodov (UZB) 6–2 1–6 7–5; Dmitri Mazur (UZB) d. James Greenhalgh (NZL) 7–6(2) 6–4. **India d. Korea 4–1, New Delhi IND; Grass (O):** Leander Paes (IND) d. Yong-Il Yoon (KOR) 6–4 6–2 6–3; Hyung-Taik Lee (KOR) d. Fazaluddin Syed (IND) 6–4 7–5 6–2; Leander Paes/Vishal Uppal (IND) d. Hyung-Taik Lee/Yong-Il Yoon (KOR) 6–7(5) 6–4 6–4 7–6(4); Leander Paes (IND) d. Hyung-Taik Lee (KOR) 6–1 3–6 7–6(3) 6–4; Fazaluddin Syed (IND) d. Seung-Hun Lee (KOR) 6–0 6–7(2) 6–2.

Uzbekistan and India qualified for World Group Qualifying Round.

SECOND ROUND/PLAYOFF: 7–9 April – *Thailand d. China PR 4–1, Tian Jin CHN; Hard (I):* Paradorn Srichaphan (THA) d. Yu Zhang (CHN) 6–3 6–2 6–1; Ben-Qiang Zhu (CHN) d. Danai Udomchoke (THA) 7–6(5) 6–2 6–0; Paradorn Srichaphan/Danai Udomchoke (THA) d. Si Li/Ran Xu (CHN) 6–2 6–7(7) 2–6 6–3 6–4; Paradorn Srichaphan (THA) d. Ben-Qiang Zhu (CHN) 7–5 6–3 6–4; Danai Udomchoke (THA) d. Yu Zhang (CHN) 6–2 6–4. **Japan d. Lebanon 4–1, Yokohamashi JPN; Carpet (I):** Yaoki Ishii (JPN) d. Jicham Zaatini (LIB) 6–4 6–3 6–3; Gouichi Motomura (JPN) d. Ali Hamadeh (LIB) 6–3 6–3 6–1; Ali Hamadeh/Jicham Zaatini (LIB) d. Satoshi Iwabuchi/Thomas Shimada (JPN) 7–6(6) 6–4 6–4; Gouichi Motomura (JPN) d. Jicham Zaatini (LIB) 6–1 5–7 6–4 6–4; Yaoki Ishii (JPN) d. Ali Hamadeh (LIB) 6–2 6–4.

3RD ROUND/PLAYOFF: 6–8 Oct – *China PR d. Lebanon 3–2, Beirut LIB; Hard (I):* Jicham Zaatini (LIB) d. Yu Wang (CHN) 2–6 6–3 6–3 7–5; Ben-Qiang Zhu (CHN) d. Ali Hamadeh (LIB) 4–6 6–4 6–3 6–4; Ran Xu/Ben-Qiang Zhu (CHN) d. Ali Hamadeh/Jicham Zaatini (LIB) 3–6 7–6(9) 6–4 7–5; Ben-Qiang Zhu (CHN) d. Jicham Zaatini (LIB) 4–6 6–3 6–4 6–4; Ali Hamadeh (LIB) d. Yu Zhang (CHN) 7–6(6) 7–5.

Lebanon relegated to Asia/Oceania Zone Group II in 2001.

GROUP II

EURO/AFRICAN ZONE

FIRST ROUND: 28–30 April – *Croatia d. Latvia 5–0, Jurmala LAT; Carpet (I):* Goran Ivanisevic (CRO) d. Girts Dzelde (LAT) 6–1 6–4 6–4; Ivan Ljubicic (CRO) d. Andris Filimonovs (LAT) 7–6(0) 7–6(6) 6–4; Goran Ivanisevic/Ivan Ljubicic (CRO) d. Girts Dzelde/Andris Filimonovs (LAT) 6–4 3–6 6–3 6–2; Mario Ancic (CRO) d. Raimonds Sproga (LAT) 6–3 6–4; Lovro Zovko (CRO) d. Ivo Lagzdins (LAT) 6–3 6–4. **Ireland d. Luxembourg 3–2, Mondorf-les-Bains LUX; Clay (O):** Scott Barron (IRL) d. Mike Scheidweiler (LUX) 6–4 6–4 6–4; Gilles Muller (LUX) d. Peter Clarke (IRL) 6–4 7–5 7–5; Scott Barron/Owen Casey (IRL) d. Johny Goudenbour/Mike Scheidweiler (LUX) 6–3 6–3 6–4; Peter Clarke (IRL) d. Mike Scheidweiler (LUX) 6–4 5–7 3–6 7–5 6–2; Gilles Muller (LUX) d. Sean Cooper (IRL) 6–2 2–6 6–3. **Denmark d. Turkey 3–2, Tarabya TUR; Hard (O):** Frederik Fetterlein (DEN) d. Erhan Oral (TUR) 6–0 6–0; Kristian Pless (DEN) d. Efe Ustundag (TUR) 6–3 7–6(5) 6–1; Mustafa Azkara/Erhan Oral (TUR) d. Kristian Pless/Jonathan Printzlau (DEN) 6–4 7–6(4) 6–3; Kristian Pless (DEN) d. Erhan Oral (TUR) 6–2 6–1 6–4; Baris Ergun (TUR) d. Bob Borella (DEN) 6–7(5) 6–3 ret. **Cote d'Ivoire**

d. Lithuania 3–2, Siauliai LTU; Carpet (I): Claude N'Goran (CIV) d. Aivaras Balzekas (LTU) 6–3 6–2 6–2; Rolandas Murashka (LTU) d. Valentin Sanon (CIV) 7–6(4) 7–5 6–3; Ilou Lonfo/Claude N'Goran (CIV) d. Paulius Jurkenas/Rolandas Murashka (LTU) 6–2 6–7(5) 6–3 6–4; Aivaras Balzekas (LTU) d. Valentin Sanon (CIV) 7–5 6–3 6–4; Claude N'Goran (CIV) d. Rolandas Murashka (LTU) 7–6(3) 4–6 6–3 6–4. *Slovenia d. Egypt, Cairo EGY, Clay (O):* Karim Maamoun (EGY) d. Marko Tkalec (SLO) 3–6 7–6(5) 7–6(2) 6–7(5) 6–4; Andrej Kracman (SLO) d. Amr Ghoneim (EGY) 4–6 7–5 4–6 7–6(6) 8–6; Andrej Kracman/Marko Tkalec (SLO) d. Amr Ghoneim/Karim Maamoun (EGY) 6–1 6–3 6–1; Marko Tkalec (SLO) d. Amr Ghoneim (EGY) 6–7(1) 6–0 5–7 6–2 6–4; Karim Maamoun (EGY) d. Miha Gregorc (SLO) 3–6 6–3 6–4. *Poland d. Estonia 4–1, Bytom POL; Clay (O):* Rene Busch (EST) d. Bartlomiej Dabrowski (POL) 7–6(5) 2–6 6–4 6–0; Krystian Pfeiffer (POL) d. Mait Kunnap (EST) 6–3 6–7(6) 6–2 6–7(5) 6–1; Marcin Matkowski/Radoslav Nijaki (POL) d. Mait Kunnap/Alti Vakhal (EST) 6–2 7–6(8) 6–7(5) 6–4; Bartlomiej Dabrowski (POL) d. Alti Vakhal (EST) 6–2 6–3 6–0; Marcin Matkowski (POL) d. Rene Busch (EST) 6–2 3–6 6–1. *Greece d. Bulgaria 3–2, Sofia BUL; Clay (O):* Ivailo Traykov (BUL) d. Solon Peppas (GRE) 6–1 6–3 7–6(2); Orlin Stanoytchev (BUL) d. Vasilis Mazarakis (GRE) 6–2 1–6 6–3 6–2; Konstantinos Economidis/Tasos Vasiliadis (GRE) d. Ivailo Traykov/Orlin Stanoytchev (BUL) 3–6 7–6(1) 6–4 7–6(5); Solon Peppas (GRE) d. Orlin Stanoytchev (BUL) 6–1 3–6 6–1 6–2; Vasilis Mazarakis (GRE) d. Milen Velev (BUL) 7–6(5) 6–2 6–0. *Norway d. Israel 3–2, Oslo NOR; Clay (O):* Christian Ruud (NOR) d. Eyal Ran (ISR) 6–2 6–2 7–5; Harel Levy (ISR) d. Jan-Frode Andersen (NOR) 7–6(6) 6–3 6–4; Christian Ruud/Helge Koll (NOR) d. Noam Behr/Andy Ram (ISR) 6–4 1–6 6–2 7–6(5); Harel Levy (ISR) d. Christian Ruud (NOR) 4–6 7–6(5) 6–2 6–7(4) 6–1; Jan-Frode Andersen (NOR) d. Andy Ram (ISR) 6–4 6–1 7–5.

SECOND ROUND: 14–16 July – *Croatia d. Ireland 5–0, Dublin IRL; Artificial Grass (O):* Goran Ivanisevic (CRO) d. Owen Casey (IRL) 7–5 4–6 6–2 6–2; Mario Ancic (CRO) d. Scott Barron (IRL) 4–6 6–1 6–4 6–4; Goran Ivanisevic/Ivo Karlovic (CRO) d. Scott Barron/Owen Casey (IRL) 6–7(5) 6–2 6–1 6–1; Ivo Karlovic (CRO) d. Conor Niland (IRL) 4–6 6–3 6–4; Lovro Zovko (CRO) d. Owen Casey (IRL) 1–6 6–4 7–6(3). **21–23 July** *Cote d'Ivoire d. Denmark 3–2, Rungsted Kyst DEN; Clay (O):* Claude N'Goran (CIV) d. Kristian Pless (DEN) 7–6(4) 6–2 6–3; Valentin Sanon (CIV) d. Frederik Fetterlein (DEN) 6–0 4–6 6–2 6–3; Illou Lonfo/Claude N'Goran (CIV) d. Frederik Fetterlein/Kristian Pless (DEN) 6–4 1–6 6–2 6–3; Patrik Langvardt (DEN) d. Valentin Sanon (CIV) 7–5 6–0; Bob Borella (DEN) d. Illou Lonfo (CIV) 6–2 6–3. *Slovenia d. Poland 3–2, Szczecin POL; Clay (O):* Marko Tkalec (SLO) d. Bartlomiej Dabrowski (POL) 6–1 7–6(3) 7–6(1); Krystian Pfeiffer (POL) d. Andrej Kracman (SLO) 6–3 6–2 4–6 3–6 6–3; Krzysztof Kwinta/Marcin Matkowski (POL) d. Andrej Kracman/Marko Tkalec (SLO) 6–4 6–4 7–6(3); Marko Tkalec (SLO) d. Krystian Pfeiffer (POL) 7–5 6–4 6–4; Andrej Kracman (SLO) d. Bartlomiej Dabrowski (POL) 6–2 4–6 7–6(5) 6–2. *Greece d. Norway 4–1, Athens GRE; Clay (O):* Solon Peppas (GRE) d. Helge Koll (NOR) 6–4 6–4 6–3; Jan-Frode Andersen (NOR) d. Vassilis Mazarakis (GRE) 6–3 6–4 6–7(5) 2–6 6–4; Konstantinos Economidis/Taso Vasiliadis (GRE) d. Stian Boretti/Helge Koll (NOR) 6–3 6–1 6–3; Solon Peppas (GRE) d. Jan-Frode Andersen (NOR) 7–5 6–2 6–2; Konstantinos Economidis (GRE) d. Stian Boretti (NOR) 6–3 6–0.

3RD ROUND: 6–8 October – *Croatia d. Cote D'Ivoire 5–0, Rijeka CRO; Hard (I):* Goran Ivanisevic (CRO) d. Claude N'Goran (CIV) 6–4 6–4 6–3; Ivan Ljubicic (CRO) d. Valentin Sanon (CIV) 6–3 7–6(6) 6–3; Goran Ivanisevic/Ivo Karlovic (CRO) d. Ilou Lonfo/Claude N'Goran (CIV) 7–6(6) 6–4 6–7(5) 4–6 6–0; Mario Ancic (CRO) d. Valentin Sanon (CIV) 7–5 6–2; Ivo Karlovic (CRO) d. Claude N'Goran (CIV) 6–4 6–1. *Slovenia d. Greece 4–1, Athens GRE; Clay (O):* Marko Tkalec (SLO) d. Nicolas Rovas (GRE) 6–2 6–3 2–6 6–1; Solon Peppas (GRE) d. Andrej Kracman (SLO) 6–4 6–4 6–4; Andrej Kracman/Borut Urh (SLO) d. Konstantinos Economidis/Taso Vasiliadis (GRE) 2–6 6–4 7–5 6–3; Marko Tkalec (SLO) d. Solon Peppas (GRE) 7–5 6–2 7–6(2); Andrej Kracman (SLO) d. Konstantinos Economidis (GRE) 6–3 2–6 6–3.

Croatia and Slovenia promoted to Euro/African Zone Group I in 2001.

SECOND ROUND/PLAYOFF: 14–16 July – *Luxembourg d. Latvia 4–1, Mondorf-les-Bains LUX; Clay (O):* Gilles Muller (LUX) d. Girts Dzelde (LAT) 6–2 6–0 6–2; Pascal Schaul (LUX) d. Andris Filimonovs (LAT) 6–4 2–6 7–6(6) 7–6(3); Johny Goudenbour/Gilles Muller (LUX) d. Girts Dzelde/Andris Filimonovs (LAT) 6–3 6–3 6–7(9) 7–5; Raimonds Sproga (LAT) d. Sacha Thoma (LUX) 6–2 7–5; Pascal Schaul (LUX) d. Ivo Lagzdins (LAT) 6–3 5–7 6–2. *Turkey d. Lithuania 4–1, Izmir TUR; Hard (O):* Rolandas Muraska (LTU) d. Efe Ustundag (TUR) 7–5 6–0 6–4; Mustafa Azkara (TUR) d. Aivaras Balzekas (LTU) 4–6 6–7(5) 6–4 6–2 9–7; Mustafa Azkara/Erhan Oral (TUR) d. Paulius Jurkenas/Rolandas Muraska (LTU) 6–4 6–3 6–1; Efe Ustundag (TUR) d. Aivaras Balzekas (LTU) 4–6 6–4 6–7(5) 6–2 6–3; Baris Ergun (TUR) d. Rolandas Muraska (LTU) 3–6 6–4 7–6(7). *Estonia d. Egypt 5–0, Tallinn EST; Wood (I):* Gert Vilms (EST) d. Karim Maamoun (EGY) 7–6(3) 6–2 6–4; Andrei Luzgin (EST) d. Hisham Hemeda (EGY) 7–6(7) 7–5 6–2 6–2; Mait Kunnap/Alti Vahkal (EST) d. Hisham Hemeda/Marwan Zewar (EGY) 7–6(3) 6–2 6–4; Andrei Luzgin (EST) d. Karim Maamoun (EGY) 6–4 7–6(5); Mait Kunnap (EST) d. Marwan Zewar (EGY) 3–6 6–4 6–3. *Israel d. Bulgaria 3–2, Sofia BUL; Clay (O):* Harel Levy (ISR) d. Milen Velev (BUL) 6–1 6–3 6–2; Ivailo Traykov (BUL) d. Lior Mor (ISR) 7–6(4) 4–6 6–4 6–4; Todor Enev/Radoslav Lukaev (BUL) d. Jonathan Erlich/Harel Levy (ISR) 4–6 7–5 7–6(5); Harel Levy (ISR) d. Ivailo Traykov (BUL) 6–7(5) 7–6(8) 7–6(3) 7–6(6); Lior Mor (ISR) d. Todor Enev (BUL) 6–3 6–3 7–5.

Latvia, Lithuania, Egypt and Bulgaria relegated to Euro/African Zone Group III in 2001.

AMERICAN ZONE

FIRST ROUND: 4–6 February – *Venezuela d. Uruguay 5–0, Caracas VEN; Hard (O):* Maurice Ruah (VEN) d. Federico Dondo (URU) 7–6(5) 6–4 6–3; Jimy Szymanski (VEN) d. Alejandro Olivera (URU) 7–6(3) 6–4 6–4; Jose De Armas/Maurice Ruah (VEN) d. Federico Dondo/Alejandro Olivera (URU) 1–6 6–4 4–6 6–3 6–4; Jose De Armas (VEN) d. Alberto Brause (URU) 6–4 7–6(5); Johny Romero (VEN) d. Alejandro Olivera (URU) 6–3 6–0. ***Paraguay d. El Salvador 5–0, San Salvador ESA; Clay (O):*** Francisco Rodriguez (PAR) d. Manuel Tejada (ESA) 7–6(1) 7–5 6–3; Paulo Carvallo (PAR) d. Yari Bernardo (ESA) 5–7 7–6(6) 6–3 6–1; Paulo Carvallo/Francisco Rodriguez (PAR) d. Yari Bernardo/Miguel Merz (ESA) 6–4 6–4 7–6(6); Paulo Carvallo (PAR) d. Manuel Tejada (ESA) 7–6(4) 6–3; Francisco Rodriguez (PAR) d. Jose Baires (ESA) 6–3 6–1. ***Guatemala d. Cuba 4–1, Guatemala City GUA; Hard (O):*** Jacobo Chavez (GUA) d. Lazaro Navarro (CUB) 7–5 4–6 4–6 6–3 6–4; Luis Perez-Chete (GUA) d. Sandor Martinez (CUB) 6–4 6–2 6–2; Daniel Chavez/Luis Perez-Chete (GUA) d. Sandor Martinez/Lazaro Navarro (CUB) 7–6(4) 6–4 6–3; Luis Perez-Chete (GUA) d. Kerlin Leon (CUB) 3–6 6–3 6–3; Sandor Martinez (CUB) d. Jorge Tejada (GUA) 6–3 7–5. ***Mexico d. Costa Rica 4–1, San Jose CRC; Hard (O):*** Rafael Brenes (CRC) d. Marco Osorio (MEX) 2–6 6–7(2) 7–6(8) 6–1 6–4; Alejandro Hernandez (MEX) d. Luis-Diego Nunez (CRC) 6–0 6–2 6–0; Oscar Ortiz/David Roditi (MEX) d. Alejandro Madrigal/Felipe Montenegro (CRC) 6–1 6–2 6–0; Alejandro Hernandez (MEX) d. Rafael Brenes (CRC) 6–3 6–2 7–6(5); Marco Osorio (MEX) d. Luis-Diego Nunez (CRC) 6–0 6–1.

SECOND ROUND: 7–9 April – *Venezuela d. Paraguay 5–0, Caracas VEN; Hard (O):* Jimy Szymanski (VEN) d. Emilio Baez-Britez (PAR) 6–2 6–1 6–2; Jose De Armas (VEN) d. Paulo Carvallo (PAR) 7–6(5) 7–5 6–3; Jose De Armas/Jimy Szymanski (VEN) d. Emilio Baez-Britez/Paulo Carvallo (PAR) 6–2 6–4 6–2; Johny Romero (VEN) d. Paulo Carvallo (PAR) 6–3 2–6 6–3; Oscar Posada (VEN) d. Emilio Baez-Britez (PAR) 6–1 6–4. ***Mexico d. Guatemala 5–0, Guatemala City GUA; Hard (O):*** Alejandro Hernandez (MEX) d. Luis Perez-Chete (GUA) 6–2 6–3 5–7 6–2; Marco Osorio (MEX) d. Jacobo Chavez (GUA) 7–5 6–3 6–4; Oscar Ortiz/David Roditi (MEX) d. Daniel Chavez/Jacobo Chavez (GUA) 6–3 7–5 6–2; Alejandro Hernandez (MEX) d. Daniel Chavez (GUA) 6–3 6–4; Marco Osorio (MEX) d. Alexander Vasquez (GUA) 6–2 6–3.

FINAL: 21–23 July – Mexico d. Venezuela 5–0, Mexico City MEX; Hard (O): Alejandro Hernandez (MEX) d. Jose De Armas (VEN) 6–2 6–1 6–4; Mariano Sanchez (MEX) d. Jimmy Szymanski (VEN) 7–6(6) 6–1 6–4; Alejandro Hernandez/David Roditi (MEX) d. Jose De Armas/Jimmy Szymanski (VEN) 7–6(4) 2–6 6–2 7–6(4); Alejandro Hernandez (MEX) d. Jimmy Szymanski (VEN) 7–6(2) 6–4; Mariano Sanchez (MEX) d. Jose De Armas (VEN) 6–0 3–6 6–2.

Mexico promoted to American Zone Group I in 2001.

PLAYOFF: 7–9 April – *Uruguay d. El Salvador 4–1, Montevideo ESA; Clay (O):* Alberto Brause (URU) d. Manuel Tejada (ESA) 6–0 6–4 6–0; Federico Dondo (URU) d. Yari Bernardo (ESA) 6–1 6–4 6–0; Miguel Merz/Augusto Sanabria (ESA) d. Federico Dondo/Alejandro Olivera (URU) 7–5 2–6 6–7(5) 6–3 7–5; Federico Dondo (URU) d. Manuel Tejada (ESA) 6–3 6–2 6–2; Marcel Felder (URU) d. Augusto Sanabria (ESA) 6–2 6–1. ***Costa Rica d. Cuba 3–2, San Rafael CRC; Hard (O):*** Lazaro Navarro (CUB) d. Rafael Brenes (CRC) 6–4 6–4 6–4; Juan Antonio Marin (CRC) d. Kerlin Leon-Zamora (CUB) 6–2 6–0 6–2; Federico Camacho/Juan Antonio Marin (CRC) d. Sandor Martinez/Lazaro Navarro (CUB) 7–6(4) 6–4 5–7 5–7 6–3; Juan Antonio Marin (CRC) d. Lazaro Navarro (CUB) 6–4 4–6 6–1 4–6 6–4; Ricardo Chile (CUB) d. Rafael Brenes (CRC) 6–4 6–0.

El Salvador and Cuba relegated to American Zone Group III in 2001.

ASIA/OCEANIA ZONE

FIRST ROUND: 28–30 January – *Pakistan d. China Hong Kong 3–2, Causeway Bay HKG; Hard (O):* Melvin Tong (HKG) d. Asim Shafik (PAK) 6–2 6–1 6–4; Aisam Qureshi (PAK) d. Wayne Wong (HKG) 6–7(7) 6–4 4–6 7–5 6–3; Aisam Qureshi/Ahmad Wahla (PAK) d. Melvin Tong/Andrew Town (HKG) 7–6(6) 4–6 4–6 6–3 6–4; Aisam Qureshi (PAK) d. Melvin Tong (HKG) 4–6 6–1 6–4 6–2; Wayne Wong (HKG) d. Aqeel Khan (PAK) 7–5 6–4. **4–6 February – *Chinese Taipei d. Kazakhstan 4–1, Almaty KAZ; Hard (I):*** Wei-Jen Cheng (TPE) d. Pavel Baranov (KAZ) 6–4 6–4 4–6 7–5; Bing-Chao Lin (TPE) d. Alexei Kedriouk (KAZ) 6–7(5) 6–1 6–4 5–7 6–4; Chih-Jung Chen/Bing-Chao Lin (TPE) d. Pavel Baranov/Alexei Kedriouk (KAZ) 6–4 6–1 4–6 6–3; Alexei Kedriouk (KAZ) d. Wei-Jen Cheng (TPE) 7–5 6–2; Chia-Yen Tsai (TPE) d. Dias Doskaraev (KAZ) 4–6 7–5 6–1. ***Malaysia d. Iran 3–2, Kuala Lumpur MAS; Hard (I):*** Ramin Raziani (IRI) d. Hazuan Hizan (MAS) 6–2 6–2 6–1; Selvam Veerasingam (MAS) d. Akbar Taheri (IRI) 5–7 7–6(4) 6–4 4–6 7–5; Ramin Raziani/Akbar Taheri (IRI) d. Vasuthevan Ortchuan/Selvam Veerasingam (MAS) 6–3 1–6 6–3 6–4; Selvam Veerasingam (MAS) d. Ramin Raziani (IRI) 6–4 6–4 6–4; Hazuan Hizan (MAS) d. Akbar Taheri (IRI) 6–4 6–2 6–3. ***Indonesia d. Philippines 4–1, Manila PHI; Hard (O):*** Suwandi Suwandi (INA) d. Johnny Arcilla (PHI) 6–4 6–2 6–2; Febi Widhiyanto (INA) d. Adelo Abadia (PHI) 6–4 6–2 6–3; Edy Kusdaryanto/Hendri-Susilo Pramono (INA) d. Adelo Abadia/Johnny Arcilla (PHI) 6–4 6–2 6–7(4) 5–7 6–1; Johnny Arcilla (PHI) d. Febi Widhiyanto (INA) 6–0 3–6 6–4; Suwandi Suwandi (INA) d. Roland Ruel (PHI) 6–4 6–1.

SECOND ROUND: 7–9 April – *Chinese Taipei d. Pakistan 3–2, Tai-Chung TPE; Clay (O):* Bing-Chao Lin (TPE) d. Asim Shafik (PAK) 6–1 6–0 6–0; Aisam-ul-Haq Qureshi (PAK) d. Chia-Yen Tsai (TPE) 6–4 7–6(2) 7–5; Aisam-ul-Haq Qureshi/Ahmed Wahla (PAK) d. Wei-Jen Cheng/Bing-Chao Lin (TPE) 6–4 6–4 6–4; Bing-Chao Lin (TPE) d. Aisam-ul-Haq Qureshi (PAK) 2–6 6–2 6–3 6–3; Chia-Yen Tsai (TPE) d. Aqeel Khan (PAK) 6–0 6–3

6–3. *Indonesia d. Malaysia 5–0, Kuala Lumpur MAS; Hard (I):* Suwandi Suwandi (INA) d. Ortchun Vasuthevan (MAS) 6–2 6–2 6–3; Febi Widhiyanto (INA) d. Selvam Veerasingam (MAS) 6–3 6–3 6–2; Sulistyo Wibowo/Bonit Wiryawan (INA) d. Mohammed-Nazreen Fuzi/Selvam Veerasingam (MAS) 6–4 6–2 6–1; Febi Widhiyanto (INA) d. Mohammed Nazreen Fuzi (MAS) 6–0 6–1; Suwandi Suwandi (INA) d. Adam Jaya (MAS) 6–1 6–1.

FINAL: 6–8 October – *Indonesia d. Chinese Taipei 4–1, Jakarta INA; Hard (O):* Suwandi Suwandi (INA) d. Wei-Jen Cheng (TPE) 6–4 6–2 6–2; Hendri-Susilo Pramono (INA) d. Chia-Yen Tsai (TPE) 6–4 7–6(3) 6–3; Sulistyo Wibowo/Bonit Wiryawan (INA) d. Wei-Ju Chen/Wei-Jen Cheng (TPE) 6–3 6–4 6–4; Suwandi Suwandi (INA) d. Chia-Yen Tsai (TPE) 6–3 5–7 6–1; Wei-Jen Cheng (TPE) d. Hendri-Susilo Pramono (INA) 6–4 6–2.

Indonesia promoted to Asia/Oceania Zone Group I for 2001.

PLAYOFF: 17–19 March – *Iran d. Philippines 3–2, Manila PHI; Clay (I):* Johnny Arcilla (PHI) d. Mohammad Reza Tavakoli (IRI) 6–3 6–4 6–3; Ramin Raziani (IRI) d. Adelo Abadia (PHI) 7–6(7) 7–6(4) 6–2; Johnny Arcilla/Michael Misa (PHI) d. Ramin Raziani/Akbar Taheri (IRI) 6–3 3–6 6–3 7–6(5); Ramin Raziani (IRI) d. Johnny Arcilla (PHI) 6–4 6–4 7–6(5); Anosha Shagholi (IRI) d. Rolando Ruel (PHI) 4–6 6–3 6–3 6–1. **7–9 April** *China Hong Kong d. Kazakhstan 3–2, Hong Kong HKG; Hard (O):* Melvin Tong (HKG) d. Pavel Baranov (KAZ) 3–6 6–3 6–4 7–5; Alexey Kedryuk (KAZ) d. Wayne Wong (HKG) 6–2 6–2 6–2; Chris Numbers/Melvin Tong (HKG) d. Pavel Baranov/Alexey Kedryuk (KAZ) 7–5 7–6(6) 6–1; Alexey Kedryuk (KAZ) d. Melvin Tong (HKG) 6–3 3–6 6–1 3–6 6–2; Wayne Wong (HKG) d. Pavel Baranov (KAZ) 6–4 4–6 7–6(5) 6–2.

Philippines and Kazakhstan relegated to Asia/Oceania Zone Group III in 2001.

GROUP III

EURO/AFRICAN ZONE – VENUE 1

Date: 24–28 May; Venue: Tunis, Tunisia; Surface: Clay (O).
Group A: Bosnia/Herzegovina, Georgia, Malta, Togo.
Group B: Botswana, Monaco, Tunisia, Yugoslavia.

GROUP A: 24 May – *Bosnia/Herzegovina d. Togo 2–1:* Haris Basalic (BIH) d. Jean-Kome Loglo (TOG) 6–3 6–1; Merid Zahirovic (BIH) d. Kossi-Essaram Loglo (TOG) 6–0 6–0; Jean-Kome Loglo/Kossi-Essaram Loglo (TOG) d. Ismar Gorcic/Merid Zahirovic (BIH) 6–1 7–5. *Georgia d. Malta 3–0:* Konstantin Burchuladze (GEO) d. Marco Cappello (MLT) 6–1 6–1; Irakli Ushangishvili (GEO) d. Mark Schembri (MLT) 6–4 2–6 6–4; Otari Enukidze/Irakli Ushangishvili (GEO) d. Luke Bonello/Matthew Debono (MLT) 2–6 6–4 6–3. **25 May –** *Bosnia/Herzegovina d. Georgia 3–0:* Haris Basalic (BHA) d. Konstantin Burchuladze (GEO) 6–0 6–2; Merid Zahirovic (BHA) d. Irakli Ushangishvili (GEO) 6–1 6–2; Ismar Gorcic/Goran Houdek (BHA) d. Konstantin Burchuladze/Otari Enukidze (GEO) 6–7(2) 6–1 7–5. *Togo d. Malta 3–0:* Komlavi Loglo (TOG) d. Matthew Debono (MLT) 6–2 6–1; Kossi-Essaram Loglo (TOG) d. Mark Schembri (MLT) 6–3 6–3; Komlavi Loglo/Kossi-Essaram Loglo (TOG) d. Luke Bonello/Matthew Debono (MLT) 6–2 6–1. **26 May –** *Bosnia/Herzegovina v Malta:* Haris Basalic (BIH) d. Luke Bonello (MLT) 6–4 6–2; second singles and doubles matches cancelled due to rain – final position in Group not affected. *Georgia d. Togo 2–1:* Jean-Kome Loglo (TOG) d. Otari Enukidze (GEO) 6–2 6–2; Irakli Ushangishvili (GEO) d. Kossi-Essaram Loglo (TOG) 6–2 6–7(4) 6–4; David Katcharava/Irakli Ushangishvili (GEO) d. Kamlavi Loglo/Kossi-Essaram Loglo (TOG) 7–5 6–2.

GROUP B: 24 May – *Botswana d. Tunisia 2–1:* Michael Judd (BOT) d. Chekib Jemai (TUN) 4–6 6–0 11–9; Fares Zaier (TUN) d. Petrus Molefe (BOT) 5–7 6–4 6–2; Michael Judd/Petrus Molefe (BOT) d. Chakib Jemai/Youssef Miled (TUN) 6–2 5–7 6–3. *Yugoslavia d. Monaco 3–0:* Nenad Zimonjic (YUG) d. Emmanuel Heussner (MON) 6–4 3–6 6–0; Dusan Vemic (YUG) d. Christophe Bosio (MON) 6–3 6–3; Relja Dulic-Fiser/Janko Tipsarevic (YUG) d. Christophe Bosio/Emmanuel Heussner (MON) 6–3 7–6(3). **25 May –** *Yugoslavia d. Botswana 3–0:* Relja Dulic-Fiser (YUG) d. Lesedi Bewlay (BOT) 6–0 6–1; Nenad Zimonjic (YUG) d. Petrus Molefe (BOT) 6–3 6–0; Janko Tipsarevic/Dusan Vemic (YUG) d. Michael Judd/Petrus Molefe (BOT) 6–4 6–0. *Monaco d. Tunisia 3–0:* Emmanuel Heussner (MON) d. Malek Jaziri (TUN) 6–1 6–2; Christophe Bosio (MON) d. Youssef Miled (TUN) 6–1 6–1; Christophe Bosio/Axel Mellet (MON) d. Chekib Jemai/Fares Zaier (TUN) 4–6 6–3 6–4. **26 May –** *Monaco d. Botswana 2–0:* Emmanuel Heussner (MON) d. Michael Judd (BOT) 7–5 6–4; Christophe Bosio (MON) d. Petrus Molefe (BOT) 6–4 6–2; doubles match cancelled due to rain – final position in Group not affected. *Yugoslavia d. Tunisia 2–0:* Janko Tipsarevic (YUG) d. Chekib Jemai (TUN) 6–3 6–2 Nenad Zimonjic (YUG) d. Youssef Miled (TUN) 6–4 6–0; doubles match cancelled due to rain – final position in Group not affected.

PLAYOFF FOR 1st–4th POSITIONS: 27 May – *Yugoslavia d. Georgia 3–0:* Nenad Zimonjic (YUG) d. Konstantin Burchuladze (GEO) 6–1 6–3; Dusan Vemic (YUG) d. Irakli Ushangishvili (GEO) 3–6 6–1; Relja Dulic-Fiser/Janko Tipsarevic (YUG) d. Konstantin Burchuladze/Otari Enukidze (GEO) 6–2 6–3. *Monaco d. Bosnia/Herzegovina 2–1:* Emmanuel Heussner (MON) d. Haris Basalic (BIH) 3–6 6–0 8–6; Merid Zahirovic (NIH) d. Christophe Bosio (MON) 3–6 6–1 6–3; Christophe Bosio/Emmanuel Heussner (MON) d. Haris Basalic/Goran Houdek (BIH) 6–3 7–6(7).

PLAYOFF FOR 1st/2nd POSITION: 28 May – *Yugoslavia d. Monaco 3–0:* Nenad Zimonjic (YUG) d. Emmanuel Heussner (MON) 6 1 6 0; Dusan Vemic (YUG) d. Christophe Bosio (MON) 6–3 6–1; Relja Dulic-Fiser/Janko Tipsarevic (YUG) d. Christophe Boggetti/Emmanuel Heussner (MON) 7–5 6–2.

PLAYOFF FOR 3rd/4th POSITION: 28 May – *Georgia d. Bosnia/Herzegovina 2–1:* Konstantin Burchuladze (GEO) d. Ismar Gorcic (BIH) 6–0 6–2; Irakli Ushangishvili (GEO) d. Goran Houdek (BIH) 7–5 6–0; Ismar Gorcic/Goran Houdek (BIH) d. Konstantin Burchuladze/Otari Enukidze (GEO) 6–4 6–2.

PLAYOFF FOR 5th–8th POSITIONS: 27 May – *Botswana d. Malta 3–0:* Michael Judd (BOT) d. Matthew Debono (MLT) 5–7 6–2 7–5; Petrus Molefe (BOT) d. Mark Schembri (MLT) 7–6(7) 6–2; Lesedi Bewlay/Karabo Makgale (BOT) d. Luke Bonello/Mark Schembri (MLT) 6–1 06 6–3. *Togo d. Tunisia 2–1:* Chekib Jemai (TUN) d. Komi Adeyo (TOG) 6–3 6–3; Komlavi Loglo (TOG) d. Youssef Miled (TUN) 6–2 1–6 6–0; Jean-Kome Loglo/Kossi-Essaram Loglo (TOG) d. Chekib Jamai/Fares Zaier (TUN) 6–3 6–1.

PLAYOFF FOR 5th/6th POSITION: 28 May – *Togo d. Botswana 3–0:* Jean-Kome Loglo (TOG) d. Michael Judd (BOT) 7–6(2) 6–2; Kossi-Essaram Loglo (TOG) d. Petrus Molefe (BOT) 7–6(4) 6–0; Komi Adeyo/Komlavi Loglo (TOG) d. Michael Judd/Karabo Makgale (BOT) 6–3 6–4.

PLAYOFF FOR 7th/8th POSITION: 28 May – *Tunisia d. Malta 2–1:* Luke Bonello (MLT) d. Malek Jaziri (TUN) 4–6 6–3 6–2; Chekib Jemai (TUN) d. Matthew Debono (MLT) 7–5 6–0; Chekib Jamai/Fares Zaier (TUN) d. Luke Bonello/Matthew Debono (MLT) 6–3 7–6(3) .

FINAL POSITIONS: 1. Yugoslavia, 2. Monaco, 3. Georgia, 4. Bosnia/Herzegovina, 5. Togo, 6. Botswana, 7. Tunisia, 8. Malta.

Yugoslavia and Monaco promoted to Euro/African Zone Group II in 2001.
Tunisia and Malta relegated to Euro/African Zone Group IV in 2001.

EURO/AFRICAN ZONE – VENUE 2
Date: 24–28 May; Venue: Antananarivo, Madagascar; Surface: Clay (O).
Group A: Benin, Iceland, Moldova, Senegal.
Group B: Armenia, FYR of Macedonia, Madagascar, Nigeria.

GROUP A: 24 May – *Moldova d. Senegal 3–0*: Yuri Gorban (MDA) d. Djadji Ka (SEN) 6–2 6–3; Evgueni Plougarev (MDA) d. Daouda Senga Ndiaye (SEN) 6–3 7–6(3); Yuri Gorban/Evgueni Plougarev (MDA) d. Djadi Ka/Daouda Senga Ndiaye (SEN) 7–5 7–5. *Iceland d. Benin 3–0:* Raj Bonifacius (ISL) d. Arnaud Segodo (BEN) 6–3 6–0; Arnar Sigurdsson (ISL) d. Alphonse Gandonou (BEN) 6–3 6–1; David Halldorsson/Arnar Sigurdsson (ISL) d. Jean-Marie Da Silva/Alphonse Gandonou (BEN) 6–4 6–4. **25 May – *Moldova d. Iceland 3–0:*** Yuri Gorban (MDA) d. David Halldorsson (ISL) 6–0 6–0; Evgueni Plougarev (MDA) d. Arnar Sigurdsson (ISL) 6–3 7–5; Andrei Gorban/Victor Ribas (MDA) d. David Halldorsson/Arnar Sigurdsson (ISL) 6–4 6–3. *Senegal d. Benin 2–1:* Wael Zeidan (SEN) d. Souron Gandonou (BEN) 6–3 6–3; Daouda Senga Ndiaye (SEN) d. Alphonse Gandonou (BEN) 6–3 6–2; Alphonse Gandonou/Arnaud Segodo (BEN) d. Djadji Ka/Wael Zeidan (SEN) 6–3 6–4. **26 May – *Moldova d. Benin 3–0:*** Yuri Gorban (MDA) d. Arnaud Segodo (BEN) 6–2 6–3; Evgueni Plougarev (MDA) d. Sourou Gandonou (BEN) 6–2 6–2; Andrei Gorban/Victor Ribas (MDA) d. Alphonse Gandonou/Jean-Marie Da Silva (BEN) 6–4 4–6 6–2. *Iceland d. Senegal 2–1:* Raj Bonifacius (ISL) d. Wael Zeidan (SEN) 6–4 7–6(3); Arnar Sigurdsson (ISL) d. Daouda Senga Ndiaye (SEN) 6–4 6–0; Daouda Senga Ndiaye/Wael Zeidan (SEN) d. David Halldorsson/Jon Axel Jonsson (ISL) 6–2 7–6(4).

GROUP B: 24 May – *FYR of Macedonia d. Nigeria 3–0:* Predrag Rusevski (MKD) d. Ganiyu Adelekan (NGR) 4–6 6–1 6–4; Zoran Sevcenko (MKD) d. Sule Ladipo (NGR) 5–7 7–5 6–2; Kristijan Mitrovski/Predrag Rusevski (MKD) d. Ganiyu Adelekan/Sule Ladipo (NGR) 6–3 6–2. *Armenia d. Madagascar 3–0:* Tsolak Gevorgyan (ARM) d. Alexis Rafidison (MAD) 6–4 3–6 6–4; Sargis Sargsian (ARM) d. Lalaina Ratsimbazafy (MAD) 7–6(3) 6–0; Tsolak Gevorgyan/Sargis Sargsian (ARM) d. Harivony Andrianafetra/Jean Marc Randriamanalina (MAD) 6–4 6–1. **25 May – *Armenia d. FYR of Macedonia 2–1:*** Zoran Sevcenko (MKD) d. Tsolak Gevorgyan (ARM) 6–3 6–3; Sargis Sargsian (ARM) d. Kristijan Mitrovski (MKD) 2–6 6–3 6–2; Tsolak Gevorgyan/Sargis Sargsian (ARM) d. Predrag Rusevski/Zoran Sevcenko (MKD) 6–1 6–1. *Madagascar d. Nigeria 2–1:* Alexis Rafidison (MAD) d. Ganiyu Adelekan (NGR) 6–2 6–1; Sule Ladipo (NGR) d. Jean Marc Randriamanalina (MAD) 7–6(6) 6–3; Harivony Andrianafetra/Alexis Rafidison (MAD) d. Ganiyu Adelekan/Sule Ladipo (NGR) 7–6(7) 6–3. **26 May – *Armenia d. Nigeria 2–1:*** Ganiyu Adelekan (NGR) d. Harutiun Sofian (ARM) 7–5 7–5; Sargis Sargsian (ARM) d. Sule Ladipo (NGR) 6–3 6–3; Tsolak Gevorgyan/Sargis Sargsian (ARM) d. Ganiyu Adelekan/Sule Ladipo (NGR) 6–4 6–4. *FYR of Macedonia d. Madagascar 2–1:* Zoran Sevcenko (MKD) d. Alexis Rafidison (MAD) 6–4 6–3; Jean Marc Randriamanalina (MAD) d. Kristijan Mitrovski (MKD) 2–6 6–3 6–4; Predrag Rusevski/Zoran Sevcenko (MKD) d. Harivony Andrianafetra/Alexis Rafidison (MAD) 6–3 1–6 6–1.

PLAYOFF FOR 1st–4th POSITIONS: 27 May – *Moldova d. FYR of Macedonia 2–1:* Yuri Gorban (MDA) d. Predrag Rusevski (MKD) 7–5 3–6 6–4; Evgueni Plougarev (MDA) d. Zoran Sevcenko (MKD 7–5 1–6 7–5; Kristijan Mitrovski/Predrag Rusevski (MKD) d. Andrei Gorban/Victor Ribas (MDA) 6–3 6–1. *Armenia d. Iceland 3–0:* Tsolak Gevorgyan (ARM) d. Raj Bonifacius (ISL) 7–6(5) 7–5; Sargis Sargsian (ARM) d. Arnar Sigurdsson (ISL) 6–3 6–2; Haik Hakobian/Harutiun Sofian (ARM) d. David Halldorsson/Arnar Sigurdsson (ISL) 6–7(5) 6–3 6–4.

PLAYOFF FOR 1st/2nd POSITION: 28 May – *Moldova d. Armenia 2–1:* Andrei Gorban (MDA) d. Harutiun Sofian (ARM) 4–6 7–6(5) 7–5; Victor Ribas (MDA) d. Tsolak Gevorgyan (ARM) 6–4 6–4; Haik Hakobian/Harutiun Sofian (ARM) d. Andrei Gorban/Victor Ribas (MDA) 5–7 7–5 6–4.

PLAYOFF FOR 3rd/4th POSITION: 28 May – *Iceland d. FYR of Macedonia 2–1:* Zoran Sevcenko (MKD) d. Raj Bonifacius (ISL) 6–2 6–2; Arnar Sigurdsson (ISL) d. Kristijan Mitrovski (MKD) 6–3 6–3; Raj Bonifacius/Arnar Sigurdsson (ISL) d. Kristijan Mitrovski/Predrag Rusevski (MKD) 6–3 6–4.

PLAYOFF FOR 5th–8th POSITIONS: 27 May – *Nigeria d. Senegal 2–1:* Ganiyu Adelekan (NGR) d. Wael Ziedan (SEN) 4–6 6–1 6–3; Sule Ladipo (NGR) d. Daouda Senga Ndiaye (SEN) 6–2 7–5; Nigeria forfeited doubles. *Madagascar d. Benin 3–0:* Alexis Rafidison (MAD) d. Arnaud Segodo (BEN) 6–1 6–2; Lalaina Ratsimbazafy (MAD) d. Alphonse Gandonou (BEN) 6–3 6–2; Jean Marc Randriamanalina/Lalaina Ratsimbazafy (MAD) d. Alphonse Gandonou/Arnaud Segodo (BEN) 4–6 6–3 6–4.

PLAYOFF FOR 5th/6th POSITION: 28 May – *Nigeria d. Madagascar 2–1:* Alexis Rafidison (MKD) d. Ganiyu Adelekan (NGR) 6–1 0–1 ret; Sule Ladipo (NGR) d. Lalaina Ratsimbazafy (MKD) 6–1 6–3; Bulus Hussaini/Sule Ladipo (NGR) d. Harivony Andrianafetra/Jean Marc Randriamanalina (MAD) 6–2 6–4.

PLAYOFF FOR 7th/8th POSITION: 2–8 May – *Benin d. Senegal 3–0:* Arnaud Segodo (BEN) d. Wael Zeidan (SEN) 6–4 6–7(3) 6–3; Alphonse Gandonou (BEN) d. Daouda Senga Ndiaye (SEN) 6–5 def; Alphonse Gandonou/Arnaud Segodo (BEN) d. Youssou Berthe/Djadji Ka (SEN) 6–3 6–1.

FINAL POSITIONS: 1. Moldova, 2. Armenia, 3. Iceland, 4. FYR of Macedonia, 5. Nigeria, 6. Madagascar, 7. Benin, 8. Senegal.

Moldova and Armenia promoted to Euro/African Zone Group II in 2001.
Benin and Senegal relegated to Euro/African Zone Group IV in 2001.

AMERICAN ZONE
Date: 24–28 March; Venue: Kingston, Jamaica; Surface: Clay (O).
Group A: Haiti, Jamaica, Panama, Puerto Rico.
Group B: Bolivia, Dominican Republic, Netherlands Antilles, Trinidad & Tobago.

GROUP A: 22 March – *Jamaica d. Panama 3–0:* Ryan Russell (JAM) d. Juan Pablo Herrera (PAN) 7–6(6) 6–1; Jermaine Smith (JAM) d. Chad Valdez (PAN) 6–3 7–6(4); Nakia Gordon/Scott Willinsky (JAM) d. Braen Aneiros/Arnulfo Courney (PAN) 6–3 7–5. *Puerto Rico d. Haiti 2–1:* Juan Carlos Fernandez (PUR) d. Joel Allen (HAI) 6–1 6–4; Gabriel Montilla (PUR) d. Jerry Joseph (HAI) 6–2 6–4; Joel Allen/Jerry Joseph (HAI) d. Stephen Diaz/Luis Haddock (PUR) 2–6 6–3 6–4. **23 March –** *Puerto Rico d. Jamaica 2–1:* Ryan Russell (JAM) d. Juan-Carlos Fernandez (PUR) 6–3 6–4; Gabriel Montilla (PUR) d. Jermaine Smith (JAM) 4–6 6–3 6–2; Stephen Diaz/Gabriel Montilla (PUR) d. Nakia Gordon/Ryan Russell (JAM) 7–6(4) 2–6 6–1. *Panama d. Haiti 2–1:* Juan Pablo Herrera (PAN) d. Joel Allen (HAI) 5–7 7–5 6–3; Chad Valdez (PAN) d. Jerry Joseph (HAI) 6–3 7–5; Joel Allen/Jerry Joseph (HAI) d. Braen Aneiros/Arnulfo Courney (PAN) 3–6 6–1 6–3. **24 March –** *Jamaica d. Haiti 3–0:* Ryan Russell (JAM) d. Carl-Henry Barthold (HAI) 6–1 6–0; Jermaine Smith (JAM) d. Jerry Joseph (HAI) 6–7(4) 6–2 6–2; Nakia Gordon/Scott Willinsky (JAM) d. Jean-Claude Augustin/Carl-Henry Barthold (HAI) 6–2 6–2. *Puerto Rico d. Panama 3–0* Luis Haddock (PUR) d. Juan Pablo Herrera (PAN) 4–6 7–6(4) 6–2; Gabriel Montilla (PUR) d. Chad Valdez (PAN) 6–0 6–2; Stephen Diaz/Juan-Carlos Fernandez (PUR) d. Braen Aneiros/Arnulfo Courney (PAN) 5–7 6–1 9–7.

GROUP B: 22 March – *Trinidad & Tobago d. Dominican Republic 2–1:* Simon Evelyn (TRI) d. Genaro De Leon (DOM) 6–2 2–6 6–4; Rodrigo Vallejo (DOM) d. Shane Stone (TRI) 1–6 7–6(3) 8–6; Shane Stone/Troy Stone (TRI) d. Sixto Camacho/Rodrigo Vallejo (DOM) 6–4 6–7(4) 6–2. *Netherlands Antilles d. Bolivia 3–0:* Elmar Gerth (AHO) d. Daniel Chavarria (BOL) 6–2 6–4; Jean-Julien Rojer (AHO) d. Jose Antelo (BOL) 6–3 6–3; Raoul Behr/Kevin Jonckheer (AHO) d. Rodrigo Navarro/Rodrigo Villarroel (BOL) 6–3 ret. **23 March –** *Dominican Republic d. Bolivia 2–1:* Daniel Chavarria (BOL) d. Victor Estrella (DOM) 6–4 6–4; Genaro de Leon (DOM) d. Jose Antelo (BOL) 6–0 6–3; Sixto Camacho/Rodrigo Vallejo (DOM) d. Daniel Chavarria/Rodrigo Villarroel (BOL) 6–4 3–6 6–1. *Netherlands Antilles d. Trinidad & Tobago 3–0:* Elmar Gerth (AHO) d. Simon Evelyn (TRI) 6–2 6–3; Jean-Julien Rojer (AHO) d. Shane Stone (TRI) 6–3 6–3; Raoul Behr/Kevin Jonckheer (AHO) d. Shane Stone/Troy Stone (TRI) 6–2 2–6 6–2. **24 March –** *Bolivia d. Trinidad & Tobago 3–0:* Rodrigo Navarro (BOL) d. Randy Hakim (TRI) 6–3 6–3; Jose Antelo (BOL) d. Simon Evelyn (TRI) 4–6 6–2 6–2; Jose Antelo/Daniel Chavarria (BOL) d. Simon Evelyn/Troy Stone (TRI) 4–6 6–1 6–4. *Netherlands Antilles d. Dominican Republic 2–1:* Elmar Gerth (AHO) d. Genaro De Leon (DOM) 6–2 6–7(1) 6–4; Jean-Julien Rojer (AHO) d. Rodrigo Vallejo (DOM) 6–1 7–6(3); Sixto Camacho/Rodrigo Vallejo (DOM) d. Raoul Behr/Kevin Jonckheer (AHO) 7–5 3–6 6–3.

PLAYOFF FOR 1st–4th POSITIONS: 25 March – *Dominican Republic d. Puerto Rico 2–1:* Genaro De Leon (DOM) d. Juan-Carlos Fernandez (PUR) 6–4 6–4; Rodrigo Vallejo (DOM) d. Stephen Diaz (PUR) 6–4 6–7(4) 6–3; Juan-Carlos Fernandez/Luis Haddock (PUR) d. Sixto Camacho/Victor Estrella (DOM) 6–2 6–4. *Netherlands Antilles d. Jamaica 2–1:* Ryan Russell (JAM) d. Elmar Gerth (AHO) 4–6 6–2 6–4; Jean-Julien Rojer (AHO) d. Jermaine Smith (JAM) 7–6(4) 6–4; Elmar Gerth/Jean-Julien Rojer (AHO) d. Ryan Russell/Jermaine Smith (JAM) 6–2 6–1.

PLAYOFF FOR 1st/2nd POSITION: 26 March – *Netherlands Antilles d. Dominican Republic 2–1:* Elmar Gerth (AHO) d. Genaro De Leon (DOM) 3–6 6–4 6–3; Jean-Julien Rojer (AHO) d. Rodrigo Vallejo (DOM) 6–3 6–2; Sixto Camacho/Victor Estrella (DOM) d. Raoul Behr/Kevin Jonckheer (AHO) 6–2 6–4.

PLAYOFF FOR 3rd/4th POSITION: 26 March – *Puerto Rico d. Jamaica 2–1:* Ryan Russell (JAM) d. Luis Haddock (PUR) 3–6 6–4 6–2; Juan-Carlos Fernandez (PUR) d. Jermaine Smith (JAM) 6–1 5–7 6–4; Juan-Carlos Fernandez/Luis Haddock (PUR) d. Nakia Gordon/Ryan Russell (PUR) 2–6 6–1 6–2.

PLAYOFF FOR 5th–8th POSITIONS: 25 March – *Trinidad & Tobago d. Panama 2–1:* Juan Pablo Herrera (PAN) d. Simon Evelyn (TRI) 6–3 6–4; Shane Stone (TRI) d. Chad Valdez (PAN) 6–4 6–3; Simon Evelyn/Troy Stone (TRI) d. Braen Aneiros/Juan Pablo Herrera (PAN) 6–3 6–4. *Bolivia d. Haiti 2–1:* Joel Allen (HAI) d. Rodrigo Villarroel (BOL) 6–1 6–3; Rodrigo Navarro (BOL) d. Jerry Joseph (HAI) 6–2 6–1; Jose Antelo/Rodrigo Navarro (BOL) d. Joel Allen/Jerry Joseph (HAI) 3–6 6–0 6–3.

PLAYOFF FOR 5th/6th POSITION: 26 March – *Bolivia d. Trinidad & Tobago 3–0:* Rodrigo Navarro (BOL) d. Randy Hakim (TRI) 6–0 6–3; Jose Antelo (BOL) d. Simon Evelyn (TRI) 7–6(5) 6–1; Rodrigo Navarro/Rodrigo Villarroel (BOL) d. Randy Hakim/Troy Stone (TRI) 6–4 6–1.

PLAYOFF FOR 7th/8th POSITION: 26 March – *Panama d. Haiti 3–0:* Juan Pablo Herrera (PAN) d. Jean-Claude Augustin (HAI) 6–1 3–6 6–3; Arnulfo Courney (PAN) d. Carl-Henry Barthold (HAI) 6–3 6–3; Arnulfo Courney/Chad Valdez (PAN) d. Joel Allen/Jerry Joseph (HAI) 6–2 6–4.

FINAL POSITIONS: 1. Netherlands Antilles, 2. Dominican Republic, 3. Puerto Rico, 4. Jamaica, 5. Bolivia, 6. Trinidad & Tobago, 7. Panama, 8. Haiti.

Netherlands Antilles and Dominican Republic promoted to American Zone Group II in 2001.
Panama and Haiti relegated to American Zone Group IV in 2001.

ASIA/OCEANIA ZONE
Date: 7–13 February; Venue: Colombo, Sri Lanka; Surface: Clay (O).
Group A: Bangladesh, Kuwait, Pacific Oceania, Qatar.
Group B: Singapore, Sri Lanka, Syria, Tajikistan.

GROUP A: 9 February – *Kuwait d. Bangladesh 3–0:* Hamed Al-Solaiteen (KUW) d. Moin-ud-din Walliullah (BAN) 3–6 6–4 6–0; Mohammed Al-Ghareeb (KUW) d. Nadeem-Kamran Khan (BAN) 6–2 6–2; Mohammed-Rashid Al-Foudari /Adel Al-Shatti (KUW) d. Dilip Passia/Moin-ud-din Walliullah (BAN) 5–7 6–2 7–5. *Qatar d. Pacific Oceania 3–0:* Nasser-Ghanim Al-Khulaifi (QAT) d. Brett Baudinet (POC) 6–4 7–5; Sultan-Khalfan Al-Alawi (QAT) d. Lency Tenai (POC) 6–3 7–5; Sultan-Khalfan Al-Alawi/Nasser-Ghanim Al-Khulaifi (QAT) d. Cyril Jacobe/Jerome Rovo (POC) 6–4 7–6(5). **10 February** – *Bangladesh d. Pacific Oceania 2–1:* Dilip Passia (BAN) d. Jerome Rovo (POC) 7–6(5) 3–6 6–1; Nadeen-Kamran Khan (BAN) d. Lency Tenai (POC) 6–3 6–3; Brett Baudinet/Cyril Jacobe (POC) d. Dilip Passia/Moin-ud-din Walliullah (BAN) 6–0 6–1. *Qatar d. Kuwait 3–0:* Nasser-Ghanim Al-Khulaifi (QAT) d. Hamed Al-Solaiteen (KUW) 6–2 6–4; Sultan-Khalfan Al-Alawi (QAT) d. Mohammed Al-Ghareeb (KUW) 6–4 3–1 ret; Sultan-Khalfan Al-Alawi/Mohammed-Ali Al-Saoud (QAT) d. Mohammed-Rashid Al-Foudari/Hammed Al-Sloulaiteen (KUW) 7–6(6) 6–7(4) 6–3. **11 February** – *Kuwait d. Pacific Oceania 2–1:* Brett Baudinet (POC) d. Hamed Al-Solaiteen (KUW) 1–6 6–4 6–3; Mohammed Al-Ghareeb (KUW) d. Lency Tenai (POC) 3–6 6–1 6–4; Mohammed-Rashid Al-Foudari/Mohammed Al-Ghareeb (KUW) d. Cyril Jacobe/Jerome Rovo (POC) 6–7(3) 6–1 6–3. *Bangladesh d. Qatar 2–1:* Moin-ud-Walliullah (BAN) d. Nasser-Ghanim Al-Khulaifi (QAT) 6–4 3–0 ret; Sultan-Khalfan Al-Alawi (QAT) d. Dilip Passia (BAN) 6–2 6–1; Dilip Passia/Moin-ud-din Walliullah (BAN) d. Sultan-Khalfan Al-Alawi /Mohammed-Ali Al-Saoud (QAT) 6–1 7–6(5).

GROUP B: 9 February – *Syria d. Tajikistan 2–1:* Samir Saad El Din (SYR) d. Sergei Makashin (TJK) 7–6(2) 6–1; Rabi Bou-Hassoun (SYR) d. Mansur Yakhyaev (TJK) 3–6 7–6(5) 6–2; Sergei Makashin/Mansur Yakhyaev (TJK) d. Rabi Bou-Hassoun/Lais Salim (SYR) 6–1 6–2. *Sri Lanka d. Singapore 3–0:* Jayendra Wijeyesekera (SRI) d. Tung-Yi Kho (SIN) 6–2 6–2; Rohan De Silva (SRI) d. Sian Yang (SIN) 6–3 6–4; Asiri Iddamalgoda/Jayendra Wijeyesekera (SRI) d. Jensen Hiu/Tung-Yi Kho (SIN) 6–3 6–2. **10 February** – *Sri Lanka d. Tajikistan 2–1:* Jayendra Wijeyesekera (SRI) d. Sergei Makashin (TJK) 6–1 6–0; Mansur Yakhyaev (TJK) d. Rohan De Silva (SRI) 6–3 6–3; Rohan De Silva/Jayendra Wijeyesekera (SRI) d. Sergei Makashin/Mansur Yakhyaev (TJK) 3–6 6–3 6–2. *Syria d. Singapore 2–1:* Lais Salim (SYR) d. Jensen Hiu (SIN) 6–0 06 6–3; Rabi Bou-Hassoun (SYR) d. Sian Yang (SIN) 6–0 6–0; Jensen Hiu/Sian Yang (SIN) d. Abdul-Rahim Salim/Lais Salim (SYR) 7–5 6–3. **11 February** – *Sri Lanka d. Syria 2–1:* Jayendra Wijeyesekera (SRI) d. Samir Saad El Din (SYR) 6–3 6–4; Rabi Bou-Hassoun (SYR) d. Rohan de Silva (SRI) 6–3 6–4; Rohan De Silva/Jayendra Wijeyesekera (SRI) d. Abdul-Rahim Salim/Lais Salim (SYR) 6–2 7–5. *Tajikistan d. Singapore 2–1:* Sergei Makashin (TJK) d. Jensen Hiu (SIN) 7–5 6–1; Mansur Yakhyaev (TJK) d. Sian Yang (SIN) 6–2 6–3; Kyoung Sik Seol/Tung-Yi Kho (SIN) d. Sergei Makashin/Sergei Sedov (TJK) 6–1 6–1.

PLAYOFF FOR 1st–4th POSITIONS: 12 February – *Syria d. Qatar 2–0:* Samir Saad El Din (SYR) d. Nasser-Ghanim Al-Khulaifi (QAT) 7–6(2) 6–3; Rabi Bou-Hassoun (SYR) d. Sultan-Khalfan Al-Alawi (QAT) 6–3 6–1; Rabi Bou-Hassoun/Lais Salim (SYR) v Sultan-Khalfan Al-Alawi/Mohammed-Ali Al-Saoud (QAT) – not played. *Kuwait d. Sri Lanka 2–1:* Jayendra Wijeyesekera (SRI) d. Hamed Al-Solaiteen (KUW) 6–3 6–7(2) 6–2; Mohammed Al-Ghareeb (KUW) d. Rohan De Silva (SRI) 6–1 6–2; Mohammed-Rashid Al-Foudari/Mohammed Al-Ghareeb (KUW) d. Rohan De Silva/Jayendra Wijeyesekera (SRI) 3–6 7–6(4).

PLAYOFF FOR 1st/2nd POSITION: 13 February – *Syria d. Kuwait 2–1:* Lais Salim (SYR) d. Hamed Al-Solaiteen (KUW) 6–2 6–1; Rabi Bou-Hassoun (SYR) d. Mohammed Al-Ghareeb (KUW) 6–4 7–6(4);

Mohammed-Rashid Al-Foudari/Adel Al-Shatti (KUW) d. Abdul-Rahim Salim/Lais Salim (SYR) 7–6(4) 2–6 6–4. **PLAYOFF FOR 3rd/4th POSITION: 13 February** – *Sri Lanka d. Qatar 2–1:* Nasser-Ghanim Al-Khulaifi (QAT) d. Sanjeev Paramanathan (SRI) 7–6(8) 6–1; Asiri Iddamalgoda (SRI) d. Sultan-Khalfan Al-Alawi (QAT) 6–4 6–2; Asiri Iddamalgoda/Rohan De Silva (SRI) d. Sultan-Khalfan Al-Alawi/Nasser-Ghanim Al-Khulaifi (QAT) 6–4 7–5.

PLAYOFF FOR 5th–8th POSITIONS: 12 February – *Singapore d. Bangladesh 2–1:* Moin-ud-din-Walliullah (BAN) d. Tung-Yi Kho (SIN) 6–3 6–4; Sian Yang (SIN) d. Nadeem-Kamran Khan (BAN) 6–4 7–6(2); Jensen Hiu/Kyoung Sik Seol (SIN) d. Dilip Passia/Moin-ud-din Walliullah (BAN) 6–2 7–6(4). *Tajikistan d. Pacific Oceania 2–0:* Sergei Makashin (TJK) d. Brett Baudinet (POC) 7–5 6–4; Mansur Yakhyaev (TJK) d. Lency Tenai (POC) 6–3 6–0; Sergei Makashin/Mansur Yakhyaev (TJK) v Brett Baudinet/Lency Tenai (POC) – not played.

PLAYOFF FOR 5th/6th POSITION: 13 February – *Tajikistan d. Singapore 2–1:* Sergei Makashin (TJK) d. Tung-Yi Kho (SIN) 3–6 4–1 ret; Mansur Yakhyaev (TJK) d. Sian Yang (SIN) 6–4 6–2; Jensen Hiu/Sian Yang (SIN) d. Sergei Makashin/Sergei Sedov (TJK) 6–3 6–4.

PLAYOFF FOR 7th/8th POSITION: 13 February – *Bangladesh d. Pacific Oceania 2–1:* Cyril Jacobe (POC) d. Dilip Passia (BAN) 6–1 6–2; Nadeem-Kamran Khan (BAN) d. Jerome Rovo (POC) 6–4 6–2; Dilip Passia/Abu-Hena-Tasawar Collins (BAN) d. Brett Baudinet/Lency Tenai (BAN) 3–6 6–4 9–7.

FINAL POSITIONS: 1. Syria, 2. Kuwait, 3. Sri Lanka, 4. Qatar, 5. Tajikistan, 6. Singapore, 7. Bangladesh, 8. Pacific Oceania.

Syria and Kuwait promoted to Asia/Oceania Group II for 2001.
Bangladesh and Pacific Oceania relegated to Asia/Oceania Group IV for 2001.

Group IV

EURO/AFRICAN ZONE – VENUE 1
Date: 14–20 February; Venue: Accra, Ghana; Surface: Hard (O).
Group A: Algeria, Andorra, Liechtenstein, Sudan.
Group B: Azerbaijan, Cameroon, Ghana, Mauritius.

GROUP A: 16 February – *Algeria d. Liechtenstein 3–0:* Noureddine Mahmoudi (ALG) d. Andreas Schweiger (LIE) 6–1 6–0; Abdelhak Hameurlaine (ALG) d. Alexander Risch (LIE) 6–3 6–0; Sid Ali Akkal/Abdel-Wahid Henni (ALG) d. Kenny Banzer/Wolfgang Strub (LIE) 6–0 6–3. *Andorra d. Sudan 3–0:* Jean-Baptiste Poux-Gautier (AND) d. Mandour Abdalla (SUD) 6–0 6–1; Joan Jimenez-Guerra (AND) d. Nour Gaafar (SUD) 6–0 6–1; Joan Jimenez-Guerra/Jean-Baptiste Poux-Gautier (AND) d. Nour Gaafar/Nour Wail (SUD) 6–0 6–1. **17 February** – *Algeria d. Sudan 3–0:* Noureddine Mahmoudi (ALG) d. Mandour Abdalla (SUD) 6–2 6–2; Abdelhak Hameurlaine (ALG) d. Nour Gaafar (SUD) 6–1 6–0; Sid Ali Akkal/Abdel-Wahid Henni (ALG) d. Nour Gaafar/Nour Wail (SUD) 7–6(2) 6–0. *Andorra d. Liechtenstein 3–0:* Jean-Baptiste Poux-Gautier (AND) d. Andreas Schweiger (LIE) 6–1 6–0; Joan Jimenez-Guerra (AND) d. Alexander Risch (LIE) 6–0 6–0; Joan Jimenez-Gautier/Kenneth Tuilier-Curco (AND) d. Kenny Banzer/Wolfgang Strub (LIE) 6–1 6–0. **18 February** – *Liechtenstein d. Sudan 2–1:* Andreas Schweiger (LIE) d. Mandour Abdalla (SUD) 4–6 6–3 7–5; Alexander Risch (LIE) d. Nour Gaafar (SUD) 6–2 6–3; Nour Gaafar/Nour Wail (SUD) d. Kenny Banzer/Wolfgang Strub (LIE) 6–1 6–3. *Algeria d. Andorra 2–1:* Noureddine Mahmoudi (ALG) d. Kenneth Tuilier-Curco (AND) 2–6 7–5 6–3; Abdelhak Hameurlaine (ALG) d. Joan Jimenez-Guerra (AND) 1–6 6–2 6–3; Kenneth Tuilier-Curco/Jean-Baptiste Poux-Gautier (AND) d. Sid Ali Akkal/Abdel-Wahid Henni (ALG) 6–1 6–1.

GROUP B: 16 February – *Ghana d. Azerbaijan 3–0:* Frank Ofori (GHA) d. Nidjat Ramazanov (AZE) 6–1 6–1; Gunther Darkey (GHA) d. Emin Agaev (AZE) 7–6(1) 6–4; Courage Anyidoho/Frank Ofori (GHA) d. Talat Rahimov/Farid Shirinov (AZE) 6–1 6–1. *Mauritius d. Cameroon 3–0:* Jean-Marcel Bourgault Du Coudray (MRI) d. Pierre Otolo-Metomo (CMR) 6–1 6–4; Kamil Patel (MRI) d. Lionel Kemajou (CMR) 6–3 6–2; Jean-Marcel Bourgault Du Coudray/ Kamil Patel (MRI) d. Luc Ondobo/Pierre Otolo-Metomo (CMR) 6–2 6–1. **17 February** – *Ghana d. Mauritius 2–1:* Frank Ofori (GHA) d. Jean-Marcel Bourgault Du Coudray (MRI) 6–4 6–4; Gunther Darkey (GHA) d. Kamil Patel (MRI) 4–6 7–6(3) 6–2; Jean-Marcel Bourgault Du Coudray/Kamil Patel (MRI) d. Courage Anyidoho/Thomas Debrah (GHA) 6–2 7–6(6). *Cameroon d. Azerbaijan 3–0:* Pierre Otolo-Metomo (CMR) d. Nidjat Ramazanov (AZE) 6–1 6–2; Lionel Kemajou (CMR) d. Emin Agaev (AZE) 6–4 6–1; Alifa Adoum/Lionel Kemajou (CMR) d. Talat Rahimov/Farid Shirinov (AZE) 6–0 6–1. **18 February** – *Ghana d. Cameroon 3–0:* Frank Ofori (GHA) d. Pierre Otolo-Metomo (CMR) 7–5 7–6(3); Gunther Darkey (GHA) d. Lionel Kemajou (CMR) 7–6(2) 7–5; Gunther Darkey/Frank Ofori (GHA) d. Alifa Adoum/Pierre Otolo-Metomo (CMR) 6–2 6–4. *Mauritius d. Azerbaijan 2–1:* Jean-Marcel Bourgault Du Coudray (MRI) d. Nidjat Ramazanov (AZE) 6–2 6–0; Emin Agaev (AZE) d. Kamil Patel (MRI) 6–7(8) 7–5 6–4; Jean-Marcel Bourgault Du Coudray/Jonathan Vencathachellum (MRI) d. Emin Agaev/Nidjat Ramazanov (AZE) 6–3 6–3.

PLAYOFF FOR 1st–4th POSITIONS: 19 February – *Mauritius d. Algeria 2–1:* Jean-Marcel Bourgault Du Coudray (MRI) d. Noureddine Mahmoudi (ALG) 6–4 6–1; Abdelhak Hameurlaine (ALG) d. Kamil Patel (MRI) 6–7(3) 6–3 6–1; Jean-Marcel Bourgault Du Coudray/Kamil Patel (MRI) d. Abdelhak Hameurlaine/Noureddine Mahmoudi (ALG) 6–3 6–1. *Ghana d. Andorra 3–0:* Frank Ofori (GHA) d. Jean-Baptiste Poux-Gautier (AND) 7–6(3) 6–3; Gunther Darkey (GHA) d. Joan Jimenez-Guerra (AND) 6–2 6–4; Courage Anyidoho/Thomas

Debrah (GHA) d. Kenneth Tuilier-Curco/Jean-Baptiste Poux-Gautier (AND) 6–3 6–3.
**PLAYOFF FOR 1st/2nd Position: 20 FEBRUARY – *Ghana d. Mauritius 3–0:* Thomas Debrah (GHA) d.
Jonathan Vencathachellum (MRI) 6–3 6–1; Courage Anyidoho (GHA) d. Jean-Marcel Bourgault Du Coudray
(MRI) 4–6 7–6(9) 6–3; Courage Anyidoho/Gunther Darkey (GHA) d. Jonathan Vencathachellum/Kenny Wong
Kee Chuan (MRI) 6–0 6–2.

**PLAYOFF FOR 3rd/4th POSITION: 20 February – *Andorra d. Algeria 2–1:* Kenneth Tuilier-Curco (AND) d.
Sid Ali Akkal (ALG) 3–6 6–2 6–1; Noureddine Mahmoudi (ALG) d. Jean-Baptiste Poux-Gautier (AND) 4–6
7–6(3) 6–4; Joan Jimenez-Guerra/Kenneth Tuilier-Curco (AND) d. Abdelhak Hameurlaine/Abdel-Wahid Henni
(ALG) 6–4 6–1.

**PLAYOFF FOR 5th–8th POSITIONS: 19 February – *Azerbaijan d. Liechtenstein 2–1:* Nidjat Ramazanov
(AZE) d. Andreas Schweiger (LIE) 6–1 2–6 6–1; Emin Agaev (AZE) d. Alexander Risch (LIE) 6–1 4–6 6–1; Kenny
Banzer/Andreas Schweiger (LIE) d. Talat Rahimov/Farid Shirinov (AZE) 6–4 6–3. *Cameroon d. Sudan 3–0:*
Alifa Adoum (CMR) d. Nour Wail (SUD) 6–4 6–3; Luc Ondobo (CMR) d. Nour Gaafar (SUD) 6–3 06 1–08; Alifa
Adoum/Luc Ondobo (CMR) d. Nour Gaafar/Nour Wail (SUD) 6–4 6–4.

**PLAYOFF FOR 5th/6th POSITION: 20 February – *Cameroon d. Azerbaijan 2–1:* Pierre Otolo-Metomo
(CMR) d. Nidjat Ramazanov (AZE) 7–6(2) 6–1; Emin Agaev (AZE) d. Lionel Kemajou (CMR) 6–4 6–3; Alifa
Adoum/Pierre Otolo-Metomo (CMR) d. Nidjat Ramazanov/Farid Shirinov (AJE) 6–3 6–2.

**PLAYOFF FOR 7th/8th POSITION: 20 February – *Liechtenstein d. Sudan 3–0:* Andreas Schweiger (LIE)
d. Nour Wail (SUD) 1–6 6–1 1–311; Alexander Risch (LIE) d. Nour Gaafar (SUD) 6–0 6–0; Kenny Banzer/Alex
Risch (LIE) d. Nour Gaafar/Abdella Jeha (SUD) 7–6(5) 7–6(1).

**Final Positions: 1. Ghana, 2. Mauritius, 3. Andorra, 4. Algeria, 5. Cameroon, 6. Azerbaijan, 7.
Liechtenstein, 8. Sudan.**

Ghana and Mauritius promoted to Euro/African Zone Group III in 2001.

EURO/AFRICAN ZONE – VENUE 2
Date: 19–23 January; Venue: Kampala, Uganda; Surface: Clay (O).
Group A: Ethiopia, Namibia, San Marino, Zambia.
Group B: Cyprus, Djibouti, Kenya, Lesotho, Uganda.

**GROUP A: 19 January – *Zambia d. San Marino 2–1:* Sidney Bwalya (ZAM) d. William Forcellini (SMR) 6–3
6–0; Domenico Vicini (SMR) d. Lighton Ndefwayi (ZAM) 7–5 6–3; Sidney Bwalya/Lighton Ndefwayi (ZAM) d.
Gabriel Francini/Domenico Vicini (SMR) 6–1 6–2. **20 January – *Zambia d. Ethiopia 2–1:* Sidney Bwalya
(ZAM) d. Yohannes Setegne (ETH) 6–2 6–1; Samuel Woldegebriel (ETH) d. Lighton Ndefwayi (ZAM) 7–5 6–3;
Sidney Bwalya/Lighton Ndefwayi (ZAM) d. Asfaw Mikaile/Yohannes Setegne (ETH) 6–3 6–2. **21 January –
Namibia d. San Marino 2–1: Jean-Pierre Huish (NAM) d. William Forcellini (SMR) 6–3 6–2; Domenico Vicini
(SMR) d. Johan Theron (NAM) 6–1 6–1; Henrico Du Plessis/Johan Theron (NAM) d. William Forcellini/
Domenico Vicini (SMR) 6–3 6–3. **22 January – *Namibia d. Ethiopia 3–0:* Jean-Pierre Huish (NAM) d.
Yohannes Setegne (ETH) 6–4 6–1; Johan Theron (NAM) d. Samuel Woldegebriel (ETH) 6–3 7–5; Henrico Du
Plessis/Kevin Wentzel (NAM) d. Asfaw Mikaile/Samuel Woldegebriel (ETH) 7–5 6–2. **23 January – *Namibia
d. Zambia 2–1:* Sidney Bwalya (ZAM) d. Jean-Pierre Huish (NAM) 6–2 3–6 6–4; Johan Theron (NAM) d.
Lighton Ndefwayi (ZAM) 6–4 6–3; Henrico Du Plessis/Johan Theron (NAM) d. Sidney Bwalya/Lighton
Ndefwayi (ZAM) 6–4 6–4. *San Marino d. Ethiopia 2–1:* Yohannes Setegne (ETH) d. William Forcellini (SMR)
6–3 6–1; Domenico Vicini (SMR) d. Samuel Woldegebriel (ETH) 6–3 6–3; Andrea Della Balda/Domenico Vicini
(SMR) d. Asfaw Mikaile/Samuel Woldegebriel (ETH) 7–5 3–6 6–3.

FINAL POSITIONS: 1. Namibia, 2. Zambia, 3. San Marino, 4. Ethiopia.

**GROUP B: 19 January – *Kenya d. Uganda 3–0:* Allan Cooper (KEN) d. Robert Buyinza (UGA) 6–3 6–1;
Trevor Kiruki (KEN) d. Bob Ndibwami (UGA) 6–4 3–6 6–1; Barry Ndinya/Norbert Oduor (KEN) d. Robert
Buyinza/Bob Ndibwami (UGA) 7–6(6) 7–6(6). *Cyprus d. Lesotho 3–0:* George Kalanov (CYP) d. Khotso Khali
(LES) 6–3 6–1; Demetrios Leondis (CYP) d. Ntsane Moeletsi (LES) 6–1 6–0; Marcos Baghdatis/Demetrios
Leondis (CYP) d. Ntsukunyane Letseka/Relebohile Motsepa (LES) 6–2 6–0. **20 January – *Kenya d. Cyprus
2–1:* Allan Cooper (KEN) d. George Kalanov (CYP) 7–5 4–6 7–5; Demetrios Leondis (CYP) d. Trevor Kiruki
(KEN) 6–4 6–4; Allan Cooper/Trevor Kiruki (KEN) d. Marcos Baghdatis/Demetrios Leondis (CYP) 6–4 6–3.
Lesotho d. Djibouti 3–0: Relebohile Motsepa (LES) d. Alla Mousa (DJI) 6–1 6–1; Ntsane Moeletsi (LES) d.
Kadar Mogueh (DJI) 6–1 6–1; Khotso Khali/Ntsukunyane Letseka (LES) d. Abdou-Rahman Aden/Kadar
Mogueh (DJI) 6–4 6–0. **21 January – *Kenya d. Lesotho 3–0:* Barry Ndinya (KEN) d. Khotso Khali (LES) 6–1
6–4; Trevor Kiruki (KEN) d. Ntsane Moeletsi (LES) 6–2 6–0; Barry Ndinya/Norbert Oduor (KEN) d. Ntsukunyane
Letseka/Relebohile Motsepa (LES) 6–2 6–4. *Uganda d. Djibouti 3–0:* Robert Buyinza (UGA) d. Alla Mousa
(DJI) 6–0 ret; Bob Ndibwami (UGA) d. Abdou-Rahman Aden (DJI) 6–1 6–0; Robert Buyinza/Bob Ndibwami
(UGA) d. Alla Mousa/Abdou-Rahman Aden (DJI) w/o. **22 January – *Uganda d. Lesotho 2–1:* Relebohile
Motsepa (LES) d. Robert Buyinza (UGA) 7–5 6–3; Bob Ndibwami (UGA) d. Ntsane Moeletsi (LES) 6–4 3–6 6–4;
Robert Buyinza/Bob Ndibwami (UGA) d. Ntsukunyane Letseka/Relebohile Motsepa (LES) 6–1 6–3. *Cyprus d.
Djibouti 3–0:* Constantinos Talianos (CYP) d. Abdou-Rahman Aden (DJI) 6–0 ret; Marcos Baghdatis (CYP) d.

Kadar Mogueh (DJI) 6–0 6–0; George Kalanov/Constantinos Talianos (CYP) d. Abdou-Rahman Aden/Kader Mogueh (DJI) 6–1 6–0. **23 January – *Cyprus d. Uganda 2–1:*** Marcos Baghdatis (CYP) d. Robert Buyinza (UGA) 6–3 6–4; George Kalanov (CYP) d. Bob Ndibwami (UGA) 6–2 6–4; Robert Buyinza/Bob Ndibwami (UGA) d. Marcos Baghdatis/Constantinos Talianos (CYP) 7–6(5) 2–6 6–3. *Kenya d. Djibouti 3–0:* Barry Ndinya (KEN) d. Abdou-Rahman Aden (DJI) 6–1 6–2; Allan Cooper (KEN) d. Kadar Mogueh (DJI) 6–0 1–0 ret; Allan Cooper/Barry Ndinya (KEN) d. Adballah Aden/Abdou-Rahman Aden (DJI) 6–0 6–1.

FINAL POSITIONS: 1. Kenya, 2. Cyprus, 3. Uganda, 4. Lesotho, 5. Djibouti.

Namibia and Kenya promoted to Euro/African Zone III in 2001.

AMERICAN ZONE
Date: 13–19 March; Venue: San Pedro Sula, Honduras; Surface: Hard (O)
Nations: Antigua & Barbuda, Bermuda, Honduras, OECS, St. Lucia, US Virgin Islands

13 March – *Honduras d. OECS 3–0:* Calton Alvarez (HON) d. Dexter Christian (ECA) 6–0 6–1; Carlos Caceres (HON) d. Kirtsen Cable (ECA) 6–3 6–1; Franklin Garcia/Cristian Kawas (HON) d. Hayden Ashton/Kirtsen Cable (ECA) 6–1 4–6 6–3. *Bermuda d. St. Lucia 2–1:* Jenson Bascome (BER) d. McCollin Fontenelle (LCA) 7–5 6–3; Kane Easter (LCA) d. James Collieson (BER) 6–3 6–3; Jenson Bascome/Richard Mallory (BER) d. Sirsean Arlain/Kane Easter (LCA) 6–4 6–4. *Barbados d. US Virgin Islands 2–1:* Lenin Mongerie (ISV) d. Duane Williams (BAR) 6–1 3–6 9–7; Kodi Lewis (BAR) d. Gregory Newton (ISV) 7–5 6–3; James Betts/Kodi Lewis (BAR) d. Lenin Mongerie/Gregory Newton (ISV) 0–6 6–4 7–5. **14 March – *Honduras d. Bermuda 3–0:*** Calton Alvarez (HON) d. Richard Mallory (BER) 7–5 3–1 ret; Carlos Caceres (HON) d. James Collieson (BER) 6–0 6–4; Carlos Caceres/Cristian Kawas (HON) d. Jenson Bascome/Dean Mello (BER) 6–2 6–1. *US Virgin Islands d. Antigua & Barbuda 2–1:* Carlton Bedminster (ANT) d. Lenin Mongerie (ISV) 6–3 4–6 6–4; Gregory Newton (ISV) d. Jerry Williams (ANT) 6–3 6–2; Gregory Newton/John Richards (ISV) d. Carlton Bedminster/Kevin Gardner (ANT) 6–1 6–1. *Barbados d. OECS 2–1:* Duane Williams (BAR) d. Dexter Christian (ECA) 7–6(4) 1–6 6–4; Kodi Lewis (BAR) d. Kirtsen Cable (ECA) 6–1 6–4; Hayden Ashton/Kirtsen Cable (ECA) d. James Betts/Michael Date (BAR) 6–4 6–2. **15 March – *St. Lucia d. Antigua/Barbuda 2–1:*** Carlton Bedminster (ANT) d. McCollin Fontenelle (LCA) 6–2 6–1; Kane Easter (LCA) d. Jerry Williams (ANT) 6–4 6–2; Sirsean Arlain/Kane Easter (LCA) d. Carlton Bedminster/Kevin Gardener (ANT) 7–6(7) 7–5. *OECS d. US Virgin Islands 2–1:* Louis Taylor (ISV) d. Dexter Christian (ECA) 6–4 6–2; Kirtsen Cable (ECA) d. Lenin Mongerie (ISV) 1–6 6–1 6–3; Hayden Ashton/Kirtsen Cable (ECA) d. Gregory Newton/John Richards (ISV) 4–6 6–3 7–5. *Bermuda d. Barbados 2–1:* Richard Mallory (BER) d. Duane Williams (BAR) 6–1 6–2; James Collieson (BER) d. Kodi Lewis (BAR) 6–4 3–6 6–4; James Betts/Duane Williams (BAR) d. Jenson Bascome/Dean Mello (BER) 7–5 2–6 7–5. **16 March – *Honduras d. St. Lucia 3–0:*** Calton Alvarez (HON) d. Sirsean Arlain (LCA) 6–1 6–1; Carlos Caceres (HON) d. Kane Easter (LCA) 6–2 7–6(5); Carlos Caceres/Cristian Kawas (HON) d. Sirsean Arlain/Jonathan Jean-Baptiste (LCA) 6–3 6–2. *Antigua & Barbuda d. OECS 3–0:* Kevin Gardener (ANT) d. Dexter Christian (ECA) 6–4 6–3; Carlton Bedminster (ANT) d. Kirtsen Cable (ECA) 3–6 7–6(3) 6–2; Jerry Williams/Gershum Philip (ANT) d. Hayden Ashton/Damian Hughes (ECA) 6–0 1–6 6–3. *Bermuda d. US Virgin Islands 2–1:* Louis Taylor (ISV) d. Richard Mallory (BER) 4–6 6–3 8–6; James Collieson (BER) d. Gregory Newton (ISV) 4–6 6–2 6–4; Dean Mello/Jenson Bascome (BER) d. Gregory Newton/John Richards (ISV) 4–6 6–4 6–4. **17 March – *Honduras d. Antigua & Barbuda 3–0:*** Calton Alvarez (HON) d. Kevin Gardner (ANT) 6–1 6–1; Carlos Caceres (HON) d. Carlton Bedminster (ANT) 6–3 6–0; Carlos Caceres/Christian Kawas (HON) d. Gershum Philip/Jerry Williams (ANT) 6–2 6–1. *Bermuda d. OECS 3–0:* Jenson Bascome (BER) d. Damian Hughes (ECA) 6–4 6–1; James Collieson (BER) d. Kirtsen Cable (ECA) 6–2 7–5; Jenson Bascome/Dean Mello (BER) d. Hayden Ashton/Damian Hughes (ECA) 6–1 ret. *St. Lucia d. Barbados 2–1:* Sirsean Arlain (LCA) d. James Betts (BAR) 6–4 6–0; Kane Easter (LCA) d. Kodi Lewis (BAR) 6–2 6–2; James Betts/Kodi Lewis (BAR) d. Sirsean Arlain/Jonathan Jean-Baptiste (LCA) 6–7(7) 6–2 7–5. **18 March – *Honduras d. Barbados 3–0:*** Calton Alvarez (HON) d. Duane Williams (BAR) 6–1 6–3; Carlos Caceres (HON) d. Kodi Lewis (BAR) 6–1 3–6 6–1; Carlos Caceres/Christian Kawas (HON) d. James Betts/Duane Williams (BAR) 6–2 3–6 6–3. *Bermuda d. Antigua & Barbuda 3–0:* Richard Mallory (BER) d. Gershum Philip (ANT) 6–1 6–1; James Collieson (BER) d. Carlton Bedminster (ANT) 6–1 7–5; Jenson Bascome/Dean Mello (BER) d. Kevin Gardner/Jerry Williams (ANT) 6–7(2) 7–6(3) 6–3. *St. Lucia d. US Virgin Islands 3–0:* Sirsean Arlain/Jonathan Jean-Baptiste (LCA) d. Louis Taylor (ISV) 6–3 7–6(5); Kane Easter (LCA) d. Lenin Mongerie (ISV) 6–2 6–1; Sirsean Arlain/Jonathan Jean-Baptiste (LCA) d. Lenin Mongerie/Gregory Newton (ISV) 7–6(3) 7–6(3). **19 March – *Honduras d. US Virgin Islands 3–0:*** Franklin Garcia (HON) d. John Richards (ISV) 7–5 6–4; Christian Kawas (HON) d. Gregory Newton (ISV) 3–6 6–1 6–2; Carlos Caceres/Christian Kawas (HON) d. Gregory Newton/John Richards (ISV) 6–4 5–7 7–5. *Antigua & Barbuda d. Barbados 3–0:* Kevin Gardner (ANT) d. Michael Date (BAR) 7–6(4) 6–0; Carlton Bedminster (ANT) d. Duane Williams (BAR) 7–5 6–2; Kevin Gardner/Jerry Williams (ANT) d. James Betts/Kodi Lewis (BAR) 3–6 7–6(5) 6–2. *St. Lucia d. OECS 3–0:* Sirsean Arlain (LCA) d. Dexter Christian (ECA) 6–2 6–2; Kane Easter (LCA) d. Kirtsen Cable (ECA) 6–4 6–2; Sirsean Arlain/Kane Easter (LCA) d. Kirtsen Cable/Hayden Ashton (ECA) 6–4 6–2.

FINAL POSITIONS: 1. Honduras, 2. Bermuda, 3. St. Lucia, 4. Antigua & Barbuda, 5. Barbados, 6. US Virgin Islands, 7. OECS.

Honduras and Bermuda promoted to American Zone Group III in 2001

ASIA/OCEANIA ZONE
Date: 24–30 April; Venue: Amman, Jordan; Surface: Hard (O).
Nations: Bahrain, Brunei, Fiji, Jordan, Oman, Saudi Arabia, United Arab Emirates.
24 April – *Jordan d. Brunei 2–1:* Ahmad Al Hadid (JOR) d. Billy Wong (BRU) 6–0 6–3; Abdalla Fada (JOR) d. Ismasufian Ibrahim (BRU) 6–4 6–1; Hardiyamin Baharuddin/Ismasufian Ibrahim (BRU) d. Ammar Al Maaytah/ Ahmad Al Hadid (JOR) 6–3 6–3. *Bahrain d. United Arab Emirates 2–1:* Essam Abdul-Aal (BRN) d. Mahmoud Al Balushi (UAE) 6–3 6–1; Abdul-Rahman Shehab (BRN) d. Omar-Bahrzrouzyan Awadhy (UAE) 6–4 7–5; Omar-Bahrzrouzyan Awadhy/Mahmoud Al Balushi (UAE) d. Nader Abdul-Aal/Fahad Sarwani (BRN) 7–6(6) 6–3. *Oman d. Fiji 3–0:* Khalid Al Nabhani (OMA) d. Hitesh Morriswala (FIJ) 6–2 7–5; Mudrik Al Rawahi (OMA) d. Sanjeev Tikaram (FIJ) 6–4 7–6(7); Khalid Al Nabhani/Mudrik Al Rawahi (OMA) d. Mohammed Jannif/Diva Gawander (FIJ) 6–0 6–3. **25 April** – *Jordan d. United Arab Emirates 2–1:* Ahmad Al Hadid (JOR) d. Mahmoud Al Balushi (UAE) 3–6 4–4 ret; Omar-Bahrzrouzyan Awadhy (UAE) d. Abdalla Fada (JOR) 6–3 2–6 6–2; Ahmad Al Hadid/Abdalla Fada (JOR) d. Omar-Bahrzrouzyan Awadhy/Abdulla Kamber (UAE) 7–6(4) 3–6 7–5. *Bahrain d. Fiji 3–0:* Essam Abdul-Aal (BRN) d. Hitesh Morriswala (FIJ) 6–2 6–0; Abdul-Rahman Shehab (BRN) d. Sanjeev Tikaram (FIJ) 6–2 6–0; Essal Abdul-Aal/Nader Abdul-Aal (BRN) d. Hitesh Morriswala/Sanjeev Tikaram (FIJ) 6–4 6–0. *Oman d. Saudi Arabia 2–1:* Badar Al Megayel (KSA) d. Khalid Al Nabhani (OMA) 6–4 6–4; Mudrik Al Rawahi (OMA) d. Abdullah Nour (KSA) 4–6 6–3 6–4; Khalid Al Nabhani (OMA)/Mudrik Al Rawahi (OMA) d. Baqer Abu Khulaif/Badar Al Megayel (KSA) 6–3 7–6(3). **26 April** – *Oman d. Jordan 3–0:* Khalid Al Nabhani (OMA) d. Ammar Al Maaytah (JOR) 7–5 6–2; Mudrik Al Rawahi (OMA) d. Ahmad Al Hadid (JOR) 4–6 6–4 7–5; Mudrik Al Rawahi/Khalid Al Nabhani (OMA) d. Abdalla Fada/Tareq Matekri (JOR) 6–2 6–2. *Fiji d. United Arab Emirates 2–1:* Omar-Bahrzrouzyan Awadhy (UAE) d. Hitesh Morriswala (FIJ) 6–2 6–3; Sanjeev Tikaram (FIJ) d. Othman Al Ulama (UAE) 6–1 7–5; Hitesh Morriswala/Sanjeev Tikaram (FIJ) d. Othman Al Ulama/Omar-Bahrzrouzyan Awadhy (UAE) 6–4 6–3. *Saudi Arabia d. Brunei 3–0:* Badar Al Megayel (KSA) d. Billy Wong (BRU) 6–0 6–0; Abdullah Nour (KSA) d. Ismasufian Ibrahim (BRU) 6–1 6–4; Badar Al Megayel/Baqer Abu Khulaif (KSA) d. Ismasufian Ibrahim/Hardiyamin Baharuddin (BRU) 6–3 6–2. **27 April** – *Saudi Arabia d. Jordan 2–1:* Badar Al Meqayel (KSA) d. Ammar Al Maaytah (JOR) 6–1 6–1; Ahmad Al Hadid (JOR) d. Abdullah Nour (KSA) 3–6 6–4 6–4; Badar Al Megayal/Baqer Abu Khulaif (KSA) d. Ahmed Al Hadid/Abdallah Fada (JOR) 6–0 4–6 6–0. *United Arab Emirates d. Brunei 3–0:* Abdulla Kamber (UAE) d. Sharill Teo (BRU) 6–1 6–2; Omar-Bahrzrouzyan Awadhy (UAE) d. Ismasufian Ibrahim (BRU) 6–2 6–4; Omar-Bahrzrouzyan Awadhy/Abdulla Kamber (UAE) d. Ismasufian Ibrahim/Hardiyamin Baharuddin (BRU) 6–0 6–3. *Bahrain d. Oman 2–1:* Essam Abdul-Aal (BRN) d. Khalid Al Nabhani (OMA) 4–6 6–3 6–1; Mudrik Al Rawahi (OMA) d. Abdul-Rahman Shehab (BRN) 6–1 6–7(5) 6–3; Essam Abdul-Aal/Abdul-Rahman Shehab (BRN) d. Khalid Al Nabhani/Mudrik Al Rawahi (OMA) 6–3 4–6 6–2. **28 April** – *Bahrain d. Jordan 2–1:* Essam Abdul-Aal (BRN) d. Tareq Matekri (JOR) 6–0 6–0; Ahmed Al-Hadid (JOR) d. Abdul-Rahman Shehab (BRN) 6–3 6–3; Essam Abdul-Aal/Abdul-Rahman Shehab (BRN) d. Ahmed Al-Hadid/Abdallah Fada (JOR) 6–1 6–3. *Saudi Arabia d. United Arab Emirates 2–1:* Badar Al Megayel (KSA) d. Asdulla Kamber (UAE) 6–0 6–1; Omar-Bahrzrouzyan Awadhy (UAE) d. Abdullah Nour (KSA) 2–6 6–4 6–1; Badar Al Megayel/Omar Al Thagib (KSA) d. Omar-Bahrzrouzyan Awadhy/Asdulla Kamber (UAE) 6–2 6–2. *Fiji d. Brunei 3–0:* Hitesh Morriswala (FIJ) d. Billy Wong (BRU) 6–1 6–1; Sanjeev Tikaram (FIJ) d. Ismafusian Ibrahim (BRU) 6–1 6–3; Mohammed Jannif/Hitesh Morriswala (FIJ) d. Sharill Teo/Billy Wong (BRU) 6–2 6–3. **29 April** – *Bahrain d. Brunei 3–0:* Fahad Sarwani (BRN) d. Sharrill Fred Teo (BRU) 6–1 6–0; Essam Abdul-Aal (BRN) d. Billy Wong (BRU) 6–0 6–0; Nader Abdul-Aal/Abdul-Rahman Shehab (BRN) d. Sharill Teo/Billy Wong (BRU) 6–0 6–0. *Saudi Arabia d. Fiji 3–0:* Badar Al Megayel (KSA) d. Mohammed Jannif (FIJ) 6–1 6–1; Abdullah Nour (KSA) d. Sanjeev Tikaram (FIJ) 6–4 4–6; Badar Al Megayel/Omar Al Thagib (KSA) d. Mohammed Jannif/Hitesh Morriswala (FIJ) 4–6 7–6(3). *United Arab Emirates d. Oman 2–1:* Omar-Bahrzrouzyan Awadhy (UAE) d. Khalid Al Nabhani (OMA) 6–4 7–6(2); Mudrik Al Rawahi (OMA) d. Othman Al Ulama (UAE) 6–3 6–4; Othman Al Ulama/Omar-Bahrzrouzyan Awadhy (UAE) d. Khalid Al Nabhani/Mudrik Al Rawahi (OMA) 7–6(3) 6–4. **30 April** – *Saudi Arabia d. Bahrain 2–1:* Badar Al Megayel (KSA) d. Essam Abdul-Aal (BRN) 6–3 6–3; Abdullah Nour (KSA) d. Abdul-Rahman Shehab (BRN) 7–6(6) 6–4; Nader Abdul-Aal/Fahad Sarwani (BRN) d. Omar Al Thagib/Baqer Abu Khulaif (KSA) 6–2 6–7(1) 6–1. *Jordan d. Fiji 2–1:* Ahmad Al Hadid (JOR) d. Hitesh Morriswala (FIJ) 6–1 6–2; Sanjeev Tikaram (FIJ) d. Abdalla Fada (JOR) 6–4 7–5; Ahmad Al Hadid/Abdalla Fada (JOR) d. Sanjeev Tikaram/Mohammed Jannif (FIJ) 6–4 7–6(6). *Oman d. Brunei 3–0:* Khalid Al Nabhani (OMA) d. Hardiyamin Baharuddin (BRU) 6–1 6–0; Mudrik Al Rawahi (OMA) d. Billy Wong (BRU) 6–0 6–1; Khalid Al Nabhani/Mohammed Al Nabhani (OMA) d. Ismasuifian Ibrahim/Billy Wong (BRU) 6–3 6–1.

FINAL POSITIONS: 1. Saudi Arabia, 2. Bahrain, 3. Oman, 4. Jordan, 5. Fiji, 6. United Arab Emirates, 7. Brunei.

Saudi Arabia and Bahrain promoted to Asia/Oceania Group III in 2001.

Fed Cup

Joanne Sirman

The new millennium marked the start of the ITF's partnership with the sports marketing company ISL to enhance the profile of the Fed Cup. The world's leading tennis team competition for women took on a new look in its elite World Group, with two restructured rounds, rather than three, to be played in the year. Including the lower level Regional Qualifying events, whose format remained the same, a record 102 nations took part in 2000.

The United States remained blithely unaffected by the changes and won the Fed Cup for the second consecutive year. The nation has now clocked up 17 wins in the competition, more than double any other, defeating old foe Spain at the Mandalay Bay Resort in Las Vegas in a dramatic and rather unexpected 5–0 sweep.

As defending champions, the United States had received a bye straight to the second round and also acted as host. This round, the Fed Cup World Finals, saw Belgium, Czech Republic and Spain join the home team in the semi-finals and final of the competition on 21–25 November. These three nations had each won a round robin contest in April. At these three events, each nation faced three other nations in best-of-three ties.

In the toughest of these round robin events, Belgium won Group C indoors in Moscow to qualify for the second round. With Australia, France and 1999 runner-up and host Russia playing, six of the world's top 20 women were in action. Four of these alone – Nathalie Dechy, Sandrine Testud, Julie Halard-Decugis and Nathalie Tauziat – were representing favourites France. Belgium, without the services of Dominique Van Roost, Sabine Appelmans and Justine Henin, chose to field the rapidly-improving Kim Clijsters in her Fed Cup debut against Australia. The 16-year-old lost an intriguing encounter with Jelena Dokic, her former junior doubles partner, 7–6 5–7 9–7. From then on however Clijsters proved to be Belgium's life-saver, winning matches against Tauziat 6–1 6–4 and Anna Kournikova 5–7 6–2 6–4 to seal victory for her country.

Hosts, the Slovak Republic, failed to take advantage of a home indoor court in Bratislava, where the Czech Republic won Group B to go through to the second week. The Czechs won

All smiles among the winning US team: (l to r) Lisa Raymond, Lindsay Davenport, Billie Jean King (capt.), Monica Seles, Jennifer Capriati. (Ron Angle)

Beaten finalists Spain: (l to r) Conchita Martinez, Virginia Ruano-Pascual, Magui Serna, Arantxa Sanchez-Vicario. (Ron Angle)

all three ties against Austria, Switzerland and the Slovak Republic, with another youngster, reigning ITF Girls' World Doubles Champion Daja Bedanova playing an important role in partnership with Kveta Hrdlickova.

In Bari, Italy hosted Croatia, Germany and Spain outdoors on clay but this only played into the hands of Spain, who used their expertise on the surface to win Group A. The Spanish had Fed Cup stalwarts Arantxa Sanchez-Vicario and Conchita Martinez at their disposal, and neither player lost a set in their singles matches as Spain swept past Italy 3–0 then Croatia 2–1. The nation took first place with a 2–1 win over Germany, with Sanchez-Vicario and Martinez teaming up for their eighteenth Fed Cup doubles victory.

With the United States and Spain through to the World Finals in Las Vegas, the old enemies looked on course to meet in the Final. The Czechs, appearing in the semi-finals for only the second time since 1991, fought hard against the Spanish, extending them to three sets in both singles matches. The more experienced nation came through 2–1 however, with Sanchez-Vicario defeating the 17-year-old Bedanova 5–7 6–4 6–3 and Martinez carving out a 7–6 6–7 6–4 win over Hrdlikova to take an insurmountable lead.

Representing the United States were world No. 2 Lindsay Davenport, No. 4 Monica Seles, Lisa Raymond and Jennifer Capriati, playing Fed Cup for the first time in four years. The nation reached its 25th Final in the event's 38-year history with a hard-won 2–1 victory over the plucky Belgians, Seles defeating Justine Henin 7–6 6–2 and Davenport winning a three-set struggle with Clijsters 7–6 4–6 6–3.

Spain had won the Fed Cup five times compared to the United States' 16 titles. Despite lacking home advantage, the recent statistics were in Spain's favour, the Europeans being the most successful Fed Cup nation of the 1990s, winning all five of their titles from seven Finals. Head-to-head, Spain had won five of the previous six meetings with the United States. Foremost in everyone's memory was their most recent showdown, in the dramatic 1998 Fed Cup semi-final which had gone to the final set of the deciding fifth rubber. Then, Martinez and Sanchez-Vicario had defeated Mary Joe Fernandez and Lisa Raymond 11–9 in the final set, en route to a Final against Switzerland and Spain's last Fed Cup title.

This time however the visitors buckled in the face of the Americans' skill and confidence. In the first of two days' play with the format reverting to a best-of-five-match format, Seles overpowered Martinez 6–2 6–3 and Davenport defeated Sanchez-Vicario 6–2 1–6 6–3. In the second match the Spaniard changed tactics to win the second set, moving inside the baseline to seize the initiative and raise the visitors' hopes. This was not enough though and Spain went into day two 0–2 down. In the first reverse singles the United States continued their devastating form and Davenport took just under an hour to defeat Martinez, who was playing with an elbow injury, 6–1 6–2 and so hand victory to her country. In the dead second singles, Capriati won when Sanchez-Vicario retired with gastroenteritis before Capriati and Raymond defeated Virginia Ruano-Pascual and Magui Serna 4–6 6–4 6–2 in the doubles to complete the sweep. For the second year running Davenport had won the decisive match for the United States. The delighted world No. 2 was thrilled to avenge the 1998 defeat: 'It's great to beat Spain again, especially after what happened in Madrid two years ago. This is my third time on a winning team, and the whole week we all had a lot of fun.' It was only the second time in the last ten years that Spain had fallen to the Americans, and the first since 1996. The Spanish had also missed out on the chance of a dream double, with their male counterparts poised on the brink of an historic Davis Cup title in Barcelona. The places of Sanchez-Vicario and Martinez in Fed Cup history remain secure, however. At the end of 2000, Sanchez-Vicario had notched up a 43–19 singles record in Fed Cup, and Martinez 41–14, meaning that both have now overtaken Chris Evert to go into second and third places on the all-time singles list, threatening Helena Sukova's 45–11 record.

Elsewhere in the 2000 Fed Cup competition there was delight for Argentina, Japan and Hungary, who won their respective Regional Qualifying events to gain promotion to the 2001 Fed Cup World Group.

At the end of the first year of their partnership, the ITF and ISL reviewed the new-look Fed Cup and decided the World Group format needed some revision to conserve its best elements. There was a feeling that, with its restructure, the competition had lost something essential, part of what makes it compelling: its home-and-away format. In 2001 therefore, there will be three rounds played during the year. The first two of these rounds will revert to a home and away contest played over a Saturday and Sunday, each tie being the best of five matches. The third and final round will be a round robin event staged over one week, ties being the best of three matches. The World Group will also be expanded from 13 nations to 16, giving more teams the chance to win the Fed Cup.

2000 FED CUP

WORLD GROUP

FIRST ROUND: 27–30 APRIL

GROUP A
Venue: Bari, Italy; Surface: Clay (O).
Nations: Croatia, Italy, Germany, Spain.

27 April – Germany d. Croatia 2–1: Jelena Kostanic (CRO) d. Andrea Glass (GER) 6–7(9) 6–1 6–3; Anke Huber (GER) d. Silvija Talaja (CRO) 6–2 6–2; Anke Huber/Barbara Rittner (GER) d. Jelena Kostanic/Silvija Talaja (CRO) 6–4 6–1. **Spain d. Italy 3–0:** Arantxa Sanchez-Vicario (ESP) d. Giulia Casoni (ITA) 6–1 6–1; Conchita Martinez (ESP) d. Tathiana Garbin (ITA) 6–3 6–3; Magui Serna/Cristina Torrens Valero (ESP) d. Giulia Casoni/Rita Grande (ITA) 6–2 3–6 6–1. **28 April – Spain d. Croatia 2–1:** Arantxa Sanchez-Vicario (ESP) d. Iva Majoli (CRO) 6–4 6–2; Conchita Martinez (ESP) d. Jelena Kostanic (CRO) 6–3 6–2; Jelena Kostanic/Iva Majoli (CRO) d. Magui Serna/Christina Torrens Valero (ESP) 6–3 7–6(3). **29 April – Italy d. Croatia 3–0:** Tathiana Garbin (ITA) d. Jelena Kostanic (CRO) 6–4 7–6(6); Silvia Farina (ITA) d. Silvija Talaja (CRO) 6–4 7–5; Giulia Casoni/Rita Grande (ITA) d. Jelena Kostanic/Silvija Talaja (CRO) 6–4 5–7 6–3. **Spain d. Germany 2–1:** Arantxa Sanchez-Vicario (ESP) d. Andrea Glass (GER) 6–3 6–3; Anke Huber (GER) d. Conchita Martinez (ESP) 6–3 6–1; Conchita Martinez/Arantxa Sanchez-Vicario (ESP) d. Anke Huber/Barbara Rittner (GER) 6–2 6–3. **30 April – Germany d. Italy 2–1:** Tathiana Garbin (ITA) d. Andrea Glass (GER) 6–2 6–3; Anke Huber (GER) d. Silvia Farina (ITA) 7–6(5) 7–5; Anke Huber/Barbara Rittner (GER) d. Silvia Farina/Rita Grande (ITA) 6–3 7–5.

FINAL STANDINGS: 1. Spain, 2. Germany, 3. Italy, 4. Croatia.

Spain qualified for World Finals. Croatia relegated to Europe/Africa Qualifying Group I.

GROUP B
Venue: Bratislava, Slovak Republic; Surface: Hard (I).
Nations: Austria, Czech Republic, Slovak Republic, Switzerland.

27 April – Czech Republic d. Austria 2–1: Kveta Hrdlickova (CZE) d. Patricia Wartusch (AUT) 6–3 1–6 6–3; Denisa Chladkova (CZE) d. Barbara Schett (AUT) 5–7 6–4 6–2; Barbara Schett/Patricia Wartusch (AUT) d. Daja Bedanova/Kveta Hrdlickova (CZE) 7–6(6) 2–6 6–3. **Switzerland d. Slovak Republic 2–1:** Emmanuelle

Gagliardi (SUI) d. Henrieta Nagyova (SVK) 5–7 6–2 6–1; Patty Schnyder (SUI) d. Karina Habsudova (SVK) 6–1 6–4; Karina Habsudova/Daniela Hantuchova (SVK) d. Patty Schnyder/Miroslava Vavrinec (SUI) 6–7(8) 6–2 7–5. **28 April – Czech Republic d. Switzerland 2–1:** Kveta Hrdlickova (CZE) d. Emmanuelle Gagliardi (SUI) 6–1 7–6(4); Patty Schnyder (SUI) d. Denisa Chladkova (CZE) 6–2 6–2; Daja Bedanova/Kveta Hrdlickova (CZE) d. Emmanuelle Gagliardi/Patty Schnyder (SUI) 4–6 6–1 6–1. **29 April – Czech Republic d. Slovak Republic 2–1:** Daniela Hantuchova (SVK) d. Kveta Hrdlickova (CZE) 6–4 6–2; Denisa Chladkova (CZE) d. Karina Habsudova (SVK) 6–4 6–4; Daja Bedanova/Kveta Hrdlickova (CZE) d. Karina Habsudova/Daniela Hantuchova (SVK) 7–5 6–3. **Switzerland d. Austria 2–1:** Emmanuelle Gagliardi (SUI) d. Patricia Wartusch (AUT) 6–2 6–4; Barbara Schett (AUT) d. Patty Schnyder (SUI) 7–6(4) 7–5; Emmanuelle Gagliardi/Patty Schnyder (SUI) d. Barbara Schett/Patricia Wartusch (AUT) 2–6 6–4 8–6. **30 April – Austria d. Slovak Republic 2–0:** Marion Maruska (AUT) d. Daniela Hantuchova (SVK) 6–4 7–6(1); Barbara Schett (AUT) d. Karina Habsudova (SVK) 6–4 7–5; doubles not played.

FINAL STANDINGS: 1. Czech Republic, 2. Switzerland, 3. Austria, 4. Slovak Republic.

Czech Republic qualified for World Finals. Slovak Republic relegated to Europe/Africa Qualifying Group I.

GROUP C
Venue: Moscow, Russia; Surface: Carpet (I).
Nations: Australia, Belgium, France, Russia.

27 April – Belgium d. Australia 2–1: Laurence Courtois (BEL) d. Nicole Pratt (AUS) 6–1 2–6 7–5; Jelena Dokic (AUS) d. Kim Clijsters (BEL) 7–6(4) 5–7 9–7; Els Callens/Laurence Courtois (BEL) d. Alicia Molik/Rennae Stubbs (AUS) 1–6 6–0 10–8. **France d. Russia 3–0:** Sandrine Testud (FRA) d. Elena Likhovtseva (RUS) 6–1 6–4; Julie Halard-Decugis (FRA) d. Anna Kournikova (RUS) 6–2 2–6 6–1; Julie Halard-Decugis/Nathalie Tauziat (FRA) d. Anna Kournikova/Elena Likhovtseva (RUS) 6–3 7–6(5). **28 April – France d. Australia 2–1:** Nathalie Dechy (FRA) d. Nicole Pratt (AUS) 6–4 5–7 6–2; Jelena Dokic (AUS) d. Sandrine Testud (FRA) 6–7(4) 7–5 6–3; Julie Halard-Decugis/Nathalie Tauziat (FRA) d. Alicia Molik/Rennae Stubbs (AUS) 6–0 7–6(3). **29 April – Russia d. Australia 2–1:** Elena Likhovtseva (RUS) d. Nicole Pratt (AUS) 6–3 6–2; Jelena Dokic (AUS) d. Anna Kournikova (RUS) 6–7(3) 7–5 6–3; Anna Kournikova/Elena Likhovtseva (RUS) d. Jelena Dokic/Rennae Stubbs (AUS) 6–3 4–6 6–1. **Belgium d. France 2–1:** Els Callens (BEL) d. Julie Halard-Decugis (FRA) 3–6 6–4 6–2; Kim Clijsters (BEL) d. Nathalie Tauziat (FRA) 6–1 6–4; Julie Halard-Decugis/Nathalie Tauziat (FRA) d. Els Callens/Laurence Courtois (BEL) 7–5 3–6 6–3. **30 April – Belgium d. Russia 2–1:** Elena Likhovtseva (RUS) d. Laurence Courtois (BEL) 6–4 6–4; Kim Clijsters (BEL) d. Anna Kournikova (RUS) 5–7 6–2 6–4; Els Callens/Laurence Courtois (BEL) d. Anna Kournikova/Elena Likhovtseva (RUS) 6–4 6–3.

FINAL STANDINGS: 1. Belgium, 2. France, 3. Russia, 4. Australia.

Belgium qualified for World Finals. Australia relegated to Asia/Oceania Qualifying Group I.

WORLD FINALS: 21–25 November
Venue: Mandalay Bay Resort, Las Vegas; Surface: Supreme (I)
Nations: Belgium, Czech Republic, Spain, USA.

SEMI-FINALS: 21 November – Spain d. Czech Republic 2–1: Arantxa Sanchez-Vicario (ESP) d. Daja Bedanova (CZE) 5–7 6–4 6–3; Conchita Martinez (ESP) d. Kveta Hrdlickova (CZE) 7–6(3) 6–7(2) 6–4; Daja Bedanova/Kveta Hrdlickova (CZE) d. Virginia Ruano Pascual/Magui Serna (ESP) 1–6 6–3 7–6(5). **22 November – USA d. Belgium 2–1:** Monica Seles (USA) d. Justine Henin (BEL) 7–6(1) 6–2; Lindsay Davenport (USA) d. Kim Clijsters (BEL) 7–6(4) 4–6 6–3; Els Callens/Dominique Van Roost (BEL) d. Jennifer Capriati/Lisa Raymond (USA) 6–3 7–5.

FINAL: 24 November – USA d. Spain 5–0: Monica Seles (USA) d. Conchita Martinez (ESP) 6–2 6–3; Lindsay Davenport (USA) d. Arantxa Sanchez-Vicario (ESP) 6–2 1–6 6–3. **(25 November)** Lindsay Davenport (USA) d. Conchita Martinez (ESP) 6–1 6–2; Jennifer Capriati (USA) d. Arantxa Sanchez-Vicario (ESP) 6–1 1–0 ret; Jennifer Capriati/Lisa Raymond (USA) d. Virginia Ruano-Pascual/Magui Serna (ESP) 4–6 6–4 6–2.

AMERICAS QUALIFYING GROUP I
Date: 25–30 April; Venue: Florianopolis, Brazil; Surface: Clay (O).
Group A: Brazil, Canada, Chile, Uruguay, Venezuela .
Group B: Argentina, Colombia, Cuba, Mexico, Paraguay.

GROUP A: 25 April – Canada d. Chile 3–0: Jana Nejedly (CAN) d. Barbara Castro (CHI) 6–1 6–3; Maureen Drake (CAN) d. Valentina Castro (CHI) 6–0 6–1; Sonya Jeyaseelan/Vanessa Webb (CAN) d. Carolina Aravena/Valentina Castro (CHI) 6–1 6–2. **Venezuela d. Uruguay 3–0:** Milagros Sequera (VEN) d. Cecilia Guillenea (URU) 4–6 6–1 6–4; Maria Alejandra Vento (VEN) d. Daniela Olivera (URU) 1–6 6–1 6–3; Milagros Sequera/Maria Alejandra Vento (VEN) d. Lucia Migliarini/Virginia Sadi (URU) 6–1 6–1. **26 April – Venezuela d. Brazil 2–1:** Milagros Sequera (VEN) d. Miriam D'Agostini (BRA) 7–6(5) 6–2; Maria Alejandra Vento (VEN) d. Joana Cortez (BRA) 7–5 3–6 6–3; Miriam D'Agostini/Carla Tiene (BRA) d. Milagros Sequera/Maria Alejandra Vento (VEN) 6–4 5–7 6–4. **Uruguay d. Chile 3–0:** Cecilia Guillenea (URU) d. Barbara Castro (CHI) 7–6(6) 6–3; Daniela Olivera (URU) d. Valentina Castro (CHI) 6–2 6–1; Daniela Olivera/Virginia Sadi (URU) d.

Carolina Aravena/Valentina Castro (CHI) 6–3 6–2. **27 April – Brazil d. Chile 3–0:** Carla Tiene (BRA) d. Carolina Aravena (CHI) 6–4 4–6 6–3; Joana Cortez (BRA) d. Barbara Castro (CHI) 6–2 6–3; Joana Cortez/Miriam D'Agostini (BRA) d. Valentina Castro/Karen Harboe (CHI) 6–4 6–2. **Canada d. Uruguay 3–0:** Sonya Jeyaseelan (CAN) d. Cecilia Guillenea (URU) 6–1 6–2; Maureen Drake (CAN) d. Daniela Olivera (URU) 7–5 6–2; Maureen Drake/Sonya Jeyaseelan (CAN) d. Lucia Migliarini/Virginia Sadi (URU) 6–0 6–2. **28 April – Canada d. Brazil 3–0:** Jana Nejedly (CAN) d. Miriam D'Agostini (BRA) 7–6(5) 6–7(5) 3–0 ret; Sonya Jeyaseelan (CAN) d. Joana Cortez (BRA) 6–0 6–4; Maureen Drake/Sonya Jeyaseelan (CAN) d. Maria Fernanda Alves/Carla Tiene (BRA) 6–1 6–3. **Venezuela d. Chile 3–0:** Milagros Sequera (VEN) d. Carolina Aravena (CHI) 4–6 6–3 6–0; Maria Alejandra Vento (VEN) d. Barbara Castro (CHI) 3–0 ret; Milagros Sequera/Maria Alejandra Vento (VEN) d. Valentina Castro/Karen Harboe (CHI) 6–2 6–1. **29 April – Canada d. Venezuela 2–1:** Jana Nejedly (CAN) d. Milagros Sequera (VEN) 2–6 7–6(1) 6–3; Maria Alejandra Vento (VEN) d. Sonya Jeyaseelan (CAN) 6–3 7–5; Maureen Drake/Sonya Jeyaseelan (CAN) d. Milagros Sequera/Maria Alejandra Vento (VEN) 6–7(4) 6–4 7–5. **Brazil d. Uruguay 2–1:** Carla Tiene (BRA) d. Cecilia Guillenea (URU) 6–3 6–4; Daniela Olivera (URU) d. Joana Cortez (BRA) 6–4 6–4; Joana Cortez/Miriam D'Agostini (BRA) d. Daniela Olivera/Virginia Sadi (URU) 6–2 6–3.

FINAL STANDINGS: 1. Canada, 2. Venezuela, 3. Brazil, 4. Uruguay, 5. Chile.

GROUP B: 25 April – Argentina d. Mexico 3–0: Maria Emilia Salerni (ARG) d. Melody Falco (MEX) 6–1 6–4; Florencia Labat (ARG) d. Jessica Fernandez (MEX) 6–3 6–2; Gisela Dulko/Laura Montalvo (ARG) d. Melody Falco/Jessica Fernandez (MEX) 6–3 7–6(2). **Paraguay d. Cuba 2–1:** Yanet Nunez (CUB) d. Alejandra Garcia (PAR) 7–5 6–1; Larissa Schaerer (PAR) d. Yoannis Montesino (CUB) 6–3 6–1; Alejandra Garcia/Larissa Schaerer (PAR) d. Yamile Fors/Yoannis Montesino (CUB) 1–6 6–2 10–8. **26 April – Argentina d. Paraguay 3–0:** Maria Emilia Salerni (ARG) d. Sarah Tami 6–0 6–3; Florencia Labat (ARG) d. Larissa Schaerer (PAR) 6–2 6–2; Florencia Labat/Laura Montalvo (ARG) d. Maria Alejandra Garcia/Sarah Tami (PAR) 6–1 6–0. **Colombia d. Mexico 2–1:** Melody Falco (MEX) d. Catalina Castano (COL) 6–2 0–6 6–2; Fabiola Zuluaga (COL) d. Jessica Fernandez (MEX) 6–3 6–1; Mariana Mesa/Fabiola Zuluaga (COL) d. Melody Falco/Jessica Fernandez (MEX) 7–5 6–1. **27 April – Colombia d. Cuba 3–0:** Catalina Castano (COL) d. Yamile Fors (CUB) 6–4 6–1; Fabiola Zuluaga (COL) d. Yanet Nunez (CUB) 6–4 6–2; Mariana Mesa/Fabiola Zuluaga (COL) d. Yamile Fors/Yoannis Montesino (CUB) 6–2 6–1. **Mexico d. Paraguay 3–0:** Melody Falco (MEX) d. Sarah Tami (PAR) 6–1 6–1; Jessica Fernandez (MEX) d. Larissa Schaerer (PAR) 7–5 7–6(5); Melody Falco/Erika Valdez (MEX) d. Maria Alejandra Garcia/Carolina Ojeda (PAR) 6–2 6–4. **28 April – Argentina d. Cuba 3–0:** Maria Emilia Salerni (ARG) d. Yanet Nunez (CUB) 6–3 6–2; Florencia Labat (ARG) d. Yoannis Montesino (CUB) 6–2 6–0; Gisela Dulko/Laura Montalvo (ARG) d. Yamile Fors/Yanet Nunez (CUB) 6–1 6–1. **Colombia d. Paraguay 3–0:** Catalina Castano (COL) d. Maria Alejandra Garcia (PAR) 6–3 6–0; Fabiola Zuluaga (COL) d. Larissa Schaerer (PAR) 6–2 4–6 6–2; Romi Farah/Mariana Mesa (COL) d. Maria Alejandra Garcia/Sarah Tami (PAR) 6–4 6–7(6) 6–2. **29 April – Argentina d. Colombia 3–0:** Maria Emilia Salerni (ARG) d. Catalina Castano (COL) 6–4 6–2; Florencia Labat (ARG) d. Fabiola Zuluaga (COL) 7–5 1–6 12–10; Gisela Dulko/Laura Montalvo (ARG) d. Romy Farah/Mariana Mesa (COL) 6–3 6–3. **Mexico d. Cuba 3–0:** Melody Falco (MEX) d. Yanet Nunez (CUB) 6–4 6–3; Jessica Fernandez (MEX) d. Yoannis Montesino (CUB) 7–5 6–4; Jessica Fernandez/Erika Valdez (MEX) d. Yamile Fors/Yanet Nunez (CUB) 6–3 4–6 6–1.

FINAL STANDINGS: 1. Argentina, 2. Colombia, 3. Mexico, 4. Paraguay, 5. Cuba.

PROMOTION PLAYOFF: 30 April – Argentina d. Canada 2–1: Jana Nejedly (CAN) d. Gisela Dulko 6–3 7–5; Maria Emilia Salerni (ARG) d. Sonya Jeyaseelan (CAN) 6–4 7–5; Laura Montalvo/Maria Emilia Salerni (ARG) d. Maureen Drake/Sonya Jeyaseelan (CAN) 6–1 6–3.

Argentina promoted to World Group for 2001.
Chile and Cuba relegated to Americas Qualifying Group II for 2001.

AMERICAS QUALIFYING GROUP II

Date: 9–13 May; Venue: La Libertad, El Salvador; Surface: Clay (O).
Group A: Barbados, Dominican Republic, Trinidad & Tobago.
Group B: Antigua & Barbuda, Bahamas, Ecuador, Panama.
Group C: Bermuda, Guatemala, Jamaica, Puerto Rico.
Group D: Bolivia, Costa Rica, El Salvador.

GROUP A: 9 May – Trinidad & Tobago d. Barbados 2–1: Ariana Marshall (BAR) d. Sheenagh Cosgrove (TRI) 7–6(4) 5–7 8–6; Anneliese Rose (TRI) d. Elena Branker (BAR) 6–0 6–0; Cindra Maharaj/Anneliese Rose (TRI) d. Elena Branker/Ariana Marshall (BAR) 6–1 6–1. **10 May – Dominican Republic d. Trinidad & Tobago 2–1:** Glenny Cepeda (DOM) d. Sheenagh Cosgrove (TRI) 6–3 6–2; Anneliese Rose (TRI) d. Joelle Schad (DOM) 6–2 6–4; Glenny Cepeda/Joelle Schad (DOM) d. Cindra Maharaj/Anneliese Rose (TRI) 6–0 6–3. **11 May – Dominican Republic d. Barbados 3–0:** Carla Prieto (DOM) d. Ariana Marshall (BAR) 6–1 6–1; Joelle Schad (DOM) d. Elena Branker 6–1 6–0; Daysi Espinal/Carla Prieto (DOM) d. Elena Branker/Ariana Marshall 6–3 6–2.

GROUP B: 9 May – Ecuador d. Bahamas 3–0: Alexandra Guzman (ECU) d. Larikah Russell (BAH) 6–0 6–0; Myriam Cueva (ECU) d. Nikkita Fountain (BAH) 6–1 6–0; Paola Guerrero/Alexandra Guzman (ECU) d. Nikkita Fountain/Larikah Russell (BAH) 6–3 6–1. **Panama d. Antigua & Barbuda 2–1:** Niki Williams (ANT) d. Lilly Cal

(PAN) 6–2 6–4; Karla Hall (PAN) d. Isoke Perry (ANT) 6–3 6–3; Lilly Cal/Karla Hall (PAN) d. Francine Harvey/Niki Williams (ANT) 6–1 6–4. **10 May – *Ecuador d. Panama 3–0:*** Alexandra Guzman (ECU) d. Lilly Cal (PAN) 6–0 6–0; Paola Guerrero (ECU) d. Karla Hall (PAN) 6–0 6–1; Paola Guerrero/Alexandra Guzman (ECU) d. Lilly Cal/Yamara Figueroa (BAH) 6–0 6–1. *Bahamas d. Antigua & Barbuda 3–0:* Larikah Russell(BAH) d. Niki Williams (ANT) 6–1 6–1; Nikkita Fountain (BAH) d. Isoke Perry (ANT) 6–4 6–2; Shaniek Pinder/Larikah Russell (BAH) d. Lorna-May Lewis/Isoke Perry (ANT) 6–2 7–5. **11 May – *Bahamas d. Panama 3–0:*** Larikah Russell (BAH) d. Lilly Cal (PAN) 6–0 6–1; Nikkita Fountain (BAH) d. Karla Hall (PAN) 1–6 6–2 6–4; Shaniek Pinder/Larikah Russell (BAH) d. Lilly Cal/ Yamara Figueroa (BAH) 6–3 6–3. *Ecuador d. Antigua & Barbuda 3–0:* Paola Guerrero (ECU) d. Niki Williams (ANT) 6–0 6–0; Myriam Cueva (ECU) d. Isoke Perry (ANT) 6–1 6–2; Paola Guerrero/Alexandra Guzman (ECU) d. Isoke Perry/Niki Williams (ANT) 6–1 6–0.

GROUP C: 9 May – *Puerto Rico d. Bermuda 3–0:* Tari Toro (PUR) d. Danielle Paynter (BER) 6–0 6–1; Mari Toro (PUR) d. Zarah De Silva (BER) 6–4 6–3; Mari Toro/Edna Vasquez (PUR) d. Danielle Downey/Tara Lambert (BER) 6–1 6–3. *Guatemala d. Jamaica 2–1:* Maria Paz Orero (GUA) d. Anya Moyston (JAM) 6–3 6–2; Luisa Lopez (GUA) d. Asha Jaja (JAM) 6–1 6–1; Anya Moyston/Tinesta Rowe (JAM) d. Lucia Henkle/Maria Paz Orero (GUA) 6–3 6–1. **10 May – *Puerto Rico d. Guatemala 3–0:*** Tari Toro (PUR) d. Maria Paz Orero (GUA) 6–2 6–3; Mari Toro (PUR) d. Luisa Lopez (GUA) 6–3 6–4; Jessica Roland/Edna Vasquez (PUR) d. Luisa Lopez/Maria Paz Orero (GUA) 6–1 6–3. *Bermuda d. Jamaica 2–1:* Danielle Paynter (BER) d. Tinesta Rowe (JAM) 6–4 6–0; Zarah De Silva (BER) d. Asha Jaja (JAM) 7–6(2) 6–4; Anya Moyston/Tinesta Rowe (JAM) d. Tara Lambert/Danielle Paynter (BER) 2–6 6–2 6–4. **11 May – *Puerto Rico d. Jamaica 3–0:*** Tari Toro (PUR) d. Tinesta Rowe (JAM) 6–4 6–0; Mari Toro (PUR) d. Anya Moyston 6–0 6–0; Jessica Roland/Mari Toro (PUR) d. Anya Moyston/Tinesta Rowe (JAM) 6–1 6–2. *Guatemala d. Bermuda 3–0:* Maria Paz Orero (GUA) d. Danielle Paynter (BER) 6–2 6–1; Luisa Lopez (GUA) d. Zarah De Silva (BER) 6–1 7–6(5); Lucia Henkle/Luisa Lopez (GUA) d. Danielle Downey/Tara Lambert (BER) 6–3 6–2.

GROUP D: 9 May – *El Salvador d. Costa Rica 2–1:* Ivon Rodezno (ESA) d. Melissa Mendieta (CRC) 6–3 4–6 6–2; Claudia Argumedo (ESA) d. Milena Leiva (CRC) 6–1 6–3; Paula Umana/Erika Villalobos (CRC) d. Liz Cruz/Ivon Rodezno (ESA) 6–3 7–6(3). **10 May – *Bolivia d. El Salvador 2–1:*** Daniela Alvarez (BOL) d. Ivon Rodezno (ESA) 6–2 6–1; Monica Poveda (BOL) d. Claudia Argumedo (ESA) 6–0 7–6(3); Liz Cruz/Ivon Rodezno (ESA) d. Viviana Rovero/Natasha Villarroel (BOL) 6–2 4–6 6–2. **11 May – *Bolivia d. Costa Rica 3–0:*** Daniela Alvarez (BOL) d. Erika Villalobos (CRC) 6–1 6–1; Viviana Rivero (BOL) d. Melissa Mendieta (CRC) 2–6 6–0 6–3; Viviana Rivero/Natasha Villarroel (BOL) d. Paula Umana/Erika Villalobos (CRC) 7–6(5) 6–1.

PLAYOFF FOR 1st–4th POSITIONS: 12 May – *Dominican Republic d. Puerto Rico 2–1:* Glenny Cepeda (DOM) d. Jessica Roland (PUR) 7–6(6) 6–1; Joelle Schad (DOM) d. Mari Toro (PUR) 7–6(2) 6–2; Tari Toro/Edna Vasquez (PUR) d. Daysi Espinal/Carla Prieto (DOM) 6–0 6–1. *Ecuador d. Bolivia 3–0:* Alexandra Guzman (ECU) d. Daniela Alvarez (BOL) 6–1 6–2; Paola Guerrero (ECU) d. Viviana Rivero (BOL) 6–0 6–1; Paola Guerrero/Nuria Niemes (ECU) d. Viviana Rivero/Natasha Villarroel (BOL) 0–6 6–4 6–1.

PLAYOFF FOR 1st/2nd POSITION: 13 May – *Ecuador d. Dominican Republic 3–0:* Paola Guerrero (ECU) d. Glenny Cepeda (DOM) 6–2 4–6 6–2; Myriam Cueva (ECU) d. Daysi Espinal (DOM) 6–2; Paola Guerrero/Alexandra Guzman (ECU) d. Daysi Espinal/Carla Prieto (DOM) 6–0 6–2.

PLAYOFF FOR 3rd/4th POSITION: 13 May – *Bolivia d. Puerto Rico 3–0:* Daniela Alvarez (BOL) d. Edna Vasquez (PUR) 6–0 6–1; Viviana Rivero (BOL) d. Jessica Roland (PUR) 6–0 6–7(4) 6–2; Viviana Rivero/Natasha Villarroel (BOL) d. Tari Toro/Edna Vasquez (PUR) 6–2 6–2.

PLAYOFF FOR 5th–8th POSITIONS: 12 May – *Bahamas d. Guatemala 3–0:* Larikah Russell (BAH) d. Maria Paz Orero (GUA) 6–2 6–1; Nikkita Fountain (BAH) d. Luisa Lopez (GUA) 6–3 3–6 7–5; Nikkita Fountain/Larikah Russell (BAH) d. Lucia Henkle/Luisa Lopez (GUA) 6–4 6–3. *El Salvador d. Trinidad & Tobago 2–1:* Ivon Rodezno (ESA) d. Sheenagh Cosgrove (TRI) 6–1 6–2; Anneliese Rose (TRI) d. Claudia Argumedo (ESA) 6–4 6–0; Liz Cruz/Ivon Rodezno (ESA) d. Sheenagh Cosgrove/Anneliese Rose (TRI) 4–6 6–4 6–4.

PLAYOFF FOR 5th/6th POSITION: 13 May – *Bahamas d. El Salvador 3–0:* Larikah Russell (BAH) d. Ivon Rodezno (ESA) 6–1 6–0; Nikkita Fountain (BAH) d. Claudia Argumedo (ESA) 6–3 6–3; Nikkita Fountain/Larikah Russell (BAH) d. Liz Cruz/Ivon Rodezno (ESA) 6–2 6–2.

PLAYOFF FOR 7th/8th POSITION: 13 May – *Trinidad & Tobago d. Guatemala 3–0:* Sheenagh Cosgrove (TRI) d. Lucia Henkle (GUA) 6–2 3–6 6–3; Anneliese Rose (TRI) d. Luisa Lopez (GUA) 6–2 6–1; Cindra Maharaj/Lisa Fung Kee Fung (TRI) d. Lucia Henkle/Luisa Lopez (GUA) 7–5 6–3.

PLAYOFF FOR 9th–12th POSITIONS: 12 May – *Costa Rica d. Barbados 3–0:* Paula Umana (CRC) d. Ariana Marshall (BAR) 6–4 6–0; Melissa Mendieta (CRC) d. Elena Branker (BAR) 6–1 6–3; Milena Leiva/Paula Umana (CRC) d. Anna-Lee Bryant/Ariana Marshall (BAR) 6–4 6–4. *Bermuda d. Panama 2–1:* Danielle Paynter (BER) d. Yamara Figueroa (PAN) 7–5 6–4; Karla Hall (PAN) d. Zarah De Silva (BER) 4–6 6–1 7–5; Zarah De Silva/Danielle Paynter (BER) d. Yamara Figueroa/Karla Hall (PAN) 7–6(0) 6–0.

PLAYOFF FOR 9th/10th POSITION: 13 May – *Costa Rica d. Bermuda 3–0:* Erika Villalobos (CRC) d. Danielle Paynter (BER) 6–0 6–1; Melissa Mendieta (CRC) d. Zarah De Silva (BER) 2–6 6–3 7–5; Milena Leiva/Erika Villalobos (CRC) d. Tara Lambert/Danielle Paynter (BER) 6–1 6–0.

PLAYOFF FOR 11th/12th POSITION: 13 May – *Panama d. Barbados 2–1:* Ariana Marshall (BAR) d. Yamara Figueroa (PAN) 6–4 6–4; Karla Hall (PAN) d. Elena Branker (BAR) 6–0 6–2; Lilly Cal/Karla Hall (PAN) d. Elena Branker/Ariana Marshall (BAR) 3–6 7–5 6–3.

PLAYOFF FOR 13th/14th POSITION: 13 May – *Jamaica d. Antigua & Barbuda 2–1:* Tinesta Rowe (JAM) d. Niki Williams (ANT) 6–4 6–4; Isoke Perry (ANT) d. Asha Jaja (JAM) 6–3 6–3; Asha Jaja/Tinesta Rowe (JAM) d. Isoke Perry/Niki Williams (ANT) 6–4 6–4.

FINAL POSITIONS: 1. Ecuador, 2. Dominican Republic, 3. Bolivia, 4. Puerto Rico, 5. Bahamas, 6. El Salvador, 7. Trinidad & Tobago, 8. Guatemala, 9. Costa Rica, 10. Bermuda, 11. Panama, 12. Barbados, 13. Jamaica, 14. Antigua & Barbuda.

Ecuador and Dominican Republic promoted to Americas Qualifying Group I for 2001.

ASIA/OCEANIA QUALIFYING GROUP I

Date: 25–30 April; Venue: Osaka, Japan; Surface: Hard (O).
Group A: China Hong Kong, India, Japan, Kazakhstan, Thailand.
Group B: China, Chinese Taipei, Indonesia, Korea, New Zealand, Singapore.

GROUP A: 25 April – *India d. Thailand 2–1:* Jayaram-Sai Jayalakshmy (IND) d. Napaporn Tongsalee (THA) 6–4 6–2; Tamarine Tanasugarn (THA) d. Nirupama Vaidyanathan (IND) 6–3 6–3; Manisha Malhotra/Nirupama Vaidyanathan (IND) d. Benjamas Sangaram/Tamarine Tanasugarn (THA) 7–6(8) 6–2. *Kazakhstan d. China Hong Kong 2–1:* Alissa Velts (KAZ) d. Olivia Graveraux (HKG) 6–4 3–6 6–4; Ka Po Tong (HKG) d. Valeriya Khazova (KAZ) 6–1 7–5; Valeriya Khazova/Alissa Velts (KAZ) d. Olivia Graveraux/Ka Po Tong (HKG) 4–6 6–3 6–4. **26 April (played on 27 April)** – *Japan d. India 2–0:* Shinobu Asagoe (JPN) d. Jayaram-Sai Jayalakshmy (IND) 6–3 6–1; Ai Sugiyama (JPN) d. Nirupama Vaidyanathan (IND) 6–2 6–3; doubles not played. *Thailand d. Kazakhstan 2–0:* Napaporn Tongsalee (THA) d. Alissa Velts (KAZ) 6–0 6–1; Tamarine Tanasugarn (THA) d. Valeriya Khazova (KAZ) 6–0 6–0; doubles not played. **27 April** – *Japan d. China Hong Kong 3–0:* Yuka Yoshida (JPN) d. Lee Chan (HKG) 6–1 6–2; Shinobu Asagoe (JPN) d. Ka-Po Tong (HKG) 6–1 6–1; Nana Miyagi/Ai Sugiyama (JPN) d. Olivia Graveraux/Ka-Po Tong (HKG) 6–1 6–0. *India d. Kazakhstan 3–0:* Jayaram-Sai Jayalakshmy (IND) d. Alissa Velts (KAZ) 6–2 6–3; Nirupama Vaidyanathan (IND) d. Valeriya Khazova (KAZ) 6–2 6–2; Manisha Malhotra/Radhika Tulpule (IND) d. Valeriya Khazova/Alissa Velts (KAZ) 7–6(5) 6–4. **28 April** – *Japan d. Kazakhstan 3–0:* Nana Miyagi (JPN) d. Alissa Velts (KAZ) 7–5 6–3; Yuka Yoshida (JPN) d. Valeriya Khazova (KAZ) 6–4 6–1; Shinobu Asagoe/Ai Sugiyama (JPN) d. Valeriya Khazova/Alissa Velts (KAZ) 6–1 6–0. *Thailand d. China Hong Kong 2–1:* Napaporn Tongsalee (THA) d. Oliva Graveraux (HKG) 6–7(5) 6–1 11–9; Tamarine Tanasugarn (THA) d. Ka-Po Tong (HKG) 6–3 6–4; Lee Chan/Po-Kuen Lam (HKG) d. Montika Anuchan/Benjamas Sangaram (THA) 7–6(2) 1–6 6–1. **29 April** – *Thailand d. Japan 2–1:* Shinobu Asagoe (JPN) d. Napaporn Tongsalee (THA) 6–1 6–0; Tamarine Tanasugarn (THA) d. Ai Sugiyama (JPN) 6–3 6–3; Benjamas Sangaram/Tamarine Tanasugarn (THA) d. Nana Miyagi/Ai Sugiyama (JPN) 5–7 6–4 7–5. *India d. China Hong Kong 3–0:* Jayaram-Sai Jayalakshmy (IND) d. Lee Chan (HKG) 6–2 6–4; Nirupama Vaidyanathan (IND) d. Ka-Po Tong (HKG) 6–1 7–5; Manisha Malhotra/Nirupama Vaidyanathan (IND) d. Lee Chan/Po-Kuen Lam (HKG) 6–3 6–2.

FINAL POSITIONS: 1. Japan, 2. India, 3. Thailand, 4. Kazakhstan, 5. China Hong Kong.

GROUP B: 25 April – *Indonesia d. New Zealand 3–0:* Yayuk Basuki (INA) d. Rewa Hudson (NZL) 6–0 6–1; Wynne Prakusya (INA) d. Leanne Baker (NZL) 6–2 7–6(7); Yayuk Basuki/Wynne Prakusya (INA) d. Rewa Hudson/Shelley Stephens (NZL) 6–4 6–2. *China d. Korea 2–1:* Na Li (CHN) d. Jin-Young Choi (KOR) 6–3 6–3; Jing-Qian Yi (CHN) d. Yoon-Jeong Cho (KOR) 6–3 6–1; Kyung-Yee Chae/Yoon-Jeong Cho (KOR) d. Na Li/Jing-Qian Yi (CHN) 6–2 6–2. *Chinese Taipei d. Singapore 3–0:* Lan-Lan Tai (TPE) d. Tina Jacob (SIN) 6–1 6–2; Janet Lee (TPE) d. Yik-Hui Leow (SIN) 6–1 6–0; Janet Lee/Shi-Ting Wang (TPE) d. Yik-Hui Leow/Simin Liu (SIN) 6–0 6–0. **26 April (played on 27 April)** – *Indonesia d. Korea 2–0:* Yayuk Basuki (INA) d. Jin-Young Choi (KOR) 6–2 6–2; Wynne Prakusya (INA) d. Yoon-Jeong Cho (KOR) 3–6 7–6(4) 6–4; doubles not played. *China d. Singapore 2–0:* Na Li (CHN) d. Tina Jacob (SIN) 6–0 6–1; Jing-Qian Yi (CHN) d. Yik-Hui Leow (SIN) 6–0 6–0; doubles not played. *Chinese Taipei d. New Zealand 2–1:* Nikki Tippins (NZL) d. Lan-Lan Tai (TPE) 6–3 3–6 6–4; Janet Lee (TPE) d. Leanne Baker (NZL) 6–2 6–4; Janet Lee/Shi-Ting Wang (TPE) d. Leanne Baker/Shelley Stephens (NZL) 7–6(2) 6–3. **27 April** – *Chinese Taipei d. Korea 2–1:* Yang-Jin Chung (KOR) d. Lan-Lan Tai (TPE) 6–1 4–6 6–1; Janet Lee (TPE) d. Kyung-Yee Chae (KOR) 6–3 6–2; Janet Lee/Shi-Ting Wang (TPE) d. Kyung-Yee Chae/Yoon-Jeong Cho (KOR) 7–5 6–4. *China d. Indonesia 2–0:* Na Li (CHN) d. Yayuk Basuki (INA) 5–7 6–1 6–2; Jing-Qian Yi (CHN) d. Wynne Prakusya (INA) 6–4 6–1; doubles not played. *New Zealand d. Singapore 3–0:* Nikki Tippins (NZL) d. Simin Liu (SIN) 6–0 6–0; Leanne Baker (NZL) d. Yik-Hui Leow (SIN) 6–0 6–0; Rewa Hudson/Shelley Stephens (NZL) d. Tina Jacob/Yik-Hui Leow (SIN) 6–0 6–0. **28 April** – *Indonesia d. Chinese Taipei 2–1:* Irawati Iskandar (INA) d. Ya-Fang Tsai (TPE) 6–0 6–4; Janet Lee (TPE) d. Wynne Prakusya (INA) 6–4 6–2; Yayuk Basuki/Wynne Prakusya (INA) d. Janet Lee/Shi-Ting Wang (TPE) 6–1 6–2. *China d. New Zealand 3–0:* Na Li (CHN) d. Nikki Tippins (NZL) 6–0 6–2; Jing-Qian Yi (CHN) d. Leanne Baker (NZL) 6–3 6–3; Fang Li/Na Li (CHN) d. Leanne Baker/Shelley Stephens (NZL) 3–6 6–3 *Singapore 3–0:* Jin-Young Choi (KOR) d. Tina Jacob (SIN) 6–0 6–0; Yang-Jin Chung (KOR) d. Yik-Hui Leow (SIN) 6–1 6–0; Kyung-Yee Chae/Yoon-Jeong Cho (KOR) d. Simin Liu/Yik-Hui Leow (SIN) 6–0 6–0. **29 April** –

Indonesia d. Singapore 3–0: Wukirasih Sawondari (INA) d. Tina Jacob (SIN) 6–0 6–0; Irawati Iskandar (INA) d. Yik-Hui Leow (SIN) 6–1 6–2; Irawati Iskandar/Wukirasih Sawondari (INA) d. Tina Jacob/Yik-Hui Leow (SIN) 6–2 6–0. *China d. Chinese Taipei 3–0:* Na Li (CHN) d. Lan-Lan Tai (TPE) 6–2 6–0; Jing-Qian Yi (CHN) d. Janet Lee (TPE) 6–4 4–6 6–4; Fang Li/Na Li (CHN) d. Lan-Lan Tai/Ya-Fang Tsai (TPE) 3–0 ret. *Korea d. New Zealand 3–0:* Kyung-Yee Chae (KOR) d. Nikki Tippins (NZL) 6–0 6–2; Yoon-Jeong Cho (KOR) d. Leanne Baker (NZL) 6–2 4–6 6–0; Kyung-Yee Chae/Yoon-Jeong Cho (KOR) d. Leanne Baker/Shelley Stephens (NZL) 6–4 7–6(4).

FINAL POSITIONS: 1. China, 2. Indonesia, 3. Chinese Taipei, 4. Korea, 5. New Zealand, 6. Singapore.

PROMOTION PLAYOFF: 30 April – *Japan d. China 2–1:* Na Li (CHN) d. Shinobu Asagoe (JPN) 7–6(6) 6–2; Ai Sugiyama (JPN) d. Jing-Qian Yi (CHN) 6–4 6–2; Nana Miyagi/Ai Sugiyama (JPN) d. Fang Li/Na Li (CHN) 1–6 6–4 6–1.

Japan promoted to World Group for 2001.
China Hong Kong and Singapore relegated to Asia/Oceania Qualifying Group II for 2001.

ASIA/OCEANIA QUALIFYING GROUP II

Date: 25–30 April; Venue: Osaka, Japan; Surface: Hard (O).
Group A: Fiji, Iraq, Malaysia, Pacific Oceania, Uzbekistan.
Group B: Jordan, Pakistan, Philippines, Sri Lanka, Syria, Tajikistan.

GROUP A: 25 April – *Uzbekistan d. Pacific Oceania 2–1:* Luisa Biktyakova (UZB) d. Davilyn Godinet (POC) 6–3 6–1; Iroda Tulyaganova (UZB) d. Tagifano So'onalole (POC) 6–3 6–2; Davilyn Godinet/Tagifano So'onalole (POC) d. Luisa Biktyakova/Iroda Tulyaganova (UZB) 6–1 5–7 6–4. *Malaysia d. Fiji 3–0:* Pei-Yuin Keng (MAS) d. Hamidan Bibi (FIJ) 6–2 6–1; Chen-Yee Liaw (MAS) d. Archana Reddy (FIJ) 6–3 6–2; Pei-Yuin Keng/Sarangam Shangamitra (MAS) d. Hamidan Bibi/Archana Reddy (FIJ) 6–3 6–4. **26 April (played on 27 April)** – *Malaysia d. Iraq 2–0:* Pei-Yuin Keng (MAS) d. Maral Khachik Awanes (IRQ) 6–0 6–0; Chen-Yee Liaw (MAS) d. Alaa AA Ali (IRQ) 6–1 6–1; doubles not played. *Pacific Oceania d. Fiji 2–0:* Nicole Anqat (POC) d. Hamidan Bibi (FIJ) 6–1 6–2; Davilyn Godinet (POC) d. Archana Reddy (FIJ) 6–1 6–1; doubles not played. **27 April** – *Pacific Oceania d. Iraq 3–0:* Davilyn Godinet (POC) d. Alaa AA Ali (IRQ) 6–1 6–0; Tagifano So'onalole (POC) d. Salima-Esmat Salman (IRQ) 6–0 6–0; Nicole Angat/Davilyn Godinet (POC) d. Alaa AA Ali/Salima-Esmat Salman (IRQ) 6–0 6–1. *Uzbekistan d. Fiji 3–0:* Luisa Biktyakova (UZB) d. Hamidan Bibi (FIJ) 6–1 6–0; Iroda Tulyaganova (UZB) d. Archana Reddy (FIJ) 6–0 6–1; Luisa Biktyakova/Anna Shchupak (UZB) d. Hamidan Bibi/Archana Reddy (FIJ) 6–3 6–4. **28 April** – *Fiji d. Iraq 3–0:* Hamidan Bibi (FIJ) d. Maral Khachik Awanes (IRQ) 6–0 6–1; Archana Reddy (FIJ) d. Salima-Esmat Salman (IRQ) 6–2 6–1; Petroena Fong/Walena White (FIJ) d. Alaa AA Ali/Maral Khachik Awanes (IRQ) 6–1 6–1. *Uzbekistan d. Malaysia 3–0:* Luisa Biktyakova (UZB) d. Pei-Yuin Keng (MAS) 6–3 6–3; Iroda Tulyaganova (UZB) d. Chen-Yee Liaw (MAS) 6–0 6–1; Luisa Biktyakova/Anna Shchupak (UZB) d. Pei-Yuin Keng/Chen-Yee Liaw (MAS) 6–4 6–2. **29 April** – *Uzbekistan d. Iraq 3–0:* Anna Shchupak (UZB) d. Alaa AA Ali (IRQ) 6–0 6–0; Luisa Biktyakova (UZB) d. Salima-Esmat Salman (IRQ) 6–0 6–0; Anna Shchupak/Iroda Tulyaganova(UZB) d. Alaa AA Ali/Maral Khachik Awanes (IRQ) 6–0 6–0. *Pacific Oceania d. Malaysia 3–0:* Davilyn Godinet (POC) d. Pei-Yuin Keng (MAS) 6–4 6–0; Tagifano So'onalole (POC) d. Chen-Yee Liaw (MAS) 6–1 6–0; Nicole Angat/Davilyn Godinet (POC) d. Pei-Yuin Keng/Sarangam Shangamitra (MAS) 6–4 6–3.

FINAL POSITIONS: 1. Uzbekistan, 2. Pacific Oceania, 3. Malaysia, 4. Fiji, 5. Iraq.

GROUP B: 25 April – *Sri Lanka d. Pakistan 2–1:* Vajira Premaratne (SRI) d. Haleema Rahim (PAK) 6–2 6–3; Nida Waseem (PAK) d. Sobhini De Silva (SRI) 6–0 6–2; Vajira Premaratne/Sobhini De Silva (SRI) d. Mehvish Chishtie/Nida Waseem (PAK) 6–1 4–6 6–2. *Tajikistan d. Syria 3–0:* Zinaida Shantalova (TJK) d. Shaza Tinawi (SYR) 6–2 7–5; Chakhlo Iboduloeva (TJK) d. Farah Dayoub (SYR) 6–2 7–6(7); Raksana Abdurakhmonova/Zinaida Shantalova (TJK) d. Farah Dayoub/Hazar Sidki (SYR) 6–1 6–1. *Philippines d. Jordan 3–0:* Czarina Mae Arevalo (PHI) d. Dina Dajani (JOR) 6–3 7–5; Maricris Fernandez (PHI) d. Dina Naffa (JOR) 6–3 6–2; Vida Alpuerto/Czarina-Mai Arevalo (PHI) d. Dina Dajani/Dina Naffa (JOR) 6–0 6–3. **26 April (played on 27 April)** – *Philippines d. Pakistan 2–0:* Czarina Mae Arevalo (PHI) d. Haleema Rahim (PAK) 6–0 6–2; Maricris Fernandez (PHI) d. Nida Waseem (PAK) 6–1 7–6(9); doubles not played. *Tajikistan d. Jordan 2–1:* Dina Dajani (JOR) d. Raksana Abdurakhmonova (TJK) 6–0 6–1; Chakhlo Iboduloeva(TJK) d. Dina Naffa (JOR) 6–2 6–1; Chakhlo Iboduloeva/Zinaida Shantalova (TJK) d. Dina Dajani/Dina Naffa (JOR) 6–4 6–4. *Sri Lanka d. Syria 2–0:* Vajira Premaratne (SRI) d. Shaza Tinawi (SYR) 6–1 6–2; Sobhini De Silva (SRI) d. Farah Dayoub (SYR) 6–3 6–1; doubles not played. **27 April** – *Philippines d. Tajikistan 3–0:* Czarina Mae Arevalo (PHI) d. Zinaida Shantalova (TJK) 6–4 6–3; Maricris Fernandez (PHI) d. Chakhlo Iboduloeva (TJK) 6–0 6–1; Vida Alpuerto/Czarina-Mai Arevalo (PHI) d. Raksana Abdurakhmonova/Zinaida Shantalova (TJK) 6–4 6–1. *Jordan d. Sri Lanka 2–1:* Dina Dajani (JOR) d. Vajira Premaratne (SRI) 6–0 6–3; Sobhini De Silva (SRI) d. Dina Naffa (JOR) 6–1 6–1; Dina Dajani/Dina Naffa (JOR) d. Sobhini De Silva/Vajira Premaratne (SRI) 4–6 6–4 6–3. *Pakistan d. Syria 2–1:* Shaza Tinawi (SYR) d. Mehvish Chishtie (PAK) 7–6(5) 6–3; Nida Waseem (PAK) d. Farah Dayoub (SYR) 6–2 6–3; Nosheen Ehtsham/Nida Waseem (PAK) d. Farah Dayoub/Hazar Sidki (SYR) 6–3 1–6 6–1. **28 April** – *Philippines d. Syria 3–0:* Czarina Mae Arevalo (PHI) d. Nivin Kezbari (SYR) 6–0 6–3; Maricris Fernandez (PHI) d. Hazar Sidki (SYR) 6–2 6–1; Vida Alpuerto/Czarina Mae Arevalo (PHI) d. Nivin Kezbari/Hazar Sidki (SYR) 6–2 6–3. *Tajikistan d. Sri Lanka 2–1:* Zinaida Shantalova (TJK) d. Vajira

Premaratne (SRI) 7–6(1) 6–3; Manihsa Abeyawardene (SRI) d. Chakhlo Iboduloeva (TJK) 6–4 6–4; Raksana Abdurakhmonova/Zinaida Shantalova (TJK) d. Manihsa Abeyawardene/Vajira Premaratne (SRI) 6–4 3–6 6–4. **Pakistan d. Jordan 2–1:** Dina Dajani (JOR) d. Mehvish Chishtie (PAK) 6–1 6–2; Nida Waseem (PAK) d. Dina Naffa (JOR) 6–0 6–1; Nosheen Ehtsham/Nida Waseem (PAK) d. Dina Dajani/Dina Naffa (JOR) 6–2 6–1. **29 April – Philippines d. Sri Lanka 3–0:** Czarina Mae Arevalo (PHI) d. Samanthi Wijesekera (SRI) 6–0 6–1; Maricris Fernandez (PHI) d. Manihsa Abeyawardene (SRI) 6–0 6–1; Vida Alpuerto/Czarina Mae Arevalo (PHI) d. Manihsa Abeyawardene/Vajira Premaratne (SRI) 7–5 2–6 6–3. **Tajikistan d. Pakistan 3–0:** Zinaida Shantalova (TJK) d. Mehvish Chishtie (PAK) 6–2 6–2; Chakhlo Iboduloeva (TJK) d. Haleema Rahim (PAK) 2–6 6–4 6–3; Raksana Abdurakhmonova/Shakhlo Iboduloeva (TJK) d. Nosheen Ehtsham/Haleema Rahim (PAK) 7–5 6–3. **Jordan d. Syria 2–1:** Dina Dajani (JOR) d. Shaza Tinawi (SYR) 6–1 6–0; Farah Dayoub (SYR) d. Dina Naffa (JOR) 4–6 6–4 7–5; Dina Dajani/Dina Naffa (JOR) d. Farah Dayoub/Hazar Sidki (SYR) 6–1 6–2.

FINAL POSITIONS: 1. Philippines, 2. Tajikistan, 3. Sri Lanka, 4. Jordan, 5. Pakistan, 6. Syria.

PROMOTION PLAYOFF: 29 April – Uzbekistan d. Tajikistan 2–0: Luisa Biktyakova (UZB) d. Zinaida Shantalova (TJK) 4–6 7–5 7–5; Iroda Tulyaganova (UZB) d. Chakhlo Iboduloeva (TJK) 6–1 6–1; doubles not played. **30 April – Pacific Oceania d. Philippines 2–0:** Davilyn Godinet (POC) d. Czarina Mae Arevalo (PHI) 0–6 7–6(6) 6–4; Tagifano So'onalole (POC) d. Maricris Fernandez (PHI) 6–1 7–6(4); doubles not played.

Uzbekistan and Pacific Oceania promoted to Asia/Oceania Qualifying Group I for 2001.

EUROPE/AFRICA QUALIFYING GROUP I
Date: 15–21 May; Venue: Murcia, Spain; Surface: Clay (O).
Group A: Bulgaria, Netherlands, Sweden, Turkey.
Group B: Greece, Hungary, Latvia, Sweden.
Group C: Belarus, Morocco, Poland, Romania, Slovenia.
Group D: Finland, Great Britain, Israel, Luxembourg, Ukraine.

GROUP A: 16 May – Netherlands d. Turkey 3–0: Seda Noorlander (NED) d. Ismet-Duygu Aksit-Oal (TUR) 6–3 7–5; Kristie Boogert (NED) d. Gulberk Gultekin (TUR) 6–1 6–0; Seda Noorlander/Miriam Oremans (NED) d. Ismet-Duygu Aksit-Oal/Gulberk Gultekin (TUR) 6–4 6–4. **Bulgaria d. Sweden 2–1:** Sofia Arvidsson (SWE) d. Antoaneta Pandjerova (BUL) 6–1 3–6 7–5; Dessislava Topalova (BUL) d. Diana Majkic (SWE) 6–2 6–7(9) 6–4; Maria Gusheva/Antoneta Pandjerova (BUL) d. Frieda Engblom/Maria Strandlund (SWE) 6–4 6–2. **17 May – Netherlands d. Sweden 3–0:** Miriam Oremans (NED) d. Sofia Arvidsson (SWE) 6–3 6–1; Seda Noorlander (NED) d. Diana Majkic (SWE) 6–3 7–5; Amanda Hopmans/Miriam Oremans (NED) d. Sofia Arvidsson/Frieda Engblom (SWE) 6–3 6–1. **Bulgaria d. Turkey 3–0:** Antoaneta Pandjerova (BUL) d. Ismet-Duygu Aksit-Oal (TUR) 6–2 6–2; Dessislava Topalova (BUL) d. Gulberk Gultekin (TUR) 6–2 6–0; Filipa Gabrovska/Maria Gusheva (BUL) d. Duygu Aksit Oal/Gulberk Gultekin (TUR) 6–4 6–4. **18 May – Netherlands d. Bulgaria 3–0:** Miriam Oremans (NED) d. Antoaneta Pandjerova (BUL) 6–3 6–4; Amanda Hopmans (NED) d. Dessislava Topalova (BUL) 7–6(6) 6–4; Kristie Boogert/Miriam Oremans (NED) d. Filipa Gabrovska/Maria Gusheva (BUL) 6–3 6–2. **Sweden d. Turkey 2–1:** Sofia Arvidsson (SWE) d. Ismet-Duygu Aksit-Oal (TUR) 6–3 3–6 6–2; Diana Majkic (SWE) d. Gulberk Gultekin (TUR) 7–5 6–3; Ismet-Duygu Aksit-Oal/Gulberk Gultekin (TUR) d. Sofia Arvidsson/Frieda Engblom (SWE) 3–6 6–2 6–3.

Final Positions: 1. Netherlands, 2. Bulgaria, 3. Sweden, 4. Turkey.

GROUP B: 1–6 May Hungary d. Latvia 3–0: Annamaria Foldenyi (HUN) d. Katrina Bandere (LAT) 6–4 6–3; Rita Kuti-Kis (HUN) d. Elena Krutko (LAT) 6–0 6–0; Petra Mandula/Katalin Marosi (HUN) d. Katrina Bandere/Larisa Neiland (LAT) 6–2 6–1. **South Africa d. Greece 2–1:** Surina de Beer (RSA) d. Maria Pavlidou (GRE) 7–5 6–3; Evagelia Roussi (GRE) d. Mariaan De Swardt (RSA) 7–5 7–6(8); Surina De Beer/Liezel Horn (RSA) d. Assimina Kaplani/Maria Pavlidou (GRE) 6–2 6–2. **17 May – Hungary d. Greece 3–0:** Katalin Marosi (HUN) d. Assimina Kaplani (GRE) 6–3 7–6(5); Rita Kuti Kis (HUN) d. Evagelia Roussi (GRE) 6–2 6–2; Annamaria Foldenyi/Petra Mandula (HUN) d. Assimina Kaplani/Maria Pavlidou (GRE) 3–6 6–2 6–4. **South Africa d. Latvia 3–0:** Nannie De Villiers (RSA) d. Katrina Bandere (LAT) 6–1 6–3; Surina De Beer (RSA) d. Elena Krutko (LAT) 6–2 6–3; Mariaan De Swardt/Liezel Horn (RSA) d. Katrina Bandere/Elena Krutko (LAT) 6–4 6–3. **18 May – Hungary d. South Africa 2–1:** Annamaria Foldenyi (HUN) d. Surina De Beer (RSA) 6–7(2) 6–1 7–5; Rita Kuti Kis (HUN) d. Mariaan De Swardt (RSA) 6–2 6–3; Nannie De Villiers/Liezel Horn (RSA) d. Rita Kuti Kis/Katalin Marosi (HUN) 6–3 6–4. **Greece d. Latvia 3–0:** Maria Pavlidou (GRE) d. Katrina Bandere (LAT) 7–6(3) 6–2; Evagelia Roussi (GRE) d. Elena Krutko (LAT) 6–3 6–4; Eleni Danilidou/Evagelia Roussi (GRE) d. Katrina Bandere/Elena Krutko (LAT) 7–5 6–4.

FINAL POSITIONS: 1. Hungary, 2. South Africa, 3. Greece, 4. Latvia.

GROUP C: 15 May – Belarus d. Poland 3–0: Nadejda Ostrovskaya (BLR) d. Joanna Sakowicz (POL) 6–1 6–4; Olga Barabanschikova (BLR) d. Katarzyna Straczy (POL) 6–0 6–3; Olga Barabanschikova/Tatiana Poutchek (BLR) d. Katarzyna Straczy/Katarzyna Teodorowicz (POL) 6–1 7–6(5). **Slovenia d. Romania 3–0:** Tina Krizan (SLO) d. Raluca Ciochina (ROM) 7–5 6–3; Katarina Srebotnik (SLO) d. Mihaela Moldovan (ROM) 6–0 6–3; Tina Krizan/Katarina Srebotnik (SLO) d. Raluca Ciochina/Mihaela Moldovan (ROM) 6–4 7–5. **16 May – Belarus d. Morocco 3–0:** Iatiana Poutchek (BLR) d. Meriam Lahlou (MAR) 6–1 6–1; Olga Barabanschikova (BLR) d. Meryem Haddad (MAR) 6–1 6–3; Nadejda Ostrovskaya/Tatiana Poutchek (BLR) d. Meryem Haddad/Meriam

Lahlou (MAR) 6–0 6–0. *Slovenia d. Poland 3–0:* Tina Hergold (SLO) d. Monika Schneider (POL) 7–5 6–2; Katarina Srebotnik (SLO) d. Katarzyna Straczy (POL) 6–3 6–2; Tina Krizan/Katarina Srebotnik (SLO) d. Joanna Sakowicz/Monika Schneider (POL) 6–3 6–1. **17 May – *Belarus d. Romania 3–0:*** Tatiana Poutchek (BLR) d. Raluca Ciochina (ROM) 6–2 6–1; Nadejda Ostrovskaya (BLR) d. Mihaela Moldovan (ROM) 6–1 7–5; Olga Barabanshikova/Tatiana Poutchek (BLR) d. Raluca Ciochina/Mihaela Moldovan (ROM) 6–2 6–3. *Poland d. Morocco 3–0:* Joanna Sakowicz (POL) d. Habiba Ifrakh (MAR) 6–1 6–1; Katarzyna Straczy (POL) d. Meryem Haddad (MAR) 5–7 6–3 6–3; Joanna Sakowicz/Katarzyna Teodorowicz (POL) d. Habiba Ifrakh/Meriam Lahlou (MAR) 6–1 6–0. **18 May – *Belarus d. Slovenia 2–1:*** Nadejda Ostrovskaya (BLR) d. Tina Krizan (SLO) 6–3 7–6(9); Katarina Srebotnik (SLO) d. Olga Barabanschikova (BLR) 6–0 3–6 6–2; Olga Barabanschikova/Tatiana Poutchek (BLR) d. Tina Krizan/Katarina Srebotnik (SLO) 7–5 2–6 7–5. *Romania d. Morocco 3–0:* Raluca Ciochina (ROM) d. Habiba Ifrakh (MAR) 6–2 6–1; Mihaela Moldovan (ROM) d. Meryem Haddad (MAR) 6–4 6–0; Raluca Ciochina/Mihaela Moldovan (ROM) d. Habiba Ifrakh/Meriam Lahlou (MAR) 6–2 6–2. **19 May – *Slovenia d. Morocco 2–0:*** Maja Matevzic (SLO) d. Meriam Lahlou (MAR) 6–2 6–1; Tina Hergold (SLO) d. Meryem Haddad (MAR) 7–5 6–2; doubles not played. *Romania d. Poland 3–0:* Raluca Ciochina (ROM) d. Joanna Sakowicz (POL) 6–2 6–0; Mihaela Moldovan (ROM) d. Katarzyna Straczy (POL) 6–4 6–4; Adriana Burz/Raluca Ciochina (ROM) d. Monika Schneider/Katarzyna Teodorowicz (POL) 4–6 6–3 6–4.

FINAL POSITIONS: 1. Belarus, 2. Slovenia, 3. Romania, 4. Poland, 5. Morocco.

GROUP D: 15 May – *Israel d. Finland 3–0:* Hila Rosen (ISR) d. Kirsi Lampinen (FIN) 6–1 6–3; Anna Smashnova (ISR) d. Petra Puheloinen (FIN) 6–4 6–2; Tzipora Obziler/Hila Rosen (ISR) d. Hanna-Katri Aalto/Kirsi Lampinen (FIN) 6–1 6–0. *Great Britain d. Ukraine 2–1:* Julie Pullin (GBR) d. Yulia Beygelzimer (UKR) 6–7(5) 6–4 6–1; Elena Tatarkova (UKR) d. Louise Latimer (GBR) 6–2 6–2; Julie Pullin/Jo Ward (GBR) d. Natalia Medvedeva/Elena Tatarkova (UKR) 6–4 6–0. **16 May – *Israel d. Luxembourg 2–1:*** Claudine Schaul (LUX) d. Tzipora Obziler (ISR) 2–6 6–3 6–3; Anna Smashnova (ISR) d. Anne Kremer (LUX) 7–6(4) 6–4; Tzipora Obziler/Hila Rosen (ISR) d. Anne Kremer/Claudine Schaul (LUX) 6–7(3) 6–3 6–4. *Great Britain d. Finland 2–1:* Hanna-Katri Aalto (FIN) d. Julie Pullin (GBR) 7–5 6–3; Louise Latimer (GBR) d. Petra Puheloinen (FIN) 7–6(3) 6–2; Julie Pullin/Jo Ward (GBR) d. Hanna-Katri Aalto/Kirsi Lampinen (FIN) 6–1 6–1. **17 May – *Ukraine d. Israel 2–1:*** Yulia Beygelzimer (UKR) d. Hila Rosen (ISR) 3–6 6–4 6–0; Anna Smashnova (ISR) d. Elena Tatarkova (UKR) 6–1 6–4; Natalia Medvedeva/Elena Tatarkova (UKR) d. Tzipora Obziler/Hila Rosen (ISR) 6–4 6–4. *Luxembourg d. Finland 3–0:* Claudine Schaul (LUX) d. Hanna-Katri Aalto (FIN) 6–0 6–2; Anne Kremer (LUX) d. Petra Puheloinen (FIN) 6–3 4–6 6–1; Celine Francois/Claudine Schaul (LUX) d. Hanna-Katri Aalto/Kirsi Lampinen (FIN) 6–3 2–6 6–1. **18 May – *Israel d. Great Britain 2–1:*** Hannah Collin (GBR) d. Tzipora Obziler (ISR) 6–1 6–1; Anna Smashnova (ISR) d. Louise Latimer (GBR) 6–1 6–3; Tzipora Obziler/Hila Rosen (ISR) d. Hannah Collin/Julie Pullin (GBR) 3–6 6–4 6–1. *Luxembourg d. Ukraine 2–1:* Claudine Schaul (LUX) d. Anna Zaporozhanova (UKR) 3–6 6–4 6–1; Anne Kremer (LUX) d. Elena Tatarkova (UKR) 6–3 6–1; Yulia Beygelzimer/Natalia Medvedeva (UKR) d. Celine Francois/Mandy Minella (LUX) 6–0 6–0. **19 May – *Luxembourg d. Great Britain 2–1:*** Claudine Schaul (LUX) d. Hannah Collin (GBR) 6–3 6–3; Anne Kremer (LUX) d. Louise Latimer (GBR) 6–4 6–0; Louise Latimer/Julie Pullin (GBR) d. Celine Francois/Mandy Minella (LUX) 6–2 6–0. *Ukraine d. Finland 3–0:* Anna Zaporozhanova (UKR) d. Hanna-Katri Aalto (FIN) 6–4 6–1; Elena Tatarkova (UKR) d. Petra Puheloinen (FIN) 6–1 6–2; Yulia Beygelzimer/Anna Zaporozhanova (UKR) d. Mariana Keranen/Kirsi Lampinen (FIN) 6–0 6–4.

FINAL POSITIONS: 1. Israel, 2. Luxembourg, 3. Ukraine, 4. Great Britain, 5. Finland.

SEMI-FINALS: 20 May – **Netherlands d. Israel 2–1:** Amanda Hopmans (NED) d. Hila Rosen (ISR) 7–6(2) 6–3; Anna Smashnova (ISR) d. Seda Noorlander (NED) 6–2 6–3; Amanda Hopmans/Miriam Oremans (NED) d. Tzipora Obziler/Hila Rosen (ISR) 6–0 3–6 6–4. **Hungary d. Belarus 2–0:** Annamaria Foldenyi (HUN) d. Nadejda Ostrovskaya (BLR) 6–3 6–4; Rita Kuti Kis (HUN) d. Olga Barabanshikova (BLR) 6–2 6–0; doubles not played.

FINAL: 21 May – **Hungary d. Netherlands 2–0:** Annamaria Foldenyi (HUN) d. Miriam Oremans (NED) 6–2 7–6(3); Rita Kuti Kis (HUN) d. Seda Noorlander (NED) 6–0 6–1; doubles not played.

Hungary promoted to World Group for 2001.
Turkey, Latvia, Morocco and Finland relegated to Europe/Africa Qualifying Group II for 2001.

EUROPE/AFRICA QUALIFYING GROUP II

Date: 27 March–2 April; Venue: Estoril, Portugal; Surface: Clay (O).
Group A: FYR Macedonia, Ireland, Kenya, Malta, Mauritius.
Group B: Bosnia/Herzegovina, Botswana, Denmark, Iceland, Liechtenstein, Tunisia.
Group C: Armenia, Cyprus, Egypt, Georgia, Lithuania, Yugoslavia.
Group D: Algeria, Estonia, Lesotho, Madagascar, Moldova, Portugal.

GROUP A: 28 March *Ireland d. Malta 2–1:* Kelly Liggan (IRL) d. Lisa Camenzuli (MLT) 7–5 6–3; Yvonne Doyle (IRL) d. Sarah Wetz (MLT) 6–4 6–4; Lisa Camenzuli/Carol Cassar Torreggiani (MLT) d. Gina Niland/Elsa O'Riain (IRL) 6–3 7–5. *FYR Macedonia d. Mauritius 3–0:* Biljana Dimovska (MKD) d. Lisa Gebert (MRI) 6–0 6–1; Marina Lazarovska (MKD) d. Corinne Ng Tung Hing (MRI) 6–0 6–1; Ana Buraku/Elena Manevska (MKD) d. Alice Lamport/Emma Taikie (MRI) 6–4 6–2. **29 March – *Ireland d. Kenya 3–0:*** Kelly Liggan (IRL) d. Esther

Mbugua (KEN) 6–0 6–1; Yvonne Doyle (IRL) d. Evelyn Otula (KEN) 6–0 6–1; Gina Niland/Elsa O'Riain (IRL) d. Christine Lukalo/Wanjiru Mbugua (KEN) 6–2 6–1. **FYR Macedonia d. Malta 2–1:** Biljana Dimovska (MKD) d. Lisa Camenzuli (MLT) 6–4 4–6 7–5; Marina Lazarovska (MKD) d. Helen Asciak (MLT) 7–5 6–0; Lisa Camenzuli/Carol Cassar Torreggiani (MLT) d. Ana Buraku/Elena Manevska (MKD) 6–0 6–1. **30 March – Ireland d. Mauritius 3–0:** Kelly Liggan (IRL) d. Lisa Gebert (MRI) 6–1 6–2; Yvonne Doyle (IRL) d. Corinne Ng Tung Hing (MRI) 6–2 6–2; Gina Niland/Elsa O'Riain (IRL) d. Alice Lamport/Emma Taikie (MRI) 6–0 6–0. **Malta d. Kenya 3–0:** Lisa Camenzuli (MLT) d. Christine Lukalo (KEN) 6–1 6–1; Carol Cassar Torreggiani (MLT) d. Evelyn Otula (KEN) 6–1 6–2; Helen Asciak/Sarah Wetz (MLT) d. Christine Lukalo/Wanjiru Mbugua (KEN) 6–4 6–1. **31 March – FYR Macedonia d. Kenya 3–0:** Biljana Dimovska (MKD) d. Esther Mbugua (KEN) 6–0 6–1; Marina Lazarovska (MKD) d. Evelyn Otula (KEN) 6–0 6–0; Biljana Dimovska/Marina Lazarovska (MKD) d. Christine Lukalo/Wanjiru Mbugua (KEN) 6–0 6–2. **Malta d. Mauritius 3–0:** Lisa Camenzuli (MLT) d. Lisa Gebert (MRI) 6–1 6–0; Helen Asciak (MLT) d. Alice Lamport (MRI) 7–6(4) 6–0; Lisa Camenzuli/Carol Cassar-Torreggiani (MLT) d. Lisa Gebert/Alice Lamport (MRI) 6–0 6–0. **1 April – FYR Macedonia d. Ireland 2–1:** Kelly Liggan (IRL) d. Biljana Dimovska (MKD) 6–2 6–2; Marina Lazarovska (MKD) d. Yvonne Doyle (IRL) 6–2 6–4; Biljana Dimovska/Marina Lazarovska (MKD) d. Yvonne Doyle/Kelly Liggan (IRL) 6–3 6–2. **Mauritius v Kenya:** Alice Lamport (MRI) d. Esther Mbugua (KEN) 6–0 6–2; Corinne Ng Tung Hing (MRI) v Evelyn Otula (KEN) 2–1 (15–0); tie not completed due to rain.

GROUP WINNERS: FYR Macedonia.

GROUP B: 28 March – Denmark d. Liechtenstein 3–0: Charlotte Aagaard (DEN) d. Angelika Schadler (LIE) 6–0 6–2; Eva Dyrberg (DEN) d. Sabrina Vogt (LIE) 6–0 6–0; Rikke Faurfelt/Karina Ildor-Jacobsgaard (DEN) d. Bettina Niedhart/Sidonia Wolfinger (LIE) 6–1 6–2. **Tunisia d. Botswana 3–0:** Mariem Bouchlaka (TUN) d. Kelesitse Makgale (BOT) 6–3 6–4; Nedia Kilani (TUN) d. Kago Phatshwane (BOT) 6–2 6–0; Azza Abbou/Nedia Kilani (TUN) d. Kelesitse Makgale/Ntswaki Mawela (BOT) 6–2 6–3. **Bosnia/Herzegovina d. Iceland 3–0:** Asja Tankic (BIH) d. Stella Kristjansdottir (ISL) 6–4 3–0 ret; Azra Resic (BIH) d. Iris Staub (ISL) 6–4 6–1; Medina Bajrambasic/Azra Resic (BIH) d. Stella Kristjansdottir/Iris Staub (ISL) w/o. **29 March – Denmark d. Botswana 3–0:** Karina Ildor-Jacobsgaard (DEN) d. Ntswaki Mawela (BOT) 6–0 6–0; Rikke Faurfelt (DEN) d. Kago Phatshwane (BOT) 6–2 6–1; Charlotte Aagaard/Eva Dyrberg (DEN) d. Kelesitse Makgale/Ntswaki Mawela (BOT) 6–0 6–2. **Bosnia/Herzegovina d. Tunisia 3–0:** Asja Tankic (BIH) d. Mariem Bouchlaka (TUN) 6–1 6–2; Azra Resic (BIH) d. Nadia Kilani (TUN) 6–0 6–1; Medina Bajrambasic/Lejla Husic (BIH) d. Azza Abbou/Mariem Bouchlaka (TUN) 6–2 2–6 7–5. **Liechtenstein d. Iceland 3–0:** Angelika Schadler (LIE) d. Sigurlaug Sigurdardottir (ISL) 6–0 6–0; Sabrina Vogt (LIE) d. Iris Staub (ISL) 6–3 6–4; Bettina Niedhart/Sidonia Wolfinger (LIE) d. Stella Kristjansdottir/Sigurlaug Sigurdardottir (ISL) 6–4 6–2. **30 March – Denmark d. Iceland 3–0:** Charlotte Aagaard (DEN) d. Sigurlaug Sigurdardottir (ISL) 6–0 6–0; Eva Dyrberg (DEN) d. Iris Staub (ISL) 6–0 6–0; Rikke Faurfelt/Karina Ildor-Jacobsgaard (DEN) d. Sigurlaug Sigurdardottir/Iris Staub (ISL) 6–0 6–1. **Tunisia d. Liechtenstein 2–1:** Angelika Schadler (LIE) d. Mariem Bouchlaka (TUN) 6–4 6–3; Selima Sfar (TUN) d. Sabrina Vogt (LIE) 6–2 6–4; Nadia Kilani/Selima Sfar (TUN) d. Angelika Schadler/Sidonia Wolfinger (LIE) 6–0 6–4. **Bosnia/Herzegovina d. Botswana 3–0:** Asja Tankic (BIH) d. Kelesitse Makgale (BOT) 6–1 6–2; Azra Resic (BIH) d. Kago Phatshwane (BOT) 6–0 6–2; Medina Bajrambasic/Lejla Husic (BIH) d. Ntswaki Mawela/Phemelo Mogapi (BOT) 6–0 6–1. **31 March – Denmark d. Bosnia/Herzegovina 3–0:** Charlotte Aagaard (DEN) d. Asja Tankic (BIH) 6–4 6–0; Eva Dyrberg (DEN) d. Azra Resic (BIH) 6–2 6–4; Charlotte Aagaard/Eva Dyrberg (DEN) d. Medina Bajrambasic/Lejla Husic (BIH) 6–1 6–1. **Tunisia d. Iceland 3–0:** Azza Abbou (TUN) d. Sigurlaug Sigurdardottir (ISL) 6–2 6–1; Selima Sfar (TUN) d. Iris Staub (ISL) 6–0 6–1; Nadia Kilani/Selima Sfar (TUN) d. Stella Kristjansdottir/Sigurlaug Sigurdardottir (ISL) 6–0 6–1. **Liechtenstein d. Botswana 3–0:** Angelika Schadler (LIE) d. Kelesitse Makgale (BOT) 6–1 6–0; Sabrina Vogt (LIE) d. Kago Phatshwane (BOT) 6–0 7–5; Bettina Niedhart/Sidonia Wolfinger (LIE) d. Ntswaki Mawela/Phemelo Mogapi (BOT) 6–4 6–0. **1 April – Denmark v Tunisia:** Charlotte Aagaard (DEN) d. Azza Abbou (TUN) 6–0 6–1; tie not completed due to rain. **Botswana v Iceland:** Kelesitse Makgale (BOT) d. Stella Kristjansdottir (ISL) 6–2 7–5; Iris Staub (ISL) v Kago Phatshwane (BOT) 2–0 (15–15); tie not completed due to rain. **Bosnia/Herzegovina v Liechtenstein:** Asja Tankic (BIH) d. Angelika Schadler (LIE) 6–1 6–2; Azra Resic (BIH) v Sabrina Vogt (LIE) 6–1 (30–30); tie not completed due to rain.

GROUP WINNERS: Denmark.

GROUP C: 28 March – Yugoslavia d. Georgia 2–1: Dragana Zaric (YUG) d. Salome Devidze (GEO) 6–2 6–4; Margalita Chakhnashvili (GEO) d. Katarina Daskovic (YUG) 7–5 6–3; Katarina Daskovic/Dragana Zaric (YUG) d. Margalita Chakhnashvili/Salome Devidze (YUG) 2–6 7–6(5) 6–1. **Egypt d. Cyprus 3–0:** Dalia El Sheikh (EGY) d. Pavlina Akritas (CYP) 2–6 6–1 6–2; Yomna Farid (EGY) d. Anita Stylianides (CYP) 6–1 6–0; Sara Omar Badran/Dalia El Sheikh (EGY) d. Pavlina Akritas/Anita Stylianides (CYP) 6–0 6–1. **Lithuania d. Armenia 2–1:** Edita Liachoviciute (LTU) d. Sona Saringulyan (ARM) 6–1 6–1; Ana Gasparyan (ARM) d. Ilona Jarkova (LTU) 6–4 6–0; Ilona Jarkova/Edita Liachoviciute (LTU) d. Ana Gasparyan/Sona Saringulyan (ARM) 6–1 6–2. **29 March – Yugoslavia d. Cyprus 3–0:** Renata Ljukovcan (YUG) d. Pavlina Akritas (CYP) 6–3 6–4; Dragana Zaric (YUG) d. Anita Stylianides (CYP) 6–0 6–0; Katarina Daskovic/Marina Petrovic (YUG) d. Pavlina Akritas/Anita Stylianides (CYP) 6–0 6–1. **Lithuania d. Egypt 3–0:** Edita Liachoviciute (LTU) d. Dina Khalil (EGY) 6–4 6–0; Ilona Jarkova (LTU) d. Yomna Farid (EGY) 6–2 6–0; Ilona Jarkova/Monika Peciulionyte (LTU) d. Sara Omar Badran/Dalia El Sheikh (EGY) 6–0 6–1. **Georgia d. Armenia 3–0:** Salome Devidze (GEO) d. Sona Saringulyan (ARM) 6–3 7–6(8); Margalita Chakhnashvili (GEO) d. Ana Gasparyan (ARM) 6–4 6–2; Salome

Devidze/Nino Esebua (GEO) d. Tatevik Babayan/Hermine Sukiasyan (ARM) 6–1 6–2. **30 March** – **Yugoslavia d. Armenia 3–0:** Marina Petrovic (YUG) d. Sona Saringulyan (ARM) 6–2 6–1; Katarina Daskovic (YUG) d. Ana Gasparyan (ARM) 6–4 6–1; Renata Ljukovcan/Dragana Zaric (YUG) d. Tatevik Babayan/Hermine Sukiasyan (ARM) 6–1 6–1. **Georgia d. Egypt 3–0:** Salome Devidze (GEO) d. Dalia El Sheikh (EGY) 6–4 6–4; Margalita Chakhnashvili (GEO) d. Yomna Farid (EGY) 6–2 6–1; Salome Devidze/Nino Esebua (GEO) d. Dalia El Sheikh/Yomna Farid (EGY) 6–1 6–3. **Lithuania d. Cyprus 3–0:** Edita Liachoviciute (LTU) d. Pavlina Akritas (CYP) 6–2 6–1; Ilona Jarkova (LTU) d. Anita Stylianides (CYP) 6–2 6–1; Ilona Jarkova/Monika Peciulionyte (LTU) d. Elya Constanta/Anita Stylianides (CYP) 6–3 6–0. **31 March** – **Yugoslavia d. Lithuania 3–0:** Dragana Zaric (YUG) d. Edita Liachoviciute (LTU) 4–6 6–1 6–3; Katarina Daskovic (YUG) d. Ilona Jarkova (LTU) 6–0 6–0; Renata Ljukovcan/Marina Petrovic (YUG) d. Monika Peciulionyte/Lina Stanciute (LTU) 4–6 6–1 6–0. **Egypt d. Armenia 2–1:** Dina Khalil (EGY) d. Sona Saringulyan (ARM) 6–3 6–0; Ana Gasparyan (ARM) d. Dalia El Sheikh (EGY) 6–0 6–4; Dina Khalil/Yomna Farid (EGY) d. Ana Gasparyan/Sona Saringulyan (ARM) 6–4 6–3. **Georgia d. Cyprus 3–0:** Nino Esebua (GEO) d. Pavlina Akritas (CYP) 3–6 6–3 6–1; Margalita Chakhnashvili (GEO) d. Anita Stylianides (CYP) 6–1 6–1; Salome Devidze/Nino Esebua (GEO) d. Elya Constanta/Pavlina Akritas (CYP) 6–0 6–1. **1 April** – **Yugoslavia d. Egypt w/o. Cyprus v Armenia:** Hermine Sukiasyan (ARM) d. Elya Constanta (CYP) 6–2 6–0; Pavlina Akritas (CYP) v Tatevik Babayan (ARM) 5–1; tie not completed due to rain. **Lithuania v Georgia:** Salome Devidze (GEO) d. Lina Stanciute (LTU) 6–0 6–3; Margalita Chakhnashvili (GEO) v Monika Peciulionyte (LTU) 4–3 (15–0); tie not completed due to rain.

GROUP WINNERS: Yugoslavia.

GROUP D: 28 March – **Estonia d. Moldova 2–1:** Kaia Kanepi (EST) d. Natalia Volcova (MDA) 6–2 6–0; Svetlana Komleva (MDA) d. Maret Ani (EST) 6–4 6–1; Maret Ani/Kaia Kanepi (EST) d. Svetlana Komleva/Natalia Volcova (MDA) 6–7(5) 6–1 6–0. **Portugal d. Lesotho 3–0:** Cristina Correia (POR) d. Tankiso Letseka (LES) 6–0 6–1; Helga Vieira (POR) d. Mamotebang Molise (LES) 6–1 6–0; Angela Cardoso/Ana-Caterina Nogueira (POR) d. Tankiso Letseka/Mamotebang Molise (LES) 6–1 6–3. **Algeria d. Madagascar 2–1:** Sihem Bennacer (ALG) d. Valisoa Rafolomanantsiatosika (MAD) 6–1 6–1; Aina Rafolomanantsiatosika (MAD) d. Feriel Esseghir (ALG) 7–5 6–4; Sihem Bennacer/Feriel Esseghir (ALG) d. Aina Rafolomanantsiatosika/Solange Rasoarivelo (MAD) 6–3 6–2. **29 March** – **Estonia d. Lesotho 3–0:** Maret Ani (EST) d. Tankiso Letseka (LES) 6–0 6–0; Liina Suurvarik (EST) d. Mamotebang Molise (LES) 6–0 6–0; Maret Ani/Liina Suurvarik (EST) d. Tankiso Letseka/Mamotebang Molise (LES) 6–1 6–1. **Portugal d. Madagascar 3–0:** Angela Cardoso (POR) d. Vonjiniaina Rasamuel (MAD) 6–1 6–4; Ana Nogueira (POR) d. Aina Rafolomanantsiatosika (MAD) 6–2 6–3; Cristina Correia/Helga Vieira (POR) d. Valisoa Rafolomanantsiatosika/Solange Rasoarivelo (MAD) 6–1 6–2. **Moldova d. Algeria 3–0:** Natalia Volcova (MDA) d. Sihem Bennacer (ALG) 6–0 6–3; Svetlana Komleva (MDA) d. Feriel Esseghir (ALG) 6–3 6–3; Svetlana Komleva/Natalia Volcova (MDA) d. Sihem Benyoucef/Feriel Esseghir (ALG) 6–1 2–6 6–3. **30 March** – **Estonia d. Algeria 3–0:** Kaia Kanepi (EST) d. Sihem Bennacer (ALG) 7–5 6–1; Maret Ani (EST) d. Feriel Esseghir (ALG) 6–4 6–1; Maret Ani/Liina Suurvarik (EST) d. Sihem Benyoucef/Feriel Esseghir (ALG) 6–3 6–1. **Moldova d. Portugal 2–1:** Angela Cardoso (POR) d. Natalia Volcova (MDA) 5–7 6–2 8–6; Svetlana Komleva (MDA) d. Ana Nogueira (POR) 6–3 6–1; Elena Arabadji/Svetlana Komleva (MDA) d. Angela Cardoso/Cristina Correia (POR) 6–2 6–2. **Madagascar d. Lesotho 2–1:** Tankiso Letseka (LES) d. Valisoa Rafolomanantsiatosika (MAD) 6–4 7–6(1); Aina Rafolomanantsiatosika (MAD) d. Mamotebang Molise (LES) 6–1 6–0; Aina Rafolomanantsiatosika/Solange Rasoarivelo (MAD) d. Tankiso Letseka/Mamotebang Molise (LES) 7–6(6) 6–3. **31 March** – **Estonia d. Madagascar 3–0:** Kaia Kanepi (EST) d. Vonjiniaina Rasamuel (MAD) 6–0 6–0; Maret Ani (EST) d. Aina Rafolomanantsiatosika (MAD) 6–2 7–5; Kaia Kanepi/Liina Suurvarik (EST) d. Valisoa Rafolomanantsiatosika/Vonjiniaina Rasamuel (MAD) 6–1 6–1. **Portugal d. Algeria 2–1:** Sihem Benyoucef (ALG) d. Helga Vieira (POR) 6–4 6–3; Ana Nogueira (POR) d. Feriel Esseghir (ALG) 6–4 3–6 6–2; Angela Cardoso/Ana Nogueira (POR) d. Sihem Benyoucef/Samira Takorabet (ALG) 6–1 6–2. **Moldova d. Lesotho 3–0:** Olga Cosic (MDA) d. Tankiso Letseka (LES) 6–0 6–1; Svetlana Komleva (MDA) d. Mamotebang Molise (LES) 6–1 6–1; Elena Arabadji/Olga Cosic (MDA) d. Tankiso Letseka/Mamotebang Molise (LES) 6–3 6–2. **1 April** – **Estonia v Portugal:** Kaia Kanepi (EST) d. Angela Cardoso (POR) 6–1 6–4; Maret Ani (EST) v Ana Nogueira (POR) 2–1; tie not completed due to rain. **Lesotho v Algeria:** Sihem Bennacer (ALG) d. Tankiso Letseka (LES) 2–6 6–3 6–0; tie not completed due to rain. **Madagascar v Moldova:** Natalia Volcova (MDA) d. Valisoa Rafolomanantsiatosika (MAD) 6–1 6–2; Svetlana Komleva (MDA) v Solange Rasoarivelo (MAD) 4–0 (15–0); tie not completed due to rain.

GROUP WINNERS: Estonia.

FYR Macedonia, Denmark, Yugoslavia and Estonia promoted to Europe/Africa Qualifying Group I for 2001.

The Hyundai Hopman Cup

Barry Wood

South Africa won the Hopman Cup at their eighth attempt when they defeated surprise challengers Thailand in a thrilling final. Amanda Coetzer, partnering Wayne Ferreira for the fifth time, held off a gallant challenge from Tamarine Tanasugarn to win 3–6 6–4 6–4 and then Wayne Ferreira resisted two set points to overcome Paradorn Srichaphan 7–6(14–12) 6–3.

Thailand, who had to qualify for the competition by beating Japan on New Year's Day, won the hearts and respect of the crowd with their efforts. Tanasugarn, who had already defeated four players with a higher ranking during the week, had Coetzer on the ropes after taking the first set and building a 3–0 lead with two breaks of serve in the second.

With Coetzer patrolling the baseline Tanasugarn often dictated from the net, and her ability to hit into the corners and keep Coetzer on the run made her look a likely winner against a perplexed opponent. 'She made me feel uncomfortable and I couldn't execute very well,' said Coetzer. 'I didn't know what to do at the start.'

The Thai held a point to lead 4–0, and although she allowed Coetzer to rally and level the match and then build a dominating 5–1 lead in the third, Tanasugarn kept the spectators on the edges of their seats as she staged a dramatic comeback. After receiving attention for an ailing back when down 1–4, Tanasugarn stormed back to 4–5 and held two points to level at 5–5 before Coetzer edged through.

Knowing South Africa had an opportunity to lift the trophy at last after finishing as runners-up to the United States three years earlier, Ferreira was in stunning form against Srichaphan. The experienced South African held seven games to love, and outside of the tiebreak dropped just nine points on his serve.

Thailand's victory over Australia in the doubles in the first round launched them on their unexpected run to the final, but Srichiphan's win over the Slovak Republic's Karol Kucera was also of great significance. However, Tanasugarn's inspired play which led to victories over Jelena

The diminutive Amanda Coetzer and Wayne Ferreira who brought South Africa their first success in the Hopman Cup. (Stephen Wake)

Dokic, Henrieta Naeyova and Barbara Schett, as well as Ai Sugiyama in the qualifying round, was the foundation of the Thai's success.

Coetzer, sporting a new braided hairstyle, remained undefeated in singles throughout the week as she overcame Dominique Van Roost, Asa Carlsson and Alexandra Stevenson – who was deputising for the injured Monica Seles – before ending Tanasugarn's run. Ferreira was almost as invincible in beating Xavier Malisse, Jonas Bjorkman and Srichaphan, but he surprisingly lost 6–4 6–4 to the injured Justin Gimelstob's replacement, James Blake.

The success of South Africa and Thailand significantly raised the profile of the game in the two nations and resulted in extensive television coverage. This was especially so in Thailand, a country unaccustomed to such international tennis acclaim. The event was front page news, and matches were still being replayed on cable television months later!

HYUNDAI HOPMAN CUP 2000
BURSWOOD DOME RESORT, PERTH, 1–8 JANUARY 2000

SEEDS: 2 Australia: Mark Philippoussis/Jelena Dokic. **3 Slovak Republic:** Karol Kucera/Henrieta Nagyova.
4 South Africa: Wayne Ferreira/Amanda Coetzer.
UNSEEDED: Austria: Stefan Koubek/Barbara Schett. **Belgium:** Xavier Malisse/Dominique Van Roost.
Sweden: Jonas Bjorkman/Asa Carlsson. **Thailand:** Paradorn Srichaphan/Tamarine Tanasugarn.
USA: James Blake/Alexandra Stevenson. **Japan:** Takao Suzuki/Ai Sugiyama.

Qualifying playoff
Thailand d. Japan 2–1: T. Tanasugarn d. A. Sugiyama 6–1 6–3; P. Srichaphan d. T. Suzuki 6–3 7–6(2); T. Suzuki/A. Sugiyama d. P. Srichaphan/T. Tanasugarn 6–3 6–4

Round Robin results
Group A
South Africa d. Belgium 3–0: A. Coetzer d. D. Van Roost 6–4 6–2; W. Ferreira d. X. Malisse 6–2 6–3; W. Ferreira/A. Coetzer d. X. Malisse/D. Van Roost 7–5 6–3.
Sweden d. USA 3–0: A. Carlsson d. A. Stevenson 6–4 6–4; J. Bjorkman d. J. Blake 6–3 7–5; J. Bjorkman/A. Carlsson d. J. Blake/A. Stevenson 6–3 6–3.
South Africa d. Sweden 2–1: A. Coetzer d. A. Carlsson 6–4 6–0; W. Ferreira d. J. Bjorkman 6–4 6–4; J. Bjorkman/A. Carlsson d. W. Ferreira/A. Coetzer 7–6(3) 6–3.
Belgium d. USA 2–1: A. Stevenson d. D. Van Roost 6–4 1–6 6–4; X. Malisse d. J. Blake 7–6(3) 3–6 6–3; X. Malisse/D. Van Roost d. J. Blake/A. Stevenson 6–4 3–6 6–2.
USA d. South Africa 2–1: A. Coetzer d. A. Stevenson 6–3 6–1; J. Blake d. W. Ferreira 6–4 6–4; J. Blake/A. Stevenson d. W. Ferreira/A. Coetzer 6–7(5) 6–3 6–2.
Sweden d. Belgium 2–1: D. Van Roost d. A. Carlsson 6–2 6–3; J. Bjorkman d. X. Malisse 6–4 6–3; J. Bjorkman/A. Carlsson d. X. Malisse/D. Van Roost 6–1 7–5.

Group B
Austria d. Slovak Republic 2–1: B. Schett d. H. Nagyova 6–2 6–3; K. Kucera d. S. Koubek 4–6 6–0 6–3; S. Koubek/B. Schett d. K. Kucera/H. Nagyova 6–2 3–6 6–3.
Thailand d. Australia 2–1: T. Tanasugarn d. J. Dokic 6–1 6–4; M. Philippoussis d. P. Srichaphan 6–1 6–4; P. Srichaphan/T. Tanasugarn d. M. Philippoussis/J. Dokic 3–6 6–3 6–4.
Australia d. Austria 2–1: J. Dokic d. B. Schett 1–6 6–2 7–5; M. Philippoussis d. S. Koubek 6–3 3–6 6–1; S. Koubek/B. Schett d. M. Philippoussis/J. Dokic 7–5 6–3.
Thailand d. Slovak Republic 3–0: T. Tanasugarn d. H. Nagyova 2–6 6–2 4–1 ret; P. Srichaphan d. K. Kucera 4–6 7–6(2) 6–2; P. Srichaphan/T. Tanasugarn d. K. Kucera/H. Nagyova w/o.
Japan (Alternate for Slovak Republic) d. Australia 3–0: A. Sugiyama d. J. Dokic 6–4 6–3; T. Suzuki d. M. Philippoussis w/o; T. Suzuki/A. Sugiyama d. M. Philippoussis/J. Dokic w/o.
Austria d. Thailand 2–1: T. Tanasugarn d. B. Schett 6–7(2) 6–3 6–3; S. Koubek d. P. Srichaphan 6–3 6–1; S. Koubek/B. Schett d. P. Srichaphan/T. Tanasugarn 8–7(3) (tie-break played at 7–7).

FINAL: South Africa d. Thailand 3-0: A. Coetzer d. T. Tanasugarn 3–6 6–4 6–4; W. Ferreira d. P. Srichaphan 7–6(12) 6–3; W. Ferreira/A. Coetzer d. P. Srichaphan/T. Tanasugarn 8–1 (pro-set).

ITF Youth Cups

Sunshine Cup & Connolly Continental Cup

Jackie Nesbitt

US Teams Excel on Home Soil

The US policy of focusing attention on the team competitions in recent years certainly appears to be bearing fruit, as the US boys' team lived up to expectations and the US girls' team exceeded expectations at the 2000 ITF Sunshine Cup and Connolly Continental Cup Finals.

Led by the 2000 Junior Boys' Singles World Champion in waiting, Andy Roddick, the US boys team fielded a strong side also featuring US Open runner-up Robby Ginepri and their doubles specialist, Tres Davis. They anticipated that their toughest challenge would come after the round robin stages. So it was to prove as the top seeds comfortably came through their group, despite a few anxious moments against unseeded South Africa, when Raven Klaasen defeated Ginepri in the opening rubber. Even Bulgaria, fielding Todor Enev, failed to halt the march as Roddick disposed of his rival for the world champion title in straight sets.

With the exception of 2nd seeded Spain, another nation that has become a great exponent of the team events in recent years, the other seeds struggled. Hearts went out to 4th seeded Chinese Taipei though, who were expected to do well, but who lost the services of their number one player, Yen-Hsun Lu just prior to the start of competition due to the sad loss of the youngster's father.

Although managing to draft in a replacement, Wei-Joe Wang, who performed remarkably well under the circumstances, the top Asian representatives were never able to mount a serious challenge. The departure of Yen-Hsun Lu left the third group wide open and in fact three teams, Australia, France and Germany ended the round robin stage level on two victories apiece. Despite Germany's win over France, it was the defending champions who progressed to the knock-out stage by virtue of a better sets won percentage.

With Spain progressing untroubled from their group, thanks to a disappointing performance by the Czech team, it was left to the teams in group two to provide the entertainment. Canada took advantage of the early retirement of Swiss number one Roman Valent to clinch a shock win over the 3rd seeds. Ecuador further complicated matters when their Davis Cup hero, the engaging Giovanni Lapentti led his team to a great win over 6th seeded Brazil. The seeds got back on track the following day, with Lapentti unable to repeat his heroics against Switzerland and Brazil pulling off a tight win against Canada. The final outcome of the group hinged on the deciding doubles between Brazil and Switzerland on the third day. The Swiss pairing of Stephane Bolhi and Michael Lammer appeared in command taking the opening set against Thiago Alves and Bruno Soares, but the higher ranked players finally proved their worth, storming back to take the next two sets for the loss of only two games.

Alves in particular kept the good form going into the semi-finals and gave the US food for thought when he defeated Ginepri in the opening rubber. Roddick levelled matters against Soares, but needed all his experience and doubles prowess to partner Davis to a tight three set win in the deciding doubles.

There was no such difficulty for Spain, led by the impressive Marc Lopez, who defeated France 3–0.

In the Final, Ginepri found his best form and was simply too good for Carlos Cuadrado demolishing his challenge 6–1 6–2. Lopez seemed to be getting the better of Roddick in the top singles rubber, despite the loss of the opening set. With Roddick a break down in the final set, the match appeared to be heading for a deciding doubles, but Roddick made several crucial ventures to the net and proved a worthy winner to clinch the title for the US in one of the best matches of the tournament.

With top seeded Slovak Republic and 2nd seeded Argentina, both fielding strong teams, the US girls initially found themselves expected to pick up a minor medal at best. The round robin group results went according to plan, although both Slovak Republic and USA were lucky to scrape by unseeded Japan and France – both 7–5 in the third set of the deciding doubles.

No such trouble for Argentina who easily defeated Spain, Italy and Germany, or for wild card entrants Estonia, who accounted for Uruguay, Chinese Taipei and a Hungarian team featuring the excellent singles and doubles player Aniko Kapros.

Estonia's fine win over Hungary gave notice of their calibre. Their semi-final against Argentina saw Maret Ani record a straight sets win over Eugenia Chialvo and Kaia Kanepi maintain her ranking superiority over Gisela Dulko to put the wild cards into the Final. The US run was expected to end at the hands of Slovak Republic, despite Ashley Harkleroad's fine opening win over Lubomira Kurhajcova. Melissa Middleton, however, produced one of her best performances of the year, having previously lost two of her round robin matches, to defeat Dlhopolcova 7–5 5–7 8–6 to give the host nation a chance of two top medals to round off the year.

Harkleroad kept her unbeaten singles record intact to destroy Ani's record in the opening match, but Kanepi proved too strong for Middleton to set the scene for an exciting doubles. Keeping faith with his doubles pairing of Harkleroad and Bethanie Mattek, Captain Jai di Louie, was rewarded by a fine late night win by the pair over Ani and Kanepi – the outstanding performance of Mattek in the doubles worthy of special mention.

The boys of the successful American Sunshine Cup team and the girls of the winning US Connolly Continental Cup team celebrate together in Key Biscayne. (Michael Baz)

In the battle for third place medals, Brazil boys were worthy winners over France and there was to be no consolation for Slovak Republic as Argentina kept up their excellent recent team record taking both singles for victory.

ITF SUNSHINE CUP 2000
Boys' 18 & Under International Team Championship
16 nations competed. Event played in Key Biscayne, Florida, USA, 4–9 December.
FINAL POSITIONS: Champion nation: USA; runners up: Spain; 3rd: Brazil; 4th: France; 5th equal: South Africa, Germany; 7th equal: Canada, Colombia; 9th: Mexico; 10th Switzerland; 11th: Slovak Republic; 12th: Australia; 13th: Czech Republic; 14th: Ecuador; 15th: Bulgaria; 16th: Chinese Taipei.
Semi-finals: USA d. Brazil 2–1; Spain d. France 3–0.
3rd place play-off: Brazil d. France 2–0: T. Alves d. C. Morel 7–5 6–3; B. Soares d. B. Balleret 6–1 6–3.
Final: USA d. Spain 2–0: R. Ginepri d. C. Cuadrado 6–1 6–2; A. Roddick d. M. Lopez 6–4 6–7(1) 6–4.

ITF CONNOLLY CONTINENTAL CUP 2000
Girls' 18 & Under International Team Championship
16 nations competed. Event played in Key Biscayne, Florida, USA, 4–9 December.
FINAL POSITIONS: Champion nation: USA; runners-up: Estonia; 3rd: Argentina; 4th: Slovak Republic; 5th equal: France, Hungary; 7th equal: Mexico, Germany; 9th: Chinese Taipei; 10th: Canada; 11th: Italy; 12th: Brazil; 13th: South Africa; 14th: Spain; 15th: Japan; 16th: Uruguay.
Semi-finals: USA d. Slovak Republic 3–0; Estonia d. Argentina 3–0.
3rd place play-off: Argentina d. Slovak Republic 2–0: E. Chialvo d. L. Kurhajcova 0–6 6–2 6–2; G. Dulko d. L. Dlhopolcova 6–3 6–4.
Final: USA d. Estonia 2–1: A. Harkleroad d. M. Ani 6–4 7–6(1); M. Middleton lost to K. Kanepi 2–6 4–6; A. Harkleroad/B. Mattek d. M. Ani/K. Kanepi 7–6(5) 6–4.

NEC World Youth Cup

Jackie Nesbitt

Australia and Czech Republic triumph in Japan

The boys' draw at the 16 & Under NEC World Youth Cup Final staged in Japan, certainly brought the best under 16 players around the world together, with a number of former junior under 14 team winners back in action. The wonderful venue in Hiroshima, with its purpose built indoor four court arena – sadly required on the final day – deserved no less.

The finals of both the boys' and girls' events proved fitting culminations to a memorable week. Australia boys emerged the surprise winners against Austria while the Czech girls outlasted Hungary to capture the girls' title.

The boys' event began with the majority of the seeds surviving the opening round except for Taipei, seeded eight, who lost to Uruguay. There was a shock in store too for 4th seeded USA, the biggest seeds to fall on day one, after they were ousted by an inspired Poland.

Richard Gasquet, a winner for France in the 14 & Under World Junior Tennis team competition in 1999, saw his top seeded team make a confident start against China. In contrast, 2nd seeded Austria fielding two former 14 & Under gold medallists in Johannes Ager and Stefan Wiespener, did not have things their own way against Chile. Wiespener opened easily enough with a straight sets win over James Knuckey, but Ager needed to recover from a first set whitewash against Jorge Aguilar to scrape home 11–9 in a gripping third set.

With the exception of Austria, all of the expected favourites had a torrid time in the quarterfinals. The top seeds, France, came unstuck at the hands of 7th seeded Sweden with Gasquet unable to level the match after Christian Johansson's victory over Marc Auradou. Fielding the silver medal winning team from the 1998 World Junior Tennis competition, third seeded Argentina had high hopes for the title. However, Argentina's Juan Monaco succumbed to Australia's Ryan Henry and despite Brian Dabul's hard fought win over Todd Reid to level matters for the South Americans, solid doubles play from the Aussies pulled them through. Having lost to Russia in the qualifying event, Poland were not expected to make an impact against the 5th seeds, but in the event brushed them aside 3–0, Michal Prziesieny performing particularly well in the opening rubber.

The Czech girls and Australian boys who were victorious in the 2000 NEC World Youth Cup, the ITF team competition for the 16-and-unders, played in Hiroshima. (Stephen Wake)

A semblance of normality was restored in the semi-finals, with Austria ending the Polish run. Johannes Ager dug deep for victory, defeating Adam Chadaj 8–6 in the third set to give Austria an expected place in the final. Australia's final berth was only secured after another decisive doubles – with Reid and Henry once again combining well to defeat Sweden's Johansson and Soderling.

The higher seeded Austria were heavy favourites in the final against Australia, which proved to be possibly the best contest of the week. But in a display of guts, Henry overcame the loss of the opening set and several breaks of serve to defeat Wiespener to get the Aussies off to the best start. Reid followed by producing his best singles form of the week to surprisingly defeat Ager in two tight sets. An unexpected win for the Aussies, but a well-deserved team effort much appreciated by a sizeable crowd. For the unfortunate Polish team there was to be no consolation in the third place play-off – they were beaten by Sweden in a tight deciding doubles.

The girls' event certainly also provided its fair share of exciting matches for the spectators. A more predictable event in terms of seeding, only two teams failed to take up their expected place in the quarter-finals. The Slovaks, the top European qualifiers, were seeded only seven following the late withdrawal of world No. 6 Lenka Dlhopolcova due to injury, proved no match for a determined French team, losing 3–0. Fifth seeded South Africa, normally so reliable in the doubles, lost out to Indonesia by the closest possible margin – Novianti Novianti and Angelique Widjaja edging past Maretha Van Niekerk and Chanelle Scheepers 8–6 in the final set of the deciding rubber.

Top seeds Hungary defeated Chinese Taipei and 2nd seeded Czech Republic took both singles against France to secure their semi-final positions. Also joining them in the last four were 3rd seeded USA, who brought Indonesia back down to earth, and 4th seeded Russia – comfortable 3–0 winners over Canada.

In the semi-finals, Hungary's Dorottya Magas and Virag Nemeth both needed three set victories to progress over USA's Ashley Harkleroad and Bethanie Mattek respectively. Joining Hungary in the final were the Czechs, 2–1 victors over Russia, but only after Petra Cetkovska and Ema Janaskova won a tense three set doubles against Anna Bastrikova and Dinara Safina.

The final was to prove the highlight of the week in the girls' event too. Eva Birnerova bettered Magas in two tight sets to put Czech Republic one up, only for Nemeth to outlast Cetkovska to level the tie. Hungarian pairing Magas and Nemeth did well to recover from losing the opening set of the doubles to take the second, but ran out of steam in the third to allow Cetkovska, partnered by Janaskova, to add to her collection of team event medals won for Czech Republic. A clean sweep for Europe was achieved when yet another dramatic deciding doubles went the way of Bastrikova and Safina as Russia defeated USA 2–1.

NEC WORLD YOUTH CUP 2000
ITF Team Championships for 16 & Under
87 nations competed, 85 taking part in the boys' event and 68 in the girls' event. Final stages took place in Hiroshima, Japan, 3–8 October.

FINAL POSITIONS – BOYS: Champion nation: Australia; runners-up: Austria; 3rd: Sweden; 4th: Poland; 5th: Russia; 6th: France; 7th: Uruguay; 8th: Argentina; 9th: USA; 10th: Japan; 11th: South Africa; 12th: Chinese Taipei; 13th: Slovak Republic; 14th: Mexico; 15th: Chile; 16th: China; **GIRLS:** Champion nation: Czech Republic; runners-up: Hungary; 3rd: Russia; 4th: USA; 5th: France; 6th: Chinese Taipei; 7th: Indonesia; 8th: Canada; 9th: South Africa; 10th: Slovak Republic; 11th: Argentina; 12th: Sweden; 13th: Japan; 14th: Brazil; 15th: Korea; 16th: Colombia.
BOYS' CHAMPIONSHIP – Semi-finals: Australia d. Sweden 2–1 (R. Henry d. C. Johansson 6–2 7–6(7); T. Reid lost to R. Soderling 4–6 6–4 1–6; R. Henry/T. Reid d. C. Johansson/R. Soderling 4–6 6–4 6–4).
Austria d. Poland 2–1 (S. Wiespeiner d. M. Przysiezny 6–1 6–2; J. Ager lost to A.Chadaj 2–6 6–4 6–8; J. Ager/S. Wiespeiner d. A. Chadaj/M.Przysiezny 4–6 7–5 6–2). **3rd place play-off: Sweden d. Poland 2–1** (C. Johansson d. M. Przysiezny 6–4 2–6 6–4; R. Soderling lost to A. Chadaj 3–6 3–6; C. Johansson/M. Ryderstedt d. A. Chadaj/M. Przysiezny 6–4 4–6 6–4). **Final: Australia d. Austria 2–0** (R. Henry d S. Wiespeiner 5–7 6–4 8–6; T. Reid d. J. Ager 6–4 7–5).
GIRLS' CHAMPIONSHIP – Semi-finals: Hungary d. USA 2–1 (D. Magas d. A. Harkleroad 0–6 6–3 6–3; V. Nemeth d. B. Mattek 6–3 4–6 6–4; I. Balazs/D. Magas lost to A. Harkleroad/K. Schlukebir 4–6 2–6). **Czech Republic d. Russia 2–1** (E. Birnerova lost to A. Bastrikova 4–6 4–6; P. Cetkovska d. G. Voskoboeva 6–4 6–1; P. Cetkovska/E. Janaskova d. A. Bastrikova/D. Safina 5–7 6–0 6–2). **3rd place play-off: Russia d. USA 2–1** (D. Safina d. K. Schlukebir 6–1 1–6 6–3; A. Bastrikova lost to A. Harkleroad 4–6 3–6; A. Bastrikova/D. Safina d. B. Mattek/K. Schlukebir 6–3 5–7 7–5). **Final: Czech Republic d. Hungary 2–1** (E. Birnerova d. D. Magas 7–6(5) 6–3; P. Cetkovska lost to V. Nemeth 5–7 6–4 6–8; P. Cetkovska/E. Janaskova d. D. Magas/ V. Nemeth 7–5 5–7 6–1).

Cesky Telecom World Junior Tennis Final

Jackie Nesbitt

Europeans dominate medals in World Junior Tennis

Much was expected of the two strong Russian teams who shared top billing at the 2000 Cesky Telecom World Junior Tennis Final, the ITF Team Championships for boys and girls of 14 & Under, held at Prostejov in Czech Republic.

The Russian girls justified their top seeding, successfully defending their title with victory over Czech Republic in the final. Russian hopes of clinching a double in the World Junior Tennis evaporated however when the Spanish boys outplayed the favourites to win the 2000 trophy.

Both competitions involved four groups of five nations with the teams in each group playing each other as a round robin. The top nation in each group would then progress to the semi-final round.

Russia girls duly opened in Group One with a victory over Argentina, but the 3–0 scoreline was very misleading as the South American team forced both singles rubbers to three sets, with Dasha Tchemarda only edging past Emilia Yorio 8–6 in the final set of the opening rubber.

The 3rd seeded home team looked far from convincing in their Group Two opener against Spain, but came through in the deciding doubles. Second seeded USA had a comfortable win in Group Four over South Africa, but 7th seeded Brazil were defeated 3–0 by Croatia. The biggest shock, however, was reserved for Group Three where 4th seeded China suffered defeat at the hands of France, with a particularly stunning performance coming from 12 year-old Tatiana Golovin, who recorded a 6–3 6–0 win over Rui Du.

Brazil's week did not improve on day two, defeated by South Africa 2–1, however, Chinese Taipei, the 5th seeds, recovered from another splendid performance from Golovin to clinch a 2–1 victory over France.

The third day of competition saw the two seeded nations in each group face each other. Canada paid the price for a lack of doubles prowess, losing 2–1 to Russia, but Barbora Strycova was on top form for Czech Republic who overcame Belarus.

Su-Wei Hsieh took the opening set from Shuai Peng, only to collapse in the ensuing two sets as Taipei lost out to regional rivals China – the 4th seeds becoming group leaders as a result.

Sure of a place in the final four, Russia dismissed the challenge by Japan, and USA emerged victorious against Croatia. Elsewhere, France easily defeated Uruguay, but needed Great Britain to claim a rubber against China to progress. Despite a fighting performance in the doubles, the British pair lost a three-setter to enable China to clinch the group by the narrowest of margins.

No doubt worn out by their struggles in the round robin matches, the USA were no match for Czech Republic in their semi-final match-up. China also lost all three rubbers against Russia, with Vera Douchevina's 7–5 6–2 win over Peng particularly impressive.

Prostejov in the Czech Republic played host to the 14-and-under teams participating in the Cesky Telecom World Junior Tennis competition, won by the boys of Spain and the Russian girls.
(Stephen Wake)

In the final, Czech Republic's Strycova took a close first set against Douchevina, but the Russian No. 1 settled into her game and was a worthy winner in three sets. When Russia's Dasha Tchemarda survived a first set tie-break against Lucie Safarova, the top seeds were celebrating for the second consecutive year. China delivered Asia its only medal of the competition by beating a valiant USA to take third spot.

With the defending boys' champions, France, failing to qualify for the Final, the way looked clear for the Russian boys to match the success of their female compatriots.

The opening day saw Russia engaged in a tight match against Australia, but they nonetheless emerged 2–1 victors. It was a tough draw for El Salvador who were forced to face second seeded USA who were far too strong for their regional opponents. Third seeded Spain triumphed easily against India – while 2nd seeded Germany also progressed against Japan. Silver medallists in 1999 and the top team in South America, Chile struggled early on against Mexico, for whom Rafael Gutierrez recorded a fine win over Matias Rojas, before the South Americans finally came through 2–1.

Day two saw Russia dispatch Peru, while Germany and Spain progressed at the expense of Morocco and Czech Republic respectiveley. USA defeated Croatia 3–0.

The quest for a semi-final position began on day three. Chile's chance of a medal was thwarted by the most convincing Russian performance to date while Germany progressed against Thailand to reach the last four. Spain managed a 3–0 scoreline over Slovak Republic. USA overcame Brazil after a tense doubles decider when Brendan Evans and Scott Oudsema reversed a set and a break down situation against Brazil's Celso Ribeiro and Bruno Rosa. The Americans will no doubt give great credit to captain Steve De Vries for convincing them they could still win.

However, the effort of the previous day proved too much for the Americans in their subsequent semi-final with Russia and they were forced to pin their hopes on a third place position. The second semi-final involved Spain against second seeded Germany. With Germany's Daniel Muller not on top form, Rafael Nadal duly won the top singles rubber for Spain. Bartolome Salva managed to frustrate the bigger hitting Sebastian Rieschick thanks to masterful clay court play to send Spain through to the final.

Facing the top seeded Russia in the final, the Spanish team nevertheless continued to be in control, with Salva recording an even more impressive win over Artem Sitak to take first blood for Spain. Nadal's performances had also caught the eye throughout the week and the Spaniard dispatched Nikolai Soloviev to give Spain its second title since 1991 – the inaugural year of the competition. A clean sweep for Europe in the boys' event was completed when Germany defeated USA 2–1 in the third place play-off.

CESKY TELECOM WORLD JUNIOR TENNIS FINAL 2000
ITF Team Championships for 14 & Under
83 nations competed, 80 taking part in the boys' event and 75 in the girls' event. Final stages took place in Prostejov, Czech Republic, 21–27 August.

FINAL POSITIONS – BOYS: Champion nation: Spain; runners-up: Russia; 3rd: Germany; 4th: USA; 5th: Slovak Republic; 6th: Brazil; 7th: Chile; 8th: Morocco; 9th: Croatia; 10th: Czech Republic; 11th: Peru; 12th: Japan; 13th: Australia; 14th: South Africa; 15th: Canada; 16th: Great Britain 17th: India; 18th: Mexico; 19th: Thailand; 20th: El Salvador. **GIRLS:** Champion nation: Russia; runners-up: Czech Republic; 3rd: China; 4th: USA; 5th: Belarus; 6th: Chinese Taipei; 7th: Croatia; 8th: Argentina; 9th: Canada; 10th: Spain; 11th: France; 12th: South Africa; 13th: Brazil; 14th: Great Britain; 15th: Japan; 16th: Egypt; 17th: Korea; 18th: Mexico; 19th: Uruguay; 20th: Bahamas.

BOYS' CHAMPIONSHIP – Semi-finals: Russia d. USA 3–0 (A. Sitak d. S. Oudsema 6–1 6–2; N. Soloviev d. B. Evans 7–5 6–4; D. Matsoukevitch/A. Sitak d. V. Mirzadeh/S. Oudsema 6–3 6–3). **Spain d. Germany 3–0** (B. Salva d. S. Rieschick 6–2 5–7 6–2; R. Nadal d. D. Muller 6–3 6–4; M. Granollers/R. Nadal d. D. Muller/S. Rieschick 7–5 6–4). **3rd place play-off: Germany d. USA 2–1** (A. Weber d. V. Mirzadeh 7–5 6–2; D. Muller lost to B. Evans 4–6 5–7; S. Rieschick/A. Weber d. B. Evans/S. Oudsema 6–4 6–3). **Final: Spain d. Russia 3–0** (B. Salva d. A. Sitak 6–3 6–3; R. Nadal d. N. Soloviev 6–3 6–2; M. Granollers/R. Nadal d. D. Matsoukevitch/A. Sitak 4–6 6–1 6–4).

GIRLS' CHAMPIONSHIP – Semi-finals: Russia d. China 3–0 (D. Tchemarda d. R. Du 6–3 6–1; V. Douchevina d. S. Peng 7–5 6–2; I. Kotkina/D. Tchemarda d. R. Du/Q. Yue 6–2 6–2). **Czech Republic d. USA 2–1** (L. Safarova d. A. Baker 6–4 6–1; B. Strycova d. A. Liles 6–3 6–0; N. Freislerova/ L. Safarova lost to A. Baker/ J. Jackson 5–7 4–6). **3rd place play-off: China d. USA 2–1** (R. Du lost to J. Jackson 6–4 0–6 5–7; S. Peng d. A. Baker 6–0 6–3; R. Du/S. Peng d. A. Baker/J. Jackson 6–4 6–2). **Final: Russia d. Czech Republic 3–0** (D. Tchemarda d. L. Safarova 7–6(3) 6–2; V. Douchevina d. B. Strycova 4–6 6–1 6–2; I. Kotkina/D. Tchemarda d. N. Freislerova/L. Safarova 6–4 6–0).

Grand Slam Championships

After a brilliant start in Australia, Andre Agassi's form fluctuated at the major Championships with a semi-final finish at Wimbledon his next best performance. (Stephen Wake)

Lindsay Davenport won convincingly in Melbourne but was thwarted in the Wimbledon and US Open finals by Venus Williams. (Stephen Wake)

Australian Open Championships

Alan Trengove

Andre Agassi unwisely waited until 1995 to play in his first Australian Open, and won at his first attempt. In 2000, at his fifth attempt, he captured the title a second time. At 29, he was fitter and more determined than at any period of his life, his tennis so relentlessly efficient that Australians were left to wonder just how many times he might have triumphed had he been similarly motivated throughout his career.

His fellow-American, Lindsay Davenport, has been less tardy in doing justice to her potential. The 23-year-old Californian became the first native-born American to win the women's title since Chris Evert in 1984. She thus ended the three-year reign of Martina Hingis, who also lost the women's doubles title she had won for three straight years with three different partners. Davenport left little doubt of her pre-eminence in the women's game. Intimidatingly strong and buoyed by the achievements of 1999 – particularly her three successive defeats of Hingis – she out-hit all opponents. 'Gosh, I just hate playing you,' said Hingis in a rueful – and revealing – tribute to her conqueror on the presentation dais after losing the final 6–1 7–5.

Always level-headed and gracious, Davenport was a popular winner, though not quite as popular as Agassi, whose charisma once again captivated Australia and was, perhaps, as much responsible as anything for a record attendance of 501,251 over the fortnight. The size of the crowds was in spite of the non-completion of the new No. 1 court, a second multi-purpose venue with a retractable roof that will augment the 15,000-seat centre court stadium, now renamed Rod Laver Arena. The new facility would have accommodated 10,000 fans had it been ready.

In the weeks before the tournament, there was keen speculation on whether we were about to see an Australian win the men's singles for the first time in almost a quarter of a century. If not Patrick Rafter, then possibly Mark Philippoussis or even young Lleyton Hewitt, it was hoped, might seize the moment. Australia, after all, had recently won the Davis Cup, and had won much else in international sport in the previous 12 months. The mood of optimism grew when Hewitt, displaying a maturity that belied his 18 years, won the lead-up tournaments at Adelaide and Sydney.

Australian dreams, alas, were just that – or, rather, pipe dreams. Rafter was unable to play because of an injured shoulder, and though Philippoussis and Hewitt were in top form and fought hard, both were eliminated in the round of 16. Thereafter, public interest centred on the rivalry between Agassi and Pete Sampras.

Agassi's dedication was evident from his thorough preparation. At Christmas, he asked his coach, Brad Gilbert, and his longtime friend and trainer, Gil Reyes, to begin supervising his campaign. His training regime comprised two solid practice sessions a day, and gruelling stints of lifting weights and road work, including lung-searing sprints up a long hill. When Agassi arrived in Australia nine days before the start of the Open, the body that a few years ago had been soft, if not decidedly flabby, was rock hard, and he possessed the cardiovascular capacity of a marathon runner. Gilbert had a new nickname for him – 'The Rock'.

Extreme physical fitness, along with the exceptional eye-to-hand coordination and the ability to produce cleanly-hit ground strokes that he has always been blessed with, were the keys to Agassi's superb performance. As he put it himself, without at all seeming to brag, he was now so fit he could turn a best-of-five-sets match into a sprint. 'Whether I'm down or whether I'm up,' he said, 'I have the platform to execute my game and not waver from it.'

After defeating defending champion Yevgeny Kafelnikov 3–6 6–3 6–2 6–4 in the final, he elaborated: 'All of us can unload on a putaway. The question is, how heavy is that rally shot, that shot you expect to make a hundred out of a hundred times. I always feel that can improve. Because the stronger you get, the better you move, [then] the more you are in position, the more snap you have on your shot, and the more you can control your opponent.'

Another possible ingredient, more difficult to assess, was his celebrated romance with Steffi Graf, who intently watched all of his matches and occasionally practised with him. While firmly declining to discuss their relationship with the media, Agassi admitted that 'you can always learn from a champion'. And since Graf had won the Australian women's singles four times, her support was probably invaluable; her own career-long commitment to physical fitness would have reinforced her boyfriend's new philosophy.

Agassi and Sampras, seeded first and third respectively, were placed in the same half of the draw and destined to clash in a semi-final, bar a major upset. That upset actually almost occurred when Sampras found himself two sets to love down against Wayne Black in the third round. The former number one, twice winner of the title, and runner-up to Agassi in 1995 a week after his then coach, Tim Gullikson, had been struck mortally ill, had complained about the 'ridiculous' speed of the Rebound Ace courts and the balls. He wasn't alone in suspecting that these had been quickened to assist the attacking styles of Rafter and Philippoussis. Sampras, one would have thought, should have benefited from the faster conditions, too, but he was having difficulty, he said, in finding his range; so much so that he'd resolved to go to the net behind first and second serves, as at Wimbledon. No doubt, he was a bit more keyed up than usual because of the chance to surpass the record of 12 Grand Slam crowns that he shared with Roy Emerson.

Sampras displayed his customary coolness and grit in eventually overcoming Black's raking passing shots. In the next two rounds he disposed of Slava Dosedel and Chris Woodruff, at which stage he appeared in sound enough form to reassert his mastery of Agassi. To turn the tables on the man who had supplanted him after six years as number one was an additional incentive.

Agassi, however, was looking ominously confident, especially after his 6–4 7–6 (4) 5–7 6–3 defeat of Philippoussis, the 16th seed. This was an engrossing match in which Agassi proved himself the greater opportunist, winning six successive points to take the second-set tie-break from 1–4, and converting three of six break-points overall. Philippoussis, by contrast, held nine break-points, but won only two. Not many could have withstood the Philippoussis blitzkrieg of powerful serves and ripping ground strokes. From the Australian's viewpoint, the fact that he could make 55 unforced errors against a player of Agassi's calibre, yet remain in close contention until the last point, boded well for the future.

The early departure of Todd Martin and Richard Krajicek meant that Agassi didn't play another seed before Sampras. Hicham Arazi, one of two Moroccans to make the quarter-finals – the other was Younes El Aynaoui, while a third, Karim Alami, reached the fourth round – presented Agassi with few problems despite some brilliant thrusts. Sampras' path, meanwhile, had been cleared of seeds by Thailand's Paradorn Srichaphan, who defeated Karol Kucera (14); Richard Fromberg, the first-round conqueror of 1999 runner-up Thomas Enqvist (6); and Woodruff a victor over Tim Henman (11).

The Agassi-Sampras semi-final was the first ever scheduled at night at any of the majors. It lived up to its billing. In a match of fierce intensity and breathtaking exchanges, Sampras served 37 aces, the most he had ever done in one match. When he went to a two sets to one lead by shutting Agassi out of the third-set tie-break, he seemed to have victory within his grasp. But Agassi was indefatigable. Not for a moment did he despair. He ran down everything he could, firing back enough deadly returns to make Sampras realise that only his best volleys would suffice. His persistence wore Sampras down, and he won 6–4 3–6 6–7 (0) 7–6 (5) 6–1. It transpired that Sampras had torn a hip flexor early in the match, though to what extent it had handicapped him was difficult to say; he himself was loath to make the injury an excuse.

In the other half of the draw the unseeded Hewitt maintained his hot streak, allowing such a hardened campaigner as Alex Corretja only one game in the second round. A Hewitt-Kafelnikov semi-final looked distinctly on the cards when, suddenly, the youngster's batteries ran dry and he was beaten in straight sets by Magnus Norman. The underestimated Swede was one of only three seeds in this half to reach the quarter-finals, the others being Kafelnikov and Nicolas Kiefer. Norman defeated Kiefer, but was outplayed by Kafelnikov, whose game improved with each match.

When he had won the title in 1999, the Russian made a point of thanking Sampras for staying at home and giving others a chance. This time, Kafelnikov may have been the only person who believed he could preserve his crown. Those who had watched him fade badly against Agassi a few months earlier at the US Open would not have backed him at long odds. He also carried some unhelpful baggage from the Davis Cup semi-final at Brisbane, where his provocative comments about the grass court and his opponents made him unpopular in Australia.

Kafelnikov regained a lot of respect, however, by the brave way he attempted to beat off Agassi's challenge. Playing all-court tennis of a very high standard, he leapt to a 4–0 lead. He unleashed some glorious winners, particularly off the backhand, and threatened to take a stranglehold. Agassi might easily have been tempted to yield to the onslaught and focus on the second set. Instead, he broke back twice before dropping service a third time. That stubbornness showed Kafelnikov that he was in for a fight; no matter how hard he battled thereafter, Agassi was able to step up the tempo and break him physically, if not mentally, as he had Sampras. Not even the unwelcome appearance in the fourth set of a so-called 'serial pest', who evaded security men and ran on the court, interfered with Awesome Andre's momentum.

Nothing could stop Davenport either. As at the 1998 US Open and Wimbledon '99 she never dropped a set. Despite a hamstring strain which had caused her to retire from the doubles, her barrage of deep, scorching drives in the final knocked the confidence out of Hingis. At one stage the former champion was in the extraordinary predicament of trailing by 1–6 1–5 and faced humiliation on the court she'd come to regard as her 'backyard'.

Hingis had shed superfluous weight, stepped up her training and learned to serve a little harder. All to no avail. 'She gets a shorter ball – and bang, boom,' Hingis said of her Nemesis. 'It is like line, line. Against some players I would be a little short, and it's not such a great return. But with Lindsay, there's no compromise. She kills you right away. No mistakes.'

The women's event inevitably developed into a showdown between the top two seeds after Venus Williams and Monica Seles withdrew before the start because of injuries. Serena Williams, who made an 11th hour decision to enter, hadn't played for three months, and although she looked spectacular in a low-cut red-and-black outfit and red shoes, her timing was awry. After three patchy performances, she lost to Elena Likhovtseva.

Amelie Mauresmo, the surprise finalist of 1999, loomed as the only other serious threat to the favourites after winning the women's title at Sydney the previous week. Unluckily, the athletic French woman faced the unseeded Patty Schnyder in the second round, and was out-served and out-smarted by the Swiss left-hander, whose rehabilitation from an emotionally troubling year seemed complete.

It was not Schnyder but another comeback player, however, who would give Davenport her toughest match. The unseeded Jennifer Capriati fought past Schnyder, as well as Dominique van Roost and Ai Sugiyama (who had eliminated Mary Pierce, the 1995 champion), to make her first Grand Slam semi-final since the 1991 US Open when she was a precocious 15-year-old. With the crowd cheering her on, Capriati forced Davenport to play at her best. 'I was hitting so many balls off my back foot because she was hitting it so hard,' said Davenport after winning 6–2 7–6.

The quarter-finals did nothing for the cause of equal prize money. Hingis routed Arantxa Sanchez-Vicario 6–1 6–1 her 13th straight victory over the Spaniard. Sugiyama also was confined to two games, while Julie Halard Decugis garnered only three from Davenport. In the only quarter-final that sustained any interest, Conchita Martinez edged out Likhovtseva. None of the last eight dominated the media as much as the highly photogenic Anna Kournikova, who was the subject of new and often wild rumours about her love life almost daily. For a week, Kournikova's tennis commanded attention, too. She won her opening match 6–0 6–0 and gave Davenport a solid workout in the fourth round.

For Australians, a major disappointment was the first-round defeat of 16-year-old Jelena Dokic by Hungary's Rita Kuti Kis. Dokic was almost unrecognisable as the uninhibited junior who had trounced Hingis in the first round at Wimbledon. More distressing to her supporters was the poor manner in which she reacted to the setback and put down Kuti Kis at a post-match press conference that she gave after first going to church for divine guidance. Her reputation suffered further when, in the company of her family, she gave an interview to a reporter in which she was alleged to have accused the WTA of rigging tournament draws against her.

More happily, two other young Aussies, Alicia Molik and Bryanne Stewart, showed rich promise in reaching the third round. Molik's serve/volley style had old-stagers reminiscing on the great attacking players of the past as she defeated Silvija Talaja, recent winner of the Gold Coast title, and Karina Habsudova. The tall blonde from Adelaide produced the fastest serve of the fortnight, a 187 km/h cannonball. Stewart – Molik's best friend – displayed a match-winning forehand, and, like Molik, an increasingly rare one-handed backhand. A wildcard from Sydney, she gave Sanchez-Vicario a scare by twice breaking the Spaniard for a 3–0 lead, but inexperience eventually told against her.

It was a very rewarding tournament for Americans. Apart from the two singles triumphs, they shared in every doubles championship. At the age of 35, Rick Leach won his fifth Grand Slam

(Continued on page 81)

Men's Singles

Winner: **A. Agassi** (USA) (1)

Holder: Y. Kafelnikov (RUS)

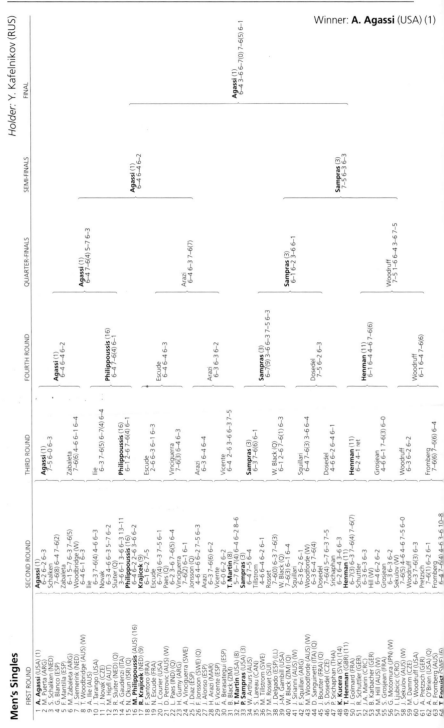

FIRST ROUND	SECOND ROUND	THIRD ROUND	FOURTH ROUND	QUARTER-FINALS	SEMI-FINALS	FINAL

FINAL

Agassi (1)
6–4 3–6 6–7(0) 7–6(5) 6–1

SEMI-FINALS

Agassi (1)
6–4 6–4 6–2

Sampras (3)
7–5 6–3 6–3

QUARTER-FINALS

Agassi (1)
6–4 7–6(4) 5–7 6–3

Arazi
6–4 6–3 7–6(7)

Sampras (3)
6–1 6–2 3–6 6–1

Woodruff
7–5 1–6 6–4 3–6 7–5

FOURTH ROUND

Agassi (1)
6–4 6–4 6–2

Philippoussis (16)
6–4 7–6(4) 6–1

Escude
6–4 6–4 6–3

Arazi
6–3 6–3 6–2

Sampras (3)
6–7(9) 3–6 6–3 7–5 6–3

Dosedel
7–5 6–2 6–3

Henman (11)
6–1 6–4–6 7–6(6)

Woodruff
6–1 6–4 7–6(6)

THIRD ROUND

Agassi (1)
7–5 6–0 6–3

Zabaleta
6–3 7–6(5) 6–7(4) 6–4

Philippoussis (16)
6–1 2–6 7–6(4) 6–1

Escude
2–6 6–3 6–1 6–3

Vinciguerra
7–6(3) 6–4 6–3

Arazi
6–3 6–4 6–4

Vicente
6–4 2–6 3–6 6–3 7–5

Sampras (3)
6–3 7–6(6) 6–1

W. Black (Q)
6–1 2–6 7–6(1) 6–3

Squillari
6–4 7–6(3) 3–6 6–4

Dosedel
4–6 6–2 6–4 6–1

Henman (11)
6–2 4–1 ret

Grosjean
4–6 6–1 7–6(3) 6–0

Woodruff
6–3 6–2 6–2

Fromberg
7–6(6) 7–6(3) 6–4

SECOND ROUND

Agassi (1)
6–2 6–2 6–3
Schalken
7–6(8) 6–4 7–6(2)
Zabaleta
6–1 5–7 6–3 7–6(5)
Woodbridge (W)
6–4 6–1 6–3
Ilie
6–3 7–6(4) 4–6 6–3
Novak
6–3 4–6 6–3 5–7 6–2
Sluiter (Q)
3–6 6–1 3–6 6–3 13–11
Philippoussis (16)
6–4 6–2 6–3 6–2
Krajicek (9)
6–1 6–2 7–5
Escude
6–7(4) 6–3 7–5 6–1
Paes (Q)
6–2 3–6 7–6(5) 6–4
Vinciguerra
7–6(2) 6–1 6–1
Jonsson (Q)
6–3 7–6(6) 6–2
Vicente
6–0 6–2 6–2
T. Martin (8)
5–7 6–7(4) 6–4 6–2 8–6
Sampras (3)
6–4 7–5 6–4
Tillstrom
4–6 6–4 6–2 6–1
Rosset
7–6(0) 6–3 7–6(3)
W. Black (Q)
7–6(3) 6–1 6–4
Squillari
6–3 6–2 6–1
Woodforde (W)
6–3 6–4 7–6(4)
Dosedel
7–6(4) 5–7 6–3 7–5
Srichaphan
6–2 6–4 3–6 6–3
Henman (11)
6–7(3) 6–3 7–6(4) 7–6(7)
Schuttler
6–3 6–3 6–3
Hill (W)
6–4 6–2 6–2
Grosjean
6–3 6–3 6–2
Sekulov (W)
7–6(5) 4–6 4–6 7–5 6–0
Woodruff
6–3 6–3 6–3
Pretzsch
7–6(1) 6–2 6–1
Fromberg
6–4 7–6(4) 4–6 3–6 10–8

FIRST ROUND

1 **A. Agassi** (USA) (1)
2 M. Puerta (ARG)
3 S. Schalken (NED)
4 G. Blanco (ESP)
5 F. Mantilla (ESP)
6 M. Zabaleta (ARG)
7 J. Siemerink (NED)
8 T. Woodbridge (AUS) (W)
9 A. Ilie (AUS)
10 J. Tarango (USA)
11 J. Novak (CZE)
12 M. Hipfl (AUT)
13 R. Sluiter (NED) (Q)
14 A. Gaudenzi (ITA)
15 N. Okun (ISR) (Q)
16 **M. Philippoussis** (AUS) (16)
17 **R. Krajicek** (NED) (9)
18 F. Santoro (FRA)
19 N. Escude (FRA)
20 J. Courier (USA)
21 D. Petrovic (AUS) (W)
22 L. Paes (IND) (Q)
23 H. Gumy (ARG)
24 A. Vinciguerra (SWE)
25 J. Diaz (ESP)
26 F. Jonsson (SWE) (Q)
27 J. Alonso (ESP)
28 Y. Arazi (MAR)
29 F. Vicente (ESP)
30 A. Berasategui (ESP)
31 B. Black (ZIM)
32 **T. Martin** (USA) (8)
33 **P. Sampras** (USA) (3)
34 W. Arthurs (AUS)
35 S. Lareau (CAN)
36 M. Tillstrom (SWE)
37 M. Rosset (SUI)
38 J. Delgado (ESP) (LL)
39 J.M. Gambill (USA)
40 W. Black (ZIM) (Q)
41 S. Sirianni (AUS) (W)
42 F. Squillari (ARG)
43 M. Woodforde (AUS) (W)
44 D. Sanguinetti (ITA) (Q)
45 J. Boutter (FRA) (Q)
46 S. Dosedel (CZE)
47 P. Srichaphan (THA)
48 **K. Kucera** (SVK) (14)
49 **T. Henman** (GBR) (11)
50 J. Golmard (FRA)
51 R. Schuttler (GER)
52 J.A. Marin (CRC)
53 B. Karbacher (GER)
54 M. Hill (AUS) (W)
55 S. Grosjean (FRA)
56 G. Motomura (JPN) (W)
57 I. Ljubicic (CRO)
58 J. Sekulov (AUS) (W)
59 M. Damm (CZE)
60 C. Woodruff (USA)
61 A. Pretzsch (GER)
62 A. O'Brien (USA) (Q)
63 R. Fromberg (AUS)
64 **T. Enqvist** (SWE) (6)

3–6 6–3 6–2 6–4

Second Quarter

No.	Player	First round	Second round	Third round	Fourth round	Quarter-final	Semi-final
65	**G. Kuerten** (BRA) (5)	Portas 4-6 4-6 6-4 7-6(8) 6-4	Voinea 6-2 6-1 6-3	Hewitt 6-2 7-5 6-3	Norman (12) 6-3 6-1 7-6(6)	Norman (12) 6-3 6-1 7-6(4)	Kafelnikov (2) 6-1 6-2 6-4
66	A Portas (ESP)	Voinea 7-6(1) 4-6 4-6 6-3 6-2					
67	A Voinea (ROM)						
68	V. Spadea (USA)						
69	L Hewitt (AUS)	Hewitt 6-2 6-7(5) 7-6(5) 6-4	Hewitt 6-0 6-0 6-1				
70	P Goldstein (USA)						
71	A. Corretja (ESP)	Corretja 7-6(5) 6-4 6-4					
72	S. Sargsian (ARM)						
73	J. Stoltenberg (AUS)	Bjorkman 6-7(6) 6-4 6-4 0-6 6-4	Bjorkman 6-4 3-6 6-4 7-6(4)	Norman (12) 6-4 6-4 7-6(8)			
74	J. Bjorkman (SWE)						
75	P. Wessels (NED)	Vanek (Q) 6-4 6-3 2-6 7-6(5)					
76	J. Vanek (CZE) (Q)						
77	T. Zib (CZE)	Pozzi 6-3 7-6(7) 6-7(5) 6-1	Norman (12) 6-4 6-3 6-4				
78	G. Pozzi (ITA)						
79	A Mamiit (USA)	Norman (12) 7-5 6-4 3-6 6-3					
80	**M Norman** (SWE) (12)						
81	**C. Pioline** (FRA) (13)	Ivanisevic 6-4 2-6 7-5 1-6 9-7	Clavet 7-6(5) 6-4 6-2	W. Ferreira 6-3 6-4 3-6 6-3	Kiefer (4) 6-3 6-4 6-2	Kiefer (4) 6-3 6-4 6-2	
82	G. Ivanisevic (CRO)						
83	F. Clavet (ESP)	Clavet 3-6 6-1 6-4 7-6(3)					
84	D. Hrbaty (SVK)						
85	Va. Ferreira (RSA)	W. Ferreira 6-3 6-3 4-6 7-6(2)	W. Ferreira 6-3 6-2 6-7(2) 4-6 6-2				
86	C. Basti (SUI)						
87	T. Johansson (SWE)	Johansson 6-1 6-2 6-4					
88	N. Kulti (SWE)						
89	G. Gaudio (ARG)	Llodra 6-3 6-2	Alami 7-6(4) 6-3 6-2	Kiefer (4) 6-3 6-4 6-2			
90	M. Llodra (FRA) (Q)						
91	K. Alami (MAR)	Alami 6-4 7-6(5) 7-5					
92	F. Meligeni (BRA)						
93	T. Behrend (GER)	Behrend 6-2 4-6 6-7(5) 6-3 6-0	Kiefer (4) 7-6(5) 6-0 6-2				
94	G. Canas (ARG)						
95	**N. Lapentti** (ECU) (7)	Kiefer (4) 4-6 6-3 6-4 6-4					
96	**N. Kiefer** (GER) (4)						
97	A. Medvedev (UKR)	Lapentti (7) 6-3 5-7 6-7(2) 6-4 8-6	Clement 3-6 7-6(3) 6-2 4-1 ret	Clement 6-1 6-4 6-3	El Aynaoui 3-6 6-3 6-4 3-6 10-8	Kafelnikov (2) 6-0 6-3 7-6(4)	
98	J. Van Lottum (NED)						
99	A. Clement (FRA)	Clement 7-6(2) 6-4 ret					
100	J. Kroslak (SVK)						
101	A. Lopez-Moron (ESP)	Kroslak 6-3 6-3 7-5	Federer 7-6(1) 6-2 6-3				
102	M. Chang (USA)						
103	R. Federer (SUI)	Federer 6-4 4-7 6(5)					
104	J. C. Ferrero (ESP)						
105	L. Tieleman (ITA)	Ferrero 7-6(3) 6-3 7-6(3)	Ferrero 7-6(5) 6-4 5-7 6-7(5) 6-4	El Aynaoui 7-6(3) 4-6 4-6 7-6(5) 6-4			
106	A. Martin (ESP)						
107	A. Parmar (GBR) (Q)	Tieleman 6-2 7-6(3) 6-7(3) 6-3					
108	Y. El Aynaoui (MAR)						
109	C. Saulnier (FRA) (Q)	El Aynaoui 6-7(8) 7-6(5) 1-6 6-3 6-1	El Aynaoui 7-5 6-3 6-3				
110	**T. Haas** (GER) (10)	Haas 7-6(2) 6-4 4-6 6-2					
111	**A. Costa** (ESP) (15)						
112	C. Rochus (BEL)	C. Rochus 6-3 6-7(8) 6-4 6-3	C. Rochus 6-4 6-4 6-3	C. Rochus (Q) 3-6 6-4 6-3 7-6(2)	Kafelnikov (2) 6-0 6-3 7-6(4)		
113	M. Tabara (CZE) (LL)						
114	K. Ulivet (ZIM) (Q)	Ulivet 6-1 7-6(6) 4-6 6-1					
115	A. Dupuis (FRA)						
116	M. Rodriguez (ARG)	Dupuis 6-4 6-4 7-6(6)	Mirnyi 6-7(3) 7-6(6) 7-6(5) 7-6(5)				
117	M. Mirnyi (BLR)						
118	R. Agenor (HAI)	Mirnyi 6-7(5) 7-6(5) 6-3 6-3					
119	R. Cadart (FRA) (Q)						
120	S. Koubek (AUT)	Koubek 6-3 5-7 6-2 6-4	Koubek 5-7 7-5 2-6 6-2 6-3	Kafelnikov (2) 6-1 6-3 7-5			
121	G. Stafford (RSA) (Q)	Stafford (Q) 7-6(4) 6-4 6-1					
122	M. Safin (RUS)						
123	S. Vacek (CZE)	Vacek 1-6 7-6(4) 7-6(11) 6-2	Kafelnikov (2) 6-3 6-0 6-1				
124	B. Stanoytchev (BUL)						
125	I. Knippschild (GER)	**Kafelnikov** (2) 6-7(4) 6-4 6-1 6-2					
126	**Y. Kafelnikov** (RUS) (2)						

Bold type denotes seeded players. Numbers following player's name gives seeding order (Q) = Qualifier, (W) = Wild Card, (LL) = Lucky Loser

Women's Singles

Winner: **Davenport** (USA) (2)

Holder: M. Hingis (SUI)

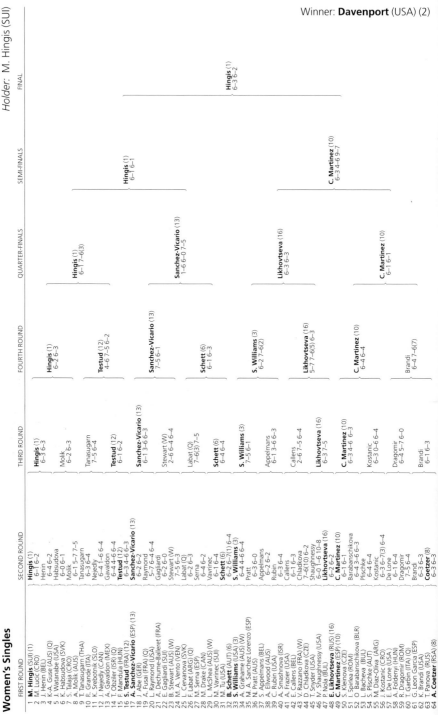

FIRST ROUND

1 **M. Hingis** (SUI) (1)
2 M Luci (CRO)
3 J. Henin (BEL)
4 K-A. Guse (AUS) (Q)
5 J. Watanabe (USA)
6 K. Habsudova (SVK)
7 S. Talaja (CRO)
8 A. Molik (AUS)
9 T. Tanasugarn (THA)
10 R. Grande (ITA)
11 K. Srebotnik (SLO)
12 A. Nejedly (CAN)
13 J. Gavaldon (MEX)
14 T. Obziler (ISR) (Q)
15 F. Mandula (HUN)
16 **S. Testud** (FRA) (12)
17 **A. Sanchez-Vicario** (ESP) (13)
18 J. Abe (GER)
19 A. Fusai (FRA) (Q)
20 L. Raymond (USA)
21 A. Dechaume-Balleret (FRA)
22 E. Gagliardi (SUI)
23 M. Stewart (AUS) (W)
24 A. Vento (VEN)
25 L. Cervanova (SVK)
26 F. Labat (ARG) (Q)
27 M. Serna (ESP)
28 M. Drake (CAN)
29 L. McShea (AUS) (W)
30 M. Vavrinec (SUI)
31 M. Tu (USA)
32 **B. Schett** (AUT) (6)
33 **S. Williams** (USA) (3)
34 A. Grahame (AUS) (W)
35 M. A. Sanchez Lorenzo (ESP)
36 N. Pratt (AUS)
37 A. Appelmans (BEL)
38 A. Ellwood (AUS)
39 C. Rubin (USA)
40 A. Smashnova (ISR)
41 A. Frazier (USA)
42 E. Callens (BEL)
43 V. Razzano (FRA) (W)
44 D. Chladkova (CZE)
45 T. Snyder (USA)
46 M. Shaughnessy (USA)
47 J. Speedy (USA)
48 **E. Likhovtseva** (RUS) (16)
49 **C. Martinez** (ESP) (10)
50 S. Klenova (CZE)
51 I. Spirlea (ROM)
52 O. Barabanschikova (BLR)
53 L. Bacheva (BUL)
54 S. Pilschke (AUT)
55 M. Diaz-Oliva (ARG)
56 J. Kostanic (CRO)
57 E. De Lone (USA)
58 A. Foldenyi (HUN)
59 R. Dragomir (ROM)
60 T. Garbin (ITA) (Q)
61 G. Leon Garcia (ESP)
62 K. Brandi (USA)
63 T. Panova (RUS)
64 **A. Coetzer** (RSA) (8)

SECOND ROUND

- **Hingis** (1) 6-1 6-2
- Henin 6-4 6-2
- Habsudova 6-0 6-1
- Molik 6-1 5-7 7-5
- Tanasugarn 6-3 6-4
- Nejedly 6-4 1-6 6-4
- Gavaldon 6-4 4-6 6-4
- Testud (12)
- **Sanchez-Vicario** (13)
- Raymond
- Gagliardi
- Stewart (W)
- Labat (Q)
- Serna
- Vavrinec
- **Schett** (6) 6-2 6-7(1) 6-4
- **S. Williams** (3) 6-4 4-6 6-4
- Appelmans 6-2 6-2
- Rubin 6-3 6-4
- Callens 6-1 6-3
- Chladkova 7-6(10) 6-2
- Shaughnessy 6-0 1-6 10-8
- **Likhovtseva** (16) 6-2 6-2
- **C. Martinez** (10) 6-1 6-1
- Barabanschikova 6-4 3-6 6-3
- Pilschke 6-4 6-4
- Kostanic 6-3 6-7(3) 6-4
- De Lone 6-1 6-4
- Dragomir 7-5 6-4
- Brandi 6-3 6-3
- **Coetzer** (8) 6-3 6-3

THIRD ROUND

- **Hingis** (1) 6-3 6-3
- Molik 6-2 6-3
- Tanasugarn 7-5 6-4
- Testud (12) 6-1 6-2
- **Sanchez-Vicario** (13) 6-1 3-6 6-3
- Stewart (W) 2-6 6-4 6-4
- Labat (Q) 7-6(3) 7-5
- **Schett** (6) 6-4 6-4
- **S. Williams** (3) 7-5 6-1
- Appelmans 6-1 3-6 6-3
- Callens 2-6 7-5 6-4
- **Likhovtseva** (16) 6-3 7-5
- **C. Martinez** (10) 6-3 4-6 6-3
- Kostanic 6-3 0-6 6-4
- Dragomir 6-4 5-7 6-0
- Brandi 6-1 6-3

FOURTH ROUND

- **Hingis** (1) 6-2 6-3
- **Testud** (12) 4-6 7-5 6-2
- **Sanchez-Vicario** (13) 7-5 6-1
- **Schett** (6) 6-1 6-3
- **S. Williams** (3) 6-2 7-6(2)
- **Likhovtseva** (16) 5-7 7-6(5) 6-3
- **C. Martinez** (10) 6-4 6-4
- Brandi 6-4 7-6(7)

QUARTER-FINALS

- **Hingis** (1) 6-1 7-6(3)
- **Sanchez-Vicario** (13) 1-6 6-0 7-5
- **Likhovtseva** (16) 6-3 6-3
- **C. Martinez** (10) 6-1 6-1

SEMI-FINALS

- **Hingis** (1) 6-1 6-1
- **C. Martinez** (10) 6-3 4-6 9-7

FINAL

- **Hingis** (1) 6-3 6-2

6–1 7–5

Winner: Davenport (2) 6–2 7–6(4)

First round

No.	Player	R64
65	**Mauresmo** (FRA) (7)	Mauresmo (7) 6–1 6–2
66	Torrens Valero (ESP)	
67	P. Schnyder (SUI)	Schnyder 6–3 6–4
68	L Osterloh (USA)	
69	N. Petrova (RUS)	Petrova 6–4 6–2
70	G. Sidot (FRA)	
71	Nemeckova (CZE)	Black 6–4 7–6(4)
72	Black (ZIM)	
73	Pullin (GBR) (Q)	Pullin 6–1 6–3
74	Chi (USA)	
75	Y. Yi (CHN) (W)	Yi (W) 7–6(5) 6–2
76	Courtois (BEL)	
77	Capriati (USA)	Capriati 6–1 7–6(1)
78	Schwartz (AUT)	
79	Clijsters (BEL)	Van Roost (14) 3–6 6–1 6–1
80	**D. Van Roost** (BEL) (14)	
81	**A. Huber** (GER) (15)	Boogert 6–4 6–4
82	K. Boogert (NED)	
83	A. Stevenson (USA)	Carlsson 7–6(6) 6–3
84	Carlsson (SWE)	
85	Sugiyama (JPN)	Sugiyama 7–6(3) 7–6(4)
86	Maleeva (BUL)	
87	S. Noorlander (NED)	Gersi 3–6 6–3 6–3
88	Gersi (CZE)	
89	Oremans (NED)	Oremans 6–2 6–2
90	A. Barna (GER)	
91	Lee (USA)	Nacuk 6–4 6–7(6) 7–5
92	S. Nacuk (YUG)	
93	Cocheteux (FRA)	Cocheteux 1–6 7–5 6–4
94	Rittner (GER)	
95	L Wild (USA) (Q)	Pierce (4) 7–5 6–3
96	**N. Pierce** (FRA) (4)	
97	**Tauziat** (FRA) (5)	Tauziat (5) 6–1 6–1
98	Nagyova (SVK)	
99	Jeyaseelan (CAN) (Q)	Jeyaseelan (Q) 6–2 3–6 6–1
100	Hopmans (NED)	
101	Kandarr (GER) (Q)	Kandarr (Q) 6–4 6–7(5) 8–6
102	Dowse (AUS) (W)	
103	Dominikovic (AUS) (W)	Loit 6–7(3) 6–4 6–2
104	Loit (FRA)	
105	McQuillan (AUS) (W)	Montolio 6–4 6–3
106	Montolio (ESP)	
107	Suarez (ARG)	Dementieva 6–0 3–6 8–6
108	Dementieva (RUS)	
109	Dechy (FRA)	Dechy 6–1 3–6 6–1
110	Zuluaga (COL)	
111	Krasnoroutskaya (RUS) (Q)	Halard-Decugis (9) 6–2 6–4
112	**Halard-Decugis** (FRA) (9)	
113	**A. Kournikova** (RUS) (11)	Kournikova (11) 6–0 6–0
114	F. Wartusch (AUT)	
115	E. Rippner (USA)	Zvereva 6–7(4) 7–5 6–2
116	Zvereva (BLR)	
117	K. Hrdlickova (CZE)	Hrdlickova 6–2 6–1
118	V. Ruano Pascual (ESP)	
119	Kut Kis (HUN)	Kut Kis 6–1 2–6 6–3
120	Dokic (AUS)	
121	Jidkova (RUS) (Q)	Jidkova (Q) 2–6 7–6(5) 6–1
122	T. Pisnik (SLO)	
123	M. Weingartner (GER)	Weingartner 6–2 2–6 6–4
124	A. Kremer (LUX)	
125	C. Morariu (USA)	Irvin (Q) 2–6 7–5 6–3
126	M. Irvin (USA) (Q)	
127	S. Pitkowski (FRA) (Q)	Davenport (2) 6–3 6–1
128	**L. Davenport** (USA) (2)	

Third round (R32)

Schnyder 6–4 6–4 · Petrova 4–6 6–4 6–4 · Yi (W) 6–3 2–6 9–7 · Capriati 6–4 6–4 · Carlsson 7–5 6–3 · Sugiyama 6–1 6–4 · Oremans 6–3 7–5 · Pierce (4) 6–2 6–2 · Jeyaseelan (Q) 7–6(3) 6–4 · Kandarr (Q) 1–6 7–5 6–3 · Dementieva 6–4 6–3 · Halard-Decugis (9) 6–3 6–3 · Kournikova (11) 6–1 6–4 · Hrdlickova 7–6(2) 6–7(5) 6–3 · Jidkova (Q) 7–5 6–3 · Davenport (2) 6–4 7–5

Fourth round (R16)

Schnyder 7–6(6) 4–6 6–2 · Capriati 6–4 6–4 · Sugiyama 6–4 4–6 6–3 · Pierce (4) 6–2 6–4 · Kandarr (Q) 6–2 0–6 6–3 · Halard-Decugis (9) 3–6 6–4 6–2 · Kournikova (11) 2–6 6–3 6–4 · Davenport (2) 6–0 6–1

Quarter-finals

Capriati 6–3 4–6 6–1 · Sugiyama 7–5 6–4 · Halard-Decugis (9) 6–1 3–0 ret · Davenport (2) 6–4 6–3

Semi-finals

Capriati 6–0 6–2 · Davenport (2) 6–1 6–2

Final

Davenport (2) 6–2 7–6(4)

Bold type denotes seeded players. Numbers following player's name gives seeding order (Q) = Qualifier, (W) = Wild Card, (LL) = Lucky Loser

Men's Doubles

Winners: **E. Ferreira** (RSA)/**Leach** (USA) (5) 6–4 3–6 6–3 3–6 18–16

Holders: Bjorkman (SWE)/Rafter (AUS)

FIRST ROUND	SECOND ROUND	THIRD ROUND	QUARTER-FINALS	SEMI-FINALS	FINAL
1 **Lareau/Paes** (1)	Grant/Waite				
2 Grant/Waite	7–6(2) 2–6 7–5				
3 Martin/Rodriguez	Barnard/Haggard	Barnard/Haggard			
4 Barnard/Haggard	6–4 6–4	7–5 2–6 10–8	Barnard/Haggard		
5 L. Jensen/M. Jensen (W)	Hrbaty/Taino		6–3 2–6 6–4		
6 Hrbaty/Taino	6–4 6–7(3) 6–2	MacPherson/Nyborg (16)			
7 Broad/Federer	**MacPherson/Nyborg** (16)	6–4 6–4			
8 **MacPherson/Nyborg** (16)	6–4 7–6(4)			**W. Black/Kratzmann** (8)	
9 Norval/Ullyett (10)	Norval/Ullyett (10)			3–6 7–6(7) 6–3	
10 Arthurs/Bracciali	6(2) 6–2(2)	Hewitt/Stolle			
11 Galbraith/MacPhie	Hewitt/Stolle	7–5 6–7(4) 6–4			
12 Hewitt/Stolle	7–6(3) 6–4		**W. Black/Kratzmann** (8)		
13 Rae/Swierk (W)	Hill/Ondruska		6–4 6–4		
14 Hill/Ondrusk	6–4 6–7(0) 6–3	**W. Black/Kratzmann** (8)			
15 Meligeni/Testa	**W. Black/Kratzmann** (8)	1–6 7–5 6–3			
16 **W. Black/Kratzmann** (8)	7–6(7) 6–4				
17 **Palmer/O'Brien** (4)	**Palmer/O'Brien** (4)				
18 Pala/Vizner	6–3 6–2	Palmer/O'Brien (4)			
19 Berasategui/Roig	Shnaida/Wakefield	6–3 6–4			
20 Shnaida/Wakefield	6–4 6–7(3) 6–3		Palmer/O'Brien (4)		
21 Bertolini/Brandi	Gambill/Humphries		3–6 6–2 9–7		
22 Gambill/Humphries	7–5 6–3	Gambill/Humphries			
23 Kilderry/Silcock	Kilderry/Silcock	6–0 6–4			
24 **Johnson/Suk** (13)	0–6 7–5 6–3			Palmer/O'Brien (4)	
25 **Novak/Rikl** (11)	**Novak/Rikl** (11)			6–1 6–3	
26 Fisher/Randjelovic (W)	6–7(9) 6–2 6–4	Novak/Rikl (11)			
27 Lopez-Moron/Portas	Lopez-Moron/Portas	6–3 6–0			
28 Garcia/Puerta	6–7(5) 6–4		Novak/Rikl (11)		
29 Aspelin/Landsberg	Aspelin/Landsberg		4–6 6–2 8–6		
30 Hood/Prieto	6–2 3–6 6–3	Aspelin/Landsberg			
31 Greenhalgh/Kohlmann	**Adams/De Jager** (6)	7–6(4) 4–6 10–8			
32 **Adams/De Jager** (6)	7–5 7–6(6)				
33 **E. Ferreira/Leach** (5)	**E. Ferreira/Leach** (5)				
34 Ivanisevic/Keil	6–3 6–4	E. Ferreira/Leach (5)			
35 Bale/Stafford	Bale/Stafford	6–3 3–6 7–5			
36 Petersson/Sell	6–3 7–6(5)		E. Ferreira/Leach (5)		
37 M. Draper/S. Draper (W)	M. Draper/S. Draper (W)		6–3 6–3		
38 Oncins/Orsanic	7–6(6) 6–4	Kulti/Tillstrom (12)			
39 Behr/Ran	**Kulti/Tillstrom** (12)	6–3 4–6 6–1			
40 **Kulti/Tillstrom** (12)	7–5 3–6 6–1			**E. Ferreira/Leach** (5)	
41 **Damm/Mirnyi** (14)	**Damm/Mirnyi** (14)			7–6(14) 5–7 7–5	
42 Goldstein/Sprengelmeyer	7–6(5) 6–4	Damm/Mirnyi (14)			
43 Ilie/Sirianni (W)	Hanley/Healey (W)	7–6(5) 6–4			
44 Hanley/Healey (W)	6–1 6–2		Eagle/Florent		
45 Eagle/Florent	Eagle/Florent		2–6 7–6(5) 6–2		
46 Knowles/Tarango	6–3 5–7 6–4	Eagle/Florent			
47 Canas/Del Rio	**Bjorkman/B. Black** (3)	5–7 6–4 6–2			
48 **Bjorkman/B. Black** (3)	6–3 6–4				
49 **Tarango/Vacek** (7)	Olhovskiy/Siemerink				
50 Olhovskiy/Siemerink	6–7(3) 6–1 6–3	Marques/Van Houdt (W)			
51 Kitnov/Manta	Marques/Van Houdt (W)	7–6(8) 6–7(5) 6–1			
52 Marques/Van Houdt (W)	6–7(6) 6–3 6–4		Marques/Van Houdt (W)		
53 Koenig/Tramacchi	Koenig/Tramacchi		3–6 6–3 6–4		
54 B. Bryan/M. Bryan	6–4 6–4	Ellwood/Tebbutt			
55 Ellwood/Tebbutt	Ellwood/Tebbutt	7–6(5) 6–2			
56 **Delaitre/Santoro** (9)	6–3 7–6(6)			Woodbridge/Woodforde (2)	
57 **W. Ferreira/Kafelnikov** (15)	**W. Ferreira/Kafelnikov** (15)			6–3 6–2	
58 Carrasco/Velasco	4–6 6–3 6–3	W. Ferreira/Kafelnikov (15)			
59 Djordjevic/Safin	Coupe/Vernic	6–4 6–3			
60 Coupe/Vernic	7–5 6–4		Woodbridge/Woodforde (2)		
61 Merklein/Montana	Bowen/Hernandez		6–3 4–6 6–3		
62 Bowen/Hernandez	7–5 6–3	Woodbridge/Woodforde (2)			
63 Coetzee/Haygarth	**Woodbridge/Woodforde** (2)	6–2 6–2			
64 **Woodbridge/Woodforde** (2)	7–6(4) 6–3				

Finals path:
- **W. Black/Kratzmann** (8) 7–6(6) 6–3
- E. Ferreira/Leach (5) 4–6 6–3 6–4

Winners:**Raymond** (USA)/**Stubbs** (AUS) (1) 6–4 5–7 6–4

Holders: Hingis (SUI)/Kournikova (RUS)

FIRST ROUND

1 **Raymond/Stubbs** (1)
2 Perning/Talaja
3 Kirventcheva/Wang
4 Csurgo/Martincova
5 Cocheteux/Husarova
6 Labat/Tanasugarn
7 Bes/Riera
8 **Rubin/Testud** (9)
9 **Arendt/Po** (1)
10 Elwood/Hiraki
11 Cristea/Dragomir
12 Dominikovic/Grahame (W)
13 De Lone/Pratt
14 Gagliardi/Reeves
15 McQuillan/McShea
16 **Martinez/Tarabini** (8)
17 **Fusai/Tauziat** (4)
18 Nacuk/Nemeckova
19 Sanchez-Vicario/Serna
20 Callens/Van Roost
21 Capriati/Dokic
22 Andres/Martinez Granados
23 Zoogeri/Oremans
24 **Habsudova/Sidot** (15)
25 **Ruano Pascual/Suarez** (14)
26 Adamczak/Watson (W)
27 Hrdlickova/Rittner
28 Jeyaseelan/Schnyder
29 Courtois/Mauresmo
30 Schwartz/Wartusch
31 Frazier/Schlukebir
32 **Kournikova/Schett** (6)
33 **Spirlea/Vis** (5)
34 Pilhatsche/Valekova
35 Graham/Miyagi
36 Basuki/Dechaume-Balleret
37 Barabanschikova/Osterloh
38 Dechy/Molik
39 Garbin/Marosi
40 **Krizan/Srebotnik** (13)
41 **Huber/Tatarkova** (12)
42 Musgrave/Stewart
43 Guse/Kunce
44 Clayton/Wheeler (W)
45 Shaughnessy/Wild
46 Clijsters/Nagyova
47 Hopmans/Noorlander
48 **Hingis/Pierce** (3)
49 **Coetzer/Likhovtseva** (7)
50 Barclay/Webb
51 Ortuno/Torrens Valero
52 Snyder/Grzybowska (W)
53 Sostanic/Prsnik
54 De Beer/Kandarr
55 De Villiers/Steck
56 **Halard-Decugis/Sugiyama** (10)
57 Appelmans/Grande
58 **Black/Selyutina** (16)
59 Dstrovskaja/Poutchek
60 Lucic/Zvereva
61 Carlsson/Loit
62 Asagoe/Yoshida
63 Ildkova/Kolbovic
64 **Davenport/Morariu** (2)

SECOND ROUND

Raymond/Stubbs (1) 4–6 7–5 6–1
Csurgo/Martincova 6–4 7–6(2)
Labat/Tanasugarn 6–2 6–2
Rubin/Testud (9) 6–3 7–5
Elwood/Hiraki 6–4 6–4
Cristea/Dragomir 3–6 7–6(10) 7–5
De Lone/Pratt 6–2 6–4
Martinez/Tarabini (8) 7–6(2) 6–7(4) 6–4
Fusai/Tauziat (4) 6–4 6–1
Callens/Van Roost 6–2 6–4
Capriati/Dokic 6–2 6–0
Habsudova/Sidot (15) 7–5 1–6 6–1
Ruano Pascual/Suarez (14) 6–4 6–1
Jeyaseelan/Schnyder 6–3 ret
Courtois/Mauresmo 6–4 3–6 6–3
Kournikova/Schett (6) 6–3 6–3
Spirlea/Vis (5) 6–3 6–2
Graham/Miyagi 4–6 6–1 6–4
Dechy/Molik 6–2 6–0
Garbin/Marosi 6–3 7–5
Musgrave/Stewart 2–6 6–1 6–4
Guse/Kunce 6–3 6–3
Shaughnessy/Wild 6–0 4–6 6–1
Hingis/Pierce (3) 6–1 6–0
Coetzer/Likhovtseva (7) 6–4 6–7(2) 6–3
De Beer/Kandarr 7–5 4–6 8–6
Halard-Decugis/Sugiyama (10) 6–2 6–3
Appelmans/Grande 6–4 6–4
Lucic/Zvereva 6–1 7–6(3)
Carlsson/Loit 6–1 7–6(3)
Davenport/Morariu (2) 6–3 6–1

THIRD ROUND

Raymond/Stubbs (1) 0–6 6–0
Labat/Tanasugarn 6–3 7–5
Ellwood/Hiraki 6–4 2–6 6–4
De Lone/Pratt 6–3 4–6 7–5
Callens/Van Roost 6–3 6–3
Capriati/Dokic 7–6(4) 6–4
Jeyaseelan/Schnyder 6–1 6–7(4) 6–3
Kournikova/Schett (6) 6–3 6–1
Graham/Miyagi 7–6(8) 6–3
Garbin/Marosi 7–6(13) 7–6(1)
Musgrave/Stewart 6–4 6–1
Hingis/Pierce (3) 6–3 6–2
Coetzer/Likhovtseva (7) 7–5 6–4
Halard-Decugis/Sugiyama (10) 2–6 1–0 RET
Appelmans/Grande 6–2 6–3
Davenport/Morariu (2) 6–1 6–0

QUARTER-FINALS

Raymond/Stubbs (1) 6–1 4–6 6–1
De Lone/Pratt 6–3 2–6 6–3
Callens/Van Roost 6–4 7–6(12)
Kournikova/Schett (6) 6–2 6–1
Graham/Miyagi 6–7(2) 7–5 6–0
Hingis/Pierce (3) 6–1 6–1
Halard-Decugis/Sugiyama (10) 4–6 6–1 7–5
Davenport/Morariu (2) 6–0 6–1

SEMI-FINALS

Raymond/Stubbs (1) 6–2 6–2
Kournikova/Schett (6) 6–1 7–6(4)
Hingis/Pierce (3) 6–3 6–1
Davenport/Morariu (2) 6–4 3–6 6–1

FINAL

Raymond/Stubbs (1) 6–4 7–6(4)
Hingis/Pierce (3) 5–0 ret

Bold type denotes seeded players. Numbers following player's name gives seeding order (Q) = Qualifier, (W) = Wild Card, (LL) = Lucky Loser

Mixed Doubles

Holders: Adams (RSA)/De Swardt (RSA)

Winners:
Palmer (USA)/**Stubbs** (AUS) (3) 7–5 7–6(3)

FIRST ROUND	SECOND ROUND	QUARTER-FINALS	SEMI-FINALS	FINAL
1 **Bjorkman/Kournikova** (1)	**Bjorkman/Kournikova** (1) 5–3 ret	**Bjorkman/Kournikova** (1) 6–3 4–1 ret	**Bjorkman/Kournikova** (1) 6–3 6–2	
2 Prieto/Tarabini				
3 Kilderry/Pleming	Hill/Morariu 6–3 6–7(14) 6–2			
4 Hill/Morariu				
5 Ilie/Pratt (W)	Koenig/Black 6–2 6–3			
6 Koenig/Black		Tarango/Likhovtseva (6) 6–4 1–6 7–6(5)		
7 E. Ferreira/Kunce	**Tarango/Likhovtseva** (6) 6–7(5) 6–3 6–2			
8 **Tarango/Likhovtseva** (6)				**Palmer/Stubbs** (3) 7–5 3–6 6–3
9 **Palmer/Stubbs** (3)	**Palmer/Stubbs** (3) 3–6 6–3 6–2	**Palmer/Stubbs** (3) 6–4 3–6 7–6(3)	**Palmer/Stubbs** (3) 7–5 ret	
10 Waite/Arendt				
11 Delaitre/Loit	Orsanic/Basuki 6–0 6–4			
12 Orsanic/Basuki				
13 Cratzmann/Dokic	Tramacchi/Barclay 6–4 7–6(5)			
14 Tramacchi/Barclay		Olhovskiy/Tatarkova (8) 6–2 6–4		
15 Norval/Srebotnik	**Olhovskiy/Tatarkova** (8) 6–4 6–4			
16 **Olhovskiy/Tatarkova** (8)				
17 **Woodforde/Zvereva** (5)	**Woodforde/Zvereva** (5) 7–6(2) 6–3	**Woodforde/Zvereva** (5) 6–4 3–6 6–3	**Woodbridge/Sanchez-Vicario** (4) (W) 4–6 7–5 6–1	
18 Leach/Coetzer				
19 Johnson/Po	Johnson/Po 6–4 4–6 6–3			
20 Arthurs/Graham				
21 MacPherson/Habsudova	MacPherson/Habsudova 7–6(7) 6–2			
22 Stolle/Molik		**Woodbridge/Sanchez-Vicario** (4) (W) 6–4 7–5		
23 Knowles/Oremans	**Woodbridge/Sanchez-Vicario** (4) (W) 4–6 6–2 6–4			
24 **Woodbridge/Sanchez-Vicario** (4) (W)				**Woodbridge/Sanchez-Vicario** (4) (W) 6–3 6–3
25 **De Jager/Vis** (7)	**De Jager/Vis** (7) 4–6 6–2 6–4	Hood/Labat 6–4 6–0	Adams/Boogert 6–3 7–5	
26 W. Black/Selyutina				
27 Nyborg/Carlsson	Hood/Labat 6–3 3–6 7–6(8)			
28 Hood/Labat				
29 Kitinov/Krizan	Haygarth/Schlukebir 6–3 7–5			
30 Haygarth/Schlukebir		Adams/Boogert 7–6(3) 6–7(5) 6–0		
31 Adams/Boogert	Adams/Boogert 7–6(7) 6–2			
32 **Paes/Raymond** (2)				

Bold type denotes seeded players. Numbers following player's name gives seeding order (Q) = Qualifier, (W) = Wild Card, (LL) = Lucky Loser

title by partnering South Africa's Ellis Ferreira to a 6–4 3–6 6–3 3–6 18–16 victory over Wayne Black of Zimbabwe and Andrew Kratzmann of Australia. Earlier, Leach and Ferreira had dashed Todd Woodbridge and Mark Woodforde's hopes of winning their last Australian Open as a team.

America's Lisa Raymond and her Australian partner, Rennae Stubbs, won the women's doubles by beating the more highly fancied Hingis and Pierce, Stubbs being the first Australian to win the event since Dianne Evers in 1979. In the mixed doubles, the 28-year-old Sydneysider succeeded again, this time alongside America's Jared Palmer. These, her first Grand Slam titles, netted her a total of $205,650.

Meanwhile, the American resurgence was underlined by Andy Roddick, the boys' winner. Aniko Kapros, a magician's daughter from Hungary, conjured up victory in the girls' event.

JUNIOR EVENTS

BOYS' SINGLES – Final: Andy Roddick (USA)(2) d. Mario Ancic (CRO)(6) 7–6 6–3.
GIRLS' SINGLES – Final: Aniko Kapros (HUN)(1) d. Aria Jose Martinez (ESP)(2) 6–2 3–6 6–2.
BOYS' DOUBLES – Final: Nicolas Mahut (FRA)/Tommy Robredo(ESP)(2) d. Tres Davis (USA)/Andy Roddick (USA)(1) 6–3 6–2 5–7 11–9.
GIRLS' DOUBLES – Final: Aniko Kapros (HUN)/Christina Wheeler (AUS) (2) d. Lauren Barnikow (USA)/Erin Burdette (USA) 6–3 6–4.

SENIOR EVENTS

LEGENDS' DOUBLES – Final: Darren Cahill (AUS)/John Fitzgerald (AUS) d. Stan Smith (USA)/Laurie Warder (AUS) 6–4 6–2.
LEGENDS' MIXED DOUBLES – Final: Fred Stolle (AUS)/Diane Balestrat (AUS) d. Ken Rosewall (AUS)/ Elizabeth Smylie (AUS) 7–6 6–4.

AUSTRALIAN OPEN CHAMPIONSHIPS 2000

PRIZE MONEY – AUS $12,420,500

MEN'S SINGLES – Winner $755,000; Runner-up $377,500; Semi-finalists $189,000; Quarter-finalists $96,500; Fourth-round losers $51,600; Third-round losers $29,500; Second-round losers $18,000; First-round losers $ 11,625.   **Total:$4,101,300**

WOMEN'S SINGLES – Winner $717,000; Runner-up $358,500; Semi-finalists $179,500; Quarter-finalists $91,800; Fourth-round losers $49,000; Third-round losers $28,000; Second-round losers $17,125; First-round losers $11,050.   **Total:$3,886,900**

MEN'S DOUBLES (per team) – Winners $314,000; Runners-up $157,000; Semi-finalists $78,000; Quarter-finalists $39,000; Third-round losers $22,000; Second-round losers $12,000; First-round losers $ 6,750.   **Total:$1,367,000**

WOMEN'S DOUBLES (per team) – Winners $298,500; Runners-up $149,250; Semi-finalists $74,000; Quarter-finalists $37,000; Third-round losers $20,900; Second-round losers $11,400; First-round losers $6,400.   **Total:$1,298,150**

MIXED DOUBLES (per team) – Winners $112,800; Runners-up $56,400; Semi-finalists $28,200; Quarter-finalists $13,000; Second-round losers $6,500; First-round losers $3,150.   **Total $311,600**

MEN'S QUALIFYING: Round of 32 losers $7,325; Round of 64 losers $3,675; First-round losers $1,825
Total $351,600

WOMEN'S QUALIFYING: Round of 32 losers $6,950; Round of 64 losers $3,500; First-round losers $1,725.
Total $250,200

LEGENDS' DOUBLES (per player) Winners(2) $10,000. Runners-up(2) $7,500. Other players(8) $5,000. Reserves(2) $3,000.   **Total $81,000**

LEGENDS' MIXED DOUBLES (per player) Winners(2) $7,500; Runners-up(2) $5,000; Other players(4) $4,000; Reserve(1) $3,000.   **Total $44,000**

MEN'S QUALIFYING (128 DRAW)	WOMEN'S QUALIFYING (64 DRAW)
Losers in round of 32 – $5,800	Losers in round of 16 – $5,400
Losers in round of 64 – $3,000	Losers in round of 32 – $2,900
Losers in round of 128 – $1,550	Losers in round of 128 – $1,400
Total:$288,000	**Total:$134,400**

Plus **PER DIEM** allowances of $170 per day per player, commencing on the day prior to the player's first match and including the day of the player's last match. Total $550,000 (estimated)

A moment of triumph for Mary Pierce whose second French Open final ended in success at the expense of Conchita Martinez. (Stephen Wake)

Roland Garros

Richard Evans

For Gustavo Kuerten, who plays with a song in his heart, the triumph had seemed pre-ordained. Three years after winning his first French Open title as a 66th ranked outsider, the Brazilian fought his way past former champions and future rivals with the fortitude expected of a favourite to beat Sweden's Magnus Norman 6–2 6–3 2–6 7–6 in a final that built towards an extraordinary climax.

But if the capacity crowds packing the re-styled Centre Court at Roland Garros – fifty percent re-built since the previous year – were merely re-assured by the maturing of a great champion, they were thrilled and shocked in almost equal measure by the sudden transformation of Mary Pierce from a pouting pretender into a serene and deserving holder of the title she had coveted for so long. Six years after losing in the final, Pierce silenced the doubters and finally won the hearts of her adopted public with an imperious 6–2 7–5 defeat of Spain's Conchita Martinez following arduous triumphs over Monica Seles and Martina Hingis in the previous rounds.

In contrast to Kuerten's seemingly effortless rise, Pierce had travelled a tortuous path, bedevilled by a violent father and a relationship with the French public that swung between suspicion, affection and bemusement. Born in Canada; raised in the United States and transformed into a 'French' player on the basis of her mother's nationality, Pierce could be forgiven if she spent many years wondering who she was. The self-conscious public mannerisms seemed to suggest vanity but, to a greater degree, they were attempts to mask the kind of insecurity that comes from an unstable upbringing.

But, having turned 25 in January; renewed her faith in God; found true love with Roberto Alomar, an American baseball star, and enlisted the help of her brother David as a travelling coach, Pierce was ready to begin a new chapter in what, until then, had been a largely unfulfilled story. True, she had won the Australian title in 1995 but Mary had allowed herself to be sidetracked by too many diversions after that and it was only in tournaments leading up to Roland Garros 2000 that Pierce started to play her best tennis again. It turned out to be better than ever before.

The bludgeoning power, generated from muscles that bulge alarmingly in pictures and make her look larger than she really is, was suddenly augmented by a greater court awareness; an understanding of angles and placement and the ability to turn the wrist for little cross court forehands that left opponents stranded in mid-court.

As a week of cool and often grey weather unfolded, Pierce swept through her early rounds with little of the fuss and fidgeting that so often accompanies her performances. Looking remarkably focused and self-assured, this tall, elegant figure detonated so many power-packed ground strokes that the likes of Tara Snyder, Barbara Rittner, French wild card Virgine Razzano and Sweden's Asa Carlsson were blown away in straight sets. In fact in her first four matches, Pierce dropped only thirteen games. It was her 6–2 6–1 demolition of Carlsson in the fourth round that alerted her some-time fickle fans that this might be the year for Mary to deliver.

Tougher work lay ahead for Pierce in a draw that quickly became top heavy. In the bottom quarter seeds fell like flies. Troubled by her back, which started to seize up at the end of the second set, No 2 seed Lindsay Davenport went down 6–3 in the third to Belgium's tenacious Dominique Van Roost who is not the sort of player to throw life lines to the sick or weary. To the disappointment of the marketing men – or, perhaps, simply men everywhere – Anna Kournikova survived only one round, failing to last the pace against Austria's Sylvia Plischke.

Meanwhile Arantxa Sanchez-Vicario had been battling in familiar fashion through a tougher section of the draw, dropping sets along the way to a promising Canadian, Sonya Jeyaseelan, Austria's 16th seeded Barbara Schett and, in the quarters, Venus Williams.

In the semi-finals, recent history between the two most successful Spanish women of the modern era counted for nought. Sanchez-Vicario had won the last seven encounters and led Martinez 13–3 in career meetings but, in one of her most disappointing displays at Roland Garros, the three time champion lost all track of what she was trying to do and allowed Martinez to stroll to a 6–1 6–2 victory.

Seles offered Pierce her first real test in the quarter-finals and harked back to her finest days with a superb performance in the first set that was liberally sprinkled with the grunting winners that used to be Monica's trademark. Pierce, to her credit, was confident enough to strike back early in the second, winning it 6–3 and going on to establish a 2–0 lead in the third. But Seles proved she still has the spirit for a fight by recovering to lead 3–2. A packed Centre Court crowd were revelling in a classic match-up between two players who believe a tennis ball is there to be hit. It was Pierce who was able to produce the telling blows in the next couple of games, opening up the court for big forehand winners with thunderous serves and continuing to go for the lines with that mighty forehand weapon. Afterwards, Seles admitted that a couple of errors at 3–3 probably cost her the match. 'You cannot afford to let mistakes creep in at those times in a match as tight as today,' she said.

It had been a fine performance from Pierce and it set up the women's match of the championship – a semi-final against Martina Hingis. The Swiss had dropped only one set – to Romania's Roxandra Dragomir – on her way to the last four, dismissing a resurgent Chanda Rubin in the quarters 6–1 6–3. Two rounds earlier Rubin had defeated No 7 seed Nathalie Tauziat in what will probably prove to be Tauziat's last appearance in the French Open after appearing at Roland Garros for 17 consecutive years.

So, after all the hysterics of the previous year when the crowd had turned against her with such vitriol during her defeat at the hands of Steffi Graf in the final, Hingis seemed to be on her way to re-establishing some kind of rapport with the Parisian public. She was never, however, going to start as favourite against Pierce. The nerves were visible right from the start when the French player double faulted twice to give Hingis a break in the first game, but at 1–3 down Pierce started to deal with the fierce wind that was swirling around the arena. Using her power to hit through it, she found a sufficient level of accuracy to win 12 of 15 points and lead 4–3. She continued to dominate from then on despite some clever retaliatory strikes from Hingis who has never allowed power to overawe her in the past. However, when Pierce came to serve for the match at 5–3 in the second, she dropped serve to love and Hingis, suddenly looking perky again, came up with her best backhand of the match, a clean winner down the line, to snatch the set 7–5.

Once again Pierce revealed a new-found self confidence by slipping easily back into her hard hitting stride at the start of the third and, helped by double faults as Hingis seemed to tire, kept a tight hold on the match despite her first ever attack of cramps as victory hove into view. She held on to reach the second Roland Garros final of her career with a thoroughly deserved 6–4 5–7 6–2 victory.

Occasionally in major finals – one thinks of Betty Stove facing Virginia Wade at Wimbledon in 1977 and Nathalie Tauziat attempting to stop the inevitable coronation of Jana Novotna – a player seems to be riding with destiny and there is nothing the underdog can do about it. So it was here. Early on Martinez seemed overwhelmed by the occasion as much as by her opponent. Pierce, moving beautifully to construct points she would never even have thought about a year before, dictated the match from all over the court. Solid and penetrating from the back, the crowd favourite would also seize the opportunity to dominate the net and won 20 of her 28 sorties to the forecourt. Martinez got into the match sufficiently to lead 2–0 in the second and have points for 3–0 but nothing was going to throw Mary out of her stride on a day that she knew would be the greatest of her career. And when she finally clinched the title on her third match point, to become the first French player since Francoise Durr in 1967 to win at Roland Garros, she drank in the cheers; held back the tears and revelled in a status that had never quite been hers before – total acceptance as a true champion.

Twenty four hours later it was Magnus Norman's turn to feel the pressure of the occasion. Until a truly extraordinary climax, the Swede found himself quite unable to produce the form that had swept him into the final after a majestic run that saw him drop only one set while winning two at 6–0 and three at 6–1. With Kuerten leading 6–2 6–3 2–6 5–4 at 15–40 on his opponent's serve, no one would have dared predict that the match would continue for a further 45 minutes with another 53 points being played – ten of them match points that Norman saved. And for that, umpire Francois Pareau can take much of the credit. Whether or not he was correct in his decision to insist that Norman's cross court winner had touched the sideline, Pareau certainly ensured a rousing finish to a match that would, otherwise, have been largely forgettable.

At the start Norman had been so unhinged by the fluency of Kuerten's shot-making that he lost the first four games. And it was only a loss of concentration on the Brazilian's part early in the third that allowed Norman to make any impression at all.

The drama started when Kuerten, at match point, watched Norman's return land and began striding to the net, arms upraised in triumph. To his astonishment, he met Pareau going the other way to check the mark. 'I was shocked,' said the personable Brazilian afterwards. 'I was thinking of shaking my opponent's hand and posing for the photographers. Then suddenly the match was not over. It was tough to take. Every time I passed that line from then on I saw that mark! It drove me crazy!'

Many observers felt Kuerten was justified and there was no doubting the man's sincerity. Already that afternoon he had underlined his reputation as one of the most sporting players in the game by rubbing out marks on the clay and giving the point to Norman. But match point is different and losing it in controversial circumstances can get into a player's head. Suddenly it became a duel of the mind and Norman showed what a fighter he can be.

Counter attacking courageously, he saved two more match points in that tenth game and a further four when he served to stay in the match a second time. It was his forehand, fearsomely potent one minute and feeble the next, that was keeping him alive as Kuerten fretted over the opportunities that were slipping by. The tie-break was surreal. Norman went 0–3 down and then recovered to 3–3 when Kuerten, fuzzy headed by this time, tried a silly drop shot. Then Norman's forehand fell apart again and it was 6–3 – three more match points for the man they call Guga. 'Now I think I cannot lose,' he smiled afterwards. 'Then I lose the next three points and I think I cannot win!'

If it was tough on Kuerten, it was heart-palpitating for the yellow-shirted Brazilians dotted around the large arena. No sooner had they waved their flags than they wanted to shred them. Ten match points gone! Would it ever end? They need not have worried. Kuerten's serve came to the rescue as it had so often during the tournament. A huge 190 km/h delivery clipped the line and it was match point No 11. This time Norman had nothing more to offer and when a return drifted wide, Roland Garros, for the second time in four years, was engulfed in the happy sound of a Brazilian beat celebrating a great Brazilian triumph.

In the broader view, the first French Open of the new century had ushered in a new generation of stars. Former champions like Agassi and Kafelnikov had failed to last the distance; Pete Sampras, having drawn the most dangerous floater, Mark Philippoussis, failed to survive the first round, going down after a brave but fruitless fight 8–6 in the fifth while even someone like Alex Corretja, champion at Indian Wells in March, was swept aside by his 20-year-old fellow countryman Juan Carlos Ferrero. Along with Marat Safin, Lleyton Hewitt and a handful of the twelve Argentineans who made the draw, Ferrero will be amongst the game's new leaders going into the next decade. After winning two titles and reaching two finals in five weeks, Safin was too exhausted to push Norman further than 7–5 in the fourth and Hewitt showed that he still has a few things to learn about clay when an expert, Albert Costa, followed up a fine win over No 7 seed Thomas Enqvist by beating the tenacious Australian 6–4 in the fourth in the round of sixteen.

Surprisingly it was Franco Squillari who carried the Argentine flag furthest. Mariano Zabaleta is generally acknowledged to be the leader of their pack but he lost to Kafelnikov after leading by two sets to one. Mariano Puerto could be described as the most skilled but he was injured and had to default against Ferrero. Juan Ignacio Chela beat Todd Martin in the first round but was then outplayed by the most consistent of the Moroccan trio, Younes El Aynaoui, while the most eye-catching performance came from Agustin Calleri who resumed his tennis career at the age of 23 after helping his father run a vineyard near Cordoba for a year. Never afraid to get in and volley, Calleri totally outplayed the previous year's semi-finalist Dominik Hrbaty to win 6–4 in the fourth before being outfoxed by Medvedev.

But there was no stopping Squillari. The sturdy left-hander had retained his Munich title a couple of weeks before and proceeded to scythe his way through the top quarter of the draw that had been reserved for Agassi. Karol Kucera, the man who beat the defending champion with embarrassing ease 2–6 7–5 6–1 6–0, was Squillari's first victim – the slender Slav simply not having enough resilience to counter a massive Argentine forehand. It was the same story with El Aynaoui and Costa until Squillari suddenly found himself in a Grand Slam semi-final. There Norman did to him what Kafelnikov had done to Norman at the same stage of the Australian Open. Squillari couldn't move for nerves at the start and barely recovered, losing 6–1 6–4 6–3.

So the Argentines are coming. And the Americans? The writing has been on the wall for a long time about the future of American tennis and now it is blinking at the USTA in red lights. For the first time in the Open era, no American reached the semi-finals in Paris in either the

(continued on page 93)

Men's Singles

Winner: **G. Kuerten** (BRA) (5)

Holder: A. Agassi (USA)

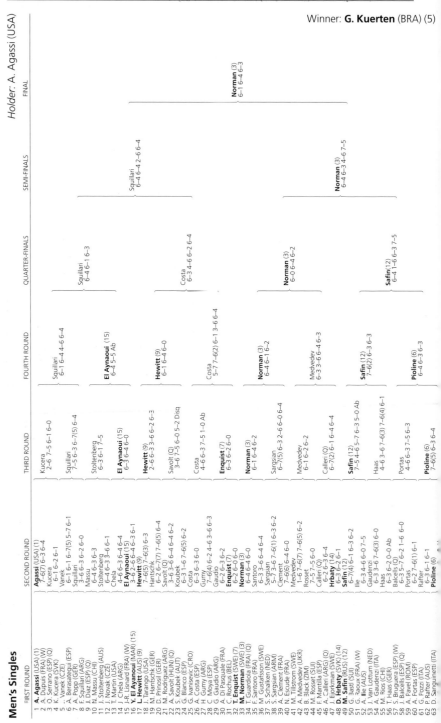

FIRST ROUND	SECOND ROUND	THIRD ROUND	FOURTH ROUND	QUARTER-FINALS	SEMI-FINALS	FINAL

1 **A. Agassi** (USA) (1) — Agassi (USA) (1) 7-6(7) 6-3 6-4 — Kucera 2-6 7-5 6-1 6-0 — Squillari 6-1 6-4 4-6 6-4 — Squillari 6-4 6-1 6-3 — Squillari 6-4 6-4 2-6 6-4 — **Norman** (3) 6-1 6-4 6-3

2 A. Dupuis (FRA) (W)
3 O. Serrano (ESP) (Q) — Kucera 6-1 6-2 6-1
4 K. Kucera (SVK)
5 ∴ Vanek (CZE) — Vanek
6 A. Berasategui (ESP) — Squillari 6-1 1-6 7(5) 5-7 6-1 — Squillari 7-5 6-3 6-7(5) 6-4
7 A. Popp (GER) — G. Squillari (ARG) 3-6 6-1 6-2 6-0
8 G. Squillari (ARG)
9 J. Diaz (ESP) (Q) — Massu
10 N. Massu (CHI) 6-4 6-3 6-3 — Stoltenberg 6-3 6-1 7-5
11 J. Stoltenberg (AUS) — Stoltenberg
12 J. Novak (CZE) 6-4 6-3 6-6-1
13 T. Martin (USA) — Chela
14 J. Chela (ARG) 4-6 6-3 6-4 6-4 — El Aynaoui (15) 6-3 6-4 6-0 — **El Aynaoui** (15) 6-4 5-5 Ab
15 J-R. Lisnard (FRA) (W) — El Aynaoui (15)
16 **Y. El Aynaoui** (MAR) (15) 3-6 2-6 6-4 6-3 6-1
17 **L. Hewitt** (AUS) (9) — Hewitt (9) 7-6(5) 7-6(3) 6-3 — Hewitt (9) 2-6 6-3 6-6 6-2 6-3 — **Hewitt** (9) 6-1 6-4 6-0 — Costa 5-7 7-6(2) 6-1 3-6 6-4
18 J. Tarango (USA)
19 M. Hantschk (GER) — Hantschk
20 D. Prinosil (GER) 6-2 6-7(7) 7-6(5) 6-4
21 M. Rodriguez (ARG) — Savolt (Q)
22 A. Savolt (HUN) (Q) 3-6 3-6 6-4 6-4 6-2 — Savolt (Q) 3-6 7-5 6-0 5-2 Disq
23 S. Koubek (AUT) — Koubek
24 G. Blanco (AUT) 6-3 1-6 7-6(5) 6-2
25 G. Ivanisevic (CRO) — Costa
26 A. Costa (ESP) 6-3 6-3 6-0 — Costa 4-6 6-3 7-5 1-0 Ab
27 H. Gumy (ARG) — Gumy
28 C. Moya (ESP) 7-6(4) 6-2 4-6 3-6 6-3
29 G. Gaudio (ARG) — Gaudio
30 A. Di Pasquale (FRA) 6-2 6-3 6-2 — Enquist (7) 6-3 6-2 6-0 — **Enquist** (7) 6-2 6-1 6-3 6-6-4
31 C. Rochus (BEL) — Enquist (7)
32 **T. Enquist** (SWE) (7) 6-2 6-5 6-0
33 **M. Norman** (SWE) (3) — Norman (3)
34 T. Guardiola (FRA) (Q) 6-4 4-6 6-0 — Norman (3) 6-1 6-4 6-2 — **Norman** (3) 6-4 6-1 6-2 — **Norman** (3) 6-0 6-4 6-2 — **Norman** (3) 6-4 6-3 4-6 7-5
35 F. Santoro (FRA) — Santoro
36 M. Gustafsson (SWE) 6-3 3-6 6-4 6-4 — Sargsian 6-7(5) 6-3 2-6 6-0 6-4
37 S. Schalken (NED) — Sargsian
38 S. Sargsian (ARM) 5-7 3-6 7-6(1) 6-3 6-2
39 A. Clement (FRA) — Clement
40 N. Escude (FRA) 7-6(6) 6-4 6-0 — Medvedev 6-1 6-2 6-2 — Medvedev 6-3 3-6 4-6 4-6-3
41 M. Tillstrom (SWE) — Medvedev
42 A. Medvedev (UKR) 1-6 7-6(7) 7-6(5) 6-2
43 B. Black (ZIM) — Rosset (SUI)
44 M. Rosset (SUI) 7-5 7-5 6-0
45 F. Mantilla (ESP) — Calleri (Q)
46 A. Calleri (ARG) (Q) 6-2 6-3 6-4 — Calleri (Q) 6-7(2) 6-1 6-4 6-4 — **Safin** (12) 7-6(2) 6-3 6-0
47 T. Ejorkman (SWE)
48 **D. Hrbaty** (SVK) (14) — Hrbaty (14) 6-3 6-2 6-4 — Safin (12) 7-5 4-6 5-7 6-3 5-0 Ab — **Safin** (12) 7-6(2) 6-3 6-3 — **Safin** (12) 6-4 1-6-2 6-3 7-5
49 **M. Safin** (RUS) (12) — Safin (12)
50 G. 3asti (SUI) 6-7(4) 6-1 6-3 6-2
51 G. Raoux (FRA) (W) — Ilie (AUS)
52 A. Ilie (AUS) 6-3 4-6 6-0 7-5 — Haas 4-6 3-6-7(3) 7-6(4) 6-1
53 A. van Lottum (NED) — Gaudenzi
54 A. Gaudenzi (ITA) 6-3 3-6-7(3) 6-0
55 M. Rios (CHI) — Haas
56 T. Haas (GER) 6-3 6-2 0-0 Ab
57 S. Bruguera (ESP) (W) — Balcells (ESP)
58 J. Balcells (ESP) (Q) 6-3 5-7 6-2 1-6 6-0 — Portas 4-6 6-3 7-5 6-3 — **Pioline** (6) 6-4 6-3 6-3
59 G. Favel (ROM) — Portas
60 A. Portas (ESP) 6-2 7-6(1) 6-1
61 G. Pozzi (ITA) — Rafter
62 P. Rafter (AUS) 6-3 6-1 6-1 — Pioline (6) 7-6(5) 6-3 6-4
63 D. Sanguinetti (ITA) — **Pioline** (6)

6–2 6–3 2–6 7–6(6)

Winner: **Kuerten** (5)
7–5 4–6 2–6 6–4 6–3

Semifinals

Kuerten (5)
6–3 3–6 4–6 4–6 6–2

Ferrero (16)
6–4 6–4 6–2

Quarterfinals

Kuerten (5)
6–3 6–4 7–6(4)

Kafelnikov (4)
5–7 6–3 5–7 7–6(4) 8–6

Corretja (10)
7–5 7–6(7) 6–2

Ferrero (16)
6–2 3–6 2–3 6 Ab

Round 4

Kuerten (5)
6–3 6–7(9) 6–1 6–4

Lapentti (11)
5–7 6–3 7–5 6–3

Vicente
7–5 4–6 4–4 6–6–3

Kafelnikov (4)
6–3 6–1 5–7 6–4

Federer
7–6(5) 6–4 2–6 6–7(4) 8–6

Corretja (10)
4–6 6–2 6–3 6–2

Ferrero (16)
6–2 3–2 Ab

Philippoussis
6–4 6–7(3) 6–0 6–2

Round 3

Kuerten (5)
7–6(5) 6–2 6–2

Chang
7–6(2) 7–6(5) 2–6 6–3

W. Ferreira
6–3 6–1 4–6 7–5

Lapentti (11)
7–6(4) 6–3 6–7(4) 6–3

Henman (13)
6–2 6–4 7–6(3)

Vicente
6–1 6–0 6–3

Grosjean
6–1 6–3 2–6 6–7(6) 6–2

Kafelnikov (4)
6–2 3–6 6–7(6) 6–4 6–4

Federer
7–6(5) 6–3 6–3

Kratochvil
6–7(6) 7–5 6–2 6–1

Krajicek
7–5 6–3 7–5

Corretja (10)
4–6 6–3 6–3 4–6 6–3

Ferrero (16)
1–6 2–6 6–2 6–4 6–4

Puerta
6–2 6–1 6–3

Arazi
6–3 3–6 5–7 6–2 6–1

Philippoussis
6–4 6–7(3) 6–0 6–2

First round draw

65	**G. Kuerten** (BRA) (5)	Kuerten (5) 6–0 6–0 6–3
66	A. Vinciguerra (SWE)	
67	K. Alami (MAR)	Charpentier (Q) 6–7(1) 6–4 6–3 1–6 6–3
68	M. Charpentier (ARG) (Q)	
69	T. Thansson (SWE)	Thansson 7–6(4) 6–3 6–3
70	C. Ruud (NOR)	
71	A. Voinea (ROM)	Chang 6–1 6–2 2–6 6–3
72	M. Tirang (USA)	
73	A. Schuttler (GER)	W. Ferreira 7–6(5) 4–6 6–3 6–2
74	W. Ferreira (RSA)	
75	G. Coria (ARG) (Q)	Coria (Q) 6–3 6–7(6) 6–4 6–4
76	M. Llodra (FRA) (W)	
77	B. Ulihrach (CZE) (Q)	Ulihrach 6–4 6–1 5–7 6–4
78	B. Phau (GER) (Q)	
79	J. Soutter (FRA) (W)	Lapentti (11) 6–4 6–2 6–0
80	**N. Lapentti** (ECU) (11)	
81	**T. Henman** (GBR) (13)	Henman (13) 7–5 7–5 6–4
82	V. Spadea (USA)	
83	J. Behrend (GER) (LL)	Vinck (Q) 6–1 6–4 6–4
84	C. Vinck (GER) (Q)	
85	F. Vicente (ESP)	Vicente 3–6 5–7 6–3 6–4 6–4
86	M. Mirnyi (BLR)	
87	R. Agenor (HAI)	Agenor 6–2 6–4 3–6 7–6(5)
88	P. Srichaphan (THA)	
89	S. Grosjean (FRA)	Grosjean 6–4 6–2 1–6 6–1
90	R. Fromberg (AUS)	
91	J. L. Marin (CRC)	Browne (LL) 6–4 6–7(3) 6–1
92	I. Browne (AUS) (LL)	
93	H. Levy (ISR) (LL)	Zabaleta 5–7 7–6(1) 6–4 6–4
94	M. Zabaleta (ARG)	
95	I. Ljubicic (CRO)	Kafelnikov (4) 6–4 6–4 3–6 3–6 6–4
96	**Y. Kafelnikov** (RUS) (4)	
97	**N. Kiefer** (GER) (8)	Gambill 6–3 7–5 6–1
98	J-M. Gambill (USA)	
99	W. Arthurs (AUS)	Federer 7–6(4) 6–3 1–6 6–3
100	R. Federer (SUI)	
101	S. Huet (FRA)(W)	Stanoytchev 4–6 6–0 6–7 5–6 4–7–5
102	E. Stanoytchev (BUL)	
103	A. Kratochvil (SUI) (Q)	Kratochvil 6–4 6–7(3) 6–3 6–1
104	J. Gimelstob (USA)	
105	A. Eschauer (AUT) (Q)	Eschauer (Q) 3–6 6–2 6–2 6–2
106	F. Saulnier (FRA) (W)	
107	S. Krajicek (NED)	Krajicek 6–3 6–1 6–2
108	T. Zib (CZE)	
109	F. Meligeni (BRA)	Meligeni 2–6 6–4 6–3 7–5
110	F. Prodon (FRA) (Q)	
111	A. Martin (ESP)	Corretja (10) 4–6 6–3 6–4 6–3
112	**J. C. Ferrero** (ESP) (16)	
113	G. Golmard (FRA)	Ferrero (16) 6–4 6–3 6–2
114	J. Riedeski (GBR)	
115	J. Dosedel (CZE)	Dosedel 6–3 6–(10) 7–6(4)
116	M. Damm (CZE)	
117	M. Puerta (ARG)	Puerta 7–6(4) 6–3 6–2
118	M. Damm (CZE)	
119	F. Clavet (ESP)	Clavet 6–2 6–0 6–3
120	G. Canas (ARG)	
121	H. Arazi (MAR)	Arazi 6–3 6–4 7–6(3)
122	C. Woodruff (USA)	
123	N. Mahut (FRA) (Q)	Hipfl 6–4 7–5 6–4
124	V. Hipfl (AUT)	
125	J. Sa (BRA)	Goldstein 6–1 6–1 7–6(7)
126	A. Goldstein (USA)	
127	M. Philippoussis (AUS)	Philippoussis 4–6 7–6(3) 7–6(4) 4–6 8–6
128	**P. Sampras** (USA) (2)	

Bold type denotes seeded players. Numbers following player's name gives seeding order (Q) = Qualifier, (W) = Wild Card, (LL) = Lucky Loser, (A) = Alternate

Women's Singles

Holder: S. Graf (GER)

Winner: **M. Pierce** (FRA) (6)

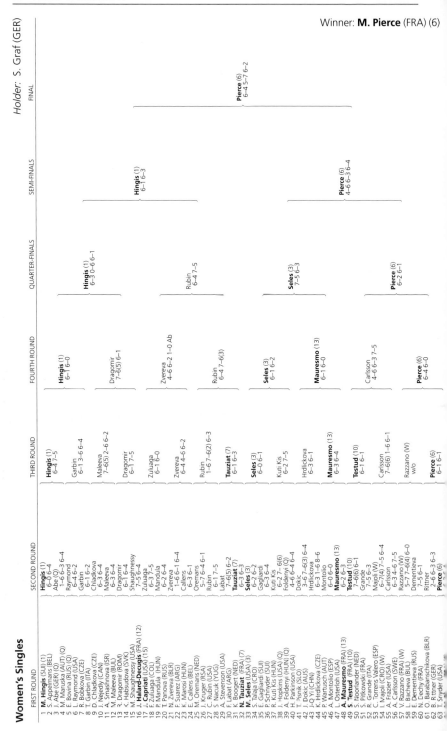

FIRST ROUND	SECOND ROUND	THIRD ROUND	FOURTH ROUND	QUARTER-FINALS	SEMI-FINALS	FINAL
1 **M. Hingis** (SUI) (1)	**Hingis** (1) 6-0 6-4	**Hingis** (1) 6-4 7-5	**Hingis** (1) 6-1 6-0	**Hingis** (1) 6-3 0-6 6-1	**Hingis** (1) 6-1 6-3	**Pierce** (6) 6-4 5-7 6-2
2 S. Appelmans (BEL)						
3 J. Abe (GER) (Q)	Abe (Q) 1-6 6-3 6-4					
4 M. Maruska (AUT) (Q)						
5 E. Bovina (RUS) (Q)	Raymond 6-4 6-2	Garbin 6-1 3-6 6-4				
6 L. Raymond (USA)						
7 R. Bobkova (CZE)	Garbin 6-1 6-2					
8 D. Garbin (ITA)						
9 D. Chladkova (CZE)	Chladkova 6-3 6-4	Maleeva 7-6(5) 2-6 6-2	Dragomir 7-6(5) 6-1			
10 J. Nejedly (CAN)						
11 A. Smashnova (ISR)	Maleeva 6-3 6-4					
12 M. Maleeva (BUL)						
13 R. Dragomir (ROM)	Dragomir 6-1 6-4	Dragomir 6-1 7-5				
14 K. Habsudova (SVK)						
15 M. Shaughnessy (USA)	Shaughnessy 7-5 6-4					
16 **J. Halard-Decugis** (FRA) (12)						
17 **J. Capriati** (USA) (15)	Zuluaga 6-3 7-5	Zuluaga 6-1 6-0	Zvereva 4-6 6-2 1-0 Ab	Rubin 6-4 7-5		
18 F. Zuluaga (COL)						
19 M. Mandula (HUN)	Mandula 6-2 6-4					
20 T. Panova (RUS)						
21 N. Zvereva (BLR)	Zvereva 1-6 6-1 6-4	Zvereva 6-4 4-6 6-2				
22 F. Suarez (ARG)						
23 K. Marosi (HUN)	Callens 6-3 6-1					
24 E. Callens (BEL)						
25 M. Oremans (NED)	Oremans 5-7 6-4 6-1	Rubin 1-6 7-6(2) 6-3	Rubin 6-4 7-6(3)			
26 J. Kruger (RSA)						
27 C. Rubin (USA)	Rubin 6-1 7-5					
28 S. Nacuk (YUG)						
29 A. Stevenson (USA)	Labat 7-6(5) 6-2	Tauziat (7) 6-1 6-3	Seles (3) 6-1 6-2	Seles (3) 7-5 6-3	**Pierce** (6) 4-6 6-3 7-5	
30 F. Labat (ARG)						
31 K. Boogert (NED)	**Tauziat** (7) 1-3 6-3					
32 **N. Tauziat** (FRA) (7)						
33 **M. Seles** (USA) (3)	**Seles** (3) 6-2 6-2	Seles (3) 6-0 6-1				
34 S. Talaja (CRO)						
35 E. Gagliardi (SUI)	Gagliardi 6-3 6-4					
36 P. Schnyder (SUI)						
37 R. Kuti Kis (HUN)	Kuti Kis 6-2 7-6(6)	Kuti Kis 6-2 7-5	Mauresmo (13) 6-1 6-0			
38 J. Hopkins (USA) (Q)						
39 A. Foldenyi (HUN) (Q)	Foldenyi (Q) 4-6 6-4 6-4					
40 H. Parkinson (USA)						
41 T. Pisnik (SLO)	Dokic 7-6(3) 6-4	Hrdlickova 6-3 6-1				
42 J. Dokic (AUS)						
43 J. Y (CHN)	Hrdlickova 6-3 1-6 8-6					
44 K. Hrdlickova (CZE)						
45 P. Wartusch (AUT)	Montolio 6-0 6-0	**Mauresmo** (13) 6-3 6-4	**Mauresmo** (13) 6-1 6-0			
46 A. Montolio (ESP)						
47 L. Osterloh (USA)	**Mauresmo** (13) 6-2 6-3					
48 **A. Mauresmo** (FRA) (13)						
49 **S. Testud** (FRA) (10)	**Testud** (10) 7-6(6) 6-1	**Testud** (10) 6-1 6-1	Carlsson 4-6 6-3 7-5	**Pierce** (6) 2-6 6-1		
50 S. Noorlander (NED)						
51 S. Pitkowski (FRA)	Grande 7-5 6-3					
52 R. Grande (ITA)						
53 C. Torrens Valero (ESP)	Majoli (W) 6-7(4) 7-5 6-4	Carlsson 7-6(6) 1-6 6-1				
54 I. Majoli (CRO) (W)						
55 A. Frazier (USA)	Carlsson 6-3 4-6 7-5					
56 A. Carlsson (SWE)						
57 V. Razzano (FRA) (W)	Razzano (W) 5-7 7-6(4) 6-0	Razzano (W) w/o	**Pierce** (6) 6-4 6-0			
58 L. Bacheva (BUL)						
59 E. Dementieva (RUS)	Dementieva 7-5 6-1					
60 N. Dechy (FRA)						
61 O. Barabanschikova (BLR)	Rittner 2-6 6-3 6-3	**Pierce** (6) 6-1 6-1				
62 B. Rittner (GER)						
63 T. Snyder (USA)	**Pierce** (6)					

6–2 7–5

Draw bracket — Roland Garros

No.	Player (seed)	Round 1	Round 2	Round 3	Round 4	Quarterfinal	Semifinal	Final
65	A. **Sanchez-Vicario** (ESP) (8)	**Sanchez-Vicario** (8) 6-1 6-1	**Sanchez-Vicario** (8) 3-6 6-2 6-2	**Sanchez-Vicario** (8) 7-5 6-4	**Sanchez-Vicario** (8) 0-6 6-4 6-2	**Sanchez-Vicario** (8) 6-0 1-6 6-2	**C. Martinez** (5) 6-1 6-2	**C. Martinez** (5) 6-1 6-2
66	P. Ivaã (BUL)							
67	S. Jeyaseelan (CAN)	Jeyaseelan 6-7(3) 6-2 6-4						
68	A. Cocheteux (FRA)							
69	H. Nagyova (SVK)	Serna 6-2 6-4	Serna 5-7 6-2					
70	M. Serna (ESP)							
71	L. Andretto (FRA) (W)	Brandi 6-2 6-1						
72	K. Brandi (USA)							
73	G. Casoni (ITA) (Q)	Casoni (Q) 1-6 7-6(3) 6-4	Casoni (Q) 6-3 7-6(5)					
74	L. Courtois (BEL)							
75	A. Kopmans (NED)	Srebotnik 4-6 7-5 6-3						
76	K. Srebotnik (SLO)							
77	J. Kostanic (CRO)	Fusai (W) 7-5 6-1	Schett (16) 6-1 6-2	Schett (16) 6-2 6-1				
78	A. Fusai (FRA) (W)							
79	S. Kleinova (CZE)	Schett (16) 6-3 6-4						
80	B. **Schett** (AUT) (16)							
81	A. **Huber** (GER) (11)	Huber (11) 3-6 6-4 7-5	Huber (11) 7-6(5) 6-1	Huber (11) 6-2 6-2	V. Williams (4) 7-6(4) 6-2			
82	N. Petrova (RUS)							
83	M. A. Vento (VEN)	Morariu 6-1 6-2						
84	C. Morariu (USA)							
85	M. Grzybowska (POL) (Q)	Grzybowska (Q) 6-0 2-6 7-5	Grzybowska (Q) 6-3 6-4					
86	E. Likhovtseva (RUS)							
87	B. Schwartz (AUT)	De Lone 6-3 6-2						
88	E. De Lone (USA)							
89	M. Babel (GER)	Babel 6-4 6-7(4) 6-1	Loit (W) 6-4 6-1	V. Williams (4) 6-2 6-2				
90	S. Cohen Aloro (FRA) (W)							
91	E. Loit (FRA) (W)	Loit (W) 6-3 6-2						
92	M. Pratt (AUS)							
93	S. Erre (FRA) (W)	Tanasugarn 7-6(6) 7-6(5)	V. Williams (4) 6-2 6-2					
94	T. Tanasugarn (THA)							
95	I. Gandarr (GER)	V. Williams (4) 6-0 6-3						
96	V. **Williams** (USA) (4)							
97	C. **Martinez** (ESP) (5)	C. Martinez (5) 6-2 6-3	C. Martinez (5) 4-6 7-5 6-4	C. Martinez (5) 6-1 6-0	C. Martinez (5) 5-7 6-3 6-4			
98	A. Jidkova (RUS)							
99	J. Black (ZIM)	Black						
100	A. Myskina (RUS)							
101	A. Molik (AUS)	Foretz (W) 6-4 6-2	Farina 6-4 6-7(4) 6-3					
102	S. Foretz (FRA) (W)							
103	S. Farina (ITA)	Farina 6-3 6-1						
104	A. Sanchez Lorenzo (ESP)							
105	A. Sugiyama (JPN)	Sugiyama 6-2 3-6 6-2	Sugiyama 6-3 7-6(5)	Sugiyama 6-4 6-1				
106	K. Clijsters (BEL)							
107	D. Gersi (CZE)	Gersi 6-4 6-3						
108	C. Cristea (ROM) (Q)							
109	A. Pliscke (AUT)	Pliscke 6-2 6-0	Pliscke 6-2 4-6 6-3					
110	M. Lucic (CRO)							
111	T. Webb (CAN)	Kournikova (14) 6-4 6-4						
112	A. **Kournikova** (RUS) (14)							
113	A. **Coetzer** (RSA) (9)	Coetzer (9) 6-0 6-4	Coetzer (9) 6-3 6-1	Coetzer (9) 6-3 6-1	Marrero (Q) 4-6 6-0 6-4			
114	M. Drake (CAN)							
115	G. Leon Garcia (ESP)	Leon Garcia 7-6(4) 6-1						
116	L. Krasnoroutskaya (RUS) (LL)							
117	M. Vavrinec (SUI)	De Los Rios (Q) 6-4 7-6(6)	De Los Rios (Q) 6-0 6-1	De Los Rios (Q) 7-5 6-7(4) 6-4				
118	R. De Los Rios (PAR) (Q)							
119	M. De Swardt (RSA)	Weingartner 1-6 7-6(2) 6-3						
120	M. Weingartner (GER)							
121	T. Kovalchuk (UKR) (Q)	Kremer 6-4 6-1	Sidot 6-4 4-6 6-1	Marrero (Q) 7-6(0) 6-2				
122	A. Kremer (LUX)							
123	A. Bachmann (GER) (Q)	Sidot 6-3 7-6(5)						
124	A.G. Sidot (FRA)							
125	M. Marrero (ESP) (Q)	Marrero (Q) 6-3 6-2	Marrero (Q) 0-6 7-5 7-5					
126	I. Spirlea (ROM)							
127	D. Van Roost (BEL)	Van Roost 6-7(5) 6-4 6-3						
128	L. **Davenport** (USA) (2)							

Bold type denotes seeded players. Numbers following player's name gives seeding order (Q) = Qualifier, (W) = Wild Card, (LL) = Lucky Loser

Men's Doubles

Winners: **T. Woodbridge** (AUS)/**M. Woodforde** (AUS) (2) 7–6(4) 6–4

Holders: Bhupathi (IND)/Paes (IND)

FIRST ROUND

1 **O'Brien/Palmer** (1)
2 Carbonell/Garcia
3 Alvarez/Vemic
4 Pala/Vizner
5 Hewitt/Rafter
6 Clement/Grosjean (W)
7 Mirnyi/Zimonjic
8 **Norval/Ullyett** (16)
9 **Bhupathi/Prinosil** (9)
10 Arthurs/Tebbutt
11 Carrasco/Velasco
12 Robichaud/Waite
13 Huet/Saulnier (W)
14 Martin/Suk
15 Gambill/Humphries
16 **W. Ferreira/Kafelnikov** (7)
17 **Haarhuis/Stolle** (3)
18 Goellner/[illegible]
19 Bowen/Coupe
20 Kilderry/Tramacchi
21 Benneteau/Mahut (W)
22 Guardiola/Prodon (W)
23 Lopez-Moron/Portas
24 **Kulti/Tillstrom** (14)
25 **E. Black/Kratzmann** (11)
26 Ellwood/Prieto
27 Appel/Landsberg
28 Godwin/Hill
29 Di Pasquale/Gilbert (W)
30 Balcells/Ivanisevic
31 Eagle/Florent
32 **Adams/De Jager** (6)
33 **Bjorkman/W. Black** (5)
34 Llodra/Nargiso
35 Hood/[illegible]
36 Oncins/Orsanic
37 Boutter/Santoro
38 Goldstein/Stark (A)
39 Lisnard/Patience (W)
40 **Gimelstob/Knowles** (12)
41 **Lareau/Nestor** (13)
42 Escude/Federer
43 Galbraith/MacPhie
44 B. Bryan/M. Bryan
45 Albano/Haggard
46 Marques/Van Houdt
47 Etlis/Rodriguez
48 **E. Ferreira/Leach** (4)
49 **Novak/Rikl** (8)
50 Bergh/Kitinov
51 Nicholas/Puentes
52 MacPherson/Nyborg
53 Forget/Raoux (W)
54 Coetzee/Haygarth
55 **Damm/Hrbaty** (10)
56 **Delaitre/Tarango** (15)
57 Shimada/Wakefield
58 [illegible]
59 Del Rio/Ran
60 Barnard/Montana
61 Arnold/Johnson
62 Bertolini/Brandi
63 Bale/Ondruska
64 **Woodbridge/Woodforde** (2)

SECOND ROUND

Carbonell/Garcia — 6–2 6–4
Pala/Vizner — 6–2 6–4
Hewitt/Rafter — 6–1 5–7 6–2
Norval/Ullyett (16) — 6–1 5–7 6–2
Bhupathi/Prinosil (9) — 6–4 7–5
Carrasco/Velasco — 7–6(7) 6–2
W. Ferreira/Kafelnikov (7) — 6–3 6–7(4) 6–1
Haarhuis/Stolle (3) — 4–6 7–5
Kilderry/Tramacchi — 6–3 6–2
Benneteau/Mahut (W) — 6–1 6–2
Kulti/Tillstrom (14) — 6–2 6–2
E. Black/Kratzmann (11) — 6–4 4–6 6–2
Godwin/Hill — 6–4 4–6 6–2
Balcells/Ivanisevic — 6–3 6–4
Eagle/Florent — 6–1 6–3
Bjorkman/W. Black (5) — 7–6(5) 6–2
Oncins/Orsanic — 7–5 6–4
Boutter/Santoro — 7–6(7) 4–6 6–2
Lisnard/Patience (W) — 6–4 6–4
Lareau/Nestor (13) — 6–4 6–3
B. Bryan/M. Bryan — 6–3 6–4
Albano/Haggard — 6–4 5–7 6–2
Etlis/Rodriguez — 3–6 6–3 6–4
Novak/Rikl (8) — 6–4 6–3
MacPherson/Nyborg — 6–1 7–6(5)
Forget/Raoux (W) — 7–5 6–3
Damm/Hrbaty (10) — 6–1 6–4
Shimada/Wakefield — 4–6 6–2 8–6
Barnard/Montana — 6–2 6–3
Woodbridge/Woodforde (2) — 6–4 6–3

THIRD ROUND

Carbonell/Garcia — 7–5 4–6 6–1
Norval/Ullyett (16) — w/o
Carrasco/Velasco — 6–4 6–7(4) 6–1
W. Ferreira/Kafelnikov (7) — 4–6 6–4 7–5
Haarhuis/Stolle (3) — 4–6 6–3 6–4
Kulti/Tillstrom (14) — 6–2 7–5
Godwin/Hill — 6–3 3–6 6–2
Eagle/Florent — 4–6 6–4 6–4
Oncins/Orsanic — 6–7(5) 6–0 11–9
Boutter/Santoro — 7–6(7) 6–1
Lareau/Nestor (13) — 6–2 6–4
Etlis/Rodriguez — 6–4 6–2
Novak/Rikl (8) — 6–3 6–3
Damm/Hrbaty (10) — 7–5 6–4
Barnard/Montana — 6–4 6–2
Woodbridge/Woodforde (2) — 6–2 4–6 6–2

QUARTER-FINALS

Carbonell/Garcia — 7–5 6–3
W. Ferreira/Kafelnikov (7) — 6–2 6–3
Haarhuis/Stolle (3) — 6–3 7–6(5)
Godwin/Hill — 6–7(5) 6–2 6–4
Oncins/Orsanic — 7–6(7) 6–2
Lareau/Nestor (13) — 4–6 6–1 8–6
Novak/Rikl (8) — 6–1 4–6 6–3
Woodbridge/Woodforde (2) — 6–4 6–2

SEMI-FINALS

Carbonell/Garcia — 5–7 6–4 7–5
Haarhuis/Stolle (3) — 6–3 6–4
Oncins/Orsanic — 6–4 4–6 6–2
Woodbridge/Woodforde (2) — 3–6 7–6(6) 6–1

FINAL

Haarhuis/Stolle (3) — 6–4 6–4
Woodbridge/Woodforde (2) — 6–4 7–6(7)

Bold type denotes seeded players. Numbers following player's name gives seeding order (Q) = Qualifier, (W) = Wild Card, (LL) = Lucky Loser, (A) = Alternate

Women's Doubles

Winners: **M. Hingis** (SUI)/**M. Pierce** (FRA) (3) 6–2 6–4

Holders: S. Williams (USA)/V. Williams (USA)

FIRST ROUND

1 Jidkova/Petrova (A)
2 Mysk na/Nagyova (A)
3 Hopmans/Torrens Valero
4 Cocheteux/Dechy (W)
5 Coetzer/McNeil
6 Black/Selyutina
7 Maunesmo/Vis
8 **Arendt/Bollegraf (11)**
9 **Po/Sidot (13)**
10 Andreu/Martinez Granados
11 Frazier/Schlukebir
12 Grzbowska/Tatarkova
13 Muscuave/Stewart
14 Cristea/Dragomir
15 Mer ga/Wagner
16 **Halard-Decugis/Sugiyama (5)**
17 **Kou~nikova/Zvereva (4)**
18 Babel/Kandarr
19 Hiralt/Yoshida
20 Barc ay/Webb
21 Gaibhl/Marosi
22 De eer/Miyagi
23 Bob czva/Krivencheva
24 **Ruano Pascual/Suarez (10)**
25 **Horn/Montalvo (16)**
26 Tarasugam/Woehr
27 McQuillan/McShea
28 De Villiers/Steck
29 Noo lander/Ortuno
30 Carepa/Casoni
31 Costanic/Pisnik
32 **Rubin/Testud (7)**
33 **C. Martinez/Tarabini (8)**
34 Boogert/Oremans
35 Bacheva/Clijsters
36 Hrd ickova/Rittner
37 Poutchek/Rampre
38 Mar k/Wild
39 Serna/Shaughnessy
40 **Ccertois/Sanchez-Vicario (9)**
41 **Callsson/Loit (14)**
42 Fa na/Habsudova
43 Krasnoroutskaya/Neiland
44 Caonato/Dokic
45 Fcretz/Razzano (W)
46 L'k -iovtseva/Tulyaganova
47 Martincova/Nacuk
48 **Hingis/Pierce (3)**
49 **Fusai/Tauziat (6)**
50 Jevaseelan/Labat
51 Bes/Riera
52 Kz ulikovskaya/Wartusch
53 Appelmans/Grande
54 Le Swardt/Navratilova (W)
55 Elwood/Osteroh
56 **Krizan/Srebotnik (12)**
57 **Huber/Schett (15)**
58 Tallin/Woodroffe
59 Callens/Van Roost
60 Bachmann/Kschwendt
61 Husarova/Zavagli
62 De Lone/Pratt
63 Chenin/Pitkowski
64 **Raymond/Stubbs (2)**

SECOND ROUND

Jidkova/Petrova (A) 5-7 6-4 7-5
Cocheteux/Dechy (W)
Black/Selyutina 6-4 6-4
Arendt/Bollegraf (11)
Po/Sidot (13) 6-3 6-1
Grzbowska/Tatarkova
Cristea/Dragomir 6-2 6-2
Halard-Decugis/Sugiyama (5)
Kournikova/Zvereva (4) 6-2 6-3
Barclay/Webb 6-1 6-2
Gaibhl/Marosi 6-3 6-3
Ruano Pascual/Suarez (10) 7-5 5-7 7-5
Horn/Montalvo (16) 6-1 6-4
McQuillan/McShea 6-4 6-2
Canepa/Casoni 6-1 4-6 7-5
Rubin/Testud (7) 6-4 6-2
C. Martinez/Tarabini (8) 6-4 4-6 6-4
Poutchek/Rampre 6-2 6-1
Serna/Shaughnessy 5-7 6-4 6-1
Ccertois/Sanchez-Vicario (9) 6-3 7-5
Farina/Habsudova 6-2 6-3
Capiati/Dokic 6-2 6-7(2) 6-4
Foretz/Razzano (W) 3-6 6-1 6-3
Hingis/Pierce (3) 6-1 6-3
Fusai/Tauziat (6) 6-1 6-0
Bes/Riera 7-5 1-6 6-4
De Swardt/Navratilova (W) 5-7 6-1 6-3
Krizan/Srebotnik (12) 6-1 6-0
Huber/Schett (15) 6-1 6-1
Callens/Van Roost 6-1 6-1
Husarova/Zavagli 0-6 6-3 8-6
Raymond/Stubbs (2) 6-2 6-1

THIRD ROUND

Cocheteux/Dechy (W) 6-4 6-3
Arendt/Bollegraf (11) 6-3 6-7(1) 10-8
Po/Sidot (13) 6-1 6-2
Halard-Decugis/Sugiyama (5) 6-1 6-1
Kournikova/Zvereva (4) 6-2 7-6(3)
Ruano Pascual/Suarez (10) 4-6 6-2 6-2
Horn/Montalvo (16) 6-3 6-2
Rubin/Testud (7) 7-6(5) 6-1
C. Martinez/Tarabini (8) 7-6(4) 4-6 6-3
Serna/Shaughnessy 6-3 6-2
Capiati/Dokic 6-3 4-6 6-2
Hingis/Pierce (3) 6-4 6-0
Fusai/Tauziat (6) 6-0 6-3
De Swardt/Navratilova (W) 7-6(2) 7-5
Huber/Schett (15) 7-5 6-4
Raymond/Stubbs (2) 6-3 6-0

QUARTER-FINALS

Cocheteux/Dechy (W) 6-1 6-4
Halard-Decugis/Sugiyama (5) 6-4 4-6 6-2
Ruano Pascual/Suarez (10) 6-3 6-4
Horn/Montalvo (16) 6-0 6-7(5) 6-4
C. Martinez/Tarabini (8) 2-6 6-2 6-4
Hingis/Pierce (3) 6-3 6-2
Fusai/Tauziat (6) 2-6 6-2 7-5
Huber/Schett (15) 6-1 6-4

SEMI-FINALS

Halard-Decugis/Sugiyama (5) 6-2 6-4
Ruano Pascual/Suarez (10) 7-6(7) 6-2
Hingis/Pierce (3) 6-1 1-0 Ab
Fusai/Tauziat (6) 6-4 6-3

FINAL

Ruano Pascual/Suarez (10) 6-4 6-2
Hingis/Pierce (3) 2-6 6-2 6-1

Bol~ type denotes seeded players. Numbers following player's name gives seeding order (Q) = Qualifier, (W) = Wild Card, (LL) = Lucky Loser, (A) = Alternate

Mixed Doubles

Winners: D. Adams (RSA)**/M. De Swardt** (RSA) (12) 6–3 3–6 6–3

Holders: Norval (RSA)/Srebotnik (SLO)

FIRST ROUND

1 **Woodbridge/Stubbs** (1)
2 bye
3 MacPherson/Habsudova
4 Bale/De Beer (A)
5 Landsberg/Kostanic
6 Hewitt/Clijsters (W)
7 bye
8 **Norval/Srebotnik** (9)
9 **Kratzmann/Oremans** (15)
10 bye
11 Haarhuis/Barclay
12 van Houdt/Van Roost
13 Riki/Husarova
14 Tramacchi/Selyutina
15 **Tarango/Likhovtseva** (5)
16 **De Jager/Sugiyama** (4)
17 bye
18 bye
19 O'Brien/Vis
20 Haygarth/Schlukebir
21 Arnold/Montalvo
22 Haggard/Callens
23 bye
24 Barnard/Steck (A)
25 **Johnson/Po** (11)
26 bye
27 Florent/McQuillan
28 Huet/Dechy (W)
29 Nyborg/Arendt
30 Waite/Tatarkova
31 bye
32 **Delaitre/Tauziat** (8)
33 **E. Ferreira/Krizan** (7)
34 bye
35 Bergh/Shaughnessy
36 Bowen/Hiraki
37 Eagle/Molik
38 Clement/Sidot (W)
39 bye
40 **Woodforde/Boogert** (10)
41 **Carbonell/Ruano Pascual** (16)
42 bye
43 Boutter/Loit (W)
44 Galbraith/Black
45 B. Bryan/Cristea
46 Garcia/Leyaseelar
47 bye
48 **Stolle/Zvereva** (3)
49 **Leach/Bollegraf** (6)
50 bye
51 Aspelin/De Villiers
52 Llodra/Halard-Decugis
53 Humphries/Dokic
54 Kitinov/Kschwendt
55 bye
56 **Kulti/Carlsson** (13)
57 **Adams/De Swardt** (12)
58 bye
59 Siemerink/Navratilova (W)
60 Suk/Nejedly
61 Ollhovskiy/Horn
62 Hill/Miyagi
63 bye
64 **Paes/Raymond** (2)

SECOND ROUND

Woodbridge/Stubbs (1)
MacPherson/Habsudova 6–3 6–1
Hewitt/Clijsters (W) 1–6 6–4 6–4
Norval/Srebotnik (9)
Kratzmann/Oremans (15)
Haarhuis/Barclay 7–6(5) 6–3
Riki/Husarova 3–6 6–1
Tarango/Likhovtseva (5) 7–5 7–5
De Jager/Sugiyama (4)
Haygarth/Schlukebir 4–6 7–6(5) 6–3
Haggard/Callens 6–4 6–2
Barnard/Steck (A)
Johnson/Po (11)
Florent/McQuillan 6–3 3–6 6–2
Waite/Tatarkova 3–6 6–1 6–3
Delaitre/Tauziat (8)
E. Ferreira/Krizan (7)
Bergh/Shaughnessy 0–0 Ab
Clement/Sidot (W) 6–3 3–6 8–6
Woodforde/Boogert (10)
Carbonell/Ruano Pascual (16)
Galbraith/Black 6–3 6–4
B. Bryan/Cristea 6–3 6–1
Stolle/Zvereva (3)
Leach/Bollegraf (6)
Aspelin/De Villiers 6–2 7–5
Humphries/Dokic 6–4 6–4
Kulti/Carlsson (13)
Adams/De Swardt (12)
Siemerink/Navratilova (W) 7–6(3) 6–3
Hill/Miyagi 6–3 1–6 6–1
Paes/Raymond (2)

THIRD ROUND

Woodbridge/Stubbs (1) 6–1 2–6 6–4
Hewitt/Clijsters (W) 3–6 6–2 6–4
Haarhuis/Barclay 6–1 6–1
Tarango/Likhovtseva (5) 6–1 7–5
De Jager/Sugiyama (4) 6–4 6–2
Haggard/Callens 4–6 6–3 6–4
Johnson/Po (11) 6–3 2–6 6–4
Waite/Tatarkova 6–4 6–4
Bergh/Shaughnessy 6–3 6–4
Woodforde/Boogert (10) 6–4 7–5
Galbraith/Black 6–3 4–6 8–6
B. Bryan/Cristea 7–5 1–6 6–4
Aspelin/De Villiers 6–4 6–4
Kulti/Carlsson (13) 6–4 6–3
Adams/De Swardt (12) 6–3 6–3
Paes/Raymond (2) 6–2 6–3

QUARTER-FINALS

Woodbridge/Stubbs (1) 6–3 6–2
Tarango/Likhovtseva (5) 6–4 6–2
De Jager/Sugiyama (4) 7–6(2) 6–4
Johnson/Po (11) 6–2 6–3
Woodforde/Boogert (10) 6–3 6–4
B. Bryan/Cristea 6–4 6–3
Aspelin/De Villiers 7–6(1) 7–6(4)
Adams/De Swardt (12) w/o

SEMI-FINALS

Woodbridge/Stubbs (1) 6–3 3–6 11–9
De Jager/Sugiyama (4) 7–5 4–6 7–5
Woodforde/Boogert (10) 6–2 6–4
Adams/De Swardt (12) 7–6(4) 3–6 6–2

FINAL

Woodbridge/Stubbs (1) 6–2 6–4
Adams/De Swardt (12) 6–3 4–6 6–2

Bold type denotes seeded players. Numbers following player's name gives seeding order (Q) = Qualifier, (W) = Wild Card, (LL) = Lucky Loser, (A) = Alternate

men's or women's singles. With Agassi a shadow of the man who had won at Melbourne Park in January, it was left to Michael Chang, a 17-year-old champion at Roland Garros in 1989, to ensure that the U.S. had at least one representative in the third round which he did by beating Thomas Johansson in a tough four-setter. But Kuerten put an end to that journey down memory lane and the Americans were gone. Hopefully, they will find some new players soon.

David Adams and Martina Navratilova's new women's double partner, Mariaan de Swardt, chalked up their second Grand Slam title by winning the mixed over Rennae Stubbs and Todd Woodbridge. But it was Woodbridge and Mark Woodforde who revised the record books by finally nailing the men's doubles. When they beat Paul Haarhuis and his new partner Sandon Stolle 7–6 6–4 in the final this was a record breaking 58th title for the famous Woodies. 'To have broken the record by winning the one Slam that had always eluded us was just perfect,' said Woodbridge.

In the women's doubles, Navratilova, making a nostalgic return for the first time in six years at the age of 43, and de Swardt survived until losing to Alexandra Fusai and Tauziat in the third round. The French pair then went down to the eventual champions Hingis and Pierce, who beat Paola Suarez and Virginia Ruano Pascual 6–2 6–4 in the final. For the new singles champion, this crowned a fortnight that exceeded her wildest dreams.

JUNIOR EVENTS

BOYS' SINGLES – Final: Paul Henri Mathieu (FRA) d. Tommy Robredo (ESP) 3–6 7–6 6–2
GIRLS' SINGLES – Final: Virginie Razzano (FRA) d. Maria Emilia Salerni (ARG) 5–7 6–4 8–6
BOYS' DOUBLES – Final: Marc Lopez (ESP)/Tommy Robredo (ESP) d. Joachim Johansson (SWE)/Andy Roddick (USA) 7–6 6–0
GIRLS' DOUBLES – Final: Maria Jose Martinez (ESP)/Anabel Medina (ESP)d. Matea Mezak (CRO)/Dinara Safina (RUS) 6–0 6–1
LEGENDS OVER 50 – Final: Manuel Santana (ESP)/Stan Smith (USA) d. Ilie Nastase (ROM)/Tom Okker (NED) 6–3 3–6 14/12 (tie-break)
LEGENDS UNDER 50 – Final: Guy Forget (FRA)/Yannick Noah (FRA) d. Mansour Bahrami (IRA)/John McEnroe (USA) 6–3 7–6(4)

FRENCH OPEN CHAMPIONSHIPS – PRIZE MONEY – 69,163,200FF

MEN – Total: 32,748,400FF
MEN'S SINGLES – Winner 4,240,000. Runner-up 2,120,000. Semi-finalists 1,060,000. Quarter-finalists 560,000. Fourth-round losers 300,000. Third-round losers 173,500. Second-round losers 105,000. First-round losers 63,000. **Total: 23,288,000FF**

MEN'S DOUBLES (per team) – Winners 1,740,000. Runners-up 870,000. Semi-finalists 435,000. Quarter-finalists 221,500. Third-round losers 126,000. Second-round losers 63,000. First-round losers 42,800. **Total: 7,751,600FF**

MEN'S QUALIFYING (each): 16 × Third-round losers 35,000. 32 × Second-round losers 17,500. 64 × First-round losers 9,200. **Total: 1,708,800FF**

WOMEN – Total: 28,808,800
WOMEN'S SINGLES – Winner 4,028,000. Runner-up 2,014,000. Semi-finalists 1,007,000. Quarter-finalists 532,000. Fourth-round losers 270,000. Third-round losers 156,150. Second-round losers 94,500. First-round losers 56,700. **Total: 21,495,200FF**

WOMEN'S DOUBLES (per team) – Winners 1,392,000. Runners-up 696,000. Semi-finalists 348,000. Quarter-finalists 177,200. Third-round losers 94,500. Second-round losers 47,250. First-round losers 32,100. **Total: 6,032,000FF**

WOMEN'S QUALIFYING (each): 12 × Third-round losers 35,000. 24 × Second-round losers 17,500. 48 × First-round losers 9,200. **Total: 1,281,600FF**

MIXED DOUBLES (per team) – Winners 380,000. Runners-up 228,000. Semi-finalists 137,000. Quarter-finalists 83,500. Second-round losers 45,000. First-round losers 20,000. **Total 1,896,000FF**

TROPHY OF THE LEGENDS, Two events: 4 teams over 50, 6 teams under 50 (per team)
Over 50: Winners 150,000. Runners-up 120,000. Third 100,000. Fourth 80,000. **Total: 450,000FF**
Under 50: Winners 150,000. Runners-up 120,000. Third 2 × 100,000. Fourth 2 × 80,000. **Total: 630,000FF**

PER DIEM allowances (estimated total) 4,630,000.

In beating both Martina Hingis and defending champion Lindsay Davenport at Wimbledon to win her first Grand Slam title, Venus Williams revealed qualities of resilience and athleticism that set her above her peers. (Stephen Wake)

The Championships – Wimbledon

John Roberts

The slim, smartly-dressed, middle-aged man rose from his seat on the Centre Court, walked to the baseline, got down on his hands and knees and kissed the ground. Bjorn Borg's gesture was not scripted for the champions' parade at Wimbledon 2000, but the Swedish pilgrim could hardly have demonstrated greater fondness and respect for the arena he once owned for five years during the 1970s.

Here, about to be introduced to the spectators for the first time since 1981, was an icon from the early years of the post-amateur era. In those days, Borg's blond tresses flowed from a headband and he was mobbed like a popstar, although his personality was as reserved as his pinstriped tennis shirts as he tortured opponents with topspin while staying as calm as his rival John McEnroe was manic.

The great stage now belonged to another maestro, the 28-year-old American Pete Sampras, who was composing himself in the wings before continuing his progress to a seventh men's singles title in eight years and a 13th Grand Slam singles title in total, breaking the record he had previously shared with Australia's Roy Emerson.

The Millennium Championships would also see the coronation of Venus Williams as the women's singles champion. Venus, 20, the older of tennis' most amazing sisters, was then detained an extra day by the weather before partnering her sibling, Serena, 18, and adding the women's doubles trophy to the silverware at their home in Florida.

But of all the vivid images from the 114th Championships – stirring matches, refreshing personalities, magnificent achievements, and resident nimbus clouds with silver linings – none encapsulated the heritage of the tournament quite like the moment Borg paused to pay homage during the pageant on the middle Saturday.

With the impressive Millennium Building providing fresh amenities for the players and the media on the site of the former Court No 1, the ambience at the All England Club was primed for triumphs and tributes. Borg, aged 44, was one of 58 former singles winners and finalists and doubles champions on parade, men and women, none prouder than the wheelchair-bound Bunny Austin, Britain's last men's singles finalist (he lost to Don Budge in 1938), making what proved to be his final public appearance (Austin died on 26 August, his 94th birthday).

The gala atmosphere of the champions' parade contrasted with a sombre mood which pervaded the All England Club on the eve of the tournament. Two male Spanish players, Alex Corretja and Albert Costa, withdrew in protest after challenging the seedings for the world's premier grass-court championships, which were decided by a Club committtee, as is customary, and did not follow ATP Tour rankings earned over a 52-week period on various court surfaces.

Wimbledon's prerogative of seeding according to grass court proficiency was complicated by the ATP Tour's new rules, which made it mandatory for leading players to compete in the four Grand Slam Championships and the nine ATP Tour Masters Series tournaments. Many players considered seedings should only be obtained by rankings.

The seeding committee nevertheless promoted six players in the men's singles above their standing in the ATP Tour entry system: Pete Sampras, from No 3 to No 1; Tim Henman, from No 14 to No 8; Mark Philippoussis, from No 17 to No 10; Richard Krajicek, from No 25 to No 11; Pat Rafter, from No 27 to No 12; and Greg Rusedski, from No 21 to No 14.

Tim Phillips, the Wimbledon chairman, said: 'There are two philosophies here: One, that you go straight down the [ATP Tour] list; the other, that you take the list and maybe make some amendments to reflect grass court, historic performance, and one or two other considerations. We could have had a situation this year, going straight down the draw, with Agassi at the top, ranked No 1, and the next five players being Rafter, Krajicek, Philippoussis, Martin and Rusedski. In a grass court tournament, that would not be a happy outcome from the seeding process. We were unwilling to revise the seedings and the draw as requested, but both organisations have agreed to work together over the next 12 months to determine a seeding system that addresses player prowess on different types of surface.'

The women's singles was seeded in accordance with the WTA Tour rankings. Nine of the 16 perished in the first two rounds, the most prominent being Mary Pierce, No 3, the new French Open champion, who was defeated in the second round by Magui Serna, of Spain, 7–6 7–6. Six seeds were eliminated in the first round, the most since 16 elite places were introduced to the women's draw in 1978. Although Martina Hingis, the 1997 champion and world No 1, was projected to meet Lindsay Davenport, the defending champion, in the final, the draw indicated a strong possibility that Hingis would be ambushed by one or other of the Williams sisters, Venus (No 5), or Serena (No 8).

Such is the strength in depth in the men's game that the slightest dip in form or fitness tends to be punished, grass or no grass. After two rounds, Sampras and Sweden's Thomas Enqvist were the only seeds remaining in the top half of the draw, and Enqvist, No 9, disappeared in the fourth round, beaten in four sets by the American Jan-Michael Gambill. Sampras, who defeated Gambill in four sets in the quarter-finals, did not have to play a seeded opponent until he met Rafter in the final, but the Californian did have to contend with an injured left shin throughout the tournament.

Much had been expected of Lleyton Hewitt, particularly since the fiesty, 19-year-old Australian had defeated Sampras in straight sets in the final of the Stella Artois Championships at Queen's Club eight days before Wimbledon. But Hewitt, ranked seventh and seeded seventh, was outplayed by Gambill in the first round, 6–3 6–2 7–5.

For Vince Spadea, from Florida, the opening day of the Championships brought to an end a record run of 21 consecutive defeats stretching back to October 1999. Spadea overcame Rusedski 6–3 6–7 6–3 6–7 9–7 after nearly four hours, plus an hour and 50 minutes' delay for rain. Rusedski, who had lost the rhythm of his mighty serve after surgery to his right foot at Christmas, hit 15 double-faults (six in one game) and converted only two of 19 break points. The British No 2 saved four match points and served for the match at 7–6 in the fifth set, but Spadea prevailed and spread his arms wide in relief. 'I just wait for the big occasions,' he joked.

Nicolas Lapentti, of Ecuador, the 16th seed, was eliminated from Sampras' section in the first round by the Czech Slava Dosedel, and three potential danger men fell in round two: Sweden's Magnus Norman, No 3, the French Open finalist, lost to Olivier Rochus, a 19-year-old Belgian qualifier, placed 179th in the ATP entry system and making his debut in the majors, 6–1 in the fifth set; Krajicek, the 1996 champion and the only player to have beaten Sampras at the All England Club in eight years, was defeated by South Africa's Wayne Ferreira in four sets; and the Frenchman Cedric Pioline, No 6, the runner-up to Sampras in 1997, lost to Vladimir Voltchkov, a qualifier from Belarus, 6–4 in the fifth set.

Voltchkov, No 237 in the entry system, went on to beat Younes El Aynaoui, of Morocco, in the third round, Ferreira in the fourth round and Byron Black, of Zimbabwe, in the quarter-finals. He thus became the first qualifier to reach the semi-finals since John McEnroe in 1977 and only the fourth qualifier in the open era to advance to the last four of a Grand Slam. None had progressed farther, and Voltchkov was not an exception. The Wimbledon boys' singles champion of 1996 found himself facing Sampras three days after his 22nd birthday. He took the title-holder to a tie-break in the opening set, but was defeated, 7–6 (4) 6–2 6–4.

Compared with the carnage in the top half of the men's draw, the bottom half was a haven for seeded players during the first week, although even here there were notable exceptions. Nicolas Kiefer, No 13, was the only casualty in the first round, defeated in four sets by fellow German, Tommy Haas, but the Russian challenge from Yevgeny Kafelnikov, No 5, and Marat Safin, No 15, was quelled in the second round, both losing in straight sets. Kafelnikov was defeated by Sweden's Thomas Johansson, Safin by the Czech Martin Damm.

Andre Agassi, the second seed, recovered from 2–5 in the fifth set against his fellow American Todd Martin, saving two match points when serving in the ninth game before prevailing, 10–8, and advancing to the third round. The match was completed on Friday afternoon, having been suspended overnight because of rain with Agassi leading by two sets to one but a break down after the opening game of the third set.

If Voltchkov provided the tournament's element of surprise, events were also enlivened by Alexander Popp, a 23-year-old German whose adventures appealed to the British press almost as much as his own media on account of his mother having been born in Wolverhampton. Popp, who stood at No 114 in the entry system and 6ft 7in in his socks, outlasted the unseeded Michael Chang in the second round, 8–6 in the fifth set, as a prelude to defeating Brazil's Gustavo Kuerten, the fourth seed and French Open champion 7–6 6–2 6–1 in round three.

Popp then had the unusual experience of beating somebody his own size, taking down Switzerland's Marc Rosset, 6–1 in the fifth set, a victory which led to a meeting with Rafter in the quarter-finals. The athletic Australian won in straight sets despite allowing his concentration to waver. Broken to love when serving for the match at 5–4 in the third set, he conceded only one point when the set went to a tie-break.

Philippoussis did his utmost to join his compatriot Rafter in the semi-finals. The 23-year-old from Melbourne needed five hours to defeat the Dutchman Sjeng Schalken in the third round, 20–18 in the fifth set of what proved to be the longest Wimbledon singles match ever completed in a day. Their labours were relieved by a few free points here and there – 74 aces in total, 44 of them from Philippoussis, who served to stay in the match 14 times.

After a day's rest, Philippoussis played Henman, the British No 1, for a place in the quarter-finals, a fascinating duel which ended with Philippoussis winning 6–4 in the fifth set, to advance to the last eight for the third year in a row. Henman, beaten by Sampras in the previous two semi-finals, made his earliest departure for five years. In the quarter-finals, Philippoussis served 22 aces, but Agassi's return of serve and court-craft proved decisive, the American winning, 7–6 (4) 6–3 6–4.

The charge of the unseeded in the women's singles led to an encouraging campaign by some and disappointment for others. Anna Kournikova beat Sandrine Testud, the 10th seed, on day one, then lost in the second round to the unseeded Anne-Gaelle Sidot; the first round win of Belgium's Kim Clijsters over Nathalie Tauziat, the seventh seed, was followed by defeat at the hands of Russia's Anastasia Myskina.

Serna capitalised on her win against Pierce by advancing to the quarter-finals, at which stage the left-hander from Barcelona was defeated in straight sets by the unseeded 17-year-old Australian Jelena Dokic, who progressed a step farther than in 1999, when she had eliminated Hingis in the first round. Not for the first time, Dokic was embarrassed by the unruly behaviour of her father/coach, Damir, who was escorted from the premises on the first Thursday, after delivering a political tirade and smashing a journalist's mobile phone, and warned that any future misdemeanours would lead to his being banned from the grounds.

Dokic Jnr's next trial was on the court, when she played Davenport, her first seeded opponent, in the semi-finals. The American No 2 seed, who was carrying a back injury, had recovered from being a set down against Russia's Elena Likhovtseva in the second round and also against Monica Seles, the sixth seed, in the quarter-finals, but Dokic was demoralised the moment Davenport loomed large on the other side of net. 'I think she intimidated me,' the Australian said. Although the pair exchanged nine breaks of serve, Davenport's greater power took her to the final, 6–4 6–2.

Venus Williams and Hingis produced a memorable contest in the quarter-finals which had the crowd marvelling at Hingis's skilful match play and wincing at the ferocity of Williams' shots. Hingis fought back after losing the first two games of the opening set, but crumbled under a welter of Williams returns to be broken for 3–5. Williams served the set out with an ace.

Hingis over-hit a crosscourt forehand on break point in the fourth game of the second set, and lost her own serve in the next game. Hingis responded by breaking back for 3–3. Three more breaks of serve decided the set: Hingis for 5–3 (after Williams tumbled at the back of the court), Williams for 5–4, and Hingis for 6–4, courtesy of one of the wilder of her opponent's drive volleys. There were five consecutive breaks in the final set before Williams held for 4–2. Hingis was unable to create another opportunity, Williams completing a 6–3 4–6 6–4 victory after two hours and 13 minutes with an ace on match point.

An air of unreality settled over the Williams family's semi-final, in which Venus defeated Serena, 6–2 7–6. Sisters had not caused such a stir at Wimbledon since Maud and Lilian Watson, the daughters of the vicar of Berkswell, Warwickshire, contested the inaugural women's final in 1884, won by Maud, the younger sibling.

Venus won the first set after 32 minutes, by three breaks to one, but Serena led 3–1 and 4–2 in the second set, only to be drawn into a tie-break after failing to convert any of three break points and then losing 11 points in a row. Serena also led in the tie-break, 3–1, but lost the last six points, finishing the match in tears after double-faulting on match point.

Davenport's prospects in the final were handicapped by a thigh injury related to her long-term back problem, whereas Williams, the victor, 6–3 7–6, had played herself into peak condition after arriving at the tournament with only 12 matches behind her after recovering from tendinitis in both wrists. Neither player served well (Davenport was broken six times, Williams five), and Davenport's frustration at losing the first set increased when she failed to capitalise on leads of 2–0 and 3–1 in the second set. Williams prolonged the contest by double-faulting twice when serving for the match at 5–4, but served the steadier in the tie-break, which she won, 7–3.

Williams, the first African-American to win the women's singles title since the pioneering Althea Gibson on 1957 and 1958, danced with delight and her father, Richard, performed a jig on the roof of the NBC commentary box, alarming its occupant, Chris Evert.

The match of the tournament was the men's singles semi-final in which Rafter, playing his first seeded opponent, defeated Agassi, 7–5 4–6 7–5 4–6 6–3. Rafter, beaten in straight sets by Agassi in the previous year's semi-finals, won this time with grace, guile and a grass-court finesse which had often eluded him in the past. Spectators were enthralled by the audacity of the shot-making of both players – finely angled volleys and half-volleys, and ground shots both pacey and feather-light, touches of masters at work – with Rafter largely dictating when Agassi would be drawn towards the net and passed.

Rafter, making his first appearance in the final, came close to taking a two sets to love lead before Sampras defied both the Australian and gathering darkness to win, 6–7 7–6 6–4 6–2, after two hours and 58 minutes. The match, which did not end until 8.57pm because of rain delays, began to turn in Sampras' favour after Rafter, who won the first set tie-break, 12–10,

On the middle Saturday 58 former singles and doubles champions paraded on the Centre Court to receive individually engraved Waterford Crystal commemorative plates from HRH The Duchess of Gloucester, GCVO, Honorary President of the LTA. (AELTC)

thanks to two double-faults by the American, who had held a set point, was unable to consolidate a 4–1 lead in the second set tie-break. Rafter double-faulted at 4–2 and Sampras went on to win the shoot-out, 7–5, on his second set point.

Sampras converted only three out of 14 break points – for 3–2 in the third set and for 3–2 and 5–2 in the fourth – and was relieved that Rafter failed to make his two opportunities count. Sampras served out to love, hitting an unreturnable serve on his first match point. 'It's just amazing how it all worked out,' he said. Tears in his eyes, Sampras hugged his parents, Sam and Georgia, who were paying their first visit to Wimbledon.

The BBC's peak viewing figure for the final was 12.5 million, nearly four and a half million more than the number who watched Sampras win against Agassi the previous year. The women's singles final attracted 7.5 million viewers, the highest audience of the past five years for a women's final.

Mark Woodforde and Todd Woodbridge won their sixth Wimbledon men's doubles title. The Australian No 1 seeds defeated the No 2 seeds, Paul Haarhuis, of the Netherlands, and Australia's Sandon Stolle, 6–3 6–4 6–1. The mixed doubles was won by the American No 8 seeds, Donald Johnson and Kimberly Po, who beat the unseeded Hewitt and Belgium's Kim Clijsters, 6–3 7–6.

A crowd of 8,729 saw the Williams sisters, seeded No 8, beat the fourth seeds, Julie Halard-Decugis, of France, and Ai Sugiyama, of Japan, in the women's doubles final on the third Monday, bringing the total attendance for the 14 days to 455,322, which was up 18,791 on the previous 14-day record of 436,531 in 1997. A wonderful Wimbledon 'for sure,' as Borg would say.

Men's Singles

Holder: P. Sampras (USA)

Winner: **P. Sampras** (USA) (1)

FIRST ROUND	SECOND ROUND	THIRD ROUND	FOURTH ROUND	QUARTER-FINALS	SEMI-FINALS	FINAL
1 **P. Sampras** (USA) (1)	**Sampras** (1) 6–4 6–4 6–2	**Sampras** (1) 7–6(9) 3–6 6–3 6–4	**Sampras** (1) 2–6 6–4 6–2 6–2	**Sampras** (1) 6–3 6–2 7–5		
2 J. Vanek (CZE)						
3 K. Kucera (SVK)	Kucera 6–2 6–2 6–4					
4 W. Black (ZIM) (LL)						
5 K. Alami (MAR)	Llodra (Q) 6–3 6–3 6–1					
6 M. Llodra (FRA) (Q)						
7 J. Gimelstob (USA)	Gimelstob 6–3 6–4 6–7(5) 6–3	Gimelstob 7–6(3) 6–3 6–4				
8 B. Cowan (GBR) (W)						
9 W. Eschauer (AUT) (LL)	A. Martin 6–4 6–4 3–6 6–2					
10 A. Martin (ESP)						
11 F. Vicente (ESP)	Godwin (Q) 6–7(6) 6–1 3–6 6–2 8–6	Godwin (Q) 7–5 6–4 6–3	Bjorkman 6–3 6–4 6–4			
12 N. Godwin (RSA) (Q)						
13 A. Medvedev (UKR)	Bjorkman 6–4 6–3 6–3					
14 J. Bjorkman (SWE)						
15 S. Dosedel (CZE)	Dosedel 6–3 6–2 0–6 6–1	Bjorkman 6–4 6–3 6–0				
16 **N. Lapentti** (ECU) (16)						
17 **T. Enqvist** (SWE) (9)	**Enqvist** (9) 6–1 6–4 6–2	**Enqvist** (9) 7–6(2) 7–6(6) 7–5	**Enqvist** (9) 6–3 6–7(4) 2–6 6–3 6–3	Gambill 7–6(5) 3–6 6–3 6–4		
18 M. Hantschk (GER)						
19 F. Clavet (ESP)	Clavet 6–3 6–3 6–3					
20 H. Gumy (ARG)						
21 J. Stoltenberg (AUS)	Levy (Q) 6–3 2–6 6–7(3) 6–4 6–4	Vinck (Q) 6–4 7–6(2) 7–5				
22 H. Levy (ISR) (Q)						
23 N. Massu (CHI)	Vinck (Q) 6–4 7–5 6(6) 3–6 6–3					
24 C. Vinck (GER) (Q)						
25 C. Boutter (FRA)	Goldstein 7–6(1) 6–3 6–4	Goldstein 3–6 6–2 5–7 6–2 12–10	Gambill 7–6(10) 6–2 6–2			
26 P. Goldstein (USA)						
27 J. Tarango (USA)	Tarango 7–6(5) 3–6 4–6 6–4					
28 S. Grosjean (FRA)						
29 A. Gaudenzi (ITA)	Santoro 6–3 6–2 6–2	Gambill 4–6 6–4 6–2 6–2				
30 F. Santoro (FRA)						
31 J-M. Gambill (USA)	Gambill 6–3 6–2 7–5					
32 **L. Hewitt** (AUS) (7)						
33 **M. Norman** (SWE) (3)	**Norman** (3) 6–4 6–2 0 ret	O. Rochus (Q) 6–4 2–6 6–4 6–7(4) 6–1	Pozzi 6–3 3–6 7–6(3) 6–2	B. Black 4–6 7–6(5) 6–2 6–4		
34 M. Woodforde (AUS) (W)						
35 R. Fromberg (AUS)	O. Rochus 6–3 6–3 6–7(4) 6–4					
36 O. Rochus (BEL) (Q)						
37 J. Novak (CZE)	Pozzi 6–3 6–4 3–6 6–1	Pozzi 7–6(6) 6–3 6–4				
38 G. Pozzi (ITA)						
39 A. O'Brien (USA) (Q)	O'Brien (Q) 5–7 6–1 7–5 7–6(4)					
40 I. Ljubicic (CRO)						
41 D. Hrbaty (SVK)	Hrbaty 6–4 2–7 5	B. Black 6–3 7–5 6–2				
42 M. Zabaleta (ARG)						
43 A. Ilie (AUS)	B. Black 6–3 5–7 7–6(4) 6–0					
44 B. Black (ZIM)						
45 A. Portas (ESP)	Portas 6–3 6–4 6–4	Portas 6–4 6–3 6–3	B. Black 6–2 6–0 6–4			
46 T. Zib (CZE)						
47 V. Spadea (USA)	Spadea 6–4 7–6(5) 6–3 6–7(8) 9–7					
48 **G. Rusedski** (GBR) (14)						
49 **R. Krajicek** (NED) (11)	**Krajicek** (11) 3–6 6–1 6–4 7–6(3)	W. Ferreira 5–7 6–3 6–3 6–7(3)	W. Ferreira 3–6 7–6(3) 7–5 6–3	Voltchkov (Q) 6–3 6–4 7–6(0)	Voltchkov (Q) 7–6(2) 7–6(2) 6–4	
50 M. Kohlmann (GER) (LL)						
51 W. Ferreira (RSA)	W. Ferreira 6–7(6) 6–3 7–6(5) 6–1					
52 W. Arthurs (AUS)						
53 A. Pavel (ROM)	Nestor 6–0 6–4 6–2	Pavel 7–6(6) 7–5 4–6 6–0				
54 A. Berasategui (ESP)						
55 D. Nestor (CAN)	Lee 4–6 7–6(3) 6–2 6–4					
56 M. MacLagan (GBR) (W)						
57 M. Lee (GBR) (W)	El Aynaoui 6–2 6–4 7–6(3)	El Aynaoui 6–7(7) 6–2 6–2 6–2	Voltchkov (Q) 7–6(4) 7–5 7–6(4)			
58 J-A. Marin (CRC)						
59 A. Martin (ESP)	Voltchkov (Q) 7–6(3) 6–3 6–4					
60 Y. El Aynaoui (MAR)						
61 V. Voltchkov (BLR) (Q)	Pioline (6) 7–6(4) 6–1 6–4 6–4	Voltchkov (Q) 6–3 6–3 2–6 3–6 6–4				
62 J. Chela (ARG)						
63 C. Ruud (NOR)						
64 **F. Pioline** (FRA) (6)						

Final: Sampras (1) 6–4 6–7(4) 6–4 6–4

6–7(10) 7–6(5) 6–4 6–2

Rafter (12)
7–5 4–6 7–5 4–6 6–3

Rafter (12)
6–3 6–2 7–6(1)

Agassi (2)
7–6(4) 6–3 6–4

Rafter (12)
6–3 6–4 6–7(4) 6–1

Popp
6–1 6–4 3–6 4–6 6–1

Philippoussis (10)
6–1 5–7 6–7(9) 6–3 6–4

Agassi (2)
6–4 6–3 6–3

Johansson
6–7(3)7–6(1) 6–4 5–7 6–3

Rafter (12)
6–2 7–6(2) 6–3

Rosset
6–4 3–6 6–3 3–6 9–7

Popp
7–6(6) 6–2 6–1

Henman (8)
6–3 6–3 6–3

Philippoussis (10)
4–6 6–3 6–7(7) 7–6(4)
20–18

Prinosil (Q)
7–6(2) 3–6 7–6(0) 6–4

Agassi (2)
6–4 6–3 6–3

Johansson
6–1 7–5(0) 6–4

Gustafsson
6–4 6–3 6–1

Schuttler
6–4 7–6(3) 7–6(5)

Rafter (12)
6–3 6–3 6–4

Haas
6–3 7–6(3) 6–3

Rosset
7–6(4) 7–5 6–3

Popp
7–6(5) 4–6 6–7(3) 6–3 8–6

Kuerten (4)
6–4 6–4 7–5

Henman (8)
6–4 6–4 6–4

Arazi
6–3 3–6 6–7(6) 6–4 9–7

Schalken
6–4 6–3 6–1

Philippoussis (10)
4–6 7–6(0) 6–3 6–0

Damm
7–5 7–6(4) 6–3

Prinosil (Q)
6–4 2–6 6–1 6–2

Golmard
7–6(4) 4–6 6–1 6–2

Agassi (2)
6–4 2–6 7–6(3) 2–6 10–8

Kafelnikov (5)
7–5 7–5 7–6(6)
Johansson
6–4 6–7(5) 6–3 6–2
Gustafsson
6–4 6–2 6–4
Mirnyi
6–2 4–0 ret
Schuttler
6–3 6–7(5) 6–3 6–2
Escude
4–6 6–4 1–6 2
Woodbridge (W)
Rafter (AUS) (12)
6–3 7–6(7) 6–1
Haas
5–5 7–6(4) 6–2 6–3
Vinciguerra
7–6(4) 6–1 6–7(7) 6–2
Rosset
7–5 6–3 7–6(4)
Parmar (W)
6–7(2) 6–3 4–6 6–2 6–3
Popp
6–7(5) 7–6(10) 6–2
Chang
6–2 6–3 6–2
Bower (Q)
Kuerten (4)
6–3 7–6(1) 4–6 7–6(1)
Kuerten (4)
6–4 6–7(5) 7–5 7–6(5)
Henman (8)
5–7 6–3 6–1 6–3
Clement
6–3 3–6 6–3 6–4
Arazi
6–2 6–4 6–0
Lareau (LL)
7–6(6) 6–2 1–6 6–2
Schalken
6–2 6–4 6–2
C. Rochus
4–6 7–6(7) 6–2 4–6 6–1
Philippoussis (10)
6–4 7–6(3) 5–7 6–4
Safin (15)
7–6(2) 6–3 6–4
Damm
6–1 6–4 6–1
Prinosil (Q)
2–6 6–1 6–2 6–4
Huet (Q)
6–7(5) 6–3 7–6(4) 6–1
Golmard
7–5 6–4 6–4
Koubek
3–3 ret
T. Martin
7–6(7) 7–6(1) 6–2
Agassi (2)
2–6 6–3 6–0 4–0 ret

65 Y. **Kafelnikov** (RUS) (5)
66 F. Federer (SUI)
67 E. Johansson (SWE)
68 M. Melgeni (BRA)
69 M. Gustafsson (SWE)
70 M. Kilderry (AUS) (Q)
71 M. Mirnyi (BLR)
72 J. Ulrich (CZE)
73 C. Moya (ESP)
74 F. Schuttler (GER)
75 H. Escude (FRA)
76 G. Canas (ARG)
77 J. Siemerink (NED)
78 A. Woodbridge (AUS) (W)
79 J. Delgado (GBR) (W)
80 P. **Rafter** (AUS) (12)
81 N. **Kiefer** (GER) (13)
82 T. Haas (GER)
83 A. Vinciguerra (SWE)
84 L. Tieleman (ITA)
85 M. Rosset (SUI)
86 E. Squillari (ARG)
87 A. Sa (BRA)
88 A. Parmar (GBR) (W)
89 A. Popp (GER)
90 M. Chang (USA)
91 J. Gaudio (ARG)
92 D. Sanguinetti (ITA)
93 J. Bower (RSA) (Q)
94 C. Woodruff (USA)
95 G. **Kuerten** (BRA) (4)
96 P. Srichaphan (THA)
97 T. **Henman** (GBR) (8)
98 G. Ivanisevic (CRO)
99 A. Clement (FRA)
100 H. Arazi (MAR)
101 L. Laudi (ITA) (Q)
102 M. Russell (USA) (Q)
103 S. Lareau (CAN) (LL)
104 S. Schalken (NED)
105 G. Basti (SUI)
106 C. Rochus (BEL)
107 M. Tillstrom (SWE)
108 N. Hipfl (AUT)
109 A. Di Pasquale (FRA)
110 J. Melzer (AUT) (Q)
111 M. **Philippoussis** (AUS) (10)
112 M. **Safin** (RUS) (15)
113 M. Bianco (ESP)
114 D. Petrovic (AUS) (Q)
115 M. Damm (CZE)
116 D. Prinosil (GER) (Q)
117 S. Sargsian (ARM)
118 M. Bhupathi (IND) (W)
119 S. Huet (FRA) (Q)
120 C. Saulnier (FRA) (LL)
121 J. Golmard (FRA)
122 A. Voinea (ROM)
123 S. Koubek (AUT)
124 F. Jonsson (SWE) (LL)
125 T. Martin (USA)
126 T. Dent (USA) (Q)
127 A. **Agassi** (USA) (2)

Bol: type denotes seeded players. Numbers following player's name gives seeding order (Q) = Qualifier, (W) = Wild Card, (LL) = Lucky Loser

Women's Singles

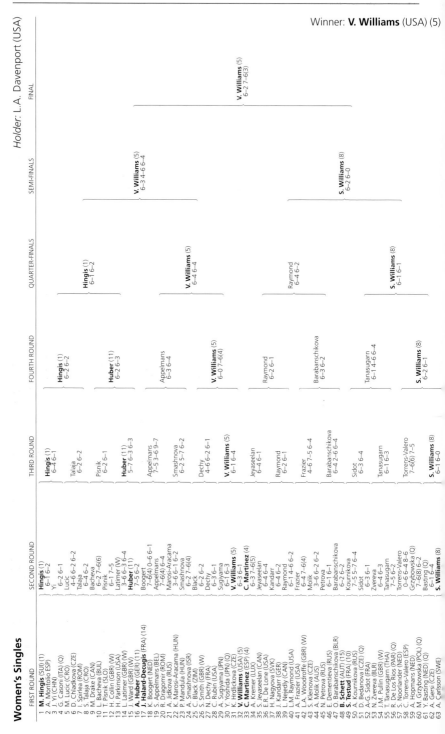

Winner: **V. Williams** (USA) (5)

Holder: L.A. Davenport (USA)

FIRST ROUND	SECOND ROUND	THIRD ROUND	FOURTH ROUND	QUARTER-FINALS	SEMI-FINALS	FINAL

FINAL: V. Williams (5) 6-2 7-6(3)

SEMI-FINALS:
- V. Williams (5) 6-3 4-6 6-4
- S. Williams (8) 6-2 6-0

QUARTER-FINALS:
- Hingis (1) 6-1 6-2
- V. Williams (5) 6-4 6-4
- Raymond 6-4 6-2
- S. Williams (8) 6-1 6-1

FOURTH ROUND:
- Hingis (1) 6-2 6-2
- Huber (11) 6-2 6-3
- Appelmans 6-3 6-4
- V. Williams (5) 6-0 7-6(4)
- Raymond 6-2 6-1
- Barabanschikova 6-3 6-2
- Tanasugarn 6-1 4-6 6-4
- S. Williams (8) 6-2 6-1

THIRD ROUND:
- Hingis (1) 6-4 6-1
- Talaja 6-2 6-2
- Pisnik 6-2 6-1
- Huber (11) 5-7 6-3 6-3
- Appelmans 7-5 3-6 9-7
- Smashnova 6-2 5-7 6-2
- Dechy 4-6 6-2 6-1
- V. Williams (5) 6-1 6-4
- Jeyaseelan 6-4 6-1
- Raymond 6-2 6-1
- Frazier 4-6 7-5 6-4
- Barabanschikova 6-4 2-6 6-4
- Sidot 6-3 6-4
- Tanasugarn 6-1 6-3
- Torrens-Valero 7-6(6) 7-5
- S. Williams (8) 6-1 6-0

SECOND ROUND:
- Hingis (1) 6-1 6-2
- Yi
- Lucic 4-6 6-2 6-2
- Talaja 6-4 6-2
- Bacheva 6-2 7-6(6)
- Pisnik
- Latimer (W) 6-1 7-5
- Huber (11) 3-6 6-3 6-4
- Boogert 7-6(4) 0-6 6-1
- Appelmans 7-6(4) 6-4
- Maros-Acaama 3-6 6-1 6-2
- Smashnova 6-2 7-6(4)
- Black 6-2 6-2
- Dechy 6-3 6-1
- Sugiyama 6-1 6-3
- V. Williams (5) 6-3 6-1
- C. Martinez (4) 6-3 7-6(5)
- Jeyaseelan 6-4 6-4
- Kandarr 6-4 6-2
- Raymond 6-1 4-6 6-2
- Frazier 6-4 7-6(4)
- Molik 6-2 6-2
- Petrova 6-1 6-1
- Barabanschikova 6-2 6-2
- Kournikova 7-5 5-7 6-4
- Sidot 6-3 6-1
- Zvereva 6-4 6-3
- Tanasugarn 7-5 6-2
- Torrens-Valero 0-6 6-4 8-6
- Grzybowska (Q) 7-6(8) 6-2
- Basting (Q) 6-1 6-4
- S. Williams (8)

FIRST ROUND:
1. M. Hingis (SUI) (1)
2. A. Montolio ESP
3. J. Yi (CHN)
4. G. Casoni (ITA) (Q)
5. M. Lucic (CRO)
6. D. Chladkova (CZE)
7. I. Spirlea (ROM)
8. S. Talaja (CRO)
9. M. Drake (CAN)
10. M. Bacheva (BUL)
11. T. Pisnik (SLO)
12. H. Collin (GBR) (W)
13. H. Parkinson (USA)
14. L. Latimer (GBR) (W)
15. J. Ward (GBR) (W)
16. **A. Huber** (GER) (11)
17. **J. Halard-Decugis** (FRA) (14)
18. K. Boogert (NED)
19. S. Appelmans (BEL)
20. R. Dragomir (ROM)
21. A. Jidkova (RUS)
22. K. Maros-Acaama (HUN)
23. P. Mandula (HUN)
24. A. Smashnova (ISR)
25. C. Black (ZIM)
26. S. Smith (GBR) (W)
27. N. Dechy (FRA)
28. C. Rubin (USA)
29. A. Sugiyama (JPN)
30. Y. Yoshida (JPN) (Q)
31. K. Hrdlickova (CZE)
32. **V. Williams** (USA) (5)
33. **C. Martinez** (ESP) (4)
34. A. Kremer (LUX)
35. S. Jeyaseelan (CAN)
36. E.R. De Lone (USA)
37. H. Nagyova (SVK)
38. J. Kandarr (GER)
39. L. Nejedly (CAN)
40. L.M. Raymond (USA)
41. A. Frazier (USA)
42. L.A. Woodroffe (GBR) (W)
43. S. Kleinova (CZE)
44. A. Molik (AUS)
45. N. Petrova (RUS)
46. E. Dementieva (RUS)
47. O. Barabanschikova (BLR)
48. **B. Schett** (AUT) (15)
49. **S. Testud** (FRA) (10)
50. A. Kournikova (RUS)
51. D. Bedanova (CZE) (Q)
52. A-G. Sidot (FRA)
53. N. Zvereva (BLR)
54. J.M. Pullin (GBR) (W)
55. T. Tanasugarn (THA)
56. G. De Los Rios (PAR) (Q)
57. B. Nacordane (NED)
58. C. Torrens-Valero (ESP)
59. A. Hopmans (NED)
60. M. Grzybowska (POL) (Q)
61. Y. Basting (NED) (Q)
62. A. Gersi (CZE)
63. A. Carlsson (SWE)

6–3 7–6(3)

Draw (second half)

Players (lower half of draw)

65	N. **Tauziat** (FRA) (7)
66	K. Clijsters (BEL)
67	L. Courtois (BEL)
68	A. Myskina (RUS)
69	J. Kruger (RSA)
70	K. Brandi (USA)
71	N. Ostrovskaya (BLR)
72	F. Labat (ARG)
73	M. de Swardt (RSA)
74	B. Rippner (USA) (Q)
75	S. Asagoe (JPN) (Q)
76	T. Snyder (USA)
77	J. Dokic (AUS)
78	G. Arn (GER) (Q)
79	S. Leon Garcia (ESP)
80	A. **Mauresmo** (FRA) (13)
81	A.. **Coetzer** (RSA) (12)
82	Iv. Washington (USA) (Q)
83	L. Osterloh (USA)
84	S. Farina (ITA)
85	R. Kuti Kis (HUN)
86	A. Stevenson (USA)
87	P. Wartusch (AUT)
88	K. Srebotnik (SLO)
89	A. Cocheteux (FRA)
90	M. Maleeva (BUL)
91	L. Krasnoroutskaya (RUS) (Q)
92	M. Oremans (NED)
93	M. Serna (ESP)
94	K. Cross (GBR) (W)
95	N. Pratt (AUS)
96	M. **Pierce** (FRA) (3)
97	M. **Seles** (USA) (6)
98	K. Habsudova (SVK)
99	E.S.H. Callens (BEL)
100	M.A. Vento (VEN)
101	E. Rittner (GER)
102	C. Cristea (ROM)
103	T. Panova (RUS)
104	S. Pitkowski (FRA)
105	J. Kostanic (CRO)
106	K. Nacuk (YUG)
107	B. Schwartz (AUT)
108	L.A. Ahl (GBR) (W)
109	B. Grande (ITA)
110	W. Schnell (AUT) (Q)
111	J. Henin (BEL)
112	A. **Sanchez-Vicario** (ESP) (9)
113	J. **Van Roost** (BEL) (16)
114	J. Capriati (USA)
115	M. Shaughnessy (USA)
116	V.A. Sanchez Lorenzo (ESP)
117	S. Reeske (AUT)
118	J. Wengartner (GER)
119	Y. Basuki (INA)
120	M. Irvin (USA)
121	P. Suarez (ARG)
122	E. Gagliardi (SUI)
123	P. Schnyder (SUI)
124	T. Garbin (ITA)
125	E. Likhovtseva (RUS)
126	M. Vavrinec (SUI)
127	C. Morariu (USA)
128	L.A. **Davenport** (USA) (2)

First round

Clijsters 6–3 3–6 6–2
Myskina 6–4 5–7 6–2
Brandi 6–3 7–5
Labat 2–6 6–4
Rippner (Q) 6–2 6–3
Asagoe (Q) 6–2 1–6 6–1
Dokic 6–1 7–6(7)
Leon Garcia 4–6 6–3 7–5
Coetzer (12) 6–4 6–2
Osterloh 6–3 5–7 6–3
Stevenson 7–5 7–6(3)
Wartusch 7–5 6–4
Maleeva 6–1 6–2
Oremans 6–7(5) 6–4 6–3
Serna 6–3 6–4
Pierce (3) 6–1 6–3
Seles (6)
Callens 3–6 6–2 7–5
Cristea 6–3 6–2
Pitkowski 7–5 2–6 9–7
Nacuk 6–3 7–6(4)
Ahl (W)
Grande 6–0 6–3
Sanchez-Vicario (9) 6–3 6–1
Capriati 6–2 6–4
Shaughnessy 7–5 6–2
Wengartner 6–4
Basuki 4–6 6–2 6–4
Suarez 6–4 6–3
Schnyder 6–3 6–2
Likhovtseva 3–6 6–3 6–1
Davenport (2) 6–3 1–0 ret

Second round

Myskina 6–4 6–2
Brandi 6–2 2–6 6–1
Rippner (Q) 6–1 6–2
Dokic 7–6(5) 6–1
Osterloh 7–6(0) 6–2
Wartusch 7–6(6) 6–3
Oremans 1–6 7–5 6–3
Serna 7–6(5) 7–6(4)
Seles (6) 6–4 6–4
Pitkowski 5–7 7–6(5) 6–2
Nacuk 6–4 6–3
Sanchez-Vicario (9) 6–3 6–1
Capriati 7–6(1) 6–2
Basuki 6–4 6–4
Suarez 6–7(5) 6–3 6–3
Davenport (2) 3–6 6–3 6–3

Third round

Brandi 4–6 6–3 6–1
Dokic 6–2 6–1
Osterloh 4–6 6–2 8–6
Serna 4–6 6–4 6–4
Seles (6) 6–0 6–3
Sanchez-Vicario (9) 3–6 7–6(5) 6–2
Capriati 7–6(4) 6–0
Davenport (2) 6–4 6–2

Fourth round

Dokic 6–1 6–3
Serna 7–6(1) 6–3
Seles (6) 6–3 6–4
Davenport (2) 6–3 6–3

Quarter-finals

Dokic 6–3 6–2
Davenport (2) 6–7(4) 6–4 6–0

Semi-final

Davenport (2) 6–4 6–2

Men's Doubles

Winners: **Woodbridge** (AUS)/**Woodforde** (AUS) (1) 6–3 6–4 6–1

Holders: Bhupathi (IND)/Paes (IND)

First Round

1 **Woodbridge/Woodforde (1)**
2 Gambill/Humphries
3 Delgado/Lee (W)
4 Shimada/Wakefield
5 Bertolini/Brandi
6 Cowan/Spencer (W)
7 Broad/Parmar (W)
8 **Eagle/Florent (15)**
9 **Lareau/Nestor (9)**
10 Barnard/Haggard
11 Pescosolido/Santopadre (Q)
12 Stafford/Tramacchi
13 Hilton/Nelson (W)
14 Pala/Vizner
15 Ellis/Rodriguez
16 **Novak/Rikl (8)**
17 **O'Brien/Palmer (3)**
18 Cibulec/Friedl
19 Davidson/Freelove (W)
20 Kildery/Martin
21 Behr/Wibauchi (Q)
22 Oncins/Suk
23 Hrbaty/Kuerten
24 **Johnson/Norval (13)**
25 **Kulti/Tillstrom (11)**
26 Macpherson/Tebbutt
27 Robichaud/Sell (Q)
28 Goellner/Siemerink
29 Llodra/Nargiso
30 Kitinov/Vemic
31 Arnold/Orsanic
32 **Bjorkman/B. Black (5)**
33 **Adams/De Jager (6)**
34 Aspelin/Landsberg
35 Marques/Vanhoudt
36 Koenig/Olhovskiy
37 Galbraith/MacPhie
38 B. Bryan/M. Bryan
39 Arthurs/Ellwood
40 **W. Black/Ullyett (12)**
41 **Gimelstob/Knowles (14)**
42 Mirnyi/Zimonjic
43 Bowen/Coupe
44 Godwin/Hill
45 Prieto/Ran
46 Rosset/Tarango
47 Albano/Lobo
48 **E. Ferreira/Leach (4)**
49 **Damm/W. Ferreira (7)**
50 Bale/Ondruska
51 Federer/Kratzmann
52 Bale/Kim (Q)
53 N colas/Puentes
54 Bergh/Nyborg
55 Hood/Prieto
56 **Bhupathi/Prinosil (10)**
57 **Cibonelli/Garcia (16)**
58 Delatre/Santoro
59 Lopez-Moron/Portas
60 Coetzee/Haygarth
61 Goldstein/Waite
62 Carrasco/Velasco
63 Stark/Taino
64 **Haarhuis/Stolle (2)**

Second Round

- **Woodbridge/Woodforde (1)** 6–2 6–3 6–2
- Shimada/Wakefield 6–3 6–1
- Bertolini/Brandi 6–4 6–3 7–5
- **Eagle/Florent (15)** 6–4 4–6 7–6(3) 3–6 6–3
- **Lareau/Nestor (9)** 4–6 3–6 4–3 6–6 1
- Pescosolido/Santopadre (Q) 6–7(2) 6–3 6–2
- Pala/Vizner 7–5 6–4 6–7(7) 7–6(4)
- **Novak/Rikl (8)** 4–6 4–6 3–3 6–9 9–7
- **O'Brien/Palmer (3)** 6–0 6–2 6–4
- Kildery/Martin 6–4 6–4 6–7(4) 7–5
- Oncins/Suk 1 6–4 4–6 4
- **Johnson/Norval (13)** 6–7(4) 7–6(4) 2–1 ret
- **Kulti/Tillstrom (11)** 7–5 6–3 6–1
- Goellner/Siemerink 7–6(4) 3–6 2–6 7–5 10–8
- Llodra/Nargiso 6–4 7–6(4) 6–3
- **Bjorkman/B. Black (5)** 6–4 7–6(4) 6–3
- **Adams/De Jager (6)** 7–6(5) 3–6 6–3 5–7 6–4
- Koenig/Olhovskiy 6–7(2) 7–6(7) 6–3 7–6(4)
- Galbraith/MacPhie
- B. Bryan/M. Bryan 6–4 7–6(4)
- Arthurs/Ellwood 5–7 6–3 7–5 6–3
- **Gimelstob/Knowles (14)** 6–3 6–2 6–4
- Prieto/Ran
- Rosset/Tarango 6–3 2–6 7–6(2) 4–6 6–3
- **E. Ferreira/Leach (4)** 4–6 7–6(5) 6–3
- **Damm/W. Ferreira (7)** 2–6 6–2 6–4
- Federer/Kratzmann 7–6(5) 6–2 3–6 6–4
- Bergh/Nyborg 6–3 7–6(5) 6–4
- **Bhupathi/Prinosil (10)**
- Delatre/Santoro 6–2 6–4 3–6 7–5
- Coetzee/Haygarth 6–3 6–1 6–7(2) 6–3
- Goldstein/Waite 6–4 4–5 7–6(5) 6–2
- **Haarhuis/Stolle (2)** 6–7(2) 7–6(7) 6–4 6–3

Third Round

- **Woodbridge/Woodforde (1)** 7–6(5) 7–6(3) 4–6 6–3
- Bertolini/Brandi 6–4 7–6(4) 3–6 6–3
- **Lareau/Nestor (9)** 6–1 6–4 6–7(2) 6–2
- **Novak/Rikl (8)** 6–1 6–2 6–4
- **O'Brien/Palmer (3)** 6–0 6–4 4–6 6–4
- Oncins/Suk 6–4 3–6 2–6 6–4 8–6
- **Kulti/Tillstrom (11)** 7–6(3) 7–6(2) 7–6(4)
- **Bjorkman/B. Black (5)** 7–6(6) 7–5 3–6 6–1
- **Adams/De Jager (6)** 7–6(7) 6–4 6–7(2) 6–4
- Arthurs/Ellwood 4–6 3–6 4–7–5(4)
- **Gimelstob/Knowles (14)** 7–5 6–3 6–4
- **E. Ferreira/Leach (4)** 4–6 6–3 6–1
- Federer/Kratzmann 7–6(5) 6–2 3–6 6–4
- **Bhupathi/Prinosil (10)** 6–4 7–6(6) 4–6 7–6(11)
- Delatre/Santoro 3–6 6–3 6–2 6–2
- **Haarhuis/Stolle (2)** 6–2 6–2 6–4

Quarter-Finals

- **Woodbridge/Woodforde (1)** 6–4 6–3 6–3
- **Lareau/Nestor (9)** 6–4 6–3 7–6(2)
- **O'Brien/Palmer (3)** 4–6 6–3 7–5 6–7(2) 7–5
- **Kulti/Tillstrom (11)** 7–6(3) 6–3 7–6(7).
- **Adams/De Jager (6)** 3–6 7–5 7–5 6–3
- **E. Ferreira/Leach (4)** 6–3 6–4 6–4
- Federer/Kratzmann 7–6(2) 6–4 6–4
- **Haarhuis/Stolle (2)** 6–3 7–6(3) 7–5

Semi-Finals

- **Woodbridge/Woodforde (1)** 6–3 6–7(4) 4–6 6–3 8–6
- **Kulti/Tillstrom (11)** 6–4 3–6 6–3 6–3
- **Adams/De Jager (6)** 6–7(5) 6–7(3) 7–6(4) 7–6(7) 8–6
- **Haarhuis/Stolle (2)** 6–7(5) 5–7 7–6(2) 6–2 6–2

Final

- **Woodbridge/Woodforde (1)** 6–4 7–6(2) 6–2
- **Haarhuis/Stolle (2)** 6–4 7–6(5) 6–7(4) 6–4

Women's Doubles

Winners: **S. Williams** (USA)/**V. Williams** (USA) (8) 6–3 6–2

Holders: Davenport (USA)/Morariu (USA)

FIRST ROUND	SECOND ROUND	THIRD ROUND	QUARTER-FINALS	SEMI-FINALS	FINAL
1 Raymond/Stubbs (1)	Raymond/Stubbs (1) 6-1 6-3	Raymond/Stubbs (1) 6-3 6-3	Raymond/Stubbs (1) 6-3 7-6(4)	Raymond/Stubbs (1) 7-6(5) 6-7(6) 6-4	
2 Applemans/Grande					
3 Cristea/Dragomir	Cristea/Dragomir 6-1 6-4				
4 Crook/Davies (Q)					
5 Barclay/Habsudova	Callens/Van Roost 6-2 6-3	Callens/Van Roost 6-4 6-1			
6 Callens/Van Roost					
7 Hopkins/Rampre (LL)	Arendt/Bollegraf (11) 6-4 6-2				
8 Arendt/Bollegraf (11)					
9 Courtois/Likhovtseva (15)	Boogert/Oremans 6-4 4-6 6-2	Boogert/Oremans 6-3 4-6 9-7	Boogert/Oremans 7-6(6) 4-6 6-2		
10 Boogert/Oremans					
11 Coetzer/McNeil	Coetzer/McNeil 6-2 6-3				
12 Heyaselan/Kostanic					
13 Irak/Noorlander	Hirak/Noorlander 6-2 6-2	Rubin/Testud (7) 6-1 7-5			
14 Ettmer/Smith (W)					
15 Duterloh/Webb	Rubin/Testud (7) 6-2 6-4				
16 Rubin/Testud (7)					
17 Halard-Decugis/Sugiyama (4)	Halard-Decugis/Sugiyama (4) 6-4 6-3	Halard-Decugis/Sugiyama (4) 6-2 6-2	Halard-Decugis/Sugiyama (4) 6-3 6-3	Halard-Decugis/Sugiyama (4) 6-4 6-2	Halard-Decugis/Sugiyama (4) 3-6 7-5 6-2
18 Kasnorutskaya/Neiland					
19 Canepa/Casoni	Clijsters/Pisnik 6-3 3-6 6-3				
20 Clijsters/Pisnik					
21 Capriati/Dokic	Capriati/Dokic 6-3 6-4	Capriati/Dokic 6-3 6-4			
22 Syzbowska/Yoshida					
23 Cosgrave/Stewart	C. Martinez/Tarabini (10) 6-3 7-5				
24 C. Martinez/Tarabini (10)					
25 Huber/Schett (14)	Huber/Schett (14) 6-3 7-5	Huber/Schett (14) 7-6(6) 6-0	Ruano Pascual/Suarez (6) 6-1 6-2		
26 McQuillan/McShea					
27 Fulin/Woodroffe (W)	Pullin/Woodroffe (W) 6-4 6-1				
28 Euth/Scott					
29 Tvartincova/Nacuk	Bachmann/Dyrberg 6-1 6-3	Ruano Pascual/Suarez (6) 7-5 2-6 6-2			
30 Bachmann/Dyrberg					
31 Star/Woehr	Ruano Pascual/Suarez (6) 6-4 6-2				
32 Ruano Pascual/Suarez (6)					
33 Kournikova/Zvereva (5)	Kournikova/Zvereva (5) 6-3 6-1	Kournikova/Zvereva (5) 6-3 6-3	Kournikova/Zvereva (5) 6-2 6-1	Kournikova/Zvereva (5) 6-4 6-4	
34 De Villiers/Steck					
35 Jolikovskaya/Wartusch	Hrdlickova/Rittner 6-2 7-5				
36 Hrdlickova/Rittner					
37 Frazier/Schlukebir	Frazier/Schlukebir 6-4 6-0	Frazier/Schlukebir 7-6(4) 7-6(10)			
38 Grant/Snyder					
39 Husarova/Zavagli	Fusai/Tauziat (9) 5-6 6-3				
40 Fusai/Tauziat (9)					
41 Krizan/Srebotnik (16)	Ellwood/Molik 6-3 6-3	Ellwood/Molik 4-6 6-4 6-4	Cocheteux/Dechy 6-4 6-3		
42 Ellwood/Molik					
43 Carlsson/Lott	Carlsson/Lott 7-6(4) 6-2				
44 Gagliardi/Schnyder					
45 Krawentcheva/Poutchek	Cocheteux/Dechy 7-5 6-1	Cocheteux/Dechy 6-4 6-3			
46 Cocheteux/Dechy					
47 Labat/Tanasugarn	Hingis/Pierce (3) 6-1 6-2				
48 Hingis/Pierce (3)					
49 S.Williams/V.Williams (8) (W)	S.Williams/V.Williams (8) (W) 6-3 6-2	S.Williams/V.Williams (8) (W) 6-2 6-3	S.Williams/V.Williams (8) (W) 6-3 6-2	S.Williams/V.Williams (8) (W) 4-6 6-2 6-1	S.Williams/V.Williams (8) (W) 6-3 7-6(4)
50 Black/Selyutina	De Beer/Miyagi 7-5 7-6(4)				
51 De Beer/Miljovic (LL)					
52 Farina/Wild	Farina/Wild 6-4 6-3				
53 De Lone/Pratt					
54 Arina/Wild	Spirlea/Vis (12) 2-6 7-5 6-1	Spirlea/Vis (12) 4-6 7-5 6-4			
55 Perzbin/Marosi-Aracama					
56 Spirlea/Vis (12)	Spirlea/Vis (12) 6-4 6-3				
57 Po/Sidot (13)	Po/Sidot (13) 6-2 6-1	De Swardt/Navratilova (W) 4-6 3-7 5	De Swardt/Navratilova (W) 6-1 6-1		
58 Deo/Riera					
59 De Swardt/Navratilova (W)	De Swardt/Navratilova (W) 7-6(4) 6-3				
60 Sachneva/Hopmans					
61 Sema/Shaughnessy	Mauresmo/Sanchez-Vicario 7-6(3) 6-7(7) 6-2	Mauresmo/Sanchez-Vicario 6-7(4) 6-3 6-3			
62 Mauresmo/Sanchez-Vicario					
63 Csapoe/Reeves (Q)	Horn/Montalvo (17) 6-1 4-6 6-4				
64 Horn/Montalvo (17)					

Bold type denotes seeded players. Numbers following player's name gives seeding order (Q) = Qualifier, (W) = Wild Card, (LL) = Lucky Loser

Mixed Doubles

Winners: **Johnson** (USA)/**Po** (USA) (8) 6–4 7–6(3)

Holders: Paes (IND)/Raymond (USA)

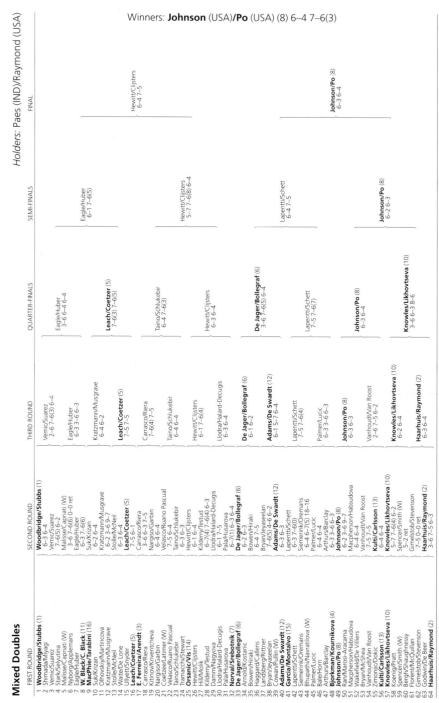

FIRST ROUND	SECOND ROUND	THIRD ROUND	QUARTER-FINALS	SEMI-FINALS	FINAL
1 **Woodbridge/Stubbs** (1)	**Woodbridge/Stubbs** (1) 6–3 6–4	Vemic/Suarez 2–6 7–6(3) 6–4	Eagle/Huber 3–6 6–4 6–4	Eagle/Huber 6–1 7–6(5)	Hewitt/Clijsters 6–4 7–5
2 Shimada/Miyagi	Vemic/Suarez 7–6(5) 6–2				
3 Vemic/Suarez					
4 Stark/Selyutina	Malisse/Capriati (W) 3–6 7–6(6) 0–0 ret	Eagle/Huber 6–3 3–6 6–3			
5 Malisse/Capriati (W)					
6 Nyborg/Appelmans					
7 Eagle/Huber	Eagle/Huber 7–6(7) 7–6				
8 W. Black/C. Black (11)					
9 **MacPhie/Tarabini** (16)	Suk/Krizan 6–2 6–4	Kratzmann/Musgrave 6–4 6–2	Leach/Coetzer (5) 7–6(3) 7–6(5)		
10 Suk/Krizan					
11 Olhovskiy/Martincova	Kratzmann/Musgrave 6–2 3–6 9–7				
12 Kratzmann/Musgrave					
13 Stolle/McNeil	Stolle/McNeil 6–3 6–4	Leach/Coetzer (5) 7–5 7–5			
14 Waite/De Lone					
15 Ullyett/Snyder	Leach/Coetzer (5) 7–5 6–1				
16 **Leach/Coetzer** (5)					
17 **E. Ferreira/Arendt** (3)	Carrasco/Riera 3–6 6–3 7–5	Carrasco/Riera 7–6(4) 7–5	Taino/Schlukebir 6–4 7–6(3)	Hewitt/Clijsters 5–7 7–6(8) 6–4	
18 Carrasco/Riera					
19 Kitinov/Kriventcheva	Nargiso/Garbin 6–4 6–4				
20 Nargiso/Garbin					
21 Coetzee/Latimer (W)	Velasco/Ruano Pascual 7–5 6–4	Taino/Schlukebir 6–4 6–4			
22 Velasco/Ruano Pascual					
23 Taino/Schlukebir	Taino/Schlukebir 6–3 6–3				
24 Tramacchi/Stewart					
25 **Orsanic/Vis** (14)	Hewitt/Clijsters 6–1 6–4	Hewitt/Clijsters 6–1 7–6(4)	Hewitt/Clijsters 6–3 6–4		
26 Hewitt/Clijsters					
27 Hill/Molik	Kilderry/Testud 6–7(4) 7–6(4) 6–3				
28 Kilderry/Testud					
29 Damm/Nagyova	Llodra/Halard-Decugis 6–1 7–5	Llodra/Halard-Decugis 6–3 6–4			
30 Llodra/Halard-Decugis					
31 Pala/Husarova	Pala/Husarova 6–7(1) 6–3 6–4				
32 **Norval/Srebotnik** (7)					
33 **De Jager/Bollegraf** (6)	De Jager/Bollegraf (6) 6–4 7–5	De Jager/Bollegraf (6) 6–1 6–2	De Jager/Bollegraf (6) 3–6 7–6(5) 6–4	Lapentti/Schett 6–4 7–5	Johnson/Po (8) 6–3 6–4
34 Arnold/Kostanic					
35 Bowen/Hiraki	Bowen/Hiraki 6–4 7–5				
36 Haggard/Callens					
37 Landsberg/Rittner	Bryan/Jeyaseelan 7–6(5) 4–6 6–2	Adams/De Swardt (12) 6–1 5–7 6–4			
38 Bryan/Jeyaseelan					
39 Cowan/Pullin (W)	Adams/De Swardt (12) 6–3 6–3				
40 **Adams/De Swardt** (12)					
41 **Garcia/Montalvo** (15)	Lapentti/Schett 6–3 7–6(0)	Lapentti/Schett 7–5 7–6(4)	Lapentti/Schett 7–5 7–6(7)		
42 Lapentti/Schett					
43 Siemerink/Oremans	Siemerink/Oremans 6–4 6–7(5) 18–16				
44 Bhupathi/Navratilova (W)					
45 Palmer/Lucic	Palmer/Lucic 6–4 6–4	Palmer/Lucic 6–3 3–6 6–3			
46 Bale/Horn					
47 Arthurs/Barclay	Arthurs/Barclay 6–3 3–6 6–3				
48 **Bjorkman/Kournikova** (4)					
49 **Johnson/Po** (8)	Johnson/Po (8) 6–3 6–9–7	Johnson/Po (8) 6–3 6–3	Johnson/Po (8) 6–3 6–4	Johnson/Po (8) 6–2 6–3	
50 Ran/Marosi-Aracama					
51 Macpherson/Habsudova	Macpherson/Habsudova 6–4 6–2				
52 Wekesa/De Villiers					
53 Bryan/McShea	Vanhoudt/Van Roost 7–5 7–5	Vanhoudt/Van Roost 2–6 7–5 6–2			
54 Vanhoudt/Van Roost					
55 Zimonjic/Dokic	Kulti/Carlsson (13) 6–4 6–4				
56 **Kulti/Carlsson** (13)					
57 **Knowles/Likhovtseva** (10)	Knowles/Likhovtseva (10) 5–7 7–6(4) 6–2	Knowles/Likhovtseva (10) 6–2 6–4	Knowles/Likhovtseva (10) 3–6 6–3 8–6		
58 Koenig/Pratt					
59 Spencer/Smith (W)	Spencer/Smith (W) 7–5 7(8) 2 ret				
60 Bergh/Shaughnessy					
61 Florent/McQuillan	Gimelstob/Stevenson 7–5 0–6 ret	Haarhuis/Raymond (2) 6–3 6–4			
62 Gimelstob/Stevenson					
63 Godwin/De Beer	Haarhuis/Raymond (2) 3–6 7–5 6–3				
64 **Haarhuis/Raymond** (2)					

Bold type denotes seeded players. Numbers following player's name gives seeding order (Q) = Qualifier, (W) = Wild Card, (LL) = Lucky Loser

JUNIOR EVENTS

BOYS' SINGLES – Final: Nicolas Mahut (FRA) (1) d. Mario Antic (CRO) (4) 3–6 6–3 7–5
GIRLS' SINGLES – Final: Maria Salerni (ARG) (4) d. Tatiana Perebiynis (UKR) (2) 6–4 7–5
BOYS' DOUBLES – Final: Dominique Coene (BEL) /Kristof Vliegen (BEL) (7) d. Andrew Banks (GBR)/Ben Riby (GBR) 6–3 1–6 6–3
GIRLS' DOUBLES – Final: Ioana Gaspar (ROM)/T Perebiynis (UKR) (2) d. Daja Bedanova (CZR) /M Salerni (ARG) (1) 7–6(3) 6–3

SENIOR EVENTS

35 AND OVER GENTLEMEN'S INVITATION DOUBLES (Round robin in 4 groups of 4 with knock-out semi-final and final) Final: Divided between Jeremy Bates (GBR)/Nick Fulwood (GBR) and Ken Flach (USA)/Robert Seguso (USA)
35 AND OVER LADIES' INVITATION DOUBLES (Round robin in 2 groups of 4 with knock-out final) – Final: Rosalyn Niedefer (RSA)/Yvonne Vermaak (RSA) d. Gretchen Magers (USA)/Virginia Wade (GBR) 6–4 6–2
45 AND OVER GENTLEMEN'S INVITATION DOUBLES (Knock-out for 16 prs.)
Final: Peter Fleming/Alexander Mayer(USA) d. Vijay Amritraj (IND)/Anand Amritraj (IND) 6–2 6–4

THE CHAMPIONSHIPS

TOTAL PRIZE MONEY – £8,056,480

MEN'S SINGLES – Winner £477,500. Runner-up £238,750. Semi-finalists £119,380. Quarter-finalists £62,080. Fourth-round losers £33,420. Third-round losers £19,330. Second-round losers £11,700. First-round losers £7,160.
Total: £2,612,610

WOMEN'S SINGLES – Winner £430,000. Runner-up £215,000. Semi-finalists £101,470. Quarter-finalists £52,760. Fourth-round losers £28,410. Third-round losers £15,460. Second-round losers £9,360. First-round losers £5,730.
Total: £2,199,860

MEN'S DOUBLES (per pair) – Winners £195,630. Runners-up £97,810. Semi-finalists £50,200. Quarter-finalists £26,060. Third-round losers £13,890. Second-round losers £7,540. First-round losers £4,420.
Total: £871,280

WOMEN'S DOUBLES (per pair) – Winners £176,070. Runners-up £88,030. Semi-finalists £42,670. Quarter-finalists £22,150. Third-round losers £11,800. Second-round losers £6,030. First-round losers £3,530.
Total: £741,880

MIXED DOUBLES (per pair) – Winners £83,100. Runners-up £41,540. Semi-finalists £20,770. Quarter-finalists £9,550. Third-round losers £4,780. Second-round losers £2,390. First-round losers £1.080.
Total: £315,420

35 AND OVER MEN'S INVITATION DOUBLES (per pair) – Winners £15,500. Runners-up £12,170. Semi-finalists £9,610. Second place in each group £7,720. Third place in each group £7,040. Fourth place in each group £6,360.
Total: £131,370

45 AND OVER MEN'S INVITATION DOUBLES (per pair) – Winners £12,170. Runners-up £9,610. Semi-finalists £7,720. Second-round losers £6,360. First-round losers £5,550.
Total: £107,060

35 AND OVER WOMEN'S INVITATION DOUBLES (per pair) – Winners £11,050. Runners-up £8,290. Second place in each group £6,360. Third place in each group £5,810. Fourth place in each group £4,960.
Total: £53,600

QUALIFYING – MEN (each): 16 × Third-round losers £4,550. 32 × Second-round losers £2,270. 64 × First-round losers £1,140.
Total £218,400

QUALIFYING – WOMEN (each): 12 × Third-round losers £3,640. 24 × Second-round losers £1,820. 48 × First-round losers £910.
Total: £131,040

PER DIEM allowances (estimated): Championship Events: £522,040. Invitation Doubles:£96,720. Qualifying Competition: £55,200.
Total: £673,960

With a breathtaking display of power and accuracy the 20-year-old Russian Marat Safin blasted his way to the US Open title with a straight sets win over Pete Sampras that was truly majestic. (Paul Zimmer)

US Open Championships

Bud Collins

Two points from defeat.

That was the precarious situation for both Millennial US Open champions, 20-year-olds Venus Williams and Marat Safin. As the loftiest couple to rule the United States (the youngest since John McEnroe, 20, and Tracy Austin, 16, in 1979) Safin, 6-feet-4, and Venus, 6-2, survived close calls such as faced by no other pair of champions in the tourney's annals.

Making more history, Venus was unique in keeping the title in her family, and Safin as the only Russian to conquer his country's former Cold War rival. She, extending a four-month winning streak to 26 matches, is the first American to seize both Wimbledon and the US Open in the same year since Martina Navratilova in 1987.

Never have there been siblings of the quality of the Sisters Sledgehammer: Venus and Serena Williams. When Serena, 18, was unable to keep the championship she won in 1999 (pummeled by Lindsay Davenport, 6–4 6–2 in the quarter-finals), big sister Venus stepped up as a worthy successor, outrunning and outgunning 1998 champ Davenport, 6–4 7–5, in the title bout.

But that was nowhere near as shocking as sixth seeded man-child Safin, the jocular Muscovite, handcuffing highly-favoured, four-time champ Pete Sampras in their final, 6–4 6–3 6–3. For 98 minutes the bulky-but-quick Safin did no wrong (merely 12 unforced errors), experiencing what Russians call a 'zvezdnyi chas,' a golden hour.

'Everybody knows how to beat Sampras. It's simple,' he had said whimsically. 'You just have to do everything better than he does.' Oh, sure. Yet that's exactly what Safin accomplished while 23,115 patrons stacked up in a concrete gulch at Flushing Meadows gawked unbelievingly and squawked 'Let's go, Pete!' – all to no avail.

Simple, as Safin suggests. Pete serves big; you return bigger. Pete crowds you at his place, the net; you pass him, 22 times. Also you serve even bigger and outduel him from the baseline. Your volleys, though less frequent, are more effective. Pete moves well; you make him seem a tortoise. Pete is slick; you are so fluid and relaxed he looks cramped. Very simple.

You have to go back a quarter-century to find a comparable throttling of a transcendant champion in the Open: Manolo Orantes baffling and dethroning Jimmy Connors by the same score in the 1975 final, the first of three played on the Har-Tru clay courts that replaced the grass at Forest Hills.

But Venus and Marat were within a couple of twitches of not making it to the finals at all. (Most recent closer calls were the weathering of match points by Sampras against Alex Corretja in the 1996 quarters, and Martina Navratilova against Steffi Graf in the 1986 semis.)

Her trial was the 4–6 6–3 7–5 semi-final over Martina Hingis, who had owned her at the Meadows: 1997 final and 1999 semi. At 3–5, 15–30 in the concluding set, Venus was wobbling so uncertainly that her father, Richard Williams, walked out. The next point was a furious exchange that Hingis should have ended with a smash. However, she failed to put it away – 'I didn't see the ball,' Martina lamented. 'I could have been at match point.' Venus converted the unimposing shot into a backhand winner.

Presto-change-o. That stroke sent the new champ into a shot-making frenzy, a reaping of 15 of the remaining 18 points.

Safin's crisis occurred at the nerve-jangling close of his rain-interrupted third round victory over Sebastian Grosjean, 6–4 7–6 (7–3) 1–6 3–6 7–6 (7–5), from a break down in the fifth. Chased for a second time by a downpour, with Safin ahead 5–4 in the decisive tie-breaker, they had to wait 1 hour 43 minutes to play the last 90 seconds. A Safin error made it 5–5. But he ripped a forehand for the mini-break, 6–5, and breathed again when Grosjean missed a forehand. After toiling for 14 sets in his first three starts, the Russian became unstoppable, losing but one set more, to Nicolas Kiefer in the quarters.

Drawing a record throng of 606,017, the tournament was excitingly disorderly in the male precinct. After the fourth round, none of the top three seeds remained, an unprecedented early purge of the upper class. Moreover, the 1997–98 champ, Patrick Rafter, who should have been seeded, was bounced by two points in the opening round by No.114 Galo Blanco, 7–6 (7–3) 2–6 6–3 1–6 7–6 (7–5).

Gustavo (Guga) Kuerten, the second seed, was gone first, dismembered at the starting gate by the left handed serving of No.102, Wayne Arthurs, 4–6 6–3 7–6 (7–4) 7–6 (7–1). Astoundingly next to vanish, in the second round, was the reigning champion, first seeded Andre Agassi, never able to get started against a swift and inspired No. 32 Arnaud Clement, 6–3 6–2 6–4.

Magnus Norman, third seeded, got through three rounds, the third a stirring fifth set tie-breaker escape from towering Max Mirnyi in which he slipped four match points, 3–6 4–6 7–6 (7–5) 6–4 7–6 (11–9). But 14th seed Kiefer nailed him, 6–2 6–7 (3–7) 6–1 6–3, in the fourth round, where fifth seed Yevgeny Kafelnikov also disappeared, ousted by Dominik Hrbaty, 6–4 7–6 (7–5) 6–1.

As he had 12 months earlier, gallant, greying Todd Martin (loser of the final in five sets to Agassi) snatched a seemingly hopeless match from the fire. In 1999 it was the quarter-final over Greg Rusedski from two sets down, a late-late show epic. This time, in the fourth round, it was later still and Todd, squelching 17 of 18 break points, was down deeper: a match point in the fourth set before subduing Carlos Moya, 6–7 (3–7) 6–7 (7–9) 6–1 7–6 (8–6) 6–2. It took 4 hours 17 minutes and endured until 1:22 the following morning.

Martin, who had beaten 10th Cedric Pioline 7–6 (7–5) 6–3 6–2 in the second round, pushed Safin hard in the semis, held a set point against the Russian's serve in the 12th game of the second but, like everyone else, couldn't hold him off and lost 6–3 7–6 (7–4) 7–6 (7–1).

Despite all the mishaps around him, fourth seeded Sampras no-problemed along into the quarters in 12 straight sets. A 7–6 (7–4) 6–2 6–4, win over the Kimchi Kid, a jovial, unknown Korean qualifier, No.182 Hyung-Taik Lee, sent Pete into rougher territory where, nonetheless, he had the look of a champion about to be crowned. His fluid mastery was underlined in a nerveless rush from ambush past his last Wimbledon superior, 1996 champ Richard Krajicek 4–6 7–6 (8–6) 6–4 6–2.

Who could imagine that Krajicek, holding four set points for a two set lead – two of them on his own serve at 6–3 and 6–4 in the breaker – would lose? Pete, that's who, reeling off six straight points from 2–6, five of them winners, during a bravura passage. A deep forehand return, then a lightning backhand passer took care of those two Krajicek serving points. Finally a forehand return knocked off the set, and turned the night starry for Nocturnal Pete. He's 15–0 under Flushing floodlights.

Losing his first set of the fortnight to another teenager, Swede Andreas Vinciguerra, the Boy Bomb, 19-year-old Aussie Lleyton Hewitt, racked the following 15. That took him to the semis and a fine fight against Sampras where he lost the last three, 7–6 (9–7) 6–4 7–6 (7–5). But not before dodging four set points in the first and holding two set points of his own in that tie-breaker. There, Safin took over.

Nevertheless, rambunctious kid Hewitt was elated by grabbing his first major title, the doubles, alongside the Belarus Mirnyi, the unseeded pair beating the fourth seeded South African-American coalition of Ellis Ferreira and Rick Leach 6–4 5–7 7–6 (7–5). They had knocked on Woodies in the second round, beating first seeded Mark Woodforde and Todd Woodbridge 6–1 4–6 7–6 (7–4). Lleyton is the youngest winner in more than a half-century, since 18-year-old American Bob Falkenburg in 1944 (with Don McNeill).

Willowy Russian 18-year-old Elena Dementieva, No. 25, was the lone outsider in the quarters, where she beat 10th seed, Anke Huber, 6–1 3–6 6–3. Huber was the beneficiary of French Open champ Mary Pierce's default (injured right shoulder) after one set in the fourth round.

Dementieva appeared ready to eclipse highly-hyped countrywoman Anna Kournikova, the 14th seed beaten by another promising kid, Belgian Justine Henin. Dementieva also eliminated seventh seed Conchita Martinez, 6–4 6–1. Lagging 2–5 in the second, she revived to shake up Davenport with two service breaks, brushing off four match points and forcing a tie-breaker before succumbing 6–2 7–6 (7–5).

A distinguished elder, 33-year-old Nathalie Tauziat, seeded eighth, joyfully lived up to it with her first triumph over ninth Arantxa Sanchez-Vicario in 12 tries over a stretch of 11 years, and then pushed Venus at the threshold of the final four, 6–4 1–6 6–1. As the last Frenchwoman standing, Nathalie also scored a moral victory over the shamefully ungrateful French Federation that refused her a deserved Olympic berth.

Nine years after, neither sixth seed Monica Seles, the 1991–92 champ, nor Jennifer Capriati could match the fireworks of their sensational three-set 1991 semi-final, Monica coming

A delighted Venus Williams after her win over Lindsay Davenport at Flushing Meadows that brought her a first US Open success – it was a repeat of the Wimbledon final. (Stephen Wake)

through comfortably to the quarters, 6–3 6–4. There she was set upon fiercely by Hingis – a 13 minute bagel – recovering somewhat though losing, 6–0 7–5.

Serena's last stand as champion came against the strong-minded Aussie, 17-year-old Jelena Dokic. She needed all her power (14 aces) to get through the 12th game and the tie-breaker, eluding two set points – the second a barely wide Dokic bid for a forehand winner – and ran eight games to win 7–6 (9–7) 6–0.

Little Sister had the speed, but Davenport had the footwork and anticipation to depose her. Lindsay, loser of her last five against Serena, kept her commuting from corner to corner with baseline blasts. Once Lindsay had manoeuvered through five deuces and three break points early, to 1–1, she began to take over. Holding to 4–4 she rattled a chain of seven consecutive games to 4–0 in the second.

Davenport continued dominantly against Big Sister, all the way to a 4–1 lead. Whereupon Venus seized five straight games to 1–0 in the second. She was stealing points with those endless, supercharged legs, not only making stunning gets, but caroming them back even harder and deeper, making Lindsay hit too many balls. Standing in daringly on the Davenport serve, she crowded Lindsay, forcing her to go for too much.

Davenport broke for 2–1 in the second, and had a point for 3–1. Venus's roaring backhand stymied that. Still, Lindsay was in it until the fifth game where she pinned Venus at 15–40 and a total of four break points in a tingling five deuce game. But her service returns flopped, as they did when Venus reached 6–5 despite two more break points.

(continued on page 119)

Men's Singles

Winner: **M. Safin** (RUS) (6)

Holder: A. Agassi (USA)

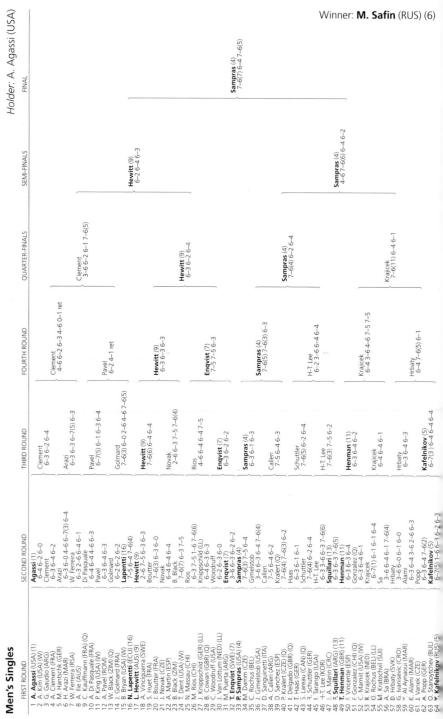

Columns: FIRST ROUND · SECOND ROUND · THIRD ROUND · FOURTH ROUND · QUARTER-FINALS · SEMI-FINALS · FINAL

First Round

1 **A. Agassi** (USA) (1)
2 A. Kim (USA) (W)
3 G. Gaudio (ARG)
4 A. Clement (FRA)
5 M. Hantschk (GER)
6 H. Arazi (MAR)
7 W. Ferreira (RSA)
8 A. Ilie (AUS)
9 C. Kaufmann (FRA) (Q)
10 D. Di Pasquale (FRA)
11 P. King (USA) (W)
12 A. Pavel (ROM)
13 W. Black (ZIM) (LL)
14 J. Golmard (FRA)
15 B. Bryan (USA) (W)
16 **N. Lapentti** (ECU) (16)
17 **L. Hewitt** (AUS) (9)
18 A. Vinciguerra (SWE)
19 S. Huet (FRA)
20 J. Boutter (FRA)
21 J. Novak (CZE)
22 A. Martin (ESP)
23 B. Black (ZIM)
24 T. Dent (USA) (W)
25 N. Massau (CHI)
26 M. Rios (CHI)
27 J. Knippschild (GER) (LL)
28 B. Cowan (GBR) (Q)
29 C. Woodruff (USA)
30 J. Van Lottum (NED) (LL)
31 M. Puerta (ARG)
32 **T. Enqvist** (SWE) (7)
33 **P. Sampras** (USA) (4)
34 M. Damm (CZE)
35 C. Rochus (BEL)
36 J. Gimelstob (USA)
37 D. Sanguinetti (ITA)
38 A. Calleri (ARG)
39 D. Sanchez (ESP)
40 P. Kralert (CZE) (Q)
41 I. Delgado (GBR) (Q)
42 T. Haas (GER)
43 S. Lareau (CAN) (Q)
44 J. Schuttler (GER)
45 J. Tarango (USA)
46 H-T. Lee (KOR)
47 J. A. Marin (CRC)
48 **S. Squillari** (ARG) (13)
49 **T. Henman** (GBR) (11)
50 F. Vincente (ESP)
51 F. Gonzalez (CHI) (Q)
52 C. Mamiit (USA) (W)
53 R. Krajicek (NED)
54 O. Rochus (BEL) (LL)
55 M. Kratochvil (SUI)
56 A. Sa (BRA)
57 D. Hrbaty (SVK)
58 G. Ivanisevic (CRO)
59 Y. Al Aynaoui (MAR)
60 K. Alami (MAR)
61 J. Vanek (CZE)
62 A. Popp (GER)
63 O. Stanoytchev (BUL)
64 **Y. Kafelnikov** (RUS) (5)

Second Round

- Agassi 6-4 6-2 6-0
- Clement 6-3 6-4 6-2
- Arazi 6-3 6-0 4-6 6-7(3) 6-4
- Di Pasquale 6-3 2-6 6-4 6-1
- Pavel 6-4 4-6 6-3
- Golmard 6-2 6-2
- Lapentti (16) 7-5 6-4 7-6(4)
- Hewitt (9)
- Boutter 7-6(3) 6-3 6-0
- Novak 6-4 6-4
- B. Black 7-6(7) 6-3 7-5
- Knippschild (LL) 6-3 7-5 1-6 7-6(6)
- Woodruff 6-4 6-3
- Enqvist (7) 6-2 6-3 6-0
- Sampras (4) 3-6 6-3 2-6
- Gimelstob
- Calleri 3-6 6-3 6-4 7-6(4)
- Kralert (Q) 7-5 6-4 6-2
- Haas 7-6(4) 6-7(3) 6-2
- Schuttler 6-3 6-1 6-1
- H-T. Lee 6-1 3-6 6-3 7-6(6)
- Squillari (13) 6-3 6-3 7-6(5)
- Henman (11) 6-3 6-4
- Gonzalez (Q) 6-3 6-4
- Krajicek 6-3 6-1
- Sa 6-4 6-1 7-6(4)
- Hrbaty 3-6 6-1 6-0
- Alami 6-3 6-4 3-6 2-6 6-3
- Popp 6-3 6-4 7-6(2)
- Kafelnikov (5) 6-7(5) 1-6 6-3 6-2 6-3

Third Round

- Clement 6-3 6-2 6-4
- Arazi 6-3 6-3 6-7(5) 6-3
- Pavel 6-7(5) 6-1 6-3 6-4
- Golmard 7-6(3) 6-0 2-6 4-6 7-6(5)
- Hewitt (9) 7-6(6) 6-4 6-4
- Novak 2-6 6-3 7-5 7-6(4)
- Rios 4-6 6-4 6-4 7-5
- Enqvist (7) 6-3 6-2 6-2
- Sampras (4) 6-3 6-1 6-3
- Calleri 7-5 6-4 6-2
- Schuttler 7-6(5) 6-2 6-4
- H-T. Lee 7-6(3) 7-5 6-2
- Henman (11) 6-3 6-4 6-2
- Krajicek 6-4 6-4 6-1
- Hrbaty 6-3 6-4 6-3
- Kafelnikov (5) 6-7(3) 6-4 6-4 6-4

Fourth Round

- Clement 4-6 6-2 6-3 4-6 0-1 ret
- Pavel 6-2 4-1 ret
- Hewitt (9) 6-3 6-3 6-3
- Enqvist (7) 7-5 7-5 6-3
- Sampras (4) 7-6(5) 7-6(3) 6-3
- H-T. Lee 6-2 3-6 6-6-4
- Krajicek 6-4 3-6 4-6 7-5 7-5
- Hrbaty 6-4 7-6(5) 6-1

Quarter-Finals

- Clement 3-6 6-2 6-1 7-6(5)
- Hewitt (9) 6-3 6-2 6-4
- Sampras (4) 7-6(4) 6-2 6-4
- Krajicek 7-6(11) 6-4 6-1

Semi-Finals

- Hewitt (9) 6-2 6-2 6-3
- Sampras (4) 4-6 7-6(6) 6-4 6-2

Final

- Sampras (4) 7-6(7) 6-4 7-6(5)

6–4 6–3 6–3

Winner: Safin (6) 6–3 7–6(4) 7–6(1)

Semi-final / quarter-final results

- Safin (6) 7–5 4–6 7–6(5) 6–3
- Safin (6) 6–1 6–2 6–2
- Kiefer (14) 6–2 6–7(3) 6–1 6–3
- T. Martin 6–4 6–4 3–6 7–5
- T. Martin 6–7(3) 6–7(7) 6–1 7–6(6) 6–2
- Johansson 6–4 6–7(7) 6–3 6–4

Round results

- Safin (6) 6–4 7–6(3) 1–6 3–6 7–6(5)
- Ferrero (12) 7–5 7–6(6) 1–6 7–6(6)
- Kiefer (14) 7–5 6–3 6–4
- Norman (3) 3–6 4–6 7–6(5) 6–4 7–6(9)
- Corretja (8) 6–3 7–6(4) 6–3
- Moya 6–3 4–6 7–5 6–2
- T. Martin 7–6(5) 6–3 6–2
- Pioline (10) 6–7(4) 3–6 6–4 7–6(6) 6–3
- Johansson 3–6 6–3 7–6(5) 7–6(1)
- Arthurs (Q) 7–6(3) 1–6 6–3 3–6 6–3

	First round scores
65 **Safin** (RUS) (6)	Safin (6) 7–5 7–(5) 6–4 6–4
66 C. Guardiola (FRA)	Pozzi
67 C. Ruud (NOR)	6–2 6–3 6–2
68 E. Pozzi (ITA)	Koubek
69 . Chela (ARG)	4–6 6–3 7–6(4) 7–6(5)
70 S. Koubek (AUT)	Grosjean
71 K. Kim (USA) (W)	6–2 6–2 4–6 6–2
72 S. Grosjean (FRA)	Nestor
73 F. Santoro (FRA)	7–6(4) 6–4 6–4
74 . Nestor (CAN)	Federer
75 . Federer (SUI)	6–1 7–5(5) 6–1
76 . Wessels (NED)	Ferrero (12)
77 . Gumy (ARG)	1–6 6–3 6–7(4) 6–2 6–3
78 V. Rossell (USA) (Q)	Kiefer (14)
79 . Meligeni (BRA)	6–1 6–4 6–3
80 **J. C. Ferrero** (ESP) (12)	Schalken
81 **N. Kiefer** (GER) (14)	6–2 6–3 6–1
82 A. Gaudenzi (ITA)	Mirnyi
83 J. Bjorkman (SWE)	6–4 6–1 6–4
84 B. Ulirhach (CZE)	Norman (3)
85 S. Schalken (NED)	6–3 6–4 6–3
86 L. Burgsmuller (GER) (Q)	Corretja (8)
87 . Pioline (FRA)	6–3 7–6(4) 6–3
88 A. Voinea (ROM)	Moya
89 J. Mirnyi (BLR)	6–3 4–6 7–5 6–2
90 K. Kucera (SVK)	T. Martin
91 A. Roddick (USA) (W)	6–4 6–2 6–4
92 A. Costa (ESP)	Pioline (10)
93 . Saulnier (FRA) (Q)	6–7(3) 3–6 6–4 7–6(6) 6–3
94 A. Savolt (HUN)	Gambill
95 . Goldlein (USA)	6–4 6–4 6–4
96 **M. Norman** (SWE) (3)	Johansson
97 **A. Corretja** (ESP) (8)	6–4 7–6(4) 6–2
98 . Srichaphan (THA)	Fromberg
99 . Rosset (SUI)	7–6(4) 4–6 6–3 7–6(2)
100 M. Vinck (GER) (Q)	Arthurs (Q)
101 . Dosedel (CZE)	2–6 7–6(2) 6–4 6–4
102 . Clavet (ESP)	

97 **A. Corretja** (ESP) (8)	Corretja (8) 7–6(2) 6–0 6–0
98 . Srichaphan (THA)	Rosset
99 . Rosset (SUI)	6–6 1–6 4
100 M. Vinck (GER) (Q)	Dosedel
101 . Dosedel (CZE)	7–6(3) 6–4 6–1
102 . Clavet (ESP)	Moya
103 . Moya (ESP)	6–4 6–2 7–5
104 M. Tillstrom (SWE)	T. Martin
105 T. Martin (USA)	6–4 6–1 1–6 6–2
106 V. Spadea (USA)	Chang
107 M. Chang (USA)	6–2 3–6 6–4 6–4
108 M. Levy (ISR)	Rusedski
109 G. Rusedski (GBR)	6–1 6–2 6–4
110 M. Gustafsson (SWE)	Sarsgian
111 . Sarsgian (ARM)	6–3 6–2 6–3
112 **C. Pioline** (FRA) (10)	Pioline (10)
113 **M. Philippoussis** (AUS) (15)	Philippoussis (15)
114 A. Portas (ESP)	6–3 6–2 6–3
115 J–M. Gambill (USA)	Gambill
116 M. Fish (USA) (W)	5–7 5–7 6–4 6–3 6–2
117 . Johansson (SWE)	Johansson
118 . Ljubicic (CRO)	7–6(1) 7–6(5) 6–3
119 . Blanco (ESP)	Blanco
120 P. Rafter (AUS)	7–6(3) 2–6 6–3 1–6 7–6(5)
121 M. Prinosil (GER)	Malisse (Q)
122 . Malisse (CZE) (Q)	7–5 6–4 6–4
123 . Bastl (SUI)	Fromberg
124 . Fromberg (AUS)	4–6 6–3 6–2
125 . Stoltenberg (AUS)	Stoltenberg
126 . Siemerink (NED) (Q)	6–0 6–4 6–1
127 N. Arthurs (AUS) (Q)	Arthurs (Q)
128 **G. Kuerten** (BRA) (2)	4–6 6–3 7–6(4) 7–6(1)

Bold type denotes seeded players. Numbers following player's name gives seeding order (Q) = Qualifier, (W) = Wild Card, (LL) = Lucky Loser

Women's Singles

Winner: **V. Williams** (USA) (3)

Holder: S. Williams (USA)

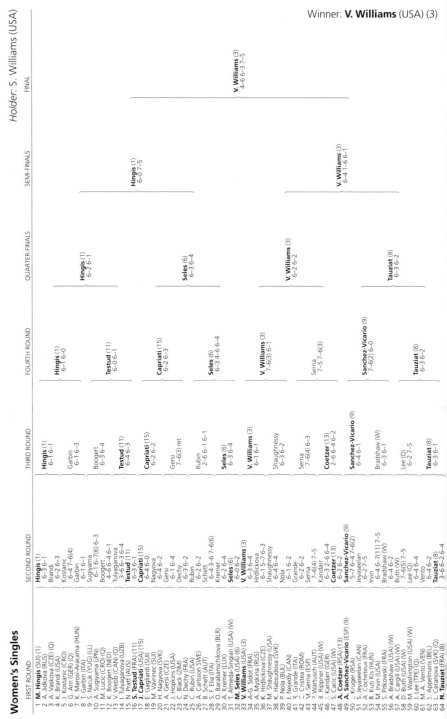

FIRST ROUND — SECOND ROUND — THIRD ROUND — FOURTH ROUND — QUARTER-FINALS — SEMI-FINALS — FINAL

1 **M. Hingis** (SUI) (1)
2 A. Jidkova (RUS)
3 A. Vaskova (CZE) (Q)
4 K. Brandi (USA)
5 J. Kostanic (CRO)
6 G. Arn (GER) (Q)
7 K. Marosi-Aracama (HUN)
8 T. Garbin (ITA)
9 S. Nacuk (YUG) (LL)
10 A. Sugiyama (JPN)
11 M. Lucic (CRO) (Q)
12 K. Boogert (NED)
13 V. Webb (CAN) (Q)
14 I. Tulyaganova (UZB)
15 N. Pratt (AUS)
16 **S. Testud** (FRA) (11)
17 **J. Capriati** (USA) (15)
18 E. Gagliardi (SUI)
19 M. Vavrinec (SUI)
20 H. Nagyova (SVK)
21 A. Gersi (CZE)
22 C. Black (ZIM)
23 J. Hopkins (USA)
24 N. Dechy (FRA)
25 C. Rubin (USA)
26 A. Carlsson (SWE)
27 B. Schett (AUT)
28 S. F. Elia (ITA)
29 O. Barabanschikova (BLR)
30 A. Kremer (LUX)
31 T. Almeda-Singian (USA) (W)
32 **M. Seles** (USA) (6)
33 **V. Williams** (USA) (3)
34 A.-G. Sidot (FRA)
35 A. Myskina (RUS)
36 K. Hrdlickova (CZE)
37 M. Shaughnessy (USA)
38 K. Habsudova (SVK)
39 P. Nola (BUL)
40 I. Nejedly (CAN)
41 R. Grande (ITA)
42 I. Cristea (ROM)
43 M. Serna (ESP)
44 P. Wartusch (AUT)
45 B. Rippner (USA) (W)
46 S. Kandarr (GER)
47 S. Cacic (USA) (W)
48 **A. Coetzer** (RSA) (13)
49 **A. Sanchez-Vicario** (ESP) (9)
50 K. Kruger (RSA)
51 S. Jeyaseelan (CAN)
52 A. Cocheteux (FRA)
53 R. Kuti Kis (HUN)
54 M. Irvin (USA)
55 S. Pitkowski (FRA)
56 A. Bradshaw (USA) (W)
57 A. Cargill (USA) (W)
58 D. Buth (USA) (W)
59 M. Washington (USA) (W)
60 J. Lee (TPE) (Q)
61 M. A. Vento (VEN)
62 S. Appelmans (BEL)
63 L. Ceranova (SVK) (Q)
64 **N. Tauziat** (FRA) (8)

SECOND ROUND
Hingis (1) 6-3 6-1
Brandi 6-2 6-3
Kostanic 6-4 7-6(4)
Garbin 6-1 6-1
Sugiyama 6-1 6-7(6) 6-3
Boogert 4-6 6-1
Tulyaganova 3-6 6-3 6-4
Testud (11)
Capriati (15)
Nagyova 6-4 6-2
Gersi 6-3 6-4
Rubin 6-3 6-2
Schett 6-4 3-6 7-6(6)
Seles (6) 6-0 6-2
V. Williams (3) 6-3 6-4
Hrdlickova 6-1 5-7 6-3
Shaughnessy 6-4 6-4
Nola 6-1 6-2
Grande 6-2 6-2
Serna 7-6(4) 7-5
Kandarr 6-3 2-6 6-4
Coetzer (13) 6-2 6-2
Sanchez-Vicario (9) 5-7 6-4 7-6(2)
Jeyaseelan 6-2 7-5
Irvin 6-4 6-7(11) 7-5
Bradshaw (W) 6-4 6-2
Buth 7-6(5) 7-5
Lee (Q) 6-4 6-4
Vento 6-4 6-2
Tauziat (8) 3-6 6-2 6-4

THIRD ROUND
Hingis (1) 6-1 6-1
Garbin 6-1 6-3
Boogert 6-3 6-4
Testud (11) 6-4 6-3
Capriati (15) 6-2 6-2
Gersi 7-6(3) ret
Rubin 2-6 6-1 6-1
Seles (6) 6-3 6-4
V. Williams (3) 6-1 6-1
Shaughnessy 6-3 6-2
Serna 7-6(4) 6-3
Coetzer (13) 2-6 4-6 6-2
Sanchez-Vicario (9) 6-4 6-1
Bradshaw (W) 6-3 6-1
Lee (Q) 6-2 7-5
Tauziat (8) 6-3 6-1

FOURTH ROUND
Hingis (1) 6-1 6-0
Testud (11) 6-0 6-1
Capriati (15) 6-2 6-3
Seles (6) 6-3 4-6 6-4
V. Williams (3) 7-6(3) 6-1
Serna 7-5 7-6(3)
Sanchez-Vicario (9) 7-6(2) 6-0
Tauziat (8) 6-3 6-2

QUARTER-FINALS
Hingis (1) 6-2 6-1
Seles (6) 6-3 6-4
V. Williams (3) 6-2 6-2
Tauziat (8) 6-3 6-2

SEMI-FINALS
Hingis (1) 6-0 7-5
V. Williams (3) 6-4 1-6 6-1

FINAL
V. Williams (3) 4-6 6-3 7-5

6–4 7–5

Women's Singles – Second Half of Draw (65–128)

First Round

- 65 **C. Martinez** (ESP) (7) — C. Martinez (7) 6–3 2–6 6–3
- 66 A. Frazier (USA)
- 67 P. Mandula (HUN) (Q) — Sanchez Lorenzo
- 68 A. Sanchez Lorenzo (ESP)
- 69 J. Snyder (USA) — Dementieva 7–5 6–1
- 70 E. Dementieva (RUS)
- 71 P. Pilschke (AUT) — Pilschke 6–3 6–3
- 72 P. Suarez (ARG)
- 73 S. Asagoe (JPN) — Asagoe 6–2 3–6 6–3
- 74 R. McQuillan (AUS) (Q)
- 75 P. Schnyder (SUI) — Schnyder 5–7 6–1 6–3
- 76 J. Craybas (USA) (Q)
- 77 L. Osterloh (USA) — Osterloh 6–0 3–6 6–3
- 78 C. Torrens-Valero (ESP)
- 79 J. Bachmann (GER) (Q) — Van Roost (14) 6–3 6–3
- 80 **D. Van Roost** (BEL) (14)
- 81 **A. Huber** (GER) (10) — Huber (10) 6–2 6–3
- 82 M. Tu (USA)
- 83 T. Panova (RUS) — Panova 6–3 6–1
- 84 S. Sfar (TUN) (Q)
- 85 E. Likhovtseva (RUS) — Likhovtseva 7–6(4) 6–4
- 86 M. Schnitzer (GER) (Q)
- 87 E. Callens (BEL) — Callens 6–1 6–1
- 88 E. de Lone (USA)
- 89 R. Dragomir (ROM) — Dragomir 6–4 6–1
- 90 R. Schlukebir (USA) (W)
- 91 L. Raymond (USA) — Raymond 6–1 6–0
- 92 V. Grzybowska (POL)
- 93 V. Maleeva (BUL) — Maleeva 6–3 6–3
- 94 I-Q Yi (CHN)
- 95 A. Stevenson (USA) — Pierce (4) 7–5 2–6 6–1
- 96 **M. Pierce** (FRA) (4)
- 97 **S. Williams** (USA) (5) — S. Williams (5) 6–3 6–2
- 98 T. Pisnik (SLO)
- 99 N. Petrova (RUS) — Petrova 6–1 6–2
- 100 D. Bedanova (CZE) (Q)
- 101 K. Nagy (HUN) (Q) — Casoni 3–6 7–6(4) 6–3
- 102 C. Casoni (ITA)
- 103 T. De Los Rios (PAR) — Bacheva 6–2 6–4
- 104 M. Bacheva (BUL)
- 105 F. Schiavone (ITA) (Q) — Schiavone (Q) 6–3 6–3
- 106 S. Talaja (CRO)
- 107 G. Pizzichini (ITA) (Q) — Pizzichini (Q) 7–6(7) 6–0
- 108 A. Hopkins (NED)
- 109 A. Smashnova (ISR) — Dokic 6–1 6–0
- 110 J. Dokic (AUS)
- 111 M. Oremans (NED) — Oremans 6–3 6–4
- 112 **J. Halard-Decugis** (FRA) (16)
- 113 **A. Kournikova** (RUS) (12) — Kournikova (12) 6–3 6–3
- 114 H. Parkinson (USA)
- 115 D. Klienova (CZE) — Klienova 7–5 7–6(4)
- 116 L. Krasnoroutskaya (RUS)
- 117 D. Chladkova (CZE) — Molik (LL) 6–1 6–2
- 118 A. Molik (AUS) (LL)
- 119 F. Labat (ARG) — Henin 6–2 6–2
- 120 J. Henin (BEL)
- 121 V. Ruano Pascual (ESP) — Ruano Pascual 4–6 6–4 6–3
- 122 K. Srebotnik (SVK)
- 123 A. Montolio (ESP) — Tanasugarn 6–1 6–1
- 124 T. Tanasugarn (THA)
- 125 K. Clijsters (BEL) — Clijsters 6–0 6–0
- 126 E. Marrero (ESP)
- 127 C. Leon Garcia (ESP) — Davenport (2) 6–0 6–1
- 128 **L. Davenport** (USA) (2)

Second Round

- C. Martinez (7) 6–3 6–2
- Dementieva 6–4 7–6(6)
- Asagoe 7–5 6–4
- Osterloh 7–6(7) 4–6 ret
- Huber (10) 6–2 6–3
- Likhovtseva 7–6(2) 4–6 6–1
- Raymond 6–4 6–2
- Pierce (4) 6–4 7–6(6)
- S. Williams (5) 6–4 6–2
- Casoni 3–6 7–6(4) 6–3
- Schiavone (Q) 6–4 6–4
- Dokic 7–6(4) 7–5
- Kournikova (12) 6–4 6–1
- Henin 6–4 6–1
- Tanasugarn 3–6 6–3 6–1
- Davenport (2) 6–2 6–1

Third Round

- Dementieva 6–4 6–1
- Osterloh 7–5 6–0
- Huber (10) 6–2 6–3
- Pierce (4) 6–4 7–6(6)
- S. Williams (5) 6–3 6–2
- Dokic 7–6(4) 7–5
- Henin 6–4 7–6(5)
- Davenport (2) 6–2 6–1

Fourth Round

- Dementieva 6–3 6–7(4) 7–6(5)
- Huber (10) 6–4 ret
- S. Williams (5) 7–6(7) 6–0
- Davenport (2) 6–0 6–4

Quarter-finals

- Dementieva 6–1 3–6 6–3
- Davenport (2) 6–4 6–2

Semi-final

- Davenport (2) 6–2 7–6(5)

Bold type denotes seeded players. Numbers following player's name gives seeding order (Q) = Qualifier, (W) = Wild Card, (LL) = Lucky Loser

Men's Doubles

Winners: Hewitt (AUS)/Mirnyi (BLR) 6–4 5–7 7–6(5)

Holders: Lareau (CAN)/O'Brien (USA)

FIRST ROUND

1 Woodbridge/Woodforde (1)
2 Mamiit/Thomas (W)
3 Hewitt/Mirnyi
4 Stark/Taino
5 Oncins/Orsanic
6 Bhupathi/Paes
7 Haggard/Van Houdt
8 Carbonell/Garcia (16)
9 Kulti/Tillstrom (9)
10 Bertolini/Brandi
11 Goldstein/Woodruff (W)
12 W. Black/Ullyett
13 Davis/Ginepri (W)
14 Albano/Arnold
15 Goellner/Kohlmann
16 Lareau/Nestor (7)
17 O'Brien/Palmer (3)
18 Gimelstob/Knowles
19 Martin/Rau
20 Bowen/Erlich
21 Gambill/Humphries
22 Bergh/Nyborg
23 Adams/De Jager (6)
24 Johnson/Norval (13)
25 Damm/Hrbaty (11)
26 Armando/Sprengelmeyer (W)
27 Manta/Tieleman (Q)
28 Kilderry/Tramacchi
29 Blake/Kim (W)
30 Pala/Vizner
31 Macpherson/Stafford
32 Novak/Rikl (5)
33 B. Bryan/M. Bryan
34 Kovacka/Kudmac (Q)
35 Etlis/S. Prieto
36 Hanley/Healey (Q)
37 Cibulec/Friedl
38 Coetzee/Haygarth
39 Bjorkman/B. Black (12)
40 Federer/Kratzmann (14)
41 Clinov/Siemerink
42 Braasch/Burgsmuller (Q)
43 Arthurs/Zimonjic
44 Hood/Waite
45 Lopez Moron/Portas
46 Jodra/Nargiso
47 T. Ferreira/Leach (4)
48 W. Ferreira/Kafelnikov (8)
49 Suk/Weiner-Smith
50 Ondruska/A. Prieto
51 Gaudenzi/Rosset
52 Godwin/Hill
53 Dent/Roddick (W)
54 Knippschild/Tarango
55 Eagle/Florent (10)
56 Dlhovsky/Prinosil (15)
57 Boutter/Santoro
58 Barnard/Koenig
59 Franklin/Oliver (W)
60 Shimada/Wakefield
61 Galbraith/MacPhie
62 Aspelin/Landsberg
63 Haarhuis/Stolle (2)

SECOND ROUND

- Woodbridge/Woodforde (1) 6–4 6–1
- Hewitt/Mirnyi 6–3 6–4
- Oncins/Orsanic 4–6 6–4 6–4
- Haggard/Van Houdt 6–4 5–7 6–4
- Kulti/Tillstrom (9) 6–3 6–4
- Goldstein/Woodruff (W) 6–2 6–7(4) 7–6(7)
- Albano/Arnold 6–7(8) 6–3 6–1
- Lareau/Nestor (7) 6–4 7–5
- O'Brien/Palmer (3) 6–3 6–2
- Balcells/Carrasco 7–6(5) 6–4
- Gambill/Humphries 7–6(1) 6–3
- Bergh/Nyborg 6–4 7–6(4) 7–5
- Damm/Hrbaty (11) 6–2 6–4
- Manta/Tieleman (Q) 7–6(6) 6–2
- Blake/Kim (W) 7–6(4) 6–1
- Macpherson/Stafford 6–3 6–4
- B. Bryan/M. Bryan 6–4 7–6(6)
- Hanley/Healey (Q) 7–6(5) 6–4
- Coetzee/Haygarth 6–7(4) 6–4 7–6(3)
- Bjorkman/B. Black (12) 6–2 6–2
- Federer/Kratzmann (14) 6–3 6–4
- Arthurs/Zimonjic 6–1 6–4
- Hood/Waite 6–4 6–4
- T. Ferreira/Leach (4) 6–3 7–6(3)
- W. Ferreira/Kafelnikov (8) 6–4 6–4
- Gaudenzi/Rosset 2–6 6–4 7–6(5)
- Dent/Roddick (W) 7–6(9) 5–7 6–4
- Knippschild/Tarango 6–3 7–6(4)
- Boutter/Santoro 8r–2 6–2
- Barnard/Koenig 5–7 7–5 6–1
- Galbraith/MacPhie 6–3 7–6(5)
- Haarhuis/Stolle (2) 4–6 7–6(6) 6–4

THIRD ROUND

- Hewitt/Mirnyi 6–1 4–6 7–6(4)
- Oncins/Orsanic 7–6(4) 6–3
- Kulti/Tillstrom (9) 7–6(5) 7–6(3)
- Lareau/Nestor (7) 6–3 6–3
- O'Brien/Palmer (3) 7–6(2) 7–6(7)
- Bergh/Nyborg 7–6(4) 6–7(4) 7–5
- Damm/Hrbaty (11) 6–2 6–4
- Macpherson/Stafford 6–4 7–6(3)
- B. Bryan/M. Bryan 6–3 7–5
- Coetzee/Haygarth 6–4 6–3
- Arthurs/Zimonjic 6–4 7–6(6)
- E. Ferreira/Leach (4) 7–6(8) 7–5
- W. Ferreira/Kafelnikov (8) 7–5 7–5
- Knippschild/Tarango 3–6 6–3 6–4
- Barnard/Koenig 7–6(5) 7–5
- Haarhuis/Stolle (2) 6–4 6–7(5) 7–5

QUARTER-FINALS

- Hewitt/Mirnyi 6–3 6–2
- Lareau/Nestor (7) 7–6(5) 6–3
- O'Brien/Palmer (3) 6–4 7–5
- Macpherson/Stafford 7–6(4) 6–7(5) 6–3
- B. Bryan/M. Bryan 6–3 2–6 6–4
- E. Ferreira/Leach (4) 6–4 3–6 7–6(5)
- W. Ferreira/Kafelnikov (8) 6–3 6–0
- Haarhuis/Stolle (2) 6–7(2) 7–6(1) 7–5

SEMI-FINALS

- Hewitt/Mirnyi 7–6(5) 6–4
- O'Brien/Palmer (3) 6–0 6–4
- E. Ferreira/Leach (4) 6–1 6–2
- W. Ferreira/Kafelnikov (8) 6–3 7–6(5)

FINAL

- Hewitt/Mirnyi 6–4 3–6 7–6(7)
- E. Ferreira/Leach (4) 6–4 5–7 6–3

Bold type denotes seeded players. Numbers following player's name gives seeding order (Q) = Qualifier, (W) = Wild Card, (LL) = Lucky Loser

Women's Doubles

Holders: S. Williams (USA)/V. Williams (USA)

Winners: **J. Halard-Decugis** (FRA)/**A. Sugiyama** (JPN) (2) 6–0 1–6 6–1

FIRST ROUND

1 **Raymond/Stubbs (1)**
2 Frac/Noorlander
3 Inun/Tu (W)
4 Bachmann/Glass (Q)
5 N Lu/J Lu
6 Martincova/Pastikova (Q)
7 de Lone/Pratt
8 **Po/Sidot (11)**
9 **C. Black/Likhovtseva (10)**
10 Pourchek/Zaporozhanova
11 De Beer/Miyagi
12 Wartusch/Webb
13 Frazier/Schlukebir
14 Diaz Oliva/Dominguez Lino (LL)
15 Garbin/Husarova
16 **Arendt/Bollegraf (8)**
17 **Rubin/Testud (4)**
18 Jiskova/Leon Garcia
19 Farina/Habsudova
20 Petrova/Schnyder
21 Serna/Shaughnessy
22 McQuillan/McShea
23 Matevzic/Schmidle (Q)
24 **Coetzer/McNeil (13)**
25 **Ruano Pascual/Suarez (5)**
26 Barclay/De Villiers
27 Clijsters/Courtois
28 Elwood/Molik
29 Boogert/Oremans
30 S Williams/V Williams (W)
31 Osterloh/Stevenson (W)
32 **Fusai/Tauziat (6)**
33 Marosi/Woodroffe
34 Pullin/Yoshida
35 Dokic/Hopmans
36 Kiaeeva/Nagyova (Q)
37 Carlsson/Jeyaseelan
38 Linettskaya/Ostrovskaya
39 **Callens/Van Roost (12)**
40 Casoni/Tulyaganova
41 **Martinez/Tarabini (9)**
42 Canepa/Dyrberg
43 Andres/Martinez Granados
44 Bacheva/Torrens-Valero
45 Musgrave/Stewart
46 Jurak/Jensen (W)
47 **Hingis/Pierce (3)**
48 **Huber/Schett (7)**
49 Cochran/Schlukebir (W)
50 Lataf/Tanasugarn
51 Graham/Srebotnik
52 Appelmans/Wild
53 Navratilova/Sanchez-Vicario
54 Navratilova/Sanchez-Vicario
55 Grande/Loit
56 **Capriati/Kournikova (14)**
57 **Krizan/Selyutina (15)**
58 De Swardt/Vis
59 Kostanic/Snyder
60 Eer/Riera
61 Hrdlickova/Rittner
62 Cristea/Dragomir
63 Razuk/Pisnik
64 **Halard-Decugis/Sugiyama (2)**

SECOND ROUND

Raymond/Stubbs (1) 6–1 6–2
Inun/Tu (W) 6–3 5–7 7–6(0)
Po/Sidot (11) 6–2 3–6 6–3
C. Black/Likhovtseva (10) 6–0 6–4
De Beer/Miyagi 6–4 2–6 6–4
Garbin/Husarova 6–4 7–5
Rubin/Testud (4) 6–4 6–3
Petrova/Schnyder 6–1 3–6 6–3
Coetzer/McNeil (13) 6–4 7–5
Horn/Montalvo (16) 1–6 6–1 6–4
Clijsters/Courtois 2–6 6–3 6–1
S Williams/V Williams (W) 2–6 7–5 6–3
Fusai/Tauziat (6) 6–3 6–4
Dokic/Hopmans 0–6 7–5 6–2
Callens/Van Roost (12) 6–1 7–6(1)
Martinez/Tarabini (9) 6–7(4) 6–4 6–2
Canepa/Dyrberg 7–6(2) 7–6(7)
Hingis/Pierce (3) 6–2 6–1
Huber/Schett (7) 4–6 6–2 6–2
Graham/Srebotnik 6–3 6–2
Navratilova/Sanchez-Vicario 7–5 6–0
Capriati/Kournikova (14) 6–4 6–2
Krizan/Selyutina (15) 6–4 6–4
Kostanic/Snyder 6–1 6–1
Hrdlickova/Rittner 6–4 6–0
Halard-Decugis/Sugiyama (2) 7–6(1) 6–4

THIRD ROUND

Raymond/Stubbs (1) 6–2 6–1
Po/Sidot (11) 6–4 6–3
C. Black/Likhovtseva (10) 3–6 7–5 6–4
Garbin/Husarova 6–2 6–1
Rubin/Testud (4) 6–1 6–2
Coetzer/McNeil (13) 6–4 6–4
Clijsters/Courtois 7–6(5) 6–7(4) 6–4
S Williams/V Williams (W) 6–2 6–1
Fusai/Tauziat (6) 6–1 6–2
Callens/Van Roost (12) 6–4 3–6 6–2
Martinez/Tarabini (9) 6–4 7–6(5)
Hingis/Pierce (3) 6–0 6–2
Huber/Schett (7) 3–6 6–4 6–3
Navratilova/Sanchez-Vicario 7–5 6–0
Krizan/Selyutina (15) 7–5 6–4
Halard-Decugis/Sugiyama (2) 6–2 6–2

QUARTER-FINALS

Raymond/Stubbs (1) 6–4 6–2
C. Black/Likhovtseva (10) 6–4 6–2
Rubin/Testud (4) 7–5 6–3
S Williams/V Williams (W) 6–1 5–7 6–1
Callens/Van Roost (12) 4–6 6–2 7–5
Martinez/Tarabini (9) w/o
Huber/Schett (7) 6–3 6–2
Halard-Decugis/Sugiyama (2) 6–3 6–3

SEMI-FINALS

C. Black/Likhovtseva (10) 6–3 6–4
S Williams/V Williams (W) 1–6 6–1 6–3
Callens/Van Roost (12) 6–3 7–6(2)
Halard-Decugis/Sugiyama (2) 3–4 ret

FINAL

C. Black/Likhovtseva (10) w/o
Halard-Decugis/Sugiyama (2) 7–5 6–1

Bold type denotes seeded players. Numbers following player's name gives seeding order (Q) = Qualifier, (W) = Wild Card, (LL) = Lucky Loser

Mixed Doubles

Holders: Bhupathi (IND)/Sugiyama (JPN)

Winners:
Palmer (USA)/**Sanchez-Vicario** (ESP) (2)
6–4 6–3

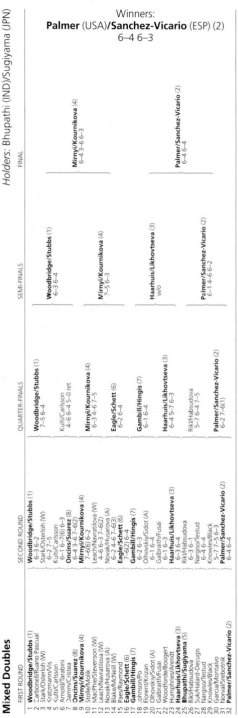

FIRST ROUND	SECOND ROUND	QUARTER-FINALS	SEMI-FINALS	FINAL
1 **Woodbridge/Stubbs** (1)	**Woodbridge/Stubbs** (1) 6–3 6–2	**Woodbridge/Stubbs** (1) 7–5 6–4	**Woodbridge/Stubbs** (1) 6–3 6–4	
2 Carbonell/Ruano Pascual				
3 Stark/Osterloh (W)	Stark/Osterloh (W) 6–2 7–5			
4 Kratzmann/Vis				
5 Kulti/Carlsson	Kulti/Carlsson 6–1 6–7(6) 6–3	Kulti/Carlsson 4–6 6–4 5–0 ret		
6 Arnold/Tarabini				
7 Damm/Cristea	**Oncins/Suarez** (8) 6–4 3–6 7–6(2)			
8 **Oncins/Suarez** (8)				
9 **Mirnyi/Kournikova** (4)	**Mirnyi/Kournikova** (4) 7–6(6) 6–2	**Mirnyi/Kournikova** (4) 6–3 4–6 7–5	**Mirnyi/Kournikova** (4) 7–5 6–3	**Mirnyi/Kournikova** (4) 6–4 3–6 6–3
10 Stolle/Molik				
11 MacPhie/Stevenson (W)	Leach/Navratilova (W) 4–6 6–3 7–6(2)			
12 Leach/Navratilova (W)				
13 Novak/Husarova (A)	Novak/Husarova (A) 6–2 4–6 7–6(3)	**Eagle/Schett** (6) 6–2 6–4		
14 Blake/McNeil (W)				
15 Paes/Raymond	**Eagle/Schett** (6) 7–6(2) 6–4			
16 **Eagle/Schett** (6)				
17 **Gambill/Hingis** (7)	**Gambill/Hingis** (7) 6–2 6–3	**Gambill/Hingis** (7) 6–1 6–4	**Haarhuis/Likhovtseva** (3) w/o	
18 Johnson/Po				
19 Florent/Krizan	Olhovskiy/Sidot (A) 6–1 6–4			
20 Olhovskiy/Sidot (A)				
21 Galbraith/Fusai	Galbraith/Fusai 6–1 6–3	**Haarhuis/Likhovtseva** (3) 6–4 5–7 6–3		
22 Woodforde/Boogert				
23 Humphries/Arendt	**Haarhuis/Likhovtseva** (3) 6–3 6–4			
24 **Haarhuis/Likhovtseva** (3)				
25 **Bhupathi/Sugiyama** (5)	**Bhupathi/Sugiyama** (5) 6–3 6–1	Riki/Habsudova 5–7 6–4 7–5	**Palmer/Sanchez-Vicario** (2) 6–1 4–6 6–2	**Palmer/Sanchez-Vicario** (2) 6–4 6–4
26 Riki/Habsudova				
27 Nargiso/Testud	Nargiso/Testud 6–4 6–4			
28 Nargiso/Testud				
29 Knowles/Black	Knowles/Black 5–7 7–5 6–3	**Palmer/Sanchez-Vicario** (2) 6–2 7–6(1)		
30 Garcia/Montalvo				
31 Norval/Srebotnik	**Palmer/Sanchez-Vicario** (2) 6–4 6–4			
32 **Palmer/Sanchez-Vicario** (2)				

Bold type denotes seeded players. Numbers following player's name gives seeding order (Q) = Qualifier, (W) = Wild Card, (LL) = Lucky Loser, (A) = Alternate

'Arantxa [Sanchez-Vicario] runs down as many balls,' said Davenport, 'but Venus doesn't just get them back. They come back as hard as you hit them, and you have to go for more.'

Venus and Serena, the French and Wimbledon champs, looked certain doubles winners, but Little Sister's sore left foot and ankle caused a semi-final walkover for the Russian-Zimbabwean entry of Elena Likhovtseva and Cara Black. And the title went to the French-Japanese blend of Julie Halard-Decugis and Ai Sugiyama 6–0 1–6 6–1. Julie was France's second victor, following Francoise Durr (1969, 1972). Japan, Russia and Zimbabwe had never previously been represented in the final.

Reappearing after an absence of six years, to the delight of her legion of fans, 43-year-old Martina Navratlilova won two rounds in doubles, with Sanchez-Vicario, and one in mixed with Rick Leach.

That event had a Spanish-American flavour as Sanchez-Vicario and Jared Palmer stopped the Russian-Belarus splicing of Kournikova and Mirnyi, 6–4 6–3. That completed a rare US triple for Arantxa, whose older brother, Emilio, won in 1987 in the company of Navratilova. It was a nifty $63,000 wedding present for the rookie bride (now Senora Juan Vehils), who won the singles in 1994, and the doubles in 1993 (with Helena Sukova) and 1994 (with Jana Novotna).

We are left wondering which of these champions will show up to compete in 2044, in the manner of the Doomsday Stroking Machine, Kenny Rosewall. Yes, gracing the super senior doubles, there was 65-year-old Rosewall, the singles champ of 1956 (and 1970), yet sporting that eternally glorious backhand.

JUNIOR EVENTS

BOYS' SINGLES – **Final:** Andy Roddick (USA) (1) d. Robby Ginepri (USA) 6–1 6–3
GIRLS' SINGLES – **Final:** Emilia Salerni (ARG) (1) d. Tatiana Perebiynis (RUS) (4) 6–3 6–4
BOYS' DOUBLES – **Final:** Lee Childs (GBR)/ James Nelson (GBR) (1) d. Tres Davis (USA)/ Robby Ginepri (USA) 6–1 6–3
GIRLS' DOUBLES – **Final:** Gisella Dulko (ARG)/ Emilia Salerni (ARG) (4) d. Aniko Kapros (HUN)/Christina Wheeler (AUS) (2) 3–6 6–2 6–2

SENIOR EVENTS

MEN'S 35s DOUBLES MASTERS (Round Robin in two groups of 4) – **Final:** Scott Davis (USA)/ David Pate (USA) d. Ken Flach (USA)/ Robert Seguso (USA) 6–3 6–3
MEN'S 45s DOUBLES MASTERS (Round Robin in four groups of 4) – **Final:** Tom Gullikson (USA)/Dick Stockton (USA) d. Sandy Mayer (USA)/Hank Pfister (USA) 6–1 5–7 7–6 (4)
WOMEN'S DOUBLES MASTERS (Round Robin in two groups of 4) – **Final:** Jo Durie (GBR)/Wendy Turnbull (AUS) d. Ilana Kloss (RSA)/ JoAnne Russell (USA) 6–4 6–1
SUPER SENIOR DOUBLES (Round Robin in two groups of 4) – **Final:** Marty Riessen (USA)/Sherwood Stewart (USA) d. Ilie Nastase (ROM)/Tom Okker (NED) 6–4 6–2

2000 US OPEN CHAMPIONSHIPS
PRIZE MONEY – Total $15,011,000

MEN'S AND WOMEN'S SINGLES – 128 draws. Winner $800,000. Runner-up $425,000. Semi-finalists $220,000. Quarter-finalists $110,000. Fourth-round losers $55,000. Third-round losers $35,000. Second-round losers $20,000. First-round losers $10,000.
Totals: MEN – $4,385,000; WOMEN – $4,385,000. ($8,790,000)

MEN'S AND WOMEN'S DOUBLES – 64 draws (per pair) – Winners $340,000. Runners-up $170,000. Semi-finalists $90,000. Quarter-finalists $45,000. Third-round losers $22,500. Second-round losers $15,000. First-round losers $9,500.
Totals: MEN $1,594,000; WOMEN $1,594,000. ($3,188,000)

MIXED DOUBLES – 32 draw (per pair) – Winners $126,000. Runners-up $63,000. Semi-finalists $31,500. Quarter- finalists $16,000. Second-round losers $11,000. First-round losers $5,500.
Total: $492,000

MEN'S AND WOMEN'S SINGLES QUALIFYING COMPETITIONS – 128 draws.
16 × Third-round losers $7,500. 32 × Second-round losers $5,500. 64 × First-round losers $3,000.
Totals: MEN $488,000; WOMEN $488,000 ($976,000)

MEN'S AND WOMEN'S DOUBLES QUALIFYING COMPETITIONS – 16 draws (per pair)
4 × Second-round losers $2,500. 8 × First-round losers $1,500.
Totals: MEN $22,000; WOMEN $22,000 ($44,000)

Total for senior events – $425,000. Total for per diem allowances and other fees – $1,076,000.

In 2000 Sampras achieved his ambition of winning more Grand Slam titles than anyone else.
(Stephen Wake)

Sampras – His Place in History

Christopher Clarey

Ask Pete Sampras if he is the greatest men's tennis player in history and his mood quickly shifts from laid-back, sneakers-on-the-coffee-table conviviality to discomfort.

'Um, it's hard for me to answer that,' he says, his eyes suddenly transformed into searchlights as if to emphasize that you really shouldn't have put him in this position. But there should be nothing wrong with asking this particular softball question at this advanced and fulfilled stage in the American's career. Sampras understands the urge to compare; he just does not want to be the one to satisfy it. He dislikes those who, in his American vernacular, 'pop off' by singing their own praises or by belittling the accomplishments of others.

So when it comes to something as tennis-weighty as his place in the game's time-line, he surveys the outer reaches of the room a bit more with his dark eyes and then happily dodges the responsibility.

'I'm not going to sit here and tell you I'm the greatest ever,' he said. 'Did you ever hear Laver say he was the greatest ever?'

At least for now it will be left to others to establish the pecking order, and while he will probably never get his deft hands on that slippery French Open trophy, there was much to recommend Sampras as 2000 came to a close. Just turned 29, he was newly married, newly at ease with his celebrity and modified priorities and newly alone in the history books as the all-time leader in Grand Slam singles titles.

In this case, 13 turned out to be a lucky number, and unsurprisingly to those who have watched Sampras routinely put pretender after pretender out to pasture in early July, his 13th major title came at Wimbledon, the anachronistic yet somehow still seminal tournament that he has dominated like no other man in the last century.

'He knows how to play big in the biggest of situations, and you can't expect anything less of him, especially here,' Andre Agassi said quite rightly after Sampras had overwhelmed him in the 1999 final.

Laurie Doherty cannot match Sampras's record at the All England Club. Nor can the debonair New Zealander Tony Wilding. Nor can Fred Perry, Rod Laver, Boris Becker or even Bjorn Borg, the unflappable Swede who won five times in a row from 1976 to 1980 and made an exceedingly rare visit as one of the returning champions in 2000.

The only man who can match Sampras's seven titles on paper is William Renshaw, a Briton who was one of the game's first main attractions and who won seven times in a nine-year span at Wimbledon in the 1880s. But tennis was more diversion than profession in that less cutthroat, infinitely less floodlit era. Furthermore, until 1922 the defending champion had to play only one match, the Challenge Round, against the winner of the All-Comers singles.

Sampras has done his dominating in the fish bowl of the modern media age with its very big cheques and proliferating messengers and mediums, and while he would have enjoyed more consistent recognition in his home country of the United States, he has endured and excelled long enough to earn himself a spot on the A list, if not quite at the top, in that sports-obsessed nation.

Though Andre Agassi would still generate more hysteria on main street or at a suburban mall, many Americans now recognize that Sampras is the gold standard: an understated champion – more athlete than celebrity – whose impact on his profession is difficult to overstate. How many other active sportsmen or sportswomen can stake a legitimate claim to being the most accomplished ever in a major international sport with a lengthy history? Tiger Woods looks like he might get there in a hurry, but he still has to sink many more clutch putts and avoid many more deep bunkers and shallow distractions. Michael Jordan has retired from the NBA, and Wayne Gretzky from the NHL.

Sampras has every intention of playing well into his thirties. Though his body has betrayed him with increasing regularity in recent seasons, he still enjoys the process more than the rewards, still relishes the feel of the ball leaving his very tightly strung racquet in a hurry; still relishes the feeling of invulnerability that invades him when his un-readable serve is on rhythm.

'When I'm playing well, tennis is easy for me,' he once conceded. It appears to be easy, as well, which goes a long way toward explaining why the public and the press long mistook his nonchalant on-court demeanor for a lack of grit. There might be an occasional ulcer lurking in his washboard stomach, but there is little visible tension in Sampras at his best: none of the sweaty, dues-paid air that was so evident in Jim Courier, Ivan Lendl, Thomas Muster or even in Agassi, whose attacking baseline style is not made for winning pressure points in too much of a hurry.

The remarkable thing about Sampras is that for all his flair and aggressive instincts and ostensibly fragile frame, his game was built to last. He is the only player, since the computer rankings were created in 1973, to have finished number one for six consecutive years, and the autumn of 1998, the season he finished off that historic streak, was one of the few times Sampras made the game look hard: grinding through every match and losing his hair and serenity in bunches. Sampras also holds the all-time record for total weeks at number one (276): a record that will never be broken now that the ranking system has been revamped.

Ask Sampras what he is proudest of in his career, and he responds, 'My consistency, and the fact that I've been at the top for pretty much my whole career. I've won a major every year now for eight years. Being consistent year after year, it's not easy. It's hard to stay on top or win majors every year when you are the man to beat, and I've been able to get through tough situations...I work my tail off, and it's definitely been worth it.'

Borg is the only other player to have won Grand Slam singles titles in eight consecutive years, and he is the only other player in the Open era to have a comparable strike rate on the biggest occasions. While Sampras was 13–3 in Grand Slam finals heading into 2001; Borg was 11–5 during his briefer career. Laver, who spanned the 'amateur' and 'open eras', was 11–6. Jimmy Connors was 8–7; Lendl, for all his consistent dominance in the late 1980s, was no better than 8–11.

Sampras, even more to his credit, is also 5–1 in finals at the year-end Tour Championship, now known as the Tennis Masters Cup and still regarded as the fifth most important individual event in the men's game.

Roy Emerson, it bears remembering and appreciating, was 12–3 in Grand Slam finals. Unlike Sampras, he won all four of the major Championships and was part of eight Davis Cup victories to Sampras's two (Sampras would certainly have more if he had not declined to commit to the event on several occasions). But what hurts Emerson's historical cause is that he won all but two of his 12 titles during a five-year span when his most dangerous rival (Laver) had turned professional.

'We could have had a pretty good competition there,' Emerson said

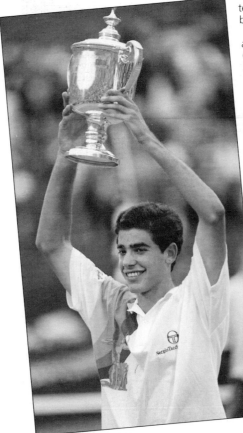

Aged 19, Pete Sampras won the US Open in 1991 to become the youngest man ever to achieve the feat. (Paul Zimmer)

Right: *Even at the age of 20, the Sampras serve was already a potent weapon and it would develop to become one of the greatest-ever. (Paul Zimmer)*

The famous Sampras forehand which would become one of the game's great shots.
(Paul Zimmer)

recently. 'Rod certainly did improve when he turned pro. He had a little bit of a glaring weakness when he first turned pro. The pros really jumped on his second serve. He tightened that up
and improved his second serve and tightened up his game. The pro game was good for Rod
because he had that tough competition week after week against those great players: Pancho
Gonzalez and all that group. But it would have been nice to have competed against Rod.'

Weaknesses or not, there can be virtually no doubt that if Laver had stayed eligible, Sampras
would still be chasing the Grand Slam titles record, which could well be as high as 18 or 19. And
what if Borg had deigned to play in the Australian Open more than once during his brilliant
career? If the Swede could win five times on grass in London, he could certainly have won a few
times against presumably weaker fields in Melbourne? And what of Big Bill Tilden, who won 10
Grand Slam singles titles and never bothered going to Australia at all?

There is no end to this sort of conjecture, of course, which is why Sampras is wise as well as
well-mannered to avoid getting drawn too far into the debate. The only strong point he will
make on his own behalf relates to the rap that he has never won the French Open: a hole in his
curriculum vitae that Emerson, fellow Australian John Newcombe and many others believe
eliminates Sampras from contention for the greatest ever.

'I don't know how fair that is,' Sampras said. 'As much as I love the Lavers and Rosewalls, the
difference now to 20 years ago, they didn't have a clay-court animal, didn't have 30 guys from
Spain who can all play. Laver basically beat guys who played like he did. He was better than
everyone, and he beat Neale Fraser and those guys. They all served and volleyed, and Laver had
to worry about a couple guys. I've got to worry about fifty guys and it's not fair for Newcombe
and those guys. You can't compare the eras.. '

It certainly is fun, though, so hopefully Sampras will forgive us having a little more of it. In
truth, there were clay-court animals in the early `60s: first and foremost Nicola Pietrangeli of
Italy who won back to back titles in Paris (1959, 1960) and then lost in two more finals there

(1961, 1964), both times to another great clay-courter, Manolo Santana. (Incidentally, the Spaniard then showed his versatility by going on to win on grass at Forest Hills in1965 and at Wimbledon in 1966).

What Sampras also might not know is how much time and thought Laver devoted to learning the intricacies of clay-court tennis – including the need to mix baseline rallies with forays to the net – before winning his first title in Paris in 1962 (after saving a match point in the quarter-finals against compatriot Martin Mulligan).

'I would say that Pete has had quite a bit more help than when we were playing,' Emerson said. 'We more or less had to do it by ourselves. And as for the tougher competition, we used to seed only eight players in most of our majors. Now they seed 16, and lots of times upsets come in the early rounds. Particularly Sampras. The only time really to beat Sampras in a major tournament is in the early rounds. If he gets through to the quarter-finals or final, he pretty much has come through. In that regard, we had it a little tougher because there were only eight seeded players.'

Yet Sampras is certainly correct when he talks about the greatly improved depth in the clay-court game and indeed the game in general. Where his case, or more accurately the case for him, gets weaker is that his principal contemporary measuring stick, Agassi, has proven (just barely) that it is possible to win all four majors in the modern era. Sampras's case is also, oddly enough, weakened by his outrageous success at Wimbledon, where he is 53–1 in the last eight years.

It had to be tougher to win at the All England Club in Laver's and Emerson's era because the bulk of leading players grew up competing on grass. Indeed, three of the four Grand Slam events were contested on the surface. Now, virtually none of today's stars – including young Australians like Lleyton Hewitt – have meaningful contact with the grasscourt game until late in their junior careers. The fact is: Sampras has won the majority of his record 13 titles on a surface that is increasingly rare and increasingly intimidating to his rivals, some of whom are as busy trying to find their footing as they are trying to get a sniff at Sampras's brutally effective first serve.

If not for the All England Club, Sampras's last Grand Slam singles title would be the 1997 Australian Open. 'Wimbledon saved my year,' has become his mantra of late. But 2000 was unquestionably a year of general resurgence for Sampras in the major championships: he lost to Agassi in a remarkable semi-final at the Australian Open and reached the final at the United States Open, where he was blown away in straight sets by an ethereal Marat Safin in much the same way Sampras blew away his more accomplished elders to win his first Grand Slam title at Flushing Meadows 10 years earlier.

En route to that breakthrough victory in 1990, the 19-year-old Sampras wore the slightly guilty smirk on court of a student who was taking a test to which he already had been handed the questions and answers. But off court, he was not prepared for the tsunami of attention: the image sticks with you of him holding out his arms reflexively to a group of curious reporters midway through the second week and saying, 'Let's not make too big a deal about this or anything.'

His athleticism was not quite so evident then. Though his sturdy legs and whipping, fluid service motion were already present, his upper body was Kuertenesque; his strong facial features still works in progress. Over the last decade, he has filled out physically and emotionally: experiencing the adult joys of professional success, wealth creation, independence and, most recently, newlywed bliss along with the adult sorrows of personal loss and suspect health.

He finally conceded in 2000 that one of his health problems has been thalassemia, an inherited blood disorder that is relatively common among people of Mediterranean descent (Sampras's mother, Georgia, was born and raised in Greece) and whose symptoms include anemia. 'It sometimes makes me feel lethargic and a little out of it – that hang-dog look is partly because of the condition – especially in any very hot weather,' Sampras told *Tennis* magazine in the United States, confirming what Canadian tennis writer Tom Tebbutt had revealed four years earlier. 'I've never admitted it until now because I didn't want my opponents to have that confidence of knowing I was playing with a deficit.'

Though he has a quick, sarcastic, occasionally profane wit in private, Sampras is not someone who relishes exhaustive analysis. But if he is not all that articulate compared to the very verbal if equally no better educated Agassi, he has grown into his role over the years, grown in off-court confidence and presence and it would be fitting if the wider public, particularly the wider American public, grew to appreciate him in the round as he approaches 30. The question is whether his increasingly fragile physique will allow him and the public that opportunity, but he seems ready, even eager, for a deeper level of communion and recognition now. There is perhaps a subliminal message in the fact that this man who would probably have defined himself as an anti-celebrity throughout the 1990s, chose to marry Hollywood actress Bridgette Wilson in 2000. Yet the Los Angeles area is home for Sampras: home to the Los Angeles Lakers basketball team he relishes following; home to his sister Stella and parents and if there was a subplot to Sampras's 10th year as a Grand Slam threat it was his return to his roots.

After losing coach Tim Gullikson to brain cancer in 1996, Sampras has re-built a professional support structure around Paul Annacone. But it took him longer to re-build a private support structure. Moving his base from sunny Florida to sunny California after the successful and not entirely happy 1998 season turned out to be the answer, and before long, his opponents were no longer the only people with family members in the stands.

Brothers, sisters; mothers, fathers. They are ubiquitous in tennis, along with bean counters, imagemeisters and massage therapists, and as classic components of the loaded term entourage the family members are often viewed as vicarious livers, as hangers-on. But no one has ever accused Sampras's parents of that – 'My parents are not tennis parents. You see a lot of cases where parents get too involved. They've always kept their distance.' Yet after a decade when they were conspicuous by their absence, they were conspicuous by their presence in 2000. They were there in the Forum in Los Angeles, where Sampras won the decisive fifth rubber of the Davis Cup quarter-final against the Czech Republic, and father Sam came on court to give his son a hug. Most poignantly, they were there in the upper reaches of Centre Court in the fading light after Sampras finished off Patrick Rafter and Emerson.

Sampras, troubled by tendinitis in his shin and perhaps by the doubts that begin to nag at so many athletes when they no longer take success for granted or a given, had not played his best all fortnight. Neither on the little points; nor on the biggest points. But he had played well enough to stand alone, and now he no longer wanted to, and the player who hardly ever glances up at the players' box was soon working his way through the crowd in the stands to embrace his parents after they had finally watched him at Wimbledon instead of on television.

'This is a moment I've dreamt about: breaking this record and my parents being there,' Sampras said later, exuding completion and weary elation. 'It's a script that I've always wanted to write, and it's happened.'

Who could begrudge him or us this? And isn't it endearing, if rather misleading, that the moment when Sampras was at his least dominant and least individualistic turned out to be the most emotional, satisfying and emblematic moment of his career. He might have been at his best between the summer of 1993 and the spring of 1994 when he won three major titles in succession. He might have been at his most courageous in Moscow in 1995, when he shrugged off cramps and the clay beneath his feet to beat the Russians nearly on his own to win back the Davis Cup for America. But this was the one for the time capsule; the one today's youngsters might still be discussing when they are old enough to feel nostalgic.

This pundit would have to agree that Sampras probably does not deserve to be considered the greatest player in history unless he holds up the silverware in Paris. After all, Laver did not just win Grand Slam events. He completed two Grand Slams. But for those of us unfortunate enough to have been born too late to watch the Rocket at work, we will always have Sampras in our memory banks, making a terribly demanding game look easy and declining to take too much credit for it.

GREATEST GRAND SLAM SINGLES WINNERS

Below are lists of all those players who have won five or more singles titles at the four Grand Slam Championships in Australia, France, Great Britain and the United States, the cornerstones of the sport. Listed separately are their combined doubles and mixed doubles totals at the four events to give a final overall total of Grand Slam titles won.

It is interesting that until the arrival of Pete Sampras, no men have totally dominated the sport during their playing spans like several of their female counterparts. That is partly because there has always been a greater strength in depth among the men and partly because from the late 1930's to the arrival of open tennis in 1968 most of the top amateur men turned professional and could not participate in the great Championships. One can only speculate how many more titles Rod Laver, for instance, might have won if he had not been barred from the Grand Slams from 1963 to 1967.

Six of the top men in the overall list are Australians who lived in an age when all the top men played doubles and many played mixed doubles too. That is not the case today. The totals for Lendl, Becker, Sampras and Agassi contain only singles victories.

Furthermore, all the players in the lists who won their titles at Wimbledon, the US Championships and the Australian Championships before 1975 won them on grass courts. In 1975 the US Open became a clay court event for three years before switching to its present hard court surface, while the Australian Open changed to another type of hard court in 1988.

In comparing players of different eras it must always be remembered that before 1939 intercontinental travel meant a sea voyage. Thus only a handful of players crossed the Atlantic each year and fewer still ventured to Australia. In considering the overall totals, also remember that the opportunities for competition were fewer in the early years. Although Wimbledon's 1877 meeting was the world's first tennis tournament, there was no ladies' doubles or mixed doubles at the All England Lawn Tennis and Croquet Club until 1913.

Furthermore, the Australian men's Championship began in 1906 and the women's in 1922 while the French Championships were open only to national players until 1924. Accordingly their international records do not begin until 1925.

MEN (winning singles span)	TOTAL SING	GR.SLM AUS	FRA	WIM	USA	Dbls	Mxd	TOTAL
1 Pete Sampras (1990–2000)	13	2	0	7	4	0	0	13
2 Roy Emerson (1961–67)	12	6	2	2	2	16	0	28 (1)
=3 Rod Laver (1960–69)	11	3	2	4	2	6	3	20 (5)
Bjorn Borg (1974–81)	11	0	6	5	0	0	0	11
5 William Tilden (1920–30)	10	0	0	3	7	6	5	21 (4)
=6 Fred Perry (1933–36)	8	1	1	3	3	2	4	14
Ken Rosewall (1953–72)	8	4	2	0	2	9	1	18
Jimmy Connors (1974–83)	8	1	0	2	5	2	0	10
Ivan Lendl (1984–90)	8	2	3	0	3	0	0	8
=10 Richard Sears (1881–87)	7	0	0	0	7	6	0	13
William Renshaw (1881–89)	7	0	0	7	0	5	0	12
William Larned (1901–11)	7	0	0	0	7	0	0	7
Rene Lacoste (1925–29)	7	0	3	2	2	3	0	10
Henri Cochet (1926–32)	7	0	4	2	1	5	3	15
John Newcombe (1967–75)	7	2	0	3	2	17	2 +	26 (2)
John McEnroe (1979–84)	7	0	0	3	4	9	1	17
Mats Wilander (1982–88)	7	3	3	0	1	1	0	8
=18 Laurence Doherty (1902–06)	6	0	0	5	1	10	0	16
Anthony Wilding (1906–13)	6	2	0	4	0	5	0	11
Don Budge (1937–38)	6	1	1	2	2	4	4	14
Jack Crawford (1931–35)	6	4	1	1	0	6	5	17
Stefan Edberg (1985–92)	6	2	0	2	2	3	0	9
Boris Becker (1985–96)	6	2	0	3	1	0	0	6
Andre Agassi (1992–2000)	6	2	1	1	2	0	0	6
=25 Frank Sedgman (1949–52)	5	2	0	1	2	9	8	22 (3)
Tony Trabert (1953–55)	5	0	2	1	2	5	0	10

WOMEN *(winning singles span)*	TOTAL SING	GR. SLM				Dbls	Mxd	TOTAL
		AUS	FRA	WIM	USA			
1 Margaret Smith Court (1960–73)	24	11	5	3	5	19	21 **+**	64 (1)
2 Steffi Graf (1987–99)	22	4	6	7	5	1	0	23
3 Helen Wills Moody (1923–38)	19	0	4	8	7	9	3	31 (5)
=4 Martina Navratilova (1978–90)	18	3	2	9	4	31	7	56 (2)
Chris Evert (1974–86)	18	2	7	3	6	3	0	21
6 Billie Jean King (1966–75)	12	1	1	6	4	16	11	39 (3)
=7 Maureen Connolly (1951–54)	9	1	2	3	3	2	1	12
Monica Seles (1990–96)	9	4	3	0	2	0	0	9
=9 Molla Bjurstedt Mallory (1915–26)	8	0	0	0	8	2	3	13
Suzanne Lenglen (1919–26) **++**	8	0	2	6	0	8	5	21
=11 Dorothea Douglass Chambers (1903–14)	7	0	0	7	0	0	0	7
Maria Bueno (1959–66)	7	0	0	3	4	11	1	19
Evonne Goolagong Cawley (1971–80)	7	4	1	2	0	6 **+++**	1	14
=14 Blanche Bingley Hillyard (1886–1900)	6	0	0	6	0	0	0	6
Nancy Wynne Bolton (1937–51)	6	6	0	0	0	10	4	20
Margaret Osborne DuPont (1946–50) ******	6	0	2	1	3	16	9	31
Louise Brough (1947–55) *****	6	1	0	4	1	17	7	30
Doris Hart (1949–55)	6	1	2	1	2	14	5	35 (4)
=19 Lottie Dod (1887–93)	5	0	0	5	0	0	0	5
Charlotte Cooper Sterry (1895–1908)	5	0	0	5	0	0	0	5
Daphne Akhurst (1925–30)	5	5	0	0	0	5	4	14
Helen Jacobs (1932–36)	5	0	0	1	4	3	1	9
Alice Marble (1936–40)	5	0	0	1	4	6	7	18
Pauline Betz (1942–46) *******	5	0	0	1	4	0	1	6
Althea Gibson (1956–58)	5	0	1	2	2	5	1	11
Martina Hingis (1997–99)	5	3	0	1	1	7	0	12
Doubles titles only								
Elizabeth Ryan (1914–34)	0	0	0	0	0	17	9	26

Notes:

+ These totals include the Australian mixed doubles finals of 1965 (Newcombe & Mrs Court) and 1969 (Mrs.Court) which were divided.

++ Suzanne Lenglen won another four French Championships before 1925 when the event was restricted to members of French clubs (1920–23).

+++ Includes the Australian women's doubles final of 1977 which was divided.

During the war years 1940–45, no Championships were staged in France or at Wimbledon. The Australian Championships were held in 1940 and the USTA continued to hold their Championships every year. During this period:

* Louise Brough won four US doubles titles (1942–45) and one US mixed doubles title (1942).

** Margaret Osborne DuPont won five US doubles titles (1941–45) and three US mixed doubles titles (1943–45).

*** Pauline Betz won three of her four US singles titles (1942–44).

DAVIS CUP by NEC

Net Results on www.daviscup.com – the official Davis Cup Web site.

Visit NEC's official Davis Cup Web site and find the hottest news, the most exciting events, videos, interviews or listen to the live radio broadcast. You're only a click away from the Net at www.daviscup.com.

Below: All seats available to the public on the new Centre Court at Homebush Bay had been sold long before the start of the Games; the fans in their thousands, well marshalled by the ever-helpful volunteers, thronged the site to create a wonderfully exciting atmosphere. *(Stephen Wake)*

Left: Rosanna de los Rios of Paraguay, one of six South Americans in the draw, received a walk over from the injured defending champion Lindsay Davenport in round two but fell to Jelena Dokic in the third. *(Stephen Wake)*

Below: Barbara Schett of Austria, seeded 12, played well to reach the quarter-finals but found the fast-improving Russian, Elena Dementieva, too strong. *(Stephen Wake)*

Below: Quarter-finalist Amanda Coetzer of South Africa, another victim of Australia's Jelena Dokic, seemed to be intimidated by the strongly patriotic crowd. *(Stephen Wake)*

Above: A silver medallist in Atlanta, Arantxa Sanchez-Vicario of Spain was one of Venus Williams' victims this time but the Spanish No.1 did take a set from the eventual champion in the quarter-finals. *(Stephen Wake)*

Right: Fabiola Zuluaga of Columbia caused a major upset by beating the much fancied No. 9 seed, Amelie Mauresmo of France, in the opening round. *(Stephen Wake)*

Far right: Eleventh-seeded Nathalie Dechy, the only member of a strong French squad to reach the third round where Monica Seles (3) proved too strong. *(Stephen Wake)*

Sydney 2000

Above: Monica Seles fell to fellow American Venus Williams in the semi-finals but went on to win the bronze medal. *(Stephen Wake)*

Below: In her last match before retirement, Dominique Van Roost (right), a quarter-finalist in the singles, teamed with Els Callens to win the bronze medal for Belgium. *(Stephen Wake)*

Right: The all-conquering Williams sisters, Venus and Serena, lost only one set in adding Olympic Gold to their Wimbledon title. *(Stephen Wake)*

Above: ITF President Francesco Ricci Bitti with the new Olympic champion Venus Williams. *(Stephen Wake)*

Left: Threatened only once, by fellow-American Monica Seles in the semi-finals, Venus Williams swept through the rest of the field to claim Olympic Gold. *(Stephen Wake)*

Left: After beating seventh seeded Tim Henman of Great Britain in the first round Karol Kucera of Slovakia was brought down by the promising young Swiss No. 1 Roger Federer. *(Stephen Wake)*

Below: Playing on the same court where he had won the Adidas Open in January, Australia's No. 4 seed Lleyton Hewitt, the home nation's chief hope for a medal, lost disappointingly in the first round to Max Mirnyi. *(Stephen Wake)*

Above: One who seized the moment was Arnaud Di Pasquale whose progress to the semi-finals was the best tennis performance by a Frenchman at the 2000 Games. *(Stephen Wake)*

Above: Being seeded 13th proved unlucky for Pat Rafter who disappointed Australian fans by losing in the second round to Daniel Nestor of Canada. *(Stephen Wake)*

Left: It was an outstanding tournament for 19-year-old Roger Federer of Switzerland whose unavailing fight for bronze against Arnaud Di Pasquale of France was one of the best matches of the competition. *(Stephen Wake)*

Above: Mark Woodforde and Todd Woodbridge (left), the world's No.1 doubles pair and gold medallists in Atlanta, were beaten by Daniel Nestor and Sebastien Lareau who brought Canada their first ever Olympic gold medal for tennis. *(Stephen Wake)*

Right: Showing remarkable consistency, Russia's Yevgeny Kafelnikov was another whose gold medal was a first for his country in tennis, a feat that meant more to him, he said, than his Grand Slam wins. *(Stephen Wake)*

Below: Germany's Tommy Haas, the silver medallist, beat two of the seeds but narrowly failed to upset Kafelnikov in a thrilling five set final. *(Stephen Wake)*

Sydney 2000

Paralympics

Above: Stephen Welch of the United States, a silver medallist in Atlanta, once again had to be content with the second prize at the highly successful Paralympics, held shortly after the Olympic Games in Sydney. *(Gordon Gillespie)*

Above right: The new Paralympic men's champion is David Hall who fulfilled a long cherished dream by winning gold on home soil and then took silver in the doubles with fellow Aussie David Johnson. *(Gordon Gillespie)*

Above: Branka Pupovac and Daniela Di Toro of Australia were silver medallists in women's doubles. *(Gordon Gillespie)*

Left: The Dutch women swept all three medals in the singles (L to R) Maaike Smit (bronze), Esther Vergeer (gold) and Sharon Walraven (silver). *(Gordon Gillespie)*

GRAND SLAM WINNERS IN THE OPEN ERA

The first figure in brackets after a player's name denotes the number of titles won at that Championship, the second figure denotes the total number of Grand Slam titles won. Several of the players winning titles in the early years of open tennis had already won some as amateurs. **GS** in bold denotes a **Grand Slam** (winning all four Championships in the same calendar year.)

YEAR	AUSTRALIAN 1968–77 (Jan) 1977–85 (Dec) 1987– (Jan)	FRENCH (May/June)	WIMBLEDON (Jun/July)	US OPEN (Aug/Sep)
1968	Bowrey (1,1) King (1,4)	Rosewall (2,5) Richey (1,2)	Laver (3,7) King (3,5)	Ashe (1,1) Wade (1,1)
1969	**Laver (3,8)** Court (8,14)	**Laver (2,9)** Court (3,15)	**Laver (4,10)** Jones (1,3)	**Laver (2,11) GS** Court (3,16)
1970	Ashe (1,2) **Court (9,17)**	Kodes (1,1) **Court (4,18)**	Newcombe (2,3) **Court (3,19)**	Rosewall (2,6) **Court (4,20) GS**
1971	Rosewall (3,7) Court (10,21)	Kodes (2,2) Goolagong(1,1)	Newcombe (3,4) Goolagong (1,2)	Smith (1,1) King (2,6)
1972	Rosewall (4,8) Wade (1,2)	Gimeno (1,1) King (1,7)	Smith (1,2) King (4,8)	Nastase (1,1) King (3,9)
1973	Newcombe (1,5) Court (11,22)	Nastase (1,2) Court (5,23)	Kodes (1,3) King (5,10)	Newcombe (2,6) Court (5,24)
1974	Connors (1,1) Goolagong (1,3)	Borg (1,1) Evert (1,1)	Connors (1,2) Evert (1,2)	Connors (1,3) King (4,11)
1975	Newcombe (2,7) Goolagong (2,4)	Borg (2,2) Evert (2,3)	Ashe (1,3) King (6,12)	Orantes (1,1) Evert (1,4)
1976	Edmondson (1,1) Cawley (3,5)	Panatta (1,1) Barker (1,1)	Borg (1,3) Evert (2,5)	Connors (2,4) Evert (2,6)
1977 Jan Dec Jan Dec	Tanner (1,1) Gerulaitis (1,1) Reid (1,1) Cawley (4,6)	Vilas (1,1) Jausovec (1,1)	Borg (2,4) Wade (1,3)	Vilas (1,2) Evert (3,7)
1978 Dec	Vilas (1,3) O'Neil (1,1)	Borg (3,5) Ruzici (1,1)	Borg (3,6) Navratilova (1,1)	Connors (3,5) Evert (4,8)
1979 Dec	Vilas (2,4) Jordan (1,1)	Borg (4,7) Evert Lloyd (3,9)	Borg (4,8) Navratilova (2,2)	McEnroe (1,1) Austin (1,1)
1980 Dec	Teacher (1,1) Mandlikova (1,1)	Borg (5,9) Evert Lloyd (4,10)	Borg (5,10) Cawley (2,7)	McEnroe (2,2) Evert Lloyd (5,11)
1981 Dec	Kriek (1,1) Navratilova (1,3)	Borg (6,11) Mandlikova (1,2)	McEnroe (1,3) Evert Lloyd (3,12)	McEnroe (3,4) Austin (2,2)
1982 Dec	Kriek (2,2) Evert Lloyd (1,14)	Wilander (1,1) Navratilova (1,4)	Connors (2,6) Navratilova (3,5)	Connors (4,7) Evert Lloyd (6,13)
1983 Dec	Wilander (1,2) Navratilova (2,8)	Noah (1,1) Evert Lloyd (5,15)	McEnroe (2,5) Navratilova (4,6)	Connors (5,8) Navratilova (1,7)
1984 Dec	Wilander (2,3) Evert Lloyd (2,16)	Lendl (1,1) Navratilova (2,9)	McEnroe (3,6) Navratilova (5,10)	McEnroe (4,7) Navratilova (2,11)
1985 Dec	Edberg (1,1) Navratilova (3,13)	Wilander (2,4) Evert Lloyd (6,17)	Becker (1,1) Navratilova (6,12)	Lendl (1,2) Mandlikova (1,3)
1986	Not Held	Lendl (2,3) Evert Lloyd (7,18)	Becker (2,2) Navratilova (7,14)	Lendl (2,4) Navratilova (3,15)
1987 Jan	Edberg (2,2) Mandlikova (2,4)	Lendl (3,5) Graf (1,1)	Cash (1,1) Navratilova (8,16)	Lendl (3,6) Navratilova (4,17)
1988	Wilander (3,5) **Graf (1,2)**	Wilander (3,6) **Graf (2,3)**	Edberg (1,3) **Graf (1,4)**	Wilander (1,7) **Graf (1,5) GS**

YEAR	AUSTRALIAN	FRENCH	WIMBLEDON	US OPEN
1989	Lendl (1,7) Graf (2,6)	Chang (1,1) Sanchez–Vicario (1,1)	Becker (3,3) Graf (2,7)	Becker (1,4) Graf (2,8)
1990	Lendl (2,8) Graf (3,9)	Gomez (1,1) Seles (1,1)	Edberg (2,4) Navratilova (9,18)	Sampras (1,1) Sabatini (1,1)
1991	Becker (1,5) Seles (1,2)	Courier (1,1) Seles (2,3)	Stich (1,1) Graf (3,10)	Edberg (1,5) Seles (1,4)
1992	Courier (1,2) Seles (2,5)	Courier (2,3) Seles (3,6)	Agassi (1,1) Graf (4,11)	Edberg (2,6) Seles (2,7)
1993	Courier (2,4) Seles (3,8)	Bruguera (1,1) Graf (3,12)	Sampras (1,2) Graf (5,13)	Sampras (2,3) Graf (3,14)
1994	Sampras (1,4) Graf (4,15)	Bruguera (2,2) Sanchez –Vicario (2,2)	Sampras (2,5) Martinez (1,1)	Agassi (1,2) Sanchez–Vicario (1,3)
1995	Agassi (1,3) Pierce (1,1)	Muster (1,1) Graf (4,16)	Sampras (3,6) Graf (6,17)	Sampras (3,7) Graf (4,18)
1996	Becker (2,6) Seles (4,9)	Kafelnikov (1,1) Graf (5,19)	Krajicek (1,1) Graf (7,20)	Sampras (4,8) Graf (5,21)
1997	Sampras (2,9) Hingis (1,1)	Kuerten (1,1) Majoli (1,1)	Sampras (4,10) Hingis (1,2)	Rafter (1,1) Hingis (1,3)
1998	Korda (1,1) Hingis (2,4)	Moya (1,1) Sanchez–Vicario (3,4)	Sampras (5,11) Novotna (1,1)	Rafter (2,2) Davenport (1,1)
1999	Kafelnikov (1,2) Hingis (3,5)	Agassi (1,4) Graf (6,22)	Sampras (6,12) Davenport (1,2)	Agassi (2,5) S.Williams (1,1)
2000	Agassi (2,6) Davenport (1, 3)	Kuerten (2, 2) Pierce (1, 2)	Sampras (7, 13) Williams V. (1, 1)	Safin (1, 1) Williams V. (1, 2)

ATP Tour

ATP Tour Year • Points Explanation and Allocation
ATP Tour Tournaments – Tennis Masters Series,
Men's International Series' 1 and 2
Tennis Masters Cup

In the very last match of the year, the final of the Tennis Masters Cup in Lisbon, Brazil's Gustavo Kuerten overtook Marat Safin to win the inaugural ATP Champions Race and become the world No. 1. (Stephen Wake)

Sweden's Magnus Norman spent seven weeks as the leader of the inaugural Champions Race but faded in the closing stages to finish in fourth place. (Paul Zimmer)

The ATP Year

John Parsons

When it was launched in Doha, Chennai and Adelaide on 3 January, 2000, not even the most enthusiastic and persuasive advocates of the new ATP Tour Champions Race could have envisaged, in their wildest dream, what a dramatic finish there would be eleven months later.

It was only in the 3,012th match of a circuit which had reached its 70th tournament of the year that Brazil's Gustavo Kuerten brilliantly achieved the 6–4 6–4 6–4 victory over Andre Agassi which not only won him the Tennis Masters Cup but also enabled him to cross the finishing line of the race in first place.

Going into Bercy, the last of the nine tournaments which comprise the Tennis Masters Series, there were still four candidates for the final two of the eight places in Lisbon, the stopping place chosen as the first venue for the new Tennis Masters Cup on what is currently proposed to be a constant worldwide tour. The favourites to join the already qualified Marat Safin, Kuerten, Pete Sampras, Magnus Norman, Yevgeny Kafelnikov and Agassi, were Lleyton Hewitt and Alex Corretja. And that is what transpired although on the opening day in Paris, there was still outside hope, mathematically, for Thomas Enqvist and Tim Henman.

When Safin beat Mark Philippoussis in a titanic final at the Palais Omnisports de Paris after Kuerten, second in the race, was beaten in the semi-finals, it sent the Russian into Lisbon with what looked to be an insuperable lead of 75 points. It meant that if Kuerten lost just one of his round-robin matches in the Green Group, then an unbeaten record for Safin in his three Red Group matches would make him the first Russian and the youngest player with the year-ending number one status since such statistics began 28 years earlier.

Kuerten's defeat by Agassi on the opening night, a few hours after Safin had beaten Corretja, prompted many to dub Safin world champion-elect, especially as the gangly 6ft 3in right hander from Brazil was needing extensive treatment from trainers Bill Norris and Alex Stober during and between every match to keep his aching body moving.

With a round-robin format, however, losers can so often become winners and when Safin was soundly walloped by Agassi in the semi-finals, Kuerten took full advantage of the reprieve the format offered by avenging that early defeat by the still charismatic American, when it mattered most in the final.

Having gone so close, 20-year-old Safin was distraught. It had been one tournament too many for his still developing body and he was already back in Moscow by the time Kuerten, the first South American to become world number one, was being hugged by his mother and laden with both the Masters Cup and the world number one trophy. To land this end-of-the-year jackpot, Kuerten had beaten Yevgeny Kafelnikov, Pete Sampras and Agassi in successive matches. He was the first player to beat the two Americans who had dominated the scene for the past decade, in back-to-back matches since Michael Chang in Toronto in 1990.

Those invaluable points Kuerten won in the final had enabled him to finish with 839 and meant he had overtaken Safin by just 15, the difference between reaching the third or fourth rounds of a Grand Slam. There was considerable sympathy for Safin. Not only had he won seven tournaments during the year, two more than Kuerten, but he reached more finals (9) than any of his rivals, won more matches (73) and the most tie-breaks (32).

His opening months of the year could hardly have been worse. By the time he reached Monte Carlo, where he suffered his sixth opening match defeat in nine tournaments, it took some tough talking from fellow countryman, Andrei Chesnokov to start turning his game round. Safin's match record was 5–11. Thereafter he won his next 11 matches and by the end of the year had improved it to 73–27, which compared more than favourably with Agassi's 63–14 while finishing as number one 12 months earlier. Kuerten's record for 2000 was 64–22. In Grand Slam terms the two front-running challengers were equal. Kuerten won the French, reclaiming the crown he first wore in 1997, while Safin gave Sampras what even the Wimbledon and former world champion called 'a humiliating defeat' in the final of the US Open.

Safin won two of the Tennis Masters Series tournaments, Toronto, as well as Paris, Bercy, and was runner-up in Hamburg, which was won by Kuerten, who in turn was runner-up in Key

Biscayne and Rome. Safin's four other titles were on clay in Barcelona, Mallorca, St Petersburg and Tashkent. Kuerten's other final triumphs were in Indianapolis (where he again beat Safin in the final) and Santiago.

In retrospect, the year also began somewhat disappointingly for Kuerten. He suffered first round defeats in Sydney and the Australian Open, as well as a surprise Davis Cup reverse against Frenchman, Nicolas Escude.Yet once he won in Santiago in early March, his form began to gather momentum and success in reaching the final at the Ericsson Open all helped to lay foundations for the major triumphs to follow, especially at Roland Garros and then the remarkable finish in Lisbon.

Although some complained that the Race was confusing for the public, in that the Race leader, particularly in the first nine months of the year, was often not the top seed in the next tournament he played, the overall verdict from most players, including some who had been sceptics back in January, was that it was a rousing success. It clearly was, especially after the interest and excitement the final stages of Race 2000 created. Those who may have found it hard to understand what the Race meant in its inaugural year, will surely now realise that it is a reflection of a player's performances in that calendar year, just as in soccer, the leaders of the Premier Division may not be the reigning champions. At the same time there is a case for going back to calling the entry system, which decides who gets into which tournaments and if and where they are seeded, the world rankings. By using both, side by side, the different figures surely tell you everything you want to know. While the ranking/entry system tells you how well a player has performed overall in relation to his peers over the previous 12 months, the Race is the more illuminating and in some cases more relevant guide to current form. This is based on a player's best 18 tournaments in that particular year, of which four must be the Grand Slams plus the nine Tennis Masters Series events. Together they account for 70 per cent of a player's end-of-the-year total, thereby placing the emphasis where it should be, on tournaments where the entryis the strongest.

The concluding event, the Tennis Masters Cup, represented the new spirit of co-operation between the International Tennis Federation, the Grand Slams and the ATP Tour. Following the ATP Tour's decision to breakaway at the end of 1989, both had staged their own year-ending tournaments. For the start of the new millenium, those two events, the Grand Slam Cup and the Tour Championships came together. The outcome? Broad smiles all round.

The ATP Tour's determined support of the Race had been handsomely justified, while the quality and status of the Slams had been underlined by the way the four winners from Australia, France, Wimbledon and the United States, filled the four semi-final places in Lisbon. It fully vindicated the decision that irrespective of their place in the Race, the winner of a Grand Slam would automatically qualify for the Masters Cup. In the event such a proviso, which upset a few players when it looked as if one of the top eight might lose out to make way for Agassi to compete, was not needed. The top three at the end of the Race were all Slam winners, Kuerten, Safin and Sampras. Agassi finished sixth. The case rests.

Seven different players had the honour of leading the Race 2000, with none more thrilled than Fabrice Santoro after he gathered more points than anyone in the first week of the year in Qatar and was happy to let everyone believe he was world number one. Successes for Hewitt on home territory in Adelaide and Sydney meant he then took over the tennis yellow jersey through the two weeks of the Australian Open, when Agassi's triumph put him on top.

Four weeks later, despite losing an acrimonious final to Marc Rosset at the London Arena, Kafelnikov surged to the top. Reaching the final had been enough to lift him above Agassi, though by only a single point. That did not matter in Russia where the headlines reflected the celebrations. A fortnight later Agassi sneaked back into the lead again by just two points – and so it went on, with Kafelnikov leapfrogging straight back into the lead at the end of the following week.Victory at the Ericsson restored Agassi's supremacy and in all during the year he was to be on top of the Race for 11 weeks, although this paled alongside the total of 16 weeks in which Kuerten was there prior to his snatch-and-grab winning raid on the last day. It was his form in winning the French Open which propelled Kuerten to the front of the pack for the first time after Magnus Norman had gone into the lead by winning Rome. Norman returned to first position after winning his third title of the year in his native Sweden (Bastad) and in all looked down on the others for a total of seven weeks.

Throughout the summer the baton continued to change hands, with Agassi and Kuerten both taking over again for a while and Sampras also on top for one week after his record-breaking seventh Wimbledon title. Yet increasingly after Safin had won his first Grand Slam title at Flushing Meadows, it always seemed likely to be a straight sprint to the finish between him and Kuerten. At the bell Safin's lead, after four weeks in front, gave him what probably ought to have been a sufficient cushion. Success in tennis, though, as those who apparently want to introduce short sets and no-ad scoring should remember is about mental, as well as physical strength allied to natural skill. That is why Kuerten's triumph based on all those qualities in abundance, was so joyously applauded and showed once again that the game does not need gimmicks which might provide short-term commercial game but will probably drive away many more customers than it might attract.

Kuerten also headed the table for the longest period of winning form during the year and was the only player during 2000 to win both singles and doubles at the same tournament – Santiago. Between 15 May and his arrival at Wimbledon where he was beaten in the first round, even though he has a more than good enough serve and volley to do better, he won 15 consecutive matches. In 1999, Sampras's best run spanned 24 matches. Hewitt was second on the 2000 list with 13 match victories in succession during January. Safin came next with 12 consecutive wins but he achieved that TWICE, first between April-May and then by winning the US Open and Tashkent back-to-back.

Safin's seven titles, were two more than anyone else managed. Apart from Kuerten, Corretja, equalling his previous best in 1998 and Norman, for the second year in succession, also won five, while there were four for Hewitt. No other player won more than two, which underlines the strength in depth of the men's game. This was further illustrated in the way Safin was the only player to win two Masters Series titles. The others were spread among seven challengers, Corretja (Indian Wells), Sampras (Key Biscayne), Cedric Pioline (Monte Carlo), Norman (Rome), Kuerten (Hamburg), Enqvist (Cincinnati), and Wayne Ferreira (Stuttgart), the only top winner to finish outside the top ten.

To add to Safin's misfortune at being pipped on the Race post, until Kuerten won the first indoor title of his career in Lisbon, he was the only player who could boast of winning tournaments on three different surfaces during the year, two on clay, three on hard and two on carpet. There were 40 different champions on the men's circuit, which for the first time officially included the Olympic Games, where Race points could be won. That was three winners fewer than last year from the same number of tournaments. They came from only 17 countries, maintaining a decline, which many will find disappointing. In 1999, the champions represented 20 countries but in 1998, the 41 different winners, admittedly from eight more events, came from 33 countries.

Swedish players had most to celebrate. With five-times champion, Norman, leading the way, they secured 11 titles, the others coming from Enqvist (2), Magnus Gustafsson, Magnus Larsson, Thomas Johansson and Andreas Vinciguerra. The United States, who had regained first place in this table in 1999, with 13 winners, slumped to sixth equal with Argentina, by far their worst rating since the advent of Open tennis in 1968. Their players won only four titles – two by Sampras and one each by Agassi and Michael Chang, although as two of the events they won included the Australian Open and Wimbledon, some might argue that quality means more than quantity.

Russia, 14th equal in 1999, soared to a best-ever second equal place, thanks entirely to Safin's seven titles and two from Kafelnikov, one of which was the gold medal which meant so much to him, at the Olympics. Sharing second with them were Spain, whose nine tiles were distrbuted much more broadly among five players – Corretja (5), and one each for Juan Balcells, Alex Calatrava, Carlos Moya and Fernando Vicente. Next were Australia with seven titles provided by four players (Hewitt, Andrew Ilie, Philippoussis and Pat Rafter), followed by France with six spread among five players, Pioline (2), Arnaud Clement, Jerome Golmard, Sebastien Grosjean and Santoro. Tim Henman's two titles in Vienna and Brighton, which happily ended his run of defeats in seven consecutive finals, left Britain 10th.

Although this time it was with one player fewer than in 1999, Spain once more led the table of 28 countries (down from 31 a year earlier) with representation in the world's top 100. Apart from Alex Corretja (7), Juan Carlos Ferrero (12), Albert Costa (26) and Juan Barcels (86) who represented them in the Davis Cup final against Australia, the others taking their total to 13, were Carlos Moya (41), Fernando Vicente (44), Francisco Clavet (46), Albert Portas (59), Alex Calatrava (63), Alberto Martin (73), Felix Mantilla (83), Sergi Bruguera (84) and Galo Blanco (94).

The United States remained in second place with nine, two fewer than the previous year, followed, as in 1999, by France and Sweden both with eight. Returning to this list, after a lengthy absence, was Israel, thanks to Harel Levy, who maintained his impressive annual rise since first stepping on to the ladder in equal 913th place in 1995, by climbing from 180 at the start of the year to 58 at the end.

No player made greater headway up the rankings during the year than Argentina's Guillermo Coria, who climbed an astonishing 641 places from 729 to 88. Belgium's Olivier Rochus was another major mover – starting the year at 364 and ending it 197 places higher on 67.

Safin hit the most aces, 921, just 14 more than Mark Philippoussis, followed by Kuerten on 742. Tim Henman's 537 placing him tenth on the list is worth noting because the British number one had pledged £100 to charity for every ace he struck during the year. That made the individual contribution by the chairman of the ATP Tour's Charities, in addition to other money he helped to raise, a handsome £53,700. Two other statistics to note: Taylor Dent, son of the former Australian Davis Cup player, Phil, hit the fastest serve timed on the Tour, with one delivery of 140mph during the US Open. Philippoussis and Switzerland's Marc Rosset shared second place, one mile an hour slower. The longest tie-break set, 16–14, was actually registered three times, while the longest match was the 4 hour 11 minutes victory by the unseeded South African, Wayne Ferreira over Lleyton Hewitt in the final of the Tennis Masters Series event in Stuttgart.

In doubles, the year brought with it the end of an era. After almost a year of supremacy, the Woodies – Mark Woodforde and Todd Woodbridge – decided to call it a day. After winning another eight titles during the year, bringing their career total together to a record 61, they left the stage vacant for others in the ATP World Doubles Championships in Bangalore but still finished as the number one pair in the year's points race.

At the age of 35 and 29 respectively, the Australians could look back on their final year with one or two disappointments, such as having to settle for silver medal in the Olympics. On the other hand there were ample compensations. Their first triumph at the French Open, not only completed their full hand of Grand Slam titles but was the one which enabled them to overtake the all-time record of doubles titles, (57), shared by John McEnroe with Peter Fleming and Bob Hewitt with Frew McMillan. Four weeks later, a record sixth Wimbledon title was the crowning glory, prompting The All England Club to recognise their enormous contribution to doubles by making them honorary members. 'When we received the letters from Wimbledon, I couldn't stop jumping up and down in the kitchen' said Woodforde. 'And then Todd rang me to say his wife was so happy she had burst into tears.'

Meanwhile as the debate continued over the significance of doubles in tour events, with some tournament directors apparently eager to cut draw sizes to the bone or even eliminate the doubles altogether, there was no lack of excitement or enthusiasm when the World Doubles Championships reached its climax.

Brilliant sunshine and large crowds were a permanent feature of the event. India's own Leander Paes and Mahesh Bhupathi, who through injuries had only played a limited circuit together during the year, began in eighth place among the seeds but first in terms of popular support. Yet there was to be no 'third time lucky' tag for the Indians, as they were beaten in the final for a third time in four years. Their conquerers were the American-South African combination of Don Johnson and Piet Norval, who stepped up their challenge for a place in the Championships during the autumn and won the final 7–6 (8) 6–3 6–4 in 2 hours 18 mins.

Norval, 30, who has been one of the most consistent doubles players for several years and had qualified for the doubles showdown a year earlier with Kevin Ullyett, was thrilled. 'I see this as a fifth major and it was a dream to win a major during my career' he said. 'I think it will take a while to sink in.'

As in Lisbon, the final was a repeat of a match-up during the round-robin section of the tournament and once again the result was reserved. In their Red Group matches Bhupathi and Paes won 6–4 6–4 but three days later they never began to play with the same authority or confidence and were well beaten. A further measure of the mental strength and determination illustrated by Johnson and Norval, who only started playing together earlier in the year and had picked up three other titles along the way (Estoril, Nottingham and Basle), was the way they recovered from being a break down in the final set of their semi-final against the new Swedish challengers, Simon Aspelin and Johan Landsberg.

Bangalore also marked the retirement of another major servant of the doubles game, Rick Leach. The 36-year-old American, who had won 14 titles with a wide variety of partners for 14 years, including nine Grand Slam doubles or mixed, won the doubles Championships with Jonathan Stark in 1997 and this time reached the semi-finals with another veteran, Ellis Ferreira.

In terms of prize money, Kuerten, appropriately enough, topped the list with $4,701,610, slightly more than Andre Agassi in the previous year though still almost $2m short of the record set by Pete Sampras in 1997. The workaholic Kafelnikov finished with $3,755,599, with a further $3,524,959 heading into the bank account of his fellow Russian, Safin. Interestingly, however, the money continued to be concentrated even more at the top, with only 13 players earning more than $1million prize money, compared with 17 a year earlier.

ATP TOUR 2000 – POINTS EXPLANATION

A new points race was introduced in 2000 – the ATP Tour Champions Race – which was designed to make it easier for the public to understand which players were setting the pace during the course of the year. All players started the year with zero points.

Alongside the new race, a modified version of the old ranking list – the ATP Entry System – continued to measure form over a moving twelve month period to determine eligibility for tournament entries and seedings. Bonus points no longer applied.

Players whose position on the ATP Entry System was high enough were obliged to participate in the four Grand Slam Championships plus all nine of the new Tennis Masters Series tournaments. Any who did not participate had to include zero points for that week among their 18 best tournament results for the year, which could include five International Series events.

ATP TOUR CHAMPIONS RACE POINTS

	W	F	SF	QF	16	32	64	128	Q
Grand Slam	200	140	90	50	30	15	7	1	+3
Tennis Masters Series	100	70	45	25	15	7	1		+3
Int. Series 1 – $1m	60	42	27	15	5	1			+2
Int. Series 1 – $800,000 – IS 2 $1m	50	35	22	12	5	1			+2
Int. Series 2 – $800,000	45	31	20	11	4	1			+2
Int. Series 2 – $600,000	40	28	18	10	3	1			+1
Int. Series 2 – $400,000	35	24	15	8	3	1			+1

Tennis Masters Cup Points: 20 points for each round robin match won
+ 40 points for a semi-final win
+ 50 points for the final win
An undefeated winner, therefore, would win 150 points

ATP ENTRY SYSTEM POINTS

	W	F	SF	QF	16	32	64	128	Q
Grand Slams (averaged)	1000	700	450	250	150	75	35	5	+15
Tennis Masters Series	500	350	225	125	75	35	5		+15
Int. Series 1 – $1m	300	210	135	75	25	5			+10
Int. Series 1 – $800,000 – IS 2 $1m	250	175	110	60	25	5			+10
Int. Series 2 – $800,000	225	155	100	55	20	5			+10
Int. Series 2 – $600,000	200	140	90	50	15	5			+5
Int. Series 2 – $400,000	175	120	75	40	15	5			+5
Challenger – $125,000+Hosp.	90	63	40	21	9	1			+3
– $125,000	80	56	36	19	8	1			+3
– $100,000	70	49	31	16	7	1			+3
– $75,000	60	42	27	14	6	1			+3
– $37,500+Hosp.	55	38	24	13	5	1			+2
– $50,000	50	35	22	12	5	1			+2
Futures – $15,000+Hosp.	24	16	8	4	1				
Futures – $15,000	18	12	6	3	1				
Futures – $10,000	12	8	4	2	1				

Points in Qualifying events:
Grand Slams   8 for losing in the last round, 4 for losing in the second round
Tennis Masters Series 8 for losing in the last round, 1 for losing in the first round
International Series 1 5 for losing in the last round, 1 for losing in the first round

Note: Int. Series 1 = International Series/Championship Series tournaments
Int. Series 2 = International Series/World Series tournaments

GRAND SLAM CHAMPIONSHIPS AND ATP TOUR 2000

Week Comm.	Venue	Surface	Singles Final	Doubles Winners
03 Jan	Doha	Hard	F. Santoro d. R. Schuttler 3–6 7–5 3–0 ret	Knowles/Mirnyi
03 Jan	Chennai	Hard	J. Golmard d. M. Hantschk 6–3 6–7 6–3	Boutter/C. Rochus
03 Jan	Adelaide	Hard	L. Hewitt d. T. Enqvist 3–6 6–3 6–2	Woodbridge/ Woodforde
10 Jan	Sydney	Hard	L. Hewitt d. J. Stoltenberg 6–4 6–0	Woodbridge/ Woodforde
10 Jan	Auckland	Hard	M. Norman d. M. Chang 3–6 6–3 7–5	E. Ferreira/Leach
17 Jan	**Australian Open**	**Hard**	**A. Agassi d. Y. Kafelnikov 3–6 6–3 6–2 6–4**	**E. Ferreira/Leach**
7 Feb	Marseille	Hard	M. Rosset d. R. Federer 2–6 6–3 7–6	Aspelin/Landsberg
7 Feb	Dubai	Hard	N. Kiefer d. J. Ferrero 7–5 4–6 6–3	Novak/Rikl
7 Feb	San Jose, CA	Hard	M. Philippoussis d. M. Tillstrom 7–5 4–6 6–3	Gambill/ Humphries
14 Feb	Memphis, TN	Hard	M. Larsson d. B. Black 6–2 1–6 6–3	Gimelstob/Lareau
14 Feb	Rotterdam	Hard	C. Pioline d. T. Henman 6–7 6–4 7–6	Adams/De Jager
21 Feb	Mexico City	Clay	J. Chela d. M. Puerta 6–4 7–6	B. Black/Johnson
21 Feb	London	Hard	M. Rosset d. Y. Kafelnikov 6–4 6–4	Adams/De Jager
28 Feb	Santiago	Clay	G. Kuerten d. M. Puerta 7–6 6–3	Kuerten/Prieto
28 Feb	Delray Beach, FL	Hard	S. Koubek d. A. Calatrava 6–1 4–6 6–4	MacPhie/Zimonjic
28 Feb	Copenhagen	Hard	A. Vinciguerra d. M. Larsson 6–3 7–6	Damm/Prinosil
06 Mar	Scottsdale, AZ	Hard	L. Hewitt d. T. Henman 6–4 7–6	Palmer/Reneberg
06 Mar	Bogota	Clay	M. Puerta d. Y. El Aynaoui 6–4 7–6	Albano/Arnold
13 Mar	Indian Wells, CA	Hard	A. Corretja d. T. Enqvist 6–4 6–4 6–3	O'Brien/Palmer
20 Mar	Miami, FL	Hard	P. Sampras d. G. Kuerten 6–1 6–7 7–6 7–6	Woodbridge/ Woodforde
10 Apr	Estoril	Clay	C. Moya d. F. Clavet 6–3 6–2	Johnson/Norval
10 Apr	Casablanca	Clay	F. Vicente d. S. Grosjean 6–4 4–6 7–6	Clement/Grosjean
10 Apr	Atlanta, GA	Clay	A. Ilie d. J. Stoltenberg 6–3 7–5	E. Ferreira/Leach
17 Apr	Monte Carlo	Clay	C. Pioline d. D. Hrbaty 6–4 7–6 7–6	W. Ferreira/ Kafelnikov
24 Apr	Barcelona	Clay	M. Safin d. J. Ferrero 6–3 6–3 6–4	Kulti/Tillstrom
01 May	Orlando, FL	Clay	F. Gonzalez d. N. Massu 6–2 6–3	Paes/Siemerink
01 May	Munich	Clay	F. Squillari d. T. Haas 6–4 6–4	Adams/De Jager
01 May	Mallorca	Clay	M. Safin d. M. Tillstrom 6–4 6–3	Llodra/Nargiso
08 May	Rome	Clay	M. Norman d. G. Kuerten 6–3 4–6 6–4 6–4	Damm/Hrbaty
15 May	Hamburg	Clay	G. Kuerten d. M. Safin 6–4 5–7 6–4 5–7 7–6	Woodbridge/ Woodforde
21 May	St. Polten	Clay	A. Pavel d. A. Ilie 7–5 3–6 6–2	Bhupathi/ Kratzmann
29 May	**Roland Garros**	**Clay**	**G. Kuerten d. M. Norman 6–2 6–3 2–6 7–6**	**Woodbridge/ Woodforde**
12 Jun	Halle	Grass	D. Prinosil d. R. Krajicek 6–3 6–2	Kulti/Tillstrom
12 Jun	Queen's	Grass	L. Hewitt d. P. Sampras 6–4 6–4	Woodbridge/ Woodforde
19 Jun	's-Hertogenbosch	Grass	P. Rafter d. N. Escude 6–1 6–3	Damm/Suk
19 Jun	Nottingham	Grass	S. Grosjean d. B. Black 7–6 6–3	Johnson/Norval
26 Jun	**Wimbledon**	**Grass**	**P. Sampras d. P. Rafter 6–7 7–6 6–4 6–2**	**Woodbridge/ Woodforde**
10 Jul	Gstaad	Clay	A. Corretja d. M. Puerta 6–1 6–3	Novak/Rikl
10 Jul	Bastad	Clay	M. Norman d. A. Vinciguerra 6–1 7–6	Kulti/Tillstrom
10 Jul	Newport, RI	Grass	P. Wessels d. J. Knippschild 7–6 6–3	Erlich/Levy
17 Jul	Stuttgart	Clay	F. Squillari d. G. Gaudio 6–2 3–6 4–6 6–4 6–2	Novak/Rikl
17 Jul	Amsterdam	Clay	M. Gustafsson d. R. Sluiter 6–7 6–3 7–6 6–1	Roitman/Schneiter
17 Jul	Umag	Clay	M. Rios d. M. Puerta 7–6 4–6 6–3	Lopez-Moron/ Portas
24 Jul	Kitzbuhel	Clay	A. Corretja d. E. Alvarez 6–3 6–1 3–0 ret	Albano/Suk
24 Jul	Los Angeles, CA	Hard	M. Chang d. J. Gambill 6–7 6–3 ret	Kilderry/Stolle
24 Jul	San Marino	Clay	A. Calatrava d. S. Bruguera 7–6 1–6 6–4	Cibulec/Friedl
31 Jul	Toronto	Hard	M. Safin d. H. Levy 6–2 6–4	Lareau/Nestor
07 Aug	Cincinnati, OH	Hard	T. Enqvist d. T. Henman 7–6 6–4	Woodbridge/ Woodforde
14 Aug	Indianapolis, IN	Hard	G. Kuerten d. M. Safin 3–6 7–6 7–6	Hewitt/Stolle
14 Aug	Washington, DC	Hard	A. Corretja d. A. Agassi 6–2 6–3	O'Brien/Palmer
21 Aug	Long Island, NY	Hard	M. Norman d. T. Enqvist 6–3 5–7 7–5	Stark/Ullyett

The 1999 finalist Todd Martin congratulates Marat Safin on his semi-final victory at Flushing Meadows, the prelude to a stunning display by the young Russian in the final. (Stephen Wake)

Week Comm.	Venue	Surface	Singles Final	Doubles Winners
28 Aug	**US Open**	**Hard**	**M. Safin d. P. Sampras 6–4 6–3 6–3**	**Hewitt/Mirnyi**
11 Sep	Tashkent	Hard	M. Safin d. D. Sanguinetti 6–3 6–4	Gimelstob/ Humphries
11 Sep	Bucharest	Clay	J. Balcells d. M. Hantschk 6–4 3–6 7–6	A. Martin/Ran
18 Sep	**Olympic Games**	**Hard**	**Y. Kafelnikov d. T. Haas 7–6 3–6 6–2 4–6 6–3**	**Lareau/Nestor**
25 Sep	Palermo	Clay	O. Rochus d. D. Nargiso 7–6 6–1	Carbonell/Garcia
02 Oct	Hong Kong	Hard	N. Kiefer d. M. Philippoussis 7–6 2–6 6–2	W. Black/Ullyett Woodforde
09 Oct	Vienna	Hard	T. Henman d. T. Haas 6–4 6–4 6–4	Kafelnikov/ Zimonjic
09 Oct	Tokyo	Hard	S. Schalken d. N. Lapentti 6–4 3–6 6–1	Bhupathi/Paes
16 Oct	Toulouse	Hard	A. Corretja d. C. Moya 6–3 6–2	Boutter/Santoro
16 Oct	Shanghai	Hard	M. Norman d. S. Schalken 6–4 4–6 6–3	Haarhuis/Schalken
23 Oct	Moscow	Carpet	Y. Kafelnikov d. D. Prinosil 6–2 7–5	Bjorkman/Prinosil
23 Oct	Basle	Carpet	T. Enqvist d. R. Federer 6–2 4–6 7–6 1–6 6–1	Johnson/Norval
30 Oct	Stuttgart	Carpet	W. Ferreira d. L. Hewitt 7–6 3–6 6–7 7–6 6–2	Novak/Rikl
06 Nov	Lyon	Carpet	A. Clement d. P. Rafter 7–6 7–6	Haarhuis/Stolle
06 Nov	St. Petersburg	Carpet	M. Safin d. D. Hrbaty 2–6 6–4 6–4	Nestor/Ullyett
13 Nov	Paris	Carpet	M. Safin d. M. Philippoussis 3–6 7–6 6–4 3–6 7–6	Kulti/Mirnyi
20 Nov	Stockholm	Hard	T. Johansson d. Y. Kafelnikov 6–2 6–4 6–4	Knowles/Nestor
20 Nov	Brighton	Hard	T. Henman d. D. Hrbaty 6–2 6–2	Hill/Tarango
27 Nov	Lisbon	Hard	G. Kuerten d. A. Agassi 6–4 6–4 6–4	
04 Dec	**David Cup Final**	**Clay**	**Spain d. Australia 3–1**	
11 Dec	Bangalore	Hard		Johnson/Norval

PLAYER NATIONALITIES AND BIRTHDAYS (MEN)

The following players have competed in the 2000 Grand Slam Championships, the ATP Tour and Davis Cup Ties. (Birthdays dd/mm/yy.)

Surname / Forename	Nation	DOB
ABADIA, Adelo	PHI	15/05/77
ABAROA, Enrique	MEX	10/01/74
ABDALLA, Mandour Rushdi-Mohammed	SUD	14/07/64
ABDUL-AAL, Essam	BRN	11/08/69
ABDUL-AAL, Nader	BRN	14/07/73
ABELSON, David	CAN	13/02/75
ABU KHULAIF, Baqer	KSA	07/03/80
ADAKTUSSON, Jacob	SWE	31/08/80
ADAMS, David	RSA	05/01/70
ADELEKAN, Ganiyu	NGR	02/10/75
ADEN, Abdallah	DJI	08/04/72
ADEN, Abdou-Rahman	DJI	28/02/70
ADEYO, Komi	TOG	07/06/79
ADOUM, Alifa	CMR	17/08/72
AGAEV, Emin	AZE	14/05/79
AGASSI, Andre	USA	29/04/70
AGENOR, Ronald	HAI	13/11/64
AL ALAWI, Sultan-Khalfan	QAT	16/03/77
AL BALUSHI, Mahmoud	UAE	30/06/80
AL FOUDARI, Mohammed-Rashid	KUW	17/06/79
AL GHAREEB, Mohammed	KUW	22/07/80
AL HADID, Ahmad	JOR	07/06/81
AL KHULAIFI, Nasser-Ghanim	QAT	12/11/73
AL MAAYTAH, Ammar	JOR	20/11/83
AL MEGAYEL, Badar	KSA	01/12/74
AL NABHANI, Khalid	OMA	02/09/82
AL NABHANI, Mohammed	OMA	01/09/85
AL RAWAHI, Mudrik	OMA	25/06/79
AL SAOUD, Mohammed-Ali	QAT	25/07/76
AL SHATTI, Adel	KUW	29/08/72
AL SOLAITEEN, Hamed	KUW	05/07/82
AL THAGIB, Omar	KSA	15/12/83
AL UMANA, Othman	UAE	12/10/76
ALAMI, Karim	MAR	24/05/73
ALBANO, Pablo	ARG	04/11/67
ALI-AKKAL, Said	ALG	02/05/74
ALLEN, Joel	HAI	09/11/81
ALMEIDA, Nelson	ANG	06/04/79
ALONSO, Julian	ESP	02/08/77
ALVAREZ, Calton	HON	10/01/75
ALVAREZ, Emilio	ESP	15/11/72
ANCIC, Mario	CRO	30/03/84
ANDERSEN, Jan-Frode	NOR	29/08/72
ANDRIANAFETRA, Harivony	MAD	15/07/69
ANEIROS-ROMERO, Braen	PAN	01/03/83
ANTELO, Jose	BOL	03/07/82
ANYIDOHO, Courage	GHA	23/06/80
ARAZI, Hicham	MAR	19/10/73
ARCILLA, Johnny	PHI	15/02/80
ARLAIN, Sirsean	LCA	01/01/81
ARMANDO, Hugo	USA	27/05/78
ARNOLD, Lucas	ARG	12/10/74
ARTHURS, Wayne	AUS	18/03/71
ASHTON, Hayden	ECA	24/07/64
ASPELIN, Simon	SWE	11/05/74
AUGUSTIN, Jean-Claude	HAI	12/11/73
AVALOS-BRENES, Rafael	CRC	21/06/61
AWADHY, Omar-Bahrouzyan	UAE	16/01/82
AZKARA, Mustafa	TUR	19/12/70

Surname / Forename	Nation	DOB
BACCANELLO, Paul	AUS	12/06/79
BACHELOT, Jean-Francois	FRA	11/06/77
BAEZ-BRITEZ, Emilio	PAR	28/05/78
BAGHDATIS, Marcos	CYP	17/06/85
BAHAR-UD-DIN, Hardiyamin	BRU	16/06/81
BAIRES, Jose	ESA	05/12/79
BALCELLS, Juan	ESP	20/06/75
BALE, Lan	RSA	07/09/69
BALZEKAS, Alvaras	LTU	08/04/82
BANZER, Kenny	LIE	11/02/86
BARANOV, Pavel	KAZ	07/11/80
BARNARD, Marius	RSA	20/01/69
BARON, Ivan	USA	12/11/72
BARRON, Scott	IRL	27/08/74
BARTHEZ, Lionel	FRA	18/05/67
BARTHOLD, Carl-Henry	HAI	27/01/77
BASALIC, Haris	BIH	01/09/79
BASCOME, Janson	BER	19/11/79
BASTL, George	SUI	01/04/75
BAUDINET, Brett	POC	01/11/81
BEARDSLEY, Jonathan	USA	08/11/75
BEDMINSTER, Carlton	ANT	08/11/82
BEHR, Noam	ISR	13/10/75
BEHR, Raoul	AHO	24/09/76
BEHREND, Tomas	GER	12/12/74
BENNETEAU, Julien	FRA	20/12/81
BERASATEGUI, Alberto	ESP	28/06/73
BERGH, Fredrik	SWE	22/04/75
BERNARDO, Yari	ESA	10/11/73
BERTHE, Youssou	SEN	14/09/85
BERTOLINI, Massimo	ITA	30/05/74
BETTS, James	BAR	17/08/78
BEWLAY, Lesedi	BOT	03/08/82
BHUPATHI, Mahesh	IND	07/06/74
BJORKMAN, Jonas	SWE	23/03/72
BLACK, Byron	ZIM	06/10/69
BLACK, Wayne	ZIM	14/11/73
BLAKE, James	USA	28/12/79
BLAKE, Ryan	USA	04/02/66
BLAKE, Thomas	USA	29/12/76
BLANCO, Galo	ESP	08/10/76
BLUMAUER, Georg	AUT	16/07/74
BOGGETTI, Christophe	MON	11/04/67
BONELLO, Luke	MLT	18/07/83
BONIFACIUS, Raj	ISL	08/11/69
BORELLA, Bob	DEN	27/06/80
BORETTI, Stian	NOR	20/12/81
BORUSZEWSKI, Jan	GER	02/10/77
BOSE, Alex	GER	13/06/76
BOSIO, Christophe	MON	11/04/77
BOU-HASSOUN, Rabi	SYR	09/06/78
BOURGAULT DU COUDRAY, Jean-Marcel	MRI	15/10/77
BOUTTER, Julien	FRA	05/04/74
BOWEN, Devin	USA	18/05/72
BOWER, Justin	RSA	23/05/78
BRAASCH, Karsten	GER	14/07/67
BRANDI, Chris	USA	11/06/82
BRANDI, Cristian	ITA	10/06/70
BRANDT, Jan-Ralph	GER	23/01/78

Surname / Forename	Nation	DOB
BRAUSE, Alberto	URU	25/08/75
BROAD, Neil	GBR	20/11/66
BROWNE, Federico	ARG	07/04/76
BRUGUERA, Sergi	ESP	16/01/71
BRYAN, Bob	USA	29/04/78
BRYAN, Mike	USA	29/04/78
BUCHMAYER, Thomas	AUT	14/02/71
BURCHULADZE, Konstantin	GEO	07/03/83
BURGSMULLER, Lars	GER	06/12/75
BURILLO, Jordi	ESP	07/12/72
BURRIEZA, Oscar	ESP	22/07/75
BUSCH, Rene	EST	19/07/71
BUYINZA, Robert	UGA	21/10/79
BWALYA, Sidney	ZAM	24/04/73
CABELLO, Francisco	ARG	06/12/72
CABLE, Kirt	ECA	26/04/77
CACERES, Carlos	HON	19/05/74
CADART, Rodolphe	FRA	08/08/78
CALATRAVA, Alex	ESP	14/06/73
CALDWELL, David	USA	13/06/74
CALLERI, Agustin	ARG	14/09/76
CAMACHO, Diego	BOL	21/05/83
CAMACHO, Federico	CRC	28/08/79
CAMACHO, Sixto	DOM	12/05/76
CANAS, Guillermo	ARG	25/11/77
CAPALIK, Kristian	BIH	03/10/78
CAPPELLO, Marco	MLT	20/08/75
CARATTI, Cristiano	ITA	24/05/70
CARBONELL, Tomas	ESP	07/08/68
CARRASCO, Juan-Ignacio	ESP	09/07/74
CARRETERO, Roberto	ESP	30/08/75
CARVALLO, Paulo	PAR	11/07/76
CASEY, Owen	IRL	22/10/69
CERDA, Juan-Ignacio	CHI	25/09/78
CHANG, Michael	USA	22/02/72
CHARPENTIER, Marcelo	ARG	11/07/73
CHAVARRIA, Daniel	BOL	12/01/78
CHAVEZ, Daniel	GUA	27/01/66
CHAVEZ, Jacobo	GUA	12/01/71
CHELA, Juan-Ignacio	ARG	30/08/79
CHEN, Chih-Jung	TPE	24/09/72
CHEN, Wei-Ju	TPE	11/04/78
CHENG, Wei-Jen	TPE	02/12/80
CHERKASOV, Andrei	RUS	04/07/70
CHILDS, Lee	GBR	11/06/82
CHILE, Ricardo	CUB	07/01/82
CHRISTIAN, Dexter	ECA	16/08/71
CHUAN, Wong-Kee	MRI	06/11/83
CHUNG, Hee-Sung	KOR	25/11/76
CIBULEC, Tomas	CZE	15/01/78
CLARKE, Peter	IRL	08/07/79
CLAVET, Francisco	ESP	24/10/68
CLEMENT, Arnaud	FRA	17/12/77
COBOLLI, Stefano	ITA	02/03/77
COETZEE, Jeff	RSA	25/04/77
COLLIESON, James	BER	22/03/77
COLLINS, Abu-Hena-Tasawar	BAN	22/01/79
COMMANDEUR, Malte	GER	09/02/78
COOPER, Allan	KEN	21/07/77
COOPER, Sean	IRL	29/06/79
CORIA, Guillermo	ARG	13/01/82
CORRETJA, Alex	ESP	11/04/74
CORTES, Jaime	COL	26/07/65
COSTA, Albert	ESP	25/06/75
COSTA, Francisco	BRA	28/06/73
COUPE, Brandon	USA	11/04/72
COURIER, Jim	USA	17/08/70

Surname / Forename	Nation	DOB
COURTNEY, Arnulfo	PAN	23/09/71
COUTELOT, Nicolas	FRA	09/02/77
COUTO, Emanuel	POR	06/08/73
COWAN, Barry	GBR	25/08/74
CRICHTON, Tim	AUS	15/04/76
CUNHA-SILVA, Joao	POR	27/11/67
DA SILVA, Jean-Marie	BEN	08/10/75
DABROWSKI, Bartlomiej	POL	20/08/72
DAMM, Martin	CZE	01/08/72
DANCEVIC, Frank	CAN	26/09/84
DARKEY, Gunther	GHA	08/06/76
DATE, Michael	BAR	05/11/82
DAVIDSON, James	GBR	16/09/73
DAVIS, Tres	USA	13/01/82
DAVYDENKO, Nikolay	RUS	02/06/81
DE ARMAS, Jose	VEN	25/03/81
DE JAGER, John-Laffnie	RSA	17/03/73
DE LEON, Genaro	DOM	19/01/71
DE SILVA, Rohan	SRI	12/02/72
DE WULF, Filip	BEL	15/03/72
DEBONO, Matthew	MLT	03/11/82
DEBRAH, Thomas	GHA	31/12/77
DECKER, Chris	USA	19/06/71
DEL RIO, Diego	ARG	04/09/72
DELAITRE, Olivier	FRA	01/06/67
DELGADO, Jamie	GBR	21/03/77
DELGADO, Ramon	PAR	14/11/76
DELLA-BALDA, Andrea	SMR	19/06/66
DENT, Taylor	USA	24/04/81
DERNOVSKIY, Andrey	UKR	23/05/82
DI PASQUALE, Arnaud	FRA	11/02/79
DIAZ, Jacobo	ESP	11/07/76
DIAZ, Stephen	PUR	28/02/68
DIER, Dirk	GER	16/02/72
DJORDJEVIC, Nebojsa	YUG	24/04/73
DONDO, Federico	URU	18/10/71
DOSCARAEV, Diaz	KAZ	09/04/84
DOSEDEL, Slava	CZE	14/08/70
DRADA, Carlos	COL	02/09/75
DRAPER, Mark	AUS	11/02/71
DRAPER, Scott	AUS	05/06/74
DU PLESSIS, Henrico	NAM	26/06/78
DU PUIS, Antony	FRA	24/02/73
DULIC-FISER, Relja	YUG	31/12/75
DZELDE, Girts	LAT	16/07/63
EAGLE, Joshua	AUS	10/05/73
EASTER, Kane	LCA	15/03/77
ECONOMIDIS, Konstantinos	GRE	02/11/77
EL AAREJ, Mounir	MAR	16/06/77
EL AYNAOUI, Younes	MAR	12/09/71
ELGIN, Mikhail	RUS	14/09/81
ELLWOOD, Ben	AUS	12/03/76
ELSNER, Daniel	GER	04/01/79
ENEV, Todor	BUL	08/02/82
ENQVIST, Thomas	SWE	13/03/74
ENUKIDZE, Otari	GEO	08/03/83
ERGUIN, Barish	TUR	11/03/75
ERLICH, Jonathan	ISR	04/05/77
ESCHAUER, Werner	AUT	26/04/74
ESCUDE, Nicolas	FRA	03/04/76
ESTRELLA, Victor	DOM	10/10/80
ETLIS, Gaston	ARG	04/11/74
EVELYN, Simon	TRI	31/05/75
FADA, Abdalla	JOR	06/01/85
FAHLKE, Andy	GER	30/05/79
FASCHING, Andreas	AUT	01/01/81
FEDERER, Roger	SUI	08/08/81

Surname / Forename	Nation	DOB
FELDER, Marcel	URU	09/09/84
FERNANDEZ, Juan-Carlos	PUR	13/03/77
FERREIRA, Ellis	RSA	19/02/70
FERREIRA, Vitor	POR	23/07/79
FERREIRA, Wayne	RSA	15/09/71
FERRERO, Juan-Carlos	ESP	12/02/80
FETTERLEIN, Frederik	DEN	11/07/70
FILIMONOVS, Andris	LAT	29/04/68
FILIPPINI, Marcelo	URU	04/08/67
FISH, Mardy	USA	09/12/81
FISHER, Ashley	AUS	25/09/75
FLEISCHFRESSER, Timo	GER	27/03/79
FLEISHMAN, Zack	USA	17/03/80
FLORENT, Andrew	AUS	24/10/70
FLYGT, Kalle	SWE	15/06/76
FONTENELLE, McCollin	LCA	09/09/73
FORCELLINI, William	SMR	06/07/81
FORGET, Guy	FRA	04/01/65
FRANCINI, Gabriel	SMR	12/12/69
FRANKLIN, Cary	USA	23/09/77
FREELOVE, Oliver	GBR	05/03/77
FRIEDL, Leos	CZE	01/01/77
FROBERG, Jonas	SWE	11/04/81
FROMBERG, Richard	AUS	28/04/70
FRONTERA, Jose	PUR	31/01/71
FRUTTERO, John-Paul	USA	30/04/81
FURLAN, Renzo	ITA	17/05/70
FUZI-NASRUDDIN, Mohammed-Nazreen	MAS	23/07/81
GAAFAR, Nour	SUD	27/09/83
GALBRAITH, Patrick	USA	16/04/67
GALIMBERTI, Giorgio	ITA	05/09/76
GAMBILL, Jan-Michael	USA	03/06/77
GAMONAL, Hermes	CHI	31/05/77
GANDONOU, Alphonse	BEN	13/01/74
GANDONOU, Sourou	BEN	13/12/79
GARCIA, Adrian	CHI	23/05/78
GARCIA, Franklin	HON	04/01/77
GARCIA, Martin	ARG	02/05/77
GARDNER, Kevin	ANT	09/02/83
GAUDENZI, Andrea	ITA	30/07/73
GAUDI, Igor	ITA	10/04/75
GAUDIO, Gaston	ARG	09/12/78
GAWANDER, Diva	FIJ	23/04/79
GERTH, Elmar	AHO	05/08/70
GEVORGYAN, Tsolak	ARM	18/08/75
GHONEIM, Amro	EGY	18/03/74
GHOUSE, Mustafa	IND	19/08/80
GILBERT, Rodolphe	FRA	12/12/68
GIMELSTOB, Justin	USA	26/01/77
GINEPRI, Robby	USA	07/10/82
GINER, Juan	ESP	28/07/78
GODWIN, Neville	RSA	31/01/75
GOELLNER, Marc-Kevin	GER	22/09/70
GOLDSTEIN, Paul	USA	04/08/76
GOLMARD, Jerome	FRA	09/09/73
GOLOVANOV, Denis	RUS	27/03/78
GOMEZ, Andres	ECU	27/02/60
GONZALEZ, Fernando	CHI	29/07/80
GONZALEZ, Pablo	COL	02/07/82
GORBAN, Andrei	MDA	19/07/83
GORBAN, Yuri	MDA	21/06/76
GORCIC, Ismar	BIH	22/05/83
GORDON, Nakia	JAM	09/02/80
GOUDENBOUR, Johnny	LUX	31/12/63
GRABB, Jim	USA	14/04/64
GRANT, Geoff	USA	16/01/70

Surname / Forename	Nation	DOB
GREENHALGH, James	NZL	19/02/75
GREGORC, Miha	SLO	15/03/79
GRILLI, Rodrigo	BRA	20/11/79
GROEN, Sander	NED	16/06/68
GROSJEAN, Sebastien	FRA	29/05/78
GROSS, Oliver	GER	17/06/73
GUARDIOLA, Thierry	FRA	07/08/71
GUBENCO, Philipe	CAN	14/03/82
GUMY, Hernan	ARG	05/03/72
GUSTAFSSON, Magnus	SWE	03/01/67
HAARHUIS, Paul	NED	19/02/66
HAAS, Tommy	GER	03/04/78
HADAD, Mauricio	COL	07/12/71
HADDOCK, Luis	PUR	11/02/82
HAGGARD, Chris	RSA	28/04/71
HAKIM, Randy	TRI	18/04/77
HAKOBIAN, Haik	ARM	27/04/80
HALLDORSSON, David	ISL	26/04/81
HAMADEH, Ali	LIB	05/09/74
HAMEURLAINE, Abdelhak	ALG	19/03/72
HANLEY, Paul	AUS	12/11/77
HANQUEZ, Jerome	FRA	11/03/74
HANSEN-DENT, Brett	USA	02/07/72
HANTSCHK, Markus	GER	19/11/77
HARPER-GRIFFITH, Levar	USA	04/09/81
HARSANYI, Paul	USA	30/12/74
HAWK, Brandon	USA	03/09/79
HAYGARTH, Brent	RSA	27/12/67
HEALEY, Nathan	AUS	27/02/80
HEMEDA, Hisham	EGY	01/05/78
HENMAN, Tim	GBR	06/09/74
HENNI, Abdel-Wahid	ALG	08/08/82
HERM-ZAHLAVA, Jakob	GER	12/05/80
HERNANDEZ, Alejandro	MEX	01/10/77
HERNYCH, Jan	CZE	07/07/79
HERRERA, Juan-Pablo	PAN	24/04/73
HEUBERGER, Ivo	SUI	19/02/76
HEUSSNER, Emmanuel	MON	03/02/71
HEWITT, Lleyton	AUS	24/02/81
HILL, Michael	AUS	30/06/74
HILPERT, Marcus	GER	01/07/71
HILTON, Mark	GBR	20/04/81
HIPFL, Markus	AUT	26/04/78
HIU, Jensen	SIN	21/06/81
HIZAN, Hazuan	MAS	12/05/78
HOOD, Mariano	ARG	14/08/73
HORNA, Luis	PER	14/09/80
HOUDEK, Goran	BIH	10/08/80
HRBATY, Dominik	SVK	04/01/78
HUET, Stephane	FRA	25/04/71
HUGHES, Damian	ECA	20/09/77
HUI, John	HKG	03/01/78
HUISH, Jean-Pierre	NAM	12/08/78
HUMPHRIES, Scott	USA	26/05/76
HUNT, Alistair	NZL	11/11/72
HUSSAINI, Bullus	NGR	01/09/55
IBRAHIM, Ismasufian	BRU	18/11/74
IDDAMALGODA, Asiri	SRI	17/06/73
ILIE, Andrew	AUS	18/04/76
ISHII, Yaoki	JPN	29/04/77
IVANISEVIC, Goran	CRO	13/09/71
IVANOV-SMOLENSKY, Kirill	RUS	19/01/81
IWABUCHI, Satoshi	JPN	07/10/75
JACOBE, Cyril	POC	31/03/83
JANNIF, Mohammed	FIJ	16/12/70
JAYA, Adam	MAS	10/01/85
JAZIRI, Malek	TUN	20/01/84

Surname / Forename	Nation	DOB
JEAN-BAPTISTE, Jonathan	LCA	04/07/72
JEHA, Abdalla	SUD	16/01/74
JEMAI, Chekib	TUN	19/01/79
JENSEN, Luke	USA	18/06/66
JENSEN, Murphy	USA	30/10/68
JIMENEZ-GUERRA, Joan	AND	24/01/78
JOHANSSON, Joakim	SWE	01/07/82
JOHANSSON, Thomas	SWE	24/03/75
JOHNSON, Donald	USA	09/09/68
JONCKHEER, Kevin	AHO	20/11/71
JONSSON, Fredrik	SWE	28/03/77
JONSSON, Jon-Axel	ISL	12/08/83
JOSEPH, Jerry	HAI	04/06/80
JUDD, Michael	BOT	15/06/77
JURKENAS, Paulius	LTU	18/02/81
KA, Djadji	SEN	18/03/81
KAFELNIKOV, Yevgeny	RUS	18/02/74
KALANOV, George	CYP	12/02/80
KAMBER, Abdulla	UAE	16/02/85
KARBACHER, Bernd	GER	03/04/68
KARLOVIC, Ivo	CRO	28/02/79
KATCHARAVA, David	GEO	28/03/69
KAUFFMANN, Cedric	FRA	01/03/76
KAWAS, Christian	HON	20/01/78
KAZHERA, Vasilly	BLR	29/01/82
KEDRIOUK, Alexey	KAZ	08/08/80
KEIL, Mark	USA	03/06/67
KEMAJOU, Lionel	CMR	04/07/70
KEMPES, Edwin	NED	23/06/76
KETOLA, Tuomas	FIN	21/02/75
KHALI, Khotso	LES	19/05/77
KHAN, Aqeel	PAK	30/01/80
KHAN, Nadeem-Kamran	BAN	27/07/82
KHO, Tung-Yi	SIN	19/01/72
KIEFER, Nicolas	GER	05/07/77
KILDERRY, Paul	AUS	11/04/73
KIM, Alex	USA	20/12/78
KIM, Kevin	USA	26/07/78
KING, Phillip	USA	19/12/81
KIRTANE, Nitin	IND	04/03/74
KIRTANE, Sandeep	IND	27/10/73
KIRUKI, Trevor	KEN	13/11/80
KISGYORGY, Gergely	HUN	08/03/76
KITINOV, Aleksandar	MKD	13/01/71
KNIPPSCHILD, Jens	GER	15/02/75
KNOWLE, Julian	AUT	29/04/74
KNOWLES, Mark	BAH	04/09/71
KOENIG, Robbie	RSA	05/07/71
KOHLMANN, Michael	GER	11/01/74
KOLL, Helge	NOR	31/05/75
KORNIENKO, Igor	RUS	16/07/72
KOUBEK, Stefan	AUT	02/01/77
KOVACKA, Petr	CZE	23/12/71
KOVES, Gabor	HUN	01/07/70
KRACMAN, Andrej	SLO	22/08/82
KRAJICEK, Richard	NED	06/12/71
KRALERT, Petr	CZE	20/10/79
KRATOCHVIL, Michel	SUI	07/04/79
KRATZMANN, Andrew	AUS	03/11/71
KROSLAK, Jan	SVK	17/10/74
KUCERA, Karol	SVK	04/03/74
KUDRNAC, Pavel	CZE	11/02/74
KUERTEN, Gustavo	BRA	10/09/76
KULTI, Nicklas	SWE	22/04/71
KUMAR, Sunil	IND	04/04/83
KUNNAP, Mait	EST	23/09/82
KUSDARYANTO, Edy	INA	09/05/75

Surname / Forename	Nation	DOB
KUTSENKO, Vadim	UZB	16/03/77
KWINTA, Krzysztof	POL	28/02/80
LADIPO, Sulieman	NGR	09/04/74
LAGZDINS, Ivo	LAT	02/09/80
LANDSBERG, Johan	SWE	30/12/74
LANGVARDT, Patrik	DEN	06/12/71
LAPENTTI, Giovanni	ECU	25/01/83
LAPENTTI, Nicolas	ECU	13/08/76
LAREAU, Sebastien	CAN	27/04/73
LAROSE, Simon	CAN	28/06/78
LARSSON, Magnus	SWE	25/03/70
LEACH, Rick	USA	28/12/64
LEE, Hyung-Taik	KOR	03/01/76
LEE, Martin	GBR	13/01/78
LEE, Seung-Hun	KOR	22/05/79
LEON-ZAMORA, Kerlin	CUB	09/05/80
LEONDIS, Demetrios	CYP	25/11/78
LETSEKA, Ntsukunyane	LES	15/02/71
LEVY, Harel	ISR	05/08/78
LEWIS, Kodi	BAR	21/01/81
LI, Si	CHN	29/04/76
LIN, Bing-Chao	TPE	28/10/73
LINDSTEDT, Robert	SWE	19/03/77
LIPSKY, Scott	USA	14/08/81
LISNARD, Jean-Rene	FRA	25/09/79
LIUKKO, Ville	FIN	24/05/74
LJUBICIC, Ivan	CRO	19/03/79
LLODRA, Michael	FRA	18/05/80
LOGLO, Jean-Kome	TOG	24/06/75
LOGLO, Komlavi	TOG	30/12/84
LOGLO, Kossi-Essaram	TOG	25/07/79
LONFO, Ilou	CIV	04/02/74
LOPES, Helder	POR	07/08/77
LOPEZ, Feliciano	ESP	20/09/81
LOPEZ-MORON, Alex	ESP	28/11/70
LOVEN, Fredrik	SWE	26/05/76
LUKAEV, Radoslav	BUL	24/04/82
LUXA, Petr	CZE	03/03/72
LUZGIN, Andrei	EST	02/02/73
LUZZI, Federico	ITA	03/01/80
MAAMOUN, Karim	EGY	18/11/79
MACLAGAN, Miles	GBR	23/09/74
MACPHERSON, David	AUS	03/07/67
MACPHIE, Brian	USA	11/05/72
MADRIGAL-ALPIZAR, Alejandro	CRC	18/02/82
MAGGI, Fabio	ITA	30/01/75
MAHMOUDI, Noureddine	ALG	27/06/73
MAHUT, Nicolas	FRA	21/01/82
MAKASHIN, Sergei	TJK	29/08/79
MAKGALE, Karabo	BOT	30/07/81
MAKHKAMOV, Abdul-Hamid	UZB	19/04/76
MALCOR, Olivier	FRA	28/01/75
MALISSE, Xavier	BEL	19/07/80
MALLORY, Richard	BER	13/07/65
MAMIIT, Cecil	USA	27/06/76
MANKAD, Harsh	IND	10/11/79
MANTA, Lorenzo	SUI	16/09/74
MANTILLA, Felix	ESP	23/09/74
MARACH, Oliver	AUT	16/07/80
MARIN, Juan-Antonio	CRC	02/03/75
MARQUES, Nuno	POR	09/04/70
MARTELLI, Marzio	ITA	14/12/71
MARTIN, Alberto	ESP	20/08/78
MARTIN, Todd	USA	08/07/70
MARTINEZ, Sandor	CUB	21/03/81
MASSU, Nicolas	CHI	10/11/79
MATA, Franco	MOZ	12/07/77

Surname / Forename	Nation	DOB
MATEKRI, Tareq	JOR	14/10/84
MATHIEU, Paul-Henri	FRA	12/01/82
MATKOWSKI, Marcin	POL	15/01/81
MAZARAKIS, Vasilis	GRE	09/02/80
MAZUR, Dmitri	UZB	08/09/79
MEDICA, Eduardo	ARG	10/02/76
MEDVEDEV, Andrei	UKR	31/08/74
MELIGENI, Fernando	BRA	12/04/71
MELLET, Axel	MON	28/12/79
MELLO, Dean	BER	14/06/61
MELZER, Jurgen	AUT	22/05/81
MERKLEIN, Mark	BAH	28/06/72
MERZ, Miguel	ESA	09/06/67
MIKAILE, Asfaw	ETH	27/11/78
MIKETA, David	CZE	04/06/75
MILED, Youssef	TUN	17/09/83
MILLIGAN, Luke	GBR	06/08/76
MIRANDA, Ivan	PER	08/03/80
MIRNYI, Max	BLR	06/07/77
MISA, Michael	PHI	31/01/74
MITROVSKI, Kristijan	MKD	02/11/82
MIYAO, Joji	JPN	15/06/81
MLYNARIK, Zbynek	AUT	24/04/77
MOELETSI, Ntsane	LES	02/04/78
MOGUEH, Kadar	DJI	01/04/76
MOLDOVAN, Ion	ROM	17/01/78
MOLEFE, Petrus	BOT	23/01/76
MONGERIE, Lenin	ISV	08/09/78
MONTANA, Francisco	USA	05/11/69
MONTENEGRO, Felipe	CRC	19/02/82
MONTILLA, Gabriel	PUR	11/08/79
MOR, Lior	ISR	29/02/76
MORARU, Gabriel	ROM	28/01/82
MOREJON, Luis-Adrian	ECU	28/03/73
MORETTI, Hector	ARG	27/01/73
MORRISON, Jeff	USA	04/02/79
MORRISWALA, Hitesh	FIJ	19/04/75
MORTIMER, Dentry	BAH	30/06/82
MOTA, Bernardo	POR	14/06/71
MOTOMURA, Goichi	JPN	25/12/73
MOTSEPA, Relebohile	LES	15/11/71
MOUSSA, Alla	DJI	03/07/82
MOYA, Carlos	ESP	27/08/76
MULLER, Gilles	LUX	09/05/83
MURASHKA, Rolandos	LTU	13/03/73
N'GORAN, Claude	CIV	18/03/75
NALBANDIAN, David	ARG	01/01/82
NARGISO, Diego	ITA	15/03/70
NAVARRO, Lazaro	CUB	28/01/74
NAVARRO, Rodrigo	BOL	22/01/74
NAVARRO, Salvador	ESP	08/01/77
NDEFWAYI, Lighton	ZAM	21/08/73
NDIAYE, Daouda	SEN	03/01/78
NDIBWAMI, Bob	UGA	06/08/78
NDINYA, Barry	KEN	17/03/77
NELSON, James	GBR	18/02/82
NESTOR, Daniel	CAN	04/09/72
NEWTON, Gregory	ISV	22/05/77
NICKLISCH, Rene	GER	31/03/76
NICOLAS, Eduardo	ESP	22/09/72
NIELSEN, Mark	NZL	08/10/77
NIEMEYER, Frederic	CAN	24/04/76
NIEMINEN, Jarkko	FIN	23/07/81
NIJAKI, Radoslav	POL	25/01/82
NILAND, Conor	IRL	19/09/81
NORMAN, Magnus	SWE	30/05/76
NORVAL, Piet	RSA	07/04/70

Surname / Forename	Nation	DOB
NOSZALY, Sandor	HUN	16/03/72
NOUR, Abdullah	KSA	17/06/83
NOVAK, Jiri	CZE	22/03/75
NOVOSSELOV, Sergei	RUS	NULL
NUMBERS, Chris	HKG	05/08/71
NUNEZ, Luis-Diego	CRC	15/12/73
NYBORG, Peter	SWE	12/12/69
NYDAHL, Tomas	SWE	21/03/68
O'BRIEN, Alex	USA	07/03/70
ODUOR, Norbert	KEN	30/04/64
OFORI, Frank	GHA	23/02/71
OGORODOV, Oleg	UZB	16/07/72
OKUN, Noam	ISR	16/04/78
OLHOVSKIY, Andrei	RUS	15/04/66
OLIVER, Graydon	USA	15/06/78
OLIVERA, Alejandro	URU	14/02/77
ONCINS, Jaime	BRA	16/06/70
ONDOBO, Luc	CMR	10/11/72
ONDRUSKA, Marcos	RSA	18/12/72
ONODA, Michihisa	JPN	31/01/78
ORAL, Erhan	TUR	19/07/71
ORSANIC, Daniel	ARG	11/06/68
ORTCHUAN, Vasuthevan	MAS	22/04/73
ORTEGREN, Johan	SWE	22/03/78
ORTIZ, Oscar	MEX	09/05/73
OSORIO, Marco	MEX	01/04/72
OSUNA, Patrick	USA	06/12/73
OTOLO-METOMO, Pierre	CMR	25/01/77
OVERHOLSER, Nathan	USA	23/06/79
PAES, Leander	IND	17/06/73
PAINTER, Andrew	AUS	18/07/75
PALA, Petr	CZE	02/10/75
PALMER, Jared	USA	02/07/71
PANJA, Saurav	IND	15/03/77
PARAMANATHAN, Niroshan	SRI	29/10/83
PARMAR, Arvind	GBR	22/03/78
PASSARELLA, Michael	USA	18/08/77
PASSIA, Dilip	BAN	10/01/73
PATEL, Kamil	MRI	03/04/79
PATIENCE, Olivier	FRA	25/03/80
PAVEL, Andrei	ROM	27/01/74
PEPPAS, Solon	GRE	25/10/74
PEREZ-CHETE, Luis	GUA	22/10/70
PERRY, Todd	AUS	17/03/76
PESCARIU, Dinu	ROM	12/04/74
PESCHEK, Denis	GER	06/01/84
PESCOSOLIDO, Stefano	ITA	13/06/71
PETERSON, Adam	USA	16/07/74
PETROVIC, Dejan	AUS	03/04/78
PEYA, Alexander	AUT	27/06/80
PFEIFFER, Krystian	POL	03/12/78
PHAU, Bjorn	GER	04/10/79
PHILIP, Gershum	ANT	08/03/82
PHILIPPOUSSIS, Mark	AUS	07/11/76
PIOLINE, Cedric	FRA	15/06/69
PISUTH-ARNONTH, Ekkarin	THA	23/01/76
PLESS, Kristian	DEN	09/02/81
PLOUGAREV, Evgueni	MDA	02/07/80
POGNON, Christophe	BEN	11/10/77
POPP, Alexander	GER	04/11/76
PORTAS, Albert	ESP	15/11/73
POSADA, Oscar	VEN	29/09/83
POUX-GAUTIER, Jean-Baptiste	AND	01/06/81
POZZI, Gianluca	ITA	17/06/65
PRAHLAD, Srinath	IND	10/01/73
PRAMONO, Hendri-Susilo	INA	05/07/79
PRETZSCH, Axel	GER	16/06/76

Surname / Forename	Nation	DOB
PRIETO, Antonio	BRA	07/09/73
PRIETO, Sebastian	ARG	19/05/75
PRINOSIL, David	GER	09/03/73
PRINTZLAU, Jonathan	DEN	07/10/76
PRODON, Eric	FRA	27/06/81
PUENTES, German	ESP	18/12/72
PUERTA, Mariano	ARG	19/09/78
QUINTERO, Michael	COL	11/07/80
QURESHI, Aisam	PAK	17/03/80
RAE, Chris	AUS	08/03/79
RAFIDISON, Alexis	MAD	19/03/80
RAFTER, Pat	AUS	28/12/72
RAHIMOV, Talat	AZE	18/05/84
RAM, Andy	ISR	10/04/80
RAMAZANOV, Nidjat	AZE	29/01/82
RAN, Eyal	ISR	21/11/72
RANDJELOVIC, Steven	AUS	21/04/75
RANDRIAMANALINA, Jean-Marc	MAD	29/02/64
RAOUX, Guillaume	FRA	14/02/70
RATSIMBAZAFY, Lalaina	MAD	26/08/73
RAZIANI, Ramin	IRI	12/04/74
RENEBERG, Richey	USA	05/10/65
RIBAS, Victor	MDA	17/08/78
RICHARDS, John	ISV	17/10/78
RIKL, David	CZE	27/02/71
RINCON, Eduardo	COL	22/03/76
RIOS, Marcelo	CHI	26/12/75
RISCH, Alex	LIE	11/01/72
ROBICHAUD, Jocelyn	CAN	08/04/78
ROBREDO, Tommy	ESP	01/05/82
ROCHUS, Christophe	BEL	15/12/78
ROCHUS, Olivier	BEL	18/01/81
RODDICK, Andy	USA	30/08/82
RODITI, David	MEX	30/11/73
RODRIGUEZ, Francisco	PAR	18/03/76
RODRIGUEZ, Martin	ARG	18/12/69
ROIG, Francisco	ESP	01/04/68
ROITMAN, Sergio	ARG	16/05/79
ROJER, Jean-Julien	AHO	25/08/81
ROMERO, Yohny	VEN	30/11/78
ROOT, Doug	USA	16/12/77
ROSNER, Paul	RSA	11/12/72
ROSSET, Marc	SUI	07/11/70
ROUX, Lionel	FRA	12/04/73
ROVAS, Nikos	GRE	20/09/77
ROVO, Jerome	POC	21/12/79
RUAH, Maurice	VEN	19/02/71
RUEL, Roland	PHI	27/02/78
RUSEDSKI, Greg	GBR	06/09/73
RUSEVSKI, Predrag	MKD	27/08/83
RUSSELL, Michael	USA	01/05/78
RUSSELL, Ryan	JAM	06/07/83
RUUD, Christian	NOR	24/08/72
RYBALKO, Andrei	UKR	05/06/72
SA, Andre	BRA	06/05/77
SAAD EL DIN, Samir	SYR	17/11/76
SABAU, Razvan	ROM	18/06/77
SAFIN, Marat	RUS	27/01/80
SALIM, Abdul-Rahim	SYR	01/01/70
SALIM, Lais	SYR	05/02/75
SALZENSTEIN, Jeff	USA	14/10/73
SAMOSEIKO, Sergei	BLR	05/02/81
SAMPRAS, Pete	USA	12/08/71
SAMREJ, Wittaya	THA	18/02/64
SANABRIA, Augusto	ESA	04/06/80
SANCHEZ, David	ESP	20/04/78
SANCHEZ, Javier	ESP	01/02/68

Surname / Forename	Nation	DOB
SANCHEZ, Mariano	MEX	03/07/78
SANGUINETTI, Davide	ITA	25/09/72
SANON, Valentin	CIV	20/05/80
SANTOPADRE, Vincenzo	ITA	11/08/71
SANTORO, Fabrice	FRA	09/12/72
SARGSIAN, Sargis	ARM	03/06/73
SARSTRAND, Marcus	SWE	24/07/78
SARWANI, Fahad	BRN	19/09/80
SAULNIER, Cyril	FRA	16/08/75
SAVOLT, Attila	HUN	05/02/76
SCHALKEN, Sjeng	NED	08/09/76
SCHALLER, Gilbert	AUT	17/03/69
SCHAUL, Pascal	LUX	11/01/79
SCHEIDWEILER, Mike	LUX	14/11/81
SCHEMBRI, Mark	MLT	15/02/75
SCHNEITER, Andres	ITA	08/04/76
SCHRANZ, Wolfgang	AUT	18/03/76
SCHUKIN, Yuri	RUS	26/06/79
SCHUTTLER, Rainer	GER	25/04/76
SCHWEIGER, Andreas	LIE	24/08/82
SEDOV, Sergei	TJK	14/03/85
SEGODO, Arnaud	BEN	12/11/84
SEKULOV, James	AUS	13/10/76
SELL, Michael	USA	23/08/72
SEOL, Kyoung-Sik	SIN	04/11/62
SERRANO, Oscar	ESP	25/05/78
SETEGNE, Yohannes	ETH	14/12/77
SEVCENKO, Zoran	MKD	21/12/69
SHAFIK, Asim	PAK	21/12/75
SHAHGHOLI, Anoosha	IRI	10/11/81
SHEHAB, Abdul-Rahman	BRN	21/03/71
SHIMADA, Thomas	JPN	10/02/75
SHIRINOV, Farid	AZE	13/06/85
SHORTALL, James	NZL	25/12/79
SHVEC, Alexander	BLR	29/06/72
SIEMERINK, Jan	NED	14/04/70
SIGURDSSON, Arnar	ISL	24/11/81
SILCOCK, Grant	AUS	21/05/75
SIMONI, Alexandre	BRA	02/07/79
SINNER, Martin	GER	07/02/68
SIRIANNI, Joseph	AUS	17/01/75
SKOCH, David	CZE	06/11/76
SLUITER, Raemon	NED	13/04/78
SMITH, Jermaine	JAM	31/01/79
SMITH, Roger	BAH	20/01/64
SOFIAN, Harutiun	ARM	12/01/83
SPADEA, Vince	USA	19/07/74
SPENCER, Kyle	GBR	26/01/76
SPOTTL, Martin	AUT	23/11/75
SPRENGELMEYER, Mitch	USA	09/01/75
SPROGA, Raimonds	LAT	12/07/81
SQUILLARI, Franco	ARG	22/08/75
SRICHAPHAN, Paradorn	THA	14/06/79
STAFFORD, Grant	RSA	27/05/71
STANOYTCHEV, Orlin	BUL	24/09/71
STARK, Jonathan	USA	03/04/71
STAUDER, Franz	GER	28/05/77
STOLIAROV, Andrei	RUS	09/01/77
STOLLE, Sandon	AUS	13/07/70
STOLTENBERG, Jason	AUS	04/04/70
STONE, Shane	TRI	03/07/77
STONE, Troy	TRI	12/05/80
STRENGBERGER, Thomas	AUT	05/10/75
STRUB, Wolfgang	LIE	03/06/58
SUK, Cyril	CZE	29/01/67
SUWANDI, Suwandi	INA	21/08/76
SUZUKI, Takao	JPN	20/09/76

Surname / Forename	Nation	DOB
SVARC, Ladislav	SVK	13/11/78
SWIERK, Sebastien	AUS	15/01/79
SYED, Fazaluddin	IND	18/10/74
SZYMANSKI, Jimy	VEN	15/09/75
TABARA, Michal	CZE	11/08/79
TAHERI, Akbar	IRI	03/11/73
TAHIRI, Mehdi	MAR	28/07/77
TAINO, Eric	USA	18/03/75
TALIANOS, Constantinos	CYP	25/02/81
TARALLO, Stefano	ITA	08/03/76
TARANGO, Jeff	USA	20/11/68
TAVAKOLI, Mohammad-Reza	IRI	12/12/71
TAYLOR, Louis	ISV	29/04/83
TEBBUTT, Michael	AUS	22/12/70
TEJADA, Jorge-Minodo	GUA	21/04/68
TEJADA, Manuel	ESA	26/11/70
TENAI, Lency	SOL	09/01/68
TEO, Sharill	BRU	05/08/82
TERESHCHUK, Orest	UKR	18/08/81
TESTA, Cristiano	BRA	23/09/73
THERON, Johan	NAM	09/09/75
THOMA, Sacha	LUX	23/11/78
THOMANN, Nicolas	FRA	29/11/72
THOMAS, Jim	USA	24/09/74
TIELEMAN, Laurence	ITA	14/11/72
TIILIKAINEN, Kim	FIN	08/07/75
TIKARAM, Sanjeev	POC	31/03/72
TILLSTROM, Mikael	SWE	05/03/72
TIMFJORD, Nicklas	SWE	18/03/77
TIPSAREVIC, Janko	YUG	22/06/84
TKALEC, Marko	SLO	17/03/77
TOBON, Miguel	COL	22/06/68
TOMASHEVICH, Dmitri	UZB	06/03/74
TONG, Melvin	HKG	19/02/75
TORRES, Ruben-Dario	COL	23/02/81
TOWN, Andrew	HKG	04/01/72
TRAMACCHI, Peter	AUS	08/11/70
TRAYKOV, Ivaylo	BUL	17/12/78
TRIFU, Gabriel	ROM	14/04/75
TRIMMEL, Clemens	AUT	08/06/78
TSAI, Chia-Yen	TPE	01/10/75
TUILIER-CURCO, Kenneth	AND	07/07/83
TUREK, Jerry	CAN	02/04/75
UDOMCHOKE, Danai	THA	11/08/81
ULIHRACH, Bohdan	CZE	23/02/75
ULLYETT, Kevin	ZIM	23/05/72
UPPAL, Vishal	IND	10/11/76
URH, Borut	SLO	28/07/74
USHANGISHVILI, Irakli	GEO	09/02/82
USTUNDAG, Efe	TUR	15/01/77
VACEK, Daniel	CZE	01/04/71
VAHKAL, Alti	EST	11/03/74
VAJDA, Ivan	CRO	04/09/78
VALDEZ, Chad	PAN	18/05/71
VALLEJO, Rodrigo	DOM	13/03/74
VAN HOUDT, Tom	BEL	28/07/72
VAN LOTTUM, John	NED	10/04/76
VAN PIETERMAN, Toni	USA	NULL
VAN SCHEPPINGEN, Dennis	NED	05/07/75
VANEK, Jiri	CZE	24/04/78
VASEK, Radomir	CZE	23/09/72
VASILIADIS, Anastasios	GRE	16/02/74
VASQUEZ, Alexander	GUA	09/12/76
VEERASINGAM, Selvam	MAS	11/08/69
VELASCO, Jairo Jr.	ESP	21/01/74
VELEV, Milen	BUL	04/09/71

Surname / Forename	Nation	DOB
VEMIC, Dusan	YUG	17/06/76
VENCATACHELLUM, Jonathan	MRI	27/11/83
VENERO-MONTES, Tupi	PER	22/02/72
VERKERK, Martin	NED	10/10/78
VICENTE, Fernando	ESP	08/03/77
VICINI, Domenico	SMR	01/09/71
VICO, Uros	ITA	19/02/81
VILLARROEL, Rodrigo	BOL	13/11/80
VILMS, Gert	EST	22/02/80
VILOCA, Juan-Albert	ESP	17/01/73
VINCIGUERRA, Andreas	SWE	19/02/81
VINCK, Christian	GER	03/09/75
VIZNER, Pavel	CZE	15/07/70
VOINEA, Adrian	ROM	06/08/74
VOLTCHKOV, Vladimir	BLR	07/04/78
WAHLA, Ahmed	PAK	16/09/82
WAIL, Nour	SUD	16/10/83
WAITE, Jack	USA	01/05/69
WAKEFIELD, Haydn	RSA	10/01/77
WAKEFIELD, Myles	RSA	13/06/74
WALLIULLAH, Moin-ud-din	BAN	22/07/75
WANG, Yu Jr.	CHN	01/08/81
WASHINGTON, Mashiska	USA	19/12/74
WASSEN, Rogier	NED	09/08/76
WEINER, Glenn	USA	27/04/76
WEIR-SMITH, Jason	RSA	08/08/75
WELGREEN, Nir	ISR	17/12/76
WENTZEL, Kevin	NAM	19/02/74
WESSELS, Peter	NED	07/05/78
WHEATON, David	USA	02/06/69
WIBOWO, Sulistyo	INA	17/02/69
WIDHIYANTO, Febi	INA	09/02/80
WIJEYESEKERA, Jayendra	SRI	12/01/70
WILLEMS, Reginald	BEL	06/09/77
WILLIAMS, Duane	BAR	14/04/79
WILLIAMS, Gareth	RSA	27/08/75
WILLIAMS, Jeff	USA	12/01/78
WILLIAMS, Jerry	ANT	29/09/62
WILLINSKY, Scott	JAM	17/12/74
WILTSCHNIG, Herbert	AUT	21/11/75
WIRYAWAN, Bonit	INA	10/02/68
WITT, Alex	USA	24/03/76
WOLDEGEBRIEL, Samuel	ETH	20/12/80
WONG, Billy	BRU	15/08/85
WONG, Wayne	HKG	21/03/81
WOODBRIDGE, Todd	AUS	02/04/71
WOODFORDE, Mark	AUS	23/09/65
WOODRUFF, Chris	USA	02/01/73
XU, Ran	CHN	10/10/80
YAKHYAEV, Mansour	TJK	01/09/76
YANG, Jing-Zhu	CHN	19/01/76
YANG, Sian	SIN	17/04/79
YOON, Yong-Il	KOR	23/09/73
YOUZHNY, Mikhail	RUS	25/06/82
ZAATINI, Jicham	LIB	17/06/76
ZABALETA, Mariano	ARG	28/02/78
ZAHIROVIC, Merid	BIH	18/03/77
ZAIER, Fares	TUN	07/02/84
ZEIDAN, Wael	SEN	18/08/81
ZEWAR, Marwan	EGY	19/01/80
ZHANG, Yu	CHN	26/09/76
ZHU, Ben-Qiang	CHN	18/03/79
ZIB, Tomas	CZE	31/01/76
ZIMONJIC, Nenad	YUG	04/06/76
ZOVKO, Lovro	CRO	18/03/81

Tennis Masters Series 2000

Formerly known as Mercedes Super 9 tournaments

TENNIS MASTERS SERIES – INDIAN WELLS ($2,450,000)

INDIAN WELLS, CA, 13–19 MARCH
MEN'S SINGLES – 1st Round: H. Arazi d. A. Agassi (1) 6–3 3–6 6–3; C. Dosedel d. F. Mantilla 6–4 6–1; M. Mirnyi (Q) d. T. Dent (WC) 6–2 3–6 6–2; G. Rusedski (15) d. J. Blake (WC) 6–2 6–0; N. Escude d. C. Pioline (9) 7–5 7–6; M. Safin d. F. Meligeni 6–2 3–6 6–2; A. Di Pasquale d. J. Courier 7–5 4–6 7–6; N. Lapentti (8) d. J. Bjorkman (WC) 6–3 6–3; F. Santoro d. N. Kiefer (4) 6–1 6–4; D. Hrbaty d. Y. El Aynaoui 7–5 6–2; A. Corretja d. K. Kucera 6–2 6–2; P. Rafter (13) d. M. Ondruska (Q) 6–3 7–6; T. Henman (11) d. K. Alami 7–5 6–2; S. Grosjean d. J. Novak 6–2 6–2; M. Chang d. J. Ferrero 7–5 6–4; M. Norman (6) d. F. Squillari 6–3 6–4; G. Kuerten (5) d. J. Gimelstob (Q) 7–5 3–6 6–3; T. Haas d. C. Saulnier (Q) 6–1 6–7 7–5; F. Clavet d. A. Ilie 6–7 6–3 6–1; M. Philippoussis (12) d. C. Woodruff 6–3 6–4; A. Costa (14) d. S. Koubek 3–6 7–5 6–3; G. Ivanisevic (WC) d. P. Goldstein (Q) 6–4 2–6 6–3; S. Schalken d. J. Kroslak (Q) 6–4 6–3; Y. Kafelnikov (3) d. V. Spadea 6–1 6–1; M. Rios (7) d. D. Vacek 7–6 6–1; M. Zabaleta d. F. Vicente 7–5 7–6; T. Johansson d. A. Clement 6–1 6–3; T. Enqvist (10) d. J. Golmard 6–1 6–4; L. Hewitt (16) d. C. Moya 6–4 3–6 6–3; B. Black (Q) d. A. Martin 6–3 6–2; W. Ferreira d. J. Gambill (Q) 6–4 6–7 6–4; P. Sampras (2) d. A. Medvedev 6–4 6–3.
2nd round: Arazi d. Dosedel 6–4 6–2; Mirnyi (Q) d. Rusedski (15) 6–4 6–4; Escude d. Safin 6–2 6–0; Lapentti (8) d. Di Pasquale 3–6 6–3 6–2; Santoro d. Hrbaty 6–7 7–6 6–4; Corretja d. Rafter (13) 7–6 5–7 6–2; Grosjean d. Henman (11) 6–3 3–6 7–5; Norman (6) d. Chang 6–4 6–4; Haas d. Kuerten (5) 7–6 7–6; Philippoussis (12) d. Clavet 7–5 6–3; A. Costa (14) Ivanisevic (WC) 6–2 6–7 6–3; Schalken d. Kafelnikov (3) 7–5 6–2; Zabaleta d. Rios (7) 7–6 6–3; Enqvist (10) d. Johansson 6–1 6–4; B. Black (Q) d. Hewitt (16) 6–3 7–6; Sampras (2) d. W. Ferreira 3–6 7–6 7–6.
3rd round: Arazi d. Mirnyi (Q) 7–5 3–6 6–4; Lapentti (8) d. Escude 3–6 6–4 7–6; Corretja d. Santoro 7–6 6–1; Norman (6) d. Grosjean 6–3 6–7 6–4; Philippoussis (12) d. Haas 6–2 6–3; Schalken d. A. Costa (14) 6–2 6–3; Enqvist (10) d. Zabaleta 6–4 7–5; Sampras (2) d. B. Black (Q) 4–6 6–3 6–2.
Quarter-finals: Lapentti (8) d. Arazi 6–2 6–0; Corretja d. Norman (6) 4–6 6–2 6–2; Philippoussis (12) d. Schalken 7–6 6–4; Enqvist (10) d. Sampras (2) 6–3 3–6 6–3.
Semi-finals: Corretja d. Lapentti (8) 6–3 6–4; Enqvist (10) d. Philippoussis (12) 6–3 6–7 7–6.
Final: Corretja d. Enqvist (10) 6–4 6–4 6–3.
MEN'S DOUBLES – Final: O'Brien/Palmer (2) d. Haarhuis/Stolle (7) 6–4 7–6.

ERICSSON OPEN ($2,700,000)

KEY BISCAYNE, FL, 23 MARCH–2 APRIL
MEN'S SINGLES – 1st Round: A. Agassi (1) bye; A. Roddick (WC) d. F. Vicente 6–4 6–0; A. Pavel d. S. Sargsian 6–1 6–3; F. Santoro (31) bye; S. Grosjean (18) bye; S. Schalken d. M. Hipfl 6–3 6–1; M. Mirnyi d. M. Tillstrom 6–1 3–6 6–4; P. Rafter (15) bye; T. Henman (10) bye; A. Calleri (Q) d. M. Rosset 5–7 6–3 7–6; R. Federer d. J. Gimelstob (WC) 7–5 6–3; M. Zabaleta (23) bye; N. Escude (26) bye; W. Arthurs (Q) d. F. Clavet 7–5 6–3; M. Chang d. J. Marin 6–3 6–4; M. Rios (8) bye; N. Kiefer (4) bye; R. Fromberg d. J. Tarango 7–6 4–6 7–5; W. Ferreira d. M. Damm (Q) 4–6 6–1 6–4; H. Arazi (29) bye; D. Hrbaty (20) bye; C. Rochus d. F. Squillari 4–6 6–3 6–4; M. Kratochvil (Q) d. J. Van Lottum 6–3 6–3; A. Costa (13) bye; A. Corretja (12) bye; J. Novak d. A. Martin 6–2 6–4; G. Pozzi (Q) d. J. Bjorkman 0–6 7–6 7–5; S. Koubek (21) bye; V. Spadea (28) bye; G. Ivanisevic d. D. Prinosil 6–3 6–2; A. Clement d. C. Woodruff 6–4 3–6 6–4; G. Kuerten (6) bye; M. Norman (5) bye; N. Massu (Q) d. A. Di Pasquale 6–4 4–6 6–0; J. Gambill d. C. Dosedel 6–4 6–1; K. Alami (27) bye; M. Philippoussis (22) bye; C. Saulnier (Q) d. T. Johansson 4–6 3–6 7–5; W. Black (Q) d. A. Berasategui 6–4 6–1; C. Pioline (11) bye; L. Hewitt (14) bye; G. Gaudio d. H. Gumy 6–3 6–3; M. Fish (WC) d. G. Blanco 6–4 0–6 4–1 ret; T. Haas (19) bye; F. Meligeni (30) bye; P. Goldstein (WC) d. C. Ruud (P) 6–2 6–1; G. Canas d. I. Ljubicic 6–4 7–5; Y. Kafelnikov (3) bye; T. Enqvist (7) bye; J. Courier d. D. Nalbandian (Q) 6–3 3–6 7–5; G. Bastl d. T. Ketola (Q) 6–4 6–4; F. Vicente (25) bye; F. Mantilla (24) bye; J. Golmard d. D. Vacek 6–4 6–2; X. Malisse (Q) d. M. Larsson 4–6 6–3; N. Lapentti (9) bye; Y. El Aynaoui (16) bye; B. Black d. R. Schuttler 6–3 7–5; A. Medvedev d. A. Ilie 7–5 6–2; G. Rusedski (17) bye; M. Safin (32) bye; A. Vinciguerra (WC) d. K. Kucera 6–1 6–3; C. Moya d. J. Viloca (Q) 6–4 6–2; P. Sampras (2) bye.
2nd round: Agassi (1) d. Roddick (WC) 6–2 6–3; Pavel d. Santoro (31) 6–3 4–6 7–6; Grosjean (18) d. Schalken 6–4 6–3; Rafter (15) d. Mirnyi 6–4 6–2; Henman (10) d. Calleri (Q) 6–3 7–6 6–4; Zabaleta (23) d. Federer 6–4 7–6; Escude (26) d. Arthurs (Q) 6–3 6–3; Rios (8) d. Chang 6–4 6–4; Fromberg d. Kiefer (4) 6–4 6–4; W. Ferreira d. Arazi (29) 7–5 6–3; Hrbaty (20) d. Rochus 6–1 6–1; Kratochvil (Q) d. A. Costa (13) 3–6 7–6 6–3; Novak d. Corretja (12) 6–7 7–6 6–1; Pozzi (Q) d. Koubek (21) 7–6 6–1; Ivanisevic d. Spadea (28) 7–5 6–2; Clement d. Kuerten (6) d. Clement 6–7 7–6 7–5; Norman (5) d. Massu (Q) 6–1 6–0; Gambill d. Alami (27) 6–4 5 7 6 1; Philippoussis (22) d. Saulnier (Q) 4–6 6–3 6–4; Pioline (11) d. W. Black (Q) 7–6 6–3; Hewitt (14) d. Gaudio 7–6

6–7 6–3; Haas (19) d. Fish (WC) 6–2 6–1; Meligeni (30) d. Goldstein (WC) 7–5 7–6; Kafelnikov (3) d. Canas 6–3 4–6 6–4; Enqvist (7) d. Courier 6–7 6–3 6–4; Bastl d. Ferrero (25) 7–6 6–4; Mantilla (24) d. Golmard 3–6 7–6 6–2; Lapentti (9) d. Malisse (Q) 6–4 6–4; B. Black d. El Aynaoui (16) 6–3 1–6 6–1; Rusedski (17) d. Medvedev 6–4 7–5; Vinciguerra (WC) d. Safin (32) 1–6 6–1 6–2; Sampras (2) d. Moya 6–1 6–4.

3rd round: Agassi (1) d. Pavel 6–3 6–4; Rafter (15) d. Grosjean (18) 2–6 6–4 6–3; Henman (10) d. Zabaleta (23) 6–3 6–3; Rios (8) d. Escude (26) 6–2 3–6 6–1; W. Ferreira d. Fromberg 6–3 6–4; Hrbaty (20) d. Kratochvil (Q) 7–6 7–6; Pozzi (Q) d. Novak 6–3 7–5; Kuerten (6) d. Ivanisevic 7–6 6–3; Gambill d. Norman (5) 6–3 3–6 6–3; Philippoussis (22) d. Pioline (11) 6–4 7–6; Hewitt (14) d. Haas (19) 6–1 6–3; Kafelnikov (3) d. Meligeni (30) 6–4 6–3; Enqvist (7) d. Bastl 6–0 7–6; Lapentti (9) d. Mantilla (24) 5–7 6–1 6–1; Rusedski (17) d. B. Black 6–1 7–6; Sampras (2) d. Vinciguerra (WC) 5–7 7–6 6–4.

4th round: Agassi (1) d. Rafter (15) d. Henman (10) d. Rios (8) 6–1 1–6 7–6; W. Ferreira d. Hrbaty (20) 2–6 6–4 6–4; Kuerten (6) d. Pozzi (Q) 6–4 7–6; Gambill d. Philippoussis (22) 6–2 6–7 6–3; Hewitt (14) d. Kafelnikov (3) 6–4 6–3; Lapentti (9) d. Enqvist (7) w/o; Sampras (2) d. Rusedski (17) 6–3 6–3.

Quarter-finals: Agassi (1) d. Henman (10) 7–5 1–6 7–6; Kuerten (6) d. W. Ferreira 6–3 6–1; Hewitt (14) d. Gambill 6–4 7–6; Sampras (2) d. Lapentti (9) 6–4 7–6.

Semi-finals: Kuerten (6) d. Agassi (1) 6–1 6–4; Sampras (2) d. Hewitt (14) 6–3 3–6 6–1.

Final: Sampras (2) d. Kuerten (6) 6–1 6–7 7–6 7–6.

MEN'S DOUBLES – Final: Woodbridge/Woodforde (3) d. O'Brien/Palmer (1) 6–3 6–4.

TENNIS MASTERS SERIES – MONTE CARLO ($2,450,000)
MONTE CARLO, 17–23 APRIL

MEN'S SINGLES – 1st Round: Y. Kafelnikov (1) d. D. Vacek 6–3 6–3; D. Hrbaty d. A. Di Pasquale 6–2 7–5; A. Clement d. G. Ivanisevic (WC) 6–0 6–7 6–4; M. Zabaleta (15) d. V. Spadea 6–2 1–6 7–5; A. Corretja (9) d. A. Berasategui (Q) 7–6 6–1; F. Santoro d. O. Stanoytchev (Q) 6–4 6–2; J. Chela (Q) d. A. Lopez-Moron (Q) 7–5 1–6 7–6; T. Henman (7) d. M. Rosset 6–3 6–2; F. Squillari d. N. Lapentti (4) 6–2 7–6; F. Meligeni d. A. Gaudenzi (WC) 7–6 6–4; J. Ferrero d. F. Clavet 6–2 6–4; H. Arazi d. T. Haas (13) 3–6 6–1 6–1; S. Sargsian d. Y. El Aynaoui (11) 7–6 4–2 ret; J. Boutter (Q) d. M. Chang 6–2 6–4; G. Gaudio d. M. Safin 7 6 6 0; F. Mantilla d. M. Rios (5) 6–4 0–6 6–2; T. Enqvist (6) d. C. Saulnier (WC) 6–3 6–2; R. Krajicek d. F. Vicente 7–5 6–1; J. Golmard d. C. Woodruff 6–4 6–2; A. Costa (12) d. R. Schuttler 6–4 6–4; W. Ferreira d. M. Philippoussis (14) 6–4 7–5; C. Ruud (Q) d. A. Vinciguerra 4–6 7–5 6–1; K. Alami d. T. Johansson 6–2 6–4; M. Norman (3) d. A. Portas (Q) 3–6 6–3 6–4; C. Pioline (8) d. M. Larsson 6–2 6–2; J. Novak d. R. Federer 6–1 2–6 7–5; N. Escude d. S. Huet (Q) 4–6 6–1 6–2; C. Dosedel d. G. Rusedski (10) 6–4 6–7 6–1; C. Moya d. S. Koubek (16) 1–6 6–3 6–0; S. Schalken d. J. Bjorkman (WC) 6–4 6–2; A. Medvedev d. S. Grosjean 2–6 6–0 6–3; K. Kucera d. G. Kuerten (2) 3–6 6–0 6–2.

2nd round: Hrbaty d. Kafelnikov (1) 6–3 5–7 6–4; Clement d. Zabaleta (15) 6–7 6–0 7–5; Corretja (9) d. Santoro 6–0 6–4; Chela (Q) d. Henman (7) 6–2 4–6 6–3; Squillari d. Meligeni 6–2 6–4; Ferrero d. Arazi 6–0 6–3; Boutter (Q) d. Sargsian 6–2 6–3; Gaudio d. Mantilla 6–3 7–5; Krajicek d. Enqvist (6) 7–5 6–1; A. Costa (12) d. Golmard 2–6 6–4 6–2; Ruud (Q) d. W. Ferreira 5–7 6–4 6–3; Alami d. Norman (3) 6–3 3–6 6–1; Pioline (8) d. Novak 6–4 6–3; Dosedel (10) d. Escude 6–0 6–2; Schalken d. Moya 6–4 4–6 6–1; Kucera d. Medvedev 7–6 6–4.

3rd round: Hrbaty d. Clement 6–4 7–5; Corretja (9) d. Chela (Q) 6–3 6–3; Ferrero d. Squillari 6–2 6–4; Gaudio d. Boutter (Q) 6–3 7–5; A. Costa (12) d. Krajicek 7–6 6–3; Alami d. Ruud (Q) 2–6 6–1 7–6; Pioline (8) d. Dosedel (10) 3–6 7–5 6–4; Kucera d. Schalken 6–2 6–4.

Quarter-finals: Hrbaty d. Corretja (9) 3–6 6–3 6–4; Gaudio d. Ferrero 6–4 6–2; Alami d. A. Costa (12) 6–4 7–5; Pioline (8) d. Kucera 6–2 6–4.

Semi-finals: Hrbaty d. Gaudio 4–6 7–5 6–2; Pioline (8) d. Alami 6–3 6–1.

Final: Pioline (8) d. Hrbaty 6–4 7–6 7–6.

MEN'S DOUBLES – Final: W. Ferreira/Kafelnikov d. Haarhuis/Stolle (3) 6–3 2–6 6–1.

TENNIS MASTERS SERIES – ROME ($2,450,000)
ROME, 8–14 MAY

MEN'S SINGLES – 1st Round: A. Agassi (1) d. T. Martin 6–2 7–6; G. Gaudio (Q) d. F. Meligeni 6–1 7–5; F. Squillari d. C. Dosedel 2–6 6–3 6–4; D. Hrbaty (15) d. J. Tarango (Q) 6–4 6–1; A. Corretja (10) d. K. Kucera 6–2 4–6 7–6; J. Novak d. T. Haas 7–6 7–6; F. Santoro d. L. Tieleman (WC) 7–5 6–3; T. Henman (8) d. B. Black 7–6 6–4; G. Kuerten (4) d. J. Golmard 6–4 6–1; M. Philippoussis d. M. Rosset 6–3 1–6 7–6; M. Zabaleta d. R. Krajicek 6–4 6–4; Y. El Aynaoui (14) d. V. Spadea 6–2 6–3; B. Ulihrach (Q) d. P. Rafter (12) 3–6 6–4 6–3; A. Costa d. A. Portas (Q) 6–2 6–3; F. Clavet d. G. Ivanisevic (Q) 6–4 3–6 7–5; N. Lapentti (6) d. T. Johansson 6–4 7–5; C. Pioline (5) d. C. Woodruff 6–1 6–1; A. Pavel (Q) d. N. Escude 6–1 4–6 6–3; F. Mantilla d. J. Chela (Q) 6–3 6–3; M. Safin d. M. Rios (11) 6–1 6–4; F. Vicente d. G. Rusedski (13) 6–3 6–1; A. Medvedev d. R. Federer 3–6 6–3 7–5; C. Moya d. C. Ruud (Q) 6–3 6–1; M. Norman (3) d. A. Di Pasquale 6–3 6–2; L. Hewitt (9) d. S. Koubek 6–4 6–2; J. Ferrero (16) d. D. Sanguinetti (WC) 6–4 6–7 7–5; H. Arazi d. S. Schalken 6–3 6–2; M. Puerta d. R. Furlan (WC) 6–2 6–3; Y. Kafelnikov (2) d. A. Gaudenzi (WC) 6–3 2–6 7–5.

2nd round: Agassi (1) d. Gaudio (Q) 6–1 6–4; Hrbaty (15) d. Squillari 6–4 7–6; Corretja (10) d. Novak 6–3 7–6; Santoro d. Henman (8) 7–6 4–6 6–4; Kuerten (4) d. Philippoussis 6–2 6–2; El Aynaoui (14) d. Zabaleta 3–6 7–6 7–6; A. Costa d. Ulihrach (Q) 6–1 6–2; Clavet d. Lapentti (6) 7–5 6–4; Pavel (Q) d. Pioline (5) 3–6 6–1

7–6; Mantilla d. Safin 7–5 6–7 6–3; Medvedev d. Vicente 6–2 7–5; Norman (3) d. Moya 6–4 6–2; Enqvist (7) d. Chang 2–6 6–4 6–2; Hewitt (9) d. Di Pasquale 6–3 6–7 6–4; Ferrero (16) d. Arazi 7–6 6–3; Puerta d. Kafelnikov (2) 6–4 6–4. **3rd round:** Hrbaty (15) d. Agassi (1) 6–4 6–4; Corretja (10) d. Santoro 6–2 6–3; Kuerten (4) El Aynaoui (14) w/o; A. Costa d. Clavet 6–3 6–2; Mantilla d. Pavel (Q) 6–4 6–2; Norman (3) d. Medvedev 7–6 6–1; Hewitt (9) d. Enqvist (7) 7–6 2–6 6–3; Puerta d. Ferrero (16) 7–6 3–6 6–4. **Quarter-finals:** Corretja (10) d. Hrbaty (15) 6–1 7–6; Kuerten (4) d. A. Costa 6–4 7–5; Norman (3) d. Mantilla 6–4 6–3; Hewitt (9) d. Puerta 6–3 6–1. **Semi-finals:** Kuerten (4) d. Corretja (10) 6–4 6–2; Norman (3) d. Hewitt (9) 6–3 6–0. **Final:** Norman (3) d. Kuerten (4) 6–3 3–6 6–4 6–4. **MEN'S DOUBLES – Final:** Damm/Hrbaty d. W. Ferreira/Kafelnikov (6) 6–4 4–6 6–3.

TENNIS MASTERS SERIES – HAMBURG ($2,450,000)
HAMBURG, 15–21 MAY
MEN'S SINGLES – 1st Round: P. Sampras (1) d. C. Woodruff 6–4 7–6; A. Di Pasquale d. C. Dosedel 7–5 1–6 6–3; A. Pavel (Q) d. R. Federer 6–4 6–3; J. Ferrero (15) d. C. Moya 3–6 6–2 7–6; L. Hewitt (10) d. M. Philippoussis 6–4 7–6; M. Zabaleta d. G. Gaudio 6–3 6–3; J. Golmard (PR) d. M. Goellner (WC) 6–3 6–1; T. Henman (8) d. H. Arazi 6–4 7–5; M. Norman (3) d. T. Johansson 6–2 6–4; R. Schuttler (WC) d. V. Spadea 6–4 3–6 6–3; A. Martin (Q) d. D. Vacek 6–4 3–6 6–1; Y. El Aynaoui (13) d. S. Huet (Q) 6–3 3–6 6–4; W. Ferreira d. P. Rafter (11) 6–4 7–5; R. Fromberg (Q) d. F. Meligeni 7–5 6–3; S. Grosjean d. F. Santoro 7–5 7–6; G. Kuerten (5) d. K. Alami 5–7 6–2 6–3; M. Rosset d. N. Lapentti (6) 7–6 6–3; B. Black d. J. Tarango (Q) 7–5 3–6 6–4; F. Mantilla d. S. Sargsian (Q) 6–3 6–4; M. Safin (12) d. A. Costa 7–6 7–6; A. Medvedev d. D. Hrbaty (14) 6–4 7–6; J. Gambill (Q) d. M. Chang 7–5 7–5; M. Mirnyi d. A. Voinea (Q) 6–3 5–7 6–4; C. Pioline (4) d. J. Novak 7–6 6–2; T. Enqvist (7) d. K. Kucera 6–3 4–6 6–4; F. Clavet d. D. Prinosil (WC) 6–4 6–2; T. Martin d. F. Vicente 6–1 6–1; A. Corretja (9) d. F. Squillari 6–3 6–2; M. Kohlmann (WC) d. T. Haas (16) 7–6 6–4; M. Rios d. N. Escude 6–4 6–1; M. Puerta d. S. Koubek 6–4 6–2; S. Schalken d. Y. Kafelnikov (2) 6–4 6–3. **2nd round:** Di Pasquale d. Sampras (1) 6–4 6–4; Pavel (Q) d. Ferrero (15) 6–4 6–4; Zabaleta d. Hewitt (10) 5–7 6–3 6–2; Henman (8) d. Golmard (PR) 2–6 6–4 6–1; Norman (3) d. Schuttler (WC) 3–6 6–3 6–1; El Aynaoui (13) d. A. Martin (Q) 6–3 6–1; W. Ferreira d. Fromberg (Q) 6–4 3–6 7–6; Kuerten (5) d. Grosjean 6–1 3–6 6–3; Rosset d. B. Black 6–3 6–2; Safin (12) d. Mantilla 6–3 6–0; Medvedev d. Gambill (Q) 1–6 7–5 6–2; Pioline (4) d. Mirnyi 7–6 6–3; Clavet d. Enqvist (7) 7–6 6–4; Corretja (9) d. T. Martin 6–3 6–2; Rios d. Kohlmann (WC) 6–1 6–0; Puerta d. Schalken 6–4 6–4. **3rd round:** Pavel (Q) d. Di Pasquale 6–3 7–6; Zabaleta d. Henman (8) 7–5 6–3; Norman (3) d. El Aynaoui (13) 3–6 6–1 6–4; Kuerten (5) d. W. Ferreira 6–1 6–2; Safin (12) d. Rosset 6–4 7–5; Pioline (4) d. Medvedev 4–6 6–2 6–3; Clavet d. Corretja (9) 6–4 6–1; Rios d. Puerta 7–6 6–0. **Quarter-finals:** Pavel (Q) d. Zabaleta 7–5 6–4; Kuerten (5) d. Norman (3) 6–4 6–2; Safin (12) d. Pioline (4) 7–6 4–6 6–3; Rios d. Clavet 6–4 6–3. **Semi-finals:** Kuerten (5) d. Pavel (Q) 6–3 6–3; Safin (12) d. Rios 7–6 6–2. **Final:** Kuerten (5) d. Safin (12) 6–4 5–7 6–4 5–7 7–6. **MEN'S DOUBLES – Final:** Woodbridge/Woodforde (3) d. Arthurs/Stolle 6–7 6–4 6–3.

TENNIS MASTERS SERIES – CANADA ($2,450,000)
TORONTO, 31 JULY–6 AUGUST
MEN'S SINGLES – 1st Round: J. Golmard (PR) d. A. Agassi (1) 7–6 7–6; P. Srichaphan (Q) d. C. Woodruff 6–3 6–4; A. Clement d. M. Puerta 6–3 6–3; M. Rios d. T. Henman (15) 6–4 3–6 6–3; S. Koubek d. N. Lapentti (10) 6–4 6–3; H. Levy (Q) d. M. Damm (LL) 7–6 4–6 6–3; S. Grosjean d. C. Mamiit (Q) 6–2 7–6; L. Hewitt (7) d. R. Federer 3–6 6–3 6–2; G. Kuerten (4) d. A. Di Pasquale 6–4 6–4; S. Lareau (WC) d. F. Santoro 6–4 6–1; K. Kucera d. J. Sekulov (LL) 6–4 6–4; P. Rafter (14) d. A. Parmar (LL) 6–1 4–6 6–3; N. Kiefer (11) d. T. Martin 6–1 7–5; J. Björkman (Q) 6–4 1–6 6–3; A. Pavel d. J. Chela 6–2 6–2; C. Saulnier (Q) d. E. Alvarez (SE) 6–2 6–3; N. Escude (17) d. M. Zabaleta 3–6 6–1; S. Sargsian d. M. Philippoussis (16) 6–4 7–6; S. Larose (WC) d. D. Wheaton (Q) 7–6 7–6; K. Alami d. P. Tramacchi (Q) 6–2 6–4; P. Sampras (2) d. M. Llodra (Q) 5–7 6–2 7–6. **2nd round:** Golmard (PR) d. Srichaphan (Q) 6–3 6–2; Rios d. Clement 6–4 7–6; Levy (Q) d. Koubek 6–1 6–3; Grosjean d. Hewitt (7) 3–6 7–6; Lareau (WC) d. Kuerten (4) 7–6 6–4; Rafter (14) d. Kucera 6–3 7–5; Novak d. Kiefer (11) 6–2 7–5; Enqvist (6) d. Ilie 6–3 6–2; Kafelnikov (5) d. Mirnyi 6–4 6–4; Ferrero (12) d. Gaudio 6–7 6–3 6–3; W. Ferreira d. Johansson 6–4 6–3; Krajicek d. Chang 6–2 7–5; Safin (8) d. Pavel 6–7 6–3 6–0; Escude (17) d. Saulnier (Q) 7–6 6–7 6–2; Sargsian d. Larose (WC) 6–3 6–2; Sampras (2) d. Alami 7–6 6–2. **3rd round:** Golmard (PR) d. Rios 2–6 7–5 7–5; Levy (Q) d. Grosjean 6–3 1–6 6–1; Rafter (14) d. Lareau (WC) 6–4 6–2; Novak d. Enqvist (6) 6–2 1–6 3–1 ret; Kafelnikov (5) d. Ferrero (12) 6–1 4–6 6–4; W. Ferreira d. Krajicek 7–5 7–6; Safin (8) d. Escude (17) 3–2 ret; Sampras (2) d. Sargsian 6–1 6–2. **Quarter-finals:** Levy (Q) d. Golmard (PR) 6–4 6–4; Novak d. Rafter (14) 3–6 7–6 6–2; W. Ferreira d. Kafelnikov (5) 6 3 7–6, Safin (8) d. Sampras (2) 6–4 3–6 7–6.

Semi-finals: Levy (Q) d. Novak 6–3 1–6 6–4; Safin (8) d. W. Ferreira 6–2 5–7 6–4.
Final: Safin (8) d. Levy (Q) 6–2 6–3.
MEN'S DOUBLES – Final: Lareau/Nestor (6) d. Eagle/Florent 6–3 7–6.

TENNIS MASTERS SERIES – CINCINNATI ($2,450,000)
CINCINNATI, OH, 7–13 AUGUST
MEN'S SINGLES – 1st Round: A. Agassi (1) d. W. Ferreira 7–6 6–1; F. Vicente d. R. Bryan (Q) 7–6 6–3; M. Rios d. M. Rosset 6–4 6–4; M. Philippoussis (16) d. A. Di Pasquale 6–4 6–2; H. Arazi d. N. Lapentti (10) 6–4 6–4; M. Mirnyi d. A. Vinciguerra 7–6 6–4; H. Levy (SE) d. A. Ilie 3–6 6–3 6–4; T. Enqvist (7) d. A. Pavel 7–5 2–6 7–6; M. Norman (3) d. J. Chela 7–6 7–6; C. Dosedel d. M. Fish (WC) 7–6 6–2; J. Novak d. L. Roux (Q) 6–1 6–0; F. Squillari (13) d. G. Gaudio 6–7 7–5 6–0; A. Clement d. J. Ferrero (12) 6–4 6–2; M. Damm (Q) d. V. Spadea (WC) 7–6 3–6 6–2; C. Woodruff d. D. Hrbaty 6–1 3–6 6–3; Y. Kafelnikov (5) d. R. Krajicek 6–3 1–6 6–3; J. Bjorkman (WC) d. A. Corretja (6) 6–4 6–4; C. Moya d. K. Alami 3 6–7 6–4; S. Schalken d. M. Chang 6–4 4–6 6–4; T. Martin d. N. Kiefer (11) 6–2 6–2; A. Gaudenzi (LL) d. A. Costa 6–3 3–6 6–1; S. Koubek d. T. Johansson 6–2 6–3; G. Pozzi (Q) d. A. Roddick (WC) 7–6 6–1; G. Kuerten (4) d. J. Golmard (PR) 6–0 6–4; M. Safin (8) d. N. Godwin (Q) 7–5 6–3; F. Clavet d. R. Federer 7–6 7–6; S. Grosjean d. K. Kucera 6–4 6–4; F. Santoro d. L. Hewitt (9) 4–6 6–4 6–4; T. Henman (15) d. C. Mamiit (Q) 6–3 5–7 6–2; M. Puerta d. V. Voltchkov (Q) 6–3 6–1; T. Dent (Q) d. J. Tarango 6–4 3–6 6–1; P. Sampras (2) d. M. Zabaleta 6–4 6–2.
2nd round: Vicente d. Agassi (1) 3–6 6–3 1–0 ret; Philippoussis (16) d. Rios 6–7 6–4 7–6; Mirnyi d. Arazi 6–3 6–3; Enqvist (7) d. Levy (SE) 6–4 6–1; Dosedel d. Norman (3) 6–7 6–3 6–3; Squillari (13) d. Novak 6–3 6–4; Clement d. Damm (Q) 7–5 6–3; Kafelnikov (5) d. Woodruff 6–4 7–6; Bjorkman (WC) d. Moya 4–6 6–2 6–1; T. Martin d. Schalken 6–4 6–4; Koubek d. Gaudenzi (14) 2–6 7–5 6–2; Kuerten (4) d. Pozzi (Q) 7–5 6–3; Safin (8) d. Clavet 7–6 6–3; Santoro d. Grosjean 6–2 6–3; Henman (15) d. Puerta 6–1 6–2; Sampras (2) d. Dent (Q) 7–6 7–6.
3rd round: Vicente d. Philippoussis (16) 3–6 7–6 7–6; Enqvist (7) d. Mirnyi 6–4 6–3; Squillari (13) d. Dosedel 6–4 7–5; Clement d. Kafelnikov (8) 6–4 6–1; T. Martin d. Bjorkman (WC) 6–2 6–4; Kuerten (4) d. Koubek 1–6 6–1 6–2; Santoro d. Safin (8) 6–1 7–6; Henman (15) d. Sampras (2) 6–3 6–4.
Quarter-finals: Enqvist (7) d. Vicente 7–5 6–1; Clement d. Squillari (13) 6–2 7–5; Kuerten (4) d. T. Martin 6–7 6–3 7–6; Henman (15) d. Santoro 6–1 6–4.
Semi-finals: Enqvist (7) d. Clement 6–2 6–2; Henman (15) d. Kuerten (4) 6–7 6–3 7–6.
Final: Enqvist (7) d. Henman (15) 7–6 6–4.
MEN'S DOUBLES – Final: Woodbridge/Woodforde (1) d. E. Ferreira/Leach (3) 7–6 6–4.

TENNIS MASTERS SERIES – STUTTGART ($2,450,000)
STUTTGART, 30 OCTOBER –5 NOVEMBER
MEN'S SINGLES - 1st Round: M. Safin (1) bye; F. Santoro d. G. Ivanisevic (WC) 6–3 7–6; G. Rusedski d. J. Golmard (PR) 6–1 6–2; M. Puerta (16) bye; T. Henman (9) bye; A. Costa d. J. Novak 7–5 6–7 7–6; R. Krajicek d. A. Martin (Q) 6–2 6–4; L. Hewitt (8) bye; M. Norman (3) bye; M. Rosset d. R. Schuttler (WC) 3–6 6–4 6–3; J. Boutter (Q) d. H. Arazi 6–4 3–6 6–1; S. Schalken (LL) bye; F. Squillari (11) bye; D. Hrbaty d. C. Moya (WC) 6–3 3–6 6–2; R. Federer d. J. Gambill 7–6 1–0 ret; Y. Kafelnikov (6) bye; T. Enqvist (5) bye; W. Ferreira d. C. Vinck (Q) 6–3 6–7 6–4; A. Clement d. A. Vinciguerra 6–2 1–6 6–4; M. Philippoussis (12) bye; P. Rafter (14) bye; A. Pavel d. G. Gaudio 6–4 4–6 6–0; T. Johansson (Q) d. F. Clavet 7–6 6–7 6–4; A. Agassi (4) bye; A. Corretja (7) bye; M. Chang d. J. Knippschild (Q) 6–3 6–7 7–6; Y. El Aynaoui d. K. Alami 7–6 3–6 6–3; J. Ferrero (10) bye; N. Lapentti (15) bye; S. Grosjean d. T. Haas (WC) 6–4 6–2; N. Escude d. B. Phau (Q) 6–3 6–4; G. Kuerten (2) bye.
2nd round: Safin (1) d. Santoro 6–2 6–2; Rusedski d. Puerta (16) 6–2 6–3; Henman (9) d. A. Costa 6–2 6–3; Hewitt (8) d. Krajicek 6–4 7–5; Norman (3) d. Rosset w/o; Schalken (LL) d. Boutter (Q) 6–1 6–3; Squillari (11) d. Hrbaty 6–7 6–3 6–3; Kafelnikov (6) d. Federer 7–5 6–3; W. Ferreira d. Enqvist (5) 6–4 7–5; Philippoussis (12) d. Clement 6–3 6–3; Pavel d. Rafter (14) 7–6 6–1; Agassi (4) d. Johansson (Q) 6–4 6–2; Chang d. Corretja (7) 1–6 7–5 6–0; El Aynaoui d. Ferrero (10) 7–6 6–4; Grosjean d. Lapentti (15) 6–1 6–0; Kuerten (2) d. Escude 7–6 7–6.
3rd round: Rusedski d. Safin (1) 7–6 6–4; Hewitt (8) d. Henman (9) 3–6 6–3 6–4; Schalken (LL) d. Norman (3) 4–6 6–3 6–3; Kafelnikov (6) d. Squillari (11) 6–3 7–5; W. Ferreira d. Philippoussis (12) 1–0 ret; Pavel d. Agassi (4) 6–3 6–4; Chang d. El Aynaoui 7–5 6–2; Grosjean d. Kuerten (2) 7–6 6–3.
Quarter-finals: Hewitt (8) d. Rusedski 6–4 6–4; Kafelnikov (6) d. Schalken (LL) 4–6 6–1 6–4; W. Ferreira d. Pavel 6–0 7–5; Grosjean d. Chang 7–5 1–6 6–2.
Semi-finals: Hewitt (8) d. Kafelnikov (6) 6–4 6–7 6–3; W. Ferreira d. Grosjean 6–4 6–2.
Final: W. Ferreira d. Hewitt (8) 7–6 3–6 6–7 7–6 6–2.
MEN'S DOUBLES – Final: Novak/Rikl (5) d. Johnson/Norval 3–6 6–3 6–4.

TENNIS MASTERS SERIES – PARIS ($2,450,000)
PARIS, 13–19 NOVEMBER
MEN'S SINGLES – 1st Round: G. Kuerten (1) bye; C. Woodruff (Q) d. J. Novak 4–6 7–5 6–3; J. Boutter (WC) d. B. Black 6–4 6–7 6–4; P. Rafter (15) bye; T. Henman (9) bye; A. Costa d. A. O'Brien (Q) 7–5 6–3; G. Pozzi (LL) d. K. Kucera 4–6 7–5 7–6; T. Enqvist (7) bye; Y. Kafelnikov (4) bye; M. Gustafsson (Q) d. J. Golmard 6–2 2–1 ret; D. Hrbaty d. R. Federer 4–6 6–2 6–2; M. Philippoussis (13) bye; F. Squillari (11) bye; D. Prinosil (Q) d.

G. Gaudio 6–2 6–1; M. Chang d. A. Di Pasquale (WC) 6–2 7–5; H. Levy (LL) bye; S. Huet (LL) bye; J. Gambill d. A. Pavel 4–1 ret; N. Lapentti d. M. Puerta 5–4 ret; J. Ferrero (12) bye; C. Pioline (14) bye; M. Rosset d. F. Vicente 6–4 6–7 6–3; F. Santoro d. C. Moya 6–7 6–4 6–3; M. Norman (3) bye; A. Corretja (8) bye; A. Clement d. G. Rusedski 7–6 7–5; M. Mirnyi d. N. Escude 3–6 6–3 6–4; W. Ferreira (10) bye; S. Grosjean (16) bye; T. Haas d. C. Rochus (Q) 7–5 6–4; G. Bastl (Q) d. M. Llodra (WC) 6–4 7–6; M. Safin (2) bye.
2nd round: Kuerten (1) d. Woodruff (Q) 6–3 7–6; Rafter (15) d. Boutter (WC) 6–3 6–2; A. Costa d. Henman (9) 6–4 6–4; Pozzi (LL) d. Enqvist (7) 6–2 1–6 7–6; Kafelnikov (4) d. Gustafsson (Q) 7–6 6–4; Philippoussis (13) d. Hrbaty 1–6 7–6 7–6; Prinosil (Q) d. Squillari (11) 6–3 6–3; Chang d. Levy (LL) 6–7 6–4 6–4; Gambill d. Huet (LL) 6–3 7–5; Ferrero (12) d. Lapentti 7–5 3–6 6–3; Rosset d. Pioline (14) 7–5 7–5; Santoro d. Norman (3) 6–2 6–4; Corretja (8) d. Clement 6–2 6–7 6–3; W. Ferreira (10) d. Mirnyi 6–4 2–6 6–4; Grosjean (16) d. Haas 7–5 6–4; Safin (2) d. Bastl (Q) 7–5 6–4.
3rd round: Kuerten (1) d. Rafter (15) 6–4 7–6; A. Costa d. Pozzi (LL) 6–2 6–4; Philippoussis (13) d. Kafelnikov (4) 6–4 6–2; Prinosil (Q) d. Chang 4–6 7–6 6–4; Ferrero (12) d. Gambill 4–6 7–5 6–4; Santoro d. Rosset 6–4 3–6 7–6; Corretja (8) d. W. Ferreira (10) 6–3 6–4; Safin (2) d. Grosjean (16) 6–2 7–6.
Quarter-finals: Kuerten (1) d. A. Costa 6–3 6–4; Philippoussis (13) d. Prinosil (Q) 4–6 6–4 7–6; Ferrero (12) d. Santoro 6–4 6–7 7–5; Safin (2) d. Corretja (8) 7–6 6–3.
Semi-finals: Philippoussis (13) d. Kuerten (1) 7–6 7–6; Safin (2) d. Ferrero (12) 6–2 6–2.
Final: Safin (2) d. Philippoussis (13) 3–6 7–6 6–4 3–6 7–6.
MEN'S DOUBLES – Final: Kulti/Mirnyi (5) d. Haarhuis/Nestor (6) 6–4 7–5.

Men's International Series 1

Formerly known as Championship Series tournaments

KROGER ST. JUDE ($700,000)
MEMPHIS, TN, 14–20 FEBRUARY
MEN'S SINGLES – 1st Round: M. Philippoussis (1) bye; B. MacPhie (Q) d. L. Manta 6–3 3–6 6–3; T. Zib d. M. Hantschk 6–3 7–6; M. Larsson (16) bye; R. Schuttler (9) bye; P. Srichaphan d. C. Caratti (Q) 4–6 6–3 6–4; O. Stanoytchev d. S. Lareau 7–6 3–6 7–6; J. Gambill (8) bye; V. Spadea (3) bye; A. Sa d. R. Agenor 6–4 6–1; D. Sanguinetti d. A. Du Puis 7–6 6–1; R. Fromberg (14) bye; S. Sargsian (11) bye; H. Levy (Q) d. J. Sekulov (LL) 6–4 6–1; L. Tieleman d. R. Bryan (WC) 6–4 3–6 7–5; J. Courier (6) bye; M. Chang (5) bye; A. Pretzsch d. M. Knowles (Q) 6–4 6–3; N. Massu d. G. Etlis 7–5 6–1; H. Gumy (12) bye; B. Black (13) bye; M. Rodriguez d. J. Gimelstob 7–6 7–6; M. Woodforde (WC) d. J. Alonso-Pintor 6–4 6–2; C. Woodruff (4) bye; W. Ferreira (7) bye; A. Popp d. T. Behrend 6–1 7–5; C. Mamiit d. L. Jensen (WC) 7–5 6–2; M. Mirnyi (10) bye; M. Tillstrom (15) bye; R. Reneberg (Q) d. P. Goldstein 6–4 6–2; J. Salzenstein (Q) d. F. Jonsson 7–6 6–1; T. Haas (2) bye.
2nd round: Philippoussis (1) d. MacPhie (Q) 6–2 6–4; Larsson (16) d. Zib 7–6 6–4; Schuttler (9) d. Srichaphan 5–7 6–3 6–3; Gambill (8) d. Stanoytchev 6–2 6–3; Sa d. Spadea (3) 6–4 6–3; Fromberg (14) d. Sanguinetti 2–6 6–3 6–3; Sargsian (11) d. Levy (Q) 6–2 6–3; Tieleman d. Courier (6) 7–6 6–0; Chang (5) d. Pretzsch 5–7 6–2 6–1; Gumy (12) d. Massu 7–5 7–6; B. Black (13) d. Rodriguez 6–2 6–2; Woodruff (4) d. Woodforde (WC) 3–6 7–5 6–3; W. Ferreira (7) d. Popp 7–5 7–5; Mamiit d. Mirnyi (10) 7–6 6–2; Tillstrom (15) d. Reneberg (Q) 6–2 6–2; Haas (2) d. Salzenstein (Q) 6–2 2–6 6–4.
3rd round: Larsson (16) d. Philippoussis (1) w/o; Schuttler (9) d. Gambill (8) 6–2 1–6 7–6; Sa d. Fromberg (14) 6–4 7–6; Sargsian (11) d. Tieleman 6–2 6–2; Chang (5) d. Gumy (12) 6–2 6–0; B. Black (13) d. Woodruff (4) 6–2 3–6 6–4; W. Ferreira (7) d. Mamiit 2–6 6–2; Haas (2) d. Tillstrom (15) 6–2 3–6 7–5.
Quarter-finals: Larsson (16) d. Schuttler (9) 2–6 7–6 6–3; Sa d. Sargsian (11) 6–4 6–4; B. Black (13) d. Chang (5) 7–5 6–2; Haas (2) d. W. Ferreira (7) 6–3 2–6 7–5.
Semi-finals: Larsson (16) d. Sa 3–6 7–6 6–4; B. Black (13) d. Haas (2) 7–6 7–6.
Final: Larsson (16) d. B. Black (13) 6–2 1–6 6–3.
MEN'S DOUBLES – Final: Gimelstob/Lareau (3) d. Grabb/Reneberg 6–2 6–4.

ABN/AMRO WORLD TENNIS TOURNAMENT ($750,000)
ROTTERDAM, 14–20 FEBRUARY
MEN'S SINGLES – 1st Round: Y. Kafelnikov (1) d. N. Kulti (LL) 6–2 6–2; N. Escude d. D. Prinosil (Q) 6–4 6–1; F. Dewulf (Q) d. G. Ivanisevic (WC) 6–3 2–6 6–4; G. Rusedski (7) d. K. Kucera 6–2 7–5; J. Bjorkman (Q) d. N. Lapentti (4) 7–6 6–2; D. Hrbaty d. M. Safin 4–6 6–1 7–6; F. Santoro d. K. Alami 7–5 6–4; T. Henman (5) d. A. Martin 6–2 6–2; J. Siemerink (WC) d. T. Enqvist (6) 6–3 7–6; J. Golmard d. M. Zabaleta 6–2 6–3; P. Wessels (WC) d. A. Pavel 6–4 6–7 6–4; M. Norman (3) d. S. Schalken 3–6 7–6 6–3; C. Pioline (8) d. A. Voinea (Q) 6–3 6–3; S. Grosjean d. A. Medvedev 7–5 6–3; J. Novak d. T. Johansson 4–6 6–3 6–2; N. Kiefer (2) d. D. Vacek 6–2 6–4.
2nd round: Kafelnikov (1) d. Escude 6–3 6–3; Rusedski (7) d. Dewulf (Q) 7–6 6–4; Hrbaty d. Bjorkman (Q) 7–6 6–3; Henman (5) d. Santoro 6 2 7 5; Golmard d. Siemerink (WC) 6 4 7 6; Norman (3) d. Wessels (WC) 6–4 6–3; Pioline (8) d. Grosjean 7–6 6–7 6–3; Kiefer (2) d. Novak 5–7 6–2 7–6.

Quarter-finals: Kafelnikov (1) d. Rusedski (7) 6–7 6–4 6–4; Henman (5) d. Hrbaty 7–6 6–2; Golmard d. Norman (3) 6–4 6–3; Pioline (8) d. Kiefer (2) 2–6 6–3 7–5.
Semi-finals: Henman (5) d. Kafelnikov (1) 6–3 4–6 6–3; Pioline (8) d. Golmard 6–3 6–4.
Final: Pioline (8) d. Henman (5) 6–7 6–4 7–6.
MEN'S DOUBLES – Final: Adams/De Jager (2) d. Henman/Kafelnikov (WC) 5–7 6–2 6–3.

ABIERTO MEXICANO DE TENIS PEGASO ($700,000)
MEXICO CITY, 21–27 FEBRUARY
MEN'S SINGLES – 1st Round: G. Kuerten (1) d. G. Etlis (Q) 6–4 3–6 6–2; J. Chela (Q) d. B. Black 6–2 6–3; M. Hantschk d. J. Marin 7–6 3–6 6–0; O. Stanoytchev (LL) d. A. Di Pasquale (8) 6–1 7–5; S. Koubek (4) d. A. Portas 6–1 6–3; R. Fromberg d. A. Sa 4–6 6–2 6–4; A. Hernandez (WC) d. L. Tieleman 6–2 6–4; G. Gaudio d. F. Clavet (5) 6–3 6–1; M. Puerta (WC) d. F. Vicente (6) 7–5 6–4; H. Gumy d. A. Dupuis 6–4 6–3; G. Canas d. N. Massu 4–1 ret; F. Meligeni (3) d. S. Bruguera (WC) 7–6 7–6; F. Squillari (7) d. G. Blanco 3–6 6–4 6–1; R. Agenor d. J. Diaz 6–3 6–4; S. Sargsian d. J. Viloca (Q) 3–6 6–4 6–1; N. Lapentti (2) d. B. Ulihrach (Q) 6–4 6–2.
2nd round: Chela (Q) d. Kuerten (1) 3–6 7–6 6–4; Hantschk d. Stanoytchev (LL) 6–3 1–6 6–2; Koubek (4) d. Fromberg 6–7 6–4 6–4; Gaudio d. Hernandez (WC) 3–6 6–3 6–3; Puerta (WC) d. Gumy 6–4 6–4; Canas d. Meligeni (3) 6–2 4–6 6–3; Squillari (7) d. Agenor 7–5 6–2; Lapentti (2) d. Sargsian 7–5 4–6 6–1.
Quarter-finals: Chela (Q) d. Hantschk 6–3 7–6; Koubek (4) d. Gaudio 7–6 6–4; Puerta (WC) d. Canas 6–2 6–3; Squillari (7) d. Lapentti (2) 6–4 7–6.
Semi-finals: Chela (Q) d. Koubek (4) 7–6 6–3; Puerta (WC) d. Squillari (7) 6–4 6–1.
Final: Chela (Q) d. Puerta (WC) 6–4 7–6.
MEN'S DOUBLES – Final: B. Black/Johnson (1) d. Etlis/Rodriguez (Q) 6–3 7–5.

AXA CUP ($700,000)
LONDON ARENA, LONDON, 21–27 FEBRUARY
MEN'S SINGLES – 1st Round: Y. Kafelnikov (1) d. A. Medvedev 6–3 6–4; D. Vacek d. T. Johansson 6–3 6–2; F. Santoro d. M. Safin 4–6 6–2 6–4; H. Arazi (8) d. J. Gambill 6–4 7–5; M. Zabaleta d. T. Henman (3) 7–6 7–5; C. Saulnier d. R. Schuttler 6–4 6–4; J. Golmard d. J. Ferrero 6–2 6–2; G. Rusedski (5) d. A. Clement 6–3 6–4; C. Pioline (6) d. A. Martin 7–5 7–6; J. Tarango (LL) d. J. Bjorkman 7–5 6–4; K. Kucera d. J. Novak 7–5 6–3; T. Enqvist (4) d. A. Voinea 6–1 6–4; D. Hrbaty (7) d. A. Pavel 6–4 6–3; M. Rosset d. I. Ljubicic 6–4 6–4; G. Ivanisevic d. W. Black 7–5 6–2; R. Federer d. N. Kiefer (2) 6–2 6–3.
2nd round: Kafelnikov (1) d. Vacek 6–2 7–5; Santoro d. Arazi (8) 4–6 6–2 6–4; Zabaleta d. Saulnier 6–4 6–1; Rusedski (5) d. Golmard 7–6 7–6; Pioline (6) d. Tarango 6–3 6–4; Enqvist (4) d. Kucera 3–6 6–3 6–4; Rosset d. Hrbaty (7) 6–3 7–6; Federer d. Ivanisevic 7–5 6–3.
Quarter-finals: Kafelnikov (1) d. Santoro 6–3 6–2; Rusedski (5) d. Zabaleta 6–4 7–5; Enqvist (4) d. Pioline (6) 7–6 4–6 7–6; Rosset d. Federer 3–6 6–4 6–4.
Semi-finals: Kafelnikov (1) d. Rusedski (5) 6–3 7–6; Rosset d. Enqvist (4) 7–6 1–6 6–3.
Final: Rosset d. Kafelnikov (1) 6–4 6–4.
MEN'S DOUBLES – Final: Adams/De Jager (3) d. Gambill/Humphries 6–3 6–7 7–6.

OPEN SEAT GODO ($900,000)
BARCELONA, 24–30 APRIL
MEN'S SINGLES – 1st Round: Y. Kafelnikov (1) bye; C. Moya d. A. Clement 6–4 4–6 6–4; M. Rosset d. B. Ulihrach (Q) 6–3 6–7 6–3; H. Arazi (15) d. R. Fromberg 6–3 6–4; T. Haas (WC) (9) d. G. Etlis (Q) 7–5 4–6 6–4; J. Marin (WC) d. A. Portas (Q) 7–6 6–3; K. Alami d. M. Mirnyi 6–3 6–7 6–2; G. Rusedski (7) bye; M. Rios (4) bye; A. Pavel d. F. Squillari 6–3 3–6 6–3; A. Vinciguerra d. V. Spadea 6–4 6–2; S. Navarro (Q) d. S. Grosjean (14) 6–3 6–4; J. Ferrero d. N. Escude (11) 6–4 7–5; F. Vicente d. H. Gumy 2–6 7–6 6–2; F. Santoro d. G. Blanco (WC) 4–6 6–3 6–3; G. Puentes (LL) bye; A. Corretja (6) bye; G. Gaudio d. A. Di Pasquale 6–1 6–3; M. Puerta d. J. Alonso-Pintor (WC) 7–5 7–6; M. Safin d. M. Zabaleta (12) 6–4 6–4; D. Hrbaty (13) d. N. Kulti (Q) 7–6 4–6 7–5; A. Berasategui d. T. Robredo (Q) 6–1 6–1; F. Mantilla d. S. Schalken 6–1 6–3; N. Lapentti (3) bye; Y. El Aynaoui (8) bye; F. Clavet d. A. Martin 7–6 6–3; S. Bruguera (WC) d. R. Federer 6–1 6–1; S. Sargsian d. A. Costa (10) 7–6 6–4; F. Meligeni (16) d. C. Rochus (Q) 6–4 6–3; R. Krajicek d. M. Tillstrom 7–6 7–6; R. Schuttler d. G. Canas 6–1 3–0 ret; M. Norman (2) bye.
2nd round: Moya d. Kafelnikov (1) 6–2 7–6; Rosset d. Arazi (15) 4–6 6–4 6–4; Haas (WC) (9) d. Marin (WC) 6–3 7–5; Rusedski (7) d. Alami 6–3 3–6 6–2; Rios (4) d. Pavel 6–3 4–6 7–6; Vinciguerra d. Navarro (Q) 6–4 7–6; Ferrero d. Vicente 7–6 6–2; Santoro d. Puentes (LL) 6–2 6–4; Gaudio d. Corretja (6) 0–6 6–3 6–3; Safin d. Puerta 6–7 7–6 6–4; Hrbaty (13) d. Berasategui 7–5 7–5; Lapentti (3) d. Mantilla 6–3 6–0; El Aynaoui (8) d. Clavet 7–5 7–6; Bruguera (WC) d. Sargsian 6–3 6–3; Krajicek d. Meligeni (16) 7–5 6–1; Norman (2) d. Schuttler 7–6 6–3.
3rd round: Moya d. Rosset 7–6 7–6; Haas (WC) (9) d. Rusedski (7) 7–6 6–3; Rios (4) d. Vinciguerra 7–6 7–5; Ferrero d. Santoro 6–3 4–6 6–0; Safin d. Gaudio 6–4 4–6 6–4; Lapentti (3) d. Hrbaty (13) 6–2 6–2; El Aynaoui (8) d. Bruguera (WC) 6–3 6–4; Norman (2) d. Krajicek 7–6 6–4.
Quarter-finals: Moya d. Haas (WC) (9) 6–4 6–4; Ferrero d. Rios (4) 6–3 6–4; Safin d. Lapentti (3) 7–6 7–5; Norman (2) d. El Aynaoui (8) 6–2 6–4.
Semi-finals: Ferrero d. Moya 6–4 6–7 6–2; Safin d. Norman (2) 2–6 7–6 6–3.
Final: Safin d. Ferrero 6–3 6–3 6–4.
MEN'S DOUBLES – Final: Kulti/Tillstrom d. Haarhuis/Stolle (2) 6–2 6–7 7–6.

MERCEDES CUP ($900,000)
STUTTGART, 17–23 JULY
MEN'S SINGLES – 1st Round: M. Norman (1) d. B. Phau (WC) 6–2 6–2; D. Elsner (WC) d. F. Clavet 6–4 4–6 6–3; F. Meligeni d. M. Hantschk 6–1 6–2; J. Novak d. D. Hrbaty (8) 6–3 7–5; Y. El Aynaoui (4) d. C. Vinck (WC) 6–1 7–6; K. Kucera d. C. Dosedel 6–2 6–1; M. Goellner (Q) d. J. Hernych (Q) 6–1 6–3; F. Squillari (5) d. F. Gonzalez (LL) 6–1 6–3; T. Haas (6) d. D. Miketa (Q) 3–6 7–5 6–2; R. Schuttler d. F. Vicente 6–4 4–6 6–3; A. Ilie d. H. Arazi 4–6 6–2 7–6; M. Safin (3) d. A. Pavel 5–7 6–3 6–3; K. Alami (7) d. F. Jonsson 0–6 7–6 6–2; G. Gaudio d. J. Diaz 6–2 7–5; A. Medvedev d. B. Karbacher (Q) 6–3 6–2; Y. Kafelnikov (2) d. J. Boutter 7–6 6–7 7–6.
2nd round: Elsner (WC) d. Norman (1) 4–6 7–6 6–4; Novak d. Meligeni 6–3 6–2; Kucera d. El Aynaoui (4) 6–3 6–2; Squillari (5) d. Goellner (Q) 4–6 6–2 6–3; Schuttler d. Haas (6) 7–5 2–1 ret; Ilie d. Safin (3) 7–6 7–6; Gaudio d. Alami (7) 5–7 6–3 6–4; Medvedev d. Kafelnikov (2) 6–7 7–5 6–3.
Quarter-finals: Elsner (WC) d. Novak 6–2 6–1; Squillari (5) d. Kucera 7–5 6–1; Ilie d. Schuttler 6–3 6–4; Gaudio d. Medvedev 6–1 7–6.
Semi-finals: Squillari (5) d. Elsner (WC) 7–6 7–6; Gaudio d. Ilie 6–2 6–4.
Final: Squillari (5) d. Gaudio 6–2 3–6 4–6 6–4 6–2.
MEN'S DOUBLES – Final: Novak/Rikl (1) d. Arnold/Johnson 5–7 6–2 6–3.

GENERALI OPEN KITZBUHEL ($700,000)
KITZBUHEL, 24–30 JULY
MEN'S SINGLES – 1st Round: Y. Kafelnikov (1) bye; H. Gumy d. A. Sa 6–3 6–4; S. Sargsian d. J. Melzer (WC) 3–6 6–3 6–1; H. Wiltschnig (LL) bye; F. Clavet (10) bye; A. Berasategui d. A. Lopez-Moron 6–1 6–4; P. Mathieu (Q) d. O. Stanoytchev 7–6 6–1; A. Costa (7) bye; N. Lapentti (4) bye; M. Kratochvil d. R. Vasek (Q) 6–3 6–3; B. Ulihrach d. M. Filippini (P) 6–1 6–3; J. Tarango (14) bye; C. Moya (12) bye; A. Voinea d. T. Guardiola 7–6 6–4; E. Alvarez d. M. Hipfl 6–4 1–0 ret; F. Costa (LL) bye; Y. El Aynaoui (6) bye; A. Martin d. F. Cabello (LL) 6–0 6–2; N. Massu d. W. Arthurs 7–6 7–6; A. Portas (11) bye; C. Dosedel (13) bye; F. Meligeni d. F. Browne 6–4 7–6; A. Calleri d. H. Moretti (Q) 6–2 6–2; M. Safin (3) bye; F. Vicente (8) bye; F. Luzzi (Q) d. G. Coria (Q) 7–6 6–3; C. Ruud d. J. Balcells 6–2 6–2; M. Zabaleta (9) bye; R. Schuttler (WC) (16) bye; I. Ljubicic d. A. Fasching (WC) 6–3 6–4; F. Gonzalez (Q) d. C. Trimmel (WC) 4–6 6–2 6–0; A. Corretja (2) bye.
2nd round: Kafelnikov (1) d. Gumy 6–4 2–6 6–2; Sargsian d. Wiltschnig (LL) 1–6 6–3 6–0; Clavet (10) d. Berasategui 6–0 7–5; A. Costa (7) d. Mathieu (Q) 6–4 7–6; N. Lapentti (4) d. Kratochvil 6–3 6–2; Ulihrach d. Tarango (14) 6–3 6–2; Voinea d. Moya (12) 2–6 6–3 6–4; Alvarez d. F. Costa (LL) 6–4 6–3; A. Martin d. El Aynaoui (6) 7–6 3–2 ret; Massu d. Portas (11) 6–4 6–4; Dosedel (13) d. Meligeni 6–1 6–3; Calleri d. Safin (3) 6–4 7–6; Luzzi (Q) d. Vicente (8) 7–6 6–7 7–6; Zabaleta (9) d. Ruud 6–3 6–2; Ljubicic d. Schuttler (WC) (16) 6–4 6–2; Corretja (2) d. Gonzalez (Q) 6–1 6–2.
3rd round: Kafelnikov (1) d. Sargsian 6–4 4–6 6–4; Clavet (10) d. A. Costa (7) 4–6 6–3 6–2; N. Lapentti (4) d. Ulihrach 6–1 6–0; Alvarez d. Voinea 6–2 6–4; A. Martin d. Massu 5–7 6–1 6–1; Calleri d. Dosedel (13) 6–0 6–1; Zabaleta (9) d. Luzzi (Q) 6–3 6–2; Corretja (2) d. Ljubicic 7–6 6–4.
Quarter-finals: Clavet (10) d. Kafelnikov (1) 6–3 6–2; Alvarez d. N. Lapentti (4) 6–4 4–6 7–6; Calleri d. A. Martin 7–5 4–6 6–4; Corretja (2) d. Zabaleta (9) 6–3 6–0.
Semi-finals: Alvarez d. Clavet (10) 6–3 7–5; Corretja (2) d. Calleri 6–3 6–7 6–2.
Final: Corretja (2) d. Alvarez 6–3 6–1 3–0 ret.
MEN'S DOUBLES – Final: Albano/Suk (8) d. Eagle/Florent (2) 6–3 3–6 6–3.

RCA CHAMPIONSHIPS ($700,000)
INDIANAPOLIS, IN, 14–20 AUGUST
MEN'S SINGLES – 1st Round: G. Kuerten (1) bye; T. Woodbridge (WC) d. J. Siemerink 6–3 6–1; T. Dent (WC) d. F. Clavet 6–3 6–4; J. Novak (16) d. G. Etlis 6–3 6–2; W. Ferreira (10) d. A. Di Pasquale 6–4 6–2; P. Mathieu (Q) d. J. Bjorkman 6–3 6–4; X. Malisse d. L. Mor (Q) 6–3 6–2; M. Rios (8) bye; T. Enqvist (4) bye; L. Roux (Q) d. S. Schalken 6–3 6–2; C. Moya d. H. Arazi 6–4 6–4; T. Martin (14) d. C. Mamiit 6–3 6–3; A. Costa (11) d. G. Ivanisevic 7–5 6–2; M. Kratochvil d. P. King (WC) 6–3 6–3; S. Koubek d. D. Wheaton (Q) 6–4 3–6 7–6; L. Hewitt (5) bye; N. Lapentti (6) bye; S. Lareau d. M. Knowles (Q) 6–4 7–5; W. Black (Q) d. K. Ullyett 6–3 6–0; S. Grosjean (12) d. M. Mirnyi 3–6 7–6 6–4; K. Alami (13) d. C. Saulnier 6–4 3–6 7–5; V. Voltchkov (WC) d. V. Spadea 3–6 6–3 6–4; H. Levy d. M. Zabaleta 6–3 6–1; M. Safin (3) bye; T. Henman (7) bye; A. Martin d. J. Blake (WC) 6–3 6–2; N. Massu d. A. Clement 1–6 6–0 6–3; Y. El Aynaoui (9) d. T. Johansson 7–6 6–4; G. Pozzi d. A. Pavel (15) 7–6 2–6 6–2; J. Sekulov d. R. Federer 6–4 7–5; M. Tillstrom d. J. Chela 7–5 5–7 6–1; Y. Kafelnikov (2) bye.
2nd round: Kuerten (1) d. Woodbridge (WC) 5–7 6–4 6–1; Dent (WC) d. Novak (16) w/o; W. Ferreira (10) d. Mathieu (Q) 6–2 1–0 ret; Malisse (Q) d. Rios (8) 6–4 ret; Enqvist (4) d. Roux (Q) 6–3 7–6; Moya d. T. Martin (14) 6–4 6–4; A. Costa (11) d. Kratochvil 6–1 6–7 6–4; Hewitt (5) d. Koubek 6–1 6–0; N. Lapentti (6) d. Lareau 6–3 3–6 6–2; Grosjean (12) d. W. Black (Q) 6–0 7–6; Alami (13) d. Voltchkov (WC) 6–4 6–3; Safin (3) d. Levy 6–4 6–2; Henman (7) d. A. Martin 6–4 6–3; El Aynaoui (9) d. Massu 6–2; Pozzi d. Sekulov 6–4; Kafelnikov (2) d. Tillstrom 6–2 6–1.
3rd round: Kuerten (1) d. Dent (WC) 6–2 7–6; W. Ferreira (10) d. Malisse (Q) 6–4 6–2; Enqvist (4) d. Moya 6–2 2–6 6–4; Hewitt (5) d. A. Costa (11) 6–2 6–4; Grosjean (12) d. N. Lapentti (6) 7–6 6–2; Safin (3) d. Alami (13) 6–4 6–4; Henman (7) d. El Aynaoui (9) 4–6 6–2 7–6; Kafelnikov (2) d. Pozzi 6–3 6–3.
Quarter-finals: Kuerten (1) d. W. Ferreira (10) 6–2 6–3; Hewitt (5) d. Enqvist (4) 6–3 6–3, Safin (3) d. Grosjean (12) 0–6 6–3 6–4; Henman (7) d. Kafelnikov (2) 7–6 6–2.

Semi-finals: Kuerten (1) d. Hewitt (5) 7–5 6–2; Safin (3) d. Henman (7) 7–5 6–4.
Final: Kuerten (1) d. Safin (3) 3–6 7–6 7–6.
MEN'S DOUBLES – Final: Hewitt/Stolle d. Bjorkman/Mirnyi (6) 6–2 3–6 6–3.

LEGG MASON TENNIS CLASSIC ($700,000)
WASHINGTON, D.C., 14–20 AUGUST
MEN'S SINGLES – 1st Round: A. Agassi (1) bye; F. Meligeni d. J. Marin 6–7 6–0 6–1; J. Vanek d. L. Burgsmuller (Q) 6–4 6–4; P. Goldstein (16) d. J. Boutter 6–2 3–6 6–3; K. Kucera (9) d. P. Harsanyi (WC) 6–0 6–1; K. Capalik (Q) d. M. Russell (Q) 1–6 6–3 6–2; A. Roddick (WC) d. A. Voinea 6–3 6–4; F. Santoro (8) bye; M. Philippoussis (4) bye; A. Sa d. A. Parmar 6–1 6–2; L. Tieleman d. B. Ulihrach 6–2 6–3; D. Prinosil (14) d. M. Damm 6–3 6–3; A. Gaudenzi d. R. Schuttler (12) 6–4 6–4; I. Ljubicic d. S. Huet 6–2 6–3; D. Sanguinetti d. A. Savolt 6–3 6–2; B. Black (6) bye; J. Gambill (5) bye; A. O'Brien (Q) d. M. Ondruska 6–7 6–4 6–3; C. Rochus d. R. Bryan (WC) 3–6 6–3 6–4; A. Ilie (11) d. R. Agenor 3–6 6–4 6–4; F. Gonzalez d. C. Woodruff (13) 6–4 1–6 6–3; L. Manta d. S. Sargsian 7–5 6–7 6–4; G. Coria (WC) d. G. Bastl 6–3 7–6; N. Kiefer (3) bye; D. Hrbaty (7) bye; W. Arthurs d. M. Washington (Q) 6–0 6–1; G. Blanco d. M. Bryan (WC) 5–7 7–6 6–1; J. Golmard (10) d. J. Kroslak 6–4 6–2; P. Srichaphan d. J. Stoltenberg (15) 6–4 6–4; B. Cowan (Q) d. I. Heuberger (LL) 6–7 6–2 6–4; K. Kim d. D. Caldwell (Q) 6–3 4–6 6–3; A. Corretja (2) bye.
2nd round: Agassi (1) d. Meligeni 6–2 6–1; Goldstein (16) d. Vanek 6–2 3–6 6–4; Kucera (9) d. Capalik (Q) 3–6 7–5 6–3; Roddick (WC) d. Santoro (8) 4–6 6–3 6–3; Sa d. Philippoussis (4) 6–1 7–6; Prinosil (14) d. Tieleman 6–1 5–7 6–3; Ljubicic d. Gaudenzi 7–5 6–3; B. Black (6) d. Sanguinetti 6–3 6–4; Gambill (5) d. O'Brien (Q) 6–3 5–7 7–5; C. Rochus d. Ilie (11) 6–3 4–6 6–4; Manta d. Gonzalez 6–3 2–6 6–4; Kiefer (3) d. Coria (WC) 4–6 6–3 6–2; Arthurs d. Hrbaty (7) 4–6 6–4 6–3; Golmard (10) d. Blanco 7–5 6–3; Srichaphan d. Cowan (Q) 6–4 6–1; Corretja (2) d. Kim 7–5 6–3.
3rd round: Agassi (1) d. Goldstein (16) 6–3 6–2; Roddick (WC) d. Kucera (9) 7–6 6–1; Prinosil (14) d. Sa 6–3 3–6 6–3; B. Black (6) d. Ljubicic 6–1 6–3; Gambill (5) d. C. Rochus 6–0 6–1; Kiefer (3) d. Manta 5–7 6–4 6–4; Arthurs d. Golmard (10) 6–3 6–2; Corretja (2) d. Srichaphan 6–3 6–1.
Quarter-finals: Agassi (1) d. Roddick (WC) 6–4 6–4; Prinosil (14) d. B. Black (6) 6–3 1–6 6–3; Kiefer (3) d. Gambill (5) 4–6 6–4 6–2; Corretja (2) d. W. Arthurs 7–6 3–6 6–3.
Semi-finals: Agassi (1) d. Prinosil (14) 6–3 6–1; Corretja (2) d. Kiefer (3) 7–6 6–2.
Final: Corretja (2) d. Agassi (1) 6–2 6–3.
MEN'S DOUBLES – Final: O'Brien/Palmer (1) d. Agassi/Sargsian 7–5 6–1.

CA TENNIS TROPHY ($700,000)
VIENNA, 9–15 OCTOBER
MEN'S SINGLES – 1st Round: N. Escude d. M. Safin (1) 5–7 6–3 7–6; S. Koubek d. C. Saulnier (LL) 6–2 6–0; A. Pavel d. T. Johansson (Q) 6–3 6–3; C. Pioline (8) d. Z. Mlynarik (WC) 6–3 6–2; C. Dosedel (Q) d. T. Enqvist (3) 5–3 ret; J. Golmard (PR) d. G. Pozzi (Q) 6–3 6–4; A. Clement d. J. Gambill 6–4 6–0; T. Haas (WC) d. A. Corretja (5) 6–1 6–0; T. Henman (6) d. M. Rosset 6–3 6–1; F. Santoro d. F. Clavet 6–4 2–6 6–4; F. Vicente d. S. Grosjean 1–6 6–4 6–2; G. Rusedski d. Y. Kafelnikov (4) 6–4 6–7 6–3; R. Krajicek d. J. Ferrero (7) 6–4 6–4; A. Vinciguerra d. J. Novak 6–1 6–4; M. Mirnyi (Q) d. A. Di Pasquale (WC) 7–5 6–3; R. Federer d. M. Norman (2) 4–6 7–6 6–4.
2nd round: Koubek d. Escude 4–6 6–3 6–2; Pioline (8) d. Pavel 7–6 7–6; Golmard (PR) d. Dosedel (Q) 2–6 7–5 6–4; Haas (WC) d. Clement 6–2 6–1; Henman (6) d. Santoro 6–3 6–2; Vicente d. Rusedski 6–2 6–7 6–2; Krajicek d. Vinciguerra 7–6 6–3; Federer d. Mirnyi (Q) 6–3 6–3.
Quarter-finals: Pioline (8) d. Koubek 6–3 6–3; Haas (WC) d. Golmard (PR) 2–6 6–3 6–1; Henman (6) d. Vicente 6–4 7–6; Federer d. Krajicek 6–4 6–3.
Semi-finals: Haas (WC) d. Pioline (8) 6–7 6–2 6–2; Henman (6) d. Federer 2–6 7–6 6–3.
Final: Henman (6) d. Haas (WC) 6–4 6–4.
MEN'S DOUBLES – Final: Kafelnikov/Zimonjic d. Novak/Rikl (2) 6–4 6–4.

JAPAN OPEN ($700,000)
TOKYO, 9–15 OCTOBER
MEN'S SINGLES – 1st Round: G. Kuerten (1) bye; N. Massu d. S. Iwabuchi (WC) 6–2 6–3; L. Paes d. F. Jonsson 7–6 6–3; A. Gaudenzi d. C. Rochus (16) 4–6 6–3 6–4; K. Kucera (9) d. P. Goldstein 6–1 6–2; L. Friedl (Q) d. D. Sanguinetti 4–6 6–1 6–4; L. Tieleman d. J. Miyao (WC) 6–4 7–5; D. Hrbaty (7) bye; N. Lapentti (4) bye; O. Rochus d. C. Woodruff 7–5 6–4; T. Suzuki d. K. Kim 3–6 6–4 6–3; J. Bjorkman (13) d. J. Tarango 6–4 3–6 7–6; K. Flygt (Q) d. M. Zabaleta (11) 7–6 3–6 6–3; A. Sa d. A. Calatrava 4–0 6–6 6–2; D. Elsner d. G. Motomura (WC) 6–4 6–4; B. Black (6) bye; M. Chang (5) bye; C. Mamiit d. J. Stoltenberg 6–3 6–4; S. Bruguera d. B. Cowan (LL) 6–4 6–3; S. Schalken (12) d. P. Srichaphan 7–5 5–7 6–2; D. Prinosil (14) d. M. Youzhny 6–2 2–6 7–6; Y. Yoon (Q) d. C. Vinck 6–4 1–6 6–2; W. Arthurs d. Y. Ishii (WC) 6–3 6–4; M. Philippoussis (3) bye; H. Arazi (8) bye; G. Bastl d. A. Stoliarov 5–7 6–1 6–0; E. Taino (Q) d. M. Onoda (WC) 6–2 6–3; V. Spadea (Q) d. A. Ilie (10) 6–2 6–1; H. Levy (15) d. J. Salzenstein (Q) 5–7 6–0 6–1; H. Lee (Q) d. O. Stanoytchev 6–1 7–6; W. Black d. M. Hantschk 6–3 7–5; T. Dent (LL) bye.
2nd round: Kuerten (1) d. Massu 7–6 6–0; Gaudenzi d. Paes 6–3 6–2; Kucera (9) d. Friedl (Q) 6–1 4–6 6–4; Hrbaty (7) d. Tieleman 7–6 7–5; Lapentti (4) d. O. Rochus 7–6 7–6; Bjorkman (13) d. Suzuki 3–6 6–1 6–1; Flygt (Q) d. Sa 6–4 6–2; B. Black (6) d. Elsner 6–2 6–1; Mamiit d. Chang (5) 7–5 6–4; Schalken (12) d. Bruguera

6–4 6–2; Yoon (Q) d. Prinosil (14) 4–6 7–5 6–1; Philippoussis (3) d. Arthurs 6–2 7–5; Arazi (8) d. Bastl 6–4 5–7 6–4; Taino (Q) d. Spadea (Q) 6–3 7–5; Levy (15) d. H. Lee (Q) 6–2 6–4; W. Black d. Dent (LL) 6–4 6–2.
3rd round: Kuerten (1) d. Gaudenzi 3–6 6–3 6–4; Hrbaty (7) d. Kucera (9) 6–4 6–4; Lapentti (4) d. Bjorkman (13) 4–6 7–5 7–6; B. Black (6) d. Flygt (Q) 6–2 6–3; Schalken (12) d. Mamiit 6–2 6–2; Philippoussis (3) d. Yoon (Q) 7–6 6–4; Arazi (8) d. Taino (Q) 6–4 6–2; W. Black d. Levy (15) 7–6 6–3.
Quarter-finals: Hrbaty (7) d. Kuerten (1) 6–7 6–2 3–0 ret; Lapentti (4) d. B. Black (6) 6–2 6–2; Schalken (12) d. Philippoussis (3) 6–3 6–2; Arazi (8) d. W. Black 6–7 6–2 6–2.
Semi-finals: Lapentti (4) d. Hrbaty (7) 6–3 6–4; Schalken (12) d. Arazi (8) 4–6 6–3 7–6.
Final: Schalken (12) d. Lapentti (4) 6–4 3–6 6–1.
MEN'S DOUBLES – Final: Bhupathi/Paes d. Hill/Tarango (5) 6–4 6–7 6–3.

Men's International Series 2

Formerly known as World Series tournaments

QATAR MOBIL OPEN ($975,000)
DOHA, 3–9 JANUARY
MEN'S SINGLES – Quarter-finals: N. Kiefer (1) d. S. Schalken (8) 6–1 6–0; F. Santoro (3) d. G. Bastl 6–2 6–4; Y. El Aynaoui (4) d. M. Tillstrom 7–5 6–3; R. Schuttler d. M. Mirnyi 6–3 6–2.
Semi-finals: Santoro (3) d. Kiefer (1) 7–5 6–4; Schuttler d. El Aynaoui (4) 6–7 6–4 6–4.
Final: Santoro (3) d. Schuttler 3–6 7–5 3–0 ret.
MEN'S DOUBLES – Final: Knowles/Mirnyi d. O'Brien/Palmer (1) 6–3 6–4.

GOLD FLAKE OPEN ($405,000)
CHENNAI, 3–9 JANUARY
MEN'S SINGLES – Quarter-finals: M. Damm d. L. Manta 6–4 6–4; J. Golmard (4) d. J. Delgado (Q) 6–3 6–4; M. Hantschk d. T. Ketola (LL) 5–7 7–5 6–2; C. Pioline (2) d. D. Sanguinetti 3–6 6–4 7–6.
Semi-finals: Golmard (4) d. Damm 3–6 6–3 6–3; Hantschk d. Pioline (2) 6–4 3–6 7–6.
Final: Golmard (4) d. Hantschk 6–3 6–7 6–3.
MEN'S DOUBLES – Final: Boutter/Rochus (WC) d. Panja/Prahlad (WC) 7–5 6–1.

AAPT CHAMPIONSHIPS ($325,000)
ADELAIDE, 3–9 JANUARY
MEN'S SINGLES – Quarter-finals: T. Enqvist (1) d. S. Grosjean (7) 7–6 7–5; M. Norman (3) d. A. Martin 6–4 6–3; L. Hewitt (6) d. J. Stoltenberg 6–2 6–2; N. Escude (8) d. T. Henman (2) 6–3 6–1.
Semi-finals: Enqvist (1) d. Norman (3) 3–6 6–2 6–2; Hewitt (6) d. Escude (8) 3–6 6–1 6–4.
Final: Hewitt (6) d. Enqvist (1) 3–6 6–3 6–2.
MEN'S DOUBLES – Final: Woodbridge/Woodforde (1) d. Hewitt/Stolle 6–4 6–2.

ADIDAS INTERNATIONAL ($325,000)
SYDNEY, 10–15 JANUARY
MEN'S SINGLES – Quarter-finals: L. Hewitt d. A. Voinea (Q) 6–3 6–4; A. Corretja d. C. Dosedel 3–6 7–5 6–3; I. Ljubicic (LL) d. K. Kucera (5) 6–3 3–6 7–5; J. Stoltenberg (WC) d. N. Lapentti (WC) (2) 4–6 7–5 6–1.
Semi-finals: Hewitt d. Corretja 6–4 6–4; Stoltenberg (WC) d. Ljubicic (LL) 6–4 6–2.
Final: Hewitt d. Stoltenberg (WC) 6–4 6–0.
MEN'S DOUBLES – Final: Woodbridge/Woodforde (1) d. Hewitt/Stolle (WC) 7–5 6–4.

HEINEKEN OPEN ($325,000)
AUCKLAND, 10–15 JANUARY
MEN'S SINGLES – Quarter-finals: J. Balcells (Q) d. J. Ferrero (7) 4–6 6–3 6–1; M. Chang d. M. Gustafsson 7–5 3–6 1–0 ret; G. Gaudio d. S. Schalken (6) 6–1 6–2; M. Norman (2) d. M. Rosset (8) 6–2 6–2.
Semi-finals: Chang d. Balcells (Q) 6–3 3–6 6–2; Norman (2) d. Gaudio 6–4 7–5.
Final: Norman (2) d. Chang 3–6 6–3 7–5.
MEN'S DOUBLES – Final: E. Ferreira/Leach (1) d. Delaitre/Tarango (2) 7–5 6–4.

MARSEILLE OPEN 13 ($475,000)
MARSEILLE, 7–13 FEBRUARY
MEN'S SINGLES – Quarter-finals: R. Federer (WC) d. I. Ljubicic 6–2 3–6 7–6; F. Santoro (6) d. T. Guardiola (Q) 6–4 7–6; S. Grosjean (4) d. A. Vinciguerra 6–4 6–4; M. Rosset d. G. Ivanisevic 6–4 3–6 6–2.
Semi-finals: Federer (WC) d. Santoro (6) 7–6 7–5; Rosset d. Grosjean (4) 6–3 6–3.
Final: Rosset d. Federer (WC) 2 6 6 3 7 6.
MEN'S DOUBLES – Final: Aspelin/Landsberg d. Carrasco/Velasco 7–6 6–4.

DUTY FREE DUBAI OPEN ($975,000)
DUBAI, 7–13 FEBRUARY
MEN'S SINGLES – Quarter-finals: N. Kiefer (1) d. J. Golmard (8) 6–3 7–6; A. Costa (4) d. Y. El Aynaoui (5) 6–2 6–4; J. Ferrero d. F. Mantilla (6) 6–3 4–6 7–6; K. Alami d. J. Novak 6–4 6–2.
Semi-finals: Kiefer (1) d. Costa (4) 6–2 6–0; Ferrero d. Alami 7–6 6–3.
Final: Kiefer (1) d. Ferrero 7–5 4–6 6–3.
MEN'S DOUBLES – Final: Novak/Rikl (3) d. Koenig/Tramacchi 6–2 7–5.

SYBASE OPEN ($350,000)
SAN JOSE, CA, 7–13 FEBRUARY
MEN'S SINGLES – Quarter-finals: W. Ferreira (7) d. M. Larsson 4–6 6–3 6–4; M. Tillstrom d. M. Chang (4) 2–6 6–3 6–3; J. Courier (5) d. P. Goldstein 6–4 6–4; M. Philippoussis (2) d. J. Gimelstob (8) 7–6 6–4.
Semi-finals: Tillstrom d. Ferreira (7) 7–6 2–6 6–3; Philippoussis (2) d. Courier (5) 4–6 6–3 6–4.
Final: Philippoussis (2) d. Tillstrom 7–5 4–6 6–3.
MEN'S DOUBLES – Final: Gambill/Humphries (4) d. Arnold/Taino 6–1 6–4.

CHEVROLET CUP BY BELLSOUTH ($350,000)
SANTIAGO, 28 FEBRUARY–5 MARCH
MEN'S SINGLES – Quarter-finals: G. Kuerten (1) d. A. Calleri (Q) 6–4 6–1; A. Portas d. M. Hood (Q) 6–4 6–4; M. Puerta d. F. Vicente (4) 6–1 7–5; G. Gaudio (8) d. B. Ulihrach 6–2 6–2.
Semi-finals: Kuerten (1) d. Portas 6–4 7–6; Puerta d. Gaudio (8) 3–6 6–4 6–2.
Final: Kuerten (1) d. Puerta 7–6 6–3.
MEN'S DOUBLES – Final: Kuerten/Prieto (WC) d. Bale/Norval (1) 6–2 6–4.

CITIRIX TENNIS CHAMPIONSHIPS ($325,000)
DELRAY BEACH, FL, 28 FEBRUARY–5 MARCH
MEN'S SINGLES – Quarter-finals: P. Goldstein d. P. Rafter (1) 4–6 6–1 6–2; A. Calatrava (Q) d. C. Woodruff (5) 6–7 6–3 6–2; S. Koubek (6) d. A. Sa 6–1 1–6 6–1; R. Fromberg d. J. Gimelstob 4–6 7–6 6–2.
Semi-finals: Calatrava (Q) d. Goldstein 6–0 5–7 7–6; Koubek (6) d. Fromberg 6–7 6–3 6–2.
Final: Koubek (6) d. Calatrava (Q) 6–1 4–6 6–4.
MEN'S DOUBLES – Final: MacPhie/Zimonjic d. Eagle/Florent 7–5 6–4.

COPENHAGEN OPEN ($325,000)
COPENHAGEN, 28 FEBRUARY–5 MARCH
MEN'S SINGLES – Quarter-finals: M. Safin (1) d. J. Bjorkman (8) 6–4 6–4; A. Vinciguerra d. M. Damm 6–3 6–1; M. Larsson (3) d. I. Ljubicic 6–4 5–7 6–4; R. Federer (7) d. G. Pozzi 4–6 6–1 6–3.
Semi-finals: Vinciguerra d. Safin (1) 6–3 6–0; Larsson (3) d. Federer (7) 6–3 7–6.
Final: Vinciguerra d. Larsson (3) 6–3 7–6.
MEN'S DOUBLES – Final: Damm/Prinosil (2) d. Bjorkman/Lareau (1) 6–1 5–7 7–5.

FRANKLIN TEMPLETON TENNIS CLASSIC ($350,000)
SCOTTSDALE, AZ, 6–12 MARCH
MEN'S SINGLES – Quarter-finals: J. Ferrero d. F. Clavet 6–4 3–6 6–3; L. Hewitt (6) d. M. Rios (3) 7–6 4–2 ret; T. Henman (5) d. N. Lapentti (4) 6–3 6–2; A. Costa (7) d. A. Corretja 6–2 4–6 7–6.
Semi-finals: Hewitt (6) d. Ferrero 6–4 6–2; Henman (5) d. Costa (7) 6–3 6–3.
Final: Hewitt (6) d. Henman (5) 6–4 7–6.
MEN'S DOUBLES – Final: Palmer/Reneberg d. Galbraith/MacPherson 6–3 7–5.

CERVEZA CLUB COLOMBIA OPEN ($350,000)
BOGOTA, 6–12 MARCH
MEN'S SINGLES – Quarter-finals: G. Kuerten (1) d. M. Hantschk 6–2 0–6 7–6; M. Puerta d. F. Mantilla (3) 7–6 6–3; F. Vicente (4) d. A. Di Pasquale (5) 6–2 6–1; Y. El Aynaoui (2) d. A. Portas 6–4 6–1.
Semi-finals: Puerta d. Kuerten (1) 3–6 6–1 7–6; El Aynaoui (2) d. Vicente (4) 1–6 7–6 7–6.
Final: Puerta d. El Aynaoui (2) 6–4 7–6.
MEN'S DOUBLES – Final: Albano/Arnold (2) d. Balcells/Hadad (WC) 7–6 1–6 6–2.

ESTORIL OPEN ($600,000)
ESTORIL, 10–16 APRIL
MEN'S SINGLES – Quarter-finals: F. Clavet d. N. Escude (8) 6–3 6–2; N. Lapentti (3) d. J. Ferrero 7–6 6–4; A. Medvedev d. T. Henman (4) 6–2 6–3; C. Moya (WC) d. B. Ulihrach (Q) 4–6 6–1 6–2.
Semi-finals: Clavet d. Lapentti (3) 6–4 6–3; Moya (WC) d. Medvedev 6–3 6–4.
Final: Moya (WC) d. Clavet 6–3 6–2.
MEN'S DOUBLES – Final: Johnson/Norval (1) d. Adams/Eagle (4) 6–4 7–5.

GRAND PRIX HASSAN II ($325,000)
CASABLANCA, 10–16 APRIL
MEN'S SINGLES – Quarter-finals: M. Puerta (7) d. Y. El Aynaoui (1) 7–6 6–4; S. Grosjean (4) d. S. Bruguera (WC) 6–0 6–0; F. Vicente (6) d. H. Arazi (3) 6–7 6–3 6–2; A. Di Pasquale (8) d. A. Vinciguerra 6–2 6–3.
Semi-finals: Grosjean (4) d. Puerta (7) 6–4 3–6 6–1; Vicente (6) d. Di Pasquale (8) 6–4 1–6 6–4.
Final: Vicente (6) d. Grosjean (4) 6–4 4–6 7–6.
MEN'S DOUBLES – Final: Clement/Grosjean (LL) d. Burgsmuller/Painter (Q) 7–6 6–2.

AT&T CHALLENGE ($350,000)
ATLANTA, GA, 10–16 APRIL
MEN'S SINGLES – Quarter-finals: J. Tarango (7) d. J. Vanek 7–6 6–2; J. Stoltenberg d. N. Massu 6–1 6–2; M. Chang (WC) (4) d. C. Woodruff (5) 7–6 6–1; A. Ilie (8) d. S. Koubek (2) 7–6 6–4.
Semi-finals: Stoltenberg d. Tarango (7) 6–2 6–4; Ilie (8) d. Chang (WC) (4) 6–3 1–6 6–2.
Final: Ilie (8) d. Stoltenberg 6–3 7–5.
MEN'S DOUBLES – Final: E. Ferreira/Leach (1) d. Gimelstob/Knowles (3) 6–3 6–4.

US MEN'S CLAY COURT CHAMPIONSHIPS ($319,230)
ORLANDO, FL, 1–7 MAY
MEN'S SINGLES – Quarter-finals: F. Gonzalez (Q) d. P. Srichaphan 6–3 6–3; M. Rodriguez d. J. Vanek 6–3 7–5; N. Massu (6) d. G. Pozzi (3) 2–6 6–2 6–2; R. Delgado (Q) d. M. Hantschk 7–5 6–4.
Semi-finals: Gonzalez (Q) d. Rodriguez 6–0 3–6 7–5; Massu (6) d. Delgado (Q) 6–4 6–4.
Final: Gonzalez (Q) d. Massu (6) 6–2 6–3.
MEN'S DOUBLES – Final: Paes/Siemerink d. Gimelstob/Lareau (2) 6–3 6–4.

BMW OPEN ($375,000)
MUNICH, 1–7 MAY
MEN'S SINGLES – Quarter-finals: T. Enqvist (1) d. J. Novak 6–3 6–4; T. Haas (3) d. F. Browne (LL) 6–3 6–4; M. Mirnyi d. F. Meligeni (6) 7–5 6–3; F. Squillari (7) d. Y. El Aynaoui (2) 2–6 6–2 7–6.
Semi-finals: Haas (3) d. Enqvist (1) 7–6 1–6 6–4; Squillari (7) d. Mirnyi 6–2 6–4.
Final: Squillari (7) d. Haas (3) 6–4 6–4.
MEN'S DOUBLES – Final: Adams/De Jager (1) d. Mirnyi/Zimonjic 6–4 6–4.

MALLORCA OPEN ($475,000)
MALLORCA, 1–7 MAY
MEN'S SINGLES – Quarter-finals: G. Blanco d. J. Chela 5–7 6–3 6–3; M. Safin (4) d. C. Moya (5) 3–6 6–4 7–6; M. Puerta (6) d. A. Martin 6–4 6–1; M. Tillstrom d. A. Portas 6–3 6–2.
Semi-finals: Safin (4) d. Blanco 6–2 6–2; Tillstrom d. Puerta (6) 3–6 7–5 6–1.
Final: Safin (4) d. Tillstrom 6–4 6–3.
MEN'S DOUBLES – Final: Llodra/Nargiso (Q) d. A. Martin/Vicente (WC) 7–6 7–6.

INTERNATIONALER RAIFFEISEN GRAND PRIX ($400,000)
ST. POLTEN, 22–27 MAY
MEN'S SINGLES – Quarter-finals: A. Portas d. G. Blanco 6–7 6–3 6–4; A. Pavel d. A. Medvedev (3) 6–4 2–6 6–2; J. Marin d. M. Hipfl 6–3 6–4; A. Ilie (7) d. J. Tarango 7–5 6–3.
Semi-finals: Pavel d. Portas 2–6 6–3 6–2; Ilie (7) d. Marin 6–1 7–6.
Final: Pavel d. Ilie (7) 7–5 3–6 6–2.
MEN'S DOUBLES – Final: Bhupathi/Kratzmann (1) d. Gaudenzi/Nargiso (WC) 7–6 6–7 6–4.

GERRY WEBER OPEN ($975,000)
HALLE, 12–18 JUNE
MEN'S SINGLES – Quarter-finals: Y. Kafelnikov (1) d. N. Escude (7) 7–6 6–3; D. Prinosil (WC) d. N. Lapentti (3) 6–3 7–6; M. Chang d. R. Federer 7–5 6–2; R. Krajicek d. N. Kiefer (2) 7–5 5–7 7–6.
Semi-finals: Prinosil (WC) d. Kafelnikov (1) 6–4 7–6; Krajicek d. Chang 6–2 6–1.
Final: Prinosil (WC) d. Krajicek 6–3 6–2.
MEN'S DOUBLES – Final: Kulti/Tillstrom (3) d. Bhupathi/Prinosil (2) 7–6 7–6.

THE STELLA ARTOIS CHAMPIONSHIPS ($775,000)
QUEEN'S, LONDON, 12–18 JUNE
MEN'S SINGLES – Quarter-finals: G. Pozzi d. M. Safin (7) 7–5 7–6; L. Hewitt (6) d. C. Pioline (4) 6–4 6–4; D. Sanguinetti d. A. Pavel (12) 3–6 7–6 6–3; P. Sampras (WC) (2) d. R. Bryan (Q) 6–4 6–4.
Semi-finals: Hewitt (6) d. Pozzi 6–1 6–4; Sampras (WC) (2) d. Sanguinetti 7–5 6–3.
Final: Hewitt (6) d. Sampras (WC) (2) 6–4 6–4.
MEN'S DOUBLES – Final: Woodbridge/Woodforde (2) d. Stark/Taino 6–7 6–3 7–6.

HEINEKEN TROPHY ($375,000)
'S-HERTOGENBOSCH, 19–25 JUNE
MEN'S SINGLES – Quarter-finals: M. Damm d. M. Gustafsson 6–3 3–6 7–5; P. Rafter (3) d. K. Alami (6) 6–3 3–6 6–3; M. Chang (5) d. K. Braasch (Q) 7–6 7–6; N. Escude (2) d. F. Clavet (8) 7–5 6–4.
Semi-finals: Rafter (3) d. Damm 2 6–1; Escude (2) d. Chang (5) 7–6 6–2.
Final: Rafter (3) d. Escude (2) 6–1 6–3.
MEN'S DOUBLES – Final: Damm/Suk (2) d. Haarhuis/Stolle (1) 6–4 6–7 7–6.

THE NOTTINGHAM OPEN ($350,000)
NOTTINGHAM, 19–24 JUNE
MEN'S SINGLES – Quarter-finals: B. Black d. A. Parmar (WC) 6–4 6–4; J. Gambill d. G. Pozzi 6–4 6–4; S. Grosjean (4) d. W. Ferreira (Q) 7–6 6–3; J. Bjorkman d. R. Fromberg 7–5 4–6 6–3.
Semi-finals: B. Black d. Gambill 7–6 6–1; Grosjean (4) d. Bjorkman 7–6 6–4.
Final: Grosjean (4) d. B. Black 7–6 6–3.
MEN'S DOUBLES – Final: Johnson/Norval d. E. Ferreira/Leach (1) 1–6 6–4 6–3.

SWEDISH OPEN ($350,000)
BASTAD, 10–16 JULY
MEN'S SINGLES – Quarter-finals: M. Norman (1) d. N. Massu 6–2 6–4; I. Ljubicic d. A. Portas (5) 7–5 6–1; A. Vinciguerra (3) d. J. Tarango (6) 6–1 6–2; M. Hipfl (Q) d. M. Gustafsson 6–7 6–1 7–5.
Semi-finals: Norman (1) d. Ljubicic 6–2 7–5; Vinciguerra (3) d. Hipfl (Q) 6–2 6–7 7–6.
Final: Norman (1) d. Vinciguerra (3) 6–1 7–6.
MEN'S DOUBLES – Final: Kulti/Tillstrom (1) d. Gaudenzi/Nargiso 4–6 6–2 6–3.

MILLER LITE HALL OF FAME TENNIS CHAMPIONSHIPS ($350,000)
NEWPORT, RI, 10–16 JULY
MEN'S SINGLES – Quarter-finals: W. Arthurs (7) d. M. Fish (Q) 6–3 6–2; P. Wessels d. J. Bjorkman (WC) (4) 7–6 6–3; J. Stoltenberg (5) d. P. Goldstein (3) 7–6 7–6; J. Knippschild d. S. Draper (Q) 6–4 6–3.
Semi-finals: Wessels d. Arthurs (7) 7–6 6–7 6–4; Knippschild d. Stoltenberg (5) 6–3 6–4.
Final: Wessels d. Knippschild 7–6 6–3.
MEN'S DOUBLES – Final: Erlich/Levy d. Spencer/Sprengelmeyer 7–6 7–5.

UBS OPEN GSTAAD ($575,000)
GSTAAD, 10–17 JULY
MEN'S SINGLES – Quarter-finals: A. Corretja (1) d. M. Rios (7) 6–7 6–1 6–3; G. Gaudio d. F. Squillari (6) 6–1 4–1 ret; A. Costa (4) d. J. Novak 7–6 6–3; M. Puerta (8) d. S. Grosjean 6–3 6–1.
Semi-finals: Corretja (1) d. Gaudio 7–5 7–5; Puerta (8) d. A. Costa (4) 6–4 6–3.
Final: Corretja (1) d. Puerta (8) 6–1 6–3.
MEN'S DOUBLES – Final: Novak/Rikl (1) d. Golmard/Kohlmann (Q) 3–6 6–3 6–4.

DUTCH OPEN ($375,000)
AMSTERDAM, 17–23 JULY
MEN'S SINGLES – Quarter-finals: E. Kempes (WC) d. C. Ruud 4–6 7–6 6–3; M. Gustafsson (4) d. N. Massu (6) 6–3 3–6 6–1; R. Sluiter d. A. Calatrava 7–6 6–4; N. Davydenko (Q) d. T. Behrend 6–2 1–6 6–4.
Semi-finals: Gustafsson (4) d. Kempes (WC) 6–4 6–4; Sluiter d. Davydenko (Q) 6–2 7–6.
Final: Gustafsson (4) d. Sluiter 6–7 6–3 7–6 6–1.
MEN'S DOUBLES – Final: Roitman/Schneiter d. Kempes/Van Scheppingen (WC) 4–6 6–4 6–1.

INTERNATIONAL CHAMPIONSHIP OF CROATIA ($375,000)
UMAG, 17–23 JULY
MEN'S SINGLES – Quarter-finals: M. Puerta (1) d. M. Damm (7) 6–3 6–2; B. Ulihrach d. A. Martin (6) 6–3 4–6 6–4; C. Moya (4) d. R. Carretero (Q) 5–7 6–3 6–4; M. Rios (2) d. D. Sanchez 7–6 6–2.
Semi-finals: Puerta (1) d. Ulihrach 4–6 6–2 6–3; Rios (2) d. Moya (4) 6–2 7–5.
Final: Rios (2) d. Puerta (1) 7–6 4–6 6–3.
MEN'S DOUBLES – Final: Lopez-Moron/Portas d. Ljubicic/Zovko (WC) 6–1 7–6.

MERCEDES-BENZ CUP ($350,000)
LOS ANGELES, CA, 24–30 JULY
MEN'S SINGLES – Quarter-finals: A. Clement (8) d. L. Roux (LL) 6–3 6–2; J. Gambill (6) d. J. Stoltenberg 6–1 3–6 6–1; M. Chang (4) d. W. Ferreira (5) 6–3 7–6; J. Gimelstob d. P. Goldstein 3–0 ret.
Semi-finals: Gambill (6) d. Clement (8) 3–6 6–0 6–3; Chang (4) d. Gimelstob 3–6 6–3 6–0.
Final: Chang (4) d. Gambill (6) 6–7 6–3 ret.
MEN'S DOUBLES – Final: Kilderry/Stolle (4) d. Gambill/Humphries (3) w/o.

INTERNAZIONALI DI TENNIS DI SAN MARINO ($325,000)
SAN MARINO, 24–30 JULY
MEN'S SINGLES – Quarter-finals: S. Bruguera (WC) d. J. Alonso-Pintor 6–2 6–4; D. Nargiso (WC) d. K. Alami (3) 7–6 6–4; A. Medvedev (5) d. J. Siemerink 6–4 7–5; A. Calatrava d. J. Vanek (8) 7–5 6–1.
Semi-finals: Bruguera (WC) d. Nargiso (WC) 6–7 6–1 6–3; Calatrava d. Medvedev (5) w/o.
Final: Calatrava d. Bruguera (WC) 7–6 1–6 6–4.
MEN'S DOUBLES – Final: Cibulec/Friedl d. Etlis/Waite (2) 7–6 7–5.

THE HAMLET CUP ($390,200)
LONG ISLAND, NY, 21–27 AUGUST
MEN'S SINGLES – Quarter-finals: M. Norman (1) d. Y. El Aynaoui (8) 6–3 2–6 6–3; R. Krajicek (11) d. C. Moya w/o; T. Enqvist (3) d. F. Santoro (12) 7–6 6–4; A. Clement (15) d. M. Chang (10) 6–3 6–2.
Semi-finals: Norman (1) d. Krajicek (11) 4–6 6–4 7–6; Enqvist (3) d. Clement (15) 7–6 6–1.
Final: Norman (1) d. Enqvist (3) 6–3 5–7 7–5.
MEN'S DOUBLES – Final: Stark/Ullyett d. Gambill/Humphries (4) 6–4 6–4.

PRESIDENT'S CUP ($500,000)
TASHKENT, 11–17 SEPTEMBER
MEN'S SINGLES – Quarter-finals: D. Sanguinetti d. J. Gimelstob 6–0 5–7 6–3; J. Boutter d. J. Golmard (6) 6–1 1–1 ret; G. Bastl d. A. Stoliarov 6–4 3–6 6–3; M. Safin (2) d. J. Delgado (Q) 6–4 6–4.
Semi-finals: Sanguinetti d. Boutter 7–6 7–6; Safin (2) d. Bastl 6–2 6–2.
Final: Safin (2) d. Sanguinetti 6–3 6–4.
MEN'S DOUBLES – Final: Gimelstob/Humphries (1) d. Barnard/Koenig (2) 6–3 6–2.

GELSOR OPEN ROMANIA ($350,000)
BUCHAREST, 11–17 SEPTEMBER
MEN'S SINGLES – Quarter-finals: J. Balcells d. A. Portas (7) 7–5 4–6 6–2; M. Gustafsson (5) d. G. Blanco 6–2 3–6 6–4; M. Hantschk d. A. Martin (6) 6–1 4–6 6–2; A. Calatrava (8) d. F. Meligeni 6–3 4–0 ret.
Semi-finals: Balcells d. Gustafsson (5) 6–4 6–4; Hantschk d. Calatrava (8) 6–4 6–1.
Final: Balcells d. Hantschk 6–4 3–6 7–6.
MEN'S DOUBLES – Final: A. Martin/Ran d. Bowen/Hood (Q) 7–6 6–1.

CAMPIONATI INTERNAZIONALI DI SICILIA ($350,000)
PALERMO, 26 SEPTEMBER–1 OCTOBER
MEN'S SINGLES – Quarter-finals: O. Rochus d. D. Sanchez 6–7 6–3 6–2; C. Rochus d. J. Balcells 7–5 7–6; D. Nargiso (WC) d. A. Martin (6) 6–4 6–3; S. Bruguera d. S. Huet 4–6 6–3 7–6.
Semi-finals: O. Rochus d. C. Rochus 7–5 6–4; Nargiso (WC) d. Bruguera 6–4 6–4.
Final: O. Rochus d. Nargiso (WC) 7–6 6–1.
MEN'S DOUBLES – Final: Carbonell/Garcia (1) d. Albano/Goellner w/o.

SALEM OPEN ($375,000)
HONG KONG, 2–8 OCTOBER
MEN'S SINGLES – Quarter-finals: P. Rafter (7) d. G. Kuerten (1) 7–6 6–4; M. Philippoussis (4) d. S. Bruguera (SE) 6–2 6–3; N. Kiefer (3) d. N. Lapentti (5) 6–2 6–4; T. Henman (2) d. M. Chang (8) 6–4 4–6 6–4.
Semi-finals: Philippoussis (4) d. Rafter (7) 7–6 6–4; Kiefer (3) d. Henman (2) 6–4 6–2.
Final: Kiefer (3) d. Philippoussis (4) 7–6 2–6 6–2.
MEN'S DOUBLES – Final: W. Black/Ullyett (2) d. Hrbaty/Prinosil (1) 6–1 6–2.

ADIDAS OPEN DE TOULOUSE ($375,000)
TOULOUSE, 16–22 OCTOBER
MEN'S SINGLES – Quarter-finals: A. Corretja (1) d. M. Tillstrom 7–5 6–3; M. Rios (3) d. J. Viloca (LL) 6–4 6–4; C. Moya d. J. Gambill (5) 6–7 7–6 6–4; M. Mirnyi d. N. Escude 3–6 7–6 6–3.
Semi-finals: Corretja (1) d. Rios (3) 7–6 6–3; Moya d. Mirnyi 6–4 7–6.
Final: Corretja (1) d. Moya 6–3 6–2.
MEN'S DOUBLES – Final: Boutter/Santoro (WC) d. Johnson/Norval (3) 7–6 4–6 7–6.

HEINEKEN OPEN SHANGHAI ($350,000)
SHANGHAI, 16–23 OCTOBER
MEN'S SINGLES – Quarter-finals: M. Norman (1) d. J. Bjorkman (8) 7–6 0–6 6–2; M. Chang (3) d. N. Massu 7–5 6–3; A. Calatrava d. B. Black (4) w/o; S. Schalken (7) d. N. Lapentti (2) 6–3 6–4.
Semi-finals: Norman (1) d. Chang (3) 6–3 6–1; Schalken (7) d. Calatrava 6–4 3–6 6–3.
Final: Norman (1) d. Schalken (7) 6–4 4–6 6–3.
MEN'S DOUBLES – Final: Haarhuis/Schalken d. Pala/Vizner 6–2 3–6 6–4.

KREMLIN CUP ($975,000)
MOSCOW, 23–29 OCTOBER
MEN'S SINGLES – Quarter-finals: M. Safin (1) d. V. Voltchkov 7–6 6–1; D. Prinosil d. J. Bjorkman 7–6 5–7 7–6; M. Rosset (4) d. M. Youzhny (WC) 6–7 6–4 7–6; Y. Kafelnikov (2) d. L. Burgsmuller (Q) 6–3 6–2.
Semi-finals: Prinosil d. Safin (1) 6–7 6–3 6–3; Kafelnikov (2) d. Rosset (4) 4–6 6–2 7–5.
Final: Kafelnikov (2) d. Prinosil 6–2 7–5.
MEN'S DOUBLES – Final: Bjorkman/Prinosil d. Novak/Rikl (1) 6–2 6–3.

DAVIDOFF SWISS INDOORS BASLE ($975,000)
BASLE, 23–29 OCTOBER
MEN'S SINGLES – Quarter-finals: R. Federer d. N. Thomann (Q) 6–4 6–4; L. Hewitt (3) d. G. Rusedski 7–6 6–2; T. Henman (4) d. H. Arazi 6–3 6–3; T. Enqvist (2) d. D. Hrbaty 4–6 6–2 6–3.
Semi-finals: Federer d. Hewitt (3) 6–4 5–7 7–6; Enqvist (2) d. Henman (4) 6–1 6–3.
Final: Enqvist (2) d. Federer 6–2 4–6 7–6 1–6 6–1.
MEN'S DOUBLES – Final: Johnson/Norval (4) d. Federer/Hrbaty 7–6 4–6 7–6.

GRAND PRIX DE TENNIS DE LYON ($775,000)
LYON, 6–12 NOVEMBER
MEN'S SINGLES – Quarter-finals: P. Rafter (8) d. G. Kuerten (1) 6–3 6–4; H. Arazi d. T. Enqvist (3) 6–7 7–6 6–4; A. Clement d. R. Sluiter (Q) 6–3 3–6 7–6; A. Agassi (2) d. K. Kucera 6–1 7–5.
Semi-finals: Rafter (8) d. Arazi 6–3 6–4; Clement d. Agassi (2) 6–3 ret.
Final: Clement d. Rafter (8) 7–6 7–6.
MEN'S DOUBLES – Final: Haarhuis/Stolle (1) d. Ljubicic/Waite (Q) 6–1 6–7 7–6.

ST. PETERSBURG OPEN ($775,000)
ST. PETERSBURG, 6–12 NOVEMBER
MEN'S SINGLES – Quarter-finals: M. Safin (1) d. R. Schuttler 6–4 1–6 6–3; J. Bjorkman d. J. Palmer (Q) 6–1 6–3; D. Hrbaty (3) d. V. Voltchkov 6–2 4–6 6–4; Y. Kafelnikov (2) d. A. Calatrava 6–3 6–4.
Semi-finals: Safin (1) d. Bjorkman 6–4 6–4; Hrbaty (3) d. Kafelnikov (2) 7–5 6–3.
Final: Safin (1) d. Hrbaty (3) 2–6 6–4 6–4.
MEN'S DOUBLES – Final: Nestor/Ullyett (4) d. Shimada/Wakefield 7–6 7–5.

SCANIA STOCKHOLM OPEN ($775,000)
STOCKHOLM, 20–26 NOVEMBER
MEN'S SINGLES – Quarter-finals: M. Norman (1) d. S. Schalken (8) 6–7 7–5 7–6; T. Johansson d. J. Bjorkman 6–7 7–6 7–5; S. Grosjean (6) d. R. Schuttler 6–1 5–7 7–6; Y. Kafelnikov (2) d. A. Vinciguerra 6–3 6–4.
Semi-finals: Johansson d. Norman (1) 7–6 6–2; Kafelnikov (2) d. Grosjean (6) w/o.
Final: Johansson d. Kafelnikov (2) 6–2 6–4 6–4.
MEN'S DOUBLES – Final: Knowles/Nestor d. Pala/Vizner 6–3 6–2.

SAMSUNG OPEN ($375,000)
BRIGHTON, 20–26 NOVEMBER
MEN'S SINGLES – Quarter-finals: T. Henman (1) d. C. Woodruff w/o; H. Lee d. R. Furlan (Q) 6–1 6–3; V. Voltchkov (5) d. I. Ljubicic 7–6 4–6 6–3; D. Hrbaty (2) d. D. Sanguinetti (7) 6–2 6–1.
Semi-finals: Henman (1) d. H. Lee 6–2 6–1; Hrbaty (2) d. Voltchkov (5) 6–1 6–0.
Final: Henman (1) d. D. Hrbaty (2) 6–2 6–2.
MEN'S DOUBLES – Final: Hill/Tarango (2) d. Goldstein/Thomas 6–3 7–5.

The Tennis Masters Cup

Barry Flatman

Five centuries ago, long before anyone came up with the idea of hitting a small furry ball back and forth over a net, the Portuguese learned how to revere brave explorers who journeyed far into the unknown in pursuit of great riches. How fitting it was therefore, that so many generations later the descendant of one of these expeditions should triumph in the greatest tennis moment Portugal had ever known.

Gustavo Kuerten's voyage, not just through the six days of the first ever Masters Cup but throughout the tennis calendar of 2000, was one of intense valour. How often during the year did he battle through the pain barrier, his wafer thin frame taken to the very edge of endurance in so many marathon encounters? Indeed, even his glorious campaign under the impressively timbered roof of Lisbon's 11,000 seater Pavilhao Atlantico seemed to have come to an abrupt halt when the back injury which had plagued him for months, flared up again in the Brazilian's opening match against Andre Agassi.

For a while after that three set defeat, the player universally known simply as 'Guga' was ready to retire. In fact, if the schedule had not presented him with a day off to recover, he would have been back home on a Florianopolis beach by the time the final came around.

However, the tender loving care of veteran physiotherapist Bill Norris and tournament doctor Paulo Bekert, plus an enormous dose of determination, kept Kuerten competitive. Amazingly he came out to exact perfect revenge over Agassi to win the title in straight sets 6–4 6–4 6–4. 'For a few hours I thought I was out of the contest,' he claimed. 'I really had a physical problem. I didn't believe I could do this and it is the best day of my life for sure.'

Yet there was much, much more to celebrate as the streamers descended on the victor, wrapped patriotically in Brazil's national flag, and the tears of emotion began to flow – and not just amongst his friends and family.

To the economically minded, Kuerten was $1,400,000 richer, taking his prize haul for the year beyond the $4.7m mark. He was also the calendar ending world number one for 2000, the only South American ever to achieve such a feat and the first player not from the United States since Sweden's Stefan Edberg nine years previously.

Tennis historians will remember this remarkable 24-year-old as the first ever winner of the Champions Race, a fitting victory for somebody who had acted as pacemaker for 17 weeks of the year. Guga was also the first man to lift the inaugural Waterford Crystal trophy after the ATP Tour and the Grand Slam Committee, together with the International Tennis Federation, had decided it was far better to amalgamate the ATP Tour Championship and the Grand Slam Cup rather than have them conflicting with one another.

Both parties were delighted with the outcome. Not only were the large and enthusiastic Lisbon crowds a credit to the game but after 69 tournaments and 3,011 singles matches, the tour's number one spot was clinched in the very last encounter of the year.

Furthermore, the Grand Slam Committee were delighted that, for the first time ever at a season-ending tournament, the four semi-final spots were filled by the champions of the Australian Open (Agassi), the French Open (Kuerten), Wimbledon (Pete Sampras) and the US Open (Marat Safin). Next year's tournament in Sydney has a shining reputation to uphold.

For the preceding few months the ATP Tour had been actively promoting their *New Balls Please* campaign, highlighting the promise of a gaggle of youngsters who had forced their way to the pinnacle of the game. Perhaps Kuerten was a somewhat tenuous member of the group having won his first French Open title more than three years previously but the likes of Safin, Magnus Norman and teenager Lleyton Hewitt were all making their debuts in the lucrative year ending finale. Representing the old guard were defending ATP champion Sampras, the previous year's No.1 Agassi, the ATP's 1998 Hanover winner Alex Corretja and Olympic gold medalist Yevgeny Kafelnikov.

Both Sampras and Agassi arrived with large question marks over their heads. The newly married king of Wimbledon had not struck a ball in anger since his emphatic defeat by Safin in the US Open final 11 weeks previously. Agassi had missed the Olympics and retired from the Lyon tournament's semi-finals with a hip injury which forced him out of the last Masters Series event of the year in Paris.

The round robin groupings kept the two Americans apart but Sampras was allotted the initial challenges of Hewitt, Corretja and Safin while Agassi had to face up to Kuerten, Kafelnikov and Norman. While Agassi has long been the most unpredictable of performers, Sampras knew he was under-prepared and the second match of the tournament provided him with the most embarrassing of reminders.

Hewitt is as ferocious and precocious as they come and he knew how to beat the winner of a record 13 Grand Slams after overcoming Sampras on his beloved London grass in the Stella Artois tournament at Queen's Club in June. Ever the record breaker, Sampras had his eyes on Ivan Lendl's long-standing record of five wins at the old Masters tournament in Madison Square Garden but reality struck as the young, pony-tailed Australian ripped the great man apart 7–5 6–0. Precise passes repeatedly scorched the line and more than a few audacious lobs flew over Sampras' head, inflicting on him a final set whitewash for the first time since Mats Wilander had done the same almost 11 years earlier.

Agassi fared considerably better than his long-time rival. Admittedly he lost the first set to Kuerten but a dash towards the net in the second saw the Brazilian pull up with the look of excruciating pain on his face; the Las Vegan is too experienced a performer not to snatch the opportunity, and ran out a 4–6 6–4 6–3 winner.

On-site replacement Thomas Enqvist must have been flexing his arm in preparation for battle as Kuerten headed for the treatment table but those ready to write Sampras' competitive obituary were made to think again when he rebounded within the space of 24 hours to beat Corretja 3–6 7–6 6–3 and then proceed to exact a 6–3 6–2 revenge on Safin for that torturous afternoon at Flushing Meadows. The US Open champion, who would have guaranteed himself the year-ending number one spot by winning, had his fearsome serve broken three times and was allowed just one break point, that when the match was almost over.

Earlier wins over Corretja and Hewitt meant Safin would join Sampras in the semi-finals as the Red Group's representatives but over in the Green Group Kuerten was making a heroic recovery at the expense of Norman and Kafelnikov. Amazingly Guga did not drop a set. His big-swinging baseline play hardly seemed affected by his injury – although Norman seemed weary from an arduous year and Kafelnikov also seemed to be paying the price for playing 100 singles matches in the space of 11 months.

In fact, one game from victory over Norman, the Russian suffered an agonising spasm of cramp in his racquet hand. Unfortunately, the win was not enough to gain him a place in the semi-finals. That honour fell to Kuerten and Agassi. The 30-year-old American might have been the oldest man in the tournament but he was the only contender to complete the round robin unbeaten. Once again the shaven-headed showman had confounded those who believe that practice makes perfect.

Another match to prove ineffectual was Corretja's win over Hewitt but, just days before the two men were expected to spearhead their respective countries' challenge in the Davis Cup final, it sparked the biggest controversy of the week.

The Australian is, of course, a man who likes to clench a fist and shout a few expletives at himself on court. Corretja believed some of the verbal attacks were directed at him and he took exception, saying: 'I don't like the way he behaves on court and I've never said that about a player before.' As it turned out, the two didn't meet in Barcelona – but that story is told on other pages.

The Lisbon tale became even more dramatic. In the first semi-final Agassi once more proved he still possesses a ruthless streak as he pounced on a brave but bruised Safin. Again the Russian missed the opportunity to cement the year-ending top ranking. Twice he stumbled awkwardly, injuring his right ankle. Safin is hardly the sort of person to give in to physical pain as he had proved in winning the Bercy title two weeks earlier with a bloodied and stitched eyebrow after an accident with his racquet. After the ankle had been strapped he gamely battled on but his chances were minimal and Agassi triumphed 6–3 6–3.

Then up stepped a rejuvenated Sampras to face Kuerten. The Brazilian, complete with supporting corset, also had a selection of pain killers knowing that one more contortion in the wrong direction would result in certain agony.

Yet Kuerten's 6–7 6–3 6–4 victory was spellbinding stuff. His go-for-broke winners – especially on his backhand side – were outrageous. His serve, always threatening, often lethal, was the foundation of his victory. Appropriately his 13th ace finished off the match after almost two

Beaten by Andre Agassi in his first round robin match, Gustavo Kuerten recovered to remain unbeaten thereafter to lift the Masters Cup trophy and snatch the year-end world No.1 ranking. (Paul Zimmer)

and a quarter hours. Amazed by his own powers, Guga looked forward to the final with the admission: 'If I'm going to win it's got to be in three sets because I don't know if I can last much longer.'

Kidology? Maybe. Prophetic? Unquestionably. From the moment Kuerten broke serve in the opening game of the match, he held the upper hand and whenever Agassi threatened, the man in the coffee coloured shirt always seemed to come up with a pin perfect big serve. Since having his service broken by Sampras early in the semi-final, Kuerten saved 16 successive break points and before too long Agassi was shaking his racquet in frustration.

A service break to love clinched the second set and an ill-timed Agassi double fault effectively sealed the match for Kuerten to win his first ever indoor title. He served another 18 aces throughout the match, a glowing testament to somebody suffering from a painful back.

The scenes of celebration were memorable. Everywhere there were jubilant supporters wearing the yellow of Brazil's football team and it is a measure of Guga's fame at home that he is now revered on a par with national sporting heroes such as the legendary Pele, Garrincha and Zico as well as Formula One's Ayrton Senna.

However, the most fitting final words came from the beaten Agassi who knows more than most about what it takes to claim tennis' finest prizes. 'There's only a few great things to accomplish in this sport – winning all the Slams, Davis Cup, the Olympic gold medal and finishing the year number one,' concluded the runner-up. 'Today Guga accomplished a truly great thing.' No-one would argue with that.

THE TENNIS MASTERS CUP 2000
Pavilhao Atlantico, Lisbon 28 November–3 December

Round Robin matches
Red Group: *First:* **Pete Sampras** (USA) (3) d. Alex Corretja (ESP) (7) 7–6(2) 7–5; d. Marat Safin (RUS) (1) 6–3 6–2; lost to Lleyton Hewitt (AUS) (6) 7–5 6–0. *Second:* **Safin** d. Corretja 6–7(6) 7–5 6–3; d. Hewitt 6–4 6–4; *Third:* **Corretja** d. Hewitt 3–6 7–6(3) 6–3; *Fourth:* **Hewitt.**
Green Group: *First:* **Andre Agassi** (USA) (8) d. Gustavo Kuerten (BRA) (2) 4–6 6–4; d. Yevgeny Kafelnikov (RUS) (5) 6–1 6–4; d. Magnus Norman (SWE) (4) 6–3 6–2. *Second:* **Kuerten** d. Norman 7–5 6–3; d. Kafelnikov 6–3 6–4; *Third:* **Kafelnikov** d. Norman 4–6 7–5 6–1. *Fourth:* **Norman.**
Semi-Finals: Agassi d. Safin 6–3 6–3; Kuerten d. Sampras 6–7(5) 6–3 6–4.
Final: Kuerten d. Agassi 6–4 6–4 6–4.
Prize Money: Kuerten $1,400,000; Agassi $820,000; Sampras $330,000; Safin $330,000; Corretja $210,000, Hewitt $210,000; Kafelnikov $210,000; Norman $90,000.

GOLD FLAKE ATP TOUR WORLD DOUBLES CHAMPIONSHIP
Bangalore, India 11–17 December

World Doubles Point Breakdown		**Prize Money Breakdown – TOTAL: $750,000**	
Round Robin Win	20 RACE points	$ 16,000	Each Round Robin Win
Semi-Finals Win	40 RACE points	$ 40,000	Semi-Finals Win
Undefeated Winners	150 RACE points	$ 62,000	Final win
		$150,000	Undefeated Winners

Red group
(1) Ellis Ferreira (RSA) /Rick Leach (USA)
(4) Josh Eagle (AUS)/Andrew Florent (AUS)
(6) Jaime Oncins (BRA)/Daniel Orsanic (ARG)
(7) Simon Aspelin (SWE)/Johan Lansberg (SWE)

Gold group
(2) Paul Haahruis (NED)/Sandon Stolle (AUS)
(3) Alex O'Brien (USA)/Jared Palmer (USA)
(5) Donald Jonson (USA)/Piet Norval (RSA)
(8) Mahesh Bhupathi (IND)/Leander Paes (IND)

Day 1 Red: Eagle/Florent d. Oncins/Orsanic 6–1 3–6 6–4; Aspelin/Landsberg d. Ferreira/Leach 6–1 3–6 6–1
Gold: Johnson/Norval d. O'Brien/Palmer 7–5 7–6(7); Bhupathi/Paes d. Haahruis/Stolle 7–5 6–4
Day 2 Red: Oncins/Orsanic d. Ferreira/Leach 1–6 7–5 7–5; Aspelin/Landsberg d. Eagle/Florent 7–5 7–6(4)
Gold: Haahruis/Stolle d. O'Brien/Palmer 5–7 6–2 6–4; Bhupathi/Paes d. Johnson/Norval 6–4 6–4
Day 3 Red: Ferreira/Leach d. Eagle/Florent 4–6 6–3 7–6(2); Aspelin/Landsberg d. Oncins/Orsanic 6–2 6–4
Gold: O'Brien/Palmer d. Bhupathi/Paes 2–6 6–4 7–6(5); Johnson/Norval d. Haahruis/Stolle 6–2 7–6(6)

FINAL GROUP STANDINGS	**Round Robin**	**Sets**	**Prize Money**
Red group	**Won/Lost**	**Won/Lost**	**Total per pair**
(7) Simon Aspelin (SWE)/Johan Lansberg (SWE)	3-0	6-1	$ 48,000
(1) Ellis Ferreira (RSA)/Rick Leach (USA)	1-2	4-5	$ 16,000
(4) Josh Eagle (AUS)/Andrew Florent (AUS)	1-2	3-5	$ 16,000
(6) Jaime Oncins (BRA)/Daniel Orsanic (ARG)	1-2	3-5	$ 16,000
Gold group			
(8) Mahesh Bhupathi (IND)/Leander Paes (IND)	2-1	7-2	$ 72,000
(5) Piet Norval (RSA)/Donald Jonson (USA)	2-1	6-3	$134,000
(3) Alex O'Brien (USA)/Jared Palmer (USA)	1-2	3-5	$ 16,000
(2) Paul Haahruis (NED)/Sandon Stolle (AUS)	1-2	2-5	$ 16,000

Day 4   Semis Johnson/Norval d. Aspelin/Landsberg 6–4 5–7 6–3; Bhupathi/Paes d. Ferreira/Leach 6–3 7–5
Day 5   Final Johnson/Norval d. Bhupathi/Paes 7–6 6–3 6–4

Philippe Chatrier – An Appreciation

Alain Deflassieux

Above: *Philippe at the Stade Roland Garros which he helped to transform into one of the world's greatest tennis stadiums.* (Sarl Sport Vision)

Left: *With Juan Antonio Samaranch – in the President's box at Roland Garros where the Spanish President of the International Olympic Committee was a frequent and popular visitor.* Below left: *Philippe would eventually be invited to become a member of the IOC.* (Russ Adams and Vladimir Sichov)

Philippe Chatrier had already been out of tennis' international scene for eight years when he passed away, aged 72, on 23rd June 2000. The disease, that terrible Alzheimer's disease, had in fact been the reason for his retirement in 1993.

During the first two or three years of his retirement, one could sometimes glimpse him, sitting in the first row of the Presidential box in Stade Roland Garros, still passionately enjoying the wonderful fights of the big matches on clay. Then, faced with the merciless progress of his disease, the President, as he was still respectfully called, discreetly remained at his home in Saint Briac, Brittany, with his wife Claudine. At first, he was happy to go back to the golf courses he had been forced to leave behind during those many years he had spent as a leading tennis figure. Sadly, those pleasures only lasted for a while. There was no miracle.

Today, all those who are involved in the world of tennis or interested in its history are well aware of Philippe's tremendous activity that he pursued relentlessly. He will remain, for a long time, the greatest leader this sport has ever known.

They also know that tennis, from its grassroots up to the topmost level, would not have

Previous page: *Philippe in front of a statue of Rene Lacoste, one of the four Musketeers' statues that adorn the Place des Mousquetaires at the Stade Roland Garros – the others are of Jean Borotra, Henri Cochet and Jacques 'Toto' Brugnon.* (Sarl Sport Vision)

A great traveller on ITF business, Philippe visited China during his Presidency to spread the tennis gospel. (Melody Braden)

developed in the same way without Philippe Chatrier, who was as keen on modernizing the sport as he was of preserving its identity and its traditions.

Everything has already been said or written about Philippe Chatrier's actions and the influence he held for more than twenty years on the world of tennis. His era began with the advent of open tennis in 1968 and included the creation of the Association of Tennis Professionals in 1971, as well as the split between the ATP and the ITF in 1990. He was a central figure during the relentless fight against private promoters and fought to defend the four Grand Slam tournaments and the Davis Cup as the pillars of the sport. Equally strong were his endeavours to develop tennis in the poorest countries and to create a real international tour for junior players.

Perhaps Philippe's greatest legacy was to have tennis returned to the Olympic Games as a full medal sport, a dream he had shared with the ITF's General Secretary at the time, David Gray. Together they persuaded IOC President, Juan Antonio Samaranch, himself a tennis lover who was often to be seen at the major Championships, that tennis deserved to be welcomed back into the Olympic family. After appearing as a demonstration sport in 1984 in Los Angeles, tennis did at last become a full medal sport again, after a gap of 64 years, at the 1988 Games in Seoul. Sadly David had died in 1983 and never saw the dream realised.

Even though everybody knows Philippe Chatrier's work, the man himself remains unknown for most people. Having been lucky enough to meet him before he became a tennis authority (he hired me in 1967 as a young reporter for *Tennis de France*, the magazine he had created in 1953), I retain many images of this dynamic man who was still in his thirties then. They come back to me like a series of flashes and I would like to describe some of them here.

The first one would have to be about a car trip we made from Paris to Vichy, where the Galea Cup finals were being held. During the journey Philippe was the target of a continuous tirade from his mother, who obviously was not very keen on his driving. After each remark, Philippe would smile and answer quietly: 'But mother, of course I had seen that truck', or, when the speedometer was showing 140 km/h: 'But of course I had the time to pass him, don't be afraid, I always drive carefully.'

It was also in Vichy that same year when, together with the lamented Marcel Bernard, I surprised him by jumping a low flower hedge that was protecting the casino's terrace to escape a boring reception being held there; he joined us and we drove 70 kilometres to have dinner at Troigros, one of the best restaurants in France!

Philippe did not usually drive his own car. At that time, he owned a black Citroën DS, and even though *Tennis de France* was not that prosperous a company, he had hired a chauffeur named Robert, who always enjoyed looking for the official motorcades of government ministers going to the Colombes stadium for the rugby matches of the Five Nations tournament. Very cleverly, Robert would slide the black DS in between two of the cars and drop his laughing but embarrassed boss just in front of the official box, to which he had no access, by the way.

During that same period, in 1967, Philippe was often seen talking at length with his great friend Jack Kramer. I still remember the two men having discussions for hours on end while walking the paths of the International Club du Lys in Chantilly. They were, of course, talking about the future of tennis and the advent of the open era. I was fascinated, but little did I know then that just a few years later, Philippe Chatrier would become the real boss of international tennis.

Also in 1967, two grass courts were inaugurated at the Lys Chantilly (a beautiful club Chatrier had created). That opening, coming just after the French Open, turned into a 16-player tournament with an entry that included such players as Roy Emerson, Charlie Pasarell, Manuel Santana and Nicola Pietrangeli, as well as youngsters like Ilie Nastase and Jan Kodes.

On the day of the finals, an exhibition doubles match took place between the four Musketeers Chatrier so admired. Out of friendship, the four living legends of French tennis – Borotra, Brugnon, Lacoste and Cochet – had agreed to come back to the courts. Never would they be seen playing together again. The expression on the faces of Emerson, Pasarell et al was a sight to behold as they sat with a delighted Philippe, who was visibly moved, to watch this memorable match.

Chatrier's passion for tennis had originated with the Musketeers. Knowing the admiration and the friendship he felt for them, it was not surprising to see him unable to control his emotions during Henri Cochet's funeral. He never managed to finish the public tribute he so wanted to pay to the man who had given him advice when he was a young tennis player. In mid-speech, he was choked with sobs and could not go on.

During his years as President of the French and International Tennis Federations, Philippe never needed the services of a media advisor to manage his relationships with the press. These were always admirable, whether the reporters were friends of his or not, and whatever countries they hailed from. Having been a reporter himself, he knew their job and was so trusting with his former colleagues that the ties between them were very strong.

For several years once every three or four months he used to organize press lunches in Paris. In the course of these meals, while only drinking Perrier and herbal tea (he was in his dieting phase), Philippe would broach all kinds of topics. Often he would unveil confidential information which should have remained secret, and about which nobody was supposed to write a single word. I don't know how many such lunches were held during these seven or eight years, but never did a reporter betray him. Given the passion for a 'scoop' which inhabits most of our colleagues, the mutual trust between the writers and Philippe really had to be very strong to allow such conversations to take place.

Regarding French tennis, the President entertained two dreams: he wished to see the Davis Cup come back to France and he yearned to see a Frenchman win the French Open. His French Open dream came true in 1983, when Yannick Noah won the tournament. The Davis Cup success happened in 1991, and the mention of that victory reminds me of the most poignant memory I keep of Philippe Chatrier. It was not so much the emotion the President felt after Captain Noah and his team had won the trophy. Rather it was the reaction he had three days later, in his office at Stade Roland Garros.

At that time, whispers were already going around about his disease. While interviewing him, I realized that his answers were blurred and that he kept repeating himself. Unfortunately, I knew the reason why. Then, as I asked him if something could have made him happier than that victory over the Americans, he replied with a vague but very lucid look:

'When I became President of the French Tennis Federation, I announced that my main objective was a Davis Cup win. It took a long time, but now it's done, the boys brought the Cup home. However, one thing saddens me. Of course, I resigned my duties as President of the ITF six months ago, but it would have been nice if my successor had asked me to present my players with the trophy instead of doing so himself. Unfortunately, he did not make that gesture. That made me sad.'

Now, Philippe was not the one who was having trouble holding back his tears.

Sanex WTA Tour

Sanex WTA Tour Year • Points Explanation and Allocation
Sanex WTA Tour Tournaments – Tiers I, II, III, IV
Chase Championships

By her own high standards it was a disappointing year for Switzerland's Martina Hingis who failed to add to her five Grand Slam successes – but she did win ten tournaments, including the Chase Championships, to consolidate her position as the undisputed world No.1. (Paul Zimmer)

Injuries contributed to a year of modest success for former US, Australian and French Open champion Monica Seles whose bronze medal at the Olympic Games was one of the highlights. (Stephen Wake)

The Sanex WTA Year

Barry Wood

Without doubt, the player to have the greatest impact during the year was Venus Williams. What makes that particularly remarkable was the fact that she did not even play for half of the season. During the first four months of the year the American was absent because of tendinitis in both wrists. She did not compete until the first week of May, and she did not play again after October, claiming anemia caused by playing so much tennis during the middle of the year.

After beating Irina Spirlea, a player who suffered an alarming loss of form and who virtually disappeared from sight as the year progressed, Williams lost to Amanda Coetzer in the quarter-finals in Hamburg. She then beat Chanda Rubin in Rome before taking just three games from Jelena Dokic. At Roland Garros, Williams reached the quarter-finals before losing to Arantxa Sanchez-Vicario, but she then remained undefeated until conceding the Linz final to Lindsay Davenport on 22nd October.

During that period this remarkable athlete won Wimbledon and Stanford, both by beating Davenport in the final, and then San Diego and New Haven, both with victory over Monica Seles. She then defeated Davenport again in the final of the US Open, and beat Elena Dementieva in the gold medal round at the Olympics. In Linz, Davenport halted her winning streak at 35 matches, the longest winning run on the Sanex WTA Tour in three years.

In fact, the Williams sisters virtually tied up the summer circuit between them, with one or the other appearing in every major final between Wimbledon and the Olympics. Serena won Manhattan Beach, and was a finalist in Montreal, retiring in the third set against Hingis. Following the US Open, the younger sister won the Princess Cup in Tokyo. But then she, too, did not play after winning the Olympic doubles with Venus. She also finished as the runner-up at the Paris Indoors, and won Hanover.

There appeared to be little doubt that, if they played consistently, the Williams sisters could dominate the game. That is a tribute to their father, Richard, who was mocked for his decision not to allow his daughters to play the junior circuit, and his assertion that they would become the top two players in the world. Although an eccentric character he is a man of great dignity and, it would seem, good judgement. He is prone to the odd outrageous comment, which interestingly his daughters always refuse to respond to or comment upon, but by now one gains the impression that what he says is often done for effect rather than with any real intent.

Certainly, the 'in your face' attitude of the sisters has attracted enormous attention both inside and outside the game and done much to promote the sport. Another positive effect is that the Williams' success has also raised the profile of the sport among the black community, especially in the United States where colour appears to be a much bigger issue than elsewhere.

Despite the successes of the Williams sisters, Martina Hingis more than held her own, and finished the year solidly entrenched as the number one. But she has failed to win a Grand Slam title since the 1999 Australian Open. The fact that Martina not only retained but strengthened her place was a reflection of a solid year in Tour events, a weaker challenge from Davenport and the absence of Venus Williams for much of the year.

Hingis won nine events, including the Ericsson Open and Chase Championships, and was runner-up at the Australian Open, Indian Wells and Philadelphia (each time to Davenport). She and Davenport were unable to play the Scottsdale final because of rain. Martina's best run came during the European indoor season, during which she won Filderstadt, Zurich and Moscow. The last time Hingis had won three straight titles was when she began 1997 by winning Sydney, the Australian Open, Tokyo Pan Pacific, Paris Indoors, Miami and Hilton Head, before finally losing to Iva Majoli in the French Open final. That ended a 39-match unbeaten run, which still stands as the longest winning streak among currently active players.

Davenport lost a little ground, largely because of injury. She was forced to retire or default in three events – the Italian Open, Montreal, and sadly at the Olympics, where she was the defending champion. But she won the Australian Open as well as the titles in Indian Wells, Linz and Philadelphia, and was the runner up in Sydney, Miami, Wimbledon, Stanford, Manhattan Beach and the US Open. She also reached the rained-off Scottsdale final.

Monica Seles, who was unable to play until the final week of February, returned to the Tour by winning Oklahoma City, and later added Amelia Island and the Italian Open. She was also runner-up in San Diego, New Haven and at the Chase Championships. All in all it was a solid if unspectacular year, with quarter-final finishes at the three Grand Slams she was able to play, an Olympic bronze medal and several semi-final placings.

Arantxa Sanchez-Vicario climbed from 17 to 9 during the year, despite the distraction of her marriage in July. She failed to win a title, but was a runner-up in Hilton Head and Hamburg, and her semi-final finishes included the French Open where she lost to Conchita Martinez. The Spaniard, whose qualities are often overlooked, had another impressive year, reaching the final of the French Open, where she lost to Mary Pierce, as well as the semi-finals of the Australian Open, where she lost to Hingis. She won the German Open in Berlin, and finished as runner-up to Seles in Amelia Island.

Pierce, as well as adding the French Open title to the Australian Open she had won in 1995, took Hilton Head for the loss of just 12 games and was a semi-finalist at Scottsdale and Indian Wells. But her season was cut short by tendinitis in her shoulder. She didn't play between Wimbledon and the US Open, where she retired in the fourth round and didn't compete for the remainder of the year.

Indeed, a disturbing number of players suffered long-term injuries, causing them to miss the last months of the season. As well as Pierce, players who failed to complete the year included Anke Huber, Venus and Serena Williams and Amelie Mauresmo.

Mauresmo, despite her strong physical appearance, is one of the most injury-prone players on the Sanex WTA Tour, a fact that has surely so far prevented her from achieving her true potential. The athletic Frenchwoman won in Sydney, beating Hingis and Davenport, and was a finalist at the Italian Open beating Pierce and Sanchez-Vicario before losing to Seles. But after being beaten by Seles in the fourth round at Roland Garros, she played just three more matches during the remainder of the year, being absent altogether between Wimbledon and the Olympics.

Several young players made an impression, none more so than Elena Dementieva. The Russian, who turned 19 in October, caught everyone's attention by reaching the semi-finals of the US Open. But she had already made her mark by reaching the semi-finals of Indian Wells and Manhattan Beach. She lost all three matches to Davenport, but then went on to win a silver medal at the Olympics after losing to Venus Williams. Beginning the year ranked 63, she finished 12.

As Dominique Van Roost announced her retirement, and Sabine Appelmans decided to make the 2001 Australian Open her last event, Belgium's future appeared to be left in capable hands by the emergence of Kim Clijsters and Justine Henin. Clijsters especially impressed, by reaching the Filderstadt final, winning Hobart and Leipzig and beating Davenport at the Chase Championships.

Jelena Dokic once again reached the semi-finals at the All England Club, and was a semi-finalist at the Olympics, losing the bronze medal match to Sanchez-Vicario. She also reached five quarter-finals, but her achievements were overshadowed by the eccentric behaviour of her father, Damir, which resulted in him being banned from Sanex WTA Tour and ITF events. Jelena, however, has always shown astonishing maturity for one so young, and she dealt with the situation with great self-assurance.

Anna Kournikova still remained without a title, but by reaching the last weekend of many events she was able to finish the year at her highest ever position of 8. Among the more experienced players, Magdalena Maleeva firmly re-established herself after her career was at one time seriously threatened by a shoulder injury. Beginning 2000 ranked 76, by year's end she had climbed to 22. Jennifer Capriati could also look back on the year with satisfaction after reaching the semi-finals of the Australian Open, her best achievement in a Grand Slam since she contested a dramatic US Open semi-final with Seles in 1991. The former American prodigy won Luxembourg and was runner-up in Quebec City towards the end of the year, and in between she was a quarter-finalist in Miami and Birmingham and a semi-finalist at 's-Hertogenbosch.

Two French veterans took contrasting decisions concerning their future. Nathalie Tauziat, who had intended to retire, decided to continue after another successful season that saw her win the Paris indoor event and reach the quarter-finals of the US Open. However, a major motivating force to play on in 2001 was her first round defeat by Clijsters at Wimbledon. Bitterly disappointed, Tauziat did not want to leave the All England Club with that match as her swansong.

Julie Halard-Decugis, meanwhile, announced during the final week of the season that she would retire immediately. Ranked one in the world in doubles, and having won the Japan Open as well as the Eastbourne title and finished as runner-up to Serena Williams at the Princess Cup in Tokyo, she felt she had achieved all her goals.

In doubles, Halard-Decugis and Ai Sugiyama ended the year as the top-ranked team, winning six titles, including their first tournament together, Sydney, and the US Open. They were also runners-up at Wimbledon and semi-finalists at Roland Garros. Towards the end of the year, Martina Hingis and Anna Kournikova re-newed their partnership with remarkable success, winning Filderstadt, Zurich, Philadelphia and the Chase Championships, and finishing as runners-up in Moscow. The Williams sisters, despite teaming up for only three events, won Wimbledon and the Olympics.

WTA TOUR RANKINGS – 2000 POINTS EXPLANATION

The Sanex WTA Tour ranking system is based on the accumulation of round points and quality points at a maximum of 18 tournaments over a moving 52-week period. The tournaments considered are those that yield the highest total points. The rankings are used to determine player acceptance and seeding at all Tour tournaments. A player's points are no longer averaged according to the number of events played.

A player's ranking in singles and doubles depends upon the points won at each tournament, according to the round reached. To these are added any quality points awarded for beating players ranked in the top 500.

RANKING POINTS (Equal points are awarded for singles and doubles).
The figures beneath each Tier heading indicate minimum prize money.

Category (draw size)	W	F	S/F	Q/F	R16	R32	R64	R128	QFR	Q3	Q2	Q1
Grand Slams	520	364	234	130	72	44	26	2	16.5	12	6	2
WTA Chps	390	273	175	97	54	—	—	—	—	—	—	—
Tier I(16) $1 million	260	182	117	65	1	—	—	—	—	—	—	—
Tier I(32) $1 million	260	182	117	65	36	1	—	—	11	6	3	1
Tier I(64) $1 million	260	182	117	65	36	22	1	—	6	—	3	1
Tier I(128) $1 million	260	182	117	65	36	22	13	1	11	6	3	1
Tier II(16) $500,000	200	140	90	50	1	—	—	—	—	—	—	—
Tier II(32) $500,000	200	140	90	50	26	1	—	—	9	5	3	1
Tier II(64) $500,000	200	140	90	50	26	14	1	—	5	—	3	1
Tier III(16) $170,000	140	98	63	35	1	—	—	—	—	—	—	—
Tier III(32) $170,000	140	98	63	35	18	1	—	—	7	3	2	1
Tier III(64) $170,000	140	98	63	35	18	10	1	—	4	—	2	1
Tier IVA(16) $140,000	110	77	50	27	1	—	—	—	—	—	—	—
Tier IVB(32) $140,000	110	77	50	27	14	1	—	—	5	3	2	1
Tier IVB(16) $110,000	80	56	36	20	1	—	—	—	5	3	2	1
Tier IVB(32) $110,000	80	56	36	20	10	1	—	—	4.5	3	2	1
Tier IVB(64) $110,000	80	56	36	20	10	6	1	—	—	—	—	—

POINTS ALLOCATION *(continued)*

Category (draw size)	W	F	S/F	Q/F	R16	R32	R64	R128	QFR	Q3	Q2	Q1
Other Tournaments												
$75,000(16)	54	38	24	14	1	—	—	—	—	—	—	—
$75,000(32)	54	38	24	14	7	1	—	—	2.5	2	1.5	1
$50,000(16)	36	25	16	9	1	—	—	—	—	—	—	—
$50,000(32)	36	25	16	9	5	1	—	—	2.5	2	1.5	1
$25,000(16)	22	15	10	6	1	—	—	—	—	—	—	—
$25,000(32)	22	15	10	6	3	1	—	—	1.5	1	0.5	0.25
$10,000(8)	10	7	5	1	—	—	—	—	—	—	—	—
$10,000M(16)	10	7	5	3	1	—	—	—	—	—	—	—
$10,000(16)	5	4	2	1.5	1	—	—	—	—	—	—	—
$10,000(32)	5	4	2	1.5	1	0.5	—	—	0.75	—	—	—
$ 5,000(8)	5	4	2	1	—	—	—	—	—	—	—	—
$ 5,000M(16)	5	4	2	1.5	1	—	—	—	—	—	—	—

QUALITY POINTS – SINGLES AND DOUBLES

Loser's Rank	Points	Grand Slam Points
1	100	200
2	75	150
3*	66	132
4	55	110
5	50	100
6–10	43	86
11–16	35	70
17–25	23	46
26–35	15	30
36–50	10	20
51–75	8	16
76–120	4	8
121–250	2	4
251–500	1	2

* Doubles quality points are awarded according to the losing team's combined ranking with 3 (three) being the lowest possible combined ranking

GRAND SLAM CHAMPIONSHIPS AND WTA TOUR 2000

Week Comm.	Venue	Surface	Singles Final	Doubles Winners
03 Jan	Auckland	Hard	A. Kremer d. C. Black 6–4 6–4	Black/Fusai
03 Jan	Gold Coast	Hard	S. Talaja d. C. Martinez 6–0 0–6 6–4	Halard-Decugis/ Kournikova
10 Jan	Hobart	Hard	K. Clijsters d. C. Rubin 2–6 6–2 6–2	Grande/Loit
10 Jan	Sydney	Hard	A. Mauresmo d. L. Davenport 7–6 6–4	Halard-Decugis/ Sugiyama
17 Jan	**Australian Open**	**Hard**	**L. Davenport d. M. Hingis 6–1 7–5**	**Raymond/Stubbs**
31 Jan	Tokyo	Carpet	M. Hingis d. S. Testud 6–3 7–5	Hingis/Pierce
07 Feb	Bogota	Clay	P. Wartusch d. T. Garbin 4–6 6–1 6–4	Montalvo/Suarez
07 Feb	Paris	Carpet	N. Tauziat d. S. Williams 7–5 6–2	Halard-Decugis/ Testud
14 Feb	Hanover	Carpet	S. Williams d. D. Chladkova 6–1 6–1	Carlsson/Zvereva
14 Feb	Sao Paulo	Clay	R. Kuti Kis d. P. Suarez 4–6 6–4 7–5	Montalvo/Suarez
21 Feb	Oklahoma City, OK	Hard	M. Seles d. N. Dechy 6–1 7–6	Morariu/Po
28 Feb	Scottsdale, AZ	Hard	L. Davenport v. M. Hingis – Final not played due to rain	Doubles event abandoned due to rain
06 Mar	Indian Wells, CA	Hard	L. Davenport d. M. Hingis 4–6 6–4 6–0	Davenport/ Morariu
20 Mar	Miami, FL	Hard	M. Hingis d. L. Davenport 6–3 6–2	Halard-Decugis/ Sugiyama

Week Comm.	Venue	Surface	Singles Final	Doubles Winners
10 Apr	Amelia Island, FL	Clay	M. Seles d. C. Martinez 6–3 6–2	Doubles event abandoned, rain
10 Apr	Estoril	Clay	A. Huber d. N. Dechy 6–2 1–6 7–5	Krizan/Srebotnik
17 Apr	Hilton Head, SC	Clay	M. Pierce d. A. Sanchez-Vicario 6–1 6–0	Ruano Pascual/ Suarez
17 Apr	Budapest	Clay	T. Garbin d. K. Boogert 6–2 7–6	Bacheva/ Torrens-Valero
01 May	Hamburg	Clay	M. Hingis d. A. Sanchez-Vicario 6–3 6–3	Kournikova/ Zvereva
01 May	Bol	Clay	T. Pisnik d. A. Mauresmo 7–6 7–6	Halard-Decugis/ Morariu
08 May	Berlin	Clay	C. Martinez d. A. Coetzer 6–1 6–2	Martinez/ Sanchez-Vicario
08 May	Warsaw	Clay	H. Nagyova d. A. Hopmans 2–6 6–4 7–5	Garbin/Husarova
15 May	Rome	Clay	M. Seles d. A. Mauresmo 6–2 7–6	Raymond/Stubbs
15 May	Antwerp	Clay	A. Coetzer d. C. Torrens-Valero 4–6 6–2 6–3	Appelmans/ Clijsters
22 May	Strasbourg	Clay	S. Talaja d. R. Kuti Kis 7–5 4–6 6–3	Jeyaseelan/Labat
22 May	Madrid	Clay	G. Leon Garcia d. F. Zuluaga 4–6 6–2 6–3	Raymond/Stubbs
29 May	**Roland Garros**	**Clay**	**M. Pierce d. C. Martinez 6–2 7–5**	**Hingis/Pierce**
12 Jun	Birmingham	Grass	L. Raymond d. T. Tanasugarn 6–2 6–7 6–4	McQuillan/McShea
12 Jun	Tashkent	Hard	I. Tulyaganova d. F. Schiavone 6–3 2–6 6–3	N. Li/T. Li
19 Jun	Eastbourne	Grass	J. Halard-Decugis d. D. Van Roost 7–6 6–4	Sugiyama/Tauziat
19 Jun	's–Hertogenbosch	Grass	M. Hingis d. R. Dragomir 6–2 3–0 ret.	De Lone/Pratt
26 Jun	**Wimbledon**	**Grass**	**V. Williams d. L. Davenport 6–3 7–6**	**S. Williams/ V. Williams**
10 Jul	Palermo	Clay	H. Nagyova d. P. Nola 6–3 7–5	Farina/Grande
10 Jul	Klagenfurt	Clay	B. Schett d. P. Schnyder 5–7 6–4 6–4	Montalvo/Suarez
17 Jul	Sopot	Clay	A. Huber d. G. Leon Garcia 7–6 6–3	Ruano Pascual/ Suarez
17 Jul	Knokke–Heist	Clay	A. Smashnova d. D. Van Roost 6–2 7–5	Casoni/ Tulyaganova
24 Jul	Stanford, CA	Hard	V. Williams d. L. Davenport 6–1 6–4	Rubin/Testud
31 Jul	San Diego, CA	Hard	V. Williams d. M. Seles 6–0 6–7 6–3	Raymond/Stubbs
07 Aug	Los Angeles, CA	Hard	S. Williams d. L. Davenport 4–6 6–4 7–6	Callens/Van Roost
14 Aug	Montreal	Hard	M. Hingis d. S. Williams 0–6 6–3 3–0 ret.	Hingis/Tauziat
21 Aug	New Haven, CT	Hard	V. Williams d. M. Seles 6–2 6–4	Halard-Decugis/ Sugiyama
28 Aug	**US Open**	**Hard**	**V. Williams d. L. Davenport 6–4 7–5**	**Halard-Decugis/ Sugiyama**
18 Sep	**Olympic Games**	**Hard**	**V. Williams d. E. Dementieva 6–2 6–4**	**S. Williams/ V. Williams**
25 Sep	Luxembourg	Carpet	J. Capriati d. M. Maleeva 4–6 6–1 6–4	Fusai/Tauziat
02 Oct	Tokyo	Hard	S. Williams d. J. Halard-Decugis 7–5 6–1	Halard-Decugis/ Sugiyama
02 Oct	Filderstadt	Hard	M. Hingis d. K. Clijsters 6–0 6–3	Hingis/Kournikova
02 Oct	Filderstadt	Hard	M. Hingis d. K. Clijsters 6–0 6–3	Hingis/Kournikova
02 Oct	Tokyo	Hard	S. Williams d. J. Halard-Decugis 7–5 6–1	Halard-Decugis/ Sugiyama
09 Oct	Zurich	Carpet	M. Hingis d. L. Davenport 6–4 4–6 7–5	Hingis/Kournikova
09 Oct	Tokyo	Hard	J. Halard-Decugis d. A. Frazier 5–7 7–5 6–4	Halard-Decugis/ Morariu
16 Oct	Linz	Carpet	L. Davenport d. V. Williams 6–4 3–6 6–2	Mauresmo/Rubin
16 Oct	Shanghai	Hard	M. Shaughnessy d. I. Tulyaganova 7–6 7–5	Osterloh/ Tanasugarn
23 Oct	Bratislava	Hard	D. Bedanova d. M. Oremans 6–1 5–7 6–3	Habsudova/ Hantuchova
23 Oct	Moscow	Carpet	M. Hingis d. A. Kournikova 6–3 6–1	Halard-Decugis/ Sugiyama
30 Oct	Leipzig	Carpet	K. Clijsters d. E. Likhovtseva 7–6 4–6 6–4	Sanchez-Vicario/ Sidot
30 Oct	Quebec City	Hard	C. Rubin d. J. Capriati 6–4 6–2	Pratt/Shaughnessy
06 Nov	Philadelphia, PA	Carpet	L. Davenport d. M. Hingis 7–6 6–4	Hingis/Kournikova
06 Nov	Kuala Lumpur	Hard	H. Nagyova d. I. Majoli 6–4 6–2	Nagyova/Plischke
13 Nov	Pattaya	Hard	A. Kremer d. T. Panova 6–1 6–4	Basuki/Vis
13 Nov	New York, NY	Carpet	M. Hingis d. M. Seles 6–7 6–4 6–4	Hingis/Kournikova
20 Nov	**Fed Cup Final**	**Carpet**	**USA d. Spain 5–0**	

PLAYER NATIONALITIES AND BIRTHDAYS (WOMEN)

The following players have competed in the 2000 Grand Slam Championships, the WTA Tour and Fed Cup Ties. (Birthdays dd/mm/yy.)

Surname / Forename	Nation	DOB	Surname / Forename	Nation	DOB
ABE, Julia	GER	21/05/76	CACIC, Sandra	USA	10/09/74
ABRAMOVIC, Ivana	CRO	03/09/83	CALLENS, Els	BEL	20/08/70
ADAMCZAK, Monique	AUS	21/01/83	CAMERIN, Maria Elena	ITA	21/03/82
AGUDELO, Maria Adelaida	COL	30/01/81	CANEPA, Alice	ITA	30/04/78
AHL, Lucie	GBR	23/07/74	CAPRIATI, Jennifer	USA	29/03/76
AKRAMOVA, Nargisa	UZB	03/12/83	CARDOSO, Angela	POR	13/05/80
ALMEDA-SINGIAN, Tracy	USA	06/10/79	CARGILL, Ansley	USA	05/01/82
ALPERT, Lindsey	USA	07/08/78	CARLOTTI, Chloe	FRA	03/03/82
ALVES, Ma. Fernanda	BRA	17/04/83	CARLSSON, Asa	SWE	16/06/75
AMANMURADOVA, Akgul	UZB	23/06/84	CASANOVA, Daniela	SUI	14/05/84
ANDRADE, Jenny	COL	16/06/82	CASONI, Giulia	ITA	19/04/78
ANDRES, Rosa M.	ESP	29/05/77	CASTANO, Catalina	COL	07/07/79
ANDRETTO, Laurence	FRA	14/05/73	CAVANAUGH, Leslie	USA	09/02/72
ANGELI, Yasmin	ITA	07/08/75	CENKOVA, Lenka	CZE	24/01/77
AOYAMA, Kaori	JPN	26/08/81	CERVANOVA, Ludmila	SVK	15/10/79
APPELMANS, Sabine	BEL	22/04/72	CHAE, Kyung Yee	KOR	02/10/80
ARENDT, Nicole	USA	26/08/69	CHANG, Kyung-Mi	KOR	25/02/82
AREVALO, Melisa	ARG	09/01/80	CHEN, Yan	CHN	11/04/77
ARN, Greta	GER	13/04/79	CHI, Jane	USA	21/06/74
ARPHANUKUL, Sunthree	THA	08/06/85	CHLADKOVA, Denisa	CZE	08/02/79
ARRIBAS, Cristina	ESP	27/03/82	CHO, Yoon Jeong	KOR	02/04/79
ASAGOE, Shinobu	JPN	28/06/76	CIOROCH, Agata	POL	20/09/81
AUER, Bettina	AUT	13/01/80	CLAYTON, Melanie	AUS	05/09/81
AUGUSTUS, Amanda	USA	19/01/78	CLIJSTERS, Kim	BEL	08/06/83
BABEL, Meike	GER	22/11/74	COCHETEUX, Amelie	FRA	27/03/78
BABILON, Julia	GER	14/07/84	COCHRAN, Tanner	USA	03/08/84
BACHEVA, Lubomira	BUL	07/03/75	COETZER, Amanda	RSA	22/10/71
BACHMANN, Angelika	GER	16/05/79	COHEN, Alyssa	USA	19/11/82
BAKER, Marilyn	USA	14/01/74	COHEN ALORO, Stephanie	FRA	18/03/83
BALTACHA, Elena	GBR	14/08/83	COLALILLO, Lauren	CAN	24/11/82
BAMMER, Sybille	AUT	20/04/80	COLLIN, Hannah	GBR	18/02/82
BANDUROWSKA, Patrycja	POL	08/04/80	CORREIA, Cristina	POR	19/02/79
BARABANSCHIKOVA, Olga	BLR	02/11/79	CORTEZ, Joana	BRA	11/01/79
BARCLAY, Catherine	AUS	12/06/73	COSTA, Diana	POR	09/02/83
BARNA, Anca	GER	14/05/77	COURTOIS, Laurence	BEL	18/01/76
BARNES, Alice	GBR	23/01/84	CRAYBAS, Jill	USA	04/07/74
BARNIKOW, Lauren	USA	21/05/82	CRISTEA, Catalina	ROM	02/06/75
BASTING, Yvette	NED	08/06/77	CROOK, Helen	GBR	22/11/71
BASTRIKOVA, Anna	RUS	15/11/85	CROSS, Karen	GBR	19/02/74
BASUKI, Yayuk	INA	30/11/70	CSURGO, Virag	HUN	10/11/72
BEDANOVA, Daja	CZE	09/03/83	CURRAN, Claire	IRL	10/03/77
BES, Eva	ESP	14/01/73	CZINK, Melinda	HUN	22/10/82
BEZVERHOVA, Kira	UZB	03/03/84	D'AGOSTINI, Miriam	BRA	15/08/78
BIKTYAKOVA, Luiza	UZB	11/04/82	DADAKHODJAEVA, Kamila	UZB	06/10/83
BLACK, Cara	ZIM	11/02/79	DANIILIDOU, Eleni	GRE	19/09/82
BLAHOTOVA, Olga	CZE	24/01/76	DASKOVIC, Katarina	YUG	05/02/76
BOBKOVA, Radka	CZE	12/02/73	DAVENPORT, Lindsay	USA	08/06/76
BOBOEDOVA, Maria	RUS	25/05/79	DAVIES, Victoria	GBR	07/08/72
BOLLEGRAF, Manon	NED	10/04/64	DE BEER, Surina	RSA	29/06/78
BOOGERT, Kristie	NED	16/12/73	DE LONE, Erika	USA	14/10/72
BORNU, Carine	FRA	28/04/75	DE LOS RIOS, Rossana	PAR	16/09/75
BOVINA, Elena	RUS	10/03/83	DE MASMAECKER, Evy	BEL	29/04/83
BRADSHAW, Allison	USA	14/11/80	DE SILVA, Sandra	SRI	16/01/75
BRANDI, Kristina	USA	29/03/77	DE SWARDT, Mariaan	RSA	18/03/71
BRAVERMAN, Brandis	USA	13/02/80	DE VILLE, Stephanie	BEL	24/07/76
BRIANTI, Alberta	ITA	05/04/80	DE VILIERS, Nannie	RSA	05/01/76
BURIC, Mia	GER	23/05/82	DECHAUME-BALLERET, Alexia	FRA	03/05/70
BUTH, Dawn	USA	29/05/76	DECHY, Nathalie	FRA	21/02/79
BUTKIEWICZ, Leslie	BEL	26/05/82	DEKMEIJERE, Liga	LAT	21/05/83

Surname / Forename	Nation	DOB
DELL'ANGELO, Laura	ITA	17/05/81
DEMENTIEVA, Elena	RUS	15/10/81
DHENIN, Caroline	FRA	13/06/73
DI NATALE, Germana	ITA	02/04/74
DIAZ-OLIVA, Mariana	ARG	11/03/76
DING, Ding	CHN	17/08/77
DITTMANN, Mireille	AUS	01/10/74
DIZDAR, Petra	CRO	30/06/84
DJORDJIO, Maria	UZB	08/06/81
DLHOPOLCOVA, Lenka	SVK	14/07/84
DOKIC, Jelena	AUS	12/04/83
DOMINGUEZ LINO, Lourdes	ESP	31/03/81
DOMINIKOVIC, Evie	AUS	29/05/80
DONG, Yanhua	CHN	18/05/83
DOWSE, Melissa	AUS	27/04/82
DOYLE, Yvonne	IRL	07/12/74
DRAGOMIR, Ruxandra	ROM	24/10/72
DRAKE, Maureen	CAN	21/03/71
DUBBERS, Nina	GER	24/06/80
DYRBERG, Eva	DEN	17/02/80
EGOROVA, Natalia	RUS	13/09/66
ELLWOOD, Annabel	AUS	02/02/78
ERRE, Sophie	FRA	06/04/79
ETIENE, Neyssa	HAI	31/10/83
FARAH, Rommy	COL	05/01/85
FARINA ELIA, Silvia	ITA	27/04/72
FARR, Heidi	GBR	04/02/82
FATTAKHETDINOVA, Goulnara	RUS	13/10/82
FAUTH, Evelyn	AUT	27/11/76
FERNANDEZ, Clarisa	ARG	28/08/81
FEYS, Debbrich	BEL	20/12/84
FISLOVA, Eva	SVK	17/03/81
FIX, Wendy	USA	31/01/75
FLORIS, Anna	ITA	15/05/82
FODERA, Karen	USA	05/12/67
FOKINA, Galina	RUS	17/01/84
FOLDENYI, Anna	HUN	22/08/74
FORETZ, Stephanie	FRA	03/05/81
FRAZIER, Amy	USA	19/09/72
FREYE, Kirstin	GER	29/05/75
FUCHS, Candice	USA	31/03/82
FUJIWARA, Rika	JPN	19/09/81
FUSAI, Alexandra	FRA	22/11/73
GAFUROVA, Firuza	UZB	19/02/82
GAGLIARDI, Emmanuelle	SUI	09/07/76
GANDIA, Julia	ESP	01/09/85
GARBIN, Tathiana	ITA	30/06/77
GARCIA, Paula	ESP	19/03/79
GARZON-ELKINS, Martha	USA	15/12/69
GAVALDON, Angelica	MEX	03/10/73
GEHRLEIN, Stefanie	GER	10/04/82
GEORGES, Sophie	FRA	08/02/77
GERARDS, Michelle	NED	08/07/84
GERS, Ilke	NZL	26/10/81
GERSI, Adriana	CZE	26/06/76
GEZNENGE, Maria	BUL	13/03/77
GHIRARDI, Lea	FRA	10/02/74
GLASS, Andrea	GER	17/07/76
GOLIMBIOSCHI, Oana-Elena	ROM	21/05/80
GOLOVIZNINA, Maria	RUS	31/12/79
GONI, Ainhoa	ESP	07/08/79
GOULET, Cynthia	CAN	15/01/84
GRAHAM, Debbie	USA	25/08/70
GRAHAME, Amanda	AUS	25/03/79
GRANDE, Rita	ITA	23/03/75

Surname / Forename	Nation	DOB
GRANT, Kim	RSA	01/05/71
GRZYBOWSKA, Magdalena	POL	22/11/78
GUBACSI, Zsofia	HUN	06/04/81
GUSE, Kerry-Anne	AUS	04/12/72
GUTIERREZ, Giana	COL	30/05/76
GUTIERREZ QUIROGA, Silvia	ESP	14/02/83
HAAK, Debby	NED	25/02/77
HABERNIGG, Christina	AUT	10/07/75
HABSUDOVA, Karina	SVK	02/08/73
HAIDNER, Stefanie	AUT	18/11/77
HALARD-DECUGIS, Julie	FRA	10/09/70
HANTUCHOVA, Daniela	SVK	23/04/83
HARKLEROAD, Ashley	USA	02/05/85
HARRIS, Briana	USA	21/12/78
HEITZ, Anne-Laure	FRA	15/03/82
HEJDOVA, Zuzana	CZE	29/04/77
HENIN, Justine	BEL	01/06/82
HENKE, Vanessa	GER	15/01/81
HERGOLD, Tina	SLO	18/10/81
HERMIDA, Paula	ESP	24/10/77
HEWITT, Jaslyn	AUS	23/02/83
HINGIS, Martina	SUI	30/09/80
HIRAKI, Rika	JPN	06/12/71
HIRANRAT, Rattiya	THA	08/11/83
HISAMATSU, Shiho	JPN	04/07/79
HLAVACKOVA, Jana	CZE	22/05/81
HOPKINS, Jennifer	USA	10/02/81
HOPMANS, Amanda	NED	11/03/76
HORN, Liezel	RSA	21/08/76
HOTTA, Tomoe	JPN	16/04/75
HRDLICKOVA, Kveta	CZE	09/07/75
HROZENSKA, Stanislava	SVK	17/06/82
HUBER, Anke	GER	04/12/74
HUDSON, Rewa	NZL	15/09/80
HUSAROVA, Janette	SVK	04/06/74
HYNDMAN, Kelley	USA	12/09/85
IIJIMA, Kumiko	JPN	22/10/82
INOUE, Haruka	JPN	07/06/77
IONESCO, Karine	CAN	08/08/83
IRVIN, Marissa	USA	23/06/80
ITO, Chisayo	JPN	10/07/81
JACKSON, Jamea	USA	07/09/86
JAGIENIAK, Karolina	FRA	04/06/79
JANKOVIC, Jelena	YUG	28/02/85
JANS, Klaudia	POL	24/09/84
JAVER, Monique	GBR	22/07/67
JENSEN, Rebecca	USA	19/11/72
JEON, Mi-Ra	KOR	06/02/78
JERABEK, Adriana	GER	28/08/83
JEYASEELAN, Sonya	CAN	24/04/76
DAN, Dan Jiang	CHN	22/11/82
JIDKOVA, Alina	RUS	18/01/77
JOHNSON, Amanda	USA	26/11/81
JURAK, Darija	CRO	05/04/84
KANDARR, Jana	GER	21/09/76
KAPROS, Aniko	HUN	11/11/83
KAWAMATA, Riei	JPN	12/05/74
YUIN, Pei Keng	MAL	29/03/82
KEOTHAVONG, Anne	GBR	16/09/83
KHODJAEVA, Gulnora	UZB	08/02/83
KIM, Eun-ha	KOR	08/03/75
KINJO, Satomi	JPN	13/10/80
KIX, Daniela	AUT	11/11/84
KLASCHKA, Sabine	GER	08/08/80
KLEINOVA, Sandra	CZE	08/05/78

Surname / Forename	Nation	DOB
KLOESEL, Sandra	GER	22/06/79
KOCHTA, Marketa	GER	14/07/75
KOLBOVIC, Renata	CAN	30/07/76
KORNIENKO, Irina	RUS	16/01/78
KOSTANIC, Jelena	CRO	06/07/81
KOUKALOVA, Klara	CZE	24/02/82
KOULIKOVSKAYA, Evgenia	RUS	21/12/78
KOURNIKOVA, Anna	RUS	07/06/81
KOVALCHUK, Tatiana	UKR	24/07/79
KOVES, Nora	HUN	13/06/71
KRASNOROUTSKAYA, Lina	RUS	29/04/84
KRASZEWSKI, Kristina	USA	11/08/79
KRAUZE, Monika	POL	11/04/84
KREJCOVA, Eva	CZE	12/11/76
KREMER, Anne	LUX	17/10/75
KRIVENTCHEVA, Svetlana	BUL	30/12/73
KRIVETS, Darya	UKR	11/01/86
KRIZAN, Tina	SLO	18/03/74
KRUGER, Joannette	RSA	03/09/73
KSCHWENDT, Karin	AUT	14/09/68
KUCEROVA, Renata	CZE	15/07/79
KUCOVA, Petra	CZE	26/02/73
KUEHN, Jenny	GER	14/01/83
KUES, Karin	BEL	17/03/83
KUNCE, Kristine	AUS	03/03/70
KURHAJCOVA, Lubomira	SVK	11/10/83
KURIOKA, Satoko	JPN	08/09/76
KUROWSKA, Agata	POL	26/04/80
KURYANOVICH, Iryna	BLR	05/10/84
KUTI, Rita Kis	HUN	13/02/78
LABAT, Florencia	ARG	12/06/71
LAMADE, Bianka	GER	30/08/82
LAMANGTHONG, Orawan	THA	08/10/81
LANDRIEUX, Nele	BEL	26/04/83
LAOSIRICHON, Pichaya	THA	01/10/85
LAROCQUE, Debbie	CAN	24/03/83
LAST, Evy	BEL	04/04/80
LASTRA, Gabriela	USA	07/06/80
LATIMER, Louise	GBR	19/01/78
LEE, Janet	TPE	22/10/76
LEE-WATERS, Lindsay	USA	28/06/77
LEFEVRE, Sophie	FRA	23/02/81
LEON, Gala Garcia	ESP	23/12/73
LEPCHENKO, Evgeniya	UZB	22/03/83
LI, Na	CHN	26/02/82
LIGGAN, Kelly	IRL	05/02/79
LIKHOVTSEVA, Elena	RUS	08/09/75
LIU, Jing-Jing	CHN	02/09/83
LLAGOSTERA, Nuria	ESP	16/05/80
LOEFFLER-CARO, Nancy	CAN	11/10/61
LOHRMANN, Susi	GER	27/03/73
LOIT, Emilie	FRA	09/06/79
LONCARIC, Anya	CAN	11/02/81
LORN ANDRADE, Marie France	CAN	12/01/84
LUBIANI, Francesca	ITA	12/07/77
LUCIC, Mirjana	CRO	09/03/82
MAES, Caroline	BEL	09/11/82
MAHLER, Marnie	GER	17/09/85
MAJOLI, Iva	CRO	12/08/77
MALEEVA, Magdalena	BUL	01/04/75
MALHOTRA, Manisha	IND	19/09/76
MALL, Anne	USA	10/12/74
MANDULA, Petra	HUN	17/01/78
MARIK, Angie	AUS	06/11/75
MARKER, Emily	USA	28/03/82

Surname / Forename	Nation	DOB
MAROIS, Melanie	CAN	10/03/84
MAROSI-ARACAMA, Katalin	HUN	12/11/79
MARRERO, Marta	ESP	16/01/83
MARSZALEK, Magdalena	POL	26/07/80
MARTINCOVA, Eva	CZE	04/03/75
MARTINEK, Veronika	GER	03/04/72
MARTINEZ, Conchita	ESP	16/04/72
MARTINEZGRANADOS, Conchita	ESP	20/01/76
MARUSKA, Marion	AUT	15/12/72
MASANTE, Luciana	ARG	04/12/78
MASSARELLA, Monica	GBR	01/08/78
MASTALIROVA, Monika	CZE	22/01/77
MATEVZIC, Maja	SLO	13/06/80
MATTEK, Bethanie	USA	23/03/85
MAURESMO, Amelie	FRA	05/07/79
MAZZOTTA, Melissa	USA	21/06/72
MCKEOWN, Jessica	CAN	26/06/83
MCCALLA, Iwalani	USA	17/06/71
MCNEIL, Lori	USA	18/12/63
MCQUILLAN, Rachel	AUS	02/12/71
MCSHEA, Lisa	AUS	29/10/74
MEDINA GARRIGUES, Ana Isabel	ESP	31/07/82
MEJIA, Marlene	USA	31/07/81
MELICHAROVA, Eva	CZE	02/02/70
MENGA, Vanessa	BRA	20/10/76
MENS, Jolanda	NED	04/02/78
MESA, Mariana	COL	01/04/80
MIDDLETON, Melissa	USA	06/06/82
MIHALACHE, Magda	ROM	06/07/81
MIHOLCEK, Lana	CRO	07/03/81
MIKAELIAN, Marie-Gaiane	SUI	03/03/84
MILLER, Annie	USA	19/01/77
MISKOLCZI, Katalin	HUN	06/08/76
MIYAGI, Nana	JPN	10/04/71
MOLIK, Alicia	AUS	27/01/81
MONTALVO, Laura	ARG	29/03/76
MONTOLIO, Angeles	ESP	06/08/75
MOORE, Joanne	GBR	09/03/76
MORARIU, Corina	USA	26/01/78
MORIGAMI, Akiko	JPN	12/01/80
MORTELLO, Giorgia	ITA	23/03/84
MOSSIAKOVA, Svetlana	RUS	29/01/82
MOUHTASSINE, Bahia	MAR	23/08/79
MULEJ, Barbara	SLO	29/05/74
MULLER, Martina	GER	11/10/82
MUSGRAVE, Trudi	AUS	10/09/77
MYSKINA, Anastasia	RUS	08/07/81
NACUK, Sandra	YUG	17/08/80
NAGY, Kyra	HUN	29/12/77
NAGYOVA, Henrieta	SVK	15/12/78
NASH, Alison	CAN	26/11/77
NAVRATILOVA, Martina	USA	18/10/56
NEILAND, Larisa	LAT	21/07/66
NEJEDLY, Jana	CAN	09/06/74
NEMECKOVA, Lenka	CZE	20/04/76
NIKITINA, Natelie	UZB	05/04/78
NIKOIAN, Lioudmila	RUS	01/08/79
NIMMERS, Katrina	USA	30/05/80
NITTINGER, Nina	GER	16/06/76
NOCIAROVA, Dominika	SVK	13/04/84
NOGUEIRA, Ana	POR	20/09/78
NOLA, Pavlina	BUL	14/07/74
NOORLANDER, Seda	NED	22/05/75
O'CONNOR, Tracey	NZL	24/09/82
O'DONOGHUE, Jane	GBR	29/03/83

Surname / Forename	Nation	DOB	Surname / Forename	Nation	DOB
OBATA, Saori	JPN	23/04/78	RYNARZEWSKA, Anna	POL	11/03/83
OBZILER, Tzipora	ISR	19/04/73	SAKOWICZ, Joanna	POL	01/05/84
ONDRASKOVA, Zuzana	CZE	03/05/80	SALAS, Ana	ESP	12/07/72
OREMANS, Miriam	NED	09/09/72	SALERNI, Ma. Emilia	ARG	14/05/83
ORTUNO, Alicia	ESP	02/05/76	SANCHEZ, Olivia	FRA	17/11/82
OSPINA, Diana	USA	04/07/77	SANCHEZ LORENZO, Ma. Antonia	ESP	07/11/77
OSTERLOH, Lilia	USA	07/04/78	SANCHEZ-VICARIO, Arantxa	ESP	18/12/71
OSTROVSKAYA, Nadejda	BLR	29/10/80	SANDU, Raluca	ROM	03/02/80
OTTOBONI, Romina	ARG	19/06/78	SANGARAM, Benjamas	THA	11/01/75
PALAVERSIC, Maja	CRO	24/03/73	SASSI, Valentina	ITA	12/07/80
PANDJEROVA, Antoaneta	BUL	22/06/77	SCHAERER, Larissa	PAR	15/04/75
PANOVA, Tatiana	RUS	13/08/76	SCHAUL, Claudine	LUX	20/08/83
PARK, Sung-Hee	KOR	17/02/75	SCHETT, Barbara	AUT	10/03/76
PARKINSON, Holly	USA	10/02/79	SCHIAVONE, Francesca	ITA	23/06/80
PASTIKOVA, Michaela	CZE	27/03/80	SCHIECHTL, Tina	AUT	15/01/84
PAULENKOVA, Alena	SVK	05/01/79	SCHLOTTERER, Nadine	AUT	02/09/82
PELIKANOVA, Radka	CZE	03/07/77	SCHLUKEBIR, Katie	USA	29/04/75
PELLETIER, Marie-Eve	CAN	18/05/82	SCHMIDLE, Syna	GER	28/11/78
PENA, Maria	ESP	31/10/83	SCHNEIDER, Caroline	GER	01/06/73
PENNETTA, Flavia	ITA	25/02/82	SCHNELL, Melanie	AUT	22/02/77
PEREBIYNIS, Tatiana	UKR	15/12/82	SCHNITZER, Miriam	GER	16/01/77
PERFETTI, Flora	ITA	29/01/69	SCHNYDER, Patty	SUI	14/12/78
PESTIEAU, Sarah	BEL	17/06/79	SCHOEFFEL, Samantha	FRA	24/01/81
PETERSON, Jewel	USA	10/09/81	SCHRUFF, Julia	GER	18/08/82
PETKES, Melinda	HUN	19/06/78	SCHWARTZ, Barbara	AUT	27/01/79
PETROVA, Nadejda	RUS	08/06/82	SCOTT, Julie	USA	16/10/75
PIEDADE, Frederica	POR	05/06/82	SEITENBECHER, Nicole	GER	03/01/80
PIERCE, Mary	FRA	15/01/75	SELES, Monica	USA	02/12/73
PIN, Camille	FRA	25/08/81	SELYUTINA, Irina	KAZ	07/11/79
PISNIK, Tina	SLO	19/02/81	SEQUERA, Milagros	VEN	30/09/80
PITKOWSKI, Sarah	FRA	13/11/75	SERNA, Magui	ESP	01/03/79
PIZZICHINI, Gloria	ITA	24/07/75	SERRA-ZANETTI, Adriana	ITA	05/03/76
PLEMING, Louise	AUS	22/06/67	SFAR, Selima	TUN	08/07/77
PLESU, Ioana	CAN	17/12/80	SHAUGHNESSY, Meghann	USA	13/04/79
PLISCHKE, Sylvia	AUT	20/07/77	SHCHUPAK, Anna	UZB	07/02/83
PO, Kimberly	USA	20/10//1	SIDOT, Anne-Gaelle	FRA	24/07/79
POOS, Martine	LUX	26/06/81	SISKOVA, Katerina	CZE	20/02/74
PORURI, Laxmi	USA	09/11/72	SMASHNOVA, Anna	ISR	16/07/76
POULIOT, Marie-Pier	CAN	31/01/84	SMITH, Samantha	GBR	27/11/71
POUTCHEK, Tatiana	BLR	09/01/79	SNYDER, Tara	USA	26/05/77
PRAKUSYA, Wynne	INA	26/04/81	SOROKOTYAGA, Alexandra	UZB	14/04/84
PRATT, Nicole	AUS	05/03/73	Spirlea, Irina	ROM	26/03/74
PRUSOVA, Libuse	CZE	13/07/79	SPREM, Karolina	CRO	25/10/84
PULLIN, Julie	GBR	05/11/75	SREBOTNIK, Katarina	SLO	12/03/81
RACEDO, Paula	ARG	21/07/77	SROMOVA, Hana	CZE	10/04/78
RAMON, Mariam	ESP	26/08/76	STECK, Jessica	RSA	06/08/78
RAMPRE, Petra	SLO	20/01/80	STEINBACH, Lydia	GER	30/07/80
RANDRIANTEFY, Dally	MAD	23/02/77	STEPHENS, Shelley	NZL	29/07/78
RAYMOND, Lisa	USA	10/08/73	STEVENSON, Alexandra	USA	15/12/80
RAZZANO, Virginie	FRA	12/05/83	STEWART, Bryanne	AUS	09/12/79
REEVES, Samantha	USA	17/01/79	STOSUR, Samantha	AUS	30/03/84
REMIS, Nicole	AUT	28/01/80	STRACZY, Katarzyna	POL	28/11/79
RIERA, Gisela	ESP	07/05/76	STUBBS, Rennae	AUS	26/03/71
RIPPNER, Brie	USA	21/01/80	SUAREZ, Paola	ARG	23/06/76
RITTNER, Barbara	GER	25/04/73	SUCHA, Martina	SVK	20/11/80
RIZZI, Stephanie	FRA	23/08/81	SUGIYAMA, Ai	JPN	05/07/75
RODIONOVA, Anastassia	RUS	12/05/82	SUN, Tian Tian	CHN	12/10/81
RODRIGUES, Katia	POR	30/11/81	SYSSOEVA, Ekaterina	RUS	03/06/81
ROESCH, Angelika	GER	08/06/77	TAGUCHI, Keiko	JPN	26/02/79
ROMERO BARRIO, Virginia	ESP	24/03/83	TAJNAI, Linda	AUS	14/09/81
ROSEN, Hila	ISR	05/09/77	TAKASE, Ayami	JPN	13/12/78
ROY, Melanie	CAN	31/03/84	TALAJA, Silvija	CRO	13/01/78
RUANO PASCUAL, Virginia	ESP	21/09/73	TAMEISHI, Keiko	JPN	22/04/77
RUBIN, Chanda	USA	18/02/76	TANASUGARN, Tamarine	THA	24/05/77
RYABTSEVA, Elena	UZB	03/09/85	TANG, Yan	CHN	05/07/79

Surname / Forename	Nation	DOB	Surname / Forename	Nation	DOB
TARABINI, Patricia	ARG	06/08/68	VIS, Caroline	NED	04/03/70
TARJAN, Rita	GER	04/11/82	VOINA, Antonela	GER	21/01/75
TATARKOVA, Elena	UKR	22/08/76	VOROPAEVA, Elena	RUS	26/07/80
TAUZIAT, Nathalie	FRA	17/10/67	VRLJIC, Ana	CRO	01/08/84
TAYLOR, Sarah	USA	06/11/81	VULETIC, Visnja	YUG	01/07/82
TESTUD, Sandrine	FRA	03/04/72	VYMETAL, Kathy	GBR	26/02/83
TIENE, Carla	BRA	15/05/81	WAGNER, Elena	GER	17/05/72
TIPPINS, Niki	NZL	15/05/76	WALKER, Sara	USA	22/10/80
TOKUDA, Keiko	USA	29/04/80	WANG, Shi-Ting	TPE	19/10/73
TONG, Ka-po	HKG	17/03/81	WARD, Jo	GBR	22/06/75
TONGSALEC, Napaporn	THA	21/10/79	WARTUSCH, Patricia	AUT	05/08/78
TOPALOVA, Dessislava	BUL	08/06/78	WASHINGTON, Mashona	USA	31/05/76
TORDOFF, Abigail	GBR	18/07/79	WATANABE, Jolene	USA	31/08/68
TORRENS VALERO, Cristina	ESP	12/09/74	WATSON, Cindy	AUS	24/03/78
TORRES, Melissa	MEX	03/02/84	WEBB, Vanessa	CAN	24/01/76
TORTI, Jorgelina	ARG	20/10/77	WEINGARTNER, Marlene	GER	03/01/80
TRICERRI, Alienor	SUI	20/03/80	WENG, Tzu-Ting	TPE	01/07/78
TU, Meilen	USA	17/01/78	WERNER, Scarlett	GER	21/11/84
TULYAGANOVA, Iroda	UZB	07/01/82	WHEELER, Christina	AUS	15/04/82
TURINSKY, Catherine	GER	06/12/72	WILD, Linda	USA	11/02/71
UMEHARA, Sachie	JPN	26/11/78	WILLIAMS, Serena	USA	26/09/81
VAIDYANATHAN, Nirupama	IND	08/12/76	WOEHR, Jasmin	GER	21/08/80
VAKULENKO, Julia	UKR	10/07/83	WOODROFFE, Lorna	GBR	18/08/76
VALEKOVA, Zuzana	SVK	23/08/79	YAO, Lan	CHN	16/03/80
VAN ACKER, Patty	BEL	21/10/76	YAVUZ, Bucke	TUR	29/06/81
VAN DE ZANDE, Daphne	RFI	21/07/74	YI, Jing-Qian	CHN	28/02/74
VAN DEN HURK, Andrea	NED	02/02/79	YOSHIDA, Yuka	JPN	01/04/76
VAN DER PERRE, Kristel	BEL	18/06/82	YU, Ji-Fei	CHN	28/01/83
VAN DOREN, Uschi	BEL	07/07/84	YUNG, Andrea	USA	13/09/83
VAN ROOST, Dominique	BEL	31/05/73	ZAPOROZHANOVA, Anna	UKR	09/08/79
VAN ROOYEN, Lara	RSA	04/12/79	ZARIC, Dragana	YUG	01/08/77
VANC, Andreea	ROM	06/10/73	ZARSKA, Anna	POL	22/07/79
VARMUZA, Ludmilla	SMR	25/02/79	PAOLA, Maria Zavagli	ITA	04/06/77
VASKOVA, Alena	CZE	08/11/75	ZDENOVCOVA, Magdalena	CZE	17/05/78
VAVRINEC, Miroslava	SUI	01/04/78	ZHANG, Yao	CHN	08/02/84
VELTS, Alissa	KAZ	26/05/80	ZIBAR, Karin	CRO	13/02/85
VENTO, Maria	VEN	24/05/74	ZIKA, Jenny	AUT	22/11/84
VIANELLO, Elena	ITA	15/02/84	ZULUAGA, Fabiola	COL	07/01/79
VIERIN, Nathalie	ITA	15/10/82	ZVEREVA, Natasha	BLR	16/04/71
VILDOVA, Helena	CZE	19/03/72	ZVONAREVA, Vera	RUS	07/08/84
VINCI, Roberta	ITA	18/02/83			

Championship Series
Tiers I and II Tournaments

ADIDAS INTERNATIONAL ($460,000)
HOMEBUSH BAY, SYDNEY, NSW, 10–15 JANUARY
WOMEN'S SINGLES – 1st Round: M. Hingis (1) bye; O. Barabanschikova (Q) d. A. Huber 6–3 3–6 6–1; D.
Van Roost d. P. Suarez (Q) 6–2 6–2; A. Coetzer (7) d. L. Raymond 7–6 6–0; M. Pierce (3) bye; C. Martinez d.
A. Kremer 5–7 7–5 6–2; S. Talaja d. N. Petrova (Q) 7–6 3–6 6–4; A. Mauresmo (6) d. A. Sugiyama 6–7 6–0
7–6; A. Kournikova (8) d. S. Appelmans 7–6 6–2; J. Capriati d. S. Testud 6–3 6–1; A. Stevenson (WC) d. A.
Sidot 6–3 6–2; B. Schett (4) bye; A. Sanchez-Vicario d. J. Halard-Decugis (5) 6–4 6–4; J. Dokic (WC) d. E.
Dominikovic (WC) 6–7 6–4 6–2; E. Likhovtseva d. S. Nacuk (Q) 6–7 7–6 6–2; L. Davenport (2) bye.
2nd round: Hingis (1) d. Barabanschikova (Q) 6–0 6–2; Van Roost d. Coetzer (7) 0–6 7–5 6–4; Pierce (3) d.
Martinez 6–1 6–4; Mauresmo (6) d. Talaja w/o; Kournikova (8) d. Capriati 6–4 7–5; Stevenson (WC) d.
Schett (4) 2–6 6–3 6–3; Sanchez-Vicario d. Dokic (WC) 6–4 6–1; Davenport (2) d. Likhovtseva 6–1 6–2.
Quarter-finals: Hingis (1) d. Van Roost 6–1 ret; Mauresmo (6) d. Pierce (3) 6–2 6–3; Kournikova (8) d.
Stevenson (WC) 4–6 6–2 6–2; Davenport (2) d. Sanchez-Vicario 6–7 6–3 6–4.
Semi-finals: Mauresmo (6) d. Hingis (1) 7–5 6–3; Davenport (2) d. Kournikova (8) 6–3 6–2.
Final: Mauresmo (6) d. Davenport (2) 7–6 6–4.
WOMEN'S DOUBLES – Final: Halard-Decugis/Sugiyama d. Hingis/Pierce (3) 6–0 6–3.

TORAY PAN PACIFIC OPEN ($1,080,000)
TOKYO, 31 JANUARY–6 FEBRUARY
WOMEN'S SINGLES – 1st Round: M. Hingis (1) bye; L. Raymond d. T. Tanasugarn (WC) 6–1 6–4; N. Pratt
d. A. Smashnova 6–0 6–1; A. Kournikova (5) d. A. Sidot 6–3 6–2; A. Coetzer (4) bye; N. Zvereva d. C.
Torrens-Valero 6–4 6–4; A. Stevenson d. M. Sanchez Lorenzo 4–1 ret; C. Rubin (7) d. T. Panova 6–0 ret; S.
Testud (6) d. K. Habsudova 6–1 6–2; C. Morariu d. T. Garbin (Q) 6–3 6–3; C. Black d. M. Maleeva (Q) 7–5
2–6 6–2; N. Tauziat (3) bye; K. Srebotnik d. A. Sugiyama (8) 6–3 6–3; I. Selyutina (Q) d. N. Petrova (Q) 6–2
6–4; L. Osterloh (LL) d. S. Asagoe (WC) 6–2 4–6 6–2; M. Pierce (2) bye.
2nd round: Hingis (1) d. Raymond 6–3 7–5; Kournikova (5) d. Pratt 6–2 1–6 6–1; Coetzer (4) d. Zvereva
7–6 6–1; Rubin (7) d. Stevenson 6–4 6–1; Testud (6) d. Morariu 6–1 4–6 6–1; Tauziat (3) d. Black 6–4 6–4;
Srebotnik d. Selyutina (Q) 7–5 2–6 6–3; Osterloh (LL) d. Pierce (2) 6–7 6–4 6–4.
Quarter-finals: Hingis (1) d. Kournikova (5) 6–0 6–2; Rubin (7) d. Coetzer (4) 6–4 6–4; Testud (6) d. Tauziat
(3) 7–6 6–0; Srebotnik d. Osterloh (LL) 7–6 6–1.
Semi-finals: Hingis (1) d. Rubin (7) 7–6 6–4; Testud (6) d. Srebotnik 3–6 7–5 6–1.
Final: Hingis (1) d. Testud (6) 6–3 7–5.
WOMEN'S DOUBLES – Final: Hingis/Pierce (3) d. Fusai/Tauziat (4) 6–4 6–1.

OPEN GAZ DE FRANCE ($535,000)
PARIS, 7–13 FEBRUARY
WOMEN'S SINGLES – 1st Round: S. Williams (1) bye; P. Schnyder d. S. Appelmans 6–4 6–3; S. Pitkowski
d. M. Serna 6–4 6–3; A. Mauresmo (5) d. R. Dragomir 6–1 6–1; J. Halard-Decugis (3) bye; L. Andretto (Q) d.
D. Chladkova (Q) 7–5 7–5; N. Dechy d. K. Habsudova 6–3 6–4; S. Farina d. E. Likhovtseva (7) 1–6 6–2 6–1;
I. Spirlea d. D. Van Roost (8) 6–4 6–2; A. Smashnova d. S. Talaja 6–4 6–4; A. Kremer d. L. Latimer (Q) 6–3
7–6; A. Kournikova (WC) (4) bye; A. Huber d. S. Testud (6) 6–1 6–2; A. Sidot d. A. Cocheteux (WC) 4–6 6–1
7–5; J. Henin (WC) d. M. Maleeva (Q) 6–4 7–6; N. Tauziat (2) bye.
2nd round: S. Williams (1) d. Schnyder 6–2 6–2; Pitkowski d. Mauresmo (5) 0–6 7–6 6–2; Halard-Decugis
(3) d. Andretto (Q) 7–5 7–6; Dechy d. Farina 6–0 6–3; Spirlea d. Smashnova 6–4 6–2; Kournikova (WC) (4)
d. Kremer 7–6 6–2; Sidot d. Huber 4–6 6–1 6–4; Tauziat (2) d. Henin (WC) 7–5 2–6 6–4.
Quarter-finals: S. Williams (1) d. Pitkowski 6–2 6–2; Halard-Decugis (3) d. Dechy 6–2 6–4; Kournikova
(WC) (4) d. Spirlea 4–6 6–4 6–2; Tauziat (2) d. Sidot 7–5 6–1.
Semi-finals: S. Williams (1) d. Halard-Decugis (3) 6–4 6–2; Tauziat (2) d. Kournikova (WC) (4) 7–6 2–6 6–4.
Final: Tauziat (2) d. S. Williams (1) 7–5 6–2.
WOMEN'S DOUBLES – Final: Halard-Decugis/Testud (3) d. Carlsson/Loit 3–6 6–3 6–4.

FABER GRAND PRIX ($535,000)
HANOVER, 14–20 FEBRUARY
WOMEN'S SINGLES – 1st Round: S. Williams (1) bye; S. Appelmans d. M. Muller (Q) 6–4 6–2; S.
Jeyaseelan (Q) d. G. Leon-Garcia 6–0 6–1; P. Schnyder (8) d. R. Sandu (WC) 6–2 7–6; A. Mauresmo (3) bye;
T. Pisnik (LL) d. S. Farina 7–6 6–3; A. Smashnova d. K. Hrdlickova 6 3 6 0; R. Dragomir (6) d. K. Habsudova
6–3 7–6; A. Kremer d. S. Talaja (7) 7–5 6–3; M. Oremans (Q) d. I. Spirlea 6–3 6–3; D. Chladkova d. A.

Hopmans (Q) 6–4 3–6 6–3; E. Likhovtseva (4) bye; K. Clijsters d. A. Huber (5) 6–1 6–7 6–3; A. Sidot d. A. Cocheteux (LL) 6–2 6–3; K. Boogert (Q) d. N. Zvereva 6–4 6–3; N. Tauziat (2) bye.

2nd round: S. Williams (1) d. Appelmans 6–1 6–3; Schnyder (8) d. Jeyaseelan (Q) 7–5 6–4; Mauresmo (3) Pisnik (LL) w/o; Smashnova d. Dragomir (6) 7–5 6–2; Kremer d. Oremans (Q) 6–2 6–4; Chladkova d. Likhovtseva (4) 3–6 6–2 6–3; Sidot d. Clijsters 6–7 6–4 6–4; Boogert (Q) d. Tauziat (2) 6–7 7–5 6–3.

Quarter-finals: S. Williams (1) d. Schnyder (8) 6–1 6–4; Mauresmo (3) d. Smashnova 6–2 6–1; Chladkova d. Kremer 6–2 6–3; Sidot d. Boogert (Q) 6–4 6–2.

Semi-finals: S. Williams (1) d. Mauresmo (3) 6–2 6–7 7–6; Chladkova d. Sidot 6–3 6–7 7–6.

Final: S. Williams (1) d. Chladkova 6–1 6–1.

WOMEN'S DOUBLES – Final: Carlsson/Zvereva (3) d. Farina/Habsudova (4) 6–3 6–4.

STATE FARM TENNIS CHAMPIONSHIPS ($535,000)

SCOTTSDALE, AZ, 28 FEBRUARY–6 MARCH

WOMEN'S SINGLES – 1st Round: M. Hingis (1) bye; C. Rubin d. C. Black (WC) 6–3 6–3; A. Frazier d. A. Huber 7–6 6–2; S. Testud (7) d. D. Van Roost 3–6 6–3 6–2; M. Pierce (3) bye; S. Nacuk (Q) d. H. Nagyova 6–2 6–0; M. Shaughnessy (WC) d. M. Lucic (WC) 6–4 6–4; N. Dechy d. C. Martinez (5) 3–6 6–3 6–4; A. Kournikova (6) d. A. Jidkova (Q) 6–2 6–1; S. Plischke (Q) d. E. Likhovtseva 6–3 2–6 7–5; A. Sugiyama d. L. Raymond 6–2 6–3; J. Halard-Decugis (4) bye; B. Schett (8) d. H. Parkinson (Q) 6–4 7–5; M. Seles d. S. Talaja 6–1 7–6; J. Capriati d. A. Stevenson 6–3 6–0; L. Davenport (2) bye.

2nd round: Hingis (1) d. Rubin 6–3 6–3; Testud (7) d. Frazier 7–5 6–0; Pierce (3) d. Nacuk (Q) 6–0 6–1; Dechy d. Shaughnessy (WC) 6–3 4–6 6–1; Kournikova (6) d. Plischke (Q) 6–1 6–1; Sugiyama d. Halard-Decugis (4) 6–4 6–2; Seles d. Schett (8) 7–6 6–1; Davenport (2) d. Capriati 3–6 6–2 6–3.

Quarter-finals: Hingis (1) d. Testud (7) 6–4 6–2; Pierce (3) d. Dechy 6–3 6–2; Kournikova (6) d. Sugiyama 6–4 6–2; Davenport (2) d. Seles 6–4 6–4.

Semi-finals: Hingis (1) d. Pierce (3) 6–4 6–3; Davenport (2) d. Kournikova (6) 6–2 6–2.

Final: Hingis (1) v. Davenport (2) – not played due to rain.

WOMEN'S DOUBLES – Final: Doubles tournament abandoned at semi-final stage due to rain.

NEWSWEEK CHAMPIONS CUP ($2,000,000)

INDIAN WELLS, CA, 10–18 MARCH

WOMEN'S SINGLES – 1st Round: M. Hingis (1) bye; A. Frazier bye; O. Barabanschikova (WC) d. M. Weingartner (Q) 6–1 6–1; A. Sugiyama bye; A. Smashnova bye; M. Grzybowska d. A. Jidkova (Q) 6–4 6–3; K. Brandi bye; B. Schett (10) bye; J. Capriati (12) bye; C. Black bye; S. Appelmans bye; T. Snyder (WC) d. A. Cocheteux 6–2 4–1 ret; M. Irvin (Q) d. T. Tanasugarn 2–6 7–6 6–1; P. Schnyder bye; S. Farina bye; M. Seles (7) bye; S. Williams (3) bye; A. Stevenson bye; P. Suarez d. J. Nejedly (Q) 6–3 3–6 7–6; R. Grande d. A. Myskina 6–2 6–4; N. Pratt bye; T. Panova bye; K. Clijsters bye; A. Mauresmo (13) bye; E. Likhovtseva (16) bye; S. Plischke bye; J. Lee (Q) d. H. Parkinson (WC) 6–2 6–3; M. Lucic bye; C. Morariu bye; C. Torrens-Valero bye; S. Jeyaseelan (Q) d. J. Steck (WC) 6–1 6–2; M. Pierce (5) bye; A. Kournikova (8) bye; D. Chladkova bye; M. Shaughnessy (LL) bye; N. Dechy bye; D. Bedanova (WC) d. T. Pisnik (Q) 4–6 7–5 6–3; M. Serna bye; E. Dementieva d. K. Srebotnik 6–0 6–3; A. Huber (14) bye; S. Testud (11) bye; S. Pitkowski bye; M. Drake d. E. De Lone 6–0 6–1; C. Rubin bye; A. Kremer bye; K. Habsudova d. A. Rippner (Q) 7–6 7–5; A. Sidot bye; N. Tauziat (4) bye; C. Martinez (6) bye; M. Maleeva d. M. Sanchez Lorenzo 6–2 6–2; J. Dokic bye; S. Talaja bye; G. Leon Garcia bye; E. Gagliardi d. H. Nagyova 6–3 6–4; D. Van Roost bye; A. Coetzer (15) bye; J. Halard-Decugis (9) bye; M. Montolio d. S. Kleinova 6–2 6–4; L. Osterloh (WC) d. R. Kuti Kis (LL) 4–6 6–4 6–3; R. Dragomir bye; N. Zvereva bye; L. Raymond bye; I. Spirlea bye; L. Davenport (2) bye.

2nd round: Hingis (1) d. Frazier 6–3 6–3; Sugiyama d. Barabanschikova (WC) 3–6 6–4 6–3; Grzybowska d. Smashnova 7–6 6–2; Schett (10) d. Brandi 6–1 6–2; Black d. Capriati (12) 5–7 6–1 6–2; Appelmans d. Snyder (WC) 6–2 7–6; Schnyder d. Irvin (Q) 6–2 6–1; Seles (7) d. Farina 6–1 6–2; S. Williams (3) d. Stevenson 7–5 3–6 6–2; Grande d. Suarez 6–1 7–6; Panova d. Pratt 6–4 6–4; Clijsters d. Mauresmo (13) 3–0 ret; Likhovtseva (16) d. Plischke 6–4 6–7 7–5; Lucic d. Lee (Q) 6–2 6–4; Morariu d. Torrens-Valero 6–2 6–2; Pierce (5) d. Jeyaseelan (Q) 6–1 6–3; Kournikova (8) d. Chladkova 7–5 6–2; Dechy d. Shaughnessy (LL) 7–5 7–6; Serna d. Bedanova (WC) 6–3 6–4; Dementieva d. Huber (14) 6–4 4–6 6–4; Testud (11) d. Pitkowski 5–7 6–2 6–4; Rubin d. Drake 6–7 6–3 6–4; Habsudova d. Kremer 7–6 6–4; Tauziat (4) d. Sidot 6–2 6–4; Martinez (6) d. Maleeva 6–3 6–3; Dokic d. Talaja 5–7 7–5 6–1; Gagliardi d. Leon Garcia 4–6 6–2 6–2; Van Roost d. Coetzer (15) 1–6 6–4 6–1; Halard-Decugis (9) d. Montolio 2–6 6–2 6–2; Dragomir d. Osterloh (WC) 6–3 6–3; Zvereva d. Raymond 1–6 6–3 6–2; Davenport (2) d. Spirlea 6–0 6–1.

3rd round: Hingis (1) d. Sugiyama 6–1 6–2; Schett (10) d. Grzybowska 6–2 6–1; Appelmans d. Black 6–3 7–6; Seles (7) d. Schnyder 6–0 6–3; S. Williams (3) d. Grande 4–6 6–1 6–2; Clijsters d. Panova 6–3 7–6; Likhovtseva (16) d. Lucic 2–6 6–4 7–5; Pierce (5) d. Morariu 6–2 6–4; Dechy d. Kournikova (8) 7–5 5–7 7–6; Dementieva d. Serna 4–6 6–4 6–4; Rubin d. Testud (11) 6–4 2–6 6–2; Habsudova d. Tauziat (4) 6–4 6–4; Martinez (6) d. Dokic 6–2 7–6; Van Roost d. Gagliardi 4–6 6–3 6–0; Halard-Decugis (9) d. Dragomir 6–3 4–6 6–3; Davenport (2) d. Zvereva 6–4 6–2.

4th round: Hingis (1) d. Schett (10) 6–1 6–1; Seles (7) d. Appelmans 3–6 6–2 6–3; S. Williams (3) d. Clijsters 6–4 6–4; Pierce (5) d. Likhovtseva (16) 6–3 5–7 7–5; Dementieva d. Dechy 7–6 6–2; Rubin d. Habsudova 6–0 6–1; Martinez (6) d. Van Roost 6–0 3–0 ret; Davenport (2) d. Halard-Decugis (9) 6–2 6–1.

Quarter-finals: Hingis (1) d. Seles (7) 6–3 6–1; Pierce (5) d. S. Williams (3) 6–2 6–1; Dementieva d. Rubin

6–4 6–1; Davenport (2) d. Martinez (6) 6–2 6–1.
Semi-finals: Hingis (1) d. Pierce (5) 6–4 6–2; Davenport (2) d. Dementieva 6–2 6–1.
Final: Davenport (2) d. Hingis (1) 4–6 6–4 6–0.
WOMEN'S DOUBLES – Final: Davenport/Morariu (3) d. Kournikova/Zvereva (4) 6–2 6–3.

ERICSSON OPEN ($2,525,000)
KEY BISCAYNE, FL, 23 MARCH–2 APRIL
WOMEN'S SINGLES – 1st Round: M. Hingis (1) bye; M. Drake d. S. Kleinova 6–3 6–2; K. Brandi d. M. Middleton (WC) 6–2 6–0; A. Sidot (29) bye; K. Clijsters (28) bye; T. Tanasugarn d. A. Jidkova (Q) 6–3 6–3; A. Gersi d. L. Nemeckova (Q) 7–5 6–1; B. Schett (11) bye; D. Van Roost (16) bye; H. Parkinson (WC) d. M. Grzybowska 4–6 6–2 7–5; D. Bedanova (WC) d. M. Weingartner 6–3 6–0; A. Coetzer (18) bye; P. Schnyder (23) bye; R. Kuti Kis d. A. Glass 4–6 6–0 6–1; J. Dokic d. N. Miyagi (Q) 6–3 6–2; C. Martinez (6) bye; N. Tauziat (4) bye; T. Snyder d. O. Barabanschikova 6–3 6–4; K. Habsudova d. J. Kruger 6–7 7–5 6–1; N. Dechy (21) bye; A. Frazier (19) bye; M. Montolio d. S. Jeyaseelan 6–2 3–6 6–2; T. Poutchek (Q) d. K. Boogert 6–1 6–2; A. Huber (14) bye; A. Kournikova (9) bye; J. Hopkins (WC) d. L. Bacheva 7–5 6–4; I. Spirlea d. K. Srebotnik 7–5 6–1; N. Zvereva (31) bye; L. Raymond (WC) (26) bye; D. Chladkova d. C. Cristea (Q) 6–3 7–5; L. Osterloh d. M. Washington (WC) 6–3 4–6 6–1; M. Seles (7) bye; S. Williams (5) bye; M. Maleeva d. R. Grande 7–6 6–4; E. De Lone d. P. Wartusch 6–3 6–2; A. Sugiyama (17) bye; C. Rubin (24) bye; A. Cocheteux d. P. Suarez 3–6 6–4 7–5; A. Rippner (WC) d. E. Callens (Q) 6–4 6–7 6–2; J. Capriati (13) bye; S. Testud (12) bye; F. Zuluaga d. I. Majoli (WC) 7–6 7–5; N. Pratt d. J. Nejedly (LL) 3–6 6–4 6–0; S. Plischke (27) bye; S. Pitkowski (32) bye; C. Black d. A. Carlsson 7–5 6–3; E. Dementieva d. D. Hantuchova (WC) 5–7 6–3 6–2; M. Pierce (3) bye; J. Halard-Decugis (8) bye; N. Petrova d. M. Serna 6–7 6–1 7–5; A. Myskina d. A. Stevenson 4–6 7–5 6–4; C. Morariu (30) bye; S. Appelmans (25) bye; S. Farina d. G. Leon Garcia 6–2 7–5; C. Torrens-Valero d. V. Webb (Q) 7–6 6–1; A. Sanchez-Vicario (10) bye; E. Likhovtseva (15) bye; M. Sanchez Lorenzo d. F. Labat (Q) 6–2 6–3; T. Panova d. E. Gagliardi 6–4 6–2; R. Dragomir (20) bye; S. Talaja (22) bye; T. Pisnik d. A. Smashnova 6–4 6–1; A. Kremer d. M. Lucic 7–6 6–2; L. Davenport (2) bye.
2nd round: Hingis (1) d. Drake 6–1 6–4; Sidot (29) d. Brandi 6–3 6–3; Clijsters (28) d. Tanasugarn 3–6 6–3 7–5; Gersi d. Schett (11) 7–6 4–6 6–1; Van Roost (16) d. Parkinson (WC) 6–7 6–1 6–0; Coetzer (18) d. Bedanova 4–6 6–2 6–3; Schnyder (23) d. Kuti Kis 7–6 7–5; Martinez (6) d. Dokic 6–4 3–6 6–3; Tauziat (4) d. Snyder 6–3 2–6 7–6; Dechy (21) d. Habsudova 6–1 6–1; Frazier (19) d. Montolio 6–3 6–1; Huber (14) d. Poutchek (Q) 6–2 6–2; Kournikova (9) d. Hopkins (WC) 6–2 6–4; Zvereva (31) d. Spirlea 6–3 6–4; Raymond (WC) (26) d. Chladkova 7–5 6–3; Seles (7) d. Osterloh 6–2 6–1; S. Williams (5) d. Maleeva 6–4 6–2; Sugiyama (17) d. De Lone 6–2 7–6; Rubin (24) d. Cocheteux 6–2 6–2; Capriati (13) d. Rippner (WC) 7–5 6–1; Testud (12) d. Zuluaga 6–4 3–6 7–6; Plischke (27) d. Pratt 7–5 7–5; Pitkowski (32) d. Black 6–2 6–0; Dementieva d. Pierce (3) 3–2 1 ret; Petrova d. Halard-Decugis (8) 6–2 6–3; Myskina d. Morariu (30) 6–4 6–4; Appelmans (25) d. Farina 7–6 6–3; Sanchez-Vicario (10) d. Torrens-Valero 7–6 6–2; Likhovtseva (15) d. Sanchez Lorenzo 6–4 6–1; Dragomir (20) d. Panova 6–4 6–1; Talaja (22) d. Pisnik 6–1 3–6 6–1; Davenport (2) d. Kremer 6–1 6–2.
3rd round: Hingis (1) d. Sidot (29) 6–0 6–3; Clijsters (28) d. Gersi 6–4 7–5; Coetzer (18) d. Van Roost (16) w/o; Martinez (6) d. Schnyder (23) 7–5 6–4; Dechy (21) d. Tauziat (4) 6–4 6–2; Frazier (19) d. Huber (14) 5–7 6–4 6–3; Kournikova (9) d. Zvereva (31) 6–1 6–4; Seles (7) d. Raymond (WC) (26) 6–3 6–2; S. Williams (5) d. Sugiyama (17) 6–3 6–0; Capriati (13) d. Rubin (24) 6–1 6–3; Testud (12) d. Plischke (27) 6–0 6–0; Dementieva d. Pitkowski (32) 6–2 6–2; Petrova d. Myskina 6–1 4–6 6–0; Appelmans (25) d. Sanchez-Vicario (10) 6–3 7–5; Likhovtseva (15) d. Dragomir (20) 6–4 2–6 7–6; Davenport (2) d. Talaja (22) 6–2 6–2.
4th round: Hingis (1) d. Clijsters (28) 6–0 6–4; Coetzer (18) d. Martinez (6) 6–1 6–2; Frazier (19) d. Dechy (21) 6–3 7–5; Seles (7) d. Kournikova (9) 6–1 3–6 6–0; Capriati (13) d. S. Williams (5) 7–6 1–6 6–3; Testud (12) d. Dementieva 5–7 6–4 6–4; Petrova d. Appelmans (25) 6–2 6–3; Davenport (2) d. Likhovtseva (15) 6–4 6–4.
Quarter-finals: Hingis (1) d. Coetzer (18) 6–3 6–1; Seles (7) d. Frazier (19) 6–0 6–3; Testud (12) d. Capriati (13) 6–3 6–4; Davenport (2) d. Petrova 6–2 6–1.
Semi-finals: Hingis (1) d. Seles (7) 6–0 6–0; Davenport (2) d. Testud (12) 6–1 6–7 7–6.
Final: Hingis (1) d. Davenport (2) 6–3 6–2.
WOMEN'S DOUBLES – Final: Halard-Decugis/Sugiyama (6) d. Arendt/Bollegraf 4–6 7–5 6–4.

BAUSCH & LOMB CHAMPIONSHIPS ($535,000)
AMELIA ISLAND, FL, 10–16 APRIL
WOMEN'S SINGLES – 1st Round: M. Pierce (1) bye; T. Singian (Q) d. L. Osterloh (WC) 6–1 6–3; A. Stevenson d. P. Nola (Q) 6–3 6–2; S. Talaja (14) d. L. Wild (Q) 6–3 6–1; E. Likhovtseva (12) d. J. Kruger 7–6 6–2; H. Nagyova d. T. Pisnik 6–0 6–2; P. Schnyder d. N. Petrova 7–5 4–6 6–2; S. Testud (5) bye; C. Martinez (4) bye; E. Dementieva d. H. Parkinson (Q) 6–1 6–2; A. Jidkova (Q) 6–0 6–4 6–3; R. Grande d. A. Frazier (9) 6–2 6–7 7–6; C. Rubin (15) d. M. Drake 7–5 6–3; A. Myskina d. E. De Lone 6–4 6–1; G. Leon Garcia d. J. Nejedly (Q) 6–1 6–1; B. Schett (8) bye; A. Sanchez-Vicario (6) bye; T. Snyder (WC) d. K. Brandi 1–6 6–4 6–4; M. Serna d. A. Glass 7–5 6–1; A. Coetzer (10) d. T. Panova 6–0 6–4; A. Carlsson d. R. Dragomir (13) 4–6 6–4 7–5; C. Morariu d. E. Gagliardi 6–4 6–4; A. Smashnova d. I. Majoli (WC) 6–3 6–1; M. Seles (3) bye; A. Kournikova (7) bye; A. Kremer d. M. Lucic 6–1 6–3; N. Pratt d. F. Zuluaga 6–4 7–6; A. Sugiyama (11) d. I. Spirlea 6–3 5–7 6–3; L. Raymond (16) d. J. Hopkins (Q) 6–4 0–6 6–1; S. Jeyaseelan d. M.

Maleeva 6–4 6–2; P. Suarez d. T. Obziler (Q) 6–1 6–1; S. Williams (2) bye.
2nd round: Pierce (1) d. Singian (Q) 6–1 6–3; Talaja (14) d. Stevenson 4–6 6–2 6–2; Likhovtseva (12) d. Nagyova 6–2 3–0 ret; Schnyder d. Testud (5) 7–6 7–6; Martinez (4) d. Dementieva 7–5 6–2; Dokic d. Grande 6–2 6–3; Rubin (15) d. Myskina 6–1 3–6 6–4; Schett (8) d. Leon Garcia 6–2 6–2; Sanchez-Vicario (6) d. T. Snyder (WC) 6–4 0–6 6–4; Coetzer (10) d. Serna 6–4 6–4; Morariu d. Carlsson 6–2 6–4; Seles (3) d. Smashnova 7–6 6–0; Kournikova (7) d. Kremer 7–5 7–6; Pratt d. Sugiyama (11) 6–1 7–5; Jeyaseelan d. Raymond (16) 6–4 6–4; Suarez d. S. Williams (2) 6–3 4–6 5–2 ret.
3rd round: Pierce (1) d. Talaja (14) 6–4 7–5; Likhovtseva (12) d. Schnyder 6–3 7–6; Martinez (4) d. Dokic 6–1 6–4; Schett (8) d. Rubin (15) 6–0 6–2; Sanchez-Vicario (6) d. Coetzer (10) 6–2 6–4; Seles (3) d. Morariu 6–3 6–1; Kournikova (7) d. Pratt 6–0 7–5; Suarez d. Jeyaseelan 6–2 6–3.
Quarter-finals: Likhovtseva (12) d. Pierce (1) 2–6 6–4 6–4; Martinez (4) d. Schett (8) 6–4 6–3; Seles (3) d. Sanchez-Vicario (6) 6–1 6–3; Suarez d. Kournikova (7) 2–6 6–2 6–4.
Semi-finals: Martinez (4) d. Likhovtseva (12) 6–3 6–2; Seles (3) d. Suarez 6–3 6–2.
Final: Seles (3) d. Martinez (4) 6–3 6–2.
WOMEN'S DOUBLES – Final: Doubles tournament abandoned at semi-final stage due to rain.

FAMILY CIRCLE CUP ($1,080,000)
HILTON HEAD ISLAND, SC, 17–23 APRIL
WOMEN'S SINGLES – 1st Round: M. Pierce (1) bye; G. Leon Garcia d. N. Miyagi (Q) 4–6 6–1 6–3; A. Smashnova d. A. Barna (Q) 6–2 6–4; C. Morariu (14) d. A. Glass 6–4 5–7 6–3; N. Pratt d. A. Kremer (16) 6–4 6–2; J. Dokic d. L. Horn (Q) 6–4 6–2; A. Rippner (Q) d. T. Panova 6–4 4–6 6–1; A. Frazier (7) bye; M. Seles (3) bye; E. De Lone d. M. Drake 6–3 6–3; H. Parkinson (Q) d. F. Zuluaga 6–4 6–3; E. Likhovtseva (9) d. L. Osterloh 6–3 4–6 6–1; R. Dragomir (11) d. E. Gagliardi 7–6 7–6; A. Myskina d. A. Stevenson 6–4 6–3; T. Snyder d. T. Pisnik 7–6 6–3; A. Kournikova (6) bye; A. Coetzer (8) bye; A. Jidkova d. J. Kruger 3–6 6–2 7–5; I. Majoli (WC) d. M. Shaughnessy 1–6 7–6 7–5; E. Dementieva (15) d. S. Noorlander 6–2 6–3; P. Schnyder (13) d. S. Jeyaseelan 6–3 6–1; M. Tu (WC) d. R. Grande 6–1 ret; P. Suarez d. H. Nagyova 7–6 6–4; A. Sanchez-Vicario (4) bye; B. Schett (5) bye; J. Nejedly d. M. Weingartner (Q) 6–2 7–5; V. Ruano Pascual (Q) d. M. Washington (Q) 6–0 7–5; L. Raymond (12) d. A. Carlsson 6–4 6–2; K. Brandi d. S. Talaja (10) 7–6 6–1; F. Labat d. M. Maleeva 6–3 6–4; M. Serna d. J. Hopkins (WC) 7–5 6–4; C. Martinez (2) bye.
2nd round: Pierce (1) d. Leon Garcia 6–1 6–1; Smashnova d. Morariu (14) 7–5 3–6 6–2; Dokic d. Pratt 6–4 6–1; Frazier (7) d. Rippner (Q) 7–6 7–5; Seles (3) d. De Lone 6–0 6–0; Likhovtseva (9) d. Parkinson (Q) 6–0 6–0; Dragomir (11) d. Myskina 3–6 7–5 6–3; Kournikova (6) d. Snyder 4–6 6–2 6–1; Coetzer (8) d. Jidkova 6–2 3–6 6–1; Dementieva (15) d. Majoli (WC) 6–1 6–1; Schnyder (13) d. Tu (WC) 6–4 6–0; Sanchez-Vicario (4) d. Suarez 6–3 7–5; Nejedly d. Schett (5) 3–6 7–6 6–2; Raymond (12) d. Ruano Pascual (Q) 7–5 3–6 6–2; Labat d. Brandi 6–4 6–2; Martinez (2) d. Hopkins (WC) 7–6 6–1.
3rd round: Pierce (1) d. Smashnova 6–1 6–2; Dokic d. Frazier (7) 6–2 6–2; Seles (3) d. Likhovtseva (9) 6–4 2–6 7–6; Dragomir (11) d. Kournikova (6) 6–7 6–3 6–3; Coetzer (8) d. Dementieva (15) 6–2 6–4; Sanchez-Vicario (4) d. Schnyder (13) 7–5 6–1; Nejedly d. Raymond (12) 6–2 6–3; Martinez (2) d. Labat 6–3 6–0.
Quarter-finals: Pierce (1) d. Dokic 6–3 6–1; Seles (3) d. Dragomir (11) 6–1 6–1; Sanchez-Vicario (4) d. Coetzer (8) 7–6 3–6 6–3; Martinez (2) d. Nejedly 6–2 6–1.
Semi-finals: Pierce (1) d. Seles (3) 6–1 6–1; Sanchez-Vicario (4) d. Martinez (2) 7–5 7–5.
Final: Pierce (1) d. Sanchez-Vicario (4) 6–1 6–0.
WOMEN'S DOUBLES – Final: Ruano-Pascual/Suarez (8) d. Martinez/Tarabini (7) 7–5 6–3.

BETTY BARCLAY CUP ($535,000)
HAMBURG, GERMANY, 2–7 MAY
WOMEN'S SINGLES – 1st Round: M. Hingis (1) bye; S. Plischke d. S. Noorlander (LL) 6–4 4–6 6–1; S. Pitkowski d. A. Hopmans (Q) 6–0 7–5; A. Kournikova (6) d. A. Smashnova 6–3 6–2; C. Martinez (3) bye; L. Bacheva (Q) d. P. Nola (Q) 6–3 6–3; S. Appelmans d. M. Diaz Oliva (Q) 6–3 7–6; A. Huber (7) d. D. Chladkova 6–3 4–6 6–0; T. Panova d. B. Schett (5) 6–3 1–0 ret; A. Glass (WC) d. A. Kremer 6–2 1–6 6–4; M. Serna (LL) d. P. Schnyder 6–4 1–6 7–6; A. Sanchez-Vicario (4) bye; A. Coetzer (WC) (8) d. R. Dragomir 6–0 6–4; A. Sidot d. M. Weingartner (WC) 5–7 6–2 7–6; I. Spirlea d. N. Zvereva 6–2 6–3; V. Williams (2) bye.
2nd round: Hingis (1) d. Plischke 6–4 6–1; Kournikova (6) d. Pitkowski 6–3 6–0; Martinez (3) d. Bacheva (Q) 6–4 5–7 6–4; Huber (7) d. Appelmans 6–1 6–3; Glass (WC) d. Panova 7–6 6–3; Sanchez-Vicario (4) d. Serna (LL) 6–3 7–6; Coetzer (WC) (8) d. Sidot 6–2 6–4; V. Williams (2) d. Spirlea 6–7 6–2 6–2.
Quarter-finals: Hingis (1) d. Kournikova (6) 3–6 6–2 6–4; Huber (7) d. Martinez (3) 6–7 7–6 6–2; Sanchez-Vicario (4) d. Glass (WC) 6–3 6–3; Coetzer (WC) (8) d. V. Williams (2) 6–3 6–4.
Semi-finals: Hingis (1) d. Huber (7) 6–3 6–2; Sanchez-Vicario (4) d. Coetzer (WC) (8) 6–3 4–6 7–6.
Final: Hingis (1) d. Sanchez-Vicario (4) 6–3 6–3.
WOMEN'S DOUBLES – Final: Kournikova/Zvereva (1) d. Arendt/Bollegraf 6–7 6–2 6–4.

GERMAN OPEN ($1,080,000)
BERLIN, 8–14 MAY
WOMEN'S SINGLES – 1st Round: M. Hingis (1) bye; E. Gagliardi d. A. Smashnova 7–6 6–4; A. Stevenson d. T. Panova 6–2 7–6; S. Talaja (12) d. A. Sidot 6–1 6–2; R. Dragomir (13) d. S. Pitkowski 7–5 7–5; D.

Chladkova d. S. Kleinova (Q) 6–2 6–1; C. Morariu d. A. Glass (WC) 6–1 6–0; S. Testud (5) bye; C. Martinez (3) bye; S. Plischke d. M. Muller (WC) 6–3 4–6 6–3; P. Suarez d. N. Llagostera (Q) 6–2 6–0; A. Mauresmo (9) d. P. Nola (Q) 6–3 6–1; C. Rubin (15) d. B. Rittner (WC) 6–1 6–4; M. Tu (Q) d. K. Habsudova 6–2 6–0; G. Leon Garcia d. F. Zuluaga 7–5 6–0; A. Kournikova (7) bye; A. Huber (8) bye; M. Montolio d. N. Ostrovskaya (Q) 6–3 6–3; M. Serna d. K. Srebotnik 7–5 7–6; C. Cristea (LL) d. A. Sugiyama (11) 7–5 3–6 6–1; A. Coetzer (10) d. T. Poutchek (Q) 6–1 6–0; A. Kremer d. M. Lucic 7–6 6–3; L. Cervanova (Q) d. A. Cocheteux 6–1 6–1; J. Halard-Decugis (4) bye; A. Sanchez-Vicario (6) bye; E. Dementieva d. C. Black 2–6 7–6 6–2; K. Hrdlickova d. M. Maleeva 4–6 6–4 6–4; R. Kuti Kis d. P. Schnyder (16) 6–3 6–4; S. Appelmans (14) d. G. Casoni (LL) 6–2 6–4; B. Lamade (Q) d. I. Spirlea 6–1 6–3; J. Kruger d. N. Zvereva 6–1 6–1; N. Tauziat (2) bye.
2nd round: Hingis (1) d. Gagliardi 6–2 6–2; Talaja (12) d. Stevenson 6–1 6–3; Chladkova d. Dragomir (13) 6–7 6–3 6–4; Testud (5) d. Morariu 6–1 7–6; Martinez (3) d. Plischke 6–0 ret; Suarez d. Mauresmo (9) 4–6 6–3 6–4; Rubin (15) d. Tu (Q) 6–3 6–1; Leon Garcia d. Kournikova (7) 6–4 4–6 6–4; Huber (8) d. Montolio 7–6 6–1; Serna d. Cristea (LL) 6–2 6–1; Coetzer (10) d. Kremer 6–3 7–6; Halard-Decugis (4) d. Cervanova (Q) 6–1 6–1; Dementieva d. Sanchez-Vicario (6) 6–4 5–7 6–2; Hrdlickova d. Kuti Kis 7–6 6–2; Lamade (Q) d. Appelmans (14) 6–3 6–4; Kruger d. Tauziat (2) 6–2 6–0.
3rd round: Hingis (1) d. Talaja (12) 7–6 6–2; Testud (5) d. Chladkova 7–6 6–2; Martinez (3) d. Suarez 6–4 6–3; Leon Garcia d. Rubin (15) 6–1 6–7 6–3; Huber (8) d. Serna 6–2 6–7 6–4; Coetzer (10) d. Halard-Decugis (4) 6–2 6–2; Dementieva d. Hrdlickova 6–2 6–1; Kruger d. Lamade (Q) 6–0 6–3.
Quarter-finals: Hingis (1) d. Testud (5) 7–5 5–7 6–2; Martinez (3) d. Leon Garcia 6–4 6–2; Coetzer (10) d. Huber (8) 6–4 6–4; Kruger d. Dementieva 2–6 6–3 7–6.
Semi-finals: Martinez (3) d. Hingis (1) 7–5 6–4; Coetzer (10) d. Kruger 6–2 6–4.
Final: Martinez (3) d. Coetzer (10) 6–1 6–2.
WOMEN'S DOUBLES – Final: Martinez/Sanchez-Vicario (6) d. Coetzer/Morariu (4) 3–6 6–2 7–6.

ITALIAN OPEN ($1,080,000)
ROME, 15–21 MAY
WOMEN'S SINGLES – 1st Round: L. Davenport (1) bye; E. Dementieva d. L. Osterloh (Q) 7–6 6–1; G. Casoni (WC) d. M. Drake (Q) 3–6 7–5 6–4; D. Van Roost (15) d. I. Spirlea 6–2 6–3; K. Brandi d. E. Likhovtseva (11) 6–2 6–1; R. Grande d. M. Lucic 6–4 6–0; C. Morariu d. C. Cristea (Q) 6–3 3–6 7–5; S. Testud (8) bye; V. Williams (3) bye; C. Rubin d. M. Serna 6–0 6–2; T. Panova d. A. Stevenson 6–0 6–2; J. Dokic d. N. Dechy (14) 6–1 4–6 6–3; A. Sidot d. J. Capriati (10) 6–3 7–5; L. Raymond d. S. Farina 6–2 6–4; M. Maleeva d. S. Pitkowski 6–4 6–4; M. Seles (5) bye; A. Sanchez-Vicario (6) bye; P. Nola (Q) d. F. Schiavone (WC) 7–5 3–6 6–2; D. Chladkova d. P. Schnyder 6–4 4–6 6–4; A. Sugiyama (13) d. J. Kruger 6–2 6–3; A. Mauresmo (12) d. G. Leon Garcia 6–1 6–3; K. Hrdlickova d. T. Pisnik (LL) 6–2 6–2; M. Weingartner (LL) d. L. Krasnoroutskaya (Q) 6–2 2–6 6–1; M. Pierce (4) bye; J. Halard-Decugis (7) bye; R. Dragomir d. C. Black 1–6 6–3 6–1; E. Martincova (Q) d. A. Fusai (Q) 6–2 6–3; F. Zuluaga (Q) d. S. Talaja (16) 6–2 6–3; A. Huber (9) d. N. Zvereva 6–4 7–5; M. Grzybowska d. E. Gagliardi 4–6 6–2 7–6; T. Garbin (WC) d. N. Pratt 7–6 6–1; N. Tauziat (2) bye.
2nd round: Davenport (1) d. Dementieva 6–3 6–2; Casoni (WC) d. Van Roost (15) 7–6 6–0; Grande d. Brandi 6–4 7–5; Morariu d. Testud (8) 7–5 4–6 6–3; V. Williams (3) d. Rubin 6–1 6–2; Dokic d. Panova 6–3 6–1; Sidot d. Raymond 6–4 3–6 6–3; Seles (5) d. Maleeva 7–5 6–1; Sanchez-Vicario (6) d. Nola (Q) 6–3 6–1; Chladkova d. Sugiyama (13) 4–6 6–3 7–6; Mauresmo (12) d. Hrdlickova 6–0 6–2; Pierce (4) d. Weingartner (LL) 7–5 6–3; Halard-Decugis (7) d. Dragomir 6–4 6–0; Zuluaga (Q) d. Martincova (Q) 6–0 6–7 6–3; Grzybowska d. Huber (9) 6–4 6–1; Tauziat (2) d. Garbin (WC) 5–7 6–2 6–4.
3rd round: Casoni (WC) d. Davenport (1) w/o; Morariu d. Grande 6–1 6–4; Dokic d. V. Williams (3) 6–1 6–2; Seles (5) d. Sidot 3–6 6–1 6–1; Sanchez-Vicario (6) d. Chladkova 6–1 6–4; Mauresmo (12) d. Pierce (4) 6–3 6–4; Zuluaga (Q) d. Halard-Decugis (7) 6–3 4–6 6–2; Tauziat (2) d. Grzybowska 6–3 3–6 7–6.
Quarter-finals: Morariu d. Casoni (WC) 3–6 6–4 7–5; Seles (5) d. Dokic 6–1 3–6 6–3; Mauresmo (12) d. Sanchez-Vicario (6) 6–1 5–7 6–4; Zuluaga (Q) d. Tauziat (2) 3–6 6–0 6–4.
Semi-finals: Seles (5) d. Morariu 6–3 6–1; Mauresmo (12) d. Zuluaga (Q) 6–1 6–2.
Final: Seles (5) d. Mauresmo (12) 6–2 7–6.
WOMEN'S DOUBLES – Final: Raymond/Stubbs (2) d. Sanchez-Vicario/Serna 6–3 4–6 6–3.

DIRECT LINE INTERNATIONAL TENNIS CHAMPIONSHIPS ($535,000)
EASTBOURNE, SUSSEX, 19–24 JUNE
WOMEN'S SINGLES – 1st Round: L. Davenport (1) bye; J. Kandarr (Q) d. A. Sidot 6–2 6–2; E. Likhovtseva d. J. Pullin (WC) 7–6 7–5; D. Van Roost (5) d. T. Pisnik (LL) 6–4 7–6; A. Coetzer (3) bye; A. Smashnova d. L. Latimer (WC) 6–1 6–3; A. Kremer d. A. Stevenson 6–7 6–1 6–4; S. Talaja d. A. Sugiyama (7) 6–3 6–2; C. Rubin (8) d. S. Pitkowski 7–5 6–3; T. Panova (Q) d. S. Plischke 6–4 1–6 6–3; N. Zvereva d. L. Raymond 7–5 6–3; A. Kournikova (4) bye; J. Halard-Decugis (WC) d. M. Vento (Q) 6–3 6–1; N. Dechy d. C. Morariu 7–6 5–7 6–1; A. Myskina (Q) d. A. Frazier 6–4 7–6; N. Tauziat (2) bye.
2nd round: Davenport (1) d. Kandarr (Q) 6–3 3–6 6–4; Van Roost (5) d. Likhovtseva 6–2 6–4; Coetzer (3) d. Smashnova 6–2 6–0; Kremer d. Talaja 2–6 6–2; Rubin (8) d. Panova (Q) 6–1 7–5; Kournikova (4) d. Zvereva 6–3 6–3; Halard-Decugis (WC) (6) d. Dechy 6–2 6–4; Tauziat (2) d. Myskina (Q) 6–4 6–2.
Quarter finals: Van Roost (5) d. Davenport (1) 4–6 6–4 6–4; Kremer d. Coetzer (3) 3–6 6–0 6–4; Rubin (8) d. Kournikova (4) 7–5 0–6 6–3; Halard-Decugis (WC) (6) d. Tauziat (2) 6–4 6–4.

Semi-finals: Van Roost (5) d. Kremer 4–6 7–5 6–1; Halard-Decugis (WC) (6) d. Rubin (8) 6–2 3–6 6–4.
Final: Halard-Decugis (WC) (6) d. Van Roost (5) 7–6 6–4.
WOMEN'S DOUBLES – Final: Sugiyama/Tauziat (4) d. Raymond/Stubbs (1) 2–6 6–3 7–6.

BANK OF THE WEST CLASSIC ($535,000)
STANFORD, CA, 24–30 JULY
WOMEN'S SINGLES – 1st Round: L. Davenport (1) bye; N. Pratt d. M. Irvin (WC) 6–3 6–7 6–4; M.
Washington (Q) d. A. Jidkova (LL) 7–6 6–2; C. Rubin (8) d. F. Zuluaga 6–4 6–2; M. Seles (4) bye; M.
Shaughnessy d. K. Clijsters 3–6 7–6 6–3; C. Black d. E. De Lone 6–1 6–4; A. Coetzer (6) d. J. Lee (Q) 6–3 6–3;
A. Kournikova (WC) (9) d. A. Miller 6–1 6–2; J. Nejedly d. P. Nola (Q) 2–6 6–1 6–0; T. Garbin d. R. De Los Rios
6–0 6–0; S. Testud (5) bye; A. Frazier (10) d. L. Osterloh (WC) 6–3 6–3; K. Brandi d. R. Kuti Kis 6–0 6–3; T.
Panova d. M. Drake (Q) 5–7 6–4 7–6; V. Williams (2) bye.
2nd round: Davenport (1) d. Pratt 6–2 6–4; Rubin (8) d. Washington (Q) 6–4 6–2; Seles (4) d. Shaughnessy
7–5 6–3; Black d. Coetzer (6) 6–2 6–1; Kournikova (WC) (9) d. Nejedly 6–1 6–0; Testud (5) d. Garbin 6–2 6–7
7–5; Frazier (10) d. Brandi 7–6 6–0; V. Williams (2) d. Panova 6–2 6–2.
Quarter-finals: Davenport (1) d. Rubin (8) 6–3 3–6 6–1; Seles (4) d. Black 6–1 6–2; Kournikova (WC) (9) d.
Testud (5) 6–3 6–2; V. Williams (2) d. Frazier (10) 6–7 6–4 7–6.
Semi-finals: Davenport (1) d. Seles (4) 7–5 7–6; V. Williams (2) d. Kournikova (WC) (9) 6–4 7–5.
Final: V. Williams (2) d. Davenport (1) 6–1 6–4.
WOMEN'S DOUBLES – Final: Rubin/Testud (1) d. Black/Frazier (4) 6–4 6–4.

ACURA CLASSIC ($535,000)
SAN DIEGO, CA, 31 JULY–6 AUGUST
WOMEN'S SINGLES – 1st Round: M. Hingis (1) bye; D. Van Roost d. A. Sugiyama 6–2 7–6; N. Dechy d. A.
Sidot 4–6 6–4 6–2; A. Frazier d. A. Huber (7) 6–0 7–6; V. Williams (3) bye; A. Coetzer d. L. Raymond 4–6 7–5
6–1; N. Pratt (Q) d. F. Zuluaga (WC) 6–2 4–6 6–2; C. Martinez (5) d. K. Clijsters (WC) 6–3 6–4; S. Testud (8) d.
C. Rubin 3–6 7–5 6–2; T. Panova (Q) d. B. Schett 4–6 6–4 7–5; M. Tu (Q) d. E. Dementieva 6–2 2–6 6–3; M.
Seles (4) bye; N. Tauziat (6) d. A. Kremer (Q) 6–4 6–3; E. Likhovtseva d. J. Capriati 6–4 6–0; A. Kournikova d.
A. Stevenson (WC) 6–2 6–3; L. Davenport (2) bye.
2nd round: Hingis (1) d. Van Roost 6–2 7–6; Frazier d. Dechy 6–3 3–6 6–1; V. Williams (3) d. Coetzer 6–0
6–4; C. Martinez (5) d. Pratt (Q) 4–6 6–0 6–3; Testud (8) d. Panova (Q) 6–2 6–3; Seles (4) d. Tu (Q) 7–5 7–5;
Tauziat (6) d. Likhovtseva 6–1 6–2; Kournikova d. Davenport (2) 2–6 6–4 7–5.
Quarter-finals: Frazier d. Hingis (1) 6–3 6–3; V. Williams (3) d. C. Martinez (5) 6–3 6–0; Seles (4) d. Testud
(8) 4–6 6–2 7–6; Kournikova d. Tauziat (6) 2–6 6–4 7–5.
Semi-finals: V. Williams (3) d. Frazier 6–2 6–3; Seles (4) d. Kournikova 6–3 7–6.
Final: V. Williams (3) d. Seles (4) 6–0 6–7 6–3.
WOMEN'S DOUBLES – Final: Raymond/Stubbs (1) d. Davenport/Kournikova (2) 4–6 6–3 7–6.

LOS ANGELES OPEN ($535,000)
LOS ANGELES, CA, 7–13 AUGUST
WOMEN'S SINGLES – 1st Round: M. Hingis (1) bye; C. Rubin d. J. Halard-Decugis 6–2 6–1; A. Frazier d. M.
Weingartner (Q) 7–6 6–2; A. Sanchez-Vicario (7) d. B. Schett 6–4 6–1; C. Martinez (4) bye; A. Stevenson (WC)
d. S. Talaja 4–6 6–4 6–2; T. Tanasugarn (Q) d. M. Serna 6–7 6–3 7–5; S. Williams (5) d. R. Dragomir 6–0 6–1;
D. Bedanova (Q) d. N. Tauziat (6) 6–3 6–4; L. Raymond d. M. Lucic (WC) 6–3 6–3; E. Dementieva d. N. Dechy
6–4 4–6 6–4; K. Brandi (LL) bye; S. Testud (8) d. E. Likhovtseva 6–2 6–4; D. Van Roost d. T. Panova (Q) 6–1
6–2; A. Sidot d. A. Sugiyama 6–3 6–4; L. Davenport (2) bye.
2nd round: Hingis (1) d. Rubin 5–7 7–5 6–1; Frazier d. Sanchez-Vicario (7) 6–3 3–6 6–3; C. Martinez (4) d.
Stevenson (WC) 6–4 7–6; S. Williams (5) d. Tanasugarn (Q) 6–2 6–2; Raymond d. Bedanova (Q) 6–4 6–4;
Dementieva d. Brandi (LL) 6–4 6–1; Testud (8) d. Van Roost 6–2 3–6 7–5; Davenport (2) d. Sidot 7–6 6–7 6–2.
Quarter-finals: Hingis (1) d. Frazier 6–2 6–1; S. Williams (5) d. C. Martinez (4) 6–2 4–6 6–2; Dementieva d.
Raymond 2–6 6–1 6–4; Davenport (2) d. Testud (8) 6–4 6–2.
Semi-finals: S. Williams (5) d. Hingis (1) 4–6 6–2 6–3; Davenport (2) d. Dementieva 6–4 6–4.
Final: S. Williams (5) d. Davenport (2) 4–6 6–4 7–5.
WOMEN'S DOUBLES – Final: Callens/Van Roost d. Po/Sidot 6–2 7–5.

DU MAURIER OPEN ($1,080,000)
MONTREAL, 14–20 AUGUST
WOMEN'S SINGLES – 1st Round: M. Hingis (1) bye; N. Petrova (Q) d. K. Brandi 7–6 6–1; J. Nejedly (WC) d.
S. Reeves (Q) 6–3 6–3; K. Hrdlickova d. D. Van Roost (12) 6–4 6–3; C. Rubin (15) d. P. Suarez 6–7 6–2 6–2; T.
Panova d. F. Zuluaga 6–4 6–1; R. Dragomir d. M. Montolio 6–1 7–5; S. Testud (8) bye; C. Martinez (3) bye; A.
Miller d. E. De Lone (Q) 6–4 3–6 6–1; S. Nacuk (Q) d. N. Pratt 7–6 6–7 6–2; J. Halard-Decugis (10) d. A. Sidot
4–6 7–6 6–3; S. Talaja d. B. Schett (14) 6–1 4–6 6–4; N. Dechy d. A. Stevenson 6–3 6–4; A. Kremer d. A.
Myskina 6–4 6–1; N. Tauziat (5) bye; A. Huber (6) bye; S. Pitkowski d. M. Serna 6–2 6–2; G. Leon-Garcia d.
A. Sugiyama 4–6 6–0 6–1; A. Frazier (16) d. E. Dementieva 6–4 6–2; A. Kournikova (11) d. C. Black 6–3 7–6;
S. Appelmans d. J. Dokic 6–7 6–4 7–6, P. Schnyder d. E. Likhovtseva 7–5 6–3; S. Williams (4) bye; A. Sanchez-
Vicario (7) bye; H. Nagyova (Q) d. D. Chladkova 2–6 7–5 6–3; V. Ruano-Pascual (Q) d. V. Webb (WC) 6–4 6–4;

J. Capriati (13) d. T. Garbin 7–6 7–6; A. Coetzer (9) d. T. Tanasugarn 6–2 6–2; M. Maleeva (Q) d. S. Jeyaseelan (WC) 6–1 6–0; J. Henin (Q) d. A. Carlsson 6–2 4–6 6–3; L. Davenport (2) bye.
2nd round: Hingis (1) d. Petrova (Q) 6–1 6–3; Hrdlickova d. Nejedly (WC) 6–3 6–0; Rubin (15) d. Panova 6–2 6–3; Testud (8) d. Dragomir 3–6 7–5 6–2; C. Martinez (3) d. A. Miller 6–0 6–1; Halard-Decugis (10) d. Nacuk (Q) 6–3 7–6; Talaja d. Dechy 7–5 6–4; Kremer d. Tauziat (5) 6–4 6–1; Huber (6) d. Pitkowski 4–6 6–1 6–4; Frazier (16) d. Leon-Garcia 3–6 6–2 6–3; Kournikova (11) d. Appelmans 6–4 6–3; S. Williams (4) d. Schnyder 6–1 6–2; Sanchez-Vicario (7) d. Nagyova (Q) 6–4 6–1; Capriati (13) d. Ruano-Pascual (Q) 3–6 6–1 6–4; Maleeva (Q) d. Coetzer (9) 6–3 6–2; Davenport (2) d. Henin (Q) 3–6 7–6 6–2.
3rd round: Hingis (1) d. Hrdlickova 6–1 6–4; Testud (8) d. Rubin (15) 6–4 6–1; C. Martinez (3) d. Halard-Decugis (10) w/o; Kremer d. Talaja 7–5 6–3; Frazier (16) d. Huber (6) 6–4 3–6 6–4; S. Williams (4) d. Kournikova (11) 6–3 6–2; Sanchez-Vicario (7) d. Capriati (13) 6–4 7–5; Maleeva (Q) d. Davenport (2) 4–3 ret.
Quarter-finals: Hingis (1) d. Testud (8) 6–4 4–6 6–3; C. Martinez (3) d. Kremer 6–2 6–4; S. Williams (4) d. Frazier (16) 6–0 6–1; Sanchez-Vicario (7) d. Maleeva (Q) 6–1 6–4.
Semi-finals: Hingis (1) d. C. Martinez (3) 6–3 6–2; S. Williams (4) d. Sanchez-Vicario (7) 6–2 6–4.
Final: Hingis (1) d. S. Williams (4) 0–6 6–3 3–0 ret.
WOMEN'S DOUBLES – Final: Hingis/Tauziat (2) d. Halard-Decugis/Sugiyama (1) 6–3 3–6 6–4.

PILOT PEN TENNIS ($535,000)
NEW HAVEN, CT, 21–27 AUGUST
WOMEN'S SINGLES – 1st Round: V. Williams (1) bye; E. Likhovtseva d. T. Garbin (Q) 6–1 6–3; E. Dementieva d. J. Dokic 6–4 6–3; P. Schnyder d. J. Halard-Decugis (8) 6–3 7–6; A. Huber (4) bye; A. Sugiyama d. J. Kandarr (Q) 6–4 6–4; J. Henin (Q) d. S. Appelmans 6–2 6–4; A. Coetzer (5) d. K. Habsudova (Q) 7–6 6–4; K. Clijsters d. B. Schett (7) 4–6 7–6 6–2; F. Zuluaga d. M. Tu (Q) 7–5 6–1; M. Shaughnessy (WC) d. R. Dragomir 6–4 6–1; N. Tauziat (3) bye; D. Van Roost (6) d. M. Maleeva (WC) 7–6 6–4; S. Talaja d. A. Sidot 6–2 5–7 6–2; K. Brandi (WC) d. A. Kremer (Q) 7–6 6–1; M. Seles (2) bye.
2nd round: V. Williams (1) d. Likhovtseva 6–3 7–5; Schnyder d. Dementieva 1–6 7–5 6–3; Huber (4) d. Sugiyama 4–6 7–5 6–2; Coetzer (5) d. Henin (Q) 6–2 4–6 6–1; Clijsters d. Zuluaga 6–1 6–1; Tauziat (3) d. Shaughnessy (WC) 6–1 4–6 6–4; Van Roost (6) d. Talaja 6–3 7–5; Seles (2) d. Brandi (WC) 6–2 6–3.
Quarter-finals: V. Williams (1) d. Schnyder 6–4 6–2; Coetzer (5) d. Huber (4) 7–6 6–1; Tauziat (3) d. Clijsters 6–2 6–4; Seles (2) d. Van Roost (6) 6–1 6–2.
Semi-finals: V. Williams (1) d. Coetzer (5) 6–3 6–4; Seles (2) d. Tauziat (3) 2–6 6–2 6–1.
Final: V. Williams (1) d. Seles (2) 6–2 6–4.
WOMEN'S DOUBLES – Final: Halard-Decugis/Sugiyama (2) d. Ruano-Pascual/Suarez (3) 6–4 5–7 6–2.

TOYOTA PRINCESS CUP ($535,000)
TOKYO, 2–8 OCTOBER
WOMEN'S SINGLES – 1st Round: M. Seles (1) bye; M. Vavrinec (Q) d. R. Kuti Kis 6–4 6–2; S. Asagoe (WC) d. Y. Yoshida (Q) 6–2 3–6 6–1; A. Sugiyama (7) d. A. Stevenson (WC) 6–3 6–3; J. Halard-Decugis (4) bye; N. Pratt d. T. Garbin 6–4 6–3; C. Morariu d. J. Kruger (Q) 7–6 2–6 6–4; K. Brandi (6) d. S. Plischke 6–3 6–4; A. Frazier (5) d. F. Zuluaga 6–2 6–1; M. Montolio d. L. Osterloh 7–5 5–7 7–6; D. Bedanova (Q) d. A. Smashnova 6–4 6–1; A. Mauresmo (3) bye; J. Dokic (8) d. M. Shaughnessy 6–4 6–2; L. Krasnoroutskaya (WC) d. R. Grande 6–3 6–4; T. Tanasugarn d. P. Suarez 6–3 7–6; S. Williams (2) bye.
2nd round: Seles (1) d. Vavrinec (Q) 6–4 6–4; Asagoe (WC) d. Sugiyama (7) 6–3 7–5; Halard-Decugis (4) d. Pratt 6–1 6–3; Brandi (6) d. Morariu 2–6 7–5 6–2; Frazier (5) d. Montolio 6–0 6–1; Bedanova (Q) d. Mauresmo (3) 5–7 6–3 6–3; Dokic (8) d. Krasnoroutskaya (WC) 6–4 7–6; S. Williams (2) d. Tanasugarn 6–1 6–4.
Quarter-finals: Seles (1) d. Asagoe (WC) 6–3 6–4; Halard-Decugis (4) d. Brandi (6) 1–6 6–1 6–4; Bedanova (Q) d. Frazier (5) 5–7 7–6 6–2; S. Williams (2) d. Dokic (8) 6–3 6–4.
Semi-finals: Halard-Decugis (4) d. Seles (1) 6–4 4–3 ret; S. Williams (2) d. Bedanova (Q) 6–1 6–4.
Final: S. Williams (2) d. Halard-Decugis (4) 7–5 6–1.
WOMEN'S DOUBLES – Final: Halard-Decugis/Sugiyama (1) d. Miyagi/Suarez (2) 6–0 6–2.

PORSCHE TENNIS GRAND PRIX ($535,000)
FILDERSTADT, STUTTGART, 2–8 OCTOBER
WOMEN'S SINGLES – 1st Round: M. Hingis (1) bye; J. Henin (Q) d. G. Leon-Garcia 6–4 6–2; A. Carlsson (Q) d. M. Serna 6–3 6–3; D. Van Roost (8) d. A. Kremer 7–5 7–6; A. Sanchez-Vicario (4) bye; C. Black d. B. Schett 7–5 6–1; P. Schnyder d. R. Dragomir 6–3 6–4; A. Coetzer (5) d. S. Talaja 6–4 6–0; C. Rubin (7) d. J. Capriati 6–0 6–7 6–2; A. Sidot d. D. Chladkova (Q) 4–6 6–3 6–4; B. Rittner (WC) d. E. Likhovtseva 6–3 7–5; N. Tauziat (3) bye; K. Clijsters (WC) d. A. Kournikova (6) 6–4 6–3; J. Kandarr (WC) d. T. Panova (Q) 6–3 6–2; M. Maleeva d. S. Appelmans 6–4 5–7 7–5; C. Martinez (2) bye.
2nd round: Hingis (1) d. Henin (Q) 6–3 3–0 ret; Van Roost (8) d. Carlsson (Q) 6–3 6–1; Sanchez-Vicario (4) d. Black 6–2 3–6 6–4; Coetzer (5) d. Schnyder 7–5 6–4; Sidot d. Rubin (7) 7–5 1–6 6–4; Tauziat (3) d. Rittner (WC) 3–6 6–2; Clijsters (WC) d. Kandarr (WC) 7–6 6–3; C. Martinez (2) d. Maleeva 4–6 6–3 7–5.
Quarter-finals: Hingis (1) d. Van Roost (8) 6–2 6–1; Sanchez-Vicario (4) d. Coetzer (5) 6–2 2–6 6–3; Tauziat (3) d. Sidot 7–5 6–2; Clijsters (WC) d. C. Martinez (2) 7–5 7–5.
Semi-finals: Hingis (1) d. Sanchez-Vicario (4) 6–1 6–0; Clijsters (WC) d. Tauziat (3) 3–6 6–4 6–1.
Final: Hingis (1) d. Clijsters (WC) 6–0 6–3.
WOMEN'S DOUBLES – Final: Hingis/Kournikova (1) d. Sanchez-Vicario/Schett (4) 6–4 6–2.

SWISSCOM CHALLENGE ($1,080,000)

ZURICH, 9–15 OCTOBER

WOMEN'S SINGLES – 1st Round: M. Hingis (1) bye; J. Dokic d. E. Gagliardi (WC) 6–3 6–0; A. Myskina (Q) d. P. Schnyder 6–4 2–6 6–1; E. Dementieva (8) d. R. Dragomir 6–3 6–4; A. Kournikova (4) bye; T. Panova d. G. Leon-Garcia 6–1 6–3; A. Sidot d. A. Glass (Q) 6–1 6–7 6–4; J. Capriati (6) d. L. Krasnoroutskaya (WC) 5–7 6–3 7–6; A. Coetzer (5) d. M. Serna 6–4 6–1; B. Schett d. E. Likhovtseva 6–0 6–1; M. Maleeva (WC) d. D. Van Roost 6–7 6–2 7–6; N. Tauziat (3) bye; Rubin (7) d. S. Talaja 2–6 6–1 6–2; J. Kandarr (Q) d. A. Kremer 6–4 6–1; S. Appelmans d. A. Sugiyama 6–2 4–6 6–2; L. Davenport (2) bye.
2nd round: Hingis (1) d. Dokic 6–3 6–2; Myskina (Q) d. Dementieva (8) 6–4 2–6 6–1; Kournikova (4) d. Panova 6–3 6–3; Capriati (6) d. Sidot 6–3 6–1; Schett d. Coetzer (5) 7–6 3–6 6–4; Tauziat (3) d. Maleeva (WC) 6–4 6–0; Rubin (7) d. Kandarr (Q) 6–2 2–0 ret; Davenport (2) d. Appelmans 6–2 6–1.
Quarter-finals: Hingis (1) d. Myskina (Q) 6–0 6–4; Capriati (6) d. Kournikova (4) 7–6 6–4; Schett d. Tauziat (3) 3–6 6–3 6–3; Davenport (2) d. Rubin (7) 6–2 6–4.
Semi-finals: Hingis (1) d. Capriati (6) 6–3 6–2; Davenport (2) d. Schett 6–2 6–1.
Final: Hingis (1) d. Davenport (2) 6–4 4–6 7–5.
WOMEN'S DOUBLES – Final: Hingis/Kournikova (2) d. Po/Sidot 6–3 6–4.

LADIES KREMLIN CUP ($1,080,000)

MOSCOW, 23–29 OCTOBER

WOMEN'S SINGLES – 1st Round: M. Hingis (1) bye; K. Hrdlickova d. J. Husarova (Q) 4–6 6–2 6–3; S. Farina-Elia d. S. Talaja 6–1 6–2; E. Dementieva (7) d. R. Dragomir 6–7 7–5 6–1; A. Sanchez-Vicario (3) bye; M. Maleeva d. L. Krasnoroutskaya (WC) 4–6 6–1 6–3; L. Raymond d. T. Poutchek (Q) 7–6 6–3; A. Mauresmo (5) d. J. Dokic 6–1 6–4; T. Panova d. J. Halard-Decugis (6) 6–4 7–6; P. Suarez d. G. Fokina (Q) 7–5 2–6 6–3; V. Zvonareva (WC) d. E. Bovina (Q) 6–7 7–5 6–2; A. Kournikova (4) bye; B. Schett (8) d. E. Likhovtseva 6–4 6–1; P. Schnyder d. M. Serna 7–6 1–6 6–3; A. Sugiyama d. S. Appelmans 6–3 7–6; N. Tauziat (2) bye.
2nd round: Hingis (1) d. Hrdlickova 6–0 6–1; Dementieva (7) d. Farina-Elia 2–6 6–4 6–4; Maleeva d. Sanchez-Vicario (3) 6–3 6–2; Mauresmo (5) d. Raymond 6–2 6–4; Panova d. Suarez 6–2 4–6 6–1; Kournikova (4) d. Zvonareva (WC) 7–6 6–4; Schett (8) d. Schnyder 6–4 6–3; Tauziat (2) d. Sugiyama 6–3 7–5.
Quarter-finals: Hingis (1) d. Dementieva (7) 6–0 6–7 7–5; Mauresmo (5) d. Maleeva 4–6 7–6 6–3; Kournikova (4) d. Panova 6–4 6–1; Tauziat (2) d. Schett (8) 7–6 6–2.
Semi-finals: Hingis (1) d. Mauresmo (5) 7–5 6–3; Kournikova (4) d. Tauziat (2) 6–2 6–1.
Final: Hingis (1) d. Kournikova (4) 6–3 6–1.
WOMEN'S DOUBLES – Final: Halard-Decugis/Sugiyama (1) d. Hingis/Kournikova (2) 4–6 6–4 7–6.

SPARKASSEN CUP INTERNATIONAL GRAND PRIX ($535,000)

LEIPZIG, 30 OCTOBER–5 NOVEMBER

WOMEN'S SINGLES – 1st Round: N. Tauziat (1) bye; T. Panova d. R. Dragomir 6–4 6–2; D. Chladkova d. A. Smashnova 6–1 6–2; B. Schett (6) d. S. Nacuk (Q) 6–4 5–7 6–4; E. Dementieva (4) bye; I. Majoli (WC) d. S. Appelmans 7–5 1–6 6–3; L. Raymond d. G. Leon Garcia 6–1 6–4; E. Likhovtseva (7) d. J. Husarova (Q) 4–6 6–3 6–3; M. Maleeva (5) d. J. Kandarr (WC) 6–2 6–2; K. Hrdlickova d. A. Sidot 6–7 6–2 7–5; S. Farina-Elia d. M. Serna 6–3 6–2; A. Kournikova (3) bye; J. Dokic (8) d. A. Glass (Q) 6–2 6–2; B. Rittner (WC) d. E. Fauth (Q) 6–3 7–5; K. Clijsters d. A. Sugiyama 6–0 6–2; A. Sanchez-Vicario (2) bye.
2nd round: Tauziat (1) d. Panova 4–6 6–4 7–5; Schett (6) d. Chladkova 6–3 6–2; Dementieva (4) d. Majoli (WC) 6–2 6–3; Likhovtseva (7) d. Raymond 6–3 6–3; Maleeva (5) d. Hrdlickova 6–4 6–0; Kournikova (3) d. Farina-Elia 6–3 6–1; Dokic (8) d. Rittner (WC) 7–6 6–2; Clijsters d. Sanchez-Vicario (2) 7–5 6–1.
Quarter-finals: Tauziat (1) d. Schett (6) 4–6 6–0 7–6; Likhovtseva (7) d. Dementieva (4) 6–3 6–0; Kournikova (3) d. Maleeva (5) 6–4 7–5; Clijsters d. Dokic (8) 4–6 6–2 7–6.
Semi-finals: Likhovtseva (7) d. Tauziat (1) 6–1 6–4; Clijsters d. Kournikova (3) 6–2 6–3.
Final: Clijsters d. Likhovtseva (7) 7–6 4–6 6–4.
WOMEN'S DOUBLES – Final: Sanchez-Vicario/Sidot (2) d. Clijsters/Courtois 6–7 7–5 6–3.

ADVANTA CHAMPIONSHIPS ($535,000)

PHILADELPHIA, PA, 6–12 NOVEMBER

WOMEN'S SINGLES – 1st Round: M. Hingis (1) bye; E. Bovina (WC) d. K. Schlukebir (LL) 6–2 6–2; N. Pratt d. A. Sugiyama 6–2 7–5; A. Kournikova (6) d. M. Washington (Q) 6–2 6–0; N. Tauziat (4) bye; D. Hantuchova (WC) d. A. Stevenson (WC) 6–3 ret; J. Halard-Decugis d. G. Arn (Q) 6–1 6–1; J. Capriati (8) d. M. Shaughnessy 3–6 7–5 6–4; C. Rubin (9) d. A. Frazier 2–6 6–2 6–3; H. Parkinson (LL) d. K. Brandi 6–1 6–3; R. Kolbovic (LL) d. M. Mikaelian (Q) 6–4 7–5; C. Martinez (3) bye; A. Coetzer (7) d. E. De Lone (LL) 6–2 6–3; J. Hopkins (LL) d. L. Osterloh 6–1 4–6 6–1; L. Raymond d. V. Henke (Q) 6–4 6–4; L. Davenport (2) bye.
2nd round: Hingis (1) d. Bovina (WC) 6–4 6–1; Kournikova (6) d. Pratt 6–0 6–2; Tauziat (4) d. Hantuchova (WC) 7–5 6–4; Halard-Decugis d. Capriati (8) 6–4 6–1; Parkinson (LL) d. Rubin (9) w/o; C. Martinez (3) d. Kolbovic (LL) 6–1 6–3; Coetzer (7) d. Hopkins (LL) 6–3 6–0; Davenport (2) d. Raymond 6–3 6–3.
Quarter-finals: Hingis (1) d. Kournikova (6) 6–4 6–0; Tauziat (4) d. Halard-Decugis 6–4 6–4; C. Martinez (3) d. Parkinson (LL) 6–2 6–0; Davenport (2) d. Coetzer (7) 6–1 1–6 6–1.
Semi-finals: Hingis (1) d. Tauziat (4) 6–1 6–2; Davenport (2) d. C. Martinez (3) 6–0 6–1.
Final: Davenport (2) d. Hingis (1) 7–6 6–4.
WOMEN'S DOUBLES – Final: Hingis/Kournikova (2) d. Raymond/Stubbs (3) 6–2 7–5.

World Series
Tiers III and IV Tournaments

THALGO AUSTRALIAN WOMEN'S HARDCOURT CHAMPIONSHIPS ($170,000)
GOLD COAST, QLD, 3–8 JANUARY
WOMEN'S SINGLES – Quarter-finals: N. Dechy (6) d. M. Maleeva 6–4 6–7 7–6; C. Martinez (3) d. S. Appelmans (8) 7–6 4–6 6–4; A. Sanchez-Vicario (4) d. P. Schnyder (5) 2–6 7–6 6–3; S. Talaja (7) d. A. Kournikova (2) 4–6 6–4 6–2.
Semi-finals: Martinez (3) d. Dechy (6) 6–3 6–1; Talaja (7) d. Sanchez-Vicario (4) 6–1 3–6 6–0.
Final: Talaja (7) d. Martinez (3) 6–0 0–6 6–4.
WOMEN'S DOUBLES – Final: Halard-Decugis/Kournikova (1) d. Appelmans/Grande 6–3 6–0.

ASB BANK CLASSIC ($110,000)
AUCKLAND, 3–8 JANUARY
WOMEN'S SINGLES – Quarter-finals: C. Black (6) d. E. Likhovtseva (1) 6–3 7–5; A. Hopmans d. M. Vavrinec 7–6 6–2; M. Shaughnessy d. A. Smashnova (5) 6–4 6–2; A. Kremer (2) d. P. Suarez 6–3 5–7 6–4.
Semi-finals: Black (6) d. Hopmans 6–3 6–3; Kremer (2) d. Shaughnessy 6–3 6–3.
Final: Kremer (2) d. Black (6) 6–4 6–4.
WOMEN'S DOUBLES – Final: Black/Fusai (1) d. Schwartz/Wartusch 3–6 6–3 6–4.

ANZ TASMANIAN INTERNATIONAL ($110,000)
HOBART, 9–15 JANUARY
WOMEN'S SINGLES – Quarter-finals: A. Frazier (1) d. C. Cristea (Q) 6–3 5–7 6–3; C. Rubin (4) d. J. Henin (Q) 7–5 0–6 6–2; M. Vento (Q) d. M. Drake 6–3 6–2; K. Clijsters d. S. Pitkowski (8) 7–5 6–1.
Semi-finals: Rubin (4) d. Frazier (1) 6–2 6–1; Clijsters d. Vento (Q) 6–2 6–3.
Final: Clijsters d. Rubin (4) 2–6 6–2 6–2.
WOMEN'S DOUBLES – Final: Grande/Loit (4) d. Clijsters/Molik 6–2 2–6 6–3.

COPA COLSANITAS ($140,000)
BOGOTA, 7–13 FEBRUARY
WOMEN'S SINGLES – Quarter-finals: S. Plischke (1) d. O. Barabanschikova (7) 6–2 6–3; P. Wartusch d. P. Suarez (6) 6–4 6–2; R. Kuti Kis d. N. Llagostera (Q) 6–3 6–0; T. Garbin d. M. Shaughnessy 6–3 6–7 6–1.
Semi-finals: Wartusch d. Plischke (1) 6–4 6–3; Garbin d. Kuti Kis 2–6 6–1 6–2.
Final: Wartusch d. Garbin 4–6 6–1 6–4.
WOMEN'S DOUBLES – Final: Montalvo/Suarez (1) d. Kuti Kis/Mandula 6–4 6–2.

BRAZIL LADIES OPEN ($140,000)
SAO PAULO, 14–20 FEBRUARY
WOMEN'S SINGLES – Quarter-finals: P. Suarez (6) d. S. Plischke (1) 6–2 4–6 6–4; J. Kruger d. C. Torrens-Valero (3) 6–4 6–7 6–3; R. Kuti Kis (9) d. A. Barna 6–1 2–6 6–1; E. Gagliardi (5) d. P. Wartusch 6–3 7–5.
Semi-finals: Suarez (6) d. Kruger 6–2 6–3; Kuti Kis (9) d. Gagliardi (5) 6–2 6–2.
Final: Kuti Kis (9) d. Suarez (6) 4–6 6–4 7–5.
WOMEN'S DOUBLES – Final: Montalvo/Suarez (1) d. Husarova/Labat (2) 5–7 6–4 6–3.

IGA SUPERTHRIFT TENNIS CLASSIC ($170,000)
OKLAHOMA CITY, OK, 21–27 FEBRUARY
WOMEN'S SINGLES – Quarter-finals: R. Grande d. T. Panova 4–6 6–3 6–4; N. Dechy (5) d. A. Frazier (4) 6–4 7–5; A. Coetzer (3) d. L. Raymond (6) 2–6 6–4 7–6; M. Seles (2) d. S. Pitkowski (8) 6–0 6–0.
Semi-finals: Dechy (5) d. Grande 6–4 6–2; Seles (2) d. Coetzer (3) 6–1 6–2.
Final: Seles (2) d. Dechy (5) 6–1 7–6.
WOMEN'S DOUBLES – Final: Morariu/Po (1) d. Tanasugarn/Tatarkova 6–4 4–6 6–2.

ESTORIL OPEN ($140,000)
ESTORIL, 10–16 APRIL
WOMEN'S SINGLES – Quarter-finals: A. Huber (1) d. C. Torrens-Valero (6) 6–3 7–6; T. Garbin d. R. Kuti Kis (7) 7–6 6–4; S. Farina (5) d. M. Vavrinec 6–3 6–2; N. Dechy (2) d. M. Montolio (8) 6–3 6–4.
Semi-finals: Huber (1) d. Garbin 6–3 6–2; Dechy (2) d. Farina (5) 6–2 6–4.
Final: Huber (1) d. Dechy (2) 6–2 1–6 7–5.
WOMEN'S DOUBLES – Final: Krizan/Srebotnik (1) d. Hopmans/Torrens-Valero 6–0 7–6

WESTEL 900 BUDAPEST OPEN ($110,000)
BUDAPEST, 17–23 APRIL
WOMEN'S SINGLES – Quarter-finals: K. Boogert (7) d. K. Marosi (Q) 3–6 6–4 6–4; M. Montolio (4) d. M. Vavrinec 6–1 6–1; T. Garbin d. O. Barabanschikova 4–6 6–0 6–1; S. Pitkowski (2) d. M. Sanchez Lorenzo 7–5 6–1.
Semi-finals: Boogert (7) d. Montolio (4) 6–4 6–2; Garbin d. Pitkowski (2) 6–3 3–0 ret.
Final: Garbin d. Boogert (7) 6–2 7–6.
WOMEN'S DOUBLES – Final: Bacheva/Torrens-Valero d. Kostanic/Nacuk 6–0 6–2.

CROATIAN BOL LADIES OPEN ($170,000)
BOL, 1–7 MAY
WOMEN'S SINGLES – Quarter-finals: G. Leon Garcia d. P. Suarez (7) 6–7 7–5 7–6; A. Mauresmo (3) d. C. Morariu (5) 4–6 7–5 6–3; T. Pisnik d. M. Montolio 6–3 6–2; M. Sanchez Lorenzo d. S. Testud (2) 6–2 6–2.
Semi-finals: Mauresmo (3) d. Leon Garcia 6–4 7–5; Pisnik d. Sanchez Lorenzo 7–6 6–4.
Final: Pisnik d. Mauresmo (3) 7–6 7–6.
WOMEN'S DOUBLES – Final: Halard-Decugis/Morariu (1) d. Krizan/Srebotnik (2) 6–2 6–2.

WARSAW CUP BY HEROS ($110,000)
WARSAW, 8–14 MAY
WOMEN'S SINGLES – Quarter-finals: J. Hopkins d. C. Torrens-Valero 6–0 6–7 6–2; H. Nagyova d. T. Garbin (3) 6–3 7–6; A. Hopmans d. O. Barabanschikova (8) 6–3 6–3; M. Oremans d. J. Kandarr 7–5 1–6 6–3.
Semi-finals: Nagyova d. Hopkins 6–0 6–4; Hopmans d. Oremans 2–6 7–5 6–0.
Final: Nagyova d. Hopmans 2–6 6–4 7–5.
WOMEN'S DOUBLES – Final: Garbin/Husarova (3) d. Tulyaganova/Zaporozhanova 6–3 6–1.

FLANDERS WOMEN'S OPEN ($140,000)
ANTWERP, 15–21 MAY
WOMEN'S SINGLES – Quarter-finals: A. Coetzer (1) d. M. Shaughnessy (8) 6–1 6–3; L. Courtois d. L. Bacheva 6–7 6–3 6–4; J. Kostanic d. M. Montolio (4) 7–6 7–6; C. Torrens-Valero d. J. Hopkins 0–6 6–4 6–4.
Semi-finals: Coetzer (1) d. Courtois 6–0 6–3; Torrens-Valero d. Kostanic 6–4 6–2.
Final: Coetzer (1) d. Torrens-Valero 4–6 6–2 6–3.
WOMEN'S DOUBLES – Final: Appelmans/Clijsters d. Hopkins/Rampre 6–1 6–1.

INTERNATIONAUX DE STRASBOURG ($170,000)
STRASBOURG, 22–27 MAY
WOMEN'S SINGLES – Quarter-finals: S. Talaja (6) d. N. Tauziat (1) 7–5 6–2; N. Dechy (4) d. C. Morariu w/o; A. Smashnova d. L. Osterloh (Q) 7–6 6–4; R. Kuti Kis d. D. Hantuchova (LL) 6–4 6–4.
Semi-finals: Talaja (6) d. Dechy (4) 6–1 1–6 6–3; Kuti Kis d. Smashnova 7–6 6–4.
Final: Talaja (6) d. Kuti Kis 7–5 4–6 6–3.
WOMEN'S DOUBLES – Final: Jeyaseelan/Labat d. Grant/Vento (Q) 6–4 6–3.

OPEN PAGINAS AMARILLAS DE MADRID ($170,000)
MADRID, 22–27 MAY
WOMEN'S SINGLES – Quarter-finals: I. Majoli (WC) d. G. Di Natale (Q) 6–1 1–0 ret; F. Zuluaga d. A. Carlsson 6–2 6–4; G. Leon Garcia (8) d. M. Montolio 6–4 6–3; V. Ruano Pascual (WC) d. N. Pratt 6–3 1–6 6–2.
Semi-finals: Zuluaga d. Majoli (WC) 6–3 6–4; Leon Garcia (8) d. Ruano Pascual (WC) 6–2 6–0.
Final: Leon-Garcia (8) d. Zuluaga 4–6 6–2 6–2.
WOMEN'S DOUBLES – Final: Raymond/Stubbs (1) d. Leon Garcia/Sanchez Lorenzo 6–1 6–3.

DFS CLASSIC ($170,000)
EDGBASTON PRIORY CLUB, BIRMINGHAM, 12–18 JUNE
WOMEN'S SINGLES – Quarter-finals: N. Tauziat (1) d. A. Sidot (7) 7–5 5–7 7–6; L. Raymond (6) d. J. Capriati (3) 6–2 4–6 7–5; C. Black d. K. Brandi (8) 6–3 7–5; T. Tanasugarn (16) d. J. Halard-Decugis (2) 6–4 6–4.
Semi-finals: Raymond (6) d. Tauziat (1) 6–4 6–2; Tanasugarn (16) d. Black 7–6 6–1.
Final: Raymond (6) d. Tanasugarn (16) 6–2 6–7 6–4.
WOMEN'S DOUBLES – Final: McQuillan/McShea d. Black/Selyutina (5) 6–3 7–6.

TASHKENT OPEN ($140,000)
TASHKENT, 12–18 JUNE
WOMEN'S SINGLES – Quarter-finals: F. Schiavone d. T. Poutchek 6–3 6–3; J. Yi (4) d. T. Obziler 6–1 6–3; I. Tulyaganova d. E. Bovina 6–3 3–0 ret; S. Pitkowski (2) d. A. Zaporozhanova (Q) 6–0 6–0.
Semi-finals: Schiavone d. Yi (4) 6–2 7–6; Tulyaganova d. Pitkowski (2) w/o.
Final: Tulyaganova d. Schiavone 6–3 2–6 6–3.
WOMEN'S DOUBLES – Final: N. Li/T. Li d. Tulyaganova/Zaporozhanova (4) 3–6 6–2 6–4.

HEINEKEN TROPHY ($170,000)
'S-HERTOGENBOSCH, 19–24 JUNE
WOMEN'S SINGLES – Quarter-finals: M. Hingis (1) d. C. Black w/o; J. Capriati (4) d. P. Schnyder 7–5 7–5; K. Brandi d. N. Pratt 6–3 7–5; R. Dragomir (8) d. S. Testud (2) 2–6 6–4 6–4.
Semi-finals: Hingis (1) d. Capriati (4) 7–5 6–2; Dragomir (8) d. Brandi 6–2 6–3.
Final: Hingis (1) d. Dragomir (8) 6–2 3–0 ret.
WOMEN'S DOUBLES – Final: De Lone/Pratt d. Barclay/Habsudova 7–6 4–3 ret.

INTERNAZIONALI FEMMINILI DE PALERMO ($110,000)
PALERMO, 10–16 JULY
WOMEN'S SINGLES – Quarter-finals: S. Farina d. M. Diaz Oliva 2–6 7–5 6–3; H. Nagyova d. J. Henin 7–5 6–4; P. Nola d. J. Husarova 5–7 6–2 6–4; A. Smashnova d. G. Pizzichini 6–4 4–6 6–1.
Semi-finals: Nagyova d. Farina 6–2 6–4; Nola d. Smashnova 6–1 6–3.
Final: Nagyova d. Nola 6–3 7–5.
WOMEN'S DOUBLES – Final: Farina/Grande (3) d. Dragomir/Ruano Pascual (2) 6–4 0–6 7–6.

UNIQA GRAND PRIX ($170,000)
KLAGENFURT, 10–16 JULY
WOMEN'S SINGLES – Quarter-finals: B. Schett (1) d. J. Kruger 6–3 6–1; M. Montolio (6) d. M. Maleeva 6–3 6–3; A. Gersi d. N. Zvereva 6–2 ret; P. Schnyder d. G. Leon Garcia 2–6 7–5 6–4.
Semi-finals: Schett (1) d. Montolio (6) 6–3 6–4; Schnyder d. Gersi 6–0 6–3.
Final: Schett (1) d. Schnyder 5–7 6–4 6–4.
WOMEN'S DOUBLES – Final: Montalvo/Suarez (1) d. Schett/Schnyder (2) 7–6 6–1.

PROKOM POLISH OPEN ($170,000)
SOPOT, 17–23 JULY
WOMEN'S SINGLES – Quarter-finals: G. Leon-Garcia (5) d. C. Martinez (1) 5–2 ret; P. Suarez d. P. Schnyder (4) 6–4 7–5; A. Myskina (8) d. B. Schett (3) 5–7 6–1 6–1; A. Huber (2) d. K. Hrdlickova 6–7 6–1 6–1.
Semi-finals: Leon-Garcia (5) d. Suarez 6–4 4–6 6–3; Huber (2) d. Myskina (8) 6–3 6–2.
Final: Huber (2) d. Leon-Garcia (5) 7–6 6–3.
WOMEN'S DOUBLES – Final: Ruano-Pascual/Suarez (1) d. Carlsson/Grande (3) 7–5 6–1.

SANEX TROPHY ($110,000)
KNOKKE-HEIST, 17–23 JULY
WOMEN'S SINGLES – Quarter-finals: D. Van Roost (1) d. D. Randriantefy (Q) 6–1 6–2; M. Serna (3) d. P. Wartusch 6–0 ret; A. Smashnova (6) d. S. Pitkowski (4) 6–1 6–1; M. Marrero (8) d. S. Appelmans (2) 6–3 5–7 6–3.
Semi-finals: Van Roost (1) d. Serna (3) 6–3 6–0; Smashnova (6) d. Marrero (8) 6–3 6–1.
Final: Smashnova (6) d. Van Roost (1) 6–2 7–5.
WOMEN'S DOUBLES – Final: Casoni/Tulyaganova (4) d. Barclay/Dyrberg 2–6 6–4 6–4.

SEAT OPEN ($170,000)
LUXEMBOURG, 25 SEPTEMBER–1 OCTOBER
WOMEN'S SINGLES – Quarter-finals: B. Rittner (WC) d. D. Hantuchova 6–7 6–1 6–2; J. Capriati (3) d. A. Sidot (6) 7–5 6–7 6–3; M. Maleeva (7) d. P. Schnyder (4) 6–3 5–7 7–6; A. Kournikova (2) d. K. Clijsters (5) 6–7 6–3 6–1.
Semi-finals: Capriati (3) d. Rittner (WC) 6–4 2–6 6–2; Maleeva (7) d. Kournikova (2) 6–2 6–4.
Final: Capriati (3) d. Maleeva (7) 4–6 6–1 6–4.
WOMEN'S DOUBLES – Final: Fusai/Tauziat (1) d. Bacheva/Torrens-Valero 6–3 7–6.

JAPAN OPEN ($170,000)
TOKYO, 9–15 OCTOBER
WOMEN'S SINGLES – Quarter-finals: J. Halard-Decugis (1) d. M. Vavrinec (Q) 3–6 6–2 6–0; T. Tanasugarn (5) d. T. Snyder (Q) 6–4 6–1; J. Kruger d. J. Lee (Q) 6–3 7–6; A. Frazier (2) d. S. Plischke 6–1 6–2.
Semi-finals: Halard-Decugis (1) d. Tanasugarn (5) 7–6 6–0; Frazier (2) d. Kruger 7–5 6–2.
Final: Halard-Decugis (1) d. Frazier (2) 5–7 7–5 6–4.
WOMEN'S DOUBLES – Final: Halard-Decugis/Morariu (1) d. Krizan/Srebotnik (3) 6–1 6–2.

GENERALI LADIES LINZ ($535,000)
LINZ, 16–22 OCTOBER
WOMEN'S SINGLES – Quarter-finals: L. Davenport (1) d. B. Schett 6–2 4–1 ret; K. Hrdlickova d. N. Tauziat (4) 6–3 6–4; C. Rubin (5) d. H. Nagyova (Q) 6–4 6–4; V. Williams (2) d. E. Likhovtseva 6–3 6–2.
Semi-finals: Davenport (1) d. Hrdlickova 6–1 6–1; V. Williams (2) d. Rubin (5) 6–4 6–0.
Final: Davenport (1) d. V. Williams (2) 6–4 3–6 6–2.
WOMEN'S DOUBLES – Final: Mauresmo/Rubin d. Sugiyama/Tauziat (1) 6–4 6–4.

HEINEKEN OPEN SHANGHAI ($140,000)
SHANGHAI, 16–22 OCTOBER
WOMEN'S SINGLES – Quarter-finals: P. Nola d. K. Brandi (1) 6–4 6–2; M. Shaughnessy (4) d. S. Obata (Q) 6–3 6–2; T. Tanasugarn (3) d. A. Smashnova (5) 6–3 6–2; I. Tulyaganova d. J. Dokic (2) 6–3 6–4.
Semi-finals: Shaughnessy (4) d. Nola 7–5 6–2; Tulyaganova d. Tanasugarn (3) 6–1 6–4.
Final: Shaughnessy (4) d. Tulyaganova 7–6 7–5.
WOMEN'S DOUBLES – Final: Osterloh/Tanasugarn d. Grande/Shaughnessy (1) 7–5 6–1.

EUROTEL SLOVAK INDOOR ($110,000)
BRATISLAVA, 23–29 OCTOBER
WOMEN'S SINGLES – Quarter-finals: M. Oremans d. A. Sidot (1) 4–6 7–6 7–6; D. Chladkova (4) d. S. Plischke (5) 7–6 6–3; D. Bedanova (WC) (6) d. J. Henin (3) 6–3 5–7 6–4; K. Habsudova d. H. Nagyova 6–4 0–6 6–3.
Semi-finals: Oremans d. Chladkova (4) 6–4 6–0; Bedanova (WC) (6) d. Habsudova 2–6 6–4 6–4.
Final: Bedanova (WC) (6) d. Oremans 6–1 5–7 6–3.
WOMEN'S DOUBLES – Final: Habsudova/Hantuchova d. Mandula/Wartusch (3) w/o.

BELL CHALLENGE ($170,000)
QUEBEC CITY, 30 OCTOBER–5 NOVEMBER
WOMEN'S SINGLES – Quarter-finals: J. Capriati (1) d. S. Jeyaseelan 7–5 6–0; A. Frazier (4) d. M. Vento (Q) 6–2 6–2; M. Tu d. T. Poutchek 6–0 5–7 6–0; C. Rubin (2) d. F. Zuluaga (9) 6–3 3–6 6–2.
Semi-finals: Capriati (1) d. Frazier (4) 3–6 7–5 7–5; Rubin (2) d. Tu 7–5 6–1.
Final: Rubin (2) d. Capriati (1) 6–4 6–2.
WOMEN'S DOUBLES – Final: Pratt/Shaughnessy (2) d. Callens/Po (1) 6–3 6–4.

WISMILAK INTERNATIONAL ($170,000)
KUALA LUMPUR, 6–12 NOVEMBER
WOMEN'S SINGLES – Quarter-finals: H. Nagyova d. C. Morariu 5–7 6–3 6–2; T. Tanasugarn (3) d. J. Kruger 6–3 5–7 6–3; T. Panova (5) d. M. Sucha (Q) 6–3 6–3; I. Majoli (WC) d. P. Nola 1–6 7–5 6–1.
Semi-finals: Nagyova d. Tanasugarn (3) 6–4 6–1; Majoli (WC) d. Panova (5) 1–6 6–4 6–2.
Final: Nagyova d. Majoli (WC) 6–4 6–2.
WOMEN'S DOUBLES – Final: Nagyova/Plischke d. Horn/Webb (4) 6–4 7–6.

VOLVO WOMEN'S OPEN ($110,000)
PATTAYA, 13–19 NOVEMBER
WOMEN'S SINGLES – Quarter-finals: H. Nagyova d. S. Farina-Elia 6–3 6–4; T. Panova (4) d. V. Webb 6–2 6–3; A. Kremer (3) d. J. Kruger (8) 6–4 6–1; N. Ostrovskaya d. T. Tanasugarn (2) 7–6 6–4.
Semi-finals: Panova (4) d. Nagyova w/o; Kremer (3) d. Ostrovskaya 6–4 6–1.
Final: Kremer (3) d. Panova (4) 6–1 6–4.
WOMEN'S DOUBLES – Final: Basuki/Vis d. Krizan/Srebotnik (1) 6–3 6–3.

The Chase Championships

John Parsons

Whatever sadness there may have been, especially in Monica Seles's mind, over the decision by the Sanex WTA Tour to move their end-of-the-year championship from Madison Square Garden, after 22 years, to Munich, was at least tempered by a final which will rank comfortably among the best.

The fact that Martina Hingis only served out for a 6–7 6–4 6–4 victory over Seles after achieving the 14th break in the 2 hours 2 minutes match, could give a totally misleading impression as to the quality of the constant high-powered hitting in a memorable contest. The 102 winners, 53 of them from the runner-up, whose double-handed backhands were once again a speciality to admire, was a more accurate reflection of what both players called 'a very high quality match.'

At one moment Seles, who had suffered a slight groin strain while breaking for 4–2 in the second set, was just five points from a triumph which would not merely have been her most cherished moment of the year – but of her career. In the preceding four weeks Monica had been suffering from a stress fracture in her left foot and it was only because she knew that this might be her last chance to complete in the Chase Championships (or whatever banner it will fly under in future), that she worked feverishly to be fit in time.

Munich may be some 350 miles from Hamburg, where Seles's career was so grotesquely interrupted for more than two years when she was stabbed during a changeover by a deranged Steffi Graf fan, but the former Yugoslav player, now an American citizen, still cannot bring herself to play again in Germany. She also expressed the view that switching the tournament to Germany, especially as she said she had not been consulted, was like a personal slap in the face.

Yet, however understandable her feelings may be, WTA Tour officials have to weigh their responsibilities to women's tennis as a whole and a Munich offer of $5m, compared with the $3m for staging the event in Madison Square Garden, was not one which could easily be dismissed, especially when the contribution by European players is so considerable.

American opposition to the move – plus the subsequent loss of what had been a highly successful tournament in Philadelphia one week earlier – might have carried more weight had two of the most prominent American players, the Williams sisters, not dropped out. Officially Venus, the Wimbledon, U.S.Open and Olympic champion, who had played only eight other tournaments during the year, was suffering from anaemia. Serena, we were told, had a stress fracture of the right foot. Yet the outburst from their father, Richard, on the eve of the Chase gave the cynics a field day. He announced that unless his daughters benefited financially from the added appeal they have brought to women's tennis, he would limit their future appearances even more. These outrageous comments were widely condemned, not just by Tour officials, but by leading players past and present.

Throughout the week Seles served probably as well as at any time in her career. She comfortably eliminated Sandrine Testud and Amanda Coetzer before forcefully bringing her added experience to bear on the 19-year-old Russian prodigy, Elena Dementieva. Throughout these encounters there were also many of those trademark backhand crosscourt winners to admire.

The Chase Championships was the biggest win of the year for Martina Hingis whose first prize of $500,000, plus the doubles prize of $200,000, took her season's earnings to $3,457,049 . (Stephen Wake)

Seles could not have given more in her effort to turn the clock back to her golden days a decade earlier. At Madison Square Garden she was unbeaten from 1990–1992. Any less mentally resilient opponent than Hingis, who is never more menacing than when her body language suggests she may be flagging, would probably have yielded.

Hingis, unlike Seles, dropped one set during her progress to the final. That was against the 33-year-old French veteran, Nathalie Tauziat, who demonstrated joyously to a 12,000 crowd that, an old-fashioned girl, in tennis terms, with old-fashioned serve and volleying ways, has much to offer. That was certainly so as Tauziat, outplayed early on, hit six clean winners in a brilliantly won 7–2 tie-break before losing 6–1 6–7 6–2.

Tauziat's appetite for tournaments showed no signs of flagging. On the other hand her fellow countryman, Julie Halard-Decugis, who had been Hingis's first round victim, 6–2 6–3, decided enough was enough and announced her retirement. 'It's time to do other things' she said 'like starting a family.'

Anna Kournikova's outfit of a figure-hugging top and short pants made sure that her photographs were regularly in the New York newspapers during the week. At the same time, though, the inescapable signs of a growing competence and maturity in her free-flowing tennis deservedly attracted attention. This was particularly true as she overcame the wily Conchita Martinez in the quarter-finals before going closer against Hingis than the 7–6 (2) 6–2 score indicated. Anna should have won the first set, in which she was twice a break up, but over-zealous hitting when she served for the set at 5–4, and similar errors as she lost the last five points of a 7–2 tie-break, cost her dearly.

In the other half of the draw, from which Seles emerged, it was the form and engaging personalities displayed by teenagers, Dementieva and Kim Clijsters which made the most impact. Clijsters, 17, made harder work than was necessary of her 7–5 6–4 win over Arantxa Sanchez-Vicario in the first round after winning the first 12 points and leading 5–2. Yet the irresistible manner in which she kept going for winners after being caught at 5–5 and again in the second set when she ended with a flurry of bold winners, made her an instant hit with the crowd.

Both Clijsters and Dementieva, who recovered from losing the first set and hit a fabulous flood of forehand winners to upset second seeded defending champion, Lindsay Davenport, 3–6 7–6 (7) 6–4, gave the admirable impression that they enjoy every minute they spend on a tennis court. Their quarter-final against each other, however, was not quite the epic contest many were expecting. With so much young personal pride at stake, the tension was clearly evident. Nevertheless the exchanges were exciting and the outcome unpredictable.

Clijsters delighted the crowd with her perfectly weighted drop shots as she romped away with the second set. She looked set to triumph when she broke for 4–2 in the third on her fourth break point but a few negative points in the next game gave Dementieva hope. The Russian, given the opportunity to rediscover the range and authority on her forehand, swept through the last four games for a thrilling 6–4 2–6 6–4 success.

CHASE CHAMPIONSHIPS ($2,000,000)
NEW YORK, NY, 13–19 NOVEMBER
WOMEN'S SINGLES – 1st Round: M. Hingis (1) d. J. Halard-Decugis 6–2 6–3; N. Tauziat (6) d. A. Frazier 6–3 6–2; C. Martinez (4) d. E. Likhovtseva (A) 2–6 6–4 6–3; A. Kournikova (7) d. J. Capriati 6–4 6–4; A. Coetzer d. C. Rubin (8) 6–2 6–1; M. Seles (3) d. S. Testud 6–3 6–4; K. Clijsters d. A. Sanchez-Vicario (5) 7–5 6–4; E. Dementieva d. L. Davenport (2) 3–6 7–6 6–4.
Quarter-finals: Hingis (1) d. Tauziat (6) 6–1 6–7 6–2; Kournikova (7) d. C. Martinez (4) 6–4 6–0; Seles (3) d. Coetzer 6–3 6–4; Dementieva d. Clijsters 6–4 2–6 6–4.
Semi-finals: Hingis (1) d. Kournikova (7) 7–6 6–2; Seles (3) d. Dementieva 6–1 7–6.
Final: Hingis (1) d. Seles (3) 6–7 6–4 6–4.
WOMEN'S DOUBLES – Final: Hingis/Kournikova (2) d. Arendt/Bollegraf 6–2 6–3.

Chase doubles champions for the second year in a row, the old team of Kournikova and Hingis found their form without any trouble. (Stephen Wake)

Other Official Pro Tournaments

Men's Challenger Tournaments
ITF Men's Circuit
ITF Women's Circuit

The promising 16-year-old Russian, Lina Krasnoroutskaya, at the start of what many observers believe will be a brilliant career, finished the year ranked 133 and with earnings of $87,185. (Stephen Wake)

Men's Challenger Tournaments

In 2000 there were more than 117 Challenger tournaments for men in some 45 countries. Where a tournament provides hospitality for its players the event is credited another US$25,000 in terms of its ranking points level. The prize money and points levels (H = plus hospitality) were:

US$125,000H	90 points to the champion
US$125,000 (or US$100,000H)	80 points to the champion
US$100,000 (or US$75,000H)	70 points to the champion
US$75,000 (or US$50,000H)	60 points to the champion
US$37,500	55 points to the champion
US$50,000 (or US$25,000H)	50 points to the champion

HEILBRONN (GER) (100H) 24–30 JANUARY – *Singles:* M. Larsson (7) d. S. Huet 6–3 7–6.
Doubles: J. Siemerink/J. Van Lottum (WC) d. M. Larsson/F. Loven (WC) 7–5 7–6.

WAIKOLOA, HI (USA) (50H) 25–30 JANUARY – *Singles:* P. Goldstein (1) d. A. Sa (7) 7–5 6–2.
Doubles: J. Grabb/R. Reneberg (2) d. J. Blake/C. Mamiit (WC) 6–2 2–6 6–4.

AMARILLO, TX (USA) (37.5H) 31 JANUARY–6 FEBRUARY – *Singles:* M. Russell d. S. Pescosolido 7–5 6–2.
Doubles: M. Hill/B. MacPhie (2) d. B. Coupe/M. Sell (4) 7–5 6–2.

HAMBURG (GER) (25H) 31 JANUARY–6 FEBRUARY – *Singles:* A. Popp (1) d. A. Fahlke 6–3 6–2.
Doubles: T. Cibulec/L. Friedl (2) d. M. Gienke/F. Jeschonek (WC) 4–6 6–3 6–2.

WOLFSBURG (GER) (25H) 7–13 FEBRUARY – *Singles:* A. Stoliarov (2) d. O. Burrieza 3–6 6–3 6–0.
Doubles: J. Brandt/M. Sinner (WC) d. T. Cibulec/L. Friedl (2) 7–5 3–6 7–6.

CALCUTTA (IND) (25H) 14–19 FEBRUARY – *Singles:* T. Ketola (3) d. A. Ram 6–3 6–1.
Doubles: A. Ram/N. Welgreen d. G. Carraz/G. Marx (WC) 2–1 ret.

HULL (GBR) (25H) 14–19 FEBRUARY – *Singles:* H. Andersson (Q) d. M. Hilton (WC) 6–4 3–6 6–4.
Doubles: B. Cowan/N. Godwin (1) d. J. Knowle/S. Pescosolido (2) 6–3 3–6 6–3.

LUBECK (GER) (25H) 14–20 FEBRUARY – *Singles:* C. Vinck (3) d. A. Fahlke (2) 6–3 6–1.
Doubles: G. Galimberti/D. Nargiso (4) d. K. Braasch/D. Dier (1) 6–4 6–4.

WROCLAW (POL) (75H) 14–20 FEBRUARY – *Singles:* M. Damm (2) d. G. Pozzi (1) 4–6 6–4 6–3.
Doubles: P. Kovacka/P. Kudrnac d. J. Robichaud/K. Spencer 3–6 7–6 6–4.

AHMEDABAD (IND) (25H) 21–26 FEBRUARY – *Singles:* V. Kutsenko (5) d. O. Motevassel (LL) 6–2 6–4.
Doubles: C. Kauffmann/F. Syed d. J. Bower/D. Roberts 3–6 6–4 6–4.

HO CHI MINH CITY (VIE) (50H) 21–27 FEBRUARY – *Singles:* J. Vanek (1) d. R. Willems 7–6 6–4.
Doubles: M. Hill/T. Woodbridge (1) d. I. Labadze/K. Ullyett 6–3 6–4.

MUMBAI (IND) (25H) 28 FEBRUARY–4 MARCH – *Singles:* L. Paes (1) d. D. Van Scheppingen (Q) 7–6 3–2 ret.
Doubles: T. Anzari/S. Iwabuchi (3) d. M. Boye/J. Erlich 7–6 6–4.

SINGAPORE (SIN) (50H) 28 FEBRUARY–5 MARCH – *Singles:* T. Woodbridge d. A. Parmar 6–3 6–3.
Doubles: N. Godwin/M. Hill (1) d. P. Hanley/N. Healey (2) 6–4 6–1.

CHERBOURG (FRA) (37.5H) 28 FEBRUARY–5 MARCH – *Singles:* J. Boutter (5) d. M. Youzhny 6–1 6–0.
Doubles: J. Boutter/M. Llodra d. J. Benneteau/N. Mahut (WC) 2–6 6–4 7–5.

BESANCON (FRA) (25H) 6–12 MARCH – *Singles:* J. Boutter d. J. Knowle (Q) 6–4 7–6.
Doubles: J. Boutter/M. Llodra (WC) d. S. Pescosolido/V. Santopadre 6–4 6–7 7–6.

KYOTO (JPN) (25H) 6–12 MARCH – *Singles:* K. Ullyett (1) d. A. Parmar 6–7 6–4 6–4.
Doubles: M. Hromec/T. Spinks d. Y. Ishii/S. Iwabuchi 6–4 7–6.

LISBON (POR) (25H) 13–19 MARCH – *Singles:* D. Sanchez d. J. Vanek (2) 6–4 3–6 6–2.
Doubles: J. Cunha-Silva/N. Marques (2) d. S. Navarro/T. Robredo 7–5 6–4.

MAGDEBURG (GER) (25H) 13 19 MARCH – *Singles:* S. Lareau (5) d. V. Voltchkov 7–6 6–3.
Doubles: K. Braasch/D. Dier d. T. Behrend/M. Kohlmann (Q) 7–5 7–6.

SALINAS (ECU) (25H) 13–19 MARCH – **Singles:** D. Sanguinetti (1) d. L. Horna 6–2 6–2.
Doubles: J. Balcells/M. Hadad (WC) d. E. Alvarez/A. Calatrava (4) w/o.

HAMILTON (NZL) (25H) 20–26 MARCH – **Singles:** M. Joyce d. G. Motomura (1) 4–6 6–4 6–4.
Doubles: N. Godwin/M. Hill (1) d. M. Joyce/J. Thomas (3) 7–6 6–4.

BARLETTA (ITA) (25H) 27 MARCH–2 APRIL – **Singles:** G. Puentes d. T. Robredo (Q) 6–4 7–6.
Doubles: P. Kovacka/P. Kudrnac d. D. Pescariu/V. Santopadre 6–7 6–2 6–0.

CAGLIARI (ITA) (75H) 3–9 APRIL – **Singles:** A. Gaudenzi (6) d. M. Rodriguez 2–6 7–5 6–2.
Doubles: T. Cibulec/L. Friedl d. A. Gaudenzi/D. Nargiso (WC) 6–1 3–6 7–5.

SAN LUIS POTOSI (MEX) (50H) 17–23 APRIL – **Singles:** A. Calleri (6) d. M. Hood 7–5 6–4.
Doubles: J. De Armas/J. Szymanski d. J. Robichaud/M. Sell (1) 5–7 6–4 6–2.

MAIA (POR) (125H) 24–30 APRIL – **Singles:** A. Gaudenzi (2) d. J. Chela (WC) (3) 3–6 7–5 6–1.
Doubles: T. Cibulec/L. Friedl d. P. Pala/P. Vizner (2) 6–3 4–6 6–4.

BERMUDA (BER) (100H) 24–30 APRIL – **Singles:** A. Ilie (1) d. M. Tabara 4–6 6–3 6–2.
Doubles: L. Paes/J. Siemerink (1) d. J. Coetzee/B. Haygarth (4) 6–3 6–2.

FERGANA (UZB) (25H) 8–13 MAY – **Singles:** V. Voltchkov (7) d. I. Kunitcin (Q) 4–6 6–0 6–4.
Doubles: J. Erlich/L. Mor (4) d. D. Melo/A. Simoni (1) 6–4 6–0.

BIRMINGHAM, AL (USA) (50) 8–14 MAY – **Singles:** R. Agenor (2) d. P. Srichaphan (4) 7–5 6–3.
Doubles: P. Kilderry/P. Tramacchi (4) d. L. Pearson/G. Silcock (Q) 6–4 6–4.

LJUBLJANA (SLO) (100H) 8–14 MAY – **Singles:** O. Gross (Q) d. J. Balcells 4–6 6–1 7–6.
Doubles: P. Rosner/J. Weir-Smith d. E. Alvarez/A. Lopez-Moron 6–3 6–4.

JERUSALEM (ISR) (50H) 15–20 MAY – **Singles:** K. Ullyett (3) d. G. Pozzi (1) 6–4 6–3.
Doubles: N. Godwin/K. Ullyett (1) d. N. Behr/E. Ran (2) 7–6 7–6.

SAMARKAND (UZB) (25H) 15–20 MAY – **Singles:** M. Youzhny (6) d. J. Andersen 7–6 2–6 7–6.
Doubles: S. Galvani/A. Stoliarov (2) d. D. Melo/A. Simoni (1) w/o.

ZAGREB (CRO) (50H) 15–21 MAY – **Singles:** G. Etlis d. A. Calleri (5) 6–3 7–5.
Doubles: M. Llodra/D. Nargiso (4) d. E. Nicolas/G. Puentes (1) 6–2 6–3.

ARMONK, NY (USA) (50) 15–21 MAY – **Singles:** S. Navarro d. A. Hernandez 6–1 3–6 6–3.
Doubles: P. Kilderry/P. Tramacchi (3) d. M. Bryan/R. Bryan (1) 2–6 7–6 6–4.

EDINBURGH (GBR) (25H) 16–21 MAY – **Singles:** F. Dewulf (7) d. M. Charpentier (Q) w/o.
Doubles: T. Robredo/M. Russell (Q) d. L. Burgsmuller/O. Fukarek (2) 6–0 6–2

BUDAPEST (HUN) (25H) 22–27 MAY – **Singles:** E. Kempes (8) d. J. Golmard (Q) (1) 6–4 ret.
Doubles: T. Shimada/M. Wakefield (1) d. I. Labadze/D. Pescariu 6–2 3–6 6–3.

TALLAHASSE, FL (USA) (50) 5–11 JUNE – **Singles:** J. Salzenstein (Q) d. K. Kim (3) 6–3 6–2.
Doubles: M. Knowles/M. Merklein (1) d. K. Gullett/B. Hawk (WC) 7–6 6–2.

PROSTEJOV (CZE) (100H) 6–11 JUNE – **Singles:** A. Vinciguerra (WC) (1) d. J. Golmard (5) w/o.
Doubles: A. Martin/E. Ran (4) d. P. Luxa/V. Santopadre 6–2 6–2.

FURTH (GER) (50H) 6–11 JUNE – **Singles:** I. Labadze (Q) d. D. Elsner (Q) 6–4 6–4.
Doubles: E. Nicolas/G. Puentes (2) d. D. Bowen/B. Coupe (1) 6–4 6–2.

SURBITON (GBR) (50) 6–11 JUNE – **Singles:** W. Arthurs d. L. Tieleman 4–6 7–6 6–4.
Doubles: J. Coetzee/M. Ondruska (3) d. J. Palmer/J. Stark (2) 7–6 7–6.

SZCZECIN (POL) (125H) 12–18 JUNE – **Singles:** B. Ulihrach (5) d. A. Martin (3) 6–0 6–2.
Doubles: A. Martin/E. Ran (2) d. M. Hood/M. Rodriguez (1) 7–6 6–7 6–2.

WEIDEN (GER) (75H) 12–18 JUNE – **Singles:** D. Elsner (SE) d. F. Dewulf (5) 6–1 7–6.
Doubles: M. Nielsen/A. Stoliarov d. D. Elsner/A. Fahlke 7–5 6–3.

ESPINHO (POR) (50) 12–18 JUNE – **Singles:** T. Robredo (4) d. J. Szymanski (6) 6–4 6–2.
Doubles: E. Couto/B. Mota (4) d. J. Cunha-Silva/N. Marques (2) 4–6 7–5 7–6.

DENVER, CO (USA) (50) 12–18 JUNE – **Singles:** L. Mor d. A. Hernandez (4) 6–3 6–4.
Doubles: J. Erlich/L. Mor (4) d. N. Behr/A. Ram 6–4 5–7 6–2.

BRAUNSCHWEIG (GER) (125H) 19–25 JUNE – **Singles:** G. Gaudio (WC) (2) d. F. Squillari (WC) (1) 6–4 6–7 6–4. **Doubles:** J. Knippschild/J. Tarango (2) d. A. Lopez-Moron/A. Portas (1) 6–2 6–2.

LUGANO (SUI) (25H) 19–25 JUNE – **Singles:** D. Sanchez (5) d. A. Savolt (2) 6–3 6–2.
Doubles: V. Kutsenko/O. Ogorodov d. F. Costa/T. Hildebrand (4) 4–6 7–6 6–0.

EISENACH (GER) (25H) 26 JUNE–2 JULY – *Singles:* J. Andersen d. F. Costa 7–6 6–3.
Doubles: D. Melo/A. Simoni (2) d. E. Abaroa/T. Crichton 6–1 6–7 6–1.

SASSUOLO (ITA) (25H) 26 JUNE–2 JULY – *Singles:* S. Tarallo (6) d. A. Calatrava (1) 7–6 3–6 7–6.
Doubles: A. Calatrava/S. Navarro (1) d. D. Bracciali/F. Luzzi (WC) 6–7 6–1 6–4.

VENICE (ITA) (100H) 4–9 JULY – *Singles:* A. Calleri (7) d. J. Diaz 6–0 6–1.
Doubles: J. Alonso-Pintor/A. Kitinov (2) d. A. Gaudenzi/D. Nargiso (3) 7–6 7–5.

ULM (GER) (50H) 4–9 JULY – *Singles:* G. Puentes d. D. Sanchez (4) 6–3 6–3.
Doubles: O. Stanoytchev/M. Youzhny (WC) d. T. Behrend/K. Braasch 6–7 7–5 6–0.

MONTAUBAN (FRA) (25H) 4–9 JULY – *Singles:* J. Lisnard (1) d. O. Serrano 6–2 6–0.
Doubles: L. Pearson/G. Silcock (1) d. T. Crichton/A. Fisher (4) 6–1 6–4.

OSTEND (BEL) (75H) 10–16 JULY – *Singles:* O. Rochus (6) d. J. Van Herck (WC) 6–4 6–4.
Doubles: T. Crichton/A. Fisher (3) d. F. Cabello/D. Furmanski (4) 6–2 2–6 6–1.

SCHEVENINGEN (NED) (75H) 10–16 July – *Singles:* N. Coutelot d. M. Rodriguez (8) 6–3 ret.
Doubles: P. Hanley/N. Healey (3) d. M. Hilpert/T. Strengberger (4) 6–2 1–6 6–3.

GRANBY (CAN) (50H) 10–16 JULY – *Singles:* T. Suzuki d. C. Mamiit (1) 6–4 6–3.
Doubles: H. Lee/Y. Yoon d. F. Niemeyer/J. Turek 7–6 6–3.

OBERSTAUFEN (GER) (25H) 10–16 JULY – *Singles:* C. Trimmel d. R. Vasek (PR) 6–4 6–1.
Doubles: H. Armando/A. Simoni (2) d. T. Behrend/K. Braasch (4) 6–4 6–3.

BRISTOL (GBR) (50) 11–16 JULY – *Singles:* A. Ram (6) d. J. Knowle (3) 6–3 6–3.
Doubles: J. Kerr/D. Roberts (1) d. N. Behr/E. Erlich 6–3 1–6 6–3.

APTOS, CA (USA) (50) 17–23 JULY – *Singles:* R. Bryan (8) d. K. Kim (7) 6–4 6–7 6–4.
Doubles: M. Bryan/R. Bryan (1) d. K. Kim/L. Smith 6–4 3–6 6–4.

CONTREXEVILLE (FRA) (37.5H) 17–23 JULY – *Singles:* V. Santopadre (SE) d. O. Patience 7–5 6–2.
Doubles: J. Benneteau/N. Mahut d. J. Lisnard/O. Patience (4) 6–3 7–6.

MANCHESTER (GBR) (50) 18–23 JULY – *Singles:* M. Navarra d. M. Lee 6–4 6–3.
Doubles: D. Petrovic/A. Ram d. Y. Allegro/I. Heuberger (Q) 6–2 7–6.

CORDOBA (ESP) (50H) 24–29 JULY – *Singles:* R. Willems d. D. Golovanov (Q) 4–6 7–5 7–6.
Doubles: D. Petrovic/A. Ram d. O. Burrieza/D. Melo 6–1 6–4.

ISTANBUL (TUR) (75) 24–30 JULY – *Singles:* W. Black (3) d. P. Kralert (6) 6–4 6–3.
Doubles: N. Behr/E. Erlich d. V. Kutsenko/O. Ogorodov (2) 6–7 6–3 6–3.

TAMPERE (FIN) (50) 24–30 JULY - *Singles:* J. Van Herck (PR) d. O. Mutis 6–3 6–2.
Doubles: V. Liukko/J. Nieminen d. S. Randjelovic/D. Vemic (1) 6–0 4–6 6–3.

WINNETKA, IL (USA) (50) 24–30 JULY – *Singles:* T. Suzuki (Q) d. Y. Yoon 6–2 6–4.
Doubles: H. Lee/Y. Yoon (3) d. M. Breen/L. Smith 2–6 7–5 6–3.

WREXHAM (GBR) (25H) 31 JULY–5 AUGUST – *Singles:* W. Arthurs (1) d. L. Svarc 6–2 6–4.
Doubles: D. Bracciali/A. Qureshi d. M. MacLagan/A. Richardson 6–4 6–2.

POZNAN (POL) (100H) 31 JULY–6 AUGUST – *Singles:* C. Rochus (4) d. A. Voinea (5) 6–4 3–6 7–6.
Doubles: P. Pala/P. Vizner (1) d. T. Cibulec/L. Friedl (3) 6–3 6–0.

LEXINGTON, KY (USA) (50) 31 JULY–6 AUGUST – *Singles:* T. Suzuki d. J. Gimelstob (WC) (1) 2–1 ret.
Doubles: L. Manta/L. Tieleman d. G. Stafford/W. Whitehouse 7–6 7–6.

SEGOVIA (ESP) (100H) 31 JULY–6 AUGUST – *Singles:* S. Bruguera (WC) d. J. Siemerink (4) 5–7 6–3 1–0
ret. *Doubles:* A. Fisher/J. Weir-Smith (1) d. J. Kerr/D. Roberts 7–6 6–1.

GRAMADO (BRA) (25H) 31 JULY–6 AUGUST – *Singles:* A. Simoni (6) d. M. Lee (3) 6–4 7–5.
Doubles: A. Sa/E. Taino (4) d. D. Melo/A. Simoni (1) 7–6 7–6.

BINGHAMTON, NY (USA) (50) 7–13 AUGUST – *Singles:* T. Suzuki d. Y. Yoon 6–1 6–4.
Doubles: J. Bower/J. Coetzee d. L. Manta/L. Tieleman 6–3 7–5.

PRAGUE (CZE) (50) 7–13 AUGUST – *Singles:* A. Montanes (8) d. F. Volandri 6–1 6–1.
Doubles: F. Cermak/O. Fukarek (4) d. T. Cibulec/L. Friedl (2) 6–4 6–3.

SOPOT (POL) (50) 7–13 AUGUST – *Singles:* H. Armando d. J. Weinzierl 6–4 6–0.
Doubles: S. Roitman/A. Schneiter (3) d. O. Hernadez-Perez/G. Puentes 6–4 6–2.

BELO HORIZONTE (BRA) (25H) 7–13 AUGUST – *Singles:* N. Zimonjic d. J. Bachelot 6–3 6–7 7–5.
Doubles: D. Melo/A. Simoni (1) d. J. Delgado/M. Lee 6–4 6–4.

TOGLIATTI (RUS) (25H) 7–13 AUGUST   *Singles:* V. Kutsenko (4) d. I. Kunitcin (G) 6–4 6–1.
Doubles: D. Vemic/L. Zovko (1) d. I. Moldovan/Y. Schukin 6–4 6–4.

KIEV (UKR) (100H) 14–20 AUGUST – **Singles:** J. Diaz (8) d. S. Peppas 6–1 6–3.
Doubles: C. Kordasz/G. Koves d. O. Ogorodov/A. Stoliarov (3) 6–4 7–5.

BRONX, NY (USA) (50) 14–20 AUGUST – **Singles:** H. Lee (LL) d. R. Willems 6–4 6–1.
Doubles: P. Luxa/W.Whitehouse d. H. Lee/Y. Yoon 3–6 6–3 6–2.

BRESSANONE (ITA) (25H) 14–20 AUGUST – **Singles:** F. Cermak d. S. Roitman 5–7 6–4 6–1.
Doubles: J. Kerr/D. Roberts (2) d. M. Charpentier/D. Del Rio 7–6 7–5.

SYLT (GER) (25H) 14–20 AUGUST – **Singles:** Y. Schukin d. J. Herm-Zahlava 6–2 6–4.
Doubles: I. Moldovan/Y. Schukin d. A. Fisher/G. Williams (2) 6–4 6–2.

GENEVA (SUI) (50H) 21–27 AUGUST – **Singles:** N. Thomann d. A. Calatrava (1) 6–4 6–7 6–1.
Doubles: D. Del Rio/E. Massa d. Y. Allegro/J. Cuaz 7–5 7–6.

MANERBIO (ITA) (25H) 21–27 AUGUST – **Singles:** S. Tarallo (2) d. K. Goossens 6–3 6–4.
Doubles: J. Kerr/D. Roberts (1) d. B. Mota/L. Svarc 7–6 6–4.

BUDAPEST (HUN) (25) 28 AUGUST–2 SEPTEMBER – **Singles:** D. Moyano d. V. Mazarakis 6–3 6–0.
Doubles: S. Roitman/A. Schneiter (1) d. D. Miketa/D. Skoch 6–3 6–3.

FREUDENSTADT (GER) (37.5) 28 AUGUST–3 SEPTEMBER – **Singles:** M. Tabara (4) d. J. Andersen 6–4 6–4.
Doubles: I. Moldovan/Y. Schukin 3–6 6–3 6–4.

MONCHENGLADBACH (GER) (25H) 21–27 AUGUST – **Singles:** N. Davydenko (5) d. E. Kempes (6) 6–3
3–6 6–3. **Doubles:** E. Alvarez/L. Horna (WC) d. F. Costa/G. Puentes (WC) 7–6 1–6 7–5.

GRAZ (AUT) (100H) 5–10 SEPTEMBER – **Singles:** M. Tabara d. D. Sanchez (6) 7–5 6–0.
Doubles: T. Cibulec/L. Friedl (2) d. P. Kovacka/P. Kudrnac 6–4 4–6 6–4.

ASCHAFFENBURG (GER) (37.5) 5–10 SEPTEMBER – **Singles:** N. Coutelot (7) d. L. Horna 6–7 6–3 6–1.
Doubles: P. Luxa/D. Skoch (4) d. M. Hilpert/V. Snyman (3) 6–2 6–3.

SOFIA (BUL) (25H) 5–10 SEPTEMBER – **Singles:** S. Tarallo (4) d. S. Galvani 6–1 6–2.
Doubles: D. Petrovic/O. Stanoytchev (3) d. R. Lukaev/L. Pampoulov (WC) 6–2 6–7 7–6.

LINZ (AUT) (75H) 11–17 SEPTEMBER – **Singles:** G. Puentes (2) d. E. Kempes 7–6 6–1.
Doubles: J. Knowle/T. Strengberger d. P. Luxa/D. Skoch 6–3 7–5.

SKOPJE (MKD) (25H) 11–17 SEPTEMBER – **Singles:** O. Gross (4) d. Y. Schukin 7–5 6–4.
Doubles: E. Artoni/S. Roitman (3) d. D. Petrovic/S. Prieto (1) 7–5 5–7 6–3.

BIELLA (ITA) (100H) 18–24 SEPTEMBER – **Singles:** F. Volandri (WC) d. H. Gumy (6) 6–3 6–2.
Doubles: M. Garcia/M. Puerta d. S. Aspelin/F. Bergh 6–2 4–6 6–4.

HOUSTON, TX (USA) (50) 18–24 SEPTEMBER – **Singles:** J. Blake (WC) d. M. Kratochvil (5) 7–6 6–7 6–3.
Doubles: B. Haygarth/M. Ondruska (1) d. J. Blake/K.Kim (3) 6–4 6–2.

BRASOV (ROM) (25H) 18–24 SEPTEMBER – **Singles:** A. Simoni d. D. Norman (Q) 7–5 6–3.
Doubles: I. Moldovan/Y. Schukin (2) d. D. Norman/W. Schranz 6–4 6–1.

SEVILLE (ESP) (37.5H) 25–30 SEPTEMBER – **Singles:** T. Robredo d. O. Serrano 6–7 6–1 6–4.
Doubles: E. Nicolas/G. Puentes (1) d. T. Robredo/S. Ventura 6–3 6–2.

SAN ANTONIO, TX (USA) (50) 25 SEPTEMBER–1 OCTOBER – **Singles:** X. Malisse (8) d. R. Agenor (6) 7–6
6–3. **Doubles:** W. Whitehouse/G. Williams d. M. Bryan/R. Bryan (1) 6–3 6–4.

TANGIERS (MAR) (25H) 2–7 OCTOBER – **Singles:** W. Eschauer (6) d. N. Thomann (5) 6–4 6–3.
Doubles: I. Moldovan/Y. Schukin (3) d. C. Kordasz/C. Testa (4) 6–4 2–6 6–2.

BRATISLAVA (SVK) (100H) 2–8 OCTOBER – **Singles:** D. Sanguinetti (Q) (6) d. R. Schuttler (1) 7–5 6–1.
Doubles: P. Hanley/P. Rosner d. J. Erlich/A. Kitinov (2) 6–4 6–4.

BARCELONA (ESP) (100) 2–8 OCTOBER – **Singles:** A. Portas (3) d. O. Serrano 3–6 6–4 6–3.
Doubles: T. Carbonell/A. Portas (1) d. M. Hilpert/J. Knippschild (4) 5–7 6–1 6–4.

AUSTIN, TX (USA) (50) 2–9 OCTOBER – **Singles:** A. Roddick (Q) d. M. Russell 6–4 6–4.
Doubles: T. Crichton/A. Fisher (4) d. R. Sluiter/D. Van Scheppingen (Q) 6–1 6–7 6–0.

GUDALAJARA (MEX) (100) 9–14 OCTOBER – **Singles:** F. Meligeni (3) d. H. Armando 7–5 4–6 6–4.
Doubles: H. Armando/A. Waske d. F. Meligeni/F. Saretta (WC) 7–6 4–6 7–6.

CAIRO (EGY) (100H) 9–15 OCTOBER – **Singles:** A. Portas (1) d. J. Vanek (3) 7–5 6–3.
Doubles: A. Lopez-Moron/A. Portas (1) d. P. Kovacka/P. Kudrnac (4) 6–4 6–3.

GRENOBLE (FRA) (75H) 9–15 OCTOBER – **Singles:** A. Dupuis d. J. Siemerink (4) 7–6 7–6.
Doubles: J. Knowle/L. Manta d. Y. Allegro/J. Cuaz 6–3 6–4.

TULSA, OK (USA) (50) 9–15 OCTOBER **Singles:** J. Szymanski (7) d. R. Sluiter (1) 7–6 6–7 7–6.
Doubles: E. Abaroa/M. Sell d. G. Trifu/G.Weiner (WC) 5–7 6–4 6–2.

BUKHARA (UZB) (25H) 9–15 OCTOBER – *Singles:* N. Behr d. A. Shvec (5) 4–6 7–6 6–0.
Doubles: V. Kutsenko/O. Ogorodov (1) d. N. Behr/A. Qureshi (2) 6–4 7–6.

LIMA (PER) (100) 16–22 OCTOBER – *Singles:* G. Coria d. J. Marin (6) 6–0 7–6.
Doubles: G. Etlis/M. Rodriguez (1) d. J. Chela/L. Horna (WC) 6–2 5–2 ret.

ECKENTAL (GER) (25H) 16–22 OCTOBER – *Singles:* J. Knippschild (3) d. O. Mutis 6–7 7–6 7–5.
Doubles: K. Braasch/J. Knippschild (1) d. I. Heuberger/M. Kohlmann (4) 7–6 6–3.

SAO PAULO (BRA) (100) 23–29 OCTOBER – *Singles:* G. Coria d. T. Behrend 7–5 6–1.
Doubles: M. Hodd/S. Prieto (4) d. T. Behrend/G. Puentes 6–3 7–6.

CHARLEROI (BEL) (100H) 30 OCTOBER–5 NOVEMBER - *Singles:* J Siemerink (8) d. P. Srichaphan (6) 7–6
7–6. *Doubles:* P. Pala/P. Vizner (4) d. A. Kitinov/L. Zovko 6–7 7–5 6–1.

LAS VEGAS, NV (USA) (50) 30 OCTOBER–5 NOVEMBER - *Singles:* N. Godwin d. C. Caratti 6–3 6–3.
Doubles: J. Coetzee/M. Ondruska (1) d. M. Fish/A. Roddick (WC) 6–7 7–6 6–1.

QUITO (ECU) (25H) 30 OCTOBER–5 NOVEMBER - *Singles:* H. Armando d. P. Arquez 6–3 6–4.
Doubles: F. Costa/I. Labadze (4) d. E. Nunez/M. Stringari (WC) 6–2 7–6.

YOKOHAMA (JPN) (25H) 30 OCTOBER–5 NOVEMBER - *Singles:* E. Taino d. J. Knowle (4) 7–6 6–4.
Doubles: Y. Allegro/J. Knowle (2) d. T. Crichton/A. Fisher (1) 6–3 7–6.

SANTIAGO (CHI) (100) 6–12 NOVEMBER - *Singles:* D. Moyano d. S. Prieto (LL) 6–3 6–2.
Doubles: I. Labadze/D. Vemic d. J. Balcells/G. Puentes (2) 6–3 6–4.

BURBANK, CA (USA) (50) 6–12 NOVEMBER - *Singles:* A. Roddick (SE) d. K. Kim 6–1 6–2.
Doubles: M. Merklein/M. Sprengelmeyer d. M. Bryan/R. Bryan (1) 7–6 7–5.

SEOUL (KOR) (50) 6–12 NOVEMBER - *Singles:* H. Lee (1) d. R. Stepanek 6–4 6–4.
Doubles: T. Crichton/A. Fisher (1) d. F. Cermak/O. Fukarek 6–4 6–4.

MONTEVIDEO (URU) (100) 13–19 NOVEMBER - *Singles:* G. Coria (6) d. J. Acasuso 6–3 6–7 6–2.
Doubles: L. Arnold/G. Etlis (1) d. J. Balcells/G. Puentes (2) 6–4 6–4.

AACHEN (GER) (50H) 13–19 NOVEMBER - *Singles:* R. Schuttler (WC) (2) d. J. Settergren (Q) 7–6 1–6 6–1.
Doubles: S. Groen/J. Siemerink d. M. Kohlmann/F. Stauder (WC) 6–7 7–6 6–3.

RANCHO MIRAGE, CA (USA) (25H) 13–19 NOVEMBER - *Singles:* J. Blake d. C. Mamiit (3) 3–6 6–4 6–2.
Doubles: M. Merklein/M. Sprengelmeyer d. M. Bryan/R. Bryan (1) 6–4 3–6 7–6.

OSAKA (JPN) (25H) 13–19 NOVEMBER - *Singles:* M. Kratochvil (2) d. H. Lee (1) 2–6 6–2 6–2.
Doubles: F. Cermak/O. Fukarek (4) d. Y. Ishi/E. Taino (3) 6–1 7–6.

BUENOS AIRES (ARG) (100) 20–26 NOVEMBER - *Singles:* G. Coria (6) d. A. Berasategui 6–1 4–6 6–4.
Doubles: P. Albano/L. Arnold (1) d. S. Roitman/A. Schneiter (4) 6–3 4–6 6–2.

KNOXVILLE, TN (USA) (50) 20–26 NOVEMBER - *Singles:* C. Caratti (7) d. A. Roddick (8) 3–6 7–6 6–4.
Doubles: K. Braasch/M. Kohlmann (3) d. J. Coetzee/M. Ondruska (2) 6–0 7–6.

BREST (FRA) (100H) 20–26 NOVEMBER - *Singles:* M. Kratochvil (4) d. J. Settergren (SE) 3–6 6–4 7–6.
Doubles: T. Ketola/L. Tieleman (3) d. F. Cermak/O. Fukarek 7–6 1–6 6–3.

PUEBLA (MEX) (25H) 20–26 NOVEMBER – *Singles:* B. Hawk d. A. Dupuis (1) 7–6 6–3.
Doubles: Z. Fleishman/J. Williams (4) d. I. Heuberger/V. Liukko (3) 6–3 6–4.

URBANA, IL (USA) (50) 27 NOVEMBER–3 DECEMBER – *Singles:* J. Salzenstein (WC) d. A. Dupuis (11) 7–6
6–4. *Doubles:* T. Dent/M. Fish (WC) d. N. Behr/M. Russell w/o.

COSTA RICA (CRC) (100) 4–10 DECEMBER – *Singles:* A. Dupuis (2) d. A. Simoni 7–6 4–6 6–3.
Doubles: G. Canas/A. Garcia (Q) d. D. Bowen/B. Coupe (4) 7–6 6–1.

MILAN (ITA) (50H) 4–10 DECEMBER – *Singles:* M. Navarra d. F. Messori 6–3 7–6.
Doubles: G. Bastl/G. Galimberti (4) d. F. Messori/V. Santopadre (3) 6–4 7–6.

PRAGUE (CZE) (25H) 4–10 DECEMBER – *Singles:* J. Vacek (7) d. I. Heuberger 6–7 7–5 6–3.
Doubles: K. Pless/A. Qureshi d. I. Heuberger/V. Liukko (4) 6–4 6–4.

ITF Men's Circuit

In 2000 there were 39 Satellite Circuits for men in 21 countries and 249 Futures tournaments for men in 55 countries. Each Satellite Circuit comprises three tournaments plus a Masters play-off at which prize money and ranking points are awarded. Single-week Futures tournaments were played for the third time in 2000, having been established in 1998 to give players more opportunities to earn ranking points and prize money.

Each Satellite Circuit and Futures tournament was organised and run by the National Association of the country in which the event took place. Below are listed the winners of each Satellite Circuit, with the ATP Tour ranking points won in brackets (based on the total number of circuit points during the four weeks). Futures results are listed on the pages that follow. Prize money of (25), (15) and (10) refers to US$25,000, US$15,000 and US$10,000 respectively.

Note: The Short Sets scoring system was used experimentally at some tournaments in 2000. For a full description please refer to The ITF Year on page 29.

MEN'S SATELLITE CIRCUITS 2000

Value Circuit + US$'000	Start	Singles Winners (+ pts)	Doubles Winners (+ pts)
Central America (25)	03 Jan	A. Waske (GER) (33)	O. Motevassel (ISR)/A. Waske (GER) (34)
Spain 1 (25)	10 Jan	D. Sanchez (ESP) (33)	E. Nicolas (ESP)/G. Puentes (ESP) (33)
Egypt 1 (25)	17 Jan	D. Lorin (FRA) (33)	I. Bozic (SLO)/M. Tkalec (SLO) (29)
Switzerland 1 (25)	24 Jan	A. Fontaine (BEL)/ L. Pampoulov (AUT) (31)	A. Fontaine (BEL)/J. Pequery (FRA) (33)
Spain 2 (50)	07 Feb	E. Nicolas (ESP)/ G. Puentes (ESP) (43)	E. Nicolas (ESP)/G. Puentes (ESP) (45)
Cuba-Mexico (25)	14 Feb	R. Mello (BRA) (33)	B. Altelaar (NED)/R. Wassen (NED) (28)
Australia (25H)	21 Feb	K. Capalik (USA)/ J. Tuckfield (AUS) (43)	M. Breen (AUS)/L. Pearson (AUS) (43)
Greece 1 (25)	28 Feb	L. Mor (ISR) (33)	A. Kreitz (GER)/A. Peya (AUT) (34)
Spain 3 (25)	06 Mar	D. Caballero (ESP) (27)	J. Giner (ESP)/E. Viuda (ESP) (34)
Italy 1 (25)	13 Mar	M. Charpentier (ARG) (35)	B. Cummings (USA)/W. McGuire (USA) (30)
Croatia 1 (25)	20 Mar	K. Tiilikainen (FIN) (29)	T. Catar (SVK)/B. Sekac (SVK) (29)
Egypt 2 (25)	20 Mar	R. Farcas (ROM) (33)	A. Ghoneim (EGY)/K. Maamoun (EGY) (34)
Australia (25H)	27 Mar	S. Draper (AUS) (43)	M. Breen (AUS)/L. Pearson (AUS) (46)
Italy 2 (25)	09 Apr	O. Hernandez (ESP) (29)	O. Hernandez (ESP)/J. Jean-Pierre (FRA) (35)
Spain 4 (25)	10 Apr	O. Martinez (ESP) (20)	J. Giner (ESP)/E. Viuda (ESP) (33)
Croatia 2 (25)	17 Apr	I. Beros (CRO) (33)	U. Vico (ITA)/R. Wassen (NED) (33)
Portugal 1 (25)	01 May	B. Mota (POR)/ R. Rake (USA) (33)	M. Bartonek (CZE)/J. Cunha-Silva (POR) (33)
Turkey 1 (25)	01 May	M. Maclagan (GBR) (35)	I. Ibrisbegovic (BIH)/O. Tereshchuk (UKR) (32)
Bulgaria (25)	08 May	R. Menendez (ESP) (33)	M. Menzler (GER)/M. Wislsperger (GER) (34)
Spain 5 (25)	08 May	M. Lopez (ESP)/M. Munoz- Bejarano (ESP) (33)	M. Lopez (ESP)/E. Viuda (ESP) (31)
Turkey 2 (25)	29 May	E. Agaev (AZE) (33)	A. Ford (AUS)/A. Laporte (FRA) (36)
India 1 (25)	05 Jun	D. Udomchoke (THA) (36)	V. Chadha (IND)/K. Majmudar (USA) (33)
South Africa/ Mauritius (25)	05 Jun	W. Moodie (RSA) (34)	W. Moodie (RSA)/S. Rudman (RSA) (36)
Netherlands (25H)	12 Jun	D. Caracciolo (ARG) (43)	D. Caracciolo (ARG)/M. Pastura (ARG) (43)
Argentina 1 (25)	12 Jun	P. Bianchi (ARG) (24)	E. Massa (ARG)/L. Olguin (ARG) (33)
Italy 3 (25H)	19 Jun	E. Grossi (ITA) (43)	D. Alvarez (ITA)/N. Fracassi (ITA) (43)
Italy 4 (25)	21 Aug	F. Messori (ITA) (36)	R. Ciruolo (ITA)/F. Messori (ITA) (28)
Slovakia (25)	21 Aug	T. Cakl (CZE) (33)	B. Sekac (SVK)/M. Stepanek (CZE) (34)
West Africa (25)	21 Aug	G. Darkey (GHA) (34)	M. Fluitt (USA)/K. Thomas (USA) (33)

Value			
Circuit + US$'000	*Start*	*Singles Winners (+ pts)*	*Doubles Winners (+ pts)*
Yugoslavia (25)	21 Aug	R. Fiser-Dulic (YUG)/ V. Pavicevic (YUG) (33)	Z. Boroczky (HUN)/R. Fiser-Dulic (YUG) (34)
Switzerland (25)	28 Aug	I. Beros (CRO) (33)	A. Anderson (RSA)/K. Dewhurst (AUS) (33)
Egypt 3 (25)	11 Sep	K. Maamoun (EGY) (36)	A. Ghoneim (EGY)/K. Maamoun (EGY) (34)
USA 1 (12.5)	11 Sep	J. Brasington (USA) (33)	L. Harper-Griffith (USA)/ R. Kendrick (USA) (32)
Australia 3 (25H)	01 Oct	A. Jones (USA) (38)	S. Huss (AUS)/L. Pearson (AUS) (45)
Italy 5 (25)	02 Oct	S. Wauters (BEL) (33)	F. Messori (ITA)/D. Scala (ITA) (35)
Portugal 2 (25)	09 Oct	E. Couto (POR) (34)	N. Marques (POR)/ A. Van Grichen (POR) (34)
Spain 6 (25)	16 Oct	D. Perez (ESP) (34)	C. Rexach-Itoiz (ESP)/G. Trujillo (ESP) (32)
South Africa (25)	16 Oct	Z. Mlynarik (AUT) (33)	A. Nisker (CAN)/T. Phillips (USA) (33)
Switzerland 3 (25)	16 Oct	C. Dillschneider (SUI) (33)	M. Chiudinelli (SUI)/J. Kato (SUI) (30)

MEN'S FUTURES TOURNAMENTS 2000

PEMBROKE PINES, FL (USA) (15) 10–16 JANUARY – *Singles:* H. Levy (1) d. R. Gilbert (2) 7–6 4–6 6–2.
Doubles: G. Williams/J. Williams (4) d. R. De Mesa/I. Labadze (WC) 6–4 6–1.

GRASSE (FRA) (10H) 10–16 JANUARY – *Singles:* F. Dewulf (8) d. N. Coutelot 6–2 6–2.
Doubles: J. Gisbert/M. Roy (1) d. N. Coutelot/A. Fontaine (2) 6–4 6–4.

SECUNDERABAD (IND) (10) 10–16 JANUARY – *Singles:* L. Svarc (3) d. D. Golovanov (Q) 6–4 6–2.
Doubles: S. Panja/S. Prahlad d. H. Pramono/F. Widhiyanto 6–4 6–2.

ALTAMONTE SPRINGS, FL (USA) (15) 17–23 JANUARY – *Singles:* E. Erlich d. R. Nicklisch 7–6 6–4.
Doubles: J. Erlich/H. Levy (1) d. O. Ortiz/J. Szymanski (2) 6–3 6–4.

ANGERS (FRA) (10H) 17–23 JANUARY – *Singles:* N. Mazany (Q) d. N. Coutelot 6–4 7–6.
Doubles: O. Rochus/R. Willems d. P. Kovacka/P. Kudrnac (1) 6–4 6–4.

BANGALORE (IND) (10) 17–23 JANUARY – *Singles:* J. Ziv d. V. Bruthans 6–2 7–6.
Doubles: A. Ram/N. Welgreen (4) d. M. MacLagan/A. Qureshi (3) 2–6 6–3 6–4.

MADRAS (IND) (10) 24–29 JANUARY – *Singles:* A. Ram (3) d. L. Svarc (1) 6–4 6–3.
Doubles: A. Ram/N. Welgreen (2) d. B. Borgula/L. Svarc (WC) 6–4 5–7 6–4.

BOCA RATON, FL (USA) (15) 24–30 JANUARY – *Singles:* I. Labadze d. M. Daniel 6–4 6–4.
Doubles: G. Williams/J. Williams (1) d. M. Daniel/M. Jorquera 7–6 6–2.

FEUCHEROLLES (FRA) (10H) 24–30 JANUARY – *Singles:* C. Auffray (Q) d. N. Coutelot 6–4 6–4.
Doubles: O. Rochus/R. Willems d. N. Coutelot/L. Olguin (3) 6–1 6–2.

EASTBOURNE (GBR) (15) 31 JANUARY–6 FEBRUARY – *Singles:* H. Koll (Q) d. I. Karlovic 7–6 7–6.
Doubles: H. Andersson/H. Koll d. O. Freelove/T. Spinks 7–5 7–5.

DEAUVILLE (FRA) (10) 31 JANUARY–6 FEBRUARY – *Singles:* C. Auffray (8) d. J. Haehnel (Q) 6–2 6–3.
Doubles: J. Gisbert/M. Roy (1) d. J. Haehnel/C. Trimmel (3) 4–6 6–4 6–4.

CHIGWELL (GBR) (15) 7–13 FEBRUARY – *Singles:* G. Elseneer (Q) d. A. Parmar (1) 7–6 6–4.
Doubles: J. Davidson/F. Loven (1) d. M. Boye/I. Karlovic (2) 7–6 7–6.

ZAGREB (CRO) (15) 14–20 FEBRUARY – *Singles:* J. Vacek (3) d. A. Witt 6–4 6–3.
Doubles: I. Ancic/M. Ancic (WC) d. R. Karanusic/Z. Krajan (WC) 6–4 5–7 7–5.

CORPUS CHRISTI, TX (USA) (15) 14–20 FEBRUARY – *Singles:* D. Furmanski (3) d. Z. Fleishman (6) 6–4 4–6 7–6. *Doubles:* R. Kokavec/C. Kordasz (3) d. M. Jorquera/E. Ustundag 6–2 6–3.

ZAGREB (CRO) (15) 21–27 FEBRUARY – *Singles:* M. Ancic (WC) d. I. Karlovic (Q) 7–6 6–4.
Doubles: I. Karlovic/C. Trimmel d. T. Nurminen/J. Ojala (1) 6–4 6–4.

JAKARTA (INA) (15) 21–27 FEBRUARY – *Singles:* Z. Mlynarik d. F. Cermak (2) 4–0 ret.
Doubles: S. Wibowo/B. Wiryawan d. E. Kusdaryanto/H. Pramono (WC) 6–4 1–6 6–3.

OSORNO (CHI) (10) 21–27 FEBRUARY – *Singles:* R. Cerdera (4) d. F. Saretta 6–2 6–2.
Doubles: A. Ferreira/F. Saretta d. G. Coria/I. Gonzalez King (4) 5–7 6–4 6–0.

MONTGOMERY, TX (USA) (15) 21–28 FEBRUARY – *Singles:* D. Melo (1) d. A. Waske (6) 7–6 6–4.
Doubles: D. Melo/L. Rosa (2) d. D. Ayala/Z. Fleishman (4) 6–3 1–6 6–3.

JAKARTA (INA) (15) 28 FEBRUARY–5 MARCH – *Singles:* Y. Yoon (4) d. O. Kwon 6–2 6–4.
Doubles: F. Cermak/R. Kukal (3) d. S. Wibowo/B. Wiryawan 6–1 6–4.

SAN ANTONIO, TX (USA) (15) 28 FEBRUARY–5 MARCH – **Singles:** T. Dent (1) d. D. Melo (2) 6–2 6–3. **Doubles:** K. Brill/C. Guy (Q) d. D. Golovanov/D. September 6–4 6–4.

TEMUCO (CHI) 28 FEBRUARY–5 MARCH – **Singles:** G. Coria (SE) d. M. Delfino (LL) 6–1 6–3. **Doubles:** E. Medica/S. Roitman (2) d. A. Olivera/J. Silva 6–4 6–4.

SANTIAGO (CHI) (10) 6–12 MARCH – **Singles:** A. Simoni (2) d. D. Moyano (1) 4–6 7–6 6–0. **Doubles:** E. Medica/S. Roitman (3) d. A. Ferreira/F. Saretta 6–3 6–2.

DOUAI (FRA) (15H) 13–19 MARCH – **Singles:** I. Karlovic (Q) d. O. Rochus (3) 7–6 7–6. **Doubles:** G. Elseneer/A. Fontaine d. A. Ram/L. Zovko (1) 6–1 6–4.

MENDOZA (ARG) (10) 13–19 MARCH – **Singles:** D. Moyano (2) d. F. Saretta 6–4 6–0. **Doubles:** E. Artoni/A. Schneiter (1) d. J. Acasuso/L. Olguin 6–1 6–3.

SHIRAKO (JPN) (10) 13–19 MARCH – **Singles:** S. Barron d. M. Hromec (2) 7–6 6–4. **Doubles:** S. Barron/J. Nieminen d. A. Matsushita/M. Takada (3) 6–3 6–3.

TAKAMORI (JPN) (10) 13–19 MARCH – **Singles:** T. Terachi (2) d. V. Bruthans (7) 6–3 6–4. **Doubles:** M. Jessup/M. Le (2) d. A. Matsushita/M. Takada (4) 7–5 3–6 7–6.

POITIERS (FRA) (15H) 20–26 MARCH – **Singles:** J. Knowle d. J. Settergren 6–3 6–3. **Doubles:** M. Boye/I. Karlovic d. R. Lindstedt/F. Loven 5–7 6–3 7–6.

CORDOBA (ARG) (10) 20–26 MARCH – **Singles:** M. Delfino (Q) d. G. Coria (WC) 6–2 6–2. **Doubles:** M. Carlsson/R. Schlachter (3) d. A. Olivera/W. Schranz 5–7 6–4 7–6.

MELUN (FRA) (15H) 27 MARCH–2 APRIL – **Singles:** J. Knowle (7) d. A. Fontaine (Q) 6–4 6–4. **Doubles:** A. Tattermusch/A. Weber d. A. Fisher/J. Frontera (1) 7–6 4–6 7–6.

MOBILE, AL (USA) (15) 27 MARCH–2 APRIL – **Singles:** D. Furmanski (6) d. P. Mathieu (Q) 5–4 ret. **Doubles:** J. Boruszewski/A. Waske d. J. Cooke/Z. Mlynarik (4) 6–4 7–6.

SANTE FE (ARG) (10) 27 MARCH–2 APRIL – **Singles:** G. Coria (SE) d. D. Moyano (3) 7–6 6–4. **Doubles:** F. Cabello/M. Wowk (3) d. D. Melo/L. Rosa (1) 6–4 6–4.

ISAWA (JPN) (10) 27 MARCH–2 APRIL – **Singles:** T. Terachi (1) d. K. Masuda (4) 7–6 6–4. **Doubles:** T. Suzuki/T. Terachi d. N. Harada/H. Sato 6–4 6–3.

LITTLE ROCK, AR (USA) (15) 3–9 APRIL – **Singles:** M. Sarstrand (Q) d. D. Furmanski (3) 1–6 6–2 6–3. **Doubles:** G. Doyle/F. Niemeyer (2) d. P. Calitz/J. Williams 6–2 6–2.

CLERMONT-FERRAND (FRA) (10H) 3–9 APRIL – **Singles:** D. Elsner (6) d. O. Mutis 6–3 6–4. **Doubles:** J. Davidson/R. Lindstedt d. M. Muller/P. Sommer 3–6 7–6 6–3.

MT PLEASANT, SC (USA) (15) 10–16 APRIL – **Singles:** D. Furmanski (6) d. F. Niemeyer (3) 6–2 5–7 6–4. **Doubles:** G. Sontag/J. Turek (Q) d. G. Doyle/J. Greenhalgh (3) 7–6 7–5.

SAINT BRIEUC (FRA) (10H) 10–16 APRIL – **Singles:** D. Elsner d. T. Clemens (Q) 6–2 6–1. **Doubles:** S. De Chaunac/O. Patience d. M. Boye/J. Hanquez (1) w/o.

ELKIN, NC (USA) (15) 17–23 APRIL – **Singles:** G. Weiner (6) d. M. Nielsen (1) 5–7 6–4 6–4. **Doubles:** W. Criswell/S. Rudman d. T. Blake/K. Thomas 6–2 7–6.

SANTIAGO (CHI) (10) 17–23 APRIL – **Singles:** S. Roitman (6) d. M. Hadad (Q) 6–4 6–3. **Doubles:** A. Ferreira/F. Saretta (2) d. E. Artoni/F. Cabello (1) 7–5 7–6.

ALGIERS (ALG) (15) 24–30 APRIL – **Singles:** A. Montanes (1) d. Y. Schukin (3) 6–0 6–3. **Doubles:** P. Neito/J. Perez-Vasques (1) d. A. Montanes/C. Rexach-Itoiz 6–1 2–0 ret.

RIEMERLING (GER) (15) 24–29 APRIL – **Singles:** D. Elsner d. J. Vacek (4) 6–2 7–5. **Doubles:** R. Stepanek/R. Vasek (2) d. M. Menzler/F. Stauder 5–7 7–6 6–3.

CHENG DU (CHN) (15) 24–30 APRIL – **Singles:** B. Zhu d. M. Nielsen (1) 6–1 6–3. **Doubles:** T. Iwami/T. Terachi d. P. Baccanello/J. Tuckfield 6–2 7–6.

BOURNEMOUTH (GBR) (15) 24–30 APRIL – **Singles:** O. Mutis d. J. Weinzierl 6–4 6–3. **Doubles:** J. Davidson/V. Liukko d. O. Freelove/M. Lee (3) 7–5 6–2.

ANDIJAN (UZB) (15) 24–30 APRIL – **Singles:** L. Dahan (7) d. A. Qureshi (8) 3–6 6–3 6–3. **Doubles:** J. Erlich/L. Mor (1) d. A. Qureshi/D. Tomashevich (2) 7–6 6–4.

SANTIAGO (CHI) (10) 24–30 APRIL – **Singles:** M. Hadad (SE) d. N. Devilder (Q) 6–2 6–2. **Doubles:** J. Guzman/E. Massa d. A. Ferreira/F. Saretta (2) 7–6 ret.

ALGIERS (ALG) (15) 1–7 MAY – **Singles:** A. Montanes (2) d. V. Mazarakis (1) 6–1 6–1. **Doubles:** P. Nieto/J. Perez-Vasques (1) d. M. Chiudinelli/T. Messmer 6–2 6–1.

CHENGDU (CHN) (15) 1–7 MAY – **Singles:** M. Nielsen (1) d. K. Ziv (6) 7–6 6–4. **Doubles:** D. Bohaboy/A. Witt (Q) R. De Voest/J. Du Randt 3–6 6–4 7–5.

ESSLINGEN (GER) (15) 1–7 MAY – *Singles:* J. Andersen d. N. Thomann (Q) 3–6 6–3 6–4.
Doubles: A. Hamadeh/J. Zaatini (3) d. J. Settergen/M. Van Gemerden 6–4 6–1.

HATFIELD (GBR) (15) 1–7 MAY – *Singles:* O. Mutis d. O. Patience (4) 6–1 6–4.
Doubles: J. Frontera/I. Moldovan d. F. Cermak/R. Svetlik (2) 7–5 6–4.

NAMANGAN (UZB) (15) 1–7 MAY – *Singles:* A. Derepasko d. K. Ivanov Smolensky 4–6 6–1 6–3.
Doubles: J. Erlich/L. Mor (3) d. Y. Ishii/S. Iwabuchi (1) 6–2 4–6 6–4.

SALZBURG (AUT) (10) 1–7 MAY – *Singles:* C. Trimmel (7) d. C. Maria 6–2 6–4.
Doubles: T. Crichton/A. Fisher (1) d. B. Dabrowski/D. Sistermans (4) 6–7 6–3 6–3.

SANTIAGO (CHI) (10) 1–7 MAY – *Singles:* S. Roitman (3) d. A. Garcia (4) 6–3 6–3.
Doubles: S. Contador/J. Guzman d. J. Fillol/A. Garcia (4) 3–6 6–4 6–1.

TEURERSHOF (GER) (15) 8–14 MAY – *Singles:* N. Davydenko (Q) d. M. Op Der Heyde (8) 7–6 7–6.
Doubles: B. Altelaar/J. Weinzierl d. Z. Krajan/L. Zovko 6–4 7–5.

NEWCASTLE (GBR) (15) 8–14 MAY – *Singles:* O. Mutis d. V. Mazarakis (3) 7–5 6–2.
Doubles: F. Cermak/R. Svetlik (4) d. T. Nurminen/J. Ojala 6–4 6–2.

FUKUOKA (JPN) (15) 8–14 MAY – *Singles* T. Terachi (2) d. Y. Yoon (3) 2–6 7–6 6–1.
Doubles: H. Lee/Y. Yoon (3) d. D. Bohaboy/A. Witt 6–7 7–5 6–2.

TAMPA, FL (USA) (15) 8–14 MAY – *Singles:* B. Rehnquist (5) d. K. Capalik 6–7 7–5 6–1.
Doubles: K. Capalik/M. Guyaux d. W. Criswell/L. Vosloo 7–6 6–7 7–5.

MENDOZA (ARG) (10) 8–14 MAY – *Singles:* S. Roitman (3) d. J. Acasuso (1) 1–6 7–6 6–2.
Doubles: J. Guzman/S. Roitman d. J. Brzezicki/M. Miranda 6–3 6–4.

TELFS (AUT) (10) 8–14 MAY – *Singles:* C. Trimmel (5) d. T. Schiessling (7) 6–4 6–4.
Doubles: S. Barron/ J. Nieminen d. S. Leiner/P. Sommer (WC) 7 6 6 1.

VERONA (ITA) (10) 8–14 MAY – *Singles:* S. Cobolli (7) d. I. Kornienko 6–4 6–4.
Doubles: F. Messori/ D. Scala (3) d. T. Messmer/J. Scherrer 6–1 6–7 6–3.

CASABLANCA (MAR) (10) 8–14 MAY – *Singles:* J. Perez-Vasquez (7) d. M. El Aarej (4) 6–4 6–1.
Doubles: C. Castellanos/J. Perez-Vasquez (2) d. D. Roberts/H. Wakefield (1) 6–2 6–4.

NECKARAU (GER) (15) 15–21 MAY – *Singles:* C. Trimmel d. N. Davydenko (Q) 2–6 6–1 6–4.
Doubles: S. Jaeger/F. Jeschonek d. M. Heppler/A. Romminger w/o.

FUKUOKA (JPN) (15) 15–21 MAY – *Singles:* Y. Yoon (3) d. P. Baccanello (7) 6–4 6–7 6–4.
Doubles: M. Takada/T. Terachi (4) d. N. Harada/M. Onoda 7–6 6–7 7–5.

VERO BEACH, FL (USA) (15) 15–21 MAY – *Singles:* J. De Armas (4) d. L. Pearson (6) 6–3 7–6.
Doubles: L. Harper-Griffith/D. Toursonov d. D. Ayala/J. De Armas (3) 6–3 6–4.

SANTA FE (ARG) (10) 15–21 MAY – *Singles:* J. Acasuso (1) d. D. Hipperdinger (7) 6–0 6–4.
Doubles: cancelled due to rain.

SCHWAZ (AUT) (10) 15–21 MAY – *Singles:* K. Pless d. S. Barron 6–3 7–5.
Doubles: F. Babej/L. Dlouhy d. G. Mandl/T. Strengberger (1) 6–3 5–7 7–6.

FORLI (ITA) (10) 15–21 MAY – *Singles:* M. Dell'Acqua (3) d. M. Colla (5) 6–2 6–2.
Doubles: F. Maggi/G. Trujillo d. G. Pacchioni/P. Pambianco (WC) 6–2 6–2.

CASABLANCA (MAR) (10) 15–21 MAY – *Singles:* R. Ramirez-Hidalgo (2) d. N. Thomann 6–3 3–6 6–0.
Doubles: A. Ford/J. Kerr (3) d. J. Pequery/N. Thomann 6–3 6–2.

SEOUL (KOR) (15) 22–28 MAY – *Singles:* S. Park (6) d. Y. Yoon (2) 7–5 7–6.
Doubles: D. Kim/C. Lee d. S. Lee/S. Oh 6–3 4–6 6–2.

BOCA RATON, FL (USA) (15) 22–28 MAY – *Singles:* K. Goossens d. M. Hadad (Q) 6–3 7–5.
Doubles: M. Breen/L. Pearson (1) d. D. Mauck/ K. Pollak 6–1 6–4.

MISIONES (ARG) (10) 22–28 MAY – *Singles:* D. Hipperdinger (4) d. J. Brzezicki 6–3 6–1.
Doubles: L. Olguin/P. Rudi (1) d. S. Gutierrez/S. Uriarte 6–2 6–4.

VITERBO (ITA) (10) 22–28 MAY – *Singles:* J. Weinzierl (3) d. G. Trujillo 1–6 7–6 6–1.
Doubles: M. Dell'Aqua/ J. Weinzierl d. F. Messori/D. Scala (1) 6–3 1–6 6–4.

AGADIR (MAR) (10) 22–28 MAY – *Singles:* M. El Aarej (5) d. R. Ramirez-Hidalgo (2) 7–6 2–6 7–5.
Doubles: A. Ford/J. Kerr (3) d. I. Navarro-Pastor/R. Ramirez-Hidalgo 7–6 6–1.

DUBLIN (IRL) (15) 29 MAY–4 JUNE – *Singles:* K. Pless (Q) d. G. Doyle 6–3 6–7 6–1.
Doubles: G. Elseneer/J. Pequerry d. J. Nieminen/K. Pless 7–6 4–6 6–3.

SEOUL (KOR) (15) 29 MAY–4 JUNE – *Singles:* H. Chung (WC) d. S. Lee (WC) 6–3 6–3.
Doubles: S. Lee/S. Sohn d. S. Chung/M. Han 6–3 6–7 6–3.

TAMPA, FL (USA) (15) 29 MAY–4 JUNE – *Singles:* C. Kauffmann d. N. Behr (6) 6–3 6–3.
Doubles: E. Abaroa/ M. Hadad (2) d. M. Arnold/J. Blake (3) 6–1 7–6.

PAVIA (ITA) (10) 29 MAY–4 JUNE – *Singles:* T. Schiessling d. E. Grossi 2–6 7–6 7–5.
Doubles: I. Gaudi/T. Suzuki (3) d. F. Messori/D. Scala (2) 6–4 6–4.

GUADALAJARA (MEX) (10) 29 MAY–4 JUNE – *Singles:* A. Hernandez (1) B. Echagaray (WC) 6–3 6–4.
Doubles: D. Roditi/L. Uribe (1) d. K. Capalik/M. Guyaux 7–6 4–6 7–5.

OBERWEIER (GER) (15H) 5–11 JUNE – *Singles:* O. Rochus (5) d. N. Thomann (Q) 5–7 6–2 7–5.
Doubles: E. Artoni/F. Cabello (2) d. O. Rochus/R. Willems 6–3 6–3.

DUBLIN (IRL) (15) 5–11 JUNE – *Singles:* O. Casey (WC) d. G. Elseneer 6–3 7–6.
Doubles: J. Kerr/D. Roberts (2) d. R. Brooks/J. Scherrer 6–3 7–5.

TORINO (ITA) (10) 5–11 JUNE – *Singles:* M. Dell'Aqua (4) d. J. Van Herck 7–5 6–2.
Doubles: J. Cuaz/G. Marx (4) d. O. Camporese/E. Grossi (1) 6–3 6–1.

CAMPECHE (MEX) (10) 5–11 JUNE – *Singles:* M. Merry (5) d. R. Samuelsson (7) 6–1 7–5.
Doubles: B. Echagarry/S. Gonzales d. J. Brasington/J. Haro (WC) 6–2 4–6 6–0.

PORTOROZ (SLO) (10) 5–11 JUNE – *Singles:* B. Sekac (Q) d. L. Azzaro (1) 2–6 7–5 7–6.
Doubles: D. Morente/K. Ritz d. F. Babej/K. Maamoun 6–2 6–4.

BERKELEY, CA (USA) (15) 12–18 JUNE – *Singles:* A. Kim d. S. Barron (4) 6–3 7–5.
Doubles: G. Abrams/A. Kim (WC) d. F. Syed/B. Zhu (4) 6–2 7–5.

VILLINGEN (GER) (10H) 12–18 JUNE – *Singles:* M. Van Gemerden (5) d. N. Davydenko 6–1 7–6.
Doubles: K. Goossens/I. Moldovan d. J. Settergren/M. Van Gemerden (2) 7–6 6–3.

MISSISSAUGA (CAN) (10) 12–18 JUNE – *Singles:* D. Ayala (4) d. T. Vilen (8) 7–6 4–6 6–3.
Doubles: M. Baron/C. Sevigny d. D. Abelson/D. Ayala (1) 6–4 6–2.

BUDAPEST (HUN) (10) 12–18 JUNE – *Singles:* T. Nurminen (1) d. S. Noszali (WC) 6–0 6–4.
Doubles: R. Diaz/ S. Duran d. Z. Nagy/M. Ott (4) 7–5 4–6 7–6.

VALDENGO (ITA) (10) 12–18 JUNE – *Singles:* M. Martelli (2, WC) d. M. El Aarej (4) 7–6 6–3.
Doubles: S. Cobolli/E. Grossi (3) d. J. Cuaz/J-C. Scherrer (2) 7–6 6–3.

SKOPJE (MKD) (10) 12–18 JUNE – *Singles:* X. Pujo (8) d. M. Velev (2) 6–2 5–7 6–3.
Doubles: Z. Boroczky/R. Fiser-Dulic (Q) d. I. Cinkus/S. Pozdnev (3) 6–7 6–4 7–5.

MERIDA (MEX) (10) 12–18 JUNE – *Singles:* R. Mello (2) d. I. Hirigoyen (5) 6–4 1–6 6–4.
Doubles: J. Gutierrez/L. Uribe (4) d. M. Merry/R. Samuelsson 7–6 6–3.

KRAKOW (POL) (10) 12–18 JUNE – *Singles:* D. Ferrer (8) d. T. Fleischfresser (5) 6–1 6–0.
Doubles: F. Maggi/E. Viuda (1) d. M. Dilaj/J. Ilowski (Q) 6–3 6–4.

MARIBOR (SLO) (10) 12–18 JUNE – *Singles:* M. Tkalec (2) d. F. Pokorny 6–4 6–0.
Doubles: A. Kracman/M. Tkalec (2) d. M. Jurman/B. Urh 6–1 7–6.

NOISY-LE-GRAND (FRA) (15H) 19–25 JUNE – *Singles:* C. Trimmel (3) d. A. Montanes (1) 6–1 7–6.
Doubles: J. Cuaz/T. Lenho (2) d. J. Haehnel/V. Lavergne (4) 4–6 6–0 6–0.

TRIER (GER) (15) 19–25 JUNE – *Singles:* M. Van Gemerden (2) d. N. Davydenko (5) (WC) 4–6 6–4 6–3.
Doubles: B. Bachert/L. Uebel d. A. Schneiter/ D. Tomashevich (1) 4–6 6–4 7–5.

REDDING, CA (USA) (15) 19–25 JUNE – *Singles:* Z. Fleishman (1) d. S. Barron (8) 6–4 6–3.
Doubles: Z. Fleishman/R. Kendrick (3) d. T. Fielding/D. Roditi 7–6 6–1.

MONTREAL (CAN) (10) 19–25 JUNE – *Singles:* S. Larose (1) d. M. Jessup 7–6 6–2.
Doubles: J. Fillol/M. Jessup (3) d. M. Fish/B. Hodge 6–3 6–0.

CHALKIDA (GRE) (10) 19–25 JUNE – *Singles:* K. Ziv (1) d. M. Kempe-Bergman 6–3 6–3.
Doubles: S. Huss/T. Vasiliadis (4) d. J. Scherrer/ K. Ziv (2) 6–2 3–6 6–3.

BUDAPEST (HUN) (10) 19–25 JUNE – *Singles:* T. Nurminen (4) M. Lopez (2) 6–3 6–1.
Doubles: Z. Nagy/M. Ott (3) d. B. Cassaigne/L. Holland 6–7 6–2 7–6.

SKOPJE (MKD) (10) 19–25 JUNE – *Singles:* X. Pujo d. R. Fiser-Dulic 5–7 6–4 6–1.
Doubles: X. Pujo/C. Saubion d. K. Mitrovski/P. Rusevski 7–6 6–1.

COZUMEL (MEX) (10) 19–25 JUNE – *Singles:* J. Brasington (Q) d. J. De Armas (1) 6–3 6–2.
Doubles: M. Gallardo/M. Amador (WC) d. B. Hansen-Dent/C. Tontz (Q) 7–5 7–6.

ZABRZE (POL) (10) 19–25 JUNE – *Singles:* D. Norman (Q) d. J. Levinsky 6–3 7–6.
Doubles: P. Szczepanik/O. Tereshchuk d. D. Ferrer/D. Lencina 6–4 6–0.

KRANJ (SLO) (10) 19–25 JUNE – *Singles:* M. Tkalec (1) d. T. Clemens (6) 6–4 6–2.
Doubles: O. Marach/M. Tkalec (2) d. A. Jones/S. Kadir 6–3 6–4.

TOULON (FRA) (15) 26 JUNE–2 JULY – *Singles:* J. Kato d. K. Goossens (7) 6–3 6–4.
Doubles: J. Cuaz/J-B. Perlant d. P. Atias/J. Sciarrino 6–3 6–3.

CHICO, CA (USA) (15) 26 JUNE–2 JULY – *Singles:* Z. Fleishman (3) d. R. Kendrick 4–6 7–5 6–4.
Doubles: M. Joyce/L. Smith (1) d. Z. Fleishman/R. Kendrick (4) 7–6 6–7 6–1.

QUEBEC (CAN) (10) 26 JUNE–2 JULY – *Singles:* M. Fish (8) d. N. Todero (Q) 4–0 ret.
Doubles: N. Harada/A. Matsushita d. B. Hodge/N. Todero 6–4 6–3.

NAFPLIO (GRE) (10) 26 JUNE–2 JULY – *Singles:* K. Economidis (2) d. F. Ventura 6–4 6–0.
Doubles: D. Mauck/K. Pollak d. M. Kempe-Bergman/D. Norberg 6–0 6–1.

BUDAPEST (HUN) (10) 26 JUNE–2 JULY – *Singles:* K. Bardoczky d. J. Hasko 6–3 0–6 6–2.
Doubles: I. Brukner/O. Marach d. Z. Nagy/M. Ott (4) 6–4 2–6 6–3.

SKOPJE (MKD) (10) 26 JUNE–2 JULY – *Singles:* I. Vajda (2) d. R. Fiser-Dulic 6–3 6–4.
Doubles: R. Fiser-Dulic/M. Velev (2) d. S. Fitz/S. Pozdnev 2–6 6–2 7–6.

KATOWICE (POL) (10) 26 JUNE–2 JULY – *Singles:* D. Norman (Q) d. K. Tiilikainen (1) 6–1 6–4.
Doubles: K. Kwinta/M. Matkowski d. M. Domka/Y. Schukin (1) 6–3 7–5.

ISTANBUL (TUR) (10) 26 JUNE–2 JULY – *Singles:* N. Welgreen (7) d. A. Kreitz 7–5 6–3.
Doubles: S. Swierk/ J. Tuckfield (3) d. A. Martin/E. Ustundag (4) 7–6 6–3.

SYROS (GRE) (10) 3–9 JULY – *Singles:* K. Economidis (3) d. S. Prahlad (5) 6–2 6–2.
Doubles: S. Huss/J. Smith d. D. Mauck/K. Pollak (3) 6–2 6–4.

ISTANBUL (TUR) (10) 3–9 JULY – *Singles:* S. Swierk d. C. Kauffmann (7) 6–2 6–3.
Doubles: C. Kauffmann/J. Kerr (1) d. S. Swierk/J. Tuckfield (3) 6–1 6–2.

BOURG-EN-BRESSE (FRA) (15) 10–16 JULY – *Singles:* S. De Chaunac (3) d. E. Couto (4) 7–5 6–2.
Doubles: T. Clemens/F. Moser d. P. Calitz/B. Cassaigne (3) 6–4 6–4.

TBILISI (GEO) (15) 10–16 JULY – *Singles:* O. Tereshchuck d. C. Ferrer 6–2 6–4.
Doubles: A. Kedriouk/O. Tereshchuck (3) d. I. Brukner/M. Hromec (1) 7–6 6–4.

ALICANTE (ESP) (15) 10–16 JULY – *Singles:* O. Hernandez-Perez (4) d. D. Ferrer 2–6 6–4 7–5.
Doubles: J. Perez-Vasquez/S. Ventura (2) d. O. Hernandez-Perez/M. Roy (1) 7–6 6–4.

ISTANBUL (TUR) (10) 10–16 JULY – *Singles:* J. Tuckfield (2) d. S. Swierk (7) 7–6 6–4.
Doubles: S. Swierk/J. Tuckfield (2) d. C. Kauffmann/E. Ustundag (1) 6–3 7–5.

TBILISI (GEO) (15) 17–23 JULY – *Singles:* A. Derepasko (1) d. D. Lorin (2) 6–1 6–1.
Doubles: I. Brukner/M. Hromec (1) d. A. Derepasko/K. Ivanov-Smolensky. (2) 6–2 6–7 7–6.

JAKARTA (INA) (15) 17–23 JULY – *Singles:* D. Udomchoke (1) d. T. Iwami 6–3 6–3.
Doubles: S. Wibowo/B. Wiryawan d. H. Pramono/F. Widhiyanto (4) 6–1 6–4.

ELCHE (ESP) (15) 17–23 JULY – *Singles:* G. Fraile (8) d. M. Lopez (6) 7–6 4–6 6–2.
Doubles: O. Hernandez/M. Roy (1) d. M. Lopez/A. Martin (3) 3–6 7–6 6–4.

KANSAS CITY, MO (USA) (15) 17–23 JULY – *Singles:* J. Crabb (6) d. D. Toursounov 6–2 6–4.
Doubles: J. Laski/J. Morrison d. T. Fielding/J. Haney (WC) 7–6 6–3.

AIX-EN-PROVENCE (FRA) (10) 17–23 JULY – *Singles:* S. De Chaunac (1) d. S. Saoudi (2) 7–6 6–3.
Doubles: F. Cardinali/A. Correa (4) d. B. Cassaigne/K. Patel (2) 6–3 2–6 7–6.

LEUN (GER) (10) 17–23 JULY – *Singles:* A. Waske (1) d. J. Weinzierl (2) 6–1 6–4.
Doubles: S. Huss/L. Pearson (2) d. C. Kauffmann/A. Waske (1) (WC) 6–4 6–4.

BUDAPEST (HUN) (15) 24–30 JULY – *Singles:* P. Snobel (3) d. R. Smotlak 4–6 6–3 6–2.
Doubles: A. Hadad/V. Platenik (1) d. L. Radovanovic/R. Ribeiro 6–2 6–7 6–4.

JAKARTA (INA) (15) 24–30 JULY – *Singles:* S. Park d. H. Pramono (WC) 7–6 1–6 7–6.
Doubles: H. Pramono/F. Widhiyanto (3) d. A. Mackin/L. Pampoupo (4) 6–3 6–3.

ST. JOSEPH, MO (USA) (15) 24–30 JULY – *Singles:* D. Toursounov (7) d. P. Luczak 6–7 6–0 6–2.
Doubles: W. Moodie/S. Rudman (3) d. N. Harada/M. Onoda 6–7 7–5 6–4.

ZELL (GER) (10H) 24–30 JULY – *Singles:* B. Vujic (Q) d. I. Rodrigo-Marin 7–6 7–6.
Doubles: S. Huss/L. Pearson (2) d. W. Neefs/D. Sistermans (3) 6–4 6–4.

CAIRO (EGY) (10) 24–30 JULY – *Singles:* A. Ghoneim (2) d. M. Mertinak (Q) 7–5 6–2.
Doubles: T. Janci/M. Mertinak (4) d. A. Ghoneim/K. Maamoun (1) 6–3 7–5.

AIX-LES-BAINS (FRA) (10) 24–30 JULY – *Singles:* X. Pujo (Q) d. P. Bianchi (2) 4–2 5–4 4–5 5–3.
Doubles: L. Bourgeois/D. Marafiote (1) d. S. Duran/D. Marrero 5–4 4–2 4–2.

JESI (ITA) (10) 24–30 JULY – *Singles:* E. Grossi (1) d. A. Di Mauro (2) 1–4 4–1 4–1 3–5 4–0.
Doubles: J. Levinsky/M. Navratil d. E. Grossi/C. Santoro (2) 4–2 4–1 2–4 4–1.

GANDIA (ESP) (10) 24–30 JULY – *Singles:* D. Ferrer d. G. Fraile (5) 6–3 6–2.
Doubles: D. Ferrer/D. Perez d. A. Martin/P. Nieto (1) 2–6 6–4 6–3.

CONCORDIA (ARG) (10) 24–31 JULY – *Singles:* J-P. Guzman (1) (WC) d. P. Arquez (3) 6–3 6–1.
Doubles: J. Brzezicki/C. Villagran d. P. Arquez/S. Decoud (4) 6–3 6–1.

BERNAU (GER) (15H) 31 JULY–6 AUGUST – *Singles:* S. Greul (Q) d. J. Settergren (8) 7–6 6–3.
Doubles: S. Huss/L. Pearson (1) d. W. Neefs/D. Sistermans (3) 6–3 6–4.

BUDAORS (HUN) (15) 31 JULY–6 AUGUST – *Singles:* K. Pless (1) d. A. Peya (8) 7–5 6–3.
Doubles: I. Brukner/M. Hromec (1) d. C. Economidis/T. Vasiliadis 6–4 6–4.

DECATUR, IL (USA) (15) 31 JULY–6 AUGUST – *Singles:* J. Williams d. D. Bohaboy 4–1 5–3 4–0.
Doubles: J. Cook/J. Williams (1) d. G. Abrams/R. Smith (WC) 2–4 4–0 4–2 2–4 5–3.

CORDOBA (ARG) (10) 31 JULY–6 AUGUST – *Singles:* R. Serpa Guinaz (6) d. J. Brzezicki (8) 7–5 6–3.
Doubles: M. Stringari/T. Tenconi d. J. Guzman/M. O'Neille (1) 6–2 6–4.

CAIRO (EGY) (10) 31 JULY–6 AUGUST – *Singles:* H. Hemeda (WC) d. M. Mertinak (SE) 7–6 3–6 6–3.
Doubles: A. Ghoneim/K. Maamoun (2) d. T. Janci/M. Mertinak 3–6 6–2 6–3.

PARNU (EST) (10) 31 JULY–6 AUGUST – *Singles:* J. Ortegren d. T. Lenho 6–4 7–5.
Doubles: A. Derepasko/O. Tereshuchuk (1) d. B. Dabrowski/P. Szczepanik (2) 4–6 7–5 6–1.

VALESCURE (FRA) (10) 31 JULY–6 AUGUST – *Singles:* J. Delinbeuf (7) d. B. Cassaigne (5) 2–4 5–3 4–0 4–5 4–2. *Doubles:* B. Cassaigne/J. Cuaz (1) d. L. Bourgeois/D. Marafiote (2) 3–5 5–3 1–4 4–2 4–1.

SAN BENEDETTO DEL TRONTO (ITA) (10) 31 JULY–6 AUGUST – *Singles:* O. Marach d. E. Grossi (2) 4–2 5–3 4–5 4–1. *Doubles:* O. Marach/G. Schaller d. G. Petrazzuolo/P. Starace 5–3 5–3 4–0.

DENIA (ESP) (10) 31 JULY–6 AUGUST – *Singles:* G. Fraile (6) d. I. Navarro-Pastor 3–6 7–6 6–4.
Doubles: D. Casquero/G. Fraile (4) d. A. Martin/C. Rexach Itoiz (1) 6–1 6–3.

CAIRO (EGY) (10) 7–13 AUGUST – *Singles:* J. Pospisil (Q) d. A. Ghoneim (2) 7–6 5–7 7–5.
Doubles: R. De Mesa/L. Uribe (3) d. M. Bartonek/L. Dlouhy (4) 6–4 6–4.

JURMALA (LAT) (10) 7–13 AUGUST – *Singles:* O. Tereshchuk (4) d. R. Sproga (WC) 6–1 6–4.
Doubles: T. Larsen/A. Tattermusch (3) d. A. Kracman/M. Tkalec (1) 7–6 6–4.

XATIVA (ESP) (10) 7–13 AUGUST – *Singles:* I. Navarro-Pastor d. J. Vicente (SE) 6–1 6–4.
Doubles: R. Menendez/G. Trujillo d. D. Casquero/F. Ventura (4) 6–3 6–7 6–3.

BATH (GBR) (15) 7–13 AUGUST – *Singles:* J. Couly (Q) d. M. Maclagan (2) 5–4 2–4 4–5 5–4 4–1.
Doubles: A. Hadad/M. Maclagan (3) d. V. Snyman/H. Wakefield (1) 5–4 5–4 5–3.

GODFREY, IL (USA) (15) 7–13 AUGUST – *Singles:* M. Merklein d. C. Kauffmann (3) 1–4 4–2 4–0 4–2.
Doubles: J. Laski/G. Sontag d. J. Cook/R. Kendrik (3) 4–2 5–4 2–4 4–2.

BUENOS AIRES (ARG) (10) 7–13 AUGUST – *Singles:* P. Bianchi (3) d. I. Gonzalez-King 5–3 4–0 4–0.
Doubles: M. Stringari/T. Tenconi d. P. Rudi/L. Vitullo 4–2 5–4 4–1.

TRANI (ITA) (10H) 7–14 AUGUST – *Singles:* O. Marach (6) d. A. Di Mauro (3) 4–2 4–1 4–2.
Doubles: T. Crichton/T. Perry (1) d. D. Scala/A. Stoppini (3) 5–3 4–2 4–2.

BERLIN (GER) (15) 7–14 AUGUST – *Singles:* J. Settergren (2) d. C. Cuadrado (Q) 6–3 6–1.
Doubles: H. Andersson/J. Settergren (1) d. W. Neefs/D. Sistermans (2) 6–3 5–7 7–5.

KASSEL (GER) (15) 14–20 AUGUST – *Singles:* G. Fraile (4) d. H. Andersson (3) 6–4 6–1.
Doubles: S. Wolpers/T. Wolpers d. S. Adamson/E. Faulk 6–1 6–1.

AMMAN (JOR) (15) 14–20 AUGUST – *Singles:* B. Cassaigne (7) d. A. Ghoneim (1) 6–3 6–4.
Doubles: A. Ghoneim/K. Maamoun (2) d. M. Slanar/D. Tomashevich 6–3 6–7 6–3.

BALASHIKHA (RUS) (15) 14–20 AUGUST – *Singles:* D. Vlasov d. A. Derepasko (1) 6–1 7–5.
Doubles: A. Kedriouk/O. Motevassel (1) d. A. Makhkamov/S. Pozdnev (4) 6–3 6–2.

VILNIUS (LTU) (10) 14–20 AUGUST – *Singles:* R. Muraska (WC) d. M. Tkalec (1) 6–1 6–4.
Doubles: A. Kracman/M. Tkalec (1) d. J. Brunstrom/T. Steinel-Hanss (Q) 6–3 6–2.

BUENOS AIRES (ARG) (10) 14–20 AUGUST – *Singles:* G. Marcaccio d. J. Guzman (2) 6–1 6–7 7–5.
Doubles: G. Marcaccio/P. Rudi (1) d. G. Carry/D. Cristin (WC) 3–6 6–1 6–1.

VIGO (ESP) (15) 14–20 AUGUST – *Singles:* O. Marach (7) d. D. Perez 4–0 1–4 4–0 5–4.
Doubles: M. Fornell/D. Perez (4) d. P. Pereira/A. Van Grichen (3) 4–2 4–1 4–2.

HAMPSTEAD (GBR) (15) 14–21 AUGUST – *Singles:* F. Fetterlein (Q) d. P. Baccanello (2) 1–4 5–4 4–2 5–4.
Doubles: J. Davidson/O. Freelove (1) d. S. Dickson/D. Sherwood 4–2 4–1 4–0.

AMMAN (JOR) (15) 21 27 AUGUST – *Singles:* B. Zhu (?) d. A. Ghoneim (1) 6–1 6–4.
Doubles: H. Hemeda/M. Zewar d. V. Bruthans/N. Karagiannis (4) 6–4 6–2.

ZHUKOVSKI (RUS) (15) 21–27 AUGUST – *Singles:* D. Vlasov d. S. Pozdnev (8) 4–6 6–3 6–3.
Doubles: M. Elgin/R. Nourmatov d. S. Krotiouk/E. Smirnov 3–6 6–3 6–0.

IRUN (ESP) (15) 21–27 AUGUST – *Singles:* P. Canovas d. R. Alvarez 4–2 4–0 4–2.
Doubles: A. Da Col/A. Martin (3) d. J. Fernandez/F. Ventura 4–5 3–5 5–4 4–1 4–1.

LUXEMBOURG (LUX) (10) 21–27 AUGUST – *Singles:* D. Norman (5) d. P. Dezort (7) 6–3 7–6.
Doubles: C. Kas/D. Norman d. R. De Voest/W. Meyer (4) 6–1 7–6.

ALPHEN A/D RIJN (NED) (15H) 28 AUGUST–3 SEPTEMBER – *Singles:* D. Van Scheppingen (2) (WC) d. M.
Merry (Q) 6–3 6–1. *Doubles:* M. Merry/D. Van Scheppingen d. L. Olguin/M. Wowk (3) 6–4 7–5.

SANTANDER (ESP) (15) 28 AUGUST–3 SEPTEMBER – *Singles:* D. Hipperdinger d. A. Martin (Q) 5–4 1–4
4–0 4–2. *Doubles:* C. Rexach-Itoiz/G. Trujillo d. E. Nicolas/M. Roy (1) 4–1 4–0 4–2.

SANTO DOMINGO (DOM) (10) 28 AUGUST–3 SEPTEMBER – *Singles:* Y. Romero (5) B. Cassaigne (4) 6–3
7–5. *Doubles:* L. Manrique/J. Rojer d. J. Layne/M. Pehar (3) 6–4 4–6 7–5.

LIMA (PER) (10) 28 AUGUST–3 SEPTEMBER – *Singles:* J. Silva (6) d. J. Peralta (Q) 7–6 3–6 6–3.
Doubles: P. Arquez/I. Gonzalez-King (2) d. C. Berlocq/F. Cardinali 7–5 6–1.

LODZ (POL) (10) 28 AUGUST–3 SEPTEMBER – *Singles:* K. Pfeiffer (1) d. J. Stasiak 6–3 7–6.
Doubles: I. Brukner/P. Dezort (1) d. J. Hajek/M. Leysek 6–1 6–4.

HILVERSUM (NED) (15H) 4–10 SEPTEMBER – *Singles:* D. Van Scheppingen (1) (SE) d. F. Saretta (6) (Q) 7–6
3–6 7–6. *Doubles:* L. Oguin/M. Wowk (4) d. P. Bianchi/D. Carracciolo 7–6 7–6.

ZNOJMO (CZE) (15) 4–10 SEPTEMBER – *Singles:* C. Kas (8) d. M. Hromec (3) 6–1 3–6 6–2.
Doubles: I. Brukner/M. Hromec (1) d. R. Dueller/C. Kas 3–6 6–1 6–4.

GALATI (ROM) (15) 4–10 SEPTEMBER – *Singles:* L. Azzaro (4) d. R. Ramirez-Hidalgo (2) 6–4 2–6 4–2 ret.
Doubles: L. Azzaro/F. Maggi (2) d. G. Cosac/C. Gard 7–5 6–2.

OVIEDO (ESP) (15) 4–10 SEPTEMBER – *Singles:* R. Menendez (4) d. J. Perez (6) 4–2 1–4 4–1 4–2.
Doubles: C. Rexach/G. Trujillo (3) d. G. Fraile/R. Menendez 0–4 1–4 5–4 5–4 4–2.

NASSAU (BAH) (10) 4–10 SEPTEMBER – *Singles:* F. Giers (4) d. Y. Ishii (2) 6–7 6–3 6–3.
Doubles: Y. Ishii/K. Majmudar (1) d. B. Cassaigne/B. Cummings 7–6 7–5.

LIMA (PER) (10) 4–10 SEPTEMBER – *Singles:* D. Veronelli d. J. Guzman (3) 3–0 ret.
Doubles: G. Marcaccio/P. Rudi (1) d. M. Miranda/J. Yanez 7–6 0–6 6–0.

SZCZECIN (POL) (10) 4–10 SEPTEMBER – *Singles:* V. Chvets (8) d. B. Dabrowski (3) 6–2 6–1.
Doubles: V. Chvets/V. Kazhera d. B. Dabrowski/M. Gawlowski (2) 6–1 6–2.

OSLO (NOR) (10) 9–16 SEPTEMBER – *Singles:* J. Settergren (2) d. H. Andersson (3) 7–6 7–5.
Doubles: H. Andersson/J. Settergren (2) d. A. Tattermusch/U. Tippenhauer (4) 6–3 7–6.

BAGNERES-DE-BIGORRE (FRA) (15H) 11–17 SEPTEMBER – *Singles:* J. Perlant d. F. Saretta (5) 4–6 6–3
6–2. *Doubles:* R. De Voest/F. Niemeyer d. D. Abelson/J. Turek (3) 6–3 6–4.

BUCHAREST (ROM) (15) 11–17 SEPTEMBER – *Singles:* D. Hipperdinger d. M. Munoz-Bejarano (2) 6–0
6–2. *Doubles:* L. Azzaro/F. Maggi (3) d. D. Alvarez/R. Ramirez-Hidalgo (1) 7–5 6–4.

WEST HAMPTON, NY (USA) (15) 11–17 SEPTEMBER – *Singles:* D. Vlasov (8) d. T. Blake 6–7 7–5 6–3.
Doubles: V. Chadha/J. Shortall d. D. Montes De Oca/J. Parker (WC) 6–4 2–6 6–3.

KARLOVY VARY (CZE) (15) 11–17 SEPTEMBER – *Singles:* Z. Mlynarik (6) d. J. Hernych (3) 6–3 7–6.
Doubles: J. Hobler/P. Snobel (3) d. T. Messmer/S. Randjelovic (2) 3–6 6–4 6–4.

KINGSTON (JAM) (10) 11–17 SEPTEMBER – *Singles:* N. Todero d. R. Russell (WC) 6–3 6–2.
Doubles: J. Smith/S. Willinsky (WC) d. J. Layne/M. Pehar (3) 6–2 7–5.

KASHIWA (JPN) (10) 11–17 SEPTEMBER – *Singles:* S. Suwandi (4) d. B. Becker (Q) 6–7 6–4 7–6.
Doubles: J. Gooding/D. McNamara d. T. Iwami/M. Takada (2) 6–7 6–4 7–6.

LIMA (PER) (10) 11–17 SEPTEMBER – *Singles:* I. Miranda d. M. O'Neille (4) 7–6 6–4.
Doubles: P. Arquez/I. Gonzalez-King (4) d. T. Alves/B. Soares 7–6 7–6.

POZNAN (POL) (10) 11–17 SEPTEMBER – *Singles:* V. Chvets d. /O. Le Jeune 6–3 6–2.
Doubles: F. Aniola/M. Fyrstenberg (3) d. S. Samoseiko/R. Sproga 4–6 6–3 6–1.

MADRID (ESP) (10) 11–17 SEPTEMBER – *Singles:* J. Couly (6) d. M. Scheidweiler 6–2 7–6.
Doubles: J. Perez-Vazquez/A. Martin (1) d. E. Couto/P. Pereira (2) 6–4 6–4.

VITORIA (BRA) (15) 18–24 SEPTEMBER – *Singles:* R. Mello (2) d. J. Silva 6–4 6–3.
Doubles: R. Ribeiro/J. Silva (4) d. M. Carlsson/A. Guevara 6–7 6–4 6–2.

ORISTANO (ITA) (15) 18–24 SEPTEMBER – *Singles:* F. Messori d. M. Dell'Acqua (1) 6–4 6–7 6–2.
Doubles: O. Camporese/I. Kornienko d. D. Bracciali/F. Messori 4–6 7–6 7–5.

GORLOVKA (UKR) (15) 18–24 SEPTEMBER – *Singles:* K. Tiilikainen (3) d. G. Kisgyorgy (5) 6–1 6–1.
Doubles: G. Kisgyorgy/K. Tiilikainen d. L. Dahan/J. Ojala (2) 6–4 6–3.

EAST SETAUKET, NY (USA) (15) 18–24 SEPTEMBER – *Singles:* D. Vlasov (6) d. I. Hirigoyen (4) 6–1 6–3.
Doubles: G. Galimberti/F. Syed (2) d. J. McGregor/N. Toroman 6–7 7–5 6–4.

LA PAZ (BOL) (10) 18–24 SEPTEMBER – *Singles:* P. Arquez (2) d. M. Miranda (4) 6–3 7–6.
Doubles: J. Fillol/M. Miranda (2) d. P. Arquez/I. Gonzalez-King (1) 6–3 6–4.

SUNDERLAND (GBR) (10) 18–24 SEPTEMBER – *Singles:* B. Parun (4) d. S. Dickson (5) 5–4 5–4 ret.
Doubles: J. Auckland/B. Fulcher d. B. Haran/N. Watts 5–4 4–2 4–5 4–1.

CHIBA (JPN) (10) 18–24 SEPTEMBER – *Singles:* L. Holland (3) d. J. Gooding 6–3 0–6 7–5.
Doubles: J. Gooding/D. McNamara d. B. Wiryawan/S. Wibowo (3) w/o.

GOTHENBURG (SWE) (10) 18–24 SEPTEMBER – *Singles:* H. Koll (1) d. K. Flygt (7) 3–6 6–2 6–4.
Doubles: R. Lindstedt/F. Loven (1) d. A. Tattermusch/U. Tippenhauer (4) 6–2 6–4.

MULHOUSE (FRA) (15H) 18–25 SEPTEMBER – *Singles:* I. Karlovic (Q) d. A. Dupuis (1) 6–7 7–6 6–4.
Doubles: V. Liukko/R. Wassen (4) d. W. Moodie/S. Rudman 7–5 6–3.

GOTHENBURG (SWE) (10) 25–30 SEPTEMBER – *Singles:* J. Settergren (1) d. K. Flygt (7) 5–7 7–5 6–1.
Doubles: A. Kreitz/A. Peya (3) d. J. Christensen/C. Hansen (Q) 6–3 7–6.

PLAISIR (FRA) (15H) 25 SEPTEMBER–1 OCTOBER – *Singles:* D. Norman d. A. Chesnokov 6–3 5–7 6–4.
Doubles: J. Benneteau/N. Mahut (2) d. N. Behr/A. Qureshi (1) 6–3 7–6.

FLORIANOPOLIS (BRA) (15) 25 SEPTEMBER–1 OCTOBER – *Singles:* D. Veronelli d. J. Acasuso 6–2 6–4.
Doubles: M. Carlsson/R. Schlachter (1) d. M. Vassallo-Arguello/D. Veronelli (2) 2–6 6–3 6–4.

SELARGIUS (ITA) (15) 25 SEPTEMBER–1 OCTOBER – *Singles:* F. Messori (1) d. R. Karanusic (Q) 6–2 6–2.
Doubles: R. De Voest/L. Pampoulov (4) d. K. Pollak/J. Williams (1) 7–6 6–7 6–4.

COCHABAMBA (BOL) (10) 25 SEPTEMBER–1 OCTOBER – *Singles:* P. Arquez (2) d. F. Parada 6–4 6–4.
Doubles: G. Marcaccio/P. Rudi (1) d. R. Daruich/C. Villagran 6–1 6–2.

GLASGOW (GBR) (10) 25 SEPTEMBER–1 OCTOBER – *Singles:* J. Scherrer d. L. Childs 5–3 5–4 4–2.
Doubles: S. Dickson/M. Hilton (3) d. N. McDonald/J. Smith 5–4 4–2 4–2.

BARCELONA (ESP) (10) 25 SEPTEMBER–1 OCTOBER – *Singles:* D. Hipperdinger (4) d. F. Fogues 6–3 6–2.
Doubles: J. Marse/G. Platel d. C. Rexach/G. Trujillo (2) 3–6 6–4 6–3.

KAWAGUCHI (JPN) (10) 25 SEPTEMBER–1 OCTOBER – *Singles:* D. Gremelmayr d. L. Holland (2) 6–1 6–2.
Doubles: T. Iwami/M. Takada (1) d. N. Harada/A. Matsushita (2) 4–6 6–3 6–4.

GULISTAN (UZB) (10) 25 SEPTEMBER–1 OCTOBER – *Singles:* A. Shvec (1) d. M. Mertinak (6) 6–7 6–1 6–4.
Doubles: J. Levinsky/B. Sekac (2) d. G. Gueit/S. Lami 3–6 6–3 6–2.

GORLOVKA (UKR) (15) 25 SEPTEMBER–2 OCTOBER – *Singles:* S. Cobolli (4) d. V. Chvets 2–6 6–3 6–2.
Doubles: V. Chvets/S. Pozdnev (4) d. S. Cobolli/S. Krotiouk (3) 6–3 7–5.

NEVERS (FRA) (15H) 2–8 OCTOBER – *Singles:* J. Haehnel d. N. Behr (2) 6–7 7–5 6–3.
Doubles: N. Behr/A. Qureshi (1) d. D. Abelson/M. Stepanek (3) 6–2 6–1.

EDINBURGH (GBR) (15) 2–8 OCTOBER – *Singles:* W. Moodie d. L. Childs (WC) 4–5 5–3 4–2 4–5 5–3.
Doubles: W. Moodie/S. Rudman (2) d. L. Milligan/G. Sontag 5–4 4–2 5–4.

SANTA CRUZ (BOL) (10) 2–8 OCTOBER – *Singles:* P. Rudi (4) d. P. Arquez (3) 6–1 6–7 7–6.
Doubles: J. Brzezicki/C. Villagran d. J. Fillol/M. Miranda (2) 7–5 6–3.

MARTOS (ESP) (10) 2–8 OCTOBER – *Singles:* F. Fogues (SE) d. J. Cook (Q) 4–6 7–6 6–2.
Doubles: J. Jimenez-Guerra/J. Perez-Vasquez (2) d. J. Garcia-Sintes/M. Roy (1) 6–1 7–5.

KARSHI (UZB) (10) 2–8 OCTOBER – *Singles:* L. Dahan (2) d. D. Tomashevich (3) 6–4 6–3.
Doubles: V. Bruthans/B. Sekac (4) d. A. Makhkamov/D. Tomashevich (1) 6–2 6–2.

LEEDS (GBR) (15) 9–15 OCTOBER – *Singles:* L. Childs (WC) d. B. Parun 5–4 5–3 5–3.
Doubles: L. Childs/J. Nelson d. J. Auckland/B. Fulcher 5–4 5–3 2–4 4–2.

ASUNCION (PAR) (15) 9–15 OCTOBER – *Singles:* J. Silva (4) d. N. Fracassi 6–4 6–1.
Doubles: J. Brzezicki/C.Villagran d M. Carlsson/R. Schlachter (1) 7–5 6–3.

FORBACH (FRA) (10) 9–15 OCTOBER – *Singles:* J. Haehnel (6) d. L. Demiliani 6–3 6–3.
Doubles: M. Muller/A. Tattermusch (2) d. D. Dier/B. Jacob (3) 6–3 7–6.

EL EJIDO (ESP) (10) 9–15 OCTOBER – *Singles:* J. Lido d. J. Jimenez Guerra 3–6 6–4 6–1.
Doubles: F. Hemmes/C. Marcote d. R. Brooks/R. Merchan 6–3 6–3.

BOGOTA (COL) (15) 16 22 OCTOBER – *Singles:* M. Hadad (2) d. I. Azzaro (1) 6–2 7–5.
Doubles: G. Lapentti/R. Torres d. G. Marcaccio/P. Rudi (1) 7–5 2–0 ret.

NEGRIL (JAM) (15) 16–22 OCTOBER – *Singles:* D. Andersson (8) d. P. Snobel (1) 7–6 6–1.
Doubles: T. Blake/M. Merklein (1) d. T. Nigri/R. Ortegren 4–6 6–3 6–2.

ASUNCION (PAR) (15) 16–22 OCTOBER – *Singles:* E. Massa (5) d. P. Arquez (2) 7–5 6–1.
Doubles: P. Arquez/I. Gonzalez-King (3) d. D. Caracciolo/N. Fracassi (2) 6–3 6–1.

WACO, TX (USA) (15) 16–22 OCTOBER – *Singles:* M. Verkerk (2) d. S. Larose 6–1 6–2.
Doubles: W. Moodie/S. Rudman (2) d. V. Luikko/K. Tiilikainen (4) 6–3 6–4.

VIERUMAKI (FIN) (10) 16–22 OCTOBER – *Singles:* A. Peya (7) d. T. Nurminen (2) 4–6 6–2 6–4.
Doubles: M. Kempe-Bergman/D. Rehnqvist d. M. Pennonen/T. Steinel-Hansson 3–6 6–2 7–5.

SAINT DIZIER (FRA) (10) 16–22 OCTOBER – *Singles:* G. Elseneer (6) d. T. Aerts (4) 6–2 6–2.
Doubles: I. Brukner/M. Hromec (1) d. N. Beirnaert/M. Sicco 6–3 7–6.

LA ROCHE SUR YON (FRA) (15H) 23–29 OCTOBER – *Singles:* J. Vacek (3) d. A. Fontaine 6–4 6–2.
Doubles: M. Hromec/W. Neefs (2) d. J. Settergren/M. Van Gemerden 6–3 1–6 7–6.

BOGOTA (COL) (15) 23–29 OCTOBER – *Singles:* M. Hadad (2) d. L. Azzaro (1) 6–1 4–2 ret.
Doubles: L. Azzaro/E. Ran (1) d. A. Falla/P. Gonzalez 6–2 6–2.

BANDUNG (INA) (15) 23–29 OCTOBER – *Singles:* L. Svarc (1) d. D. September (5) 6–1 6–3.
Doubles: G. Gueit/L. Svarc d. S. Wibowo/B. Wiryawan (4) 7–6 2–6 6–2.

NEGRIL (JAM) (15) 23–29 OCTOBER – *Singles:* J. Hajek (Q) d. J. Ortegren (3) 6–3 6–1.
Doubles: J. Kareld/J. Ortegren d. S. Martinez/L. Navarro (2) 7–5 6–2.

HOUSTON, TX (USA) (15) 23–29 OCTOBER – *Singles:* W. Moodie d. A. Waske (1) 6–3 6–3.
Doubles: W. Moodie/S. Rudman (1) d. E. Carter/B. Hawk 6–3 6–4.

HELSINKI (FIN) (10) 23–29 OCTOBER – *Singles:* T. Nurminen (3) d. M. Sarstrand (4) 6–4 7–5.
Doubles: K. Beck/I. Zelenay d. J. Nieminen/T. Vilen 6–2 6–4.

CHANIA (GRE) (10) 23–29 OCTOBER – *Singles:* K. Economidis (2) d. I. Vajda (6) 4–6 6–4 6–4.
Doubles: V. Bruthans/B. Sekac (3) d. I. Cinkus/K. Ritz 3–6 6–2 6–3.

RODEZ (FRA) (10) 30 OCTOBER–4 NOVEMBER – *Singles:* J. Pequery (2) d. M. Hromec (5) 6–7 6–3 6–4.
Doubles: M. Bauer/S. Lami d. N. Beirnaert/M. Sicco 6–4 7–5.

JAKARTA (INA) (15) 30 OCTOBER–5 NOVEMBER – *Singles:* L. Svarc (1) d. L. Holland (6) 6–2 6–0.
Doubles: H. Pramono/F. Widhiyanto (3) d. S. Wibowo/B.Wiryawan (4) 3–6 6–2 7–5.

HATTIESBURG, MS (USA) (15) 30 OCTOBER–5 NOVEMBER – *Singles:* S. Barron (3) d. D. Toursounov (6) 6–7 7–6 6–3. *Doubles:* W. Moodie/S. Rudman (3) d. T. Blake/V. Snyman (2) 7–6 6–7 6–1.

HELSINKI (FIN) (10) 30 OCTOBER–5 NOVEMBER – *Singles:* A. Peya (4) d. J. Adaktusson 6–2 6–2.
Doubles: A. Kreitz/A. Peya (2) d. L. Kiiski/T. Nieminen 6–4 6–1.

ERAKLIO (GRE) (10) 30 OCTOBER–5 NOVEMBER – *Singles:* F. Jeschonek d. K. Economidis (2) 7–5 3–6 6–4.
Doubles: I. Cinkus/ K. Ritz d. J. Ager/K. Gruber (Q) 3–6 6–2 6–3.

ZACATECAS (MEX) (10) 30 OCTOBER–5 NOVEMBER – *Singles:* G. Kisgyorgy (1) d. R. Carvalho 6–4 7–6.
Doubles: E. Bergmann/G. Kisgyorgy (1) d. E. Morones/O. Ortiz (WC) 7–6 7–5.

LUCKNOW (IND) (10) 6–11 NOVEMBER – *Singles:* J. Marray (Q) d. L. Demiliani (4) 7–5 0–6 7–5.
Doubles: L. Demiliani/D. Pizzato d. N. Kirtane/V. Uppal (2) 6–2 6–4.

BEAUMARIS (AUS) (15) 6–12 NOVEMBER – *Singles:* R. Zitko d. P. Hanley 6–2 6–4.
Doubles: J. Gooding/D. McNamara 6–2 3–6 6–4.

LAFAYETTE, LA (USA) (15) 6–12 NOVEMBER – *Singles:* J. Bower (2) d. J. Morrison 6–7 6–3 6–0.
Doubles: J. Brasington/D. Root (3) d. T. Blake/J. Morrison (2) w/o.

NICOSIA (CYP) (10) 6–12 NOVEMBER – *Singles:* O. Marach (2) d. T. Cakl (5) 6–2 6–4.
Doubles: A. Kracman/M. Tkalec (2) d. I. Cinkus/K. Ritz w/o.

LEON (MEX) (10) 6–12 NOVEMBER – *Singles:* M. Sanchez (WC) d. T. Boniecki 6–7 6–3 6–3.
Doubles: G. Maldonado/M. Sanchez (WC) d. R. Royt/J. Vrbka w/o.

NONTHABURI (THA) (10) 6–12 NOVEMBER – *Singles:* D. Tomashevich (3) d. D. Mazur (7) 6–4 3–6 6–3.
Doubles: V. Samrej/N. Srichaphan d. L. Radovanovich/D. September (4) 7–6 6–1.

CHANDIGARH (IND) (10) 13–18 NOVEMBER – *Singles:* S. Krotiouk d. J. Doran (Q) 6–2 6–2.
Doubles: T. Janci/M. Mertinak d. V. Bruthans/B. Sekac (4) 6–4 6–1.

FRANKSTON (AUS) (15) 13–19 NOVEMBER – *Singles:* T. Larkham (Q) d. P. Hanley (SE) 6–4 6–3.
Doubles: P. Baccanello/J. Tuckfield (4) d. S. Huss/L. Pearson (3) 7–6 4–6 6–1.

CLEARWATER, FL (USA) (15) 13–19 NOVEMBER – *Singles:* J. Bower (2) d. I. Hirigoyen (5) 6–1 6–3.
Doubles: J. Bower/V. Snyman (1) d. M. Pehar/L. Zovko (2) w/o.

TORREON (MEX) (10) 13–19 NOVEMBER – *Singles:* M. Sanchez d. M. Amador 6–1 6–1.
Doubles: G. Maldonado/M. Sanchez d. M. Fluitt/K. Thomas (2) 6–2 6–1.

PATTAYA (THA) (10) 13–19 NOVEMBER – *Singles:* D. Tomashevich (2) d. D. September (1) 6–4 6–2.
Doubles: V. Samrej/N. Srichaphan d. J. Smith/S. Smith 6–4 6–2.

BERRI (AUS) (15) 19–26 NOVEMBER – *Singles:* D. Petrovic (1) d. P. Baccanello (3) 6–3 6–4.
Doubles: P. Baccanello/D. Petrovic (2) d. S. Huss/L. Pearson (1) 6–3 6–4.

MUMBAI (IND) (10) 20–25 NOVEMBER – *Singles:* J. Doran (Q) d. J. Hasko (1) 6–2 6–2.
Doubles: V. Bruthans/B. Sekac (1) d. J. Doran/K. Shah (WC) 6–4 7–5.

LAS PALOMAS (ESP) (15) 20–26 NOVEMBER – *Singles:* T. Nurminen (6) d. D. Hipperdinger (2) 6–3 5–7 7–5. *Doubles:* T. Cakl/D. Hipperdinger d. M. Chiudinelli/J. Kato (3) 6–2 6–2.

HO CHI MINH CITY (VIE) 20–26 NOVEMBER – *Singles:* A. Qureshi (2) d. J. Levinsky (8) 3–6 6–2 6–3.
Doubles: A. Fisher/A. Qureshi (1) d. J. Levinsky/M. Naratil 6–4 6–4.

SANTIAGO (CHI) (10) 20–26 NOVEMBER – *Singles:* H. Gamonal (Q) d. M. Miranda 7–5 6–3.
Doubles: J. Fillol/I Gonzalez-King (2) d. M. Carlsson/ R. Schlachter (1) 6–4 6–7 7–5.

MALIBU, CA (USA) (15) 20–26 NOVEMBER – *Singles:* D. Toursounov (6) d. J. De Armas (7) (Q) 6–2 6–1.
Doubles: J. De Armas/D. Sistermans (1) d. S. Graeff/A. Ross (WC) 7–6 6–4.

BARMERA (AUS) (15) 26 NOVEMBER–3 DECEMBER – *Singles:* L. Smith d. P. Hanley (WC) 3–6 6–4 7–5.
Doubles: T. Crichton/T. Perry (2) d. S. Huss/L. Pearson (3) 4–6 7–6 7–6.

VINA DEL MAR (CHI) (10) 27 NOVEMBER–3 DECEMBER – *Singles:* H. Gamonal (SE) 3–6 7–5 6–2. *Doubles:* R. Schlachter/J. Yanez d. H. Gamonal/P. Harboe (WC) 3–6 7–5 6–3.

MASPALOMAS (ESP) (15) 27 NOVEMBER–3 DECEMBER – *Singles:* D. Hipperdinger (3) d. G. Fraile (2) 6–3 6–3. *Doubles:* D. Perez/F. Ventura d. F. Betencourt/F. Serra 6–5 ret.

MANILA (PHI) (15) 27 NOVEMBER–3 DECEMBER – *Singles:* Z. Mlynarik (3) d. Y. Yoon (1) 4–6 6–0 6–2.
Doubles: A. Anderson/R. De Voest (3) d. D. Marafiote/L. Radovanovich 7–5 6–7 6–2.

LAGUNA NIGUEL, CA (USA) (15) 28 NOVEMBER–3 DECEMBER – *Singles:* J. Bower (6) d. A. Kim 7–5 6–0.
Doubles: K. Beck/C. Kauffmann d. K. Gullett/D. Sistermans 6–2 6–3.

SANTIAGO (CHI) (10) 4–10 DECEMBER – *Singles:* P. Rudi (6) d. J. Peralta (Q) 3–6 7–6 6–0.
Doubles: M. O'Neille/P. Rudi (4) d. M. Vassallo/D. Veronelli 6–4 1–0 ret.

MANILA (PHI) (15) 4–10 DECEMBER – *Singles:* D. Udomchoke (2) d. Y. Yoon (1) 6–3 3–6 7–5.
Doubles: D. September/D. Udomchoke d. D. Marafiote/L. Radovanovic (3) 6–4 6–3.

SCOTTSDALE, AZ (USA) (15) 4–10 DECEMBER – *Singles:* D. Toursounov d. S. Wauters 6–4 7–5.
Doubles: G. Sontag/J. Turek (2) d. Z. Fleishman/J. Williams (1) 6–4 6–0.

ITF Women's Circuit

The ITF Women's Circuit currently offers tournaments in 52 countries worldwide. These events enable players to gain experience and earn the ranking points necessary to enter professional events and ultimately play on the Sanex WTA Tour. The ITF Women's Circuit is the vital link between Junior tennis, the Tour and the Grand Slams.

Women's Circuit Events are categorised as follows:

$20,000 Circuits
A circuit of 3 tournaments plus a Masters tournament, each offering $5,000 in prize money. Only the Masters tournament offers ranking points.

$40,000 Circuits
A circuit of 3 tournaments plus a Masters tournament, each offering $10,000 in prize money.

$10,000, $25,000, $50,000 and $75,000 tournaments
Individual tournaments with $10,000, $25,000, $50,000 or $75,000 prize money.

$50,000+H and $75,000+H tournaments
Individual tournaments of $50,000 or $75,000 prize money which offer hospitality.

During 2000 overall totals of prize money and tournaments have risen to record levels with $5.89 million in prize money available and 309 events scheduled on the calendar.

The country by country breakdown of events for 2000 shows good global representation, with the majority of the events (162) on the Circuit taking place in Europe. North America continues to provide many playing opportunities, with 45 tournaments taking place in the USA alone. A total of 49 events took place in Asia with 28 tournaments in South and Central America.

One of the goals of the Women's Circuit remains to provide balance in the calendar, giving players around the world the best access to tournaments upon which to build their careers.

The ITF Women's Circuit programmes continue to be successful. The Junior Exempt Project, where the year-end top ten female Junior players are given places in the Main Draws of three selected ITF $25,000, $50,000 and $75,000 events has now been in effect for four years. The programme brings great benefit to the participating players in terms of gaining important experience on the senior circuit. The Feed Up system has been in place for many years and offers the winner of selected $25,000 ITF Women's Circuit events the opportunity of securing a spot in the qualifying draw of a designated Sanex WTA Tour tournament. The winner of selected $50,000/$75,000 ITF Women's Circuit events has the opportunity of securing a spot in the main draw of a designated Sanex WTA Tour tournament.

As well as serving the needs of its players, the Women's Circuit has an obligation to encourage the growth and development of tournaments, both through its National Associations and private promoters. With this in mind, the Department is compiling a set of comprehensive guidelines to assist organisers of all levels of Women's Circuit events with the planning and preparation of an international women's tennis tournament.

It remains the ITF Women's Circuit's aim to continue to strive towards raising the profile and improving standards at all Women's Circuit events and to promote tennis in general to the benefit of all women tennis players and the National Associations.

Note: The Short Sets scoring system was used experimentally at some tournaments in 2000. For a full description please refer to The ITF Year on page 29.

ITF WOMEN'S $20,000 TOURNAMENTS

Reynosa, Mexico – 31 January (Week 1) – ***Singles:*** A. Nefedova (RUS) d. C. Novoa (ARG) 6–2 6–2.
Doubles: B. Freudenberg (USA)/S. Uberoi (USA) d. E. Clarke (MEX)/E. Juricich (URU) 6–2 6–1.

Monterrey, Mexico – 7 February (Week 2) – ***Singles:*** A. Nefedova (RUS) d. S. Uberoi (USA) 7–6 6–1.
Doubles: B. Freudenberg (USA)/S. Uberoi (USA) d. N. Uberoi (USA)/F. Sanchez-Rezende (BRA) 7–6 6–2.

Matamoros, Mexico –14 February (Week 3) – ***Singles:*** A. Nefedova (RUS) d. S. Uberoi (USA) 6–1 6–2.
Doubles: E. Clarke (USA)/A. Nefedova (RUS) d. B. Freudenberg (USA)/S. Uberoi (USA) 6–4 7–5.

C. D. Victoria, Mexico – 21 February (Masters) – ***Singles:*** A. Nefedova (RUS) d. M. Brito (MEX) 7–6 6–0.
Doubles: B. Freudenberg (USA)/S. Uberoi (USA) d. M. Brito (MEX)/A. Rivero (MEX) 6–1 6–1.

Indora, India – 8 May (Week 1) – ***Singles:*** S. Phadke (IND) d. Archana Venkataraman (IND) 5–7 6–4 7–6.
Doubles: Archana Venkataraman (IND)/Arthi Venkataraman (IND) d. S. Goutham (IND)/L. Pereira (IND) 6–4 6–4.

Mumbai, India – 15 May (Week 2) – ***Singles:*** Archana Venkataraman (IND) d. S. Phadke (IND) 6–4 6–4.
Doubles: Archana Venkataraman (IND)/Arthi Venkataraman (IND) d. S. Thakur (IND)/K. Patel (IND) 1–6 6–3 6–0.

Pune, India – 22 May (Week 3) – ***Singles:*** M. Vakharia (IND) d. Archana Venkataraman (IND) 6–4 7–5.
Doubles: Archana Venkataraman (IND)/Arthi Venkataraman (IND) d. I. Lakhani (IND)/M. Vakharia (IND) 6–3 1–6 6–2.

New Delhi, India – 29 May (Masters) – ***Singles:*** S. Phadke (IND) d. M. Vakharia (IND) 6–1 6–3.
Doubles: M. Vakharia (IND)/I. Lakhani (IND) d. S. Goutham (IND)/L. Pereira (IND) 7–5 6–2.

ITF WOMEN'S $40,000 TOURNAMENTS

Warranbool, Australia – 6 March (Week 1) – ***Singles:*** A. Morigami (JPN) d. M. Dittmann (AUS) 6–4 5–7 6–1. ***Doubles:*** J. Belobrajdic (AUS)/K. Van Elden (AUS) d. N. Grandin (RSA)/N. Rencken (RSA) 6–3 6–4.

Benalla, Australia –13 March (Week 2) – ***Singles:*** J. Belobrajdic (AUS) d. K. Van Elden (AUS) 6–3 6–1.
Doubles: K. Hunt (AUS)/M. Joubert (RSA) d. N. Grandin (RSA)/N. Rencken (RSA) 6–3 6–2.

Wodonga, Australia – 20 March (Week 3) – ***Singles:*** A. Morigami (JPN) d. M. Joubert (RSA) 6–1 6–1.
Doubles: N. Grandin (RSA)/N. Rencken (RSA) d. K. Hunt (AUS)/M. Joubert (RSA) 6–4 6–4.

Corowa, Australia – 27 March (Masters) – ***Singles:*** M. Clayton (AUS) d. M. Joubert (RSA) 5–7 6–3 6–1.
Doubles: C. Watson (AUS)/C. Wheeler (AUS) d. N. Grandin (RSA)/N. Rencken (RSA) 6–3 7–6.

ITF WOMEN'S $10,000 TOURNAMENTS

Boca Raton, FL, USA – 10 January – ***Singles:*** L. Lee (USA) d. O. Blahotova (CZE) 6–2 3–6 6–3.
Doubles: T. Li (CHN)/M. Inoue (JPN) d. O. Blahotova (CZE)/G. Navratilova (CZE) 4–6 6–2 6–3.

Boca Raton, FL, USA – 17 January – ***Singles:*** N. Li (CHN) d. S. Cacic (USA) 6–4 6–3.
Doubles: S. Cacic (USA)/L. Lee (USA) d. N. Li (CHN)/T. Li (CHN) 6–4 7–5.

Bastad, Sweden – 24 January – ***Singles:*** M. Zdenovcova (CZE) d. H. Vildova (CZE) 6–3 0–6 6–4.
Doubles: H. Vildova (CZE)/M. Zdenovcova (CZE) d. F. Engblom (SWE)/E. Ohlsson (SWE) 6–4 6–2.

Hollandale Beach, FL, USA – 24 January – ***Singles:*** H. Sromova (CZE) d. D. Buth (USA) 3–6 6–0 6–2.
Doubles: N. Li (CHN)/T. Li (CHN) d. J. Okada (USA)/H. Sromova (CZE) 6–3 7–5.

Istanbul, Turkey – 31 January – ***Singles:*** C. Raba (GER) d. A. Brianti (ITA) 6–2 6–4.
Doubles: I. Kornienko (RUS)/A. Yaryshka (BLR) d. N. Cahana (ISR)/K. Daskovic (YUG) 6–3 3–6 6–4.

Wellington, New Zealand – 31 January – ***Singles:*** M. Dittmann (AUS) d. L. Baker (NZL) 7–6 1–6 7–6.
Doubles: M. Dittmann (AUS)/K. Van Elden (AUS) d. J. Belobrajdic (AUS)/K. Tong (HKG) 7–6 6–4.

Jersey, Great Britain – 31 January – ***Singles:*** E. Bovina (RUS) d. H. Reesby (GBR) 6–2 6–3.
Doubles: E. Bovina (UKR)/A. Zaporozhanova (RUS) d. S. Sfar (TUN)/J. Ward (GBR) 6–3 6–2.

Mallorca 1, Spain – 31 January – ***Singles:*** G. Navratilova (CZE) d. P. Garcia (ESP) 6–1 2–6 6–3.
Doubles: D. Haak (NED)/S. Haidner (AUT) d. A. Vedy (FRA)/M. Wolfbrandt (SWE) 6–4 3–6 6–4.

Mallorca 2, Spain – 7 February – ***Singles:*** D. Van De Zande (BEL) d. A. Sebova (SVK) 4–6 6–3 6–0.
Doubles: J. Macurova (CZE)/G. Navratilova (CZE) d. A. Paulenkova (SVK)/A. Sebova (SVK) 6–2 6–1.

Birmingham, Great Britain – 7 February – ***Singles:*** E. Bovina (RUS) d. A. Zaporozhanova (UKR) 6–1 6–2.
Doubles: E. Bovina (RUS)/A. Zaporozhanova (UKR) d. N. Egorova (RUS)/E. Syssoeva (RUS) 6–3 6–4.

Jakarta, Indonesia – 14 February – ***Singles:*** Y. Chung (KOR) d. L. Van Rooyen (RSA) 7–6 7–5.
Doubles: N. Basuki (INA)/I. Iskandar (INA) d. Y. Choi (KOR)/E. Kim (KOR) 7–5 7–5.

Faro, Portugal – 14 February – *Singles:* Z. Valekova (SVK) d. C. Pin (FRA) 6–4 6–3.
Doubles: N. Galouza (NED)/S. Stephens (NZL) d. M. Geznenge (BUL)/A. Pandjerova (BUL) 7–6 6–3.

Pec, Hungary – 14 February – *Singles:* P. Kucova (CZE) d. K. Koukalova (CZE) 6–4 7–6.
Doubles: P. Kucova (CZE)/B. Kumbarova (CZE) d. K. Berecz (HUN)/Z. Ondraskova (CZE) 7–5 6–2.

Jakarta, Indonesia – 21 February – *Singles:* K. Chae (KOR) d. Y. Choi (KOR) 1–6 6–3 6–1.
Doubles: Y. Basuki(INA)/W. Prakusya (INA) d. I. Iskandar (INA)/W. Sawondari (INA) 6–4 6–2.

Montechoro, Portugal – 21 February – *Singles:* C. Pin (FRA) d. M. Samoilenko (RUS) 6–0 6–2.
Doubles: M. Camerin (ITA)/B. Hellwig (AUT) d. A. Nogueira (POR)/N. Payne(GBR) 6–2 6–0.

Buchen, Germany – 21 February – *Singles:* R. Pelikanova (CZE) d. Z. Ondraskova (CZE) 6–3 7–5.
Doubles: A. Hegedus (HUN)/M. Koutstaal (NED) d. M. Kucerova (GER)/L. Richterova (CZE) 6–4 6–2.

Lisbon, Portugal – 13 March – *Singles:* E. Dyrberg (DEN) d. M. Samoilenko (RUS) 6–3 6–0.
Doubles: O. Blahotova (CZE)/G. Navratilova (CZE) d. E. Kozhokina (RUS)/M. Samoilenko (RUS) 6–1 6–0.

Nanjing, China – 20 March – *Singles:* N. Li (CHN) d. M. Pelletier (CAN) 7–6 6–2.
Doubles: N. Li (CHN)/T. Li(CHN) d. K. Chae (KOR)/R. Takemura (JPN) 7–6 6–1.

Santiago, Chile – 27 March – *Singles:* M. Arevalo (ARG) d. M. D'Agostini (BRA) 3–6 6–3 6–0.
Doubles: M. D'Agostini (BRA)/J. Torti (ARG) d. M. Arevalo (ARG)/P. Racedo (ARG) 6–3 7–6.

Kalamata, Greece – 27 March – *Singles:* E. Kozhokina (RUS) d. A. Bondarenko (UKR) 7–5 7–5.
Doubles: R. Hudson (NZL)/S. Stephens (NZL) d. A. Burz (ROM)/L. Miholcek (CRO) 6–1 6–0.

Pontevedra, Spain – 27 March – *Singles:* A. Salas (ESP) d. V. Krauth (ARG) 6–1 6–4.
Doubles: N. Galouza (NED)/V. Krauth (ARG) d. H. Crook (GBR)/V. Davies (GBR) 6–3 2–6 6–2.

Nanjing, China – 27 March – *Singles:* N. Li (CHN) d. D. Ding (CHN) 6–2 6–2.
Doubles: N. Li (CHN)/T. Li (CHN) d. Y. Lin (CHN)/D. Ding (CHN) 6–1 7–6.

Quartu S'Elena, Italy – 27 March – *Singles:* E. Fislova (SVK) d. L. Pena (ESP) 4–6 6–1 7–5.
Doubles: S. Kriventcheva (BUL)/A. Pandjerova (BUL) d. M. Pastikova (CZE)/H. Vildova (CZE) 7–5 7–6.

Amiens, France – 27 March – *Singles:* K. De Weille (NED) d. M. Mihalache (ROM) 6–2 6–3.
Doubles: M. Mihalche (ROM)/Z. Valekova (SVK) d. M. Diaz Oliva (ARG)/A. Tricerri (SUI) 6–2 6–4.

Makarska, Croatia – 3 April – *Singles:* Z. Ondraskova (CZE) d. Y. Beygelzimer (UKR) 6–2 6–3.
Doubles: I. Albers (GER)/N. Galouza (NED) d. P. Kucova (CZE)/G. Navratilova (CZE) 6–1 6–2.

Mumbai, India – 10 April – *Singles:* J. Jayalakshmy (IND) d. S. Phadke (IND) 6–2 6–3.
Doubles: J. Jayalakshmy (IND)/R. Chakravarthi (IND) d. M. Malhotra (IND)/S. Kinjo (JPN) 6–4 4–6 2–1 ret.

Hvar, Croatia – 10 April – *Singles:* M. Moldovan (ROM) d. P. Slitrova (CZE) 6–4 2–6 6–3.
Doubles: M. Kovacevic (CRO)/M. Santangelo (ITA) d. Z. Hejdova (CZE)/P. Kucova (CZE) 6–3 4–6 6–3.

Shenyang, China – 10 April – *Singles:* N. Li (CHN) d. T. Sun (CHN) 6–0 6–4.
Doubles: T. Sun (CHN)/Y. Chen (CHN) d. Q. Tuo (CHN)/Y. Chen (CHN) 6–2 6–4.

Belo Horizonte, Brazil – 10 April – *Singles:* J. Cortez (BRA) d. B. Miringoff (USA) 6–3 6–7 6–3.
Doubles: M. D'Agostini (BRA)/J. Cortez (BRA) d. T. Sono (BRA)/C. Tiene (BRA) 6–4 6–1.

New Delhi, India – 17 April – *Singles:* N. Vaidyanathan (IND) d. J. Jayalakshmy (IND) 6–3 6–2.
Doubles: J. Jayalakshmy (IND)/N. Vaidyanathan (IND) d. R. Chakravarthi (IND)/R. Tulpule (IND) 6–4 6–2.

San Savero, Italy – 17 April – *Singles:* M. Salerni (ARG) d. V. Krauth (ARG) 6–4 6–1.
Doubles: D. Haak (NED)/L. Seelen (NED) d. O. Golimbioschi (ROM)/S. Kriventcheva (BUL) 6–4 6–3.

Dalian, China – 17 April – *Singles:* N. Li (CHN) d. L. Chen (CHN) 6–4 6–4.
Doubles: D. Ding (CHN)/N. Li (CHN) d. K. Chang (KOR)/S. Kurioka (JPN) 7–5 6–3.

Athens, Greece – 17 April – *Singles:* A. Hegedus (HUN) d. M. Lazarovska (MKD) 7–6 6–1.
Doubles: M. Mihalache (ROM)/A. Tricerri (SUI) d. K. Berecz (HUN)/A. Hegedus (HUN) 6–2 5–7 7–5.

Talence, France – 24 April – *Singles:* B. Mouhtassine (MAR) d. A. Heitz (FRA) 7–6 7–6.
Doubles: S. Beltrame (FRA)/S. Schoeffel (FRA) d. A. Desert (FRA)/M. Lamarre (FRA) 6–2 6–2.

Bournemouth, Great Britain – 24 April – *Singles:* S. Sfar (TUN) d. D. Zaric (YUG) 7–5 6–2.
Doubles: S. Sfar (TUN)/L. Woodroffe (GBR) d. H. Collin (GBR)/Z. Gubacsi (HUN) 6–1 6–0.

Cerignola, Italy – 24 April – *Singles:* I. Gaspar (ROM) d. A. Tricerri (SUI) 4–6 6–3 6–1.
Doubles: M. Boboedova (RUS)/L. Nikoian (RUS) d. M. Camerin (ITA)/M. Santangelo (ITA) w/o.

Angiulli, Italy – 1 May – *Singles:* N. Gussoni (ARG) d. V. Sassi (ITA) 0–6 6–4 6–2.
Doubles: V. Krauth (ARG)/A. Tricerri (SUI) d. N. Gussoni (ARG)/S. Valenti (ARG) 7–5 6–4.

Itajai, Brazil – 1 May – *Singles:* J. Cravero (ARG) d. N. Garbellotto (ARG) 6–3 6–3.
Doubles: J. Cravero (ARG)/C. Salgues (URU) d. N. Bellizia (BRA)/L. Sobral (BRA) 6–3 6–2.

Hatfield, Great Britain – 1 May – **Singles:** D. Zaric (YUG) d. C. Pin (FRA) 7–6 6–4.
Doubles: S. Sfar (TUN)/J. Ward (GBR) d. Z. Gubacsi (HUN)/J. Wohr (GER) 7–6 6–2.

Tampico, Mexico – 8 May – **Singles:** N. Johnston (AUS) d. D. Olivera (URU) 6–3 6–0.
Doubles: M. Falco (MEX)/C. Tiene (BRA) d. H. Crook (GBR)/V. Davies (GBR) 6–4 6–3.

Caserta, Italy – 8 May – **Singles:** M. Salerni (ARG) d. V. Essaadi (MAR) 6–4 6–1.
Doubles: S. Urickova (SVK)/E. Voropaeva (RUS) d. N. Gussoni (ARG)/S. Valenti (ARG) 7–6 2–6 7–5.

Tortosa, Spain – 8 May – **Singles:** V. Krauth (ARG) d. A. Salas (ESP) 2–6 6–3 6–1.
Doubles: E. Krauth (ARG)/V. Krauth (ARG) d. B. Rosenberger (GER)/L. Tallo (SUI) 6–3 7–5.

Swansea, Great Britain – 8 May – **Singles:** C. Wheeler (AUS) d. D. Zaric (YUG) 6–4 7–6.
Doubles: N. Koves (HUN)/D. Zaric (YUG) d. N. Egorova (RUS)/E. Syssoeva (RUS) 2–6 6–4 6–3.

Casale, Italy – 15 May – **Singles:** S. Rizzi (FRA) d. O. Golimbioschi (ROM) 6–3 7–6.
Doubles: C. Carlotti (FRA)/E. Fislova (SVK) d. M. Mihalache (ROM)/B. Pavlova (BUL) 6–1 6–4.

Barcelona, Spain – 15 May – **Singles:** M. Gajo-Torrell (ESP) d. B. Cabrera-Rosendo (ESP) 6–7 6–3 6–2.
Doubles: E. Krauth (ARG)/V. Krauth (ARG) d. R. Gonzalez (ESP)/M. Sitja (ESP) 7–6 6–3.

Poza Rica, Mexico – 15 May – **Singles:** D. Olivera (URU) d. M. Arevalo (ARG) 6–1 6–4.
Doubles: M. Falco (MEX)/C. Tiene (BRA) d. C. De La Torre (USA)/N. Johnston (AUS) 4–6 6–2 6–3.

Biella, Italy – 22 May – **Singles:** M. Matevzic (SLO) d. N. Vierin (ITA) 6–0 6–2.
Doubles: K. Freye (GER)/A. Hegedus (HUN) d. E. Fislova (SVK)/Z. Hejdova (CZE) 6–2 6–4.

Warsaw, Poland – 22 May – **Singles:** P. Slitrova (CZE) d. N. Dubbers (GER) 6–1 6–4.
Doubles: A. Plackova (CZE)/P. Plackova (CZE) d. O. Antypina (UKR)/D. Panova (RUS) w/o.

Jaffa, Israel – 22 May – **Singles:** H. Bargil (ISR) d. Y. Glitsen (ISR) 6–4 6–4.
Doubles: S. Arghire (ROM)/M. Pavlidou (GRE) d. I. Kornienko (RUS)/E. Voropaeva (RUS) 6–1 6–2.

El Paso, TX, USA – 22 May – **Singles:** E. Burdette (USA) d. L. Baker (NZL) 6–1 6–3.
Doubles: L. Baker (NZL)/M. Malhotra (IND) d. K. Smashey (USA)/V. Sureephong (USA) 6–2 7–6.

Stare Splavy, Czech Republic – 29 May – **Singles:** J. Schonfeldova (CZE) d. R. Voracova (CZE) 6–4 7–6.
Doubles: A. Plackova (CZE)/P. Slitrova (CZE) d. J. Macurova (CZE)/M. Nekvapilova (CZE) 6–3 6–4.

San Antonio, TX, USA – 29 May – **Singles:** L. Skavronskaia (RUS) d. J. Moore (GBR) 6–2 4–6 6–4.
Doubles: M. Clayton (AUS)/E. Gott (AUS) d. L. Baker (NZL)/M. Malhotra (IND) 3–6 7–6 7–5.

Skopje, Macedonia – 29 May – **Singles:** K. Daskovic (YUG) d. N. Schlotterer (AUT) 6–2 6–2.
Doubles: K. Daskovic (YUG)/M. Lazarovska (MKD) d. L. Nanusevic (YUG)/B. Pavlova (BUL) 7–6 6–3.

Inchon, Korea – 5 June – **Singles:** Y. Choi (KOR) d. Y. Chung (KOR) 6–1 6–2.
Doubles: K. Chae (KOR)/K. Chang (KOR) d. E. Lee (KOR)/Y. Chung (KOR) 6–3 4–6 7–5.

Pretoria, South Africa – 5 June – **Singles:** A. Mojzis (RSA) d. A. Anastasiu (RSA) 7–5 6–2.
Doubles: N. Grandin (RSA)/N. Rencken (RSA) d. C. Scheepers (RSA)/C. Venter (RSA) 7–6 6–2.

Vaduz, Liechtenstein – 5 June – **Singles:** Z. Hejdova (CZE) d. S. Stephens (NZL) 6–7 6–2 6–2.
Doubles: R. Hudson (NZL)/S. Stephens (NZL) d. Z. Hejdova (CZE)/J. Macurova (CZE) 6–2 2–6 6–2.

Hilton Head Island, SC, USA – 5 June – **Singles:** A. Bradshaw (USA) d. J. Trail (USA) 6–3 7–5.
Doubles: W. Fix (USA)/M. Malhotra (IND) d. M. Sequera (VEN)/G. Volekova (SVK) 6–4 7–6.

Antalya 1, Turkey – 5 June – **Singles:** M. Wolfbrandt (SWE) d. A. Tricerri (SUI) 6–2 6–0.
Doubles: S. Filipp (AUT)/M. Wolfbrandt (SWE) d. A. Kurowska (POL)/A. Yaryshka (BLR) 6–2 6–4.

Hoorn, Netherlands – 12 June – **Singles:** A. Van Exel (NED) d. M. Czink (HUN) 7–5 7–6.
Doubles: M. Chialvo (ARG)/P. Racedo (ARG) d. D. Gherghi (ROM)/K. Van Elden (AUS) 4–6 6–2 6–0.

Kedzierzyn-Kozle, Poland – 12 June – **Singles:** Z. Ondraskova (CZE) d. O. Lazarchuk (UKR) 7–5 6–4.
Doubles: A. Bondarenko (UKR)/V. Bondarenko (UKR) d. E. Kovalchuk (UKR)/O. Lazarchuk (UKR) 6–4 6–2.

Seoul, Korea – 12 June – **Singles:** Y. Chung (KOR) d. E. Lee (KOR) 6–4 6–2.
Doubles: Y. Choi (KOR)/E. Kim (KOR) d. K. Chang (KOR)/K. Chae (KOR) 6–0 6–0.

Benoni, South Africa – 12 June – **Singles:** A. Mojzis (RSA) d. A. Anastasiu (RSA) 6–3 6–1.
Doubles: L. Gibbs (RSA)/G. Swart (RSA) d. N. Grandin (RSA)/N. Renckrn (RSA) 2–6 6–4 6–4.

Ankara, Turkey – 12 June – **Singles:** S. Weis (GER) d. M. Jugic (BIH) 6–7 6–3 6–2.
Doubles: M. Jugic (BIH)/M. Lazarovska (MKD) d. K. Diankova (BUL)/I. Benoglu (TUR) 6–2 0–6 6–4.

Montreal, Canada – 19 June – **Singles:** K. Liggan (IRL) d. J. Embry (USA) 6–3 6–2.
Doubles: A. Augustus (USA)/A. Jensen (AUS) d. J. Embry (USA)/K. Kraszewski (USA) 3–6 7–5 6–0.

Easton, MD, USA – 19 June – **Singles:** J. Trail (USA) d. A. Engel (USA) 4–6 6–2 6–1.
Doubles: K. Nimmers (USA)/V. Vuletic (USA) d. W. Laiho (USA)/J. Walker (USA) 6–4 6–4.

Montemor, Portugal – 19 June – **Singles:** E. Nunes (FRA) d. D. Brunel (FRA) 6–4 6–4.
Doubles: V. Courmes (FRA)/E. Lebescond (FRA) d. A. Floris (ITA)/G. Meruzzi (ITA) 4–6 6–4 7–6.

Tallinn, Estonia – 19 June – **Singles:** K. Kanepi (EST) d. M. Ruutel (EST) 6–1 6–2.
Doubles: A. Kurowska (POL)/M. Wolfbrandt (SWE) d. K. Kanepi (EST)/S. Werner (GER) 7–6 6–4.

Alkmaar, Netherlands – 19 June – **Singles:** M. Chialvo (ARG) d. E. Krauth (ARG) 5–5 ret.
Doubles: M. Joubert (RSA)/N. Sewell (AUS) d. E. Krauth (ARG)/V. Krauth (ARG) w/o.

Velp, Netherlands – 26 June – **Singles:** S. De Ville (BEL) d. E. Molnar (HUN) 7–6 6–1.
Doubles: J. Belobrajdic (AUS)/K. Van Elden (AUS) d. C. Kremer (LUX)/K. Miskolczi (HUN) 6–1 6–2.

Elvas, Portugal – 26 June – **Singles:** D. Brunel (FRA) d. E. Morel (FRA) 6–4 6–3.
Doubles: D. Brunel (FRA)/E. Nunes (FRA) d. F. Piedade (POR)/C. Santos (POR) 7–5 6–2.

Istanbul, Turkey – 26 June – **Singles:** A. Tricerri (SUI) d. L. Steflova (CZE) 6–4 7–6.
Doubles: V. Bondarenko (UKR)/G. Fattakhetdinova (RUS) d. I. Kornienko (RUS)/A. Yaryshka (BLR) 6–2 4–6 6–3.

Springfield, MO, USA – 26 June – **Singles:** A. Engel (USA) d. K. Chang (KOR) 6–2 6–3.
Doubles: L. Barnikow (USA)/E. Burdette (USA) d. E. Schmidt (USA)/A. Spears (USA) 3–6 6–3 7–6.

Lachine, Canada – 26 June – **Singles:** K. Liggan (IRL) d. R. Tezuka (JPN) 7–5 6–0.
Doubles: J. Embry (USA)/K. Kraszewski (USA) d. A. Augustus (USA)/A. Jensen (AUS) 6–1 7–5.

Bastad, Sweden – 26 June – **Singles:** M. Wolfbrandt (SWE) d. C. Aagaard (DEN) 6–0 6–2.
Doubles: S. Arvidsson (SWE)/K. Bengtsson (SWE) d. S. Filipp (AUT)/M. Wolfbrandt (SWE) 6–4 7–5.

Edmond, OK, USA – 3 July – **Singles:** A. Spears (USA) d. K. Chang (KOR) 1–6 6–4 6–3.
Doubles: K. Chang (KOR)/C. Khoo (MAS) d. J. Trail (USA)/C. Watson (AUS) 6–4 6–4.

Amersfoort, Netherlands – 3 July – **Singles:** Z. Hejdova (CZE) d. A. Van Exel (NED) w/o.
Doubles: Final not played due to bad weather.

Brussels, Belgium – 10 July – **Singles:** A. Heitz (FRA) d. E. Roussi (GRE) 7–6 6–1.
Doubles: I. Kozhokina (RUS)/C. Maes (BEL) d. K. Aoyama (JPN)/K Iljima (JPN) 6–1 6–4.

Sezze, Italy – 10 July – **Singles:** E. Villa (ITA) d. D. Olivera (URU) 6–1 6–1.
Doubles: S. Disderi (ITA)/M. Zavagli (ITA) d. D. Milosevic (YUG)/L. Tvarovskova (SVK) 6–4 0–6 7–6.

Jakarta, Indonesia –10 July – **Singles:** J. Choi (KOR) d. K. Chae (KOR) w/o.
Doubles: I. Iskandar (INA)/W. Sawondari (INA) d. K. Chae (KOR)/M. Jeon (KOR) w/o.

Baltimore, MD, USA – 17 July – **Singles:** M. Malhotra (IND) d. K. Fujiwara (JPN) 7–6 6–7 6–2.
Doubles: T. Hotta (JPN)/R. Takemura (JPN) d. C. Chapman (USA)/T. Weng (TPE) 6–3 6–2.

Frinton, Great Britain – 17 July – **Singles:** S. Smith (GBR) d. H. Crook (GBR) 6–3 6–0.
Doubles: H. Crook (GBR)/V. Davies (GBR) d. M. Joubert (RSA)/N. Sewell (AUS) 6–2 6–4.

Vancouver, Canada – 17 July – **Singles:** K. Chang (KOR) d. A. Nash (CAN) 6–1 2–6 6–0.
Doubles: S. Kinjo (JPN)/R. Tezuka (JPN) d. N. Havlicek (CAN)/M. Summerside (AUS) 2–6 7–6 6–4.

Jakarta, Indonesia – 17 July – **Singles:** K. Chae (KOR) d. S. Umehara (JPN) 6–0 6–0.
Doubles: M. Jeon (KOR)/W. Sawondari (INA) d. J. Choi (KOR)/A. Kinebuchi (JPN) 3–6 7–5 7–6.

Brussels, Belgium – 17 July – **Singles:** A. Van Axel (NED) d. M. Zdenovcova (CZE) 6–4 6–0.
Doubles: S. Urickova (CZE)/M. Zdenovcova (CZE) d. G. Aizenberg (ARG)/ S. Stephens (NZL) 7–6 3–6 6–1.

Vancouver, Canada – 24 July – **Singles:** A. Cooper (USA) d. A. Nogueira (POR) 6–2 6–1.
Doubles: A. Cooper (USA)/B. Freudenberg (USA) d. K. Chang (KOR)/ A. Matic (GER) 6–4 6–2.

Caracas, Venezuela – 24 July – **Singles:** M. Alves (BRA) d. S. Schaer (VEN) 6–3 6–2.
Doubles: M. Francesa (VEN)/M. Vento (VEN) d. C. De La Torre (USA)/G. Volekova (SVK) 6–1 6–4.

Evansville, IN, USA – 24 July – **Singles:** K. McCain (USA) d. S. Hazlett (USA) 6–3 6–4.
Doubles: T. Hotta (JPN)/R. Takemura (JPN) d. R. Fujiwara (JPN)/A. Plessinger (USA) 6–4 6–1

Lido di Camaiore, Italy – 24 July – **Singles:** M. Chialvo (ARG) d. M. Ani (EST) 6–1 2–6 7–5.
Doubles: M. Chialvo (ARG)/J. Cravero (ARG) d. A. Brianti (ITA)/G. Meruzzi (ITA) 2–6 6–1.

Horb, Germany – 24 July – **Singles:** M. Salerni (ARG) d. A. Jerabek (GER) 6–3 2–6 6–2.
Doubles: P. Bandurowska (POL)/M. Salerni (ARG) d. Z. Hejdova (CZE)/K. Van Elden (AUS) 6–3 6–4.

Torun, Poland – 31 July – **Singles:** Z. Ondraskova (CZE) d. G. Navratilova (CZE) 6–0 6–4.
Doubles: Y. Benesova (CZE)/L. Novotna (CZE) d. J. Macurova (CZE)/G. Navratilova (CZE) 6–1 6–4.

Harrisonburg, VA, USA – 31 July – **Singles:** M. Dasso (USA) d. R. Viollet (GBR) 6–3 6–4.
Doubles: R. Fujiwara (JPN)/C. Watson (AUS) d. L. Kalvaria (USA)/G. Lastra (USA) 6–4 5–7 7–5.

Vigo, Spain – 31 July – **Singles:** M. Mimo (ESP) d. S. Delgado (ESP) 6–2 6–1.
Doubles: P. Aznar (ESP)/Y. Clemot (ESP) d. M. Escobar (ESP)/R. Temez (ESP) 6–2 6–1.

Bucharest, Romania – 31 July – **Singles:** E. Gallovits (ROM) d. R. Ciochina (ROM) 6–3 6–3.
Doubles: L. Balaci (ROM)/E. Gallovits (ROM) d. Z. Kucova (SVK)/D. Luzarova (CZE) 7–5 4–0 ret.

Guayaquil, Ecuador – 31 July – **Singles:** H. Vieira (POR) d. G. Volekova (SVK) 6–1 7–6.
Doubles: C. De La Torre (ECU)/G. Volekova (SVK) d. M. Evangelista (BRA)/P. Ortega (BRA) 6–4 6–2.

Rabat, Morrocco – 31 July – **Singles:** S. Klemenschits (AUT) d. E. Kozhokina (RUS) 7–5 6–1.
Doubles: D. Klemenschits (AUT)/S. Klemenschits (AUT) d. B. Kamper (AUT)/E. Kozhokina (RUS) 7–6 6–0.

Perigueux, France – 7 August – **Singles:** C. Beigbeder (FRA) d. V. Pichet (FRA) 6–1 6–1.
Doubles: D. Brunel (FRA)/E. Nunes (FRA) d. C. Carlotti (FRA)/V. Pichet (FRA) 6–3 6–4.

Istanbul, Turkey – 7 August – **Singles:** G. Fattakhetdinova (RUS) d. I. Aksit-Oal (TUR) 6–0 6–4.
Doubles: G. Fattakhetdinova (RUS)/E. Voropaeva (RUS) d. S. Ozlu (TUR)/A. Yaryshka (BLR) 1–6 6–3 6–4.

Nonthabuiri, Thailand – 7 August – **Singles:** M. Jeon (KOR) d. Y. Choi (KOR) 6–1 6–3.
Dobles: K. Chae (KOR)/M. Jeon (KOR) d. Y. Choi (KOR)/E. Kim (KOR) 6–3 6–2.

Rimini, Italy – 7 August – **Singles:** Z. Gubacsi (HUN) d. M. Ani (EST) 6–2 6–2.
Doubles: M. Ani (EST)/M. Ruutel (EST) d. Z. Gubacsi (HUN)/N. Remis (AUT) 3–6 6–3 7–5.

Bath, Great Britain – 7 August – **Singles:** S. Bensch (GER) d. J. O'Donoghue (GBR) 6–4 6–7 6–2.
Doubles: M. Joubert (RSA)/N. Sewell (AUS) d. J. Belobrajdic (AUS)/A. Takase (JPN) 6–2 6–2.

Lima, Peru – 7 August – **Singles:** C. Guillenea (URU) d. P. Collantes (ESP) 6–2 6–1.
Doubles: T. Dabek (USA)/C. Guillenea (URU) d. C. Salgues (URU)/V. Garcia-Sokol (ARG) 7–6 6–2.

Rebecq, Belgium – 7 August – **Singles:** C. Maes (BEL) d. C. Schaul (LUX) 1–6 7–6 6–3.
Doubles: J. Pandzic (CRO)/L. Snajdrova (CZE) d. D. Feys (BEL)/K. Kues (BEL) 6–7 6–2 6–4.

Nonthabuiri, Thailand – 14 August – Singles: S. Viratprasert (THA) d. M. Jeon (KOR) 7–5 1–6 6–1.
Doubles: Y. Choi (KOR)/E. Kim (KOR) d. K. Chae (KOR)/M. Jeon (KOR) 1–6 6–1 6–1.

Cuernavaca, Mexico – 14 August – **Singles:** S. Mabry (USA) d. G. Volekova (SVK) 6–2 6–1.
Doubles: S. Mabry (USA)/M. Summerside (AUS) d. M. Torres (MEX)/E. Valdes (MEX) 6–2 6–3.

Aosta, Italy –14 August – **Singles:** M. Santangelo (ITA) d. A. Vanc (ROM) 1–6 6–0 6–1.
Doubles: M. Camerin (ITA)/M. Santangelo (ITA) d. O. Golimbioschi (ROM)/A. Vanc (ROM) 7–5 4–6 6–1.

Valasske Mezirici, Czech Republic – 14 August – **Singles:** Z. Ondraskova (CZE) d. L. Steflova (CZE) 6–4 6–1.
Doubles: P. Cetkovska (CZE)/P. Ticha (CZE) d. A. Plackova (CZE)/P. Plackova (CZE) 6–4 6–2.

Koksijde, Belgium –14 August – **Singles:** A. Van Exel (NED) d. M. Wolfbrandt (SWE) 6–3 6–4.
Doubles: L. Butkiewicz (BEL)/L. Snajdrova (CZE) d. M. Bartoli (FRA)/M. Gajo-Torrell (ESP) 6–3 6–4.

La Paz, Bolivia – 14 August – **Singles:** C. Guillenea (URU) d. S. Eisenberg (ARG) 2–6 6–2 6–3.
Doubles: T. Dabek (USA)/C. Guillenea (URU) d. N. Bellizia (BRA)/A. Novaes (BRA) 6–3 6–3.

London, Great Britain -14 August – **Singles:** P. Van Acker (BEL) d. M. Joubert (RSA) 6–4 6–1.
Doubles: N. Grandin (RSA)/N. Rencken (RSA) d. S. Bensch (GER)/M. Malhotra (IND) 6–2 5–7 7–6.

Cuneo, Italy – 21 August – **Singles:** M. Santangelo (ITA) d. E. Nunes (FRA) 6–2 3–6 6–3.
Doubles: M. Camerin/M. Santagelo (ITA) d. S. Disderi (ITA)/A. Floris (ITA) 7–5 6–2.

Buenos Aires, Argentina – 21 August – **Singles:** L. Masante (ARG) d. L. Schaerer (PAR) 6–3 6–0.
Doubles: G. Aizenberg (ARG)/L. Masante (ARG) d. M. Arevalo (ARG)/P. Racedo (ARG) 6–2 6–2.

Kastoria, Greece - 21 August – **Singles:** E. Danilidou (GRE) d. J. Mens (NED) 6–3 6–1.
Doubles: E. Danilidou/E. Roussi (GRE) d. D. Klemenschits/S. Klemenschits (AUT) 6–3 6–4.

Bucharest, Romania – 21 August – **Singles:** R. Ciochina (ROM) d. A. Burz (ROM) 6–2 5–7 6–4.
Doubles: V. Raimrova (CZE)/D. Luzarova (CZE) d. M. Moldovan (ROM)/A. Orasanu (ROM) 2–6 7–5 7–5.

Westend, Belgium – 21 August – **Singles:** L. Fritz (GER) d. J. Pandzic (CRO) 6–2 3–6 6–4.
Doubles: N. Galouza (NED)/A. Sterk (NED) d. E. Clijsters (BEL)/C. Maes (BEL) 6–1 6–0.

Toluco, Mexico – 21 August – **Singles:** E. Valdes (MEX) d. O. Kalioujnaia (RUS) 6–4 4–6 7–6.
Doubles: K. Blumberg (USA)/A. Plessinger (USA) d. M. Torres (MEX)/E. Valdes (MEX) w/o.

Buenos Aires, Argentina – 28 August – **Singles:** R. Ottoboni (ARG) d. M. Mesa (COL) 7–6 6–2.
Doubles: M. Arevalo (ARG)/P. Racedo (ARG) d. M. Mesa (COL)/L. Schaerer (PAR) 6–3 7–5.

Kugayama, Japan – 28 August – **Singles:** K. Tong (HKG) d. K. Chang (KOR) 7–6 7–5.
Doubles: Y. Chen (TPE)/K. Tong (HKG) d. K. Chae (KOR)/K. Chang (KOR) 6–3 6–1.

Istanbul, Turkey – 28 August – **Singles:** S. Bensch (GER) d. A. Yaryshka (BLR) 6–4 7–5.
Doubles: S. Bensch (GER)/ L. Tallo (SUI) d. Y. Glitsenstein (ISR)/T. Luzanska (ISR) 6–2 6–4.

Jaipur, India – 28 August – **Singles:** M. Adamczak (AUS) d. M. Malhotra (IND) 6–2 2 6 6–3.
Doubles: M. Adamczak (AUS)/J. Schmidt (AUT) d. R. Chakravarthi (IND)/J. Jayalakshmy (IND) 6–3 1–6 7–5.

Ciudad Juarez, Mexico – 28 August – **Singles:** S. Mabry (USA) d. M. Brito (MEX) 6–1 6–3.
Doubles: M. Brito (MEX)/E. Clarke (MEX) d. M. Garzon-Elkins (COL)/S. Mabry (USA) 6–3 7–6.

Saulgau, Germany – 28 August – **Singles:** S. Lohrmann (GER) d. T. Plivelitsch (GER) 6–1 6–7 6–4.
Doubles: Z. Hejdova (CZE)/P. Novotnikova (CZE) d. L. Finlayson (NZL)/R. Hudson (NZL) 6–0 6–4.

Spoleto, Italy – 28 August – **Singles:** M. Camerin (ITA) d. M. Ani (EST) 6–2 7–6.
Doubles: M. Camerin (ITA)/M. Santangelo (ITA) d. O. Golimbioschi (ROM)/A. Vanc (ROM) w/o.

Mostar, Bosnia/Herzegovina – 28 August – **Singles:** M. Palaversic (CRO) d. A. Basaric (BIH) 6–3 7–5.
Doubles: M. Kovacevic (CRO)/M. Palaversic (CRO) d. M. Marszalek (POL)/D. Panova (RUS) 6–2 6–0.

New Delhi, India – 4 September – **Singles:** M. Malhotra (IND) d. V. Raimrova (CZE) 4–6 6–1 6–3.
Doubles: R. Chakravarthi (IND)/S. Jayalakshmy (IND) d. I. Wang (TPE)/O. Wongkamalasai (THA) 6–3 6–2.

Zhejiang, China – 4 September – **Singles:** T. Sun (CHN) d. J. Zheng (CHN) 6–2 6–2.
Doubles: Y. Chen (CHN)/T. Sun (CHN) d. Z. Yan (CHN)/J. Zheng (CHN) 6–3 7–5.

Ibaraki, Japan – 4 September – **Singles:** S. Hisamatsu (JPN) d. K. Chang (KOR) 7–5 6–7 6–2.
Doubles: S. Hisamatsu (JPN)/M. Jeon (KOR) d. K. Chae (KOR)/K. Chang (KOR) 6–3 6–3.

Zadar, Croatia – 4 September – **Singles:** M. Casanova (SUI) d. Z. Kucova (SVK) 6–4 6–1.
Doubles: P. Dizdar (CRO)/M. Marovic (CRO) d. M. Kovacevic (CRO)/I. Visic (CRO) 6–2 6–3.

Mollerusa, Spain – 4 September – **Singles:** H. Collin (GBR) d. L. Shen (CHN) 6–2 6–3.
Doubles: M. Losey (SUI)/L. Tallo (SUI) d. H. Collin (GBR)/J. Mens (NED) 7–5 6–3.

Osaka, Japan – 11 September – **Singles:** M. Jeon (KOR) d. K. Chang (KOR) 7–6 6–1.
Doubles: A. Augustus (USA)/A. Jensen (AUS) d. S. Hisamatsu (JPN)/M. Jeon (KOR) 6–3 6–2.

Bangalore, India – 11 September – **Singles:** R. Chakravarthi (IND) v. R. Tulpule (IND) 7–6 1–3 –
abandoned due to rain. **Doubles:** R. Chakravarthi (IND)/J. Jayalakshmy (IND) v. J. Vasisht (IND)/K. Patel (IND)
– no match due to rain.

Odessa, Ukraine – 11 September – **Singles:** D. Gherghi (ROM) d. J. Ustyuzhanina (UKR) 7–5 6–1.
Doubles: E. Bryoukhovets (UKR)/I. Bryukhovets (UKR) d. N. Bogdanova (UKR)/J. Semenets (UKR) 6–3 6–3.

Hohhot, China – 11 September – **Singles:** T. Sun (CHN) d. D. Ding (CHN) 6–4 6–3.
Doubles: Y. Chen (CHN)/T. Sun (CHN) d. D. Ding (CHN)/Y. Tang (CHN) 6–0 6–3.

Buenos Aires, Argentina – 11 September – **Singles:** R. Ottoboni (ARG) d. N. Gussoni (ARG) 6–3 6–0.
Doubles: G. Aizenberg (ARG)/P. Racedo (ARG) d. N. Gussoni (ARG)/S. Valenti (ARG) 6–2 6–2.

Biograd, Croatia – 11 September – **Singles:** D. Casanova (SUI) d. M. Kovacevic (CRO) 1–6 6–1 6–4.
Doubles: S. Haidner (AUT)/B. Kamper (AUT) d. M. Jugic (BIH)/L. Nanusevic (YUG) 6–3 5–7 7–5.

Madrid, Spain – 11 September – **Singles:** M. Wolfbrandt (SWE) d. C. Rodriguez (ESP) 6–1 6–1.
Doubles: A. Floris (ESP)/E. Morel (FRA) d. M. Losey (SUI)/L. Tallo (SUI) 7–6 6–1.

Antalya, Turkey – 18 September – **Singles:** U. Vesenjak (SLO) d. M. Vesenjak (SLO) 6–3 6–3.
Doubles: B. Cremer (GER)/A. Hegedus (HUN) d. M. Vesenjak (SLO)/U. Vesenjak (SLO) 6–4 6–4.

Asuncion, Paraguay – 18 September – **Singles:** L. Schaerer (PAR) d. J. Cravero (ARG) 6–4 6–3.
Doubles: J. Cravero (ARG)/G. Dulko (ARG) d. L. Schaerer (PAR)/S. Tami (PAR) 4–6 6–3 6–3.

Makarska, Croatia – 18 September – **Singles:** M. Jugic (BIH) d. A. Navratilova (CZE) 6–4 6–2.
Doubles: A. Sinnige (NED)/A. Sterk (NED) d. O. Golimbioschi (ROM)/E. Molnar (HUN) 6–4 7–6.

Sunderland, Great Britain – 18 September – **Singles:** H. Collin (GBR) d. O. Sanchez (FRA) 6–3 6–3.
Doubles: S. Bensch (GER)/N. Payne (GBR) d. E. Morel (FRA)/P. Spaar (SUI) 6–4 6–4.

Kyoto, Japan – 18 September – **Singles:** K. Chang (KOR) d. S. Hisamatsu (JPN) 6–2 5–7 6–2.
Doubles: S. Hisamatsu (JPN)/M. Jeon (KOR) d. K. Chae (KOR)/K. Chang (KOR) 7–6 7–5.

Moscow, Russia –18 September – **Singles:** V. Zvonareva (RUS) d. M. Goloviznina (RUS) 6–4 6–2.
Doubles: G. Fokina (RUS)/R. Gourevich (RUS) d. D. Kustava (BLR)/A. Zerkalova (RUS) 6–1 6–0.

Greenville, SC, USA – 18 September – **Singles:** C. De La Torre (USA) d. K. Blumberg (USA) 6–2 6–1.
Doubles: N. Kriz (AUS)/E. Subbotina (BLR) d. K. Blumberg (USA)/E. Schmidt (USA) 6–2 6–2.

Lerida, Spain – 25 September – **Singles:** M. Wolfbrandt (SWE) d. S. Beltrame (FRA) 6–3 6–4.
Doubles: P. Aznar (ESP)/B. Navarro (ESP) d. C. Basu (GER)/A. Timotic (YUG) 6–1 6–3.

Raleigh, NC, USA – 25 September – **Singles:** C. Avants (USA) d. E. Subbotina (BLR) 5–7 6–4 6–3.
Doubles: N. Kriz (AUS)/E. Subbotina (BLR) d. A. Plessinger (USA)/J. Trail (USA) 7–5 6–1.

Makarska, Croatia – 25 September – **Singles:** Z. Ondraskova (CZE) d. O. Golimbioschi (ROM) 6–2 6–0.
Doubles: N. Galouza (NED)/Z. Hejdova (CZE) d. R. But (ROM)/E. Gallovits (ROM) 7–5 6–3.

Antalya, Turkey – 25 September – **Singles:** A. Hegedus (HUN) d. A. Yaryshka (BLR) 7–6 7–5.
Doubles: M. Vesenjak (SLO)/U. Vesenjak (SLO) d. B. Cremer (GER)/A. Hegedus (HUN) 6–1 2–6 6–2.

Glasgow, Great Britain – 25 September – **Singles:** S. Bensch (GER) d. S. Gehrlein (GER) 4–6 6–2 6–3. **Doubles:** A. Hawkins (GBR)/A. Tordoff (GBR) d. J. Smith (GBR)/R. Tezuka (JPN) 6–2 6–2.

Montevideo, Uruguay – 25 September – **Singles:** G. Dulko (ARG) d. G. Aizenberg (ARG) 6–1 6–2. **Doubles:** J. Cravero (ARG)/G. Dulko (ARG) d. G. Aizenberg (ARG)/P. Racedo (ARG) 6–1 6–4.

Mexico City, Mexico – 2 October – **Singles:** S. Mabry (USA) d. A. Rivero (MEX) 4–1 4–2 4–1. **Doubles:** B. Bojovic (YUG)/M. Mesa (COL) d. Z. Reyes (MEX)/ A. Rivero (MEX) 5–3 4–0 3–5 2–4 4–2.

Cairo, Egypt – 2 October – **Singles:** S. Klemenschits (AUT) d. Z. Kucova (SVK) 1–4 2–4 4–1 5–4 5–3. **Doubles:** D. Klemenshchits (AUT)/S. Klemenschits (AUT) d. A. Masarykova (SVK)/A. Tricerri (SUI) 4–1 4–1 4–2.

Fiumicino, Italy – 2 October – **Singles:** A. Vanc (ROM) d. M. Ani (EST) 4–1 4–1 3–5 4–1. **Doubles:** M. Babakova (SVK)/S. Werner (GER) d. A. Kaplani (GRE)/M. Pavlidou (GRE) 4–1 4–1 4–2.

Hallandale Beach, FL, USA – 2 October – **Singles:** T. Dabek (USA) d. G. Volekova (SVK) 5–3 2–4 4–2 3–5 4–2. **Doubles:** K. Blumberg (USA)/A. Soukup (CAN) d. A. Plessinger (USA)/N. Rojas (CHI) 4–0 4–1 4–1.

Cairo, Egypt – 9 October – **Singles:** A. Tricerri (SUI) d. D. Klemenschits (AUT) 5–4 5–4 4–2. **Doubles**: D. Klemenschits (AUT)/ S. Klemenschits (AUT) d. B. Blahutiakova (SVK)/ Z. Kucova (SVK) 4–0 4–0 4–0.

Sofia, Bulgaria – 9 October – **Singles:** N. Bogdanova (UKR) d. D. Krastevitch (BUL) 4–2 4–1 4–0. **Doubles:** F. Gabrovska (BUL)/N. Mihneva (BUL) d. D. Alexandrov (BUL)/V. Trifonova (BUL) 4–1 2–4 4–1 0–4 4–2.

Ciampino, Italy – 9 October – **Singles:** I. Gaspar (ROM) d. A. Vanc (ROM) 5–4 4–1 4–1. **Doubles:** A. Burz (ROM)/A. Vanc (ROM) d. A. Kaplani (GRE)/M. Pavlidou (GRE) 4–2 4–5 4–2 4–1.

Ciampino, Italy – 16 October – **Singles:** M. Wolfbrandt (SWE) d. L. Bao (SUI) 3–5 5–4 2–4 5–3. **Doubles:** E. Krauth (ARG)/V. Krauth (ARG) d. O. Golimbioschi (ROM)/A. Vanc (ROM) 4–5 4–1 4–2 4–1.

Gwalior, India – 16 October – **Singles:** J. Jayalakshmy (IND) d. A. Van Den Hurk (NED) 4–1 5–3 4–0. **Doubles:** M. Acosta (PAR)/L. Schaerer (PAR) d. R. Chakravarthi (IND)/J. Jayalakshmy (IND) 4–2 4–1 0–4 5–3.

New Delhi, India – 23 October – **Singles:** U. Vesenjak (SLO) d. M. Vesenjak (SLO) 4–1 4–5 4–2 5–4. **Doubles:** R. Chakravarthi (IND)/J. Jayalakshmy (IND) d. M. Vesenjak (SLO)/U. Vesenjak (SLO) 4–2 4–5 4–1 4–0.

Cairo, Egypt – 30 October – **Singles:** A. Hegedus (HUN) d. D. Klemenschits (AUT) 4–0 4–1 5–3. **Doubles:** K. Basternakova (SVK)/A. Paulenkova (SVK) d. D. Klemenschits (AUT)/A. Suzuki (JPN) 1–4 5–4 4–1 4–0.

Ashkelon, Israel – 30 October – **Singles:** T. Obziler (ISR) d. T. Luzanska (ISR) 4–1 3–5 4–1 4–1. **Doubles:** L. Akkerman (NED)/A. Sinnige (NED) d. Y. Glitsenstein (ISR)/T. Luzanska (ISR) 4–1 5–4 4–2.

Jakarta, Indonesia – 30 October – **Singles:** K. Chae (KOR) d. R. Tedjakusuma (INA) 5–4 4–1 1–4 4–1. **Doubles:** L. Andriyani (INA)/A. Widjaja (INA) d. K. Chae (KOR)/J. Kim (KOR) 2–4 5–3 4–2 0–4 4–0.

Minsk, Belarus – 30 October – **Singles:** A. Yaryshka (BLR) d. A. Bastrikova (RUS) 4–1 5–3 4–1. **Doubles:** E. Birnerova (CZE)/A. Zerkalova (RUS) d. R. Gourevich (RUS)/L. Nikoian (RUS) 2–4 3–5 5–3 4–2 4–0.

Stockholm, Sweden – 30 October – **Singles:** S. Jolk (GER) d. S. Arvidsson (SWE) 4–2 0–4 4–2 4–2. **Doubles:** J. Lindstrom (SWE)/M. Wolfbrandt (SWE) d. S. Arvidsson (SWE)/K. Jarkenstedt (SWE) 4–0 5–3 4–0.

Bandung, Indonesia – 6 November – **Singles:** R. Tedjakusuma (INA) d. K. Chae (KOR) 2–4 5–3 4–2 4–5 4–1. **Doubles:** L. Andriyani (INA)/A. Widjaja (INA) d. R. Chakravarthi (IND)/J. Jayalakshmy (IND) 4–1 4–2 4–0.

Elmansoura, Egypt – 6 November – **Singles:** A. Hegedus (HUN) d. G. Meruzzi (ITA) 4–2 5–3 4–1. **Doubles:** A. Hegedus (HUN)/D. Klemenschits (AUT) d. G. Meruzzi (ITA)/M. Scartoni (ITA) 5–4 4–2 4–0.

Granada, Spain – 6 November – **Singles:** C. Martinez Granados (ESP) d. V. Devesa (ESP) 1–4 3–5 5–4 4–1 4–2. **Doubles:** E. Krauth (ARG)/V. Krauth (ARG) d. B. Bojovic (YUG)/C. Martinez Granados (ESP) 4–0 4–2 4–1.

Villenaue D'Ornon, France – 6 November – **Singles:** C. Maes (BEL) d. C. Schaul (LUX) 4–0 4–1 4–5 4–1. **Doubles:** C. Maes (BEL)/S. Stephens (NZL) d. D. Brunel (FRA)/E. Nunes (FRA) 4–1 1–4 4–2 4–0.

Haibara, Japan – 13 November – **Singles:** S. Umehara (JPN) d. K. Ishida (JPN) 4–2 4–2 5–3. **Doubles:** S. Okamoto (JPN)/K. Taguchi (JPN) d. A. Gunji (JPN)/K. Ishida (JPN) 2–4 4–0 5–3 3–5 4–2.

Manila, Philippines – 13 November – **Singles:** M. Saeki (JPN) d. R. Tedjakusuma (INA) 4–0 4–1 4–0. **Doubles:** K. Chae (KOR)/J. Kim (KOR) d. C. Turinsky (GER)/A. Van Den Hurk (NED) 4–2 4–2 4–0.

Stupava, Slovak Republic – 13 November – **Singles:** I. Gaspar (ROM) d. M. Zdenovcova (CZE) 5–3 5–4 4–2. **Doubles:** S. Bensch (GER)/S. Weis (GER) d. O. Blahotova (CZE)/G. Navratilova (CZE) 4–1 5–4 5–3.

Le Havre, France – 13 November – *Singles:* E. Villa (ITA) d. N. Vierin (ITA) 4–1 5–3 4–2.
Doubles: B. Pavlova (BUL)/I. Poljakova (EST) d. L. Shen (CHN)/A. Zotta (ROM) 4–0 4–1 4–1.

San Salvador, El Salvador – 13 November – *Singles:* M. Alves (BRA) d. A. Rivero (MEX) 4–2 4–2 4–2.
Doubles: M. Alvarez (BOL)/F. Salvadores (ARG) d. M. Brito/R. Clarke (MEX) 5–4 4–1 5–3.

Mallorca 3, Spain – 20 November – *Singles:* R. Andres (ESP) d. D. Safina (RUS) 5–3 4–2 0–4 2–4 5–3.
Doubles: E. Krauth (ARG)/V. Krauth (ARG) d. D. Ilic (YUG)/A. Paulenkova (SVK) 4–0 4–1 4–0.

Manila, Philippines – 20 November – *Singles:* A. Ortuno (ESP) d. K. Chae (KOR) 5–3 4–0 4–2.
Doubles: R. Chakravarthi (IND)/J. Jayalakshmy (IND) d. M. Saeki (JPN)/R. Uda (JPN) 5–3 4–1 4–2.

Deauville, France – 20 November – *Singles:* N. Vierin (ITA) d. C. Leclere (FRA) 5–3 2–4 4–2 5–4.
Doubles: D. Brunel (FRA)/E. Nunes (FRA) d. B. Pavlova (BUL)/M. Zdenovcova (CZE) 5–3 0–4 4–2 4–0.

Kofu, Japan – 20 November – *Singles:* S. Okamoto (JPN) d. K. Taguchi (JPN) 4–1 1–4 4–1 5–3.
Doubles: S. Okamoto (JPN)/K. Taguchi (JPN) d. Y. Arai (JPN)/K. Iijima (JPN) 3–5 4–1 5–4 4–1.

Beersheba, Israel – 20 November – *Singles:* T. Obziler (ISR) d. Y. Savransky (ISR) 4–1 4–0 2–4 4–0.
Doubles: D. Klemenschits (AUT)/S. Klemenschits (AUT) d. G. Meruzzi (ITA)/L. Muller Van Moppe (NED) 4–0 4–0 5–3.

Mallorca 4, Spain – 27 November – *Singles:* R. Andres (ESP) d. D. Luzarova (CZE) 4–1 4–0 4–0.
Doubles: G. Navratilova (CZE)/L. Novotna (CZE) d. E. Krauth (ARG)/V. Krauth (ARG) 4–1 4–2 5–3.

Arad, Israel – 27 November – *Singles:* H. Collin (GBR) d. D. Klemenschits (AUT) 5–3 4–0 4–0.
Doubles: G. Meruzzi (ITA)/L. Muller Van Moppe (NED) d. D. Klemenschits (AUT)/S. Klemenschits (AUT) 5–4 4–1 4–2.

Prague, Czech Republic – 11 December – *Singles:* R. Kucerova (CZE) d. E. Morel (FRA) 4–1 4–2 4–1.
Doubles: O. Blahotova (CZE)/G. Navratilova (CZE) d. I. Benesova (CZE)/L. Novotna (CZE) 5–3 2–4 0–4 4–1 4–2.

ITF WOMEN'S $25,000 TOURNAMENTS

Clearwater, FL, USA – 31 January – *Singles:* M. Irvin (USA) d. A. Ellwood (AUS) 6–4 6–3.
Doubles: Y. Cho (KOR)/J. Yi (CHN) d. S. Cacic (USA)/L. Lee (USA) 6–4 7–6.

Ljubljana, Slovenia – 7 February – *Singles:* T. Krizan (SLO) d. M. Schnitzer (GER) 6–2 6–3.
Doubles: A. Hegedus (HUN)/N. Ostrovskaya (BLR) d. O. Blahotova (CZE)/H. Sromova (CZE) 7–5 6–3.

Rockford, IL, USA – 7 February – *Singles:* D. Bedanova (CZE) d. F. Schiavone (ITA) 2–6 6–3 6–1.
Doubles: D. Buth (USA)/R. Jensen (USA) d. A. Ellwood (AUS)/ J. Steck (RSA) 7–6 7–5.

Redbridge, Great Britain – 14 February – *Singles:* E. Bovina (RUS) d. J. Pullin (GBR) 2–6 6–0 6–1.
Doubles: A. Fusai (FRA)/T. Krizan (SLO) d. J. Pullin (GBR)/L. Woodroffe (GBR) 7–6 3–6 7–6.

Bushey, Great Britain – 21 February – *Singles:* N. Ostrovskaya (BLR) d. S. Erre (FRA) 3–6 6–3 7–6.
Doubles: A. Ellwood (AUS)/N. Ostrovskaya (BLR) d. J. Pullin (GBR)/L. Woodroffe (GBR) 6–1 6–1.

Chengdu City, China – 28 February – *Singles:* J. Yi (CHN) d. E. Bovina (RUS) 6–1 6–2.
Doubles: N. Li (CHN)/T. Li (CHN) d. J. Cortez (BRA)/K. Marosi (HUN) 6–1 6–3.

Benigo, Australia – 28 February – *Singles:* R. McQuillan (AUS) d. J. Hewitt (AUS) 7–5 4–6 7–5.
Doubles: E. Dominikovic (AUS)/A. Grahame (AUS) d. T. Musgrave (AUS)/B. Stewart (AUS) 6–4 6–1.

Haikou, China – 6 March – *Singles:* J. Yi (CHN) d. K. Marosi (HUN) 4–6 6–0 6–1.
Doubles: G. Arn (GER)/J. Pullin (GBR) d. K. Chae (KOR)/R. Takemura (JPN) 7–5 6–4.

Ortisei, Italy – 6 March – *Singles:* N. Ostrovskaya (BLR) d. T. Poutchek (BLR) 4–6 6–1 7–6.
Doubles: G. Casoni (ITA)/Antonella Serra-Zanetti (ITA) d. A. Bachmann (GER)/E. Dyrberg (DEN) 7–6 6–2.

Taranto, Italy – 20 March – *Singles:* M. Marrero (ESP) d. G. Pizzichini (ESP) 6–4 6–4.
Doubles: E. Bes (ESP)/G. Riera (ESP) d. S. Foretz (FRA)/Antonella Serra-Zanetti (ITA) 6–7 6–2 6–2.

Stone Mountain, GA, USA – 20 March – *Singles:* D. Buth (USA) d. L. Lee (USA) 6–3 4–6 6–1.
Doubles: T. Musgrave (AUS)/B. Stewart (AUS) d. H. Inoue (JPN)/M. Inoue (JPN) 6–4 2–6 7–6.

Norcross, GA, USA – 27 March – *Singles:* M. Irvin (USA) d. P. Nola (BUL) 6–2 6–3.
Doubles: J. Abe (GER)/T. Obziler (ISR) d. L. Lee (USA)/J. Steck (RSA) 5–7 7–6 6–4.

Cagliari, Italy – 3 April – *Singles:* L. Pena (ESP) d. A. Canepa (ITA) 6–2 6–4.
Doubles: L. Dominguez Lino (ESP)/A. Ortuno (ESP) d. M. Pastikova (CZE)/J. Woehr (GER) 7–5 3–6 6–3.

Dinan, France – 3 April – *Singles:* M. Schnell (AUT) d. J. Vakulenko (UKR) 2–6 6–1 6–2.
Doubles: V. Henke (GER)/S. Schmidle (GER) d. S. Foretz (FRA)/P. Van Acker (BEL) 6–7 6–4 6–2.

Magli, Italy – 10 April – *Singles:* A. Pandjerova (BUL) d. P. Mandula (HUN) 6–4 2–6 7–5.
Doubles: A. Canepa (ITA)/M. Zavagli (ITA) d. S. Kriventcheva (BUL)/T. Poutchek (BLR) 6–1 6–4.

Cagnes sur Mer, France – 10 April – **Singles:** I. Tulyaganova (UZB) d. G. Casoni (ITA) 6–2 6–3.
Doubles: A. Bachmann (GER)/G. Casoni (ITA) d. I. Tulyaganova (UZB)/A. Zaporozhanova (UKR) 7–5 6–1.

La Canada, CA, USA – 10 April – **Singles:** J. Yi (CHN) d. R. De Los Rios (PAR) 3–6 7–5 6–3.
Doubles: A. Augustus (USA)/J. Scott (USA) d. J. Lee (TPE)/W. Prakusya (INA) 6–3 6–1.

Prostejov, Czech Republic – 17 April – **Singles:** D. Topalova (BUL) d. D. Van De Zande (BEL) 6–4 6–1.
Doubles: M. Pastikova (CZE)/J. Woehr (GER) d. H. Vildova (CZE)/M. Zdenovcova (CZE) 3–6 6–1 7–6.

Gelos, France – 17 April – **Singles:** M. Marrero (ESP) d. A. Medina Garrigues (ESP) 2–6 7–5 7–5.
Doubles: E. Bes (ESP)/M. Marrero (ESP) d. L. Dominguez Lino (ESP)/A. Medina Garrigues (ESP) 6–3 6–4.

Fresno, CA, USA – 17 April – **Singles:** R. McQuillan (AUS) d. M. Pelletier (CAN) 6–1 6–1.
Doubles: R. McQuilan (AUS)/L. McShea (AUS) d. E. Dominikovic (AUS)/A. Grahame (AUS) 6–4 6–4.

San Luis Potosi, Mexico – 17 April – **Singles:** M. Sequera (VEN) d. C. Castano (COL) 6–4 3–6 7–5.
Doubles: M. Landa (ARG)/R. Ottoboni (ARG) d. H. Crook (GBR)/V. Davies (GBR) 6–4 7–6.

Coatzacoalcos, Mexico – 1 May – **Singles:** M. D'Agostini (BRA) d. J. Cortez (BRA) 6–4 2–6 6–1.
Doubles: M. Sequera (VEN)/G. Volekova (SVK) d. J. Cortez (BRA)/M. D'Agostini (BRA) 6–3 7–5.

Virginia Beach, VA, USA – 1 May – **Singles:** M. Pelletier (CAN) d. R. De Los Rios (PAR) 7–6 6–2.
Doubles: D. Buth (USA)/M. Washington (USA) d. L. McShea (AUS)/J. Steck (RSA) 1–6 6–3 7–6.

Midlothian, VA, USA – 8 May – **Singles:** C. Castano (COL) d. E. Fauth (AUT) 6–3 7–5.
Doubles: D. Buth (USA)/J. Scott (USA) d. J. Cortez (BRA)/M. D'Agostini (BRA) 6–3 6–2.

Edinburgh, Great Britain – 15 May – **Singles:** M. Martinez (ESP) d. Z. Gubacsi (HUN) 6–2 6–3.
Doubles: N. Grandin (RSA)/N. Rencken (RSA) d. S. Sfar (TUN)/L. Woodroffe (GBR) 0–6 6–3 6–4.

Jackson, MS, USA – 15 May – **Singles:** J. Steck (RSA) d. D. Buth (USA) 6–1 7–6.
Doubles: J. Cortez (BRA)/M. D'Agostini (BRA) d. K. Miller (USA)/J. Steck (RSA) 6–4 5–7 6–1.

Guimaraes, Portugal – 22 May – **Singles:** K. Nagy (HUN) d. B. Mouhtassine (MAR) 6–0 5–7 7–6.
Doubles: N. Grandin (RSA)/N. Rencken (RSA) d. A. Cardoso (POR)/C. Santos (POR) 7–6 2–6 6–2.

Ho Chi Minh City, Vietnam – 22 May – **Singles:** N. Li (CHN) d. W. Prakusya (INA) 6–1 6–2.
Doubles: Y. Cho (KOR)/S. Obata (JPN) d. N. Li (CHN)/T. Li (CHN) 6–1 6–2.

Modena, Italy – 29 May – **Singles:** L. Dominguez Lino (ESP) d. M. Martinez (ESP) 4–6 6–4 7–5.
Doubles: L. Dominguez Lino (ESP)/M. Martinez (ESP) d. T. Hergold (SLO)/M. Matevzic (SLO) 6–4 4–6 6–3.

Shenzhen, China – 29 May – **Singles:** E. Kim (KOR) d. T. Sun (CHN) 6–4 6–3.
Doubles: E. Kim (KOR)/S. Obata (JPN) d. N. Li (CHN)/T. Li (CHN) 6–1 6–2.

Surbiton, Great Britain – 5 June – **Singles:** L. Latimer (GBR) d. T. Tanasugarn (THA) 7–5 6–3.
Doubles: T. Musgrave (AUS)/B. Stewart (AUS) d. C. Dhenin (FRA)/F. Lubiani (ITA) 3–6 6–3 6–1.

Galatina, Italy – 5 June – **Singles:** Antonella Serra-Zanetti (ITA) d. M. Sucha (SVK) 7–5 1–6 6–3.
Doubles: A. Canepa (ITA)/M. Diaz Oliva (ARG) d. J. Cortez (BRA)/M. D'Agostini (BRA) 6–4 4–6 6–4.

Mount Pleasant, GA, USA – 12 June – **Singles:** S. Cacic (USA) d. J. Watanabe (USA) 6–2 6–2.
Doubles: M. Clayton (AUS)/N. Johnston (AUS) d. M. Palaversic (CRO)/J. Trail (USA) 4–6 6–3 6–2.

Grado, Italy – 12 June – **Singles:** G. Riera (ESP) d. F. Perfetti (ITA) 6–2 6–4.
Doubles: V. Menga (BRA)/A. Ortuno (ESP) d. L. Dominguez Lino (ESP)/M. Martinez (ESP) 3–6 7–5 6–1.

Lenzerheide, Switzerland – 12 June – **Singles:** K. Nagy (HUN) d. J. Vakulenko (UKR) 6–2 3–6 7–6.
Doubles: M. Buric (GER)/B. Lamade (GER) d. Y. Basting (NED)/A. Van Den Hurk (NED) 7–5 6–3.

Sopot, Poland – 19 June – **Singles:** K. Koukalova (CZE) d. S. Schmidle (GER) 7–6 6–3.
Doubles: M. Nekvapilova (CZE)/H. Sromova (CZE) d. M. Kochta (GER)/L. Richterova (CZE) 6–3 6–2.

Gorizia, Italy – 19 June – **Singles:** M. Ramon (ESP) d. D. Randriantefy (MAD) 6–2 6–1.
Doubles: V. Menga (BRA)/A. Ortuno (ESP) d. M. Matevzic (SLO)/D. Zaric (YUG) 4–6 6–4 6–1.

Orbetello, Italy – 26 June – **Singles:** N. Llagostera (ESP) d. L. Dominguez Lino (ESP) 6–4 6–2.
Doubles: N. Li (CHN)/T. Li (CHN) d. J. Cortez (BRA)/M. D'Agostini (BRA) 6–3 7–6.

Mont-de-Marsan, France – 3 July – **Singles:** S. Foretz (FRA) d. D. Randriantefy (MAD) 6–2 6–3.
Doubles: E. Bes (ESP)/A. Ortuno (ESP) d. E. Chialvo (ARG)/J. Cravero (ARG) 6–2 6–2.

Vaihingen, Germany – 3 July – **Singles:** M. Schnitzer (GER) d. M. Buric (GER) 6–3 6–4.
Doubles: V. Csurgo (HUN)/E. Martincova (CZE) d. A. Glass (GER)/J. Woehr (GER) 6–2 2–6 6–4.

Civitanova, Italy – 3 July – **Singles:** N. Li (CHN) d. E. Gagliardi (SUI) 6–3 4–6 7–6.
Doubles: R. Andres (ESP)/C. Martinez Granados (ESP) d. E. Koulikovskaya (RUS)/T. Poutchek (BLR) 6–2 6–3.

Darmstadt, Germany – 10 July – **Singles:** M. Schnitzer (GER) d. R. Kucerova (CZE) 6 4 6–3.
Doubles: M. Matevzic (SLO)/M. Zavagli (ITA) d. Adriana Barna (GER)/A. Zaporozhanova (UKR) 7–6 6–7 6–4.

Felixstowe, Great Britain – 10 July – *Singles:* R. Vinci (ITA) d. L. Woodroffe (GBR) 6–2 6–2.
Doubles: T. Musgrave (AUS)/L. Woodroffe (GBR) d. L. Ahl (GBR)/N. Egorova (RUS) 6–4 3–6 6–4.

Gexto, Spain – 10 July – *Singles:* M. Martinez (ESP) d. J. Vakulenko (UKR) 6–4 6–0.
Doubles: A. Ortuno (ESP)/M. Palaversic (CRO) d. L. Dominguez Lino (ESP)/M. Martinez (ESP) 6–1 6–2.

Winnipeg, Canada – 10 July – *Singles:* K. Kraszewski (USA) d. V. Webb (CAN) 6–3 3–6 7–6.
Doubles: R. Kolbovic (CAN)/V. Webb (CAN) d. K. Freye (GER)/K. Tong (HKG) 6–1 6–4.

Peachtree City, GA, USA –10 July – *Singles:* S. Cacic (USA) d. A. Jidkova (RUS) 6–0 4–2 ret.
Doubles: D. Buth (USA)/L. McShea (AUS) d. A. Bradshaw (USA)/A. Spears (USA) 2–6 6–4 6–4.

Pucheim, Germany – 17 July – *Singles:* A. Vaskova (CZE) d. V. Henke (GER) 6–1 6–1.
Doubles: S. Kriventcheva (BUL)/Z. Valekova (SVK) d. A. Bachmann (GER)/M. Schnell (AUT) 7–5 3–6 7–5.

Fontanafredda, Italy – 17 July – *Singles:* E. Bes (ESP) d. G. Pizzichini (ITA) 6–4 6–1.
Doubles: R. Andres (ESP)/C. Martinez Granados (ESP) d. M. Matevzic (SLO)/Antonella Serra-Zanetti (ITA) 4–6 6–2 6–4.

Valladolid, Spain – 17 July – *Singles:* M. Martinez (ESP) d. P. Hermida (ESP) 6–4 6–2.
Doubles: M. Martinez (ESP)/A. Ortuno (ESP) d. T. Musgrave (AUS)/L. Woodroffe (GBR) 6–2 6–4.

Le Touquet, France – 17 July – *Singles:* B. Lamade (GER) d. S. Sfar (TUN) 7–5 6–4.
Doubles: B. Lamade (GER)/J. Woehr (GER) d. M. Chialvo (ARG)/L. Dominguez Lino (ESP) 6–3 7–5.

Pampalona, Spain – 24 July – *Singles:* Y. Basting (NED) d. A. Rodionova (RUS) 6–4 6–1.
Doubles: Y. Basting (NED)/M. Buric (GER) d. L. Baker (NZL)/M. Mesa (COL) 6–2 6–0.

Les Contamines, France – 24 July – *Singles:* B. Lamade (GER) d. D. Randriantefy (MAD) 6–2 6–1.
Doubles: C. Dhenin (FRA)/B. Lamade (GER) d. C. Bornu (FRA)/K. De Weille (NED) 6–7 6–4 6–4.

Dublin, Ireland – 24 July – *Singles:* L. Ahl (GBR) d. M. Joubert (RSA) 6–2 6–4.
Doubles: C. Barclay (AUS)/A. Van Den Hurk (NED) d. T. Musgrave (AUS)/L. Woodroffe (GBR) 6–4 7–5.

Alghero, Italy – 31 July – *Singles:* F. Lubiani (ITA) d. Z. Gubacsi (HUN) 6–1 6–0.
Doubles: K. Tong (HKG)/A. Takase (JPN) d. A. Canepa (ITA)/V. Sassi (ITA) 3–6 6–3 6–1.

Saint Gaudens, France – 31 July – *Singles:* E. Tatarkova (UKR) d. S. Sfar (TUN) 6–4 6–4.
Doubles: S. Kriventcheva (BUL)/E. Tatarkova (UKR) d. E. Molnar (HUN)/M. Palaversic (CRO) 3–6 7–5 6–3.

Carthage, Tunisia –7 August – *Singles:* K. Daskovic (YUG) d. M. Vesenjak (SLO) 6–1 6–4.
Doubles: V. Menga (BRA)/A. Ortuno (ESP) d. B. Kamper (AUT)/E. Kozhokina (RUS) 6–2 6–1.

Maribor, Slovenia – 21 August – *Singles:* K. Koukalova (CZE) d. A. Roesch (GER) 7–5 6–4.
Doubles: A. Roesch (GER)/J. Woehr (GER) d. V. Krauth (ARG)/A. Tricerri (SUI) 6–4 4–6 7–6.

Bucharest, Romania – 4 September – *Singles:* Z. Gubacsi (HUN) d. A. Pandjerova (BUL) 6–3 6–4.
Doubles: A. Pandjerova (BUL)/D. Topalova (BUL) d. K. Daskovic (YUG)/M. Kochta (GER) 6–4 6–2.

Fano, Italy – 4 September – *Singles:* F. Perfetti (ITA) d. M. Matevzic (SLO) 6–3 6–4.
Doubles: R. Andres (ESP)/C. Martinez Granados (ESP) d. E. Danilidou (GRE)/A. Ortuno (ESP) 6–2 6–4.

Reggio Calabria, Italy –11 September – *Singles:* Antonella Serra-Zanetti (ITA) d. M. Camerin (ITA) 6–4 6–4. *Doubles:* T. Kovalchuk (UKR)/S. Schmidle (GER) d. A. Vanc (ROM)/M. Zavagli (ITA) w/o.

Hopewell Junction, NY, USA –11 September – *Singles:* A. Jidkova (RUS) d. J. Hopkins (USA) 6–3 6–0.
Doubles: J. Hopkins (USA)/P. Rampre (SLO) d. E. Koulikovskaya (RUS)/J. Watanabe (USA) 6–3 6–1.

Sofia, Bulgaria – 11 September – *Singles:* A. Pandjerova (BUL) d. E. Fauth (AUT) 7–5 6–4.
Doubles: A. Pandjerova (BUL)/D. Topalova (BUL) d. N. Galouza (NED)/S. Stephens (NZL) 6–1 7–6.

Lecce, Italy –18 September – *Singles:* M. Palaversic (CRO) d. L. Nemeckova (CZE) 6–2 6–2.
Doubles: E. Bes (ESP)/A. Ortuno (ESP) d. A. Roesch (GER)/ S. Schmidle (GER) 6–4 6–0.

Saga, Japan –25 September – *Singles:* E. Krejcova (CZE) d. R. Fujiwara (JPN) 7–6 6–2.
Doubles: A. Augustus (USA)/A. Jensen (AUS) d. N. De Villiers (RSA)/E. Krejcova (CZE) 6–4 6–3.

Tbilisi, Georgia – 25 September – *Singles:* M. Diaz Oliva (ARG) d. M. Goloviznina (RUS) 3–6 6–2 6–2.
Doubles: M. Diaz Oliva (ARG)/M. Santangelo (ITA) d. J. Mens (NED)/A. Paulenkova (SVK) 4–6 6–3 6–2.

Verona, Italy – 25 September – *Singles:* A. Vaskova (CZE) d. M. Pastikova (CZE) 6–3 6–0.
Doubles: M. Camerin (ITA)/A.Vanc (ROM) d. M. Chialvo (ARG)/L. Dominguez Lino (ESP) 7–6 6–2.

Girona, Spain – 2 October – *Singles:* L. Dominguez Lino (ESP) d. L. Masante (ARG) 0–4 4–5 4–0 4–2 4–1.
Doubles: E. Bes (ESP)/L. Dominguez (ESP) d. M. Ramon (ESP)/G. Riera (ESP) 4–2 5–4 4–2.

Makarska, Croatia – 2 October – *Singles:* Z. Ondraskova (CZE) d. I. Gaspar (ROM) 4–0 2–4 1 4 4–0 4–1.
Doubles: E. Martincova (CZE)/A. Vaskova (CZE) d. M. Matevzic (SLO)/M. Palaversic (CRO) 4–2 4–1 2–4 4–2.

Plzen, Czech Republic – 9 October – **Singles:** A. Vaskova (CZE) d. A. Hegedus (HUN) 5–4 4–2 4–1.
Doubles: E. Krejcova (CZE)/H. Vildova (CZE) d. G. Navratilova (CZE)/A. Vaskova (CZE) 5–3 4–1 4–2.

Welwyn, Great Britain – 9 October – **Singles:** L. Ahl (GBR) d. Antonella Serra-Zanetti (ITA) 4–2 4–2 4–1.
Doubles: S. Stephens (NZL)/D. Zaric (YUG) d. Adriana Serra-Zanetti (ITA)/Antonella Serra-Zanetti (ITA) 4–0 5–3 4–1.

Mexico City, Mexico – 9 October – **Singles:** S. Taylor (USA) d. K. Freye (GER) 4–1 4–2 3–5 4–2.
Doubles: J. Cortez (BRA)/V. Menga (BRA) d. K. Freye (GER)/K. Liggan (IRL) 5–3 5–4 4–0.

Miramer, FL, USA – 9 October – **Singles:** A. Jidkova (RUS) d. R. De Los Rios (PAR) 4–1 5–4 4–2.
Doubles: L. Horn (RSA)/ L. McShea (AUS) d. R. De Los Rios (PAR)/S. Reeves (USA) 5–3 4–1 4–1.

Brisbane, Australia – 16 October – **Singles:** R. McQuillan (AUS) d. E. Dominikovic (AUS) 5–4 4–1 2–4 4–2.
Doubles: E. De Villiers (RSA)/A. Ellwood (AUS) d. K. Guse (AUS)/R. McQuillan (AUS) 3–5 4–2 5–3 4–1.

Joue-Les-Tours, France – 16 October – **Singles:** D. Randriantefy (MAD) d. L. Steinbach (GER) 4–0 4–1 4–1.
Doubles: E. Danilidou (GRE)/M. Geznenge (BUL) d. M. Buric (GER)/L. Dell'Angelo (ITA) 5–3 4–1 4–0.

Dalby, Australia – 23 October – **Singles:** E. Dominikovic (AUS) d. R. McQuillan (AUS) 6–2 7–5.
Doubles: K. Guse (AUS)/R. McQuillan (AUS) d. M. Clayton (AUS)/N. Johnston (AUS) 3–0 ret.

Saint Raphael, France – 23 October – **Singles:** M. Buric (GER) d. M. Ani (EST) 4–2 1–4 2–4 5–3 5–3.
Doubles: A. Goni (ESP)/N. Llagostera (ESP) d. K. Chevalier (FRA)/S. Trik (NED) 4–1 5–4 3–1 ret.

Gold Coast, Australia – 30 October – **Singles:** E. Dominikovic (AUS) d. R. McQuillan (AUS) 6–2 6–4.
Doubles: A. Augustus (USA)/A. Jensen (AUS) d. N. Grandin (RSA)/N. Rencken (RSA) 6–4 6–3.

Haywood, CA, USA – 30 October – **Singles:** A. Barna (GER) d. D. Buth (USA) 5–3 4–2 5–3.
Doubles: N. Miyagi (JPN)/N. Vaidyanathan (IND) d. K. Liggan (IRL)/M. Sequera (VEN) 4–2 4–0 4–2.

Hull, Great Britain – 30 October – **Singles:** L. Latimer (GBR) d. J. Pullin (GBR) 4–2 4–2 4–1.
Doubles: J. Pullin (GBR)/L. Woodroffe (GBR) d. M. Buric (GER)/S. Schmidle (GER) 4–1 1–4 4–1 5–4.

New Delhi, India – 30 October – **Singles:** L. Dlhopolcova (SVK) d. O. Kaliojnaia (RUS) 4–1 1–4 5–4 4–2.
Doubles: R. Chakravarthi (IND)/J. Jayalakshmy (IND) d. M. Vesenjak (SLO)/U. Vesenjak (SLO) 5–3 4–2 5–3.

Port Pirie, Australia – 13 November – **Singles:** E. Dominikovic (AUS) d. C. Wheeler (AUS) 6–4 6–4.
Doubles: E. De Villiers (RSA)/A. Ellwood (AUS) d. E. Dominikovic (AUS)/A. Grahame (AUS) 3–6 6–2 6–4.

Nuriootpa, Australia – 20 November – **Singles:** R. McQuillan (AUS) d. M. Weingartner (GER) 6–4 6–3.
Doubles: E. De Villiers (RSA)/A. Ellwood (AUS) d. R. McQuillan (AUS)/L. McShea (AUS) 7–6 6–3.

ITF WOMEN'S $50,000 TOURNAMENTS

Gifu, Japan – 1 May – **Singles:** T. Tanasugarn (THA) d. S. Asagoe (JPN) 7–5 6–4.
Doubles: S. Asagoe (JPN)/Y. Yoshida (JPN) d. S. De Beer (RSA)/N. De Villiers (RSA) 6–3 6–1.

Seoul, Korea – 8 May – **Singles:** N. Li (CHN) d. E. Kim (KOR) 6–3 7–6.
Doubles: S. Asagoe (JPN)/S. Obata (JPN) d. N. Li (CHN)/T. Li (CHN) 6–1 6–3.

Marseille, France – 12 June – **Singles:** A. Montolio (ESP) d. A. Medina Garrigues (ESP) 6–2 6–7 6–4.
Doubles: A. Canepa (ITA)/M. Diaz Oliva (ARG) d. S. Kriventcheva (BUL)/A. Zarska (POL) 6–2 6–3.

Los Gatos, CA, USA – 3 July – **Singles:** M. Tu (USA) d. M Irvin (USA) 1–6 7–5 6–4.
Doubles: J. Lee (TPE)/V. Webb (CAN) d. S. Cacic (USA)/R. Kolbovic (CAN) 6–4 6–1.

Mahwah, NJ, USA – 17 July – **Singles:** S. Cacic (USA) d. T. Almeda-Singian (USA) 6–2 6–7 7–5.
Doubles: E. Dominikovic (AUS)/N. Vaidyanathan (IND) d. L. McShea (AUS)/I. Selyutina (KAZ) 6–4 6–4.

Liege, Belgium – 24 July – **Singles:** J. Henin (BEL) d. B. Rittner (GER) 6–0 3–1 ret.
Doubles: V. Csurgo (HUN)/P. Mandula (HUN) d. E. Bes (ESP)/G. Riera (ESP) 7–6 6–1.

Salt Lake City, UT, USA – 24 July – **Singles:** W. Prakusya (INA) d. J. Steck (RSA) 4–6 6–4 7–6.
Doubles: L. McShea (AUS)/I. Selyutina (KAZ) d. S. Reeves (USA)/J. Steck (RSA) w/o.

Ettenheim, Germany – 31 July – **Singles:** M. Salerni (ARG) d. M. Sucha (SVK) 6–4 6–2.
Doubles: N. Ostrovskaya (BLR)/A. Zaporozhanova (UKR) d. M. Diaz Oliva (ARG)/M. Salerni (ARG) 6–4 6–2.

Lexington, KY, USA – 31 July – **Singles:** J. Hopkins (USA) d. D. Buth (USA) 6–3 6–1.
Doubles: J. Lee (TPE)/W. Prakusya (INA) d. S. Cacic (USA)/R. Kolbovic (CAN) 6–2 3–6 6–2.

Bronx, NY, USA – 14 August – **Singles:** D. Hantuchova (SVK) d. J. Yi (CHN) 6–4 6–4.
Doubles: S. De Beer (RSA)/N. Miyagi (JPN) d. A. Fusai (FRA)/E. Loit (FRA) 5–7 6–4 6–4.

Istanbul, Turkey – 14 August – **Singles:** T. Perebiynis (UKR) d. M. Vavrinec (SUI) 6–4 6–3.
Doubles: M. Mihalache (ROM)/K. Tong (HKG) d. M. Goloviznina (RUS)/E. Koulikovskaya (RUS) 6–1 6–2.

Denain, France – 4 September – *Singles:* A. Medina Garrigues (ESP) d. M. Martinez (ESP) 2–6 7–5 6–0.
Doubles: L. Dominguez Lino (ESP)/M. Martinez (ESP) d. E. Bovina (RUS)/M. Diaz Oliva (ARG) 6–4 6–0.

Albuquerque, NM, USA – 2 October – *Singles:* B. Rippner (USA) d. M. Vento (VEN) 6–0 6–0.
Doubles: B. Rippner (USA)/ E. Tatarkova (UKR) d. L. McShea (AUS)/ N. Vaidyanathan (IND) 6–4 6–4.

Largo, FL, USA – 16 October – *Singles:* A. Rippner (USA) d. T. Hergold (SLO) 6–2 6–1.
Doubles: A. Rippner (USA)/E. Tatarkova (UKR) d. D. Buth (USA)/S. Cacic (USA) 6–2 6–4.

Cardiff, Great Britain – 16 October – *Singles:* D. Zaric (YUG) d. L. Courtois (BEL) 7–5 5–7 6–4.
Doubles: J. Pullin (GBR)/L. Woodroffe (GBR) d. G. Casoni (ITA)/L. Courtois (BEL) 0–6 6–1 6–3.

Dallas, TX, USA – 23 October – *Singles:* J. Hopkins (USA) d. M. Sequera (VEN) 6–2 6–1.
Doubles: A. Rippner (USA)/E. Tatarkova (UKR) d. N. Miyagi (JPN)/N. Vaidyanathan (IND) 6–3 3–6 6–3.

Seoul, Korea – 23 October – *Singles:* V. Webb (CAN) d. M. Weingartner (GER) 4–2 5–3 1–4 5–3.
Doubles: S. De Beer (RSA)/M. Weingartner (GER) d. Y. Cho (KOR)/M. Jeon (KOR) 4–2 4–1 1–4 3–5 4–2.

Pittsburgh, PA, USA – 6 November – *Singles:* S. Cacic (USA) d. R. De Los Rios (PAR) 7–5 1–6 6–2.
Doubles: N. Miyagi (JPN)/N. Vaidyanathan (IND) d. K. Freye (GER)/S. Noorlander (NED) 5–7 6–4 6–0.

Naples, FL, USA – 13 November – *Singles:* Y. Basting (NED) d. C. Castano (COL) 4–0 4–1 4–2.
Doubles: N. Miyagi (JPN)/E. Tatarkova (UKR) d. M. Ani (EST)/V. Sassi (ITA) 5–3 2–4 2–4 5–3 4–1.

Mount Gambier, Australia – 27 November – *Singles:* E. Dominikovic (AUS) d. R. McQuillan (AUS) 6–2 6–1. *Doubles:* E. De Villiers (RSA)/A. Ellwood (AUS) d. E. Dominikovic (AUS)/A. Grahame (AUS) 6–2 6–2.

Tucson, AZ, USA – 27 November – *Singles:* K. Marosi (HUN) d. A. Jidkova (RUS) 6–7 6–4 6–3.
Doubles: L. Horn (RSA)/K. Marosi (HUN) d. D. Buth (USA)/J. Watanabe (USA) 6–4 6–2.

Santa Fe de Bogota, Columbia – 4 December – *Singles:* C. Castano (COL) d. F. Zuluaga (COL) 4–1 ret.
Doubles: J. Cortez (BRA)/M. Diaz Oliva (ARG) d. C. Fernandez (ARG)/C. Martinez (ESP) 3–6 6–1 6–2.

ITF WOMEN'S $75,000 TOURNAMENTS

Midland, MI, USA – 14 February – *Singles:* N. Pratt (AUS) d. Y. Yoshida (JPN) 6–4 6–3.
Doubles: E. De Villiers (RSA)/R. Hiraki (JPN) d. S. De Beer (RSA)/T. Obziler (ISR) 6–1 1–6 6–1.

West Palm, FL, USA – 3 April – *Singles:* M. Shaughnessy (USA) d. H. Nagyova (SVK) 4–6 7–5 7–6.
Doubles: R. Hiraki (JPN)/Y. Yoshida (JPN) d. E. De Lone (USA)/N. Pratt (AUS) 1–6 6–0 7–6.

Dubai, United Arab Emirates – 3 April – *Singles:* A. Gersi (CZE) d. T. Garbin (ITA) 6–4 6–3.
Doubles: T. Garbin (ITA)/K. Marosi (HUN) d. A. Bachmann (GER)/T. Krizan (SLO) 7–6 6–3.

Sarasota, FL, USA – 24 April – *Singles:* M. Shaughnessy (USA) d. K. Brandi (USA) 6–1 6–3.
Doubles: S. Cacic (USA)/M. Shaughnessy (USA) d. E. Dominikovic (AUS)/A. Grahame (AUS) 6–4 6–2.

Oporto, Portugal – 15 May – *Singles:* M. Sanchez Lorenzo (ESP) d. V. Ruano Pascual (ESP) 6–4 4–6 6–3.
Doubles: E. Bes (ESP)/G. Riera (ESP) d. R. Andres (ESP)/C. Martinez Granados (ESP) 6–3 6–3.

Bordeaux, France – 11 September – *Singles:* E. Loit (FRA) d. L. Bacheva 7–5 6–2.
Doubles: V. Razzano (FRA)/M. Schnell (AUT) d. L. Dominguez Lino (ESP)/M. Sanchez Lorenzo (ESP) 2–6 7–5 6–3.

Kirkland, NY, USA – 18 September – *Singles:* A. Rippner (USA) d. Y. Yoshida (JPN) 6–3 6–2.
Doubles: L. McShea (AUS)/K. Schlukebir (USA) d. A. Bradshaw (USA)/A. Spears (USA) 3–6 6–2 6–3.

Santa Clara, CA, USA – 25 September – *Singles:* M. Tu (USA) d. R. Kolbovic (CAN) 6–7 6–2 6–2.
Doubles: K. Freye (GER)/S. Noorlander (NED) d. D. Buth (USA)/P. Rampre (SLO) 6–1 6–4.

Batumi, GA, USA – 2 October – *Singles:* T. Poutchek (BLR) d. N. Ostrovskaya (BLR) 4–1 4–1 2–4 1–4 5–4.
Doubles: T. Peribiynis (UKR)/T. Poutchek (BLR) d. M. Diaz Oliva (ARG)/ E. Dyrberg (DEN) 1–4 4–2 4–1 4–2.

Poitiers, France – 9 October – *Singles:* L. Cervanova (SVK) d. I. Majoli (CRO) 4–6 6–3 6–2.
Doubles: Y. Basting (NED)/ K. Marosi (HUN) d. P. Mandula (HUN)/ P. Wartusch (AUT) 7–6 6–1.

Cergy Pontoise, France – 4 December – *Singles:* V. Razzano (FRA) d. I. Majoli (CRO) 3–6 6–4 6–3.
Doubles: J. Henin (BEL)/V. Razzano (FRA) d. M. Matevzic (SLO)/C. Schneider (GER) 6–2 6–4.

Australian Open Championships

Left: Sweden's Magnus Norman won five tournaments during 2000 and was a semi-finalist in Melbourne – his best year since turning professional in 1995. *(Paul Zimmer)*

Below: With a devastating display of power hitting, Lindsay Davenport ended the three-year reign of Martina Hingis in Melbourne. *(Paul Zimmer)*

Below: The victory of Australia's Rennae Stubbs and her American partner Lisa Raymond was a first Grand Slam success for this popular pair. *(Stephen Wake)*

Above: Title-holder Yevgeny Kafelnikov reached the final for the second year in a row but was outhit by Andre Agassi. *(Paul Zimmer)*

Right: After a gap of four years Andre Agassi returned to the winner's enclosure in Melbourne, his sixth career Grand Slam success. *(Paul Zimmer)*

Roland Garros – The French Open Championships

Left: A finalist in Paris six years ago, Mary Pierce at last fulfilled the hopes of her loyal French fans by beating Conchita Martinez to claim her national title. *(Paul Zimmer)*

Below left: America's Chanda Rubin had an impressive win over local favourite and No.7 seed, Nathalie Tauziat, to reach the quarter-finals in Paris for the second time. *(Paul Zimmer)*

Below right: By reaching the semi-finals at the French Open for the first time, the unseeded left-hander, Franco Squillari of Argentina, recorded a career-best performance. *(Paul Zimmer)*

Above: Gustavo Kuerten, the 1997 champion, beat Magnus Norman to claim a second title at Roland Garros, a win that lifted him to the top of the ATP Tour Champions Race. *(Paul Zimmer)*

Left: In their last year on the Tour, Australia's "Woodies", Todd Woodbridge and Mark Woodforde, added the missing French title to their collection – a 58th doubles title together that surpassed the record they has shared with Hewitt/McMillan and Fleming/McEnroe. *(Paul Zimmer)*

The Championships – Wimbledon

Left: By winning his semi-final against Andre Agassi, who had beaten him at the same stage in 1999, Australia's Pat Rafter reached the Wimbledon final for the first time and was within a few points of upsetting Pete Sampras. *(Stephen Wake)*

Below: Nursing an injured leg, Pete Sampras won an historic seventh victory in eight years on the Centre Court. His dramatic win over Pat Rafter ended in near darkness and gave the 28-year-old American a record 13th career Grand Slam title. *(Paul Zimmer)*

Below: The 1992 champion Andre Agassi, a finalist in 1999, lost a thrilling semi-final to Australia's Pat Rafter in the match of the tournament. *(Paul Zimmer)*

Right: The remarkable American sisters, Venus and Serena Williams, lost only one set in winning their third Grand Slam title together. *(Paul Zimmer)*

Far right: By winning the singles at Wimbledon, Venus Williams joined her sister Serena, the reigning US Open champion, in the exclusive club of Grand Slam champions. *(Paul Zimmer)*

US Open Championships

Left: After a season of spectacular improvement the 20-year-old Russian, Marat Safin won his first Grand Slam title by thrashing the four-time former champion Pete Sampras in an unexpectedly one-sided final. *(Paul Zimmer)*

Below: Until he ran into a red-hot Safin in the final, Pete Sampras seemed ready to claim a 14th Grand Slam success. *(Paul Zimmer)*

Below right: Much is expected of Andy Roddick, winner of the boy's singles at Flushing Meadows and world No. 1 junior, who was attached to the US Davis Cup team during the year. *(Stephen Wake)*

Left: By following her sister as the US Open champion Venus Williams was writing a new page in the history of Grand Slam tennis. *(Stephen Wake)*

Right: Lindsay Davenport had won the singles in 1998 but in 2000, like Martina Hingis the year before, she found it impossible to beat both Williams sisters in the same Championships. *(Paul Zimmer)*

Rest of the year...

Left: Alex Corretja of Spain, who won five titles and led his country to the final of the Davis Cup, where they beat the holders Australia to win the team trophy for the first time. *(Paul Zimmer)*

Below: The champion in Cincinnati and Basel, Sweden's Thomas Enqvist ended the year at No.9 in the ATP Champions Race, then took time out for surgery on his shoulder and foot, delaying his start in 2001. *(Paul Zimmer)*

Above: With a spectacular run of success at Wimbledon, qualifier Alexander Voltchkov went through to the semi-finals unseeded, a feat last achieved by John McEnroe in 1977. *(Paul Zimmer)*

Above: Arnaud Clement, one of eight Frenchmen in the world's top 70, beat Andre Agassi at the US Open on his way to the quarter-finals, his best-ever Grand Slam finish. *(Paul Zimmer)*

Left: Australia's feisty battler Lleyton Hewitt won five tournaments during the year. *(Paul Zimmer)*

Left: At the US Open the 18-year-old Russian Elena Dementieva reached the semi-finals unseeded and pushed the 1998 champion Lindsay Davenport to the limit. *(Paul Zimmer)*

Below: Despite some unwelcome publicity generated by her volatile father Damir, Jelena Dokic enjoyed another year of significant progress with a semi-final finish at Wimbledon and at the Olympic Games, both times unseeded. *(Stephen Wake)*

Above: Without a Grand Slam title in 2000, the first blank year since 1996, Martina Hingis nevertheless won nine tournaments and consolidated her position as the world No.1. *(Paul Zimmer)*

Above: The winner of four tournaments, including a first Australian Open, Lindsay Davenport's year was interrupted by injury which forced her to retire after winning one round at the Olympic Games, a sad end for the title-holder. *(Stephen Wake)*

Left: The Japanese/French pairing of Ai Sugiyama and Julie Halard-Decugis won their first Grand Slam title together at the US Open, a career breakthrough for both. *(Stephen Wake)*

Left: Argentina's Maria Emilia Salerni, winner of the Wimbledon and US Open junior titles and a finalist in Paris, was the No. 1 player of the year. *(Paul Zimmer)*

Below: Aniko Kapros of Hungary started the year well with victory at the Australian Open junior event. *(Stephen Wake)*

Below: The junior doubles win by Lee Childs and James Nelson at the US Open was the first by a British pair. *(Stephen Wake)*

Above: A semi-finalist in Paris, Nicolas Mahut of France showed his versatility by winning the junior title at Wimbledon on unaccustomed grass. *(Paul Zimmer)*

Left: Paul-Henri Mathieu of France, very much at home on the red clay, won the junior title in Paris against the favourite, Tommy Robredo of Spain. *(Paul Zimmer)*

Left: Virginie Razzano of France won a marathon final in Paris against Maria Emilia Salerni to keep the French junior title at home. *(Paul Zimmer)*

LACOSTE

BECOME WHAT YOU ARE

www.lacoste.fr

International Team Competitions

European Cups – Men and Women
World Team Cup

Dominik Hrbaty, with Karol Kucera, captured the World Team Cup for Slovakia and ended the year with a ranking of 17, a career high. (Paul Zimmer)

EUROPEAN CUP

EUROPEAN MEN'S TEAM CHAMPIONSHIPS
Champions Division (29 November–3 December 2000, Montecatini, Italy)

First Round: **Slovenia d. Italy 2–1:** F. Volandri (ITA) d. A. Kracman (SLO) 6–1 6–4; M. Tkalec (SLO) d. S. Tarallo (ITA) 7–6(2) 6–4; A. Kracman/B. Urh (SLO) d. D. Bracciali/M. Dell'Acqua (ITA) 6–1 6–7(5) 6–3. **Sweden d. Croatia 2–1:** J. Adaktusson (SWE) d. M. Ancic (CRO) 2–6 7–6(6) 6–0; I. Karlovic (CRO) d. J. Froberg (SWE) 7–6(7) 6–2; J. Adaktusson/ D. Norberg (SWE) d.I. Karlovic/R. Karanusic (CRO) 7–6(4) 6–4. **Czech Republic d. Spain 3–0:** O. Fukarek (CZE) d. J. Lido (ESP) 6–3 3–6 6–3; J. Vacek (CZE) d. D. Caballero (ESP) 6–3 6–1; O. Fukarek/M. Stepanek (CZE) d. D. Caballero/P. Rico (ESP) 6–4 6–4. **Bulgaria d. Great Britain 2–1:** I. Bratanov (BUL) d. L. Childs (GBR) 6–4 6–2; M. Velev (BUL) d. J. Delgado (GBR) 6–2 7–5; J. Nelson/O. Freelove (GBR) d. I. Bratanov/ V. Ivanchev (BUL) 6–3 6–7(6) 6–1.
Semi-finals: **Slovenia d. Sweden 2–0:** A. Kracman (SLO) d. J. Adaktusson (SWE) 6–4 6–4; M. Tkalec (SLO) d. J. Froberg (SWE) 2–6 6–2 6–1; **Czech Republic d. Bulgaria 2–0:** O. Fukarek (CZE) d. I. Bratanov (BUL) 6–3 6–2; J. Vacek (CZE) d. M. Velev (BUL) 4–6 6–1 7–5.
Final: **Czech Republic d. Slovenia 2–0:** O. Fukarek (CZE) d. A. Kracman (SLO) 6–4 6–1; J. Vacek (CZE) d. M. Tkalec (SLO) 6–2 6–2.
Croatia, Great Britain and Spain are relegated to the 2001 First Division.

FIRST DIVISION GROUP ONE (Sopot, Poland)
Round Robin: Monaco d. Poland 2–1; Luxembourg d. Belarus 3–0; Poland d. Belarus 2–1; Luxembourg d. Monaco 2–1; Monaco d. Belarus 2–1; Poland d. Luxembourg 3–0.
Poland is promoted to the 2001 Champions Division.

FIRST DIVISION GROUP TWO (Filothei, Greece)
Preliminary Round: Ireland d. Yugoslavia 3–0.
Semi-finals: Greece d. Yugoslavia 2–1; Slovak Republic d. Malta 3–0.
Final: Greece d. Slovak Republic 3–0.
Greece is promoted to the 2001 Champions Division.

FIRST DIVISION GROUP THREE (Istanbul, Turkey)
Round Robin: Belgium d. Portugal 2–1; Portugal d. Turkey 2–1; Belgium d. Turkey 3–0.
Belgium is promoted to 2001 Champions Division.

EUROPEAN WOMEN'S TEAM CHAMPIONSHIPS
Champions Division (15–26 November 2000, Cesky Krumlov, Czech Republic)

First Round: **Great Britain d. Poland 2–1:** K. Straczy (POL) d. E. Baltacha (GBR) 1–6 6–4 6–3; L. Latimer (GBR) d. A. Zarska (POL) 6–3 3–6 6–1 E. Baltacha/Pullin (GBR) d. K. Straczy/A. Zarska (POL) 6–1 5–7 6–3. **Spain d. Belarus 3–0:** P. Hermida (ESP) d. O. Glouschenko (BLR) 6–2 6–3; Ma. J. Martinez (ESP) d. D. Kustava (BLR) 6–1 6–1; E. Bes/ Ma. J Martinez (ESP) d. D. Kustava/T. Uvarova (BLR) 6–1 6–2. **Czech Republic d. Croatia 2–1:** L. Nemeckova (CZE) d. D. Jurak (CRO) 6–1 6–4; M. Mezak (CRO) d. A. Vaskova (CZE) 5–7 6–1 6–2; L. Nemeckova/A. Vaskova (CZE) d. D. Jurak/M. Mezak (CRO) 6–1 6–0. **Italy d. Greece 2–1:** G. Casoni (ITA) d. E.Roussi (GRE) 6–3 6–3; E. Daniilidou (GRE) d. F. Schiavone (ITA) 1–6 6–3 6–4; G. Casoni/F.Schiavone (ITA) d. E. Daniilidou/E. Roussi (GRE) 6–0 6–2.
Semi-finals: **Italy d. Czech Republic 2–1:** G. Casoni (ITA) d. L. Nemeckova (CZE) 6–1 7–6(3); F. Schiavone (ITA) d. A. Vaskova (CZE) 7–6(5) 6–4; K. Koukalova/L. Nemeckova (CZE) d. M.E. Camerin/L. Dell'Angelo (ITA) 6–2 6–4. **Great Britain d. Spain 2–1:** P. Hermida (ESP) d. H. Collin (GBR) 4–6 6–4 6–2; L. Latimer (GBR) d. Ma. J Martinez (ESP) 7–6(5) 1–6 7–6(3); E. Baltacha/J. Pullin (GBR) d. E. Bes/ Ma. J Martinez (ESP) 6–7(6) 6–4 6–3.
Final: **Italy d. Great Britain 2–1:** E. Baltacha (GBR) d. G. Casoni (ITA) 3–6 6–3 7–5; F. Schiavone (ITA) d. L. Latimer (GBR) 6–3 6–2; G. Casoni/F. Schiavone (ITA) d. E. Baltache/J. Pullin (GBR) 6–1 6–2.
Belarus and Croatia are relegated to the 2001 First Division.

First Division Group One (Lomma, Sweden)
Round Robin: **Group A:** Denmark d. Netherlands 2–1; Ukraine d. Denmark 2–1; Ukraine d. Netherlands 3–0. **Group B:** Ireland d. Luxembourg 2–1; Sweden d. Ireland 3–0; Sweden d. Luxembourg 3–0.
Final: Sweden d. Ukraine 2–0.
Sweden is promoted to the 2001 Champions Division.

First Division Group Two (Espinho, Portugal)
Round Robin: **Group A:** Yugoslavia d. Malta 3–0; Belgium d. Malta 3–0; Yugoslavia d. Belgium 2–1. **Group B:** Slovenia d. Portugal 2–1; Turkey d. Portugal 2–1; Slovenia d. Turkey 2:1.
Final: Yugoslavia d. Slovenia 2–1.
Yugoslavia is promoted to the 2001 Champions Division.

World Team Cup

Barry Wood

The 2000 World Team Cup was won by Slovakia, who defeated Russia 3–0 in the final. Dominik Hrbaty, who had won four of five previous matches against Yevgeny Kafelnikov, beat him again 6–4 7–6, and Karol Kucera won perhaps the best match of the week as he dismissed Marat Safin 6–3 6–2. Hrbaty joined with Jan Kroslak to beat Kafelnikov and Safin 6–4 6–2 in the doubles.

It was a particularly fine week for Kucera, who also defeated Vince Spadea, Mikael Tillstrom and Rainer Schuttler for the loss of only 12 games. Afterwards, he described the victory as 'probably the best win in my career so far. It's a great feeling to be the world champions, a great success.'

Slovakia topped the group that also included Sweden, Germany and the United States. The Americans, despite the presence of Pete Sampras, finished bottom of the group, winning only three of their nine matches. Sampras was first beaten by Hrbaty after rain at the end of the first set had robbed him of the momentum gained from a fine start. The score, 0–6 6–4 6–4.

Then he was defeated 7–5 6–2 by Tommy Haas. His only win came, surprisingly, at the expense of the Champions Race leader at the time, Magnus Norman, although the Swede did confess after his 6–3 6–4 defeat that he had not gone to sleep until 4am after watching a replay of the Champions League soccer final.

The Americans were also hindered by the struggling Vince Spadea, who entered the tournament having lost his previous 15 matches stretching back some six months. The best he could do was win a set, against Mikael Tillstrom. Alex O'Brien and Jared Palmer gave the Americans some respectability, winning two of their three doubles matches.

Russia easily won their group over Australia, Spain and Chile, conceding only one match when Kafelnikov lost 6–3 6–3 to Felix Mantilla. Perhaps the biggest stir was caused by the wild card team, Chile. The only impression they left was a negative one, as despite having the former world number one, Marcelo Rios, in their team they lost all nine of their matches. In fact, they salvaged just one set, when Nicolas Massu took a set from Patrick Rafter. Both Rios and Massu retired from matches when trailing 0–5, Rios against Lleyton Hewitt and Massu against Alberto Martin. Hewitt only played five games in each of his first two matches, as Albert Costa also retired against him when 1–4 behind.

During the week, tournament chairman Horst Klosterkemper announced that consideration was being given to not only increasing the field from eight teams to 12 after 2002, but also having two sessions a day, with the first being played outdoors at the present location, the Rochusclub, and the second indoors in the evening. Quite what the ATP would make of playing indoors in the week preceding Roland Garros remains to be seen.

Karol Kucera's win over Russia's Marat Safin clinched victory for Slovakia in the final.
(Paul Zimmer)

ROUND ROBIN COMPETITION

Red Group:
Sunday – **Germany d. Sweden 2–1**: Tommy Haas (GER) d. Thomas Enqvist 5–7 6–2 6–2; Mikael Tillstrom (SWE) d. Rainer Schuttler (GER) 6–4 7–6 (Rain) *Monday* – Tommy Haas/David Prinosil (GER) d. Nicklas Kulti/Mikael Tillstrom (SWE) 6–2 6–2 (postponed from Sunday).
Slovakia d. USA 2–1: Karol Kucera (SVK) d. Vince Spadea (USA) 6–3 6–3; Dominik Hrbaty (SVK) d. Pete Sampras (USA) 0–6 6–4 6–4 (rain) *Monday* – Alex O'Brien/Jared Palmer (USA) d. Dominik Hrbaty/Jan Kroslak (SVK) 6–1 7–6(6) (postponed from Sunday).
Tuesday – **Germany d. USA 2–1**: Tommy Haas (GER) d. Pete Sampras (USA) 7–5 6–2; Rainer Schuttler (GER) d. Vincent Spadea (USA) 7–5 3–6 6–1; Alex O'Brien/Jared Palmer (USA) d. Tommy Haas/David Prinosil (GER) 7–6(3) 6–7(5) 6–3.
Sweden d. Slovakia 2–1: Magnus Norman (SWE) d. Dominik Hrbaty (SVK) 3–6 7–6(5) 6–3; Karol Kucera (SVK) d. Mikael Tillstrom (SWE) 6–0 6–2; Mikael Tillstrom/Nicklas Kulti (SWE) d. Dominik Hrbaty/Karol Kucera (SVK) 6–4 7–6(4).
Thursday – **Slovakia d. Germany 2–1**: Dominik Hrbaty (SVK) d. Tommy Haas (GER) 6–2 4–6 6–2; Karol Kucera (SVK) d. Rainer Schuttler (GER) 6–2 6–2; Tommy Haas/David Prinosil (GER) d. Karol Kucera/Dominik Hrbaty (SVK) 6–3 4–6 6–1.
Sweden d. USA 2–1: Pete Sampras (USA) d. Magnus Norman (SWE) 6–3 6–4; Mikael Tillstrom (SWE) d. Vincent Spadea (USA) 6–3 6–3; Nicklas Kulti/Mikael Tillstrom (SWE) d. Alex O'Brien/Jared Palmer (USA) 6–3 4–6 6–3.

Blue Group:
Monday – **Australia d. Spain 2–1**: Lleyton Hewitt (AUS) d. Albert Costa (ESP) 4–1 ret (back – muscle contraction); Felix Mantilla (ESP) d. Patrick Rafter (AUS) 6–2 6–4; Lleyton Hewitt/Sandon Stolle (AUS) d. Jairo Velasco Jr/Juan Carrasco (ESP) 6–2 6–2.
Russia d. Chile 3–0: Yevgeny Kafelnikov (RUS) d. Marcelo Rios (CHI) 6–3 7–5; Marat Safin (RUS) d Nicolas Massu (CHI) 7–6(7) 6–4; Yevgeny Kafelnikov/Marat Safin (RUS) d. Nicolas Massu/Hermes Gamonal (CHI) 6–3 6–4.
Wednesday – **Australia d. Chile 3–0**: Lleyton Hewitt (AUS) d. Marcelo Rios (CHI) 5–0 ret.; Patrick Rafter (AUS) d. Nicolas Massu (CHI) 4–6 7–6(4) 6–1; Lleyton Hewitt/Sandon Stolle (AUS) d. Hermes Gamonal/Nicolas Massu (CHI) 6–1 6–0.
Russia d. Spain 2–1: Marat Safin (RUS) d. Alberto Martin (ESP) 7–6(2) 6–1; Felix Mantilla (ESP) d. Yevgeny Kafelnikov (RUS) 6–3 6–3; Yevgeny Kafelnikov/Marat Safin (RUS) d. Juan Carrasco/Jairo Velasco Jr (ESP) 7–6(5) 6–4.
Friday – **Russia d. Australia 3–0**: Yevgeny Kafelnikov (RUS) d. Lleyton Hewitt (AUS) 6–1 6–2; Marat Safin (RUS) d. Richard Fromberg (AUS) 6–2 6–4; Yevgeny Kafelnikov/Marat Safin (RUS) d. Patrick Rafter/Sandon Stolle (AUS) 6–4 6–1.
Spain d. Chile 3–0: Alberto Martin (ESP) d. Nicolas Massu (CHI) 5–0 ret. (right ankle); Felix Mantilla (ESP) d. Marcelo Rios (CHI) 6–4 6–1; Juan Carrasco/Jairo Velasco Jr (ESP) d. Hermes Gamonal/Marcelo Rios (CHI) 6–2 6–3.

FINAL STANDINGS

Red Group

	Ties	Matches	Sets	Prize Money
Slovakia	2:1	5:4	12:10	$500,000
Sweden	2:1	5:4	11:10	$150,000
Germany	2:1	5:4	12:11	$100,000
USA	0:3	3:6	9:13	$ 60,000

Blue Group

	Ties	Matches	Sets	Prize Money
Russia	3:0	8:1	16:2	$300,000
Australia	2:1	5:4	10:9	$150,000
Spain	1:2	5:4	10:8	$100,000
Chile	0:3	0:9	1:18	$ 60,000

FINAL – *Sunday 27 May* – **Slovakia d. Russia 3–0**: Dominik Hrbaty (SVK) d. Yevgeny Kafelnikov (RUS) 6–4 7–6(1); Karol Kucera (SVK) d. Marat Safin (RUS) 6–3 6–2; Dominik Hrbaty/Jan Kroslak (SVK) d. Yevgeny Kafelnikov/Marat Safin (RUS) 6–4 6–2.

Rankings

ATP Tour Rankings and Prize Money
History of the ATP Tour No. 1 Men's Ranking
WTA Tour Rankings and Prize Money
History of the WTA Tour No. 1 Women's Ranking

Injuries contributed to a fall in the rankings for Nicolas Kiefer of Germany from No. 6 at the end of 1999 to 20. (Paul Zimmer)

ATP Tour Rankings and Prize Money 2000

In 2000 a new ranking concept was introduced. The Champions Race began on 1st January with all players on zero points. Week by week they accumulated points according to the round reached at tournaments. All players eligible on the Entry Rankings (see below) were automatically entered in the four Grand Slam Championships and the nine Masters Series tournaments. Regardless of whether a player competed, all 13 were counted. A further five International group tournaments could be selected by the player to bring his total to 18. Points were also given for the Olympic Games and for the season-ending Tennis Masters Cup, a new event for the top eight players in the Race, replacing the old ATP Tour World Championship and the Grand Slam Cup.

Behind the scenes the ATP Entry Rankings, used to determine eligibility for tournament entries and seedings, measured a player's form over a moving twelve month period, though now without any bonus points for beating a higher ranked player. The following tables show the year-end entry rankings of the top 200 men in singles, the top 130 in doubles and the top 150 on the prize money list based on a player's best 18 results, plus those players whose career earnings exceed $1 million.

Besides the tournaments mentioned above, all official ATP Tour Challenger Series events and the Satellite Circuits administered by member nations of the ITF, were eligible for ranking purposes. (Statistics supplied by ATP Tour)

(The nationalities and birthdays of players can be found on pp 140–146)

SINGLES (As at 4 December)

Rank	Player	Tourns Played	Total Points	Rank	Player	Tourns Played	Total Points
1	Gustavo Kuerten	23	4195	33	Jan-Michael Gambill	26	1030
2	Marat Safin	30	4120	34	Gaston Gaudio	26	995
3	Pete Sampras	16	3385	35	Byron Black	26	960
4	Magnus Norman	26	3110	36	Richard Krajicek	19	950
5	Yevgeny Kafelnikov	32	2935	37	Marcelo Rios	25	950
6	Andre Agassi	19	2765	38	David Prinosil	21	945
7	Lleyton Hewitt	21	2625	39	Thomas Johansson	28	930
8	Alex Corretja	25	2475	40	Max Mirnyi	29	880
9	Thomas Enqvist	25	2210	41	Carlos Moya	24	870
10	Tim Henman	26	2020	42	Jerome Golmard	27	856
11	Mark Philippoussis	23	1865	43	Gianluca Pozzi	30	854
12	Juan Carlos Ferrero	27	1840	44	Jonas Bjorkman	27	845
13	Wayne Ferreira	23	1770	45	Rainer Schuettler	29	835
14	Franco Squillari	27	1598	46	Vladimir Voltchkov	16	830
15	Patrick Rafter	21	1535	47	Fernando Vicente	34	825
16	Cedric Pioline	24	1520	48	Nicolas Escude	25	805
17	Dominik Hrbaty	29	1395	49	Francisco Clavet	31	795
18	Arnaud Clement	29	1360	50	Andrew Ilie	30	775
19	Sebastien Grosjean	28	1325	51	Albert Portas	28	760
20	Nicolas Kiefer	23	1265	52	Andreas Vinciguerra	25	760
21	Mariano Puerta	23	1235	53	Jiri Novak	26	755
22	Sjeng Schalken	27	1163	54	Stefan Koubek	28	755
23	Tommy Haas	23	1145	55	Todd Martin	16	740
24	Nicolas Lapentti	28	1130	56	Alex Calatrava	28	731
25	Younes El Aynaoui	29	1125	57	Karim Alami	30	725
26	Albert Costa	25	1115	58	Andrei Medvedev	20	680
27	Andrei Pavel	30	1105	59	Harel Levy	26	677
28	Marc Rosset	27	1080	60	Arnaud Di Pasquale	29	660
29	Roger Federer	29	1080	61	Mariano Zabaleta	28	645
30	Hicham Arazi	27	1060	62	Agustin Calleri	17	633
31	Fabrice Santoro	28	1040	63	Juan Ignacio Chela	21	632
32	Michael Chang	27	1040	64	Slava Dosedel	23	619

Rank	Player	Tourns Played	Total Points	Rank	Player	Tourns Played	Total Points
65	Davide Sanguinetti	33	609	133	Bob Bryan	25	285
66	Jason Stoltenberg	15	606	134	Nikolay Davydenko	23	283
67	Olivier Rochus	26	596	135	Diego Nargiso	13	280
68	Chris Woodruff	23	590	136	Cristiano Caratti	27	279
69	Greg Rusedski	24	575	137	Laurence Tieleman	34	278
70	Julien Boutter	27	575	138	Ronald Agenor	37	278
71	Juan Balcells	23	566	139	Martin Rodriguez	25	278
72	Markus Hantschk	27	562	140	Nicolas Thomann	25	278
73	Karol Kucera	22	555	141	Tomas Behrend	29	271
74	Christophe Rochus	30	540	142	Diego Moyano	23	271
75	Magnus Larsson	16	540	143	Christian Ruud	19	269
76	Bohdan Ulihrach	27	536	144	Attila Savolt	22	268
77	Jiri Vanek	29	532	145	Tuomas Ketola	29	268
78	Martin Damm	23	530	146	Orlin Stanoytchev	32	262
79	Paul Goldstein	28	519	147	Peter Wessels	13	262
80	Alberto Martin	32	518	148	Oliver Gross	18	262
81	Mikael Tillstrom	18	518	149	Nicolas Coutelot	21	262
82	Magnus Gustafsson	20	515	150	Gaston Etlis	23	261
83	Wayne Arthurs	26	513	151	Yong-Il Yoon	19	255
84	Richard Fromberg	25	507	152	Alberto Berasategui	27	254
85	Sergi Bruguera	21	504	153	Leander Paes	12	253
86	Alexander Popp	21	500	154	Julian Knowle	22	251
87	Nicolas Massu	29	496	155	Arvind Parmar	19	250
88	Guillermo Coria	18	492	156	Michael Russell	33	250
89	David Sanchez	21	490	157	Federico Browne	25	250
90	Hyung-Taik Lee	21	484	158	Andy Roddick	10	250
91	Ivan Ljubicic	27	484	159	Jan Kroslak	25	249
92	German Puentes	30	451	160	Kevin Kim	27	249
93	Michel Kratochvil	29	440	161	Kevin Ullyett	15	248
94	Sargis Sargsian	29	433	162	Michael Llodra	19	245
95	Raemon Sluiter	25	433	163	Takao Suzuki	10	244
96	Michal Tabara	21	424	164	Filip Dewulf	18	244
97	Justin Gimelstob	21	420	165	Stefano Tarallo	23	242
98	Daniel Elsner	23	412	166	Marcelo Charpentier	18	239
99	Felix Mantilla	17	410	167	Filippo Volandri	23	239
100	Fernando Meligeni	27	409	168	Barry Cowan	25	238
101	Andrea Gaudenzi	27	404	169	Irakli Labadze	26	236
102	Christian Vinck	21	398	170	Reginald Willems	22	235
103	Jan Siemerink	25	391	171	Werner Eschauer	23	234
104	George Bastl	31	390	172	Hugo Armando	17	231
105	Paradorn Srichaphan	26	387	173	Julian Alonso	28	227
106	Andre Sa	30	385	174	Thierry Guardiola	28	226
107	Wayne Black	16	382	175	Albert Montanes	22	225
108	Jens Knippschild	24	374	176	Jose Acasuso	22	222
109	Cecil Mamiit	29	363	177	Jamie Delgado	25	217
110	Adrian Voinea	25	361	178	Vincenzo Santopadre	25	217
111	Jacobo Diaz	35	350	179	Taylor Dent	17	216
112	Jeff Tarango	26	349	180	Martin Lee	25	216
113	Mikhail Youzhny	23	347	181	Lars Burgsmuller	26	212
114	Galo Blanco	29	342	182	Olivier Mutis	18	210
115	Fernando Gonzalez	15	338	183	Alejandro Hernandez	20	209
116	Stephane Huet	29	333	184	Johan Settergren	19	207
117	Anthony Dupuis	28	328	185	Salvador Navarro	19	207
118	Tomas Zib	32	327	186	Razvan Sabau	29	207
119	Hernan Gumy	27	321	187	Lorenzo Manta	27	205
120	Markus Hipfl	22	318	188	Francisco Costa	34	205
121	Juan Antonio Marin	33	316	189	Todd Woodbridge	12	204
122	Andrei Stoliarov	35	315	190	Marc-Kevin Goellner	17	202
123	Neville Godwin	19	314	191	Petr Luxa	27	201
124	Sebastien Lareau	24	311	192	Jean-Rene Lisnard	27	196
125	Emilio Alvarez	21	310	193	Jeff Salzenstein	19	196
126	Edwin Kempes	23	308	194	Alexandre Simoni	20	196
127	Xavier Malisse	21	307	195	Petr Kralert	25	195
128	Oscar Serrano	26	306	196	Marcos Ondruska	25	195
129	Goran Ivanisevic	24	298	197	Solon Peppas	29	195
130	Cyril Saulnier	22	294	198	Juan Albert Viloca	15	192
131	Tommy Robredo	17	291	199	Andrei Cherkasov	26	192
132	Luis Horna	21	289	200	Clemens Trimmel	22	190

DOUBLES

Rank	Player	Tourns Played	Total Points	Rank	Player	Tourns Played	Total Points
1	Mark Woodforde	19	4985	66=	Tomas Cibulec	28	949
2	Todd Woodbridge	16	4970	66=	Leos Friedl	28	949
3	Sandon Stolle	25	4085	68	Myles Wakefield	31	945
4	Paul Haarhuis	16	3850	69	Thomas Shimada	32	936
5	Ellis Ferreira	20	3565	70	Cristian Brandi	26	930
6	Rick Leach	21	3565	71	Massimo Bertolini	24	895
7	Jared Palmer	25	3260	72	Peter Nyborg	25	890
8	Alex O'Brien	20	3020	73	Patrick Galbraith	20	860
9	Max Mirnyi	23	2990	74	Peter Tramacchi	28	830
10	Jiri Novak	22	2960	75	Jan Siemerink	21	791
11	David Rikl	24	2960	76	Andrea Gaudenzi	16	787
12	Yevgeny Kafelnikov	17	2800	77	Paul Kilderry	22	787
13	Daniel Nestor	14	2630	78	Jack Waite	32	785
14	Wayne Ferreira	20	2520	79	Paul Goldstein	22	780
15	Nicklas Kulti	17	2455	80	Alex Lopez Moron	24	774
16	Dominik Hrbaty	21	2285	81	Eyal Ran	31	772
17	Sebastien Lareau	15	2265	82	Neville Godwin	19	771
18	Donald Johnson	27	2265	83	Martin Rodriguez	22	770
19	David Adams	34	2255	84	Juan Ignacio Carrasco	23	764
20	Lleyton Hewitt	12	2155	85	Leander Paes	14	749
21	Martin Damm	19	2134	86	Alberto Martin	20	740
22	John-Laffnie de Jager	25	2095	87	Jeff Coetzee	22	732
23	Piet Norval	30	2065	88	Albert Portas	20	718
24	Mikael Tillstrom	16	1960	89	Brent Haygarth	23	716
25	Joshua Eagle	29	1955	90	Eric Taino	25	709
26	Jonas Bjorkman	23	1915	91	Andrei Olhovskiy	21	700
27	Andrew Florent	31	1875	92	Michael Llodra	18	685
28	Wayne Arthurs	22	1750	93	Devin Bowen	33	671
29	Nenad Zimonjic	25	1655	94	Nicolas Lapentti	11	665
30	Martin Garcia	26	1621	95	Michael Kohlmann	25	662
31	Andrew Kratzmann	22	1595	96	Jairo Velasco Jr	24	661
32	Roger Federer	20	1570	97	Jonathan Stark	20	655
33	Jaime Oncins	22	1555	98	Juan Balcells	21	640
34	Kevin Ullyett	26	1530	99	Nuno Marques	13	630
35	Scott Humphries	37	1500	100	Jens Knippschild	15	624
36	Tomas Carbonell	32	1485	101	Marc-Kevin Goellner	19	609
37	Jeff Tarango	31	1465	102	Grant Stafford	16	599
38	Michael Hill	27	1390	103	Jim Thomas	28	591
39	Mahesh Bhupathi	19	1380	104	Aleksandar Kitinov	38	590
40	David Prinosil	14	1330	105	Chris Woodruff	13	580
41	Jan-Michael Gambill	24	1330	106	Mariano Hood	23	571
42	Wayne Black	17	1315	107	Olivier Delaitre	15	560
43	David Macpherson	27	1280	108	Marat Safin	13	555
44	Pablo Albano	26	1275	109	German Puentes	23	550
45	Diego Nargiso	24	1255	110	Jonathan Erlich	22	544
46	Lucas Arnold	22	1250	111	Jason Weir Smith	27	541
47	Daniel Orsanic	26	1250	112	Paul Hanley	29	536
48	Mark Knowles	21	1225	113	Paul Rosner	27	535
49	Chris Haggard	35	1215	114	Sergio Roitman	24	532
50	Robbie Koenig	29	1205	115	Antonio Prieto	24	530
51	Simon Aspelin	24	1157	116	Marcos Ondruska	24	524
52	Tom Vanhoudt	29	1140	117	Arnaud Clement	11	520
53	Byron Black	19	1135	118	Ashley Fisher	29	516
54	Marius Barnard	30	1125	119	Dusan Vemic	26	515
55	Justin Gimelstob	13	1045	120	Andres Schneiter	27	507
56	Petr Pala	32	1023	121	Patrick Rafter	8	501
57	Johan Landsberg	26	1010	122	Petr Kovacka	30	501
58	Mike Bryan	28	989	123	Pavel Kudrnac	28	493
59	Bob Bryan	29	989	124	Yuri Schukin	25	488
60	Pavel Vizner	33	988	125	Alexandre Simoni	21	477
61	Fabrice Santoro	22	985	126	Mitch Sprengelmeyer	19	474
62	Cyril Suk	27	981	127	Goran Ivanisevic	15	470
63	Brian MacPhie	23	980	128	Karsten Braasch	21	469
64	Gaston Etlis	23	958	129	Laurence Tieleman	16	465
65	Julien Boutter	20	953	130	Gustavo Kuerten	11	460

PRIZE MONEY 2000

With a second French Open success plus four tournament wins from seven finals (including a victory in the inaugural Tennis Masters Cup) Gustavo Kuerten not surprisingly heads the earnings table for 2000. Altogether 13 men earned more than a million dollars during the year, four fewer than in 1999, a reflection of the growing concentration of success among the upper echelon of players. There were 37 men who earned at least $500,000, against 42 the previous year.

Note: Prize money figures issued by the ATP Tour represent all earnings from official sources, including circuit bonuses, play-offs and team events where entry is based purely on merit. They do not include income from the Davis Cup, invitation tournaments, special events or exhibitions, nor income from commercial contracts or endorsements. (Figures supplied by ATP Tour)

(The nationalities and birthdays of players can be found on pp 140–146)

1	Gustavo Kuerten	$4,701,610		51	Karim Alami	407,346
2	Yevgeny Kafelnikov	3,755,599		52	Mikael Tillstrom	404,467
3	Marat Safin	3,524,959		53	Martin Damm	400,811
4	Thomas Enqvist	2,381,060		54	Francisco Clavet	400,202
5	Pete Sampras	2,254,598		55	Alex O'Brien	399,063
6	Andre Agassi	1,884,443		56	Nicolas Escude	393,359
7	Magnus Norman	1,846,269		57	Paul Haarhuis	391,668
8	Lleyton Hewitt	1,642,572		58	Harel Levy	390,664
9	Alex Corretja	1,530,062		59	Jared Palmer	388,645
10	Wayne Ferreira	1,237,864		60	Todd Martin	378,849
11	Dominik Hrbaty	1,195,760		61	Daniel Nestor	374,904
12	Nicolas Lapentti	1,126,305		62	Rick Leach	367,405
13	Tim Henman	1,057,823		63	Ellis Ferreira	363,155
14	Cedric Pioline	888,789		64	Stefan Koubek	359,379
15	Mark Philippoussis	839,567		65	David Rikl	347,913
16	Patrick Rafter	814,586		66	Wayne Arthurs	341,729
17	Juan Carlos Ferrero	812,636		67	Andrew Ilie	336,021
18	Jiri Novak	776,933		68	Jeff Tarango	333,855
19	Max Mirnyi	760,368		69	Albert Portas	331,173
20	Franco Squillari	754,458		70	Sebastien Lareau	325,199
21	Arnaud Clement	671,815		71	Nicklas Kulti	324,218
22	Todd Woodbridge	662,871		72	Gianluca Pozzi	320,931
23	Sebastien Grosjean	655,280		73	Greg Rusedski	320,358
24	Fabrice Santoro	652,131		74	Alberto Martin	317,170
25	Mark Woodforde	649,410		75	Chris Woodruff	311,129
26	David Prinosil	625,811		76	Andr Vinciguerra	310,365
27	Roger Federer	623,782		77	Mariano Zabaleta	302,875
28	Sjeng Schalken	596,918		78	Felix Mantilla	294,662
29	Nicolas Kiefer	591,749		79	Juan Ignacio Chela	287,172
30	Marc Rosset	583,636		80	Vladimir Voltchkov	274,488
31	Albert Costa	557,589		81	Andrei Medvedev	272,385
32	Jan-Michael Gambill	553,778		82	Julien Boutter	271,453
33	Andrei Pavel	550,061		83	David Adams	264,913
34	Jonas Bjorkman	541,965		84	Slava Dosedel	260,538
35	Mariano Puerta	529,893		85	Paul Goldstein	258,563
36	Sandon Stolle	516,942		86	Donald Johnson	257,426
37	Byron Black	516,347		87	Arnaud Di Pasquale	251,539
38	Thomas Johansson	497,170		88	Justin Gimelstob	251,092
39	Michael Chang	494,488		89	Richard Fromberg	247,876
40	Marcelo Rios	493,816		90	Sargis Sargsian	238,289
41	Younes El Aynaoui	491,615		91	Goran Ivanisevic	234,736
42	Hicham Arazi	491,221		92	Davide Sanguinetti	232,317
43	Karol Kucera	487,608		93	George Bastl	232,127
44	Gaston Gaudio	484,576		94	Ivan Ljubicic	228,057
45	Jerome Golmard	483,495		95	Piet Norval	225,086
46	Tommy Haas	437,436		96	John-Laffnie de Jager	222,783
47	Rainer Schuettler	435,201		97	Wayne Black	221,478
48	Carlos Moya	422,106		98	Jan Kroslak	219,527
49	Fernando Vicente	419,729		99	Christophe Rochus	217,184
50	Richard Krajicek	410,641		100	Andrea Gaudenzi	215,886

101	Markus Hantschk	215,517		126	Stephane Huet	159,542
102	Magnus Larsson	210,290		127	Agustin Calleri	157,693
103	Nicolas Massu	209,422		128	Mark Knowles	157,588
104	Fernando Meligeni	208,557		129	Christian Ruud	153,413
105	Magnus Gustafsson	201,781		130	Hernan Gumy	152,896
106	Alex Calatrava	200,269		131	Sergi Bruguera	152,761
107	Jan Siemerink	194,790		132	Michael Llodra	146,617
108	Kevin Ullyett	194,583		133	Olivier Rochus	145,981
109	Bohdan Ulihrach	187,707		134	Jiri Vanek	145,664
110	Jason Stoltenberg	185,314		135	Cyril Saulnier	144,727
111	Galo Blanco	183,632		136	Orlin Stanoytchev	142,734
112	Juan Balcells	177,336		137	Daniel Vacek	142,623
113	Juan Antonio Marin	176,422		138	Alberto Berasategui	141,458
114	Joshua Eagle	175,115		139	Mahesh Bhupathi	139,531
115	Andrew Florent	172,365		140	Michel Kratochvil	138,730
116	Diego Nargiso	171,015		141	Emilio Alvarez	136,904
117	Nenad Zimonjic	169,194		142	Martin Garcia	136,728
118	Alexander Popp	168,387		143	Parad Srichaphan	135,075
119	Vincent Spadea	166,411		144	Andrew Kratzmann	134,789
120	Andre Sa	164,873		145	Marc-Kev Goellner	134,173
121	Adrian Voinea	164,581		146	Michael Hill	134,015
122	Scott Humphries	164,313		147	Martin Rodriguez	133,581
123	Laurence Tieleman	163,858		148	Gaston Etlis	131,829
124	Jens Knippschild	161,529		149	Ronald Agenor	128,296
125	Bob Bryan	160,233		150	Christian Vinck	127,877

THE MILLIONAIRES

Below is a list of players who, by the 4th December 2000, had won at leaast $1 million during the course of their careers. A further 23 men (marked *) achieved the one million dollar plateau during 2000. The totals do not include income from the Davis Cup, nor from special events, exhibitions or commercial endorsements.

1	Pete Sampras	USA	$41,063,159		32	Marc Rosset	SUI	6,135,419
2	Boris Becker	GER	25,079,456		33	Carlos Moya	ESP	6,005,976
3	Ivan Lendl	USA	21,262,417		34	Jakob Hlasek	SUI	5,892,962
4	Andre Agassi	USA	21,140,724		35	Tim Henman	GBR	5,869,480
5	Stefan Edberg	SWE	20,630,941		36	Guy Forget	FRA	5,666,692
6	Michael Chang	USA	18,651,206		37	Magnus Larsson	SWE	5,603,707
7	Goran Ivanisevic	CRO	18,437,580		38	Brad Gilbert	USA	5,509,060
8	Yevgeny Kafelnikov	RUS	18,184,646		39	Anders Jarryd	SWE	5,374,736
9	Jim Courier	USA	14,033,132		40	Emilio Sanchez	ESP	5,333,851
10	Michael Stich	GER	12,590,152		41	David Wheaton	USA	5,217,915
11	John McEnroe	USA	12,539,622		42	Mark Philippoussis	AUS	4,957,710
12	Thomas Muster	AUT	12,224,410		43	Guillermo Vilas	ARG	4,923,882
13	Sergi Bruguera	ESP	11,421,046		44	Jacco Eltingh	NED	4,841,162
14	Petr Korda	CZE	10,448,085		45	Byron Black	ZIM	4,836,286
15	Richard Krajicek	NED	9,814,581		46	Alberto Berasategui	ESP	4,671,997
16	Patrick Rafter	AUS	9,432,719		47	Daniel Vacek	CZE	4,585,003
17	Gustavo Kuerten	BRA	8,923,321		48	Marat Safin	RUS	4,475,663
18	Thomas Enqvist	SWE	8,680,378		49	Javier Sanchez	ESP	4,427,811
19	Jimmy Connors	USA	8,641,040		50	Richey Reneberg	USA	4,424,535
20	Marcelo Rios	CHI	8,423,663		51	Albert Costa	ESP	4,414,006
21	Mark Woodforde	AUS	8,324,401		52	Andres Gomez	ECU	4,385,040
22	Wayne Ferreira	RSA	8,189,242		53	Magnus Gustafsson	SWE	4,336,641
23	Alex Corretja	ESP	8,150,134		54	Jan Siemerink	NED	4,125,334
24	Mats Wilander	SWE	7,976,256		55	Fabrice Santoro	FRA	4,095,861
25	Todd Woodbridge	AUS	7,715,042		56	Karol Kucera	SVK	3,996,330
26	Jonas Bjorkman	SWE	7,502,600		57	Henri Leconte	FRA	3,917,596
27	Paul Haarhuis	NED	7,264,084		58	Karel Novacek	CZE	3,731,838
28	Todd Martin	USA	7,153,598		59	Aaron Krickstein	USA	3,710,447
29	Greg Rusedski	GBR	6,937,169		60	Tomas Smid	CZE	3,699,738
30	Andrei Medvedev	UKR	6,580,136		61	Rick Leach	USA	3,677,044
31	Cedric Pioline	FRA	6,395,573		62	Francisco Clavet	ESP	3,668,834

63	Bjorn Borg	SWE	3,655,751
64	Magnus Norman	SWE	3,580,972
65	Yannick Noah	FRA	3,440,660
66	Alex O'Brien	USA	3,437,004
67	Felix Mantilla	ESP	3,418,169
68	Alexander Volkov	RUS	3,362,786
69	Martin Damm	CZE	3,272,557
70	David Prinosil	GER	3,266,181
71	Jeff Tarango	USA	3,255,475
72	MaliVai Washington	USA	3,239,865
73	Jim Grabb	USA	3,237,237
74	Jason Stoltenberg	AUS	3,224,751
75	John Fitzgerald	AUS	3,204,941
76	Nicolas Lapentti	ECU	3,188,897
77	Carlos Costa	ESP	3,134,189
78	Wally Masur	AUS	3,130,742
79	Jonathan Stark	USA	3,129,019
80	Nicklas Kulti	SWE	3,125,787
81	Sandon Stolle	AUS	3,123,643
82	Patrick McEnroe	USA	3,115,985
83	Andrei Chesnokov	RUS	3,084,188
84	Tomas Carbonell	ESP	3,062,724
85	Kevin Curren	USA	3,055,510
86	Arnaud Boetsch	FRA	3,031,247
87	Nicolas Kiefer	GER	2,993,112
88	Andrei Olhovskiy	RUS	2,966,190
89	Tommy Haas	GER	2,913,578
90	Grant Connell	CAN	2,853,907
91	Jiri Novak	CZE	2,829,781
92	Brian Gottfried	USA	2,782,514
93	Olivier Delaitre	FRA	2,781,686
94	Vitas Gerulaitis	USA	2,778,748
95	Sebastien Lareau	CAN	2,746,614
96	Daniel Nestor	CAN	2,740,119
97	Wojtek Fibak	POL	2,725,403
98	Dominik Hrbaty	SVK	2,672,170
99	Tim Mayotte	USA	2,663,672
100	Miloslav Mecir	CZE	2,632,538
101	Patrick Galbraith	USA	2,622,275
102	Thomas Johansson	SWE	2,568,361
103	Richard Fromberg	AUS	2,539,750
104	Marc-Kevin Goellner	GER	2,536,066
105	Andrea Gaudenzi	ITA	2,488,147
106	Cyril Suk	CZE	2,481,872
107	Guillaume Raoux	FRA	2,445,864
108	Jonas Svensson	SWE	2,439,702
109	Amos Mansdorf	ISR	2,427,691
110	Brett Steven	NZL	2,420,416
111	Leander Paes	IND	2,415,018
112	Johan Kriek	USA	2,383,794
113	Slava Dosedel	CZE	2,330,435
114	Renzo Furlan	ITA	2,328,265
115	Carl-Uwe Steeb	GER	2,320,082
116	Mark Knowles	BAH	2,318,956
117	Sjeng Schalken	NED	2,299,936
118	Jared Palmer	USA	2,292,804
119	Scott Davis	USA	2,274,730
120	Jaime Yzaga	PER	2,235,560
121	Andrei Cherkasov	RUS	2,226,626
122	Raul Ramirez	MEX	2,217,971
123*	Lleyton Hewitt	AUS	2,197,797
124	Bohdan Ulihrach	CZE	2,173,389
125	David Adams	RSA	2,136,796
126	Sergio Casal	ESP	2,105,414
127	Vincent Spadea	USA	2,093,899
128	Ilie Nastase	ROM	2,076,761

129	Joakim Nystrom	SWE	2,074,947
130	Ken Flach	USA	2,062,815
131	Bernd Karbacher	GER	2,043,057
132	Gianluca Pozzi	ITA	2,039,819
133	Marcelo Filippini	URU	2,034,890
134	Mikael Tillstrom	SWE	2,029,070
135	David Pate	USA	2,025,747
136	Fernando Meligeni	BRA	2,019,308
137	Eddie Dibbs	USA	2,016,426
138	David Rikl	CZE	1,991,798
139	Hicham Arazi	MAR	1,990,294
140	Jose-Luis Clerc	ARG	1,987,036
141	Peter Fleming	USA	1,986,799
142	Ronald Agenor	HAI	1,959,237
143	Pat Cash	AUS	1,946,128
144	Christo Van Rensburg	RSA	1,918,911
145	Ellis Ferreira	RSA	1,911,908
146	Karim Alami	MAR	1,909,251
147	Robert Seguso	USA	1,888,353
148	Martin Jaite	ARG	1,873,881
149	Jordi Arrese	ESP	1,846,849
150	Jimmy Arias	USA	1,834,140
151	Piet Norval	RSA	1,808,733
152	Harold Solomon	USA	1,802,769
153	Diego Nargiso	ITA	1,798,232

After a brilliant year, Australia's Davis Cup hero, Lleyton Hewitt, leaped from $555,225 at the end of 1999 to a staggering $2,197,797 twelve months later. (Stephen Wake)

154	Mahesh Bhupathi	IND	1,782,824
155	Jim Pugh	USA	1,776,490
156	Stan Smith	USA	1,774,811
157	Marcos Ondruska	RSA	1,761,217
158	Chris Woodruff	USA	1,712,529
159	Roscoe Tanner	USA	1,696,108
160	Younes El Aynaoui	MAR	1,691,001
161	Javier Frana	ARG	1,687,872
162	Henrik Holm	SWE	1,686,056
163	Guillermo Perez-Roldan	ARG	1,685,921
164	Eliot Teltscher	USA	1,653,997
165	Horst Skoff	AUT	1,651,858
166	Paul Annacone	USA	1,645,351
167	Patrik Kuhnen	GER	1,643,997
168	Jerome Golmard	FRA	1,627,768
169	Derrick Rostagno	USA	1,621,535
170	Omar Camporese	ITA	1,608,644
171	Sherwood Stewart	USA	1,602,565
172	Ken Rosewall	AUS	1,600,300
173	Arthur Ashe	USA	1,584,909
174	Kenneth Carlsen	DEN	1,566,249
175	Rod Laver	AUS	1,564,213
176	Heinz Gunthardt	SUI	1,550,007
177	Alberto Mancini	ARG	1,543,120
178	Danie Visser	RSA	1,524,225
179*	Andrei Pavel	ROM	1,519,509
180	David Macpherson	AUS	1,508,365
181	Libor Pimek	BEL	1,503,445
182	Filip Dewulf	BEL	1,503,077
183	Luiz Mattar	BRA	1,493,136
184*	Sebastien Grosjean	FRA	1,476,381
185	Stefano Pescosolido	ITA	1,471,462
186*	Franco Squillari	ARG	1,455,763
187	Tom Nijssen	NED	1,454,739
188	Mark Edmondson	AUS	1,451,680
189	Slobodan Zivojinovic	YUG	1,450,654
190	Wayne Black	ZIM	1,447,833
191	Francisco Roig	ESP	1,440,475
192	Gary Muller	RSA	1,439,570
193	Balazs Taroczy	HUN	1,437,443
194	Bill Scanlon	USA	1,427,007
195	Brian Teacher	USA	1,426,514
196	Todd Witsken	USA	1,420,910
197*	Jan-Michael Gambill	USA	1,407,313
198	Jose Higueras	ESP	1,406,355
199	Manuel Orantes	ESP	1,398,303
200	Jan Apell	SWE	1,397,620
201*	Nicolas Escude	FRA	1,388,389
202*	Arnaud Clement	FRA	1,382,941
203	Gene Mayer	USA	1,381,562
204	Mark Kratzmann	AUS	1,376,605
205	Christian Ruud	NOR	1,363,963
206	Mikael Pernfors	SWE	1,363,793
207	Donald Johnson	USA	1,351,294
208	Jean-Philippe Fleurian	FRA	1,349,735
209	Darren Cahill	AUS	1,346,916
210	Hendrik Dreekmann	GER	1,344,648
211	Jeremy Bates	GBR	1,335,989
212	Vijay Amritraj	IND	1,331,913
213	Gilbert Schaller	AUT	1,316,283
214	Goran Prpic	CRO	1,303,639
215	Adrian Voinea	ROM	1,298,235
216	Luke Jensen	USA	1,294,957
217	Tim Wilkison	USA	1,289,085
218	Jan Gunnarsson	SWE	1,285,040
219	Ramesh Krishnan	IND	1,263,130
220	Christian Bergstrom	SWE	1,262,792
221	Tom Okker	NED	1,257,200
222	Thierry Champion	FRA	1,254,369
223	Grant Stafford	RSA	1,254,044
224	Cristiano Caratti	ITA	1,244,242
225*	Justin Gimelstob	USA	1,235,019
226	Horacio De La Pena	ARG	1,234,768
227	Paul McNamee	AUS	1,233,615
228	Bryan Shelton	USA	1,226,771
229	Francisco Montana	USA	1,224,493
230*	Max Mirnyi	BLR	1,221,069
231	John Alexander	AUS	1,214,079
232	Hernan Gumy	ARG	1,212,668
233	Lionel Roux	FRA	1,207,151
234*	John-Laffnie de Jager	RSA	1,206,042
235	Jordi Burillo	ESP	1,197,761
236	Karsten Braasch	GER	1,196,640
237	Scott Draper	AUS	1,192,207
238	Neil Broad	GBR	1,186,440
239*	Albert Portas	ESP	1,174,189
240	Robert Lutz	USA	1,165,276
241	Kelly Jones	USA	1,160,067
242*	Fernando Vicente	ESP	1,140,185
243*	Rodolphe Gilbert	FRA	1,137,011
244*	Jaime Oncins	BRA	1,133,989
245*	Mariano Zabaleta	ARG	1,133,341
246	Peter Lundgren	SWE	1,130,516
247	Michiel Schapers	NED	1,124,730
248	Tim Gullikson	USA	1,121,880
249	Shuzo Matsuoka	JPN	1,117,112
250*	Mariano Puerta	ARG	1,111,212
251*	Jan Kroslak	SVK	1,110,559
252	Franco Davin	ARG	1,108,860
253*	Sargis Sargsian	ARM	1,106,340
254	Eric Jelen	GER	1,100,059
255	Steve Denton	USA	1,084,664
256	Glenn Michibata	CAN	1,081,667
257*	Rainer Schuettler	GER	1,080,057
258*	Wayne Arthurs	AUS	1,079,242
259	Michael Tebbutt	AUS	1,078,481
260	Nicolas Pereira	VEN	1,074,564
261	Dick Stockton	USA	1,063,385
262	John Newcombe	AUS	1,062,408
263	Thierry Tulasne	FRA	1,058,412
264	Sandy Mayer	USA	1,057,783
265	Peter McNamara	AUS	1,046,935
266	Diego Perez	URU	1,042,224
267	Menno Oosting	NED	1,036,152
268*	Kevin Ullyett	ZIM	1,033,902
269*	Galo Blanco	ESP	1,032,994
270*	Juan Carlos Ferrero	ESP	1,028,181
271	Alex Antonitsch	AUT	1,024,171

ATP TOUR BOARD OF DIRECTORS 2000–2001
(Chief Executive Officer: Mark Miles)

Tournament representatives:
Franco Bartoni (Europe)
Charlie Pasarell (North America)
Graham Pearce (Rest of the world)

Player Representatives:
David Felgate
John Fitzgerald
Harold Solomon

ATP TOUR PLAYER COUNCIL
President: Jonas Bjorkman   **Vice President:** David Adams
Members: (1–10) Nicolas Lapentti ; **(11–25)** Younes El Aynaoui; **(26–50)** Fernando
Meligeni; **(1–50 Doubles)** David Adams; **(Div.2)** Antonio Prieto; **Alumni:** Ricardo Acioly;
(At Large) Jonas Bjorkman, Marc Rosset, Jared Palmer, Jack Waite.

ATP TOUR TOURNAMENT COUNCIL
Europe: Franco Bartoni (Chairman), Wim Buitendijk, Jacques Hermenjat, Leo Huemer,
Gunther Sanders
International: Sanji Arisawa, Ayman Azmy, Graham Pearce, (one TBA)
Americas: Tom Buford, Paul Flory, Bob Kramer, Charlie Pasarell

ADDRESSES – ATP TOUR OFFICES (Web Site Address: **http://www.atptour.com**)

United States:	Europe:	International Group:
201 ATP Tour Boulevard,	Monte Carlo Sun,	Level 6,
Ponte Vedra Beach,	74 Boulevard D'Italie,	20 Alfred Street,
Florida,	98000, Monaco	Milsons Point
32082, U.S.A.	Tel: 377-97-97-04-04	NSW, 2061, Australia
Tel:1-904-285 8000	Fax: 377-97-97-04-00	Tel: 61-2 9964 9900
Fax:1-904-285 5966		Fax: 61-2 9964 9977

ANNUAL ATP TOUR AWARDS FOR 2000 (for performances in 1999)
For the fifth time in six years, the ATP TOUR Awards Gala was held on Tuesday, 18th
April at the Monte Carlo Sporting Club where the following individuals and
organisations were recognised for outstanding performances in 1999.

Player of the Year:	Andre Agassi
Doubles Team of the Year:	Mahesh Bhupathi and Leander Paes
Most Improved Player:	Nicolas Lapentti
Newcomer of the Year:	Juan Carlos Ferrero
Comeback Player of the Year:	Chris Woodruff
Stefan Edberg Sportsmanship Award:	Patrick Rafter
Delta Airlines Senior Circuit Player of the Year:	John McEnroe
Ron Bookman Media Excellence Award:	L'Equipe
Arthur Ashe Humanitarian Award:	International Series event in Memphis
Championship Series Tournament of the Year:	Ericsson Open
World Series Tournament of the Year:	Lyon and Scottsdale
Milestone Awards: Sixtieth title:	Pete Sampras
Fortieth title:	Andre Agassi
Twentieth title:	Yevgeny Kafelnikov
Tenth title:	Albert Costa
Fifth title:	Karol Kucera, Gustavo Kuerten, Magnus Norman
First-time winners:	Galo Blanco, Arnaud Di Pasquale, Younes El Aynaoui, Nicolas Escude, Juan Carlos Ferrero, Jan-Michael Gambill, Jerome Golmard, Tommy Haas, Stefan Koubek, Juan Antonio Marin, Alberto Martin, Marat Safin, Rainer Schuttler, Franco Squillari, Fernando Vicente and Adrian Voinea

History of the ATP Tour
No.1 World Ranking

August 23 1973 – December 31 2000
(Figures supplied by ATP Tour)

Up to and including the end of 1999 the world No.1 ranking changed whenever a new player arrived at the top of the rankings. With the introduction of the Champions Race in 2000, the player in the lead at the end of the year became the world No.1.

	Player	Age	First date No.1	Total Weeks
1	Pete Sampras	21.8	12 Apr 1993	276
2	Ivan Lendl	22.11	28 Feb 1983	270
3	Jimmy Connors	21.11	29 July 1974	268
4	John McEnroe	21 (& 15 days)	3 Mar 1980	170
5	Bjorn Borg	21.2	23 Aug 1977	109
6	Stefan Edberg	24.9	13 Aug 1990	72
7	Jim Courier	21.5	10 Feb 1992	58
9	Andre Agassi	24.11	10 Apr 1995	51
8	Ilie Nastase	27.1	23 Aug 1973	40
10	Mats Wilander	24.1	12 Sep 1988	20
11	Boris Becker	23.2	28 Jan 1991	12
12	John Newcombe	30 (& 11 days)	3 Jun 1974	8
13	Thomas Muster	28.4	12 Feb 1996	6
14	Marcelo Rios	22.3	30 Mar 1998	6
15	Yevgeny Kafelnikov	25.2	3 May 1999	6
16	Carlos Moya	22.6	15 Mar 1999	2
17	Patrick Rafter	26.6	26 July 1999	1
18	Gustavo Kuerten	24.3	4 Dec 2000	N/A

HISTORY OF THE NO.1 RANKING

Ranking date	Player	Weeks at No.1
1973 23 August	Ilie Nastase (1)	40
1974 3 June	John Newcombe (2)	8
1974 29 July	Jimmy Connors (3)	160
1975		
1976		
1977 23 August	Bjorn Borg (4)	1
1977 30 August	Connors	84
1978		
1979 9 April	Borg	6
1979 21 May	Connors	7
1979 9 July	Borg	34
1980 3 March	John McEnroe (5)	3
1980 24 March	Borg	20
1980 11 August	McEnroe	1
1980 18 August	Borg	46
1981 6 July	McEnroe	2
1981 20 July	Borg	2
1981 3 August	McEnroe	58
1982 13 September	Connors	7
1982 1 November	McEnroe	1
1982 8 November	Connors	1
1982 15 November	McEnroe	11
1983 31 January	Connors	1
1983 7 February	McEnroe	1

HISTORY OF THE NO.1 RANKING (continued)

Ranking date	Player	Weeks at No.1
1983 14 February	Connors	2
1983 28 February	**Ivan Lendl (6)**	**11**
1983 16 May	Connors	3
1983 6 June	McEnroe	1
1983 13 June	Connors	3
1983 4 July	McEnroe	17
1983 31 October	Lendl	6
1983 12 December	McEnroe	4
1984 9 January	Lendl	9
1984 12 March	McEnroe	13
1984 11 June	Lendl	1
1984 18 June	McEnroe	3
1984 9 July	Lendl	5
1984 13 August	McEnroe	53
1985 19 August	Lendl	1
1985 26 August	McEnroe	2
1985 9 September	Lendl	157
1986		
1987		
1988 12 September	**Mats Wilander (7)**	**20**
1989 30 January	Lendl	80
1990 13 August	**Stefan Edberg (8)**	**24**
1991 28 January	**Boris Becker (9)**	**3**
1991 18 February	Edberg	20
1991 8 July	Becker	9
1991 9 September	Edberg	22
1992 10 February	**Jim Courier (10)**	**6**
1992 23 March	Edberg	3
1992 13 April	Courier	22
1992 14 September	Edberg	3
1992 5 October	Courier	27
1993 12 April	**Pete Sampras (11)**	**19**
1993 23 August	Courier	3
1993 13 September	Sampras	82
1994		
1995 10 April	**Andre Agassi (12)**	**30**
1995 6 November	Sampras	12
1996 29 January	Agassi	2
1996 12 February	**Thomas Muster (13)**	**1**
1996 19 February	Sampras	3
1996 11 March	Muster	5
1996 15 April	Sampras	102
1997		
1998 30 March	**Marcelo Rios S(14)**	4
1998 27 April	Sampras	15
1998 10 August	Rios	2
1998 24 August	Sampras	29
1999 15 March	**Carlos Moya (15)**	**2**
1999 29 March	Sampras	5
1999 3 May	**Yevgeny Kafelnikov (16)**	6
1999 14 June	Sampras	3
1999 5 July	Agassi	3
1999 26 July	**Patrick Rafter (17)**	**1**
1999 2 August	Sampras	6
1999 13 September	Agassi	16

Year End No.1

2000 4 December	**Gustavo Kuerten (18)**	

Sanex WTA Tour Rankings and Prize Money 2000

RANKINGS

The following tables show the season-ending rankings in singles and doubles. The rankings, updated weekly, are based on points won on the Sanex WTA Tour, including the four Grand Slam Championships. (Statistics supplied by Sanex WTA Tour).

(The nationalities and birthdays of players can be found on pp 176–180)

SINGLES

Rank	Player	Tourns Played	Total Points	Rank	Player	Tourns Played	Total Points
1	Martina Hingis	20	6180.00	49	Sonya Jeyaseelan	22	649.00
2	Lindsay Davenport	18	5022.00	50	Sabine Appelmans	22	649.00
3	Venus Williams	9	3694.00	51	Denisa Chladkova	22	633.00
4	Monica Seles	15	3255.00	52	Corina Morariu	19	630.00
5	Conchita Martinez	20	2795.00	53	Sylvia Plischke	27	612.00
6	Serena Williams	11	2306.00	54	Daja Bedanova	16	610.00
7	Mary Pierce	13	2162.00	55	Nicole Pratt	26	609.00
8	Anna Kournikova	26	2158.00	56	Rita Kuti Kis	19	596.00
9	Arantxa Sanchez-Vicario	18	2132.00	57	Asa Carlsson	21	573.00
10	Nathalie Tauziat	26	1963.00	58	Anastasia Myskina	21	573.00
11	Amanda Coetzer	23	1798.00	59	Joannette Kruger	19	570.00
12	Elena Dementieva	22	1774.00	60	Angeles Montolio	23	561.00
13	Chanda Rubin	23	1760.00	61	Jana Kandarr	22	528.00
14	Jennifer Capriati	20	1664.00	62	Nadejda Petrova	18	526.00
15	Julie Halard-Decugis	24	1436.00	63	Silvia Farina Elia	21	500.00
16	Amelie Mauresmo	13	1426.00	64	Miriam Oremans	18	497.00
17	Sandrine Testud	20	1414.00	65	Sarah Pitkowski	21	495.00
18	Kim Clijsters	17	1398.00	66	Kristie Boogert	20	483.00
19	Anke Huber	18	1370.00	67	Meilen Tu	26	478.00
20	Amy Frazier	22	1255.00	68	Adriana Gersi	22	476.00
21	Elena Likhovtseva	27	1216.00	69	Jana Nejedly	29	474.00
22	Magdalena Maleeva	26	1108.00	70	Marta Marrero	15	451.00
23	Barbara Schett	23	1065.00	71	Brie Rippner	25	445.50
24	Dominique Van Roost	19	1056.00	72	Shinobu Asagoe	23	444.00
25	Patty Schnyder	25	1056.00	73	Iva Majoli	14	441.50
26	Jelena Dokic	19	1054.00	74	Olga Barabanschikova	17	436.00
27	Nathalie Dechy	19	1020.00	75	Iroda Tulyaganova	21	434.00
28	Kristina Brandi	29	956.00	76	Tina Pisnik	25	433.00
29	Tamarine Tanasugarn	25	954.00	77	Rossana De Los Rios	18	427.00
30	Silvija Talaja	29	935.00	78	Rita Grande	24	410.00
31	Lisa Raymond	21	931.00	79	Natasha Zvereva	12	407.00
32	Gala Leon Garcia	21	879.00	80	Francesca Schiavone	22	402.00
33	Ai Sugiyama	24	876.00	81	Jennifer Hopkins	33	397.00
34	Tatiana Panova	30	860.00	82	Pavlina Nola	26	392.00
35	Anne Kremer	27	854.00	83	Magdalena Grzybowska	16	390.00
36	Anne-Gaelle Sidot	27	842.00	84	Alina Jidkova	31	383.00
37	Paola Suarez	23	840.00	85	Holly Parkinson	30	382.50
38	Magui Serna	25	826.00	86	Karina Habsudova	23	381.00
39	Meghann Shaughnessy	28	825.00	87	Tatiana Poutchek	27	378.00
40	Tathiana Garbin	26	789.00	88	Vavrinec Miroslava	26	374.00
41	Henrieta Nagyova	22	756.00	89	Virginia Ruano Pascual	18	370.00
42	Fabiola Zuluaga	20	755.00	90	Patricia Wartusch	25	364.00
43	Cara Black	23	748.00	91	Giulia Casoni	24	363.00
44	Lilia Osterloh	28	710.00	92	Marissa Irvin	16	359.00
45	Ruxandra Dragomir	24	706.00	93	Alexandra Stevenson	26	353.00
46	Anna Smashnova	27	700.00	94	Cristina Torrens Valero	26	353.00
47	Kveta Hrdlickova	17	690.00	95	Marlene Weingartner	25	347.00
48	Justine Henin	14	661.50	96	Jing-Qian Yi	22	346.00

Rank	Player	Tourns Played	Total Points	Rank	Player	Tourns Played	Total Points
97	Emmanuelle Gagliardi	25	344.00	166	Seda Noorlander	26	160.00
98	Lubomira Bacheva	26	344.00	167	Irina Spirlea	12	155.00
99	Maria Antonia Sanchez Lorenzo	22	344.00	168	Bryanne Stewart	29	154.00
100	Sandra Nacuk	23	343.00	169	Saori Obata	24	152.50
101	Barbara Rittner	17	342.00	170	Petra Rampre	24	152.00
102	Emilie Loit	27	339.50	171	Melanie Schnell	22	151.50
103	Nadejda Ostrovskaya	26	337.00	172	Jeong Cho Yoon	26	151.50
104	Amanda Hopmans	21	328.00	173	Samantha Reeves	29	151.00
105	Maria Vento	23	318.50	174	Michaela Pastikova	29	149.50
106	Florencia Labat	16	317.50	175	Nirupama Vaidyanathan	18	143.50
107	Els Callens	20	316.00	176	Antoaneta Pandjerova	23	142.00
108	Daniela Hantuchova	15	309.50	177	Dragana Zaric	14	141.50
109	Martina Sucha	23	302.00	178	Gisela Riera	21	141.00
110	Rachel Mcquillan	21	299.00	179	Amelie Cocheteux	25	138.00
111	Louise Latimer	32	296.00	180	Mariam Ramon	25	137.00
112	Vanessa Webb	25	295.50	181	Laurence Andretto	29	136.50
113	Jelena Kostanic	24	286.50	182	Selima Sfar	26	134.75
114	Ana I Garrigues Medina	15	285.25	183	Klara Koukalova	21	134.50
115	Alicia Molik	20	285.00	184	Antonell Serra-Zanetti	29	134.50
116	Janet Lee	26	279.00	185	Lucie Ahl	30	134.50
117	Catalina Cristea	22	276.50	186	Zsofia Gubacsi	26	134.00
118	Mariana Diaz-Oliva	30	276.00	187	Maja Palaversic	19	133.75
119	Katarina Srebotnik	25	273.50	188	Tatiana Perebiynis	13	132.25
120	Erika De Lone	31	273.00	189	Marion Maruska	25	132.00
121	Ludmila Cervanova	25	272.00	190	Evelyn Fauth	27	132.00
122	Sandra Kleinova	29	268.00	191	Irina Selyutina	19	132.00
123	Yvette Basting	25	260.50	192	Libuse Prusova	27	131.50
124	Dawn Buth	27	256.00	193	Dessislava Topalova	25	131.00
125	Wynne Prakusya	24	253.50	194	Maja Matevzic	22	130.50
126	Yuka Yoshida	25	250.00	195	Alice Canepa	28	130.50
127	Bianka Lamade	18	249.50	196	Daphne Van de Zande	25	129.50
128	Katalin Marosi-Aracama	29	243.50	197	Germana Di Natale	23	129.00
129	Tara Snyder	24	241.00	198	Ainhoa Goni	26	129.00
130	Laurence Courtois	23	239.00	199	Bahia Mouhtassine	23	126.75
131	Andrea Glass	20	238.50	200	Anna Foldenyi	14	126.00
132	Nuria Llagostera	27	237.50	201	Eva Martincova	21	125.50
133	Lina Krasnoroutskaya	14	234.50	202	Miriam D'agostini	23	125.00
134	Na Li	23	234.50	203	Tzipora Obziler	12	120.00
135	Elena Bovina	17	233.50	204	Virginie Razzano	13	119.00
136	Gloria Pizzichini	18	232.50	205	Tatiana Kovalchuk	19	118.50
137	Allison Bradshaw	14	226.25	206	Emilia Maria Salerni	8	118.00
138	Julie Pullin	29	224.50	207	Mirjana Lucic	14	118.00
139	Milagros Sequera	24	223.50	208	Eva Krejcova	26	118.00
140	Sandra Cacic	20	220.00	209	Eun-Ha Kim	25	117.50
141	Lourdes Dominguez Lino	21	217.00	210	Marie-Eve Pelletier	18	116.00
142	Mashona Washington	23	216.00	211	Tina Krizan	21	115.50
143	Catalina Castano	26	216.00	212	Zuzana Ondraskova	17	115.50
144	Anca Barna	33	213.50	213	Jessica Steck	15	115.50
145	Evie Dominikovic	30	207.50	214	Anna Zarska	31	113.50
146	Alexandra Fusai	21	206.50	215	Vanessa Henke	25	113.50
147	Greta Arn	26	202.00	216	Angelika Roesch	28	113.50
148	Maureen Drake	18	198.00	217	Tracy Almeda-Singian	27	113.50
149	Angelika Bachmann	26	196.00	218	Anna Zaporozhanova	13	113.00
150	Jill Craybas	25	193.50	219	Hila Rosen	21	110.50
151	Janette Husarova	20	188.00	220	Sarah Taylor	24	110.00
152	Alena Vaskova	20	185.00	221	Mia Buric	14	106.75
153	Maria Jose Martinez	15	184.00	222	Annabel Ellwood	27	106.00
154	Francesca Lubiani	24	179.00	223	Nana Miyagi	18	104.50
155	Lisa Mcshea	30	176.00	224	Laura Dell'Angelo	29	104.50
156	Stephanie Foretz	22	170.50	225	Sophie Georges	23	103.50
157	Lenka Nemeckova	29	170.00	226	Julia Vakulenko	12	102.50
158	Petra Mandula	22	170.00	227	Karolina Jagieniak	30	102.00
159	Tina Hergold	21	169.50	228	Julia Abe	12	100.00
160	Kyra Nagy	25	169.00	229	Elena Camerin Maria	22	100.00
161	Miriam Schnitzer	19	166.00	230	Amanda Grahame	26	97.50
162	Renata Kolbovic	26	164.00	231	Lorna Woodroffe	27	96.50
163	Dally Randriantefy	16	162.50	232	Jana Hlavackova	22	95.50
164	Eva Bes	22	161.00	233	Jolene Watanabe	26	95.00
165	Eva Dyrberg	27	161.00	234	Anastassia Rodionova	16	93.75

Rank	Player	Tourns Played	Total Points
235	Karin Miller	25	91.50
236	Adriana Barna	25	90.50
237	Kristina Kraszewski	10	90.50
238	Kelly Liggan	31	90.50
239	Trudi Musgrave	24	89.50
240	Katarina Daskovic	27	88.50
241	Flora Perfetti	7	88.00
242	Lea Ghirardi	19	87.50

Rank	Player	Tourns Played	Total Points
243	Joana Cortez	24	87.00
244	Zuzana Valekova	21	86.00
245	Svetlana Kriventcheva	24	86.00
246	Rika Fujiwara	24	86.00
247	Renata Kucerova	21	85.00
248	Conchita Martinez Granados	21	84.50
249	Hana Sromova	20	83.50
250	Adrienn Hegedus	25	83.50

DOUBLES

Rank	Player	Tourns Played	Total Points
1	Julie Halard-Decugis	21	3807.00
2	Ai Sugiyama	24	3755.00
3	Martina Hingis	15	3709.00
4	Anna Kournikova	20	2921.00
5	Lisa Raymond	20	2739.00
6	Rennae Stubbs	20	2727.00
7	Paola Suarez	20	2290.00
8	Nathalie Tauziat	24	2051.00
9	Mary Pierce	10	2024.00
10	Virginia Ruano Pascual	16	1907.00
11	Nicole Arendt	23	1734.00
12	Barbara Schett	16	1693.00
13	Cara Black	23	1689.00
14	Corina Morariu	15	1667.00
15	Els Callens	21	1621.00
16	Arantxa Sanchez-Vicario	17	1517.00
17	Manon Bollegraf	17	1467.00
18	Elena Likhovtseva	26	1455.00
19	Alexandra Fusai	22	1445.00
20	Kimberly Po	26	1433.00
21	Dominique Van Roost	16	1404.00
22	Chanda Rubin	17	1322.00
23	Sandrine Testud	15	1300.00
24	Anne-Gaelle Sidot	23	1294.00
25	Natasha Zvereva	10	1255.00
26	Lindsay Davenport	9	1174.00
27	Amanda Coetzer	19	1161.00
28	Laura Montalvo	21	1122.00
29	Conchita Martinez	13	1114.00
30	Asa Carlsson	21	1002.00
31	Irina Selyutina	21	932.00
32	Tina Krizan	24	926.00
33	Katarina Srebotnik	23	924.00
34	Patricia Tarabini	18	911.00
35	Rita Grande	23	909.00
36	Meghann Shaughnessy	25	898.00
37	Nicole Pratt	24	866.00
38	Nana Miyagi	23	856.00
39	Kristie Boogert	20	832.00
40	Anke Huber	12	830.00
41	Ruxandra Dragomir	23	822.00
42	Karina Habsudova	23	809.00
43	Liezel Horn	17	794.00
44	Laurence Courtois	19	785.00
45	Miriam Oremans	19	781.00
46	Erika de Lone	26	773.00
47	Patty Schnyder	21	757.00
48	Kim Clijsters	12	733.00
49	Sonya Jeyaseelan	23	727.00
50	Catalina Cristea	23	711.00

Rank	Player	Tourns Played	Total Points
51	Jelena Dokic	18	666.00
52	Tathiana Garbin	21	663.00
53	Amelie Mauresmo	8	648.00
54	Surina De Beer	18	640.00
55	Janette Husarova	20	636.00
56	Caroline Vis	24	633.00
57	Emilie Loit	16	625.00
58	Jennifer Capriati	9	624.00
59	Lori Mcneil	12	622.00
60	Amy Frazier	19	616.00
61	Nathalie Dechy	12	601.00
62	Lisa Mcshea	28	596.00
63	Magui Serna	14	567.00
64	Rika Hiraki	25	559.00
65	Silvia Farina Elia	14	551.00
66	Martina Navratilova	7	538.00
67	Amelie Cocheteux	15	529.00
68	Katie Schlukebir	20	510.00
69	Alicia Molik	17	504.00
70	Tamarine Tanasugarn	14	500.00
71	Cristin Torrens Valero	19	493.00
72	Tatiana Poutchek	25	489.00
73	Lubomira Bacheva	15	486.00
74	Rachel Mcquillan	19	434.00
75	Sandra Nacuk	17	431.00
76	Alina Jidkova	22	430.00
77	Elena Tatarkova	11	423.00
78	Sabine Appelmans	18	423.00
79	Giulia Casoni	16	419.00
80	Eva Bes	21	415.00
81	Petra Mandula	14	409.00
82	Jelena Kostanic	20	408.00
83	Alexandra Stevenson	16	396.00
84	Petra Rampre	23	394.00
85	Andrea Glass	9	389.00
86	Patricia Wartusch	20	389.00
87	Florencia Labat	13	385.00
88	Ting Li	23	384.00
89	Na Li	23	384.00
90	Katalin Marosi-Aracama	26	383.00
91	Tina Pisnik	19	382.00
92	Angelika Bachmann	19	382.00
93	Yuka Yoshida	21	378.00
94	Catherine Barclay	20	370.00
95	Eva Dyrberg	23	369.00
96	Iroda Tulyaganova	16	369.00
97	Nannie De Villiers	21	368.00
98	Annabel Ellwood	24	366.00
99	Vanessa Webb	26	365.00
100	Rosa M. Andres	23	362.00

PRIZE MONEY (As at 20 November 2000)

The following table shows the prize money (including bonuses) won at all recognised tournament which adopted the WTA guidelines, where direct entry was based solely upon merit. It does not include income from Fed Cup, other team events, exhibitions, special events or commercial contracts. (Figures supplied by Sanex WTA Tour)

(The nationalities and birthdays of players can be found on pp 176–180)

1	Martina Hingis	$3,457,049	59	Katarina Srebotnik	165,860
2	Lindsay Davenport	2,444,734	60	Miriam Oremans	164,242
3	Venus Williams	2,074,150	61	Anna Smashnova	161,935
4	Mary Pierce	1,208,018	62	Tina Pisnik	161,496
5	Monica Seles	1,140,850	63	Alexandra Fusai	161,379
6	Conchita Martinez	1,067,930	64	Rita Grande	159,347
7	Serena Williams	1,001,818	65	Silvia Farina Elia	158,997
8	Anna Kournikova	984,930	66	Nicole Arendt	158,237
9	Julie Halard-Decugis	879,570	67	Denisa Chladkova	157,673
10	Arantxa Sanchez-Vicario	819,689	68	Nadejda Petrova	153,760
11	Nathalie Tauziat	761,211	69	Sylvia Plischke	149,698
12	Ai Sugiyama	729,635	70	Erika De Lone	144,047
13	Elena Dementieva	613,627	71	Manon Bollegraf	140,914
14	Amanda Coetzer	593,357	72	Fabiola Zuluaga	137,549
15	Lisa Raymond	560,474	73	Jana Kandarr	132,276
16	Sandrine Testud	547,384	74	Anastasia Myskina	130,662
17	Elena Likhovtseva	536,014	75	Cristina Torrens Valero	129,784
18	Chanda Rubin	528,020	76	Rita Kuti Kis	129,536
19	Jennifer Capriati	488,861	77	Sarah Pitkowski	128,655
20	Barbara Schett	470,987	78	Patricia Wartusch	128,147
21	Anke Huber	447,441	79	Giulia Casoni	126,814
22	Jelena Dokic	429,880	80	Catalina Cristea	125,693
23	Kim Clijsters	418,503	81	Justine Henin	122,798
24	Amelie Mauresmo	365,074	82	Sandra Nacuk	122,342
25	Dominique Van Roost	351,854	83	Joannette Kruger	121,911
26	Rennae Stubbs	340,407	84	Alina Jidkova	120,994
27	Paola Suarez	333,084	85	Lubomira Bacheva	118,066
28	Cara Black	316,153	86	Adriana Gersi	117,448
29	Anne-Gaelle Sidot	312,537	87	Emilie Loit	116,317
30	Magui Serna	311,384	88	Amelie Cocheteux	115,000
31	Amy Frazier	306,059	89	Brie Rippner	114,901
32	Patty Schnyder	263,318	90	Marta Marrero	114,054
33	Ruxandra Dragomir	260,704	91	Laurence Courtois	113,097
34	Corina Morariu	259,817	92	Jelena Kostanic	112,891
35	Sabine Appelmans	243,748	93	Alicia Molik	112,374
36	Natasha Zvereva	239,710	94	Angeles Montolio	111,761
37	Meghann Shaughnessy	238,659	95	Emmanuelle Gagliardi	111,182
38	Nathalie Dechy	234,074	96	Jana Nejedly	111,114
39	Tamarine Tanasugarn	232,786	97	Florencia Labat	110,617
40	Els Callens	227,188	98	Olga Barabanschikova	110,312
41	Lilia Osterloh	226,653	99	Shinobu Asagoe	109,563
42	Silvija Talaja	224,103	100	Amanda Hopmans	104,903
43	Magdalena Maleeva	221,384	101	Meilen Tu	104,252
44	Virginia Ruano Pascual	217,099	102	Maria Antonia Sanchez Lorenzo	104,056
45	Kristina Brandi	208,367	103	Barbara Rittner	100,899
46	Anne Kremer	207,639	104	Tara Snyder	98,332
47	Tatiana Panova	203,867	105	Pavlina Nola	97,143
48	Tathiana Garbin	201,925	106	Tatiana Poutchek	93,916
49	Asa Carlsson	194,089	107	Magdalena Grzybowska	92,664
50	Nicole Pratt	191,309	108	Daja Bedanova	92,333
51	Kristie Boogert	181,481	109	Irina Spirlea	92,259
52	Alexandra Stevenson	180,948	110	Holly Parkinson	90,765
53	Karina Habsudova	179,914	111	Jennifer Hopkins	90,660
54	Sonya Jeyaseelan	179,657	112	Marlene Weingartner	90,431
55	Kveta Hrdlickova	176,701	113	Iroda Tulyaganova	90,427
56	Kimberly Po	175,059	114	Vanessa Webb	89,601
57	Gala Leon Garcia	174,004	115	Katalin Marosi Aracama	89,454
58	Henrieta Nagyova	172,942	116	Mirjana Lucic	89,178

117	Mariaan De Swardt	88,855	184	Nannie De Villiers	38,917
118	Tina Krizan	88,831	185	Stephanie Foretz	38,242
119	Janet Lee	88,421	186	Nuria Llagostera	38,142
120	Patricia Tarabini	88,027	187	Trudi Musgrave	38,139
121	Sandra Kleinova	87,436	188	Lourdes Dominguez Lino	37,494
122	Lina Krasnoroutskaya	87,185	189	Lorna Woodroffe	37,251
123	Janette Husarova	87,005	190	Lucie Ahl	36,977
124	Nana Miyagi	84,902	191	Jill Craybas	36,275
125	Irina Selyutina	83,912	192	Tracy Almeda-Singian	36,197
126	Rossana De Los Rios	82,797	193	Laurence Andretto	36,194
127	Maria Vento	82,552	194	Milagros Sequera	35,715
128	Andrea Glass	82,484	195	Jessica Steck	33,898
129	Jing-Qian Yi	81,486	196	Francesca Lubiani	33,861
130	Marissa Irvin	79,864	197	Conchita Martinez Granados	33,738
131	Seda Noorlander	78,500	198	Jolene Watanabe	33,522
132	Miroslava Vavrinec	77,626	199	Elena Tatarkova	33,177
133	Yuka Yoshida	76,866	200	Marion Maruska	32,534
134	Laura Montalvo	75,797	201	Anna Zarska	31,312
135	Francesca Schiavone	75,210	202	Debbie Graham	31,300
136	Maureen Drake	71,017	203	Svetlana Kriventcheva	31,213
137	Julie Pullin	71,003	204	Ana Medina Garrigues	30,853
138	Rachel Mcquillan	69,945	205	Barbara Schwartz	30,572
139	Louise Latimer	69,662	206	Melanie Schnell	30,425
140	Iva Majoli	69,320	207	Michaela Pastikova	30,398
141	Lisa Mcshea	69,131	208	Tina Hergold	29,235
142	Nadejda Ostrovskaya	69,005	209	Catalina Castano	29,079
143	Angelika Bachmann	68,640	210	Anna Foldenyi	29,026
144	Annabel Ellwood	67,509	211	Maja Matevzic	28,941
145	Mashona Washington	64,306	212	Bianka Lamade	28,808
146	Mariana Diaz-Oliva	64,009	213	Nirupama Vaidyanathan	28,783
147	Bryanne Stewart	63,860	214	Selima Sfar	28,481
148	Caroline Vis	63,840	215	Anna Zaporozhanova	27,944
149	Petra Mandula	62,952	216	Amanda Grahame	27,876
150	Liezel Horn	60,460	217	Julia Abe	27,865
151	Katie Schlukebir	59,351	218	Miriam Schnitzer	27,755
152	Dawn Buth	57,806	219	Maria Jose Martinez	27,429
153	Surina De Beer	56,177	220	Alena Vaskova	27,413
154	Ludmila Cervanova	53,305	221	Kyra Nagy	27,325
155	Allison Bradshaw	53,225	222	Adriana Serra-Zanetti	26,850
156	Na Li	52,604	223	Evelyn Fauth	26,438
157	Elena Bovina	52,538	224	Ainhoa Goni	25,586
158	Martina Navratilova	52,338	225	Daphne Van De Zande	25,494
159	Samantha Reeves	52,233	226	Evgenia Koulikovskaya	25,451
160	Gisela Riera	52,110	227	Jo Ward	25,252
161	Anca Barna	51,566	228	Yoon Jeong Cho	25,224
162	Eva Bes	50,890	229	Tatiana Kovalchuk	24,679
163	Daniela Hantuchova	49,740	230	Ting Li	24,597
164	Sandra Cacic	49,150	231	Saori Obata	24,450
165	Virginie Razzano	49,006	232	Antonella Serra-Zanetti	24,376
166	Eva Dyrberg	48,680	233	Eun-Ha Kim	24,275
167	Greta Arn	48,664	234	Alicia Ortuno	23,872
168	Renata Kolbovic	48,303	235	Dessislava Topalova	23,804
169	Linda Wild	48,010	236	Tzipora Obziler	23,603
170	Yvette Basting	47,057	237	Zsofia Gubacsi	23,189
171	Petra Rampre	46,602	238	Mariam Ramon	22,993
172	Lori Mcneil	46,180	239	Vanessa Henke	22,871
173	Yayuk Basuki	45,625	240	Marie-Eve Pelletier	22,869
174	Evie Dominikovic	44,092	241	Karin Kschwendt	22,851
175	Martina Sucha	43,799	242	Laura Dell'Angelo	22,424
176	Wynne Prakusya	43,629	243	Libuse Prusova	22,323
177	Rika Hiraki	43,351	244	Adriana Barna	22,253
178	Eva Martincova	43,000	245	Samantha Smith	21,940
179	Alice Canepa	42,950	246	Meike Babel	21,804
180	Gloria Pizzichini	41,221	247	Syna Schmidle	21,748
181	Lenka Nemeckova	41,207	248	Maria Paola Zavagli	21,651
182	Catherine Barclay	40,990	249	Ansley Cargill	21,550
183	Rosa Maria Andres	39,279	250	Hannah Collin	21,522

THE MILLIONAIRESSES

Below is a list of players who, by the end of November 2000, had won at least $1 million during the course of their careers. The totals include earnings at all official tournaments recognised by the WTA Tour, as well as official bonuses. They do not include income from Fed Cup, special events, exhibitions or commercial endorsements.

NOTE: * indicates the 2 players who appear for the first time.

1	Steffi Graf	$21,895,277		55	Ruxandra Dragomir	$1,667,496
2	Martina Navratilova	$20,396,399		56	Rennae Stubbs	$1,651,786
3	Arantxa Sanchez-Vicario	$15,747,252		57	Yayuk Basuki	$1,613,527
4	Martina Hingis	$15,080,325		58	Kathy Jordan	$1,592,111
5	Monica Seles	$12,891,708		59	Patty Fendick	$1,574,956
6	Lindsay Davenport	$11,934,628		60	Virginia Wade	$1,542,278
7	Jana Novotna	$11,249,134		61	Kimberly Po	$1,518,798
8	Conchita Martinez	$9,335,263		62	Meredith McGrath	$1,448,132
9	Chris Evert	$8,896,195		63	Silvia Farina Elia	$1,443,469
10	Gabriela Sabatini	$8,785,850		64	Kathy Rinaldi Stunkel	$1,417,273
11	Natasha Zvereva	$7,714,430		65	Evonne Goolagong	$1,399,431
12	Venus Williams	$6,656,727		66	Andrea Jaeger	$1,379,066
13	Helena Sukova	$6,391,245		67	Barbara Potter	$1,376,580
14	Mary Pierce	$6,169,661		68	Alexandra Fusai	$1,371,277
15	Nathalie Tauziat	$5,707,942		69	Miriam Oremans	$1,368,357
16	Pam Shriver	$5,460,566		70	Nicole Arendt	$1,367,467
17	Mary Joe Fernandez	$5,258,471		71	Rosie Casals	$1,364,955
18	Gigi Fernandez	$4,681,906		72	Florencia Labat	$1,350,630
19	Zina Garrison Jackson	$4,590,816		73	Rachel McQuillan	$1,332,585
20	Amanda Coetzer	$4,252,428		74	Sandra Cecchini	$1,319,152
21	Anke Huber	$4,251,770		75	Patricia Tarabini	$1,301,918
22	Larisa Neiland	$4,083,936		76	Nicole Bradtke	$1,298,972
23	Serena Williams	$3,970,061		77	Sylvia Hanika	$1,296,560
24	Iva Majoli	$3,604,806		78	Barbara Paulus	$1,294,445
25	Lori Mcneil	$3,475,690		79	Katrina Adams	$1,294,235
26	Hana Mandlikova	$3,340,959		80	Barbara Rittner	$1,279,297
27	Manuela Maleeva-Fragniere	$3,244,811		81	Linda Wild	$1,237,931
28	Julie Halard-Decugis	$3,096,734		82	Jo Durie	$1,224,016
29	Lisa Raymond	$2,797,956		83	Amelie Mauresmo	$1,223,127
30	Wendy Turnbull	$2,769,024		84	Virginia Ruzici	$1,183,728
31	Anna Kournikova	$2,692,929		85	Leila Meskhi	$1,179,720
32	Irina Spirlea	$2,652,068		86	Robin White	$1,174,349
33	Brenda Schultz-McCarthy	$2,562,281		87	Mercedes Paz	$1,163,693
34	Sandrine Testud	$2,560,220		88	Andrea Temesvari	$1,162,635
35	Chanda Rubin	$2,488,798		89	Anne Smith	$1,159,717
36	Jennifer Capriati	$2,488,000		90	Dianne Balestrat	$1,145,377
37	Amy Frazier	$2,280,003		91	Ann Wunderlich	$1,138,377
38	Ai Sugiyama	$2,264,798		92	Kristie Boogert	$1,137,466
39	Claudia Kohde-Kilsch	$2,227,116		93	Mariaan De Swardt	$1,127,365
40	Katerina Maleeva	$2,220,371		94	Catarina Lindqvist	$1,126,665
41	Elena Likhovtseva	$2,209,665		95	Bettina Bunge	$1,126,424
42	Manon Bollegraf	$2,112,117		96	Elna Reinach	$1,114,668
43	Magdalena Maleeva	$2,111,543		97	Naoko Sawamatsu	$1,107,264
44	Sabine Appelmans	$2,041,247		98	Radka Zrubakova	$1,074,479
45	Dominique Van Roost	$2,013,032		99	Virginia Ruano Pascual	$1,070,124
46	Tracy Austin	$1,992,380		100	Asa Carlsson	$1,059,819
47	Kimiko Date	$1,974,253		101	Betty Stove	$1,047,356
48	Billie Jean King	$1,966,487		102	Marianne Werdel Witmeyer	$1,045,983
49	Barbara Schett	$1,891,782		103	Corina Morariu	$1,040,262
50	Patty Schnyder	$1,852,192		104	Betsy Nagelsen	$1,016,519
51	Judith Wiesner	$1,738,253		105	Laura Golarsa	$1,012,453
52	Rosalyn Nideffer	$1,701,944		106	Patricia Hy-Boulais	$1,011,116
53	Elizabeth Smylie	$1,701,837		107	* Laura Arraya	$1,005,589
54	Karina Habsudova	$1,698,164		108	* Anne-Gaelle Sidot	$1,005,360

2001 SANEX WTA TOUR – Tour Board

Chief Executive Officer:	Bart McGuire
Tournament Representatives:	Ivan Brixi
	Jim Curley
	Gunter Sanders
Player Representatives:	Lisa Grattan
	Kathy Jordan
	Harold Solomon
International Tennis Federation:	Debbie Jevans
Non-Affiliated:	Claude de Jouvencel
	Jan Soderstrom
Alternate Directors:	Richarde Legrande (Tournament)
	Ilana Kloss (Player)
	Francesco Ricci Bitti (ITF)
Non-Voting Observors:	Mark Selva (Championships)
	Judy Levering, Bill Babcock (Grand Slams)
	Frank Meysman (Sara Lee)

2001 SANEX WTA TOUR PLAYERS' COUNCIL

Top 20 Representatives:	Lindsay Davenport
	Sandrine Testud
	Amilie Mauresmo
	Venus Williams
Top 51–100 Representative:	Nicole Pratt
Top 21–50 Representative:	Mary Joe Fernandez
Top 21–100 Representative:	Joannette Kruger
101 +	Erika de Lone
Business Advisors:	Harold Solomon (Chairperson)
	Kathy Jordan (Top 21–100 Rep)
	Lisa Grattan (Top 20 Rep)
	Ilana Kloss (Alternate)

2001 SANEX WTA TOUR PLAYERS' COMMITTEE

Sabine Appelmans	Nicole Arendt
Mariana Diaz-Oliva	Debbie Graham
Karina Habsudova	Rika Hiraki
Joannette Kruger	Miriam Oremans
Sylvia Plischke	Katie Schlukebir
Elena Wagner	

SANEX WTA TOUR ANNUAL AWARDS, Miami, 22nd March 2000
Presented for performances in 1999

Player of the Year:	Lindsay Davenport
Doubles Team of the Year:	Martina Hingis/Anna Kournikova
Most Improved Player:	Serena Williams
Most Impressive Newcomer:	Kim Clijsters
Comeback Player of the Year:	Sabine Appelmans
Karen Krantzcke Sportsmanship:	Ai Sugiyama
Player Service Award:	Nicole Pratt
Ted Tinling Broadcast Media of the Year:	Eurosport
Sanex WTA Tour Employee of the Year:	Linda Christensen
Eurosport Spirit of Cooperation Award:	Jennifer Capriati
David Gray Special Service:	Butch Buchholz
Most Exciting Player Award:	Steffi Graf
Diamond ACES Award:	Lindsay Davenport
Ted Tinling Print Media of the Year:	John Parsons, Daily Telegraph
Tier I/II Tournament of the Year:	du Maurier Open, Toronto, Canada
Tier III/IV Tournament of the Year:	Bell Challenge, Quebec City, Canada
Tournament Achievement Award:	German Open, Berlin, Germany

History of the WTA Tour
No.1 World Ranking

November 1 1975 – November 20 2000

(Figures supplied by WTA Tour)

	Player	Age	First date No.1		Total Weeks
1	Steffi Graf (+)	18.2	17 Aug	1987	377
2	Martina Navratilova	21.9	10 Jul	1978	331
3	Chris Evert	20.11	1 Nov	1975	262
4	Monica Seles (+)	17.3	11 Mar	1991	178
5	Martina Hingis	16.6	31 Mar	1997	155
6	Lindsay Davenport	22.4	12 Oct	1998	28
7	Tracy Austin	17.3	7 Apr	1980	22
8	Arantxa Sanchez-Vicario	23.2	6 Feb	1995	12

(+) including 65 weeks as joint No.1

HISTORY OF THE NO.1 RANKING

Ranking date		Player	Weeks at No.1
1975	**1 November**	**Chris Evert (1)**	**140**
1976			
1977			
1978	**10 July**	**Martina Navratilova (2)**	**27**
1979	14 January	Chris Evert	2
1979	28 January	Martina Navratilova	4
1979	25 February	Chris Evert	7
1979	16 April	Martina Navratilova	10
1979	25 June	Chris Evert	11
1979	10 September	Martina Navratilova	30
1980	**7 April**	**Tracy Austin (3)***	**2**
1980	21 April	Martina Navratilova	10
1980	1 July	Tracy Austin	20
1980	18 November	Chris Evert	76
1981			
1982	3 May	Martina Navratilova	2
1982	17 May	Chris Evert	4
1982	14 June	Martina Navratilova +	156
1983			
1984			
1985	10 June	Chris Evert	18
1985	14 October	Martina Navratilova	2
1985	28 October	Chris Evert	4
1985	25 November	Martina Navratilova	90
1986			
1987	**17 August**	**Steffi Graf (4) ++**	**186**
1988			
1989			
1990			
1991	**11 March**	**Monica Seles (5)****	**21**
1991	5 August	Steffi Graf	1
1991	12 August	Monica Seles	1
1991	19 August	Steffi Graf	3
1991	9 September	Monica Seles	91
1992			
1993	7 June	Steffi Graf	87

HISTORY OF THE NO.1 RANKING (continued)

Ranking date	Player	Weeks at No.1
1994		
1995 6 February	**Arantxa Sanchez-Vicario (6)**	**2**
1995 20 February	Steffi Graf	1
1995 27 February	Arantxa Sanchez-Vicario	6
1995 10 April	Steffi Graf	5
1995 15 May	Arantxa Sanchez-Vicario	4
1995 12 June	Steffi Graf	9
1995 14 August	Steffi Graf	64
	and Monica Seles +++	64
1996 4 November	Steffi Graf	2
1996 18 November	Steffi Graf	1
	and Monica Seles +++	1
1996 25 November	Steffi Graf	18
1997 31 March	**Martina Hingis (7) *****	**80**
1998 12 October	**Lindsay Davenport (8)**	**17**
1999 8 February	Martina Hingis	20
1999 5 July	Lindsay Davenport	5
1999 9 August	Martina Hingis	30
2000 3 April	Lindsay Davenport	5
2000 8 May	Martina Hingis	1
2000 15 May	Lindsay Davenport	1
2000 22 May	Martina Hingis	24

* In April 1980 Tracy Austin is the youngest player to reach No. 1 at 17 years, 3 months, 26 days.

** In March 1991 Monica Seles becomes No.1 aged 17 years, 3 months, 19 days, 7 days younger than Austin.

*** In March 1997 Martina Hingis becomes the youngest woman ever to be ranked No.1, aged exactly 16 years and 6 months.

\+ Martina Navratilova held the No.1 position for 156 weeks consecutively.

\++ Steffi Graf held the No.1 position for a record 186 weeks consecutively, more than any man or woman.

\+++ Steffi Graf and Monica Seles co-ranked No. 1.

Second in the list of all-time world No. 1's, Martina Navratilova, having retired from singles, returned to competition in doubles with Marianne de Swardt of South Africa. (Paul Zimmer)

Twenty-Five Years of Wheelchair Tennis

Wendy Kewley

'To paraphrase Michael Jordan, it is not that you fall down that is important, but whether you get back up that is significant'. Typically emotive words from wheelchair tennis legend and motivational speaker Randy Snow.

Metaphorically speaking, 'getting back up' is perhaps the most gut wrenching thing a disabled person can do. It takes character. For some, 'getting back up' might involve an intellectual activity but for others it is sport. And since it was first founded in 1976, wheelchair tennis has become the fastest growing disabled sport. But much more than just an activity, wheelchair tennis gives people the chance to regain self-belief, to push the limits, and, perhaps most importantly, to smile again. From its humble beginnings as a leisure activity, wheelchair tennis is now conducted on a professional basis with its own tournament circuit, ranking system and prize money. Yet 25 years ago, the sport barely existed.

Commonly considered the founder of wheelchair tennis, Brad Parks was injured in a local free-style snow ski competition when he was 18. Realising that he would be in a wheelchair for the rest of his life, Parks began to find out about the sports that he could play. The Californian recalls, 'Shortly after I started playing I met a guy who was building sports wheelchairs and playing wheelchair tennis named Jeff Minnenbraker. He was playing with two bounces on his side of the court. I tried it and it made sense.'

Parks also realised that Minnenbraker's wheelchair was lighter and more mobile than his heavy hospital version. The extra lightness and different frame made the sport much easier to play and also meant that more athletes with higher level injuries could participate. Over the years, the evolution of the wheelchair has transformed the game. Many players adopted baseline games at the beginning but the introduction of a lighter wheelchair with one small front wheel has encouraged more attacking and faster play.

Enthusiastic and dynamic, Parks and Minnenbraker encouraged many others to participate, playing in exhibitions and tournaments in order to promote the sport on the west coast of the US. They also decided that the two-bounce rule should remain and that the court dimensions should be the same as a standard able-bodied tennis court.

A successful wheelchair racer, in 1980 Parks chose to stop racing in order to develop tennis. As Snow remembers, 'He could have gone on and pursued a racing career yet he believed in the sport – so he threw out his racing career and invested his time in wheelchair tennis and didn't get paid for a long, long time.'

In December 1979, Parks joined with David Saltz in founding the National Foundation of Wheelchair Tennis. The board of directors – the missionaries of wheelchair tennis – were Parks, Saltz, Jim Worth and Dave Kiley.

These were thrilling times. In March 1980, Parks, Worth and Saltz met John Newcombe, Fred Stolle and Charlie Pasarell and were invited to do exhibition matches in Australia. The same year they produced a circuit of ten tournaments in the US including the first US Open Championships in September. By 1981 the Wheelchair Tennis Players Association (WTPA) had been formed to represent the growing numbers of keen tennis athletes. Wheelchair tennis was on the move.

The enthusiastic and skilful American, Brad Parks who is considered to be the founder of wheelchair tennis. (ITF)

In 1981, a Frenchman named Jean Paul Limborg came over to the United States in search of a light wheelchair and visited Minnenbraker's factory. He found more than he could have ever dreamed. Meeting Minnenbraker, Limborg was told about a wheelchair tennis event happening in Las Vegas. Little did he realise he would end up competing in the women's draw – a way of easing his introduction to the sport! 'I really enjoyed the game and atmosphere between the players so I decided to stay in California for four months,' remembers Limborg.

Inspired by his new found pastime, he finally returned to France where he met former tennis teacher Pierre Fusade and tried to elicit his support. 'It's impossible to play tennis in a chair,' came the response. However, the future president of the IWTF was soon persuaded that wheelchair tennis was feasible – with the two bounce rule. The first wheelchair tennis club opened its doors in Antony, Paris and by 1984 it was hosting the first international competition in Europe. Amongst the eager competitors was a girl called Chantal Vandierendonck, whose father had accompanied her on their journey from the Netherlands. A very talented national tennis player, Vandierendonck had been paralysed in a car accident when she was 18 and was curious to find out about the new sport. After having her first ever wheelchair tennis rally with Fusade and Limborg, Vandierendonck was ecstatic at having a chance to play the sport she loved once again. Not only did she promote it in the Netherlands but she went on to spearhead the Dutch wheelchair tennis success, winning three ITF World Champion awards and collecting four Paralympic medals, including two golds in doubles.

In 1985, to cater for the rapid globalisation of wheelchair tennis, an international team competition was established for men with six countries participating in the first event. Called the World Team Cup, the women's equivalent was introduced in 1986 with a US and a combined Dutch/French team entering the inaugural event. The Dutch/French team comprised Vandierendonck and Martine Pickard.

Originally conceived as a warm up tournament for the US Open Wheelchair Tennis Championships in order to foster international camaraderie, the World Team Cup has become one of the highlights on the tennis calendar with 44 countries (including Regional Qualifying) participating in 2000.

In 1988, the ITF adopted the two-bounce rule in the official Rules of Tennis, sanctioning the new sport. Recognising the widening appeal of wheelchair tennis, Parks founded the International Wheelchair Tennis Federation (IWTF) at a meeting attended by representatives from Australia, Canada, France, Great Britain, Holland, Israel, Japan and the USA. The formation of the IWTF represented a huge leap forward – it gave the sport an international focus and allowed many countries to develop and organise the game.

Wheelchair tennis players were included in the able-bodied Lipton Championships, providing the perfect international spotlight for the game. As France's Laurent Giammartini put it at the time, 'Being accepted and being able to compete as part of an important event like the Lipton with its crowd, its atmosphere and media attention is what really counts.'

At the 1994 Lipton Championships, an unexpected promotional opportunity arose when Pete Sampras needed time out for medical treatment before playing Andre Agassi in the final. To fill the gap, wheelchair tennis players were asked to play an exhibition match. Brad Parks and David Hall teamed up with Fred Stolle and Sherwood Stewart and succeeded in entertaining the capacity crowds.

While the sport was receiving greater promotion, there had also been advances in coaching and playing techniques, vital in improving the standard of the game. In early 1989, leading US college tennis coach, Bal Moore, happened to meet Randy Snow as he conducted a wheelchair tennis clinic. After studying biomechanics and kinesiology at university, Moore was well qualified and knew that his knowledge could improve wheelchair tennis. With 30 years of coaching to his name, Moore was looking for a fresh direction – wheelchair tennis was the answer. Before long, Moore and Snow had started the first wheelchair tennis camp series in the US because as Snow explained, 'Wheelchair tennis camps are needed for proper development in mobility, mental toughness and stroke production.' Emphasising the point, the USA won the World Team Cup while Snow lifted the US Open trophy a week later – both achievements were under Moore's guidance.

In 1991, wheelchair tennis reached another watershed with the entrance of former world No. 2, Ellen de Lange. The Dutchwoman was appointed as Executive Secretary to the IWTF and was based at the ITF's offices in London. For the first time, wheelchair tennis had a full-time administrator. Doug MacCurdy, ITF General Manager at the time, recalls, 'I felt that it seemed logical to include wheelchair tennis in the development efforts of the ITF.'

Chantal Vandierendonck (NED) and Randy Snow (USA) join the other ITF World Champions on stage in 1991. (ITF)

Newly appointed ITF President at the time, Brian Tobin, calls de Lange's appointment 'the catalyst which set the sport on an exciting course of expansion – from the grass roots level to the top (now professional) echelons of the game.' He adds, 'Having been a highly ranked player in women's wheelchair tennis, Ellen knew what the game needed to grow and possessed the qualities that made others – players, coaches etc want to help and support her.'

According to Fusade, the ITF's decision helped wheelchair tennis as no other sport federation has helped other disabled sports ever in recognising it as part of the family of tennis.

In 1991, the IWTF had 12 member nations compared with 57 today. One of the main problems facing wheelchair tennis was the lack of equipment in some of the newly developing countries. In the first IWTF newsletter, de Lange appealed to readers to check their attic or garage for unwanted wheelchairs. Anything spare might help to get a wheelchair tennis programme underway. One thing was clear, she meant business.

A further boost came when NEC announced its support, generously providing a grant for three years from their Social Contribution Programmes Department. With most of the funds being used to develop the game by sponsoring clinics in countries new to wheelchair tennis, sponsorship enabled many more people to enjoy the sport. NEC's support also prompted a formalised tournament system with all the major events opting to join the NEC Wheelchair Tennis Tour. When the IWTF took over the ranking system from the NFWT, the ranking became known as the NEC Wheelchair Tennis Ranking.

Nineteen ninety-one also achieved some other notable firsts. The US Open had prize money for the first time ever. The ITF also recognised wheelchair tennis world champions for the first time, honouring Snow and Vandierendonck at Roland Garros, in the company of the able bodied champions. Thanking the ITF afterwards, Snow wrote, 'This recognition is important because it reminds me of the hours of training and travelling I put into the sport... To join the stage with Seles and Edberg and the other champions was superb.'

Another milestone was achieved when wheelchair tennis became a full medal sport at the 1992 Paralympics in Barcelona. Near capacity crowds watched 48 players from 15 different countries competing for tennis medals. The competition received live television coverage and was held at the Vall D'Hebron site where the able bodied players had participated in the Olympic Tennis Event beforehand. One of the best matches of the event featured eventual gold medallist Snow playing Abde Naili in a gripping semi-final match, enjoyed by a crowd of over 6000. More people than ever were enjoying wheelchair tennis.

With an international competitive structure firmly in place, de Lange turned her attention to developing the sport in countries new to wheelchair tennis. Setting up wheelchair tennis programmes in Asia and Latin America was high on the agenda.

So in 1993, clinics were held in South America – the first time something had been officially organised there. The IWTF met officials from the national associations of Argentina, Brazil and Mexico which resulted in the latter two countries joining the IWTF while the Argentina Tennis Association took over the membership of the Disabled Sports Association.

De Lange also visited China, Sri Lanka and Korea. In Sri Lanka, she saw an army hospital and a rehab centre was organised to meet the many soldiers who had a disability that would end their army careers. The workshop showed how important sport could be in the rehab process. Moved by her experience, de Lange promised a return trip, writing, 'More than anywhere else, these young people need something which gives them hope and joy for the rest of their lives.'

There were some thorns lurking amongst the roses though. A 1996 visit to Cambodia, Indonesia and Malaysia prompted Limborg to say, 'Working in Cambodia has been a fantastic but terrible experience and definitely not an easy one. This country has been through years of wars and the people are now mentally broken.' Nevertheless, the Frenchman managed to set up the first federation in Cambodia and $3000 was spent on tennis rackets and wheelchairs. Limborg returned to Cambodia last year – only to find that everything had disappeared.

Despite experiencing difficulties in some countries, de Lange's frequent visits to foreign parts combined with NEC's funding did reap positive results overall. In 1993, 22 nations took part in the World Team Cup – 60 per cent more than in the previous year. Similarly, wheelchair tennis was played in 50 countries in 1992 – incredibly, this number was to double by 2000. Word was getting around.

Development received a further injection of enthusiasm with the appointment of the first Development/Tournament Officer, Marko Polic. His work took him to some of the most destitute regions in South East Asia, Africa and South America. He says, 'In countries like Malaysia, Peru, Zimbabwe and Korea where polio and other debilitating diseases are still rampant, learning how to play tennis should probably be placed at the bottom of their list of priorities, falling well below finding that day's meal or a roof to sleep under.'

In war ravaged countries where years of conflict has ripped the spirit from its victims, Polic hoped to introduce them to an alternative from a life of depression, or at least a momentary break from it via a sport. He simply says, 'I realise that although I have educated people about wheelchair tennis, I am the one who has been given the most important lesson about life: that the fire that fuels man's will to not just exist but also achieve is unquenchable.'

Another important ingredient in the development of the game has been the creation of junior camps, organised by the ITF since 1994. Dutch players Esther Vergeer, Sonja Peters and Angela Maas have all benefited from these camps – so much so that Vergeer was the year-end world No. 1 in 2000 while Peters and Maas were ranked third and sixth respectively.

From the grass roots to the professional game: in 1994, the first elite year-end event – the NEC Wheelchair Tennis Masters – was held. Featuring the top eight men and top eight women on the NEC Wheelchair Tennis World Ranking, the inaugural competition took place at the Eindhoven Indoor Sports Centre. The Paralympic champions showed their pedigree with Snow beating Steven Welch in the men's final while Kalkman defeated Vandierendonck for the women's title.

In 1995, the World Team Cup obtained a title sponsor in the Invacare Corporation, the world's leading manufacturer and distributor of home health care and mobility products. The event became known as the Action World Team Cup after the name of Invacare's ultra light sports wheelchairs. In 1998 the competition was renamed the Invacare World Team Cup. In the same year a quad division was included in the team competition for the first time – an important marker in the ITF's plans to incorporate a quad division in a future Paralympic Games. By 1999, it had become necessary to introduce qualification for the men's draw of the World Team Cup, so popular had the event become. In 2000, a junior competition was also held for the first time providing greater competitive opportunities for the next generation of wheelchair tennis players.

Wheelchair tennis received further recognition when it was integrated into the ITF from January 1998 becoming the first disabled sport to do so. The IWTF was replaced by the IWTA, which has its own membership (the wheelchair tennis association, national tennis association and the disabled sport association) and acts as the advisory body to the ITF. The ITF encourages its member nations to include wheelchair tennis in their national federation's programme. It is hoped that one day it will be possible to dissolve the IWTA when all the ITF member nations

The Dutch, winners of the World Team Cup in 1991; (l to r) Monique Kalkman, Chantal Vandierendonck, Ellen de Lange and Maaike Smit, with coach Gert Bolk. (ITF)

have included wheelchair tennis as an integral part of their tennis association. ITF President Francesco Ricci Bitti says, 'The aim of the ITF is to make our 198 National Associations realise that wheelchair tennis is an important part of the sport. We will do everything possible to allow them to achieve this goal.'

Another historic decision was taken in 1998, when the ITF's AGM allowed wheelchair tennis players to compete using two bounces, both in wheelchair tournaments and able-bodied events.

With 116 international tournaments on the NEC Wheelchair Tennis Tour, the sport is prospering at the start of the new millennium. A doubles event was introduced at the 2000 NEC Tennis Masters, adding to the on-court drama. But in 2000 the highlight was undoubtedly the Sydney Paralympic Tennis Event. Hailed as the most successful event ever, the nine day Paralympic competition attracted record crowds with 20,000 people visiting the NSW tennis venue on the first Sunday of the tournament. Ten thousand fans watched home hero David Hall outplay Steven Welch in the men's final which unfolded into the most thrilling showdown of the tournament. Australia's Branka Pupovac sums up the occasion best, 'This is history in the making. Wheelchair tennis has never had so many people attend and it's just sensational.'

Reflecting on how far wheelchair tennis has come since those heady days in 1976, Parks says, 'I didn't think it would have developed to the point it is at today. I hoped it would, but it has surpassed my dreams and hopes.'

But there is still more to be done. Over to Snow, 'People need to see it. The players are here, the personalities are available so it's packaged and ready to go.' However dramatic the action may be on court, wheelchair tennis remains relatively unnoticed by the media.

While some, like Limborg, believe that it will take a long time for the performance of tennis athletes to be watched for their performances alone – rather than because of their disabilities – others disagree. The Paralympic Tennis Event was an amazing sports extravaganza, highlighting the enormous marketing potential of the game but unfortunately this spotlight is only there once every four years. But as de Lange says, 'Our task now is to channel the amazing energy created by the Paralympics so that wheelchair tennis can benefit from the incredible success of Sydney.'

Reference Section

Biographies • All-Time Greats
Obituaries • Championship Rolls

INDEX TO BIOGRAPHIES

The top 50 singles and leading doubles players on both the ATP and WTA tours are shown, together with senior and junior Grand Slam winners and all those who competed in the season-ending championships. Players ranked in the top 10 in singles are shown in bold. Figures following players' names indicate their singles ranking, junior ranking where applicable and those in brackets show the doubles ranking where appropriate.

MEN

WOMEN

Biographies

Christine Forrest

Abbreviations used in this section:

f	final	1r	first round	Champ	Champion/
sf	semi-final	2s	second set		Championship
qf	quarter-final	RH	right-handed	GP	Grand Prix
r/u	runner-up	LH	left-handed	Jun	Junior
def	defaulted	2HB	2-handed backhand	Nat	National
ret	retired	2HF	2-handed forehand	Pro	Professional
fs	final set	US CC	US Clay Court	Tourn	Tournament
rr	round-robin		Championships	HC	Hard Court
bp	break-point	LIPC	Lipton International	VS	Virginia Slims
sp	set-point		Players Championships	WT Cup	World Team Cup
mp	match-point	FC Cup	Family Circle Cup	D Cup	Davis Cup
tb	tie-break	GS Cup	Grand Slam Cup		

TOP TEN

Full biographical and statistical details of the top ten men and top ten women head separate men's and women's sections. Each individual's record contains personal details, followed by his or her 2000 prize money, career prize money, the number of career titles won and year-end rankings. A paragraph on style is followed by annual notes of career highlights, beginning with the tournaments won each year. A section giving principal singles results in full for 2000 includes all matches where a player has reached at least the semi-final. There follows a complete career record of every singles match played at each of the four Grand Slam Championships, at the Olympic Games and in Davis Cup or Fed Cup ties, in the Grand Slam Cup and in the season ending Tour Championships.

REMAINING BIOGRAPHIES

Within the two sections are the principal 2000 results, the annual notes and the career highlights of the next 50 ranked singles players of each sex, the leading doubles players, all Grand Slam winners and the juniors who have won Grand Slam titles. The final ranking for each year is shown in brackets following the year.

John Barrett's annual world rankings, as well as the year-end rankings published by the ATP Tour and the WTA Tour, and total prize money together with lists of the men and women whose career earnings exceed $1 million, can be found in the Rankings Section (pp 230–248).

We gratefully acknowledge the assistance of the ATP Tour, especially Nathalie Durot, the WTA Tour, and the WTA European office in supplying statistical information.

1 GUSTAVO KUERTEN (BRA)

Born: Florianapolis, 10 September 1976. **Lives:** Florianapolis.
Father: Deceased. **Mother:** Alice. **Brothers:** Rafael (older);
Guilherme (younger).

Agent: Octagon Athlete Representation (Jorg Salkeld).
Coach: Larri Passos. **Turned Pro:** 1995.
Height: 6ft 3in (1.90m). **Weight:** 165lb (75kg).

Rankings: 1993: 665; **1994:** 421; **1995:** 187;
1996: 88; **1997:** 14; **1998:** 23; **1999:** 5; **2000:** 1.
Highest: 1 (3 December 2000).

2000 Prize Money: $4,701,610.
Career Earnings: $8,923,321. **Career Titles:** 9.

Style: A heavy hitter from the baseline whose single-handed backhand is one of the game's great shots. He mixes deft touch with intimidating power, a subtle mixture that surprises many opponents and makes him a master on clay. His improving volleying skills have allowed him to shine on fast surfaces, where his serve is a potent weapon.

CAREER HIGHLIGHTS (year: (titles))
Known as Guga. **1994:** Won French Open Jun doubles with Lapentti, to whom he was r/u Orange Bowl 18s. **1995:** Made an impact on the satellite circuits. **1996:** Reached qf Umag (d. Berasategui) and Beijing and finished the season by winning Campinas Challenger. In doubles he won Santiago with Meligeni. **1997: (1)** *FRENCH OPEN.* The title at Curitiba Challenger restored his confidence after a poor start to the year, which gave no hint of what was to come at French Open. There he upset CC specialists Muster, Medvedev, Kafelnikov and Bruguera to win his 1st title, having never before passed qf. He was the 1st Brazilian to win a GS title (or even to pass qf in GS), 3rd unseeded player to win French Open, and 1st since Wilander in 1982 to win his 1st career title in GS. Only Mark Edmondson, winning Australian Open in 1976 from a ranking of 212, had won a GS ranked lower than his 66. However, that triumph saw him become the 1st Brazilian to break into top 20 at No. 15, and after r/u showing at Montreal (d. M. Chang), he moved into top 10. He also reached f Bologna (d. Berasategui) and qf Cincinnati, as well as recording other useful upsets during the year, including Agassi at Memphis and W. Ferreira at Indian Wells. In doubles with Meligeni, he played and won 3 f. **1998: (2)** *Stuttgart Mercedes, Mallorca.* Emerging from a slump, he won his 2nd career title at Stuttgart Mercedes in July and followed with Mallorca (d. Moya), as well as reaching sf Memphis and Rome, plus qf LIPC, Hamburg, Umag and Long Island (d. Rios). In doubles with Meligeni he won Gstaad, but was involved in an unsavoury incident at French Open: in an argument over a call on serve, he threw his racket at umpire Bruno Rebeuh, who ducked, and the racket hit a spectator. The match was awarded to his opponents, Bjorkman/Rafter, Kuerten being disqualified and fined for unsportsmanlike behaviour. **1999: (2)** *Monte Carlo, Rome.* Having his hair cut short in spring seemed to have a good effect on him, for shortly afterwards he won Monte Carlo, following with Rome (d. Kafelnikov, Kucera, Corretja and Rafter). Adding sf finishes at Indian Wells (d. Kafelnikov) and Lyon (d. T. Martin) and qf Sydney, Dubai, Estoril, Hamburg, Cincinnati and Indianapolis, he became the 1st Brazilian to qualify for season-ending champs, although he did not progress beyond rr. In doubles he won Adelaide with Lapentti. **2000: (5)** *FRENCH OPEN, Santiago, Hamburg, Indianapolis, Masters Cup.* Until the glorious climax to his season at Masters Cup, the highlight of his year had been winning a second French Open title over M. Norman, a performance that took him to the top of the Champions Race for the 1st of several times during the year. On the Entry System he moved to a career-high No. 2 behind Sampras at end Aug. after winning his 4th title of year and 1st of his career on HC at Indianapolis. His earlier titles had all been on clay – at Santiago, where he also took the doubles with Prieto, Hamburg and French Open. He was r/u at 2 more Masters Series events at Ericsson Open (d. Agassi) and Rome, and reached sf Bogota, Cincinnati and Paris Masters and qf Hong Kong, Tokyo Japan Open, Lyon and Olympics. He had threatened to withdrew BRA Olympic team in dispute over which sponsor's kit he should wear – his or the Olympic sponsor's. In other GS he was disappointing, losing 1r at

Australian and US Opens and 3r Wimbledon, but when it came to Masters Cup at end of year, he was magnificent. Despite a recurrence of the back injury that had troubled him on and off from mid-March, he overcame that and a hamstring injury to take not only the title – his 1st indoors – but also the No. 1 year-end ranking for 1st time. Although Agassi beat him in rr, when it came to the knockout stages he was superb in beating Sampras in sf and sweeping past an in-form Agassi in ss in f, clinching the No. 1 spot only in the last match of the season.

PRINCIPAL 2000 RESULTS – won 5, r/u 2, sf 3 (detailed Grand Slam results follow)
won French Open, **won** Santiago (d. Lisnard 7–5 6–1, Stanoytchev 6–3 6–4, Calleri 6–4 6–1, Portas 6–4 7–6, Puerta 7–6 6–3), **won** Hamburg (d. Alami 5–7 6–2 6–3, Grosjean 6–1 3–6 6–3, W. Ferreira 6–1 6–2, M. Norman 6–4 6–2, Pavel 6–3 6–3, Safin 6–4 5–7 6–4 5–7 7–6), **won** Indianapolis (d. Woodbridge 5–7 6–4 6–1, Dent 6–2 7–6, W. Ferreira 6–2 6–3, Hewitt 7–5 6–2, Safin 3–6 7–6 7–6), **won** Masters Cup; **r/u** Ericsson Open (d. Clement 6–7 7–6 7–5, Ivanisevic 7–6 6–3, Pozzi 6–4 7–6, W. Ferreira 6–3 6–1, Agassi 6–1 6–4, lost Sampras 6–1 6–7 7–6 7–6), **r/u** Rome (d. Golmard 6–4 6–1, Philippoussis 6–2 6–2, El Aynaoui w/o, A. Costa 6–4 7–5, Corretja 6–4 6–2, lost M. Norman 6–3 4–6 6–4 6–4); **sf** Bogota (d. Bruguera 6–4 6–1, Prieto 6–3 7–5, Hantschk 6–2 0–6 7–6, lost Puerta 3–6 6–1 7–6), **sf** Cincinnati (d. Golmard 6–0 6–4, Pozzi 7–5 6–3, Koubek 1–6 6–1 6–2, T. Martin 6–7 6–3 7–6, lost Henman 6–7 6–3 7–6), **sf** Paris Masters (d. Woodruff 6–3 7–6, Rafter 6–4 7–6, A. Costa 6–4 7–6, lost Philippoussis 7–6 7–6). **2000 HIGHLIGHTS – DOUBLES:** (with Prieto) **won** Santiago (d. Bale/Norval 6–2 6–4).

CAREER GRAND SLAM RECORD
AUSTRALIAN OPEN – Played 4
1997: 2r d. Tillstrom 7–5 7–6 3–6 6–4, lost Godwin 6–7 6–0 6–1 6–0. **1998: 2r** [seed 12] d. Diaz 6–3 3–6 6–3 6–2, lost Escude 5–7 6–3 6–1 7–5. **1999: 2r** d. Ondruska 6–4 6–3 6–3, lost Safin 6–3 6–7 4–6 6–3 6–4. **2000: 1r** [seed 5] lost Portas 4–6 4–6 6–4 7–6 6–4.
FRENCH OPEN – Played 5, won 2, qf 1
1996: 1r lost W. Ferreira [10] 6–4 7–5 7–6. **1997: won** [unseeded] d. Dosedel 6–0 7–5 6–1, Bjorkman 6–4 6–2 4–6 7–5, Muster [5] 6–7 6–1 6–3 3–6 6–4, Medvedev 5–7 6–1 6–2 1–6 7–5, Kafelnikov [3] 6–2 5–7 2–6 6–0 6–4, Dewulf 6–1 3–6 6–1 7–6, Bruguera 6–3 6–4 6–2. **1998: 2r** [seed 8] d. Auffray 6–0 6–2 6–2, lost Safin 3–6 7–6 3–6 6–1 6–4. **1999: qf** [seed 8] d. Blanco 6–4 6–4 6–3, Canas 6–2 6–3 6–2, Schalken 6–2 6–4 6–3, Ulihrach 6–4 6–4 6–2, lost Medvedev 7–5 6–4 6–4. **2000: won** [seed 5] d. Vinciguerra 6–0 6–0 6–3, Charpentier 7–6 6–2 6–2, Chang 6–3 6–7 6–1 6–4, N. Lapentti [11] 6–3 6–4 7–6, Kafelnikov [4] 6–3 3–6 4–6 6–4 6–2, Ferrero 7–5 4–6 2–6 6–4 6–3, M. Norman [3] 6–1 6–4 6–3.
WIMBLEDON – Played 4, qf 1
1997: 1r [seed 11] lost Gimelstob 6–3 6–4 4–6 1–6 6–4. **1998: 1r** lost Stoltenberg 4–6 6–3 6–1 4–6 10–8. **1999: qf** [seed 11] d. Wilkinson 6–4 6–4 6–4, Prinosil 6–3 6–3 6–2, Zimonjic 6–4 6–4 6–2, Manta 7–5 6–4 5–7 6–3, lost Agassi [seed 4] 6–3 6–4 6–4. **2000: 3r** [seed 5] d. Woodruff 6–4 6–7 7–5 7–6, Bower 6–4 6–4 7–5, lost Popp 7–6 6–2 6–1.
US OPEN – Played 4, qf 1
1997: 3r [seed 9] d. Grant 6–4 3–6 6–7 6–2 6–2, Schalken 6–4 6–4 6–2, lost Bjorkman 6–3 6–1 7–5. **1998: 2r** d. Behr 4–6 6–4 6–3 6–4, lost Nainkin 2–6 6–4 6–3 6–4. **1999: qf** [seed 5] d. Ulihrach 6–4 6–4 6–3, Haarhuis 6–3 7–6 3–6 6–2, Ivanisevic 6–4 6–2 6–4, Norman 7–6 ret, lost Pioline 4–6 7–6 7–6 7–6. **2000: 1r** [seed 2] lost Arthurs 4–6 6–3 7–6 7–6.

OLYMPIC RECORD
2000: (Sydney) qf [seed 2] d. Pognon 6–1 6–1, Schuttler 6–4 6–4, Ljubicic 7–6 6–3, lost Kafelnikov [5] 6–4 7–5.

CAREER DAVIS CUP RECORD
1996: February – *American Zone 1r BRA d. CHI 3–2 in CHI (Clay).* R3 (with J. Oncins) d. M. Rebolledo/M. Rios 7–5 6–3 4–6 6–2. **April** – *American Zone 2r BRA d. VEN 4–1 in BRA (Clay).* R1 d. N. Pereira 6–2 6–7 6–1 6–2; R5 d. J. Szymanski 6–2 6–7 6–0. **September** – *World Group Qualifying BRA d. AUT 4–1 in BRA (Carpet).* R2 d. M. Hipfl 4–6 3–6 7–6 7–6 6–1; R3 (with J. Oncins) d. T. Muster/U. Plamberger 7–6 4–6 6–3 3–6 2–0 ret. R4 w/o Plamberger. **1997: February** – *World Group 1r BRA d. BRA 4–1 in BRA (Clay).* R1 lost MaliVai Washington 3–6 7–6 7–6 6–3. R3 (with J. Oncins) d. A. O'Brien/R. Reneberg 6–2 6–4 7–5. R4 lost J. Courier 6–3 6–2 5–7 7–6. **September** – *World Group Qualifying BRA d. NZL 5–0 in BRA (Clay).* R1 d. A. Hunt 7–5 6–3 6–2; R3 (with J. Oncins) d. Hunt/B. Steven 6–0 6–2 6–0; R4 d. Steven 6–1 6–0. **1998: April** – *World Group 1r ESP d. BRA 3–2 in BRA (Clay).* R1 d. C. Moya 5–7 1–6 6–4 6–4 6–4; R3 (with J. Oncins) d. A. Corretja/J. Sanchez 6–1 7–5 3–6 6–2; R4 lost Corretja 6–3 7–5 4–6 6–4. **September** – *World Group Qualifying BRA d. ROM 3–0 in BRA (Clay).* R2 d. A. Pavel 7–5 6–3 6–3; R3 (with Oncins) d. Pavel/G. Trifu 7–5 6–4 6–4; R4 v A. Voinea not played. **1999: April** – *World Group 1r BRA d. ESP 3–2 in ESP (Clay).* R2 d. A. Corretja 6–3 6–4 7–5; R3 (with J. Oncins) d. Corretja/A. Costa 6–2 5–7 4–6 6–4 6–3; R4 d. C. Moya 6–2 6–4 6–1. **July** – *World Group qf FRA d. BRA 3–2 in FRA (Carpet).* R1 d. S. Grosjean 6–2 6–7 7–6 6–2 7–5; R3 (with Oncins) lost O. Delaitre/F. Santoro 7–6 6–4 6–4; R4 lost C. Pioline 6–3 6–4 6–4 **2000: February** – *World Group 1r BRA d. FRA 4–1 in BRA (Clay).* R2 d. J. Golmard 6–3 3–6 6–3 6–2. R3 (with J. Oncins) d. N. Escude/C.

Gustavo Kuerten, the first South American to become World No. 1. (Paul Zimmer)

Pioline 6–4 6–4 6–4; R4 lost Escude 6–2 7–6. **April** – *World Group qf BRA d. SVK 3–2 in BRA (Clay).* R2 d. K. Kucera 2–6 6–3 4–6 7–5 6–1; R3 (with Oncins) d. D. Hrbaty/Kucera 6–3 2–6 6–2 6–3; R4 lost Hrbaty 7–5 6–4 7–6. **July** – *World Group sf AUS d. BRA 5–0 in AUS (Grass).* R1 lost P. Rafter 6–3 6–2 6–3; R3 (with Oncins) lost S. Stolle/M. Woodforde 6–7 6–4 3–6 6–3 6–4.

GRAND SLAM CUP RECORD – Played 2
1997: 1r [seed 3] lost Korda 6–3 5–3 ret. **1998:** Did not play. **1999: 1r** lost Rusedski 6–3 3–6 6–3.

ATP TOUR CHAMPIONSHIP/MASTERS CUP – Played 2, won 1
1999: 3rd in rr lost Sampras 6–2 6–3, d. Lapentti 6–1 6–2, lost Agassi 6–4 7–5. **2000: won** in rr lost Agassi 4 6 6 4 6 3, d. M. Norman 7 5 6 3, d. Kafelnikov 6 3 6 4 in rr; sf d. Sampras 6 7 6 3 6 4; f d. Agassi 6–4 6–4 6–4.

2 MARAT SAFIN (RUS)

Born: Moscow, 27 January 1980.
Lives: Moscow and Valencia, Spain.
Father: Misha. **Mother:** Rausa Islanova, who played French Open Jun and Wimbledon Jun. **Sister:** Dinara, 6 years younger, now beginning to play Jun circuit.

Agent: Elite Management (Gerard Tsobanian). **Coach:** Rafael Mensua; formerly his mother, and, briefly, by Andrei Chesnokov, Alexander Volkov and Tony Pickard.
Turned Pro: 1997. **Height:** 6ft 4in (1.93cm).
Weight: 180lb (81kg).

Rankings: 1996: 441; **1997:** 194; **1998:** 48; **1999:** 25; **2000:** 2. **Highest:** 1 (September 2000).
2000 Prize Money: $3,524,959. **Career Earnings:** 4,475,663. **Career titles:** 8.

Style: A powerful hitter from the baseline where control of length and the ability to take the ball early make him a formidable opponent. Using his height well he serves with great power and is learning to vary the spin and placement to keep opponents guessing. For a big man he covers the court well and is becoming a fine volleyer. His weakness in the past has been a volatile temperament which led him to quit during matches occasionally. With growing maturity this happens less frequently.

CAREER HIGHLIGHTS (Year: (titles))
1997: Won Espinho Challenger. **1998:** The 4 years he spent working on Spanish clay in Valencia paid off as he sprang to prominence at French Open. There, a qualifier, he upset Agassi and Kuerten – the 1st time in the open era that a defending champion had lost to a qualifier – and bowed out only after extending Pioline to 5s. These results took him into the top 100. Having won Napoli Challenger in April, he reached his 1st sf on the main tour at Long Island (d. Berasategui) in August, as well as reaching qf Tashkent and recording upsets of Korda at Ostrava and Larsson at Barcelona, being voted Player to Watch. **1999: (1)** *Boston.* Won his 1st main tour title at Boston, playing in his 1st f, and finished the year in the top 25 after r/u showing at Paris Open (unseeded, d. Kuerten). He also reached sf St Petersburg, Rotterdam (d. Corretja) and Amsterdam, while other notable upsets included Enqvist at Indian Wells, Philippoussis at LIPC and Henman at Vienna. **2000: (7)** *US OPEN, Barcelona, Mallorca, Toronto, Tashkent, St Petersburg, Paris Masters.* After a frustrating period when his game seemed to fall apart and he was fined for not trying in his 1r def by Stafford at Australian Open, he joined forces in April with Chesnokov, who spurred him on with some straight talking. Until then he had not passed 2r but immediately his season took off as he won 2 titles: first he upset N. Lapentti and M. Norman on his way to the title at Barcelona, unseeded, and was in the winner's circle again a week later when he won Mallorca. He followed with r/u Hamburg (d. Pioline), where he lost to Kuerten only 7–6 5s, moving into top 10 Champions Race, and upset Rios at Rome. Then at Toronto he won his 1st Tennis Masters Series title, saving 3 mps in tb to upset Sampras on the way. But the best was still to come, for at US Open he upset Sampras again in ss in f to capture his 1st GS title. When he added the title at Tashkent a week later, he took over the No. 1 spot in the Champions Race, although Kuerten displaced him after Olympics. However, Safin was back on top again on 13 Nov. after winning St Petersburg, and when he took his 2nd Masters Series title of the year at Paris the following week, he also moved to the top of the Entry System rankings, ahead of Sampras. Going into his 1st season-ending champs at Masters Cup he was in with a chance of becoming the youngest to finish the year ranked No. 1, but when he lost sf to Agassi and Kuerten took the title, he was beaten into 2nd place. In other tourns he was r/u Indianapolis, reached sf Copenhagen and Moscow, and appeared in qf French Open (d. Pioline) and Queen's. He was hard on rackets during the year, smashing almost 100 during tourns, and during f v Hrbaty at St Petersburg he needed attention after one such incident left him with graphite in his arm. Back with Mensua and ready to listen to advice, he seemed set for great things again in 2001.

PRINCIPAL 2000 RESULTS – won 7, r/u 2, sf 3 (detailed Grand Slam results follow)
won Barcelona (d. Zabaleta 6–4 6–4, Puerta 6–7 7–6 6–4, Gaudio 6–4 4–6 6–4, N. Lapentti 7–6 7–5, M. Norman 2–6 7–6 6–3, Ferrero 6–3 6–3 6–4), **won** Mallorca (d. Voinea 6–4 7–6, Ruud 3–6 7–5 7–5, Moya 3–6 6–4 7–6, Blanco 6–2 6–2, Tillstrom 3–6 7–5 6–1), **won** Toronto (d. Bjorkman 6–4 1–6 6–3, Pavel 6–7 6–3 6–0, Escude 3–2 ret, Sampras 6–4 3–6 7–6, W. Ferreira 6–2 5–7 6–4, Levy 6–3 1–6 6–4), **won** US Open, **won** Tashkent (d. Ogorodov 6–4 6–4, Kratochvil 4–6 6–1 6–3, J. Delgado 6–4 6–4, Bastl 6–2 6–2, Sanguinetti 6–3 6–4), **won** St Petersburg (d. Kornienko 7–6 6–1, Woodruff 6–3 6–1, Schuttler 6–4 1–6 6–3, Bjorkman 6–4 6–4, Hrbaty 2–6 6–4 6–4), **won** Paris Masters (d. Bastl 7–5 6–4, Grosjean 6–2 7–6, Corretja 7–6 6–3, Ferrero 6–2 6–2); **r/u** Hamburg (d. A. Costa 7–6 7–6, Mantilla 6–3 6–0, Rosset 6–4 7–5, Pioline 7–6 4–6 6–3, Rios 7–6 6–2, lost Kuerten 6–4 5–7 6–4 5–7 7–6), **r/u** Indianapolis (d. Levy 6–4 6–2, Alami 6–4 6–4, Grosjean 0–6 6–3 6–4, Henman 7–5 6–4, lost Corretja 3–6 7–6 7–6); **sf** Copenhagen (d. Lareau 6–4 7–6, Kroslak 3–6 6–0 7–6, Bjorkman 6–4 6–4, lost Vinciguerra 6–3 6–0), **sf** Moscow (d. Schuttler 6–4 6–4, Pozzi 6–1 7–5, Voltchkov 7–6 6–1, lost Prinosil 6–7 6–3 6–3); **sf** Masters Cup.

CAREER GRAND SLAM RECORD
AUSTRALIAN OPEN – Played 2
1999: 3r d. Prinosil 6–2 7–6 7–6, Kuerten 6–3 5–7 4–6 6–3 6–4, lost Kucera [7] 6–2 6–3 6–2. **2000: 1r** lost Stafford 7–6 6–4 6–1.
FRENCH OPEN – Played 3, qf 1
1998: last 16 [unseeded] d. Agassi 5–7 7–5 6–3 3–6 6–2, Kuerten [8] 3–6 7–6 3–6 6–1 6–4, Vacek 6–3 3–6 6–3 7–5, lost Pioline 7–5 4–6 6–7 6–4 6–4. **1999: last 16** [unseeded] d. Kroslak 6–2 4–6 6–3 3–6 6–2, Knippschild 6–3 4–3 ret, Arazi 7–6 3–6 6–4 6–3, lost Hrbaty 6–4 3–6 7–6 6–3. **2000: qf** [seed 12] d. Bastl 6–7 6–1 6–3 6–2, Ilie 7–5 4–6 5–7 6–3 5–0 ret, Haas 7–6 3–6 6–3, Pioline [6] 6–4 1–6 6–3 6–3 7–5, lost M. Norman [3] 6–4 6–3 4–6 7–5.
WIMBLEDON – Played 2
1998: 1r lost Medvedev 6–3 6–4 3–6 6–4. **1999:** Did not play. **2000: 2r** [seed 15] d. Blanco 7–6 6–3 6–4, lost Damm 7–5 7–6 6–3.
US OPEN – Played 3, won 1
1998: last 16 [unseeded] d. Gustafsson 6–2 3–6 6–3 7–6, Dent 6–3 6–1 7–6, Muster 6–4 6–4 1–6 6–3, lost Sampras [1] 6–4 6–3 6–2. **1999: 2r** d. Tillstrom 6–2 5–7 6–4 2–6 6–4, lost Novak 6–2 5–7 6–4 3–6 6–2. **2000: won** [seed 6] d. Guardiola 7–5 6–7 6–4 6–4, Pozzi 6–3 3–6 6–3 3–6 6–4, Grosjean 6–4 7–6 1–6 3–6 7–6, Ferrero [12] 6–1 6–2 6–2, Kiefer [14] 7–5 4–6 7–6 6–3, T. Martin 6–3 7–6 7–6, Sampras [4] 6–4 6–3 6–3.

OLYMPIC RECORD
2000: (Sydney) 1r [seed 1] lost Santoro 1–6 6–1 6–4.

CAREER DAVIS CUP RECORD
1998: April – *World Group 1r USA d. RUS 3–2 in USA (Hard).* R2 lost A. Agassi 6–3 6–3 6–3; R3 (with Y. Kafelnikov) lost T. Martin/R. Reneberg 7–6 6–1 2–6 6–1; R5 lost J. Courier 0–6 6–4 4–6 6–1 6–4. **1998: September** – *World Group qualifying RUS d. JPN 3–1 in JPN (Hard).* R2 d. T. Suzuki 7–6 6–2 6–3; R3 (with Y. Kafelnikov) d. G. Motomura/Suzuki 7–5 6–3 4–6 6–2. **1999: April** – *World Group 1r RUS d. GER 3–2 in GER (Carpet).* R1 lost T. Haas 6–7 6–4 6–3 2–6 9–7; R5 d. N. Kiefer 7–6 6–4 6–4. **July** – *World Group qf RUS d. SVK 3–2 in RUS (Clay).* R1 d. K. Kucera 2–6 6–4 6–2 6–4; R5 d. D. Hrbaty 6–3 4–6 7–5 6–7 6–4. **September** – *World Group sf AUS d. RUS 4–1 in Aus (Grass).* R1 lost L. Hewitt 7–6 6–2 4–6 6–3; R5 lost W. Arthurs 6–3 6–2. **2000: February** – *World Group 1r RUS d. BEL 4–1 in RUS (Carpet).* R2 d. C. Rochus 7–5 3–6 6–2 6–4; R3 (with A. Cherkasov) d. C./O. Rochus 4–6 7–6 1–6 6–1 6–3. **April** – *World Group 2r ESP d. RUS 4–1 in ESP (Clay).* R1 lost A. Corretja 6–4 6–3 5–7 6–1; R3 (with Y. Kafelnikov) d. J. Balcells/Corretja 7–6 2–6 7–6 6–4; R5 lost J. Ferrero 6–0 6–3.

GRAND SLAM CUP RECORD
Has never played.

MASTERS CUP – Played 1, sf 1
2000: sf in rr d. Corretja 6–7 7–5 6–3, d. Hewitt 6–4 6–4, lost Sampras 6–3 6–2 in rr; sf lost Agassi 6–3 6–3.

3 PETE SAMPRAS (USA)

Born: Washington, DC, 12 August 1971. **Lives:** Tampa, Fla. Son of Greek immigrants. **Father:** Sam. **Mother:** Georgia. **Sisters:** Stella and Marion. **Brother:** Gus (older). **Wife:** Bridgette Wilson (married 30 September 2000).

Agent: AMG Sports (Jeff Schwartz). **Coaches:** Paul Annacone; formerly the late Tim Gullikson. Coached first by Dr Pete Fischer and after they split in 1989 Robert Lansdorp coached him on forehand, Larry Easley on volley and Del Little on footwork. Went to Bollettieri Academy and worked with Joe Brandi. They parted in Dec. 1990, to be reunited briefly during 1991, and Sampras started working with Pat Etcheberry for strength.
Personal Trainer: Walter Landers (occasionally).
Turned Pro: 1988.
Height: 6ft 1in (1.83m). **Weight:** 175lb (79kg).

Rankings: 1988: 97; **1989:** 81; **1990:** 5; **1991:** 6; **1992:** 3; **1993:** 1; **1994:** 1; **1995:** 1; **1996:** 1; **1997:** 1; **1998:** 1; **1999:** 3; **2000:** 3. **Highest:** 1 (12 April 1993).

2000 Prize Money: $2,254,598. **Career Earnings:** $41,063,159. **Career Titles:** 63.

Style: Right-handed, ever since changing from 2HB to 1HB in 1987 on advice of his then coach, Dr Pete Fischer. Sampras is one of the finest servers and volleyers on the tour and has flat, orthodox groundstrokes, hit on the rise with awesome power. He is vulnerable to shin splints that have affected his career at important moments, and his stamina is questionable. This is because he suffers from thalassemia minor, a blood disorder in which the sufferer has a low haemoglobin count meaning he will be short of oxygen when exerting himself. Latterly other injuries have affected him (see below).

CAREER HIGHLIGHTS (year: (titles))
1988: Reached sf Schenectady and qf Detroit (d. Mayotte). **1989:** Upset Wilander *en route* to last 16 US Open and reached qf Adelaide. In doubles with Courier won Italian Open, and took 7th place at Masters. **1990: (4)** *US OPEN, Philadelphia, Manchester, GS Cup.* Upset Mayotte in 70-game struggle 1r Australian Open on his way to last 16, unseeded, and in Feb. won his 1st tour title at Philadelphia. In Sept. he won his 1st GS title at US Open and moved into the top 10. At 19 yrs 28 days he was the youngest champion there (the previous youngest was Oliver Campbell, who won in 1890 aged 19 yrs 6 mths). Shin splints had been troubling him since US Open, and although he was able to play ATP World Champ, he did not progress beyond rr. Won inaugural GS Cup and 1st prize $2m. Voted Most Improved Player of The Year. **1991: (4)** *Los Angeles, Indianapolis, Lyon, IBM/ATP World Champ.* Suffered a string of injuries to shin, foot and hamstring, returning to action in Feb. He finished the year in tremendous style by winning ATP World Champ in Frankfurt, the youngest since J. McEnroe in 1979. After Frankfurt sacked Brandi again and sought new coach on eve of D Cup f v France in Lyon where, in his 1st ever tie, he was humiliated by an inspired Leconte on opening day and lost decisive 3rd rubber to Forget. **1992: (5)** *Philadelphia, Kitzbuhel, Cincinnati, Indianapolis, Lyon.* Broke into top 3 after winning Philadelphia and on 5 Oct. took 2nd place ahead of Edberg. In US Open he upset Courier but lost f to Edberg in 4s. In July he won his 1st title on clay at Kitzbuhel. **1993: (8)** *WIMBLEDON, US OPEN, Sydney Outdoor, LIPC, Tokyo Japan Open, Hong Kong, Lyon, Antwerp.* Ousted Edberg from the No. 2 position after Australian Open, closed the gap behind Courier after winning LIPC and finally took over the top spot on 12 April, the 11th man to reach the top since rankings began in 1973. He lost the No. 1 position to Courier again on 22 Aug. after 19 weeks, but regained it 13 Sept. He won his 1st Wimbledon and 2nd US Open to take 8 titles across the year, including 3 in succession with LIPC, Tokyo Japan Open and Hong Kong. His 83 matches won in the year were the most since Lendl's 84 in 1985 and 8 titles the most since Lendl's 10 in 1989. He was also r/u in IBM/ATP World Champ, where he lost to an inspired Stich, and reached sf GS Cup where Korda beat him in an exhausting 4½ hour match. He appeared

in 5 other sf and was in winning US WT Cup squad. **1994: (10)** *AUSTRALIAN OPEN, WIMBLE-DON, Sydney NSW Open, Indian Wells, LIPC, Osaka, Tokyo Japan Open, Italian Open, Antwerp, IBM/ATP Champ.* It was another extraordinary year in which he won 10 tourns – 3 more than anyone else – including a 1st Australian Open, 2nd Wimbledon and 2nd IBM/ATP Champ. After Wimbledon he looked unassailable at the top of the rankings by the biggest margin ever and was the 1st man since Lendl in 1987 to remain unmoved at No.1 all year. He was also the only player in 1994 to win titles on all 4 surfaces. Yet he began surprisingly by losing to qualifier Alami in 1r Qatar, his 1st tourn of the year, but then overcame a stomach upset to retain his LIPC title over Agassi, who agreed to delay their f for 50 mins to allow Sampras to recover. He took a 4-week break from the tour in spring, returning to win Italian Open in May, his 5th consec. tourn success, and extended to 29 matches his winning streak (the longest since Lendl's 31 in 1985), which was ended by Stich at WT Cup after Sampras had held 2 mps. He then lost to Courier in qf French Open, 3 matches short of becoming the 1st man to win a GS on 4 different surfaces. Martin beat him in f Queen's, but at Wimbledon he was superb, sweeping to f, where he demolished Ivanisevic in ss to retain the title. In addition to the quality of his tennis, for which he was voted Player of the Year, his outfits attracted attention, for he wore baggy, knee-length shorts specially designed for him by Nike. By the end of Wimbledon, he had already qualified for the year-end IBM/ATP World Champ – the earliest ever. However, thereafter he was plagued by injury. He withdrew from Washington suffering from tendinitis in left ankle, was out for 6 weeks before US Open and was not fully fit there, suffering from exhaustion, dehydration and blisters as he lost to Yzaga in 5s in last 16. There was further disappointment when US lost D Cup sf to SWE after he was forced to retire v Edberg with hamstring injury, after having hurt his knee beating Larsson on the 1st day. He suffered a rare defeat at the hands of an inspired Becker in sf Stockholm in Oct. and his victory at Antwerp was his 1st since Wimbledon. He was still not invincible at IBM/ATP Champ, where Becker beat him in rr, although the tables were turned in their f. After beating Ivanisevic in magnificent 5s sf in GS Cup, he lost f to Larsson, again affected by fatigue. **1995: (5)** *WIMBLEDON, US OPEN, Indian Wells, Queen's, Paris Open.* His year was overshadowed by the illness of his coach, Tim Gullikson, who was receiving treatment throughout for 4 brain tumours. When the diagnosis was first made and Gullikson was flown back to US during the Australian Open, Sampras broke down during an emotional qf v Courier, recovering from 2 sets down to win the match, although he eventually lost the f to Agassi. It was an unsettled year for him as he flew back and forth over the Atlantic to visit Gullikson between tourns and he was coached on the spot at Wimbledon by Paul Annacone. Won his 1st title of the year at Indian Wells in March, but lost the No.1 ranking to Agassi 10 April after 82 consec. weeks. He regained the top spot on 6 Nov. after winning Paris Open, from which Agassi had withdrawn injured, and with Agassi sidelined for the rest of the year with a chest muscle injury, he finished the year at the top – the 1st since Lendl in 1987 to hold that position for 3 years in succession. Withdrew 2r Monte Carlo v Haarhuis with right ankle injury, returning at Hamburg in May. In an attempt to become only the 5th man to win all 4 GS titles, he changed his schedule to allow himself 2 months on European clay in preparation for French Open, but fell there 1r to Schaller. However, he retained his Wimbledon crown and won a 3rd US Open, taking 5 titles in all from 9 f and was named ATP Player of the Year. He was disappointing at IBM/ATP Champ, where it seemed that, once he had secured his year-end position at the top of the rankings, he lost interest, losing his 3rd rr match to W. Ferreira and capitulating tamely to Chang in ss in sf. In D Cup f, however, he played a heroic part, winning both his singles and then doubles (with Martin) as USA d. RUS 3–2 in Moscow. **1996: (8)** *US OPEN, San Jose, Memphis, Hong Kong, Tokyo Japan Open, Indianapolis, Basle, ATP Champ.* It was a year in which he was challenged for the top ranking at different times by Agassi, Muster, M. Chang and Kafelnikov, although he finished as No. 1 for the 4th time in succession and was again voted Player of the Year. On 29 Jan., after losing 3r Australian Open to Philippoussis, he dropped behind Agassi and Muster to be ranked as low as No. 3 for 1st time since Jan. 1993. He was back at No. 2 on 12 Feb. and returned to the top a week later after winning San Jose. The title at Memphis the following week consolidated his position, but he slipped again after withdrawing qf Rotterdam with a metatarsal sprain of his right ankle. Back-to-back titles at Hong Kong and Tokyo Japan Open saw him return to the top on 14 April and become the 10th man to win 40 titles. Withdrew from Italian Open after the death of his former coach, Tim Gullikson, and missed some of WT Cup with back spasms, although he was back later in the tourn, losing to Kafelnikov. He had played only 2 CC matches before French Open, where he recovered from 2 sets to 0 down v Courier, but was exhausted when losing sf to Kafelnikov again and withdrew from Queen's to recover. He was still below his best at Wimbledon, where Krajicek beat him in qf, and although he claimed to be feeling better at Indianapolis in August, where he won his 1st title since April, he was struggling again at US Open. In 5s of his 3 hr 52 min qf v Corretja, he was ill from severe dehydration, vomiting on court and leaning on his racket between points. However, he saved mp at 7–6 in 5s tb and then, hardly able to stand with stomach pains, produced an ace to take an 8–7 lead, where-upon Corretja served a double-fault. He was almost certainly saved by the US Open rule of play-ing 5s tb. Amazingly, he went on to beat Ivanisevic in 4s sf 2 days later and take the title over M. Chang 2 days after that. His final victory was particularly poignant, coming as it did on what would have been Tim Gullikson's 45th birthday, and he paid tribute to his former coach. He added the title at Basle, r/u Stuttgart Eurocard and sf LIPC, plus 3 qf, and was already con-firmed as World Champion before ATP Champ. There his year finished in triumph as he and Becker played a magnificent f, which Sampras eventually took in 5s, in front of Becker's home crowd. Withdrew from GS Cup with bilateral peroneal tendinitis and ankle pain. **1997: (8)** AUS-TRALIAN OPEN, WIMBLEDON, San Jose, Philadelphia, Cincinnati, GS Cup, Paris Open, ATP Champ. On 28 April he had been at No. 1 for 171 weeks, overtaking J. McEnroe to become 3rd on the all-time list (after Lendl, 270, and Connors, 268), and was still at the top at end of year – only 2nd after Connors to finish No. 1 for 5th consec. year. He won his 1st 17 matches of the year, including a 2nd Australian Open, before a 2r defeat by Ulihrach at Indian Wells heralded a relatively lean patch. He was hampered at LIPC by a wrist injury, although he refused to blame that for his sf defeat by Bruguera, and missed 2 tourns with the injury thereafter. After being beaten qf Queen's by Bjorkman, he went into Wimbledon having failed to reach f in previous 7 tourns. However, he was back on top there, winning the Championships for a 4th time. When he won his next tourn at Cincinnati, his 49th career title, he drew level with Becker at the top amongst active players, moving ahead on his own after taking a 50th at GS Cup. He finished the season with 52 titles, having won all 8 f he played. In French Open, however, he lost to M. Norman 3r while suffering from a stomach upset (although, in his usual style, he refused to make that an excuse for his defeat) and at US Open he fell in 5s tb in last 16 to Korda, who had also stretched him to 5s at Wimbledon. In his 8th consec ATP Champ, he lost 1st match to Moya, but was magnificent thereafter as he swept to his 4th title there, finishing the year head and shoulders above the rest of the pack. After leading US to f of D Cup, he was forced to retire injured v Larsson in 2nd rubber when trailing 6–3 6–7 1–2 as USA went down 5–0 to SWE. Voted ATP Player of the Year. **1998: (4)** WIMBLEDON, Philadelphia, Atlanta, Vienna. Having been No. 1 for 102 consecutive weeks, 3rd-longest behind Connors (160) and Lendl (157), he was displaced at the top of the rankings on 30 March by Rios. Although he returned to the top on 27 April, his position was never totally secure and he slipped down again on 10 Aug. after losing qf Toronto to Agassi in his 1st tourn back after minor surgery on his foot in July to remove a plantar's wart. He was back at the top on 31 August, but with both Moya and Rafter close behind, he found himself by Oct. needing every win he could muster to achieve a new record of finishing the year at No. 1 for 6 consec. seasons. He did manage it, but the record was not certain until the very last moment, and he owed much to Becker, who gave up his WC at Vienna to enable Sampras to play there – and win the title. By ATP Champ only Rios was threatening his position, and when the No. 2 withdrew after 1 match and Sampras won all his matches in rr, he had achieved his goal, whereupon he lost sf 7–6 fs to Corretja. That battle for the top year-end ranking put a tremendous strain on him and he faced an increasing struggle to find motivation for anything other than GS; even in those tourns he could not always give his best, except for Wimbledon, where he confirmed his supremacy with his 5th Championship title. Underprepared for Australian Open following the calf injury suffered in D Cup final, he fell to Kucera in qf; at French Open he lost 2r to Delgado, ranked 98 at the time; and at US Open he was leading in 3s sf v Rafter when he injured his leg, losing mobility and eventually the match. Fitness was often elusive during the year and he withdrew Hong Kong with a shoulder injury suffered at LIPC; indeed, a back injury might have prevented him from playing ATP Champ had the top ranking not been at stake. Atlanta was his 1st CC title since Rome 1994 and only 3rd of career, but his 3r loss to Santoro at Monte Carlo was his worst since Svensson defeated him at Munich in 1990. He also won Philadelphia, was r/u San Jose and Cincinnati, and reached sf Stuttgart Eurocard, plus qf Los Angeles and Lyon. **1999: (5)** WIMBLEDON, Queen's, Los Angeles, Cincinnati, ATP Champ. By any other standards his year would have been considered an exceptional one, but by his own it was fraught with frustration. His position at the top of the rankings became ever less certain and by Nov., having been out of action for most of the previous three months, he had tumbled as low as No. 5, although he ended the season back at No. 3, behind Agassi and Kafelnikov. It was Moya who first displaced him on 15 March – for 2 weeks – and then Kafelnikov on 3 May. A poor showing at French Open, where he fell 2r to Medvedev, resulted in a slide to No. 3 behind Kafelnikov and Rafter, but with the grass season he came into his own, returning to No. 1 on 14 June after winning Queen's. The climax of his year followed when he won his 6th Wimbledon – a record for the open era and just 1 behind William Renshaw in the all-time records – and equalled Emerson's record of 12 GS titles, overtaking Borg and Laver. He was probably lucky at Wimbledon that Philippoussis ret with a knee injury when ahead in their qf, but in f v Agassi there was no doubt about Sampras's supremacy. Ironically it was Agassi who next replaced him at the top of the rankings on 5 July as Sampras took 3rd place again behind Rafter. When he returned to the top again on 2 Aug., it was his 271st week in total as No. 1, overtaking Lendl's record, but injury prevented him remaining there for long. He struggled all year with exhaustion, which kept him out of Australian Open, a leg injury, right hip flexor strain and a herniated disc, which prevented him playing US Open and GS Cup and threatened to keep him out of ATP Champ, for which he comfortably qualified. In the event, not only was he fit, but he finished the year on a high note by winning the title, again imposing a convincing defeat in f on Agassi, who had beaten him equally convincingly in rr. In addition to Wimbledon, Queen's and ATP Champ, he won Los Angeles and Cincinnati and reached sf San Jose (ret with left leg injury) and qf LIPC and Indianapolis (ret right hip strain). As he had in 1998, he declined to play D Cup until persuaded to play doubles rubber in qf v. Australia, which he won – playing with O'Brien. **2000: (2)** *WIMBLEDON, Ericsson Open.* He was again restricted by a string of injuries to his hip, lower back, foot and ankle, as well as apparent lack of motivation for all but the GS tourns, so that, despite the ATP ruling that all Masters Series events are mandatory, he played only 5 – and only 13 tourns all year. Once more the climax of his year came at Wimbledon, where his 7th title equalled William Renshaw's record and his 13th GS title in all beat Emerson's career record. He managed it despite tendinitis in left foot and ankle which left him unable to practise between matches. Earlier Agassi had beaten him in sf Australian Open and his hopes of capturing an elusive 1st French Open were dashed when he lost 8–6 fs 1r to Philippoussis. He dropped as low as No. 4 in the Entry System behind Agassi, M. Norman and Kuerten after that, although he was back at the top after US Open, where he was r/u to Safin, who eventually displaced him on 20 Nov. His only other title came at Ericsson Open, with r/u showing at Queen's as well as US Open, and appearances in sf Australian Open, plus qf Indian Wells and Toronto, where he let slip 3 mps in fs tb v Safin. At Masters Cup, where he continued his unbroken sequence of appearances since 1990, he lost a close sf to an inspired Kuerten.

PRINCIPAL 2000 RESULTS – won 2, r/u 2, sf 1 (detailed Grand Slam results follow)
won Ericsson Open (d. Moya 6–1 6–4, Vinciguerra 5–7 7–6 6–4, Rusedski 6–3 6–3, N. Lapentti 6–4 7–6, Hewitt 6–3 3–6 6–1, Kuerten 6–1 6–7 7–6 7–6), **won** Wimbledon; **r/u** Queen's (d. Parmar 6–7 6–4 6–3, Llodra 6–1 7–6, B. Bryan 6–4 6–4, Sanguinetti 7–5 6–3, lost Hewitt 6–4 6–4), **r/u** US Open; **sf** Australian Open.

CAREER GRAND SLAM RECORD
AUSTRALIAN OPEN – Played 9, won 2, r/u 1, sf 2, qf 1
1989: 1r lost Saceanu 6–4 6–4 7–6. **1990: last 16** d. Mayotte [6] 7–6 6–7 4–6 7–5 12–10, Arrese 0–6 6–2 3–6 6–1 6–3, Woodbridge 7–5 6–4 6–2, lost Noah [12] 6–3 6–4 3–6 6–2. **1991–92:** Did not play. **1993: sf** [seed 3] d. Steeb 6–1 6–2 6–1, Larsson 6–3 3–6 6–3 6–4, Antonitsch 6–7 6–4 6–2, Washington [13] 6–3 6–4 6–4, Steven 6–3 6–2 6–3, lost Edberg [2] 7–6 6–3 7–6. **1994: won** [seed 1] d. Eagle 6–4 6–0 7–6, Kafelnikov 6–3 2–6 6–3 1–6 9–7, Simian 7–5 6–1 1–6 6–4, Lendl [15] 7–6 6–2 7–5, Gustafsson [10] 7–6 2–6 6–3 7–6, Courier [3] 6–3 6–4 6–4, Martin [9] 7–6 6–4 6–4). **1995: r/u** [seed 1] d. Pozzi 6–3 6–2 6–0, Kroslak 6–2 6–0 6–1, Jonsson 6–1 6–2 6–4, Larsson [15] 4–6 6–7 7–5 6–4 6–4, Courier [9] 6–7 6–7 6–3 6–4 6–3, Chang [5] 6–7 6–3 6–4 6–4, lost Agassi [2] 4–6 6–1 7–6 6–4. **1996: 3r** seed 1. d. Fromberg 7–5 6–3 6–2, Joyce 3–6 6–3 6–4 6–4, lost Philippoussis 6–4 7–6 7–6. **1997: won** [seed 1] d. Pescariu 6–2 6–4 6–2, Voinea 3–6 6–2 6–3 6–2, Woodforde 6–1 6–0 6–1, Hrbaty 6–7 6–3 6–4 3–6 6–4, A. Costa [10] 6–3 6–7 6–1 3–6 6–2, Muster [5] 6–1 7–6 6–3, Moya 6–2 6–3 6–3. **1998: qf** [seed 1] d. Schalken 7–5 6–4 6–2, Sanguinetti 6–2 6–1 6–2, Gustafsson 7–5 6–3 6–4, Arazi 7–6 6–4 6–4, lost Kucera 6–4 6–2 6–7 6–3. **1999:** Did not play. **2000: sf** [seed 3] d. Arthurs 6–4 7–5 6–4, Tillstrom 3–6 7–6 6–1, W. Black 6–3 6–3 7–5 6–3, Dosedel 6–1 6–2 3–6 6–1, Woodruff 7–5 6–3 6–3, lost Agassi [1] 6–4 3–6 6–7 7–6 6–1.
FRENCH OPEN – Played 11, sf 1, qf 3
1989: 2r d. Lozano 6–3 6–2 6–4, lost Chang [15] 6–1 6–1 6–1. **1991: 2r** [seed 0] d. Muster 4–6 4–6 6–4 6–1 6–4, lost Champion 6–3 6–1 6–1. **1992: qf** [seed 3] d. Rosset 7–6 4–6 6–4 3–6 6–3, Prades 7–6 6–4 7–6, R.

Gilbert 6–3 6–2 6–3, Steeb 6–4 6–3 6–2, lost Agassi [11] 7–6 6–2 6–1. **1993: qf** [seed 1] d. Cherkasov 6–1 6–2 3–6 6–1, Ondruska 7–5 6–0 6–3, Svensson 6–4 6–4 6–2, Washington [16] 6–3 7–6 6–1, lost Bruguera [10] 6–3 4–6 6–1 6–4. **1994: qf** [seed 1] d. A. Costa 6–3 6–4 6–4, Rios 7–6 7–6 6–4, Haarhuis 6–1 6–4 6–1, Tillstroem 6–4 6–4 1–6 6–4, lost Courier [7] 6–4 5–7 6–4 6–4. **1995: 1r** [seed 2] lost Schaller 7–6 4–6 6–7 6–2 6–4. **1996: sf** [seed 1] d. Gustafsson 6–1 7–5 7–6, Bruguera 6–3 6–4 6–7 2–6 6–3, Martin 3–6 6–4 7–5 4–6 6–2, Draper 6–4 7–5 6–2, Courier [7] 6–7 4–6 6–4 6–4 6–4, lost Kafelnikov [6] 7–6 6–0 6–2. **1997: 3r** [seed 1] d. Santoro 6–3 7–5 6–1, Clavet 6–1 6–2 6–2, lost M. Norman 6–2 6–4 2–6 6–4. **1998: 2r** [seed 1] d. T. Martin 6–4 6–3 6–3, lost Delgado 7–6 6–3 6–4. **1999: 2r** [seed 2] d. Marin 6–7 6–4 7–5 6–7 6–4, lost Medvedev 7–5 1–6 6–4 6–3. **2000: 1r** [seed 2] lost Philippoussis 4–6 7–5 7–6 4–6 8–6.

WIMBLEDON – Played 12, won 7, sf 1, qf 1

1989: 1r lost Woodbridge 7–5 7–6 5–7 6–3. **1990: 1r** lost Van Rensburg 7–6 7–5 7–6. **1991: 2r** [seed 8] d. Marcellino 6–1 6–2 6–2, lost Rostagno 6–4 3–6 7–6 6–4. **1992: sf** [seed 5] d. Cherkasov 6–1 6–3 6–3, Woodbridge 7–6 7–6 6–7 6–4, S. Davis 6–1 6–0 6–2, Boetsch 6–3 7–5 7–6, Stich [3] 6–3 6–2 6–4, lost Ivanisevic [8] 6–7 7–6 6–4 6–2. **1993: won** [seed 1] d. Borwick 6–7 6–3 7–6 6–3, Morgan 6–4 7–6 6–4, Black 6–4 6–1 6–1, Foster 6–1 6–2 7–6, Agassi [8] 6–2 6–2 3–6 6–4, Becker [4] 7–6 6–4 6–4, Courier [3] 7–6 7–6 3–6 6–3. **1994: won** [seed 1] d. Palmer 7–6 7–5 6–3, Reneberg 6–3 6–4 6–2, C. Adams 6–1 6–2 6–4, Vacek 6–4 6–1 7–6, Chang [10] 6–4 6–1 6–3, Martin [6] 6–4 6–4 3–6 6–3, Ivanisevic [4] 7–6 7–6 6–0. **1995: won** [seed 2] d. Braasch 7–6 6–7 6–4 6–1, Henman 6–2 6–3 7–6, Palmer 4–6 6–4 6–1 6–2, Rusedski 6–4 6–3 7–5, Matsuoka 6–7 6–3 6–4 6–2, Ivanisevic [4] 7–6 4–6 7–6. **1996: qf** [seed 1] d. Reneberg 4–6 6–4 6–3 6–3, Philippoussis 7–6 6–4 6–4, Kucera 6–4 6–3 6–7 7–6, Pioline [16] 6–4 6–4 6–2, lost Krajicek 7–5 7–6 6–4. **1997: won** [seed 1] d. Tillstrom 6–4 6–4 6–2, Dreekmann 7–6 7–5 7–5, B. Black 6–1 6–2 6–2, Korda [16] 6–4 6–3 6–7 6–7 6–4, Becker [8] 6–1 6–7 6–1 6–4, Woodbridge 6–2 6–1 7–6, Pioline 6–4 6–2 6–4. **1998: won** [seed 1] d. Hrbaty 6–3 6–3 6–2, Tillstrom 6–4 6–4 7–6, Enqvist 6–3 7–6 7–6, Grosjean 6–3 6–4 6–4, Philippoussis 7–6 6–4 6–4, Henman [12] 6–3 4–6 7–5 6–3, Ivanisevic [14] 6–7 7–6 6–4 3–6 6–2. **1999: won** [seed 1] d. S. Draper 6–3 6–4 6–4, Lareau 6–4 6–2 6–3, Sapsford 3–6 6–4 7–5, Nestor 6–3 6–4 6–2, Philippoussis [7] 4–6 2–1 ret, Henman [6] 3–6 6–4 6–3 6–4, Agassi [4] 6–3 6–4 7–5. **2000: won** [seed 1] d. Vanek 6–4 6–4 6–2, Kucera 6–3 6–3 6–4, Gimelstob 2–6 6–4 6–2 6–2, Bjorkman 6–3 6–2 7–5, Gambill 6–4 7–6 6–4, Voltchkov 7–6 6–2 6–4, Rafter [12] 6–7 7–6 6–4 6–2.

US OPEN – Played 12, won 4, r/u 2, sf 1, qf 1

1988: 1r lost Yzaga 6–7 6–7 6–4 7–5 6–2. **1989: last 16** d. Moreno 6–3 5–7 6–4 6–1, Wilander [5] 5–7 6–3 1–6 6–1 6–4, Yzaga 4–6 6–4 6–3 6–2, lost Berger [11] 7–5 6–2 6–1. **1990: won** [seed 12] d. Goldie 6–1 7–5 6–1, Lundgren 6–4 6–3 6–3, Hlasek 6–3 6–4 6–4, Muster [6] 6–7 6–4 6–3, Lendl [3] 6–4 7–6 3–6 4–6 6–2, J. McEnroe 6–2 6–4 3–6 6–3, Agassi [4] 6–4 6–3 6–2. **1991: qf** [seed 6] d. van Rensburg 6–0 6–3 6–2, Ferreira 6–1 6–2 2–2 ret'd, Simian 7–6 6–4 6–3, Wheaton [11] 3–6 6–2 6–2 6–4, lost Courier [4] 6–2 7–6 7–6. **1992: r/u** [seed 3] d. di Lucia 6–3 7–5 6–2, Damm 7–5 6–1 6–2, Martin 7–6 2–6 4–6 7–5 6–4, Forget [13] 6–3 1–6 1–6 6–4 6–0, Courier [1] 6–1 3–6 6–2 6–2, lost Edberg [2] 3–6 6–4 7–6 6–2. **1993: won** [seed 2] d. Santoro 6–3 6–1 6–2, Vacek 6–4 5–7 6–2 7–6, Boetsch 6–4 6–4 7–6, Enqvist 6–4 6–4 7–6, M. Chang [7] 6–7 7–6 6–1 6–1, Volkov [14] 6–4 6–3 6–2, Pioline [15] 6–4 6–4 6–3. **1994: last 16** [seed 1] d. Ullyett 6–2 6–2 6–2, Vacek 6–3 6–4 6–4, Smith 4–6 6–2 6–4 6–3, lost Yzaga 3–6 6–3 4–6 7–6 7–5. **1995: won** [seed 2] d. Meligeni 6–0 6–3 6–4, Yzaga 6–1 6–4 6–3, Philippoussis 6–7 7–5 7–5 6–3, Martin [15] 7–6 6–3 6–4, B. Black 7–6 6–4 6–0, Courier [14] 7–5 4–6 6–4 7–5, Agassi [1] 6–4 6–3 4–6 7–5. **1996: won** [seed 1] d. Szymanski 6–2 6–2 6–1, Novak 6–3 1–6 6–3 4–6 6–4, Volkov 6–3 6–4 6–2, Philippoussis 6–3 6–3 6–4, Corretja 7–6 5–7 5–7 6–4 7–6, Ivanisevic [4] 6–3 6–4 6–7 6–3, M. Chang [2] 6–1 6–4 7–6. **1997: last 16** [seed 1] d. Larkham 6–3 6–1 6–3, Baur 7–5 6–4 6–3, Radulescu 6–3 6–4 6–4, lost Korda [15] 6–7 7–5 7–6 3–6 7–6. **1998: sf** [seed 1] d. Goellner 6–3 6–2 6–2, Goldstein 7–6 2–6 6–3 6–3, Tillstrom 6–2 6–3 6–1, Safin 6–4 6–3 6–2, Kucera [9] 6–3 7–5 6–4, lost Rafter [3] 6–7 6–4 2–6 6–4 6–3. **1999: Did not play. 2000: r/u** [seed 4] d. Damm 7–6 7–5 6–4, Gimelstob 6–3 6–1 6–3, Calleri 7–6 7–6 6–3, H. T. Lee 7–6 6–2 6–4, Krajicek 4–6 7–6 6–4 6–2, Hewitt [9] 7–6 6–4 7–6, lost Safin [6] 6–4 6–3 6–3.

OLYMPIC RECORD

1992: (Barcelona) last 16 [seed 3] d. Masur 6–1 7–6 6–4, Yzaga 6–3 6–0 3–6 6–1, lost Cherkasov [13] 6–7 1–6 7–5 6–0 6–3.

CAREER DAVIS CUP RECORD

1991: November – *World Group Final FRA d. USA 3–1 in FRA (Carpet).* R2 lost H. Leconte 6–4 7–5 6–4; R4 lost G. Forget 7–6 3–6 6–3 6–4. **1992: January** – *World Group 1R USA d. ARG 5–0 in USA (Hard).* R1 d. M. Jaite 3–6 6–4 6–2 6–4; R4 d. A. Mancini 6–4 6–1. **March** – *World Group qf USA d. TCH 3–2 in USA (Hard).* R1 d. K. Novacek 6–3 6–4 6–2; R4 lost P. Korda 6–4 3–6 2–6 6–3. **September** – *World Group sf USA d. SWE 4–1 in USA (Clay).* R3 (with J. McEnroe) d. S. Edberg/A. Jarryd 6–1 6–7 4–6 6–3 6–3. **December** – *World Group Final USA d. SWZ 3–1 in USA (Hard).* R3 (with J. McEnroe) d. J. Hlasek/M. Rosset 6–7 6–7 7–5 6–1 6–2. **1994: July** – *World Group 2r USA d. NED 3–2 in NED (Hard).* R2 d. J. Eltingh 6–2 6–2 6–0; R4 lost R. Krajicek 2–6 7–5 7–6 7–5. **September** – *World Group sf SWE d. USA 3–2 in SWE (Carpet).* R2 d. M. Larsson 6–7 6–4 6–2 7–6; R4 lost S. Edberg 6–3 ret'd. **1995: March** – *World Group qf USA d. ITA 5–0 in ITA (Clay).* R2 d. R. furlan 7–6 6–3 6–0; R 4 d. A. Gaudenzi 6–3 1–6 6–3. **September** – *World Group sf USA d. SWE 4–1 in USA (Hard).* R1 d. T. Enqvist 6–3 6–4 3–6 6–3; R5 d. M. Wilander 2–6 7–6 6–3. **December** – *World Group Final USA d. RUS 3–2 in Moscow (Clay).* R1 d. A. Chesnokov 3–6 6–4 6–3 6–7 6–4. R3 (+ T. Martin) d. Y.

Kafelnikov/A. Olhovskiy) 7–5 6–4 6–3; R4 d. Kafelnikov 6–2 6–4 7–6. **1997: September** – *World Group sf USA d. AUS 4–1 in USA (Hard).* R2 d. M. Philippoussis 6–1 6–2 7–6; R3 (with T. Martin) lost T. Woodbridge/M. Woodforde 3–6 7–6 6–2 6–4; R4 d. P. Rafter 6–7 6–1 6–1 6–4. **November** – *World Group Final SWE d. USA 5–0 in SWE (Hard).* R2 lost M. Larsson 3–6 7–6 2–1 ret. **1999: July** – *World Group qf AUS d. USA 4–1 in USA (Hard).* R3 (with A. O'Brien) d. S. Stolle/M. Woodforde 6–4 6–3 3–6 4–6 6–3. **2000: April** – *World Group qf USA d. CZE 3–2 in USA (Carpet).* R1 lost J. Novak 7–6 6–3 6–2; R5 d. C. Dosedel 6–4 6–4 7–6.

GRAND SLAM CUP RECORD – Played 6, won 2, r/u 1, sf 1, qf 1

1990: won [seed 4] d. Cherkasov 5–7 6–2 7–5, Ivanisevic [5] 7–6 6–7 8–6, Chang 6–3 6–4 6–4, Gilbert 6–3 6–4 6–2. **1992: sf** [seed 3] d. Volkov 6–3 6–4, Leconte 7–6 6–4, lost Stich 7–6 7–6 3–6 7–6. **1993: sf** [seed 1] d. Muster 6–3 6–1, Chang 7–6 6–3, lost Korda 3–6 7–6 3–6 7–6 13–11. **1994: r/u** [seed 1] d. Yzaga 6–2 6–4, Chang [8] 6–4 6–3, Ivanisevic [6] 5–7 6–3 6–4 6–7 10–8, lost Larsson 7–6 4–6 7–6 6–4. **1995: qf** [seed 1] d. P. McEnroe 6–1 7–6, lost Ivanisevic [8] def. **1997: won** [seed 1] d. Mantilla 6–4 3–6 6–2, Bjorkman [8] 7–6 6–4, Rusedski [4] 3–6 7–6 7–6 6–2, Rafter [2] 6–2 6–4 7–5.

GRAND PRIX MASTERS/ATP TOUR CHAMPIONSHIP/MASTERS CUP – Played 11, won 5, r/u 1, sf 4

1990: 3rd in rr lost Edberg 7–5 6–4, lost Agassi 6–4 6–2, d. E. Sanchez 6–2 6–4. **1991: won** in rr d. Stich 6–2 7–6, d. Agassi 6–3 1–6 6–3, lost Becker 6–4 6–7 6–1; sf d. Lendl 6–2 6–3; f d. Courier 3–6 7–6 6–3 6–4. **1992: sf** in rr d. Becker 7–6 7–6, d. Edberg 6–3 3–6 7–5, d. Korda 3–6 6–3 6–3; sf lost Courier 7–6 7–6. **1993: r/u** in rr d. Ivanisevic 6–3 4–6 6–2, d. Edberg 6–3 7–6, d. Bruguera 6–3 1–6 6–3; sf d. Medvedev 6–3 6–0; f lost Stich 7–6 2–6 7–6 6–2. **1994: won** in rr lost Becker 7–5 7–5, d. Edberg 4–6 6–3 7–6, d. Ivanisevic 6–3 6–4; sf d. Agassi 4–6 7–6 6–3; f d. Becker 4–6 6–3 7–5 6–4. **1995: sf** in rr d. Kafelnikov 6–3 6–3, d. Becker 6–2 7–6, lost W. Ferreira 7–6 6–3; sf lost M. Chang 6–4 6–4. **1996: won** in rr d. Agassi 6–2 6–1, lost Becker 7–6 7–6, d. Kafelnikov 6–4 6–4; sf d. Ivanisevic 6–7 7–6 7–5; f d. Becker 3–6 7–6 7–6 6–7 6–4. **1997: won** in rr lost Moya 6–3 6–7 6–2, d. Rusedski 6–4 7–5, d. Rafter 6–4 6–1; sf d. Bjorkman 6–3 6–4; f d. Kafelnikov 6–3 6–2 6–2. **1998: sf** in rr d. Moya 6–3 6–3, d. Kucera 6–2 6–1, d. Kafelnikov 6–2 6–4; sf lost Corretja 4–6 6–3 7–6. **1999: won** in rr d. Kuerten 6–2 6–3, lost Agassi 6–2 6–2, d. Lapentti 7–6 7–6; sf d. Kiefer 6–3 6–3, f d. Agassi 6–1 7–5 6–4. **2000: sf** in rr lost Hewitt 7–5 6–0, d. Corretja 7–6 7–5, d. Safin 6–3 6–2; sf lost Kuerten 6–7 6–3 6–4.

It was quite a year for Pete Sampras with marriage and a 13th Grand Slam title as the highlights. (Stephen Wake)

4 MAGNUS NORMAN (SWE)

Born: Filipstad, 30 May 1976. **Lives:** Monte Carlo, Monaco.
Father: Leif. **Mother:** Lena, formerly a Swedish national
swimmer.
Brother: Marcus (younger).
Girlfriend: Martina Hingis for much of 2000.
Agent: IMG (Per Hjertqvist). **Coach:** Fredrik Rosengren;
formerly Martin Bohm and Thomas Hogstedt.
Turned Pro: 1995. **Height:** 6ft 2in (1.88m).
Weight: 165lb (74kg).
Rankings: 1992: 679; **1993:** 733; **1994:** 686; **1995:** 174;
1996: 86; **1997:** 22; **1998:** 52; **1999:** 15; **2000:** 4.
Highest: 2 (12 June 2000).
2000 Prize Money: $1,846,269.
Career Earnings: $3,580,972. **Career Titles:** 12.

Style: A strong baseliner, typical of today's players, with a powerful forehand and penetrating double-handed backhand, he pounds away relentlessly, endeavouring to wear his opponents down with consistency, accuracy, power and stamina. His phenomenal work rate makes him one of the strongest and fittest men on the Tour and his mental strength is equally impressive.

CAREER HIGHLIGHTS (Year: (titles))
He might have concentrated on Bandy (a form of ice-hockey) in which he was a member of the national under-16 team, but decided in the end to concentrate on tennis. **1995:** He reached his qf on the main tour at Bastad and upset Berasategui at Palermo, as well as making his mark on the satellite circuits. **1996:** Reached sf Bournemouth and Stockholm, qf Casablanca and won 2 Challenger titles. **1997: (1)** *Bastad.* He caused one of the upsets of the year at French Open when he removed Sampras 3r, following with Rosset to reach qf, unseeded. He upset Agassi and Korda *en route* to sf Atlanta, then at Wimbledon surprised Ivanisevic in an epic 2r battle, prevailing 14–12 5s. He followed with his 1st tour title at Bastad, having saved mp when 1–5 down 3s v Voinea. He continued to challenge top players by upsetting Bruguera and Muster on his way to f Ostrava, where he was forced to retire with a thigh injury that also kept him out of Stuttgart. He reached sf St Polten and Amsterdam, plus qf St Petersburg, Chennai and Basle (d. Bjorkman), finishing the year in top 25. During his long fs v Ivanisevic at Wimbledon that went to 14–12, he suffered irregular heartbeat for 3rd time in his career, although this time it lasted only 30 sec. (as opposed to 40 min. before), and he was able to continue after receiving treatment on court. He underwent surgery later in year to correct this irregular heartbeat/heart murmur, which relates to a hereditary condition and was not considered to be dangerous. **1998: (1)** *Amsterdam.* Finding it hard to cope with the pressure after his successes the previous season, he struggled somewhat. He won Amsterdam and was r/u Umag, but his only other qf appearance was at Halle (d. Siemerink). In his D Cup debut year he was part of the SWE team that won the title over ITA. **1999: (5)** *Orlando, Stuttgart Mercedes, Umag, Long Island, Shanghai.* Inspired by his new coach Rosengren, he regained his perspective and enthusiasm. After winning Orlando in April he added Stuttgart Mercedes and Umag (d. Moya) back-to-back in July, then 4 weeks later took his 1st HC title at Long Island (unseeded, d. Kafelnikov and Corretja). In Oct. he collected a 5th title at Shanghai, saving 4 mps to d. Rios on the way, and broke into top 20 1st time. Only Sampras and Agassi, also with 5 titles in the year, won as many as he did. In what seemed to be an all-or-nothing year, his only other qf appearance was at Bastad, until Nov. when he reached sf Stockholm (d. Lapentti). At US Open, where he was unseeded, he upset Mantilla 1r, but was forced to withdraw 4r with a back strain. **2000: (5)** *Auckland, Rome, Bastad, Long Island, Shanghai.* He continued his fine form by following sf Adelaide with the title at Auckland and sf appearance at Australian Open, where he upset Kiefer, but 'froze' v Kafelnikov. These results took him into top 10 in the Entry System rankings 1st time, and his 1st Masters Series title in Rome gave him the lead in the Champions Race, overtaking Agassi. He then swept to his 1st GS f at French Open, where he put up a spirited but unsuccessful fight v Kuerten, who displaced him at the head of the Champions Race. He was back at the top for a while after winning Bastad, until a poor showing in Toronto saw him slip

back down again. In the Entry System rankings he went to No. 3 behind Agassi and Sampras, displacing Kafelnikov, and on 12 June reached his highest point at No. 2 ahead of Sampras. However, he was unable to maintain that level as his form fell away later in year, apart from a return to his winning ways with the title at Shanghai in Oct. He made 2 other sf appearances across the year at Barcelona and Stockholm and also reached qf Rotterdam, Indian Wells and Hamburg. His best year yet finished on a disappointing note as he failed to win a single match at Masters Cup, in his 1st season-ending champs, and he settled at No. 4 in the rankings, having at one time looked a potential No. 1.

PRINCIPAL 2000 RESULTS – won 5, r/u 1, sf 4 (detailed Grand Slam results follow)
won Auckland (d. F. Costa 6–2 7–5, Gambill 6–3 6–3, Rosset 6–2 6–2, Gaudio 6–4 7–5, M. Chang 3–6 6–3 7–5), **won** Rome (d. Grosjean 6–3 7–6, Moya 6–4 6–2, Medvedev 7–6 6–1, Mantilla 6–4 6–3, Hewitt 6–3 6–0, Kuerten 6–4 6–2), **won** Bastad (d. C. Rochus 6–2 6–1, Vanek 6–2 6–2, Massu 6–2 6–4, Ljubicic 6–2 7–5, Vinciguerra 6–2 6–7 7–6), **won** Long Island (d. Bjorkman 6–4 6–1, Taino 6–4 6–1, El Aynaoui 6–3 2–6 6–3, Krajicek 4–6 6–4 7–6, Enqvist 6–3 5–7 7–5), **won** Shanghai (d. Gaudenzi 6–3 6–7 6–4, Sa 6–4 6–2, Bjorkman 7–6 0–6 6–2, Chang 6–3 6–1, Schalken 6–4 4–6 6–3); **r/u** French Open; **sf** Adelaide (d. S. Draper 6–4 6–4, Fromberg 7–5 6–4, A. Martin 6–4 6–3, lost Enqvist 3–6 6–2 6–2), **sf** Australian Open, **sf** Barcelona (d. Schuttler 7–6 6–3, Krajicek 7–6 6–4, El Aynaoui 6–2 6–4, lost Safin 2–6 7–6 6–3), **sf** Stockholm (d. Ruud 6–1 6–2, Gambill w/o, Schalken 6–7 7–5 7–6, lost Johansson 7–6 6–2).

CAREER GRAND SLAM RECORD
AUSTRALIAN OPEN – Played 5, sf 1
1996: 1r lost Raoux 6–3 7–6 6–1. **1997: 1r** lost Woodruff 6–4 6–1 6–1. **1998: 1r** lost Lareau 6–4 6–7 7–6 6–7 7–5. **1999: 2r** d. Van Lottum 6–4 5–7 2–6 6–2 7–5, lost Lapentti 7–6 3–6 2–6 6–3 6–4. **2000: sf** [seed 12] d. Mamiit 7–5 6–4 3–6 6–3, Pozzi 6–4 6–3 6–4, Bjorkman 6–4 6–4 7–6, Hewitt 6–3 6–1 7–6, Kiefer [4] 3–6 6–3 6–1 7–6, lost Kafelnikov [2] 6–1 6–2 6–4.
FRENCH OPEN – Played 5, r/u 1, qf 1
1996: 2r d. Hadad 4–6 6–3 6–2 6–0, lost Kucera 7–6 6–4 6–7 4–6 6–2. **1997: qf** [unseeded] d. Rusedski 6–3 6–2 3–6 4–6 9–7, Paes 6–3 6–2 3–6 6–3, Sampras [1] 6–2 6–4 2–6 6–4, Rosset [15] 4–6 6–3 7–6 6–3, lost Dewulf 6–2 6–7 6–4 6–3. **1998: 2r** d. Karbacher 6–2 1–6 6–3 6–1, lost W. Ferreira 6–4 6–4 6–4. **1999: 1r** lost Karbacher 7–6 4–6 6–2 6–4. **2000: r/u** [seed 3] d. Guardiola 6–4 6–4 6–0, Santoro 6–1 6–4 6–2, Sargsian 6–4 6–1 6–2, Medvedev 6–0 6–4 6–2, Safin [12] 6–4 6–3 4–6 7–5, Squillari 6–1 6–4 6–3, lost Kuerten [5] 6–2 6–3 2–6 7–6.
WIMBLEDON – Played 4
1997: 3r d. Herrera 7–6 6–1 6–4, Ivanisevic [2] 6–3 2–6 7–6 4–6 14–12, lost Steven 6–7 6–2 6–3 6–1. **1998: 1r** lost A. Costa 7–5 7–5 7–6. **1999: 3r** d. Gaudio 6–4 7–5 7–5, Santoro 6–2 6–3 7–6, lost Rusedski [9] 6–3 6–4 7–5. **2000: 2r** [seed 3] d. Woodforde 6–4 6–2 2–0 ret, lost O. Rochus 6–4 2–6 6–4 6–7 6–1.
US OPEN – Played 4
1997: 2r d. Kucera 6–7 6–4 6–2 6–3, lost Rafter [13] 6–2 6–1 6–2. **1998: 2r** d. Nestor 7–6 6–7 6–7 6–4 6–4, lost Gambill 6–4 6–2 6–7 6–3. **1999: last 16** [unseeded] d. Mantilla 1–6 6–1 6–2 6–4, Pozzi 6–4 6–3 6–4, Fromberg 4–6 6–3 6–1 6–3, lost Kuerten [5] 7–6 ret. **2000: last 16** [seed 3] d. Goldstein 7–5 6–4 6–4, Saulnier 6–3 6–4 6–3, Mirnyi 3–6 4–6 7–6 6–4 7–6, lost Kiefer [seed 14] 6–2 6–7 6–1 6–3.

OLYMPIC RECORD
2000: (Sydney) 3r [seed 3] d. Pavel 6–7 6–3 10–8, Srichaphan 7–5 6–2, lost Di Pasquale 7–6 7–6.

CAREER DAVIS CUP RECORD
1998: April – *World Group 1r SWE d. SVK 3–2 in SVK (Clay).* R1 lost D. Hrbaty 7–6 4–6 6–4 3–6 6–2; R4 d. K. Kucera 6–3 4–6 6–3 3–6 6–3. **December** – *World Group final SWE d. ITA 4–1 in ITA (Clay).* R1 d. A. Gaudenzi 6–7 7–6 4–6 6–3 6–6 ret; R5 lost D. Nargiso 6–2 6–3. **1999: September** – *World Group qualifying AUT d. SWE 3–2 in AUT (Clay).* R1 lost M. Hipfl 6–4 6–3 6–4; R4 d. S. Koubek 6–7 6–1 6–4 6–2. **2000: April** – *Zone 1 2r SWE d. FIN 3–2 in FIN (Hard).* R1 d. V. Liukko 6–3 4–6 6–1 7–6; R4 d. T. Ketola 6–2 6–4 6–1.

GRAND SLAM CUP RECORD
Has never played.

MASTERS CUP – Played 1
2000: 4th in rr lost Kafelnikov 4–6 7–5 6–1, lost Kuerten 7–5 6–3, lost Agassi 6–3 6–2.

5 YEVGENY KAFELNIKOV (RUS)

Born: Sochi, 18 February 1974. **Lives:** Sochi.
Father: Aleksandre. **Mother:** Valentina. **Wife:** Mascha
(married 11 July 1998). **Daughter:** Aleysa (born 23 October
1998).

Agent: IMG (Bill Ryan). **Coach:** Larry Stefanki; formerly Anatoli
Lepeshin. **Turned Pro:** 1992.
Height: 6ft 3in (1.90m). **Weight:** 185lb (83kg).

Rankings: 1992: 314; **1993:** 104; **1994:** 11; **1995:** 6;
1996: 3; **1997:** 5; **1998:** 11; **1999:** 2; **2000:** 5 singles, 12
doubles. **Highest:** 1 (3 May 1999).

2000 Prize Money: $3,755,599.
Career Earnings: $18,184,646. **Career Titles:** 22.

Style: An elegant groundstroke artist whose returns of serve on both wings, single-handed on
forehand, double on backhand, are the foundation of his powerful game. A sound serve-and-
volley technique makes him a threat on any surface, in singles or doubles.

CAREER HIGHLIGHTS (year: (titles))
1990: In winning USSR World Youth Cup team. **1992:** Began to make his mark on the Eastern
European satellite circuits. **1993:** Upset Stich on his way to qf Barcelona in spring and again at
Lyon in autumn. **1994: (3)** *Adelaide, Copenhagen, Long Island*. He sprang to prominence and
the top 100 by winning his 1st tour title in his 1st f at Adelaide on HC. In 2r Australian Open he
took Sampras to 9–7 5s, followed with the title at Copenhagen on carpet in Feb. and was ranked
as high as 36 by March. In April he upset Agassi and Stich to reach sf Monte Carlo; in May he
upset Ivanisevic and Stich on his way to f Hamburg, moving into the top 20, and in June he surprised Courier to reach sf Halle. He continued his winning ways by upsetting M. Chang on his
way to the title at Long Island in Aug., upset Muster *en route* to sf Gstaad, Edberg and Bruguera
to reach sf Stockholm and appeared in the same stage New Haven, plus 5 more qf across the
year, to finish the year poised just outside the top 10. He was also a successful doubles player,
winning 4 titles from 6 f with various partners. Led RUS to their first ever D Cup f and was voted
Most Improved Player of the Year. He played the busiest schedule of any player on the tour with
171 matches. **1995: (4)** *Milan, St Petersburg, Gstaad, Long Island*. Broke into the top 10 after
his qf appearance at Australian Open. Upset Agassi, who was injured, at French Open and
removed both Ivanisevic and Becker on his way to the title at Milan, going on to win St Petersburg, Gstaad and Long Island. He was r/u Nice, and reached sf Rotterdam, Barcelona, Gstaad,
New Haven and Lyon, plus 6 more qf. In doubles played 6 f with various partners, winning 3, and
was the 1st player since E. Sanchez in 1990 to end the year in top 10 both singles and doubles.
In D Cup with Olhovskiy saved 5 mps to upset Becker and Stich, although he won only 1 of his 3
matches in f as RUS lost 3–2 to USA. **1996: (4)** *FRENCH OPEN, Adelaide, Prague, Lyon*. The high
point of his career came with a magnificent performance at French Open, where he won both
singles and doubles (with Vacek, in only their 3rd tourn together). He became 1st Russian since
Metreveli in 1973 to reach GS f and 1st player since Rosewall in 1968 to win both singles and
doubles there. He played a heavy schedule, winning Adelaide, Prague and Lyon, as well as r/u
Rotterdam, St Petersburg, Halle, Stuttgart, Paris Open and Moscow, plus sf Milan, Hamburg,
Gstaad, Basel and GS Cup (lost in 5s to Ivanisevic), and 4 qf, including Australian Open. Upset
Sampras at both WT Cup and French Open (although the No. 1 was below his best on both occasions) and had hoped to overtake him at the top of the rankings by the end of HC season. However, he threw away an outside chance of achieving that when he withdrew from US Open,
offended at being seeded lower than his ranking and using a slight injury as a legitimate excuse.
He might still have been in with a chance had he not lost f Paris Open to Enqvist, although he
reached career-high No. 3 on 4 Nov. The only man to qualify for end-of-season champs in both
singles and doubles (with Vacek), he decided not to compete in the doubles, which were played
in US in the week before the singles in Hannover. There, in a tough group, he won only 1 match in
rr. He and Vacek played 7 f together, winning 4, and he also took a 5th with Olhovskiy. In all he

played 171 matches, which for the 3rd straight year was the busiest schedule of the tour. **1997: (3)** *Halle, New Haven, Moscow.* Broke a finger on right hand in gym the week before Australian Open and was out 3 months, returning at end April – still not fully fit but missing the game and keen to play again. He was back to form by June, when he won his 1st GC title at Halle, following with New Haven and Moscow to qualify for ATP Champs, where he was r/u to Sampras. Across the year he also reached sf Hamburg, Montreal, Tashkent, Lyon and Paris Open, plus qf French Open, Stuttgart Mercedes, Kitzbuhel, Cincinnati, Basel and GS Cup, although he was generally disappointing in GS singles. In doubles with Vacek, he won all 3 f he played – at French Open, US Open and Gstaad – and was again the only man to qualify for the season-ending champs in both singles and doubles, although injury prevented him from taking up his doubles place. **1998: (3)** *London, Halle, Moscow.* Having missed Australian Open with a sprained knee, he struggled for motivation for much of the year, in which he won London, Halle and Moscow, was r/u Marseille, Tashkent and Stuttgart Eurocard, and reached sf Cincinnati, New Haven and Paris Open, plus qf Barcelona and Toronto. He squeezed into ATP Champ, taking the last place ahead of Rusedski only by virtue of his victory at Moscow and the absence of the injured Krajicek and Rafter. However, he won only 1 match there and, having managed all year to hold on to his top 10 ranking, he finished the season just outside. He appeared in 4 doubles f, winning Antwerp with W. Ferreira and Vienna with Vacek. In all he played 150 matches, which for the 4th year in 5 was more than anyone else. **1999: (2)** *AUSTRALIAN OPEN, Rotterdam.* His enthusiasm rekindled by new coach Stefanki, he began the year in terrific style with the title at Australian Open. After winning Rotterdam in Feb., he went into the tourn at London the following week with the chance of overtaking Sampras as No. 1, but fell 1 match short in qf there and had to wait until 3 May to head the rankings for 1st time – ironically immediately after losing 7 consec. matches. On 14 June he slipped from the top spot to No. 3 behind Sampras and Rafter and thereafter the top places shifted between those three and Agassi. It was a see-saw year with another high point in Aug. when in 4 consec. tourns he was r/u Montreal and Washington in between sf Kitzbuhel and Cincinnati, followed by sf appearance at US Open. He lost there to Agassi, who beat him to the No. 1 year-end ranking and consolidated their respective positions by removing him in sf ATP Champ. He also reached sf St Polten and qf London, Long Island, GS Cup, Basel, Vienna and Lyon, but at Wimbledon was forced to retire 3r with severe dehydration. In doubles he won Barcelona with Haarhuis. **2000: (2)** *OLYMPICS, Moscow.* His best performances came in Australia, where he began the year with r/u finish at Australian Open and followed in Oct. with Olympic gold, overcoming Haas in 5s f to take his 1st title of the year in tremendous style. He added Moscow to his tally of titles, with 2 more r/u finishes at London and Stockholm, sf Rotterdam, Halle, Stuttgart Masters and St Petersburg, plus qf French Open, Kitzbuhel, Toronto and Indianapolis. Having settled for some months at No. 3 in the Entry System rankings behind Agassi and Sampras, he dropped to No. 4 behind M. Norman at end May before Safin's progress pushed him back to No. 5. He finished the year on a disappointing note when he failed to pass rr at Masters Cup. When he won Monte Carlo doubles with W. Ferreira he became 20th player to win 20 doubles and 20 singles titles in the open era, adding Vienna doubles with Zimonjic from 3 other f. He qualified for World Doubles Champ with W. Ferreira as 6th pairing – again the only player to qualify for season-ending champs in both singles and doubles – but they did not take up their place.

PRINCIPAL 2000 RESULTS – won 2, r/u 3, sf 4 (detailed Grand Slam results follow)
won Olympics, **won** Moscow (d. Golovanov 7–6 6–4, A. Martin 6–3 6–1, Burgsmuller 6–3 6–2, Rosset 4–6 6–2 7–5, Prinosil 6–2 7–5); **r/u** Australian Open, **r/u** London (d. Medvedev 6–3 6–4, Vacek 6–2 7–5, Santoro 6–3 6–2, Rusedski 6–3 7–6, lost Rosset 6–4 6–4), **r/u** Stockholm (d. Bastl 6–2 6–2, Fromberg 6–4 6–2, Vinciguerra 6–3 6–4, Grosjean w/o, lost Johansson 6–2 6–4 6–4); **sf** Rotterdam (d. Kulti 6–2 6–2, Escude 6–3 6–3, Rusedski 6–7 6–4 6–4, lost Henman 6–3 4–6 6–3); **sf** Halle (d. Vicente 6–7 7–6 6–4, Burrieza 6–7 7–6 6–3, Escude 7–6 6–3, lost Prinosil 6–4 7–6), **sf** Stuttgart Masters (d. Federer 7–5 6–3, Squillari 6–3 7–5, Schalken 4–6 6–1 6–4, lost Hewitt 4–6 7–6 6–3); **sf** St Petersburg (d. Ulihrach 6–3 6–1, Ruud 6–1 7–6, Calatrava 6–3 6–4, lost Hrbaty 7–5 6–3). **DOUBLES:** (with W. Ferreira unless stated) **won** Monte Carlo (d. Haarhuis/Stolle 6–3 2–6 6–1), (with Zimonjic) **won** Vienna (d. Novak/Rikl 6–4 6–4); **r/u** Rome (lost Damm/Hrbaty 6–4 4–6 6–3), (with Henman) **r/u** Rotterdam (lost Adams/De Jager 5–7 6–2 6–3).

CAREER GRAND SLAM RECORD
AUSTRALIAN OPEN – Played 5, won 1, r/u 1, qf 2
1994: 2r d. Bryan 4–6 ret, lost Sampras [1] 6–3 2–6 6–3 1–6 9–7. **1995: qf** [seed 10] d. Larkham 6–3 6–0 6–1, Carlsen 4–6 6–3 6–1 6–3, Bjorkman 4–6 6–1 6–2 7–6, Martin 6 1 6 4 6 2, lost Agassi [2] 6 2 7 5 6 0. **1996: qf** [seed 6] d. Santoro 6–1 6–1 7–5, Corretja 6–1 6–2 6–3, Tebbutt 7–5 5–7 6–4 6–2, MaliVai

Washington 6–3 6–2 6–4, lost Becker [4] 6–4 7–6 6–1. **1997–98:** Did not play. **1999: won** [seed 10] d. Bjorkman 6–3 6–4 6–2, Stoltenberg 7–5 3–6 7–6 7–6, Courier 6–7 6–4 6–2 3–0 ret, Pavel 6–3 7–6 6–7 3–6 6–4, T. Martin [15] 6–2 7–6 6–2, Haas 6–3 6–4 7–5, Enqvist 4–6 6–0 6–3 7–6. **2000: r/u** [seed 2] d. Knippschild 6–7 6–4 6–1 6–2, Vacek 6–3 6–0 6–1, Koubek 6–3 6–3 6–4, Rochus 6–1 6–3 7–5, El Aynaoui 6–0 6–3 7–6, M. Norman [12] 6–1 6–2 6–4, lost Agassi [1] 3–6 6–3 6–2 6–4.

FRENCH OPEN – Played 8, won 1, sf 1, qf 2
1993: 2r d. Kucera 6–3 6–4 6–4, lost Dosedel 6–3 6–1 6–0). **1994: 3r** d. Guardiola 4–6 7–5 6–4 4–6 6–4, Karbacher 6–2 1–6 6–2 6–2, lost Berasategui 6–3 6–2 6–2. **1995: sf** [seed 9] d. Siemerink 6–1 6–2 6–7 6–3, Gustafsson 6–3 6–7 6–1 7–5, Wheaton 6–2 6–1 4–6 6–3, Corretja 6–3 6–2 6–2, Agassi [1] 6–4 6–3 7–5, lost Muster [5] 6–4 6–0 6–4. **1996: won** [seed 6] d. Blanco 6–1 6–3 6–3, Johansson 6–2 7–5 6–3, Mantilla 6–4 6–2 6–2, Clavet 6–4 6–3 6–3, Krajicek [13] 6–3 6–4 6–7 6–2, Sampras [1] 7–6 6–0 6–2, Stich [15] 7–6 7–5 7–6. **1997: qf** [seed 3] d. Damm 6–2 6–4 6–4, Raoux 7–5 6–3 6–4, Pioline 7–5 6–4 6–7 1–6 6–4, Philippoussis 6–2 6–3 7–5, lost Kuerten 6–2 5–7 2–6 6–0 6–4. **1998: 2r** [seed 6] d. Navarra 6–4 4–6 6–1 6–4, lost Enqvist 4–6 7–6 7–6 6–1. **1999: 2r** [seed 1] d. M. Chang 6–2 5–7 6–0 7–6, lost Hrbaty 6–4 6–1 6–4. **2000: qf** [seed 4] d. Ljubicic 6–4 6–4 3–6 3–6 6–4, Zabaleta 6–2 3–6 6–7 6–4 6–4, Grosjean 6–3 6–1 5–7 6–4, Vicente 5–7 6–3 5–7 7–6 8–6, lost Kuerten [5] 6–3 3–6 4–6 6–4 6–2.

WIMBLEDON – Played 7, qf 1
1994 3r [seed 16] d. Tieleman 7–5 6–7 7–5 6–7 11–9, Braasch 6–1 6–1 6–3, lost Vacek 4–6 7–5 6–4 3–6 6–4. **1995: qf** d. Dewulf 6–3 7–5 6–3, Karbacher 6–4 6–4 7–5, Volkov 7–6 6–2 6–4, Krickstein 6–3 6–3 6–2, lost Ivanisevic [4] 7–5 7–6 6–3. **1996: 1r** [seed 5] lost Henman 7–6 6–3 6–7 4–6 7–5. **1997: last 16** [seed 3] d. Marin 6–4 6–2 6–0, J. Sanchez 6–2 4–6 6–3 6–4, Stoltenberg 6–3 7–6 4–6 6–3, lost Kiefer 6–2 7–5 2–6 6–1. **1998: 1r** [seed 7] lost Philippoussis 6–7 7–6 6–4 6–2. **1999: 3r** [seed 3] d. Larsson 6–7 7–5 7–6 4–6 7–5, Srichaphan 6–7 6–4 7–6 6–4, lost Pioline 3–6 6–4 1–0 ret. **2000: 2r** [seed 5] d. Federer 7–5 5–7 7–6 ret, lost T. Johansson 6–1 7–6 6–4.

US OPEN – Played 6, sf 1
1994: last 16 [seed 14] d. Eltingh 7–6 7–5 6–3, Damm 6–3 7–6 7–6, C. Costa 6–3 6–4 6–2, lost Stich [4] 7–6 6–3 6–2. **1995: 3r** [seed /] d. Iarango 6–0 6–4 /–5, Marques 6–3 6–4 6–4, lost Spadea 6–2 6–4 6–4. **1996:** Did not play. **1997: 2r** [seed 3] d. Caratti 6–2 6–4 7–6, lost Woodforde 6–3 6–4 7–6. **1998: last 16** [seed 11] d. Van Scheppingen 6–1 6–2 6–4, Haas 7–5 6–2 1–6 7–5, Kiefer 6–4 6–0 6–2, lost Johansson 3–6 6–3 6–3 7–6. **1999: sf** [seed 3] d. A. Martin 6–1 3–6 6–3 6–4, Mirnyi 7–5 6–1 6–7 6–3, Bjorkman 6–1 6–4 6–4, Medvedev 7–6 6–1 6–0, Krajicek [12] 7–6 7–6 3–6 1–6 7–6, lost Agassi [2] 1–6 6–3 6–3 6–3. **2000: 3r** [seed 5] d. Stanoytchev 6–7 1–6 6–3 6–2 6–3, Popp 6–7 6–4 6–4 6–4, lost Hrbaty 6–4 7–6 6–1.

OLYMPIC RECORD
2000: (Sydney) won gold medal [seed 5] d. Marin 6–0 6–1, Chela 7–6 6–4, Philippoussis [11] 7–6 6–3, Kuerten [2] 6–4 7–5, Di Pasquale 6–4 6–4, Haas 7–6 3–6 6–2 4–6 6–3.

CAREER DAVIS CUP RECORD
1993: March – *World Group 1r GER d. RUS 4–1 in RUS (Carpet).* R5 lost M. Stich 6–3 6–4. **September** – *World Group qualifying RUS d. CUB 5–0 in RUS (Carpet).* R1 d. M. Tabares 6–2 6–3 6–2; R5 d. J. Pino 7–6 6–7 6–2. **1994: March** – *World Group 1r RUS d. AUS 4–1 in RUS (Carpet).* R1 P. Rafter 6–3 6–0 6–4; R3 (+ A. Olhovskiy) d. T. Woodbridge/M. Woodforde 6–4 6–0 3–6 4–6 6–3; R5 d. J. Morgan 6–3 6–7 7–5. **July** – *World Group qf RUS d. CZE 3–2 in RUS (Carpet).* R1 d. C. Dosedel 6–2 6–3 6–4; R3 (+ Olhovskiy) lost P. Korda/C. Suk 3–6 6–4 4–6 6–3 7–5; R4 d. Korda 6–4 6–1 2–6 6–4. **September** – *World Group sf RUS d. GER 4–1 in GER (Hard).* R1 d. B. Karbacher 7–6 6–1 2–6 6–4; R3 (+ Olhovskiy) d. K. Braasch/M. Stich 6–4 7–6 3–6 6–7 10–8; R4 d. Stich 7–5 6–3. **December** – *World Group Final SWE d. RUS 4–1 in RUS (Carpet).* R2 lost M. Larsson 6–0 6–2 3–6 2–6 6–3; R3 (+ Olhovskiy) lost J. Apell/J. Bjorkman 6–7 6–2 3–6 1–6 8–6; R4 d. S. Edberg 4–6 6–4 6–0. **1995: February** – *World Group 1r RUS d. BEL 4–1 in BEL (Clay).* R2 d. K. Goossens 4–6 6–4 6–3 6–4; R3 (+ A. Olhovskiy) d. F. Dewulf/L. Pimek 2–6 7–5 7–5 6–3; R4 lost J. van Herck 7–6 6–3 6–1. **March** – *World Group qf RUS d. RSA 4–1 in RUS (Carpet).* R1 d. M. Ondruska 6–1 6–4 6–4; R3 (+ Olhovskiy) d. W. Ferreira/G. Muller 4–6 4–6 7–6 7–6 6–3; R4 d. Ferreira 6–4 7–5 6–1. **September** – *World Group sf RUS d. GER 3–2 in RUS (Clay).* R2 lost M. Stich 6–1 4–6 6–3 6–4; R3 (+ Olhovskiy) d. B. Becker/Stich 7–6 6–4 2–6 6–7 7–5; R4 d. B. Karbacher 6–1 7–6 6–2. **December** – *World Group Final USA d. RUS 3–2 in RUS (Clay).* R2 d. J. Courier 7–6 7–5 6–3; R3 (+ Olhovskiy) lost T. Martin/P. Sampras 7–5 6–4 6–3; R4 lost Sampras 6–2 6–4 7–6. **1996: February** – *World Group 1r ITA d. RUS 3–2 in ITA (Clay).* R2 d. R. Furlan 6–3 5–7 6–4 6–3; R3 (+ A. Olhovskiy) lost A. Gaudenzi/R. Furlan 6–4 2–6 5–7 7–6 6–4; R4 d. Gaudenzi 6–3 3–6 7–6 7–5. **September** – *World Group Qualifying RUS d. HUN 4–1 in RUS (Carpet).* R1 d. A. Savolt 7–5 3–6 6–3 6–4; R3 (+ A. Olhovskiy) d. G. Koves/S. Noszaly 7–6 6–3 6–1; R4 d. J. Krocsko 6–0 6–3). **1997: September** – *World Group Qualifying RUS d. ROM 3–2 in ROM (Carpet).* R2 d. I. Moldovan 6–4 7–6 6–4; R3 (with A. Olhovskiy) lost A. Pavel/G. Trifu 6–4 6–4 6–4. R4 lost Pavel 6–4 3–6 6–4 6–1. **1998: April** – *World Group 1r RUS d. USA 3–2 in USA (Hard).* R1 d. J. Courier 6–2 5–7 6–7 6–4 6–4; R3 (with M. Safin) lost T. Martin/R. Reneberg 7–6 6–1 2–6 6–1; R4 d. A. Agassi 6–3 6–0 7–6. **September** – *World Group Qualifying RUS d. JPN 3–1 in JPN (Hard).* R1 d. G. Motomura 4–6 6–2 6–3 6–2; R3 (with Safin) d. Motomura/T. Suzuki 7–5 6–3 4–6 6–2. **1999: April** – *World Group 1r RUS d. GER 3–2 in GER (Carpet).* R2 d. N. Kiefer 7–6 6–4 6–4; R3 (with A. Olhovskiy) lost B. Becker/D. Prinosil 6 7 6 2 6 3 4 6 10 8; R4 d. T. Haas 6–3 6–4 6–2. **July** – *World Group qf RUS d. SVK 3–2 in RUS (Clay).* R2 d. D. Hrbaty 2–6 6–2 6–7 6–1 7–5; R3 (with Olhovskiy) lost Hrbaty/Kucera 6–2 6–2 6–2; R4

The new Olympic Champion, Yevgeny Kafelnikov was making history for Russia.
(Stephen Wake)

lost Kucera 6–1 6–1 6–4. **September** – *World Group sf AUS d. RUS 4–1 in AUS (Grass).* R2 lost W. Arthurs 6–2 6–7 6–2 6–0; (with Olhovskiy) d. S. Stolle/M. Woodforde 6–1 6–4 4–6 4–6 8–6; R4 lost L. Hewitt 6–4 7–5 6–2. **2000: February** – *World Group 1r RUS d. BEL 4–1 in RUS (Carpet).* R 1 d. F. De Wulf 6–7 6–4 7–5 6–2. **April** – *World Group qf ESP d. RUS 4–1 in ESP (Clay).* R2 lost J. Ferrero 6–2 6–2 6–2; R3 (with M. Safin) d. J. Balcells/A. Corretja 7–6 2–6 7–6 6–4; R4 lost A. Costa 6–0 6–3 6–0.

GRAND SLAM CUP RECORD – Played 4, sf 2, qf 2
1995: sf [seed 6] d. Furlan 6–4 6–1, Eltingh 3–6 6–3 6–2, lost Ivanisevic [8] 7–6 4–6 6–3 6–4. **1996: sf** [seed 3] d. Corretja 6–4 7–6, d. Courier 2–6 6–4 8–6, last Ivanisevic 6–7 2–6 6–3 6–2 6–4. **1997: qf** d. Bruguera [5] 6–4 6–3, lost Rusedski [4] 6–7 6–3 6–1. **1999: qf** [seed 2] bye, lost Rusedski 7–5 7–6.

ATP TOUR CHAMPIONSHIP/MASTERS CUP – Played 5, r/u 1
1995: 4th in rr lost Sampras 6–3 6–3, lost W. Ferreira 3–6 7–6 6–1, lost Becker 6–4 7–5. **1996: Equal 3rd in rr** lost Becker 6–4 7–5, d. Enqvist 6–3 7–6, lost Sampras 6–4 6–4. **1997: r/u** in rr d. Bjorkman 6–3 7–6, d. M. Chang 6–3 6–0, lost Henman 6–4 6–4; sf d. Moya 7–6 7–6; f lost Sampras 6–3 6–2 6–2. **1998:** Did not play. **1999: sf** in rr d. T. Martin 6–4 1–6 6–1, d. Enqvist 7–5 3–6 6–4, lost Kiefer 6–1 4–6 6–2; sf lost Agassi 6–4 7–6. **2000: 3rd in rr** d. M. Norman 4–6 7–5 6–1, lost Agassi 6–1 6–4, lost Kuerten 6–3 6–4.

6 ANDRE AGASSI (USA)

Born: Las Vegas, 29 April 1970. **Lives:** Las Vegas.
Father: Emanuel Agassian, who boxed for Iran in the 1952
Olympics, and became Mike Agassi.
Mother: Elizabeth. **Brother:** Philip, who occasionally travels
with him. **Sisters:** Tammee and Rita, who was married to
Pancho Gonzales. **Girlfriend:** Steffi Graf.

Agent: Perry Rodgers of Agassi Enterprises.
Coach: Brad Gilbert. Formerly coached by Nick Bollettieri
(from age 13 until 1993). Formerly assisted by Pat Etcheberry
for movement and from 1990 by Gil Reyes for strength.
Turned Pro: 1986 (aged 16).
Height: 5ft 11in (1.80m). **Weight:** 170lb (77kg).

Rankings: 1985: 618; **1986:** 91; **1987:** 5; **1988:** 3; **1989:** 7; **1990:** 4; **1991:** 10; **1992:** 9; **1993:**
24; **1994:** 2; **1995:** 2; **1996:** 8; **1997:** 122; **1998:** 6; **1999:** 1; **2000:** 6. **Highest:** 1 (April 1995).

2000 Prize Money: $1,884,443. **Career Earnings:** $21,140,724. **Career Titles:** 45

Style: A go-for-broke right-handed hitter from the back of the court with early-ball forehands
and double-handed backhands that are amongst the hardest-hit strokes in tennis. A fine serve
and improving volleys, added to his agility and speed about the court, make him a fearsome
opponent. Inevitably he hits many unforced errors and these sometimes contribute to unexpected losses.

CAREER HIGHLIGHTS (year: (titles))
Andre is a born-again Christian who collects motor cars. As a child, he suffered from Osgood
Schlatter's disease, which causes a bone in the knee to grow improperly. **1984:** Ranked 4 in US
Boys' 14s and won Nat 14s. **1985:** Receiving expert counsel from brother-in-law Pancho
Gonzales, he tested the waters of men's circuit. **1986:** Downed Mayotte and S. Davis on his way
to qf Stratton Mountain. **1987: (1)** *Itaparica*. Reached first GP f at Seoul, won his 1st GP title at
Itaparica at end of season and d. Jarryd *en route* to sf Basle. **1988: (6)** *Memphis, Charleston,
Forest Hills, Stuttgart, Stratton Mountain, Livingston*. Began the year by winning 2nd consec.
tourn at Memphis, adding 5 more during the year. After reaching 1st GS sf in Paris, he took a
month's rest, missing Wimbledon. Made D Cup debut and qualified for Masters, but was
restricted by a hand injury. **1989: (1)** *Orlando*. Could not maintain the high standards of 1988,
having to wait until Orlando in Oct. for his 1st title for 14 months. R/u Italian Open; reached 2nd
GS sf at US Open and appeared in 4 other sf to qualify for Masters, but won no match there.
1990: (4) *San Francisco, LIPC, Washington, ATP Champ*. His year finished on a high note when
he beat world No. 1, Edberg, to win ATP Tour World Champ in Nov. Reached 1st GS f at French
Open, where he shocked traditionalists with his lurid outfits, which included luminous cycling
shorts under black denim shorts. Did not play Wimbledon or Australian Open, but was also r/u
at US Open, where he was fined $3,000 for his conduct in 2r match v Korda. In autumn was
fined 20% of total earnings on ATP tour (excluding GS) for falling 2 tourns short of his commitment to the tour and was fined a further $25,000 at end of year for withdrawing from GS
Cup after submitting an entry. Played in US D Cup team v AUS in f but withdrew with pulled
stomach muscle in 4th rubber. **1991: (2)** *Orlando, Washington*. Reached his 3rd GS f at French
Open, but in losing to Courier he again cast doubts on his ability to win a title at the highest
level. Known generally for his garish outfits, he delighted both officials and crowds at
Wimbledon with his pristine white attire and his enthusiasm. He reached qf there, but disappointed at US Open, falling in ss 1r to Krickstein. At ATP World Champ he reached sf but fell to
Courier to finish the year with just 2 titles. Again led USA to f D Cup. **1992: (3)** *WIMBLEDON,
Atlanta, Toronto*. In Jan. dropped out of top 10 for 1st time since May 1988 and reached no sf
until winning Atlanta in May for his 1st title since July 1991. But everything came right for him
at Wimbledon, where he removed Becker in 5s and outlasted Ivanisevic in a pulsating 5-set f to
take his 1st GS title and return to top 10. Reached sf French Open and qf US Open, where he
wore Wimbledon colours, and won Toronto in summer. Qualified for ATP World Champ but

was forced to withdraw with an injury to his left thigh. **1993: (2)** *San Francisco, Scottsdale.* Missed Australian Open with bronchitis and returned to play with a new commitment and discipline, winning San Francisco. However, he was forced to miss French Open with tendinitis of right wrist and returned to Wimbledon to defend his title after very little practice. He fell there to Sampras in 5s qf and surprised fans by revealing that he had trimmed his body hair 'to make him more aerodynamic'. Split with Bollettieri in July – when his former coach resigned, saying the distance between Agassi in Las Vegas and Bollettieri at his academy in Florida was too far. Joined with Pancho Segura in Aug., agreeing to work together at least through the US Open. Won Scottsdale and reached sf New Haven and Cincinnati, where he won the 1st doubles title of his career with Korda. He missed the last 3 tourns of the year with a wrist injury (dorsal capsulitis), undergoing surgery on 20 Dec. and for the 1st time since 1987 he finished outside the top 20. However, psychotherapy, which he underwent while recovering from wrist surgery at end of year, enabled him to come to terms with the harsh discipline of his upbringing, in which he was groomed for tennis from babyhood. **1994: (5)** *US OPEN, Scottsdale, Toronto, Vienna, Paris Open.* After joining forces with Brad Gilbert, who helped him restore belief in himself and his game, he enjoyed a remarkable year, the climax coming in Sept. with his 1st US Open. Ranked as low as 32 when he returned in Feb., he won Scottsdale in his 1st tourn back. Then in March he upset Becker and Edberg on his way to r/u LIPC, having agreed to delay f 50 minutes in order to let his opponent, Sampras, recover more from a stomach virus. He escaped punishment for obscene outbursts at Italian Open but at French Open, where he was not seeded, was fined $750 for an audible obscenity and $1,500 for verbal abuse. He was again a popular competitor at Wimbledon, where he lost in 5s to Martin in last 16, but his next GS outing was the highlight, when, unseeded at US Open for the 1st time since 1987, he became the 1st unseeded winner there since Fred Stolle in 1966. Playing better than ever on European carpet, where he hadn't prospered before, he upset Ivanisevic and Stich to take the title at Vienna, and beat Sampras and Bruguera in winning Paris Open – a victory that took him to a career-high ranking of No. 2. He retained that ranking at year's end, after sf showing at IBM/ATP World Champ, where he was a set up v Sampras, and was 1st man to climb to No. 2 from outside the top 20 within a year. At GS Cup he was fined $6,000 for verbal obscenity during his losing qf against ultimate winner, Larsson. **1995: (7)** *AUSTRALIAN OPEN, San Jose, LIPC, Washington, Montreal, Cincinnati, New Haven.* Startled fans by appearing at his 1st Australian Open looking rather plump and sporting a new look with his unbleached hair close-cropped and receding. He won that and 6 more titles across the year from a total of 10 f. On 10 April he replaced Sampras as No. 1, becoming the 12th player to top the rankings. He was then unexpectedly beaten by Courier in Tokyo Japan Open and the next week incurred a $5,000 fine for withdrawing from Hong Kong, owing to a lower back strain. At French Open he injured his hip when he fell in 4th game qf v Kafelnikov and lost the match. At Wimbledon he lost sf to Becker in one of the best matches of the tourn and at US Open he gained revenge in a similarly fine sf, but lost f to Sampras. In the summer he had a sequence of 4 successive titles, saving 2 mps v Krajicek at New Haven. Suffering from a chest injury incurred when he was helping USA beat SWE in D Cup in Sept., he lost 3r Essen to MaliVai Washington and was forced to withdraw from Paris Open, then IBM/ATP Champ and D Cup f. With Sampras still in action and winning in Paris, he lost the No. 1 ranking in Nov. Won the 1995 Arthur Ashe Humanitarian Award for his work with the Andre Agassi Foundation to benefit disadvantaged youth. **1996: (3)** *OLYMPICS, LIPC, Cincinnati.* Winning an Olympic gold medal was the high point of his career and an outstanding moment in a mixed year, in which he often seemed to have lost interest, concentrating too much on commercial matters and not enough on his tennis. He returned to No. 1 on 29 Jan. after Australian Open, where he appeared with his head newly shaven. The highlight there was his dramatic 5s qf win over Courier, in which he recovered from 2s down for the 1st time in his career; he came from behind in 4 of his matches there, but could not do so again v M. Chang in sf. Fell from the top spot again on 19 Feb. after losing f San Jose to Sampras, won LIPC when Ivanisevic retired in their f, but was booed off court at Monte Carlo after a sloppy performance v A. Costa 3r. He was again disappointing at French Open, where he appeared to be overweight and unfit; he let slip a 2–1 sets lead against Woodruff and was fined £2,000 for failing to appear at the press conference afterwards. He had flu just before Wimbledon – arriving there underprepared, still overweight and having played in only 4 matches since March – and was beaten by qualifier D. Flach. His subsequent fall to No. 6 on 22 July saw him ranked outside the top 5 for 1st time since Oct. 1994. Although his game eventually came good at Olympics, he struggled in the early rounds and narrowly escaped disqualification for an obscenity v W. Ferreira in an ill-tempered qf. He was then defaulted at Indianapolis for racket abuse and an expletive, subsequently being fined $4,000 for the misdemeanour. The umpire there had been advised by the ATP supervisor, but Agassi complained that the usual procedure of warning, point penalty, default was not followed. He reached sf US Open, where M. Chang removed him again, and qf Indian Wells and Stuttgart Eurocard. He declined to play D Cup in Prague, where USA lost to CZE. His year finished on an unsatisfactory note, when, again underprepared and suffering from a heavy cold, he put up a dismal performance v Sampras at ATP Champ, winning only 3 games, and then withdrew from the tourn. He was fined $35,000 (5% of his tour earnings, excluding GS) for failing to appear at the draw. His 1r loss at GS Cup to Woodforde did nothing to restore his reputation. **1997:** The downhill slide continued as he pulled out of Australian Open lacking motivation, fell from top 20 after his 4th consec. 1r defeat at LIPC (to Draper), and withdrew from Wimbledon, where he was unseeded, complaining of a recurring wrist injury. In his 1st year since 1986 without a title, he played 24 matches in 12 tourns, reaching sf San Jose and qf Indianapolis and extending his D Cup record to 15 consec. wins. Otherwise he seemed to have lost his way and dropped outside top 100 for 1st time since 1986, reaching a low of 141 in Nov. However, rediscovering motivation towards the end of year, he vowed to return to his previous form, and began playing in lower-level tournaments. He started with Las Vegas Challenger, where he was r/u to Vinck, and continued the upward trend with the title at Burbank Challenger. On 19 April he married Brooke Shields, whose grandfather, Frank Shields, was the 1st unseeded finalist at US Open in 1930. **1998: (5)** *San Jose, Scottsdale, Washington, Los Angeles, Ostrava.* As the season opened he was already showing signs of his old form, following sf finish at Adelaide with an upset of A. Costa at Australian Open, where he was unseeded. From there he simply took off, rising swiftly through the rankings to make the top 20 again on 27 April and finish the year in his old place in the top 10 and voted Most Improved Player of the Year. When he won his 5th title of the season at Ostrava in Oct., he returned to the top 5 – and was even in contention for the No. 1 year-end ranking until his qf defeat by T. Martin at Paris Open. Still ranked low enough to be unseeded at San Jose in Feb., he removed Kuerten, M. Chang and Sampras (all in ss) to take his 1st title since August 1996, and added Scottsdale 3 weeks later. He was disappointing at both French Open and Wimbledon, but hit the HC season in style with a 3-week run in which he swept to the title at Washington, took Los Angeles a week later and then upset Sampras again to reach sf Toronto. In other tourns he was r/u LIPC, Munich, Indianapolis, Basle and GS Cup, where he was controversially awarded a WC and lost f only in 5s to Rios. He qualified for ATP Champ, but suffered a back injury during practice the day before and was unable to complete his 1st match. He was not available for vital D Cup sf v Italy. **1999: (5)** *FRENCH OPEN, US OPEN, Hong Kong, Washington, Paris Open.* After separating from his wife, Brooke Shields, in April, he appeared to take on a new lease of life, winning his 1st title of the year at Hong Kong at the beginning of that month. At French Open he became only the 2nd man in the open era and the 5th of all time after Perry, Budge, Laver and Emerson to win all 4 GS tourns – and the first ever to do so on all surfaces, the others having played only on grass and clay. In f v Medvedev he came from 1–6 2–6 down to win his 1st GS for 4 years in an emotional climax. After Wimbledon, where he was r/u to Sampras, he returned to No. 1 on 5 July for 1st time since 1995, although Rafter displaced him 3 weeks later. He dropped to No. 3 for a time and the top ranking shifted from player to player through the summer. Eventually, though, he returned to the top after winning a 2nd US Open title – and his 2nd GS of the season – in yet another terrific performance. It was back in Paris again in Nov. that he clinched the year-end No. 1 ranking during Paris Open, finishing the season at the top for 1st time in his career. At ATP Champ he conceded no set on his way to f, but lost there to Sampras, whom he had convincingly beaten in rr. In all he won 5 titles, having added Washington in Aug., was r/u Los Angeles as well as Wimbledon and ATP Champ, and reached sf Scottsdale, Montreal, Cincinnati and Stuttgart Eurocard plus qf Basel and GS Cup. He was an obvious choice for the Player of the Year award. **2000: (1)** *AUSTRALIAN OPEN.* He began the year where he left off the previous season by winning Australian Open to become the 1st since Laver in 1969 to reach 4 consec. GS f. However, things went downhill after that as he was plagued by a string of injuries and distracted by the illness of his mother and sister, who were both suffering from cancer. He withdrew Olympics to be with them and was clearly affected for much of the year by his concern. He withdrew San Jose in Feb. with lower back strain, then at 2r Scottsdale in March Clavet inflicted a 6–1 6–2 drubbing that was his worst HC defeat since April 1987. He damaged an ankle ligament at Ericsson Open later that month and at Atlanta in April ret v Vanek 2r with pulled hamstring. In June he withdrew

Queen's after bruising his back in a fall, but was able to play Wimbledon, where he saved 2 mps
v T. Martin before winning their 2r match only 10–8 fs, eventually losing sf to Rafter in 5s.
Returning home from Wimbledon in July, his car was tail-ended and he suffered a strained
back, right side and arm, which kept him out of D Cup sf v ESP. He ret Cincinnati with an ongoing back injury, but was back as r/u both singles and doubles at Washington a week later. It
was a hip injury that caused him to ret sf Lyon in Nov. and he missed Paris Masters in order to
rest it before Masters Cup. That obviously paid off, for he swept through rr there, the only
player to win all his matches and following with ss defeat of Safin in sf. It was only an inspired
Kuerten, on his way to the year-end No. 1 ranking, who stopped him in f. In between the
injuries he could perform with the old magic, and his tally for the year was the Australian Open
title, r/u Masters Cup and Washington, plus sf Wimbledon, Ericsson Open and Lyon. At French
Open, where Kucera beat him 2r, he was fined $10,000 for missing post-match conference.

PRINCIPAL 2000 RESULTS – won 1, r/u 2, sf 3 (detailed Grand Slam results follow)
won Australian Open; **r/u** Washington (d. Meligeni 6–2 6–1, Goldstein 6–3 6–2, Roddick 6–4 6–4, Prinosil
6–1 6–3, lost Corretja 6–2 6–3), **r/u** Masters Cup; **sf** Ericsson Open (d. Roddick 6–2 6–3, Pavel 6–4 6–3,
Rafter 6–4 6–4, Henman 7–5 1–6 7–6, lost Kuerten 6–1 6–4), **sf** Wimbledon, **sf** Lyon (d. Sargsian 6–7 6–1
6–4, Haas 6–2 6–3, Kucera 6–1 7–5, lost Clement 6–3 ret.). **2000 HIGHLIGHTS – DOUBLES:** (with Sargsian)
r/u Washington (lost O'Brien/Palmer 7–5 6–1).

CAREER GRAND SLAM RECORD
AUSTRALIAN OPEN – Played 5, won 2, sf 1
1987–1994: Did not play. **1995: won** [seed 2] d. Stafford 6–2 6–4 6–2, Golmard 6–2 6–3 6–1, Rusedski 6–2
6–4 6–2, Rafter 6–3 6–4 6–0, Kafelnikov [10] 6–2 7–5 6–0, Krickstein 6–4 6–4 3–0 ret'd, Sampras [1] 4–6 6–1
7–6 6–4. **1996: sf** [seed 2] d. Etlis 3–6 7–6 4–6 7–6 6–3, Spadea 4–6 6–2 6–3, Bryan 4–6 6–0 6–2 6–1,
Bjorkman 4–6 6–2 4–6 6–1 6–2, Courier [8] 6–7 2–6 6–3 6–4 6–2, lost M. Chang [5] 6–1 6–4 7–6. **1997:** Did
not play. **1998: last 16** [unseeded] d. Martelli 3–6 7–6 6–2 6–2, A. Costa [16] 6–4 6–4 2–6 7–5, Gaudenzi
6–2 6–2 6–0, lost Berasategui 3–6 3–6 6–2 6–2 6–3. **1999: last 16** [seed 5] d. Gumy 6–0 6–3 6–0, Dosedel
7–6 6–2 6–0, Novak 6–3 6–2 6–1, lost Spadea 6–1 7–5 6–7 6–3. **2000: won** [seed 1] d. Puerta 6–2 6–2 6–3,
Schalken 7–5 6–0 6–3, Zabaleta 6–2 6–2 6–2, Philippoussis [16] 6–4 7–6 5–7 6–3, Arazi 6–4 6–4 6–2,
Sampras [3] 6–4 3–6 6–7 7–6 6–1, Kafelnikov 3–6 6–3 6–2 6–4.
FRENCH OPEN Played 12, won 1, r/u 2, sf 2, qf 1
1987: 2r d. Arraya 6–2 4–6 6–1 7–5, lost Kuchna 6–4 6–3 6–3. **1988: sf** [seed 9] d. Cane 6–4 6–1 6–2,
Narducci 6–1 6–2 6–2, Vysand 7–5 3–6 3–6 6–2, Gustafsson 6–4 6–2 4–6 6–0, Perez Roldan [15] 6–2 6–2 6–4,
lost Wilander [3] 4–6 6–2 7–5 5–7 6–0. **1989: 3r** [seed 5] d. J. Carlsson 6–4 6–4 6–1, Cane 6–2 6–2 6–3, lost
Courier 7–6 4–6 6–3 6–2. **1990: r/u** [seed 3] d. Wostenholme 4–6 7–6 6–0 6–1, Woodbridge 7–5 6–1 6–3,
Boetsch 6–3 6–2 6–0, Courier [13] 6–7 6–1 6–4 6–0, Chang [11] 6–1 6–2 4–6 6–2, Svensson 6–1 6–4 3–6
6–3, lost Gomez [4] 6–3 2–6 6–4 6–4. **1991: r/u** [seed 4] d. Rosset 3–6 7–5 6–4 6–3, Korda 6–1 6–2 6–2, P.
McEnroe 6–2 6–2 6–0, Mancini 6–3 6–3 5–7 6–1, Hlasek 6–3 6–1 6–1, Becker [2] 7–5 6–3 3–6 6–1, lost
Courier [9] 3–6 6–4 2–6 6–1 6–4. **1992: sf** [seed 11] d. Frana 6–1 6–4 6–4, Pozzi 6–0 6–2 6–1, Prpic 2–6 6–4
6–1 7–6, E. Sanchez 6–1 6–3 7–5, Sampras [3] 7–6 6–2 6–1, lost Courier [1] 6–3 6–2 6–2. **1993:** Did not play.
1994: 2r d. Wilander 6–2 7–5 6–1, lost Muster [11] 6–3 6–7 7–5 2–6 7–5. **1995: qf** [seed 1] d. Braasch 6–1
6–4 6–4, Woodbridge 7–6 6–1 6–0, Clavet 6–1 6–2 6–0, El Aynaoui 6–4 6–2 6–2, lost Kafelnikov [9] 6–4 6–3
7–5. **1996: 2r** [seed 3] d. Diaz 6–1 6–7 6–4 6–4, lost Woodruff 4–6 6–4 6–7 6–3 6–2. **1997:** Did not play.
1998: 1r lost Safin 5–7 7–5 6–2 3–6 6–2. **1999: won** [seed 13] d. Squillari 3–6 7–5 7–5 6–3, Clement 6–2
4–6 2–6 7–5 6–0, Woodruff 6–4 6–4 6–3, Moya [4] 4–6 7–5 7–5 6–1, Filippini 6–2 6–2 6–0, Hrbaty 6–4 7–6
3–6 6–4, Medvedev 1–6 2–6 6–4 6–3 6–4. **2000: 2r** [seed 1] d. Dupuis 7–6 6–3 6–4, lost Kucera 2–6 7–5 6–1
6–0.
WIMBLEDON – Played 10, won 1, r/u 1, sf 2, qf 2
1987: 1r lost Leconte [9] 6–2 6–1 6–2. **1988–90:** Did not play. **1991: qf** [seed 5] d. Connell 4–6 6–1 6–7 7–5
6–3, Prpic 7–6 3–6 6–4 6–2, Krajicek 7–6 6–4 6–3, Eltingh 6–3 3–6 6–3 6–4, lost Wheaton 6–2 0–6 3–6 7–6
6–2). **1992: won** [seed 12] d. Chesnokov 5–7 6–1 7–5 7–5, Masso 4–6 6–1 6–3 6–3, Rostagno 6–3 7–6 7–5,
Saceanu 7–6 6–1 7–6, Becker [4] 4–6 6–2 6–2 4–6 6–3, J. McEnroe 6–4 6–2 6–3 Ivanisevic [8] 6–7 6–4 6–4
1–6 6–4. **1993: qf** [seed 8] d. Karbacher 7–5 6–4 6–0, Cunha–Silva 5–7 6–3 6–2 6–0, Rafter 6–1 6–2 6–0
6–3, Krajicek [9] 7–5 7–6 7–6, lost Sampras [1] 6–2 6–2 3–6 3–6 6–4). **1994: last 16** [seed 12] d. Gaudenzi
6–2 6–7 6–3 6–2, Pereira 6–7 6–3 6–4 6–7 6–4, Krickstein 6–4 6–3 7–6, lost Martin [6] 6–3 7–5 6–7 4–6 6–1.
1995: sf [seed 1] d. Painter 6–2 6–2 6–1, P. McEnroe 6–1 6–1 6–3, Wheaton 6–2 3–6 6–4 6–2, Mronz 6–3
6–3 6–3, Eltingh 6–2 6–3 6–4, lost Becker [3] 2–6 7–6 6–4 7–6. **1996: 1r** [seed 3] lost D. Flach 2–6 7–6 6–4
7–6. **1997:** Did not play. **1998: 2r** [seed 13] d. Calatrava 6–1 6–3 6–2, lost Haas 4–6 6–1 7–6 6–4. **1999: r/u**
[seed 4] d. Pavel 6–1 6–2 6–3, Canas 6–3 6–4 6–3, A. Martin 6–2 6–0 2–6 6–3, Arthurs 6–7 7–6 6–1 6–4,
Kuerten [11] 6–3 4 6 4, Rafter [2] 7–5 7–6 6 ?, lost Sampras [1] 6–3 6–4 7–5. **2000: sf** [seed 2] d. Dent
2–6 6–3 6–0 4–0 ret, T. Martin 6–4 2–6 7–6 2–6 10–8, Golmard 6–3 6–3 6–4, Prinosil 6–4 6–3 6–3,
Philippoussis [10] 7–6 6–3 6–4, lost Rafter [12] 7–5 4–6 7–5 4–6 6–3.

US OPEN – Played 15, won 2, r/u 2, sf 3, qf 1

1986: 1r lost Bates 7–6 6–3 3–6 6–4. **1987: 1r** lost Leconte [11] 6–4 7–6 4–6 6–3. **1988: sf** [seed 4] d. Johnson 7–6 6–3 6–3, Leach 4–6 6–2 6–3 6–4, Kriek 6–3 6–1 2–6 6–0, Chang 7–5 6–3 6–2, Connors [6] 6–2 7–6 6–1, lost Lendl [1] 4–6 6–2 6–3 6–4. **1989: sf** [seed 6] d. Weiss 6–3 7–6 6–0, Broad 6–3 6–2 6–3, Johnson 6–1 7–5 6–2, Grabb 6–1 7–5 6–3, Connors [13] 6–1 4–6 0–6 6–3 6–4, lost Lendl [1] 7–6 6–1 3–6 6–1. **1990: r/u** [seed 4] d. Connell 6–4 6–2 6–2, Korda 7–5 5–7 6–0 6–4, Davin 7–5 6–4 6–0, Berger [13] 7–5 6–0 6–2, Cherkasov 6–2 6–2 6–3, Becker [2] 6–7 6–3 6–2 6–3, lost Sampras [12] 6–4 6–3 6–2). **1991: 1r** [seed 8] lost Krickstein 7–5 7–6 6–2. **1992: qf** [seed 8] d. Pernfors 6–2 6–4 6–1, Roig 6–1 6–3 6–2, Siemerink 6–2 6–3 6–3, Costa [10] 6–4 6–3 6–2, lost Courier [1] 6–3 6–7 6–1 6–4). **1993: 1r** [seed 16] lost Enqvist 6–4 6–4 3–6 6–7 6–2. **1994: won** [unseeded] d. Eriksson 6–3 6–2 6–0, Forget 6–3 7–5 6–7 6–2, W. Ferreira [12] 7–5 6–1 7–5, Chang [6] 6–1 6–7 6–3 3–6 6–1, Muster [13] 7–6 6–3 6–0, Martin [9] 6–3 4–6 6–2 6–3, Stich [4] 6–1 7–6 7–5). **1995: r/u** [seed 1] d. Shelton 6–2 6–2 6–2, Corretja 5–7 6–3 5–7 6–0 6–2, Edberg 6–4 6–3 6–1, Palmer 7–5 6–3 6–2, Korda 6–4 6–2 1–6 7–5, Becker [4] 7–6 7–6 4–6 6–4, lost Sampras [2] 6–4 6–3 4–6 7–5. **1996: sf** [seed 6] d. Hadad 6–3 6–3 6–2, Paes 3–6 6–4 6–1 6–0, Siemerink 6–4 6–2 7–6, Wheaton 4–6 6–2 6–3 6–4, Muster [3] 6–2 7–5 4–6 6–2, lost M. Chang [2] 6–3 6–2 6–2. **1997: last 16** [unseeded] d. Campbell 6–1 6–1 4–6 6–3, Voinea 6–0 6–2 6–2, Woodforde 6–2 6–2 6–4, lost Rafter [13] 6–3 7–6 4–6 6–3. **1998: last 16** [seed 8] d. Grosjean 6–4 6–1 6–4, Raoux 6–3 6–2 6–7 3–6 6–1, Sanguinetti 6–2 6–3 6–0, lost Kucera [9] 6–3 6–3 6–7 1–6 6–3. **1999: won** [seed 2] d. Kulti 6–0 6–1 6–3, Pretzsch 6–3 6–2 6–1, Gimelstob 6–1 4–6 6–3 6–4, Clement 6–2 6–4 6–3, Escude 7–6 6–3 6–4, Kafelnikov [3] 1–6 6–3 6–3 6–3, T. Martin [7] 6–4 6–7 6–7 6–3 6–2. **2000: 2r** [seed 1] d. Kim 6–4 6–2 6–0, lost Clement 6–3 6–2 6–4.

OLYMPIC RECORD

1996: (Atlanta) won gold medal [seed 1] d. Bjorkman 7–6 7–6, Kucera 6–4 6–4, Gaudenzi 2–6 6–4 6–2, W. Ferreira [5] 7–5 4–6 7–5, Paes 7–6 6–3, Bruguera 6–2 6–3 6–1.

CAREER DAVIS CUP RECORD

1988: April – *Zone 1 sf USA d. PER 5–0 in PER (Clay).* R2 d. Yzaga 6–8 7–5 6–1 6–2; R5 v P. Arraya not played. **July** – *Zone 1 Final USA d. ARG 4–1 in ARG (Clay).* R2 d. M. Jaite 6–2 6–2 6–1; R4 d. G. Perez–Roldan 2–6 6–2 8–6. **1989: February** – *World Group 1r USA d. PAR 5–0 in USA (Hard).* R2 d. H. Chapacu 6–2 6–1 6–1; R5 d. F. Gonzalez 6–2 6–4. **April** – *World Group qf USA d. FRA 5–0 in USA (Carpet).* R2 d. H. Leconte 6–1 6–2 5–7 6–1; R4 d. Y. Noah 6–3 7–6. **July** – *World Group sf FRG d. USA 3–2 in FRG (Carpet).* R2 lost B. Becker 6–7 6–7 7–6 6–3 6–4; R4 lost C. Steeb 4–6 6–4 6–4 6–2. **1990: September** – *World Group sf USA d. AUT 3–2 in AUT (Clay).* R2 d. H. Skoff 7–6 6–0 6–1; R4 lost T. Muster 6–2 6–2 7–6. **December** – *World Group Final USA d. AUS 3–2 in USA (Clay).* R1 d. R. Fromberg 4–6 6–2 4–6 6–2 6–4; R4 lost D. Cahill 6–4 4–4 6 ret'd. **1991: September** – *World Group sf USA d. GER 3–2 in USA (Clay).* R1 d. M. Stich 6–3 6–1 6–4; R5 d. C. Steeb 6–2 6–2 6–3. **November** – *World Group Final FRA d. USA 3–1 (Carpet).* R1 d. G. Forget 6–7 6–2 6–1 6–2; R5 v H. Leconte not played. **1992: January** – *World Group 1r USA d. ARG 5–0 in USA (Hard).* R2 d. A. Mancini 6–4 6–4 6–4; R5 d. M. Jaite 7–5 6–3. **March** – *World Group qf USA d. TCH 3–2 in USA (Hard).* R2 d. P. Korda 6–2 6–4 6–1; R5 d. K. Novacek 7–5 6–0 6–0. **September** – *World Group sf USA d. SWE 4–1 in USA (Clay).* R2 d. S. Edberg 5–7 6–3 7–6 6–3; R5 d. N. Kulti 6–7 6–2 6–2. **December** – *World Group Final USA d. SUI 3–1 in USA (Hard).* R1 d. J. Hlasek 6–1 6–2 6–2; R5 v M. Rosset not played. **1993: September** – *World Group Qualifying USA d. BAH 5–0 in USA (Hard).* R1 d. R. Smith 6–2 6–2 6–3. **1995: March** – *World Group qf USA d. ITA 5–0 in ITA (Clay).* R1 d. A. Gaudenzi 6–4 6–4 6–1. **September** – *World Group sf USA d. SWE 4–1 in USA (Hard).* R2 d. M. Wilander 7–6 6–2 6–2. **1997: April** – *World Group qf USA d. NED 4–1 in USA (Hard).* R1 d. S. Schalken 7–6 6–4 7–6; R4 d. J. Siemerink 3–6 6–3 6–3 6–3. **1998: April** – *World Group 1r USA d. RUS 3–2 in USA (Hard).* R2 d. M. Safin 6–3 6–3 6–3; R4 lost Y. Kafelnikov 6–3 6–0 7–6. **July** – *World Group qf USA d. BEL 4–1 in USA (Hard).* R2 d. C. Van Garsse 6–2 6–2 6–2. **2000: February** – *World Group 1r USA d. ZIM 3–2 in ZIM (Hard).* R1 d. W. Black 7–5 6–3 7–5; R4 d. B. Black 6–2 6–3 7–6. **April** – *World Group qf USA d. CZE 3–2 in USA (Carpet).* R2 d. S. Dosedel 6–3 6–3 6–3; R4 d. J. Novak 6–3 6–3 6–1.

GRAND SLAM CUP RECORD – Played 5, r/u 1, qf 2

1992: 1r [seed 2] lost Chang 6–4 6–2. **1994: qf** [seed 2] d. Muster 6–3 7–5, lost Larsson 6–3 1–6 6–0. **1996: 1r** [seed 8] lost Woodforde 6–3 6–4. **1998: r/u** d. Pioline 6–0 6–0, Korda [1] 4–6 6–0 6–1, Kucera 7–6 6–7 2–6 7–5 6–0, lost Rios [2] 6–4 2–6 7–6 5–7 6–3. **1999: qf** [seed 1] bye, lost Haas 6–0 6–7 6–4.

GRAND PRIX MASTERS/ATP TOUR CHAMPIONSHIP/MASTERS CUP – Played 8, won 1, r/u 2, sf 2

1989: 4th in rr lost Becker 6–1 6–3, lost Edberg 6–4 6–2, lost Gilbert 3–6 6–3 6–3. **1990: won** in rr d. Sampras 6–4 6–2, d. E. Sanchez 6–0 6–3, lost Edberg 7–6 4–6 7–6; sf d. Becker 6–2 6–4; f d. Edberg 5–7 7–6 7–5 6–2. **1991: sf** in rr d. Becker 6–3 7–5, lost Sampras 6–3 1–6 6–3, d. Stich 7–5 6–3; sf lost Courier 6–3 7–5. **1994: sf** in rr d. Berasategui 6–2 6–0, d. Chang 6–4 6–4, d. Bruguera 6–4 1–6 6–3; sf lost Sampras 4–6 7–6 6–3. **1996:** lost Sampras 6–2 6–1 ret in rr **1998:** lost Corretja 5–7 6–3 2–1 ret in rr. **1999: r/u** in rr d. Lapentti 6–1 6–2, Sampras 6–2 6–2, Kuerten 6–4 7–5; sf d. Kafelnikov 6–4 7–6; f lost Sampras 6–1 7–5 6–4. **2000: r/u;** in rr d. Kuerten 4–6 6–4 6–3, d. Kafelnikov 6–1 6–4, d. M. Norman 6–3 6–2; sf d. Satin 6–3 6–3; f lost Kuerten 6–4 6–4 6–4.

7 LLEYTON HEWITT (AUS)

Born: Adelaide, 24 February 1981. **Lives:** Adelaide.
Father: Glynn, who travels with him. **Mother:** Sherilyn.
Sister: Jaslyn (younger), who plays the junior circuit.
Girlfriend: Kim Clijsters, who plays the women's circuit.

Agent: Octagon (Tom Ross).
Coach: Darren Cahill; formerly Peter Smith.
Turned Pro: 1998. **Height:** 5ft 11in (1.80cm).
Weight: 145lb (65kg).

Rankings: 1997: 722; **1998:** 113; **1999:** 22;
2000: 7 singles, 20 doubles. **Highest:** 6 (2000).

2000 Prize Money: $1,642,572.
Career Earnings: $2,197,797. **Career Titles:** 6.

Style: A feisty battler who never knows when he is beaten. One of the quickest men about the court his counter-hitting passes on the run are at times breathtaking. His early-hit returns of serve are among the best in the game and he despatches mid-court balls for winners with commendable regularity.

CAREER HIGHLIGHTS (year: (titles))
Former nat 18s GC and HC champ. **1997:** Although he had not taken up tennis until age 15, at 15 years 11 months he was the youngest qualifier ever at Australian Open. **1998: (1)** *Adelaide.* A wild-card entry at Adelaide, he upset Woodforde, Agassi and Stoltenberg to win his 1st career title, becoming, at 16 years 10 months, the youngest to win a tourn since Chang (16 years 7 months) at San Francisco in 1988. The following week he upset Bjorkman 1r Sydney and went on to reach qf Singapore as a qualifier. **1999: (1)** *Delray Beach.* After breaking into the top 100 he moved up into the top 25 during the year, in which his 2nd main tour title came at Delray Beach. It was another exciting year in which he was also r/u Adelaide (d. Kiefer), Scottsdale (d. Rafter) and Lyon; reached sf Queen's, where he extended Sampras to 7–6 fs on grass, and Singapore; appeared in qf Sydney (d. Rafter), Nottingham, Los Angeles; upset Kafelnikov at Paris Open; and won Perth Challenger. In his debut year he helped take AUS to D Cup f, although he lost both his matches there as AUS d. FRA 3–2. **2000: (4)** *Adelaide, Sydney, Scottsdale, Queen's.* He began the year in style again, with the titles at Adelaide and Sydney back-to-back, unseeded and r/u in doubles both times with Stolle. He added Scottsdale in March (d. Rios and Henman), breaking into top 10 Entry System 1st time on 15 May and consolidating his position with upsets of Pioline and Sampras on grass to win Queen's. At Stuttgart Masters he upset Kafelnikov to reach his 1st f at that level, but withdrew Paris Masters with a mystery virus/allergy. Kafelnikov had also been his victim *en route* to sf Ericsson Open, and he upset Enqvist on his way to same stage Rome, Indianapolis and US Open, also reaching sf Basel. Qualifying for his 1st season-ending champs, he upset Sampras in rr Masters Cup, but did not progress beyond rr. His 1st GS title came at US Open, where, pairing for 1st time with Mirnyi and unseeded, he became the youngest male in the open era to win a GS doubles title. He also won Indianapolis from 3 f with Stolle and in mixed was r/u Wimbledon with his girlfriend, Clijsters. In D Cup he helped AUS to f, where he d. A. Costa in a 5s, 4hr battle, but could not overcome Ferrero as ESP won 3–1 in Barcelona.

PRINCIPAL 2000 RESULTS – won 4, r/u 1, sf 5 (detailed Grand Slam results follow)
won Adelaide (d. Woodforde 6–3 2–6 6–1, Petrovic 6–0 6–2, Stoltenberg 6–2 6–2, Escude 3–6 6–1 6–4, Enqvist 3–6 6–3 6–2), **won** Sydney (d. Grosjean 6–4 6–4, Clavet 6–3 6–2, Voinea 6–3 6–4, Corretja 6–4 6–4, Stoltenberg 6–4 6–0), **won** Scottsdale (d. Vacek 6–1 6–7 6–2, Woodruff 3–6 6–2 6–3, Rios 7–6 4–2 ret, Ferrero 6–4 6–2, Henman 6–4 7–6), **won** Queen's (d. Wheaton 6–4 6–4, Ivanisevic 6–4 6–4, Pioline 6–4 6–4, Pozzi 6–1 6–4, Sampras 6–4 6–4); **r/u** Stuttgart Masters (d. Krajicek 6–4 7–5, Henman 3–6 6–3 6–4, Rusedski 6–4 6–4, Kafelnikov 6–4 6–7 6–3, lost W. Ferreira 7–6 3–6 6–7 7–6 6–2); **sf** Ericsson Open (d. Gaudio 7–6 6–7 6–3, Haas 6–1 6–3, Kafelnikov 6–4 6–3, Gambill 6–4 7–6, lost Sampras 6–3 3–6 6–1), **sf** Rome (d. Koubek 6–4 6–2, Di Pasquale 6–3 6–7 6–4, Enqvist 7–6 2–6 6–3, Puerta 6–3 3–6 6–1, lost M. Norman 6–3 6–0), **sf** Indianapolis (d. Koubek 6–1 6–0, A. Costa 6–2 6–4, Enqvist 6–3 6–3, lost Kuerten 7–5 6–2), **sf** US Open, **sf** Basel (d. Saulnier 6–2 6–2, Vinciguerra 6–3 7–5, Rusedski 7–6 6–2, lost Federer 6–4 5–7 7–6).

Australia's Lleyton Hewitt, who showed typical courage on day one of the Davis Cup Final.
(Paul Zimmer)

DOUBLES: (with Stolle unless stated) (with Mirnyi) **won US Open** (d. E. Ferreira/Leach 6–4 5–7 7–6); **won** Indianapolis (d. Bjorkman/Mirnyi 6–2 3–6 6–3); **r/u** Adelaide (lost Woodbridge/Woodforde 6–4 6–2), **r/u** Sydney (lost Woodbridge/Woodforde 7–5 6–4). **MIXED DOUBLES:** (with Clijsters) **r/u Wimbledon** (lost Johnson/Po 6–4 7–6).

CAREER GRAND SLAM RECORD
AUSTRALIAN OPEN – Played 4
1997: 1r lost Bruguera 6–3 6–4 6–3. **1998: 1r** lost Vacek 6–2 6–4 1–6 2–6 6–3. **1999: 2r** d. Pioline [12] 6–3 6–1 6–1, lost Haas 4–6 6–4 6–3 6–4. **2000: last 16** [unseeded] d. Goldstein 6–2 6–7 7–6 6–4, Corretja 6–0 6–0 6–1, Voinea 6–2 7–5 6–3, lost M. Norman [seed 12] 6–3 6–1 7–6.

FRENCH OPEN – Played 2
1999: 1r lost Rodriguez 4–6 6–4 6–4 4–6 6–4. **2000: last 16** [seed 9] d. Tarango 7–6 7–6 6–3, Hantschk 2–6 6–3 3–6 6–2 6–3, Savolt 6–1 6–4 6–0, lost A. Costa 6–3 4–6 6–2 6–4.

WIMBLEDON – Played 2
1999: 3r d. Filippini 6–2 6–2 6–1, Alami 6–1 6–4 4–6 6–4, lost Becker 6–1 6–4 7–6. **2000: 1r** [seed 7] lost Gambill 6–3 6–2 7–5.

US OPEN – Played 2, sf 1
1999: 3r d. Rosset 6–2 6–2 6–0, Arthurs 6–2 6–4 6–7 6–4, lost Medvedev 3–6 6–3 3–6 6–4 6–3. **2000: sf** [seed 9] d. Vinciguerra 2–6 7–5 6–3 6–3, Boutter 7–6 6–4 6–4, Novak 6–3 6–3 6–3, Enqvist [7] 6–3 6–2 6–4, Clement 6–2 6–4 6–3, lost Sampras [4] 7–6 6–4 7–6.

OLYMPIC RECORD
2000: (Sydney) 1r [seed 4] lost Mirnyi 6–3 6–3.

CAREER DAVIS CUP RECORD
1999: July – *World Group qf AUS d. USA 4–1 in USA (Hard).* R1 d. T. Martin 6–4 6–7 6–3 6–0; R5 d. A. O'Brien 7–5 6–4. **September** – *World Group sf AUS d. RUS 4–1 in AUS (Grass).* R1 d. M. Safin 7–6 6–2 4–6 6–3; R4 d. Y. Kafelnikov 6–4 7–5 6–2. **December** – *World Group final AUS d. FRA 3–2 in FRA (Clay).* R2 lost C. Pioline 7–6 7–6 7–5; R5 lost S. Grosjean 6–4 6–3. **2000: February** – *World Group 1r AUS d. SUI 3–2 in SUI (Hard).* R1 d. G. Bastl 4–6 6–3 6–2 6–4; R4 d. R. Federer 6–2 3–6 7–6 6–1. **April** – *World Group qf AUS d. GER 3–2 in AUS (Grass).* R1 d. M. Kohlmann 6–1 6–1 6–2; R4 lost R. Schuttler 2–6 6–3 6–4. **July** – *World Group sf AUS d. BRA 5–0 in AUS (Grass).* R2 d. F. Meligeni 6–4 6–2 6–3; R4 d. A. Sa 6–4 6–1. **December** – *World Group final ESP d. AUS 3–1 in ESP (Clay).* R1 d. A. Costa 3–6 6–1 2–6 6–4 6–4; R4 lost J.C. Ferrero 6–2 7–6 4–6 6–4.

GRAND SLAM CUP RECORD
Has never played.

MASTERS CUP – Played 1
2000: 3rd in rr d. Sampras 7–5 6–0, lost Corretja 3–6 7–6 6–3, lost Safin 6–4 6–4.

8 ALEX CORRETJA (ESP)

Born: Barcelona, 11 April 1974. **Lives:** Andorra
Father: Luis. **Mother:** Luisa. **Brothers:** Sergio and Ivan.
Agent: ProServ. **Coach:** Javier Duarte. **Trainer:** Patrick Feijula.
Turned Pro: 1991. **Height:** 5ft 11in (1.80cm). **Weight:** 155lb
(70kg).

Rankings: 1991: 234; **1992:** 86; **1993:** 76; **1994:** 22;
1995: 48; **1996:** 23; **1997:** 12; **1998:** 3; **1999:** 26; **2000:** 6.
Highest: 2 (1 February 1999).

2000 Prize Money: $1,530,062.
Career Earnings: $8,150,134. **Career titles:** 14.

Style: A fine baseliner with heavy, topspin forehand and backhand that make him a formidable CC player. He has developed his game on other surfaces by improving his volleying technique and by adopting a more aggressive attitude. Superb fitness and the ability to concentrate over long spells make him one of the best all-rounders in the game.

CAREER HIGHLIGHTS (year: (titles))
1990: Won Orange Bowl 16s. **1991:** Began to make his mark on the satellite circuits. **1992:** Reached his 1st tour f at Guaruja in Nov. and moved into top 100. Upset E. Sanchez 1r Hamburg. **1993:** Reached sf Florence and Sao Paulo, plus qf Monte Carlo. **1994: (1)** *Buenos Aires*. His 1st tour title came at the very end of the season – at Buenos Aires, in his 3rd career f. He had scored some big upsets during the year on his way to f Palermo (where he held 2 mps v Berasategui), sf Mexico City (d. Berasategui), Barcelona (d. Courier), Madrid (d. Berasategui again), Indianapolis (d. Courier and Edberg), Athens and Santiago, as well as beating Becker at Hamburg. At French Open, he was 2-sets-to-love up v Ivanisevic 3r before letting the match slip away. **1995:** Upset W. Ferreira at French Open and at Gstaad he ended Muster's 40-match CC winning streak. He also reached sf Mexico City, Munich and Buenos Aires and in doubles won Palermo with Santoro. **1996:** He was again a dangerous opponent, as he confirmed on his way to r/u Hamburg (d. A. Costa, Rosset and Rios), Kitzbuhel and Marbella, sf Estoril (d. A. Costa and took a set off Muster) and Stuttgart Eurocard (d. Moya), plus qf Indianapolis (d. Reneberg) and Palermo. He reached the same stage at US Open, where, unseeded, he was on the verge of causing the upset of the year v Sampras: he held mp at 7–6 in fs tb, with Sampras suffering so severely from dehydration that he was hardly able to stand. However, the No. 1 drew level, served an ace for 8–7 and Corretja let the match go with a double-fault after 3 hr 52 min. Won the Stefan Edberg Sportsmanship award. **1997: (3)** *Estoril, Rome, Stuttgart Mercedes*. In his best year to date, he broke into top 10 for a while with titles at Estoril, Rome (d. Ivanisevic and Rios) and Stuttgart Mercedes. He also reached f Monte Carlo and Munich (where he won the doubles with Albano), sf Gstaad and Palermo and qf Boston. In GS he overruled an 'out' call on a crucial bp when losing to Dewulf at French Open, and withdrew 3r US Open after injuring his left thigh while warming up. **1998: (5)** *Dubai, Gstaad, Indianapolis, Lyon, ATP Champ*. He crowned an excellent year with the title at his 1st ATP Champ, earned in dramatic style: in sf he saved 3 mps v Sampras before winning 7–6 fs, then in f he pulled back from 2-sets-to-love down to d. Moya 7–5 fs in a 4-hour struggle. He became the 1st Spaniard since Orantes in 1976 to win the event and the 1st player since McEnroe in 1978 to win on his 1st appearance there. This triumph took him into the top 3, ahead of Rafter, Moya and Agassi. His 1st HC title at Dubai (d. Bjorkman) had already underlined what a complete player he was becoming, although he was no exception among the CC specialists in finding GC a puzzle. He also won Gstaad, Indianapolis (d. Agassi for his 1st title in US) and Lyon (saving mp v Haas in 2s tb in f). He reached his 1st GS f at French Open, where he met no seeded player until that stage and on the way needed 5 hr 31 min – the longest recorded GS match – to d. Gumy 3r (9–7 fs). Earlier at Hamburg another string of gruelling matches had left him too exhausted to complete his f v A. Costa, obliging him to ret 3s. In other tourns he reached sf Indian Wells and Palermo and qualified for GS Cup, although he did not take up his place. **1999:** Although he won no title, he was consistent with r/u Sydney, Long Island and Mallorca, sf Rome and Stuttgart Mercedes,

and qf French Open (where he was restricted by an allergic reaction, worsened by medication), Bucharest and Palermo, and won all his matches in WT Cup. However, it was not enough to maintain his ranking and, hampered by a string of injuries and illnesses, he dropped out of top 10 in Oct. and out of top 25 by end of year. **2000: (5)** *Indian Wells, Gstaad, Kitzbuhel, Washington, Toulouse.* His 1st title since ATP Champ 1998 came at Indian Wells (d. M. Norman, N. Lapentti and Enqvist) and was followed across the year by Gstaad, Kitzbuhel, Washington (d. Agassi) and Toulouse, returning him to his place in the top 10. He was disappointing in GS, with qf French Open his best showing, and pulled out of Wimbledon in protest at seeding arrangements, but was not fined as he withdrew before starting. At Masters Cup, too, he won only 1 match and did not progress beyond rr. However, he led ESP to their 1st D Cup f for 33 years and their 1st title ever. In f, where he was surprisingly not called on to play either 1st or 2nd singles, he won doubles with Balcells, then his 5th-rubber singles v Rafter (injured) was cancelled as ESP triumphed 3–1 in Barcelona. Elsewhere he reached sf Sydney and Rome and qf French Open, Scottsdale, Monte Carlo and Paris Masters and won Olympic bronze in doubles with A. Costa.

PRINCIPAL 2000 RESULTS – won 5, sf 2 (detailed Grand Slam results follow)
won Indian Wells (d. Kucera 6–2 6–2, Rafter 7–6 5–7 6–2, Santoro 7–6 6–1, M. Norman 4–6 6–2 6–2, N. Lapentti 6–3 6–4, Enqvist 6–4 6–4 6–3), **won** Gstaad (d. Federer 6–4 4–6 6–4, Spadea 6–2 6–2, Rios 6–7 6–1 6–3, Gaudio 7–5 7–5, Puerta 6–1 6–3), **won** Kitzbuhel (d. Gonzalez 6–1 6–2, Ljubicic 7–6 6–4, Zabaleta 6–3 6–0, Calleri 6–3 6–7 6–2, Alvarez 6–3 6–1 3–0 ret), **won** Washington (d. Kim 7–5 6–3, Srichaphan 6–3 6–1, Arthurs 7–6 3–6 6–3, Kiefer 7–6 6–2, Agassi 6–2 6–3), **won** Toulouse (d. Pozzi 6–1 6–2, Popp 6–1 6–4, Tillstrom 7–5 6–3, Rios 7–6 6–3, Moya 6–3 6–2); **sf** Sydney (d. Pioline 6–4 6–4, Arazi 3–6 6–3 7–6, Dosedel 3–6 7–5 6–3, lost Hewitt 6–4 6–4), **sf** Rome (d. Kucera 6–2 4–6 7–6, Novak 6–3 7–6, Santoro 6–2 6–3, Hrbaty 6–1 7–6, lost Kuerten 6–4 6–2). **DOUBLES:** (with A. Costa) **Olympics bronze medal.**

CAREER GRAND SLAM RECORD
AUSTRALIAN OPEN – Played 5
1996: 2r d. Jonsson 6–3 6–3 6–0, lost Kafelnikov [6] 6–1 6–2 6–3. **1997: 2r** d. Mitchell 7–6 6–0 6–2, lost Schaller 4–6 6–3 6–3 4–6 6–3. **1998: 3r** [seed 11] d. Arnold 6–4 7–5 2–6 6–3, Prinosil 6–4 6–3 6–0, lost Pioline 6–2 6–1 6–4. **1999: 2r** [seed 2] d. Suzuki 6–3 4–6 3–6 7–6 6–2, lost Ruud 3–6 6–3 6–4 6–4. **2000: 2r** d. Sargsian 7–6 6–4 6–4, lost Hewitt 6–0 6–0 6–1.
FRENCH OPEN – Played 9, r/u 1, qf 2
1992: 1r lost Mancini 6–4 1–6 6–4 6–7 6–3. **1993: 1r** lost M. Larsson 2–6 6–3 7–6 7–6. **1994: 3r** d. Meligeni 6–3 6–1 1–6 5–7 6–3, O'Brien 6–4 6–6–2 6–4, lost Ivanisevic [5] 6–7 3–6 6–1 6–2 6–3. **1995: last 16** [unseeded] d. Golmard 6–4 7–5 6–0, Forget 6–2 6–3 6–3, W. Ferreira [8] 6–4 7–5 6–2, lost Kafelnikov [9] 6–3 6–2 6–2. **1996: 2r** d. Woodforde 6–3 6–4 0–6 6–4, lost Mantilla 7–6 6–2 6–4. **1997: last 16** [seed 8] d. Alami 6–3 6–4 6–1, Knippschild 4–6 6–1 6–1 7–6, Champion 6–1 3–0 ret, lost Dewulf 5–7 6–1 6–4 7–5. **1998: r/u** [seed 14] d. Alami 6–3 6–2 0–6 6–4, Vicente 6–3 6–2 6–3, Gumy 6–1 5–7 6–7 7–5 9–7, Stoltenberg 6–4 6–4 6–3, Dewulf 7–5 6–4 6–3, Pioline 6–3 6–4 6–2, lost Moya [12] 6–3 7–5 6–3. **1999: qf** [seed 6] d. Puentes 7–6 6–4 6–2, Vicente 6–3 6–4 3–6 6–7 6–2, Gaudio 6–4 6–3 6–3, Koubek 6–2 6–3 7–5, lost Meligeni 6–2 6–2 6–0. **2000: qf** [seed 10] d. A. Martin 6–3 6–4 6–4, Meligeni 4–6 6–3 6–3 4–6 6–3, Krajicek 4–6 6–2 6–3 6–2, Federer 7–5 7–6 6–2, lost Ferrero 6–4 6–4 6–2.
WIMBLEDON – Played 3
1994: 2r d. Leconte 2–6 4–6 7–5 7–6 3–2 ret, lost Fromberg 6–2 7–6 7–5. **1995: Did not play. 1996: 2r** d. Tebbutt 3–6 7–6 6–4 6–4, lost Hlasek 4–6 6–3 6–4 6–4. **1997: Did not play. 1998: 1r** [seed 10] lost Gimelstob 7–6 6–2 6–3. **1999–2000:** Did not play.
US OPEN – Played 9, qf 1
1992: 1r lost Woodbridge 6–2 6–2 6–2. **1993: 1r** lost Muster [12] 6–4 6–4 6–3. **1994: 1r** lost Enqvist 4–6 6–3 6–4 6–7 6–1. **1995: 2r** d. O'Brien 6–4 6–4 6–3, lost Agassi [1] 5–7 6–3 5–7 6–0 6–2. **1996: qf** [unseeded] d. B. Black 7–6 6–6 6–2 6–2, Veglio 6–7 6–4 6–4 6–0, Bjorkman 6–2 4–6 4–6 6–4 6–3, Forget 6–4 6–3 7–6, lost Sampras [1] 7–6 5–7 5–7 6–4 7–6. **1997: 3r** [seed 8] d. Rosset 4–6 6–3 6–2 6–2, Ulihrach 7–5 6–4 3–6 6–4, lost Krajicek w/o. **1998: last 16** [seed 7] d. Pozzi 2–6 6–3 7–5 7–5, Perlant 6–4 5–7 6–7 6–1 6–0, B. Black 6–3 4–6 6–2 7–6, lost Moya [10] 7–6 7–5 6–3. **1999: 1r** [seed 13] lost Arthurs 6–3 6–4 1–6 4–6 7–6. **2000: 3r** [seed 8] d. Srichaphan 7–6 6–0 6–0, Rosset 6–3 7–6 6–3, lost Moya 7–6 6–3 4–6 6–4.

OLYMPIC RECORD
2000: (Sydney) 3r [seed 6] d. Ivanisevic 7–6 7–6, Clement 6–7 6–4 6–4, lost Haas 7–6 6–3. **DOUBLES:** (with A. Costa) **2000: (Sydney) bronze medal** d. Adams/De Jager 2–6 6–4 6–3 in play-off.

CAREER DAVIS CUP RECORD
1996: April – *Zone 1 2r ESP d. ISR 4–1 in ISR (Hard).* R3 (with E. Sanchez) lost N. Behr/E. Erlich 7–5 4–6 4–6 7–6 6–3. **September** – *World Group Qualifying ESP d. DEN 4–1 in ESP (Clay).* R3 (with T. Carbonell) d. K. Carlsen/T. Fetterlein 6–4 7–5 4–6 5–7 6–3). **1997: February** – *World Group 1r ESP d. GER 4–1 in ESP (Clay).* R3 (with C. Costa) lost M. Goellner/D. Prinosil 6–2 6–2 6–3. **1998: April** – *World Group 1r ESP d. BRA 3–2 in*

Spanish No. 1, Alex Corretja, whose role in the successful Davis Cup Final against Australia was restricted to doubles. (Paul Zimmer)

BRA (Clay). R2 d. F. Meligeni 4–6 6–4 3–6 6–4 6–4; R3 (with J. Sanchez) lost G. Kuerten/J. Oncins 6–1 5–7 6–3 6–2; R4 d. Kuerten 6–3 7–5 4–6 6–4. **July** – *World Group qf ESP d. SUI 4–1 in ESP (Clay).* R2 d. M. Rosset 6–1 6–2 6–2; R5 d. G. Bastl 6–0 7–5. **September** – *World Group sf SWE d. ESP 4–1 in SWE (Carpet).* R1 lost J. Bjorkman 6–3 7–5 6–7 6–3. **1999: April** – *World Group 1r BRA d. ESP 3–2 in ESP (Clay).* R2 lost G. Kuerten 6–3 6–4 7–5; R3 (with A. Costa) lost Kuerten/J. Oncins 6–2 5–7 4–6 6–4 6–3; R5 d. M. Carlsson 6–1 6–2. **2000: February** – *World Group 1r ESP d. ITA 4–1 in ESP (Clay).* R2 d. A. Gaudenzi 4–6 6–1 6–1 6–1; R3 (with J. Balcells) d. Gaudenzi/D. Nargiso 6–3 6–4 6–1. **April** – *World Group qf ESP d. RUS 4–1 in ESP (Clay).* R1 d. M. Safin 6–4 6–3 5–7 6–1; R3 (with Balcells) lost Y. Kafelnikov/Safin 7–6 2–6 7–6 6–4. **July** – *World Group sf ESP d. USA 5–0 in ESP (Clay).* R2 d. J. Gambill 1–6 6–3 6–4 6–4; R3 (with Balcells) d. T. Martin/C. Woodruff 7–6 2–6 6–3 6–7 6–3. **December** – *World Group final ESP d. AUS 3–1 in ESP* (Clay). R3 (with J. Balcells) d. S. Stolle/M. Woodforde 6–4 6–4 6–4. R5 v P. Rafter cancelled.

GRAND SLAM CUP RECORD – Played 1
1996: 1r lost Kafelnikov [3] 6–4 7–6.

ATP TOUR CHAMPIONSHIP/MASTERS CUP – Played 2, won 1
1998: won in rr d. Agassi 5 7 6–3 2–1 ret, lost Henman 7–6 6–7 6–2, d. A. Costa 6–2 6–4; sf d. Sampras 4–6 6–3 7–6; f d. Moya 3–6 3–6 7–5 6–3 7–5. **2000: 4th In rr** lost Safin 6–7 7–5 6–3, lost Sampras 7 6 7 5, d. Hewitt 3–6 7–6 6–3.

9 THOMAS ENQVIST (SWE)

Born: Stockholm, 13 March 1974. **Lives:** Monte Carlo, Monaco. **Father:** Folke. **Mother:** Birgitta. **Brother:** Torbjorn 'Toby' (older). **Sister:** Maria (younger). **Fiancée:** Daniela.

Agent: IMG (Bill Ryan). **Coach:** Mikael Stripple; formerly Joakim Nystrom. **Turned Pro:** 1991.
Height: 6ft 3in (1.91m). **Weight:** 192lb (87kg).

Rankings: 1989: 1103; **1990:** 472; **1991:** 229; **1992:** 63; **1993:** 87; **1994:** 60; **1995:** 7; **1996:** 9; **1997:** 28; **1998:** 22; **1999:** 4; **2000:** 9. **Highest:** 4 (1999).

2000 Prize Money: $2,381,060.
Career Earnings: $8,680,378. **Career Titles:** 18

Style: With a very powerful game based on a match-winning forehand and effective two-handed backhand, he has improved his serve to the extent that it, too, has become a match-winning shot. Great determination and concentration make him a formidable opponent.

CAREER HIGHLIGHTS (year: (titles))

Won Donald Duck Cup in 1985, 1987 and 1988. **1988:** Won European 14s. **1990:** (472) R/u French Open Jun to Gaudenzi. **1991:** (229) In Jun singles won Australian Open over Gleeson, Wimbledon over Joyce and was r/u French Open to Medvedev to finish the year at No. 1 in the ITF Jun singles rankings. In Jun doubles won French Open with Martinelle. **1992: (1)** *Bolzano.* Made his mark in the senior game right from the start of the year at Australian Open, where he was the only player apart from Edberg to take a set off Courier. Reached qf Adelaide, Bastad and Indianapolis and in autumn won his 1st tour title at Bolzano. **1993: (1)** *Schenectady.* Having failed to pass 2r all year to date, he won Schenectady in Aug., upsetting Lendl on the way, and followed with sf Vienna (d. Volkov) and qf Bordeaux. Upset Agassi at US Open, where he was unseeded. **1994:** Hampered by knee problems through the year: he underwent surgery for patella tendinitis of the left knee in March, took 3 months to get back into shape, and underwent surgery on the right knee in Nov. However, he still managed to reach sf Auckland, qf Memphis (d. MaliVai Washington), Toronto (d. Korda and Yzaga), Washington (d. Yzaga again), Indianapolis and Schenectady; upset Korda 1r Australian Open and Kafelnikov at Cincinnati. **1995: (5)** *Auckland, Philadelphia, Indianapolis, US CC, Stockholm.* He continued to cause some big upsets: he beat Volkov on his way to the title at Auckland, Agassi and M. Chang to take Philadelphia, Ivanisevic and M. Chang at Montreal (where he lost sf to Sampras only 7–6 fs), and surprised Ivanisevic three times more on his way to f Los Angeles, sf Cincinnati and then the title at Indianapolis. That last result took him into the top 10 and ahead of Larsson to the No. 1 slot in Sweden. He also won US CC and reached 6 more qf to qualify for his 1st IBM/ATP Champ. There he was inspired, being the only player unbeaten in rr and falling only 7–5 fs to Becker in sf. Voted ATP Most Improved Player of the Year. **1996: (3)** *New Delhi, Paris Open, Stockholm.* After taking the title at New Delhi in April, without losing a set, he was less consistent and dropped out of the top 10 in July. However, he found form again later in the year, upsetting Sampras *en route* to sf Cincinnati, removing Kafelnikov on the way to his 1st Mercedes Super 9 title at Paris Open in Nov., which saw him back in the top 10, and confirming his position with the title at Stockholm. He also appeared in sf Lyon and qf Australian Open, Dubai, Memphis, Tokyo Japan Open, Indianapolis and Toronto. Playing at ATP Champs as alternate when Agassi withdrew after 1 match, he d. Becker in ss but lost to Kafelnikov. **1997: (1)** *Marseille.* Hampered during the year by infected blisters, an arm injury, ankle injury and flu, he played only Australian Open of GS and slipped out of the top 25. However, he won both singles and doubles at Marseille (with Larsson), reached f Los Angeles and sf Zagreb, Rotterdam and Paris Open, plus qf Montreal, Basle and Lyon. **1998: (2)** *Marseille, Munich.* Returning to form after a 4-month absence with various injuries, he upset Kafelnikov and Krajicek on his way to the title at Marseille, following with a defeat of Agassi to win Munich. However, he was out again for 3 months in the summer, undergoing ankle surgery to remove a bone chip on 11 Aug. In addition to his 2 titles, he was r/u Philadelphia, and reached sf Ostrava, qf Sydney (d. Moya),

Memphis, Indian Wells, LIPC (d. Kucera and Rusedski) and Queen's. **1999: (3)** *Adelaide, Stuttgart Eurocard, Stockholm.* He began the year in tremendous style by following the title at Adelaide with upsets of Rafter and Philippoussis on his way to f Australian Open, unseeded. Unsurprisingly his year was less spectacular thereafter until Oct., when he won Stuttgart Eurocard (d. Kuerten, Rios, Agassi and Krajicek) and added Stockholm a fortnight later. He also reached sf LIPC, Bournemouth and GS Cup, appeared in qf London, Tokyo and Long Island, and upset T. Martin at Paris Open. Going into ATP Champ he had won 1st and last tourns of season, but there he could win only 1 match so that his season ended after all on an anticlimax. **2000: (2)** *Cincinnati, Basel.* Although it was a less spectacular year, he maintained his top 10 ranking with titles at Cincinnati and Basel, plus r/u Adelaide, Indian Wells (upset Sampras, who was returning from injury) and Long Island, as well as sf London and Munich and qf Indianapolis and Lyon. He settled into the Champions Race top 10 from Aug., but just missed qualification for Masters Cup, where he was 1st alternate but not called on to play.

PRINCIPAL 2000 RESULTS – won 2, r/u 3, sf 2 (detailed Grand Slam results follow)
won Cincinnati (d. Pavel 7–5 2–6 7–6, Levy 6–4 6–1, Mirnyi 6–4 6–3, Vicente 7–5 6–1, Clement 6–2 6–2, Henman 7–6 6–4), **won** Basel (d. Gambill 7–6 7–6, Golmard 6–4 6–2, Hrbaty 4–6 6–2 6–3, Henman 6–1 6–3, Federer 6–2 4–6 7–6 1–6 6–1); **r/u** Adelaide (d. Clement 6–3 6–4, Federer 7–6 6–4, Grosjean 7–6 7–5, M. Norman 3–6 6–2 6–2, lost Hewitt 3–6 6–3 6–2), **r/u** Indian Wells (d. Golmard 6–1 6–4, T. Johansson 6–1 6–4, Zabaleta 6–4 7–5, Sampras 6–3 3–6 6–3, Philippoussis 6–3 6–7 7–6, lost Corretja 6–4 6–4 6–3), **r/u** Long Island (d. Goldstein 6–3 6–2, Santoro 7–6 6–4, Clement 7–6 6–1, lost M. Norman 3 5–7 7–5); **sf** London (d. Voinea 6–1 6–4, Kucera 6–3 3–6 6–4, Pioline 7–6 4–6 7–6, lost Rosset 7–5 1–6 6–3), **sf** Munich (d. Pavel 3–6 6–4 6–2, Ljubicic 6–2 6–7 7–6, Novak 6–3 6–4, lost Haas 7–6 1–6 6–4).

CAREER GRAND SLAM RECORD
AUSTRALIAN OPEN – Played 9, r/u 1, qf 1
1992: 2r d. Larsson 7–5 7–6 7–5, lost Courier [2] 2–6 6–3 6–1 6–4. **1993: 1r** lost Bruguera [15] 6–3 6–7 4–6 6–1 6–2. **1994: 2r** d. Korda [6] 6–3 6–4 7–6, lost Daufresne 6–3 6–2 7–6. **1995: 3r** d. Haarhuis 6–2 6–1 6–1, Nestor 6–4 6–4 7–5, lost Larsson w.o. **1996: qf** [seed 7] d. Goellner 6–3 6–2 6–4, Voinea 6–4 6–4 6–4, Gumy 6–2 7–6 3–6 6–1, Furlan 7–5 6–0 6–3, lost Woodforde 6–4 6–4 6–4. **1997: last 16** [seed 7] d. Pereira 6–1 6–2 6–4, Fromberg 6–4 6–4 7–5, Bruguera 7–6 7–5 6–2, lost Rios [9] 4–6 7–6 6–7 6–3. **1998: 2r** d. Marin 6–3 6–4 6–3, lost Rios [9] 6–4 7–6 4–6 6–4. **1999: r/u** [unseeded] d. Gambill 6–3 7–6 6–4, B. Black 7–6 7–6 6–0, Rafter [3] 6–4 4–6 6–4 6–4, Philippoussis [14] 6–2 6–7 4–6 6–2, Rosset 6–3 6–4 6–4, Lapentti 6–3 7–6 6–1, lost Kafelnikov [10] 4–6 6–0 6–3 7–6. **2000: 1r** [seed 6] lost Fromberg 6–4 7–6 4–6 3–6 10–8.
FRENCH OPEN – Played 7
1993: 1r lost Arriens 6–3 6–4 2–6 6–7 6–0. **1994: 1r** lost Wheaton 7–6 6–0 6–3. **1995: 1r** lost Boetsch 6–4 6–3 6–2. **1996: 1r** [seed 8] lost Reneberg 6–2 3–6 2–6 6–4 6–4. **1997:** Did not play. **1998: 3r** d. Pescariu 7–6 6–4 6–4, Kafelnikov [6] 4–6 7–6 6–1. **1999: 2r** [16] d. Moretti 6–4 6–2, lost Ruud 7–6 4–6 6–3. **2000: 3r** [seed 7] d. C. Rochus 6–2 6–0 6–0, Gaudio 6–3 6–2 6–0, lost A. Costa 5–7 7–6 6–1 3–6 6–4.
WIMBLEDON – Played 6
1993: 1r lost Foster 4–6 6–3 6–2 3–6 6–3. **1995: 1r** lost Jarryd 1–6 6–3 6–4 6–2. **1996: 2r** [seed 9] (d. A. Chang 6–4 6–2 6–1, lost MaliVai Washington 6–4 7–6 6–3. **1997:** Did not play. **1998: 3r** d. Nestor 6–7 6–7 6–4 6–0 6–0, S. Draper 6–7 6–1 6–4 6–3, lost Sampras [1] 6–3 7–6 7–6. **1999: 3r** d. Gumy 6–1 6–4 7–6, Schuttler 6–2 6–4 7–5, lost Rafter [2] 7–6 6–3 6–3. **2000: last 16** [seed 9] d. Hantschk 6–1 6–4 6–2, Clavet 7–6 7–6 7–5, Vinck 6–3 6–7 2–6 6–3 6–3, lost Gambill 7–6 3–6 6–3 6–4.
US OPEN – Played 6
1993: last 16 [unseeded] d. Agassi [16] 6–4 6–4 3–6 6–7 6–2, Bale 6–2 4–6 6–3 6–3, Black 6–3 6–1 6–1, lost Sampras [2] 6–4 6–7 7–6. **1994: 3r** d. Corretja 4–6 6–3 6–4 6–7 6–1, Dreekmann 7–6 7–6 6–7 7–5, lost Muster [seed 13] 6–0 6–4 6–2. **1995: 2r** [seed 9] d. Rios 2–6 6–2 4–6 6–3 7–6, lost B. Black 6–4 6–4 3–6 6–3. **1996: last 16** [seed 13] d. Simian 6–3 6–1 6–4, Raoux 6–3 6–2 6–3, Campana 6–4 6–4 6–2, lost Muster [3] 7–6 6–2 4–6 6–1. **1997–98:** Did not play. **1999: 1r** lost Haas [14] 6–2 6–4 7–6. **2000: last 16** [seed 7] d. Puerta 3–6 6–3 6–2, Woodruff 6–3 6–2 6–2, Rios 7–5 7–5 6–3, lost Hewitt 6–3 6–2 6–4.

OLYMPIC RECORD
1996: (Atlanta) 3r [seed 3] d. Goellner 7–6 4–6 6–4, Sargsian 4–6 7–6 6–4, lost Paes 7–5 7–6.

CAREER DAVIS CUP RECORD
1995: September – *World Group sf USA d. SWE 4–1 in USA (Hard).* R1 lost P. Sampras 6–3 6–4 3–6 6–3; R4 d. T. Martin 7–5 7–5 7–6. **1996: February** – *World Group 1r SWE d. BEL 4–1 in SWE (Carpet).* R2 d. D. Norman 6–4 6–3 6–1. R4 lost J. van Herck 7–5 6–2. **April** – *World Group qf SWE d. IND 5–0 in IND (Grass).* R2 d. M. Bhupathi 6–7 7–6 6–1 6–1. **September** – *World Group sf SWE d. CZE 4–1 in CZE (Carpet).* R1 d. P. Korda 6 4 6 3 7 6; R4 d. D. Vacek 6–3 6–7 4–6 7–5 6–3. **1997: February** – *World Group 1r SWE d. SUI 4–1 in SWE (Hard).* R2 d. L. Manta 7–6 7–6 6–2; R4 d. M. Rosset 6–3 6–2 3–6 6–2. **April** – *World Group qf SWE d. RSA 3–2 in SWE (Carpet).* R1 d. G. Stafford 7–5 2–6 6–4 6–1; R4 lost W. Ferreira 6–4 6–4 6–4. **September**

Forced to miss the Olympic Games through injury, Sweden's Thomas Enqvist completed his season at the Masters Cup and then faced surgery. (Paul Zimmer)

– World Group sf SWE d. ITA 4–1 in SWE (Carpet). R2 lost R. Furlan 3–6 6–3 6–4 3–6 6–3. R5 d. O. Camporese 6–3 6–7 6–3. **1998: July** *– World Group qf SWE d. GER 3–2 in GER (Hard).* R2 d. N. Kiefer 6–3 6–3 7–5. **1999: April** *– World Group 1r SVK d. SWE 3–2 in SWE (Carpet).* R2 lost D. Hrbaty 7–5 4–6 2–6 6–2 6–4; R4 lost K. Kucera 1–6 6–3 6–2 6–4.

GRAND SLAM CUP RECORD – Played 1, sf 1
1999: sf [seed 4] bye, d. Lapentti 6–3 6–2, lost Haas 6–3 6–4 6–7 6–4.

ATP TOUR CHAMPIONSHIP – Played 3, sf 1
1995: sf in rr d. Courier 6–3 6–2, d. M. Chang 6–1 6–4, d. Muster 6–4 6–7 6–4; sf lost Becker 6–4 6–7 7–5. **1996: 4th in rr** lost Kafelnikov 6–3 7–6, d. Becker 6–3 7–6. **1997-98:** Did not play. **1999: 4th in rr** d. Kiefer 6–4 7–5, lost Kafelnikov 7–5 3–6 6–4, lost T. Martin 6–4 6–1.

10 TIM HENMAN (GBR)

Born: Oxford, 6 September 1974. **Lives:** London.
Father: Anthony. **Mother:** Jane.
Brothers: Michael and Richard (both older).
Wife: Lucy Heald (married 11 December 1999).

Agent: Jan Felgate of IMG. **Coach:** David Felgate.
Physical Trainer: Tim Newenham. **Turned Pro:** 1993.
Height: 6ft 1in (1.85cm). **Weight:** 167lb (76kg).

Rankings: 1992: 771; **1993:** 434; **1994:** 161; **1995:** 99;
1996: 29; **1997:** 17; **1998:** 7; **1999:** 12; **2000:** 10.
Highest: 5 (26 July, 1999).

2000 Prize Money: $1,057,823.
Career Earnings: $5,869,480. **Career titles:** 6.

Style: One of the best serve-volleyers in the game, whose instinct is to attack from the net at every opportunity. His chip-and-charge tactics and excellent touch on the volley, together with speedy court coverage (much improved through tough physical training regime) make him an attractive player to watch. His powerful but erratic first serve is backed up by a much improved kicking second delivery. His naturally strong backhand is a match-winner, and the forehand, once erratic, is now a reliable weapon.

CAREER HIGHLIGHTS (year: (titles))
Great-grandson of Ellen Stawell-Brown, the 1st woman to serve overarm in the ladies' singles at Wimbledon, and grandson of Henry Billington, who played at Wimbledon in 1940s and 1950s. At age 12 suffered from Osteochondritis Dissecans, leaving him with permanently bent left arm. **1992:** Nat Jun champ in singles and doubles. **1994:** Began to make an impact on the satellite circuits and made his D Cup debut, but in September he broke his leg in 3 places and was out 5 months. **1995:** A mixed year finished on a high note when he broke into the top 100 after winning both singles and doubles at Seoul Challenger in Oct., following with Nat Champs and singles title at Reunion Challenger. On the main tour he reached his 1st qf at Nottingham, but hit a low point at Wimbledon, where he was disqualified and fined $3,000 after a ball he hit in frustration during a doubles match accidentally hit a ball-girl on the head. **1996:** In contrast to the previous year, Wimbledon provided the highlight of his career to date. Against Kafelnikov in 1r, he squandered a 2-set lead and stood 2 mps down at 3–5 fs, but served 2 aces before going on to win 7–5. He further thrilled his home crowds by progressing to qf, unseeded, a performance which took him into top 50 1st time. He went on to take an Olympic silver medal in doubles with Broad – Britain's 1st in tennis since 1924 – and at US Open he avenged his Wimbledon defeat by T. Martin en route to last 16, again unseeded. He also reached sf Shanghai, Rotterdam (d. Siemerink and Moya), Copenhagen, Seoul, Lyon (d. Siemerink again), Ostrava (d. W. Ferreira) and GS Cup (as alternate) and qf Nottingham (d. MaliVai Washington), moving into top 25 in Oct., although he slipped down again as he struggled at end of year. He took over No. 1 British ranking from Rusedski on 29 April and confirmed his position by winning Nat Champ in Nov. Won Most Improved Player award. **1997: (2)** *Sydney, Tashkent*. He began the year in style with his 1st f on the main tour at Qatar, following the next week with his 1st title at Sydney (d. Ivanisevic) and then a 3rd consec. f at Antwerp. After Qatar he became 1st GBR player since Mottram in 1983 to reach the top 20, progressing to No. 14 after Antwerp. However, he was restricted at LIPC by an elbow injury, which required arthroscopic surgery on 26 March to remove pieces of bone from the elbow joint, causing him to miss D Cup tie v Zimbabwe. At Wimbledon he reached qf again, inspired by the middle-Sunday home crowd as he d. Haarhuis 14–12 5s before upsetting Krajicek. After that, he hit a low point in losing 1r Montreal to LeBlanc, ranked more than 800 places below him, was brilliant in beating Muster 1r US Open, but dreadful in losing to W. Ferreira 2r. Avoiding clay at home at Bournemouth, he then opted instead to play in Tashkent, where he won his 2nd title of the year. By then, though, Rusedski had overtaken him as No. 1 in GBR and confirmed his

dominance by winning their sf at Vienna. He reached the same stage at Nottingham and Basle (where he won the doubles with Rosset) and qf New Haven and Stockholm. Played 1 match at ATP Champ (d. Kafelnikov, who had already qualified for sf) as alternate when Bruguera withdrew after playing 2. **1998: (2)** *Tashkent, Basle.* Working with physical trainer Tim Newenham, he gained bulk without losing agility and enjoyed his best year yet, although consistency was still a problem. He broke into top 10 1st time on 17 Aug., and although he wobbled in and out of the top ranks during the rest of the year, he finished the season there and as the No. 1 British player. His 1st 2 GS tourns were disappointing as Golmard removed him 11–9 fs 1r Australian Open and he was forced to retire 1r French Open with a back injury, suffered in practice the day before and believed to be the result of having played 33 tourns in 12 months. However, he came into his own again at Wimbledon, playing the tennis of his life to upset Rafter and Korda en route to sf, where he became the 1st player of the tourn to take a set off Sampras, with whom he practises. His 1st title of the year was Tashkent in Sept., followed 3 weeks later by Basle (d. Agassi). He was r/u Sydney (d. Rafter) and Los Angeles, reached sf LIPC (d. Moya, Korda and Kuerten), Toronto and Stockholm, as well as Wimbledon, and played qf Qatar, Tokyo Japan Open, Queen's, New Haven and Vienna. His 1st official berth at ATP Champ was clinched only at the last minute when he reached sf Stockholm, and because Krajicek and Rafter, who were ahead of him, had withdrawn. There he reached sf before losing 7–5 fs to Moya; had he won that match he could have finished the year in the top 5. GBR qualified for WT Cup 1st time in 20 years, but he declined to play, thus depriving Rusedski of the chance to compete and further straining relations between the top 2 GBR players. Led GBR into World Group of D Cup with 2 key wins v IND. **1999:** He excelled on grass again, extending Sampras to 7–6 fs in f Queen's and taking a set off the same player in sf Wimbledon. However, his early loss at US Open, followed immediately by 1r defeat at Bournemouth, persuaded him to seek the help of a sports psychologist, and in a vain attempt to retain his top 10 ranking he missed GS Cup to chase points in Toulouse. However, he dropped out of the top ranks on 18 Oct., returned briefly a week later after a morale-boosting r/u showing at Basel, but slipped out again on 15 Nov., finishing his season with neither a berth at ATP Champ nor a top 10 ranking. There were other high points, though, with two more r/u showings at Qatar and Rotterdam and qf Dubai, Indian Wells, Hamburg and Cincinnati, while in doubles he won London with Rusedski and Monte Carlo with Delaitre. **2000: (2)** *Vienna, Brighton.* Vienna was his 1st title for 2 years, ending a sequence of 7 consec. f losses, and he finished the year triumphantly with his 1st title in GBR at Brighton. Although it still left him 2 places short of a berth at Masters Cup, he finished the year in top 10 again, having moved in and out during the season. Other r/u showings were at Rotterdam (d. Kafelnikov, with whom he was r/u doubles), Scottsdale (d. N. Lapentti) and Cincinnati, where he d Sampras 1st time (in ss) and followed with an upset of Kuerten to reach his 1st Masters Series f. He also reached sf Indianapolis (d. Kafelnikov), Hong Kong and Basel, and qf Adelaide, Ericsson Open and Estoril. He was disappointing in GS, with last 16 Australian Open and Wimbledon his best efforts, and at US Open he lost to Krajicek on double fault after being 2–1 sets up. His frustration there may have given him the spur he needed, for his 2 titles came after that episode.

PRINCIPAL 2000 RESULTS – won 2, r/u 3, sf 3 (detailed Grand Slam results follow)

won Vienna (d. Rosset 6–3 6–1, Santoro 6–3 6–2, Vicente 6–4 7–6, Federer 2–6 7–6 6–3, Haas 6–4 6–4 6–4), **won** Brighton (d. Tabara 6–0 6–2, Sluiter 7–6 6–1, Woodruff w/o, H. T. Lee 6–2 6–1, Hrbaty 6–2 6–2); **r/u** Rotterdam (d. A. Martin 6–2 6–2, Santoro 6–2 7–5, Hrbaty 7–6 6–2, Kafelnikov 6–3 4–6 6–3, lost Pioline 6–7 6–4 7–6), **r/u** Scottsdale (d. Koubek 6–3 7–6, B. Black 6–1 6–4, N. Lapentti 6–3 6–2, A. Costa 6–3 6–3, lost Hewitt 6–4 7–6), **r/u** Cincinnati (d. Mamiit 6–3 5–7 6–2, Puerta 6–1 6–2, Sampras 6–3 6–4, Santoro 6–1 6–4, Kuerten 6–7 6–3 7–6, lost Enqvist 7–6 6–4); **sf** Indianapolis (d. A. Martin 6–4 6–3, El Aynaoui 4–6 6–2 7–6, Kafelnikov 7–6 6–2, lost Safin 7–5 6–4), **sf** Hong Kong (d. Levy 4–6 6–1 6–4, Zabaleta 6–2 6–4, Chang 6–4 4–6 6–4, lost Kiefer 6–4 6–2), **sf** Basel (d. Robredo 6–3 6–4, Clement 6–3 6–4, Arazi 6–3 6–3, lost Enqvist 6–1 6–3). **2000 HIGHLIGHTS – DOUBLES:** (with Kafelnikov) **r/u** Rotterdam (lost Adams/De Jager 5–7 6–2 6–3).

CAREER GRAND SLAM RECORD
AUSTRALIAN OPEN – Played 5
1996: 2r d. Korda 5–7 7–6 6–3 6–4, lost Bjorkman 6–1 6–3 6–2. **1997: 3r** d. Pavel 7–5 6–4 6–2, Raoux 6–3 6–3 6–4, lost M. Chang [2] 6–1 7–6 6–3. **1998: 1r** lost Golmard 6–3 6–7 6–2 3–6 11–9. **1999: 3r** [seed 6] d. Alami 6–3 6–2 6–1, Stolle 4–6 7–5 4–6 6–1 6–4, lost Rosset 7–6 6–3 7–5. **2000: last 16** [seed 11] d. Golmard 6–7 6–3 7–6 7–6, Schuttler 6–2 4–1 ret, Grosjean 6–1 6–4 4–6 7–6, lost Woodruff 7–5 1–6 6–4 3–6 7–5.

FRENCH OPEN – Played 5
1996: 1r lost Goossens 6–4 6–4 7–5. **1997: 1r** [seed 14] lost Delaitre 6–2 2–6 1–6 6–2 6–4. **1998: 1r** lost Sargsian 5–2 ret. **1999 3r** [seed 7] d. Alami 6–4 3–6 4–6 6–3 6–4, Novak 5–7 6–1 7–5 6–2, lost Berasategui 4–6 4–6 6–4 7–5 6–4. **2000: 3r** [seed 13] d. Spadea 7–5 7–5 6–4, Vinck 6–2 6–4 7–6, lost Vicente 7–5 4–6 6–4 4–6 6–3.

WIMBLEDON – Played 7, sf 2, qf 2
1994: 1r lost Prinosil 4–6 6–3 6–2 6–2. **1995: 2r** d. Wekesa 7–6 6–0 6–4, lost Sampras [2] 6–2 6–3 7–6. **1996: qf** [unseeded] d. Kafelnikov [5] 7–6 6–3 6–7 4–6 7–5, Sapsford 6–1 6–7 6–0 6–1, Milligan 6–1 6–3 6–4, Gustafsson 7–6 6–4 7–6, lost Martin [13] 7–6 7–6 6–4; **1997: qf** [seed 14] d. Nestor 7–6 6–1 6–4, Golmard 7–6 6–3 6–3, Haarhuis 6–7 6–3 6–2 4–6 14–12, Krajicek [4] 7–6 6–7 7–6 6–4, lost Stich 6–3 6–2 6–4. **1998: sf** [seed 12] d. Novak 7–6 7–5 5–7 4–6 6–2, Nainkin 6–3 5–7 6–4 6–2, B. Black 6–4 6–4 3–6 7–5, Rafter [G] 6–3 6–7 6–3 6–2, Korda [3] 6–3 6–4 6–2, lost Sampras [1] 6–3 4–6 7–5 6–3. **1999: sf** [seed 6] d. Di Pasquale 6–4 6–0 3–6 7–6, Woodruff 6–4 6–3 7–6, Grosjean 6–1 6–7 6–3 6–2, Courier 4–6 7–5 7–5 6–7 9–7, Pioline 6–4 6–2 4–6 6–3, lost Sampras [1] 3–6 6–4 6–3 6–4. **2000: last 16** [seed 8] (d. Srichaphan 5–7 6–3 6–1 6–3, Clement 6–4 6–4 6–4, Arazi 6–3 6–3 6–3, lost Philippoussis [10] 6–1 5–7 6–7 6–3 6–4.

US OPEN – Played 6
1995: 2r d. Viloca 6–3 4–6 6–3 6–2, lost Palmer 6–4 6–7 6–3 6–1. **1996: last 16** [unseeded] d. Jabali 6–2 6–3 6–4, D. Flach 6–3 6–4 6–2, Martin [12] 6–2 7–6 6–4, lost Edberg 6–7 7–6 6–4 6–4. **1997: 2r** d. Muster [5] 6–3 7–6 4–6 6–4, lost W. Ferreira 6–3 6–2 6–4. **1998: last 16** [seed 13] d. S. Draper 6–3 7–6 7–6, Mantilla 6–3 5–7 7–5 6–4, Kohlmann 6–3 7–5 1–6 6–4, lost Philippoussis 7–5 0–6 6–4 6–1. **1999: 1r** [seed 6] lost Canas 7–6 6–4 6–3. **2000: 3r** [seed 11] (d. Vicente 6–3 6–3 6–4, Gonzalez 6–3 6–4 6–2, lost Krajicek 6–4 3–6 4–6 7–5 7–5.

OLYMPIC RECORD
1996: (Atlanta) 2r d. Matsuoka 7–6 6–3, lost Woodbridge 7–6 7–6. **2000: (Sydney) 1r** [seed 7] lost Kucera 6–3 6–2). **DOUBLES:** (with Broad) **1996: (Atlanta) r/u silver medal** lost Woodbridge/Woodforde 6–4 6–4 6–2.

CAREER DAVIS CUP RECORD
1994: July – *Zone 1 Relegation ROM d. GBR 3–2 in GBR (Grass).* R3 (with J. Bates) d. G. Cosac/D. Pescariu 6–2 6–7 5–7 6–2 6–1. **1995: April** – *Zone 2 1r SVK d. GBR 5–0 in SVK (Clay).* R1 lost J. Kroslak 7–5 6–3 4–6 6–3; R3 (with N. Broad) lost Kroslak/K. Kucera 3–6 6–4 6–4 2–6 6–2; R4 lost Kucera 6–4 6–2. **July** – *Zone 2 Relegation GBR d. MON 5–0 in GBR (Grass).* R2 d. S. Graeff 6–0 6–3 6–2; R5 d. C. Boggetti 6–1 6–4. **1996: July** – *Zone 2 2r GBR d. GHA 5–0 in GHA (Hard)* R1 d. I. Donkor 6–2 6–0 6–2; R4 d. D. Omaboe 6–3 4–6 6–0. **September** – *Zone 2 sf GBR d. EGY 5–0 in GBR (Grass).* R2 d. A. Ghoneim 6–0 6–4 7–5; R4 d. T. El Savvy 6–7 6–2 6–2). **1997: July** – *Zone 1 Relegation GBR d. UKR 3–2 in UKR (Clay).* R1 d. A. Rybalko 2–6 6–4 6–3 4–6 6–4; R3 (with G. Rusedski) d. A. Medvedev/A. Poliakov 6–1 6–4 7–6; R4 lost Medvedev 6–7 6–3 6–4 6–4. **1998: April** – *Zone 1 2r GBR d. UKR 5–0 in GBR (Carpet).* R2 d. A. Medvedev 6–2 6–7 6–4 1–6 6–1; R3 (with G. Rusedski) d. Medvedev/A. Rybalko 6–4 7–5 7–6; R5 d. Rybalko 6–1 2–6 6–2. **September** – *World Group Qualifying GBR d. IND 3–2 in GBR (Hard).* R2 d. M. Bhupathi 4–6 6–3 6–3 6–3; R3 (with N. Broad) lost Bhupathi/L. Paes 7–6 6–3 7–6; R4 d. Paes 7–6 6–2 6–2. **1999: April** – *World Group 1r USA d. GBR 3–2 in GBR (Hard).* R1 lost J. Courier 7–6 2–6 7–6 6–7 7–5; R3 (with G. Rusedski) d. T. Martin/A. O'Brien 3–6 7–5 6–3 6–7 6–3; R4 d. Martin 4–6 7–5 6–3 7–6. **September** – *World Group qualifying GBR d. RSA 4–1 in GBR (Hard).* R2 d. G. Stafford 6–3 7–5 7–6; R3 (with N. Broad) lost D. Adams/J. De Jager 6–3 7–6 6–4; R4 d. N. Godwin 6–2 6–2 6–2. **2000: February** – *World Group 1r CZE d. GBR 4–1 in CZE (Clay).* R1 d. C. Dosedel 6–7 5–7 6–1 7–5 6–3; R3 (with N. Broad) lost J. Novak/D. Rikl 7–6 6–4 6–7 6–2; R4 lost Novak 6–4 6–2 6–2. **July** – *World Group qualifying ECU d. GBR 3–2 in GBR (Grass).* R2 d. L. Morejon 6–2 6–1 6–4; R3 (with A. Parmar) lost G./N. Lapentti 6–3 7–5 6–3; R4 d. N. Lapentti 6–1 6–4 6–4.

GRAND SLAM CUP RECORD – Played 2, sf 1
1996: sf d. Stich [11] 6–3 6–3, MaliVai Washington 7–6 6–3, lost Becker [4] 7–6 6–3 6–1. **1998: 1r** lost Bjorkman 7–5 6–3.

ATP TOUR CHAMPIONSHIP – Played 2, sf 1
1997: as alt d. Kafelnikov 6–4 6–4. **1998: sf** in rr d. Corretja 7–6 6–7 6–2, Rios 7–5 6–1, lost Rusedski 6–2 6–4; sf lost Moya 6–4 3–6 7–5.

REMAINING MEN'S BIOGRAPHIES

The following biographies show the players' progress each year in the four Grand Slam Championships. It is shown thus: A (Australian Open), F (French Open), W (Wimbledon), US (US Open), followed by the round reached, or '–' if a player did not compete.

DAVID ADAMS (RSA) [Prize money to come after World Doubles]
Born Durban, South Africa, 5 January 1970; lives Cape Town; RH; 6ft 2in; 175lb; turned pro 1989; career singles titles 0; final 2000 ATP ranking 19 doubles; 2000 prize money $264,913; career prize money $2,136,796.
Coached by Lance Lockhart-Ross. Father, Peter, is South African who remained in SA when his Australian wife, Ann, took their son to Australia at age 17. **1987:** (954). **1988:** (701) South African Jun GC champ. **1989:** (556) Played on the satellite circuits, specialising in doubles. **1990:** (546) Concentrated on the Challenger circuit. **1991:** (516) Won 1st doubles title at Lisbon Challenger. **1992:** (450) Burst into prominence as a doubles specialist on the main tour, reaching 1st GS f at French Open with Olhovskiy and winning Munich with Oosting. **1993:** (257) In doubles with Olhovskiy won Copenhagen and Estoril from 6 f. They qualified for ATP World Doubles but fell sf to Woodbridge/Woodforde, whom they had beaten at US Open. **1994:** (138) At Rosmalen he reached sf after qualifying (d. Volkov 1r) and appeared at the same stage Beijing. He continued to excel in doubles, reaching 7 f with various partners, winning 2 with Olhovskiy and 1 with Oosting, and qualifying for World Doubles with Olhovskiy. **1995:** (257) Won doubles titles at Jakarta and Marseille with Olhovskiy. **1996:** (607) A 1, F –, W –, US –. Won Rotterdam doubles with Barnard as LL and was r/u in 4 other f with Oosting. Joined RSA D Cup team. **1997:** (752) A –, F –, W –, US –. Played 4 doubles f with different partners, winning Antwerp with Delaitre. **1998:** (–) A –, F –, W –, US –. He appeared in 4 doubles with different partners, but won no title. **1999:** A –, F –, W –, US –. From 9 doubles f with 4 different partners, he won 2 with Tarango and 1 with De Jager, with whom he qualified for World Doubles Champ; there, however, De Jager was suffering with flu and they withdrew after losing their 1st 2 matches. In mixed he won Australian Open with De Swardt. **2000:** A –, F –, W –, US –. He won 3 men's doubles titles with De Jager, was r/u once with Eagle and added French Open mixed with De Swardt. He and De Jager qualified for World Doubles Champ but could not take up their place, owing to a wrist injury suffered by De Jager. **2000 HIGHLIGHTS – DOUBLES:** (with De Jager unless stated) **won** London (d. Gambill/Humphries 6–3 6–7 7–6), **won** Rotterdam (d. Henman/Kafelnikov 4–6 6–3 6–4), **won** Munich (d. Mirnyi/Zimonjic 6–4 6–4); (with Eagle) **r/u** Estoril (lost Johnson/Norval 6–4 7–5). **MIXED DOUBLES:** (with De Swardt) **won French Open** (d. Woodbridge/Stubbs 6–3 3–6 6–3). **CAREER HIGHLIGHTS – DOUBLES:** (with Olhovskiy) **French Open – r/u 1992** (lost Hlasek/Rosset 7–6 6–7 7–5). **MIXED DOUBLES:** (with De Swardt) **Australian Open – won 1999** (d. Mirnyi/S. Williams 6–4 4–6 7–6)**, French Open – won 2000.**

MARIO ANCIC (CRO)
Born Split, 30 March 1984, and lives there; RH; 2HB; 6ft 3in; 165lb; career singles titles 0.
Coached by Bob Brett. In CRO team r/u Under-16 World Youth Cup. **2000:** R/u Australian Open Jun to Roddick and Wimbledon Jun to Mahut.

HICHAM ARAZI (MAR)
Born Casablanca, 19 October 1973; lives Monte Carlo, Monaco; LH; 5ft 9in; 143lb; turned pro 1993; career singles titles 1; final 2000 ATP ranking 30, junior ranking 4; 2000 prize money $491,221; career prize money $1,990,294.
Coached by Patrick Charton. Moved to France at age 2. **1991:** (1093). **1992:** (533). **1993:** (340) Began to make his mark on the satellite circuits. **1994:** (185). **1995:** (148) A –, F –, W –, US 1. Reached 3 f on the Challenger circuit. **1996:** (78) A –, F –, W 2, US 1. Won 2 Challenger titles and on the main tour reached qf Palermo and Toulouse, breaking into the top 100. **1997:** (38) A 1, F qf, W 1, US 1. He began the year with his 1st sf at Qatar, then delighted the home crowds at Casablanca by winning his 1st career singles title there. At French Open he upset Rios to reach qf, unseeded, and reached the same stage Hamburg (d. Muster), Bologna and Tashkent. Played 2 doubles f, but won no title. **1998:** (36) A 4, F qf, W 3, US 1. He made his mark in GS again (unseeded each time) with upsets of Philippoussis at Australian Open, Berasategui *en route* to qf French Open, where he extended Pioline to 5s, and Moya at Wimbledon. He also appeared in qf Casablanca and Indianapolis (d. Mantilla) as well as upsetting Kafelnikov at Dubai, Korda at Rome and Ivanisevic at Long Island. He played GS Cup, but lost 1r to Kucera. **1999:** (36) A 1, F 3, W 1, US 3. He was r/u Merano, letting slip 3 mps v Vicente in f, and reached sf London (d. Ivanisevic), plus qf Qatar (d. Kafelnikov) and Amsterdam (d. Medvedev). He upset Ivanisevic again at Monte Carlo and French Open and removed Krajicek at Hamburg. **2000:** A qf, F 3, W 3, US 3. His best performances were reaching sf Tokyo Japan Open and Lyon (d. Philippoussis and Enqvist), with qf appearances at Australian Open (unseeded), Indian Wells (d. Agassi), Casablanca and Basel. Other notable upsets included Haas at Monte Carlo, N. Lapentti at Cincinnati and W. Ferreira at US Open. **2000 HIGHLIGHTS – SINGLES: Australian Open qf** [unseeded] (d. Alonso 6–3 7–6 6–2, F. Jonsson 6–3 6–4 6–4, Vicente 6–3 6–3 6–2, Escude 6–4 6–3 7–6, lost Agassi [seed 1] 6–4 6–4 6–2), **French Open 3r** (d. Woodruff 6–3 6–4 7–6, Hipfl 6–3 3–6 5–7 6–2 6–1, lost Philippoussis 6–2 6–1 3–6 6–3), **Wimbledon 3r** (d. Gaudio 6–2 6–4 6–0, Lareau 6–3 3–6 6–7 6–4 9–7, lost Henman [seed 8] 6–3 6–3

6–3), **US Open 3r** (d. Hantschk 6–3 6–0 4–6 6–7 6–4, W. Ferreira 6–3 6–3 6–7 6–3, lost Clement 4–6 6–2 6–2 4–6 0–1 ret); **sf** Tokyo Japan Open (d. Bastl 6–4 5–7 6–4, Taino 6–4 6–2, W. Black 6–7 6–2 6–2, lost Schalken 4–6 6–3 7–6), **sf** Lyon (d. Boutter 6–3 3–6 6–4, Philippoussis 6–3 3–6 7–5, Enqvist 6–7 7–6 6–4, lost Rafter 6–3 6–4). **CAREER HIGHLIGHTS – SINGLES: Australian Open – qf 2000.**

MAHESH BHUPATHI (IND)

Born Madras, 7 June 1974; lives Bangalore; RH; 6ft 1in; 183lb; turned pro 1995; career singles titles 0; final 2000 ATP ranking 39 doubles; 2000 prize money $175,531; career prize money $1,782,824.

Coached by Enrico Piperno. **1992:** (944). **1993:** (532). **1994:** (284). **1995:** (350) A –, F –, W –, US 1. All-American in both singles and doubles at Univ. of Mississippi, where he was No. 3 in singles and No. 1 in doubles, winning NCAA Champ with Hamadeh. Joined IND D Cup squad. **1996:** (418). **1997:** (228) A –, F –, W 1, US –. He formed a successful doubles partnership with Paes, winning the 6 f they played together and qualifying for a first World Doubles Champ. There they squeaked past Lareau/O'Brien in sf before denting their record of f won by losing to Leach/Stark. In mixed, he won French Open with Hiraki, becoming the 1st Indian to win a GS title. **1998:** (372) A –, F –, W 1, US –. His partnership with Paes continued to flourish as they won 5 of 7 f played to qualify for World Doubles Champ. There, however, a bone spur injury to Paes' hand forced them to withdraw after losing 2 matches, but they still finished the year as No. 2 pairing behind Eltingh/Haarhuis and ahead of Woodbridge/Woodforde. In mixed doubles he was r/u Wimbledon with V. Williams. **1999:** (297) A –, F –, W –, US –. On 26 April, he became the 1st Indian to top the rankings when he took over as No. 1 in doubles, although by end of season he was No. 2 behind Paes. Together they won their 1st GS men's title at French Open, following with Wimbledon. Also r/u at Australian Open and US Open, they became the 1st pairing since McGregor/Sedgman in 1952 to appear in all 4 GS f in a year. In other tourns they also won Chennai and qualified for World Doubles Champ, where they were r/u to Lareau/O'Brien, and finished the season as top pairing, voted Doubles Team of the Year. In mixed he won US Open with Sugiyama. **2000:** A –, F –, W 1, US –. Split for a while with Paes because of a disagreement over coaching, but they joined together again towards end of year, winning Tokyo Japan Open at only their 5th tourn of the year together and gaining WC entry to World Doubles Champ in Bangalore where they were r/u to Johnson/Norval. Earlier he had won St Polten with Kratzmann. **2000 HIGHLIGHTS – SINGLES: Wimbledon 1r** (lost Huet 6–7 6–3 7–6 6–1). **2000 HIGHLIGHTS – DOUBLES:** (with Kratzmann) **won** St Polten (d. Gaudenzi/Nargiso 7–6 6–7 6–4), (with Paes) **won** Tokyo Japan Open (d. Hill/Tarango 6–4 6–7 6–3); (with Prinosil) **r/u** Halle (lost Kulti/Tillstrom 7–6 7–6), (with Paes) **r/u** World Doubles Champ (lost Johnson/Norval 7–6 6–3 6–4). **CAREER HIGHLIGHTS – DOUBLES:** (with Paes) **French Open – won 1999** (d. Ivanisevic/Tarango 6–2 7–5)**; Wimbledon – won 1999** (d. Haarhuis/Palmer 6–7 6–3 6–4 7–6); **Australian Open – r/u 1999** (lost Bjorkman/Rafter 6–3 4–6 6–4 6–7 6–4)**; US Open – r/u 1999** (lost Lareau/O'Brien 7–6 6–4)**; World Doubles Champ – r/u 1997** (lost Leach/Stark 3–6 3–6 4–7–6), **r/u 1999** (lost Lareau/O'Brien 6–2 6–2 6–2), **r/u 2000. CAREER HIGHLIGHTS – MIXED DOUBLES: French Open –** (with Hiraki) **won 1997** (d. Galbraith/Raymond 6–4 6–1); **US Open –** (with Sugiyama) **won 1999** (d. Johnson/Po 6–4 6–4).

JONAS BJORKMAN (SWE)

Born Vaxjo, 23 March 1972; lives Monte Carlo, Monaco; RH; 2HB; 6ft; 180lb; turned pro 1991; career singles titles 4; final 2000 ATP ranking 44; 2000 prize money $541,965; career prize money $7,502,600.

Coached by Peter Carlsson. Former Nat Jun champ. **1991:** (691). **1992:** (331) Began to make his mark on the satellite circuits. **1993:** (95) A –, F –, W –, US 2. Reached qf Kuala Lumpur Salem Open and won 3 Challenger titles, which took him into the top 100. **1994:** (50) A 2, F 3, W 4, US qf. Unseeded at Wimbledon, he took advantage of the removal of Edberg by Carlsen and the Dane's retirement during their encounter next day to reach last 16, and at US Open he upset Edberg himself on his way to qf, again unseeded. Reached sf Schenectady (d. Bruguera) plus qf Marseille, Tel Aviv and Antwerp. In doubles he appeared in his 1st GS f at French Open with Apell and with various partners he won 8 titles from 11 other f. He and Apell won 6 titles on 4 different surfaces during the year, including their 1st World Doubles Champ. Member of victorious SWE D Cup team, winning doubles with Apell. **1995:** (30) A 3, F 1, W 2, US 3. In singles he broke into top 25 after reaching his 1st f at Hong Kong. He also reached sf LIPC and Vienna, plus 4 more qf, and played on winning SWE WT Cup team. He played 5 doubles f, winning 1 with regular partner Apell and 1 each with De Jager and Frana after Apell underwent shoulder surgery in Sept. **1996:** (69) A 4, F 4, W 1, US 3. Although it was a less impressive year in singles, he reached sf Rosmalen (d. Siemerink) and qf US CC and Los Angeles. At Australian Open, where he was unseeded, he upset Martin and extended Agassi to 5s. Played 7 doubles f with 3 different partners, winning Antwerp and New Delhi with Kulti, with whom he qualified for World Doubles Champ, although they did not pass rr. **1997:** (4) A 4, F 2, W 1, US sf. In by far his best year to date, he won his 1st career singles title at Auckland and broke into the top 20 after taking his 2nd at Indianapolis. He moved into the top 5 in Oct., progressing to a career-high No. 4 after winning Stockholm. Playing more matches than anyone else (158), he was consistent through the year with r/u Coral Springs and Paris Open, sf Memphis (d. Haarhuis), Scottsdale (d. Rafter and A. Costa), Indian Wells, Queen's (d. Sampras), Rosmalen, Stuttgart Eurocard, US Open (unseeded, extended Rusedski to 7–5 fs), plus qf Adelaide (losing 15–17 on tb v Tarango), LIPC (d. Rios) and GS Cup (d. Becker). Qualifying for his 1st ATP Champ, he reached sf before losing in ss to Sampras, and finished the year in triumph on winning SWE D Cup team. From 4 doubles f he won Atlanta and was r/u US

Open, both with Kulti. **1998:** (24) A qf, F 1, W 3, US qf. Although it was a less spectacular year, he remained consistent, winning his 1st GC title at Nottingham and reaching sf Dubai and Stuttgart Eurocard, plus qf Australian Open, US Open, Munich, Toronto, Boston, GS Cup, Vienna and Moscow. In doubles he won his 1st GS title at Australian Open with Eltingh, and with Rafter won Indian Wells. In D Cup f won doubles with Kulti to give SWE 3–0 win v ITA. **1999:** (74) A 1, F 1, W 2, US 3. It was a less successful year in singles, in which his best performances were sf Tokyo (d. Krajicek) and Shanghai, plus qf Hong Kong, 's-Hertogenbosch and Boston. In doubles he won Australian Open plus 2 other titles with Rafter, took 2 more with B. Black, and in mixed he was r/u Wimbledon with Kournikova. He and Rafter qualified for World Doubles Champ, but were unable to take their place, owing to Rafter's shoulder injury. **2000:** A 3, F 1, W 4, US 2. In singles he upset Henman *en route* to sf Nottingham and reached same stage St Petersburg, qf Copenhagen, Newport, Shanghai, Moscow and Stockholm, as well as upsetting N. Lapentti 1r Rotterdam and Corretja at Cincinnati. In doubles he played 3 f with different partners, winning Moscow with Prinosil, and planned to team with Woodbridge in 2001. **2000 HIGHLIGHTS – SINGLES: Australian Open 3r** (d. Stoltenberg 6–7 6–4 6–4 0–6 6–4, Vanek 6–4 3–6 6–4 7–6, lost M. Norman [seed 12] 6–4 6–4 7–6), **French Open 1r** (lost Hrbaty [seed 14] 6–3 6–2 6–1), **Wimbledon last 16** [unseeded] (d. Medvedev 6–4 6–3 6–3, Dosedel 6–4 6–3 6–0, Godwin 6–3 6–4 6–4, lost Sampras [seed 1] 6–3 6–2 7–5), **US Open 2r** (d. Ulihrach 2–6 7–6 7–6 6–1, lost Kiefer [seed 14] 6–1 6–4 6–3); **sf** Nottingham (d. Henman 5–7 6–4 7–5, Mirnyi 6–4 6–4, Fromberg 7–5 4–6 6–3, lost Grosjean 7–6 6–4), **sf** St Petersburg (d. Portas 6–2 6–2, Stoliarov 6–4 6–3, Palmer 6–1 6–3, lost Safin 6–4 6–4). **2000 HIGHLIGHTS – DOUBLES:** (with Prinosil) **won** Moscow (d. Novak/Rikl 6–2 6–3); (with Lareau) **r/u** Copenhagen (lost Damm/Prinosil 6–1 5–7 7–5), (with Mirnyi) **r/u** Indianapolis (lost Hewitt/Stolle 6–2 3–6 6–3). **CAREER HIGHLIGHTS – SINGLES: US Open – sf 1997** (d. Clavet 6–2 6–4 6–4, T. Martin 7–5 6–4 6–0, Kuerten 6–3 6–1 7–5, Draper 6–3 6–3 1–6 7–6, Korda 7–6 6–2 1–0 ret, lost Rusedski 6–1 3–6 3–6 7–6 7–5), **qf 1994** [unseeded] (d. Stark 6–2 6–2 7–5, O'Brien 6–2 6–3 6–4, Edberg 6–4 6–4 6–3, Renzenbrink 3–6 6–3 7–6 3, lost Stich 6–4 6–4 6–7 6–3), **qf 1998** (d. Pioline 6–2 4–6 6–1 6–7 6–2, Stark 6–2 6–3 6–1, Santoro 3 6–1 6–2, Siemerink 6–4 2–6 6–2 6–2, lost Rafter 6–2 6–3 7–5); **ATP Champ – sf 1997** (lost Kafelnikov 6–3 7–6, d. Bruguera 6–3 6–1, d. M. Chang 6–4 7–5 in rr, lost Sampras 6–3 6–4); **Australian Open – qf 1998** (d. Beldbradjic 2–6 6–1 6–1 6–1, W. Ferreira 6 7 4 6 6 4 6 2 6 3, Santoro 7–5 6–3 6–4, B. Black 6–2 6–1 6–4, lost Korda 3–6 6–7 6–3 6–4 6–2). **CAREER HIGHLIGHTS – DOUBLES:** (with Apell unless stated) **Australian Open –** (with Eltingh) **won 1998** (d. Woodbridge/Woodforde 6–2 5–7 2–6 6–4 6–3)**,** (with Rafter) **won 1999** (d. Bhupathi/Paes 6–3 4–6 6–4 6–7 6–4); **World Doubles Champ – won 1994** (d. Woodbridge/Woodforde 6–4 4–6 4–6 7–6); **French Open – r/u 1994** (lost B. Black/Stark 6–4 7–6); **US Open –** (with Kulti) **r/u 1997** (lost Kafelnikov/Vacek 7–6 6–3).

BYRON BLACK (ZIM)

Born Harare, 6 October 1969, and lives there and Wimbledon, England; RH; 2HF; 2HB; 5ft 10in; 155lb; turned pro 1991; career singles titles 2; final 2000 ATP ranking 35; 2000 prize money $516,347; career prize money $4,836,286.

Coached by Brett Stephens. Wife Fiona (married 14 December 1996); daughter Shawn (born 27 July 2000). Brother of Wayne, with whom he competed in Olympic doubles, and of Cara, who plays the women's circuit; father Don competed at Wimbledon in the 1950s. Learned to play tennis barefoot on his father's avocado plantation. Won All-African Jun Champs aged 15 and was 1st beneficiary of GS Development Fund to qualify for GS Cup. **1988:** Gold medallist in singles and doubles at All-Africa Games. **1989:** Won NCAA doubles title with Amend. **1990:** (453) Won Arthur Ashe Sportsmanship award. **1991:** (122) An All-American 3 times in singles and 4 times in doubles, he helped USC to nat team title over Georgia. On the Challenger circuit he won Winnetka and Madeira and was voted Newcomer of the Year. **1992:** (143) A 1, F 1, W 2, US 1. Upset Krajicek 1r Singapore. **1993:** (81) A 3, F –, W 3, US 3. In singles he reached sf New Haven, upset Lendl at Queen's and surprised Washington on his way to qf Vienna, as well as winning Wellington Challenger. In doubles he reached 8 f with 5 different partners, winning 6 titles. **1994:** (67) A 1, F 1, W 1, US 3. Reached sf Washington (d. W. Ferreira) and Newport, qf Antwerp (d. Yzaga) and upset Martin at LIPC. In doubles with Stark he won French Open, was r/u Australian Open and won 2 more titles from a total of 9 f with him and 1 with D. Adams. Qualified with Stark for his 1st World Doubles Champ and teamed with his brother Wayne to beat Hlasek/Rosset in D Cup. **1995:** (40) A 1, F 2, W 2, US qf. He made his mark at US Open where, unseeded, he upset Enqvist and Stich on his way to qf. Reached sf Johannesburg, Nottingham and Newport, qf Tokyo Seiko (d. Bruguera) and Moscow and won Bombay Challenger. Played 4 doubles f with different partners, winning Bologna with Stark and Moscow with Palmer. **1996:** (44) A 2, F 1, W 2, US 1. He began the year with his 1st career singles f at Adelaide and followed in April with his 1st title at Seoul. He was also r/u New Delhi and reached sf Beijing and qf Philadelphia, Newport and Moscow (d. Rosset). From 7 doubles f, he won 4 with Connell, with whom he was also r/u Wimbledon. They qualified together for World Doubles Champ, where they were the only pairing to win all their rr matches, but lost sf to Woodbridge/Woodforde. **1997:** (77) A 1, F 2, W 3, US 1. Although he did not pass qf all year, he reached that stage at Sydney, Philadelphia, Scottsdale (d. Rios), Indian Wells (d. A. Costa), Orlando, Los Angeles and Beijing. **1998:** (28) A 4, F 2, W 3, US 3. He moved back into top 30 with r/u Hong Kong Salem Open (where he won the doubles with O'Brien), Tokyo Japan Open and Nottingham, sf Auckland and Queen's (d. Bjorkman), and qf Los Angeles and Indianapolis. Other notable upsets included Mantilla at Australian Open, where he was unseeded, and Rafter at St Polten. **1999:** (65) A 2, F 3, W 1, US 1. He began the year with qf Adelaide, followed by sf Copenhagen and then the title at Chennai in March, which took him into top 25. After that, his year in singles fell away until Nov. when he ended the season on a high note with r/u Moscow, unseeded. In doubles he played 5 f, winning 2 with Bjorkman and 1 with W. Ferreira. **2000:** A 1, F 1, W qf, US 2. He upset Haas to reach f Memphis and reached same stage Nottingham, plus qf Wimbledon (unseeded), Washington and Tokyo Japan Open. It was a quieter year in doubles, with the title at Mexico City with Johnson coming from his only f. **2000 HIGHLIGHTS – SINGLES: Australian Open 1r** (lost T. Martin [seed 8] 5–7 6–7 6–4 2–6 8–6), **French Open 1r** (lost Rosset 7–5 7–5 6–0), **Wimbledon qf** [unseeded] (d. Ilie 6–3 5–7 7–6 6–0, Hrbaty 6–3 7–5 6–2, Portas 6–2 6–0 6–4, Pozzi 4–6 7–6 6–2 6–4, lost Voltchkov 7–6 7–6 6–4), **US Open 2r** (d. Dent 7–6 6–3 7–5, lost Novak 2–6 6–3 7–5 7–6); **r/u** Memphis (d. Rodriguez 6–2 6–2, Woodruff 6–2 3–6 6–4, Chang 7–5 6–2, Haas 7–6 7–6, lost Larsson 6–2 1–6 6–3), **r/u** Nottingham (d. Sa 6–1 6–7 6–1, Sargsian 6–3 2–6 6–4, Parmar 6–4 6–4, Gambill 7–6 6–1, lost Grosjean 7–6 6–3). **2000 HIGHLIGHTS – DOUBLES:** (with Johnson) **won** Mexico City (d. Etlis/Rodriguez 6–3 7–5). **CAREER HIGHLIGHTS – SINGLES: Wimbledon – qf 2000; US Open – qf 1995** unseeded (d. Boetsch 7–6 6–3 6–3, Enqvist 6–4 6–4 3–6 6–3, Bjorkman 6–3 7–6 6–1, Stich 6–4 6–4 3–6 2–6 6–3, lost Sampras 7–6 6–4 6–0). **CAREER HIGHLIGHTS – DOUBLES:** (with Stark unless stated) **French Open – won 1994** (d. Apell/ Bjorkman 6–4 7–6); **Australian Open – r/u 1994** (lost Eltingh/Haarhuis 6–7 6–3 6–4 6–3); (with Connell) **Wimbledon – r/u 1996** (lost Woodbridge/ Woodforde 4–6 6–4 6–3 6–2).

MICHAEL CHANG (USA)

Born Hoboken, NJ, 22 February 1972; lives Mercer Island, Wash.; RH; 2HB; 5ft 9in; 160lb; turned pro 1988; career singles titles 34; final 2000 ATP ranking 32; 2000 prize money $494,488; career prize money $18,651,206.

Coached by his brother, Carl. **1987:** (163) A –, F –, W –, US 2. At 15 yrs 6 mths he was the youngest player to compete in men's singles at US Open since 1918, and was the youngest ever to win a match in GS tourn, having been granted a wild card after winning US 18s at Kalamazoo. At 15 yrs 7 mths was youngest to win a pro tourn at Las Vegas Challenger and was the youngest ever GP semi-finalist at Scottsdale. **1988:** (30) A –, F 3, W 2, US 4. At 16 yrs 4 mths was the youngest for 60 years to win a match in Wimbledon main draw, and when he won his 1st title at San Francisco at 16 yrs 7 mths, he was youngest to win a SS event and second-youngest after Krickstein to win a GP title. **1989:** (5) A –, F won, W 4, US 4. At the French Open aged 17 yrs 3 mths, he became the youngest male winner of a GS tourn and the 1st American since Trabert in 1955 to win that title. In 5s of his 4r match v Lendl, he was so badly affected with cramp that he had to serve under-arm. He also won Wembley and was r/u Los Angeles, qualifying for Masters 1st time, although he failed to win a match there. Became the youngest to play D Cup for USA, making his debut v PAR, and the youngest to break into top 5. **1990:** (15) A –, F qf, W 4, US 3. Out until March with stress fracture of cup of left hip suffered Dec. 1989. He did not reach the heights of the previous year, but won his 1st HC title at Canadian Open, was r/u Los Angeles and Wembley and reached sf Washington and GS Cup, as well as playing in winning US D Cup team. **1991:** (15) A –, F qf, W 1, US 4. Although he reached sf Memphis, Tokyo Suntory and Paris Open (d. Edberg) and played 7 more qf, he had to wait until Nov. before winning his 1st title of the year at Birmingham, following with r/u to Wheaton in GS Cup. **1992:** (6) A 3, F 3, W 1, US sf. Returned to top 10 1st time since July 1991 after winning Indian Wells, following with LIPC (d. Sampras and Courier) and San Francisco (d. Courier again). Was also r/u Hong Kong and appeared in sf Tokyo Suntory (losing both times to Courier) and reached same stage Cincinnati, Long Island, Tokyo Seiko (losing all 3 to Lendl) and US Open. There he survived 5s matches v Washington and W. Ferreira, but lost a 3rd over the same length v Edberg. Qualified for ATP World Champ, but won no match there. Wore spectacles on court 1st time at Gstaad in July, switching from contact lenses after suffering build-up problems. **1993:** (8) A 2, F 2, W 3, US qf. He beat Agassi and Edberg back-to-back to win Cincinnati in Aug., but enjoyed his greatest success in Asia, where he won Jakarta, Osaka, Kuala Lumpur Salem Open and Beijing. A member of the winning US World Team Cup squad, he was r/u Los Angeles and Long Island (d. Edberg) and reached 4 more sf to qualify for IBM/ATP World Champ where he won only match 1 (v Courier) in rr. **1994:** (6) A –, F 3, W qf, US 4. After winning Jakarta in Jan., he took a 3-month break, missing Australian Open, to work on fitness and strength. He returned to take 5 more titles at Philadelphia, Hong Kong, Atlanta, Cincinnati and Beijing – his 7th title in Asia. He was r/u both Tokyo tourns and San Jose, and at Antwerp beat Ivanisevic for the 1st time. However, he disappointed again at IBM/ATP World Champ, where he beat only Berasategui. **1995:** (5) A sf, F r/u, W 2, US qf. Continued his success in Asia, winning Hong Kong, Tokyo Seiko and Beijing, with his 4th title of year coming at Atlanta. He played during the year with a slightly longer-handled racket, and, working on his serve to make it more of a weapon, he rediscovered his CC form in reaching f French Open – his best performance since he won in 1989. He also reached f San Jose, Philadelphia and Cincinnati, sf Australian Open and Tokyo Japan Open and 4 more qf. His year finished on a high note when he upset Sampras in sf IBM/ATP Champ and finished r/u to Becker, never before having progressed beyond rr. **1996:** (2) A r/u, F 3, W 1, US r/u. At Australian Open he defied a stomach injury to beat Agassi in ss and extend Becker to 4s in f, then upset Agassi again on his way to the title at Indian Wells. However, at French Open he could not overcome a pulled abdominal muscle as he lost to an inspired Edberg in 3r, and at Wimbledon A. Costa beat him 1r. Things looked up again after that as he reached the top 3 1st time after winning Washington. He then won his next tourn at Los Angeles and reached f the following week at Cincinnati. At US Open, where he was controversially seeded 2 ahead of Muster, who was ranked above him, he upset Agassi again and was r/u to Sampras. This result took him to the No. 2 slot, and had he beaten Sampras, he would have passed him at the top of the rankings. Although his results in Asia were less impressive than before, he was r/u Hong Kong and Singapore, and also reached sf San Jose, Memphis, Atlanta and Stuttgart Eurocard, plus 3 more qf. His season tailed off in disappointment at ATP Champ, where he won only 1 rr match, and he missed GS Cup 1st time after withdrawing with tendinitis in ankle. **1997:** (3) A sf, F 4, W 1, US sf. Although he never looked likely to displace Sampras at the top of the rankings, he held on to his 2nd position until the last week of the season. He won all 5 f he played, taking Memphis, Indian Wells, Hong Kong (his 11th title in Asia), Orlando and Washington. He also appeared in sf Australian Open, US Open, Rosmalen, Montreal and Cincinnati, plus qf San Jose and Long Island. Yet again he was disappointing at ATP Champ, winning only 1 match, and lost his No. 2 ranking to Rafter. **1998:** (29) A 2, F 3, W 2, US 2. Seeming only a shadow of his former self, he dropped out of the top 10 after LIPC and by June had slipped so far down the rankings that he was unseeded at Wimbledon and US Open. On the positive side, Boston in Aug. was his 1st title for 13 months and Shanghai his 12th in total in Asia. He also reached f Memphis and Orlando, sf San Jose and Washington, and qf Rome (d. Sampras). Injury again featured in his year: he was out of action for 6 weeks from early March following the partial tear of a ligament in his knee, and returned at Hong Kong wearing a brace; then from May he was affected by tendinitis of the wrist, which caused him to retire at Washington and hampered him for rest of year. **1999:** (50) A 2, F 1, W –, US 2. With no title during the year, he ended his run of at least 1 title in each of the past 11 years – the longest streak at the time among current players. It was another disappointing season, in which he had slipped far enough down the rankings to be unseeded at GS, dropped out of top 50, and missed the entire GC season with back spasms. His best performance came at Paris Open, where he played through the qualifying then d. Rios and Pioline to reach sf. He also appeared in same stage San Jose and Shanghai, plus qf Los Angeles and Cincinnati (d. Corretja). **2000:** A 1, F 3, W 2, US 2. At Auckland in Jan. he reached his 1st f since October 1998 and followed in Aug. at Los Angeles with his 1st title since that date. With sf appearances in Atlanta, Halle, 's-Hertogenbosch and Shanghai, plus qf San Jose, Memphis, Long Island (d. Rafter), Hong Kong and Stuttgart Masters (d. Corretja), he crept back up the rankings, although he was still low enough to be unseeded at all GS. **2000 HIGHLIGHTS – SINGLES: Australian Open 1r** (lost Federer 6–4 6–4 7–6), **French Open 3r** (d. Voinea 6–1 6–2 2–6 6–3, T. Johansson 7–6 7–6 2–6 6–3, lost Kuerten 6–3 6–7 6–1 6–4), **Wimbledon 2r** (d. Gaudio 6–2 6–3 6–2, lost Popp 7–6 4–6 6–7 6–3 8–6), **US Open 2r** (d. Levy 6–2 3–6 6–4 6–4, lost T. Martin 6 4 6 2 6 4), **Olympics 1r** [seed 16] (lost Lareau 7–6 6–3); **won** Los Angeles (d. Kilderry 6–4 6–2, Ullyett 6–1 6–3, W. Ferreira 6–3 7–6, Gimelstob 3–6 6–3 6–0, Gambill 6–7 6–3 ret); **r/u** Auckland (d. B. Black 7–5 4–6 7–6, Sell 4–6 6–4 7–6, Gustafsson 7–5 3–6 1–0 ret, Balcells 6–3 3–6 6–2, lost M. Norman 3–6 6–3 7–5); **sf** Atlanta (d. Sanguinetti 7–5 6–3, Alonso 7–5 6–7 6–3, Woodruff 7–6 6–1, lost Ilie 6–3 1–6 6–2), **sf** Halle (d. Tillstrom 6–3 3–6 6–3, Medvedev 2–6 7–6 6–4, Federer 7–5 6–2, lost Krajicek 6–2 6–1), **sf** 's-Hertogenbosch (d. Srichaphan 6–3 6–2, Golmard 1–6 6–4 6–3, Braasch 7–6 7–6, lost Escude 7–6 6–2), **sf** Shanghai (d. Levy 4–6 6–4 6–1, Goldstein 6–3 6–4, Massu 7–5 6–3, lost M. Norman 6–3 6–1). **CAREER HIGHLIGHTS – SINGLES: French Open – won** 1989 (d. Masso 6–7 6–3 6–0 6–3, Sampras 6–1 6–1 6–1, Roig 6–0 7–5 6–3, Lendl 4–6 4–6 6–3 6–3, Agenor 6–4 2–6 6–4 7–6, Chesnokov 6–1 5–7 7–6 7–5, Edberg 6–1 2–6 4–6 6–4 6–2), **r/u** 1995 (d. Nargiso 6–3 6–4 6–1, Vacek 6–3 5–7 6–4 6–4, Carbonell 6–1 6–2 7–6, Stich 1–6 6–0 6–2 6–3, Voinea 7–5 6–0 6–1, Bruguera 6–4 7–6 7–6, lost Muster 7–5 6–2 6–4); **Australian Open – r/u** 1996 (d. Rikl 6–2 6–1 6–2, Hlasek 6–1 6–3 6–3, Raoux 6–2 6–2 7–6, Fleurian 6–3 6–3 6–4, Tillstrom 6–0 6–2 6–4, Agassi 6–1 6–4 7–6, lost Becker 6–4 2–6 6–2), **sf** 1995 (d. Kilderry 6–2 6–4 5–7 6–2, Alami 6–3 6–4 6–1, Damm 6–3 7–5 6–3, Delaitre 6–3 6–2 6–4, Medvedev 7–6 7–5 6–3, lost Sampras 6–7 6–3 6–4 6–4), **sf** 1997 (d. Goossens 6–0 6–3 6–1, Reneberg 6–3 7–5 6–1, Henman 6–1 7–6 6–3, Medvedev 4–6 6–2 6–2 6–1, Rios 7–5 6–1 6–4, lost Moya 7–5 6–2 6–4); **US Open – r/u** 1996 (d. Oncins 3–6 6–1 6–0 7–6, Godwin 6–1 6–3 6–1, Spadea 6–4 5–7 2–6 7–5 6–3, Hlasek 6–3 6–4 6–2, J. Sanchez 7–5 6–3 6–7 6–3, Agassi 6–3 6–2 6–2, lost Sampras 6–1 6–4 7–6), **sf** 1992 (d. E. Ferreira 6–3 6–4 7–6, P. McEnroe 6–3 6–3 6–4, Boetsch 6–3 6–3 6–1, Washington 6–2 2–6 3–6 6–3 6–1, W. Ferreira 7–5 2–6 6–3 6–7 6–1, lost Edberg 6–7 7–5 7–6 5–7 6–4), **sf** 1997 (d. Fredriksson 6–3 6–4 6–2, Salzenstein 4–6 6–2 6–3 6–4, Sargsian 6–1 6–3 7–5, Pioline 6–3 0–6 5–7 7–5 6–1, Rios 7–5 6–2 4–6 4–6 6–3, lost Rafter 6–3 6–3 6–4); **ATP Champ – r/u** 1995 (d. Muster 4–6 6–2 6–3, lost Enqvist 6–1 6–4, d. Courier 6–2 7–5 in rr, d. Sampras 6–4 6–4, lost Becker 7–6 6–0 7–6); **GS Cup – r/u** 1991 (d. Courier 6–4 6–2, P. McEnroe 6–2 6–4, Lendl 2–6 4–6 6–4 7–6 9–7, lost Wheaton 7–5 6–2 6–4), **r/u** 1992 (d. Agassi 6–4 6–2, Korda 6–3 6–4, Ivanisevic 6–7 6–2 6–4 3–6 6–3, lost Stich 6–2 6–3 6–2), **sf** 1990 (d. Edberg 6–4 4–6 7–5, Leconte 7–6 6–3, lost Sampras 3–6 4–6 6–4).

LEE CHILDS (GBR)

Born Yeovil, 11 June 1982; lives Bridgewater; RH; 6ft; 174lb; career singles titles 0; final 2000 junior doubles ranking 1. Coached by Danny Sapsford. **2000:** Won US Open Jun doubles with Nelson and won both singles and doubles at European Jun Champs.

FRANCISCO CLAVET (ESP)

Born Aranjuez, 24 October 1968; lives Madrid; LH; 6ft; 156lb; turned pro 1988; career singles titles 7; final 2000 ATP ranking 49; 2000 prize money $400,202; career prize money $3,668,834. Coached by Jose Miguel Morales; formerly by his older brother Pepo (Jose), who used to play the circuit. **1986:** (870). **1987:** (638). **1988:** (290). **1989:** (188) Qf Kitzbuhel. **1990:** (90) A –, F 1, W –, US –. Won his 1st tour title at Hilversum as a lucky loser, upsetting Jaite on the way. **1991:** (30) A 2, F 4, W 1, US 3. Reached sf Stuttgart Mercedes Mercedes (d. Muster and Gomez), Kitzbuhel, Schenectady, Athens and Sao Paulo, plus 3 more qf and last 16 French Open, unseeded. **1992:** (22) A 2, F 1, W 1, US 1. Enjoying another consistent year, he was r/u Gstaad and San Marino and reached sf Philadelphia, Indian Wells, Madrid, Athens and Palermo. **1993:** (99) A –, F 2, W –, US 1. In a less successful year, his best showing was sf Genova, plus qf Hilversum, Bucharest and Sao Paulo (d. Yzaga) and an upset of Novacek at Buenos Aires. **1994:** (38) A –, F 2, W –, US 2. On the main tour he was r/u Santiago and Montevideo (losing both to Berasategui) and reached sf Athens and Buenos Aires (d. Berasategui on clay), plus qf Pinehurst, Florence, St Polten and Palermo. He also won 2 titles on the Challenger circuit. **1995:** (49) A –, F 3, W –, US 3. At Palermo he won his 1st title since 1990, as well as reaching sf Mexico City, Oporto, Umag and Montevideo. **1996:** (34) A 3, F 4, W 1, US 1. In another productive year, he won Amsterdam and appeared in sf Mexico City and Bologna, plus qf Antwerp, Estoril, St Polten, Gstaad (d. MaliVai Washington), Stuttgart Eurocard, Bucharest and Palermo. Upset A. Costa at French Open, where he was unseeded. **1997:** (33) A –, F 2, W 2, US 1. His best performances came in Oct., when he won Mexico City and Bogota back-to-back, having earlier reached f Estoril (d. Kuerten, Moya and Mantilla), sf Tashkent and Bucharest, and qf Antwerp (d. Enqvist), Rosmalen, Amsterdam and Palermo. **1998:** (30) A 3, F 4, W 4, US 2. Again he performed best later in the season, winning Bucharest in Sept. and Santiago in Nov. In other tourns he reached sf Kitzbuhel and Mexico City, qf St Polten and Gstaad (d. Berasategui), and, in GS, unseeded each time, he upset M. Chang at French Open and Rios at Wimbledon. **1999:** (38) A 1, F 2, W 3, US 1. It was a consistent if unspectacular year in which he reached sf LIPC and Barcelona (d. Henman) and qf Dubai (d. Rusedski), St Polten, Gstaad, Umag and Mallorca. **2000:** A 3, F 2, W 2, US 1. He was always a dangerous opponent as he moved to f Estoril (d. Kafelnikov and N. Lapentti), sf Kitzbuhel (d. Kafelnikov), qf Scottsdale (where he inflicted Agassi's worst HC defeat for nearly 13 years), Hamburg (d. Enqvist) and 's-Hertogenbosch, and upset N. Lapentti again at Rome. **2000 HIGHLIGHTS – SINGLES: Australian Open 3r** (d. Hrbaty 3–6 6–1 6–4 ret, Ivanisevic 7–6 6–4 6–2, lost W. Ferreira 6–3 6–4 3–6 6–3), **French Open 2r** (d. Canas 6–2 6–0 6–3, lost Puerta 6–2 6–1 6–3), **Wimbledon 2r** (d. Gumy 6–3 6–3 6–3, lost Enqvist [seed 9] 7–6 7–6 7–5), **US Open 1r** (lost Dosedel 7–6 6–4 6–1); **r/u** Estoril (d. Kafelnikov 6–7 7–6 6–2, Chela 6–4 7–5, Escude 6–3 6–2, N. Lapentti 6–4 6–3, lost Moya 6–3 6–2); **sf** Kitzbuhel (d. Berasategui 6–0 7–5, A. Costa 4–6 6–3 6–2, Kafelnikov 6–3 6–2, lost Alvarez 6–3 7–5).

ARNAUD CLEMENT (FRA)

Born Aix-en-Provence, 17 December 1977; lives Geneva, Switzerland; RH; 5ft 8in; 142lb; turned pro 1996; career singles titles 1; final 2000 ATP ranking 18; 2000 prize money $671,815; career prize money $1,382,941.

Coached by Philippe Rosant; trained by Daniel Gibert. **1995:** (655). **1996:** (341) Won Bulgaria satellite circuit. **1997:** (101) A –, F 1, W 3, US –. He reached his 1st qf on the main tour at St Petersburg, following with same stage Toulouse (d. Larsson), as well as upsetting Bruguera at Vienna and Rafter at Lyon. **1998:** (105) A 1, F 1, W 1, US 1. Reached his 1st sf in his last tourn of the year at Moscow, having earlier reached qf Marseille, Bournemouth and Toulouse and upset Siemerink at Rome, breaking into top 100. **1999:** (56) A 2, F 2, W 2, US 4. He progressed to his 1st f at Marseille and sf Boston (d. Mantilla and extended Rusedski to 3s). He also upset Kiefer at US Open, where he was unseeded, removed Enqvist at Montreal, Johansson at Indianapolis and extended Agassi to 5s 2r French Open. **2000:** A 4, F 2, W 2, US qf. His year finished on a high note at Lyon in Nov. as he won his 1st title, unseeded, with upsets of Squillari and Rafter. He had earlier broken into top 20 with a successful spell in summer when he reached sf Los Angeles, Cincinnati (d. Ferrero, Kafelnikov and Squillari) and Long Island. At US Open he upset Agassi on his way to qf, unseeded, and Rusedski was his victim at Olympics. In doubles he won Casablanca with Grosjean. **2000 HIGHLIGHTS – SINGLES: Australian Open last 16** [unseeded] (d. Van Lottum 7–6 6–4 ret, N. Lapentti [seed 7] 3–6 7–6 6–2 4–1 ret, Federer 6–1 6–4 6–3, lost El Aynaoui 3–6 6–3 6–4 3–6 10–8), **French Open 2r** (d. Escude 7–6 6–4 6–0, lost Sargsian 6–7 6–3 2–6 6–0 6–4), **Wimbledon 2r** (d. Ivanisevic 6–3 3–6 6–3 6–4, lost Henman 6–4 6–4 6–4), **US Open qf** [unseeded] (d. Gaudio 6–3 6–4 6–2, Agassi [seed 1] 6–3 6–2 6–4, Arazi 4–6 6–2 6–2 4–6 0–1 ret, Pavel 3–6 6–2 6–1 7–6 ret, lost Hewitt [seed 9] 6–2 6–4 6–3), **Olympics 2r** (d. Rusedski 6–2 6–3, lost Corretja [seed 6] 6–7 6–4 6–4); **won** Lyon (d. Guardiola 7–5 4–6 6–1, Squillari 3–6 6–2 6–3, Sluiter 6–3 3–6 7–6, Agassi 6–3 ret, Rafter 7–6 7–6); **sf** Los Angeles (d. Ondruska 6–3 6–2, Godwin 6–4 4–6 6–3, Roux 6–3 6–2, lost Gambill 3–6 6–0 6–3), **sf** Cincinnati (d. Ferrero 6–4 6–2, Damm 7–5 6–3, Kafelnikov 6–4 6–1, Squillari 6–2 7–5, lost Enqvist 6–2 6–2), **sf** Long Island (d. Bastl 6–4 5–7 7–6, Kucera 7–6 6–2, Chang 6–3 6–2, lost Enqvist 7–6 6–1). **2000 HIGHLIGHTS – DOUBLES:** (with Grosjean) **won** Casablanca (d. Burgsmuller/Painter 7–6 6–4).

DOMINIQUE COENE (BEL)

Born Brugge, 23 January 1982; lives Meldegem; RH; 2HB; 5ft 9in; 163lb; career singles titles 0.

Coached by Christophe Delmeille. **2000:** Won Wimbledon Jun doubles with Vliegen.

ALBERT COSTA (ESP)

Born Lerida, 25 June 1975; lives Monte Carlo, Monaco; RH; 5ft 11in; 163lb; turned pro 1993; career singles titles 11; final 2000 ATP ranking 26; 2000 prize money $557,589; career prize money $4,414,006.

Coached by Jose Perlas; trained by Mariano Montecillas. A Catalan, he prefers to be known as Albert, rather than Alberto. No relation to Carlos Costa. **1991:** On winning ESP World Youth Cup team. **1993:** Ranked No.

4 in ITF Jun rankings, he won Orange Bowl and was r/u French Open Jun to Carretero. In the senior game he reached qf Santiago (d. Berasategui) after qualifying. **1994:** (52) A –, F 1, W 1, US 1. He was voted Newcomer of the Year, in which he reached sf Estoril, Prague (d. Chesnokov) and Bucharest (d. Gaudenzi), and won 2 Challenger titles. **1995:** (24) A –, F qf, W –, US –. Unseeded at French Open, he upset Courier and was the only player to take a set off Muster, whom he extended to 5s. At Casablanca he reached his 1st f on the main tour, following with the same stage Estoril (d. Medvedev) and in Aug. won his 1st title at Kitzbuhel, upsetting Muster on clay. He also reached sf Nice and Santiago, plus 2 qf, to break into top 25. **1996:** (13) A 2, F 2, W 2, US 1. He continued his march through the rankings with the titles at Gstaad (d. Kafelnikov), San Marino and Bournemouth. He removed Agassi on the way to f Monte Carlo, where he extended Muster to 5s, reached his 1st HC f at Dubai and upset M. Chang at Wimbledon in only his 4th tourn on grass as he developed his skills on surfaces other than clay. He also appeared in sf Italian Open and Tel Aviv, plus qf Scottsdale and Umag. **1997:** (19) A qf, F 3, W –, US 1. Broke into top 10 after winning Barcelona and consolidated with the title at Marbella, although he was unable to maintain that position, despite reaching sf Sydney, Stuttgart Mercedes (d. Kafelnikov), Cincinnati (d. Corretja) and Boston, and qf Australian Open (extended Sampras to 5s), Scottsdale and Hamburg. Played in winning ESP WT Cup team. **1998:** (14) A 2, F 4, W 2, US 1. He maintained his top 20 ranking with the titles at Hamburg (where both his sf and f opponents were forced to retire) and Kitzbuhel, r/u Rome (d. M. Chang but withdrew before f with wrist injury) and Bournemouth, and played qf Sydney, Scottsdale, Gstaad and Stuttgart Mercedes. Coming into ATP Champ as 2nd alternate when Rios withdrew, he lost both his matches there. **1999:** (18) A 1, F 3, W 1, US 1. He won Estoril (d. T. Martin), Gstaad (d. Lapentti) and Kitzbuhel (d. Kafelnikov) on the main tour, adding Birmingham on the Challenger circuit. In other tourns he reached sf Palermo and Bucharest, plus qf Sydney (where he retired after damaging a tendon on right knee), Barcelona (d. Rios), Monte Carlo and Paris Masters (d. Henman). **2000:** A 1, F qf, W –, US 2. His best performances were sf Dubai, Scottsdale (d. Corretja) and Gstaad, and qf Monte Carlo, Rome and French Open (unseeded, d. Enqvist and Hewitt). In D Cup he upset Kafelnikov as ESP d. RUS 4–1 in qf on their way to 1st f in 33 years, and although he lost to Hewitt in 5s in f, ESP d. AUS 3–1 in Barcelona to win D Cup 1st time. Also on the international stage he won Olympic bronze in doubles with Corretja. He pulled out of Wimbledon in protest at not being seeded, but was not fined, having withdrawn in time for a LL to take his place. **2000 HIGHLIGHTS – SINGLES: Australian Open 1r** (lost C. Rochus 6–3 6–7 6–4 6–3), **French Open qf** [unseeded] (d. Ivanisevic 6–3 6–3 6–0, Gumy 4–6 6–3 7–5 1–0 ret, Enqvist [seed 7] 5–7 7–6 3–6 6–4, Hewitt [seed 15] 6–3 4–6 6–2 6–4, lost Squillari 6–4 6–4 2–6 6–4), **US Open 2r** (d. Roddick 6–3 6–7 6–1 6–4, lost Mirnyi 6–4 6–1 6–4), **Olympics 1r** [seed 15] (lost Ullyett 6–3 3–6 11–9); **sf** Dubai (d. Berasategui 6–4 7–5, Koubek 6–0 6–1, El Aynaoui 6–2 6–4, lost Kiefer 6–2 6–0), **sf** Scottsdale (d. Goldstein 6–3 6–1, Pavel 6–2 6–4, Corretja 6–2 4–6 7–6, lost Henman 6–3 6–3), **sf** Gstaad (d. Koubek 4–6 6–3 6–3, Golmard 6–4 6–3, Novak 6–3 6–4, lost Puerta 6–4 6–3). **2000 HIGHLIGHTS – DOUBLES:** (with Corretja) **Olympics bronze medal** (d. Adams/De Jager in play-off). **CAREER HIGHLIGHTS – SINGLES: Australian Open – qf 1997** (d. Rafter 7–5 6–2 7–5, Kroslak 6–1 7–6 7–6, Draper 6–4 6–2 7–5, W. Ferreira 6–3 6–2 3–2 ret, lost Sampras 6–3 6–7 6–1 3–6 6–2); **French Open – qf 1995** [unseeded] (d. Renzenbrink 6–3 6–4 6–0, Raoux 6–4 6–4 6–4, Karbacher 7–5 6–2 6–2, Courier 6–4 1–6 7–6 6–4, lost Muster 6–2 3–6 6–7 7–5 6–2), **qf 2000.**

JOHN-LAFFNIE DE JAGER (RSA)

Born Johannesburg, 17 March 1973; lives Ermelo; RH; 6ft 4in; 180lb; turned pro 1992; career singles titles 0; final 2000 ATP ranking 22 doubles; 2000 prize money $22,783; career prize money $1,206,042.

Coached by Craig Tiley. Won Orange Bowl 12s. **1989:** (872). **1990:** (854). **1991:** (–) Won US Open Jun doubles with Alami. **1992:** (341) A –, F –, W 1, US –. Won Moscow doubles with Barnard. **1993:** (890) A –, F –, W –, US –. R/u Lyon doubles with Kruger. **1994:** (–) A –, F –, W –, US –. Played 2 doubles f with Bale, winning Tel Aviv. **1995:** (–) A –, F –, W –, US –. Won Toulouse doubles with Bjorkman and was r/u Lyon with W. Ferreira. In mixed he was r/u French Open with Hetherington. **1996:** (–) A –, F –, W –, US –. **1997:** (–) A –, F –, W –, US –. R/u Australian Open mixed doubles with Neiland. **1998:** (–) A –, F –, W –, US –. He appeared in 2 doubles f with different partners but won no title. **1999:** (–) A –, F –, W –, US –. In doubles with Adams he won Rotterdam and was r/u in 5 other tourns, qualifying for World Doubles Champ, although there he was suffering from flu and they withdrew after losing their 1st 2 matches. **2000:** A –, F –, W –, US –. His doubles partnership with Adams brought titles in London, Rotterdam and Munich as well as a place at World Doubles Champ, although they were unable to compete at the last minute when he suffered a wrist injury. **2000 HIGHLIGHTS – DOUBLES:** (with Adams) **won** London (d. Gambill/Humphries 6–3 6–7 7–6), **won** Rotterdam (d. Henman/Kafelnikov 4–6 6–3 6–4), **won** Munich (d. Mirnyi/Zimonjic 6–4 6–4).

YOUNES EL AYNAOUI (MAR)

Born Rabat, 12 September 1971, and lives there; RH; 6ft 4in; 185lb; turned pro 1990; career singles titles 1; final 2000 ATP ranking 25; 2000 prize money $491,615; career prize money $1,691,001.

Coached by Koen Gonnissen and trains every winter at Bollettieri Academy in Florida. Wife Anne Sophie Rocher (married 13 September 1997); son Ewen Marwan (born 11 August 1997). A three-times winner of nat champs, he has been ranked No. 1 in Morocco since 1990. **1992:** (307) Upset Muster on his way to qf

Casablanca. **1993:** (51) Was a finalist at Casablanca and won Oporto Challenger, a result which took him into the top 100. Also reached qf Kitzbuhel (d. E. Sanchez), San Marino, Toulouse (d. Bruguera), Sao Paulo and Buenos Aires. **1994:** (115) A 2, F 1, W 1, US 1. Although he broke into the top 50 in March, he had slipped out of the top 100 by the end of a year in which his best performances were sf Jakarta and Casablanca, qf Schenectady and the Challenger title at Agadir. **1995:** (112) A 1, F 4, W –, US –. Although he reached no qf on the main tour, he won Challenger titles at Geneva and Siracusa. **1996:** A –, F 1, W 1, US 1. He began the year in style with r/u Qatar (d. Enqvist and Muster before losing to Korda in 3s tb) and following the next week with the same stage Jakarta (d. Haarhuis), unseeded both times. Then followed a slump in which he won only 1 match in 12 tours until, again unseeded, he played his 3rd f of the year at Amsterdam, upsetting A. Costa on the way. He underwent surgery for an ankle injury in Nov. **1997:** (237) A –, F –, W –, US –. He returned in Feb. to reach qf Casablanca and win Guadalajara Challenger, but missed the last 7 months with a recurrence of the ankle injury. **1998:** (49) A –, F –, W –, US –. Further surgery on his right ankle in Feb. kept him out until June. He returned in style, though, winning 6 Challenger titles across the year, including Szczecin and Oporto back-to-back in autumn, and burst back on to the main tour in Nov. to take r/u slot at Santiago, upsetting Berasategui, Puerta and Mantilla on the way, finishing back in the top 50 and voted Comeback Player of Year. **1999:** (34) A 2, F 2, W 2, US 2. At Amsterdam he won his 1st title on the main tour in his 6th f, as well as reaching sf St Polten, Gstaad (d. Rios) and Bournemouth and qf Bucharest, and upsetting Corretja at Barcelona. On the Challenger circuit he added Ulm to his collection of titles. **2000:** A qf, F 4, W 3, US 1. He was consistent through the year with r/u Bogota, sf Qatar, and qf Australian Open (unseeded, d. Haas and Ferrero), Dubai, Casablanca, Barcelona, Munich and Long Island. **2000 HIGHLIGHTS – SINGLES: Australian Open qf** [unseeded] (d. Parmar 6–7 7–6 1–6 6–3 6–1, Haas [seed 10] 7–5 6–3 6–3, Ferrero 7–6 4–6 4–6 7–6 6–4, Clement 3–6 6–3 6–4 3–6 10–8, lost Kafelnikov [seed 2] 6–0 6–3 7–6), **French Open last 16** [seed 15] (d. Lisnard 3–6 2–6 6–4 6–3 6–1, Chela 6–3 6–4 6–0, Stoltenberg 6–4 5–5 ret, lost Squillari 6–4 6–1 6–3), **Wimbledon 3r** (d. Mantilla 7–6 6–3 6–4, M. Lee 6–7 6–2 6–2 6–2, lost Voltchkov 7–6 7–5 7–6), **US Open 1r** (lost Alami 6–3 6–4 3–6 2–6 6–3); **r/u** Bogota (d. Lisnard 6–4 6–2, Etlis 6–4 4–6 7–6, Portas 6–4 6–1, Vicente 1–6 7–6 7–6); **sf** Qatar (d. Dupuis 4–6 6–3 6–2, Gaudio 6–4 6–4, Tillstrom 7–5 6–3, lost Schuttler 6–7 6–4 6–4).

NICOLAS ESCUDE (FRA)

Born Chartres, 3 April 1976; lives Geneva, Switzerland; RH; 6ft 1in; 155lb; turned pro 1995; career singles titles 1; final 2000 ATP ranking 48; 2000 prize money $393,359; career prize money $1,388,389.

Coached by Arnaud Casagrande. A natural left-hander, he was trained from childhood to play right-handed. **1993:** (617) A –, F 1, W –, US –. Began to play the satellite circuits. **1994:** (646) A –, F –, W –, US –. **1995:** (193) A –, F –, W –, US –. Won Morocco satellite. **1996:** (406) A –, F –, W –, US –. He was restricted for most of the season by a herniated disk. **1997:** (93) A –, F 3, W –, US 2. Success on the satellites and main-tour upsets of Berasategui and Kuerten at Paris Indoor took him into the top 100 1st time. **1998:** (37) A sf, F 2, W 2, US 1. A change of racket in an attempt to ease arm/shoulder problems reduced his injuries but restricted his form, so he changed back to the old racket and put up with the aches and pains. He sprang to prominence at Australian Open, where he survived 3 5s matches, becoming the 1st player to recover from 2s down 3 times in GS, and removed Kuerten on his way to sf, unseeded. He reached the same stage at Tashkent, plus qf Adelaide, Munich (d. Philippoussis) and Long Island, and upset Corretja at Halle. He qualified for GS Cup 1st time, but lost 1r to Mantilla. **1999:** (37) A –, F 2, W –, US qf. Marseille had been his only qf appearance until US Open, where, unseeded, he upset Rios to reach same stage there. He followed that with his 1st main tour title at Toulouse, unseeded again and with upsets of Henman and Rosset, and finished the year on another high note with sf Moscow. **2000:** A 4, F 1, W 2, US –. He followed sf appearance at Adelaide with an upset of Krajicek at Australian Open, where he was unseeded. His best showing was r/u 's-Hertogenbosch, and he reached qf Estoril, Halle and Toulouse, as well as upsetting Pioline at Indian Wells, Safin at Vienna and Kuerten in D Cup. **2000 HIGHLIGHTS – SINGLES: Australian Open last 16** [unseeded] (d. Courier 6–7 6–3 7–5 6–1, Krajicek [seed 9] 2–6 6–3 6–1 6–3, Vinciguerra 6–4 6–4 6–3, lost Arazi 6–4 6–3 7–6), **French Open 1r** (lost Clement 7–6 6–4 6–0), **Wimbledon 2r** (d. Canas 4–6 6–4 6–1 6–2, lost Schuttler 6–4 7–6 7–6), **Olympics 1r** (lost Chela 6–7 7–5 6–1); **r/u** 's-Hertogenbosch (d. Van Lottum 6–1 6–2, Youzhny 7–5 6–2, Clavet 7–5 6–4, M. Chang 7–6 6–2, lost Rafter 6–1 6–3); **sf** Adelaide (d. Baccanello 6–7 7–5 6–3, Dosedel 7–6 6–4, Henman 6–3 6–1, lost Hewitt 3–6 6–1 6–4). **CAREER HIGHLIGHTS – SINGLES: Australian Open – sf 1998** [unseeded] (d. Larsson 5–7 4–6 7–5 6–1 10–8, Kuerten 5–7 6–3 6–1 7–5, Reneberg 1–6 6–7 6–2 7–5 6–4, Woodbridge 7–6 6–3 6–2, Kiefer 4–6 3–6 6–4 6–1 6–2, lost Rios 6–1 6–3 6–2), **US Open – qf 1999** [unseeded] (d. Gustafsson 4–6 4–6 7–6 6–2 6–4, Moya 6–1 6–4 0–1 ret, Malisse 6–3 6–2 6–1, Rios 6–2 6–3 7–5, lost Agassi 7–6 6–3 6–4).

ROGER FEDERER (SUI)

Born Basle, 8 August 1981; lives Munchenstein; RH; 6ft 1in; 177lb; career singles titles 0; final 2000 ATP ranking 29; 2000 prize money $623,782.

Coached by Peter Carter and Peter Lundgren. **1998:** (302) At Wimbledon he won both Jun singles (over Labadze) and doubles (with Rochus), at US Open was r/u singles to Nalbandian, and he won Orange Bowl. In the senior game he reached qf Toulouse (d. Raoux and Fromberg) after qualifying. **1999:** (64) A –, F 1, W

1, US –. Moving effectively into the men's game, he reached his 1st sf at Vienna, and qf Marseille (d. Moya), Rotterdam and Basel, as well as winning Brest Challenger. **2000:** A 3, F 4, W 1, US 3. Although a 1st title still eluded him, he was r/u Marseille and Basel, where he upset Hewitt and extended Enqvist to 5s, going on to play another long f as he and Hrbaty lost the doubles there on fs tb. He also reached sf Copenhagen, Vienna (d. M. Norman) and Olympics (losing bronze medal play-off to Di Pasquale), plus qf London (d. Kiefer) and Halle, and upset Philippoussis in D Cup. **2000 HIGHLIGHTS – SINGLES: Australian Open 3r** (d. M. Chang 6–4 6–4 7–6, Kroslak 7–6 6–2 6–3, lost Clement 6–1 6–4 6–3), **French Open last 16** [unseeded] (d. Arthurs 7–6 6–3 1–6 6–3, Gambill 7–6 6–3 6–3, Kratochvil 7–6 6–4 2–6 6–7 8–6, lost Corretja [seed 10] 7–5 7–6 6–2), **Wimbledon 1r** (lost Kafelnikov [seed 5] 7–5 5–7 7–6 ret), **US Open 3r** (d. Wessels 4–6 4–6 6–3 7–5 3–4 ret, Nestor 6–1 7–6 6–1, lost Ferrero [seed 12] 7–5 7–6 1–6 7–6), **Olympics sf** [unseeded] (d. Prinosil 6–2 6–2, Kucera 6–4 7–6, Tillstrom 6–1 6–2, Alami 7–6 6–1, lost Haas 6–3 6–2; bronze medal play-off lost Di Pasquale 7–6 6–7 6–3); **r/u** Marseille (d. Dupuis 6–4 6–4, T. Johansson 6–3 6–2, Ljubicic 6–2 3–6 7–6, Santoro 7–6 7–5, lost Rosset 2–6 6–3 7–6), **r/u** Basel (d. Haas 6–3 6–3, Pavel 7–6 6–4, Thomann 6–4 6–4, Hewitt 6–4 5–7 7–6, lost Enqvist 6–2 4–6 7–6 1–6 6–1); **sf** Copenhagen (d. Dewulf 6–4 4–6 6–3, Jonsson 6–4 6–4, Pozzi 4–6 6–1 6–3, lost Larsson 6–3 7–6), **sf** Vienna (d. M. Norman 4–6 7–6 6–4, Mirnyi 6–3 6–3, Krajicek 6–4 6–3, lost Henman 2–6 7–6 6–3). **2000 HIGHLIGHTS – DOUBLES:** (with Hrbaty) **r/u** Basel (lost Johnsson/Norval 7–6 4–6 7–6).

ELLIS FERREIRA (RSA)

Born Pretoria, 19 February 1970; lives Atlanta, Ga.; LH; 6ft 2in; 190lb; turned pro 1992; career singles titles 0; final 2000 ATP ranking 5 doubles; 2000 prize money $421,155; career prize money $1,911.908.

Wife Ashley (married 19 September 1992); daughter Camden Lanier (born 24 July 1997); son Sullivan Paige born 22 March 2000. No relation to Wayne Ferreira. **1991:** (503) All-American in doubles for 3rd year at Univ. of Alabama. **1992:** (387) A –, F –, W –, US 1. **1993:** (362) A –, F –, W –, US –. **1994:** (240) A –, F –, W 1, US 2. R/u Sun City doubles with Stafford. **1995:** (519) A –, F –, W –, US –. In doubles with Siemerink won Vienna and r/u Stuttgart Mercedes. **1996:** (–) A –, F –, W –, US –. Played 3 doubles f, winning Sydney and Monte Carlo with Siemerink. **1997:** (–) A –, F –, W –, US –. Won 5 doubles titles from 7 f with Galbraith, with whom he qualified for his 1st World Doubles Champ, where they won only 1 match. **1998:** (–) A –, F –, W –, US –. From 8 doubles f with 3 different partners, he won 2 with Leach and 1 with Haygarth. It was with Leach that he qualified for World Doubles Champ, but they did not progress beyond rr. **1999:** (–) A –, F –, W –, US –. From 3 doubles f he shared 's-Hertogenbosch with Rikl and won Rome with Leach, with whom he qualified for World Doubles Champ, where they won only 1 match. **2000:** A –, F –, W –, US –. In doubles with Leach he won Australian Open (in a match lasting 4hr 21min and decided only 18–16 fs), r/u US Open (losing fs tb), and also took Auckland and Atlanta from 4 other f. They qualified for World Doubles Champ again, but were unable to send Leach into retirement with a final title as they lost sf to Bhupathi/Paes. However, they finished the season as No. 2 pairing behind Woodbridge/Woodforde. **2000 HIGHLIGHTS – DOUBLES:** (with Leach) **won Australian Open** (d. W. Black/Kratzmann 6–4 3–6 6–3 3–6 18–16), **r/u US Open** (lost Hewitt/Mirnyi 6–4 5–7 7–6); **won** Auckland (d. Delaitre/Tarango 7–5 6–4), **won** Atlanta (d. Gimelstob/Knowles 6–3 6–4); **r/u** Nottingham (lost Johnson/Norval 1–6 6–4 6–3), **r/u** Cincinnati (lost Woodbridge/Woodforde 7–6 6–4).

WAYNE FERREIRA (RSA)

Born Johannesburg, 15 September 1971, and lives there; RH; 2HB; 6ft 1in; 187lb; turned pro 1989; career singles titles 14; final 2000 ATP ranking 13 singles, 14 doubles; 2000 prize money $1,237,864; career prize money $8,189,242.

Coached and trained by Kieron Vorster. Wife Liesl (married 16 Dec. 1994); son Marcus William (born 15 September 1999). No relation to Ellis Ferreira. Has represented Transvaal at cricket, football and badminton. **1989:** (229) Finished the year No. 1 doubles player in ITF Jun Rankings, having won US Open Jun with Stafford and r/u Wimbledon Jun with De Jager. **1990:** (173) A –, F –, W 2, US –. Upset Noah 1r Wimbledon. **1991:** (50) A 4, F 2, W 2, US 2. In singles reached last 16 Australian Open after qualifying and qf Sydney Indoor (d. Lendl), Brisbane and Birmingham. In doubles won LIPC with Norval and Adelaide with Kruger. **1992:** (12) A sf, F 3, W 4, US qf. Having never before progressed beyond qf on the main tour, he put in a tremendous performance at Australian Open, where he upset Wheaton and Novacek *en route* to sf, unseeded. Took his 1st tour title at Queen's in June and broke into top 20, progressing to top 10 in Sept. after reaching qf US Open. Won a second title at Schenectady, r/u Memphis and Stuttgart Mercedes and sf Johannesburg. Played 4 doubles f, winning Olympic silver medal with Norval and taking Auckland with Grabb. **1993:** (22) A 4, F 2, W 4, US 4. It was a less spectacular year in which he slipped out of the top 20 and was unseeded at US Open, where he survived 3 5s matches. He won no title but was r/u Indian Wells and Queen's and reached sf Durban and Sydney Indoor. **1994:** (12) A 4, F 1, W qf, US 3. Won Hawaii, Indianapolis, Bordeaux, Basle, Tel Aviv; r/u Rotterdam (d. Ivanisevic), Manchester; sf Dubai and Toronto. Unseeded at Wimbledon, he upset Rosset on his way to qf, where he took Martin to 7–5 5s. **1995:** (9) A 2, F 3, W 4, US 1. Returned to top 10 after winning his 1st CC title at Munich in May, although he slipped out again later in year. Was asked to try a different racket, but did not get on with it and lost 1r or 2r of 5 tourns before returning to his old type, whereupon he won Ostrava 2 weeks later, following the next week with Lyon, where he beat Sampras in f. He also won Dubai and reached sf Tokyo Japan Open, Italian Open and Paris Open, plus 4 qf. **1996:** (10) A 2, F 4, W 3, US 1. He edged up the rankings in what was a solid, if not spectacular, year. Although his GS performances were disappointing, he won the titles at Scottsdale and Toronto, was r/u Washington and reached sf Italian Open, Queen's and New Haven, as well as qf Dubai, Indian Wells, Hamburg, Cincinnati, Ostrava and Olympics. **1997:** (43) A –, F 3, W 3, US 4. He began the year by winning Hopman Cup singles and followed with sf Gstaad and Indianapolis and qf Dubai. However, restricted by a thigh strain, he missed Australian Open, then withdrew during French Open and struggled for much of the year before undergoing ankle surgery. **1998:** (26) A 2, F 3, W 4, US 1. Although he did not achieve his aim of making it back into the top 10 during the year, he scored some significant upsets in reaching sf London (d. Ivanisevic and Rafter), Dubai, Washington and Lyon (d. Rafter and Pioline) and qf Indianapolis. Other important scalps included Sampras twice – at LIPC and Basle – and Rios at Hamburg, while at US Open he twice had mps v Rusedski before losing in 5s. From 2 doubles f he won Antwerp with Kafelnikov. **1999:** (53) A 4, F 2, W 1, US 1. Apart from Tokyo, where he was r/u, he did not pass qf all year, although he reached that stage at Rotterdam (d. Enqvist) and Los Angeles. In doubles he appeared in 4 f, winning Los Angeles with B. Black. In GS he upset Krajicek at Australian Open, where he was unseeded, and after US Open he tied with Raoux and Woodforde on the longest streak of consec. GS singles draws with 36. However, he missed D Cup tie v GBR in Sept. to be with his wife for the birth of their son. **2000:** A 4, F 3, W 4, US 2. The highlight of his year came in Nov. at Stuttgart Masters, when he upset Enqvist and then d. Hewitt in 5s to take his 1st title since 1996, unseeded. He began the year by winning Hopman Cup with Coetzer, following with sf San Jose and Toronto, plus qf Memphis, Ericsson Open, Nottingham, Los Angeles and Indianapolis. He removed Rafter at Hamburg and upset Krajicek at Wimbledon, where he was unseeded. In that match, he was fined a total of £1,500 for foul language and racket abuse following an outburst v the umpire who overruled a crucial call on sp. In doubles with Kafelnikov (whom he beat at both Toronto and Indianapolis), he played 2 f, winning Rome and qualifying for World Doubles Champ as 6th pairing, although they did not take up their place. **2000 HIGHLIGHTS – SINGLES: Australian Open last 16** [unseeded] (d. Bastl 6–3 6–3 4–6 7–6, T. Johansson 6–3 6–2 6–7 4–6 6–2, Clavet 6–3 6–4 3–6 6–3, lost Kiefer [seed 4] 6–3 6–4 6–2), **French Open 3r** (d. Schuttler 7–6 4–6 6–3 6–2, Coria 6–3 6–1 4–6 7–5, lost N. Lapentti [seed 11] 5–7 6–3 7–5 6–3), **Wimbledon last 16** [unseeded] (d. Arthurs 6–7 6–3 7–6 6–1, Krajicek [seed 11] 5–7 6–3 6–3 7–6, Pavel 3–6 7–6 7–5 6–3, lost Voltchkov 6–3 6–4 7–6), **US Open 2r** (d. Ilie 6–3 2–6 6–4 6–1, lost Arazi 6–3 6–3 6–7 6–3), **Olympics 1r** [seed 16] (lost Haas 7–5 6–2); **won** Stuttgart Masters (d. Vinck 6–3 6–7 6–4, Enqvist 6–2 7–5, Philippoussis 1–0 ret, Pavel 6–0 7–5, Grosjean 6–4 6–2, Hewitt 7–6 3–6 6–7 7–6 6–2); **sf** San Jose (d. Salzenstein 6–4 6–4, Liukko 6–3 6–3, Larsson 4–6 6–3 6–4, lost Tillstrom 7–6 2–6 6–3), **sf** Toronto (d. Squillari 7–6 6–4, T. Johansson 6–4 6–3, Krajicek 7–5 7–6, Kafelnikov 6–3 7–6, lost Safin 6–2 5–7 6–4). **2000 HIGHLIGHTS – DOUBLES:** (with Kafelnikov) **won** Monte Carlo (d. Haarhuis/Stolle 6–3 2–6 6–1); **r/u** Rome (lost Damm/Hrbaty 6–4 4–6 6–3). **CAREER HIGHLIGHTS – SINGLES: Australian Open – sf 1992** (d. Lavalle 6–2 6–4 1–6 6–3, Novacek 3–6 6–3 7–6 7–6, Woodforde 4–6 6–3 6–2 6–2, Wheaton 7–6 6–4 6–2, J. McEnroe 6–4 6–4 6–4, lost Edberg 7–6 6–1 6–2); **Wimbledon – qf 1994** (d. Hadad 6–4 3–6 7–5 6–3, Rosset [14] 6–7 6–3 6–4 6–4, Wilkinson 6–2 6–2 6–3, Bjorkman 6–3 6–7 6–4 6–3, lost Martin 6–3 6–2 3–6 5–7 7–5); **US Open – qf 1992** (d. Arrese 3–6 7–5 6–3 6–3, Bruguera 6–7 6–2 3–6 6–1 6–2, Masur 6–4 6–4 6–2, E. Sanchez 6–2 6–4 2–6 6–4, lost Chang 7–5 2–6 6–3 6–7 6–1).

JUAN-CARLOS FERRERO (ESP)

Born Onteniente, 12 February 1980; lives Villena; RH; 2HB; 6ft; 160lb; turned pro 1998; career singles titles 1; final 2000 ATP ranking 12; 2000 prize money $812,636; career prize money $1,028,181.

Coached by Antonio Martinez; trained by Miguel Maeso. **1997:** Began to play the satellite circuits. **1998:** Played in winning ESP Sunshine Cup team and won 2 titles on the Spanish satellite circuit. **1999:** (43) A –, F –, W –, US 1. He reached sf Casablanca in his 1st main draw event, having won all 4 legs of Murcia satellite circuit. In only his 5th main-tour tourn and 1st f, he won the title at Mallorca as a qualifier, breaking into top 50. He also reached qf Kitzbuhel (d. Gustafsson, Haas), and on the Challenger circuit won Napoli and Oporto, moving more than 300 places up the rankings during the year in which he was voted Newcomer of the Year. **2000:** A 3, F sf, W –, US 4. He upset N. Lapentti and Mantilla on his way to f Dubai, removed Rios and Moya to reach same stage Barcelona and surprised Kafelnikov and Safin in D Cup debut year as ESP d. RUS. He excelled again in f in Barcelona as ESP d. AUS 3–1 to take D Cup 1st time; he won 1st singles when Rafter ret 4s and clinched the deciding 5s encounter with Hewitt. Elsewhere he reached sf Scottsdale, French Open (upset Corretja and extended Kuerten to 5s) and Paris Masters, plus qf Auckland, Estoril, Monte Carlo and Olympics to finish the year poised just outside the top 10. Pulled out of Wimbledon with a leg injury (also protesting at seeding arrangements). **2000 HIGHLIGHTS – SINGLES: Australian Open 3r** (d. S. Draper 7–6 6–3 7–6, Tieleman 7–6 6–4 5–7 6–7 6–4, lost El Aynaoui 7–6 4–6 4–6 7–6 6–4), **French Open sf** [seed 16] (d. Golmard 6–4 6–3 6–2, Dosedel 1–6 2–6 6–2 6–4 6–4, Puerta 6–2 3–2 ret, Philippoussis 6–2 6–2 3–6 6–3, Corretja [seed 10] 6–4 6–4 6–2, lost Kuerten [seed 5] 7–5 4–6 2–6 6–4 6–3), **US Open last 16** [seed 12] (d. Meligeni 6–3 6–4 6–7 6–2, Gumy 1–6 6–3 6–7 6–2 6–3, Federer 7–5 7–6 1–6 7–6, lost Safin [seed 6] 6–4 7–6 2–6 6–2), **Olympics qf** [seed 8] (d. H. Lee 6–7 7–6 7–5, Massu 6–4 7–6, Nestor 7–6 6–3, lost Di Pasquale 6–2 6–1), **r/u** Dubai (d. Damm 6–3 7–6, N. Lapentti 6–4 6–3, Mantilla 6–3 4–6 7–6, Alami 7–6 6–3, lost Kiefer 7–5 4–6 6–3), **r/u** Barcelona (d. Escude 6–4 7–5, Vicente 7–6 6–2, Santoro 6–3 4–6 6–0, Rios 6–3 6–4, Moya

6–4 6–7 6–2, lost Safin 6–3 6–3 6–4); **sf** Scottsdale (d. Rafter 6–4 6–2, Moya 6–1 7–6, Clavet 6–4 3–6 6–3, lost Hewitt 6–4 6–2), **sf** Paris Masters (d. N. Lapentti 7–5 3–6 6–3, Gambill 4–6 7–5 6–4, Santoro 6–4 6–7 7–5, lost Safin 6–2 6–2).

JAN-MICHAEL GAMBILL (USA)

Born Spokane, Wash., 3 June 1977; lives Colbert, Wash.; RH; 2HF; 2HB; 6ft 3in; 195lb; turned pro 1996; career singles titles 1; final 2000 ATP ranking 33; 2000 prize money $553,778; career prize money $1,407,313.

Coached by his father, Chuck. His younger brother, Torrey, also plays on the circuit. **1994:** (1192). **1995:** (554). **1996:** (474). **1997:** (176) A –, F –, W –, US 1. Won Aptos Challenger and on the main tour reached qf Auckland. **1998:** (38) A 1, F 2, W 2, US 3. It was a significant year in which he made his D Cup debut and broke into top 50 after US Open. He caused some notable upsets in reaching his 1st sf at Indian Wells (d. Philippoussis and Agassi) and following with the same stage Tokyo Japan Open (d. Henman), plus qf Singapore and Stuttgart Eurocard (d. Corretja and Henman). He also surprised Pioline at Cincinnati, and at US Open extended Moya to 5s tb. **1999:** (58) A 1, F 1, W 2, US 2. He upset Sampras on the way to his 1st title on the main tour at Scottsdale and reached sf Stockholm (d. Henman and Philippoussis) and qf Memphis, Shanghai and Singapore. In doubles he played 3 f but won no title. **2000:** A 1, F 2, W qf, US 3. Following a slow start to the year, in which he did not pass 2r in 1st 8 tourns, he upset M. Norman *en route* to qf Ericsson Open, removed Kiefer at French Open, progressed to sf Nottingham, then at Wimbledon removed Hewitt and Enqvist before taking a set off Sampras in qf. Sampras, impressed, suggested he might be America's next rising star. Despite being hindered by tendinitis in left knee and a sprained ankle, he was r/u Los Angeles, following with an upset of Philippoussis at US Open. Other qf appearances came at Washington and Toulouse, and from 3 doubles he won San Jose with Humphries. **2000 HIGHLIGHTS – SINGLES: Australian Open 1r** (lost W. Black 7–6 6–1 6–4), **French Open 2r** (d. Kiefer [seed 8] 6–3 7–5 6–1, lost Federer 7–6 6–3 6–3), **Wimbledon qf** [unseeded] (d. Hewitt [seed 7] 6–3 6–2 7–5, Santoro 4–6 6–4 6–2 6–2, Goldstein 7–6 6–2 6–2, Enqvist [seed 9] 7–6 3–6 6–3 6–4, lost Sampras [seed 1] 6–4 6–7 6–4 6–4), **US Open 3r** (d. Fish 5–7 5–7 6–4 6–3 6–2, Philippoussis [seed 15] 6–4 6–4 6–4, lost T. Johansson 3–6 6–3 7–6 7–6); **r/u** Los Angeles (d. Mamiit 6–3 6–2, Tieleman 7–6 6–2, Stoltenberg 6–1 3–6 6–1, Clement 3–6 6–0 6–3, lost Chang 6–7 6–3); **sf** Nottingham (d. Lee 6–3 6–3, Santoro 7–6 6–1, Pozzi 6–4 6–4, lost B. Black 7–6 6–1). **2000 HIGHLIGHTS – DOUBLES:** (with Humphries) **won** San Jose (d. Arnold/Taino 6–1 6–4); **r/u** London (lost Adams/De Jager 6–3 6–7 7–6), **r/u** Long Island (lost Stark/Ullyett 6–4 6–4). **CAREER HIGHLIGHTS – SINGLES: Wimbledon – qf 2000.**

GASTON GAUDIO (ARG)

Born Buenos Aires 9 December 1978, and lives there; RH; 5ft 9in; 155lb; turned pro 1996; career singles titles 0; final 2000 ATP ranking 34; 2000 prize money $484,576.

Coached by Jorge Gerosi. **1999:** (807). **1996:** (437). **1997:** (406) He began to make his mark on the satellite circuits. **1998:** (168) Won his 1st Challenger titles at Santa Cruz and Santiago. **1999:** (69) A –, F 3, W 1, US 1. On the Challenger circuit he won Santiago, Nice and Espinho, breaking into top 100 1st time in April. **2000:** A 1, F 2, W 1, US 1. Emerging on to the main tour, he broke into top 50 with his 1st f at that level at Stuttgart Mercedes, sf Auckland (d. Novak), Santiago, Monte Carlo (d. Safin and Ferrero) and Gstaad (d. Ferrero again), as well as qf Mexico City and the Challenger title at Braunschweig. **2000 HIGHLIGHTS – SINGLES: Australian Open 1r** (lost Llodra 6–3 6–3 6–2), **French Open 2r** (d. Di Pasquale 6–2 6–3 6–2, lost Enqvist [seed 7] 6–3 6–2 6–0), **Wimbledon 1r** (lost M. Chang 6–2 6–3 6–2), **US Open 1r** (lost Clement 6–3 6–4 6–2), **Olympics 1r** (lost Voltchkov 7–6 4–6 6–1); **won** Braunschweig Challenger (d. Squillari 6–4 6–7 6–4); **r/u** Stuttgart Mercedes (d. Diaz 6–2 7–5, Alami 5–7 6–3 6–4, Medvedev 6–1 7–6, lile 6–2 6–4, lost Squillari 6–2 3–6 4–6 6–4 6–2); **sf** Auckland (d. Sargsian 7–5 4–6 7–5, Novak 6–4 6–7 7–6, Schalken 6–1 6–2, lost M. Norman 6–4 7–5); **sf** Santiago (d. Spottl 6–4 7–6, Garcia 7–5 7–6, Ulihrach 6–2 6–2, lost Puerta 3–6 6–4 6–2); **sf** Monte Carlo (d. Safin 7–6 6–0, Mantilla 6–3 7–5, Boutter 6–3 7–5, Ferrero 6–4 6–2, lost Hrbaty 4–6 7–5 6–2); **sf** Gstaad (d. Ferrero 6–4 7–6, Mirnyi 6–2 4–6 7–5, Squillari 6–1 4–1 ret, lost Corretja 7–5 7–5).

ROBBY GINEPRI (USA)

Born Florida, 7 October 1982; lives Marietta, Ga; RH; 2HB; 5ft 9in; 152lb; career singles titles 0; final 2000 junior doubles ranking 14.

Coached by Jerry Baskin. **2000:** At US Open Jun he was r/u singles to Roddick and r/u doubles with Davis.

JEROME GOLMARD (FRA)

Born Dijon, 9 September 1973; lives Boca Raton, Fla; LH; 6ft 2in; 170lb; turned pro 1993; career singles titles 2; final 2000 ATP ranking 42; 2000 prize money $483,495; career prize money $1,627,768.

Coached by Eric Deblicker. **1993:** (425). **1994:** (205) Won Campinas Challenger. **1995:** (90) A 2, F 1, W –, US 2. Qf Indianapolis (d. Courier), upset W. Ferreira 1r US Open and won 2 Challenger titles. Out of action from Oct. with stress fracture of left femur. **1996:** (142) A –, F 1, W 1, US –. Returning to action in March, he reached qf New Delhi a month later and won Segovia Challenger. **1997:** (117) A –, F 2, W 2, US 2. He reached qf Shanghai, Scottsdale (d. W. Ferreira) and Queen's (d. Rosset). **1998:** (46) A 3, F 1, W 3, US 2. His 1st sf appearance on the main tour came at Nottingham, and he also reached qf Adelaide (d. M. Norman) and Bastad, as well as winning 2 Challenger titles. These results, plus upsets of Moya at Cincinnati and A. Costa at Paris Open, took him back into the top 100. **1999:** (35) A 2, F –, W –, US –. He was often a dangerous opponent, upsetting Kucera, Henman and Moya on the way to his 1st title on the main tour at Dubai, and removing Moya again before extending Rios to 3s sf Monte Carlo. He also reached sf Estoril and qf Scottsdale and LIPC, where Henman and Kucera were his victims. However, he suffered a string of injuries and missed 7 months with knee problems, **2000:** A 1, F 1, W 3, US 3. With the help of an alternative therapist and stretching exercises, he was back on form again to win Chennai in Jan. and reach sf Rotterdam in Feb. He also appeared in qf Dubai, Toronto (d. Agassi), Tashkent and Vienna, and upset N. Lapentti in 5s tb at US Open before retiring v Pavel with ongoing tendinitis of right knee. **2000 HIGHLIGHTS – SINGLES: Australian Open 1r** (lost Henman [seed 11] 6–7 6–3 7–6 7–6), **French Open 1r** (lost Ferrero [seed 16] 6–4 6–3 6–2), **Wimbledon 3r** (d. Saulnier 7–5 6–4 6–4, Koubek 7–6 4–6 6–1 6–2, lost Agassi [seed 2] 6–3 6–3 6–4), **US Open 3r** (d. W. Black 6–2 6–2 6–2, N. Lapentti [seed 16] 7–6 6–0 2–6 4–6 7–6, lost Pavel 6–2 4–1 ret); **won** Chennai (d. Spottl 6–3 6–4, Jonsson 6–2 6–3, Delgado 6–3 6–4, Damm 3–6 6–3 6–3, Hantschk 6–3 6–7 6–3); **sf** Rotterdam (d. Zabaleta 6–2 6–3, Siemerink 6–4 7–6, M. Norman 6–4 6–3, lost Pioline 6–3 6–4). **2000 HIGHLIGHTS – DOUBLES:** (with Kohlmann) **r/u** Gstaad (lost Novak/Rikl 3–6 6–3 6–4).

SEBASTIEN GROSJEAN (FRA)
Born Marseille, 29 May 1978; lives Boca Raton, Fla; RH; 5ft 9in; 145lb; turned pro 1996; career singles titles 1; final 2000 ATP ranking 19; 2000 prize money $655,280; career prize money $1,476,381.
Coached by Eric Deblicker; trained by Daniel Gilbert. Wife Marie-Pierre (married 16 November 1998); daughter Lola (born 11 October 1998). **1995:** (855) Nat Jun champ. **1996:** (397) Won European Jun singles, took French Open Jun doubles with Mutis, and led FRA to victory in the Sunshine Cup, finishing the year ranked No. 1 in ITF Jun singles and doubles. **1997:** (141) A –, F -, W –, US –. Made his presence felt on the Challenger circuit, playing 3 f and winning Bratislava. **1998:** (89) A –, F –, W 4, US 1. Emerging on to the senior tour, he reached his 1st sf at Boston, plus qf Coral Springs and Casablanca, and upset Mantilla at Wimbledon after qualifying. **1999:** (27) A 1, F 3, W 3, US 1. He progressed to his 1st tour f at LIPC, upsetting Kuerten, Moya and Clavet on the way and extending Krajicek to 7–5 4s, then followed with same stage Atlanta. He also reached sf Copenhagen, Delray Beach and Indianapolis (d. A. Costa, Rios and Kuerten), plus qf Boston and Vienna, and won Cherbourg Challenger. Member of FRA D Cup team that reached f, but lost opening rubber to Philippoussis as AUS won 3–2 in Nice. **2000:** A 3, F 3, W 1, US 3. He won his 1st tour title at Nottingham, despite not being a GC specialist and finding the surface difficult. He was also r/u Casablanca, where he won doubles with Clement, and reached sf Marseille, Stuttgart Masters (d. N. Lapentti and Kuerten) and Stockholm (ret owing to death of his grandmother), qf Adelaide, Gstaad (d. Kiefer) and Indianapolis (d. N. Lapentti). He could be a dangerous opponent, other upsets including Henman at Indian Wells, Hewitt at Toronto and extending Safin to fs tb at US Open. **2000 HIGHLIGHTS – SINGLES: Australian Open 3r** (d. Motomura 6–3 6–3 6–2, Hill 4–6 6–1 7–6 6–0, lost Henman [seed 11] 6–1 6–4 4–6 7–6), **French Open 3r** (d. Fromberg 6–3 6–2 1–6 6–1, Browne 6–1 6–3 2–6 7–6 6–2, lost Kafelnikov 6–3 6–1 5–7 6–4), **Wimbledon 1r** (lost Tarango 7–6 3–6 4–6 6–4), **US Open 3r** (d. Kim 6–3 6–2 6–4, Koubek 6–2 4–6 6–2, lost Safin [seed 6] 6–4 7–6 1–6 3–6 7–6); **won** Nottingham (d. Spadea 6–1 4–6 7–5, Arthurs 7–6 7–6, W. Ferreira 7–6 6–3, Bjorkman 7–6 6–4, B. Black 7–6 6–3); **r/u** Casablanca (d. Pozzi 6–3 6–0, Willems 6–3 6–2, Bruguera 6–0 6–0, Puerta 6–4 3–6 6–1, lost Vicente 6–4 4–6 7–6); **sf** Marseille (d. Di Pasquale 7–6 6–1, Roux 6–4 3–6 6–4, Vinciguerra 6–4 6–4, lost Rosset 6–3 6–3), **sf** Stuttgart Masters (d. Haas 6–4 6–2, N. Lapentti 6–1 6–0, Kuerten 7–6 6–3, Chang 7–5 1–6 6–2, lost W. Ferreira 6–4 6–2), **sf** Stockholm Id. Nestor 6–4 6–4, Ortegren 6–1 6–2, Schuttler 6–7 5–7 7–6, lost Kafelnikov w/o). **2000 HIGHLIGHTS – DOUBLES:** (with Clement) **won** Casablanca (d. Burgsmuller/Painter 7–6 6–4).

PAUL HAARHUIS (NED)
Born Eindhoven, 19 February 1966; lives Monte Carlo, Monaco; RH; 2HB; 6ft 2in; 177lb; turned pro 1989; career singles titles 1; final 2000 ATP ranking 4 doubles; 2000 prize money $434,668; career prize money $7,264,084.
Coached by Alex Reynders. Wife Anja (married 12 September 1996); son Daan (born 3 February 1998). **1987:** (397) Finished 2nd on Dutch satellite circuit. **1988:** (462) Graduated from Florida State Univ. **1989:** (57) A –, F 3, W –, US 4. After winning Lagos Challenger, he qualified for French Open, where he upset Zivojinovic 1r, and again as a qualifier upset J. McEnroe at US Open. Qf Hilversum (d. K. Carlsson) and Itaparica. **1990:** (54) A 1, F 3, W 3, US 1. Qf Philadelphia (d. Gilbert and took Gomez to 3s) and Estoril. Reached 4 f in doubles with various partners, winning Moscow. **1991:** (37) A 2, F 3, W 1, US qf. He again excelled at US Open, upsetting top seed Becker *en route* to qf, unseeded. Reached sf Rotterdam, won Lagos Challenger and scored some other big upsets – E. Sanchez at Estoril and Ivanisevic at Italian Open and French Open. In doubles reached 5 f, winning 3 with different partners, and was r/u French Open mixed with Vis. **1992:** (39) A 2, F 1, W 2, US 2. Scored some useful upsets during the year on his way to f Singapore, sf Rotterdam (d. Lendl) and qf Wellington, Memphis (d. Wheaton), Philadelphia (d. Wheaton again), Hamburg (d. Muster and Chang), Schenectady and Sydney Indoor. Reached 4 doubles f, winning Hilversum with Koevermans and

Schenectady with Eltingh. **1993:** (42) A 1, F 4, W 1, US 2. He was still a dangerous opponent, surprising W. Ferreira at French Open, where he was unseeded, and removing Ivanisevic and Medvedev on his way to sf Tokyo Seiko. He reached the same stage at Kuala Lumpur Malaysian Open and Jakarta, plus qf at Prague, Hilversum (d. Bruguera) and Moscow and upset Volkov at LIPC. In doubles he reached 11 f, winning 1 with Koevermans and 6 with Eltingh, including IBM/ATP World Doubles where they beat Woodbridge/Woodforde in ss. **1994:** (37) A 3, F 3, W 1, US 1. In singles r/u Qatar (d. Ivanisevic) and Philadelphia and reached sf Rotterdam (d. Becker and Volkov). Voted Doubles Team of the Year with Eltingh: their partnership flourished as they won their 1st GS title at Australian Open, following with US Open, and won a total of 8 titles from 12 f to qualify for World Doubles Champ as top pairing, but lost to Woodbridge/Woodforde. **1995:** (19) A 1, F 1, W 2, US 2. Won his 1st career singles title at Jakarta, r/u Memphis and Rotterdam (d. Kafelnikov) and reached sf Philadelphia (d. Sampras) and Halle (d. Kafelnikov again), plus 2 qf. Then after upsetting Ivanisevic at Paris Open in Nov., he broke into the top 20. In doubles with Eltingh, he won French Open and all 6 other f they played to qualify for World Doubles Champ. There they advanced to f without dropping a set before being surprisingly beaten by Connell/Galbraith. **1996:** (26) A 1, F 3, W 4, US 3. R/u Indian Wells (d. Enqvist, Sampras and Ivanisevic), sf Jakarta, Estoril and Rosmalen (d. Krajicek) and qf Washington and Paris Open (d. Ivanisevic and Martin). Other upsets across the year included Boetsch at French Open and Enqvist again at Halle. His regular doubles partner, Eltingh, was restricted for much of the year by tendinitis in both knees, but they still won 2 of 5 doubles f, were r/u US Open and qualified for World Doubles Champ. He took a 3rd title with Galbraith. **1997:** (71) A 1, F 1, W 3, US 2. Reached sf Halle (d. Medvedev) and qf Memphis and Umag, as well as upsetting A. Costa at Toulouse and Muster at Stuttgart Eurocard. In 3r Wimbledon he served for the match v Henman at 5–4 40–30 5s, but double-faulted, going on to lose 12–14. He played 9 doubles f in all, 8 of them with Eltingh, with whom he won 5 titles – but not the 1st Wimbledon title they needed to complete their collection of GS, losing f there in 4s to Woodbridge/Woodforde. They qualified for World Doubles Champ again, and were the only duo to win all their rr matches, but lost sf to Leach/Stark. However, they still finished the year as the season's 2nd pairing. **1998:** (73) A –, F 2, W 1, US 3. He missed 1st 6 weeks of year to be with his wife for the birth of their 1st child, and was out again for 2 weeks after Monte Carlo with inflamed tendon in wrist. By missing Australian Open, he broke his sequence of 33 consec. GS tourns – the longest amongst active players. In singles he was r/u Boston and reached sf Halle and Shanghai, plus qf Umag (d. Moya), as well as upsetting Mantilla at LIPC and Korda at Halle. He won 9 doubles titles with Eltingh, including French Open and their 1st Wimbledon – winning f 10–8 fs over Woodbridge/Woodforde, whom they thus overtook as top doubles pairing – to become the only team in the open era to have won all 4 GS titles in their careers. They missed the chance of a calendar year GS when Eltingh left US Open early to be with his wife for the birth of their son. However, their season finished in triumph at World Doubles Champ, where they won all their matches to take the title and finish the year well ahead as top pairing, and being voted Doubles Team of the Year. **1999:** (174) A 2, F 1, W 3, US 2. In singles he passed 2r only at Wimbledon, a highlight being his upset of A. Costa at Indian Wells. However, he was still a force in doubles, being r/u Wimbledon with Palmer, and from 7 other f with 4 partners he won 1 each with Kafelnikov, Schalken and Palmer. It was with Palmer that he qualified for World Doubles Champ, but they did not progress beyond rr. **2000:** A –, F –, W –, US –. He reached 9 doubles f during the year, including French Open and Wimbledon with Stolle, but did not clinch a title until joining forces with Schalken at Shanghai in Oct., then added Lyon with Stolle a month later. It was with Stolle that he qualified for World Doubles Champ, but they did not progress beyond rr. **2000 HIGHLIGHTS – DOUBLES:** (with Stolle unless stated) **r/u French Open** (lost Woodbridge/Woodforde 7–6 6–4), **r/u Wimbledon** (lost Woodbridge/Woodforde 6–3 6–4 6–1); (with Schalken) **won** Shanghai (d. Pala/Vizner 6–2 3–6 6–4), **won** Lyon (d. Ljubicic/Waite 6–1 6–7 7–6); **r/u** Indian Wells (lost O'Brien/Palmer 6–4 7–6), **r/u** Monte Carlo (lost W. Ferreira/Kafelnikov 6–3 2–6 6–1), **r/u** Barcelona (lost Kulti/Tillstrom 6–2 6–7 7–6), **r/u** 's-Hertogenbosch (lost Damm/Suk 6–4 6–7 7–6), (with Nestor) **r/u** Paris Masters (lost Kulti/Mirnyi 6–4 7–5). **CAREER HIGHLIGHTS – SINGLES:** US Open – qf 1991 [unseeded] (d. Jelen 2–6 6–2 6–1 3–6 6–2, Chesnokov 6–1 4–6 6–2 7–6, Becker 6–3 6–4 6–2, Steeb 6–3 6–2, lost Connors 4–6 7–6 6–4 6–2). **CAREER HIGHLIGHTS – DOUBLES:** (with Eltingh unless stated) **Australian Open – won 1994** (d. B. Black/ Stark 6–7 6–3 6–4 6–3); **French Open – won 1995** (d. Kulti/Larsson 6–7 6–4 6–1), **won 1998** (d. Knowles/Nestor 6–3 3–6 6–3), (with Stolle) **r/u 2000**; **Wimbledon – won 1998** (d. Woodbridge/Woodforde 2–6 6–4 7–6 5–7 10–8), **r/u 1997** (lost Woodbridge/Woodforde 7–6 7–6 5–7 6–3) (with Palmer) **r/u 1999** (lost Bhupathi/Paes 6–7 6–3 6–4 7–6), (with Stolle) **r/u 2000**; **US Open – won 1994** (d. Woodbridge/Woodforde 6–3 7–6), **r/u 1996** (lost Woodbridge/ Woodforde 4–6 7–6 7–6); **IBM/ATP World Doubles Champ – won 1993** (d. Woodbridge/Woodforde 7–6 7–6 6–4), **won 1998** (d. Knowles/Nestor 6–4 6–2 7–5), **r/u 1995** (lost Connell/Galbraith 7–6 7–6 3–6 7–6).

TOMMY HAAS (GER)

Born Hamburg, 3 April 1978; lives Bradenton, Fla and Kitzbuhel, Austria; RH; 6ft 2in; 182lb; turned pro 1996; career singles titles 1; final 2000 ATP ranking 23; 2000 prize money $437,436; career prize money $2,913,578.
Coached by Nick Bollettieri; travels with David (Red) Ayme. **1993:** (1072). **1994:** (1192). **1995:** (–) R/u Orange Bowl to Zabaleta. Broke his right ankle in Dec. **1996:** (196) A –, F –, W –, US 1. Upset Furlan and Woodforde *en route* to qf Indianapolis and extended Stich to 4s at US Open. He finished the season in the same way as the previous year, with a broken ankle – the left this time, and as before requiring surgery. **1997:** (41) A –, F

–, W 2, US 3. Played his 1st career sf at Hamburg (d. Moya and Berasategui) and followed in Oct. at Lyon with his 1st f (unseeded, d. Enqvist and Kafelnikov), breaking into top 50. His other qf appearances came at Washington and Toulouse. **1998:** (34) A 1, F 1, W 3, US 2. At Lyon, where he reached f by virtue of Sampras withdrawing and Rios retiring, he held mp in 2s tb v Corretja before letting the match and title slip away. He also appeared in sf Philadelphia and Scottsdale (d. Philippoussis) and qf San Jose and Mallorca (d. Berasategui), as well as upsetting Agassi 2r Wimbledon, A. Costa at Cincinnati and Corretja at Paris Open. Played in victorious GER WT Cup team, winning all his matches, made his D Cup debut and took over No. 1 ranking in his country for 1st time. **1999:** (11) A sf, F 3, W 3, US 4. In his 1st 3 tourns, he was r/u Auckland (d. Mantilla), reached sf Australian Open, where he was unseeded, then at Memphis in Feb. he won his 1st tour title in his 4th f. Although he could not maintain that pace, he was r/u both Stuttgart Mercedes (d. Moya and Corretja) and GS Cup (d. Agassi and Enqvist) and appeared in sf 's-Hertogenbosch and qf Hamburg, Halle and Paris Open, looking a strong contender for the top 10. **2000:** A 2, F 3, W 3, US 2. The high point of his year was winning a silver medal at the Olympics, where, unseeded, he upset Corretja and extended Kafelnikov to 5s in f. Elsewhere he was r/u Munich (d. Enqvist) and Vienna (d. Corretja and Pioline), reached sf Memphis and qf Barcelona (d. Rusedski) and recorded more significant upsets including Kiefer at Wimbledon, Kuerten at Indian Wells, and Enqvist and Sampras in WT Cup. **2000 HIGHLIGHTS – SINGLES: Australian Open 2r** [seed 10] (d. Saulnier 7–6 6–4 4–6 6–2, lost El Aynaoui 7–5 6–3 6–3), **French Open 3r** (d. Rios 6–3 6–2 ret, Gaudenzi 4–6 3–6 7–6 7–6 6–1, lost Safin [seed 12] 7–6 6–3 6–3), **Wimbledon 3r** (d. Kiefer [seed 13] 5–7 6–4 6–2 6–3, Vinciguerra 6–3 7–6 6–3, lost Rosset 6–4 3–6 6–3 3–6 9–7), **US Open 2r** (d. J. Delgado 6–3 6–1 6–1, lost Schuttler 7–6 6–2 6–4), **r/u Olympics silver medal** [unseeded] (d. W. Ferreira 7–5 6–2, Vinciguerra 4–6 6–4 6–2, Corretja [seed 6] 7–6 6–3, Mirnyi 4–6 7–5 6–3, Federer 6–3 6–2, lost Kafelnikov [seed 5] 7–6 3–6 6–2 4–6 6–3); **r/u** Munich (d. Prinosil 6–1 4–2 ret, Ulihrach 7–5 3–6 6–3, Browne 6–3 6–4, Enqvist 7–6 1–6 6–4, lost Squillari 6–4 6–4); **r/u** Vienna (d. Corretja 6–1 6–0, Clement 6–2 6–1, Golmard 2–6 6–3 6–1, Pioline 6–7 6–2 6–2, lost Henman 6–4 6–4 6–4); **sf** Memphis (d. Salzenstein 6–2 2–6 6–4, Tillstrom 6–2 3–6 7–5, W. Ferreira 6–3 2–6 7–5, lost B. Black 7–6 7–6). **CAREER HIGHLIGHTS – SINGLES: GS Cup – r/u 1999** (d. Hrbaty 6–3 6–2, Agassi 6–0 6–7 6–4 6–0 6–7 6–4, Enqvist 6–3 6–4 6–7 6–4, lost Rusedski 6–3 6–4 6–7 7–6); **Olympics – silver medal 2000; Australian Open – sf 1999** [unseeded] (d. Kohlmann 7–6 6–2 7–5, Hewitt 4–6 6–4 6–3 6–4, Nestor 7–5 4–6 6–3 6–4, Santoro 6–2 6–3 7–5, Spadea 7–6 7–5 6–3, lost Kafelnikov 7–3 6–4 7–5).

MARKUS HANTSCHK (GER)
Born Dachau, 19 November 1977; lives Bobrach; RH; 6ft 2in; 187lb; turned pro 1996; career singles titles 0; final 2000 ATP ranking 72; 2000 prize money $215,517.
Coached by his older brother, Alfred. **1994:** (938). **1995:** (693). **1996:** (473). **1997:** (295) Began to make his mark on the Challenger circuit. **1998:** (197). **1999:** (127) A –, F 2, W –, US –. Won Magdeburg Challenger and on the main tour upset Ivanisevic 1r Prague. **2000:** A –, F 2, W 1, US 1. Emerging from the satellite circuits, he began the year with an appearance in his 1st f at Chennai (d. Pioline), followed by same stage Bucharest in Sept. In between he reached qf Mexico City, Bogota and Orlando, extended Hewitt to 5s at French Open and broke into top 100 1st time. **2000 HIGHLIGHTS – SINGLES: French Open 2r** (d. Prinosil 6–2 6–7 7–6 6–4, lost Hewitt [seed 9] 2–6 6–3 3–6 6–2 6–3), **Wimbledon 1r** (lost Enqvist [seed 9] 6–1 6–4 6–2), **US Open 1r** (lost Arazi 6–3 6–0 4–6 6–7 6–4); **r/u** Chennai (d. Tieleman 7–6 6–3, Behrend 3–6 4–6 6–3, Ketola 5–7 7–5 6–2, Pioline 6–4 3–6 7–6, lost Golmard 6–3 6–7 6–3), **r/u** Bucharest (d. Voinea 6–3 6–3, Pescariu 6–3 6–2, A. Martin 6–1 4–6 6–2, Calatrava 6–4 6–1, lost Balcells 6–4 3–6 7–6).

DOMINIK HRBATY (SVK)
Born Bratislava, 4 January 1978; lives Monte Carlo, Monaco; RH; 6ft; 165lb; turned pro 1996; career singles titles 2; final 2000 ATP ranking 17 singles, 16 doubles; 2000 prize money $1,195,760; career prize money $2,672,170.
Coached by Marian Vajda. **1994:** (1024). **1995:** (364) Enjoyed some success on the satellite circuits. **1996:** (77) Joined his country's D Cup squad and was voted Player to Watch after winning 2 Challenger titles from 6 f. **1997:** (42) A 4, F 1, W 1, US 1. In May, he upset Kafelnikov as he swept to his 1st sf on the main tour at St Polten, following in Oct. with an upset of Corretja to reach his 1st f, before missing the last month of the season with right wrist injury. Other highlights were sf San Marino and Marbella, and qf Umag, as well as the title at Kosice Challenger. At Australian Open, unseeded in his 1st GS, he led 4–2 and 15–40 on Sampras's serve in 5s last 16. **1998:** (45) A 1, F 3, W 1, US 2. His 1st tour title came at San Marino, and he also appeared in sf Bologna and Bastad, plus qf Auckland, St Petersburg, Barcelona (d. Kucera and Gustafsson) and Amsterdam, where he was r/u doubles with Kucera. On the Challenger circuit he won the title at Kosice. **1999:** (21) A 1, F sf, W 1, US 1. Going into French Open, he had already reached qf of 6 of his 1st 8 tourns of year and won the title at Prague; at Roland Garros, where he was unseeded, he upset Kafelnikov and Rios before taking a set off Agassi in sf. He broke into top 20 after reaching sf Merano in June and added same stage Mallorca to his qf appearances at Adelaide, Auckland (d. Meligeni), Marseille (d. Kafelnikov), St Petersburg, London, LIPC (d. Agassi and Rios) and Umag. He upset Enqvist in D Cup and qualified for GS Cup, losing 1r to Haas. **2000:** A 1, F 2, W 2, US 4. On clay he upset Kuerten in D Cup, then Sampras, Haas and Kafelnikov as SVK won WT Cup 1st time. Also on European clay he upset Kafelnikov at Monte Carlo en route to his 1st f at Masters level and surprised Agassi at Rome. In Nov. he reached 2 more f at St Petersburg and

Brighton, where he was restricted by inflammation of a disc – an ongoing injury that strikes suddenly, requires massage and manipulation on court to enable him to continue, and had kept him out 3 weeks in summer. He also reached sf Tokyo Japan Open, qf Rotterdam (d. Safin), Rome (d. Agassi) and Basel, and he upset Kafelnikov again at US Open, where he was unseeded. In doubles he played 4 f with 3 different partners, winning Rome with Damm. **2000 HIGHLIGHTS – SINGLES: Australian Open 1r** (lost Clavet 3–6 6–1 6–4 7–6), **French Open 2r** [seed 14] (d. Bjorkman 6–3 6–2 6–1, lost Calleri 6–7 6–1 6–4 6–4), **Wimbledon 2r** (d. Zabaleta 6–4 6–2 7–5, lost B. Black 6–3 7–5 6–2), **US Open last 16** [unseeded] (d. Ivanisevic 3–6 6–0 6–1 6–0, Alami 6–3 6–4 6–3, Kafelnikov [seed 5] 6–4 7–6 6–1, lost Krajicek 7–6 6–4 6–1), **Olympics 1r** (lost Ljubicic 6–1 1–6 6–3); **r/u** Monte Carlo (d. Di Pasquale 6–2 7–5, Kafelnikov 6–3 5–7 6–4, Clement 6–4 7–5, Corretja 3–6 6–3 6–4, Gaudio 4–6 7–5 6–2, lost Pioline 6–4 7–6 7–6), **r/u** St Petersburg (d. Massu 6–3 6–4, T. Johansson 6–4 6–3, Voltchkov 6–2 4–6 6–3, Kafelnikov 7–5 6–3, lost Safin 2–6 6–4 6–4), **r/u** Brighton (d. Spadea 6–1 6–2, Popp 4–6 6–1 6–0, Sanguinetti 6–2 6–1, Voltchkov 6–1 6–0, lost Henman 6–2 6–2); **sf** Tokyo Japan Open (d. Tieleman 7–6 7–5, Kucera 6–4 6–4, Kuerten 6–7 6–2 3–0 ret, lost N. Lapentti 6–3 6–4). **2000 HIGHLIGHTS – DOUBLES:** (with Damm unless stated) **won** Rome (d. W. Ferreira/Kafelnikov 6–4 4–6 6–3); **r/u** Ericsson Open (lost Woodbridge/Woodforde 6–3 6–4), (with Prinosil) **r/u** Hong Kong (lost W. Black/Ullyett 6–1 6–2), (with Federer) **r/u** Basel (lost Johnsson/Norval 7–6 4–6 7–6). **CAREER HIGHLIGHTS – SINGLES: French Open – sf 1999** [unseeded] (d. Boutter 5–7 6–4 7–5 7–5, Kafelnikov 6–4 6–1 6–4, Ilie 3–6 7–5 6–2 4–6 6–2, Safin 6–4 3–6 7–6 6–3, Rios 7–6 6–2 6–7 6–3, lost Agassi 6–4 7–6 3–6 6–4).

ANDREW ILIE (AUS)

Born Bucharest, Romania, 18 April 1996; lives Melbourne; RH; 5ft 11in; 172lb; turned pro 1994; career singles titles 2; final 2000 ATP ranking 50; 2000 prize money $336,021.
Coached by Craig Tyzzer. Emigrated from Romania to Australia in 1988. **1992:** (913). **1993:** (917). **1994:** (303) R/u Australian Jun singles to Ellwood. **1995:** (165) A 1, F 3, W –, US –. Upset Krajicek 2r French Open after qualifying and won Lillehammer Challenger. **1996:** (346) A 1, F –, W 1, US –. Hampered by back problems, he was out completely from July 1996 to Dec. 1997. **1997:** (–) A –, F –, W –, US –. He was out all year. **1998:** (59) A 3, F 3, W –, US 1. Returning to action, he reached his 1st qf on the main tour at Orlando, then at Coral Springs, after qualifying, he upset Stoltenberg *en route* to his 1st career title in his 1st f. He added Biella Challenger and broke into top 100. **1999:** (54) A 4, F 3, W 2, US 1. He upset Corretja, Korda and Kuerten to reach sf Dubai and removed Ivanisevic on his way to same stage Los Angeles, also reaching qf Memphis, Nottingham, Newport and Singapore. **2000:** A 3, F 2, W 2, US 1. He won Atlanta on the main tour and Bermuda on the Challenger circuit, as well as reaching f St Polten and sf Stuttgart Mercedes (d. Safin). **2000 HIGHLIGHTS – SINGLES: Australian Open 3r** (d. Tarango 6–3 7–6 4–6 6–3, Novak 6–3 7–6 6–7 6–4, lost Philippoussis [seed 16] 6–4 7–6 6–1), **French Open 2r** (d. Raoux 6–3 4–6 6–0 7–5, lost Safin [seed 12] 7–5 4–6 5–7 6–3 5–0 ret), **Wimbledon 1r** (lost B. Black 6–3 5–7 7–6 6–0), **US Open 1r** (lost W. Ferreira 6–3 2–6 6–4 6–1), **Olympics 1r** (lost Vicente 6–3 6–3); **won** Atlanta (d. Zib 6–4 6–2, Huet 6–3 7–5, Koubek 7–6 6–4, Chang 6–3 1–6 6–2, Stoltenberg 6–3 7–5), **won** Bermuda Challenger (d. Tabara 4–6 6–3 6–2); **r/u** St Polten (d. Melzer 6–4 7–6, Stanoytchev 4–6 6–3 6–2, Tarango 7–5 6–3, Marin 6–1 7–6, lost Pavel 7–5 3–6 6–2); **sf** Stuttgart Mercedes (d. Arazi 4–6 6–2 7–6, Safin 7–6 7–6, Schuttler 6–3 6–4, lost Gaudio 6–2 6–4).

THOMAS JOHANSSON (SWE)

Born Linkoping, 24 March 1975; lives Monte Carlo, Monaco; RH; 5ft 11in; 165lb; turned pro 1994; career singles titles 4; final 2000 ATP ranking 39; 2000 prize money $497,170; career prize money $2,568,361.
Coached by Magnus Tideman. **1989:** European 14s champ in singles and doubles (with M. Norman). **1991:** R/u Orange Bowl 16s to Corrales. **1992:** Underwent surgery in Oct. and did not play for rest of year. **1993:** (418) Unranked at the time, he upset Novacek *en route* to qf Bolzano in his 1st ATP tourn. **1994:** (485) A 1, F –, W –, US –. **1995:** (126) A –, F 1, W –, US –. Won Jerusalem and Napoli on the Challenger circuit. **1996:** (60) A 2, F 2, W 4, US 3. He attracted attention at Australian Open, where he led Becker 2-sets-to-love 2r, before letting the match slip from his grasp, and at Wimbledon, where he was unseeded, he removed Eltingh in 5s before taking a set off Martin. Moved into top 100 with sf finishes at Singapore, Beijing and Moscow (d. Haarhuis), and qf Gstaad and Long Island, looking ready to crack the top 50 in 1997. **1997:** (39) A 2, F 1, W 2, US 1. His best performances came in spring, beginning with his 1st singles title at Copenhagen, in his 1st f. He followed the next week with St Petersburg, upsetting Stich on the way, and reached sf of his next 2 tourns at Hong Kong and Tokyo Japan Open. After a quieter summer, he appeared in 2 more Asian sf at Beijing and Singapore. **1998:** (17) A 1, A 1, W 3, US qf. In another impressive year he moved into the top 20 with r/u Rotterdam (d. Kafelnikov) and Stockholm (d. Rusedski); sf St Petersburg, Hong Kong Salem Open, Den Bosch, Toulouse, Bastad and Basle; qf Cincinnati, Antwerp (d. Bjorkman) and Ostrava. He upset Moya at Indianapolis, Korda at Stuttgart Eurocard; and at US Open, where he was unseeded, he upset Kafelnikov and extended eventual finalist Philippoussis to 5s tb. He took over the No. 1 ranking in SWE and made his D Cup debut, helping SWE d. ESP in sf, but he did not play in f v ITA. **1999:** (40) A 1, F –, W 2, US –. Although he fell back in the rankings, he none the less took his 1st Super 9 title at Montreal (d. Kiefer and Kafelnikov) and reached sf London (d. Kafelnikov), Tokyo and Toulouse, plus qf Long Island. **2000:** A 2, F 2, W 4, US qf. He saved his best for last, upsetting Enqvist, M. Norman and Kafelnikov to win Stockholm, unseeded and delighting his home fans. Until then his best performances had came in GS, unseeded each time, as he upset

Kafelnikov at Wimbledon and reached his only other qf of year at US Open. **2000 HIGHLIGHTS – SINGLES: Australian Open 2r** (d. Kulti 6–1 6–2 6–4, lost W. Ferreira 6–3 6–2 6–7 4–6 6–2), **French Open 2r** (d. Ruud 7–6 6–3 6–3, lost Chang 7–6 7–6 2–6 6–3), **Wimbledon last 16** [unseeded] (d. Meligeni 6–4 6–7 6–3 6–2, Kafelnikov [seed 5] 6–1 7–6 6–4, Gustafsson 6–7 7–6 6–4 5–7 6–3, lost Rafter [seed 12] 6–3 6–4 6–7 6–1), **US Open qf** [unseeded] (d. Ljubicic 7–6 7–6 6–3, Blanco 6–4 7–6 6–2, Gambill 3–6 6–3 7–6 7–6, Arthurs 6–4 6–7 6–3 6–4, lost T. Martin 6–4 6–4 3–6 7–5), **Olympics 1r** (lost Philippoussis [seed 11] 7–6 6–4); **won** Stockholm (d. Enqvist 6–2 6–2, Vinck 6–4 6–2, Bjorkman 6–7 7–6 7–5, M. Norman 7–6 6–2, Kafelnikov 6–2 6–4 6–4). **CAREER HIGHLIGHTS – SINGLES: US Open – qf 1998** [unseeded] (d. Meligeni 7–6 6–3 7–6, Dreekmann 2–6 7–5 6–2 6–3, Krajicek 6–7 5–4 ret, Kafelnikov 3–6 6–3 6–3 7–6, lost Philippoussis 4–6 6–3 6–7 6–3 7–6), **qf 2000**.

DONALD JOHNSON (USA)

Born Bethlehem, Pa, 9 September 1968; lives Chapel Hill, NC; LH; 6ft 3in; 185lb; turned pro 1992; career singles titles 0; final 2000 ATP ranking 18 doubles; 2000 prize money $349,426; career prize money $1,351,294.

Coached by Sam Paul in NC and travels with Juan Barcelo. Wife Krista (married 21 May 1995). **1989:** (943). **1990:** (–). **1991:** (518). **1992:** (295) Won his 1st doubles titles on the Challenger circuit. **1993:** (415) Won 3 more Challenger doubles titles. **1994:** (320). **1995:** (199) A –, F 2, W –, US –. Spent his honeymoon playing through qualifying at French Open. **1996:** (460) A –, F –, W –, US –. Emerging from the satellite circuits, he extended Sampras to 3s 1r Indianapolis. Won his 1st doubles title on the main tour when he took Mexico City with Montana, following with Amsterdam – and 5 more on the Challenger circuit. **1997:** (517) A –, F –, W –, US –. Appeared in 3 doubles f with Montana, winning Monte Carlo. They played as alternates at World Doubles Champ when Kafelnikov/Vacek withdrew, but lost all 3 rr matches. **1998:** (545) A –, F –, W –, US –. Missed 1st part of season with torn tendon in left wrist, but returned to win 4 out of 5 doubles f played with Montana, with whom he qualified 1st time for World Doubles Champ, where they reached sf before bowing to Eltingh/Haarhuis. **1999:** (–) A –, F –, W –, US –. In doubles he won Estoril with Carbonell and Gstaad with Suk, while in mixed he was r/u US Open with Po. **2000:** A –, F –, W –, US –. His 1st GS title came at Wimbledon, where he won the mixed doubles with Po. In men's doubles he played 7 f, winning 4 with Norval and 1 with B. Black. These results took him to World Doubles Champ, with Norval, where they finished the season in style by taking the title in their first season in partnership. **2000 HIGHLIGHTS – DOUBLES:** (with Norval unless stated) (with B. Black) **won** Mexico City (d. Etlis/Rodriguez 6–3 7–5), **won** Estoril (d. Adams/Eagle 6–4 7–5), **won** Nottingham (d. E. Ferreira/Leach 1–6 6–4 6–3), **won** Basel (d. Federer/Hrbaty 7–6 4–6 7–6); won World Doubles Champ (d. Bhupathi/Paes 7–6 6–3 6–4); (with Arnold) **r/u** Stuttgart Mercedes (lost Novak/Rikl 5–7 6–2 6–3), **r/u** Toulouse (lost Boutter/Santoro 7–6 4–6 7–6), **r/u** Stuttgart Masters (lost Novak/Rikl 3–6 6–3 6–4). **MIXED DOUBLES:** (with Po) **won Wimbledon** (d. Hewitt/Clijsters 6–4 7–6). **CAREER HIGHLIGHTS – DOUBLES:** (with Norval) **World Doubles Champ – won 2000. CAREER HIGHLIGHTS – MIXED DOUBLES:** (with Po) **Wimbledon – won 2000.**

NICOLAS KIEFER (GER)

Born Holzminden, 5 July 1977; lives Sievershausen; RH; 6ft; 177lb; turned pro 1995; career singles titles 6; final 2000 ATP ranking 20; 2000 prize money $591,749; career prize money $2,993,112.

Coached by Sven Groeneveld; formerly by Bob Brett. **1993:** Won Nat Jun Champ. **1994:** (1212). **1995:** (202) No. 2 in ITF Jun rankings after winning Australian Open over J. Lee, US Open over Seetzen, and r/u Wimbledon to Mutis. In the senior game he followed the title at Garmisch Challenger with qf St Petersburg on the main tour. **1996:** (127) A 1, F –, W –, US –. Qf Kitzbuhel. **1997:** (32) A –, F 1, W qf, US –. Reached his 1st sf at Milan, then upset Medvedev and Kafelnikov back-to-back on his way to qf Wimbledon, unseeded. A severe ankle injury suffered at Stuttgart Mercedes in July kept him out until Sept., but 2 weeks after his return he upset Henman and Philippoussis to take his 1st tour title in his 1st f at Toulouse, following with f Singapore (d. Rios). He also played qf Gstaad and Stuttgart Eurocard (d. Rusedski) and overtook Becker as No. 1 in GER. **1998:** (35) A qf, F 2, W 3, US 3. Although he reached no f, he appeared in sf Toulouse and qf Australian Open (unseeded), Gstaad and Basle (d. Korda). Frequently a dangerous opponent, he upset Bruguera at Sydney, Muster at Dubai, Kuerten at Indian Wells and Bjorkman at LIPC. He also won Ostrava doubles with Prinosil and played in the winning GER WT Cup team, finishing year as No. 2 in GER behind Haas. **1999:** (6) A 3, F 1, W 2, US 3. He really came into his own during the year, breaking into top 20 in June and cracking the top 10 in Nov. when he found himself poised just outside the top 5 and, for a time, next behind Sampras. He won Tokyo (d. Enqvist), Halle and Tashkent; was r/u Dubai and Vienna, where he upset Kafelnikov but let slip a 2-sets lead v Rusedski; and reached sf Montreal (d. Haas and Rafter), Washington and Basel (d. Rusedski), qf LIPC (d. Rafter and Rusedski) and Hong Kong. Other upsets included Moya at Australian Open, Rafter at Indian Wells and Krajicek at Rome. In an attempt to qualify 1st time for the season-ending champs, he played at Paris Open with a sprained ankle. The gamble paid off, for not only did he qualify for ATP Champ but he reached sf there before falling to Sampras. **2000:** A qf, F 1, W 1, US qf. Although it was a less spectacular year, in which he was restricted by a sequence of ankle injuries, he won Dubai and Hong Kong, reached sf Qatar and Washington, and appeared in qf Australian Open, US Open (d. M. Norman), Rotterdam and Halle. **2000 HIGHLIGHTS – SINGLES: Australian Open qf** [seed 4] (d. Canas 4–6

6–3 6–4 6–4, Behrend 7–6 6–0 6–2, Alami 6–3 6–4 6–2, W. Ferreira 6–3 6–4 6–2, lost M. Norman [seed 12] 3–6 6–3 6–1 7–6), **French Open 1r** [seed 8] (lost Gambill 6–3 7–5 6–1), **Wimbledon 1r** [seed 13] (lost Haas 5–7 6–4 6–2 6–3), **US Open qf** [seed 14] (d. Gaudenzi 7–5 6–4 0–6 6–1, Bjorkman 6–1 6–4 6–3, Schalken 7–5 6–3 6–4, M. Norman [seed 3] 6–2 6–7 6–1 6–3, lost Safin [seed 6] 7–5 4–6 7–6 6–3), **Olympics 1r** [seed 9] (lost Di Pasquale 6–4 6–3); **won** Dubai (d. Burgsmuller 6–1 2–6 6–4, A. Martin 6–3 5–7 6–0, Golmard 6–3 7–6, A. Costa 6–2 6–0, Ferrero 7–5 4–6 6–3), **won** Hong Kong (d. Bastl 6–2 6–4, Stoltenberg 6–3 6–2, N. Lapentti 6–2 6–4, Henman 6–4 6–2, Philippoussis 7–6 2–6 6–2); **sf** Qatar (d. Tarango 7–6 7–6, Caratti 6–1 6–1, Schalken 6–1 6–0, lost Santoro 7–5 6–4), **sf** Washington (d. Coria 4–6 6–3 6–2, Manta 5–7 6–4 6–4, Gambill 4–6 6–4 6–2, lost Corretja 7–6 6–2). **CAREER HIGHLIGHTS – SINGLES: Australian Open – qf 1998** [unseeded] (d. M. Draper 6–4 6–4 6–0, Wheaton 2–6 1–6 6–2 7–6 6–2, Golmard 7–5 4–0 ret, Raoux 6–3 6–4 7–5, lost Escude 4–6 3–6 6–4 6–1 6–2), **qf 2000; Wimbledon – qf 1997** [unseeded] (d. Volkov 6–4 6–4 6–2, Baur 7–5 7–6 6–1, Medvedev 6–4 6–2 6–7 6–4, Kafelnikov 6–2 7–5 2–6 6–1, lost Woodbridge 7–6 2–6 6–0 6–4); **US Open – qf 2000.**

RICHARD KRAJICEK (NED)

Born Rotterdam, 6 December 1971; lives Muiderberg; RH; 6ft 5in; 195lb; turned pro 1989; career singles titles 17; final 2000 ATP ranking 36; 2000 prize money $410,641; career prize money $9,814,581.

Coached by Rohan Goetzke. Son of Czech immigrants. Wife Daphne Deckers (married 7 July 1999); daughter Emma (born 26 March 1998); son Alec born May 2000. Switched from 2HB to 1HB at age 12. Won Nat 12s and 14s. **1990:** (129) Won Verona and Casablanca Challengers. **1991:** (40) A 4, F 2, W 3, US 1. Reached last 16 Australian Open, unseeded, then at Hong Kong in April he won his 1st tour title in his 1st f. At New Haven he upset Edberg *en route* to qf (where he retired) and Hlasek and J. McEnroe in reaching sf Toulouse. At US Open held 2 mps v Lendl 1r before losing in 5s, and in doubles reached 2 f with Siemerink, winning Hilversum. **1992:** (10) A sf, F 3, W 3, US 4. Upset Lendl 1r Sydney NSW Open, then made a tremendous impact at Australian Open where, unseeded, he surprised Chang and Stich before being forced to def. sf v Courier with tendinitis of right shoulder. He followed by winning Los Angeles and Antwerp (d. Courier), r/u Tokyo Suntory (d. Stich and Edberg) and sf Sydney Indoor (d. Lendl again). These performances saw him become the 1st Dutchman in the top 20 since Tom Okker in 1976 and at end of year he broke into the top 10. His late surge at Antwerp gained him the last place at his 1st ATP Champs when Agassi and Lendl were forced to withdraw, but he won only 1 match there (v Chang). **1993:** (15) A 2, F sf, W 4, US 4. At French Open he outlasted 3 opponents in consec. 5s encounters before falling to Courier in 4s and at US Open he saved 2 mps in 3s v Martin in a match lasting 5 hr 10 min. Won Los Angeles, r/u Stuttgart Eurocard (d. Becker) and upset Agassi *en route* to qf LIPC, where he won the doubles with Siemerink. Out of action from Nov. with tendinitis in both knees. **1994:** (17) A –, F 3, W 1, US 2. He returned from injury to play doubles only at Estoril in March; then in his 1st singles start at Barcelona in April, he won his 1st ever CC title, upsetting Bruguera on the way. Won 1st GC title at Rosmalen in June and in Sept. won Sydney Indoor, for his 3rd title on a different surface during the year. This last success and sf finish at Los Angeles took him back to the top 20. **1995:** (11) A 2, F 2, W 1, US 3. Upset W. Ferreira and Stich on his way on his way to the title at Stuttgart Eurocard, took Rotterdam the following week, and upset Kafelnikov and Becker to reach f New Haven. He also reached sf Adelaide and 7 more qf, including Essen, where he upset Becker again. Won Rosmalen doubles with Siemerink. **1996:** (7) A 3, F qf, W won, US 1. The climax of his career came at Wimbledon, where, unseeded owing to his previous disappointing performances there and record of injury, he became the 1st Dutchman to win a GS title. He upset Stich and Sampras and lost only one set along the way, returning to top 10. The rest of the year was less spectacular, with no other title, but r/u showings at Italian Open (unseeded, d. W. Ferreira) and Los Angeles, sf ATP Champs and qf appearances at French Open, Antwerp, Hong Kong, Tokyo Japan Open, Rosmalen, New Haven and Singapore. He also upset Bruguera at LIPC and was the only player to take a set off Kafelnikov at French Open. After he withdrew 3r Australian Open with a back injury, Agassi had remarked that every time Krajicek thought about tennis, he was mysteriously injured; thereafter he changed his attitude, became less worried about getting injured and thus relieved the pressure on himself. However, it was not all plain sailing and he retired from qf Singapore in Oct. with a right knee injury and pulled out of Stockholm with recurring knee problems. At GS Cup he lost tamely 1r to MaliVai Washington, his victim in Wimbledon f, and immediately sought a solution to his knee problem, undergoing surgery to repair torn meniscus on 9 Dec. **1997:** (11) A –, F 3, W 4, US qf. After returning in Feb., he won Rotterdam (d. Enqvist), Tokyo Japan Open and Rosmalen (d. Chang), but by US Open (d. Mantilla) had slipped far enough down the rankings to be unseeded. However, he picked up again, upsetting Sampras in ss *en route* to f Stuttgart Eurocard and returning to top 10. He also reached sf Vienna and qf Dubai, Monte Carlo, Los Angeles, Montreal, New Haven and Paris Open, where he withdrew with a knee injury – the 10th time in his career he'd pulled out mid-tourn. **1998:** (10) A –, F 3, W sf, US 3. His best performance came in Oct. at Stuttgart Eurocard, where he put together an amazing run to d. Agassi, Ivanisevic, Sampras and Kafelnikov and return to the top 10 for season's end. One of the few players to have the measure of Sampras, he beat the No. 1 there for a 5th time in 7 meetings, seriously denting Sampras' hopes of finishing the year at No. 1 for a record 6th successive season. Once again the highlight in GS was at Wimbledon, where he recovered from 2 sets to love down v Ivanisevic in sf only to lose the match 15–13 5s. In the process he aggravated a knee injury, which then caused him to withdraw from US Open and miss GS Cup, and it became obvious that he would require surgery for a torn cartilage. Having unexpectedly qualified for ATP Champ after Stuttgart, he had been undecided whether to delay the surgery in order to play there, but eventually the decision was made for him when he was forced to retire yet again 5–2 up fs v Rosset at Paris Open and he had surgery the following week. In other tourns across the year he won St Petersburg, was r/u Toronto (d. Kafelnikov and Agassi) and reached sf Marseille, Rotterdam, Monte Carlo (d. Korda), New Haven and qf Rome (d. Kafelnikov and Den Bosch (withdrew with knee injury). He had missed Australian Open for personal reasons, rather than because of injury, and was hoping to recover in time to play there in 1999. **1999:** (10) A 3, F 2, W 3, US qf. He dedicated his 1st title of the season at London to countryman Menno Oosting, whose funeral he had attended between qf and sf matches. He followed that title with LIPC (d. Sampras again), which took him to a career-high No. 4, although he could not maintain that level and had dropped to 13 by US Open. There he extended Kafelnikov to 5s tb in qf and moved back towards the top 10, where he finished the year. His 48 aces in that match were a record for ATP Tour/GS. In other tourns he was r/u Stuttgart Eurocard and reached sf Vienna and qf Indian Wells, Hong Kong, Tokyo, 's-Hertogenbosch, Cincinnati and GS Cup. **2000:** A 2, F 3, W 2, US qf. He was again hampered by knee problems and, becoming more of a family man, felt less intense about his tennis. His best performances were r/u Halle (d. Kiefer), sf Long Island (extended M. Norman to 7–6 fs), qf US Open (unseeded, d. Henman) and Vienna (d. Ferrero), while other upsets included Enqvist at Monte Carlo, M. Norman 1r Toronto, and Ferrero at Basel. **2000 HIGHLIGHTS – SINGLES: Australian Open 2r** [seed 9] (d. Santoro 6–1 6–2 7–5, lost Escude 2–6 6–3 6–1 6–3), **French Open 3r** (d. Zib 6–3 6–1 6–2, Eschauer 7–5 6–3 7–5, lost Corretja [seed 10] 4–6 6–2 6–3 6–2), **Wimbledon 2r** [seed 11] (d. Kohlmann 3–6 6–1 6–4 7–6, lost W. Ferreira 5–7 6–3 6–3 7–6), **US Open qf** [unseeded] (d. O. Rochus 6–7 6–1 6–1 6–4, Sa 6–4 6–4 6–1, Henman [seed 11] 6–4 3–6 4–6 7–5 7–5, Hrbaty 7–6 6–4 6–1, lost Sampras [seed 4] 4–6 7–6 6–4 6–2); **r/u** Halle (d. Tarango 6–7 6–4 6–4, Rafter 6–7 7–6 6–2, Kiefer 7–5 5–7 7–6, M. Chang 6–2 6–1, lost Prinosil 6–3 6–2); **sf** Long Island (d. Ulihrach 6–4 6–1, Ferrero 6–3 6–4, Moya w/o, lost M. Norman 4–6 6–4 7–6). **CAREER HIGHLIGHTS – SINGLES: Wimbledon – won 1996** [unseeded] (d. J. Sanchez 6–4 6–3 6–4, Rostagno 6–4 6–3 6–3, Steven 7–6 6–7 6–4 6–2, Stich 6–4 7–6 6–4, Sampras 7–5 7–6 6–4, Stoltenberg 7–5 6–2 6–1, MaliVai Washington 6–3 6–4 6–3), **sf 1998** (d. Steven 6–3 7–6 4–6 6–2, Pescariu 6–1 6–3 6–2, Kiefer 6–4 7–6 7–6, W. Ferreira 6–3 6–3 7–5, Sanguinetti 6–2 6–3 6–4, lost Ivanisevic 6–3 6–4 5–7 6–7 15–13); **Australian Open – sf 1992** [unseeded] (d. Saceanu 6–3 6–3 6–3, Grabb 6–2 7–6 6–1, Chang 6–4 6–1 5–7 1–6 6–3, Bergstrom 7–5 7–6 6–3, Stich 5–7 7–6 6–7 6–4 6–4, lost Courier w.o.); **French Open – sf 1993** (d. Bergstrom 7–5 6–3 7–5, Rosset 6–2 6–3 6–1, Arrese 2–6 6–2 6–2 6–7 6–2, C. Costa 7–5 3–6 6–3 5–7 10–8, Novacek 3–6 6–3 3–6 6–3 6–4, lost Courier 6–1 6–7 7–5 6–2), **qf 1996** (d. Noszaly 4–6 6–4 6–4 7–6, Carbonell 6–2 4–6 7–6 6–2, Woodbridge 7–5 6–2 6–2, Bjorkman 6–3 6–2 6–4, lost Kafelnikov 6–3 6–4 6–7 6–2). **US OPEN – qf 1997** (d. W. Black 6–4 6–2 6–2, Filippini 7–6 6–2 7–5, Corretja w.o., Mantilla 7–5 6–3 6–4, lost Rusedski 7–5 7–6 7–6), **qf 1999** (d. King 6–1 6–4 6–0, Manta 6–2 6–4 6–1, Van Lottum 6–4 6–1 6–4, Spadea 6–2 7–6 6–2, lost Kafelnikov 7–6 7–6 3–6 1–6 7–6), **qf 2000**.

NICKLAS KULTI (SWE)

Born Stockholm, 22 April 1971, and liver there; RH; 6ft 3in; 195lb; turned pro 1989; career singles titles 3; final 2000 ATP ranking 15 doubles; 2000 prize money $324,218; career prize money $3,125,787.

Coached by Martin Bohm. Girlfriend Malin; daughters Mikaela (born 24 March 1998) and Emma (born 15 March 2000). Won 11 Nat Jun titles. **1985:** Won Orange Bowl 14s. **1986:** Won European Jun doubles with Larsson. **1988:** (176) R/u US Open Jun to Pereira. **1989:** (110) A 3, F 1, W –, US –. In Jun tennis won Australian Open and Wimbledon, r/u US Open to Stark and finished the year ranked No. 1 in ITF Jun rankings. On the senior tour reached sf Bastad. **1990:** (57) A 1, F 3, W –, US –. Reached 1st tour f at Prague and sf San Marino. **1991:** (79) A 1, F 2, W 1, US 1. Won his 1st tour title at Adelaide. **1992:** (79) A 2, F qf, W 2, US 1. Upset Chang in reaching his 1st GS qf at French Open, where he took Leconte to 5s. He appeared at the same stage in Copenhagen and Munich and won 2 doubles titles. **1993:** (46) A 2, F 1, W 1, US 2. Won Adelaide again (d. Volkov), r/u Copenhagen and reached qf Sydney Indoor, Munich, Bastad, Prague and Antwerp. **1994:** (98) A 3, F 2, W 1, US 2. In singles he reached sf Adelaide (d. Rosset) and qf Sydney NSW Open (d. MaliVai Washington and Chesnokov). In doubles he played 3 f with different partners, winning Monte Carlo with Larsson. **1995:** (173) A 2, F –, W –, US 1. Reached his 1st GS f at French Open doubles with Larsson and in singles appeared in sf Prague. However, in Sept. he underwent surgery to repair inflamed tendon on left foot and was out for rest of year. **1996:** (64) A 3, F 1, W 1 US 1. Returning in Jan., he was back in the top 100 after r/u showing at Atlanta in May (d. Reneberg), then at Halle he upset Kafelnikov en route to his 1st GC title after qualifying. At Stockholm, Edberg's last tourn, he beat the former No. 1 in 5s. From 6 doubles f he won Antwerp and New Delhi with Bjorkman, with whom he qualified for his 1st World Doubles Champ. After losing doubles with Bjorkman in D Cup f v FRA, he played as substitute for Edberg in decisive 5th rubber, held 3 Cup points as Boetsch served at 6–7 0–40 in 5s, but lost 10–8 after 4 hrs 48 min of drama. **1997:** (153) A 2, F 1, W 2, US –. Reached no qf in singles, but in doubles played 4 f, winning Bastad with Tillstrom and Atlanta with Bjorkman, with whom he was r/u US Open. **1998:** (290) A –, F –, W –, US –. Qf Ostrava was his best singles showing. In doubles he played 3 f, winning St Petersburg and Moscow with Tillstrom. **1999:** (117) A –, F –, W –, US 1. He upset Moya on his way to f Halle as LL and followed with sf Bastad and qf 's-Hertogenbosch. He appeared in 2 doubles f but won no title. **2000:** A 1, F –, W –, US –. He played 4 doubles f, winning 3 with Tillstrom and 1 with Mirnyi. **2000 HIGHLIGHTS – SINGLES: Australian Open 1r** (lost T.

Johansson 6–1 6–2 6–4). **2000 HIGHLIGHTS – DOUBLES:** (with Tillstrom unless stated) **won** Barcelona (d. Haarhuis/Stolle 6–2 6–7 7–6), **won** Halle (d. Bhupathi/Prinosil 7–6 7–6), **won** Bastad (d. Gaudenzi/Nargiso 4–6 6–2 6–3), (with Mirnyi) **won** Paris Masters (d. Haarhuis/Nestor 6–4 7–5). **CAREER HIGHLIGHTS – SINGLES: French Open – qf 1992** (d. J. McEnroe 6–2 7–5 6–7 7–5, Zillner 4–6 6–1 2–6 7–6 6–2, Chang 7–6 2–6 6–3 8–6, Perez 6–0 3–6 7–5 6–4, lost Leconte 6–7 3–6 6–3 6–3 6–3). **CAREER HIGHLIGHTS – DOUBLES: French Open –** (with Larsson) **r/u 1955** (lost Eltingh/ Haarhuis 6–7 6–4 6–1), **US Open –** (with Bjorkman) **r/u 1997** (lost Kafelnikov/Vacek 7–6 6–3).

NICOLAS LAPENTTI (ECU)

Born Guyaquil, 13 August 1976, and lives there; RH; 6ft 2in; 185lb; turned pro 1995; career singles titles 3; final 2000 ATP ranking 24; 2000 prize money $1,126,305; career prize money $3,188,897.

Coached by Patricio Rodriguez. Younger brother, Giovanni, also plays the circuit; cousin of Andres Gomez. **1991:** (922). **1992:** (–) Joined his country's D Cup squad. **1993:** (323) Began to make his mark on the satellite circuits and made his D Cup debut. **1994:** (632) Won Orange Bowl 18s over Kuerten; in Jun doubles won French Open with him and US Open with Ellwood, finishing No. 2 in ITF Jun rankings in both singles and doubles. **1995:** (125) On the satellite circuits he won all his singles matches in 4 weeks on the Colombia satellite, following with the 1st 2 on the Ecuador circuit. Five days later he qualified for his 1st main tour event at Bogota and won the title. He then rounded off his season by winning Santiago Challenger. **1996:** (121) A 1, F 1, W 2, US 1. R/u Bogota in both singles and doubles (with Campana). **1997:** (64) A –, F 2, W 1, US 2. Bogota again saw him at his best: he was r/u there, having reached sf Mexico City the week before and qf Bologna and Bucharest (d. Berasategui) earlier in year. Played 3 doubles f with different partners, winning Amsterdam with Kilderry and Mexico City with Orsanic. **1998:** (92) A 2, F 1, W 1, US 1. His best showing was sf Prague, and he also reached qf Kitzbuhel (d. Kafelnikov), Palermo and Santiago (d. Kuerten). **1999:** (8) A sf, F 2, W 2, US 2. He began the year in style at Australian Open, where, unseeded, he upset Johansson and Kucera (8–6 fs) in 2 of 4 5s matches *en route* to sf. Some consistent results followed as he won Indianapolis (d. Moya) and Lyon (d. Kuerten on carpet, never before having won a match on that surface), was r/u Gstaad, and reached sf Hamburg, Amsterdam and Paris Open, in addition to Australian Open, plus qf Rome (d. Rusedski), Stuttgart Mercedes, Kitzbuhel, GS Cup and Stockholm. These results took him into top 10 in Nov. and earned him his 1st berth at ATP Champ, although he was unable to win a single match there. He played 2 doubles f with Kuerten, winning Adelaide. Voted Most Improved Player. **2000:** A 2, F 4, W 1, US 2. Although it was a less impressive year in which he won no title, he was consistent with r/u Tokyo Japan Open, sf Indian Wells and Estoril, and qf Sydney, Mexico City, Scottsdale, Ericsson Open, Barcelona, Halle, Kitzbuhel, Hong Kong and Shanghai. With his brother he took ECU to 1st D Cup win outside Americas, beating GBR in GBR on grass. **2000 HIGHLIGHTS – SINGLES: Australian Open 2r** [seed 7] (d. Medvedev 6–3 5–7 6–7 6–4 8–6, lost Clement 3–6 7–6 6–2 4–1 ret), **French Open last 16** [seed 11] (d. Boutter 6–4 6–2 6–0, Ulihrach 7–6 6–3 6–7 6–3, W. Ferreira 5–7 6–3 7–5 6–3, lost Kuerten [seed 5] 6–3 6–4 7–6), **Wimbledon 1r** [seed 16] (lost Dosedel 6–3 6–2 0–6 6–1), **US Open 2r** [seed 16] (d. B. Bryan 7–5 6–4 7–6, lost Golmard 7–6 6–0 2–6 4–6 7–6); **r/u** Tokyo Japan Open (d. O. Rochus 7–6 7–6, Bjorkman 4–6 7–5 7–6, B. Black 6–2 6–2, Hrbaty 6–3 6–4, lost Schalken 6–4 3–6 6–1); **sf** Indian Wells (d. Bjorkman 6–3 6–3, Di Pasquale 3–6 6–3 6–2, Escude 3–6 6–4 7–6, Arazi 6–2 6–0, lost Corretja 6–3 6–4), **sf** Estoril (d. Ljubicic 6–4 6–3, Fromberg 6–3 6–3 6–2, Ferrero 7–6 6–4, lost Clavet 6–4 6–3). **CAREER HIGHLIGHTS – SINGLES: Australian Open – sf 1999** (d. Johansson 6–3 3–6 3–6 7–6 6–0, M. Norman 7–6 3–6 2–6 6–3 6–4, Tillstrom 4–6 7–6 2–6 6–4 6–2, Ilie 6–4 6–2 4–6 6–2, Kucera 7–6 6–7 6–2 0–6 8–6, lost Enqvist 6–3 7–5 6–1).

SEBASTIEN LAREAU (CAN)

Born Montreal, 27 April 1973; lives Boucherville, Quebec; RH; 6ft; 175lb; turned pro 1991; career singles titles 0; final 2000 ATP ranking 124 singles, 17 doubles; 2000 prize money $325,199; career prize money $2,746,614.

Coached by Yann Lefebvre. Won Nat 12s, 16s and 18s in singles and doubles. **1989:** (1015). **1990:** (633) Won French Open and Wimbledon Jun doubles with LeBlanc. **1991:** (348) Began to make his mark on the satellite circuits and joined his country's D Cup squad. **1992:** (193) Won Nova Scotia Challenger. **1993:** (167) Won Calgary Challenger in singles and doubles. **1994:** (102) He reached his 1st qf on the main tour at Antwerp (d. Stich) and won 2 Challenger titles. R/u 3 times in doubles with different partners. Won Nat singles and doubles and took over the No. 1 ranking in Canada. **1995:** (138) A 2, F 1, W 1, US 2. In singles he moved into top 100 1st time with qf showings at Philadelphia and St Petersburg, and in doubles he won Seoul with Tarango and Beijing with Ho. **1996:** (104) A 2, F –, W –, US –. In doubles with O'Brien he reached his 1st GS f at Australian Open and from 3 more f won Stuttgart Eurocard. Qualifying as 8th pairing for World Doubles Champ, they d. Woodbridge/Woodforde in rr but lost f to them 7–6 4s. **1997:** (155) A 1, F 2, W 1, US –. Qf Hong Kong was his best singles performance. Played 4 doubles f with O'Brien, winning Philadelphia and Los Angeles and r/u Australian Open, to qualify for World Doubles Champ. In their last rr match there, needing to d. Woodbridge/Woodforde on set or game percentage, they did so, but then lost in 3s to Bhupathi/Paes. **1998:** (79) A 3, F 1, W 2, US 2. In singles he reached sf Philadelphia (d. Courier) and Hong Kong/Salem Open, plus qf Scottsdale, Washington and Moscow (d. Corretja). From 4 doubles f he won Tokyo/Japan Open with Nestor and Stuttgart with O'Brien. **1999:** (107) A 1, F –, W 2, US 2. Singles highlights were qf Tokyo (d. B. Black), an upset of Krajicek at Montreal and the Challenger title at Laguna Hills. He won US Open in partnership with O'Brien to take his 1st GS title in his 3rd f, and from 6 other f with 3 different partners he won 3 more with O'Brien, 2 with Nestor and 1 with Gimelstob. It was with O'Brien that he qualified for and won World Doubles Champ, over Bhupathi/Paes, finishing the season as No. 2 pairing behind the Indian duo. Their partnership ended on that high point as they agreed to prepare separately for Sydney Olympics. **2000:** A 1, F –, W 2, US 1. His Olympic preparation paid off as he and Nestor spoiled the finale of Woodbridge/Woodforde by beating them 7–6 fs to take Canada's first tennis gold medal. Earlier they had triumphed in front of a home crowd in Toronto, and he also won Memphis with Gimelstob from a total of 5 f with 3 different partners. In singles he won Magdeburg Challenger as well as upsetting Kuerten at Toronto and Chang at Olympics. **2000 HIGHLIGHTS – SINGLES: Australian Open 1r** (lost Tillstrom 4–6 6–4 6–2 6–1), **Wimbledon 2r** (d. Russell 7–6 6–2 1–6 6–7, lost Arazi 6–3 3–6 6–7 6–4 9–7), **US Open 1r** (lost Schuttler 7–6 6–2 6–4), **Olympics 2r** (d. Chang [seed 16] 7–6 6–3, lost Tillstrom 6–1 3–6 6–3); **won** Magdeburg Challenger (d. Voltchkov 7–6 6–3). **2000 HIGHLIGHTS – DOUBLES:** (with Nestor unless stated) **won Olympic gold medal** (d. Woodbridge/Woodforde 5–7 6–3 7–6); (with Gimelstob) **won** Memphis (d. Grabb/Reneberg 6–3 7–6), **won** Toronto (d. Eagle/Florent 6–3 7–6); (with Bjorkman) **r/u** Copenhagen (lost Damm/Prinosil 6–1 5–7 7–5), (with Gimelstob) **r/u** Orlando (lost Paes/Siemerink 6–3 6–4). **CAREER HIGHLIGHTS – DOUBLES:** (with O'Brien unless stated) **US Open – won 1999** (d. Bhupathi/Paes 7–6 6–4); (with Nestor) **Olympics – won gold medal 2000; World Doubles Champ – won 1999** (d. Bhupathi/Paes 6–3 6–2 6–2), **r/u 1996** (lost Woodbridge/Woodforde 6–4 5–7 6–2 7–6); **Australian Open – r/u 1996** (lost Edberg/Korda 7–5 7–5 4–6 6–1), **r/u 1997** (lost Woodbridge/Woodforde 4–6 7–5 7–5 6–3).

RICK LEACH (USA)

Born Arcadia, Cal., 28 December 1964; lives Laguna Beach, Cal.; LH; 6ft 2in; 185lb; turned pro 1987; career singles titles 0; final 2000 ATP ranking 6 doubles; 2000 prize money $425,405; career prize money $3,677,044.

Wife Christi Bondra (married 26 December 1992); daughter Paulina Christine (born 23 February 1994). Won 19 nat jun titles. **1986:** (201) Coached by his father, Dick, at USC, where he was an All-American. Won NCAA doubles with Pawsat and took 3 singles titles on USTA circuit. **1987:** (148) A –, F –, W –, US 2. Won NCAA doubles again (with Melville) and won 2 GP doubles titles. **1988:** (258) A 2, F –, W –, US 2. In doubles with Pugh won Australian Open and Masters doubles on 1st appearance there but, suffering from flu and food poisoning, was forced to default US Open doubles f. Won 6 other titles (1 with Goldie). **1989:** (195) A 1, F –, W –, US 2. In doubles with Pugh won Australian Open, r/u Wimbledon and took 4 other titles to qualify for Masters, where they surprisingly took only 6th place. **1990:** (279) A –, F –, W 1, US 2. In doubles with Pugh won a 1st Wimbledon title, plus LIPC and Philadelphia, to qualify for IBM/ATP World Doubles, where they failed to reach sf, and played together in winning US D Cup team. In mixed doubles with Garrison won Wimbledon and r/u US Open. **1991:** (402) A –, F –, W –, US 1. Won 2 doubles titles with Pugh and r/u French Open. **1992:** (429) A –, F –, W 1, US –. In doubles with Jones was r/u Australian Open and US Open, won Tokyo Suntory and New Haven and qualified for World Doubles final. **1993:** (632) A –, F –, W –, US –. Teamed with K. Flach to win his 1st US Open doubles. They won another 2 titles together, just missing IBM/ATP World Doubles, and he had a 4th win with Black. **1994:** (536) A –, F –, W –, US –. Won 2 doubles titles with different partners. **1995:** (–) A –, F –, W –, US –. Won New Haven doubles with Melville, with whom he qualified for World Doubles Champ, although they did not progress beyond rr. In mixed he took Australian Open with Zvereva. **1996:** (–) A –, F –, W –, US –. In men's doubles he won 4 of 5 f, each with a different partner, and in mixed he was r/u US Open with Bollegraf. **1997:** (–) A –, F –, W –, US –. Until the World Doubles f he had won no doubles title, although he had played 7 f – 5 with Stark and 1 each with Bjorkman and Bhupathi. However, playing his 7th season-ending champ in 10 years and with his 5th different partner (Stark), he won the title for the 2nd time. It was a triumphant end for the partnership, for he and Stark had decided in Aug. to part company and end of year. He also collected 2 mixed doubles titles, taking Australian Open and US Open with Bollegraf. **1998:** (–) A –, F –, W –, US –. He played 6 doubles f with E. Ferreira, winning LIPC and Halle to extend to 12 his run of consec. seasons with at least 1 title to his name. Ferreira became the 6th different partner with whom he qualified for World Doubles Champ, but they did not progress beyond rr. **1999:** (–) A –, F –, W –, US –. His win at Rome with E. Ferreira extended to 13 his run of consec. seasons with a title and was instrumental in their qualifying for World Doubles Champ, where they won only 1 match. In mixed doubles he was r/u French Open with Neiland. **2000:** A –, F –, W –, US –. The doubles crown at Auckland in Jan. ensured a title for a 14th consec. year – his last before retirement – and was followed by his 5th GS title when he and E. Ferreira won Australian Open in a match lasting 4hr 21min and finishing 18–16 fs. They added a 3rd title at Atlanta and played 3 other f, including US Open. They finished the year as No. 2 pairing behind Woodbridge/Woodforde, having qualified again for World Doubles Champ, where they reached sf before Bhupathi/Paes ended hopes of his career finishing with the title again. **2000 HIGHLIGHTS – DOUBLES:** (with E. Ferreira) **won Australian Open** (d. W. Black/Kratzmann 6–4 3–6 6–3 3–6 18–16), **r/u US Open** (lost Hewitt/Mirnyi 6–4 5–7 7–6); **won** Auckland (d. Delaitre/Tarango 7–5 6–4), **won** Atlanta (d. Gimelstob/Knowles 6–3 6–4); **r/u** Nottingham (lost Johnson/Norval 1–6 6–4 6–3), **r/u** Cincinnati (lost Woodbridge/Woodforde 7–6 6–4). **CAREER HIGHLIGHTS – DOUBLES:** (with Pugh unless stated) **Australian Open – won 1988** (d. Bates/Lundgren 6–3 6–2 6–3), **won 1989** (d. Cahill/Kratzmann 6–4 6–4 6–4), (with E. Ferreira) **won 2000**, (with Jones) **r/u 1992** (lost Woodbridge/Woodforde 6 4 6 3 6–4), **Wimbledon – won 1990** (d. Aldrich/Visser 7–6 7–6 7–6), **r/u 1989** (lost Fitzgerald/Jarryd 3–6 7–6 6–4 7–6);

US Open – (with Flach) **won 1993** (d. Damm/Novacek 6–7 6–4 6–2), **r/u 1988** (lost Casal/E. Sanchez def), (with Jones) **r/u 1992** (lost Grabb/Reneberg 3–6 7–6 6–3 6–3), (with E. Ferreira) **r/u 2000**; **Masters/World Doubles Champ – won 1988** (d. Casal/E. Sanchez 6-4 6-3 2-6 6-0), (with Stark) **won 1997** (d. Bhupathi/Paes 6–3 6–4 7–6); **French Open – r/u 1991** (lost Fitzgerald/Jarryd 6–0 7–6). **MIXED DOUBLES:** (with Bollegraf unless stated) **Australian Open** – (with Zvereva) **won 1995** (d. Suk/G. Fernandez 7–6 6–7 6–4), **won 1997** (d. de Jager/Neiland 6–3 6–7 7–5); **Wimbledon** – (with Garrison) **won 1990** (d. Smylie/Fitzgerald 7–5 6–2), **US Open – won 1997** (d. Albano/Paz 3–6 7–5 7–6).

MARC LOPEZ (ESP)
Born Barcelona, 31 July 1982, and lives there; RH; 2HB; career singles titles 0.
Coached by Moises Pozo. **2000:** Won French Open Jun doubles with Robredo.

NICOLAS MAHUT (FRA)
Born Angers, 21 January 1982, and lives there; RH; 6ft 2in; 165lb; career singles titles 0.
Coached by Louis Borfiga and Olivier Soules. **1999:** In Jun doubles he won US Open and Orange Bowl with Benneteau, with whom he headed ITF Jun rankings. Led FRA to victory in Sunshine Cup. **2000:** A –, F 1, W –, US –. Won Wimbledon Jun over Ancic and took Australian Jun doubles with Robredo. **2000 HIGHLIGHTS – SINGLES: French Open 1r** (lost Hipfl 6–4 7–5 6–4).

TODD MARTIN (USA)
Born Hinsdale, Ill., 8 July 1970; lives Ponte Vedra Beach, Fla.; RH; 6ft 6in; 205lb; turned pro 1990; career singles titles 8; final 2000 ATP ranking 55; 2000 prize money $378,849; career prize money $7,153,598.
Coached by Dean Goldfine; trained by Todd Snyder. Wife Amy Barbato (married 17 December 2000). **1989:** (257) Won New Haven Challenger. **1990:** (269) A –, F –, W –, US 1. All-American at Northwestern (Illinois) Univ. **1991:** (133) A –, F 4, W –, US 3. Won no match all year until winning 7 in a row through qualifying to last 16 French Open and followed with upset of Lundgren *en route* to 1st tour sf at Newport. **1992:** (87) A –, F –, W 2, US 3. Extended Sampras to 5s 3r US Open and reached sf Indianapolis, breaking into top 100. **1993:** (13) A 1, F 1, W qf, US 3. He burst into the top 20 with some impressive performances and some stunning upsets. He surprised Agassi and M. Chang back-to-back on his way to f Memphis, where he took a set off Courier and extended him to 2 tb, then in May won his 1st career singles title at Coral Springs. He was also r/u Washington, Montreal (d. Becker and Agassi), Tokyo Seiko (d. Edberg) and reached sf US CC and Queen's. In GS he upset Ivanisevic on his way to qf Wimbledon, unseeded, and at US Open held 2 mps v Krajicek before losing in 5 hr 10 min. **1994:** (10) A r/u, F 3, W sf, US sf. Broke into the top 10 after his 1st appearance in GS f at Australian Open, upsetting Edberg on the way. He won Memphis in Feb. and at Queen's took his 1st GC title, surprising Edberg in qf and Sampras in f. He made his mark at Wimbledon, where he played 4 5s matches, removed Agassi and was the only player to take a set off Sampras. This result took him briefly into top 5. He was also r/u Atlanta and Pinehurst and reached sf Sydney NSW Open. He made his D Cup debut in March and upset Edberg in his 2nd tie in Sept. Won Adidas Sportsmanship Award for 2nd successive year. **1995:** (18) A 4, F 3, W 4, US 4. Although it was a less spectacular year, he finished in style as r/u to Ivanisevic at GS Cup. Earlier he upset Sampras on his way to the title at Memphis and reached sf Scottsdale, Atlanta, Washington and Lyon, plus qf Indian Wells. In doubles he won 2 titles from 4 f with different partners and in D Cup f partnered Sampras to key victory over Kafelnikov/Olhovskiy as USA d. RUS 3–2 in Moscow. **1996:** (12) A 3, F 3, W sf, US 3. Aiming to return to the top 10 in 1996, he began well with the title at Sydney over Ivanisevic, following during the year with r/u Memphis and Stockholm, sf Wimbledon, Indianapolis, Toronto and Vienna (d. Ivanisevic again), plus 4 qf. He extended Sampras to 5s at French Open and came close to his 2nd GS f at Wimbledon, where, serving for the sf at 5–1 fs v MaliVai Washington, he missed his chance and eventually lost 10–8. He played US Open with his right arm heavily strapped, although he refused to blame that for his 3r defeat by Henman. **1997:** (81) A –, F –, W –, US 2. Missed Australian Open with tendinitis in right knee, and was restricted all year by shin and elbow injuries. Up to US Open, he had played only 2 tourns, reaching sf both San Jose and Memphis, then added qf Vienna (d. Muster) and Stuttgart Eurocard (d. Moya) in autumn, as well as winning Delray Beach Challenger. **1998:** (16) A 2, F 1, W 4, US 2. Unseeded at Barcelona, he upset Muster and Berasategui on the way to his first title for more than 2 years, and in Nov., again unseeded, he won Stockholm (d. Henman). It was an excellent end to the season for him, following his performance the previous week at Paris Open, where he upset Ivanisevic, Rafter and Agassi to reach sf and regain his old place in the top 20. He also reached sf Indianapolis and Vienna (d. Korda), and played qf Sydney (d. Pioline) and San Jose (d. Woodbridge). In other tourns he upset Kucera at Stuttgart Eurocard and extended Rafter to 5s at Australian Open. **1999:** (7) He began the new season where he had ended the previous one – in the winner's circle. Although Sydney was his only title, he enjoyed his best year to date, the highlight coming at US Open where he was r/u. In 4r there, he recovered from 2s down v Rusedski to win 3s tb and go on to take the match on his way to f where he extended Agassi to 5s after letting slip a 2-sets-to-1 lead. That performance took him to a career-high No. 4. Elsewhere he was r/u Estoril, reached sf Memphis, Barcelona and Washington, qf Australian Open, Wimbledon, Indian Wells (d. Rios), Montreal and Stuttgart Eurocard to qualify for his 1st ATP Champ, although he won only 1 match there. He also qualified for GS Cup, but did not take up his place. Long-term arm and stomach muscle injuries were still a problem for him, and he was on a drip the night before his match

v Rusedski at US Open. In D Cup he won important rubber v Rusedski as USA d. GBR 3–2. **2000:** A 2, F 1, W 2, US sf. He was out of action from Feb. to May with an ankle injury and struggled to regain his form. Having done no better than qf Cincinnati all year, at US Open, where he was unseeded, he upset Pioline and outlasted Moya in 5s *en route* to sf. At Wimbledon he had failed to capitalise on 2 mps v Agassi and eventually lost their match 10–8 fs (as he had v Washington in 1996), although Agassi was amongst those anxious to state that he hadn't choked. **2000 HIGHLIGHTS – SINGLES: Australian Open 2r** [seed 8] (d. B. Black 5–7 6–7 6–4 6–2 8–6, lost Vicente 6–4 2–6 3–6 6–3 7–5), **French Open 1r** (lost Chela 4–6 6–3 6–4 6–4), **Wimbledon 2r** (d. Jonsson 7–6 7–6 6–2, lost Agassi [seed 2] 6–4 2–6 7–6 2–6 10–8), **US Open sf** [unseeded] (d. Spadea 6–4 6–1 1–6 6–2, Chang 6–4 6–2 6–2, Pioline [seed 10] 7–6 6–3 6–2, Moya 6–7 6–7 6–1 7–6 6–2, T. Johansson 6–4 6–4 3–6 7–5, lost Safin [seed 5] 6–3 7–6 7–6), **Olympics 1r** (lost Schuttler 6–2 6–0). **CAREER HIGHLIGHTS – SINGLES: Australian Open – r/u 1994** (d. Yzaga 6–3 7–6 6–2, Bjorkman 6–3 6–4 6–0, Svensson 6–1 5–7 6–2 6–2, Daufresne 6–7 7–6 6–3 6–3, MaliVai Washington 6–2 7–6 7–6, Edberg 3–6 7–6 7–6 7–6, lost Sampras 7–6 6–4 6–4), **qf 1999** (d. Meligeni 3–6 4–6 6–3 6–4 6–1, Dreekmann 4–6 6–2 7–6 6–2, Korda 7–5 4–6 7–6 5–7 6–4, W. Black 7–6 6–4 6–4, lost Kafelnikov 6–2 7–6 6–2); **US Open – r/u 1999** (d. Huet 6–4 6–3 6–7 6–7 7–6, Reneberg 6–4 6–3 3–6 6–1, Larsson 6–3 ret, Rusedski 5–7 0–6 7–6 6–4 6–4, Dosedel 6–3 5–7 6–4 6–4, Pioline 6–4 6–1 6–2, lost Agassi 6–4 6–7 6–7 6–3 6–2), **sf 1994** (d. Raoux 6–7 4–6 6–3 6–4 7–6, Chesnokov 6–3 6–2 7–5, Rafter 7–5 6–3 6–7 6–2, Reneberg 3–6 3–0 ret, Karbacher 6–2 4–6 7–6, lost Agassi 6–3 4–6 6–2 6–3), **sf 2000; GS Cup – r/u 1995** (d. Bruguera 7–6 6–4, Medvedev 6–3 1–6 4–0 ret, Becker 5–7 6–3 6–4 7–6, lost Ivanisevic 7–6 6–3 6–4); **Wimbledon – sf 1994** (d. Stafford 6–4 6–2 6–7 6–7 6–1, Kuhnen 6–2 6–2 6–4, Damm 6–2 6–7 4–6 6–3 11–9, Agassi 6–3 7–5 6–7 4–6 6–1, W. Ferreira 6–3 6–2 3–6 5–7 7–5, lost Sampras 6–4 6–4 3–6 6–3), **sf 1996** (d. Ondruska 6–3 6–4 6–3, Grabb 6–2 6–4 7–6, Furlan 7–6 6–4 6–2, Johansson 3–6 6–3 7–5 6–2, Henman 7–6 7–6 6–4, lost MaliVai Washington 5–7 6–4 6–7 6–3 10–8), **qf 1999** (d. Dreekmann 6–7 6–7 6–3 6–2 6–4, Novak 7–6 6–4 6–4, Knippschild 6–7 6–1 7–6 7–5, Ivanisevic 7–6 6–3 6–4, lost Rafter 6–3 6–7 7–6 7–6).

PAUL-HENRI MATHIEU (FRA)

Born Strasbourg, 12 January 1982, and lives there; RH; 6ft; 163lb; career singles titles 0; final 2000 ATP ranking 272
Coached by Thierry Champion. **2000:** Won French Open Jun over Robredo.

MAX MIRNYI (BLR)

Born Minsk, 6 July 1977, and lives there and Bradenton, Fla; RH; 6ft 5in; 200lb; turned pro 1996; career singles titles 0; final 2000 ATP ranking 40 singles, 9 doubles; 2000 prize money $760,368; career prize money $1,221,069.
Coached by his father, Nikolai, a former member of the Russian nat jun Olympic volleyball team, and trains at Nick Bollettieri Academy. **1993:** (1186). **1994:** (1212) Joined his country's D Cup squad. **1995:** (399). **1996:** (310). **1997:** (491) From 2 doubles f he won Shanghai with Ullyett. **1998:** (264) A –, F –, W –, US –. In mixed doubles w S. Williams he won Wimbledon and US Open. **1999:** (75) A –, F 2, W –, US 2. He upset Courier on the way to his 1st tour sf at Orlando (as a qualifier) and reached qf Copenhagen. In doubles he won 2 titles with Olhovskiy and 1 each with Zimonjic and Taino, while in mixed he was r/u Australian Open with S. Williams. **2000:** A 3, F 1, W 2, US 3. In his best year to date, he broke into top 50 with sf Munich and Toulouse, qf Qatar and Olympics (d. Hewitt), and upsets of Rusedski at Indian Wells and T. Martin at Queen's. At US Open he was 2 sets up v M. Norman before losing 3s tb and finally the match in 5s tb. He won the doubles there, pairing Hewitt 1st time, and was r/u mixed with Kournikova. From 4 other f with different partners, he won Qatar with Knowles and Paris Masters with Mirnyi. **2000 HIGHLIGHTS – SINGLES: Australian Open 3r** (d. Agenor 6–7 7–6 6–3 6–3, Dupuis 6–7 7–6 7–6 7–6, lost C. Rochus 3–6 6–4 6–3 7–6), **French Open 1r** (lost Vicente 3–6 5–7 6–3 6–4 6–4), **Wimbledon 2r** (d. Ulihrach 6–2 4–0 ret, lost Gustafsson 6–4 6–3 6–1), **US Open 3r** (d. Kucera 7–6 6–3 7–6, A. Costa 6–4 6–1 6–4, lost M. Norman [seed 3] 3–6 4–6 7–6 6–4 7–6), **Olympics qf** [unseeded] (d. Hewitt [seed 4] 6–3 6–3, Vanek 6–7 6–4 11–9, Zabaleta 7–6 6–2, lost Haas 6–4 7–5 6–3); **sf** Munich (d. Zabaleta 6–7 6–3 7–5, Gumy 6–0 6–0, Meligeni 7–5 6–3, lost Squillari 6–2 6–4); **sf** Toulouse (d. Nargiso 3–2 ret, Vinciguerra 6–3 6–0 ret, Escude 3–6 7–6 6–3, lost Moya 6–4 7–6). **2000 HIGHLIGHTS – DOUBLES:** (with Hewitt) **won** US Open (d. E. Ferreira/Leach 6–4 5–7 7–6), (with Kulti) **won** Paris Masters (d. Haarhuis/Nestor 6–4 7–5); (with Knowles) **won** Qatar (d. O'Brien/Palmer 6–3 6–4); (with Zimonjic) **r/u** Munich (lost Adams/De Jager 6–4 6–3), (with Bjorkman) **r/u** Indianapolis (lost Hewitt/Stolle 6–2 3–6 6–3). **MIXED DOUBLES:** (with Kournikova) **r/u** US Open (lost Palmer/Sanchez-Vicario 6–4 6–3). **CARER HIGHLIGHTS – SINGLES: Olympics – qf 2000. CAREER HIGH-LIGHTS – DOUBLES:** (with Hewitt) US Open – won 2000. **MIXED DOUBLES:** (with S. Williams) **won** Wimbledon (d. Bhupathi/V. Williams 6–4 6–4), **won US Open** (d. Raymond/Galbraith 6–2 6–2).

CARLOS MOYA (ESP)

Born Palma de Mallorca, 27 August 1976; lives Geneva, Switzerland, and Monte Carlo, Monaco; RH; 6ft 3in; 177lb; turned pro 1995; career singles titles 6; final 2000 ATP ranking 41; 2000 prize money $422,106; career prize money $6,005,976.
Coached by Jose Perlas, trained by Luis Miguel Morales. **1994:** (346) European Jun champ in singles and dou-bles and played on winning Galea Cup team. A qualifier at St Polten, he upset Clavet on the way to his 1st

main tour qf. **1995:** (63) After taking 2 Challenger titles, he finished the year in style with his 1st success on the senior tour at Buenos Aires, unseeded and without dropping a set. **1996:** (28) A 1, F 2, W 1, US 2. He recorded some significant upsets on his way to the title at Umag; r/u Munich (d. MaliVai Washington, Ivanisevic and Muster) and Bucharest; sf Barcelona (d. Rosset and Berasategui and took a set off Muster) and Oporto; and qf Casablanca and Amsterdam. He also surprised MaliVai Washington again at Italian Open, breaking into the top 20 in May, and removed Becker at Paris Open. **1997:** (7) A r/u, F 2, W 2, US 1. He began the year in style by upsetting W. Ferreira and A. Costa on the way to f Sydney, and followed with the high point of his career to date at Australian Open where, unseeded, he was r/u, upsetting Becker and M. Chang on the way. This performance took him into top 10, and he moved on up to top 5 in autumn. He became 1st Spaniard since Higueras in 1983 to win a title in US when he took Long Island in Aug., and also reached f Amsterdam, Indianapolis and Bournemouth, sf Barcelona, Monte Carlo and Umag, plus qf Scottsdale, Estoril and Munich. These results took him to his 1st ATP Champ, where he upset Sampras in rr and qualified for sf, where he lost to Kafelnikov. **1998:** (5) A 2, F won, W 2, US sf. The climax of his year and career came at French Open, where he swept to his 1st GS title, having earlier given warning of his form by upsetting Kafelnikov, Corretja and Krajicek on the way to his 1st Super 9 title at Monte Carlo. He came close to ending his year on a similarly high note at ATP Champ, when he led Corretja by 2 sets to love at 5–all 3s in f, but his countryman fought back, leaving Moya as r/u, but still in the top 5. Already a force to be reckoned with on CC and having proved his prowess on HC in 1997, he was aiming to become a complete player on all surfaces, and played a full schedule on grass at Halle and Nottingham before Wimbledon. He was less successful there, but upset Corretja on his way to sf US Open, and reached the same stage at Estoril, Barcelona, Stuttgart Mercedes and Mallorca, plus qf Dubai. **1999:** (24) A 1, F 4, W 2, US 2. On 15 March, after reaching f Indian Wells, he became the 1st Spaniard to reach No. 1, although he slipped back behind Sampras after 2 weeks, out of top 10 by autumn, and out of top 20 by end of year, when he was restricted by the back injury that forced his retirement at US Open. He reached no other f, but appeared in sf Dubai, Hamburg and Halle, as well as qf Chennai, Barcelona, Monte Carlo, Stuttgart Mercedes, Umag and Indianapolis. **2000:** A –, F 2, W 1, US 4. His back injury still troubled him and kept him out of Australian Open. However, he returned to the winner's circle at Estoril (d. M. Norman) and reached f Toulouse, sf Barcelona (d. Kafelnikov) and qf Mallorca and Long Island. At US Open, where he was unseeded, he upset Corretja and extended T. Martin to 5s, but these performances were not enough to maintain even a top 25 ranking. **2000 HIGHLIGHTS – SINGLES: French Open 1r** (lost Gumy 7–6 6–2 4–6 3–6 6–3), **Wimbledon 1r** (lost Schuttler 6–3 6–7 6–3 6–2), **US Open last 16** [unseeded] (d. Tillstrom 6–4 6–2 7–5, Dosedel 6–3 4–6 7–5 6–2, Corretja [seed 8] 7–6 6–3 4–6 6–4, lost T. Martin 6–7 6–7 6–1 7–6 6–2); **won** Estoril (d. Voinea 6–4 6–4, M. Norman 6–1 6–3, Ulihrach 4–6 6–1 6–2, Medvedev 6–3 6–4, Clavet 6–3 6–2); **r/u** Toulouse (d. El Aynaoui 6–7 6–4 6–2, Rosset 7–6 6–7 7–6, Gambill 6–7 7–6 6–4, Mirnyi 6–4 7–6, lost Corretja 6–3 6–2); **sf** Barcelona (d. Clement 6–4 4–6 6–4, Kafelnikov 6–2 7–6, Rosset 7–6 7–6, Haas 6–4 6–4, lost Ferrero 6–4 6–7 6–2), **sf** Umag (d. Vajda 6–3 6–1, Marin 6–3 6–3, Carretero 5–7 6–3 6–4, lost Rios 6–2 7–5). **CAREER HIGHLIGHTS – SINGLES: French Open – won 1998** (d. Grosjean 7–5 6–1 6–4, Imaz 6–4 7–6 6–2, Ilie 6–2 7–6 6–3, Knippschild 6–3 7–5 3–6 6–4, Rios 6–1 2–6 6–2 6–4, Mantilla 5–7 6–2 6–4 6–2, Corretja 6–3 7–5 6–3); **Australian Open – r/u 1997** [unseeded] (d. Becker 5–7 7–6 3–6 6–1 6–4, McEnroe 3–6 6–0 6–3 6–1, Karbacher 6–2 6–2 6–2, Bjorkman 6–3 1–6 3–6 6–2 6–4, Mantilla 7–5 6–2 6–7 6–2, M. Chang 7–5 6–2 6–4, lost Sampras 6–2 6–3 6–3); **US Open – sf 1998** (d. Puerta 6–1 7–6 6–7 4–4 ret, M. Chang 3–6 1–6 7–6 6–4 6–3, Gambill 6–2 3–6 3–6 6–3 7–6, Corretja 7–6 7–5 6–3, Larsson 6–4 6–3 6–3, lost Philippoussis 6–1 6–4 5–7 6–4).

JAMES NELSON (GBR)

Born Newcastle-upon-Tyne, 18 February 1982, and lives there; RH; 2HB; 5ft 10in; 174lb; career singles titles 0; final 2000 junior doubles ranking 1.
Coached by Colin Beecher. **2000:** Won US Open Jun doubles with Childs.

DANIEL NESTOR (CAN)

Born Belgrade, Yugoslavia, 4 September 1972; lives Willowdale, Ontario; LH; 6ft 3in; 180lb; turned pro 1991; career singles titles 0; final 2000 ATP ranking 219 singles, 13 doubles; 2000 prize money $374,904; career prize money $2,740,119.
Coached by Brian Teacher. Moved to Canada in 1976 and is ranked No. 1 there. **1989:** (823). **1990:** (741). **1991:** (247) Won Nat doubles with Pridham. **1992:** (239) A 1, F –, W –, US –. Upset Edberg in D Cup and began to make his mark on the satellite circuit. **1993:** (186) A –, F –, W –, US 1. Out of action April to July with tendinitis of left wrist. R/u Nat singles and won doubles with Lareau. **1994:** (169) A –, F –, W –, US –. Upset Volkov at Toronto and reached qf Bogota, where he won the doubles with Knowles. **1995:** (180) A 2, F –, W 2, US 2. In singles he won Aptos Challenger but reached no qf on the main tour. In partnership with Knowles, upset Woodbridge/Woodforde on the way to a 1st GS f at Australian Open and won Indianapolis from 2 more f to qualify for World Doubles Champ, although they won no match there. **1996:** (114) A 1, F –, W 1, US –. Reached sf Newport and upset Muster at Toronto. In doubles he played 6 f, winning Qatar, Memphis, Hamburg and Cincinnati with Knowles. They qualified for World Doubles Champ, but were forced to withdraw after 2 rr matches when Nestor suffered a rib injury. **1997:** (112) A 1, F 1, W 1, US 1. In singles he reached sf Moscow, upset Enqvist at LIPC, and won San Antonio Challenger. From 4 doubles f with Knowles, he won Indian Wells and Rome to take the last berth at World Doubles Champ. There they lost their

1st 2 matches and were forced to withdraw when Knowles aggravated a rib injury. **1998:** (107) A 3, F 1, W 1, US 1. In autumn he won 2 Challenger singles titles back-to-back and upset Pioline to reach qf Stockholm, breaking into top 100 singles 1st time. Despite being hampered by a rib injury during the year, he played 7 doubles f with 3 different partners, winning Tokyo Japan Open with Lareau and Cincinnati with Knowles, with whom he was also r/u French Open, US Open and World Doubles Champ. **1999:** (85) A 3, F 1, W 4, US 1. His best singles performances were qf Memphis (d. Philippoussis) and Copenhagen (d. Rosset), while in doubles he won 2 titles with Lareau. **2000:** A –, F –, W 2, US 2. The highlight of his year came at Olympics, where he and Lareau won Canada's first tennis gold medal with a 7–6 fs upset of Woodbridge/Woodforde, playing their last match together. Earlier he and Lareau had thrilled the home crowds by taking the title at Toronto and at end of year he added titles at St Petersburg with Ullyett and Stockholm with Knowles, plus r/u Paris Masters with Haarhuis. In singles his best performance was also at Olympics, where he upset Rafter. **2000 HIGHLIGHTS – SINGLES: Wimbledon 2r** (d. MacLagan 4–6 7–6 6–2 6–4, lost Pavel 7–6 7–5 4–6 6–0), **US Open 2r** (d. Santoro 7–6 6–4 6–4, lost Federer 6–1 7–6 6–1), **Olympics 3r** (d. Cowan 5–7 6–1 6–4, Rafter 7–5 7–6 [seed 13], lost Ferrero 7–6 6–3). **2000 HIGHLIGHTS – DOUBLES:** (with Lareau unless stated) **won Olympic gold medal** (d. Woodbridge/Woodforde 5–7 6–3 7–6); **won** Toronto (d. Eagle/Florent 6–3 7–6), (with Ullyett) **won** St Petersburg (d. Shimada/Wakefield 7–6 7–5), (with Knowles) **won** Stockholm (d. Pala/Vizner 6–3 6–2), (with Haarhuis) **r/u** Paris Masters (lost Kulti/Mirnyi 6–4 7–5). **CAREER HIGHLIGHTS – DOUBLES:** (with Knowles unless stated) **Olympics** – (with Lareau) **won gold medal 2000; Australian Open – r/u 1995** (lost Palmer/ Reneberg 6–3 3–6 6–3 6–2); **French Open – r/u 1998** (lost Eltingh/Haarhuis 6–3 3–6 6–3); **US Open – r/u 1998** (lost Stolle/Suk 4–6 7–6 6–2); **World Doubles Champ – r/u 1998** (lost Eltingh/Haarhuis 6–4 6–2 7–5).

PIET NORVAL (RSA)

Born Belville, 7 April 1970; lives Cape Town; RH; 6ft; 165lb; turned pro 1988; career singles titles 0; final 2000 ATP ranking 23 doubles; 2000 prize money $317,086; career prize money $1,808,733.

Wife Nolde (married 11 December 1993). **1985:** (794). **1986:** (870). **1987:** (356) Nat Jun Champ. **1988:** (194) Nat Jun Champ again. **1989:** (273) A 1, F –, W 1, US –. Out of action for 7 months with right arm and wrist injuries. Won Johannesburg Challenger. **1990:** (427) A –, F –, W –, US –. **1991:** (437) A –, F –, W –, US –. Won LIPC doubles with W. Ferreira. **1992:** (467) A –, F –, W –, US –. Continuing his partnership with W. Ferreira, he won an Olympic silver medal and r/u Johannesburg. **1993:** (582) A –, F –, W –, US –. Played 4 doubles f, winning Casablanca with Bauer and Bolzano with Davids. **1994:** (–) A –, F –, W –, US –. From 5 f with various partners, he won Hamburg and Stuttgart Mercedes with Melville. **1995:** (913) A –, F –, W –, US –. Reached 1 doubles f each with Muller and Davids, but won no title. **1996:** (594) A –, F –, W –, US –. Played 5 doubles f, winning Newport and Los Angeles with Barnard. R/u 3 times with Broad, with whom he qualified as alternates for World Doubles Champ, replacing Knowles/Nestor after 2 matches. **1997:** (761) A –, F –, W –, US –. Reached only 1 doubles f and won no title. **1998:** (789) He played 4 doubles f with 3 different partners, winning Umag with Broad. **1999:** (–) A –, F –, W – US –. In doubles with Ullyett he won Lyon and Stockholm from 4 f to qualify for World Doubles Champ, where they won only 1 match. In mixed he won a 1st GS title at French Open with Srebotnik. **2000:** A –, F –, W –, US –. From 6 doubles f he won 4 with Johnson to qualify for World Doubles Champ again, where they crowned their year with a 4th title, and their ist season-ending champs in their first year in partnership. **2000 HIGHLIGHTS – DOUBLES:** (with Johnson unless stated) **won** Estoril (d. Adams/Eagle 6–4 7–5), **won** Nottingham (d. E. Ferreira/Leach 1–6 6–4 6–3), **won** Basel (d. Federer/Hrbaty 7–6 4–6 7–6); (with Bale) **r/u** Santiago (lost Kuerten/Prieto 6–2 6–4), **r/u** Toulouse (lost Boutter/Santoro 7–6 4–6 7–6), **r/u** Stuttgart Masters (lost Novak/Rikl 3–6 6–3 6–4). **CAREER HIGHLIGHTS – DOUBLES: World Doubles Champ** – (with Johnson) **won 2000; Olympics** – (with W. Ferreira) **silver medal 1992** (lost Becker/Stich 7–6 4–6 7–6 6–3). **MIXED DOUBLES:** (with Srebotnik) **French Open – won 1999** (d. Leach/Neiland 6–3 3–6 6–3).

ALEX O'BRIEN (USA)

Born Amarillo, Texas, 7 March 1970, and lives there; RH; 6ft 1in; 185lb; turned pro 1992; career singles titles 1; final 2000 ATP ranking 213 singles, 8 doubles; 2000 prize money $437,063; career prize money $3,437,004.

Coached by Keith Diepraam. **1989:** (666). **1990:** (689). **1991:** (256) Won New Haven Challenger. **1992:** (127) A –, F –, W –, US 1. All-American at Stanford for 3rd year in singles and 4th in doubles, he led them to NCAA team title and won NCAA individual singles and doubles titles – the 1st player to take all 3 in a season. On the Challenger circuit, he won Monterrey singles and both singles and doubles at Aptos. **1993:** (121) A 1, F 2, W 1, US 1. Won Fairfield Challenger and on the senior tour appeared in qf Adelaide (d. Krajicek) and Coral Springs. **1994:** (90) A 1, F 2, W 1, US 2. Reached his 1st sf on the main tour at Memphis, plus qf Manchester and Cincinnati (as LL), and upset Forget at New Haven. From 3 doubles f, he won Cincinnati with Stolle. **1995:** (210) A 2, F –, W 1, US 1. Appeared in 3 doubles f with Stolle, including a 1st in GS at US Open, but won no title. **1996:** (38) A –, F –, W –, US 3. Upset Kafelnikov, Boetsch and Siemerink on the way to his 1st singles title, unseeded, at New Haven, a result which enabled him to rise more than 200 places to 76 in 4 weeks. He also appeared in sf Moscow (d. Corretja), qf Los Angeles (d. Enqvist) and Toronto and upset MaliVai Washington at US Open. In doubles with Lareau he played 3 f, including Australian Open, and won

Stuttgart Eurocard, qualifying for World Doubles Champ as 8th pairing. There they were surprise finalists, losing 7–6 4s to Woodbridge/Woodforde, whom they had beaten in rr. **1997:** (98) A 1, F –, W 3, US 1. Extended Korda to 5s at Wimbledon and reached qf Adelaide, Sydney, Orlando, Nottingham, Beijing and Moscow in singles. Played 7 doubles f with various partners, winning Philadelphia and Los Angeles and r/u Australian Open with Lareau, with whom he qualified for World Doubles Champ. In their last rr match there, needing to d. Woodbridge/Woodforde in ss to qualify for sf on game percentage, they did so, but then lost 7–6 fs to Bhupathi/Paes. Suffering from a stress fracture of the left foot, he was forced to withdraw from D Cup f the following week, having made his debut earlier in season. **1998:** (147) A 2, F 1, W 2, US 2. Upset Kucera at Toronto and won Bloomfield Challenger. From 5 doubles f with 4 different partners he won Hong Kong with B. Black and Stuttgart with Lareau. **1999:** (178) A –, F –, W –, US –. He won his 1st GS title in his 4th f when he took US Open with Lareau, with whom he also won Queen's and Paris Open before crowning their year with World Doubles Champ. There they d. Bhupathi/Paes in f and finished the season as No. 2 pairing behind the Indian duo before splitting to prepare separately for Sydney Olympics. He also added a 5th title at Qatar with Palmer. His best singles performance was taking the title at Winnetka Challenger. **2000:** A 1, F –, W 2, US –. Pairing with Palmer, he won Indian Wells and Washington from 3 doubles f. They qualified for World Doubles Champ but won only 1 match in rr. **2000 HIGHLIGHTS – SINGLES: Australian Open 1r** (lost Pretzsch 7–6 6–2 6–1), **Wimbledon 2r** (d. Ljubicic 5–7 6–1 7–5 7–6, lost Pozzi 7–6 6–3 6–4). **2000 HIGHLIGHTS – DOUBLES:** (with Palmer) **won** Indian Wells (d. Haarhuis/Stolle 6–4 7–6), **won** Washington (d. Agassi/Sargsian 7–5 6–1); **r/u** Qatar (lost Knowles/Mirnyi 6–3 6–4). **CAREER HIGHLIGHTS – DOUBLES:** (with Lareau unless stated) **US Open – won 1999** (d. Bhupathi/Paes 7–6 6–4), (with Stolle) **r/u 1995** (lost Woodbridge/ Woodforde 6–3 6–3); **World Doubles Champ – won 1999** (d. Bhupathi/Paes 6–3 6–2 6–2), **r/u 1996** (lost Woodbridge/Woodforde 6–4 5–7 6–2 7–6); **Australian Open – r/u 1996** (lost Edberg/Korda 7–5 7–5 4–6 6–1), **r/u 1997** (lost Woodbridge/ Woodforde 4–6 7–5 7–5 6–3).

JARED PALMER (USA)

Born New York, 2 July 1971; lives Palo Alto, Cal.; RH; 6ft 3in; 180lb; turned pro 1991; career singles titles 1; final 2000 ATP ranking 7 doubles; 2000 prize money $426,645; career prize money $2,292,804.

Coached by Jeff Arons. **1987:** Won USTA CC 16s and HC 18s. **1988:** (517) A –, F –, W –, US 2. **1989:** (240) A –, F –, W –, US 2. R/u French Open Jun to Santoro and won Wimbledon Jun doubles with college teammate Stark. **1990:** (564) A –, F –, W –, US –. All-American at Stanford Univ. and won Collegiate doubles title with Stark. **1991:** (425) A –, F –, W –, US 1. Won NCAA singles title over Arnold and r/u doubles with Stark. **1992:** (148) A 1, F –, W –, US 2. In singles won Fairfield Challenger, and in doubles played 4 f, winning Washington with Garnett. **1993:** (101) A –, F –, W 2, US 2. Reached sf Atlanta and extended Pioline to 5s US Open. **1994:** (35) A 2, F 2, W 1, US 1. Broke into the top 100 and then top 50 in singles with some useful upsets. Won his 1st main tour singles title at Pinehurst (d. MaliVai Washington and Martin), r/u Toulouse (d. Volkov and Karbacher) and reached sf Birmingham and Antwerp (d. Rafter), qf Coral Springs (d. Martin again), Los Angeles (d. B. Gilbert) and Basel. He reached 10 doubles f with 5 partners, winning 3. **1995:** (123) A 1, F 2, W 3, US 4. His best singles showings were qf US CC, Toulouse and Tel Aviv. The highlight of his year came in doubles, when he won a 1st GS doubles title at Australian Open with Reneberg. He played another 4 f, winning 1 more with Reneberg and 1 each with B. Black and Grabb. **1996:** (214) A –, F 1, W 2, US 2. Upset Rosset at US Open. **1997:** (890) A –, F –, W –, US –. **1998:** (172) A –, F –, W –, US –. **1999:** (424) A –, F –, W –, US –. He was back as a force in doubles, partnering Haarhuis in 5 f, from which they won Indianapolis and were r/u Wimbledon, and he also won Qatar with O'Brien. He and Haarhuis qualified for World Doubles Champ but did not progress beyond rr stage. **2000:** A –, F –, W –, US –. His only qf appearance in singles came in Nov. at St Petersburg. After Indian Wells, which he won in partnership with O'Brien, he topped the individual doubles Entry System for the 1st time, becoming the 37th man to make No. 1. They also won Washington and he joined with Reneberg to win Scottsdale. It was with O'Brien that he qualified for World Doubles Champ, but again did not pass rr. In mixed he won Australian Open with Stubbs and US Open with Sanchez-Vicario. **2000 HIGHLIGHTS – DOUBLES:** (with O'Brien unless stated) (with Reneberg) **won** Scottsdale (d. Galbraith/MacPherson 6–3 7–5), **won** Indian Wells (d. Haarhuis/Stolle 6–4 7–6), **won** Washington (d. Agassi/Sargsian 7–5 6–1); **r/u** Qatar (lost Knowles/Mirnyi 6–3 6–4). **MIXED DOUBLES:** (with Stubbs) **won** Australian Open (d. Woodbridge/Sanchez-Vicario 7–5 7–6), (with Sanchez-Vicario) **won US Open** (d. Mirnyi/Kournikova 6–4 6–3). **CAREER HIGHLIGHTS – DOUBLES: Australian Open –** (with Reneberg) **won 1995** (d. Knowles/Nestor 6–3 3–6 6–3 6–2); **Wimbledon –** (with Haarhuis) **r/u 1999** (lost Bhupathi/Paes 6–7 6–3 6–4 7–6). **MIXED DOUBLES: Australian Open –** (with Stubbs) **won 2000; US Open –** (with Sanchez-Vicario) **won 2000.**

ANDREI PAVEL (ROM)

Born Constanta, 27 January 1974; lives Borgholzhausen, Germany; RH; 6ft; 184lb; turned pro 1990; career singles titles 2; final 2000 ATP ranking 27; 2000 prize money $550,061; career prize money $1,519,509.

Coached by Radu Popescu; fitness coach Gavrila Ionut. Wife Simone (married 19 August 1994); daughter Caroline Elena (born 19 July 1999). Moved to Germany at age 16, but plays D Cup for Romania. **1990:** (460) Won European 16s (d. Enqvist) and in the senior game won Romanian satellite. **1991:** (536). **1992:** (493)

Won French Open Jun over Navarra. **1993:** (307). **1994:** (406). **1995:** (213) Continued to make his mark on the satellite circuits. **1996:** (140) Emerging from the satellite circuit he reached his 1st sf on the main tour at Bucharest (d. Novak), and on the Challenger circuit he won Montauban. **1997:** (109) A 1, F 2, W 2, US 1. During the year in which he broke into top 100 1st time he upset Krajicek *en route* to sf Chennai, Berasategui on his way to qf San Marino, and Kafelnikov in D Cup. **1998:** (66) A –, F –, W 1, US 1. After winning Magdeburg Challenger, he went on to take his 1st title on the main tour at Tokyo Japan Open, becoming the 1st Romanian to win a pro title at that level since Nastase in 1978. He added sf Atlanta and qf Bucharest, where he won the doubles with Trifu. **1999:** (42) A 4, F 1, W 1, US 1. He was r/u Munich and 's-Hertogenbosch (d. Kucera and held mp v Rafter before losing in 3s). He also appeared in qf Auckland, St Petersburg (where he was r/u doubles with Oosting) and Stuttgart Eurocard, upset Kafelnikov at Estoril, having earlier extended him to 5s at Australian Open, and won Venice Challenger. **2000:** A –, F 1, W 3, US 4. His work with new fitness coach Gavrila Ionut paid off as he enjoyed his best year to date, winning St Polten (unseeded) and reaching sf Hamburg (unseeded again and upsetting Ferrero) and qf Queen's and Stuttgart Masters (d. Rafter and Agassi). He upset Pioline at both Rome and Long Island and extended M. Norman to 10–8 fs at Olympics. **2000 HIGHLIGHTS – SINGLES: French Open 1r** (lost Portas 6–2 7–6 6–1), **Wimbledon 3r** (d. Berasategui 6–0 6–4 6–2, Nestor 7–6 7–5 4–6 6–0, lost W. Ferreira 3–6 7–6 7–5 6–3), **US Open last 16** [unseeded] (d. King 6–3 6–4 6–3, Di Pasquale 6–7 6–1 6–3 6–4, Golmard 6–2 4–1 ret, lost Clement 3–6 6–2 6–1 7–6), **Olympics 1r** (lost M. Norman [seed 3] 6–7 6–3 10–8); **won** St Polten (d. Vicente 6–4 7–5, Gambill 6–3 7–5, Medvedev 6–4 2–6 6–2, Portas 2–6 6–3 6–2, Ilie 7–5 3–6 6–2); **sf** Hamburg (d. Federer 6–4 6–3, Ferrero 6–4 6–4, Di Pasquale 6–3 7–6, Zabaleta 7–5 6–4 lost Kuerten 6–3 6–3).

MARK PHILIPPOUSSIS (AUS)
Born Melbourne, 7 November 1976; lives there and Miami, Fla.; RH; 6ft 4in; 205lb; turned pro 1994; career singles titles 8; final 2000 ATP ranking 11; 2000 prize money $839,567; career prize money $4,957,710.
Coached by Peter McNamara; advised by Pat Cash and Boris Becker; works on fitness with Todd Viney. Speaks fluent Greek but has been to Greece only once – as a baby. **1993:** (1072) Won Victorian satellite. **1994:** (304) A 1, F –, W –, US –. R/u Wimbledon Jun singles to Humphries and in Jun doubles won Australian Open and Wimbledon with Ellwood. **1995:** (32) A 1, F –, W –, US 3. After qualifying and having never before reached qf, he upset Martin on his way to f Scottsdale in only his 5th main tour event. Upset Haarhuis on his way to f Kuala Lumpur, following the next week with f Tokyo Seiko (d. Edberg), and also reached sf Bologna. Missed Wimbledon because he did not get the wild card he had requested and his father would not let him try to qualify. Won 2 doubles titles with different partners and was voted Player to Watch. **1996:** (30) A 4, F 2, W 2, US 4. Played near-perfect tennis to beat Sampras in ss at Australian Open and upset Pioline at US Open, unseeded both times. He won his 1st ATP tour title at Toulouse in the week his manager, Brad Robinson, died of lymphoma; reached sf Memphis (d. Haarhuis) and New Haven (d. Courier and Rosset); qf Olympics (d. Haarhuis again) Munich and Toronto (d. Rosset). **1997:** (18) A –, F 4, W 1, US 3. Missed Australian Open with tendinitis in right arm, returning to win Scottsdale, unseeded. At Munich he played and won his 1st CC f, and followed with his 1st GC title at Queen's, where he also won the doubles with Rafter. It was an anticlimax when he drew, and lost to, Rusedski 1r Wimbledon. He reached f Toulouse and Basle (d. Kafelnikov), sf Lyon and qf Indian Wells (d. Agassi and Moya), Los Angeles and Montreal. **1998:** (15) A 2, F 2, W qf, US r/u. His year began badly when he announced that he would not be available for D Cup until qf and was dropped from the squad by captain Newcombe. He won Memphis (d. Rios and M. Chang) but otherwise struggled for motivation and consistency until, as summer began, he asked Cash to help him sort out his mind. Cash turned out to be a major force in his revival, and the subsequent improvement was already noticeable at Wimbledon, where, unseeded, he upset Kafelnikov on his way to qf. He then went on to achieve new heights at US Open, where he was r/u, unseeded, with upsets of Henman and Moya. He followed with qf GS round, losing to Rios, and qf Paris Open (d. Korda and Kucera). **1999:** (19) A 4, F 1, W qf, US –. With a new-found resolve that he attributed to going for each match 100%, rather than heading for high ranking, he broke into top 10 1st time 29 March after winning San Jose and Indian Wells. However, in Wimbledon qf, when he appeared to be dominating Sampras, he suffered a torn cartilage in his left knee and could not continue. On 7 July he underwent arthroscopic surgery to repair the lateral meniscus tear, and although he had recovered in time for US Open, he withdrew again with an ankle injury. In other tourns he reached qf Monte Carlo, Paris Open (d. Krajicek and Henman) and Moscow and played in winning Australian WT Cup team. In D Cup f he won both singles to lead AUS to 3–2 win over FRA in Nice. **2000:** A 4, F 4, W qf, US 2. He won San Jose, was r/u Hong Kong and Paris Masters (d. Kafelnikov and Kuerten and lost f to Safin only on 5s tb) and reached sf Indian Wells, qf Wimbledon (d. Henman) and Tokyo Japan Open. At French Open, where he was unseeded, he upset Sampras 1r, and was again prominent at Wimbledon. His 3r match there v Schalken went to 20–18 fs and, lasting 5hr 1min, was the longest singles match to be completed in a day, 11 min short of Gonzales v Pasarell in 1969, which spread over 2 days in the era before tie-breaks were played. Two days after that marathon he d. Henman in 5s, but suffered a knee injury during qf v Agassi and took 2 weeks off to recover. Although he did not quite manage a year-end ranking in the top 10, he finished poised just outside. **2000 HIGHLIGHTS – SINGLES: Australian Open last 16** [seed 16] (d. Okun 6 4 6 2 2 6 3–6 6–2, Sluiter 6–1 2–6 7–6 6–1, Ilie 6 4 7–6 6–1, lost Agassi [seed 1] 6–4 7–6 5–7 6–3), **French Open last 16** [unseeded] (d. Sampras [seed 2] 4–6 7–5 7–6 4–6 8–6, Goldstein 6–4 6–7 6–0 6–2, Arazi 6–2 6–1 3–6 6–3, lost Ferrero [seed 16] 6–2 6–2 3–6 6–3), **Wimbledon qf** [seed 10] (d. Melzer 6–4 7–6

5–7 6–4, Di Pasquale 4–6 7–6 6–3 6–0, Schalken 4–6 6–3 6–7 7–6 20–18, Henman [seed 8] 6–1 5–7 6–7 6–3 6–4, lost Agassi [seed 2] 7–6 6–3 6–4), **US Open 2r** [seed 15] (d. Portas 6–3 6–2 6–3, lost Gambill 6–4 6–4 6–4), **Olympics 3r** (d. T. Johansson 7–6 6–4, Pless 6–4 6–4, lost Kafelnikov [seed 5] 7–6 6–3); **won** San Jose (d. Canas 7–6 4–6 7–6, Agenor 6–3 6–4, Gimelstob 7–6 6–4, Courier 4–6 6–3 6–4, Tillstrom 7–5 4–6 6–3); **r/u** Hong Kong (d. B. Black 7–6 7–6, Woodruff 6–7 7–5 6–3, Bruguera 6–2 6–3, Rafter 7–6 6–4, lost Kiefer 7–6 2–6 6–2), **r/u** Paris Masters (d. Hrbaty 1–6 7–6 7–6, Kafelnikov 6–4 6–2, Prinosil 4–6 6–4 7–6, Kuerten 7–6 7–6, lost Safin 3–6 7–6 6–4 3–6 7–6); **sf** Indian Wells (d. Woodruff 6–3 6–4, Clavet 7–5 6–3, Haas 6–2 6–3, Schalken 7–6 6–4, lost Enqvist 6–3 6–7 7–6). **CAREER HIGHLIGHTS – SINGLES: US Open** – r/u 1998 (d. Ruud 7–5 6–4 6–3, Lareau 6–7 6–3 6–3 6–4, Arnold 7–6 6–3 6–3, Henman 7–5 0–6 6–4 6–1, Johansson 4–6 6–3 6–7 6–3 7–6, Moya 6–1 6–4 5–7 6–4, lost Rafter 6–3 3–6 6–2 6–0); **GS Cup – sf 1998** (d. Bjorkman 4–6 7–6 6–1, lost Rios 7–6 6–3 6–4); **Wimbledon – qf 1998** (d. Kafelnikov 6–7 7–6 6–4 6–2, O'Brien 6–7 6–4 7–6 6–3, Bracciali 6–3 6–4 6–4, Stoltenberg 5–7 6–1 6–3 6–3, lost Sampras 7–6 6–4 6–4), **qf 1999** (d. Malisse 6–7 6–4 6–3 6–4, Woodforde 6–7 7–6 7–6 6–4, Clavet 7–5 6–4 6–4, Rusedski 3–6 7–6 6–3 6–1, lost Sampras 4–6 2–1 ret), **qf 2000.**

CEDRIC PIOLINE (FRA)

Born Neuilly-sur-Seine, 15 June 1969; lives Geneva, Switzerland; RH; 6ft 2in; 175lb; turned pro 1989; career singles titles 5; final 2000 ATP ranking 16; 2000 prize money $888,789; career prize money $6,395,573.

Coached by childhood friend Pierre Cherret; physical trainer Luc Pausicles. Working with sports psychologist since Dec. 1999 to try to improve relationship/communication with coach. Wife Mireille Bercot; son Andrea (born 14 March 1993). His mother was a member of Romania's World Championship volleyball squad, and he might have concentrated on that sport, but took up tennis instead after undergoing surgery to shorten one leg to match the other. **1987:** (954) R/u Nat Jun Champ. **1988:** (461). **1989:** (202) A –, F 1, W –, US –. Enjoyed some success on the Challenger circuit. **1990:** (118) A 1, F 1, W –, US –. Won his 1st pro title at Brest Challenger. **1991:** (51) A 1, F 2, W 2, US 1. Broke into top 100 after reaching sf Nice (d. Volkov and Leconte back-to-back). **1992:** (33) A 2, F 4, W 2, US 3. He reached the 16 French Open, unseeded. His HL (d. Forget) and upset B. Gilbert on his way to last 16 French Open, unseeded. **1993:** (10) A 2, F 2, W qf, US r/u. The highlight of his career came at US Open, where he swept aside Courier and Medvedev to become the 1st Frenchman since Cochet in 1932 to reach f there, eventually losing to Sampras. R/u Monte Carlo (d. Edberg), Toulouse, Bolzano and Lyon; sf Munich and Antwerp (d. Ivanisevic); upset Medvedev *en route* to qf Wimbledon, unseeded. He broke into top 10 in Oct., becoming only 2nd player after Pernfors to reach top 10 without a title. **1994:** (51) A 1, F 2, W 1, US 3. That 1st title still evaded him as he slipped out of the top 50. He was a finalist at Long Island, but otherwise reached qf only in Milan and Bordeaux. **1995:** (56) A 1, F 2, W qf, US 2. His best showing was sf Toulouse, plus qf Auckland, Nice, Long Island, Lyon and Wimbledon, where, unseeded, he upset Courier and recovered from 2s down to extend Becker to 9–7 5s. **1996:** (21) A –, F qf, W 4, US 3. After reaching f Zagreb and Marseille, he had played 9 f without winning that elusive 1st title: it came at last at Copenhagen in March, in his 10th f. He also appeared in sf Monte Carlo (d. Kafelnikov) and qf Rotterdam (d. Krajicek), Toulouse and French Open (d. Rios), where he was unseeded. Member of winning FRA D Cup team v SWE, he d. an injured Edberg in 1st rubber and served for the tie at 5–3 in 5s 4th, but lost to Enqvist 9–7. Took over No. 1 ranking in France. **1997:** (20) A –, F 3, W r/u, US 4. The highlight of his year came at Wimbledon, where, ranked 44 and unseeded, he became the 1st French finalist there since Petra in 1946. He had missed Australian Open with a back injury and in other GS lost only in 5s to both Kafelnikov at French Open and M. Chang at US Open. He won his 2nd career title at Prague, but otherwise did not pass qf, although he reached that stage at Indian Wells, Barcelona (d. Muster), GS Cup, Ostrava and Stockholm, and upset M. Chang at Stuttgart Eurocard. **1998:** (18) A 4, F sf, W 1, US 1. He began the year with an upset of Corretja at Australian Open, where he was unseeded, and followed with r/u London (d. Korda) and Monte Carlo. He withdrew from Rome with back problems, but returned at French Open, again unseeded, to upset Krajicek and survive 3 5s matches before bowing out to Corretja in sf. He also reached sf St Petersburg, Boston and Tashkent and qf Vienna (d. Krajicek). He qualified for GS Cup, but could not salvage a single game v Agassi. **1999:** (13) A 1, F 1, W qf, US sf. Again he made his mark in GS, upsetting Kucera at Wimbledon *en route* to qf, then going a stage further at US Open by removing Haas and Kuerten (whom he had earlier upset in D Cup) to reach sf – unseeded both times. He also won Nottingham (d. Rusedski) and reached sf Qatar and Marseille, qf Rotterdam (d. Krajicek), Scottsdale, Queen's and Paris Open, but chose not to play GS Cup for which he had qualified. Led FRA to f D Cup but lost decisive rubber to Philippoussis as AUS won 3–2 in Nice. **2000:** A 1, F 4, W 2, US 3. Concentrating on a more positive approach, thanks to the influence of a sports psychologist, he won Rotterdam and Monte Carlo and reached sf Chennai and Vienna, plus qf London, Hamburg and Queen's. In July he broke 3 metacarpal bones in left hand playing volleyball and underwent surgery, playing only 1 match between Wimbledon and US Open, where he recovered from 2 sets down v Rusedski and saved 2 mps. He returned to Entry System top 10 in April, but finished the year outside again. **2000 HIGHLIGHTS – SINGLES: Australian Open 1r** [seed 13] (lost Ivanisevic 6–4 2–6 7–5 1–6 9–7), **French Open last 16** [seed 6] (d. Sanguinetti 4–6 6–0 4–0 ret, Rafter 7–6 6–3 6–4, Portas 6–4 6–3 6–3, lost Safin [seed 12] 6–4 1–6 6–3 7–5), **Wimbledon 2r** [seed 6] (d. Ruud 7–6 6–1 4–6 6–3, lost Voltchkov 6–3 6–3 2–6 3–6 6–4), **US Open 3r** [seed 10] (d. Sargsian 6–3 6–3 6–1, Rusedski 6–7 3–6 6–4 7–6 6–3, lost T. Martin 7–6 6–3 6–2); **won** Rotterdam (d. Voinea 6–2 6–3, Grosjean 7–6 6–7 6–3, Kiefer 2–6 6–3 7–5, Golmard 6–3 6–4, Henman 6–7 6–4 7–6), **won** Monte Carlo (d. Larsson 6–2 6–2, Novak 6–4 6–3, Dosedel 3–6 7–5 6–4, Kucera 6–2 6–4,

Alami 6–3 6–1, Hrbaty 6–4 7–6 7–6); **sf** Chennai (d. Ran 6–3 6–1, Paes 6–3 6–4, Sanguinetti 3–6 6–4 7–6, lost Hantschk 6–4 3–6 7–6), **sf** Vienna (d. Mlynarik 6–3 6–2, Pavel 7–6 7–6, Koubek 6–3 6–3, lost Haas 6–7 6–2 6–2). **CAREER HIGHLIGHTS – SINGLES: Wimbledon – r/u 1997** (d. Charpentier 5–7 6–3 7–5 6–2, Frana w/o, W. Ferreira 6–4 6–3 6–3, Steven 3–6 6–3 6–4 7–5, Rusedski 6–4 4–6 6–4 6–3, Stich 6–7 6–2 6–1 5–7 6–4, lost Sampras 6–4 6–2 6–4), **qf 1993** (d. Damm 6–4 7–5 3–6 7–5, Medvedev 6–7 7–6 6–3 6–4, Carlsen 6–4 6–4 6–3, Masur 6–3 6–2 3–6 6–7 8–6, lost Edberg 7–5 7–5 6–3), **qf 1995** (d. Lopez–Moron 6–1 6–2 6–4, Courier 6–4 6–4 6–4, Baur 6–4 6–4 6–3, Korda 7–6 6–3 6–2, lost Becker 6–3 6–1 6–7 6–7 9–7), **qf 1999** [unseeded] (d. Damm 7–6 6–4 6–2, Clement 6–3 6–1 6–3, Kafelnikov 3–6 6–4 1–0 ret, Kucera 6–4 5–7 7–6 4–6 6–3, lost Henman 6–4 6–2 4–6 6–3); **US Open – r/u 1993** (d. Prinosil 6–7 7–5 6–4 3–6 6–1, Palmer 6–4 3–6 5–7 7–5 6–1, Wilander 6–4 6–4 6–4, Courier 7–5 6–7 6–4 6–4, Medvedev 6–3 6–1 3–6 6–2, Masur 6–1 6–7 7–6 6–1, lost Sampras 6–4 6–4 6–3), **sf 1999** [unseeded] (d. Rafter 4–6 4–6 6–3 7–5 1–0 ret, Burgsmuller 7–6 1–6 6–3 3–6 6–2, Wessels 7–6 7–5 4–6 7–4, Haas 6–4 7–5 6–3, Kuerten 4–6 7–6 7–6 7–6, lost T. Martin 6–4 6–1 6–2); **French Open – sf 1998** [unseeded] (d. Filippini 6–1 3–6 7–5 6–7 6–4, Boutter 7–5 6–0 3–6 6–2 7–5, Safin 7–5 6–4 6–7 6–4 6–4, Arazi 3–6 6–2 7–6 4–6 6–3, lost Corretja 6–3 6–4 6–2), **qf 1996** [unseeded] (d. Frana 6–1 6–3 6–2, Reneberg 7–5 6–2 6–3, Berasategui 4–6 6–1 6–4 6–0, Rios 6–4 6–1 6–2, lost Stich 6–4 4–6 6–3 6–2).

ALBERT PORTAS (ESP)

Born Barcelona, 15 November 1973; lives Andorra; RH; 6ft 2in; 172lb; turned pro 1993; career singles titles 0; final 2000 ATP ranking 51; 2000 prize money $331,173; career prize money $1,174,189.

Coached by Victor Lopez-Moron. **1991:** (732). **1992:** (502). **1993:** (388). **1994:** (263) Began to make an impression on the satellite circuits. **1995:** (120) He enjoyed his greatest success in Prague, where he reached sf main tour event and won Challenger. **1996:** (180) Out of action until May, following right knee surgery previous Dec. R/u Santiago doubles with Pescariu. **1997:** (35) A –, F 3, W –, US 1. He burst into prominence in the spring when he upset Rios and Berasategui on the way to his 1st career f at Barcelona, after qualifying, reached qf Prague (again as a qualifier), and (still a qualifier) upset Moya 2r French Open. He followed that with sf Stuttgart Mercedes (d. Muster and Mantilla) and also reached qf Umag, Bucharest and Palermo, as well as winning Prague Challenger again. **1998:** (84) A 1, F 1, W 1, US –. On the main tour he reached sf Bucharest and qf Casablanca, while on the Challenger circuit he won both singles and doubles at Cairo. **1999:** (88) A –, F 2, W 1, US 1. He reached his 2nd f on the main tour at San Marino, as well as sf Umag (d. Mantilla) and qf Casablanca again. **2000:** A 2, F 3, W 3, US 1. On the main tour his best showings were sf Santiago and St Polten and qf Bogota, Mallorca (d. Rios), Bastad and Bucharest. At Australian Open he recovered from 2 sets down to upset Kuerten and on the Challenger circuit he won both singles and doubles at Barcelona and Cairo back-to-back in Oct. On the main tour he won the doubles at Umag with Lopez-Moron, brother of his coach. **2000 HIGHLIGHTS – SINGLES: Australian Open 2r** (d. Kuerten [seed 5] 4–6 4–6 6–4 7–6 6–4, lost Voinea 6–2 6–1 6–3), **French Open 3r** (d. Pavel 6–2 7–6 6–1, Balcells 4–6 6–3 7–5 6–3, lost Pioline [seed 6] 6–4 6–3 6–3), **Wimbledon 3r** (d. Zib 6–3 6–4 6–4, Spadea 6–4 6–3 6–3, lost B. Black 6–2 6–0 6–4), **US Open 1r** (lost Philippoussis [seed 15] 6–3 6–2 6–3); **won** Barcelona Challenger (d. Serrano 3–6 6–4 6–3), **won** Cairo Challenger (d. Vanck 7–5 6–3); **sf** Santiago (d. Sanguinetti 6–2 6–3, Canas 6–4 6–4, Hood 6–4 6–4, lost Kuerten 6–4 7–6), **sf** St Polten (d. Giner 4–6 6–1 6–2, Gaudenzi 6–2 6–0, Blanco 6–7 6–3 6–4, lost Pavel 2–6 6–3 6–2). **2000 HIGHLIGHTS – DOUBLES:** (with Lopez-Moron) **won** Umag (d. Ljubicic/Zovko 6–1 7–6)

GIANLUCA POZZI (ITA)

Born Bari, 17 June 1965, and lives there; LH; 5ft 11in; 176lb; turned pro 1984; career singles titles 1; final 2000 ATP ranking 43; 2000 prize money $320,931; career prize money $2,039,819.

Wife Cristina (married 29 November 1997). **1982:** (831). **1984:** (355). **1985:** (330). **1986:** (277) Began to play the satellite circuits. **1987:** (153) A –, F –, W –, US 2. Took his 1st Challenger title at Dublin. **1988:** (165) A 2, F –, W –, US 2. **1989:** (179) A 2, F –, W –, US 1. **1990:** (185) A 1, F –, W –, US –. **1991:** (72) A –, F –, W 2, US –. Captured his 1st main-tour title at Brisbane and took Newport doubles with Steven. **1992:** (68) A 2, F 2, W 1, US 2. R/u Vienna (d. Bruguera and Chesnokov) as a qualifier, having entered the draw only because Cairo Challenger, where he had intended to play, was cancelled. Also reached sf Seoul, qf Milan and Los Angeles. **1993:** (114) A 1, F 1, W 1, US 1. He reached qf Qatar, Marseille (d. Lendl), Rosmalen (d. Medvedev) and Washington (d. Holm) and won Kuala Lumpur Challenger. **1994:** (84) A 1, F –, W 1, US 4. On the main tour he played qf Zaragoza and Kuala Lumpur and on the Challenger circuit he won Taipei. **1995:** (143) A 1, F 1, W 2, US 1. He won Cherbourg Challenger, but Beijing was his only qf appearance on the main tour. **1996:** (106) A –, F –, W 2, US 1. He reached qf Seoul, upset Gaudenzi at Queen's and won 2 Challenger titles. Underwent surgery on 2 Dec. for removal of a small tumour on the bone of his leg. **1997:** (96) A –, F –, W –, US –. He returned to the top 100 with qf Beijing on the main tour and 3 Challenger titles across the year, including 2 from 4 f in 5 consec. tourns. **1998:** (62) A 2, F 2, W 1, US 1. Although he did not pass qf all year, he reached that stage at Hong Kong Salem Open, Halle, Nottingham (d. Rios) and Lyon, upset Siemerink at Lyon and collected 2 more Challenger titles. Made D Cup debut as member of ITA team that reached f, losing 4–1 to SWE. **1999:** (93) A 3, F 1, W 2, US 2. He made only 2 qf appearances – at Marseille and Halle

(d. Mantilla). **2000:** A 2, F 1, W 4, US 2. In his best year yet, at age 35, he returned to top 50 with sf appearance at Queen's, upsetting Safin, whom he extended to 5s at US Open, plus qf Copenhagen, Orlando and Nottingham and an upset of Enqvist at Paris Masters. **2000 HIGHLIGHTS – SINGLES: Australian Open 2r** (d. Zib 6–3 7–6 6–7 6–1, lost M. Norman [seed 12] 6–4 6–3 6–4), **French Open 1r** (lost Rafter 6–3 6–1 6–1), **Wimbledon last 16** (d. Novak 6–3 6–4 3–6 6–1, O'Brien 7–6 6–3 6–4, O. Rochus 6–3 3–6 7–6 6–2, lost B. Black 4–6 7–6 6–2 6–4), **US Open 2r** (d. Ruud 6–2 6–3 6–2, lost Safin [seed 6] 6–3 3–6 6–3 3–6 6–4), **Olympics 2r** (d. Novak 6–1 6–2, lost Alami 6–2 4–6 8–6); **sf** Queen's (d. Siemerink 6–3 4–6 6–1, Agenor 6–3 4–6 6–0, Agassi 4–6 3–2 ret, Safin 7–5 7–6, lost Hewitt 6–1 6–4).

DAVID PRINOSIL (GER)

Born Olmutz, Czechoslovakia, 9 March 1973; lives Munich; RH; 6ft 1in; 180lb; turned pro 1991; career singles titles 3; final 2000 ATP ranking 38; 2000 prize money $625,811; career prize money $3,226,181.

Coached by his father, Jiri. Moved with his family to Germany from Czechoslovakia at age 14 and is now a German citizen. **1989:** In winning German World Youth Cup team. **1990:** (389). **1991:** (238) Made progress on the satellite circuits. **1992:** (123) A –, F 3, W –, US –. Moving on to the main tour, he reached qf Vienna in singles. Won Rotterdam doubles with Goellner as lucky loser and Umag with Vogel. **1993:** (74) A 2, F 2, W 2, US 1. Won 2 Challenger titles and on the senior tour reached qf Kuala Lumpur Malaysian Open, Jakarta, Copenhagen (d. Holm), Basel (d. Volkov), Athens and Bolzano (d. Hlasek). Teamed with Goellner in doubles at French Open, where, unseeded, they upset Woodbridge/Woodforde to reach f, and played 3 more f with various partners, winning Long Island with Goellner. **1994:** (127) A 1, F 2, W 3, US –. Reached qf Zaragoza (d. Svensson) and Newport and won Dublin Challenger. At French Open his 2r match v Agenor lasted 71 games (14–12 5s), the longest in tourn since introduction of tb. **1995:** (50) A 3, F 1, W 1, US 1. After taking 2 singles titles on the Challenger circuit, he collected his 1st on the main tour at Newport in July, upsetting Frana and Wheaton on the way, and finished the year with an upset of Courier to reach sf Stockholm. **1996:** (39) A 1, F 1, W 1, US 2. He had been in a slump from April, but regained his form to upset Krajicek and Martin on his way to the title at Ostrava. He also reached sf Qatar, Dubai (d. Edberg and Enqvist) and Moscow, qf St Petersburg and Hong Kong (took a set off Sampras) and surprised Ivanisevic at Basel. In doubles he won an Olympic bronze medal with Goellner. **1997:** (88) A 1, F 1, W –, US 1. Upset Stich and Korda *en route* to sf Milan and reached qf Hong Kong and Tokyo Japan Open. He appeared in 3 doubles f with different partners, winning Long Island with Ondruska. **1998:** (77) A 2, F 2, W 2, US 1. He was r/u Copenhagen and progressed to qf Nottingham, Long Island (d. Moya) and Basel (d. Rusedski). Played doubles with Becker in victorious GER WT Cup squad, winning all their matches, and won Ostrava with Kiefer. **1999:** (66) A 1, F 1, W 2, US 2. His best performance was r/u St Petersburg, and he also reached sf Nottingham and qf Rome (d. Rios) and Boston (d. Pioline). From 2 doubles f with different partners he won Vienna with Stolle. **2000:** A –, F 1, W 4, US 1. Having failed to pass 1r all year, he upset N. Lapentti and Kafelnikov on his way to the title at Halle, unseeded. He followed in Oct. with an upset of Safin to reach f Moscow, again unseeded, and appeared in sf Washington and qf Paris Masters (d. Squillari). With a different partner each time he played 4 doubles f, winning Copenhagen with Damm and Moscow with Bjorkman. **2000 HIGHLIGHTS – SINGLES: French Open 1r** (lost Hantschk 6–2 6–7 7–6 6–4), **Wimbledon last 16** [unseeded] (d. Sargsian 2–6 6–1 6–2 6–4, Huet 6–4 2–6 6–1 6–2, Damm 7–6 3–6 7–6 6–4, lost Agassi [seed 2] 6–4 6–3 6–3), **US Open 1r** (lost Malisse 7–5 6–4 6–4), **Olympics 1r** (lost Federer 6–2 6–2); **won** Halle (d. T. Johansson 7–5 6–1, Ljubicic 6–4 6–7 6–4, N. Lapentti 6–3 7–6, Kafelnikov 6–4 7–6, Krajicek 6–3 6–2); **r/u** Moscow (d. Nestor 6–7 6–3 6–3, Levy 6–3 6–0, Bjorkman 7–6 5–7 7–6, Safin 6–7 6–3 6–3, lost Kafelnikov 6–2 7–5); **sf** Washington (d. Damm 6–3 6–3, Teileman 6–1 5–7 6–3, Sa 6–3 3–6 6–3, B. Black 6–3 1–6 6–3, lost Agassi 6–1 6–3). **2000 HIGHLIGHTS – DOUBLES:** (with Damm) **won** Copenhagen (d. Bjorkman/Lareau 6–1 5–7 7–5), (with Bjorkman) **won** Moscow (d. Novak/Rikl 6–2 6–3); (with Bhupathi) **r/u** Halle (lost Kulti/Tillstrom 7–6 7–6), (with Hrbaty) **r/u** Hong Kong (lost W. Black/Ullyett 6–1 6–2). **CAREER HIGHLIGHTS – DOUBLES:** (with Goellner) **French Open – r/u 1993** (lost L./M. Jensen 6–4 6–7 6–4).

MARIANO PUERTA (ARG)

Born Buenos Aires, 19 September 1978, and lives there; LH; 5ft 10in; 165lb; turned pro 1995; career singles titles 2; final 2000 ATP ranking 21; 2000 prize money $529,893; career prize money $1,111,212.

Coached by his father, Ruben. **1995:** (756) R/u French Open Jun to Zabaleta and won South American Champs. **1996:** (419) Began to make an impression on the satellite circuits. **1997:** (147) Moving on to the Challenger circuit, he won Quito, then finished the year with qf Santiago in his 1st main tour event. **1998:** (39) A –, F –, W 1, US 1. He upset Kuerten on his way to sf Umag, following with r/u spot at San Marino in only his 6th tourn, and then his 1st title at Palermo (d. Corretja), bursting into the top 50. He also reached sf Mexico City, qf Bologna and Santiago, won Bogota doubles with Del Rio and took the Challenger title in Nice. **1999:** (99) A 2, F 2, W –, US 2. In a quieter year qf Memphis was his best singles performance, while in doubles he won Munich with Orsanic and Umag with J. Sanchez. **2000:** A 1, F 3, W –, US 1. In his best year yet, he appeared in consec. f at Mexico City, Santiago and Bogota, where he upset Kuerten *en route* to the title, unseeded. He moved into top 20 Entry System in July after reaching consec. finals again at Gstaad and Umag in July, although he could not add another title. In other tourns he reached sf Casablanca and

Mallorca, plus qf Rome (d. Ferrero and Kafelnikov). **2000 HIGHLIGHTS – SINGLES: Australian Open 1r** (lost Agassi [seed 1] 6–2 6–2 6–3), **French Open 3r** (d. Damm 7–6 6–3 6–2, Clavet 6–2 6–1 6–3, lost Ferrero [seed 16] 6–2 3–2 ret), **US Open 1r** (lost Enqvist [seed 7] 3–6 6–3 6–2 6–2); **won** Bogota (d. Cortes 6–1 6–2, Sanguinetti 6–4 6–3, Mantilla 7–6 6–3, Kuerten 3–6 6–1 7–6, El Aynaoui 6–4 7–6); **r/u** Mexico City (d. Vicente 7–5 6–4, Gumy 6–4 6–4, Canas 6–2 6–3, Squillari 6–4 6–1, lost Chela 6–4 7–6), **r/u** Santiago (d. Squillari 6–2 6–2, Chela 6–3 2–6 6–3, Vicente 6–1 7–5, Gaudio 3–6 6–4 6–2, lost Kuerten 7–6 6–3), **r/u** Gstaad (d. Di Pasquale 6–3 6–4, Mantilla 6–0 6–2, Grosjean 7–6 6–3, A. Costa 6–4 6–3, lost Corretja 6–1 6–3), **r/u** Umag (d. Alonso 6–4 6–1, Ljubicic 6–4 4–6 6–4, Damm 6–3 6–2, Ulirhach 4–6 6–2 6–3, lost Rios 7–6 4–6 6–3); **sf** Casablanca (d. Hantschk 6–4 6–2, Coutelot 6–2 6–4, El Aynaoui 7–6 6–4, lost Grosjean 6–4 3–6 6–1), **sf** Mallorca (d. Hipfl 6–2 6–3, Marin 6–1 6–2, A. Martin 6–4 6–1, lost Tillstrom 3–6 7–5 6–1).

PATRICK RAFTER (AUS)

Born Mount Isa, 28 December 1972; lives Pembroke, Bermuda; RH; 6ft 1in; 190lb; turned pro 1991; career singles titles 1; final 2000 ATP ranking 15; 2000 prize money $814,586; career prize money $9,432,719.

Has no formal coach but is helped by Tony Roche. **1991:** (294) Began to make his mark on the Satellite circuits. **1992:** (301) A 1, F –, W –, US –. **1993:** (57) A 1, F –, W 3, US 1. Emerging from the Challenger circuit, where he won Aptos, he broke into top 100 after reaching sf Indianapolis, where he upset Chesnokov, Ferreira and Sampras. Voted ATP Newcomer of the Year. **1994:** (21) A 2, F 4, W 2, US 3. In a remarkable 18-month period he moved from 301 to 21 in the rankings. He upset Courier 1r Indian Wells, surprised Rosset and M. Chang on his way to sf LIPC, and broke into top 25 after reaching his 1st tour f at Hong Kong in April, where the match was delayed 1 hour to allow him to recover from food poisoning. He upset Muster at French Open, where he was unseeded, and after he had won his 1st title at Manchester, he played a 5-set marathon v Bruguera in 2r Wimbledon, succumbing only 13–11 after being overtaken by cramp. He also reached sf Adelaide and Sydney Indoor, 4 more qf and last 16 French Open, unseeded. Played 3 doubles f, winning Bologna with Fitzgerald. **1995:** (68) A 4, F 1, W 1, US 2. Having achieved so much so fast, he felt somewhat drained and disillusioned, as well as being hampered during the year by a torn cartilage in his racket wrist, for which he underwent surgery on 30 Oct., missing the rest of the season. His best performances were sf Washington, qf Adelaide, Los Angeles, Ostrava and Lyon and an upset of Medvedev at Cincinnati. Played 2 doubles f, winning Adelaide with Courier. **1996:** (62) A 2, F 1, W 4, US 1. Returning at Australian Open, he was forced to retire 2r with a recurrence of the wrist injury, and was out with that and an ankle injury until April. However, he felt more optimistic and under less pressure once Philippoussis had replaced him at the top of the Australian rankings. He did not progress beyond qf, but reached that stage at US CC (where he won the doubles with Cash), Queen's, Washington (d. Agassi) and Toronto (d. MaliVai Washington) and upset Rosset at Wimbledon, where he was unseeded. **1997:** (2) A 1, F sf, W 4, US won. The climax of an superb season came at US Open, where, playing his 3rd f in consec. tourns and his 6th of the year, he won his 1st title of the year in tremendous style. He was the 1st Australian since Cash at Wimbledon in 1987 to win a GS title and the 1st to win US Open since Newcombe in 1973. It was his 1st title for 3 years. Hampered by a sore shoulder, he had not even been sure of competing and was grateful for his Wednesday start. His success swept him through the rankings to No. 3, the highest by an Australian since Laver was No. 2 in 1975, and at end of season he ousted M. Chang to take the No. 2 slot himself. He also performed well on clay in spring: unseeded at French Open, he upset Krajicek on his way to becoming the 1st Australian man to reach qf there since Phil Dent in 1977 and progressing to sf, unseeded. In other tourns, he was r/u Philadelphia, Hong Kong, St Polten (d. Muster on clay), New Haven, Long Island (d. M. Chang and Enqvist) and GS Cup, adding sf Tokyo Japan Open, Stuttgart Eurocard and Stockholm and qf Sydney (d. Haarhuis) and Queen's (d. Courier). Qualified for his 1st ATP Champ, where he was just beaten to sf by Moya, whom he had beaten in rr. In doubles he played 5 f with 3 different partners, winning Adelaide with Shelton and Queen's with Philippoussis. When he was playing Pioline at Paris Open, a laser beam was shone in his eyes from the crowd, but he went on to save 3 mps and win the match. Voted ATP Most Improved Player and won Stefan Edberg Sportsmanship award. **1998:** (4) A 3, F 2, W 4, US won. At the beginning of the year he struggled to cope with the extra pressure after winning US Open; it seemed to crush his morale, and he found he was no longer enjoying the game – as well as being hindered by injury. He took a 4-week break and, helped by John Newcombe's advice to put less pressure on himself and to have fun, he took off again after returning at Rome. He won his 1st Super 9 tourn at Toronto, following with his 2nd at Cincinnati, where he d. Sampras in f. He beat Sampras again at US Open, returning 21 hours after their gruelling 5s sf to retain the title over Philippoussis and challenge for the top ranking. He also won titles at Chennai, Den Bosch and Long Island, reached sf Sydney and Antwerp and qf Rotterdam, Los Angeles and Vienna. Although he qualified for ATP Champ, and would still have been in with a chance of ending the year at No. 1 had he played and won, he decided to withdraw to nurse a knee injury and prepare for Australian Open. In doubles he won Los Angeles with Stolle and Indian Wells with Bjorkman, with whom he also shared Queen's. He also won Arthur Ashe Humanitarian of Year award. **1999:** (16) A 3, F 3, W sf, US 1. After a poor start to the year, in which he won only 7 of 15 matches, he hit form again with r/u Rome (d. Agassi), followed by the title at 's-Hertogenbosch (d. Kafelnikov) and sf showing at Wimbledon. He had moved to No. 2 ahead of Sampras and behind Kafelnikov at beginning June, and on 26 July he displaced Agassi to take the top spot for 1st time, although Sampras overtook him again after only a week. He won a 2nd title at Cincinnati in Aug., and reached qf Montreal and Indianapolis, where he withdrew with tendinitis of right shoulder, an injury that had caused him also to pull out of Wimbledon doubles. The same injury forced him to withdraw from US Open, where he was booed off the court, and in Oct. he underwent arthroscopic surgery on his right rotator cuff, missing GS Cup, D Cup f and World Doubles Champ, for which he qualified with Bjorkman. He played in winning AUS WT Cup team (d. Sampras) and in doubles with Bjorkman won Australian Open and 2 other titles. For a second year he won the Stefan Edberg Sportsmanship award. **2000:** A –, F 2, W r/u, US 1. Although he returned to play doubles at Sydney, he missed Australian Open and did not return completely until Feb. The climax of his year came at Wimbledon when, fully fit, he upset Agassi in 5s sf to reach f, where he lost to Sampras in 4s. He suffered a recurrence of the shoulder injury at Toronto and was unseeded at US Open, where he lost in 5s tb to Blanco. Other highlights of his year were the title at 's-Hertogenbosch, r/u Lyon (d. Kuerten), sf Hong Kong (d. Kuerten), qf Delray Beach and Toronto, and carrying the Olympic torch at Sydney. Played in AUS D Cup team that reached f v ESP in Barcelona, but there he was severely affected by cramp and had to ret. in crucial match v Ferrero. ESP went on to win 3–1 as his last match – v Corretja – was cancelled. **2000 HIGHLIGHTS – SINGLES: French Open 2r** (d. Pozzi 6–3 6–1 6–1, lost Pioline [seed 6] 7–6 6–3 6–4), **r/u Wimbledon** [seed 12] (d. J. Delgado 6–3 7–6 6–1, Woodbridge 6–3 6–3 6–4, Schuttler 6–2 7–6 6–3, T. Johansson 6–3 6–4 6–7 6–1, Popp 6–3 6–2 7–6, Agassi [seed 2] 7–5 4–6 7–5 4–6 6–3, lost Sampras [seed 1] 6–7 7–6 6–4 6–2), **US Open 1r** (lost Blanco 7–6 2–6 6–3 1–6 7–6), **Olympics 2r** [seed 13] (d. Spadea 6–4 6–3, lost Nestor 7–5 7–6); **won** 's-Hertogenbosch (d. Van Scheppingen 6–3 6–4, Schalken 6–3 6–2, Alami 6–3 3–6 6–3, Damm 6–2 6–1, Escude 6–1 6–3); **r/u** Lyon (d. Gaudio 6–4 4–6 6–4, El Aynaoui 7–6 6–2, Kuerten 6–3 6–4, Arazi 6–3 6–4, lost Clement 7–6 7–6); **sf** Hong Kong (d. Pless 6–4 7–5, Bjorkman 6–4 5–7 6–3, Kuerten 7–6 6–4, lost Philippoussis 7–6 6–4). **CAREER HIGHLIGHTS – US Open – won 1997** (d. Medvedev 6–3 6–4 7–5, M. Norman 6–2 6–1 6–2, Roux 6–1 6–1 6–2, Agassi 6–3 7–6 4–6 6–3, Larsson 7–6 6–4 6–2, M. Chang 6–3 6–3 6–4, Rusedski 6–3 6–2 4–6 7–5), **won 1998** (d. Arazi 4–6 4–6 6–3 6–3 6–1, Gumy 6–4 6–1 6–2, Nainkin 6–1 6–1 6–1, Ivanisevic 6–3 6–4 4–6 6–1, Bjorkman 6–2 6–3 7–5, Sampras 6–7 6–4 2–6 6–4 6–3, Philippoussis 6–3 3–6 6–2 6–0); **Wimbledon – r/u 2000, sf 1999** (d. Caratti 6–3 6–2 6–2, Bjorkman 6–2 7–6 6–7 6–2, Enqvist 7–6 6–2 6–2, Becker 6–3 6–2 6–3, T. Martin 6–3 6–7 7–6 7–6, lost Agassi 7–5 7–6 6–2); **GS Cup – r/u 1997** (d. Muster 6–2 6–3, Rios 6–1 7–6, Korda 7–5 3–6 6 7 7–6 9–7, lost Sampras 6–2 6 4 7–5); **French Open – sf 1997** [unseeded] (d. Gaudenzi 3–6 7–6 6–3 6–4, Fontang 6–3 6–4 6–3, Krajicek 6–3 4–6 6–4 6–2, Woodforde 6–2 5–7 6–1 6–2, Blanco 6–3 7–6 6–3, lost Bruguera 6–7 6–1 7–5 7–6). **CAREER HIGHLIGHTS – DOUBLES:** (with Bjorkman) **Australian Open – won 1999** (d. Bhupathi/Paes 6–3 4–6 6–4 6–7 6–4).

DAVID RIKL (CZE)

Born Brandys, 27 February 1971; lives London, England; LH; 5ft 10in; 150lb; turned pro 1989; career singles titles 0; final 2000 ATP ranking 11 doubles; 2000 prize money $347,913; career prize money $1,991,798.
Coached by Petr Vanicek. Wife Alice a former Czech WTA player (married 5 May 1994); sons Filip (born 12 March 1996) and Patrik (born 6 January 1999). **1987:** (878). **1988:** (774) R/u Wimbledon Jun doubles with Zdrazila, with whom he shared 1st place in ITF Jun Doubles Rankings. **1989:** (400). **1990:** (313) A –, F –, W – US –. In partnership with Zdrazila, he enjoyed a second year of success on the satellite circuits. **1991:** (161) A –, F –, W –, US –. Won his 1st title on the main tour when he took Tel Aviv with Schapers. **1992:** (150) A –, F –, W –, W 3, US –. Reached his 1st singles sf at Prague and won Newport doubles with Deppe. **1993:** (102) A –, F –, W –, US –. Having won 2 Challenger titles, he reached sf San Marino on the main tour in Aug. **1994:** (73) A 2, F 2, W 1, US 1. Reached his 1st tour f at Jakarta in Jan. and appeared in qf Adelaide (d. Mansdorf), Marseille, Mexico City, Monte Carlo (d. Pioline, Chesnokov and Skoff) and Munich (d. Pioline). In doubles he won 3 titles with Kafelnikov and 1 with Bauer. **1995:** (87) A 1, F 2, W –, US –. He reached qf Marseille and Santiago, as well as winning Pilsen Challenger. In doubles with Novak he won 2 titles from 5 f. **1996:** (148) A 1, F 2, W 1, US 2. From 3 doubles f he won Casablanca with Novak and Bogota with Pereira. **1997:** (171) A –, F –, W 3, US –. He won Ostrava doubles with Novak. **1998:** (869) A –, F –, W –, US –. In doubles with Novak he won 2 titles from 3 f. **1999:** (–) A –, F –, W –, US –. In doubles he shared 's-Hertogenbosch in partnership with E. Ferreira and was r/u 4 times with Novak, with whom he was 1st alternate for World Doubles Champ, playing (and losing) just one match. **2000:** A –, F –, W –, US –. From 6 doubles f with Novak he won Dubai, Gstaad and both Stuttgart tourns. They qualified for World Doubles Champ but did not take up their place. **2000 HIGHLIGHTS – DOUBLES:** (with Novak) **won** Dubai (d. Koenig/Tramacchi 6–2 7–5), **won** Gstaad (d. Golmard/Kohlmann 3–6 6–3 6–4), **won** Stuttgart Mercedes (d. Arnold/Johnson 5–7 6–2 6–3), **won** Stuttgart Masters (d. Johnson/Norval 3–6 6–3 6–4); **r/u** Vienna (lost Kafelnikov/Zimonjic 6–4 6–4), **r/u** Moscow (lost Bjorkman/Prinosil 6–2 6–3).

MARCELO RIOS (CHI)

Born Santiago, 26 December 1975, and lives there; LH; 2HB; 5ft 9in; 160lb; turned pro 1994; career singles titles 16; final 2000 ATP ranking 37; 2000 prize money $493,816; career prize money $8,423,663.
Wife Juliana Sotela (married 26 December 2000). As a junior worked from Nick Bollettieri's Academy. **1992:** (487) Won Chilean satellite aged 16. **1993:** (549) No. 1 in ITF Jun rankings after winning US Open Jun over Downs. Joined the Chilean D Cup squad and was named his country's Athlete of the Year. **1994:** (107) A –, F 2, W –, US 2. He reached sf Hilversum and qf Gstaad and at French Open, after qualifying, he kept Sampras

on court more than 2½ hours in 2r. Took over the No. 1 ranking in Chile from Sergio Cortes in summer. **1995:** (25) A –, F 2, W 1, US 1. Won his 1st tour title at Bologna and broke into the top 50, becoming the 1st Chilean to reach that level since Acuna in 1986. In July he won both singles and doubles titles at Amsterdam, having played through the qualifying after applying too late for a regular place in the draw, and in Oct. reached top 25 after winning a 3rd title in Kuala Lumpur and r/u Santiago. **1996:** (11) A 1, F 4, W –, US 2. In an impressive year he continued to shoot up the rankings, becoming in May the 1st Chilean to appear in the top 10. Won St Polten; r/u Scottsdale, Barcelona (d. Courier and took a set off Muster) and Santiago; sf Indian Wells (d. W. Ferreira), Monte Carlo (d. Becker), Hamburg (d. W. Ferreira again), Toronto and Toulouse; and reached 4 more qf. **1997:** (10) Performing consistently he maintained his ranking, finishing just inside the top 10, and narrowly missed a berth at the season-ending champ. He won Monte Carlo, was r/u Marseille (retired with leg injury), Rome, Boston and Santiago, and reached qf Australian Open (d. Enqvist), US Open (d. Bruguera and extended M. Chang to 5s), GS Cup, Auckland, Prague, Singapore and Stuttgart Eurocard (d. Kafelnikov). **1998:** (2) In a spectacular year he won more titles than anyone else and for a time knocked Sampras off the top of the rankings. He began at Australian Open by becoming the 1st Chilean to reach a GS f since Ayala at French Open 38 years earlier, and the 1st in the open era, although he followed that achievement with a lacklustre performance in losing f to Korda. He confirmed his all-round ability with a successful HC season, and on 30 March, after winning his 3rd title of the year at LIPC, he became the 14th player to be ranked No. 1 – the 1st Chilean and 1st South American to reach that position. On 27 April Sampras regained his top ranking, with Korda at No. 2 and Rios 3, but Rios was back to the top on 10 Aug., dropping again 2 weeks later to 2nd place, where he finished the season. By 9 Nov. he was the only player left who could still challenge Sampras for the top year-end ranking, but his last chance to do so disappeared when he withdrew from ATP Champ with a back injury after playing only one match. Rome was his 3rd Super 9 title of the calendar year and on 17 Aug. he was 1st to qualify for ATP Champ – despite a relatively miserable summer, as a result of which he acrimoniously split with his coach, Stefanki. He won 7 titles in all at Auckland, Indian Wells, LIPC, Rome, St Polten, Singapore and GS Cup and reached sf Memphis, Gstaad, Stuttgart Mercedes and Lyon, plus qf French Open, Stuttgart Eurocard, Paris Open and Santiago. He had his share of injury problems, being forced to retire at Lyon with a left hamstring injury and to withdraw from Barcelona and Monte Carlo with an inflammation in left elbow – possibly the result of using a larger racket. **1999:** (9) He continued to be plagued by injury: having retired 1r Auckland with a right hamstring strain, he withdrew Australian Open with stress fracture of vertebra, which kept him out of action until March; he retired again in f Monte Carlo with a right thigh injury; and was unable to take up his place as 1st alternate at ATP Champ because of a groin injury. In Nov. he underwent surgery to alleviate pain of adductor muscle injury in both legs. Between injuries, though, he managed to maintain his top 10 ranking with titles at Hamburg, St Polten and Singapore, r/u Monte Carlo and Shanghai (where he let slip 4 mps v M. Norman in f), sf Estoril and qf French Open, Stuttgart Mercedes, Boston and Stuttgart Eurocard. **2000:** A –, F 1, W –, US 3. He returned to action at Santiago in Feb., but was still not 100 per cent, retiring lame at French Open and withdrawing from Wimbledon. His only title of the year came at Umag, with sf finishes at Hamburg and Toulouse, plus qf Scottsdale, Barcelona and Gstaad. **2000 HIGHLIGHTS – SINGLES: French Open 1r** (lost Haas 6–3 6–2 ret), **US Open 3r** (d. Massu 6–3 7–5 1–6 7–6, Knippschild 4–6 6–4 6–4 7–5, lost Enqvist [seed 7] 7–5 7–5 6–3), **Olympics 1r** [seed 12] (lost Zabaleta 6–7 6–4 7–5); **won** Umag (d. Kroslak 6–3 6–1, Puentes 6–3 6–2, D. Sanchez 7–6 6–2, Moya 6–2 7–5, Puerta 7–6 4–6 6–3); **sf** Hamburg (d. Escude 6–4 6–1, Kohlmann 6–1 6–0, Puerta 7–6 6–0, Clavet 6–4 6–3, lost Safin 7–6 6–2), **sf** Toulouse (d. Vicente 6–4 3–6 6–1, Alami 6–7 6–3 6–4, Viloca 6–4 6–4, lost Corretja 7–6 6–3). **CAREER HIGHLIGHTS – SINGLES: GS Cup – won 1998** (d. Mantilla 7–6 7–5, Philippoussis 7–6 6–3 6–4, Agassi 6–4 2–6 7–6 5–7 6–3); **Australian Open – r/u 1998** (d. Stafford 6–1 6–0 6–3, Enqvist 6–4 7–6 4–6 6–4, Ilie 6–2 6–3 6–2, Roux 6–2 4–6 6–2 6–4, Berasategui 6–7 6–4 6–4 6–0, Escude 6–1 6–3 6–2, lost Korda 6–2 6–2 6–2), **qf 1997** (d. Korda 7–6 6–3 6–3, Joyce 6–0 6–4 6–2, Schaller 4–6 7–6 6–1 6–1, Enqvist 4–6 6–4 7–6 6–7 6–3, lost M. Chang 7–5 6–1 6–4); **French Open – qf 1998** (d. Steven 7–5 6–2 3–6 6–3, Alvarez 6–4 6–2 6–2, W. Ferreira 6–1 3–3 ret, A. Costa 4–6 6–3 6–3, lost Moya 6–1 2–6 6–4), **qf 1999** (d. Pretzsch 6–3 6–2 7–5, Boetsch 6–2 6–3 7–5, A. Costa 7–5 6–4 7–5, Berasategui 3–6 3–6 6–3 6–4 6–3, lost Hrbaty 7–6 6–2 6–7 6–3); **US Open – qf 1997** (d. Smith 6–1 6–1 6–4, Carlsen 6–4 5–7 3–6 6–1 7–6, Haas 6–4 3–6 6–3 1–6 6–1, Bruguera 7–5 6–2 6–4, lost M. Chang 7–5 6–2 4–6 4–6 6–3).

TOMMY ROBREDO (ESP)

Born Girona, 1 May 1982; lives Barcelona; RH; 5ft 11in; 152lb; career singles titles 0; final 2000 ATP ranking 131.

Coached by Joan Auendione and Miguel Sanchez. **1998:** Played in ESP teams that won Under-16 World Youth Cup and Under-18 Sunshine Cup. **2000:** In Jun tennis he was r/u French Open singles to Mathieu, winning the doubles there with Lopez and at Australian Open with Mahut. In the men's game he won Challenger titles in Espinho and Seville. **2000 HIGHLIGHTS – SINGLES: won** Espinho Challenger d. Szymanski 6–4 6–2), **won** Seville Challenger (d. Serrano 6–7 6–1 6–4).

ANDY RODDICK (USA)

Born Omaha, Nebraska, 30 August 1982; lives Boca Raton, Fla; RH; 2HB; 6ft 1in; 180lb; turned pro 2000; career singles titles 0; final 2000 ATP ranking 158, junior ranking 1.

Coached by Tarik Benhabiles. **1999:** Won Orange Bowl over Abel. **2000:** A –, F –, W –, US 1. In Jun tennis he won Australian Open over Ancic and US Open over Ginepri, being r/u Australian Open doubles with Davis and French Open with J. Johansson. In the men's game he reached qf Washington (d. Kucera) on the main tour and won Challenger titles at Austin and Burbank. **2000 HIGHLIGHTS – SINGLES: US Open 1r** (lost A. Costa 6–3 6–7 6–1 6–4); **won** Austin Challenger (d. Russell 6–4 6–4), **won** Burbank Challenger (d. K. Kim 6–1 6–2).

MARC ROSSET (SUI)

Born Geneva, 7 November 1970; lives Monte Carlo, Monaco; RH; 2HB; 6ft 7in; 194lb; turned pro 1988; career singles titles 15; final 2000 ATP ranking 28; 2000 prize money $583,636; career prize money $6,135,419.
Coached by Pierre Simsolo. **1988:** (474) Won Orange Bowl and was No. 4 on ITF Jun Rankings. **1989:** (45) Progressing from the Challenger circuit, on which he won 2 titles and reached qf or better in 8 more tourns, he won his 1st main tour title at Geneva and cracked the top 100 in Sept. **1990:** (22) A 1, F 2, W 3, US 1. Broke into the top 25 in autumn, following some big upsets during the year. Won Lyon (d. Wilander); r/u Madrid (d. E. Sanchez) and Bologna; sf Nice (d. Noah), Gstaad (d. E. Sanchez) and Geneva. **1991:** (60) A 1, F 1, W 1, US 1. Sf New Haven (d. Lendl and Chang back-to-back); qf Brussels, LIPC and Hilversum. **1992:** (35) A 4, F 1, W 3, US 1. The highlight of his career came in August when he won an Olympic gold medal, unseeded, upsetting Courier (in ss), E. Sanchez and Ivanisevic. He also won Moscow in Nov., reached last 16 Australian Open, unseeded (d. Gustafsson), sf Basle and qf Adelaide, Scottsdale (d. Agassi) and Madrid (d. E. Sanchez). In partnership with Hlasek won his 1st GS title at French Open, plus Italian Open and Lyon, and took Adelaide with Ivanisevic. Played in D Cup squad as SUI reached f, upsetting FRA in qf. **1993:** (16) A –, F 2, W 1, US 1. Began the year slowly, suffering from tonsillitis, and struggled to find his best form until Feb. when he won Marseille, following with Long Island (d. Ivanisevic and M. Chang) and then Moscow at end of year. He reached sf Bordeaux, Basle and Stockholm (d. Courier), and upset Agassi at Indian Wells, Becker at Monte Carlo and Muster at Italian Open. **1994:** (14) A 3, F 1, W 2, US 3. Still a dangerous opponent, he scored some big upsets during the year as he won Marseille (d. Stich) and Lyon (d. Courier), r/u New Haven (d. Lendl and Medvedev) and Paris Open (d. Becker and Chang) and reached sf Nice, Bordeaux and Moscow (d. Kafelnikov). **1995:** (15) A 1, F 2, W 1, US 4. Out 2 months early in year after fracturing a bone in his right foot in D Cup tie v NED in Feb. He returned to win Nice in his 1st tourn back, following with Halle (saving 7 mps v Stich), and sf Gstaad, Long Island, Toulouse and Moscow and 3 more qf. Broke into top 10 1st time in July but could not maintain his position. **1996:** (22) A –, F sf, W 3, US 1. At French Open, where he recovered from 2s down v Karbacher to win their qf, he became 1st Swiss to reach sf any GS. In WT Cup, he was undefeated in winning Swiss squad, having never before won any of his 9 matches in the competition. In other tourns he upset Kafelnikov *en route* to f Milan and reached qf Antwerp, Rotterdam, New Haven, Vienna (d. W. Ferreira) and Paris Open (d. Sampras in ss). At Hopman Cup in Jan. he injured his hand in a gesture of frustration after he and Hingis wasted 4 champ points in mixed doubles and was forced to def after playing 2 more points. **1997:** (31) A 2, F 4, W 2, US 1. He recorded some notable upsets on his way to winning Antwerp (d. Korda), r/u Tashkent (d. Kafelnikov), sf Munich (d. Moya) and qf Marseille and Gstaad (d. Kafelnikov). In doubles he won Basle with Henman. **1998:** (32) A 2, F 1, W 2, US 1. He was r/u St Petersburg and Antwerp (d. Kafelnikov and Rafter), reached sf Split (extended Rusedski to 7–6 fs), Basle and Moscow and qf Toulouse and upset Pioline at Wimbledon (13–11 fs). **1999:** (39) A qf, F 1, W 2, US 1. He showed his liking for St Petersburg again by winning the title there. Elsewhere he reached sf Marseille and Toulouse and qf Australian Open (unseeded, d. Henman) and Moscow, adding upsets of Rusedski at Gstaad and Corretja at Paris Open. In doubles he won Tashkent with Ogorodov. **2000:** A 2, F 2, W 4, US 2. He began the year with qf Auckland, going on in Feb. to win Marseille and London (d. Enqvist and Kafelnikov) back-to-back. Thereafter, though, his best showing was sf Moscow, and he reached no other qf. **2000 HIGHLIGHTS – SINGLES: Australian Open 2r** (d. Delgado 7–6 6–3 7–6, lost W. Black 6–1 2–6 7–6 6–2), **French Open 2r** (d. B. Black 7–5 7–5 6–0, lost Medvedev 6–1 6–2 6–2), **Wimbledon last 16** [unseeded] (d. Squillari 7–5 6–3 7–6, Parmar 7–6 7–5 6–3, Haas 6–4 3–6 6–3 3–6 9–7, lost Popp 6–1 6–4 3–6 4–6 6–1), **US Open 2r** (d. Vinck 6–4 6–1 6–4, lost Corretja [seed 8] 6–3 7–6 6–3); **won** Marseille (d. Arthurs 6–3, Clement 6–4 7–5, Ivanisevic 6–4 3–6 6–2, Grosjean 6–3 6–3, Federer 2–6 6–3 7–6), **won** London (d. Ljubicic 6–4 6–4, Hrbaty 6–3 7–6, Federer 3–6 6–4 6–4, Enqvist 7–5 1–6 6–3, Kafelnikov 6–4 6–4); **sf** Moscow (d. Cherkasov 6–2 6–4, Gustafsson 6–3 6–4, Youzhny 6–7 6–4 7–6, lost Kafelnikov 4–6 6–2 7–5). **CAREER HIGHLIGHTS – SINGLES: Olympics – gold medal 1992** [unseeded] (d. Alami 6–2 4–6 2–1 ret, W. Ferreira 6–4 6–0 6–2, Courier 6–4 6–2 6–1, E. Sanchez 6–4 7–6 3–6 7–6, Ivanisevic 6–3 7–5 6–2, Arrese 7–6 6–3 3–6 4–6 8–6); **French Open – sf 1996** (d. Steeb 6–4 7–6 6–0, Novak 6–2 6–3, Hlasek 6–4 6–4 6–1, Edberg 7–6 6–3 6–3, Karbacher 4–6 4–6 6–3 7–5 6–0, lost Stich 6–3 6–4 6–2), **Australian Open – qf 1999** [unseeded] (d. Woodbridge 6–4 6–2 6–4, Knippschild 6–7 7–6 6–1 6–3, Henman 7–6 6–3 7–5, Ulihrach 6–3 6–4 6–2, lost Enqvist 6–3 6–4 6–4). **CAREER HIGHLIGHTS – DOUBLES:** (with Hlasek) **French Open – won 1992** (d. D. Adams/Olhovskiy 7–6 6–7 7–5).

FABRICE SANTORO (FRA)

Born Tahiti, 7 December 1972; lives London, England; RH; 2HF; 2HB; 5ft 10in; 160lb; turned pro 1989; career singles titles 3; final 2000 ATP ranking 31; 2000 prize money $652,131; career prize money $4,095,861.
Coached by his father, Marcel. Nat champ in 12s, 14s and 16s. **1988:** (571) Won Orange Bowl 16s. **1989:** (235) A –, F 1, W –, US –. Won French Open Jun over Palmer and was No. 2 in ITF Jun rankings. Upset Gomez

at Stuttgart. **1990:** (62) A –, F 2, W 1, US 3. After winning Telford Challenger, he upset Gomez again *en route* to his 1st tour f at Toulouse. Qf Nice (d. Chesnokov) and Bordeaux. Voted Newcomer of the Year. **1991:** (43) A 1, F 4, W –, US 1. Won Brest Challenger, and on the main tour reached qf Adelaide, Sydney, Italian Open, Florence, Indianapolis and Bordeaux and reached last 16 French Open, unseeded. **1992:** (43) A –, F 1, W –, US 1. Made his mark at the Olympics, where he upset Becker and extended Ivanisevic to 8–6 fs in qf. Scored other big upsets during the year as he moved to sf Nice (d. Chesnokov), Gstaad (d. Novacek), Hilversum and New Haven (d. Korda). **1993:** (55) A 2, F 1, W –, US 1. Upset Volkov on his way to f Dubai and appeared in sf Nice (d. Krickstein) plus 3 more qf, including Indian Wells, where he upset Stich. Out 4 months from May to Aug. with a serious thumb injury. **1994:** (47) A 3, F 3, W –, US –. His best performance came at Kitzbuhel, where he upset Gaudenzi and Muster and extended Ivanisevic to 5s in f. He also won Venice Challenger and reached sf Tel Aviv, plus qf Pinehurst, Bordeaux and Montevideo. **1995:** (104) A 2, F 1, W 1, US 1. Reached sf Estoril and qf Palermo, where he won the doubles with Corretja, as well as upsetting Edberg 1r Monte Carlo and Sampras 1r Italian Open. Military service left him with limited opportunities for training and practice. **1996:** (118) A 1, F –, W –, US –. Military service again restricted his schedule. **1997:** (29) A –, F 1, W 1, US 1. After winning Newcastle Challenger, he went on in Oct. to take his 1st title on the main tour at Lyon, unseeded and upsetting Krajicek, Mantilla and Philippoussis. He scored other big upsets on his way to sf Marseille (d. Korda), Monte Carlo (d. Muster and Bruguera), Prague (d. Kuerten and Rios), qf Estoril and Montreal (d. Muster) and removed Bruguera at Stuttgart Eurocard. In doubles he played 2 f with Delaitre and 1 with D. Adams, but won no title. **1998:** (41) A 3, F 3, W –, US 3. He began the year in style at Qatar, where he upset Rusedski and Ivanisevic *en route* to f, unseeded. Although he did not pass qf again, he reached that stage at St Petersburg, Monte Carlo (d. Sampras 6–1 6–1), Hamburg (d. Krajicek) and Basle. He became a force in doubles with Delaitre, winning 4 titles from 6 f and qualifying for a 1st World Doubles Champ, where they reached sf before bowing to Knowles/Nestor. **1999:** (33) A 4, F 1, W 2, US 3. He won Marseille, unseeded, and was r/u Copenhagen, as well as reaching qf Nottingham, Montreal, Washington and Toulouse. In doubles he won the only f he played – Long Island with Delaitre, with whom he played in FRA D Cup team that lost 3–2 to AUS in f. **2000:** (31) A 1, F 2, W 2, US 1. Qatar was again his most successful tourn as he won the title, upsetting Kiefer on the way. He also did well again at Marseille, reaching sf, and added qf appearances at London, Cincinnati (d. Hewitt and Safin), Long Island and Paris Masters, with other notable upsets including Kiefer at Indian Wells, Henman at Rome and Safin at Olympics. In doubles he won Toulouse with Boutter. **2000 HIGHLIGHTS – SINGLES: Australian Open 1r** (lost Krajicek [seed 9] 6–1 6–2 7–5), **French Open 2r** (d. Gustafsson 6–3 3–6 6–4 6–4, lost M. Norman [seed 3] 6–1 6–4 6–2), **Wimbledon 2r** (d. Gaudenzi 6–3 6–2 6–2, lost Gambill 4–6 6–4 6–2 6–2), **US Open 1r** (lost Nestor 7–6 6–4 6–4), **Olympics 3r** (d. Safin [seed 1] 1–6 6–1 6–4); **won** Qatar (d. Burgsmuller 6–4 6–1, Van Lottum 7–6 6–1, Bastl 6–2 6–4, Kiefer 7–5 6–4, Schuttler 3–6 7–5 3–0 ret); **sf** Marseille (d. Wessels 7–5 6–2, Siemerink 6–4 1–6 6–2, Guardiola 6–4 7–6, lost Federer 7–6 7–5). **2000 HIGHLIGHTS – DOUBLES:** (with Boutter) **won** Toulouse (d. Johnson/Norval 7–6 4–6 7–6).

SJENG SCHALKEN (NED)

Born Weert, 8 September 1976; lives Monte Carlo, Monaco; RH; 6ft 3in; 185lb; turned pro 1994; career singles titles 5; final 2000 ATP ranking 22; 2000 prize money $596,918; career prize money $2,292,804.

Coached by Henk van Hulst and Alex Reynders. Won Nat 14s, 16s and 18s. **1994:** (187) Won US Open Jun over Tahiri. In the men's game he won Guayaquil Challenger and upset Vacek at Rosmalen. **1995:** (54) A –, F –, W 1, US 1. Upset Berasategui at Valencia on the way to his 1st title from his 1st f on the senior tour; reached sf Casablanca, qf Rotterdam (as LL) Munich (d. Korda), Palermo (d. Gaudenzi) and Santiago and won Monte Carlo Challenger. In doubles he won Amsterdam with Rios. **1996:** (65) A 1, F 2, W 1, US 3. Won Jakarta and reached qf Monte Carlo (d. Enqvist), Bogota, Beijing and Moscow (d. Courier). **1997:** (60) A 1, F 1, W 1, US 2. A qualifier at Philadelphia, he upset Stoltenberg and took a set off Sampras in sf. Then at Boston in Aug., unseeded and defying a knee injury that had almost caused him to withdraw, he upset Corretja, A. Costa and Rios back-to-back to win the title. In other tourns he reached qf St Polten (d. Henman) and Rosmalen and extended Courier to 8–6 5s at Australian Open. **1998:** (67) A 1, F 1, W 1, US 1. Although he won no title, he reached sf Scottsdale (d. A. Costa) and Singapore, qf Qatar, Philadelphia, St Polten and Boston, and upset Rafter at Rome as LL. **1999:** (45) A 2, F 3, W 3, US 1. He began the year with the title at Auckland (d. Haas), adding sf Boston (d. Rios) and qf Halle, and at Wimbledon he let slip 2 mps v Courier, to whom he lost only 13–11 fs. In doubles he won Amsterdam with Haarhuis. Underwent arthroscopic surgery on right knee 9 Nov. **2000:** A 2, F 1, W 3, US 3. His best performances came in Oct. when he won Tokyo Japan Open (d. Philippoussis and N. Lapentti) and followed the next week with r/u Shanghai (d. N. Lapentti again), where he won the doubles with Haarhuis. Elsewhere he reached qf Qatar, Auckland, Indian Wells (d. Kafelnikov and A. Costa), Stuttgart Masters (d. M. Norman) and Stockholm, and upset Kafelnikov at Hamburg. His 3r match at Wimbledon v Philippoussis went to 20–18 fs and lasted 5hr 1min – the longest singles match to be completed in a day and just 11 min short of Gonzales v Passarell in 1969, in the era before tie-breaks were played. **2000 HIGHLIGHTS – SINGLES: Australian Open 2r** (d. Blanco 7–6 6–4 7–6, lost Agassi [seed 1] 7–5 6–0 6–3), **French Open 1r** (lost Sargsian 5–7 3–6 7–6 6–3 6–2), **Wimbledon 3r** (d. Bastl 6–2 6–4 6–2, C Rochus 6–4 6–3 6–1, lost Philippoussis [seed 10] 4–6 6–3 6–7 7 6 20 18), **US Open 3r** (d. Burgsmuller 6–1 7–6 6–2, Voinea 6–2 6–3 6–1, lost Kiefer [seed 14] 7–5 6–3 6–4); **won** Tokyo Japan Open (d. Srichaphan 7–5 5–7 6–2, Bruguera 6–4 6–2, Mamiit 6–2 6–2, Philippoussis 6–2 6–3, Arazi 4–6 6–3 7–6,

N. Lapentti 6–4 3–6 6–1); **r/u** Shanghai (d. C. Rochus 6–2 6–4, Stoltenberg 1–6 6–3 6–4, N. Lapentti 6–3 6–4, Calatrava 6–3 3–6 6–3, lost M. Norman 6–4 4–6 6–3). **2000 HIGHLIGHTS – DOUBLES:** (with Haarhuis) **won** Shanghai (d. Pala/Vizner 6–2 3–6 6–4).

RAINER SCHUTTLER (GER)
Born Korbach, 25 April 1976; lives Bad Homburg; RH; 5ft 11in; 155lb; turned pro 1995; career singles titles 1; final 2000 ATP ranking 45; 2000 prize money $435,201; career prize money $1,080,057.
Coached by Dirk Hordoff. **1994:** (772). **1995:** (445). **1996:** (329) He made progress on the satellite circuits. **1997:** (123) His 1st qf on the main tour came at Chennai (d. Enqvist), followed by same stage Washington, while on the Challenger circuit he won Echental. **1998:** (111) A –, F –, W 1, US –. He reached qf Split (d. Henman) and Newport and finished the season with the Challenger title at Potorov. **1999:** (48) A 1, F 1, W 2, US 1. Continuing his winning streak, he began the year with his 1st title on the main tour at Qatar as a qualifier (d. Ivanisevic, Pioline and Henman), a result which took him into the top 100. In other tourns he was r/u Chennai, reached qf Copenhagen, upset Ivanisevic at Hamburg, and made his D Cup debut. **2000:** A 2, F 1, W 3, US 3. He played through the qualifying to f Qatar, where he was forced to ret 3s with cramp, and at Australian Open he ret v Henman with stomach injury. Elsewhere he reached qf Memphis, Stuttgart Mercedes, St Petersburg and Stockholm, upset Hewitt in D Cup and removed Haas at US Open. He finished the season by taking the Challenger title at Aachen. **2000 HIGHLIGHTS – SINGLES: Australian Open 2r** (d. Marin 6–3 6–3 6–3, lost Henman [seed 11] 6–2 4–1 ret), **French Open 1r** (lost W. Ferreira 7–6 4–6 6–3 6–2), **Wimbledon 3r** (d. Moya 6–3 6–7 6–3 6–2, Escude 6–4 7–6 7–6, lost Rafter [seed 12] 6–2 7–6 6–3), **US Open 3r** (d. Lareau 7–6 6–2 6–4, Haas 7–6 6–2 6–4, lost H. Lee 6–2 3–6 6–4 6–4), **Olympics 2r** (d. T. Martin 6–2 6–0, lost Kuerten [seed 2] 6–4 6–4); **won** Aachen Challenger (d. Settergren 7–6 1–6 6–1); **r/u** Qatar (d. J. Sanchez 6–2 7–6, Vacek 6–3 6–2, Mirnyi 6–3 6–2, El Aynaoui 6–7 6–4 6–4, lost Santoro 3–6 7–5 3–0 ret).

FRANCO SQUILLARI (ARG)
Born Buenos Aires, 22 August 1975, and lives there; LH; 6ft; 168lb; turned pro 1994; career singles titles 3; final 2000 ATP ranking 14; 2000 prize money $754,458; career prize money $1,455,763.
Coached by Horacio De La Pena. **1992:** (944). **1993:** (391) Won South American Jun Champs. **1994:** (305). **1995:** (433) Began to make an impression on ARG satellite circuits. **1996:** (137) A –, F 2, W –, US –. Upset Moya on the way to qf Kitzbuhel after qualifying. **1997:** (106) A –, F 1, W –, US –. His 1st f on the main tour at Casablanca and his 1st Challenger title at Puerto Rico took him into the top 100 1st time. **1998:** (60) A 2, F –, W 2, US 1. He made his D Cup debut and moved into the top 50 for a while with r/u Palermo, sf Kitzbuhel, qf Atlanta and Bologna (d. Clavet) and the Braunschweig Challenger title. **1999:** (52) A 2, F 1, W 1, US 1. He won his 1st title on the main tour at Munich, unseeded (d. Haas), reached qf Rome as LL (d. Moya) and upset Kafelnikov 2r Barcelona, before finishing the year with the Challenger title in Buenos Aires. **2000:** A 3, F sf, W 1, US 2. He moved into the top 20 with titles at Munich (d. El Aynaoui) and Stuttgart Mercedes, sf Mexico City (d. N. Lapentti) and French Open (unseeded, d. El Aynaoui), plus qf Gstaad and Cincinnati and another upset of N. Lapentti at Monte Carlo. **2000 HIGHLIGHTS – SINGLES: Australian Open 3r** (d. Sirianni 6–3 6–2 6–1, Woodforde 6–4 7–6 3–6 6–4, lost Dosedel 7–5 6–2 6–3), **French Open sf** [unseeded] (d. Popp 3–6 6–3 6–2 6–0, Vanek 7–5 6–3 6–7 6–4, Kucera 6–1 6–4 4–6 6–4, El Aynaoui [seed 15] 6–4 6–1 6–3, A. Costa 6–4 6–4 2–6 6–4, lost M. Norman [seed 3] 6–1 6–4 6–3), **Wimbledon 1r** (lost Rosset 7–5 6–3 7–6), **US Open 2r** [seed 13] (d. Marin 6–3 6–3 7–6, lost H. T. Lee 7–6 7–5 6–2), **Olympics 1r** [seed 10] (lost Alami 6–2 4–6 8–6); **won** Munich (d. Knippschild 6–7 6–4 6–1, Damm 6–2 6–2, El Aynaoui 2–6 6–2 7–6, Mirnyi 6–2 6–4, Haas 6–4 6–4), **won** Stuttgart Mercedes (d. Gonzalez 6–1 6–3, Goellner 4–6 6–2 6–3, Kucera 7–5 6–1, Elsner 7–6 7–6, Gaudio 6–3 3–6 4–6 6–4 6–2); **sf** Mexico City (d. Blanco 3–6 6–4 6–1, Agenor 7–5 6–2, N. Lapentti 6–4 7–6, lost Puerta 6–4 6–1).

SANDON STOLLE (AUS)
Born Sydney, 13 July 1970; lives there and Aventura, Fla; RH; 6ft 4in; 175lb; turned pro 1991; career singles titles 0; final 2000 ATP ranking 3 doubles; 2000 prize money $559,942; career prize money $3,123,643.
Fitness coach Brett Stevens. Son of Fred Stolle. Studied under Harry Hopman in his freshman year of high school; also helped by TCU coach 'Tut' Bartzen. **1989:** (813). **1990:** (228) All-American in doubles with Ruette at Texas Christian Univ. **1991:** (169) A 1, F –, W 2, US –. Qf Brasilia. **1992:** A 2, F –, W 3, US 2. Broke into top 100 May after winning Kuala Lumpur and Taipei Challengers, going on to reach sf Los Angeles on the main tour. **1993:** (199) A 1, F 1, W 2, US –. Won Sydney Outdoor doubles with Stoltenberg, but reached no singles qf all year. **1994:** (182) A2, F –, W –, US –. His strength was again in doubles, in which he won 3 titles with different partners. **1995:** (182) A 1, F –, W 1, US –. Reached qf Queen's (d. Bjorkman) and upset Edberg at Cincinnati. Played 4 doubles f, including his 1st GS at US Open with O'Brien, but won no title. **1996:** (58) A 2, F 1, W 3, US 1. It was a stronger year in singles, in which he reached his 1st f on the main tour at Nottingham and appeared in sf Scottsdale (d. Edberg) and Los Angeles (d. Siemerink), plus qf Dubai (d. Muster), New Delhi and Coral Springs. From 4 doubles f with 3 different partners, he won Ostrava with Suk. **1997:** (84) A 1, F 2, W 3, US –. In singles he reached sf Nottingham, qf Sydney, Philadelphia, Atlanta (d.

Bjorkman) and Newport, and in doubles played 3 f with Suk but won no title. **1998:** (237) A 1, F –, W –, US –. He won his 1st GS title in partnership with Suk at US Open, as well as taking Newport and Los Angeles with Rafter. It was with Suk that he qualified for his 1st World Doubles Champ, although they did not pass rr. In singles his best showings were qf Hong Kong Salem Open and Los Angeles. **1999:** (–) A 2, F –, W 2, US –. He extended Henman to 5s at Australian Open, took a set off Ivanisevic at Wimbledon, and played in winning AUS WT Cup team. Continuing to specialise in doubles, he appeared in 6 f with 4 different partners, winning 1 with Prinosil and 3 with W. Black, with whom he qualified for World Doubles Champ and reached sf. **2000:** A –, F –, W –, US –. He played a total of 12 doubles f with 4 different partners, winning the last 3 – Los Angeles with Kilderry, Indianapolis with Hewitt and Lyon with Haarhuis, with whom he was also r/u French Open and Wimbledon. It was with Haarhuis that he qualified for World Doubles Champ, although they did not progress beyond rr. **2000 HIGHLIGHTS – DOUBLES:** (with Haarhuis unless stated) **r/u French Open** (lost Woodbridge/Woodforde 7–6 6–4), **r/u Wimbledon** (lost Woodbridge/Woodforde 6–3 6–4 6–1); (with Kilderry) **won** Los Angeles (d. Gambill/Humphries w/o), (with Hewitt) **won** Indianapolis (d. Bjorkman/Mirnyi 6–2 3–6 6–3), **won** Lyon (d. Ljubicic/Waite 6–1 6–7 7–6); (with Hewitt) **r/u** Adelaide (lost Woodbridge/Woodforde 6–4 6–2), (with Hewitt) **r/u** Sydney (lost Woodbridge/Woodforde 7–5 6–4), **r/u** Indian Wells (lost O'Brien/Palmer 6–4 7–6), **r/u** Monte Carlo (lost W. Ferreira/Kafelnikov 6–3 2–6 6–1), **r/u** Barcelona (lost Kulti/Tillstrom 6–2 6–7 7–6), (with Arthurs) **r/u** Hamburg (lost Woodbridge/Woodforde 6–7 6–4 6–3), **r/u** 's-Hertogenbosch (lost Damm/Suk 6–4 6–7 7–6). **CAREER HIGHLIGHTS – DOUBLES: US Open** – (with Suk) **won 1998** (d. Knowles/Nestor 4–6 7–6 6–2), (with O'Brien) **r/u 1995** (lost Woodbridge/Woodforde 6–3 6–3); **French Open** – (with Haarhuis) **r/u 2000; Wimbledon** – (with Haarhuis) **r/u 2000.**

FERNANDO VICENTE (ESP)

Born Benicarlo, 8 March 1977; lives Barcelona; RH; 5ft 11in; 165lb; turned pro 1996; career singles titles 2; final 2000 ATP ranking 47; 2000 prize money $419,729; career prize money $1,140,185.

Coached by Alvaro Margets. His twin brother, Jose Maria, also plays the circuit. **1994:** (391) Began to compete on the Spanish satellites. **1995:** (589). **1996:** (151) Reached his 1st qf on the main tour at Marbella. **1997:** (121) Appeared in qf Casablanca, upset Siemerink at Barcelona and broke into top 100 1st time in Aug. **1998:** (54) A –, F 2, W –, US 2. In a productive year he progressed to sf Mallorca (d. A. Costa), played qf Casablanca, Prague, Rome (after qualifying), Stuttgart Mercedes (d. Muster) and Palermo (d. Kuerten), and won 2 Challenger titles. **1999:** (49) A 1, F 2, W 2, US 2. He reached his 1st tour f at Casablanca and followed in June with his 1st title at Merano, unseeded and saving 3 mps in f v Arazi. He went on to reach a 3rd f, being r/u Kitzbuhel (d. Corretja and Lapentti), and on the Challenger circuit won Barcelona. **2000:** A 3, F 4, W 1, US 1. He retained his title at Casablanca and appeared in sf Bogota and qf Santiago, Cincinnati (d. Philippoussis) and Vienna. At Australian Open he upset T. Martin, then at French Open, where he was unseeded, he upset Henman and extended Kafelnikov to 8–6 fs, while Rusedski was his victim in Rome. **2000 HIGHLIGHTS – SINGLES: Australian Open 3r** (d. Berasategui 6–0 6–2 6–2, T. Martin [seed 8] 6–4 2–6 3–6 6–3 7–5, lost Arazi 6–3 6–3 6–2), **French Open last 16** [unseeded] (d. Mirnyi 3–6 5–7 6–3 6–4 6–3, Agenor 6–1 6–0 6–3, Henman [seed 13] 7–5 4–6 6–4 4–6 6–3, lost Kafelnikov [seed 4] 5–7 6–3 5–7 7–6 8–6), **Wimbledon 1r** (lost Godwin 6–7 6–1 3–6 6–2 8–6), **US Open 1r** (lost Henman [seed 11] 6–3 6–3 6–4), **Olympics 2r** (d. Ilie 6–3 6–3, lost Santoro 6–1 6–7 7–5); **won** Casablanca (d. Youzhny 3–6 6–1 6–1, Wiltschnig 6–2 6–3, Arazi 6–7 6–3 6–2, Di Pasquale 6–4 1–6 6–4, Grosjean 6–4 4–6 7–6); **sf** Bogota (d. Tieleman 6–3 6–1, Rodriguez 7–5 7–5, Di Pasquale 6–2 6–1, lost El Aynaoui 1–6 7–6 7–6). **2000 HIGHLIGHTS – DOUBLES:** (with A. Martin) **r/u** Mallorca (lost Llodra/Nargiso 7–6 7–6).

ANDREAS VINCIGUERRA (SWE)

Born Malmo, 19 February 1981, and lives there; LH; 2HB; 5ft 10in; turned pro 1998; career singles titles 1; final 2000 ATP ranking 52; 2000 prize money $310,365.

Coached by Anders Henricsson. He is Swedish but both parents are Italian. **1997:** (1102). **1998:** (637) R/u Australian Open Jun to Jeanpierre and won European Jun Champ. In the senior game he won Oulu Futures. **1999:** (96) He shot through the rankings into the top 100, still being ranked only 390 when he reached f Bastad. Elsewhere he appeared in qf Shanghai (d. Schalken) and Stockholm and won his 1st Challenger title at Szczecin. **2000:** A 3, F 1, W 2, US 1. He won his 1st tour title at Copenhagen in March (unseeded, d. Safin) and was r/u Bastad again. In other tourns he reached qf Marseille, Casablanca (d. Alami) and Stockholm (d. Federer), extended Sampras to 3s at Ericsson Open and won Prostejov Challenger. **2000 HIGHLIGHTS – SINGLES: Australian Open 3r** (d. Gumy 7–6 6–1 6–1, Paes 7–6 6–4 6–3, lost Escude 6–4 6–4 6–3), **French Open 1r** (lost Kuerten [seed 5] 6–0 6–0 6–3), **Wimbledon 2r** (d. Tieleman 7–6 6–1 6–7 6–2, lost Haas 6–3 7–6 6–3), **US Open 1r** (lost Hewitt [seed 9] 2–6 7–5 6–3 6–3), **Olympics 2r** (d. Ruud 6–2 6–4, lost Haas 4–6 6–4 6–2); **won** Copenhagen (d. Rochus 6–2 6–1, Schuttler 3–6 6–4 6–1, Damm 6–3 6–1, Safin 6–3 6–0, Larsson 6–3 7–6), **won** Prostejov Challenger (d. Golmard w/o); **r/u** Bastad (d. Marin 6–4 6–4, Gaudenzi 6–2 7–6, Tarango 6–1 6–2, Hipfl 6–2 6–7 7–6, lost M. Norman 6–1 7–6).

KRISTOF VLIEGEN (BEL)

Born 22 June 1982; lives Maaseik; RH; 2HB; 6ft 2in; 143lb; career singles titles 0.

Coached by Bob Bierkens. **2000:** Won Wimbledon Jun doubles with Coene.

VLADIMIR VOLTCHKOV (BLR)

Born Minsk, 4 July 1978, and lives there; RH; 5ft 11in; 167lb; turned pro 1995; career singles titles 0; final 2000 ATP ranking 46; 2000 prize money $274,488.

Coached by Sergei Srakoun. **1995:** (670). **1996:** (422) Won Wimbledon Jun over Ljubicic. **1997:** (394). **1998:** (151) A –, F –, W 3, US –. Upset Kucera 1r Wimbledon. **1999:** (170) A 1, F 1, W 1, US –. On the Challenger circuit he won Hamburg and Ljubliana. **2000:** A –, F –, W sf, US –. At Wimbledon, ranked 237 and wearing kit borrowed from Safin, he became 1st qualifier to reach sf since McEnroe in 1977, upsetting Pioline along the way. He broke into top 100 and consolidated his position by end of year with sf Brighton, qf Moscow (d. Vicente) and St Petersburg and the Challenger title at Fergana. **2000 HIGHLIGHTS – SINGLES: Wimbledon sf** [unseeded] (d. Chela 6–7 6–3 3–6 6–3 6–0, Pioline 6–3 6–3 2–6 3–6 6–4, El Aynaoui 7–6 7–5 7–6, W. Ferreira 6–3 6–4 7–5, B. Black 7–6 7–6 6–4, lost Sampras [seed 1] 7–6 6–2 6–4), **Olympics 2r** (d. Gaudio 7–6 4–6 6–1, lost Di Pasquale 6–2 6–2); **won** Fergana Challenger (d. Kunitcin 4–6 6–0 6–4); **sf** Brighton (d. Milligan 6–3 6–1, Nargiso w/o, Ljubicic 7–6 4–6 6–3, lost Hrbaty 6–1 6–0).

TODD WOODBRIDGE (AUS)

Born Sydney, 2 April 1971; lives there and Orlando, Fla; RH; 5ft 10in; 165lb; turned pro 1988; career singles titles 2; final 2000 ATP ranking 189 singles, 2 doubles; 2000 prize money $662,871; career prize money $7,715,042.

Coached by Desmond Tyson; trained by Mark Waters. Wife Natasha Provis (sister of Nicole Bradtke who plays women's tour; married 8 April 1995); daughter Zara Rose (born 12 December 2000). **1987:** (420) R/u Australian Open Jun to Stoltenberg, with whom he won the doubles there and at Wimbledon, and in winning AUS World Youth Cup team for 2nd straight year. **1988:** (213) A 2, F 1, W 1, US –. Won Tasmania and in Jun doubles with Stoltenberg won Australian Open, French Open and Wimbledon. **1989:** (131) A 2, F –, W 2, US –. Won Brisbane Challenger, upset Fitzgerald *en route* to sf GP event there and finished the year by winning Hobart Challenger. In Jun doubles won Australian and French Open with J. Anderson and in Jun singles was r/u Wimbledon to Kulti. **1990:** (50) A 2, F 2, W 1, US 1. Upset Chang on the way to his 1st tour f at New Haven and Gilbert *en route* to sf Sydney Indoor. In doubles with various partners he reached 4 f, winning 2, and took US Open mixed with Smylie. **1991:** (77) A 4, F 2, W 3, US 3. Upset Svensson at Australian Open, where he was unseeded, and at French Open extended Becker to 5s. In doubles won 6 titles, 4 with Woodforde, with whom he qualified for ATP Doubles Champ. **1992:** (54) A 1, F 3, W 2, US 2. R/u Seoul (d. Chang), sf Hong Kong, qf Tokyo Suntory and upset Stich at Sydney NSW Open. In doubles with Woodforde won a 1st men's GS title at Australian Open, World Doubles Final and 6 other titles, winning every f they played to finish the year as the top-ranked pairing and were voted ATP Doubles Team of year. In mixed doubles with Sanchez-Vicario won French Open and r/u Australian Open. **1993:** (107) A 3, F 2, W 2, US 2. Was r/u Seoul and reached qf Tokyo Japan Open (d. M. Chang) in singles and continued to excel in doubles. Won his 1st Wimbledon and 4 other titles with Woodforde, took Hong Kong with Wheaton and qualified for ATP World Doubles with Woodforde. They were beaten there in f by Eltingh/Haarhuis, thus ending their record of having won all 17 finals they played since Feb. 1991, equalling McEnroe/Fleming's string in 1979–80. This defeat also ended Woodbridge's personal sequence of winning 21 consec. doubles f, which overtook J. McEnroe's record of 19. Their year ended on another disappointing note when they lost their match in 4–1 D Cup defeat by GER. In mixed doubles he won Australian Open with Sanchez-Vicario and US Open with Sukova. **1994:** (91) A 2, F –, W –, US 3. In singles he was r/u Newport, reached sf Kuala Lumpur and won Wellington Challenger. His year began badly, with a slide down the singles rankings and a lacklustre performance in doubles with Woodforde, notably when they were defeated in D Cup 1r v RUS as AUS were eliminated. However, they regained form to win Wimbledon and finished the year with a total of 5 titles and r/u US Open to qualify for World Doubles Champ where they were r/u. In mixed doubles with Sukova he won Wimbledon and was r/u Australian Open. **1995:** (34) A 1, F 2, W 3, US 3. Won his 1st tour singles title at Coral Springs, where he also took the doubles; was r/u Nottingham and reached sf Vienna, plus 3 more qf. In doubles with Woodforde he won a 3rd Wimbledon, 1st US Open and 5 other titles to qualify for World Doubles Champ, where they lost sf to Connell/Galbraith, although they retained their position as top-ranked pairing and were named Doubles Team of the Year. **1996:** (36) A 3, F 3, W 2, US 1. In singles he was r/u Toronto (d. Rios), reached sf Sydney, Philadelphia, Hong Kong (d. Krajicek) and Nottingham, and upset Siemerink at Olympics, breaking into top 25 in March. He enjoyed another spectacular year in doubles with Woodforde, with whom he was named Doubles Team of the Year again. Despite missing that elusive 1st French Open crown, they won a 4th consec. Wimbledon, and after winning US Open, they tied with Newcombe/Roche and Fleming/J. McEnroe on a record 7 GS titles as a pairing. They crowned their year with Olympic gold, surviving some close matches along the way and playing an Olympic record 34-game 3rd set v Goellner/Prinosil. Their record of 12 titles from 13 f during the year was the most since Fleming/McEnroe's 15 in 1979 and included a 2nd World Doubles Champ. **1997:** (26) A 3, F 2, W sf, US 2. A good year in singles brought him a 2nd career title at Adelaide, r/u Memphis, sf Wimbledon and qf Hong Kong and Tokyo Japan Open, with an upset of Moya at Paris Open. Wimbledon saw him in superb form as he upset M. Chang (8–6 fs) and Rafter in the singles, unseeded, and won the doubles with Woodforde. They were again the season's top doubles pairing, overtaking Fleming/McEnroe and Newcombe/Roche when they won their 8th GS title at Australian Open. A 1st French Open title still eluded them, despite their 1st f there, but their 5th consec. Wimbledon equalled the record of the Dohertys in 1897–1901 and their 9th GS title as a pairing was a record in the open era. With

5 titles across the year, they overtook Casal/E. Sanchez on the all-time list and finished the year with 50 titles, in 3rd place behind Fleming/McEnroe and Hewitt/McMillan on 57. At World Doubles Champ, they needed only to win 1s v Leach/Stark in their last rr match to qualify for sf, but lost in ss. However, they were still clearly the season's top doubles team and were voted ATP Doubles Team of the Year for the 3rd consec. season. **1998:** (65) A 4, F 3, W 3, US 1. In a less profitable year, his best performances in singles were sf Adelaide and Chennai, qf Shanghai, and upsets of Rusedski at Australian Open (where he was unseeded) and Kucera at French Open. He and Woodforde reached 10 doubles f, winning 5 and sharing 1, but taking no GS, although they were r/u Australian Open and Wimbledon. They slipped behind Eltingh/Haarhuis as the top doubles pairing and by end of year Bhupathi/Paes pushed them into 3rd place. However, they continued to set records by becoming the 1st pairing to qualify for the season-ending champ for 8 consec. years, although surprisingly they won no match there. **1999:** (194) A 1, F 1, W 2, US –. In singles his only qf appearance was in Shanghai. Although he was still a force in doubles, appearing in 8 f, he was less dominant, winning just 2 with Woodforde and 1 with Courier. The 2 titles he and Woodforde won were their fewest since 1990, in which they played only 2 tourns together. However, they qualified for a record 9th consec. World Doubles Champ and reached sf where they lost to Lareau/O'Brien, behind whom they finished as No. 3 pairing for the season. His year ended on a high note when he and Woodforde won crucial doubles rubber in D Cup f as AUS d. FRA 3–2 in Nice. **2000:** A 2, F –, W 2, US –. This was his last season with Woodforde, who had announced his intention to retire at end of year, wanting to go out while still on top. They won their 1st 2 tourns of year at Adelaide and Sydney, added Ericsson Open in March, and when they took Hamburg in May they equalled Fleming/McEnroe and Hewitt/McMillan's record 57 titles. Their 1st French Open title took them past the record to stand alone on 58, and they improved on that by adding a 6th Wimbledon and 2 other titles to finish with 61. However, there were disappointments when Hewitt/Mirnyi knocked them out 2r US Open and they failed to crown their final season with Olympic gold when Lareau/Nestor beat them in f 7–6 fs in f. Although they qualified for World Doubles Champ as top pairing, they did not take up their place owing to the impending birth of his first child. He was planning to team with Bjorkman for 2001. In mixed he was r/u Australian Open with Sanchez-Vicario, and the highlight in singles was winning Singapore Challenger. **2000 HIGHLIGHTS – SINGLES: Australian Open 2r** (d. Siemerink 6–4 6–1 6–3, lost Zabaleta 7–6 4–6 6–1 6–4) , **Wimbledon 2r** (d. Siemerink 6–4 3–6 7–6 6–2, lost Rafter [seed 12] 6–3 6–3 6–4); **won** Singapore Challenger (d. Parmar 6–3 6–3). **2000 HIGHLIGHTS – DOUBLES:** (with Woodforde) **won French Open** (d. Haarhuis/Stolle 7–6 6–4), **won Wimbledon** (d. Haarhuis/Stolle 6–3 6–4 6–1), **r/u Olympics silver medal** (lost Lareau/Nestor 5–7 6–3 7–6); **won** Adelaide (d. Hewitt/Stolle 6–4 6–2), **won** Sydney (d. Hewitt/Stolle 7–5 6–4), **won** Ericsson Open (d. Damm/Hrbaty 3–6 6–3 7–5), **won** Hamburg (d. Arthurs/Stolle 6–7 6–4 6–3), **won** Queen's (d. Stark/Taino 6–7 6–3 7–6), **won** Cincinnati (d. E. Ferreira/Leach 7–6 6–4). **MIXED DOUBLES:** (with Sanchez-Vicario) **r/u Australian Open** (lost Palmer/Stubbs 7–5 7–6). **CAREER HIGH- LIGHTS – DOUBLES:** (with Woodforde) **Australian Open – won 1992** (d. Jones/Leach 6–4 6–3 6–4), **won 1997** (d. Lareau/O'Brien 4–6 7–5 7–5 6–3), **r/u 1998** (lost Bjorkman/Eltingh 6–2 5–7 2–6 6–4 6–3); **French Open – won 2000, r/u 1997** (lost Kafelnikov/Vacek 7–6 4–6 6–3); **Wimbledon – won 1993** (d. Connell/Galbraith 6–3 6–4 6–4), **won 1994** (d. Connell/Galbraith 7–6 6–3 6–1), **won 1995** (d. Leach/Melville 7–5 7–6 7–6), **won 1996** (d. B. Black/Connell 4–6 6–4 6–3 6–2), **won 2000, r/u 1998** (lost Eltingh/Haarhuis 2–6 6–4 5–7 10–8); **US Open – won 1995** (d. O'Brien/Stolle 6–3 6–3), **won 1996** (d. Eltingh/Haarhuis 4–6 7–6 7–6), **r/u 1994** (lost Eltingh/Haarhuis 6–3 7–6); **Olympics – won 1996** (d. Broad/Henman 6–4 6–4 6–2); **World Doubles Final – won 1992** (d. Fitzgerald/Jarryd 6–2 7–6 5–7 3–6 6–2), **won 1996** (d. Lareau/O'Brien 6–4 5–7 6–2 7–6), **r/u 1993** (lost Eltingh/Haarhuis 7–6 7–6 6–4), **r/u 1994** (lost Apell/Bjorkman 6–4 4–6 4–6 7–6 6–3). **CAREER HIGHLIGHTS – MIXED DOUBLES:** (with Sanchez-Vicario unless stated) **Australian Open – won 1993** (d. Leach/Garrison-Jackson 7–5 6–4); **French Open – won 1992** (d. Shelton/McNeil 6–2 6–3); **Wimbledon – (with Sukova) won 1994** (d. Middleton/McNeil 3–6 7–5 6–3); **US Open – (with Smylie) won 1990** (d. Pugh/Zvereva 6–4 6–2), (with Sukova) **won 1993** (d. Woodforde/Navratilova 7–5 6–3).

MARK WOODFORDE (AUS)

Born Adelaide, 23 September 1965; lives Rancho Mirage, Cal.; LH; 2HB; 6ft 1in; 175lb; turned pro 1984; career singles titles 4; final 2000 ATP ranking singles, 1 doubles; 2000 prize money $649,410; career prize money $8,324,401.

Coached by John Newcombe and Tony Roche; trained by Mark Waters and also works part-time with Tommy Tucker. Wife Erin (married 15 September 1999). **1984:** (385). **1985:** (127) A 3, F –, W –, US –. **1986:** (181) A –, F 1, W 1, US 1. Won 1st pro title at Auckland and reached sf Bristol. **1987:** (67) A 2, F –, W 2, US 4. Upset Mayotte on his way to last 16 US Open after qualifying. **1988:** (42) A 2, F 2, W 4, US 4. Enjoyed a remarkable year, with success on all surfaces, in which he extended Lendl to 5 close sets in 4 hr 46 min match at Wimbledon, conceding only 10–8 in 5s, upset Edberg and J. McEnroe to reach sf Toronto and beat McEnroe again at US Open, where he was unseeded. Formed a useful doubles partnership with J. McEnroe in autumn. **1989:** (75) A 3, F 3, W 1, US 2. In singles won Adelaide and r/u Brisbane. In doubles won US Open with J. McEnroe and Monte Carlo with Smid. **1990:** (101) A 3, F –, W 4, US –. Upset Chesnokov 2r Australian Open, but was forced to retire in 3r v Wheaton when he tore 2 ligaments in his ankle, requiring surgery. Out of action until June, when he progressed to last 16 Wimbledon, unseeded and a wild card, and in Aug. reached sf New Haven. **1991:** (101) A 4, F 1, W 1, US 1. Upset E. Sanchez at Australian Open (unseeded), Chesnokov in reaching qf Copenhagen and Korda 1r Moscow. Won 4 doubles titles with Woodbridge to qualify for ATP Doubles Champ. **1992:** (40) A 3, F 1, W 2, US 3. In singles he was r/u Los Angeles and Antwerp (d. Lendl and Chang) and reached qf Singapore, Tampa and US CC. With Woodbridge took Australian Open doubles, World Doubles Final and 6 other titles, winning every f they played to finish the year as the top pairing and voted ATP Doubles Team of year. In mixed doubles with Provis, he won Australian Open and US Open. **1993:** (28) A 2, F 3, W 2, US 1. Won Philadelphia singles, beating Clavet and M. Chang on his way to f, where Lendl was forced to retire, and followed with an upset of Washington *en route* to sf Scottsdale. He also appeared in qf Sydney (d. Medvedev), LIPC (d. Courier), New Haven and Paris Open and broke into the top 25. At Wimbledon he won a 2nd men's doubles GS title with Woodbridge and took mixed with Navratilova. After Stockholm he and Woodbridge had won all 17 finals they played since Feb. 1991, equalling McEnroe/Fleming's string in 1979–80, but their run was ended by Eltingh/Haarhuis in f ATP World Doubles. Further disappointment followed when they lost in D Cup f as GER beat AUS 4–1. **1994:** (43) A 1, F 3, W 2, US 1. Upset Krajicek *en route* to f Los Angeles, Costa at LIPC, Lendl on his way to sf Coral Springs, Muster at Cincinnati, Ivanisevic at Indianapolis, and Courier at Paris Open, as well as reaching sf Pinehurst and Sydney Indoor. In doubles he and Woodbridge made a poor start to the year with failure again in D Cup as AUS lost to RUS, but they went on to win Wimbledon and r/u US Open. With various partners, he won 7 titles from 10 f, qualifying with Woodbridge for World Doubles Champ, where they were r/u. **1995:** (51) A 3, F 2, W 3, US 2. In singles he reached sf Adelaide (d. Kafelnikov), Coral Springs and Nottingham, played 3 more qf and upset Courier at LIPC. In doubles with Woodbridge he won Wimbledon, US Open and 5 other titles to qualify for World Doubles Champ, where they lost sf to Connell/Galbraith, although they still finished the year as top-ranked pairing and were named Doubles Team of the Year. When he won French Open mixed with Neiland, he had won a mixed title at all 4 GS tourns. **1996:** (27) A sf, F 1, W 1, US 1. The highlight of his singles year came at Australian Open where, unseeded, he took advantage of Sampras's removal from his half of the draw to sweep to sf, upsetting Enqvist on the way. He reached the same stage Philadelphia, Tokyo Japan Open (d. Enqvist again) and Toulouse, plus qf Sydney, Memphis and Queen's and made a 1st appearance in the top 20 on 22 April. In doubles with Woodbridge won a record 4th consec. Wimbledon and, after winning US Open, they tied with Newcombe/Roche and Fleming/J. McEnroe on a record 7 GS titles as a pairing. They also won Olympic gold, surviving some close matches along the way and playing an Olympic record 34-game 3rd set v Goellner/Prinosil. They finished a superb season with the World Doubles title, taking to 12 their titles from 13 f during the year – the most since Fleming/McEnroe's 15 in 1979 – and were voted Doubles Team of the Year again. In mixed doubles with Neiland he won Australian Open (where he and Woodbridge were surprisingly beaten 1r) and was r/u Wimbledon. **1997:** (46) A 3, F 4, W 4, US 3. Although it was a quieter year in singles, he reached sf Indianapolis (d. Rios and Agassi), qf Tokyo Japan Open (d. Rosset), Coral Springs and Newport, as well as upsetting A. Costa at French Open and Kafelnikov at US Open. He and Woodbridge were again the season's top duo with 5 titles across the year, which took them to 50, ahead of Casal/E. Sanchez and into 3rd place on the all-time list behind Fleming/McEnroe and Hewitt/McMillan on 57. Their 8th GS title at Australian Open took them ahead of Fleming/McEnroe and Newcombe/Roche in GS titles, and their 5th consec. Wimbledon, equalled the record of the Dohertys in 1897–1901. This 9th GS title as a pairing was a record in the open era, but they were still unable to add an elusive 1st French Open title, despite reaching f there 1st time. At World Doubles Champ they needed only to take a set off Leach/Stark in their last rr match to qualify for sf, but they were beaten in ss. However, they still finished the season head and shoulders above any other pairing and were voted ATP Doubles Team of the Year for the 3rd consec. season. **1998:** (58) A 1, F 1, W 3, US 1. At Singapore in Oct. he reached his 1st singles f since 1994 (d. Ivanisevic and won the doubles). He also upset Sampras *en route* to sf Queen's, and appeared in qf San Jose, Memphis, Chennai and Shanghai. He and Woodbridge played 10 doubles f, winning 5 and sharing 1, but they did not add to their collection of GS, although they were r/u Australian Open and Wimbledon. They were displaced as top pairing by Eltingh/Haarhuis, and then Bhupathi/Paes pushed them down to 3rd place. However, they continued to set records as the 1st pair to qualify for the season-ending champs for 8 consec. years, although surprisingly they won no match there. **1999:** (128) A 2, F 1, W 2, US 2. Singles highlights were sf finish at Scottsdale and qf San Jose. His appearance at US Open was his 36th consec. in GS singles, tying as the most among current players with W. Ferreira and Raoux. He and Woodbridge were still a considerable force in doubles, although less invincible, winning just 2 of the 7 f they reached. They qualified for World Doubles Champ for a record 9th consec. season, losing there to Lareau/O'Brien, behind whom they finished as No. 3 pairing for the season. The season finished in triumph as he and Woodbridge won crucial doubles rubber in D Cup f as AUS d. FRA 3–2 in Nice. **2000:** A 2, F –, W 1, US –. He announced his intention to retire at end of year, wanting to go out while still on top – and it proved to be an excellent year. He and Woodbridge won their 1st 2 tourns of year at Adelaide and Sydney, added Ericsson Open in March, and when they took a 4th title at Hamburg, they equalled Fleming/McEnroe's and Hewitt/McMillan's record of 57 in a career. Their 1st French Open took them past the record to stand alone on 58 and after adding a 6th Wimbledon and 2 other titles, they finished on 61. However, it wasn't quite the perfect finish as Hewitt/Mirnyi knocked them out 2r US Open and they failed to crown their final season with Olympic gold when Lareau/Nestor beat them in 7–6 fs in f. Although they qualified as first pairing for World Doubles Champ, they did not take up their place because of the impending birth of Woodbridge's first child. His last D Cup appearance also failed to provide a dream finale; partnered by Stolle in the absence of Woodbridge, they were beaten by Balcello/Corretja as ESP won f 3–1 in Barcelona. So he finished his career with a further 8 men's doubles titles, taking his total to 67, with 5 mixed and 4 singles. **2000 HIGHLIGHTS**

– SINGLES: Australian Open 2r (d. Sanguinetti 6–3 6–4 7–6, lost Squillari 6–4 7–6 3–6 6–4), **Wimbledon 1r** (lost M. Norman [seed 3] 6–4 6–2 2–0 ret). **2000 HIGHLIGHTS – DOUBLES:** (with Woodbridge) **won French Open** (d. Haarhuis/Stolle 7–6 6–4), **won Wimbledon** (d. Haarhuis/Stolle 6–3 6–4 6–1), **Olympics silver medal** (lost Lareau/Nestor 5–7 6–3 7–6); **won** Adelaide (d. Hewitt/Stolle 6–4 6–2), **won** Sydney (d. Hewitt/Stolle 7–5 6–4), **won** Ericsson Open (d. Damm/Hrbaty 3–6 6–3 7–5), **won** Hamburg (d. Arthurs/Stolle 6–7 6–4 6–3), **won** Queen's (d. Stark/Taino 6–7 6–3 7–6), **won** Cincinnati (d. E. Ferreira/Leach 7–6 6–4). **CAREER HIGHLIGHTS – SINGLES: Australian Open – sf 1996** [unseeded] (d. Matsuoka 2–1 ret, Sinner 6–4 6–1 6–4, Clavet 4–6 7–6 6–2 6–4, Philippoussis 6–2 6–2 6–2, Enqvist 6–4 6–4 6–4, lost Becker 6–4 6–2 6–0). **CAREER HIGHLIGHTS – DOUBLES:** (with Woodbridge unless stated) **Australian Open – won 1992** (d. Jones/Leach 6–4 6–3 6–4), **won 1997** (d. Lareau/O'Brien 4–6 7–5 7–5 6–3), **r/u 1998** (lost Bjorkman/Eltingh 6–2 5–7 2–6 6–4 6–3); **French Open – won 2000, r/u 1997** (lost Kafelnikov/Vacek 7–6 4–6 6–3) **Wimbledon – won 1993** (d. Connell/ Galbraith 6–3 6–4 6–4), **won 1994** (d. Connell/Galbraith 7–6 6–3 6–1), **won 1995** (d. Leach/Melville 7–5 7–6 7–6), **won 1996** (d. B. Black/Connell 4–6 6–4 6–3 6–2), **won 1997** (d. Eltingh/Haarhuis 7–6 7–6 5–7 6–3), **won 2000, r/u 1998** (lost Eltingh/Haarhuis 2–6 6–4 7–6 5–7 10–8); **US Open** – (with J. McEnroe) **won 1989** (d. Flach/Seguso 6–4 4–6 6–3 6–3), **won 1995** (d. O'Brien/Stolle 6–3 6–3), **won 1996** (d. Eltingh/Haarhuis 4–6 7–6 7–6), **r/u 1994** (lost Eltingh/Haarhuis 6–3 7–6); **Olympics – won 1996** (d. Broad/Henman 6–4 6–4 6–2); **World Doubles Final – won 1992** (d. Fitzgerald/Jarryd 6–2 7–6 5–7 3–6 6–3), **won 1996** (d. Lareau/O'Brien 6–4 5–7 6–2 7–6), **r/u 1993** (lost Eltingh/Haarhuis 7–6 7–6 6–4), **r/u 1994** (lost Apell/Bjorkman 6–4 4–6 4–6 7–6 7–6). **CAREER HIGHLIGHTS – MIXED DOUBLES:** (with Provis unless stated) **Australian Open – won 1992** (d. Woodbridge/Sanchez-Vicario 6–3 4–6 11–9), (with Neiland) **won 1996** (d. L. Jensen/Arendt 4–6 7–5 6–0); **French Open** – (with Neiland) **won 1995** (d. De Jager/Hetherington 7–6 7–6); **Wimbledon** – (with Navratilova) **won 1993** (d. Nijssen/Bollegraf 6–3 6–4); **US Open – won 1992** (d. Nijssen/Sukova 4–6 6–3 6–3).

1 MARTINA HINGIS (SUI)

Born: Kosice, Czechoslovakia, 30 September 1980.
Lives: Trubbach (moved to Switzerland at age 7).
Father: Karol. **Mother:** Melanie Molitor, a former Czech champion, who named her daughter after Martina Navratilova. **Boyfriend:** Magnus Norman, for much of 2000.

Agent: Octagon. **Coach:** Her mother, Melanie Molitor.
Turned pro: 1994.
Height: 5ft 7in (1.70m). **Weight:** 130lb (59kg).

Rankings: 1994: 87; **1995:** 16; **1996:** 4; **1997:** 1; **1998:** 2; **1999:** 1; **2000:** 1 singles, 3 doubles. **Highest:** 1 (31 March 1997).

2000 Prize Money: $3,457,049. **Career Earnings:** $15,080,325. **Career Titles:** 36.

Style: Despite an apparent frailty of physique, she hits her groundstrokes with intimidating power and accuracy, thanks to the natural gift of split-second timing which allows her to take the ball on the rise. Her control of the racket face allows her to project the ball at unexpected angles so that her opponents are continually surprised and appear off balance. Her natural volleying skills make her an exceptional doubles player. Even stronger and fitter in 2000 she still struggled to hold her own against bigger and better-trained athletes. Although a natural winner, with confidence bordering on arrogance, she no longer dominates her peers.

CAREER HIGHLIGHTS (year: (titles))
1993: Won French Open Jun over Courtois, becoming, at age 12, the youngest to win a Jun GS title. Won the title at Langentha in her 1st Futures event. **1994:** Ranked No. 1 in ITF Jun singles after she won French Open over Jeyaseelan and Wimbledon over Jeon (becoming the youngest Jun champ there at 13 years 276 days), was r/u US Open to Tu and won European Champs; in Jun doubles, she won French Open with Nagyova. Having played 3 satellite events, she made her debut on the senior tour earlier than expected in Oct., in order to beat the new eligibility rules coming into effect in Jan. 1995. She was allowed to play only 3 tourns before returning to her private school. Her 1st appearance was at Zurich, where she beat Fendick (becoming, at 14 years 3 months 17 days, the youngest player to win a singles match in Open era) before losing to Pierce. She followed with qf at both Filderstadt and Essen where she beat Hack. **1995:** In a year in which she was voted Most Impressive Newcomer, she reached her 1st tour f at Hamburg, upsetting Novotna and Huber, surprised M. Maleeva at US Open and broke into top 20 in June, only 8 months after joining the tour. She also reached qf Paris Open (d. Halard) and played 2 doubles f, winning Hamburg with G. Fernandez. When she beat Watanabe at Australian Open, she became the youngest to win a singles match there in the Open era. **1996: (2)** *Filderstadt, Oakland*. At 15 years 3 months 22 days and unseeded, she became the youngest to reach qf Australian Open, upsetting Schultz-McCarthy on the way, and followed in May with one of the major upsets of the year when she removed Graf on her way to f Italian Open. At Wimbledon, aged 15 years 282 days, she became the youngest to win a title there when she and Sukova took the doubles – being 3 days younger than Lottie Dod when she won the singles in 1887 – and was the 1st Swiss woman to win a title at Wimbledon. She broke into the top 10 on 7 Oct., took her 1st title on the main tour at Filderstadt a week later (upsetting Sanchez-Vicario, Davenport and Huber back-to-back), and played her next f the week after that, losing in Zurich to Novotna. Her 2nd title came in tremendous style at Oakland, where she upset Seles 6–2 6–0 in f, inflicting the most lop-sided defeat of the former No. 1's career. After qualifying for her 1st Chase Champs in both singles and doubles (with Sukova), she extended Graf to 5s in f, but was virtually immobilised towards the end by cramp and was unable to take advantage of Graf's back and knee injuries. She also reached sf Tokyo Toray (d. Sabatini), following with the same stage at US Open (d. Sanchez-Vicario and Novotna) and Chicago (d. Davenport), plus qf Hamburg and the title at Prostejov Futures. At 16 years 1 month and 11 days, she became the youngest player, male or female, to pass $1m in earnings in a season.

Voted Most Improved Player of the Year. **1997: (12)** *AUSTRALIAN OPEN, WIMBLEDON, US OPEN, Sydney, Tokyo Pan Pacific, Paris Open, LIPC, FC Cup, Stanford, San Diego, Filderstadt, Philadelphia.* Her remarkable year began in tremendous style at Australian Open, where she became the youngest GS winner this century, losing no set on her way to the title, and was the 1st to win both singles and doubles there since Navratilova in 1985. On 31 March, she overtook the injured Graf at the top of the rankings, becoming the 7th woman to be ranked No. 1, and the youngest of all, aged 16 years 6 months and 1 day. At LIPC she d. Seles in f in 44 mins, becoming the 1st woman to have earned $1m by end March. She beat Seles again in f FC Cup, coming from 2–5 down in 3s tb having earlier led 5–2 fs. In April she fell from a horse and suffered a slight tear of the posterior cruciate ligament in her left knee, for which she underwent arthroscopic surgery on 21 April. She was back in action at French Open, where Majoli inflicted her 1st defeat of the year in f. She interrupted their match with a 5-minute bathroom break and later incurred a code violation for slamming down her racket. This ended her winning streak of 37 matches, but by end of French Open she had already qualified for Chase Champs. At Wimbledon she became the youngest singles champion there this century. Until Chase Champs, she had failed to reach sf only at Zurich in Oct., when Raymond beat her in qf, and through the year she had been beaten only by Majoli, Davenport, Coetzer and Raymond. However, towards the end of the year, she was showing signs of tiring both physically and mentally, missing Chicago with an injury to her right heel and being extended to 3s in all 4 matches at Philadelphia. At Chase Champs, Schultz-McCarthy stretched her before retiring and Pierce was eventually too much for her, winning their qf 7–5 3s. So Hingis finished an extraordinary year firmly at the top of the rankings, but looking less invincible than she had in the summer. In addition to her singles triumphs, she was also a considerable force in doubles. She had been approached by Navratilova, who suggested that they might play GS doubles together, but she turned down the invitation from her former idol, wanting to pair with someone with whom she could play more often, although in fact she played with 6 different partners in reaching 9 doubles f. She won both singles and doubles at Australian Open (with Zvereva), Paris Open (Novotna), FC Cup (M. J. Fernandez), Stanford (Davenport), plus San Diego and Filderstadt (both with Sanchez-Vicario), and also took doubles titles at Leipzig (with Novotna) and Zurich (with Sanchez-Vicario). It was with Sanchez-Vicario that she qualified for Chase Champs, but they fared little better than she had in the singles, losing 1r to finish the year on a surprisingly downbeat note. **1998: (5)** *AUSTRALIAN OPEN, Indian Wells, Hamburg, Rome, Chase Champs.* She began the year at Sydney sporting a new look, with her hair darkened and browning contact lenses, seeming flat and lacking *joie de vivre* as she lost 2r to V. Williams. At Australian Open, though, she was more her old self as she became the youngest to retain a GS title, taking the doubles as well with Lucic. And that was much the pattern of her year, with ups and downs, but rarely reaching the heights of the previous year. The ups saw her qualify for the season-ending champs after only 23 weeks – the fastest ever – and her part in taking SUI to 1st ever Fed Cup f. The downs included the loss of her No. 1 ranking on 12 Oct. to Davenport and failure to add any more to her collection of GS singles titles, losing French Open sf to Seles, Wimbledon same stage to Novotna and US Open f to Davenport. However, her season ended on another high note when she added a 1st Chase Champs title to her collection, defeating Davenport in a lacklustre f to finish her year in triumph, albeit at No. 2 in the rankings. Her other titles all came in the first half of the year, and in the second half she seemed more vulnerable, as well as being affected by injury – she ret with leg cramps at 5–5 fs v Schnyder at GS Cup and missed Zurich with an ankle strain. However, she remained firmly at No. 2 with her 5 titles; r/u Tokyo Pan Pacific and Los Angeles; sf LIPC, San Diego, Montreal and GS Cup; qf Berlin, Filderstadt and Philadelphia. She had another terrific year in doubles, winning 9 of 10 f with 4 different partners and collecting a calendar year GS as she took Australian Open with Lucic and added French Open, Wimbledon and US Open with Novotna, with whom she was voted Doubles Team of the Year. They qualified together for Chase Champs, but disappointingly lost 1r to Basuki/Vis. **1999: (7)** *AUSTRALIAN OPEN, Tokyo Toray, FC Cup, Berlin, San Diego, Toronto, Filderstadt.* The year began positively at Australian Open, where, for the 3rd time in succession she won both singles and doubles – with Kournikova. She returned to No. 1 on 8 Feb. after winning Tokyo Toray, to which she added FC Cup, Berlin, San Diego, Toronto and Filderstadt during the year. In f French Open, with an extraordinary display of petulance and gamesmanship, she was awarded a point penalty for unsportsmanlike conduct, and took her defeat by and the crowd's support of Graf very badly. She then separated from her mother, saying she wanted to go it alone and to be more independent without anyone telling her what to do. However,

Wimbledon, her 1st tourn without her mother, was disastrous: she could salvage only 2 games in her 1r defeat by Dokic and withdrew from the doubles with 'a recurring medical problem'. She lost the No. 1 position again on 5 July but, reunited with her mother, she returned to the top on 9 Aug. after winning San Diego. At US Open she was r/u to S. Williams and at Chase Champs it was Davenport who got the better of her in f. However, in the rankings she managed to keep Davenport at bay to finish the year as No. 1, with her 7 titles, r/u French Open, US Open, Sydney, Zurich, Philadelphia and Chase Champs, plus sf LIPC, Rome, Manhattan Beach and GS Cup and qf Paris Open and Indian Wells. In doubles she played 8 f, winning 1 with Novotna (whom she later discarded as a partner, describing her as 'too old and slow') and 5 with Kournikova, including Chase Champs. **2000: (10)** *Tokyo Pan Pacific, Ericsson Open, Hamburg, 's-Hertogenbosch, Montreal, Filderstadt, Zurich, Moscow, Philadelphia, Chase Champs.* Her loss to Davenport in f Australian Open was her 1st defeat there since qf 1996 and left her for 1st time in 4 years without a current GS title. That situation did not change all year, as she lost sf French Open to Pierce and both qf Wimbledon and sf US Open to V. Williams. However, she was the undoubted No. 1 and finished the year with the title at Chase Champs, as well as 9 others. She won both singles and doubles at Tokyo Pan Pacific (with Pierce), Montreal (with Tauziat), Filderstadt (losing only 10 games on her way to the title), Zurich (for her 1st home title), followed the next week by Philadelphia and finally Chase Champs (all with Kournikova). She also took the singles at Ericsson Open, Hamburg, 's-Hertogenbosch and Moscow and the doubles at French Open with Pierce, with whom she was r/u Australian Open. Her defeat by Davenport at Indian Wells was the 5th in succession at the hands of her rival for the top rank-ing, although she gained her revenge at Ericsson Open. However, it was at that point that Davenport replaced her at the top of the rankings, although she was back as No. 1 on 8 May, and stayed there for rest of year. Elsewhere she shared Scottsdale with Davenport when their final was not played, was r/u Indian Wells and reached sf Sydney, Berlin, Los Angeles, French Open and US Open, plus qf Wimbledon and San Diego. She withdrew Rome with Plantar Fascitis (aggravated inflammation) of left foot, resting it and receiving treatment in TCH before French Open. At Chase Champs she played through cramps to become 1st since Novotna 1997 to take both singles and doubles there.

PRINCIPAL 2000 RESULTS – won 10, shared 1, r/u 2, sf 5 (detailed Grand Slam results follow) **won** Tokyo Pan Pacific (d. Raymond 6–3 7–5, Kournikova 6–0 6–2, Rubin 7–6 6–4, Testud 6–3 7–5), **won** Ericsson Open (d. Drake 6–1 6–4, Sidot 6–0 6–3, Clijsters 6–0 6–4, Coetzer 6–3 6–1, Seles 6–0 6–0, Davenport 6–3 6–2), **won** Hamburg (d. Plischke 6–4 6–1, Kournikova 3–6 6–2 6–4, Huber 6–3 6–2, Sanchez-Vicario 6–3 6–3), **won** 's-Hertogenbosch (d. Nejedly 6–0 6–2, Black w/o, Capriati 7–5 6–2, Dragomir 6–2 3–0 ret), **won** Montreal (d. Petrova 6–1 6–3, Hrdlickova 6–1 6–4, Testud 6–4 4–6 6–3, C. Martinez 6–3 6–2, S. Williams 0–6 6–3 3–0 ret), **won** Filderstadt (d. Henin 6–3 3–0 ret, Van Roost 6–2 6–1, Sanchez-Vicario 6–1 6–0, Clijsters 6–0 6–3), **won** Zurich (d. Dokic 6–3 6–2, Myskina 6–0 6–4, Capriati 6–3 6–2, Davenport 6–4 4–6 7–5), **won** Moscow (d. Hrdlickova 6–0 6–1, Dementieva 6–0 6–7 7–5, Mauresmo 7–5 6–3, Kournikova 6–3 6–1), **won** Philadelphia (d. Bovina 6–4 6–1, Kournikova 6–4 6–0, Tauziat 6–1 6–2, lost Davenport 7–6 6–4), **won** Chase Champs; **shared** Scottsdale (d. Rubin 6–3 6–3, Testud 6–4 6–2, Pierce 6–4 6–3, final v Davenport not played); **r/u** Australian Open, **r/u** Indian Wells (d. Frazier 6–3 6–3, Sugiyama 6–1 6–2, Schett 6–1 6–1, Seles 6–3 6–1, Pierce 6–4 6–2, lost Davenport 4–6 6–4 6–0); **sf** French Open, **sf** US Open, **sf** Sydney (d. Barabanschikova 6–0 6–2, Van Roost 6–1 ret, lost Mauresmo 7–5 6–3), **sf** Berlin (d. Gagliardi 6–2 6–2, Talaja 7–6 6–3, Testud 7–5 5–7 6–2, lost C. Martinez 6–4 6–4), **sf** Los Angeles (d. Rubin 5–7 7–5 6–1, Frazier 6–2 6–1, lost S. Williams 4–6 6–2 6–3). **DOUBLES:** (with Kournikova unless stated) (with Pierce) **r/u** **Australian Open** (lost Raymond/Stubbs 5–0 ret), (with Pierce) **won French Open** (d. Ruano Pascual/Suarez 6–2 6–4); (with Pierce) **won** Tokyo Pan Pacific (d. Fusai/Tauziat 6–4 6–1), (with Tauziat) **won** Montreal (d. Halard-Decugis/Sugiyama 6–3 3–6 6–4), **won** Filderstadt (d. Sanchez-Vicario/Schett 6–4 6–2), **won** Zurich (d. Po/Sidot 6–3 6–4), **won** Philadelphia (d. Raymond/Stubbs 6–2 7–5), **won** Chase Champs (d. Arendt/Bollegraf 6–2 6–3); (with Pierce) **r/u** Sydney (lost Halard-Decugis/Sugiyama 6–0 6–3), **r/u** Moscow (lost Halard-Decugis/Sugiyama 4–6 6–4 7–6).

CAREER GRAND SLAM RECORD
AUSTRALIAN OPEN – Played 6, won 3, r/u 1, qf 1
1995: 2r d. Watanabe 6–0 7–6, lost Nagatsuka 6–3 6–4. **1996: qf** [unseeded] d. Nejedly 6–1 6–1, Paulus 6–1 6–4, Endo 6–1 6–4, Schultz-McCarthy [11] 6–1 6–4, lost Coetzer [16] 7–5 4–6 6–1. **1997: won** [seed 4] d. Rittner 6–1 7–5, Raymond 6–4 6–2, Schett 6–2 6–1, Dragomir 7–6 6–1, Spirlea [8] 7–5 6–2, M. J. Fernandez [14] 6–1 6–3, Pierce 6–2 6–2. **1998: won** [seed 1] d. Probst 6–1 6–2, Rittner 7–5 6–1, Kournikova 6–4 4–6 6–4, Basuki 6–0 6–0, Pierce [5] 6–2 6–3, Huber [10] 6–1 2–6 6–1, Martinez [8] 6–2 6–3. **1999: won** [seed 2] d. Osterloh 6–1 6–2, Dementieva 6–3 6–2, Dokic 6–1 6–2, Coetzer [16] 6–3 6–7 6–1, Pierce [7] 6–3 6–4, Seles [6] 6–2 6–4, Mauresmo 6–2 6–3. **2000: r/u** [seed 1] d. Lucic 6–1 6–2, Henin 6–3 6–3, Molik 6–2 6–3,

Testud [12] 6–1 7–6, Sanchez-Vicario [13] 6–1 6–1, C. Martinez [10] 6–3 6–2, lost Davenport [2] 6–1 7–5.

FRENCH OPEN – Played 6, r/u 2, sf 2
1995: 3r d. Wiesner 2–6 6–3 7–5, De Swardt 6–1 6–7 6–2, lost Davenport [7] 4–6 6–2 6–2. **1996: 3r** [seed 15] d. Schett 6–3 6–0, Begerow 7–5 7–5, lost Habsudova 4–6 7–5 6–4. **1997: r/u** [seed 1] d. Nagyova 6–0 6–2, Pizzichini 3–6 6–4 6–1, Kournikova 6–1 6–3, Paulus [16] 6–3 0–6 6–0, Sanchez-Vicario [6] 6–2 6–2, Seles [3] 6–7 7–5 6–4, lost Majoli [9] 6–4 6–2. **1998: sf** [seed 1] d. Sanchez Lorenzo 6–2 6–1, Babel 6–1 6–2, Habsudova 6–3 6–2, Smashnova 6–1 6–2, V. Williams [8] 6–3 6–4, lost Seles [6] 6–3 6–2. **1999: r/u** [seed 1] d. Hopmans 6–1 6–4, Mauresmo 6–3 6–3, Hrdlickova 6–3 6–4, Dragomir 6–3 7–6, Schwartz 6–2 6–2, Sanchez-Vicario [7] 6–3 6–2, lost Graf [6] 4–6 7–5 6–3. **2000: sf** [seed 1] d. Appelmans 6–0 6–1, Abe 6–4 7–5, Garbin 6–1 6–0, Dragomir 6–3 0–6 6–1, Rubin 6–1 6–3, lost Pierce [6] 6–4 5–7 6–2.

WIMBLEDON – Played 6, won 1, sf 1, qf 1
1995: 1r lost Graf [1] 6–3 6–1. **1996: last 16** [seed 16] d. Nejedly 6–2 6–2, Viollet 6–1 6–1, Wild 6–3 2–6 6–1, lost Graf [1] 6–1 6–4. **1997: won** [seed 1] d. Kremer 6–4 6–4, Barabanschikova 6–2 6–2, Arendt 6–1 6–3, Appelmans 6–1 6–3, Chladkova 6–3 6–2, Kournikova 6–3 6–2, Novotna [3] 2–6 6–3 6–3. **1998: sf** [seed 1] d. Raymond 7–5 6–3, Makarova 7–6 6–4, Likhovtseva 6–2 6–1, Tanasugarn 6–3 6–2, Sanchez-Vicario [5] 6–3 3–6 6–3, lost Novotna [3] 6–4 6–4. **1999: 1r** [seed 1] lost Dokic 6–2 6–0. **2000: qf** [seed 1] d. Montolio 6–1 6–2, Yi 6–4 6–1, Talaja 6–2 6–2, Huber [11] 6–1 6–2, lost V. Williams [5] 6–3 4–6 6–4.

US OPEN – Played 6, won 1, r/u 2, sf 2
1995: [unseeded] d. Feber 6–2 6–3, M. Maleeva [8] 4–6 6–4 6–2, Hy-Boulais 4–6 6–1 6–4, lost Sabatini [9] 6–2 6–4. **1996: sf** [seed 16] d. Montolio 6–1 6–0, Oremans 6–4 6–4, Kijimuta 6–2 6–2, Sanchez-Vicario [3] 6–1 3–6 6–4, Novotna [7] 7–6 6–4, lost Graf [1] 7–5 6–3. **1997: won** [seed 1] d. Whitlinger-Jones 6–0 6–1, Chladkova 6–1 6–2, Likhovtseva 7–5 6–2, Labat 6–0 6–2, Sanchez-Vicario [10] 6–3 6–2, Davenport [6] 6–2 6–4, V. Williams 6–0 6–4. **1998: r/u** [seed 1] d. Olsza 6–2 6–0, Majoli 7–6 6–0, Mauresmo 4–6 6–2 6–2, Dechy 6–4 6–4, Seles 6–4 6–4, Novotna [3] 3–6 6–1 6–4, lost Davenport [2] 6–3 7–5. **1999: r/u** [seed 1] d. Hrdlickova 6–1 7–5, Pitkowski 6–1 6–1, Kloesel 6–3 6–1, Sanchez-Vicario [10] 6–4 7–5, Huber 6–2 6–0, V. Williams [3] 6–1 4–6 6–3, lost S. Williams [7] 6–3 7–6. **2000: sf** [seed 1] d. Jidkova 6–3 6–1, Brandi 6–1 6–1, Garbin 6–1 6–0, Testud [11] 6–2 6–1, Seles [6] 6–0 7–5, lost V. Williams [3] 4–6 6–3 7–5.

OLYMPIC RECORD
1996: (Atlanta) 2r [seed 15] d. Schad 6–0 6–1, lost Sugiyama 6–4 6–4.

CAREER FED CUP RECORD
1995: April *(Euro/Africa Group 1 in ESP, Clay): Round-robin LAT d. SUI 2–1.* R2 d. L. Neiland 6–1 6–2; R3 (with G. Dondit) lost A. Blumberga/Neiland 7–5 5–7 7–5. *Round-robin SUI d. FIN 3–0.* R2 d. N. Dahlman 6–1 7–6; R3 (with J. Manta) d. H. Aalto/Dahlman 6–1 6–1. *Round-robin BLR d. SUI 2–1.* R2 lost N. Zvereva 6–3 3–6 6–3; R3 (with Manta) d. M. Stets/V. Zhukovets 6–1 6–1. **1996: April** *(Euro/Africa Group 1 in ESP, Clay): Round-robin SUI d. YUG 3–0.* R2 d. B. Ivanovic 6–2 6–1; R3 (with A. Burgis) d. S. Nacuk/D. Zaric 6–1 6–3. *Round-robin SUI d. GEO 3–0.* R2 d. N. Louarsabishvili 6–1 6–1. *Round-robin SUI d. CRO 2–1.* R2 d. I. Majoli 5–7 6–1 6–1; R3 (with Burgis) d. M. Lucic/Majoli 6–1 7–5. *Qf SUI d. HUN 2–1.* R2 d. A. Temesvari 6–0 6–3. *Final SUI d. RUS 2–1.* R2 d. E. Likhovtseva 6–3 6–0. **July** – *World Group II play-off SUI d. INA 3–2 in INA (Hard).* R2 d. L. Andriyani 6–0 6–0; R3 lost Y. Basuki 5–7 6–3 6–1; R5 (with P. Schnyder) d. Basuki/Tedjakusuma 6–3 6–2. **1997: March** – *World Group II qf SUI d. SVK 3–2 in SVK (Carpet).* R1 d. K. Studenikova 6–1 6–3; R3 d. K. Habsudova 6–2 6–0. R5 (with P. Schnyder) d. Habsudova/R. Zrubakova 6–0 6–1. **July** – *World Group play-off SUI d. ARG 5–0 in SUI (Carpet).* R1 d. M. Gaidano 6–1 6–2; R3 d. F. Labat 6–2 6–1. R5 (with E. Gagliardi) d. L. Montalvo/M. Paz 6–3 6–4. **1998: April** – *World Group qf SUI d. CZE 4–1 in CZE (Carpet).* R2 d. A. Gersi 6–2 6–1; R3 d. J. Novotna 4–6 6–3 6–2; R5 d. D. Chladkova/L. Richterova 6–0 6–1. **July** – *World Group sf SUI d. FRA 5–0 in SUI (Clay).* R1 d. Halard-Decugis 7–5 6–1; R3 d. A. Mauresmo 6–7 6–4 6–2. **September** – *World Group Final ESP d. SUI 3–2 in SUI (Hard).* R2. d. C. Martinez 6–4 6–4; R3 d. A. Sanchez-Vicario 7–6 6–3; R5 (with P. Schnyder) lost Martinez/Sanchez-Vicario 6–0 6–2))

GRAND SLAM CUP RECORD – Played 2, sf 2
1998: sf d. Martinez 6–2 7–5, lost Schnyder 5–7 7–5 5–5 ret. **1999: sf** [seed 1] d. Mauresmo 7–6 6–2, lost V. Williams 6–2 6–7 9–7.

SEASON ENDING CHAMPIONSHIPS – Played 5, won 2, r/u 2, qf 1
(1996–2000 Chase)
1996: r/u d. Spirlea 6–1 6–2, Date 6–1 6–2, Majoli 6–2 4–6 6–1, lost Graf 6–3 4–6 6–0 4–6 6–0. **1997: qf** d. Schultz-McCarthy 7–6 5–7 ret, lost Pierce 6–3 2–6 7–5. **1998: won** d. Schnyder 4–6 6–0 6–3, Pierce 7–6 6–4, Spirlea 6–2 7–6, Davenport 7–5 6–4 4–6 6–2. **1999: r/u** d. Testud 7–6 7–6, Pierce 6–1 6–2, V. Williams 6–4 7–6, lost Davenport 6–4 6–2. **2000: won** d. Halard-Decugis 6–2 6–3, Tauziat 6–1 6–7 6–2, Kournikova 7–6 6–2, Seles 6–7 6–4 6–4.

2 LINDSAY DAVENPORT (USA)

Born: Palos Verdes, Cal., 8 June 1976. **Lives:** Newport Beach, Cal. **Father:** Wink, a former Olympic volleyball player. **Mother:** Ann. **Sisters:** Shannon and Leiann (both older).

Agent: ProServ. **Coaches:** Robert Van't Hof since Jan. 1996. Formerly Lynn Rolley and Craig Kardon. **Turned pro:** 22 February 1993. **Height:** 6ft 2½in (1.89m). **Weight:** 175lb (79kg).

Rankings: 1991: 339; **1992:** 159; **1993:** 20; **1994:** 6; **1995:** 12; **1996:** 9; **1997:** 3; **1998:** 1; **1999:** 2; **2000:** 2. **Highest:** 1 (12 October 1998).

2000 Prize Money: $2,444,734. **Career Earnings:** $11,934,628. **Career Titles:** 30.

Style: With a powerful, match-winning forehand, a double-handed backhand of almost equal ferocity and an intimidating serve, she likes to dominate from the baseline. Her agility is much improved, now that she has shed excess pounds, thanks to the influence of Billie Jean King, who encouraged her to work and train harder. She has also improved her volleying, and her serve has become a potent weapon. Altogether more confident as a result of getting to more balls in time to make forceful shots.

CAREER HIGHLIGHTS (year: (titles))
1991: Won USTA 18s singles and doubles. **1992:** Ranked No. 1 in Nat 18s, in Jun tennis she won US Open over Steven, was r/u Australian Open to Limmer and won Australian Open and US Open doubles with London. **1993: (1)** *Lucerne.* She burst into prominence on the senior tour and swept up the rankings, improving by more than 100 places to 25 in May when she won her 1st title at Lucerne, and breaking into top 20 by autumn. She reached sf Oakland, where she took a set off Navratilova, plus qf VS Florida (d. Sabatini), Indian Wells (d. Schultz) and Tokyo Nicherei. At US Open, unseeded, she upset Coetzer on her way to last 16, where she extended Sabatini to 3s. Made her Fed Cup debut. **1994: (2)** *Brisbane, Lucerne.* In the year in which she graduated from high school, she established herself as one of the top women players. She broke into the top 20 in Jan. after winning Brisbane and moved into top 10 in spring, winning Lucerne in May. At Australian Open she upset M. J. Fernandez to reach qf and reached the same stage Wimbledon, removing Sabatini and taking a set off eventual champ Martinez. She also appeared in sf Indian Wells, LIPC (d. Sabatini), Amelia Island (d. Martinez) and Oakland, plus 4 more qf. These results took her to her 1st VS Champs, where she removed Novotna and Pierce before Sabatini demolished her in f. In doubles she was r/u French Open and won Indian Wells with Raymond, with whom she qualified for VS Champs, and took Oakland with Sanchez-Vicario. **1995: (1)** *Strasbourg.* She won both singles and doubles titles at Strasbourg, and achieved r/u finish at Sydney and Tokyo Pan Pacific, sf Oakland and qf Indian Wells, Manhattan Beach and Tokyo Nicherei. Qualified for VS Champs, but lost 1r to Sabatini. In doubles she played 5 f, winning 2 with M. J. Fernandez and 1 each with Novotna and Raymond. Injury restricted her towards the end of the year: she withdrew from San Diego with a tendon injury in her left leg and from Oakland with back problems, and dropped out of the top 10. **1996: (3)** *OLYMPICS, Strasbourg, Los Angeles.* She enjoyed the performance of her life at the Olympics, where she upset Huber, Majoli, M. J. Fernandez and Sanchez-Vicario – for the 1st time in 6 meetings – to take the gold medal, never before having progressed beyond qf in GS. Yet, discouraged by injury, illness and lack of self-belief, she had come close to quitting towards the end of the previous year, before being talked out of it by M. J. Fernandez. Her rehabilitation and motivation were completed by Billie Jean King in her role as coach to the US Fed Cup and Olympic squads. Fitter and 20lb lighter, she learned how to use her size and strength to advantage, playing with renewed dedication after her split with Craig Kardon. She began the year on a high note at Sydney, where she upset Date and came near to doing the same to Seles in f (letting slip mp in 2s), as well as winning the doubles with M. J. Fernandez. At Indian Wells in March she extended Graf to 2 tb in sf before losing in 3s, following with the title at Strasbourg. Then at LA, where she

won both singles and doubles (with Zvereva), she became the 1st player since 1994 to d. Graf in ss. She also reached sf LIPC and Filderstadt, plus qf French Open, Tokyo Toray, Leipzig and Chicago. In other doubles tourns, she and M. J. Fernandez won French Open (upsetting Novotna/Sanchez-Vicario and G. Fernandez/Zvereva on the way), Sydney and Oakland and were r/u Australian Open. Her year ended less dramatically in singles, as she fell to Wild at US Open and Graf 2r Chase Champs, but she finished on a high note by taking the doubles there with M. J. Fernandez. **1997: (6)** *Oklahoma City, Indian Wells, Amelia Island, Atlanta, Zurich, Chicago.* After winning Oklahoma City in Feb., she followed the next week by taking both singles and doubles at Indian Wells, coming from 1–4 and 5–6 behind in 3s qf v V. Williams. A month later she won both singles and doubles at Amelia Island, adding singles titles at Atlanta, Zurich (d. Novotna) and Chicago. Only Hingis won more tournaments across the year. She was always a dangerous opponent: at Los Angeles she became the 2nd of only 5 players all year to beat Hingis, before extending Seles to 3s in f; at French Open she was 7–5 4–0 up v Majoli, before letting the match slip away; and at US Open she upset Novotna to reach sf. She seriously challenged Hingis again at Philadelphia, losing their f only 7–5 6–7 7–6. She had upset Novotna a 3rd time there and immediately replaced her as No. 2 in the rankings on 17 Nov. However, at Chase Champs the following week, Novotna's triumph and Davenport's 1r defeat by M. J. Fernandez reversed their positions again. She had also reached sf Sydney and Stanford (where she extended Hingis to 3s) and 3 more qf, as well as being a major force in doubles. When M. J. Fernandez talked of retiring at end 1996, Davenport established a new doubles partnership with Novotna, causing some bad feeling for a while between the former best friends. During the year she reached 12 f in all with 5 different partners, winning 3 with Novotna (including US Open), 2 with Zvereva and 1 with Hingis, as well as being r/u Australian Open with Raymond. She qualified for Chase Champs in both singles and doubles, falling 1r singles to M. J. Fernandez but winning the doubles with Novotna. **1998: (6)** *US OPEN, Tokyo Pan Pacific, Stanford, San Diego, Los Angeles, Zurich.* An amazing season saw her win her 1st GS at US Open, where she was magnificent, sweeping to the title without dropping a set and for the loss of only 32 games. That triumph was followed on 12 Oct. by her arrival at the top of the rankings as she overtook Hingis and became the 8th woman to take the No. 1 spot. She had enjoyed a remarkable summer, in which she won both singles and doubles at Stanford and San Diego back-to-back, following the next week with Los Angeles (where she did not play doubles). In winning these 3 HC events in Aug., she became the 1st player since Navratilova in 1988 to win 3 titles in a month and the 1st since Graf in 1994 to win 3 consec. events. Her US Open triumph then silenced any critics who doubted her ability to go all the way in GS, having fallen sf Australian Open and French Open and qf Wimbledon, and she finished the year still at the very top. She did not manage to crown her year with the singles title at Chase Champs, losing a lacklustre f to Hingis – unsurprisingly she was drained by winning her long sf v Graf and then a long doubles f the day before – but she did hold on to her top ranking and was voted WTA Player of the Year. In other tourns she won Tokyo Japan Open and Zurich, was r/u Indian Wells, Filderstadt and Philadelphia, and reached sf Oklahoma City, Amelia Island and New Haven, plus qf Sydney (in which she served at 6–1 5–2 v S. Williams before losing the match), LIPC and FC Cup. She excelled again in doubles, too, pairing with Zvereva to win 6 titles, including Chase Champs, and being r/u 5 times, including all 4 GS. **1999: (7)** *WIMBLEDON, Sydney, Madrid, Stanford, Tokyo Toyota, Philadelphia, Chase Champs.* The highlight of her year and career to date came when she exceeded even the heights of the previous year with her 1st Wimbledon singles title, achieved without the loss of a set and to which she added the doubles with Morariu. Her year ended on another high note when she overcame a hamstring injury to take her 1st Chase Champs title over Hingis, her rival for the No. 1 spot throughout the year. Hingis had overtaken her on 8 Feb., and although Davenport took control again on 5 July, she dropped back again on 9 Aug. and at end of year was still at No. 2. She was restricted by a virus in Feb–March and by a recurring wrist injury throughout the year, which limited her participation in winning Fed Cup team to 2 rubbers in f. In addition to her two major titles, she won Sydney, Madrid, Stanford (where she also won the doubles), Tokyo Toyota and Philadelphia, was r/u New Haven, and appeared in sf Australian Open, US Open, San Diego, Manhattan Beach and GS Cup, plus qf French Open, Tokyo Toray, LIPC and Filderstadt. In doubles, as well as Wimbledon, she won another 2 titles with Morariu and 1 with Zvereva, with whom she was also r/u Australian Open. It was with Morariu that she qualified for Chase Champs, where they reached sf. **2000: (4)** *AUSTRALIAN OPEN, Indian Wells, Linz, Philadelphia.* Although it was a difficult year in which she was plagued by a string of injuries, she still managed to maintain her No. 2 ranking. It was a left hamstring strain, suffered in sf on her way to a 1st

Australian Open title, that saw her withdraw doubles there, and she was sidelined 6 weeks from Ericsson Open by both a foot injury and burnout. Returning at Rome, she withdrew after suffering lower back injury while practising for 3r match. She had not fully recovered by French Open, where she seemed to give up v Van Roost 1r and withdrew doubles. At Wimbledon she lost her singles crown to V. Williams, hampered in f by head cold and the leg and back injuries that had also left her with little match practice beforehand. Even had she been fit, she lost the chance to contest the doubles when her partner, Morariu, was injured in their 1r singles match. Then left foot injuries saw her retire at both Montreal and Olympics. However, despite these handicaps, she won Australian Open, Indian Wells, where she also won the doubles, Linz, where she ended V. Williams's 35-match winning streak, and Philadelphia the following week. Her defeat of Hingis at Indian Wells was the 5th in succession and although it was still not enough to win back the No. 1 singles ranking, she moved back to the top in doubles and was back at No. 1 in singles on 3 April, despite losing f Ericsson Open to Hingis, whom she displaced from the top ranking – but only for 5 weeks. She was r/u Wimbledon, US Open, Sydney, Ericsson Open, Stanford, Los Angeles and Zurich, shared Scottsdale with Hingis when their f was not played, and reached qf Eastbourne. Her year ended disappointingly when she lost 1r Chase Champs to Dementieva after holding mp, although there was compensation in winning all her matches as USA d. ESP 5–0 in Fed Cup f the following week.

PRINCIPAL 2000 RESULTS – won 4, shared 1, r/u 7 (detailed Grand Slam results follow)
won Australian Open, **won** Indian Wells (d. Spirlea 6–0 6–1, Zvereva 6–4 6–2, Halard-Decugis 6–2 6–1, Martinez 6–2 6–1, Dementieva 6–2 6–1, Hingis 4–6 6–4 6–0), **won** Linz (d. Hopmans 6–1 6–1, Schett 6–2 4–1 ret, Hrdlickova 6–1 6–1, V. Williams 6–4 3–6 6–2), **won** Philadelphia (d. Raymond 6–3 6–3, Coetzer 6–1 1–6 6–1, Martinez 6–0 6–1, Hingis 7–6 6–4); **shared** Scottsdale (d. Capriati 3–6 6–2 6–3, Seles 6–4 6–4, Kournikova 6–2 6–2, final v Hingis not played); **r/u** Wimbledon, **r/u** US Open, **r/u** Sydney (d. Likhovtseva 6–1 6–2, Sanchez-Vicario 6–7 6–3 6–4, Kournikova 6–3 6–2, lost Mauresmo 7–6 6–4), **r/u** Ericsson Open (d. Kremer 6–1 6–2, Talaja 6–2 6–2, Likhovtseva 6–4 6–4, Petrova 6–2 6–1, Testud 6–1 6–7 7–6, lost Hingis 6–3 6–2), **r/u** Stanford (d. Pratt 6–2 6–4, Rubin 6–3 3–6 6–1, Seles 7–5 7–6, lost V. Williams 6–1 6–4), **r/u** Los Angeles (d. Sidot 7–6 6–7 6–2, Testud 6–4 6–2, Dementieva 6–4 6–4, lost S. Williams 4–6 6–4 7–6), **r/u** Zurich (d. Appelmans 6–2 6–1, Rubin 6–2 6–4, Schett 6–2 6–1, lost Hingis 6–4 4–6 7–5). **DOUBLES:** (with Morariu) **won** Indian Wells (d. Kournikova/Zvereva 6–2 6–3); (with Kournikova) **r/u** San Diego (lost Raymond/Stubbs 4–6 6–3 7–6).

CAREER GRAND SLAM RECORD
AUSTRALIAN OPEN – Played 8, won 1, sf 2, qf 2
1993: 3r d. Fusai 7–5 6–1, Kiene 7–5 6–4, lost Pierce [10] 6–3 6–0. **1994: qf** [seed 16] d. Hy 3–6 6–2 7–5, Probst 6–1 7–5, Makarova 6–1 6–2, M. J. Fernandez [6] 6–2 6–7 6–2, lost Graf [1] 6–3 6–2. **1995: qf** [seed 6] d. Graham 4–6 6–3 6–2, Probst 6–2 6–2, Testud 6–3 6–4, Schultz [12] 6–2 3–6 6–2, lost Martinez [2] 6–3 4–6 6–3. **1996: last 16** [seed 10] d. Singer 6–1 6–2, Stubbs 7–6 6–3, N. Dahlman 6–4 7–5, lost Martinez [2] 6–3 6–1. **1997: last 16** [seed 7] d. Dechy 4–6 6–1 6–1, Perfetti 6–2 7–5, Tanasugarn 6–1 6–0, lost Po 7–6 6–4. **1998: sf** [seed 2] d. Cocheteux 6–2 6–3, Habsudova 2–6 6–0 9–7, Perfetti 6–2 6–2, Dragomir [15] 6–0 6–0, V. Williams 1–6 7–5 6–3, lost Martinez [8] 4–6 6–3 6–3. **1999: sf** [seed 1] d. Leon-Garcia 6–2 6–2, Labat 6–2 6–1, Habsudova 6–0 6–4, Drake 6–1 6–3, V. Williams [5] 6–4 6–0, lost Mauresmo 4–6 7–5 7–5. **2000: won** [seed 2] d. Pitkowski 6–3 6–1, Irvin 6–4 7–5, Jidkova 6–0 6–1, Kournikova [11] 6–4 6–3, Halard-Decugis [9] 6–1 6–2, Capriati 6–4 7–6, Hingis [1] 6–1 7–5.
FRENCH OPEN – Played 8, sf 1, qf 2
1993: 1r lost Wiesner 6–3 6–1. **1994: 3r** [seed 9] d. Rubin 6–7 6–4 6–3, Nowak 6–4 6–2, lost Halard 6–4 6–2. **1995: last 16** [seed 7] d. Tang 7–6 6–0, Testud 6–3 7–5, Hingis 4–6 6–2 6–2, lost Date [9] 6–4 6–3. **1996: qf** [seed 9] d. Perfetti 6–4 6–1, Park 6–1 6–2, Basuki 6–3 6–2, Date [7] 3–6 6–4 8–6, lost Martinez [3] 6–1 6–3). **1997: last 16** [seed 5] d. Kruger 6–2 6–3, Makarova 6–1 6–1, Schnyder 4–6 6–3 9–7, lost Majoli [9] 5–7 6–4 6–2. **1998: sf** [seed 2] d. Po 6–2 6–2, Horn 6–2 6–0, Likhovtseva 7–5 7–5, Testud [14] 6–3 4–6 6–2, Majoli [10] 6–1 5–7 6–3, lost Sanchez-Vicario [4] 6–3 7–6. **1999: qf** [seed 2] d. Chi 6–3 6–1, Henin 6–3 2–6 7–5, Zuluaga 6–3 6–3, Capriati 6–2 6–3, lost Graf [6] 6–1 6–7 6–3. **2000: 1r** [seed 2] lost Van Roost 6–7 6–4 6–3.
WIMBLEDON – Played 8, won 1, r/u 1, qf 2
1993: 3r d. Martinek 6–0 4–6 7–5, Rittner 6–0 7–6, lost Tauziat [16] 6–3 7–6. **1994: qf** [seed 9] d. Halard 6–1 6–4, Price 6–4 6–2, Rittner 6–4 3–6 6–1, Sabatini [10] 6–1 6–3, lost Martinez [3] 6–2 6–7 6–3. **1995: last 16** [seed 7] d. G. Fernandez 6–2 4–6 7–5, Labat 6–1 6–1, Singer 6–7 6–3 6–2, lost M. J. Fernandez [seed 13] 7–6 6–1. **1996: 2r** [seed 8] d. Schnell 6–4 6–1, lost Neiland 6–3 6–2. **1997: 2r** [seed 5] d. Whitlinger-Jones 5–7 6–2 6–2, lost Chladkova 7–5 6–2. **1998: qf** [seed 2] d. Labat 6–2 6–2, Neiland 6–1 7–5, Vento 6–3 1–6 6–2, Serna 6–1 6–0, lost Tauziat [16] 6–3 6–3. **1999: won** [seed 3] d. Fusai 6–0 6–3, Habsudova 6–2 6–2, Golarsa 6–3 6–2, Schett [14] 7–6 6–1, Novotna [5] 6–3 6–4, Stevenson 6–1 6–1, Graf [2] 6–4 7–5. **2000: r/u** [seed 2] d. Morariu 6–3 1–0 ret, Likhovtseva 3–6 6–3 6–3, Suarez 6–4 6–2, Capriati 6–3 6–3, Seles [6] 6–7 6–4 6–0, Dokic 6–4 6–2, lost V. Williams [5] 6–3 7–6.

US OPEN – Played 10, won 1, r/u 1, sf 2
1991: 1r lost Graham 6–3 6–2. **1992: 2r** d. Basuki 6–4 6–4, lost Sanchez-Vicario [5] 6–2 6–1). **1993: last 16** [unseeded] d. Probst 6–4 6–2, Hy 6–4 6–2, Coetzer [15] 6–1 6–2, lost Sabatini [5] 6–7 6–4 6–4. **1994: 3r** [seed 6] d. Grossi 6–1 6–1, Shriver 6–1 6–2, lost Endo 6–3 7–6. **1995: 2r** [seed 10] d. Kamstra 6–2 6–2, lost Garrison-Jackson 6–1 6–3. **1996: last 16** [seed 8] d. Serra-Zanetti 6–2 6–1, Nagyova 6–0 6–4, Sidot 6–0 6–3, lost Wild 6–2 3–6 6–0. **1997 sf** [seed 6] d. McNeil 6–2 7–6, Probst 6–2 6–3, Schnyder 1–6 6–1 6–4, Serna 6–0 6–3, Novotna [3] 6–2 4–6 7–6, lost Hingis [1] 6–2 6–4. **1998: won** [seed 2] d. Cristea 6–0 6–2, McNeil 6–1 6–1, Ruano Pascual 6–2 6–1, Tauziat [10] 6–1 6–4, Coetzer [13] 6–0 6–4, V. Williams [5] 6–4 6–4, Hingis [1] 6–3 7–5. **1999: sf** [seed 2] d. Morariu 6–0 6–3, Dragomir 6–0 6–2, Frazier 6–1 6–1, Halard-Decugis [seed 9] 6–1 6–2, Pierce [5] 6–2 3–6 7–5, lost S. Williams [7] 6–4 1–6 6–4. **2000: r/u** [seed 2] d. Leon Garcia 6–0 6–1, Clijsters 4–6 6–2 6–2, Tanasugarn 6–2 6–1, Henin 6–0 6–4, S. Williams 6–4 6–2 [5], Dementieva 6–2 7–6, lost V. Williams [3] 6–4 7–5.

OLYMPIC RECORD
1996: (Atlanta) won gold medal [seed 9] d. Kremer 6–2 6–1, Sawamatsu 6–2 6–2, Huber [5] 6–1 3–6 6–3, Majoli [4] 7–5 6–3, M. J. Fernandez [7] 6–2 7–6, Sanchez-Vicario [3] 7–6 6–2. **2000: (Sydney) 2r** [seed 1] d. Suarez 6–2 6–2, lost De Los Rios w/o.

CAREER FED CUP RECORD
1993 (in GER, Clay): *1r USA d. SUI 3–0.* R1 d. C. Fauche 6–4 6–3. *2r USA d. CHN 2–1.* R1 d. Y. Bi 6–1 6–3; R3 (+ L. McNeil) d. L. Chen/F. Li 6–3 6–0. *Qf ARG d. USA 2–1.* R1 lost I. Gorrochategui 7–6 5–7 5–7. **1994 (in GER, Clay):** *1r USA d. CZE 3–0.* R2 d. L. Richterova 4–6 6–1 6–4. *2r USA d. CAN 3–0.* R2 d. P. Hy 6–2 6–4. *Qf USA d. AUT 3–0.* R2 d. J. Wiesner 2–6 6–2 6–2. *Sf USA d. FRA 3–0.* R2 d. M. Pierce 5–7 6–2 6–2. *Final ESP d. USA 3–0.* R2 lost A. Sanchez-Vicario 6–2 6–1. **1995: July** *– World Group sf USA d. FRA 3–2 in USA (Carpet).* R2 d. J. Halard-Decugis 7–6 7–5; R3 d. M. Pierce 6–3 4–6 6–0; R5 (+ G. Fernandez) d. Halard-Decugis/N. Tauziat 6–1 7–6. **November** *– World Group Final ESP d. USA 3–2 in ESP (Clay).* (+ G. Fernandez) R5 D. Ruano-Pascual/ M. Sanchez Lorenzo 6–3 7–6. **1996: July** *– World Group I sf USA d. JPN 5–0 in JPN (Carpet).* R1 d. K. Date 6–2 6–1; R4 d. A. Sugiyama 7–6 7–5; R5 (+ L. Wild) d. K. Nagatsuka/A. Sugiyama 6–2 6–1. **September** *– World Group I Final USA d. ESP 5–0 in USA (Carpet).* R2 d. A. Sanchez-Vicario 7–5 6–1; R4 d. G. Leon-Garcia 7–5 6–2. **1997: July** *– World Group play-off USA d. JPN 5–0 in USA (Hard).* R2 d. N. Sawamatsu 6–1 6–3; R3 d. A. Sugiyama 6–4 7–6; R5 (with L. Raymond) d. N. Kijimuta/N. Miyagi 6–4 6–4. **1998: April** *– World Group qf USA d. NED 5–0 in USA (Clay).* R1 d. A. Hopmans 6–4 6–1; R3 d. M. Oremans 6–1 6–2. **1999: September** *– World Group f USA d. RUS 4–1 in USA (Hard).* R2 d. E. Dementieva 6–4 6–0; R3 d. E. Likhovtseva 6–4 6–4. **2000: November (in USA, Carpet):** *World Group sf USA d. BEL 2–1.* R2 d. K. Clijsters 7–6 4–6 6–3. *Final USA d. ESP 5–0.* R2 d. A. Sanchez-Vicario 6–2 1–6 6–3; R3 d. C. Martinez 6–1 6–2.

GRAND SLAM CUP RECORD – Played 2, sf 1
1998: 1r [seed 2] lost Tauziat 4–6 6–1 7–5. **1999: sf** [seed 2] d. Pierce 3–6 6–2 6–4, lost S. Williams 6–3 6–4.

SEASON ENDING CHAMPIONSHIPS – Played 7, won 1, r/u 2
(1983–94 Virginia Slims, 1995 Corel, 1996–2000 Chase)
1994: r/u d. Huber 6–2 6–3, Novotna 6–2 6–2, Pierce 6–3 6–2, lost Sabatini 6–3 6–2 6–4. **1995: 1r** lost Sabatini 6–4 6–3. **1996: 2r** d. Paulus 6–3 6–2, lost Graf 6–4 7–6. **1997: 1r** lost M. J. Fernandez 2–6 6–4 7–6. **1998: r/u** d. Testud 4–6 7–6 6–0, Tauziat 6–0 6–3, Graf 6–1 2–6 6–3, lost Hingis 7–5 6–4 4–6 6–2. **1999: won** d. Mauresmo 3–6 6–3 6–2, Huber 6–3 6 1, Tauziat 7–6 6–0, Hingis 6–4 6–2. **2000: 1r** lost Dementieva 3–6 7–6 6–4.

3 VENUS WILLIAMS (USA)

Born: Lynwood, Cal., 17 June 1980. **Lives:** Palm Beach
Gardens, Fla. **Father:** Richard. **Mother:** Oracene.
Sisters: Isha, Lyndrea, Yelunde (older) and Serena (younger).

Agent: Keven Davis Esq., Garvey, Schubert and Barer.
Coach: Her parents, Richard and Oracene; formerly
Rick Macci. **Trainer:** Kerrie Brooks. **Turned pro:** 1994.
Height: 6ft 1in (1.86m). **Weight:** 160lb (72kg).

Rankings: 1995: 204; **1996:** 204; **1997:** 22; **1998:** 5;
1999: 3; **2000:** 3. **Highest:** 3 (August 1999).

2000 Prize Money: $2,074,150.
Career Earnings: $6,656,727. **Career Titles:** 15.

Style: A wonderful natural athlete, who hits the ball as hard as any woman ever has, she
attacks relentlessly, even recklessly at times. This makes every match she plays an exciting spec-
tacle. She has no technical weakness with a single-handed forehand and a double-handed
backhand that are the foundations of her powerful game. One of the best-ever servers and a
skilful volleyer, she is gaining in experience, and has the potential to improve still further.

CAREER HIGHLIGHTS (year: (titles))

In her 1st year as a pro, her father allowed her to play only 4 tourns to prevent burnout and to
concentrate on education, which he considers very important. **1995:** Reached her 1st qf at
Oakland (d. Frazier) and joined US Fed Cup squad. **1996:** Upset Wild at Los Angeles. **1997:** She
produced an extraordinary performance to reach f US Open, upsetting Huber and Spirlea
(saving 2 mps in 3s tb) along the way to becoming the 1st unseeded women's finalist there
since Darlene Hard in 1958. Until then her best performance had been at Indian Wells, where
she qualified, upset Majoli and was 4–1 and 6–5 up in 3s qf v Davenport before losing their tb.
After US Open, she failed to qualify at Filderstadt, but reached qf Zurich (as a qualifier) the next
week and followed with the same stage Moscow. She was voted Most Impressive Newcomer
in her 1st full year on the circuit. **1998: (3)** *Oklahoma City, LIPC, GS Cup.* Having vowed to
avenge her one-sided defeat by Hingis at US Open at their next meeting, she did just that on
her way to f Sydney in Jan. Then at end Feb. she upset Davenport on the way to her 1st tour
title at Oklahoma City, where she also won the doubles with her sister, Serena. She followed
with the title at LIPC (beating Hingis again in sf), a result which took her into the top 10.
However, she was bothered all year with knee problems: it was patella tendinitis of the left knee
that kept her out for a month in spring; in summer she was given a diagnosis of chronic
patellofemoral syndrome of the right knee; and it was the left knee again that kept her out of
Chase Champs. She was back to play US Open and outlasted Schnyder to win the inaugural
women's GS Cup, but was unable to play Chase Champs. In other tourns she was r/u Rome (d.
Sanchez-Vicario), Stanford (d. Seles) and Zurich (where she won a 2nd doubles title with
Serena) and reached sf Indian Wells, Moscow and US Open, plus qf Australian Open
(unseeded), French Open and San Diego. Her 125 mph serve to Schett at Wimbledon was the
fastest recorded by a woman until her 127 mph serve v Davenport at Zurich. In mixed doubles
she won Australian Open and French Open with Gimelstob and was r/u Wimbledon with
Bhupathi. **1999: (6)** *Oklahoma City, LIPC, Hamburg, Rome, New Haven, Zurich.* In another
impressive year she moved into the top 3 and was challenging for the place she had predicted
for herself at the very top, beating Hingis 3 times and Davenport twice during the year.
Although the majors eluded her in singles, she won titles at Oklahoma City, LIPC, Hamburg (her
1st on clay) and Rome back-to-back, New Haven and Zurich, as well as being r/u Hannover,
Stanford, San Diego and GS Cup, and reaching sf Philadelphia US Open and Chase Champs,
plus qf Sydney, Australian Open and Wimbledon. In doubles she won French Open, US Open
and Hannover from 4 f in partnership with her sister, Serena, who beat her to a 1st GS singles
title and was seriously challenging her in the rankings. They both played in the winning US Fed
Cup team. **2000: (6)** *WIMBLEDON, US OPEN, OLYMPICS, Stanford, San Diego, New Haven.*

Studying fashion design at college in Florida since summer 1999, and with some 'personal issues' to sort out, she was absent until May with tendinitis in both wrists. There was speculation that her defeat by Hingis at US Open in 1999 had seriously dented her confidence and, coinciding with her sister Serena's continuing success, she appeared to have lost her mental toughness for a while. When she first returned to action, during her sister's absence with a knee injury, she reached qf Hamburg, but gave a lacklustre performance v Dokic in Rome and lost qf French Open to Sanchez-Vicario. She didn't play between then and Wimbledon, but at Wimbledon she hit the high spot of her career to date and began a remarkable summer of success. She began by triumphantly winning her 1st GS singles title, beating first Hingis, then her sister Serena in sf and finally overpowering Davenport in ss, before adding the doubles title (with Serena). She followed her triumph at Wimbledon with another defeat of Davenport to take Stanford in Aug. and made it 4 in a row by winning San Diego the following week, and then New Haven. Still on an unbroken winning streak, she won her second consec. GS at US Open, squeezing past Hingis in sf – thus gaining revenge for that defeat at the same stage a year earlier – and overcoming Davenport again in f. She missed her chance to do the double again at US Open when Serena's left foot injury caused them to withdraw from sf doubles. However, she won gold in both singles and doubles (with Serena) at Olympics, becoming only the second woman to do so after Wills in 1924. She was undefeated from qf French Open to that triumph in Sydney, and until Davenport finally beat her in f Linz, inflicting only her 4th loss of year in 46 matches, she had put together a winning streak of 35 matches, the longest in women's tennis for 3 years. She then retired from the circuit for a while to complete her design studies and missed Chase Champs suffering from anaemia. Her prolonged absences followed by a return with a different style continue to cause problems for her opponents, who find that they no sooner work out how to beat her than she disappears again, returning with something different.

PRINCIPAL 2000 RESULTS – won 6, r/u 1 (detailed Grand Slam results follow)
won Wimbledon, **won** US Open, **won** Olympics, **won** Stanford (d. Panova 6–2 6–2, Frazier 6–7 6–4 7–6, Kournikova 6–4 7–5, Davenport 6–1 6–4), **won** San Diego (d. Coetzer 6–0 6–4, C. Martinez 6–3 6–0, Frazier 6–2 6–3, Seles 6–0 6–7 6–3), **won** New Haven (d. Likhovtseva 6–3 7–5, Schnyder 6–4 6–2, Coetzer 6–3 6–4, Seles 6–2 6–4); **r/u** Linz (d. Sugiyama 7–5 6–2, Likhovtseva 6–3 6–2, Rubin 6–4 6–0, lost Davenport 6–4 3–6 6–2). **DOUBLES:** (with S. Williams) **won Wimbledon** (d. Halard-Decugis/Sugiyama 6–3 6–2), **won Olympic gold medal** (d. Boogert/Oremans 6–1 6–1).

CAREER GRAND SLAM RECORD
AUSTRALIAN OPEN – Played 2, qf 2
1998: qf [unseeded] d. Dechaume-Balleret 6–3 6–0, S. Williams 7–6 6–1, Mauresmo 6–1 6–4, Schnyder 6–4 6–1, lost Davenport [2] 1–6 7–5 6–3. **1999: qf** [seed 5] d. Talaja 3–6 6–3 9–7, Carlsson 6–2 6–1, Dragomir 6–3 6–4, Rubin 7–6 6–4, lost Davenport [1] 6–4 6–0. **2000:** Did not play.
FRENCH OPEN – Played 4, qf 2
1997: 2r d. Sawamatsu 6–2 6–7 7–5, lost Tauziat 5–7 6–3 7–5. **1998: qf** [seed 8] d. Tanasugarn 6–3 6–1, Sugiyama 6–0 6–2, Dechaume-Balleret 6–2 6–1, Nagyova 6–1 6–3, lost Hingis [1] 6–3 6–4. **1999: last 16** [seed 5] d. Fusai 6–1 6–1, Zvereva 7–6 6–0, Molik 6–3 6–1, lost Schwartz 2–6 7–6 6–3. **2000: qf** [seed 4] d. Kandarr 6–0 6–3, Tanasugarn 6–2 6–2, Loit 6–2 6–2, Huber [11] 7–6 6–2, lost Sanchez-Vicario [8] 6–0 1–6 6–2.
WIMBLEDON – Played 4, won 1
1997: 1r lost Grzybowska 4–6 6–2 6–4. **1998: qf** [seed 7] d. Nejedly 6–3 6–3, Schett 6–1 6–2, Rubin 6–3 6–4, Ruano-Pascual 6–3 6–1, lost Novotna [3] 7–5 7–6. **1999: qf** [seed 6] d. Oremans 6–1 7–5, Tatarkova 6–3 6–4, Pitkowski 6–1 6–1, Kournikova [17] 3–6 6–3 6–2, lost Graf [2] 6–2 3–6 6–4. **2000: won** [seed 5] d. Hrdlickova 6–3 6–1, Sugiyama 6–1 6–4, Dechy 6–0 7–6, Appelmans 6–4 6–4, Hingis [1] 6–3 4–6 6–4, S. Williams 6–2 7–6, Davenport [2] 6–3 7–6.
US OPEN – Played 4, won 1, r/u 1, sf 2
1997: r/u [unseeded] d. Neiland 5–7 6–0 6–1, Leon-Garcia 6–0 6–1, Huber [8] 6–3 6–4, Kruger 6–2 6–3, Testud 7–5 7–5, Spirlea [11] 7–6 4–6 7–6, lost Hingis [1] 6–0 6–4. **1998: sf** [seed 5] d. Wagner 6–1 6–0, Kremer 6–1 6–3, Neiland 5–0 ret, Pierce [12] 6–1 7–6, Sanchez-Vicario [4] 2–6 6–1 6–1, lost Davenport [2] 6–4 6–4. **1999: sf** [seed 3] d. Poutchek 6–1 6–2, Sidot 6–4 6–3, Nagyova w/o, Fernandez 2–6 6–1 6–0, Schett [12] 6–4 6–3, lost Hingis [1] 6–1 4–6 6–3. **2000: won** [seed 3] d. Sidot 6–3 6–4, Hrdlickova 6–1 6–1, Shaughnessy 7–6 6–1, Serna 6–2 6–1, Tauziat [8] 6–4 1–6 6–1, Hingis [seed 1] 4–6 6–3 7–5, Davenport [2] 6–4 7–5.

OLYMPIC RECORD
2000: (Sydney) won gold medal [seed 2] d. Nagyova 6 ? 6–2, Tanasugarn 6–2 6–3, Kandarr 6–2 6–2, Sanchez-Vicario [5] 3–6 6–2 6–4, Seles [3] 6–1 4–6 6–3, Dementieva [10] 6–2 6–4.

Venus Williams produced the best tennis of all the women in 2000 with success at Wimbledon and the US Open, plus two Olympic gold medals in Sydney. (Paul Zimmer)

CAREER FED CUP RECORD
1999: July – *World Group sf – USA d. ITA 4–1 in ITA (Clay).* R1 d. R. Grande 6–2 6–3; R3 d. S. Farina 6–1 6–1; R5 (with S. Williams) d. T. Garbin/Adriana Serra-Zanetti 6–2 6–2. **September** – *World Group Final – USA d. RUS 4–1 in USA (Hard).* R1 d. E. Likhovtseva 6–3 6–4; R4 lost E. Dementieva 1–6 6–3 7–6; R5 (with S. Williams) d. Dementieva/Makarova 6–2 6–1.

CAREER GRAND SLAM CUP RECORD – Played 2, won 1, r/u 1
1998: won [unseeded] d. Sanchez-Vicario [3] 6–3 6–2, Tauziat 6–4 6–0, Schnyder 6–2 3–6 6–2. **1999: r/u** [seed 4] (d. Schett 6–3 6–4, Hingis [1] 6–2 6–7 9–7, lost S. Williams [3] 6–1 3–6 6–3).

SEASON ENDING CHAMPIONSHIPS – Played 1, sf 1
(Chase)
1999: sf [seed 3] d. Martinez 6–2 5–7 6–4, Schett 6–4 7–6 [7], lost Hingis [1] 6–4 7–6. **2000:** Did not play.

4 MONICA SELES (USA)

Born: Novi Sad, 2 December 1973. **Lives:** Sarasota, Fla.
Father: The late Karolj was cartoonist and TV director.
Mother: Esther. **Brother:** Zoltan (older), who helps to train
her. Discovered at 1985 Orange Bowl by Nick Bollettieri, who
moved her family to USA from Yugoslavia in 1986.

Agent: IMG. **Coach:** Bobby Banck since Oct. 1999; formerly
her father, Karolj; Gavin Hopper from March–December
1998. **Fitness coach:** Chris Milesky.
Turned pro: 1989.
Height: 5ft 10in (1.79m). **Weight:** 155lb (70kg).

Rankings: 1988: 86; **1989:** 6; **1990:** 2; **1991:** 1; **1992:** 1;
1993: 8; **1994:** Not ranked; **1995:** 1 (jointly with Graf);
1996: 2 (jointly with Sanchez-Vicario); **1997:** 5; **1998:** 6;
1999: 6; **2000:** 4. **Highest:** 1 (March 1991).

2000 Prize Money: $1,140,850. **Career Earnings:** $12,891,708. **Career Titles:** 47.

Style: A naturally competitive left-hander who hits with two hands on both forehand and
backhand. Her ability to hit a rising ball with perfect timing allows her to project thunderous
drives on both wings that can destroy all opposition. An improving serve that is now the equal
of most women, plus a greater willingness to volley, allied to an acute tactical awareness, make
her arguably among the finest match players of all time. Since her return in 1995, she has lost
some of her speed of shot and of movement.

Ranking: Her ranking was protected when she returned in 1995, an arrangement set to last
until she had played 14 tourns or after 18 months. During that time, she was co-ranked with
the player whose average was immediately below hers (calculated by dividing points total by
tourns played in past 52 weeks, but a minimum of 6).

CAREER HIGHLIGHTS (year: (titles))
Became a US citizen 16 March 1994. **1983:** At age 9, reached last 16 Sport Goofy singles. **1984:**
Won Sport Goofy singles. **1985:** Won Sport Goofy singles and doubles. **1988:** Upset Kelesi at VS
Florida in 1st pro match, took Sabatini to 1s tb 1r LIPC and upset Magers and McNeil to reach sf
New Orleans. **1989: (1)** *Houston.* Won Houston over Evert and was r/u Dallas and Brighton.
Unseeded at French Open, she upset Garrison and Manuela Maleeva before extending Graf to
3s sf. **1990: (9)** *FRENCH OPEN, Berlin, Los Angeles, Oakland, VS Champs, LIPC, San Antonio,
Tampa, Italian Open.* Following her acrimonious split in March with Bollettieri, who she consid-
ered was spending too much time coaching Agassi, she was coached only by her father. At 16
years 6 months became the youngest French Open women's champion and second-youngest
GS champion (after Lottie Dod, who was 15 years 10 months when she won Wimbledon in
1887). She went into the French Open having won 5 consec. tourns without dropping a set, but
her unbeaten run of 36 matches was ended by Garrison in qf Wimbledon. She in turn had ended
Graf's 66-match unbeaten run at Berlin. Her season finished in triumph when she beat Sabatini
in 5s in f VS Champs to finish with 9 titles. She beat Graf twice and Navratilova 3 times and by
year's end had displaced Navratilova to finish ranked 2. Won WTA Most Improved Player award.
1991: (10) *AUSTRALIAN OPEN, FRENCH OPEN, US OPEN, VS Champs, LIPC, Houston, Los Angeles, Tokyo Nicherei, Milan, Philadelphia.* Enjoyed a spectacular year in which she reached f in all
16 tourns she entered. At 17 years 2 months she became the youngest to take the Australian
Open, being 4 months younger than Margaret Smith in 1960, and in March she ousted Graf
from the top ranking to become the youngest (17 years 3 months) to reach that spot (Tracy
Austin had been 1 month older). Although Graf overtook her again briefly on and off during the
summer, Seles finished the year firmly fixed at the top, was voted WTA Singles Player of the Year
and was the youngest to be named Official World Champion. She pulled out of Wimbledon 72
hours before the start, losing her chance of completing a GS. She first said she had suffered 'a
minor accident' but eventually she claimed she had panicked after being given conflicting advice

that the shin splints from which she was suffering might keep her out of the game for 6 months or a year. She was fined $6,000 for withdrawing and $20,000 for subsequently appearing in an exhibition tournament. She also missed Fed Cup, claiming injury, although she played an exhibition tournament at the same time. **1992: (10)** *AUSTRALIAN OPEN, FRENCH OPEN, US OPEN, VS Champs, Essen, Indian Wells, Houston, Barcelona, Tokyo Nicherei, Oakland.* After she had won Australian Open and become the 1st woman since Hilde Sperling in 1937 to win 3 consec French Opens, she seemed on course for a GS. But Graf, who had stretched her to 10–8 fs in Paris, demolished her in Wimbledon f and thereafter she seemed less invincible, although she won her 3rd GS title of the year at US Open and finished the season with ss win over Navratilova in f of VS Champs. She was beaten all year only 5 times – by Capriati at LIPC (the only tourn she entered in which she failed to reach the f), by Sabatini at Italian Open, Graf at Wimbledon, Navratilova at Los Angeles and by Sanchez-Vicario at Montreal. She took a total of 10 titles, including Houston for the loss of only 8 games, and when she won Barcelona at 18 years 4 months, she beat Tracy Austin's record of 18 years 8 months as youngest to achieve 25 singles titles. Controversy was never far away, and in 1992 it was her grunting which was the main subject. She played the Wimbledon final almost silently (refusing to make that an excuse for her defeat) and for the rest of the year made an attempt to control the noise, which players and spectators alike found distasteful and disturbing. She was voted Player of Year for the second straight year and set a new record for prize money won in one season, beating Edberg's record $2,363,575 in 1991. **1993: (2)** *AUSTRALIAN OPEN, VS Chicago.* She suffered a nightmare year, at the end of which there was still some question whether she would return to competitive play. Having taken a 2-month break, she returned to win Australian Open but was then sidelined for 2 months with a viral infection, missing LIPC. She returned to action at Hamburg where, on 30 April, during a changeover after she had recovered from 0–3 down to 4–3 v Magdalena Maleeva, she was stabbed in the back by Gunther Parche, a German who wanted to put her out of action to enable Steffi Graf to return to the No. 1 position. She and the rest of the world were horrified when Parche was given only a two-year suspended sentence in autumn, while Seles was sidelined for more than 2 years as the injury, which required only 2 stitches, was worse than first thought – and the psychological damage was considerable, requiring more than 100 hours of therapy. In the other 2 tourns she played, she won VS Chicago and was r/u Paris Open to Navratilova. **1994:** She did not play at all and dropped off the rankings on 14 Feb., a month before becoming a US citizen. **1995: (1)** *Toronto.* She returned to the public arena in a much-publicised exhibition match v Navratilova at Atlantic City on 29 July, which she won 6–3 6–2. Two inches taller, 10lb heavier and with some new one-handed strokes in her repertoire, she was co-ranked No. 1 with Graf when she returned to the tour, a position it was agreed she should hold for her 1st 6 tourns. Despite her extra weight and suffering from tendinitis in her left knee, she was still head and shoulders above anyone else apart from Graf, sweeping to the title at her 1st tourn back at Toronto, where she dropped only 14 games in 5 matches. She then moved as convincingly to f US Open, losing no set until Graf beat her there, and was given a special invitation to play in WTA Champs. However, when her knee and ankle problems flared up again, despite a rest until end Oct., she was forced to withdraw first from Oakland and then from WTA Champs. Voted Comeback Player of the Year and Most Exciting Player. **1996: (5)** *AUSTRALIAN OPEN, Sydney, Eastbourne, Montreal, Tokyo Nicherei.* Having won her 1st 2 tourns of year at Sydney and Australian Open, she suffered only the 2nd defeat since her return when Majoli upset her in qf Tokyo Toray. At Australian Open she had recovered from 2–5 down in 3s sf v Rubin and maintained her record of never having lost a match at the event. However, she suffered tendinitis and a small tear to the lining of the shoulder socket, which may in the long term require surgery and in the short term caused her to withdraw from Indian Wells, LIPC, FC Cup and before sf Madrid. That was her 1st tourn on European red clay since her stabbing on that surface in Hamburg, and although not fully fit, she had wanted to overcome the mental barrier of returning to Europe before French Open. She was determined to play in Paris, regardless of her injury, and was magnificent in beating M. Maleeva, whom she had been playing when stabbed, but was below par (particularly her serve) when losing to Novotna. It ended her run of 25 consec. match wins there since 1989, and was only her 5th defeat on clay. Still receiving 2 hours' treatment a day on her shoulder, she won her 1st title on grass at Eastbourne, but her timing deserted her at Wimbledon and she fell 2r to Studenikova. Novotna inflicted a second defeat in qf Olympics and Graf beat her again in f US Open, but she won Montreal and Tokyo Nicherei and was in the winning USA Fed Cup team that d. ESP 5–0 in f, after making her debut in Japan in July. In Oct. she began a rehabilitation programme for her shoulder in the hope of avoiding

Monica Seles, an Olympic bronze medallist and a member of the winning US Fed Cup team. (Stephen Wake)

surgery, returning at the end of the month at Chicago, where she lost sf to Capriati. On 4 Nov. she slipped from the top to No. 2, co-ranked with Sanchez-Vicario, and at Oakland suffered the most one-sided defeat of her career at the hands of Hingis. Losing 6–2 6–0, she recorded her 1st set lost to love since Nov. 1990 and only the 4th of her pro career. The year ended in further disappointment when her shoulder injury forced her to retire v Date 1r Chase Champs, and she was left seriously considering surgery. That, however, would necessitate an absence of several months from the tour and another setback in her psychological rehabilitation. Then in Dec., warming up for an exhibition match, she broke a finger on her right hand. **1997: (3)** *Los Angeles, Toronto, Tokyo Nicherei.* Having missed 4 tourns, including Australian Open, she returned in March at LIPC, where she appeared overwhelmed both physically and mentally by Hingis in f, losing in 44 mins. She lost to the same player in 3s tb in f FC Cup, having recovered from 2–5 down in 3s, and withdrew from Amelia Island with bronchitis. She was further distracted by the absence of her father, fighting in US against stomach cancer and unable to be with her for French Open, where she lost sf in 3s to Hingis, and Wimbledon, where she was beaten 3r by Testud. From 21 July, however, she played 7 tourns in 9 weeks, winning her 1st title of the year at Los Angeles in Aug. She followed with Toronto the next week and then Tokyo Nicherei, where she also took the doubles with Sugiyama (the 5th doubles title of her career – each won with a different partner). She was also r/u Madrid and San Diego, and played qf Eastbourne, Stanford, Atlanta, Chicago and Philadelphia, qualifying for Chase Champs by end Sept. At US Open, she held mp in 2s v Spirlea, but went on to lose the match. She was encouraged by having played through 4 months without injury, and although she withdrew Moscow in Oct. with a shoulder injury, she was back in action the following week at Chicago, where she was r/u doubles with

Davenport. At the start of Chase Champs, where she fell 1r to Sanchez-Vicario, she had slipped to No. 5 in the rankings. **1998: (2)** *Montreal, Tokyo Toyota*. Preferring to be with her father as much as possible, she played only sporadically at start of year, LIPC in March being her 1st tourn in 4 months. For 2 years she had been hampered by lack of practice and her concentration interrupted by thoughts of her dying father, but after his death on 14 May, she returned looking leaner and fully committed. At French Open, putting her grief behind her for a while, she upset Hingis in ss to reach her 1st GS f since 1996. Her 1st title of the year came at Montreal, where she upset Hingis and Sanchez-Vicario to take her 4th straight title there, and she followed with both singles and doubles (with Kournikova) at Tokyo Toyota. In other tourns she was r/u Moscow and reached sf FC Cup, Stanford, San Diego, Los Angeles and Philadelphia, plus qf Wimbledon and US Open. By then she had regained some of the excess weight lost when she returned after the death of her father, and injury was still a threat as she suffered back and shoulder problems during the year, in which she was voted WTA Comeback Player of the Year. At Chase Champs, despite being debilitated by a virus, she d. Kournikova before losing a thrilling qf v Graf. In doubles she played 2 f, winning Tokyo Toyota with Kournikova. **1999: (1)** *Amelia Island*. Her only title came at Amelia Island, followed by 2 more f appearances at Toronto and Tokyo Toyota. In other tourns she reached sf Australian Open, French Open, Tokyo Toray, New Haven and US Open. Her defeat by Hingis at Australian Open was her first ever there and ended a record unbeaten run there of 33 matches – the most in a GS by any player, male or female, since Navratilova's 48 at Wimbledon from 1982–88. Injuries again hampered her as she withdrew Stanford with tendinitis of right arm and was out of action from Oct. with a stress fracture of the right foot, which prevented her taking up her place at Chase Champs. She played in winning US Fed Cup team, but was unable to participate in f. **2000: (3)** *Oklahoma City, Amelia Island, Rome*. Her ongoing foot injury kept her out of Australian Open, but she was soon back in action, winning Oklahoma City at her 1st tourn back. However, a twisted ankle at Ericsson Open was instrumental in her suffering the worst loss of her career there – 6–0 6–0 to Hingis. Between then and French Open she lost weight and gained fitness, but injuries were never far away and she was out of action again in Aug. with tendinitis of the left arm, and once more in Oct. with tendinitis of the feet. In between she was as formidable as ever, adding the titles at Amelia Island and Rome, r/u San Diego, New Haven and Chase Champs, sf Ericsson Open, FC Cup, Stanford, Tokyo Toyota and Olympics, plus qf French Open, Wimbledon, US Open, Scottsdale and Indian Wells. At Olympics she swept through for the loss of only 10 games before falling in 3s sf to V. Williams, and at Chase Champs she looked a potential champion until Hingis eventually overpowered her in 3s in f. Despite carrying a foot injury, she was particularly determined to do well at that tourn, feeling hurt and aggrieved that in 2001 it was scheduled to be held in Munich where, having vowed that she would never again play in Germany after she was stabbed on court there in 1993, she would be unable to compete. She ended the year on the victorious USA Fed Cup team that d. ESP 5–0 in f.

PRINCIPAL 2000 RESULTS – won 3, r/u 3, sf 5 (detailed Grand Slam results follow)
won Oklahoma City (d. Lubiani 6–3 6–3, Pitkowski 6–0 6–0, Coetzer 6–1 6–2, Dechy 6–1 7–6), **won** Amelia Island (d. Smashnova 7–6 6–0, Morariu 6–3 6–1, Sanchez-Vicario 6–1 6–3, Suarez 6–3 6–2, Martinez 6–3 6–2), **won** Rome (d. Maleeva 7–5 6–1, Sidot 3–6 6–1 6–1, Dokic 6–1 2–6 6–3, Morariu 6–3 6–1, Mauresmo 6–2 7–6); **r/u** San Diego (d. Tu 7–5 7–5, Testud 4–6 6–2 7–6, Kournikova 6–3 7–6, lost V. Williams 6–0 6–7 6–3), **r/u** New Haven (d. Brandi 6–2 6–3, Van Roost 6–1 6–2, Tauziat 2–6 6–2 6–1, lost V. Williams 6–2 6–4), **r/u** Chase Champs; **sf** Ericsson Open (d. Osterloh 6–2 6–1, Raymond 6–3 6–2, Kournikova 6–1 3–6 6–0, Frazier 6–0 6–2, lost Hingis 6–0 6–0), **sf** FC Cup (d. De Lone 6–0 6–0, Likhovtseva 6–4 2–6 7–6, Dragomir 6–4 6–1, lost Pierce 6–1 6–1), **sf** Stanford (d. Shaughnessy 7–5 6–3, Black 6–1 6–2, lost Davenport 7–5 7–6), **sf** Tokyo Toyota (d. Vavrinec 6–4 6–4, Asagoe 6–3 6–4, lost Halard-Decugis 6–3 4–3 ret), **sf** Olympics.

CAREER GRAND SLAM RECORD
AUSTRALIAN OPEN – Played 5, won 4, sf 1
1991: won [seed 2] d. Hack 6–0 6–0, Caverzasio 6–1 6–0, Kschwendt 6–3 6–1, Tanvier 6–2 6–1, Huber 6–3 6–1, Fernandez [3] 6–3 0–6 9–7, Novotna [10] 5–7 6–3 6–1. **1992: won** [seed 1] d. Kijimuta 6–2 6–0, Date 6–2 7–5, Basuki 6–1 6–1, Meskhi [13] 6–4 4–6 6–2, Huber [12] 7–5 6–3, Sanchez-Vicario [4] 6–2 6–2, M. J. Fernandez [7] 6–2 6–3. **1993: won** [seed 1] d. Pizzichini 6–1 6–2, Strandlund 6–2 6–0, Fendick 6–1 6–0, Tauziat [13] 6–2 6–0, Halard 6–2 6–7 6–0, Sabatini [3] 6–1 6–2, Graf [2] 4–6 6–3 6–2. **1994–95:** Did not play. **1996: won** [seed 1] d. J. Lee 6–3 6–0, Studenikova 6–1 6–1, Halard-Decugis 7–5 6–0, Sawamatsu [15] 6–1 6–3, Majoli [7] 6–1 6–2, Rubin [13] 6–7 6–1 7–5, Huber [8] 6–4 6–1. **1997–98:** Did not play. **1999: sf** [seed 6] d. Krizan 6–1 6–0, Dechaume-Balleret 6–1 6–4, Appelmans 6–3 3–6 6–4, Testud 6–0 6–3 [14], Graf 6–0 6–3 [10], 7–5 6–1, lost Hingis [2] 6–2 6–4. **2000:** Did not play.

FRENCH OPEN – Played 9, won 3, r/u 1, sf 3, qf 2
1989: sf d. Reis 6–4 6–1, Martin 6–0 6–2, Garrison [4] 6–3 6–2, Faull 6–3 6–2, M. Maleeva [6] 6–3 7–5, lost Graf [1] 6–3 3–6 6–3. **1990: won** [seed 2] d. Piccolini 6–0 6–0, Kelesi 4–6 6–4 6–4, Meskhi 7–6 7–6, Gildemeister [16] 6–4 6–0, Maleeva-Fragniere [6] 3–6 6–1 7–5, Capriati 6–2 6–2, Graf [1] 7–6 6–4. **1991: won** [seed 1] d. Zrubakova 6–3 6–0, De Swardt 6–0 6–2, Quentrec 6–1 6–2, Cecchini 3–6 6–3 6–0, Martinez [7] 6–0 7–5, Sabatini [3] 6–4 6–1, Sanchez-Vicario [5] 6–3 6–4. **1992: won** [seed 1] d. Mothes 6–1 6–0, Kschwendt 6–2 6–2, McNeil 6–0 6–1, Kijimuta 6–1 3–6 6–4, Capriati [5] 6–2 6–2, Sabatini [3] 6–3 4–6 6–4, Graf [2] 6–2 3–6 10–8. **1993–95:** Did not play. **1996: qf** [seed 1] d. Chenin 6–1 6–1, Sawamatsu 7–6 6–2, Appelmans 6–2 7–5, M. Maleeva [13] 6–1 6–1, lost Novotna [10] 7–6 6–3. **1997: sf** [seed 3] d. Saeki 6–0 6–3, Pitkowski 6–3 7–5, Tauziat 6–0 6–1, Pierce [10] 6–4 7–5, M. J. Fernandez [12] 3–6 6–2 7–5, lost Hingis [1] 6–7 7–5 6–4. **1998: r/u** [seed 6] d. Ellwood 6–0 6–2, Maruska 2–6 6–1 6–0, Schwartz 6–1 7–5, Rubin 6–1 6–4, Novotna [3] 4–6 6–3 6–3, Hingis [1] 6–3 6–2, lost Sanchez-Vicario [4] 7–6 0–6 6–2. **1999: sf** [seed 3] d. Li 6–2 6–4, Bacheva 6–3 6–4, Sanchez-Lorenzo 6–1 6–4, Halard-Decugis [16] 6–1 7–5, Martinez 6–1 6–4, lost Graf [6] 6–7 6–3 6–4. **2000: qf** [seed 3] d. Talaja 6–2 6–2, Gagliardi 6–0 6–1, Kuti Kis 6–1 6–2, Mauresmo [13] 7–5 6–3, lost Pierce [6] 4–6 6–3 6–4.

WIMBLEDON – Played 8, r/u 1, qf 3
1989: last 16 [seed 11] d. Schultz 7–6 1–6 6–4, Porwik 6–2 6–4, Sviglerova 6–4 6–3, lost Graf [1] 6–0 6–1. **1990: qf** [seed 3] d. Strandlund 6–2 6–0, Benjamin 6–3 7–5, A. Minter 6–3 6–3, Henricksson 6–1 6–0, lost Garrison [5] 3–6 6–3 9–7. **1991:** Did not play. **1992: r/u** [seed 1] d. Byrne 6–2 6–2, Appelmans 6–3 6–2, Gildemeister 6–4 6–1, G. Fernandez 6–4 6–2, Tauziat [14] 6–1 6–3, Navratilova [4] 6–2 6–7 6–4, lost Graf [2] 6–2 6–1. **1993–95:** Did not play. **1996: 2r** [seed 2] d. Grossman 6–1 6–2, lost Studenikova 7–5 6–7 6–4. **1997: 3r** [seed 2] d. McQuillan 6–0 6–2, Brandi 5–7 6–3 6–3, lost Testud 0–6 6–4 8–6. **1998: qf** [seed 6] d. Sanchez Lorenzo 6–3 6–4, Fusai 6–1 6–1, Basuki 6–2 6–3, Testud [14] 6–3 6–2. lost Zvereva 7–6 6–2. **1999: 3r** [seed 4] d. Torrens-Valero 6–3 6–1, Weingartner 6–0 6–0, lost Lucic 7–6 7–6. **2000: qf** [seed 6] d. Habsudova 3–6 6–2 7–5, Callens 6–4 6–4, Pitkowski 6–0 6–3, Sanchez-Vicario [9] 6–3 6–4, lost Davenport [2] 6–7 6–4 6–0.

US OPEN – Played 10, won 2, r/u 2, qf 4
1989: last 16 [seed 12] d. Henricksson 4–6 6–2 6–2, A. Smith 7–5 6–2, Stafford 7–6 6–2, lost Evert [4] 6–0 6–2. **1990: 3r** [seed 3] d. Pampoulova 6–0 6–0, Fairbank-Nideffer 6–2 6–2, lost Ferrando 1–6 6–1 7–6. **1991: won** [seed 2] d. Arendt 6–2 6–0, Zardo 6–0 4–6 6–0, Gomer 6–1 6–4, Rajchrtova 6–1 6–1, G. Fernandez 6–1 6–2, Capriati [7] 6–3 3–6–7–6, Navratilova [6] 7–6 6–1. **1992: won** [seed 1] d. Keller 6–1 6–0, Raymond 7–5 6–0, Porwik 6–4 6–0, G. Fernandez 6–1 6–2, Hy 6–1 6–2, M. J. Fernandez [7] 6–3 6–2, Sanchez-Vicario [5] 6–3 6–3. **1993–94:** Did not play. **1995: r/u** [seed 2] d. Dragomir 6–3 6–1, De Lone 6–2 6–1, Kamio 6–1 6–1, Huber [11] 6–1 6–4, Novotna [seed 5] 7–6 6–2, Martinez [4] 6–2 6–2, lost Graf [1] 7–6 0–6 6–3. **1996: r/u** [seed 2] d. Miller 6–0 6–1, Courtois w/o, Randriantefy 6–0 6–2, Testud 7–5 6–0, Coetzer 6–0 6–3, Martinez [4] 6–4 6–3, lost Graf [1] 7–5 6–4. **1997: qf** [seed 2] d. Boogert 6–1 6–2, Snyder 6–2 6–3, Oremans 6–1 6–1, Pierce [9] 1–6 6–2 6–2, lost Spirlea [seed 11] 6–7 7–6 6–3. **1998: qf** [seed 6] d. Labat 7–6 6–2, Kruger 6–2 6–3, A. Miller 6–3 6–3, Po 6–2 4–6 6–3, lost Hingis [1] 6–4 6–4. **1999: qf** [seed 4] d. Rittner 6–1 6–1, Farina 6–2 6–3, Sugiyama 6–2 6–3, Capriati 6–4 6–3, lost S. Williams [7] 4–6 6–3 6–2). **2000: qf** [seed 6] d. Almeda-Singian 6–0 6–2, Kremer 6–3 6–4, Rubin 6–3 4–6 6–4, Capriati [15] 6–3 6–4, lost Hingis [1] 6–0 7–5.

OLYMPIC RECORD
1996: (Atlanta) qf [seed 1] d. Chen 6–0 6–4, Hy-Boulais 6–3 6–2, Sabatini 6–3 6–3, lost Novotna [6] 7–5 3–6 8–6). **2000: (Sydney) sf** [seed 3] d. Marosi-Aracama 6–0 6–1, Oremans 6–1 6–1, Dechy 6–3 6–2, Van Roost [8] 6–0 6–2, lost V. Williams [2] 6–1 4–6 6–3. Won silver medal, d. Dokic 6–1 6–4.

CAREER FED CUP RECORD
1996: July – *World Group sf USA d. JPN 5–0 in JPN (Carpet).* R2 d. A. Sugiyama 6–2 6–2; R3 d. K. Date 6–0 6–2. **September** – *World Group Final USA d. ESP 5–0 in USA (Carpet).* R1 d. C. Martinez 6–2 6–4; R3 d. A. Sanchez-Vicario 3–6 6–3 6–1. **1998: April** – *World Group qf USA d. NED 5–0 in USA (Clay).* R2 d. M. Oremans 6–1 6–2; R4 d. A. Hopmans 6–1 6–2. **July** – *World Group sf ESP d. USA 3–2 in ESP (Clay).* R2 d. C. Martinez 6–3 3–6 6–1; R3 d. A. Sanchez-Vicario 6–4 6–0. **1999: April** – *World Group qf USA d. CRO 5–0 in USA (Clay)* R2 d. S. Talaja 6–3 6–1; R3 d. I. Majoli 6–0 6–3; R5 (with C. Rubin) d. Majoli/Talaja 6–3 6–2. **July** – *World Group sf USA d. ITA 4–1 in ITA (Clay).* R2 lost S. Farina 6–4 4–6 6–4. **2000: November (in USA, Carpet):** *World Group sf USA d. BEL 2–1.* R1 d. J. Henin 7–6 6–2. *Final USA d. ESP 5–0.* R1 d. C. Martinez 6–2 6–3.

SEASON ENDING CHAMPIONSHIPS – Played 8, won 3, r/u 1, qf 1
(1983–94 Virginia Slims, 1995 Corel, 1996–2000 Chase)
1989: qf lost Navratilova 6–3 5–7 7–5. **1990: won** d. Paulus 6–2 6–2, Sanchez-Vicario 5–7 7–6 6–4, M. J. Fernandez 6–3 6–4, Sabatini 6–4 5–7 3–6 6–4 6–2. **1991: won** d. Halard 6–1 6–0, M. J. Fernandez 6–3 6–2, Sabatini 6–1 6–1, Navratilova 6–4 3–6 7–5 6–0. **1992: won** d. Tauziat 6–1 6–2, Novotna 3–6 6–4 6–1, Sabatini 7–6 6–1, Navratilova 7–5 6–3 6–1. **1993–95:** Did not play. **1996: 1r** lost Date 5–4 ret. **1997: 1r** lost Sanchez-Vicario 3–6 6–4 6–4. **1998: qf** d. Kournikova 6–4 6–3, lost Graf 1–6 6–4 6–4. **1999:** Did not play. **2000: r/u** d. Testud 6–3 6–4, Coetzer 6–3 6–4, Dementieva 6–1 7–6, lost Hingis 6–7 6–4 6–4.

5 CONCHITA MARTINEZ (ESP)

Born: Monzon, 16 April 1972. **Lives:** Barcelona and San Diego, Cal. **Father:** Cecilio. **Mother:** Conchita. **Brothers:** Fernando and Roberto (both older). **Agent:** Advantage International; Elvira Vazquez. **Coach:** Patricia Tarabini; formerly Eric Van Harpen, Carlos Kirmayr and Gabriel Urpi. **Trainer:** Miguel Mir. **Turned pro:** 1988. **Height:** 5ft 7in (1.70m). **Weight:** 132lb (59kg).

Rankings: 1988: 40; **1989:** 7; **1990:** 11; **1991:** 9; **1992:** 8; **1993:** 4; **1994:** 3; **1995:** 2; **1996:** 5; **1997:** 12; **1998:** 8; **1999:** 15; **2000:** 5. **Highest:** 2 (30 October 1995).

2000 Prize Money: $1,067,930. **Career Earnings:** $9,335,263. **Career Titles:** 32.

Style: A right-hander with a formidable backhand who hits with topspin on both wings. She is one of the most experienced groundstrokers whose strength is her consistency. Despite an above average volley (which makes her a good doubles player) she rarely chooses to advance to the net in singles.

CAREER HIGHLIGHTS (year: (titles))
1988: (1) *Sofia.* Upset McNeil en route to last 16 French Open after qualifying and won 1st pro title in both singles and doubles (with Paulus) at Sofia. Won Nat Champs over Sanchez and played Fed Cup. **1989: (3)** *Wellington, Tampa, VS Arizona.* Beat Sabatini on her way to the title at VS Arizona; r/u Geneva and Bayonne; qf French Open and qualified for 1st VS Champs. Voted WTA Most Impressive Newcomer. **1990: (3)** *Clarins, Scottsdale, Indianapolis.* Reached sf LIPC (d. Sabatini again), Tampa and Leipzig and appeared in qf French Open again. **1991: (3)** *Barcelona, Kitzbuhel, Clarins.* She again won 3 titles, upset Navratilova on her way to sf Italian Open, and reached the same stage Geneva, San Diego and Milan. Played in the successful Spanish Fed Cup team and qualified for VS Champs, where she fell 1r to Graf. In GS reached qf French Open again and US Open. **1992: (1)** *Kitzbuhel.* Although Kitzbuhel was her only title, she was r/u Indian Wells, VS Florida, FC Cup and San Diego and appeared in sf Amelia Island and Barcelona. She extended Sabatini to 3s in her 4th French Open qf and reached the same stage at Olympics. Qualified for VS Champs, where she beat K. Maleeva but lost qf to McNeil. In doubles with Sanchez-Vicario she was r/u French Open and Olympic Games (silver medal) and won Barcelona, reaching 4 more f with various partners. **1993: (5)** *Brisbane, VS Houston, Italian Open, Stratton Mountain, VS Philadelphia.* When she won Italian Open, with defeats of Navratilova and Sabatini, she became the 1st Spanish woman to win the title since 1930. She also won Brisbane, VS Houston (d. Sabatini), Stratton Mountain and VS Philadelphia (ending Graf's 9-match winning streak against her), was r/u Linz, Barcelona and Essen and reached 4 more sf. Qualified for VS Champs, where she lost qf to Huber and played in winning Spanish Fed Cup team. In doubles she won 2 titles from 4 f with 3 different partners. **1994: (4)** *WIMBLEDON, FC Cup, Italian Open, Stratton Mountain.* The highlight of an excellent year came when she won her first GS title at Wimbledon, ending Navratilova's dream of a 10th title in a thrilling f, where the Spaniard overcame a leg injury to play superb tennis. She was the 1st Spaniard to reach Wimbledon f since De Alvarez lost to Wills-Moody in 1928. She won 3 more titles and reached sf French Open, VS Houston and San Diego, plus qf Australian Open and same stage at 6 other tourns. One of these was Brighton, where she was accused of throwing the match v Neiland, the day before she was due to attend her coach's wedding in Switzerland. Played on the victorious Spanish Fed Cup team for the third time, and qualified for VS Champs, where she lost qf to Date. **1995: (6)** *FC Cup, Amelia Island, Hamburg, Italian Open, San Diego, Manhattan Beach.* After splitting with Van Harpen, who left 'for family reasons', she was coached by Carlos Kirmayr from March 1995, whereupon her fortunes changed and she won FC Cup, Amelia Island, Hamburg and Italian Open (d. Pierce and Sanchez-Vicario) back-to-back, following with San Diego and Manhattan Beach. She was also r/u Delray Beach and reached sf of all 4 GS tourns. She had slipped down the rankings behind Pierce, but after beating her again at San

Diego, she regained the No. 3 position and at end Oct. overtook Sanchez-Vicario to take 2nd place (behind Graf and Seles jointly). Qualified for WTA Champs in both singles and doubles (with Tarabini), but was restricted by a neck injury, losing qf singles to Schultz-McCarthy and 1r doubles to Novotna/Sanchez-Vicario. Contributed two singles wins as Spain d. USA 3–2 in f Fed Cup. **1996: (2)** *Italian Open, Moscow.* She became the 1st to win 4 consec. Italian Open titles, following in autumn with Moscow, and was r/u Indian Wells and Hamburg, as well as reaching sf French Open, US Open, Tokyo Toray, FC Cup and San Diego. Her ranking fluctuated for much of the year between 2nd and 3rd spot: on 15 April she slipped to No. 3 behind Sanchez-Vicario again, returned to No. 2 for 1 week on 29 April, but dropped back again after letting slip a 4–1 lead in 2s to lose f Hamburg to her countrywoman. She returned briefly to 2nd spot in Aug., before settling back at No. 3 then dropping to No. 5 in Nov. She finished the year on a sour note, losing to Majoli in a 2r encounter in which she received a warning for racket abuse and a point penalty for a visible obscenity. In doubles, she took an Olympic bronze medal with Sanchez-Vicario and won San Diego with G. Fernandez. **1997:** She struggled to hold on to her top 10 ranking, slipping in and out of the elite before finishing the season just outside after another disappointing performance at Chase Champs, where Novotna beat her 1r. A highlight was at Stanford, where she was r/u, upsetting Seles (1st time in 12 meetings) and Coetzer. She reached no other f, but appeared in sf FC Cup, Toronto and Moscow, as well as qf Tokyo Pan Pacific, Oklahoma City, Amelia Island, Hamburg, San Diego and Tokyo Nicherei. She also qualified for Chase Champs in doubles with Tarabini, despite having reached no f all year. **1998: (2)** *Berlin, Warsaw.* Looking fitter and more enthusiastic than for some time, she began the year on a high note with r/u slot at Australian Open, upsetting Davenport on the way and returning to the top 10. She followed in May with her 1st title for 18 months at Berlin, adding Warsaw in July. She was also r/u Amelia Island and Rome, reached qf Indian Wells, Montreal and Moscow, and played in winning ESP Fed Cup team. When she d. Perfetti 2r Rome, she became 16th woman in pro tennis to win 500 singles matches, but the later part of the year was disappointing as she lost 1r GS Cup to Hingis and fell at the same stage to Van Roost at Chase Champs. In doubles she won FC Cup with Tarabini, with whom she qualified again for Chase Champs, although they lost 1r to Raymond/Stubbs. **1999: (1)** *Sopot.* She not only dropped out of the top 10, but had slipped far enough down the rankings to be unseeded at the French Open, where she upset Pierce to reach qf. Her season continued to improve as she won Sopot, and also across the year reached sf Amelia Island and qf Hamburg, Manhattan Beach, Tokyo Toyota and Leipzig to qualify for Chase Champs, where she lost in 3s 1r to V. Williams. In doubles she won Amelia Island and Tokyo Toyota with Tarabini to qualify for Chase Champs, where they did not pass 1r. **2000: (1)** *Berlin.* Benefiting from the advice of sports psychologist Guillermo Perez, she regained her place in the top 5. Her best performance came at Berlin, where she upset Hingis *en route* to the singles title and won the doubles with Sanchez-Vicario – despite having already announced her withdrawal from Rome the following week, citing an achilles tendon injury. She was back in action to reach her 1st French Open f, where she lost to Pierce, having begun the year in GS with sf showing at Australian Open. Although she was less impressive at Wimbledon, US Open and Olympics, she was consistent through the year as r/u Gold Coast and Amelia Island and appearing in sf FC Cup (where she was r/u doubles with Tarabini), Montreal, Philadelphia and qf Indian Wells, Hamburg, Sopot (ret with wrist injury), San Diego, Los Angeles, Filderstadt and Chase Champs.

PRINCIPAL 2000 RESULTS – won 1, r/u 3, sf 4 (detailed Grand Slam results follow)
won Berlin (d. Plischke 6–0 ret, Suarez 6–4 6–3, Leon Garcia 6–4 6–2, Hingis 6–4 6–4, Coetzer 6–1 6–2); **r/u** French Open, **r/u** Gold Coast (d. Plischke 6–3 6–4, Rittner 6–2 1–0 ret, Appelmans 7–6 4–6 6–4, Dechy 6–3 6–1, lost Talaja 6–0 0–6 6–4), **r/u** Amelia Island (d. Dementieva 7–6 6–2, Dokic 6–1 6–4, Schett 6–4 6–3, Likhovtseva 6–3 6–2, lost Seles 6–3 6–2); **sf** Australian Open, **sf** FC Cup (d. Serna 7–6 6–1, Nejedly 6–2 6–1, lost Sanchez-Vicario 7–5 7–5), **sf** Montreal (d. A. Miller 6–0 6–1, Halard-Decugis w/o, Kremer 6–2 6–3, lost Hingis 6–3 6–2), **sf** Philadelphia (d. Kolbovic 6–1 6–3, Parkinson 6–2 6–0, lost Davenport 6–0 6–1). **2000 HIGHLIGHTS – DOUBLES:** (with Sanchez-Vicario) **won** Berlin (d. Coetzer/Morariu 3–6 6–2 7–6); (with Tarabini) **r/u** FC Cup (lost Ruano Pascual/Suarez 7–5 6–3).

CAREER GRAND SLAM RECORD
AUSTRALIAN OPEN – Played 10, r/u 1, sf 2, qf 2
1989: 2r d. Sviglerova 6–0 6–0, lost Sabatini [3] 3 6 6–1 0–2. **1992 last 16** [seed 8] d. Stafford 6–3 6–1, Rehe 6–1 6–2, R. White 7–5 6–0, lost Maleeva-Fragniere [9] 6–4 2–6 6–2. **1993: last 16** [seed 6] d. Rottier 2–6 6–4 6–1, Javer 7–5 6–1, Oremans 6–3 4–6 6–4, lost Halard 6–4 6–3. **1994: qf** [seed 3] d. Zvereva 5–7 6–4 6–3,

Fendick 6–7 6–1 6–4, Frazier 6–3 6–0, Rubin 7–6 6–3, lost Date [10] 6–2 4–6 6–3. **1995: sf** [seed 2] d. Rittner 6–3 6–2, Martinek 6–1 6–3, Boogert 6–3 2–6 6–3, Spirlea 6–2 6–7 6–2, Davenport [6] 6–3 4–6 6–3, lost Pierce [4] 6–3 6–1. **1996: qf** [seed 2] d. Wood 6–4 6–1, Labat 6–2 6–4, Kandarr 6–3 6–0, Davenport [10] 6–3 6–1, lost Huber [8] 4–6 6–2 6–1. **1997: last 16** [seed 3] d. Oremans 6–0 6–2, Gersi 6–2 7–6, Carlsson 6–0 6–1, lost Appelmans [16] 2–6 7–5 6–1. **1998: r/u** [seed 8] d. Kloesel 6–2 6–2, Oremans 7–5 6–2, Sidot 3–6 6–0 6–3, Schett 6–3 6–3, Testud [9] 6–3 6–2, Davenport [2] 4–6 6–3 6–3, lost Hingis [1] 6–3 6–3. **1999: 3r** [seed 9] d. Gersi 6–3 6–3, Rippner 6–0 6–4, lost Loit 7–5 6–1. **2000: sf** [seed 10] d. Kleinova 6–1 6–1, Barabanschikova 6–3 4–6 6–3, Kostanic 6–4 6–4, Brandi 6–1 6–1, Likhovtseva [16] 6–3 4–6 9–7, lost Hingis [1] 6–3 6–2.

FRENCH OPEN – Played 13, r/u, sf 3, qf 6
1988: last 16 d. Dechaume 6–0 6–2, Scheuer Larsen 6–2 6–0, McNeil [9] 1–6 6–3 6–1, lost Fulco 6–2 6–4. **1989: qf** [seed 8] d. Herr 6–3 6–2, Pospisilova 6–0 6–4, Amiach 6–3 6–3, K. Maleeva [9] 6–0 6–1, lost Graf [1] 6–0 6–4. **1990: qf** [seed 9] d. Thompson 7–5 6–1, Etchemendy 7–6 6–3, Zrubakova 6–1 6–3, Probst 6–3 6–3, lost Graf [1] 6–1 6–3. **1991: qf** [seed 7] d. Wiesner 6–4 6–3, Rehe 6–1 7–6, Cunningham, 6–1 6–4, Capriati [10] 6–3 6–3, lost Seles [1] 6–0 7–5. **1992: qf** [seed 7] d. Gildemeister 6–2 7–6, Martinek 6–2 6–0, Grossman 6–2 6–2, Meskhi [15] 6–4 7–6, lost Sabatini [3] 3–6 6–3 6–2. **1993: qf** [seed 4] d. Ghirardi 7–5 3–6 6–4, Helgeson 7–5 6–2, Baudone 6–0 7–5, Wiesner 6–3 6–3, lost Huber [8] 6–7 6–4 6–4. **1994: sf** [seed 3] d. Neiland 6–2 6–3, Helgeson 6–2 6–3, Schultz 7–5 6–3, Dechaume-Balleret 6–1 6–2, Hack [16] 2–6 6–0 6–2, lost Sanchez-Vicario [2] 6–3 6–1). **1995: sf** [seed 4] d. Hack 6–0 6–0, Oremans 6–2 6–3, Halard 6–1 6–2, Serra-Zanetti 6–0 6–1, Ruano Pascual 6–0 6–4, lost Graf [2] 6–3 6–7 6–3. **1996: sf** [seed 3] d. Callens 6–1 6–1, Zrubakova 6–3 7–5, Grossman 6–2 6–1, Coetzer [14] 6–2 6–3, Davenport [9] 6–1 6–3, lost Graf [1] 6–3 6–1). **1997: last 16** [seed 7] d. Loic 6–4 6–2 6–3, Rubin 6–3 6–0, Dhenin 6–2 6–1, lost Coetzer [11] 6–7 6–4 6–3. **1998: last 16** [seed 7] d. Lamarre 6–1 6–1, Grande 6–1 6–2, Ruano Pascual 6–1 6–0, lost Majoli [10] 7–6 6–7 6–3. **1999: qf** [unseeded] d. Black 2–6 6–3 6–3, Pierce [8] 4–6 6–3 6–3, Smashnova 6–2 7–5, Leon Garcia 6–2 6–1, lost Seles [3] 6–1 6–4. **2000: r/u** [seed 5] d. Jidkova 6–2 6–3, Black 4–6 7–5 6–4, Farina-Elia 6–1 6–0, Sugiyama 5–7 6–3 6–4, Marrero 7–6 6–1, Sanchez-Vicario [8] 6–1 6–2, lost Pierce [6] 6–2 7–5.

WIMBLEDON – Played 9, won 1, sf 2
1992: 2r [seed 8] d. Daniels 6–1 6–0, lost Zvereva 6–3 5–7 6–4. **1993: sf** [seed 6] d. Helgeson 7–5 6–3, Wiesner 6–1 4–6 6–1, Paradis-Mangon 7–5 6–0, Basuki 3–6 6–2 6–2, Sukova [15] 6–1 6–4, lost Graf [1] 7–6 6–3. **1994: won** [seed 3] d. Simpson-Alter 6–1 6–3, Miyagi 6–1 7–6, Tauziat 6–1 6–3, Radford 3–6 6–3 6–4, Davenport [9] 6–2 6–7 6–3, McNeil 3–6 6–2 10–8, Navratilova [4] 6–4 3–6 6–3. **1995: sf** [seed 4] d. Carlsson 6–1 6–1, Kandarr 6–4 6–3, Stafford 6–1 6–1, Kamstra 6–2 6–3, Sabatini [8] 7–5 7–6, lost Sanchez-Vicario [2] 6–3 6–7 6–1. **1996: last 16** [seed 3] d. Farina 6–0 6–0, Raymond 7–5 7–5, McNeil 7–5 7–6, lost Date [12] 6–7 7–6 6–3. **1997: 3r** [seed 10] d. Habsudova 6–1 6–2, Yoshida 6–0 6–0, lost Sukova 6–4 6–2. **1998: 3r** [seed 8] d. Farina 6–1 6–0, Boogert 7–5 7–5, lost Smith 2–6 6–3 7–5. **1999:** d. Kuti Kis 6–2 6–1, Snyder 6–4 6–1, lost Raymond 6–3 7–6, lost Jeyaseelan 6–4 6–1. **2000: 2r** [seed 4] d. Kremer 6–3 7–6, lost Jeyaseelan 6–4 6–1.

US OPEN – Played 13, sf 2, qf 1
1988: 1r lost Evert [3] 6–4 6–1. **1989: last 16** [seed 15] d. Birch 6–3 6–2, Amiach 6–3 6–4, Hanika 7–5 6–1, lost Sabatini [3] 6–1 6–1. **1990: 3r** [seed 10] d. Werdel 2–6 7–5 6–2, Bartos 6–0 6–4, lost Tauziat 6–2 6–1. **1991: qf** [seed 8] d. Dahlman 6–1 6–1, Basuki 6–3 6–4, Fendick 7–5 6–3, Garrison, [12] 6–4 6–4, lost Graf [1] 6–1 6–3. **1992: 1r** [seed 8] lost Grossman 6–3 2–6 6–4. **1993: last 16** [seed 4] d. Testud 6–2 6–3, Frazier 6–1 6–0, Muns-Jagerman 6–3 6–1, lost Maleeva-Fragniere [11] 1–6 6–0 6–2. **1994: 3r** [seed 3] d. Martinek 6–1 6–0, Arendt 6–3 6–3, lost Helgeson 3–6 6–4 6–1. **1995: sf** [seed 4] d. Rinaldi-Stunkel 6–2 6–2, Po 6–1 6–4, Sawamatsu 6–1 6–2, Garrison-Jackson 7–6 7–5, Schultz-McCarthy [16] 3–6 7–6 6–2, lost Seles [2] 6–2 6–2. **1996: sf** [seed 4] d. Dragomir 6–2 6–0, Tauziat 6–1 6–3, Sukova 6–4 6–3, Carlsson 6–2 6–1, Wild 7–6 6–0, lost Seles [2] 6–4 6–3. **1997: 3r** [seed 7] d. Capriati 6–1 6–2, Smith 6–1 6–0, lost McQuillan 6–7 7–5. **1998: last 16** [seed 7] d. Oremans 6–1 6–2, Trail 7–6 6–1, Raymond 6–3 3–6 6–2, lost Coetzer [13] 6–4 4–6 6–2. **1999: last 16** [seed 16] d. Rubin 6–2 6–3, Dechaume-Balleret 6–0 6–0, Dementieva 6–2 2–6 6–4, lost S. Williams [7] 4–6 6–2 6–2. **2000: 3r** [seed 7] d. Frazier 6–3 2–6 6–3, Sanchez Lorenzo 6–3 6–2, lost Dementieva 6–4 6–1.

OLYMPIC RECORD
1992: (Barcelona) qf [seed 5] d. Wiesner 4–6 6–1 6–2, Cecchini 6–4 6–3, Coetzer 6–4 6–3, lost Sanchez-Vicario [2] 6–4 6–4. **1996: (Atlanta) qf** [seed 2] d. Schnyder 6–1 6–2, Zrubakova 6–1 6–4, Zvereva 6–2 7–5, lost M. J. Fernandez [7] 3–6 6–2 6–3. **2000: (Sydney) 2r** [seed 4] d. Mandula 6–1 6–0, lost Habsudova 1–6 6–0 6–4). **DOUBLES:** (with Sanchez-Vicario) **1992: (Barcelona) r/u silver medal** d. McQuillan/ Provis 6–3 6–3, lost G./M. J. Fernandez 7–5 2–6 6–2. **1996: (Atlanta) sf bronze medal** lost Novotna/Sukova; bronze medal play-off d. Bollegraf/Schultz-McCarthy 6–1 6–3. **2000: (Sydney)** 2r [seed 2] d. Bedanova/Hrdlickova 6–4 6–3; lost Barabanschikova/Zvereva 6–4 7–5.

CAREER FEDERATION CUP RECORD
1988 (in AUS, Hard): 1r *ESP d. NED 3–0*. R1 d. M. Bollegraf 6–2 6–4; R3 (with A. Sanchez-Vicario) d. Bollegraf/C. Vis 5–7 6–4 6–4. *2r ESP d. INA 3–0*. R1 d. W. Walalangi 6–0 6–1; R3 (with Sanchez-Vicario) d. S. Anggarkusuma/N. Basuki 6–0 5–7 6–2. *Qf URS d. ESP 2–1*. R1 lost L. Savchenko 7–6 6–2; R3 (with Sanchez-Vicario) lost Savchenko/N. Zvereva 4–6 6–4 6–4. **1989 (in JPN, Hard): 1r** *ESP d. FRA 2–0.* d. I. Demongeot 6–7 7–6 6–4. *2r ESP d. NED 2–0.* R1 d. N. Jagerman 6–4 7–5. *Qf ESP d. URS 2–1.* R1 d. L. Savchenko 6–1 6–1;

R3 (with A. Sanchez-Vicario) lost Savchenko/N. Zvereva 6–4 2–6 6–1. *Sf ESP d. AUS 2–0.* R1 d. E. Smylie 6–3 6–2. *Final USA d. ESP 3–0.* R1 lost C. Evert 6–3 6–2; R3 (with Sanchez-Vicario) lost Z. Garrison/P. Shriver (USA) 7–5 6–1. **1990 (in USA, Hard):** *1r ESP d. CAN 2–1.* R1 d. J. Hetherington 6–1 6–4; R3 (with P. Perez) lost J. Hetherington/R. Simpson 7–5 2–6 6–2. *2r ESP d. ISR 3–0.* R1 (d. I. Berger 6–3 6–2; (with A. Sanchez-Vicario) d. Berger/L. Zaltz 6–3 6–4. *Qf ESP d. FRA 3–0.* R1 d. J. Halard 6–0 6–3; R3 (with Sanchez-Vicario) d. I. Demongeot/M. Pierce 6–4 6–4. *Sf ESP d. URS 2–1.* R1 d. L. Meshki 6–3 7–5; R3 (with Perez) lost L. Savchenko/N. Zvereva 6–2 6–3. **1991 (in GBR, Hard):** *1r ESP d. BEL 2–0.* 1R d. D. Monami 6–3 6–1. *2r ESP d. AUS 3–0.* R1 d. N. Provis 6–0 2–6 7–5; R3 (with A. Sanchez-Vicario) d. K. Godridge/E. Smylie 6–3 6–4. *Qf ESP d. INA 2–0.* R1 d. S. Wibowo 6–2 6–0. *Sf ESP d. GER 3–0.* R1 d. B. Rittner 6–4 6–1; R3 (with Sanchez-Vicario) d. Rittner/A. Huber 6–1 6–1. *Final ESP d. USA 2–1.* R1 lost J. Capriati 4–6 7–6 6–1; R3 (with Sanchez-Vicario) d. Z. Garrison/G. Fernandez 3–6 6–1 6–1. **1992 (in GER, Clay):** *1r ESP d. BEL 2–1.* R1 d. D. Monami 6–1 6–4. *2r ESP d. CAN 2–1.* R1 lost H. Kelesi 7–6 6–2; R3 (with A. Sanchez-Vicario) d. J. Hetherington/P. Hy 6–4 6–0. *Qf ESP d. ARG 2–1.* R1 d. F. Labat 6–0 6–1. *Sf ESP d. AUS 3–0.* R1 d. R. McQuillan 6–1 6–4. *Final GER d. ESP 2–1.* R1 lost A. Huber 6–3 6–7 6–1; R3 (with Sanchez-Vicario) d. Huber/B. Rittner 6–1 6–2. **1993 (in GER, Clay):** *1r ESP d. GBR 3–0.* R1 d. J. Durie 6–2 6–1; (with A. Sanchez-Vicario) d. Durie/C. Wood 6–1 4–6 6–1). *2r ESP d. INA 3–0.* R1 d. R. Tedjakusuma 6–1 6–1. *Qf ESP d. NED 3–0.* R1 d. S. Rottier 7–6 6–3. *Sf ESP d. FRA 2–1.* R1 d. J. Halard 6–1 3–6 6–3. *Final ESP d. AUS 3–0.* R1 d. M. Jaggard-Lai 6–0 6–2; R3 (with Sanchez-Vicario) d. E. Smylie/R. Stubbs 3–6 6–1 6–3). **1994 (in GER, Clay):** *1r ESP d. CHI 3–0.* R1 d. M. Quezada 6–1 6–0; R3 (with A. Sanchez-Vicario) d. P. Cabezas/B. Castro 6–0 6–1. *2r ESP d. ARG 3–0.* R1 d. P. Tarabini 6–3 6–7 6–2). *Qf ESP d. JPN 3–0.* R1 d. N. Sawamatsu 6–3 6–4. *Sf ESP d. GER 2–1.* R1 lost S. Hack 2–6 7–5 6–4; R3 (with Sanchez-Vicario) d. B. Rittner/C. Singer 7–5 6–1. *Final ESP d. USA 3–0.* R1 d. M. J. Fernandez 6–2 6–2; R3 (with Sanchez-Vicario) d. G./M. J. Fernandez 6–3 6–4. **1995: April** – World Group qf ESP d. BUL 3–2 in BUL (Carpet). R2 d. M. Maleeva 6–2 6–4; R4 d. K. Maleeva 6–2 6–1. **July** – World Group sf ESP d. GER 3–2 in ESP (Clay). R1 d. A Huber 6–2 2–6 6–0; R4 d. S. Hack 6–0 6–0. **November** – World Group Final ESP d. USA 3–2 in ESP (Clay). R1 d. C. Rubin 7–5 7–6; R3 d. M. J. Fernandez 6–3 6–4. **1996: April** – World Group qf ESP d. RSA 3–2 in ESP (Clay). R2 d. A. Coetzer 7–5 6–3; R4 d. M. De Swardt 6–2 6–3. **July** – World Group sf ESP d. FRA 3–2 in FRA (Carpet). R1 d. J. Halard-Decugis 1–6 6–4 6–2; R3 d. M. Pierce 7–5 6–1; R5 (with A. Sanchez-Vicario) d. Halard-Decugis/N. Tauziat 6–4 6–1). **September** – World Group Final USA d. ESP 5–0 in USA (Carpet). R1 lost M. Seles 6–2 6–4. **1998: April** – World Group qf ESP d. GER 3–2 in GER (Carpet). R2 lost J. Kandarr 6–1 1–6 7–5; R3 lost A. Glass 3–6 6–3 6–2; R5 (with M. Serna) d. Glass/W. Probst 6–4 7–6). **July** – World Group sf ESP d. USA 3–2 in ESP (Clay). R2 lost M. Seles 6–3 3–6 6–1; R4 d. L. Raymond 7–6 6–4; R5 (with A. Sanchez-Vicario) d. M. J. Fernandez/Raymond 6–4 6–7 11–9. **September** – World Group Final ESP d. SUI 3–2 in SUI (Hard). R2 lost M. Hingis 6–4 6–4; R4 d. P. Schnyder 6–3 2–6 9–7; R5 (with Sanchez-Vicario) d. Hingis/Schnyder 6–0 6–2. **2000: April (in ITA, Clay):** World Group rr ESP d. ITA 3–0 in ITA (Clay). R2 d. T. Garbin 6–3 6–3. ESP d. CRO 2–1. R 2. d. J. Kostanic 6–3 6–2. ESP d. GER 2–1. R2 lost A. Huber 6–3 6–1; R3 (with A. Sanchez-Vicario) d. Huber/B. Rittner 6–2 6–3. **November (in USA, Carpet):** World Group sf ESP d. CZE 2–1. R2 d. K. Hrdlickova 7–6 6–7 6–4. *Final USA d. ESP 5–0.* R1 lost M. Seles 6–2 6–3; R3 lost L. Davenport 6–1 6–2.

GRAND SLAM CUP RECORD – Played 1
1998: 1r lost Hingis [1] 6–2 7–5.

SEASON ENDING CHAMPIONSHIPS – Played 11, qf 4
(1983–94 Virginia Slims, 1995 Corel, 1996–2000 Chase)
1990: 1r lost Garrison 6–3 6–0. **1991: 1r** lost Graf 6–0 6–3. **1992: qf** d. K. Maleeva 6–4 6–3, lost McNeil 3–6 6–3 6–2. **1993: qf** d. Maleeva-Fragniere 7–5 6–2, lost Huber 6–3 6–3. **1994: qf** d. Zvereva 2–6 6–2 6–4, lost Date 2–6 6–4 7–6. **1995: qf** d. Majoli 1–6 7–5 6–0, lost Schultz-McCarthy 7–5 6–2. **1996: 2r** d. Wiesner 6–1 3–6 6–4, lost Majoli 7–6 7–6. **1997: 1r** lost Novotna 6–4 6–4. **1998: 1r** lost Van Roost 7–6 6–2. **1999: 1r** lost V. Williams 6–2 5–7 6–4. **2000: qf** d. Likhovtseva 2–6 6–4 6–3, lost Kournikova 6–4 6–0.

6 SERENA WILLIAMS (USA)

Born: Saginaw, Mich., 26 September 1981. **Lives:** Palm Beach Gardens, Fla. **Father:** Richard. **Mother:** Oracene. **Sisters:** Isha, Lyndrea, Yelunde, Venus (all older).

Agent: Keven Davis Esq., Garvey, Schubert and Barer.
Coach: Her parents, Richard and Oracene; formerly Rick Macci. **Turned pro:** 1997.
Height: 5ft 10in (1.78m). **Weight:** 145lb (65kg).

Rankings: 1997: 99; **1998:** 20; **1999:** 4; **2000:** 6. **Highest:** 4 (1999).

2000 Prize Money: $1,001,818. **Career Earnings:** $3,970,061. **Career Titles:** 8.

Style: An even stronger athlete than her sister, Venus, and equally fit and well-trained, she hits the ball with intimidating power from the baseline, right-handed on forehand, two-handed on backhand. She serves well and volleys at selected moments to pose serious problems for her opponents, who are surprised by her speed about the court.

CAREER HIGHLIGHTS (year: (titles))

1997: She burst into prominence at Chicago, where, in only her 2nd tourn, she upset Pierce and Seles back-to-back on her way to sf. **1998:** Aiming for the top 10 by year's end, she began by upsetting Spirlea at Australian Open and again at LIPC, where she went on to extend Hingis to 7–6 fs. These results took her into the top 50, and she cracked the top 20 after French Open where, unseeded, she upset Van Roost and extended Sanchez-Vicario to 3s, as well as being r/u mixed doubles with Lobo. At Wimbledon she withdrew from singles with a calf injury when losing to Ruano-Pascual, but continued to play mixed doubles and went on to win the title with Mirnyi, with whom she also won US Open mixed. Although she did not quite reach the heights she had hoped for, she was always a threat to the top players and caused more significant upsets on her way to sf Sydney (d. Davenport) and qf Oklahoma City, LIPC (d. Spirlea and Schnyder), Rome (d. Tauziat and Martinez), Eastbourne (d. Sugiyama), Los Angeles (d. Testud) and Filderstadt (d. Novotna). In women's doubles she won Oklahoma City and Zurich with her sister, Venus, and was voted WTA Newcomer of the Year. **1999: (5)** *US OPEN, Paris Open, Indian Wells, Manhattan Beach, GS Cup.* The highlight of her career to date came at US Open, where she won her 1st GS title, beating her sister, Venus, to that distinction. After a wobble in 4r, when Clijsters served for the match before Williams won next 12 points to win, she removed Seles, Davenport and finally Hingis to take the title as the lowest-seeded woman (7) to win US Open in the open era. This took her to a career-high No. 4, where she remained at end of year, despite having played only 12 tourns, compared to Hingis's 21 and her sister's 19. Her triumphs began in Feb. when she upset Tauziat and Mauresmo to win her 1st tour title at Paris Open, unseeded, and followed with Indian Wells (again unseeded) in her next tourn, upsetting Davenport, Pierce, Testud and Graf. She followed that with r/u LIPC to her sister, Venus, including upsets of Seles and Hingis, to break into top 10 1st time on 5 April. She upset Hingis again *en route* to a 3rd title at Manhattan Beach, followed by US Open and finally GS Cup, in which she d. her sister, Venus, in f. She also reached qf Rome and Berlin and played in winning USA Fed Cup team. A back injury prevented her taking up her place at Chase Champs, and she was troubled by injury and ailments during the year, patella tendinitis of the right knee affecting her in spring, an arm injury in May, her back in Nov. and severe flu keeping her out of Wimbledon. In doubles with Venus she won French Open, US Open and Hannover from 4 f and in mixed was r/u Australian Open with Mirnyi. **2000: (3)** *Hannover, Los Angeles, Tokyo Toyota.* Her 1st title of the year came at Hannover after she had been r/u Paris Open the previous week. At Amelia Island she ret with a meniscus tear in left knee at 5–2 15–0 down fs v Suarez, and withdrew FC Cup the following week in support of the National Association for the Advancement of Coloured People's boycott of South Carolina for flying the Confederate flag from the Civic Hall. In fact the knee injury kept her out until June, sidelining her for French Open. Returning at

Wimbledon, she swept to sf for the loss of only 13 games before falling to her sister – the 1st seed she had encountered. At Los Angeles, where Venus was not playing, she upset Hingis and Davenport back-to-back to win the title, and at f Montreal the following week she took the 1st set v Hingis before retiring 0–3 down in 3s with sesmoiditis (inflammation) at base of left foot. She played at US Open but, having lost sf singles to Davenport, she withdrew from sf doubles (with Venus) with the same injury, and although they went on to win Olympic gold together, and she was able to play and win Tokyo Toyota the following week, it was that same left foot injury that prevented her taking her place at Chase Champs.

PRINCIPAL 2000 RESULTS – won 3, r/u 2, sf 2 (detailed Grand Slam results follow)
won Hannover (d. Appelmans 6–1 6–3, Schnyder 6–1 6–4, Mauresmo 6–2 6–7 7–6, Chladkova 6–1 6–1), **won** Los Angeles (d. Dragomir 6–0 6–1, Tanasugarn 6–2 6–2, C. Martinez 6–2 4–6 6–2, Hingis 4–6 6–2 6–3, Davenport 4–6 6–4 7–6), **won** Tokyo Toyota (d. Tanasugarn 6–1 6–4, Dokic 6–3 6–4, Bedanova 6–1 6–4, Halard-Decugis 7–5 6–1); **r/u** Paris Open (d. Schnyder 6–2 6–2, Pitkowski 6–1 6–1, Halard-Decugis 6–4 6–2, lost Tauziat 7–5 6–2), **r/u** Montreal (d. Schnyder 6–1 6–2, Kournikova 6–4 6–3, Frazier 6–0 6–1, Sanchez-Vicario ??, lost Hingis 0–6 6–3 3–0 ret); **sf** Wimbledon, **sf** US Open. **DOUBLES:** (with V. Williams) **won Wimbledon** (d. Halard-Decugis/Sugiyama 6–3 6–2), **won Olympic gold medal**.

CAREER GRAND SLAM RECORD
AUSTRALIAN OPEN – Played 3
1998: 2r d. Spirlea [6] 6–7 6–3 6–1, lost V. Williams 7–6 6–1. **1999: 3r** d. Sandu 6–2 6–3, Serna 6–1 6–3, lost Testud [14] 6–2 2–6 9–7. **2000: last 16** [seed 3] d. Grahame 6–4 4–6 6–4, Pratt 7–5 6–1, Appelmans 6–2 7–6, lost Likhovtseva [16] 6–3 6–3.
FRENCH OPEN – Played 2
1998: last 16 [unseeded] (d. Nejedly 6–2 1–6 6–4, Morariu 6–1 6–0, Van Roost 6–1 6–1, lost Sanchez-Vicario [4] 4–6 7–5 6–3. **1999: 3r** [seed 10] d. Courtois 6–4 6–0, Diaz-Oliva 6–3 6–4, lost Fernandez 6–3 1–6 6–0. **2000:** Did not play.
WIMBLEDON – Played 2, sf 1
1998: 3r d. Golarsa 6–4 6–3, Lucic 6–3 6–0, lost Ruano-Pascual 7–5 4–1 ret. **1999:** Did not play. **2000: sf** [seed 8] d. Carlsson 6–3 6–2, Basting 6–1 6–0, Torrens-Valero 6–2 6–1, Tanasugarn 6–1 6–1, Raymond 6–2 6–0, lost V. Williams [5] 6–2 7–6.
US OPEN – Played 3, won 1, sf 2
1998: 3r d. Pratt 6–3 3–6 6–4, Stoyanova 6–2 6–1, lost Spirlea [9] 6–3 0–6 7–5. **1999: won** [seed 7] d. Po 6–1 6–0, Kostanic 6–4 6–2, Clijsters 4–6 6–2 7–5, Martinez [16] 4–6 6–2 6–2, Seles [4] 4–6 6–3 6–2, Davenport [2] 6–4 1–6 6–4, Hingis [1] 6–3 7–6. **2000: sf** [seed 5] d. Pisnik 6–3 6–2, Petrova 6–3 6–2, Casoni 6–4 6–2, Dokic 7–6 6–0, lost Davenport [2] 6–4 6–2.

OLYMPIC RECORD
Has never played singles. **DOUBLES:** (with V. Williams) **2000: (Sydney) won gold medal** d. Boogert/Oremans 6–1 6–1.

CAREER FED CUP RECORD
1999: July – *World Group sf USA d. ITA 4–1 in ITA (Clay).* R4 d. R. Grande 6–1 6–1; R5 (with V. Williams) d. T. Garbin/Adriana Serra-Zanetti 6–2 6–2). **September** – *World Group Final USA d. RUS 4–1 in USA (Hard).* R5 (with V. Williams) d. E. Dementieva/E. Makarova 6–2 6–1. **1999: July** – *World Group rr USA d. ITA 4–1 in ITA (Clay).* R4 d. R. Grande 6–1 6–1; R5 (with V. Williams) d. T. Garbin/Ad. Serra-Zanetti 6–2 6–2. **September** – *World Group Final USA d. RUS 4–1 in USA (Hard).* R5 (with V. Williams) d. E. Dementieva/E. Makarova 6–2 6–1.

CAREER GRAND SLAM CUP RECORD – Played 1, won 1
1999: won [seed 3] d. Sanchez-Vicario 6–3 6–1, Davenport [2] 6–3 6–4, V. Williams [4] 6–1 3–6 6–3.

SEASON ENDING CHAMPIONSHIPS
Has never played.

7 MARY PIERCE (FRA)

Born: Montreal, Canada, 15 January 1975. **Lives:** Paris and Bradenton, Fla., USA. **Father:** Jim. **Mother:** Yannick, who is French. **Brother:** David (younger). **Fiance:** Roberto Alomar, a Cleveland Indians baseball player.

Agent: IMG. **Coach:** Her brother David; formerly her father, then Nick Bollettieri, Sven Groeneveld, Joe Giuliano, Brad Gilbert, Craig Kardon, Michael De Jongh and Craig Wildey. **Trainer:** Jose Rincon and her brother David.
Turned pro: March 1989.
Height: 5ft 10in (1.80m). **Weight:** 150lb (64kg).

Rankings: 1989: 236; **1990:** 106; **1991:** 26; **1992:** 13; **1993:** 12; **1994:** 5; **1995:** 5; **1996:** 20; **1997:** 7; **1998:** 7; **1999:** 5; **2000:** 7 singles, 9 doubles. **Highest:** 3 (February 1995).

2000 Prize Money: $1,208,018. **Career Earnings:** $6,169,661. **Career Titles:** 14.

Style: An exciting, forceful baseliner with uncompromising attitude whose forehand is as powerful as Graf's used to be. Her two-handed backhand is also powerful, though somewhat erratic. Not a natural volleyer. Has improved her movement and also her awareness of when to take risks.

CAREER HIGHLIGHTS (year: (titles))
Decided to play for France, her mother's country, when the USTA, put off by her father's aggressive manner, were not interested in supporting her. He was banned indefinitely from all her tournaments from French Open 1993 – mainly as a consequence of his disruptive behaviour, but also after bruises on her arms and shoulders, which he had inflicted, were noticed. Free from his dominance, she gained in confidence and was advised until Feb. 1996 by Nick Bollettieri. **1989:** At 14 yrs 2 mths at Hilton Head, she was the youngest to make her pro debut – a record broken the following year by Capriati. Won York on the USTA satellite circuit. **1990:** Reached sf Athens and moved to France, representing that country in Fed Cup. **1991: (1)** *Palermo.* At Palermo she won both singles and doubles for her 1st career title, which took her into the top 50. Upset Fairbank-Nideffer *en route* to last 16 LIPC and appeared in sf Puerto Rico. **1992: (3)** *Cesena, Palermo, Puerto Rico.* Broke into the top 20 after winning Cesena and followed with Palermo and Puerto Rico, plus sf Essen. Reached last 16 French Open and US Open, but was forced to withdraw from LIPC with leg and back strains. **1993: (1)** *Filderstadt.* She won Filderstadt, was r/u Palermo and reached sf Brighton plus 6 more qf, including Australian Open, where she extended Sabatini to 3s. From May onwards, once her aggressive father was excluded from her affairs, she was noticeably more relaxed in her game. She confirmed this improvement and crowned her year by upsetting Sabatini and Navratilova (her 1st victories over top 10 players) on her way to sf VS Champs, for which she qualified 1st time. **1994:** The highlight of her career came at French Open, where she swept to f with the loss of only 10 games – 4 in her sf v Graf, whom she demolished, having managed to win only one game against the same opponent in 1993 US Open. Her loss of only 6 games to qf was a modern-day record. Playing Under-21 at Eastbourne to get used to grass (which she finds difficult to play on), she lost 1r and then announced her withdrawal from Wimbledon 'for reasons beyond my control', later claiming that she could not face the threat that her father might appear there, brought over by a British tabloid newspaper. Although she won no title, she was r/u Houston, Leipzig, Filderstadt, Philadelphia and reached sf FC Cup (upsetting Sanchez-Vicario) and Montreal. At VS Champs she again made her mark, upsetting Graf before falling to Davenport in sf. **1995: (2)** *AUSTRALIAN OPEN, Tokyo Nicherei.* She began the year in tremendous style at Australian Open when she took her 1st GS title without losing a set. However, things went downhill thereafter as she was restricted by a series of illness and injury problems. She suffered a groin pull in Feb., then a bad reaction to antibiotics for a kidney infection caused her to withdraw 2r Hamburg, so that the French Open was only her 7th tourn of the year. Despite complaining of shoulder and groin injuries after her defeat in last 16 there, she did appear at Wimbledon for

1st time, although Tauziat beat her 2r. She upset Sanchez-Vicario to win Tokyo Nicherei and appeared in f Paris Open and Zurich, as well as sf Italian Open and San Diego, plus 4 more qf. She moved as high as No. 3 behind Sanchez-Vicario in Feb., although she had slipped back to No. 6 by Nov. Qualified for WTA Champs but lost 1r to Huber. **1996:** She seemed to have lost her way in what turned out to be a disappointing year in which she was affected by injuries. She began the year badly when she became the 1st defending Australian Open champ in the Open era to lose before qf. Her 2r loss saw her fall from the top 10 for 1st time since June 1994, and Nick Bollettieri resigned as her coach in an acrimonious split. She was booed off the court after her defeat at the hands of Rittner 3r French Open and departed without waiting for her opponent after a display of stalling and gamesmanship. Her best performances were at Amelia Island, where she upset Martinez *en route* to f, and Hamburg, where she upset Hingis to reach sf. Otherwise her only qf appearances were at Tokyo Nicherei and at Wimbledon, where, on her least favourite surface, she performed better than expected. On that occasion, she wore a demure white outfit, in contrast to the low-cut black number that aroused such interest at the French Open. She withdrew from Filderstadt, Zurich and Oakland to rest her right shoulder, which had been troubling her for much of the year. **1997: (1)** *Rome.* Returning after 3 months' absence, she had slipped so far down the rankings that she was unseeded at Australian Open, where she upset Huber and Coetzer on her way to f. Then she withdrew Indian Wells with a right calf strain suffered at Fed Cup and was out for another 5 weeks. On her return, she upset Sanchez-Vicario and Majoli on her way to f Amelia Island and surprised Majoli again to reach the same stage Berlin, following with the only title of her year at Rome, upsetting Seles and Martinez on the way. She also reached sf San Diego and qf Paris Open, Hamburg and Rosmalen, and played in winning FRA Fed Cup team in Oct., although an elbow injury had kept her out of sf in July. After missing another 3 tourns in autumn with a kidney infection, she was beaten by S. Williams at Chicago on her return and withdrew from Philadelphia to recover and prepare for Chase Champs. She obviously did that to good effect, for in qf she became only the 5th player all year to beat Hingis. In her 1st f there, she seriously challenged Novotna for 1s, but went on to lose in ss. Played 2 doubles f, winning Hamburg with Huber. **1998: (4)** *Paris Open, Amelia Island, Moscow, Luxembourg.* Her 1st title in France came at Paris Open (d. Novotna) and was followed by Amelia Island, where she upset Davenport and also won the doubles with Cacic. She upset V. Williams and Seles back-to-back to take Moscow (again adding the doubles – with Zvereva), and won Luxembourg the following week. Martinez and Hingis were her victims at San Diego, where she was hampered in f by a leg injury, and she also appeared in qf Australian Open, Zurich and Chase Champs. She generally lost French support as her regular home is not in France and she is apparently not committed to Fed Cup, although it was captain Noah who dropped her from the squad after her Amelia Island triumphs, saying he felt that she hadn't played enough in the year and would not have time to adapt to the faster surface. **1999: (1)** *Linz.* The title at Linz in Oct. was her 1st for 13 months and her only one of the year, although she was r/u Hope Island, Hamburg, Rome and Filderstadt and reached sf Toronto (won doubles with Novotna), Zurich and Leipzig (won doubles with Neiland), plus qf Australian Open, Indian Wells, Amelia Island, Cairo, Manhattan Beach, US Open and Chase Champs. These consistent results took her back to the top 5, where she finished the year, and although she did not upset any of the very top players during the year, she was usually a threat. She appeared in April looking surprisingly muscular as a result of using creatine and played with added power. **2000: (2)** *FRENCH OPEN, Indian Wells.* She appeared calmer under the stabilising influence of her fiance Roberto Alomar and seemed generally more at peace with herself. The climax of her career came at French Open, where she beat C. Martinez in f to became the 1st Frenchwoman for 33 years to win the title there, crowning her triumph by adding the doubles with Hingis, whom she beat in sf singles. That match left her suffering so severely from dehydration and cramp that she required a drip immediately afterwards. She also won FC Cup and reached sf Scottsdale and Indian Wells, plus qf Sydney and Amelia Island. However, she was troubled with right shoulder rotator cuff tendinitis, which kept her out between Wimbledon and US Open, forced her to retire there and prevented her taking her place at Chase Champs. In doubles she and Hingis played 4 f, winning Tokyo Pan Pacific in addition to French Open and r/u Australian Open.

PRINCIPAL 2000 RESULTS – won 2, sf 2 (detailed Grand Slam results follow)
won French Open, **won** FC Cup (d. Leon Garcia 6–1 6–1, Smashnova 6–1 6–2, Dokic 6 3 6–1, Seles 6–1 6–1, Sanchez Vicario 6–1 6 0); **sf** Scottsdale (d. Nacuk 6–0 6–1, Dechy 6–3 6–2, lost Hingis 6–4 6–3), **sf**

Indian Wells (d. Jeyaseelan 6–1 6–3, Morariu 6–2 4–6 6–2, Likhovtseva 6–3 5–7 7–5, S. Williams 6–2 6–1, lost Hingis 6–4 6–2). **DOUBLES:** (with Hingis) **r/u Australian Open** (lost Raymond/Stubbs 5–0 ret), **won French Open** (d. Ruano Pascual/Suarez 6–2 6–4); **won** Tokyo Pan Pacific (d. Fusai/Tauziat 6–4 6–1); **r/u** Sydney (lost Halard-Decugis/Sugiyama 6–0 6–3).

CAREER GRAND SLAM RECORD
AUSTRALIAN OPEN – Played 8, won 1, r/u 1, qf 3
1993: qf [seed 10] d. Byrne 6–2 6–2, Date 6–1 6–1, Davenport 6–3 6–0, G. Fernandez 6–0 6–0, lost Sabatini [3] 4–6 7–6 6–0). **1994: last 16** [seed 9] d. Baudone 6–2 6–1, Harvey-Wild 6–7 7–5 6–3, Appelmans 6–3 6–2, lost Sabatini [4] 6–3 6–3. **1995: won** [seed 4] d. Krizan 6–1 6–0, Reinach 6–1 6–2, Randriantefy 6–3 6–3, Huber [10] 6–2 6–4, Zvereva [8] 6–1 6–4, Martinez [2] 6–3 6–1, Sanchez-Vicario [1] 6–3 6–2. **1996: 2r** [seed 4] d. Schwarz 6–3 6–1, lost Likhovtseva 6–4 6–4. **1997: r/u** [unseeded] d. Likhovtseva [13] 3–6 6–2 6–4, Medvedeva 6–2 6–2, Kochta 6–0 6–2, Huber [5] 6–2 6–3, Appelmans [16] 1–6 6–4 6–4, Coetzer [12] 7–5 6–1, lost Hingis [4] 6–2 6–2. **1998: qf** [seed 5] d. Li 6–0 6–0, Torrens-Valero 6–1 6–2, Barabanschikova 7–5 6–3, Nagyova 6–0 6–0, lost Hingis [1] 6–2 6–3. **1999: qf** [seed 7] d. Watson 6–2 6–1, Kremer 6–2 6–1, Grande 6–2 6–2, Kournikova [12] 6–0 6–4, lost Hingis [2] 6–3 6–4. **2000: last 16** [seed 4] d. Wild 7–5 6–3, Cocheteux 6–2 6–2, Oremans 6–2 6–4, lost Sugiyama 7–5 6–4.
FRENCH OPEN – Played 11, won 1, r/u 1
1990: 2r d. Fulco 6–0 6–1, lost M. J. Fernandez [7] 6–4 6–4. **1991: 3r** d. Dahlman 7–6 6–0, Martinek 6–3 6–0, lost Sabatini [3] 6–2 6–1. **1992: last 16** [seed 13] d. Rajchrtova 6–1 6–1, Savchenko Neiland 6–2 6–3, Strnadova 7–6 6–4, lost Capriati [5] 6–4 6–3. **1993: last 16** [seed 12] d. Mothes 6–0 6–0, McQuillan 6–4 6–0, Po 6–7 6–3 6–3, lost Capriati [6] 6–4 7–6. **1994: r/u** [seed 12] d. Provis 6–1 6–0, Bentivoglio 6–0 6–1, McNeil 6–0 6–0, Coetzer 6–1 6–1, Ritter 6–0 6–2, Graf [1] 6–2 6–2, lost Sanchez-Vicario [2] 6–4 6–4). **1995: last 16** [seed 3] d. Bradtke 6–1 6–3, Singer 7–5 6–0, Labat 6–2 6–2, lost Majoli [12] 6–2 6–3. **1996: 3r** [seed 12] d. Schnell 7–5 6–2, Randriantefy 6–3 2–6 6–2, lost Rittner 6–4 6–2. **1997: last 16** [seed 10] d. Panova 6–2 4–6 6–4, Hy-Boulais 6–1 6–3, Testud 6–1 6–3, lost Seles [3] 6–4 7–5. **1998: 2r** [seed 11] d. Appelmans 6–2 6–3, lost Serna 7–5 6–2. **1999: 2r** [seed 8] d. Kruger 6–4 6–3, lost Martinez 4–6 6–3 6–3. **2000: won** [seed 6] d. Snyder 6–3 6–1, Rittner 6–1 6–1, Razzano 6–4 6–0, Carlsson 6–2 6–1, Seles [3] 4–6 6–3 6–4, Hingis [1] 6–4 5–7 6–2, C. Martinez [5] 6–2 7–5.
WIMBLEDON – Played 6, qf 1
1995: 2r [seed 5] d. Dopfer 6–1 6–2, lost Tauziat 6–4 3–6 6–1. **1996: qf** [seed 13] d. Schnyder 6–3 6–2, Taylor 6–4 6–2, Medvedeva 6–4 6–1, Likhovtseva 6–2 6–3, lost Date [12] 3–6 6–3 6–1. **1997: last 16** [seed 9] d. Van Roost 6–3 6–4, Ruano Pascual 6–0 2–6 6–3, Serna 6–4 6–3, lost Sanchez-Vicario [8] 6–1 6–3. **1998: 1r** [seed 11] lost Tatarkova 7–6 6–3. **1999: last 16** [seed 9] d. Zuluaga 6–3 6–2, Grande 6–1 6–3, Wagner 6–3 6–0, lost Dokic 6–4 6–3. **2000: 2r** [seed 3] d. Pratt 6–1 6–3, lost Serna 7–6 7–6.
US OPEN – Played 9, qf 2
1991: 3r d. Garrone 4–6 6–0 7–6, McNeil 6–3 3–6 7–6, lost Maleeva-Fragniere [10] 4–6 6–1 5–1 ret. **1992: last 16** [seed 16] d. Vento 6–2 6–2, L. Ferrando 7–5 6–4, R. White 6–2 6–1, lost M. J. Fernandez [7] 6–0 6–4. **1993: last 16** [seed 13] d. Baudone 6–0 6–7 7–6, Arendt 6–2 6–4, Schultz 7–5 7–6, lost Graf [1] 6–1 6–0. **1994: qf** [seed 4] d. Temesvari 6–3 6–2, Studenikova 6–3 2–6 6–4, Wiesner 6–2 6–4, Majoli 6–1 6–2, lost Novotna [7] 6–4 6–0. **1995: 3r** [seed 6] d. De Swardt 6–4 6–1, Jecmenica 6–3 6–0, lost Frazier 6–3 7–6. **1996: Did not play. 1997: last 16** [seed 9] d. G. Fernandez 6–1 6–2, Farina 6–2 3–0 ret, Zvereva 7–6 6–1, lost Seles [2] 1–6 6–2 6–2. **1998: last 16** [seed 12] d. Babel 6–1 4–6 6–2, Black 6–1 6–1, Golarsa 6–1 6–0, lost V. Williams [5] 6–1 7–6. **1999: qf** [seed 5] d. Nacuk 6–4 7–6, Leon Garcia 6–2 6–3, Montolio 6–0 7–6, Appelmans 6–3 7–6, lost Davenport [2] 6–2 3–6 7–5. **2000: last 16** [seed 4] d. Stevenson 6–3 6–4, Maleeva 7–5 2–6 6–1, Raymond 6–4 7–6, lost Huber [10] 6–4 ret.

OLYMPIC RECORD
1996: (Atlanta) 2r [seed 12] d. Barabanschikova 7–5 7–6, lost Gorrochategui 6–4 1–6 7–5.

CAREER FED CUP RECORD
1990 (in USA, Hard): *1r FRA d. TPE 3–0.* R3 (with I. Demongeot) d. S. Lai/Y. Lin 6–2 6–2. *2r FRA d. NZL 3–0.* R3 (with Demongeot) d. B. Cordwell/J. Richardson 6–3 6–4. *Qf ESP d. FRA 3–0.* R3 (with Demongeot) lost C. Martinez/A. Sanchez-Vicario 6–4 6–4. **1991 (in GBR, Hard):** *1r POL d. FRA 2–1.* R1 d. M. Mroz 6–4 6–2; R3 (with N. Tauziat) lost Mroz/K. Teodorowicz 6–4 6–4. *Play–off FRA d. YUG 2–0.* R1 d. L. Pavlov 6–0 6–4. **1992 (in GER, Clay):** *1r FRA d. CHN 2–1.* R1 d. L. Chen 6–2 6–2. *2r FRA d. RUS 3–0.* R1 d. E. Makarova 6–1 6–2. *Qf USA d. FRA 2–1.* R1 lost G. Fernandez 6–1 6–4. **1994 (in GER, Clay):** *1r FRA d. KOR 3–0.* R2 d. S. Park 6–3 6–1. *2r FRA d. ITA 3–0.* R2 d. S. Cecchini 6–0 6–3. *Qf FRA d. BUL 2–1.* R2 lost Mag. Maleeva 6–7 6–4 6–4. *Sf USA d. FRA 3–0.* R2 lost Davenport 5–7 6–2 6–3. **1995: April –** *World Group qf FRA d. RSA 3–2 in FRA (Clay).* R2 d. J. Kruger 6–4 6–3; R3 lost A. Coetzer 6–4 6–3. **July –** *World Group sf USA d. FRA 3–2 in USA (Carpet).* R1 d. M. J. Fernandez 7–6 6–3; R3 lost L. Davenport 6–3 4–6 6–0. **1996: July –** *World Group sf ESP d. FRA 3–2 in ESP (Carpet).* R1 d. A. Sanchez-Vicario 6–3 6–4; R3 lost C. Martinez 7–5 2–1. **1997: March –** *World Group qf FRA d. JPN 4–1 in JPN (Hard).* R1 d. N. Sawamatsu 6–0 7–6; R3 lost A. Sugiyama 7–5 6–7 6–4 **October –** *World Group Final FRA d. NED 4–1 in NED (Carpet).* R2 d. M. Oremans 6–4 6–1; R3 lost B. Schultz-McCarthy 4–6 6–3 6–4.

For Mary Pierce the capture of a first French Open singles title was a dream come true.
(Paul Zimmer)

GRAND SLAM CUP CAREER RECORD – Played 1
1999: 1r lost Davenport 3–6 6–2 6–4.

SEASON ENDING CHAMPIONSHIPS – Played 6, r/u 1, sf 2, qf 2
(1983–94 Virginia Slims, 1995 Corel, 1996–2000 Chase)
1993: sf d. Sabatini 7–6 6–3, Navratilova 6–1 3–6 6–4, lost Sanchez-Vicario 6–2 5–7 6–3. **1994: sf** d. Coetzer 5–7 6–3 6–3, Graf 6–4 6–4, lost Davenport 6–3 6–2. **1995: 1r** lost Huber 6–2 6–3. **1996:** Did not play. **1997: r/u** d. Appelmans 6–3 6–4, Hingis 6–3 2–6 7–5, Tauziat 6–2 5–7 6–4, lost Novotna 7–6 6–2 6–3. **1998: qf** d. Coetzer 6–1 6–0, lost Hingis 7–6 6–4. **1999: qf** d. Kournikova 6–7 7–6 6–0, lost Hingis 6–1 6–2. **2000:** Did not play.

8 ANNA KOURNIKOVA (RUS)

Born: Moscow, 7 June 1981. **Lives:** Miami, Fla.
Father: Sergei. **Mother:** Alla.

Agent: IMG **Coach:** Eric Van Harpen; formerly
Nick Bollettieri and Pavel Slozil.
Turned pro: 1995. **Height:** 5ft 8in (1.73m).
Weight: 123lb (55.5kg).

Rankings: 1995: 281; **1996:** 57; **1997:** 32; **1998:** 13;
1999: 12; **2000:** 8 singles, 4 doubles. **Highest:** 8 (2000).
2000 Prize Money: $984,930.
Career Earnings: $2,692,929.
Career Titles: 0.

Style: With uncompromising groundstrokes, single-handed on the forehand, double-handed on the backhand, she hits as hard as any of the women (a habit developed at the Bollettieri Academy in Florida) but lacks consistency. While admiring her go-for-broke courage, one has to question her wisdom. Her quick reflexes make her a good volleyer and she enjoys the doubles game at which she excels.

CAREER HIGHLIGHTS (year: (titles)
1995: No. 1 in ITF Jun rankings after winning Orange Bowl and European Champs. **1996:** At US Open, having played through the qualifying in only her 2nd main draw event, she upset Paulus to reach last 16. She surprised Coetzer at Zurich and won 2 titles on the Futures circuit. Aged 14, she became the youngest to win a Fed Cup match when she helped RUS d. SWE 3–0. Voted Most Impressive Newcomer. **1997:** Playing the compulsorily restricted schedule according to her age, she found it hard to maintain her form. None the less, she upset Coetzer at LIPC and Sanchez-Vicario on her way to qf Berlin, before impressing at Wimbledon, where, unseeded, she upset Huber and Majoli on her way to sf. **1998:** She gave the performance of her life at LIPC, where she became the first to beat 4 top 10 players in succession (Seles, Martinez, Davenport, Sanchez-Vicario) on the way to her 1st career f, in which she was a set up v V. Williams before losing. She followed in May with upsets of Sanchez-Vicario and Hingis to reach sf Berlin, and removed Graf to reach the same stage Eastbourne, but was forced to withdraw with a torn ligament in her thumb, which kept her out 8 weeks, missing Wimbledon. These results were enough to take her into the top 10 on 22 June, although she slipped out again during her absence from the game and, with her serve falling apart in autumn, she could not regain her place. In other tourns she reached sf Hannover (d. Huber) and qf Linz, Amelia Island, Rome (d. Majoli) and Tokyo Toyota, qualifying for her 1st Chase Champs in both singles and doubles, falling 1r in both. She played 4 doubles f with 3 different partners, winning Tokyo Toyota with Seles, although it was Neiland with whom she qualified for Chase Champs. **1999:** Once she had ironed out some problems with her serve, she enjoyed another successful year in which she was r/u FC Cup, and reached sf Oklahoma City, Amelia Island (d. Davenport) and Eastbourne, and qf Tokyo Toray, Stanford and Leipzig. She upset Schnyder 3 times, including French Open, where she was unseeded, and removed Halard-Decugis at LIPC, but a mild stress fracture of right foot suffered in Aug. caused her to withdraw from both US Open and Fed Cup f v USA. Qualifying again for Chase Champs in both singles and doubles, she fell 1r singles to Pierce after taking the 1st set, but won the doubles with Hingis. In all they collected 5 titles together, including Australian Open, and were r/u French Open. She reached a 7th doubles f with Likhovtseva and in mixed with Bjorkman was r/u Wimbledon. **2000:** Although a 1st title continued to elude her, she was r/u Moscow and appeared in sf Sydney, Paris Open, Scottsdale, Stanford, San Diego (d. Davenport), Luxembourg, Leipzig and Chase Champs, plus qf Gold Coast, Tokyo Pan Pacific, Amelia Island, Hamburg, Eastbourne, Zurich and Philadelphia. These results rooted her firmly in top 10 singles, and she was also a force in doubles, in which she played a total of 9 f with 4 different partners, winning 4 (including Chase Champs) with Hingis and 1 each with Halard-Decugis and Zvereva. In mixed she was r/u US Open with Mirnyi.

PRINCIPAL 2000 RESULTS – r/u 1, sf 8 (detailed Grand Slam results follow)
r/u Moscow (d. Zvonareva 7–6 6–4, Panova 6–4 6–1, Tauziat 6–2 6–1, lost Hingis 6–3 6–1); **sf** Sydney (d. Appelmans 7–6 6–2, Capriati 6–4 7–5, Stevenson 4–6 6–2 6–2, lost Davenport 6–3 6–2), **sf** Paris Open (d. Kremer 7–6 6–2, Spirlea 4–6 6–4 6–2, lost Tauziat 7–6 2–6 6–4), **sf** Scottsdale (d. Jidkova 6–2 6–1, Plischke 6–1 6–1, Sugiyama 6–4 6–2, lost Davenport 6–2 6–2), **sf** Stanford (d. A. Miller 6–1 6–2, Nejedly 6–1 6–0, Testud 6–3 6–2, lost V. Williams 6–4 7–5), **sf** San Diego (d. Stevenson 6–2 6–3, Davenport 2–6 6–4 7–5, Tauziat 2–6 6–4 7–5, lost Seles 6–3 7–6), **sf** Luxembourg (d. Petrova 1–6 7–5 4–1 ret, Clijsters 6–7 6–3 6–1, lost Maleeva 6–2 6–4), **sf** Leipzig (d. Farina-Elia 6–3 6–1, Maleeva 6–4 7–5, lost Clijsters 6–2 6–3), **sf** Chase Champs. **DOUBLES:** (with Hingis unless stated) (with Halard-Decugis) **won** Gold Coast (d. Appelmans/Grande 6–3 6–0), (with Zvereva) **won** Hamburg (d. Arendt/Bollegraf 6–7 6–2 6–4), **won** Filderstadt (d. Sanchez-Vicario/Schett 6–4 6–2), **won** Zurich (d. Po/Sidot 6–3 6–4), **won** Philadelphia (d. Raymond/Stubbs 6–2 7–5), **won** Chase Champs (d. Arendt/Bollegraf 6–2 6–3); (with Zvereva) **r/u** Indian Wells (lost Davenport/Morariu 6–2 6–3), (with Davenport) **r/u** San Diego (lost Raymond/Stubbs 4–6 6–3 7–6), **r/u** Moscow (lost Halard-Decugis/Sugiyama 4–6 6–4 7–6). **MIXED DOUBLES:** (with Mirnyi) **r/u US Open** (lost Palmer/Sanchez-Vicario 6–4 6–3).

CAREER GRAND SLAM RECORD
AUSTRALIAN OPEN – Played 4
1997: 1r lost Coetzer [12] 6–2 6–2. **1998: 3r** d. Studenikova 6–2 6–1, Morariu 7–5 6–2, lost Hingis [1] 6–4 4–6 6–4. **1999: last 16** [seed 12] d. Craybas 7–6 7–5, Saeki 1–6 6–4 10–8, Glass 4–6 6–2 6–3, lost Pierce [7] 6–0 6–4. **2000: last 16** [seed 11] d. Wartusch 6–0 6–0, Zvereva 6–1 6–4, Hrdlickova 2–6 6–3 6–4, lost Davenport [2] 6–4 6–3.
FRENCH OPEN – Played 4
1997: 3r d. Zrubakova 6–3 6–2, Cecchini 6–2 6–2, lost Hingis [1] 6–1 6–3. **1998: last 16** [seed 13] d. Mauresmo 6–2 6–4, Studenikova 6–2 7–6, Carlsson 6–0 6–0, lost Novotna [3] 6–7 6–3 6–3. **1999: last 16** [unseeded] d. Tanasugarn 6–3 6–3, Frazier 6–4 6–1, Schnyder [11] 6–1 3–6 6–0, lost Graf [6] 6–3 7–6. **2000: 2r** [seed 14] d. Webb 6–4 6–4, lost Plischke 6–2 4–6 6–3.
WIMBLEDON – Played 3, sf 1
1997: sf [unseeded] d. Rubin 6–1 6–1, Rittner 4–6 7–6 6–3, Huber [7] 3–6 6–4 6–4, Sukova 2–6 6–2 6–3, Majoli [4] 7–6 6–4, lost Hingis [1] 6–3 6–2. **1998: Did not play. 1999: last 16** [seed 17] d. Schwartz 7–6 4–6 6–2, Vento 7–5 6–4, Gorrochategui 7–5 3–1 ret., lost V. Williams 3–6 6–3 6–2. **2000: 2r** d. Testud [10], lost Sidot 6–3 6–4.
US OPEN – Played 4
1996: last 16 [unseeded] d. Richterova 7–6 6–3, Baudone 6–3 6–3, Paulus 3–6 6–2 6–4 [14], lost Graf [1] 6–2 6–1. **1997: 2r** d. Appelmans 6–2 6–0, lost Spirlea [11] 6–1 3–6 6–3. **1998: last 16** [seed 15] d. Ghirardi 6–1 6–3, Bobkova 6–3 6–4, Farina 6–4 6–1, lost Sanchez-Vicario [4] 7–6 6–3. **1999: Did not play. 2000: 3r** [seed 12] d. Parkinson 6–2 6–3, Kleinova 6–4 6–1, lost Henin 6–4 7–6.

OLYMPIC RECORD
1996: (Atlanta) 1r lost Courtois 1–6 6–2 6–2.

CAREER FED CUP RECORD
1996: April (in ESP, Clay): Euro/Africa Group 1 rr RUS d. SLO 3–0. R3 (with E. Makarova) d. T. Jezernik/T. Krizan 6–4 5–7 7–5. RUS d. GBR 3–0. R3 (with Makarova) d. S. Smith/C. Wood 7–6 6–1. BLR d. RUS 2–1. R3 (with Makarova) d. T. Ignatieva/N. Zvereva 6–3 4–6 6–4. Qf RUS d. SWE 3–0. R2 d. A. Svensson 6–0 6–3; R3 (with Makarova) d. A. Carlsson/M. Lindstrom 6–3 6–3. Final SUI d. RUS 2–1. R1 lost P. Schnyder 6–4 6–3. R3 (with Makarova) d. A. Buergis/E. Zardo 7–5 6–1. **1997: April (in ITA, Clay):** Euro/Africa Group 1 rr RUS d. GRE 3–0. R1 d. C. Zachariadou 6–3 6–4; R3 (with E. Likhovtseva) d. C. Papadaki/Zachariadou 7–5 6–1. RUS d. BUL 2–1. R3 (with Likhovtseva) d. T. Nevada/P. Topalova 6–2 6–7 6–0. Qf RUS d. ISR 2–1. R1 lost H. Rosen 6–1 7–6. R3 (with Likhovtseva) d. T. Obziler/Rosen 7–5 6–3. Sf RUS d. BLR 3–0. R3 (with Likhovtseva) d. O. Barabanschikova/T. Poutchek 6–3 7–5. **2000: April (in RUS, Carpet):** World Group rr FRA d. RUS 3–0. R2 lost J. Halard-Decugis 6–2 2–6 6–1; R3 (with E. Likhovtseva) lost Halard-Decugis/N. Tauziat 6–3 7–6. RUS d. AUS 2–1. R2 lost J. Dokic 6–7 7–5 6–3; R3 (with Likhovtseva) d. Dokic/R. Stubbs 6–3 4–6 6–1. BEL d. RUS 2–1. R2 lost K. Clijsters 5–7 6–2 6–4; R3 (with Likhovtseva) lost E. Callens/L. Courtois 6–4 6–3.

SEASON ENDING CHAMPIONSHIPS – Played 3, sf 1
(Chase)
1998: 1r lost Seles 6–4 6–3. **1999: 1r** lost Pierce 6–7 7–5 6–0. **2000: sf** d. Capriati 6–4 6–4, C. Martinez 6–4 6–0, lost Hingis 7–6 6–2.

9 ARANTXA SANCHEZ-VICARIO (ESP)

Born: Barcelona, 18 December 1971. **Lives:** Andorra.
Husband: Juan Vehils (married 21 July 2000).
Father: Emilio. **Mother:** Marisa, whose maiden name,
Vicario, she added to her own.
Sister: Marisa (older). **Brothers:** Emilio and Javier (both older)
who compete on the men's tour.
Agent: IMG. **Coach:** Her brother Emilio, formerly Angel
Giminez, Gabriel Urpi, Mervyn Rose, Carlos Kirmayr, Juan
Nunez, Mike Estep, Eduardo Osta, Sven Groeneveld and
David De Migues.
Turned pro: 1986. **Height:** 5ft 6½in (1.69m).
Weight: 124lb (56kg).

Rankings: 1986: 124; **1987:** 47; **1988:** 18; **1989:** 5; **1990:** 7; **1991:** 5; **1992:** 4; **1993:** 2;
1994: 2; **1995:** 3; **1996:** 2 (jointly with Seles); **1997:** 9; **1998:** 4; **1999:** 17;
2000: 9 singles, 16 doubles. **Highest:** 1 (February 1995).

2000 Prize Money: $819,689. **Career Earnings:** $15,747,252. **Career Titles:** 27.

Style: One of the fastest movers on a tennis court whose attacking, all-round game and cheerful demeanour have created an enormous following round the world. A right-hander with a good forehand, accurate double-handed backhand and excellent touch on the volley, Arantxa has enjoyed outstanding success both in singles and doubles.

CAREER HIGHLIGHTS (year: (titles))
1986: Emerging from the satellite circuits, she reached sf Spanish Open and played Fed Cup.
1987: Qf French Open in 1st GS appearance. **1988: (1)** *Brussels.* Upset Evert (suffering from a foot injury) at French Open en route to qf again and reached last 16 US Open. Won her 1st pro singles title at Brussels and was r/u Tampa. **1989: (2)** *FRENCH OPEN, Barcelona.* At 17 yrs 6 mths became the youngest woman and the 1st Spaniard to win French Open women's title. Qf Wimbledon and US Open, won Barcelona and was r/u Italian Open and Canadian Open, qualifying for 1st VS Champs, where she reached sf. Voted WTA Most Improved Player for 2nd year running. **1990: (2)** *Barcelona, Newport.* In some disappointing performances she fell to Harvey-Wild 1r VS Chicago, to Paz 2r French Open and to Nagelsen 1r Wimbledon. Won 2 titles, r/u Tokyo Toray, VS Houston, Amelia Island, Leipzig and Hamburg, where she d. Navratilova and took Graf to 3s. She lost qf VS Champs to Seles and in GS her best showing was sf US Open, but she won French Open mixed doubles with Lozano. In women's doubles won 1 title with Navratilova and 3 with Paz, with whom she was r/u VS Champs. **1991: (1)** *Washington.* Upset Sabatini en route to sf Australian Open and Graf on her way to f French Open, inflicting on the former No. 1 her worst defeat and 1st love set since 1984. In other GS lost qf Wimbledon to M. J. Fernandez and same round US Open to Navratilova, who also stopped her at that stage VS Champs. Had to wait until late Aug. to win her 1st title of the year at VS Washington, although she had reached qf or better in all 13 tourns until then. R/u Sydney, Berlin, Eastbourne, VS Philadelphia and appeared in 6 more sf. Played in the victorious Spanish Fed Cup team, winning all her matches. In doubles won Barcelona with Navratilova and took Sydney and Amelia Island with Sukova, with whom she qualified for VS Champs. In mixed doubles r/u US Open with her brother, Emilio. **1992: (2)** *LIPC, Montreal.* Again she was remarkably consistent if not spectacular. She upset Graf qf US Open on her way to f, where she lost to Seles, whom she had beaten 3 weeks earlier at Montreal – one of only 5 defeats the No. 1 suffered all year. Reached sf Australian Open and French Open and won an Olympic bronze medal; took 2 titles and was r/u Sydney, Barcelona, Hamburg, Berlin and Philadelphia, reaching 4 more sf and losing qf VS Champs to Navratilova. She enjoyed a terrific year in doubles, winning Australian Open, VS Champs and 4 more titles with Sukova; r/u French Open, Olympic silver medal and 1 title with Martinez; plus 3 more titles with other partners. In mixed with Woodbridge won French Open and r/u Australian Open. **1993: (4)** *LIPC, Amelia Island, Barcelona, Hamburg.* Following a heavy schedule which left her exhausted and struggling to finish her f v Graf at VS Champs, she

moved up to No. 2 in the rankings. She beat Graf twice during the year in winning LIPC and Hamburg (ending the German's unbeaten record there), and also won Amelia Island and Barcelona. She was r/u VS Florida, FC Cup, San Diego, VS Los Angeles and VS Champs and appeared in 4 more sf. In GS she reached sf Australian Open, French Open and US Open and played in winning Spanish Fed Cup team, unbeaten in all her matches. She also played 7 women's doubles f, winning US Open and two others with Sukova, with whom she reached sf VS Champs, and one each with Martinez and Novotna. In mixed, she took Australian Open with Woodbridge. **1994: (8)** FRENCH OPEN, US OPEN, Amelia Island, Barcelona, Hamburg, Montreal, Tokyo Nicherei, Oakland. In a great year for her and for Spanish tennis, she won French Open and a 1st US Open and, with new Wimbledon champion Martinez, took ESP to victory in Fed Cup. Graf was the only player to beat her 3 times, including f Australian Open, although she beat the German in Hamburg and Montreal, both matches being decided in 3s tb, and in 3s at US Open. She was r/u VS Florida, Stratton Mountain and San Diego, but her Wimbledon singles bid ended at last 16 stage, when she lost to Garrison-Jackson, and at VS Champs she surprisingly fell 1r to Halard. She played 16 doubles f with various partners, winning 11 – including US Open with Novotna, with whom she was also r/u Wimbledon and VS Champs – and 7 times she won both singles and doubles titles at same tourn, most notably at US Open. The only woman to earn more than $2m prize money in 1994, she won almost $3m. **1995: (2)** Barcelona, Berlin. Took over the No. 1 ranking for the 1st time on 6 Feb., becoming the 1st Spanish player and only the 6th woman to hold that position since rankings began, and on 13 Feb. she became the 1st since Navratilova in August 1987 to top both singles and doubles rankings. However, Graf deposed her again a week later, and when she regained the top singles spot on 27 Feb., Zvereva had replaced her at the top of the doubles. She topped both rankings again twice more, on 27 March and 1 May, but Graf took over the top singles spot after French Open and by Oct. she had slipped to No. 3 behind Martinez, although she finished the year No. 1 in doubles. She had to wait until 30 April before winning her 1st title of year at Barcelona, where she also won the doubles, and Berlin was her only other singles title, although she was r/u Australian Open, French Open, Wimbledon, Italian Open and Tokyo Nicherei and reached 2 more sf. The outcome of her memorable f v Graf at Wimbledon hung on the result of a remarkable game on her serve at 5–5 fs, which covered 32 points and 20 min. For the 1st time in her 10-year career she was restricted by illness and injury, suffering a stomach virus at French Open, withdrawing qf FC Cup with a badly sprained right ankle and tenderness to the fibula and taking a break in autumn, suffering from fatigue. She still seemed below her best at WTA Champs, where she lost 1r singles to Zvereva, although she and Novotna won the doubles. Also with Novotna she won Australian Open and Wimbledon, was r/u French Open and took 2 more titles, plus a 5th with Neiland. Contributed 1 singles win as ESP d. USA 3–2 in f Fed Cup. **1996: (2)** FC Cup, Hamburg. Between April and August, her ranking fluctuated with that of Martinez between No. 2 and No. 3, before she settled at No. 2 on 5 Aug. after taking a silver medal at the Olympics, and was co-ranked in that spot with Seles from 4 Nov. She won both singles and doubles in 2 tourns – at FC Cup (with Novotna) and Hamburg (with Schultz-McCarthy). At French Open, she lost f to Graf only 10–8 fs in what was probably the match of the year. Earlier, though, she had been booed off the court after a disappointing display of gamesmanship in qf v Habsudova; after missing 2 mps at 5–4 in 2s, she lost tb and played dolly-shots in 3s, which she eventually won 10–8. Apparently forgetting the need to entertain, she claimed she was simply doing her job by winning. In contrast to their French Open f, her Wimbledon f defeat by Graf was disappointingly one-sided. She was also r/u Tokyo Toray, Montreal, San Diego and Tokyo Nicherei, reaching 2 more sf and 5 more qf, including Chase Champs, where she lost in ss to Novotna. In qf Australian Open v Rubin, she played (and lost) the longest women's match in the history of the tourn; it lasted 3 hours 33 min, comprising the most games in a set (30) and most in a woman's match (48) and being the 6th-longest on the WTA tour. The pair then joined together to win the doubles. Retaining her top doubles ranking, she took 9 titles from 12 f, winning a total of 4 with Novotna – with whom she was also r/u US Open and Chase Champs – 2 with Rubin and 1 each with Schultz-McCarthy, Spirlea and Neiland, as well as an Olympic bronze medal with Martinez. Her Fed Cup record suffered a set-back as she won only one singles and one doubles match, losing to players she would normally expect to beat. She was restricted in the spring by a shoulder injury, caused by playing too much tennis, and in autumn took a 3-week break, feeling physically and mentally exhausted by the game. **1997:** It was another generally disappointing year in which she dropped out of the top 10 for a while and was seeded as low as 10 at US Open. She won no title, although she shared

Eastbourne (where f was rained off) with Novotna and in f Tokyo Nicherei was 3–1 up in 3s v Seles before letting the match slip away. In November, she showed her old form again at Philadelphia, where she upset Coetzer in ss and was on the point of doing the same to Hingis in sf before losing 2s tb and eventually the match. Then at Chase Champs, where she qualified in both singles and doubles, she upset Seles before losing qf in 3s to her former doubles partner Novotna, and, in partnership with Hingis, fell 1r doubles to Fusai/Tauziat. Her best GS performance was sf Wimbledon, and she reached the same stage Indian Wells, Madrid and Philadelphia, as well as qf French Open, US Open, Amelia Island, Los Angeles, Filderstadt and Moscow. In doubles she played and won 7 f, taking 3 titles with Hingis, 2 with Zvereva and 1 each with G. Fernandez and M. J. Fernandez. **1998: (2)** *FRENCH OPEN, Sydney.* Back to something like her old form again, she began the year in style at Sydney by winning her 1st title for more than a year. The climax of her season came in May when she won her 3rd French Open crown over Davenport and Seles. Although she did not win another title, she was r/u Eastbourne, Montreal and Tokyo Toyota, reached sf LIPC, Rome, Los Angeles and Filderstadt, qf Australian Open, Hamburg, Wimbledon and US Open, and played in the victorious ESP Fed Cup team. Her season tailed off rather as she was beaten 1r GS Cup by V. Williams and fell 1r Chase Champs to Spirlea, although she finished comfortably back in the top 5. In doubles she played 5 f with 4 different partners, but won no title. **1999: (1)** *Cairo.* She won both singles and doubles (with Courtois) at Cairo and reached sf Hamburg (where she won doubles with Neiland) and Berlin, plus qf Sydney, Manhattan Beach (won doubles with Neiland) and Toronto. She qualified for GS Cup, but lost 1r to S. Williams, and at Chase Champs lost 1r to Schett. She and Neiland were r/u doubles there to Hingis/Kournikova, leaving her with 3 titles from her 6 doubles f. **2000:** Although she won no title she was consistent through the year and regained her top 10 place with r/u FC Cup and Hamburg, sf French Open, Gold Coast, Montreal and Filderstadt and qf Australian Open, Sydney, Amelia Island, Rome and Olympics. However, she failed again at Chase Champs, losing 1r Clijsters. In doubles she played 4 f with different partners, winning Berlin with C. Martinez and Leipzig with Sidot, while in mixed she won US Open with Palmer and was r/u Australian Open with Woodbridge. Took time out after Wimbledon for her marriage to Juan Vehils.

PRINCIPAL 2000 RESULTS – r/u 2, sf 4 (detailed Grand Slam results follow)
r/u FC Cup (d. Suarez 6–3 7–5, Schnyder 7–5 6–1, Coetzer 7–6 3–6 6–3, Martinez 7–5 7–5, lost Pierce 6–1 6–0), **r/u** Hamburg (d. Serna 6–3 7–6, Glass 6–3 6–3, Coetzer 6–3 4–6 7–6, lost Hingis 6–3 6–3); **sf** French Open, **sf** Gold Coast (d. Montolio 6–1 6–1, Grande 6–3 6–1, Schnyder 2–6 7–6 6–3, lost Talaja 6–1 3–6 6–0), **sf** Montreal (d. Nagyova 6–4 6–1, Capriati 6–4 7–5, Maleeva 6–1 6–4, lost S. Williams ??), **sf** Filderstadt (d. Black 6–2 3–6 6–4, Coetzer 6–2 2–6 6–3, lost Hingis 6–1 6–0). **DOUBLES:** (with C. Martinez) **won** Berlin (d. Coetzer/Morariu 3–6 6–2 7–6), (with Sidot) **won** Leipzig (d. Clijsters/Courtois 6–7 7–5 6–3); (with Serna) **r/u** Rome (lost Raymond/Stubbs 6–3 4–6 6–3), (with Schett) **r/u** Filderstadt (lost Hingis/Kournikova 6–4 6–2). **MIXED DOUBLES:** (with Woodbridge) **r/u** **Australian Open** (lost Palmer/Stubbs 7–5 7–6), (with Palmer) **won US Open** (d. Mirnyi/Kournikova 6–4 6–3).

CAREER GRAND SLAM RECORD
AUSTRALIAN OPEN – Played 10, r/u 2, sf 3, qf 9
1991: sf [seed 6] d. Medvedeva 6–0 6–2, Javer 4–6 6–4 6–2, McNeil 6–4 3–6 6–0, Frazier [13] 6–3 6–2, Sabatini [4] 6–1 6–3, lost Novotna [10] 6–2 6–4. **1992: sf** [seed 4] d. Provis 6–2 6–1, Testud 6–1 6–1, Strnadova 1–6 6–0 6–3, Savchenko-Neiland 6–1 7–6, Maleeva-Fragniere [9] def, lost Seles [1] 6–2 6–2. **1993: sf** [seed 4] d. Van Lottum 6–2 6–3, Arraya 6–0 6–1, Zrubakova 6–1 6–3, Huber [11] 7–5 6–2, M. J. Fernandez [5] 7–5 6–4, lost Graf [2] 7–5 6–4. **1994: r/u** [seed 2] d. Habsudova 6–1 6–3, Wang 6–2 6–4, Grossman 6–2 6–3, Mag. Maleeva [14] 4–6 6–1 6–3, Maleeva-Fragniere [8] 7–6 6–4, Sabatini [4] 6–1 6–2, lost Graf [1] 6–0 6–2. **1995: r/u** [seed 1] d. Li 6–2 6–0, Whitlinger-Jones 6–2 6–1, Garrison-Jackson 6–1 6–3, Habsudova 7–5 6–0, Sawamatsu 6–1 6–3, Werdel-Witmeyer 6–4 6–1, lost Pierce [4] 6–3 6–2. **1996: qf** [seed 3] d. Reinstadler 6–2 6–2, Rittner 6–3 6–2, Cacic 6–3 6–3, M. J. Fernandez [9] 6–3 6–1, lost Rubin [13] 6–4 2–6 16–14. **1997: 3r** [seed 2] d. Pizzichini 6–4 6–4, De Ville 1–0 ret, lost Van Roost 1–6 6–4 8–6. **1998: qf** [seed 7] d. J. Lee 6–0 6–4, Makarova 6–0 6–0, Hiraki 6–2 6–3, Sugiyama [16] 6–2 6–4, lost Huber [10] 7–6 7–5. **1999: 2r** [seed 4] d. De Swardt 6–2 6–2, lost Schett 6–2 6–2. **2000: qf** [seed 13] d. Abe 6–2 6–2, Raymond 6–1 3–6 6–3, Stewart 7–5 6–1, Schett [6] 1–6 6–0 7–5, lost Hingis [1] 6–1 6–1.

FRENCH OPEN – Played 14, won 3, r/u 3, sf 4, qf 3
1987: qf d. Burgin 7–5 6–3, Dinu 6–0 6–2, Paulus 6–4 6–2, Karlsson 6–1 6–4, lost Sabatini [7] 6–4 6–0. **1988: qf** d. Kuczynska 6–2 6–0, Meier 7–5 6–0, Evert [3] 6–1 7–6, Tanvier 6–2 6–0, lost Provis 7–5 3–6 6–4. **1989: won** [seed 7] d. Rajchrtova 6–2 6–1, Demongeot 6–4 6–4, Medvedeva 6–0 3–6 6–2, Coetzer 6–3 6–2, Novotna [11] 6–2 6–2, M. J. Fernandez [15] 6–2 6–2, Graf [1] 7–6 3–6 7–5. **1990: 2r** [seed 3] d. Van Lottum 6–1 6–3, lost Paz 7–5 3–6 6–1. **1991: r/u** [seed 5] d. McNeil 6–2 6–2, Godridge 6–1 6–2, Fulco 6–1 6–1, Tami

Whitlinger 6–2 6–1, M. J. Fernandez [4] 6–3 6–2, Graf [2] 6–0 6–2, lost Seles [1] 6–3 6–4. **1992: sf** [seed 4] d. Oeljeklaus 6–0 6–2, Zardo 6–3 6–2, Wiesner 6–3 6–1, Date [14] 6–1 6–2, Bollegraf 6–2 6–3, lost Graf [2] 0–6 6–2 6–2. **1993: sf** [seed 2] d. Kiene 6–3 7–6, Sawamatsu 6–0 6–0, Meskhi 6–3 6–0, Dragomir 6–0 6–1, Novotna [7] 6–2 7–5, lost M. J. Fernandez [5] 6–2 6–2. **1994: won** [seed 2] d. Labat 6–4 6–1, Van Lottum 6–1 6–0, Rittner 6–4 6–2, Huber [11] 6–3 6–2, Halard 6–1 7–6, Martinez [3] 6–3 6–1, Pierce [12] 6–4 6–4. **1995: r/u** [seed 1] d. Park 6–1 6–0, Pitkowski 6–3 6–0, Reinstadler 6–3 6–1, Smashnova 6–4 6–0, Rubin 6–3 6–1, Date [9] 7–5 6–3, lost Graf [2] 7–5 4–6 6–0. **1996: r/u** [seed 4] d. Glass 6–2 6–3, Martinek 6–0 6–1, Likhovtseva 6–0 6–0, Rittner 6–3 6–4, Habsudova 6–2 6–7 10–8, Novotna [10] 6–3 7–5, lost Graf [1] 6–3 6–7 10–8. **1997: qf** [seed 6] d. Jagieniak 6–0 6–2, Sugiyama 6–3 6–1, Van Roost 6–0 6–3, Zvereva 6–4 6–2, lost Hingis [1] 6–2 6–2. **1998: won** [seed 4] d. Kandarr 6–2 7–5, Cristea 6–2 6–3, Fusai 6–2 6–1, S. Williams 4–6 7–5 6–3, Schnyder 6–2 6–7 6–0, Davenport [2] 6–3 7–6, Seles [6] 7–6 0–6 6–2. **1999: sf** [seed 7] d. Lucic 6–2 6–2, Srebotnik 6–1 6–2, Spirlea 6–4 6–1, Fernandez w/o, Plischke 6–2 6–4, lost Hingis [1] 6–3 6–2. **2000: sf** [seed 8] d. Nola 6–1 6–1, Jeyaseelan 3–6 6–2 6–2, Serna 7–5 6–4, Schett 0–6 6–4 6–2, V. Williams 6–0 1–6 6–2 [4], lost Martinez [6] 6–1 6–2.

WIMBLEDON – Played 14, r/u 2, sf 1, qf 3
1987: 1r lost Cordwell 6–1 2–6 6–4. **1988: 1r** lost Okamoto 6–3 6–4. **1989: qf** [seed 7] d. Pospisilova 6–2 7–5, Halard 6–4 6–3, Reggi 4–6 6–3 7–5, McNeil [15] 6–3 2–6 6–1, lost Graf [1] 7–5 6–1. **1990: 1r** [seed 6] lost Nagelsen 1–6 7–6 9–7. **1991: qf** [seed 4] d. Rittner 6–1 6–2, Coetzer 6–4 6–1, McNeil 6–2 6–4, A. Minter 7–5 3–6 6–1, lost M. J. Fernandez [5] 6–2 7–5. **1992: 2r** [seed 5] d. Meskhi 6–3 7–6, lost Halard 6–3 2–6 6–3). **1993: last 16** [seed 3] d. Zrubakova 6–1 6–1, Neiland 7–6 6–0, Fendick 6–3 6–2, lost Sukova [15] 6–3 6–4. **1994: last 16** [seed 2] d. K. Maleeva 6–1 6–2, Gaidano 6–2 6–1, Feber 6–2 6–1, lost Garrison-Jackson [13] 7–5 4–6 6–3. **1995: r/u** [seed 2] d. Studenikova 6–2 6–1, Endo 7–5 6–2, Garrison-Jackson 6–1 6–2, Huber [9] 7–5 6–4, Schultz-McCarthy [15] 6–4 6–1, Martinez [3] 6–3 6–7 6–1, lost Graf [1] 4–6 6–1 7–5. **1996: r/u** [seed 4] d. Serra-Zanetti 6–3 6–4, Oremans 7–6 6–3, Sawamatsu 6–4 6–1, Appelmans 3–6 6–2 6–1, Wiesner 6–4 6–0, McGrath 6–2 6–1, lost Graf [1] 6–3 7–5. **1997: sf** [seed 8] d. Wood 6–0 6–0 Gagliardi 6–4 6–2, Labat 6–1 6–2, Pierce [9] 6–1 6–3, Tauziat 6–2 7–5, lost Novotna [3] 6–4 6–2. **1998: qf** [seed 5] d. Cristea 5–7 6–2 6–0, Grzybowska 4–6 6–4 6–3, Plischke 7–5 6–2, Van Roost [15] 3–6 6–3 6–2, lost Hingis [1] 6–3 3–6 6–3. **1999: 2r** [seed 7] d. Foldenyi 4–6 6–3 6–4, lost Raymond 7–6 6–1. **2000: last 16** [seed 9] d. Henin 1–6 6–1, Grande 6–3 6–1, Nacuk 3–6 7–6 6–2, lost Seles [6] 6–3 6–4.

US OPEN – Played 13, won 1, r/u 1, sf 2, qf 2
1987: 1r lost Dias 6–4 6–2. **1988: last 16** d. Keil 6–3 6–0, Steinmetz 6–2 6–2, Sloane 6–3 6–3, lost Garrison [11] 4–6 7–5 6–2. **1989: qf** [seed 6] d. Faull 3–6 6–1, Cammy Macgregor 6–1 6–3, Wasserman 6–1 2–6 6–4, Paulus 6–2 6–2, lost Sabatini [3] 3–6 6–4 6–1. **1990: sf** [seed 6] d. Provis 6–0 6–3, Kuhlman 6–1 6–2, Fendick 6–2 6–1, Paulus [16] 6–4 6–3, Garrison [4] 6–2 6–2, lost Graf [1] 6–1 6–2. **1991: qf** [seed 4] d. Piccolini 6–0 6–1, Godridge 6–1 6–1, Herreman 6–2 6–2, Zvereva 6–3 7–6, lost Navratilova [6] 6–7 7–6 6–2. **1992: r/u** [seed 5] d. Savchenko-Neiland 5–7 6–2 6–2, Davenport 6–2 6–1, Sawamatsu 6–1 6–3, Garrison [14] 6–0 6–1, Graf [2] 7–6 6–3, Maleeva-Fragniere [9] 6–2 6–1, lost Seles [1] 6–3 6–3. **1993: sf** [seed 2] d. Labat 6–4 6–3, Harvey-Wild 6–2 6–4, Rubin 6–0 6–1, Tauziat [14] 6–4 6–3, Zvereva 3–0 ret, lost Sukova [12] 6–7 7–5 6–2. **1994: won** [seed 2] d. Ferrando 7–5 6–1, Tauziat 6–2 7–6, Cecchini 6–2 6–1, Grossman 6–2 6–0, Date [5] 6–3 6–0, Sabatini [8] 6–1 7–6, Graf [1] 1–6 7–6 6–4. **1995: last 16** [seed 3] d. Cristea 6–1 6–1, Kruger 6–4 6–3, Gaidano 6–3 6–0, lost M. J. Fernandez [14] 1–6 6–4 6–4. **1996: last 16** [seed 3] d. Poruri 6–2 6–1, Arendt 6–2 6–2, Likhovtseva 6–1 6–0, lost Hingis [16] 6–1 3–6 6–4. **1997: qf** [seed 10] d. Guse 6–2 6–4, Tu 6–2 5–7 6–2, Fusai 6–2 6–1, McQuillan 6–1 6–2, lost Hingis [seed 1] 6–3 6–2. **1998: qf** [seed 4] d. Brandi 6–2 6–2, Zuluaga 6–3 6–2, Pitkowski 6–2 6–1, Kournikova [15] 7–6 6–3, lost V. Williams [5] 2–6 6–1 6–1. **1999: last 16** [seed 10] d. Dokic 7–5 6–1, Pratt 6–2 6–2, Schnyder 6–2 6–2, lost Hingis [1] 6–4 7–5. **2000: last 16** [seed 9] d. Kruger 5–7 6–4 7–6, Jeyaseelan 6–4 6–1, Bradshaw 7–6 6–0, lost Tauziat [8] 6–3 6–2.

OLYMPIC RECORD
SINGLES: 1988: (Seoul) 1r lost Goles 6–4 6–2. **1992: (Barcelona) sf bronze medal** [seed 2] d. Spirlea 6–1 6–3, Endo 6–0 6–1, Rittner 4–6 6–3 6–1, Martinez [5] 6–4 6–4, lost Capriati [3] 6–3 3–6 6–1. **1996: (Atlanta) r/u silver medal** [seed 3] d. Van Roost 6–1 7–5, Farina 6–1 6–3, Schultz-McCarthy [11] 6–4 7–6, Date [8] 4–6 6–3 10–8, Novotna [6] 6–4 1–6 6–3, lost Davenport [9] 7–6 6–2). **2000: (Sydney) qf** [seed 5] d. N. Li 6–1 7–5, Wartusch 6–2 6–4, Zuluaga 6–2 6–0, lost V. Williams [2] 3–6 6–2 6–4. **DOUBLES:** (with Martinez): **1992: (Barcelona) r/u silver medal** d. McQuillan/Provis 6–3 6–3, lost G. Fernandez/M. J. Fernandez 7–5 2–6 6–2. **1996: (Atlanta) sf bronze medal** lost Novotna/Sukova 6–2 7–6; bronze medal play-off d. Bollegraf/Schultz-McCarthy 6–1 6–3. **2000: (Sydney) 2r** [seed 2] d. Bedanova/Hrdlickova 6–4 6–3; lost Barabanschikova/Zvereva 6–4 7–5.

CAREER FED CUP RECORD
1986 (in TCH, Clay): 1r ESP d. INA 2–1. R2 d. S. Anggarkusuma 7–6 6–3. R3 (with A. Almansa) d. Anggarkusuma/Y. Basuki 7–5 6–4. 2r USA d. ESP 3–0. R2 lost M. Navratilova 6–3 6–0. **1987 (in CAN, Hard):** 1r ESP d. JAM 3–0. R2 d. J. Van Ryck De Groot 6–3 6–1; R3 (with M. J. Llorca) d. H. Harris/van Ryck De Groot 7–6 6–2. 2r AUS d. ESP 2–1. R2 lost E. Smylie 6–1 4–6 6–1; R3 (with Llorca) lost Smylie/W. Turnbull 6–1 6–2. **1988 (in AUS, Hard):** 1r ESP d. NED 3–0. R2 d. R. Schultz 6–2 7–6; R3 (with C. Martinez) d. M. Bollegraf/C. Vis 5–7 6–1 6–4. 2r ESP d. INA 3–0. R2 d. Y. Basuki 6–1 6–1; R3 (with Martinez) d. S. Anggarkusuma/Basuki 6–0 5–7 6–2. Qf URS d. ESP 2–1. R2 d. N. Zvereva 7–6 6–1; R3 (with Martinez) lost L. Savchenko/Zvereva 4–6

6–4 6–4. **1989 (in JPN, Hard):** *1r ESP d. FRA 2–0.* R2 d. N. Tauziat 6–4 6–2. *2r ESP d. NED 2–0.* R2 d. B. Schultz 2–6 6–4 10–8. *Qf ESP d. URS 2–1.* R2 d. N. Zvereva 7–5 6–3; R3 (with C. Martinez) lost L. Savchenko/Zvereva 6–4 2–6 6–1. *Sf ESP d. AUS 2–0.* R2 d. A. Minter 6–1 4–6 6–2. *Final USA d. ESP 3–0.* R2 lost M. Navratilova (USA) 0–6 6–3 6–4; R3 (with Martinez) lost Z. Garrison/P. Shriver 7–5 6–1. **1990 (in USA, Hard):** *1r ESP d. CAN 2–1.* R2 d. H. Kelesi 6–3 6–2. *2r ESP d. ISR 3–0.* R2 d. Y. Segal 6–0 6–0; R3 (with C. Martinez) d. I. Berger/L. Zaltz 6–3 6–4. *Qf ESP d. FRA 3–0.* R2 d. N. Tauziat 7–6 6–1; R3 (with Martinez) d. I. Demongeot/M. Pierce 6–4 6–4. *Sf URS d. ESP 2–1.* R2 lost N. Zvereva 6–4 2–0 ret. **1991 (in GBR, Hard):** *1r ESP d. BEL 2–0.* R2 d. S. Appelmans 7–6 6–3. *2r ESP d. AUS 3–0.* R2 d. R. McQuillan 6–1 3–6 6–2; R3 (with C. Martinez) d. K. Godridge/E. Smylie 6–3 6–4. *Qf ESP d. FRA 3–0.* R2 d. Y. Basuki 4–6 7–5 6–4. *Sf ESP d. GER 3–0.* R2 d. A. Huber 6–1 2–6 6–2; R3 (with Martinez) d. B. Rittner/Huber 6–1 6–1. *Final ESP d. USA 2–1.* R2 d. M. J. Fernandez 6–3 6–4; R3 (with Martinez) d. Z. Garrison/G. Fernandez 3–6 6–1 6–1. **1992 (in GER, Clay):** *1r ESP d. BEL 2–1.* R2 d. S. Appelmans 6–1 6–2; R3 (with N. Perez) lost D. Monami/S. Wasserman 7–5 6–4. *2r ESP d. CAN 2–1.* R2 d. P. Hy 6–4 6–2; R3 (with C. Martinez) d. J. Hetherington/Hy 6–4 6–0. *Qf ESP d. ARG 2–1.* R2 d. M. Paz 6–2 6–1. *Sf ESP d. AUS 3–0.* R2 d. N. Provis 6–2 6–0; R3 (with V. Ruano-Pascual) d. J. Byrne/R. Stubbs 6–3 6–3. *Final GER d. ESP 2–1.* R2 lost S. Graf 6–4 6–2; R3 (with Martinez) d. A. Huber/B. Rittner 6–1 6–2. **1993 (in GER, Clay):** *1r ESP d. GBR 3–0.* R2 d. C. Wood 6–3 6–0; R3 (with C. Martinez) d. J. Durie/Wood 6–1 4–6 6–1. *2r ESP d. INA 3–0.* R2 d. N. Basuki 6–1 6–2. *Qf ESP d. NED 3–0.* R2 d. M. Oremans 7–6 6–0. *Sf ESP d. FRA 2–1.* R2 d. N. Tauziat 6–1 6–4. *Final ESP d. AUS 3–0.* R2 d. N. Provis 6–2 6–3; R3 (with Martinez) d. E. Smylie/R. Stubbs 3–6 6–1 6–3. **1994 (in GER, Clay):** *1r ESP d. CHI 3–0.* R2 d. P. Cabezas 6–1 6–0; R3 (with C. Martinez) d. Cabezas/Castro 6–0 6–1. *2r ESP d. ARG 3–0.* R2 d. F. Labat 6–1 6–4. *Qf ESP d. JPN 3–0.* R2 d. K. Date 6–3 2–6 8–6. *Sf ESP d. GER 2–1.* R2 d. A. Huber 4–6 6–0 7–5; R3 (with Martinez) d. B. Rittner/C. Singer 7–6 6–3. *Final ESP d. USA 3–0.* R2 d. L. Davenport 6–2 6–1; R3 (with Martinez) d. G./ M. J. Fernandez 6–3 6–4. **1995: April** – *World Group qf ESP d. BUL 3–2 in BUL (Carpet).* R1 d. K. Maleeva 6–3 6–3; R3 lost M. Maleeva 6–3 6–3). **July** – *World Group sf ESP d. GER 3–2 in ESP (Clay).* R2 lost S. Hack 6–4 6–2; R3 d. A. Huber 6–3 1–6 6–2. **November** – *World Group Final ESP d. USA 3–2 in ESP (Clay).* R2 d. M. J. Fernandez 6–3 6–2; R4 lost C. Rubin 1–6 6–4 6–4. **1996: April** – *World Group qf ESP d. RSA 3–2 in ESP (Clay).* R1 d. J. Kruger 6–3 6–1; R3 lost A. Coetzer 6–4 6–1. **July** – *World Group sf ESP d. FRA 3–2 in FRA (Carpet).* R2 lost M. Pierce 6–3 6–4; R4 lost J. Halard-Decugis 2–6 6–4 7–5; R5 (with C. Martinez) d. Halard-Decugis/N. Tauziat 6–4 2–1 ret. **September** – *World Group Final USA d. ESP 5–0 in USA (Carpet).* R2 lost L. Davenport 7–5 6–1; R3 lost M. Seles 3–6 6–3 6–0. **1997: March** – *World Group qf BEL d. ESP 5–0 in BEL (Hard).* R1 lost E. Callens 6–3 7–6; R3 lost S. Appelmans 6–3 2–6 8–6. **July** – *World Group play-off ESP d. AUS 3–2 in AUS (Hard).* R1 d. R. McQuillan 6–2 6–1; R3 d. A. Ellwood 6–2 6–0. **1998: July** – *World Group sf ESP d. USA 3–2 in ESP (Clay).* R1 d. L. Raymond 6–7 6–3 6–0; R3 lost M. Seles 6–4 6–0; R5 (with C. Martinez) d. M. J. Fernandez/Raymond 6–4 6–7 11–9. **September** – *World Group Final ESP d. SUI 3–2 in SUI (Hard).* R1 d. P. Schnyder 6–2 3–6 6–2; R3 lost M. Hingis 7–6 6–3; R5 (with Martinez) d. Hingis/Schnyder 6–0 6–2. **2000: April (in ITA, Clay):** *World Group rr ESP d. ITA 3–0.* R1 d. G. Casoni 6–1 6–1. *ESP d. CRO 2–1.* R 1 d. I. Majoli 6–4 6–2. *ESP d. CRO 2–1.* R1 d. A. Glass 6–3 6–3. R3 (with C. Martinez) d. A. Huber/B. Rittner 6–2 6–3. **November: (in USA, Carpet):** *Sf ESP d. CZE 2–1.* R1 d. D. Bedanova 5–7 6–4 6–3. *Final USA d. ESP 5–0.* R2 lost L. Davenport 6–2 1–6 6–3; R4 lost J. Capriati 6–1 1–0 ret.

GRAND SLAM CUP RECORD – Played 2
1998: 1r lost V. Williams 6–3 6–2. **1999: 1r** lost S. Williams 6–3 6–1.

SEASON ENDING CHAMPIONSHIPS – Played 12, r/u 1, sf 1, qf 5
(1983–94 Virginia Slims, 1995 Corel, 1996–2000 Chase)
1989: sf d. Lindqvist 7–6 6–3, Man. Maleeva 7–5 7–6, lost Navratilova 6–2 6–2. **1990: qf** d. Zvereva 6–2 7–5, lost Seles 5–7 7–6 6–4. **1991: qf** d. Garrison 4–6 6–1 6–0, lost Navratilova 1–6 6–4 6–2. **1992: qf** d. Garrison-Jackson 7–6 6–1, lost Navratilova 6–1 2–6 6–2. **1993: r/u** d. Sukova 7–5 6–2, Novotna 6–7 7–6 6–4, Pierce 6–2 5–7 6–2, lost Graf 6–1 6–4 3–6 6–1. **1994: 1r** lost Halard 6–2 1–6 7–6. **1995: 1r** lost Zvereva 4–6 6–4 6–4. **1996: qf** d. Schultz-McCarthy 6–4 7–6, lost Novotna 6–0 6–3. **1997: qf** d. Seles 3–6 6–4 6–4, lost Novotna 6–3 3–6 6–1. **1998: 1r** lost Spirlea 7–6 6–1. **1999: 1r** lost Schett 6–1 6–4. **2000: 1r** lost Clijsters 7–5 6–4.

10 NATHALIE TAUZIAT (FRA)

Born: Bangui, Central African Republic, 17 October 1967.
Lives: Bayonne. **Father:** Bernard. **Mother:** Regine.
Brother: Eric.

Agent: Benoite Lardy. **Coach:** Regis DeCamaret; formerly
Francois Xavier D'Eau.
Turned pro: 1984.
Height: 5ft 5in (1.65m). **Weight:** 120lb (54kg).

Rankings: 1984: 296; **1985:** 112; **1986:** 67; **1987:** 25;
1988: 27; **1989;** 25; **1990:** 18; **1991:** 13; **1992:** 14; **1993:** 18;
1994: 35; **1995;** 27; **1996:** 30; **1997:** 11; **1998:** 10; **1999:** 7;
2000: 10 singles, 8 doubles. **Highest:** 5 (13 February 2000).

2000 Prize Money: $761,211. **Career Earnings:** $5,707,942. **Career Titles:** 7.

Style: A fine all-court right-hander whose volleying ability makes her particularly effective on fast courts. She is equally at home on the baseline or at the net and can adapt her game to suit different opponents or surfaces. A natural athlete, she moves well but is no longer as fast about court as she used to be.

CAREER HIGHLIGHTS (year: (titles))
1985: Upset Casale at French Open and played Fed Cup. **1986:** Qf Hilversum. **1987:** Reached sf Strasbourg, San Diego and Zurich, last 16 French Open (unseeded) and d. Rinaldi to reach qf LIPC. **1988:** R/u Nice, upset Zvereva and K. Maleeva *en route* to f Mahwah. In doubles with Demongeot upset Kohde-Kilsch/Sukova to win both Berlin and Zurich and qualified for VS Champs. **1989:** Sf Italian Open (d. Man. Maleeva) and San Diego. **1990: (1)** *Bayonne.* Won her 1st primary circuit title at Bayonne; r/u Wichita and reached sf LIPC, Birmingham and Canadian Open (d. Maleeva-Fragniere) to qualify for VS Champs, where she fell 1r to M. J. Fernandez. In GS she reached last 16 in all 3 tourns she entered, unseeded at both Wimbledon and US Open. **1991:** She scored some major upsets in reaching f Zurich (d. Sabatini), sf VS Palm Springs, VS Florida (d. M. J. Fernandez), Barcelona (d. Navratilova), San Diego and Bayonne and was close to beating Capriati at VS Champs, eventually losing her 1r match in 3s tb. She also reached her 1st GS qf at French Open. Played 3 doubles f, winning Bayonne with Tarabini. **1992:** R/u San Antonio and Bayonne and reached 9 more qf, including Wimbledon. Qualified for VS Champs, but lost 1r to Seles. **1993: (1)** *Quebec City.* Won Quebec City in Nov., having earlier appeared in sf Schenectady and Filderstadt plus 8 more qf, upsetting Maleeva-Fragniere at Tokyo Pan Pacific. Qualified for VS Champs but fell 1r again – to Navratilova. **1994:** Although she did not progress beyond sf, she reached that stage at Birmingham, Schenectady and Quebec City, plus qf Italian Open and Brighton (d. Huber), and upset Martinez 1r Philadelphia. From 3 doubles f she won Quebec City with Reinach and Los Angeles with Halard, with whom she qualified for VS Champs. **1995: (1)** *Eastbourne.* Upset Zvereva on her way to the title at Eastbourne, surprised M. Maleeva at French Open and Pierce at Wimbledon and reached qf Barcelona. In doubles she won Linz with McGrath. **1996:** Confirming her liking for grass, she was r/u Birmingham, reached sf Eastbourne and upset M. Maleeva at Wimbledon. Otherwise she could not pass qf, although she reached that stage at Indian Wells (d. M. J. Fernandez), Italian Open, Berlin, Strasbourg and San Diego. In doubles she played 6 f with 4 different partners, winning Leipzig and Luxembourg with Boogert. **1997: (1)** *Birmingham.* She excelled at Birmingham again, winning the title. Her 2nd f of year came at Zurich and she was r/u again at Chicago, where she upset Novotna and Majoli back-to-back and took the doubles. Her only other sf was a big one, as she upset Coetzer and Majoli to reach that stage at Chase Champs, where she extended Pierce to 3s. She also reached qf Linz, Paris Open, Indian Wells, Eastbourne (d. M. J. Fernandez), Los Angeles and Wimbledon, where she was unseeded. She enjoyed a lucky escape in last 16 there, trailing 4–5 15–40 on Testud's serve in 3s when rain interrupted play: on the resumption 75 minutes later, she took 10 points in a row and finally won 12–10. fs. A member of the winning FRA Fed Cup team, she d. Sawamatsu 7–5 4 6 17 15 in that competition, playing the longest singles set and equalling the longest rubber (Baldovonis d. Connor

6–4 11–13 11–9 in 1974). She played 6 doubles f with 3 different partners, winning Linz and Chicago with Fusai. She qualified for Chase Champs in both singles and doubles, joining with Fusai to upset Hingis/Sanchez-Vicario in ss and extend Davenport/Novotna to 3s in f. **1998:** The highlight of her career came at Wimbledon, where she was r/u, playing her 1st GS f and becoming the 1st Frenchwoman for 73 years and at 15 the lowest-ranked woman in the open era to reach f Wimbledon. She had removed Davenport in ss on the way and upset her again *en route* to sf GS Cup. She broke into the top 10 1st time in Jan., slipped out again for a while in spring, but returned after Wimbledon, moving up to a career-high 8 in Aug. Although she won no title, she was consistent in progressing to qf or better in 15 tourns with a 2nd f of year at Leipzig (d. Spirlea) and reaching sf Paris Open, Birmingham (tourn cancelled at that stage), GS Cup, Zurich, Luxembourg and Philadelphia, as well as qf Hannover, Linz, Strasbourg, San Diego, Los Angeles, Filderstadt and Chase Champs. Her partnership with Fusai continued to flourish, bringing 3 titles and a berth at Chase Champs, where they narrowly lost to Davenport/Zvereva in their 7th f of season. **1999: (2)** *Moscow, Leipzig.* Having won only 8 matches in 12 tourns, she came into her own in GC season, reaching f both Birmingham and Eastbourne (where she recovered from 1–5 down fs v Kournikova in sf) and qf Wimbledon. Then in autumn she won Moscow – in contrast to her visit there earlier in year when she had lost all 3 Fed Cup matches as RUS d. FRA 3–2 – and followed 3 weeks later with Leipzig. She also reached sf Zurich (d. Coetzer and extended Hingis to 3s), Philadelphia and VS Champs, plus qf Strasbourg and Linz. She played 6 doubles f, 1 with Zvereva and 5 with Fusai, with whom she won Prostejov and Berlin and qualified for Chase Champs, where they extended Hingis/Kournikova to 7–5 fs in 1r. **2000: (1)** *Paris Open.* She broke into top 5 1st time after winning her only title of the year at Paris Open. Although she played no other f, she reached sf Birmingham, New Haven, Filderstadt, Moscow, Leipzig and Philadelphia and qf Tokyo Pan Pacific, Rome, Strasbourg, Eastbourne, San Diego, Zurich, Linz, US Open and Chase Champs, where she extended Hingis to 3s. She offended many people with personal comments and views expressed in a book and was omitted from French Olympic squad after her compatriots objected to criticisms she had written; her appeal against the decision was rejected. In doubles she played 5 f with 3 different partners, winning Eastbourne with Sugiyama, Montreal with Hingis and Luxembourg with Fusai, with whom she qualified for Chase Champs. She had talked of retiring at end of year, but in the end decided to continue with a selected schedule in 2001.

PRINCIPAL 2000 RESULTS – won 1, sf 6 (detailed Grand Slam results follow)
won Paris Open (d. Henin 7–6 2–6 6–4, Sidot 7–5 6–1, Kournikova 7–6 2–6 6–4, S. Williams 7–5 6–2); **sf** Birmingham (d. De Lone 6–1 6–1, Rittner 6–2 6–2, Sidot 7–5 5–7 7–6, lost Raymond 6–4 6–2), **sf** New Haven (d. Shaughnessy 6–1 4–6 6–4, Clijsters 6–2 6–4, lost Seles 2–6 6–2 6–1), **sf** Filderstadt (d. Rittner 3–6 6–3 6–3, Sidot 7–5 6–2, lost Clijsters 3–6 6–4 6–1), **sf** Moscow (d. Sugiyama 6–3 7–5, Schett 7–6 6–2, lost Kournikova 6–2 6–1), **sf** Leipzig (d. Panova 4–6 6–4 7–5, Schett 4–6 6–0 7–6, lost Likhovtseva 6–1 6–4), **sf** Philadelphia (d. Hantuchova 7–5 6–4, Halard-Decugis 6–4 6–4, lost Hingis 6–1 6–2). **DOUBLES:** (with Sugiyama) **won** Eastbourne (d. Raymond/Stubbs 2–6 6–3 7–6), (with Hingis) **won** Montreal (d. Halard-Decugis/Sugiyama 6–3 3–6 6–4), (with Fusai) **won** Luxembourg (d. Bacheva/Torrens-Valero 6–3 7–6); (with Fusai) **r/u** Tokyo Pan Pacific (lost Hingis/Pierce 6–4 6–1), (with Sugiyama) **r/u** Linz (lost Mauresmo/Rubin 6–4 6–4).

CAREER GRAND SLAM RECORD
AUSTRALIAN OPEN – Played 3
1993: last 16 [seed 13] d. Meskhi 5–7 6–4 6–4, Probst 6–2 4–6 6–2, N. Dahlman 6–2 6–1, lost Seles [1] 6–2 6–0. **1994: 1r** [seed 15] lost Basuki 6–4 7–6. **1995-99:** Did not play. **2000: 2r** [seed 5] d. Nagyova 6–1 2–6 6–1, lost Jeyaseelan 7–6 6–4.

FRENCH OPEN – Played 17, qf 1
1984: 1r lost Navratilova [1] 6–1 6–2. **1985: 3r** d. W. White 6–0 6–7 6–2, Casale [16] 6–7 7–6 6–2, lost Phelps 6–3 1–6 6–2. **1986: 2r** d. Niox-Chateau 5–7 6–3 9–7, lost A. Smith 1–6 6–2 6–2. **1987: last 16** [unseeded] d. Byrne 7–5 3–6 6–3, Cueto 6–2 0–6 6–3, Rinaldi [10] 6–1 6–3, lost Kohde-Kilsch [8] 6–1 3–6 6–0. **1988: last 16** [seed 16] d. Bollegraf 6–3 6–2, Corsato 6–3 6–0, Byrne 7–5 6–2, lost Graf [1] 6–1 6–3. **1989: 1r** lost McNeil [12] 6–4 6–4. **1990: last 16** [seed 15] d. Godridge 6–3 7–5, Hack 6–2 3–6 6–3, Lapi 6–1 2–6 6–1, lost Graf [1] 6–1 6–4. **1991: qf** [seed 13] d. Etchemendy 6–3 6–1, Guerree 6–2 6–1, Jagerman 6–4 6–0, Sawamatsu 7–5 2–6 12–10, lost Graf [2] 6–3 6–2. **1992: last 16** [seed 12] d. Gorrochategui 7–5 6–1, Helgeson 3–6 6–1 6–3, Wasserman 6–4 6–2, lost Bollegraf 6–4 1–6 6–2. **1993: 3r** [seed 13] d. Grossi 6–4 5–7 6–1, Boogert 6–3 1–6 6–4, lost Wiesner 6–3 7–6. **1994: 2r** d. Reinstadler 7–5 6–2, lost Ritter 6–3 6–1. **1995: 3r** d. Kamio 6–1 6–2, M. Maleeva [6] 4–6 6–4 7–5, lost Ruano-Pascual 6–2 7–6. **1996: 2r** d. A. Miller 6–1 6–1, lost Habsudova 6–2 4–6 8–6. **1997: 3r** d. Simpson 6–3 6–2, V. Williams 5–7 6–3 7–5, lost Seles [3] 6–0 6–1. **1998: 1r** [seed 12] lost Gagliardi 4–6 7–5 6–4. **1999: 2r** [seed 9] d. Cocheteux 6–4 6–3, lost Leon Garcia 6–2 6–4. **2000: 3r** [seed 7] d. Boogert 6–3 6–3, Labat 6–1 6–3, lost Rubin 6–4 7–6.

WIMBLEDON – Played 15, r/u 1, qf 3

1986: 2r d. Nelson-Dunbar 6–1 6–2, lost K. Maleeva 6–4 6–2. **1987: 2r** d. Paulus 2–6 6–1 6–1, lost Henricksson 6–4 6–4. **1988: 2r** d. Devries 6–2 6–4, lost K. Adams 2–6 6–4 6–4. **1989: 1r** lost Kohde-Kilsch 6–4 6–2. **1990: last 16** [unseeded] d. Field 6–1 6–1, Pfaff 6–2 6–1, Frazier 3–6 6–2 7–5, lost Sabatini [4] 6–2 7–6. **1991: last 16** [seed 11] d. Rajchrtova 6–4 7–5, Kijimuta 3–6 6–2 6–2, L. Ferrando 6–1 6–1, lost Sabatini [2] 7–6 6–3. **1992: qf** [seed 14] d. Schultz 6-4 6-0, Medvedeva 7-5 2-6 6-3, Provis 4-6 7-5 6-3, Frazier 6-0 6-3, lost Seles [1] 6-1 6-3. **1993: last 16** [seed 16] d. Stubbs 7–5 6–4, Javer 6–1 6–2, Davenport 6–3 7–6, lost Navratilova [2] 6–1 6–3. **1994: 3r** d. Carlsson 6–2 6–1, Reinach 6–3 6–7 6–2, lost Martinez [3] 6–1 6–3. **1995: 3r** d. Vento 6–1 4–6 7–5, Pierce [seed 5] 6–4 3–6 6–1, lost Basuki 6–7 6–3 6–4. **1996: 3r** d. Kamstra 6–2 3–6 6–1, M. Maleeva [10] 7–6 3–6 9–7, lost Hy-Boulais 6–3 3–6 6–4. **1997: qf** [unseeded] d. Miyagi 6–3 6–4, Guse 6–0 6–3, Wiesner 3–6 6–3 6–2, Testud 4–6 7–5 12–10, lost Sanchez-Vicario [8] 6–2 7–5. **1998: r/u** [seed 16] d. Inoue 2–6 6–1 6–3, Majoli 6–0 6–1, Halard-Decugis 7–6 3–6 6–4, Smith 6–3 6–1, Davenport [2] 6–3 6–3, Zvereva 1–6 7–6 6–3, lost Novotna [3] 6–4 7–6. **1999: qf** [seed 8] d. Ahl 6–3 6–2, Hopmans 6–3 6–4, Noorlander 6–1 6–1, Van Roost [15] 6–3 3–6 6–3, lost Lucic 4–6 6–4 7–5. **2000:** [seed 7] lost Clijsters 6–3 3–6 6–2.

US OPEN – Played 15, qf 1

1986: 1r lost Sabatini [11] 6–3 6–2. **1987: 2r** d. Ludloff 6–4 6–2, lost M. Maleeva [10] 6–1 6–3. **1988: 2r** d. Louie-Harper 1–6 7–6 6–1, lost M. J. Fernandez [13] 6–4 6–4. **1989: 3r** d. Farley 6–1 6–3, Rinaldi 6–2 6–1, lost Man. Maleeva [7] 6–1 6–3. **1990: last 16** [unseeded] d. Dahlman 7–5 6–2, Zardo 6–4 4–6 6–2, Martinez [seed 10] 6–2 6–1, lost Garrison [4] 6–1 7–5. **1991: 1r** [seed 14] lost Labat 7–5 6–4. **1992: 2r** [seed 12] d. Ercegovic 6-3 6-2, Coetzer 6-0 6-0. **1993: last 16** [seed 14] d. Brioukhovets 1–6 6–4 6–1, Boogert 6–1 6–4, Singer 6–3 6–2, lost Sanchez-Vicario [2] 6–4 6–3. **1994: 2r** d. Rottier 7–5 2–6 7–5, lost Sanchez-Vicario [2] 6–2 7–6. **1995: 3r** d. Bradtke 6–3 6–1, Shriver 6–4 6–3, lost Graf [1] 6–3 6–3. **1996: 2r** d. Gavaldon 7–6 6–2, lost Martinez [4] 6–1 6–3. **1997: 1r** lost Habsudova 7–5 7–6. **1998: last 16** [seed 10] d. Perfetti 6–3 6–2, Barabanschikova 6–7 6–2 6–3, Nagyova 6–1 6–1, lost Davenport [2] 6–1 6–4. **1999: 3r** [seed 11] d. Stevenson 6–2 6–2, Sanchez-Lorenzo 7–5 4–6 6–1, lost Capriati 6–3 1–6 6–1. **2000 qf** [seed 8] d. Cervanova 3–6 6–2 6–4, Vento 6–3 6–1, J. Lee 6–3 6–2, Sanchez-Vicario [9] 6–3 6–2, lost V. Williams [3] 6–4 1–6 6–1.

OLYMPIC RECORD

1992: (Barcelona) 2r [seed 10] d. Zrubakova 6-3 6-2, lost Rittner 6-3 6-2. **1996: (Atlanta) 1r** lost Sabatini [13] 7–5 6–2.

CAREER FED CUP RECORD

1985: October (in JPN, Hard): *World Group 1r NZL d. FRA 2–1.* R1 d. J. Richardson 3–6 6–3 6–2; R3 (with I. Demongeot) lost B. Cordwell/Richardson 6–0 7–5. *Consolation Plate 2r FRA d. URU 3–0.* R3 (with Demongeot) d. M. Clavijo/L. Rodriguez 6–1 6–0. *Consolation Plate qf RUS d. FRA 2–1.* R1 d. N. Bykova 5–7 6–4 6–4; R3 (with Demongeot) lost S. Cherneva/L. Savchenko 6–3 6–1. **1986: July (in TCH, Clay):** *World Group 1r FRA d. SWE 3–0.* R3 (with P. Paradis) d. H. Dahlstrom/M. Lundqvist 6–3 5–7 6–2). *World Group 2r BUL d. FRA 2–1.* R1 lost K. Maleeva 7–6 7–6. **1987: August (in CAN, Hard):** *World Group 1r FRA d. AUT 3–0.* R2 d. J. Wiesner 6–3 7–5. *World Group 2r USA d. FRA 3–0.* R2 lost C. Evert 6–1 6–0. **1989: October (in JPN, Hard):** *World Group 1r ESP d. FRA 2–0.* R2 lost A. Sanchez-Vicario 6–4 6–2. **1990: July (in USA, Hard):** *World Group 1r FRA d. TPE 3–0.* R2 d. S. Wang 6–3 6–2. *World Group 2r FRA d. NZL 3–0.* R2 d. B. Cordwell 6–1 6–2. *World Group qf ESP d. FRA 2–0.* R2 lost A. Sanchez-Vicario 7–6 6–1. **1991: July (in GBR, Hard):** *World Group 1r POL d. FRA 2–1.* R2 lost K. Nowak 4–6 6–4 6–4; R3 (with M. Pierce) lost M. Mroz/K. Teodorowicz 6–4 6–4). *World Group Play-off FRA d. YUG 2–0.* R2 d. N. Ercegovic 6–2 5–7 6–2. **1992: July (in GER, Clay):** *World Group 1r FRA d. CHN 2–1.* R2 lost F. Li 6–1 6–7 6–3; R3 (with I. Demongeot) d. Li/M. Tang 6–3 7–6). *World Group 2r FRA d. RUS 3–0.* R2 d. E. Maniokova 6–1 6–3; R3 (with Demongeot) d. E. Makarova/E. Pogorelova 6–3 6–3. *World Group qf USA d. FRA 2–1.* R2 d. L. McNeil 6–4 7–5; R3 (with Demongeot) lost G. Fernandez/P. Shriver 6–4 6–2. **1993: July (in GER, Clay):** *World Group 1r FRA d. CAN 2–1.* R2 d. P. Hy 6–4 6–1; R3 (with J. Halard) d. J. Hetherington/Hy 7–5 7–6. *World Group 2r FRA d. SWE 3–0.* R2 d. C. Dahlman 6–1 7–6; R3 (with Halard) d. M. Lindstrom/M. Strandlund 6–2 6–3. *World Group qf FRA d. TCH 3–0.* R2 d. J. Novotna 6–1 0–6 6–3. *World Group sf ESP d. FRA 2–1.* R2 lost A. Sanchez-Vicario 6–1 6–4. **1994: July (in GER, Clay):** *World Group 1r FRA d. KOR 3–0.* R3 (with A. Fusai) d. J. Choi/S. Park 6–4 6–4. *World Group 2r FRA d. ITA 3–0.* R3 (with J. Halard) d. R. Grande/M. Grossi 6–4 6–1. *World Group qf FRA d. BUL 2–1.* R3 (with Halard) d. K./M. Maleeva 6–2 3–6 6–2. *World Group sf USA d. FRA 3–0.* R3 (with Halard) lost G. Fernandez/Z. Garrison 3–6 6–3 6–1. **1995: April** – *World Group qf FRA d. ARG 3–2 in FRA (Clay).* R5 (with J. Halard) d. M. De Swardt/E. Reinach 7–5 6–2. **July** – *World Group sf USA d. FRA 3–2 in USA (Carpet).* R5 (with Halard) lost L. Davenport/G. Fernandez 6–1 7–6. **1996: April** – *World Group qf FRA d. ARG 3–2 in FRA (Clay).* R1 lost F. Labat 6–3 6–4; R4 lost P. Suarez 7–6 6–1; R5 (with J. Halard-Decugis) d. Labat/P. Tarabini 6–2 6–4. **July:** – *World Group sf ESP d. FRA 3–2 in FRA (Carpet).* R5 (with Halard-Decugis) lost C. Martinez/A. Sanchez-Vicario 6–4 2–1 ret. **1997: March** – *World Group qf FRA d. JPN 4–1 in JPN (Hard).* R2 d. A. Sugiyama 4–6 7–5 6–4; R4 d. N. Sawamatsu 7–5 4–6 17–15. **July** – *World Group sf FRA d. BEL 3–2 in BEL (Clay).* R5 (with A. Fusai) d. E. Callens/D. Van Roost 3–6 6–2 7–5. **October** – *World Group Final FRA d. NED 4–1 in NED (Carpet).* R5 (with Fusai) d. M. Bollegraf/C. Vis 6–3 6–4 . **1998: April** – *World Group sf FRA d. BEL 3–2 in BEL (Hard).* R5 (with A. Fusai) d. E. Callens/L. Courtois 6–4 6–0. **July** *World Group sf SUI d. FRA 5–0 in SUI (Clay).* R5 (with Fusai) lost E. Gagliardi/P. Schnyder 2–6 6–3 6–3. **1999: October** – *World Group qf RUS d. FRA 3–2*

Nathalie Tauziat, a quarter-finalist at the US Open for the first time. (Paul Zimmer)

in RUS (Carpet). R2 lost T. Panova 6–4 6–2; R3 lost E. Likhovtseva 6–2 6–4; R5 (with Mauresmo) lost Likhovtseva/E. Makarova 6–0 7–6. **2000: April (in RUS, Carpet):** *World Group rr FRA d. RUS 3–0*. R3 (with J. Halard-Decugis) d. A. Kournikova/E. Likhovtseva 6–3 7–6. *FRA d. AUS 2–1*. R3 (with Halard-Decugis) d. A. Molik/R. Stubbs 6–0 7–6. *BEL d. FRA 2–1*. R2 lost K. Clijsters 6–1 6–4. R3 (with Halard-Decugis) d. E. Callens/L. Courtois 7–5 3–6 6–3.

GRAND SLAM CUP RECORD – Played 1, sf 1
1998: sf d. Davenport [2] 4–6 6–1 7–5, lost V. Williams 6–4 6–0.

SEASON ENDING CHAMPIONSHIPS – Played 8, sf 2, qf 2
(1983-94 Virginia Slims, 1995 Corel, 1996-2000 Chase)
1990: 1r lost M. J. Fernandez 6–1 7–6. **1991: 1r** lost Capriati 5–7 6–0 7–6. **1992: 1r** lost Seles 6–1 6–2. **1993: 1r** lost Navratilova 6–4 6–4. **1994-96:** Did not play. **1997: sf** d. Coetzer 6–3 6–3, Majoli 7–6 7–6, lost Pierce 6–2 5–7 6–4. **1998: qf** d. Zvereva 6–3 6–1, lost Davenport 6–0 6–3. **1999: sf** d. Coetzer 6–3 7–6, Van Roost 6–3 6–2, lost Davenport 7–6 6–0. **2000: qf** [seed 6] (d. Frazier 6–3 6–2, lost Hingis [1] 6–1 6–7 6–2.

REMAINING WOMEN'S BIOGRAPHIES

The following biographies show the players' progress each year in the four Grand Slam Championships. It is shown thus: A (Australian Open), F (French Open), W (Wimbledon), US (US Open), followed by the round reached, or '–' if a player did not compete.

SABINE APPELMANS (BEL)
Born Aalst, 22 April 1972; lives Asse; LH; 2HB; 5ft 6in; 127lb; turned pro 1989; career singles titles 7; final 2000 WTA ranking 50; 2000 prize money $243,748; career prize money $2,041,247.
Coached by Steve Martens. Husband Serge Haubourdin (married 20 September 1997). She is naturally right-handed, but chose to join a left-handed group when learning to play tennis in order to be with a friend. **1987:** (283). **1988:** (215) A –, F 2, W –, US –. Enjoyed some success on the European satellite circuits and upset Burgin 1r French Open. **1989:** (149) A –, F –, W –, US –. Reached her 1st primary circuit qf at Taipei. **1990:** (22) A 3, F 1, W –, US 3. R/u Auckland (d. Cordwell) and reached sf Wellington and Singapore, breaking into top 100 and finishing the year in the top 25. **1991:** (18) A 4, F 4, W 1, US 1. Won her 1st singles title at Phoenix, following with VS Nashville; was r/u Tokyo Suntory, reached sf Oslo and Puerto Rico and appeared in 3 doubles f. Voted Belgian Sports Celebrity of the Year. **1992:** (26) A 1, F 2, W 2, US 4. Won Pattaya City and r/u Tokyo Suntory, as well as reaching qf Olympics, Essen, Berlin and Leipzig. In GS upset Huber *en route* to last 16 US Open, unseeded. **1993:** (36) A 1, F 2, W 3, US 2. Having won Porto Challenger but reached no qf on the main tour, she was r/u Budapest (d. Wiesner) in Oct. and followed the next week with sf Essen (d. Maleeva-Fragniere). **1994:** (27) A 3, F 2, W 1, US 1. Won Linz (d. Huber) and Pattaya City and reached sf Tokyo Japan Open, Los Angeles (d. Novotna) and Moscow. Ranked No. 1 in Belgium, she reached her highest world ranking of 17 in May, before slipping back out of the top 20. **1995:** (31) A 3, F 3, W 1, US 3. Won Zagreb and reached qf Paris Open, Linz, Strasbourg (d. Frazier) and Tokyo Nicherei. **1996:** (21) A 4, F 3, W 4, US 1. Upset Novotna, Sukova and Halard-Decugis on her way to the title at Linz and reached sf Moscow, plus qf Jakarta, Zurich (d. Martinez) and Luxembourg. She made her mark in GS: at French Open she was 5–2 up in 2s v Seles, but won no more games, and at Wimbledon, where she was unseeded, she scraped past Schultz-McCarthy 12–10 fs before extending Sanchez-Vicario to 3s. In doubles she reached 2 f with Oremans, but won no title. **1997:** (16) A qf, F 1, W 4, US 1. She was r/u Budapest, and although she reached no other f, she appeared in qf Australian Open, Gold Coast, Berlin, Strasbourg, Rosmalen, Leipzig, Zurich (d. Schultz-McCarthy and Majoli) and Luxembourg. Once again she impressed in GS, removing Martinez at Australian Open and Schultz-McCarthy at Wimbledon, where she was unseeded. Upset M. J. Fernandez at Chicago and surprised Sanchez-Vicario in Fed Cup as BEL d. ESP. Qualified for Chase Champs 1st time, but fell 1r to Pierce at her best. **1998:** (49) A 1, F 1, W 3, US –. Her best singles performances were an upset of Graf (returning from injury) *en route* to sf Hannover, and qf appearance at Linz. In doubles she won Paris Open and 's-Hertogenbosch with Oremans. **1999:** (30) A 3, F 1, W 2, US 4. Until Sept., she had reached qf only twice and had dropped out of top 50. However, a useful performance at US Open, where she was unseeded, followed by sf Luxembourg, saw her return to her accustomed place, and by end of year she had appeared in qf Antwerp, Knokke-Heist, Filderstadt (d. Coetzer), Bratislava and Quebec City. **2000:** A 3, F 1, W 4, US 1. In singles she reached qf only twice – at Gold Coast, where she was r/u doubles with Grande, and Knokke-Heist. She also upset Sanchez-Vicario at Ericsson Open and won Antwerp doubles with Clijsters. She announced in Nov. that she would be retiring after Australian Open 2001. **2000 HIGHLIGHTS – SINGLES: Australian Open 3r** (d. Ellwood 6–2 6–2, Rubin 6–1 3–6 6–3, lost S. Williams [seed 3] 6–2 7–6), **French Open 1r** (lost Hingis [seed 1] 6–0 6–4), **Wimbledon last 16** [unseeded] (d. Dragomir 7–6 6–4, Boogert 7–5 3–6 9–7, Smashnova 6–3 6–4, lost V. Williams [seed 5] 6–4 6–4), **US Open 1r** (lost Vento 6–4 6–2), **Olympics 3r** [seed 16] (d. Jeyaseelan 7–5 6–2, Vento 6–2 6–2, lost Coetzer [seed 7] 6–3 6–1). **2000 HIGHLIGHTS – DOUBLES:** (with Clijsters) **won** Antwerp (d. Hopkins/Rampre 6–1 6–1); (with Grande) **r/u** Gold Coast (lost Halard-Decugis/Kournikova 6–3 6–0). **CAREER HIGHLIGHTS – Australian Open – qf 1997** (d. Sukova 6–2 6–2, Grossman 6–4 6–1, Boogert 6–1 3–0 ret, Martinez 2–6 7–5 6–1, lost Pierce 1–6 6–4 6–4).

NICOLE ARENDT (USA)
Born Somerville, NJ, 26 August 1969; lives Gainsville, Fla; LH; 5ft 9in; 150lb; turned pro 1991; career singles titles 0; final 2000 WTA ranking – singles, 11 doubles; 2000 prize money $158,237; career prize money $1,367,467.
Coached by Charlton Eagle. **1986:** (–) A –, F –, W –, US 2. Won San Antonio Futures. **1987:** (366) A –, F –, W –, US 1. **1988:** (451) A –, F –, W –, US –. Began 3-year career at Univ. of Florida-Gainesville, where she was an All-American 8 times. **1989:** (–) A –, F –, W –, US –. R/u NCAA Champs **1990:** (388) A –, F –, W –, US –. R/u NCAA Champs and won Lady Lake Futures. **1991:** (211) A –, F –, W –, US 1. Won NCAA Champs and on the Futures circuit took Sanibel and Greensboro. **1992:** (126) A 2, F –, W –, US 2. At Puerto Rico she reached her 1st qf on the senior tour. **1993:** (88) A 2, F –, W 2, US 2. Reached sf Jakarta, where she won the doubles with Radford and upset Paradis-Mangon on her way to qf Pattaya City. Won Karen Krantzcke Sportsmanship Award. **1994:** (73) A 1, F –, W 2, US 2. Upset Appelmans at Eastbourne, and appeared in sf Singapore and qf Pattaya City (d. Basuki) and Jakarta, where she won the doubles again with Radford. Sidelined for 2 months with pulled

stomach muscle, suffered at Filderstadt. **1995:** A 1, F 1, W 1, US 3. In singles qf Birmingham was her best showing, but she made her mark in doubles, winning 3 titles with Bollegraf, with whom she qualified for WTA Champs, and 1 with Golarsa. **1996:** (70) A 3, F 1, W 3, US 2. From 4 women's doubles f with different partners, she won Edinburgh with Bollegraf and Filderstadt with Novotna. In mixed r/u Australian Open and French Open with L. Jensen. **1997:** (63) A 1, F 4, W 3, US 1. Upset Novotna at French Open, where she was unseeded. In doubles with Bollegraf, she was r/u Wimbledon and reached 7 other f, winning Hannover, Rome, Edinburgh and Atlanta and sharing Eastbourne. They qualified together for Chase Champs and reached sf before retiring v Fusai/Tauziat. **1998:** (–) She was out all season following right shoulder surgery and spent the year continuing with her studies. **1999:** (142) A –, F 2, W 2, US –. She returned to play doubles at Australian Open and in singles reached qf Birmingham. **2000:** A –, F –, W –, US –. In doubles with Bollegraf she played 3 f, including Chase Champs, but won no title. **2000 HIGHLIGHTS – DOUBLES:** (with Bollegraf) **r/u** Ericsson Open (lost Halard-Decugis/Sugiyama 4–6 7–5 6–4), **r/u** Hamburg (lost Kournikova/Zvereva 6–7 6–2 6–4), **r/u** Chase Champs (lost Hingis/Kournikova 6–2 6–3). **CAREER HIGHLIGHTS – DOUBLES:** (with Bollegraf) **Wimbledon – r/u 1997** (lost G. Fernandez/Zvereva 7–6 6–4).

CARA BLACK (ZIM)

Born Harare, 17 February 1979, and lives there; RH; 2HB; 5ft 6in; 122lb; turned pro 1998; career singles titles 0; final 2000 WTA ranking 43 singles, 13 doubles; 2000 prize money $316,153.

Coached by her father, Don Black, a former pro player, and Daria Kopsic-Segal. Her brothers, Byron and Wayne, play the men's circuit. **1992:** All-Africa champ. **1994:** Won Nat Jun Champ in singles and doubles. **1995:** (489) Won Wimbledon Jun doubles with Olsza and Nat Jun Champ in singles and doubles again. In the women's game won 2 Futures singles titles, being r/u in both doubles. **1996:** (337) Played Fed Cup and won Nitra Futures. **1997:** (189) Missed Australian Open Jun, but in other Jun GS was r/u French Open to Henin, won Wimbledon over Rippner and US Open over Chevalier, as well as taking French Open and Wimbledon doubles with Selyutina. These results placed her at No. 1 in ITF Jun rankings at year's end in both singles and doubles. In the women's game, she won Futures titles at Dinard and Mission. **1998:** (44) A –, F 2, W 3, US 2. Playing her 1st full year on the main circuit, she broke into the top 50 with her 1st career sf at Boston (d. Farina and Likhovtseva) and also upset Schnyder 2r Wimbledon. **1999:** (51) A 1, F 1, W 1, US 1. She reached sf Birmingham as well as qf Hobart, Oklahoma City and Quebec City, adding upsets of Huber and Spirlea at Indian Wells and Halard-Decugis at Tokyo Japan Open. On the ITF circuit she won the $75,000 tourn at Santa Carla. **2000:** A 2, F 2, W 2, US 1. She began the year by appearing in her 1st f on the main tour at Auckland, where she won the doubles with Fusai. She also reached sf Birmingham (d. Talaja), and qf 's-Hertogenbosch (d. Appelmans) and Stanford, as well as upsetting Capriati at Indian Wells and Dementieva at Linz. In doubles she played 4 f with different partners, being r/u 3 times, including at US Open with Likhovtseva, with whom she qualified for Chase Champs after Rubin/Testud withdrew. **2000 HIGHLIGHTS – SINGLES: Australian Open 2r** (d. Nemeckova 6–4 7–6, lost Petrova 4–6 6–4 6–4), **French Open 2r** (d. Myskina 2–6 7–6 6–2, lost C. Martinez [seed 5] 4–6 7–5 6–4), **Wimbledon 2r** (d. Smith 6–2 6–2, lost Dechy 4–6 6–2 6–1), **US Open 1r** (lost Dechy 6–3 6–2), **Olympics 1r** (lost Farina-Elia 6–2 3–6 6–3); **r/u** Auckland (d. Noorlander 6–0 6–1, Nejedly 6–1 7–6, Likhovtseva 6–3 7–5, Hopmans 6–3 6–3, lost Kremer 6–4 6–4); **sf** Birmingham (d. Panova 6–1 6–4, Molik 6–3 5–7 6–3, Talaja 6–3 6–4, Brandi 6–3 7–5, lost Tanasugarn 6–4 6–4). **2000 HIGH-LIGHTS – DOUBLES:** (with Likhovtseva) **r/u US Open** (lost Halard-Decugis/Sugiyama 6–0 1–6 6–1); (with Fusai) **won** Auckland (d. Schwartz/Wartusch 3–6 6–3 6–4); (with Selyutina) **r/u** Birmingham (lost McQuillan/McShea 6–3 7–6), (with Frazier) **r/u** Stanford (lost Rubin/Testud 6–4 6–4). **CAREER HIGHLIGHTS – DOUBLES:** (with Likhovtseva) **US Open – r/u 2000.**

MANON BOLLEGRAF (NED)

Born Den Bosch, 10 April 1964; lives Ermelo; RH; 2HB; 5ft 8in; 150lb; turned pro 1985; career singles titles 1; final 2000 WTA ranking – singles, 17 doubles; 2000 prize money $140,914; career prize money $2,112,117.

Coached by Ron Timmermans and at tournaments by Charlton Eagle. **1986:** (148) Qf Singapore. **1987:** (120) A 2, F 2, W –, US –. Qf Little Rock and took over the No. 1 ranking in her country. **1988:** (117) A 2, F 1, W 2, US 2. Qf Brisbane. **1989:** (38) A 3, F 3, W 1, US 2. In singles won 1st primary circuit title at Oklahoma (unseeded), reached sf Brussels and Nashville and upset McNeil 2r French Open. In doubles won 4 women's titles plus French Open mixed with Nijssen. **1990:** (32) A 2, F 1, W 1, US 2. In singles r/u VS Oklahoma and reached sf Strasbourg. Appeared in 5 doubles f with various partners, winning Wichita with McGrath and Zurich with Pfaff. **1991:** (49) A 1, F 1, W 3, US 1. R/u Colorado and sf Oklahoma in singles, won Leipzig with Demongeot in doubles and took US Open mixed with Nijssen. **1992:** (44) A 1, F qf, W 2, US –. In singles she upset Maleeva-Fragniere and Tauziat in reaching qf French Open, unseeded, and reached sf VS Oklahoma and qf Chicago. In doubles she reached 4 f with different partners, winning Waregem with Vis. Missed Olympics and US Open after tearing several ligaments at Frankfurt, for which she underwent surgery, and was out for rest of year. **1993:** (161) A 1, F 1, W 1, US 1. At US Open she extended eventual finalist Sukova to 3s tb 1r, but it was in doubles that she excelled. In mixed she was r/u French Open with Nijssen and in partnership with Adams she played 5 women's f, winning 3 and qualifying for VS Champs, where they failed to pass 1r. **1994:** (109) A 1, F 1, W 1, US 1. She upset Garrison-Jackson at FC Cup, but reached no qf in singles.

Again her strength lay in doubles, in which she appeared in 10 f with various partners, winning 1 with Neiland and 2 with Navratilova, with whom she reached sf VS Champs. **1995:** (158) A 2, F –, W –, US 2. Played 9 doubles f with various partners, winning 4 with Arendt, with whom she qualified for WTA Champs, and 1 with Stubbs. **1996:** (–) A –, F –, W –, US –. In doubles she won Linz with McGrath and Edinburgh with Arendt; in mixed was r/u US Open with Leach. Underwent arthroscopic surgery on her left knee at end Sept., which prevented her playing at Chase Champs, for which she qualified in doubles. **1997:** (–) A –, F –, W –, US –. Returning in time for Australian Open, she won the mixed doubles there with Leach, adding US Open later in year. In women's doubles with Arendt, she was r/u Wimbledon and from 7 other f won 4 titles and shared another, qualifying for Chase Champs. There, however, they were forced to retire sf v Fusai/Tauziat. **1998:** (–) A –, F –, W –, US –. Playing doubles only, she was r/u Leipzig with Spirlea. **1999:** (–) A –, F –, W –, US –. **2000:** Although she won no title, she appeared in 3 doubles f with Arendt, including Chase Champs, after which she retired from the tour. **2000 HIGHLIGHTS – DOUBLES:** (with Arendt) **r/u** Ericsson Open (lost Halard-Decugis/Sugiyama 4–6 7–5 6–4), **r/u** Hamburg (lost Kournikova/Zvereva 6–7 6–2 6–4). **CAREER HIGHLIGHTS – SINGLES: French Open – qf 1992** [unseeded] (d. Maniokova 6–2 6–3, Thoren 6–2 4–6 7–5, Maleeva-Fragniere 7–5 6–2, Tauziat 6–4 1–6 6–2, lost Sanchez-Vicario 6–2 6–3). **CAREER HIGHLIGHTS – DOUBLES:** (with Arendt) **Wimbledon – r/u 1997** (lost G. Fernandez/Zvereva 7–6 6–4). **CAREER HIGH-LIGHTS – MIXED DOUBLES:** (with Nijssen unless stated) **Australian Open –** (with Leach) **won 1997** (d. De Jager/Neiland 6–3 6–7 7–5); **French Open – won 1989** (d. De La Pena/Sanchez-Vicario 3–6 6–7 6–2); **US Open – won 1991** (d. E. Sanchez/Sanchez-Vicario 6–2 7–6), (with Leach) **won 1997** (d. Albano/Paz 3–6 7–5 7–6).

KRISTINA BRANDI (USA)

Born San Juan, Puerto Rico, 29 March 1977; lives Tampa, Fla; RH; 2HB; 5ft 6in; 130lb; turned pro 1995; career singles titles 1; final 2000 WTA ranking 28; 2000 prize money $208,367.
Coached by her father, Joe, who formerly coached Sampras; sponsored by Gigi Fernandez. Moved to Florida aged 3. Won Nat CC 14s. **1992:** (559). **1993:** (558). **1994:** (268) Won Indianapolis Futures. **1995:** (191). **1996:** (148) A –, F –, W –, US 2. **1997:** (78) A 3, F 1, W 2, US 1. Took a set off Seles at Wimbledon. **1998:** (70) A 1, F 1, W 1, US 1. Emerging from the ITF circuit, where she won Peachtree $25,000 and Austin $50,000, she finished the year in style with her 1st sf on the main tour at Pattaya. **1999:** (55) A 2, F 1, W 1, US 1. On the senior tour she won her 1st title at 's-Hertogenbosch (unseeded, d. Van Roost) and reached qf Auckland and Kuala Lumpur; on the $50,000 ITF circuit she won Salt Lake City. **2000:** A 4, F 2, W 4, US 2. Her best performance was again at 's-Hertogenbosch, where she upset Dokic *en route* to her only sf of year. Elsewhere she played qf Birmingham, Tokyo Toyota and Shanghai, as well as upsetting Nagyova at Hobart, Coetzer at Australian Open, where she was unseeded, Talaja at FC Cup and Likhovtseva at Rome. **2000 HIGHLIGHTS – SINGLES: Australian Open last 16** [unseeded] (d. Leon Garcia 6–3 6–3, Coetzer [seed 8] 6–1 6–3, Dragomir 6–4 7–6, lost C. Martinez [seed 10] 6–1 6–1), **French Open 2r** (d. Andretto 6–2 6–1, lost Serna 5–7 6–2 6–2), **Wimbledon last 16** [unseeded] (d. Kruger 6–3 7–5, Labat 6–2 2–6 6–1, Myskina 4–6 6–3 6–1, lost Dokic 6–1 6–3), **US Open 2r** (d. Vaskova 6–2 6–3, lost Hingis [seed 1] 6–1 6–1); **sf** 's-Hertogenbosch (d. Schwartz 6–3 6–1, Dokic 6–0 6–1, Pratt 6–3 7–5, lost Dragomir 6–2 6–3).

JENNIFER CAPRIATI (USA)

Born New York, 29 March 1976; lives Wesley Chapel, Fla.; RH; 2HB; 5ft 8½in; 135lb; turned pro 1990; career singles titles 9; final 2000 WTA ranking 14; 2000 prize money $488,861; career prize money $2,488,000.
Coached again by her father, Stefano. Fitness trainer Karen Burnett. **1988:** Won Nat 18s at age 12. **1989:** Won French Open Jun (losing no set, and being the youngest to win that title), US Open Jun, plus Wimbledon and US Open Jun doubles with McGrath, as well as US 18s HC and CC. At 13 years 6 months was youngest to play W Cup, making a sparkling debut with a 6–0 6–0 drubbing of Wood, but was still too young to compete on the pro tour until March. **1990:** (8) A –, F sf, W 4, US 4. At age 13 she became the 1st female to reach f of her 1st pro tourn at VS Florida, Boca Raton. She upset Sukova there and at LIPC, where she reached last 16, stunned Sanchez-Vicario and Zvereva *en route* to 2nd tour f at FC Cup, and in Oct. beat Garrison at Puerto Rico to win her 1st tour title. Reached sf in 1st GS tourn at French Open, becoming youngest (at 14 years 66 days) to reach that stage; youngest seed at Wimbledon, youngest to win singles match at US Open, and youngest to qualify for VS Champs, where she lost 1r to Graf. Also youngest to reach top 10 at 14 years 235 days. She was a member of the winning US Fed Cup team and won WTA Most Impressive Newcomer award. **1991:** (6) A –, F 4, W sf, US sf. Caused the upset of the Championships when she stunned Navratilova in ss to become youngest semi-finalist at Wimbledon, and at US Open d. Sabatini to reach the same stage and took Seles to 3s tb. She had earlier upset the No. 1 as she won San Diego, following with Toronto and r/u VS Philadelphia. Also reached sf VS Florida and Berlin and qualified for VS Champs, where she lost qf to Sabatini. In doubles won Italian Open with Seles. **1992:** (7) A qf, F qf, W qf, US 3. Found it a hard year on the tour, despite winning the Olympic gold medal. She struggled to recapture her enjoyment of the game and early in the year was rumoured to be contemplating retirement. By year's end she was beginning to feel more positive again and reached sf VS Champs, where she lost to Sabatini. Won San Diego and reached sf Berlin, Philadelphia and LIPC where, in qf, she became one of a handful of players to beat Seles during the year. **1993:** (9) A qf, F qf, W qf, US 1. She struggled again and, feeling more and more jaded and less interested in

the game, she withdrew from VS Champs, lacking motivation. Her only title came at Sydney, with r/u Toronto and sf FC Cup, plus 5 more qf, including Australian Open, French Open and Wimbledon, but at US Open fell 1r to Meskhi. **1994:** (–) A –, F –, W –, US –. In Jan. she dropped out of the top 10 for 1st time since July 1991. Disillusioned with life on the circuit and showing behavioural problems, she was arrested on drug charges in mid-May and voluntarily entered a Miami drug abuse rehabilitation centre, uncertain whether she would ever return to the tennis circuit. However, she was back in action for her only tourn of the year at Philadelphia in Nov., where she lost 1r to Huber, but was still vague about her future plans. **1995:** (–) A –, F –, W –, US –. Still struggling with behavioural problems and motivation, she was out of action all year. **1996:** (24) A –, F 1, W –, US 1. At Paris Open in Feb. she was expected back for her 1st event since Nov. 1994, but withdrew citing a strained gluteal muscle sustained during practice. She eventually ended her absence of 1 year 9 months and 4 weeks on 19 Feb. at Essen, where she won 2 matches and extended Novotna to 3s in qf. Upset Coetzer at LIPC, after losing 2nd set to love, in her 3rd tourn back and still unranked, and played Fed Cup in April. Returned to the rankings at 103 on 1 April – for the first time since she fell off on 26 June 1994 – was back in the top 50 in Oct., and top 25 in Nov. Withdrew from Wimbledon, not feeling ready to compete at that level, and at Montreal retired 3r with a gluteal strain on her left side, after upsetting Spirlea 1r. She followed qf appearance at Zurich (d. M. Maleeva) with the high point of her year at sf Chicago, where she upset Seles in ss, before losing to Novotna in her 1st f since Toronto 1993. She was voted Comeback Player of the Year. Low points were her disappointing performance at Fed Cup qf, losing both her singles in ss v AUT, and occasional behavioural problems. **1997:** (66) A 1, F –, W –, US 1. She began the year well by upsetting Davenport *en route* to f Sydney, where she extended Hingis to 3s. Thereafter, though, her best showing was qf Oklahoma City, as she withdrew from Amelia Island with a left hip adductor strain, sprained her right ankle during practice in Rome and withdrew from French Open and Wimbledon. **1998:** (101) A –, F –, W 2, US 1. She was troubled at start of year by a chronic shoulder injury before making another comeback in spring, featuring an improved backhand. In her 3rd tourn, at Amelia Island, she notched her 1st match win since Aug. 1997, and went on to reach qf Hamburg and Palermo. **1999:** (23) A 2, F 4, W 2, US 4. At Strasbourg, unseeded, she removed Tauziat and Likhovtseva to take her 1st title since 1993, and followed with a 2nd at Quebec City in Nov. She reached no other qf, but upset Martinez at Stanford and Tauziat at both Toronto and US Open, where she was unseeded, and finished the year back in the top 25. **2000:** A sf, F 1, W 4, US 4. More muscular and bulky after a weight training regime, she became stronger and faster during the year, having appeared at Rome looking overweight and short of training after tendinitis of right achilles tendon had kept her out of action for a while in spring. She began the year well, beating Hingis in an exhibition event in Hong Kong, and gave her best performance in a major tourn since 1991 at Australian Open, where she was unseeded. Having split with Harold Solomon in May, and being coached once more by her father, she was back in form again to upset Van Roost at Wimbledon, where she was unseeded. Across the year she won Luxembourg, was r/u Quebec City, reached sf Australian Open, 's-Hertogenbosch and Zurich (d. Kournikova) and qf Ericsson Open (d. S. Williams in ss) and Birmingham. She qualified for Chase Champs for 1st time since 1992, but fell 1r to Kournikova. However, the following week she was celebrating her part in the USA Fed Cup team that d. ESP 5–0 in f. **2000 HIGHLIGHTS – SINGLES: Australian Open sf** [unseeded] (d. Schwartz 6–1 7–6, Van Roost [seed 14] 6–1 4–6 8–6, Yi 6–4 6–4, Schnyder 6–3 4–6 6–1, Sugiyama 6–0 6–2, lost Davenport 6–2 7–6), **French Open 1r** [seed 15] (lost Zuluaga 6–3 7–5), **Wimbledon last 16** [unseeded] (d. Van Roost [seed 16] 7–5 6–2, Shaughnessy 7–6 6–2, Basuki 7–6 6–0, lost Davenport [seed 2] 6–3 6–3), **US Open last 16** [seed 15] (d. Gagliardi 6–4 6–0, Nagyova 6–2 6–2, Gersi 6–2 6–3, lost Seles [seed 6] 6–3 6–4); **won** Luxembourg (d. Kostanic 6–4 6–2, Sanchez Lorenzo 6–2 7–5, Sidot 7–5 5–7 6–3, Rittner 6–4 6–2, Maleeva 4–6 6–1 6–4); **r/u** Quebec City (d. Nejedly 6–4 7–6, Jeyaseelan 7–5 6–0, Frazier 3–6 7–5 7–5, lost Rubin 6–4 6–2); **sf** 's-Hertogenbosch (d. Maleeva 6–3 6–1, De Lone 6–1 5–7 6–1, Schnyder 7–5 7–5, lost Hingis 7–5 6–2), **sf** Zurich (d. Krasnoroutskaia 5–7 6–3 7–6, Sidot 6–3 6–1, Kournikova 7–6 6–4, lost Hingis 6–3 6–2). **CAREER HIGHLIGHTS – SINGLES: Olympics – won gold medal 1992** (d. Reinach 6–1 6–0, Tarabini 6–4 6–1, Basuki 6–3 6–4, Huber 6–3 7–6, Sanchez-Vicario 6–3 3–6 6–1, Graf 3–6 6–3 6–4); **Australian Open – sf 2000; French Open – sf 1990** (d. Testud 6–1 6–1, Cammy Macgregor 6–1 6–0, Wiesner 6–4 6–4, Paz 6–0 6–3, M. J. Fernandez 6–2 6–4, lost Seles 6–2 6–2), **qf** 1992 (d. Reinstadler 6–1 6–7 6–3, Testud 6–4 6–4, Habsudova 4–6 6–4 6–3, Pierce 6–4 6–3, lost Seles 6–2 6–2), **qf** 1993 (d. Herreman 6–0 6–1, Fusai 6–1 7–5, Labat 6–0 3–6 6–4, Pierce 6–4 7–6, lost Graf 6–3 7–5); **Wimbledon – sf 1991** (d. Stafford 6–0 7–5, Zrubakova 6–2 6–3, Probst 6–3 1–6 6–3, Schultz 3–6 6–1 6–1, Navratilova 6–4 7–5, lost Sabatini 6–4 6–4), **qf** 1992 (d. Rubin 6–0 7–5, Shriver 6–2 6–4, Hy 6–3 6–1, Sawamatsu 6–3 4–6 6–4, lost Sabatini 6–1 3–6 6–3), **qf** 1993 (d. Siddall 6–7 6–2 6–1, Smylie 4–6 6–3 6–2, Schultz 7–5 4–6 6–2, Raymond 4–6 6–3 8–6, lost Graf 7–6 6–1); **US Open – sf 1991** (d. Pfaff 6–1 6–0, Ritter 6–3 6–0, Hy 6–1 6–4, Durie 6–1 6–2, Sabatini 6–3 7–6, lost Seles 3–6 6–3 7–6); **Australian Open – qf 1992** (d. Medvedeva 6–2 6–0, van Lottum 6–3 6–4, Adams 6–0 6–0, Garrison Jackson 6–4 6–4, lost Sabatini 6–4 7–6), **qf** 1993 (d. Harvey-Wild 6–0 6–1, Labat 6–7 7–5 6–2, Zvereva 7–5 7–5, K. Maleeva 6–7 6–3 6–1, lost Graf 7–5 6–2).

DENISA CHLADKOVA (CZE)

Born Prague, 8 February 1979, and lives there; RH; 5ft 8½in; 126lb; turned pro 1994; career singles titles 0; final 2000 WTA ranking 51; 2000 prize money $157,673.
Coached by Michael Kopriva. **1995:** (276) A member of winning World Youth Cup team, she began to make an impact on the satellite circuits. **1996:** (99) Reached her 1st tour sf at Pattaya at end of year (d. Park and Labat) and broke into top 100. **1997:** (50) A 1, F 1, W qf, US 2. Upset Davenport on her way to qf

Wimbledon, where she was unseeded, and reached the same stage at Prague. **1998:** (134) A 1, F 1, W 1, US –. Her only success was on the ITF circuit, where she won Edinburgh. **1999:** (57) A –, F 1, W 1, US 1. At Knokke-Heist, she reached her 1st f on the main tour (d. Habsudova and Talaja). In other tourns she appeared in sf Budapest, Strasbourg (d. Raymond and Sugiyama after qualifying) and Pattaya and qf Linz (d. Schett). **2000:** A 2, F 2, W 1, US 1. She surprised Likhovtseva on her way to f Hannover, unseeded, and reached sf Bratislava, adding upsets of Dragomir at Berlin, Sugiyama at Rome and Talaja at Linz. **2000 HIGHLIGHTS – SINGLES: Australian Open 2r** (d. Razzano 7–6 6–2, lost Callens 2–6 7–5 6–4), **French Open 2r** (d. Nejedly 6–3 6–4, lost Maleeva 7–6 2–6 6–2), **Wimbledon 1r** (lost Lucic 4–6 6–2 6–2), **US Open 1r** (lost Molik 6–1 6–2); **r/u** Hannover (d. Hopmans 6–4 3–6 6–3, Likhovtseva 3–6 6–2 6–3, Kremer 6–2 6–3, Sidot 6–3 6–7 7–6, lost S. Williams 6–1 6–1); **sf** Bratislava (d. Bobkova 7–5 6–3, Srebotnik 6–4 6–3, Plischke 7–6 6–3, lost Oremans 6–2 6–0).

KIM CLIJSTERS (BEL)
Born Bilzen, 8 June 1983, and lives there; RH; 2HB; 5ft 8in; 151lb; pro; career singles titles 3; final 2000 WTA ranking 18; 2000 prize money $418,503.
Coached by Carl Maes. **1996:** Played in winning BEL Europa Cup squad with her sister, Elke. **1998:** (409) In Jun tennis she reached Wimbledon singles to Srebotnik, won French Open doubles with Dokic and US Open doubles with Dyrberg. In the women's game, on the ITF $10,000 circuit, she won both singles and doubles at Brussels I and took Koksijde singles. **1999:** (47) A –, F –, W 4, US 3. At Luxembourg she played through the qualifying and upset Appelmans and Van Roost to take her 1st title on the main tour, aged 16. She followed with r/u Bratislava (d. Appelmans and Dechy, and won doubles with Courtois) to consolidate her position in the top 50 in her 1st season, and also reached qf Antwerp, playing as LL in her 1st main draw. In GS she upset Coetzer at Wimbledon, where she was unseeded, and at US Open, against eventual champ S. Williams, she served for the match at 5–3 fs, but lost her nerve, allowing Williams to take 12 points in a row for the match. On the ITF circuit she won the $10,000 tourn at Sheffield. **2000:** A 1, F 1, W 2, US 2. She began the year in style by winning Hobart, unseeded, and finished the year in top 20 1st time after taking the title at Leipzig in Nov., again unseeded and including upsets of Sanchez-Vicario, Dokic (saving mp), Kournikova and Likhovtseva. She also reached qf Luxembourg and her 1st Chase Champs, where she d. Sanchez-Vicario and was 4–2 up fs v Dementieva before losing. Other notable upsets during the year included Kournikova, C. Martinez and Tauziat *en route* to f Filderstadt, Huber at Hannover, Tauziat and Kournikova in Fed Cup as BEL d. FRA and RUS, and Schett at New Haven. In doubles she played 3 f with different partners, winning Antwerp with Appelmans, and in mixed she was r/u Wimbledon with Hewitt, her boyfriend. **2000 HIGH-LIGHTS – SINGLES: Australian Open 1r** (lost Van Roost [seed 14] 3–6 6–1 6–1), **French Open 1r** (lost Sugiyama 6–2 3–6 6–2), **Wimbledon 2r** (d. Tauziat 6–3 3–6 6–2, lost Myskina 6–4 6–2), **US Open 2r** (d. Marrero 6–0 6–0, lost Davenport [seed 2] 4–6 6–2 6–2); **won** Hobart (d. Dragomir 4–6 6–1 6–2, Oremans 6–2 6–4, Pitkowski 7–5 6–1, Vento 6–3 6–2, Rubin 2–6 6–2 6–2), **won** Leipzig (d. Sugiyama 6–0 6–2, Sanchez-Vicario 7–5 6–1, Dokic 4–6 6–2 7–6, Kournikova 6–2 6–3, Likhovtseva 7–6 4–6 6–4); **r/u** Filderstadt (d. Kournikova 6–4 6–3, Kandarr 7–6 6–3, C. Martinez 7–5 7–5, Tauziat 3–6 6–4, lost Hingis 6–0 6–3). **2000 HIGHLIGHTS – DOUBLES:** (with Appelmans) **won** Antwerp (d. Hopkins/Rampre 6–1 6–1); (with Molik) **r/u** Hobart (lost Grande/Loit 6–4 4–6 6–4), (with Courtois) **r/u** Leipzig (lost Sanchez-Vicario/Sidot 6–7 7–5 6–3). **MIXED DOUBLES:** (with Hewitt) **r/u Wimbledon** (lost Johnson/Po 6–4 7–6).

AMANDA COETZER (RSA)
Born Hoopstad, 22 October 1971, and lives there; RH; 2HB; 5ft 2in; 120lb; turned pro 1988; career singles titles 7; final 2000 WTA ranking 11; 2000 prize money $593,357; career prize money $4,252,428.
Coached by Nigel Sears; boyfriend and hitting partner is Mike Newell. Shares a great-grandmother with Elna Reinach. **1987:** (442). **1988:** (153) Won 4 titles on the satellite circuits. **1989:** (63) A –, F 4, W 1, US 1. Made an unexpected appearance in last 16 French Open and reached sf VS Arizona. **1990:** (75) A –, F 1, W 2, US 1. Qf VS Florida, Geneva and VS Albuquerque. **1991:** (67) A –, F 2, W 2, US 1. Upset K. Maleeva at Berlin and G. Fernandez on the way to her 1st primary circuit f at Puerto Rico. **1992:** (17) A –, F 3, W –, US 3. Scored some big upsets during the year, surprising Garrison en route to last 16 Olympics, unseeded, Wiesner and Sabatini *en route* to sf VS Florida, Capriati and Zvereva in reaching the same stage Italian Open and Tauziat at US Open. She also appeared in sf Kitzbuhel and Taipei, plus 5 more qf. In doubles she played 4 f with different partners, winning Taranto with Gorrochategui and Puerto Rico with Reinach. **1993:** (15) A 1, F 2, W 2, US 3. Won her 1st Kraft tour title at Melbourne Open, following in autumn with Tokyo Nicherei (d. Sanchez-Vicario). She was r/u Indian Wells, where she extended M. J. Fernandez to 3s tb and reached sf VS Florida, Amelia Island (d. Capriati) and Barcelona. In doubles she was r/u US Open with Gorrochategui and reached 3 other f. Qualified for VS Champs 1st time in both singles, where she upset M. J. Fernandez before falling qf to Graf, and doubles, in which she and Gorrochategui lost 1r. **1994:** (18) A 2, F 4, W 4, US qf. Won both singles and doubles (with Harvey-Wild) at Prague in May, was r/u Indian Wells (d. M. J. Fernandez and Davenport) and reached sf Stratton Mountain and Schenectady. Unseeded at French Open, she upset Date as she embarked on her best year yet in GS. She qualified for VS Champs singles, but fell 1r to Pierce. **1995:** (19) A 3, F 2, W 2, US 1. Her best moments came at Toronto, where she was unseeded: after becoming the 1st of only 2 players all year to beat Graf, ending her 32-match winning streak 1r, she went on to upset Pierce and Novotna before losing f to Seles, who was playing in her 1st tourn for 2_2 years. She met Graf again 1r

US Open, where she held 7 sps before taking 1s tb, but lost the next 2 sets. She was also r/u Brighton (d. M. Maleeva), reached sf Barcelona and Tokyo Nicherei plus 2 more qf, upset Pierce in Fed Cup and qualified for WTA Champs, where she lost 1r to Graf. In doubles she played 3 f, winning 2 with Gorrochategui. She won the Karen Krantzcke Sportsmanship Award. **1996:** (17) A sf, F 4, W 2, US qf. She made her mark in GS, at Australian Open becoming the 1st South African in the open era to reach that stage in GS, and upsetting Huber at US Open, where she was unseeded. In other tourns she was r/u Oklahoma and appeared in qf Indian Wells, Madrid, Los Angeles and Tokyo Nicherei to qualify for Chase Champs, where Novotna removed her 1r. **1997:** (4) A sf, F sf, W 2, US 4. In her best year to date, she became only the 2nd South African woman to crack the top 10, after Greer Stevens in 1979, and in Nov. overtook Seles to reach a career-high No. 4. She continued to cause many significant upsets on her way to the titles at Budapest (singles and doubles, with Fusai) and Luxembourg, r/u Leipzig and sf Australian Open, French Open, Amelia Island, Bol, Berlin, Strasbourg, Stanford, San Diego, Atlanta and Filderstadt, plus qf Tokyo Pan Pacific, Oklahoma City, FC Cup (d. Sanchez-Vicario), Toronto and Philadelphia. At Australian Open she ended Graf's run of 45 GS matches won, she beat her again at Berlin 6–0 6–1 (inflicting the worst defeat of her career in 57 mins on the former No. 1, who was returning from injury), and upset her a third time at French Open, before extending Majoli to 7–5 3s in their sf. At Leipzig she became only the 3rd of 5 players all year to beat Hingis, and other upsets included Novotna at Amelia Island and Atlanta, M. J. Fernandez at Amelia Island, Martinez at French Open and Sanchez-Vicario at FC Cup. At Chase Champs, however, she was unexpectedly beaten 1r by Tauziat. **1998:** (17) A 4, F 1, W 2, US qf. Although she could not reach the heights of the previous season, she won her 1st Tier I singles title at FC Cup, as well as reaching sf Tokyo Pan Pacific and Amelia Island, plus qf Indian Wells, Strasbourg, Boston, New Haven, Zurich, Philadelphia (d. Sanchez-Vicario) and US Open (d. Martinez). These results took her to Chase Champs, where she fell 1r again – to Pierce. She had 3 coaches during the year: Gavin Hopper left to coach Seles and Philippoussis; she was briefly with Michael De Jongh until he moved to coach Pierce; and she finished the year with Nigel Sears. **1999:** (11) A 4, F 1, W 3, US 1. Her best performance came at Tokyo Toray where she upset Davenport and Seles back-to-back on her way to f. She reached same stage Oklahoma City, as well as sf Eastbourne, Stanford and San Diego and qf LIPC, Amelia Island, Hamburg, Toronto, Tokyo Toyota, New Haven and Zurich and extended Hingis to 3s at Australian Open. She returned to the top 10 for a while, although she slipped out again after Chase Champs, where she lost 1r to Tauziat. In doubles she played 3 f with different partners, but won no title. **2000:** A 2, F 3, W 2, US 3. She began the year by winning Hopman Cup with W. Ferreira. At Berlin she was r/u both singles and doubles, then the following week, in Antwerp, she won her 1st title for 2 years. She also appeared in sf Oklahoma City, Hamburg (d. V. Williams) and New Haven, plus qf Olympics, Tokyo Pan Pacific, Ericsson Open, FC Cup, Eastbourne, Filderstadt, Philadelphia and Chase Champs. **2000 HIGHLIGHTS – SINGLES: Australian Open 2r** [seed 8] (d. Panova 6–3 6–3, lost Brandi 6–1 6–3), **French Open 3r** [seed 9] (d. Drake 6–0 6–4, Leon Garcia 6–3 6–1, lost De Los Rios 7–5 6–7 6–4), **Wimbledon 2r** [seed 13] (d. Washington 6–4 6–2, lost Osterloh 7–6 6–2), **US Open 3r** [seed 12] (d. Cacic 6–2 6–2, Kandarr 2–6 6–4 6–2, lost Serna 7–5 7–6), **Olympics qf** [seed 7] (d. Kuti Kis 6–1 6–1, Kremer 4–6 6–3 6–4, Appelmans [seed 16] 6–3 6–1, lost Dokic 6–1 1–6 6–1); **won** Antwerp (d. Callens 7–5 6–2, Vavrinec 6–1 6–2, Shaughnessy 6–1 6–3, Courtois 6–0 6–3, Torrens-Valero 4–6 6–2 6–3); **r/u** Berlin (d. Poutchek 6–1 6–0, Kremer 6–3 7–6, Halard-Decugis 6–2 6–2, Huber 6–4 6–4, Kruger 6–2 6–4, lost Martinez 6–1 6–2); **sf** Oklahoma City (d. Myskina 7–5 6–2, Tanasugarn 7–6 7–6, Raymond 2–6 6–4 7–6, lost Seles 6–1 6–2); **sf** Hamburg (d. Dragomir 6–0 6–4, Sidot 6–2 6–4, V. Williams 6–3 6–4, lost Sanchez-Vicario 6–3 4–6 7–6); **sf** New Haven (d. Habsudova 7–6 6–4, Henin 6–2 4–6 6–1, Huber 7–6 6–1, lost V. Williams 6–3 6–4). **2000 HIGHLIGHTS – DOUBLES:** (with Morariu) **r/u** Berlin (lost C. Martinez/Sanchez-Vicario 3–6 6–2 7–6). **CAREER HIGHLIGHTS – SINGLES: Australian Open – sf 1996** (d. Schnell 6–2 6–2, Hack 6–1 6–1, Hiraki 6–3 6–3, Likhovtseva 6–3 6–3, Hingis 7–5 4–6 6–1, lost Huber 4–6 6–4 6–2); **qf 1997** (d. Kournikova 6–2 6–2, Kandarr 6–2 7–6, Serna 6–3 6–2, Graf 6–2 7–5, Po 6–4 6–1, lost Pierce 7–5 6–1); **French Open – sf 1997** (d. Grande 6–4 6–0, Frazier 7–6 6–4, Babel 6–4 6–2, Martinez 6–7 6–4 6–3, Graf 6–1 6–4, lost Majoli 6–3 4–6 7–5); **US Open – qf 1994** (d. Ritter 6–1 7–6, Maniokova 6–2 6–0, De Swardt 6–1 6–3, Endo 6–3 6–0, lost Graf 6–0 6–2), **qf 1996** (d. Huber 6–1 2–6 6–2, De Swardt 6–2 7–5, Spirlea 7–6 7–5, Raymond 6–4 6–1, lost Seles 6–0 6–3), **qf 1998** (d. Cacic 6–1 7–6, Sandu 6–0 6–2, Schett 3–6 6–0 6–3, Martinez 6–4 4–6 6–2, lost Davenport 6–0 6–4); **Olympics – qf 2000. CAREER HIGHLIGHTS – DOUBLES:** (with Gorrochategui) **US Open – r/u 1993** (lost Sanchez-Vicario/Sukova 6–4 6–2).

NATHALIE DECHY (FRA)

Born Abimes, Guadeloupe, 21 February 1979; lives Villeneuf d'Ascq; RH; 2HB; 5ft 10in; 132lb; career singles titles 0; final 2000 WTA ranking 27; 2000 prize money $234,074.
Coached by Loic Courteau and Georges Goven. Won Orange Bowl 16s and Nat 16s in singles and doubles. **1994:** (586) Enjoyed some success on the satellite circuits. **1995:** (294) A –, F 1, W –, US –. **1996:** (102) A –, F 2, W 1, US 2. R/u Australian Open Jun to Grzybowska and won Eastbourne Under-21. In the senior game, she reached qf Paris Open (d. Tauziat) after qualifying and appeared at same stage Surabaya. **1997:** (90) A 1, F 1, W 2, US 2. Upset V. Williams 1r Toronto and broke into top 100. **1998:** (48) A 1, F 3, W 1, US 4. She moved into the top 50 with her 1st sf on the main tour at Quebec City and an upset of Paulus at US Open, where she was unseeded. **1999:** (25) A 1, F 3, W 4, US 1. She proved to be a dangerous opponent, upsetting Testud and Majoli to reach sf Paris Open and removing Mauresmo at FC Cup. She also reached sf Bratislava and qf Hope Island (d. Likhovtseva), Hobart (d. De Swardt), Prostejov, Strasbourg, Eastbourne (d. Sanchez-

Vicario), Filderstadt (d. Testud), continuing her march through the rankings to top 25. **2000:** A 1, F 1, W 3, US 2. She was r/u Oklahoma City and Estoril and reached sf Gold Coast and Strasbourg, plus qf Paris Open and Scottsdale (d. C. Martinez), with other upsets including Kournikova at Indian Wells and Tauziat at Ericsson Open. She ret US Open with recurrent abdominal strain, which restricted her at Olympics, and sidelined her for rest of year. **2000 HIGHLIGHTS – SINGLES: Australian Open 1r** (lost Zuluaga 6–1 3–6 6–1), **French Open 1r** (lost Dementieva 7–5 6–1), **Wimbledon 3r** (d. Rubin 6–3 6–1, Black 4–6 6–2 6–1, lost V. Williams [seed 5] 6–0 7–6), **US Open 2r** (d. Black 6–3 6–2, lost Gersi 7–6 ret), **Olympics 3r** [seed 11] (d. Serna 6–1 6–2, Pratt 6–3 6–1, lost Seles [seed 3 6–3 6–2); **r/u** Oklahoma City (d. Molik 7–5 6–0, Pratt 6–4 6–3, Frazier 6–4 7–5, Grande 6–4 6–2, lost Seles 6–1 7–6), **r/u** Estoril (d. Llagostera 7–5 5–7 6–3, Courtois 7–6 7–5, Montolio 6–3 6–4, Farina-Elia 6–2 6–4, lost Huber 6–2 1–6 7–5); **sf** Gold Coast (d. Pratt 6–0 6–2, Garbin 6–3 6–3, Maleeva 6–4 6–7 7–6, lost C. Martinez 6–3 6–1), **sf** Strasbourg (d. Tu 6–4 6–2, Myskina 4–6 6–2 6–2, Morariu w/o, lost Talaja 6–1 1–6 6–3).

ELENA DEMENTIEVA (RUS)
Born Moscow, 15 October 1981, and lives there; RH; 2HB; 5ft 11in; 142lb; turned pro 1998; career singles titles 0; final 2000 WTA ranking 12; 2000 prize money $613,627.
Coached by Sergey Pashkov. **1996:** (624) Won Orange Bowl 16s. **1997:** (355). **1998:** (109) Played in RUS team that won Connolly Continental Cup. **1999:** (62) A 2, F 2, W 1, US 3. She broke into top 100 after sf appearance at Palermo (d. Pitkowski), also reaching qf Tashkent and upsetting V. Williams in Fed Cup f. A Member of winning RUS Sunshine Cup team. **2000:** A 3, F 2, W 1, US sf. Having earlier reached sf Indian Wells (d. Huber and Rubin) and Los Angeles, she upset C. Martinez and Huber to reach same stage US Open, where she was unseeded. She crowned her year with an Olympic silver medal, followed by sf showing at her 1st Chase Champs, where she saved mp v Davenport 1r and recovered from 2–4 down fs v Clijsters. She also reached qf Berlin (d. Sanchez-Vicario), Moscow and Leipzig, but in spring was hampered by stress fracture of rib, which caused her to ret 2r French Open. **2000 HIGHLIGHTS – SINGLES: Australian Open 3r** (d. Suarez 6–0 3–6 8–6, Montolio 6–4 6–3, lost Halard-Decugis [seed 9] 3–6 6–4 6–2), **French Open 2r** (d. Dechy 7–5 6–1, lost Razzano w/o), **Wimbledon 1r** (lost Petrova 6–1 6–1), **US Open sf** [unseeded] (d. Snyder 7–5 6–1, Plischke 6–4 7–6, C. Martinez [seed 7] 6–4 6–1, Osterloh 6–3 6–7 7–6, Huber [seed 10] 6–1 3–6 6–3, lost Davenport [seed 2] 6–2 7–6), **Olympics silver medal** [seed 10] (d. Vavrinec 6–1 6–1, Boogert 6–2 4–6 7–5, Habsudova 6–2 6–1, Schett [seed 12] 2–6 6–2 6–1, Dokic 6–1 1–6 6–1, lost V. Williams [seed 2] 6–2 6–4); **sf** Indian Wells (d. Srebotnik 6–0 6–3, Huber 6–4 4–6 6–4, Serna 4–6 6–4 6–4, Dechy 7–6 6–2, Rubin 6–4 6–1, lost Davenport 6–2 6–1), **sf** Los Angeles (d. Dechy 6–4 4–6 6–4, Brandi 6–4 6–1, Raymond 2–6 6–1 6–4, lost Davenport 6–4 6–4), **sf** Chase Champs (d. Davenport 3–6 7–6 6–4, Clijsters 6–4 2–6 6–4, lost Seles 6–1 7–6).
CAREER HIGHLIGHTS – SINGLES: Olympics – silver medal 2000; US Open – sf 2000.

JELENA DOKIC (AUS)
Born Belgrade, Yugoslavia, 12 April 1983; lives Sydney; RH; 2HB; 5ft 6in; 126lb; turned pro 1998; career singles titles 0; final 2000 WTA ranking 26; 2000 prize money $429,880.
Her family moved from Serbia to Australia in 1994. Coached by her father Damir, who has a strong influence on her and has caused trouble on the circuit with his noisy behaviour. **1998:** (341) At French Open she was r/u singles to Petrova and won doubles with Clijsters; then at US Open she won singles over Srebotnik and was r/u doubles with Dominikovic, finishing the year at No. 1 in ITF Jun rankings. **1999:** (43) A 3, F 1, W qf, US 1. After winning Hopman Cup for Australia with Philippoussis (d. Sanchez-Vicario and Testud), she impressed Hingis, who invited her to join her for a week in Switzerland, where they practised together. It obviously paid off, for at Wimbledon she played through the qualifying, caused the upset of the tournament by upsetting Hingis 1r, then added Pierce to her victims *en route* to qf – a performance that took her into top 50. In other tourns she reached qf Cairo (d. Serna) and Warsaw and upset Schett in Fed Cup. **2000:** A 1, F 2, W sf, US 4. She excelled in the big events, reaching sf at Wimbledon and Olympics (d. Sugiyama and Coetzer), unseeded both times. Although she did not pass qf anywhere else, she reached that stage at FC Cup (d. Frazier), Rome (d. Dechy and V. Williams before extending Seles to 3s), Tokyo Toyota, Shanghai and Leipzig. **2000 HIGHLIGHTS – SINGLES: Australian Open 1r** (lost Kuti Kis 6–1 2–6 6–3), **French Open 2r** (d. Pisnik 3–6 7–6 6–4, lost Hrdlickova 6–3 6–1), **Wimbledon sf** [unseeded] (d. Arn 6–1 7–6, Leon Garcia 7–6 6–1, Rippner 6–3, Brandi 6–1 6–3, Serna 6–3 6–2, lost Davenport [seed 4] 6–4 6–2), **US Open last 16** [unseeded] (d. Smashnova 6–1 6–0, Oremans 6–1 6–4, Schiavone 7–6 7–5, lost S. Williams [seed 5] 7–6 6–0), **Olympics sf** [unseeded] (d. Sugiyama [seed 14] 6–0 7–6, Grande 5–7 6–3 6–3, De Los Rios 7–6 7–5, Coetzer [seed 7] 6–1 1–6 6–1, lost Dementieva [seed 10] 2–6 6–4 6–4). **CAREER HIGHLIGHTS – SINGLES: Wimbledon – sf 2000, qf 1999** [unseeded] (d. Hingis 6–2 6–0, Studenikova 6–0 4–6 8–6, Kremer 6–7 6–1 6–4, Pierce 6–4 6–3, lost Stevenson 6–3 1–6 6–3)**; Olympics – sf 2000.**

RUXANDRA DRAGOMIR (ROM)
Born Pitesti, 24 October 1972; lives Bucharest; RH; 2HB; 5ft 6in; 127lb; pro; career singles titles 4; final 2000 WTA ranking 45; 2000 prize money $260,704; career prize money $1,667,496.
Coached by Ad Luttikhuis. **1990:** (294) Won 3 titles on the Futures circuits and took French Open Jun doubles with Spirlea. **1991:** (322) Won Supetar Challenger and joined her country's Fed Cup squad. **1992:** (175) Won Klagenfurt and Le Havre Challengers. **1993:** (74) A –, F 4, W 2, US 1. Upset Date on her way to an unex-

pected appearance in last 16 French Open and reached sf Curitiba. **1994:** (82) A 1, F 4, W 2, US 2. Upset Mag. Maleeva at French Open, where she was unseeded, and reached qf Prague. **1995:** (54) A 2, F 4, W 1, US 1. Still unseeded at French Open, she again made her mark and upset Sawamatsu. Reached her 1st f on the main tour at Styrian Open, appeared in qf Barcelona and won Bournemouth doubles with De Swardt. **1996:** (25) A 2, F 2, W 3, US 1. Won her 1st title on the main tour at Budapest (d. Halard-Decugis), followed in Sept. with Karlovy Vary at her 2nd tourn back after a hamstring injury suffered 1r Olympics, and finished the year on a high note with the title at Pattaya. She also reached sf Rosmalen and qf Hamburg and Moscow, breaking into top 25 1st time by end of year. **1997:** (19) A 4, F qf, W 1, US 1. She moved into the top 20 with the title at Rosmalen, r/u Hamburg, sf Warsaw and Pattaya, as well as upsets of Wiesner at Australian Open and Habsudova at French Open, unseeded both times. In doubles she reached 4 f with different partners, winning Prague with Habsudova and Warsaw with Gorrochategui. **1998:** (38) A 4, F 3, W 1, US 1. Although her only qf appearance was at Gold Coast, she upset Testud at FC Cup and Coetzer at Rome, and won Prostejov on the ITF $75,000 circuit. **1999:** (20) A 3, F 4, W 2, US 2. She upset Serna, Schett and Kournikova to reach f Amelia Island, unseeded, removed Novotna, Mauresmo and Schnyder back-to-back on her way to sf Berlin, and upset Novotna and Testud to reach sf New Haven, where she extended Davenport to 3s. **2000:** A 3, F 4, W 1, US 2. She upset Testud *en route* to f 's-Hertogenbosch, but withdrew during that last match with a toe injury, wanting to protect it for Wimbledon. Her only other qf appearance was at FC Cup (d. Kournikova), but she made her mark by taking a set off Hingis at French Open, where she was unseeded. **2000 HIGHLIGHTS – SINGLES: Australian Open 3r** (d. Garbin 7–5 6–4, De Lone 6–4 5–7 6–0, lost Brandi 6–4 7–6), **French Open last 16** [unseeded] (d. Habsudova 6–1 6–4, Shaughnessy 6–1 7–5, Maleeva 7–6 6–1, lost Hingis [seed 1] 6–3 0–6 6–1), **Wimbledon 1r** (lost Appelmans 7–6 6–4), **US Open 2r** (d. Schlukebir 6–4 6–1), **Olympics 1r** (lost Pratt 6–3 6–3); **r/u** 's-Hertogenbosch (d. Petrova 4–6 6–4 6–4, Nagyova 6–4 6–0, Testud 2–6 6–4 6–4, Brandi 6–2 6–3, lost Hingis 6–2 4–0 ret). **2000 HIGHLIGHTS – DOUBLES:** (with Ruano Pascual) **r/u** Palermo (lost Farina-Elia/Grande 6–4 0–6 7–6). **CAREER HIGHLIGHTS – French Open – qf 1997** (d. Jeyaseelan 6–3 6–2, Basuki 7–5 4–6 8–6, Habsudova 6–3 6–2, Arendt 6–1 6–1, lost Majoli 6–3 5–7 6–2).

GISELA DULKO (ARG)

Born Buenos Aires, 30 January 1985, and lives there; RH; 2HB; 5ft 6in; 121lb; career singles titles 0; final 2000 WTA ranking 585, junior ranking 12.
Coached by Billy Czerner. **1999:** In winning ARG Jun World Cup team. **2000:** Won US Open Jun doubles with Salerni.

AMY FRAZIER (USA)

Born St Louis, Mo., 19 September 1972; lives Rochester Hills, Mich.; RH; 2HB; 5ft 8in; 140lb; turned pro 1990; career singles titles 6; final 2000 WTA ranking 20; 2000 prize money $306,059; career prize money $2,280,003.
Coached by John Austin and Wayne Jackson. Won 7 Nat Jun titles. **1986:** (331). **1987:** (202) A –, F –, W –, US 1. Won Kona on USTA circuit. **1988:** (55) A 1, F 1, W 1, US 3. Appeared in sf Guaruja, plus qf LA (d. Shriver and Magers), Kansas and Indianapolis (d. Kelesi). **1989:** (33) A 3, F 1, W 2, US 1. Won 1st primary circuit singles title at VS Kansas as well as reaching sf Albuquerque (d. Maleeva-Fragniere) and VS Indianapolis. **1990:** (16) A 1, F –, W 3, US 1. Won VS Oklahoma and was r/u Tokyo Nicherei, where she beat Seles and K. Maleeva back-to-back and extended M. J. Fernandez to 3s. In other tourns reached sf Indian Wells and Sydney, where she upset Novotna and took Zvereva to 3s, and upset Fairbank-Nideffer at Wimbledon. **1991:** (28) A 4, F –, W 4, US 2. Although she won no title, she reached sf Tokyo Nicherei and qf VS Chicago, Tokyo Suntory, Toronto and VS California. **1992:** (19) A qf, F 2, W 4, US 1. Taking advantage of Graf's withdrawal from her part of the draw, she made an unexpected appearance in qf Australian Open, and, again unseeded, upset M. J. Fernandez at Wimbledon. Won both singles and doubles titles at Lucerne and also took the doubles at Tokyo Suntory. She reached sf doubles there, as well as at VS Oklahoma and San Antonio, and qualified for VS Champs 1st time, losing 1r to Sabatini. **1993:** (39) A 1, F –, W –, US 2. Out of action for 6 months from Feb. with a chronic form of flu, she had a quieter year, in which her best showings were sf Sydney and VS Philadelphia (d. Pierce and Sabatini) and qf Tokyo Nicherei (d. K. Maleeva). **1994:** (16) A 3, F 1, W 1, US 2. At Tokyo Japan Open she reached her 1st f for 2 years, a result which took her back to the top 20. She upset Huber and Martinez on her way to the title at Los Angeles, surprised Sabatini again *en route* to f Tokyo Nicherei and reached sf Oklahoma and Lucerne. **1995:** (18) A 3, F 3, W 2, US qf. She was still a dangerous opponent, upsetting Pierce and Zvereva back-to-back at US Open, where she was unseeded, and removing Date to take the title at Tokyo Japan Open. She also reached sf Oklahoma, qf Chicago and Tokyo Nicherei. **1996:** (29) A 1, F 1, W 4, US 2. R/u Tokyo Japan Open and reached qf Oklahoma, Montreal (d. Pierce) and Los Angeles. Played 3 doubles f with Po, but won no title. **1997:** (37) A 1, F 2, W 2, US 1. She began the year with an upset of Sanchez-Vicario to reach qf Sydney, following with r/u Tokyo Japan Open and sf Los Angeles (d. Coetzer and Sanchez-Vicario again). **1998:** (42) A –, F –, W 1, US 1. Her best performances came in Tokyo: at Japan Open she reached sf singles and was r/u doubles with Hiraki, and at the Toyota tourn she rallied from love set down to upset Coetzer *en route* to qf. Schnyder was her victim on her way to the same stage Philadelphia, and on the ITF $50,000 circuit she won both singles and doubles at Mahwah. **1999:** (19) A 2, F 2, W 1, US 3. She continued to excel in Tokyo, winning Japan Open and reaching sf at the Toyota tourn there

(d. Coetzer). She also appeared in sf Hobart, Madrid, Stanford (d. Schett) and Quebec City (where she won doubles with Schlukebir), as well as qf San Diego and Philadelphia. **2000:** A 1, F 1, W 3, US 1. Once again Tokyo saw her at her best as she played the only f of her year there at Japan Open. Elsewhere she reached sf Hobart, San Diego (d. Huber and Hingis in ss) and Quebec City, plus qf Oklahoma City, Ericsson Open, Stanford, Los Angeles (d. Sanchez-Vicario), Montreal and Tokyo Toyota. She qualified 1st time for Chase Champs, but lost 1r to Tauziat. **2000 HIGHLIGHTS – SINGLES: Australian Open 1r** (lost Callens 6–1 6–3), **French Open 1r** (lost Carlsson 6–3 4–6 7–5), **Wimbledon 3r** (d. Woodroffe 6–4 7–6, Molik 4–6 7–5 6–4, lost Barabanschikova 6–3 6–2), **US Open 1r** (lost Sanchez Lorenzo 6–3 7–5, lost C. Martinez [seed 7] 6–3 6–2); **r/u** Tokyo Japan Open (d. Morariu 7–6 7–6, Plischke 6–1 6–2, Kruger 7–5 6–2, lost Halard-Decugis 5–7 7–5 6–4); **sf** Hobart (d. Panova 6–4 6–4, Parkinson 3–6 6–0 6–4, Cristea 6–3 5–7 6–3, lost Rubin 6–2 6–1), **sf** San Diego (d. Huber 6–0 7–6, Dechy 6–3 3–6 6–1, Hingis 6–3 6–3, lost V. Williams 6–2 6–3), **sf** Quebec City (d. Callens 6–7 6–4 7–5, Snyder 6–4 6–1, Vento 6–2 6–2, lost Capriati 3–6 7–5 7–5). **2000 HIGHLIGHTS – DOUBLES:** (with Black) **r/u** Stanford (lost Rubin/Testud 6–4 6–4). **CAREER HIGHLIGHTS – SINGLES: Australian Open – qf 1992** [unseeded] (d. Cunningham 6–3 7–5, De Vries 6–1 7–6, Hack 6–1 3–6 6–2, Monami 6–3 6–4, lost M. J. Fernandez 6–4 7–6); **US Open – qf 1995** [unseeded] (d. Rottier 6–0 6–0, Phebus 6–2 6–1, Pierce 6–3 7–6, Zvereva 6–4 4–6 6–3, lost Graf 6–2 6–3).

TATHIANA GARBIN (ITA)
Born Mestre, 30 June 1977, and lives there; RH; 5ft 8in; 136lb; turned pro 1996; career singles titles 1; final 2000 WTA ranking 40; 2000 prize money $201,295.
Coached by Polidori Carlo and Max Trevisan. **1994:** (26). **1995:** (709). **1996:** (553) Won ITF Catania. **1997:** (206) Won ITF Novi Sad. **1998:** (152) Won Delhi on the ITF circuit. **1999:** A 1, F –, W –, US –. Won ITF Civitanova and on the main tour reached qf Bogota and Tashkent. **2000:** A 1, F 3, W 1, US 3. Having reached her 1st f on the main tour at Bogota in Feb., she followed with her 1st tour title at Budapest in April, unseeded both times. She also reached sf Estoril and qf Warsaw, where she won the doubles with Husarova. **2000 HIGHLIGHTS – SINGLES: Australian Open 1r** (lost Dragomir 7–5 6–4), **French Open 3r** (d. Bobkova 6–1 6–2, Raymond 6–1 3–6 6–4, lost Hingis [seed 1] 6–1 6–0), **Wimbledon 1r** (lost Schnyder 6–3 6–2), **US Open 3r** (d. Marosi-Aracama 6–1 6–1, Kostanic 6–1 6–3, lost Hingis [seed 1] 6–1 6–0), **Olympics 1r** (lost Halard-Decugis 6–4 6–2); **won** Budapest (d. Torrens-Valero 6–2 7–5, Molik 3–6 6–3 6–1, Barabanschikova 4–6 6–0 6–1, Pitkowski 6–3 3–0 ret, Boogert 6–2 7–6); **r/u** Bogota (d. Vento 6–3 6–7 6–3, Zuluaga 6–1 6–4, Shaughnessy 6–3 6–7 6–1, Kuti Kis 2–6 6–1 6–2, lost Wartusch 4–6 6–1 6–4); **sf** Estoril (d. Hopmans 7–6 3–6 6–3, Sidot 7–6 6–4, Kuti Kis 7–6 6–4, lost Huber 6–3 6–2). **2000 HIGHLIGHTS – DOUBLES:** (with Husarova) **won** Warsaw (d. Tulyaganova/Zaporozhanova 6–3 6–1).

IOANA GASPAR (ROM)
Born Timisoara, 17 April 1983, and lives there; RH; 2HB; 5ft 5in; 117lb; career singles titles 0; final 2000 WTA ranking 353, junior ranking 6.
Coached by Ducian Dudas. Member of ITF touring Team, funded by GS Development Fund. **2000:** Won Wimbledon Jun doubles with Perebiynis. In the women's game she won Cerignola on the $10,000 ITF circuit. **2000 HIGHLIGHTS – SINGLES: won** Cerignola ITF (d. Tricerri 4–6 6–3 6–1).

JULIE HALARD-DECUGIS (FRA)
Born Versailles, 10 September 1970; lives Pully, Switzerland; RH; 2HB; 5ft 8in; 125lb; turned pro 1986; career singles titles 12; final 2000 WTA ranking 15 singles, 1 doubles; 2000 prize money $879,570; career prize money $3,096,734.
Married her coach, Arnaud Decugis, a distant relative of 8-times French champion Max Decugis, 22 September 1995. **1986:** Won French Open Jun. **1987:** (62) A –, F 2, W –, US 3. R/u Wimbledon Jun to Zvereva and reached f Athens. **1988:** (75) A 2, F 2, W 1, US 1. Won French Open Jun over Farley. **1989:** (119) A 1, F 1, W 2, US 2. Upset Shriver en route to qf Moscow. **1990:** (41) A 3, F 3, W 2, US 2. Sf Clarins, qf Sydney and Barcelona, and upset Garrison on her way to last 16 LIPC. **1991:** (20) A 2, F 2, W 2, US 2. Won her 1st primary circuit title at Puerto Rico; r/u VS Albuquerque; sf San Antonio, Clarins and Phoenix; and upset M. J. Fernandez at Berlin. Qualified for her 1st VS Champs, but fell 1r to Seles. **1992:** (27) A 1, F 3, W 4 US 2. Won Taranto, reached sf Clarins and upset Sanchez-Vicario en route to last 16 Wimbledon, unseeded. **1993:** (29) A qf, F 3, W 1, US 2. At Australian Open, unseeded, she upset Garrison-Jackson and Martinez before reaching Seles to 3s in qf. She followed with appearances at the same stage Paris Open and Toronto (d. Sabatini), then in autumn progressed to sf Tokyo Nicherei and Budapest. **1994:** (21) A 2, F qf, W 1, US 2. It was another solid year in which she won Taranto, was r/u Paris Open (d. K. Maleeva) and reached sf Auckland, Los Angeles and Brighton, plus 3 more qf. In GS she thrilled her home crowds at French Open by upsetting Davenport and Zvereva on her way to qf. Qualified for VS Champs in both singles and doubles, upsetting Sanchez-Vicario in singles and taking a set off Sabatini in qf. In doubles she played 3 f, winning Los Angeles with Tauziat, with whom she qualified for VS Champs, and Tokyo Nicherei with Sanchez-Vicario. **1995:** (51) A 1, F 3, W 1, US 2. Although she moved to a career-high ranking of 15 in Jan., it turned out to be a quieter year in which she won Prague, but otherwise reached qf only at Auckland and Quebec City. **1996:** (15) A 3, F 2, W –, US –. She returned to the top 20 with her best year yet. Unseeded both times, she won Hobart in Jan. and Paris Open in Feb. (d. Sukova, Huber and Majoli) – the 1st time she'd won 2 tourns in a year. Linz at beginning of March

was her 3rd f from 5 tourns and she also reached sf Hamburg (d. Schultz-McCarthy), plus qf Auckland (d. Spirlea) and Budapest. Upset Sanchez-Vicario in sf Fed Cup, but was forced to abandon the deciding doubles (with Tauziat) when she tore a ligament in her right wrist. The same injury kept her out of Wimbledon and US Open. In doubles, she played 3 f, winning Auckland with Callens. **1997:** (–) A –, F –, W –, US –. It was an injury-plagued year in which she was restricted by knee, shoulder and wrist injuries and a strained abdominal muscle. **1998:** (22) A –, F 2, W –, US 1. Her year ended on a high note at Pattaya, where she won both singles and doubles titles. Earlier she had returned to action and the top 25 with some useful upsets on her way to her 1st title for 2 years at Hertogenbosch, r/u Strasbourg (d. Coetzer), sf New Haven (d. Sanchez-Vicario) and qf Auckland, Budapest and Tokyo Toyota. In doubles she won Birmingham and Pattaya with Callens and reached 2 other f with Husarova. **1999:** (9) A 2, F 4, W 3, US 4. Having won her last tourn of 1998, she continued the streak by taking her 1st of 1999 at Auckland, and at Hobart the following week she reached sf before being forced to ret with a stomach muscle strain. Her 2nd title of the year came at Birmingham and she also reached f Bol, Berlin (d. Graf) and Manhattan Beach (d. Pierce and Davenport). Adding qf Paris Open, Tokyo Toyota, Zurich, Moscow and Philadelphia, she broke into top 10 1st time at age 29 and qualified for Chase Champs, where she fell 1r to Huber, with whom she was r/u Moscow doubles. **2000:** A qf, F 1, W 1, US 1. She won singles titles at Eastbourne and Tokyo Japan Open, where she also took the doubles with Morariu. A week earlier, also in Tokyo, she had been r/u Toyota singles and won the doubles with Sugiyama. Elsewhere she reached sf Paris Open and qf Birmingham and Philadelphia. A major force in doubles, she appeared in 12 f, winning 7 with regular partner Sugiyama, 2 with Morariu and 1 with Kournikova. It was with Sugiyama, with whom she won US Open and was r/u Wimbledon, that she qualified for Chase Champs as 1st pairing, although they lost 1r to Callens/Van Roost. She also qualified in singles, but lost at same stage to Hingis. **2000 HIGHLIGHTS – SINGLES: Australian Open qf** [seed 9] (d. Krasnoroutskaia 6–2 6–4, Zuluaga 6–3 6–3, Dementieva 3–6 6–4 6–2, Kandarr 6–1 3–0 ret, lost Davenport [seed 2] 6–1 6–2), **French Open 1r** [seed 12] (lost Shaughnessy 7–6 6–4), **Wimbledon 1r** [seed 14] (lost Boogert 7–6 0–6 6–1), **US Open 1r** [seed 16] (lost Oremans 6–3 6–4), **Olympics 3r** (d. Garbin 6–4 6–2, Bedanova 6–3 6–4, lost Schett [seed 12] 2–6 6–2 6–1); **won** Eastbourne (d. Vento 6–3 6–1, Dechy 6–2 6–4, Tauziat 6–4 6–4, Rubin 6–2 3–6 6–4, Van Roost 7–6 6–4), **won** Tokyo Japan Open (d. Asagoe 6–2 3–6 7–5, Vavrinec 3–6 6–2 6–0, Tanasugarn 7–6 6–0, Frazier 5–7 7–5 6–4); **r/u** Tokyo Toyota (d. Pratt 6–1 6–3, Brandi 1–6 6–1 6–4, Seles 6–4 4–3 ret, lost S. Williams 7–5 6–1); **sf** Paris Open (d. Andretto 7–5 7–6, Dechy 6–2 6–4, lost S. Williams 6–4 6–2). **2000 HIGHLIGHTS – DOUBLES:** (with Sugiyama unless stated) **r/u Wimbledon** (lost S./V. Williams 6–3 6–2), **won US Open** (d. Black/Likhovtseva 6–0 1–6 6–1); (with Kournikova) **won** Gold Coast (d. Appelmans/Grande 6–3 6–0), **won** Sydney (d. Hingis/Pierce 6–0 6–3), (with Testud) **won** Paris Open (d. Carlsson/Loit 3–6 6–3 6–4), **won** Ericsson Open (d. Arendt/Bollegraf 4–6 7–5 6–4), (with Morariu) **won** Bol (d. Krizan/Srebotnik 6–2 6–2), **won** New Haven (d. Ruano Pascual/Suarez 6–4 5–7 6–2), **won** Tokyo Toyota (d. Miyagi/Suarez 6–0 6–2), (with Morariu) **won** Tokyo Japan Open (d. Krizan/Srebotnik 6–1 6–2), **won** Moscow (d. Hingis/Kournikova 4–6 6–4 7–6); **r/u** Montreal (lost Hingis/Tauziat 6–3 3–6 6–4). **CAREER HIGHLIGHTS – SINGLES: Australian Open – qf 1993** [unseeded] (d. Kidowaki 6–0 6–0, Kschwendt 6–4 1–6 6–4, Garrison-Jackson 6–4 7–5, Martinez 6–4 6–3, lost Seles 6–2 6–7 6–0); **French Open – qf 1994** [unseeded] (d. Tarabini 6–3 6–2, Begerow 7–5 4–6 6–4, Davenport 6–4 6–2, Zvereva 7–6 7–5, lost Sanchez-Vicario 6–1 7–6). **CAREER HIGHLIGHTS – DOUBLES:** (with Sugiyama) **US Open – won 2000; Wimbledon – r/u 2000**.

JUSTINE HENIN (BEL)

Born Liege, 1 June 1982; lives Rochefort; RH; 5ft 6in; 126lb; turned pro 1999; career singles titles 1; final 2000 WTA ranking 48; 2000 prize money $122,798.

Coached by Carlos Rodriguez; her father, Jose, travels with her. **1996:** Won Orange Bowl 14s and European 14s. **1997:** Won French Open Jun over Black and became youngest-ever nat champ at 15 years 2 months. **1999:** (69) A –, F 2, W –, US 1. At Antwerp, playing in her 1st main tour event, she won the title, adding qf Luxembourg and Quebec City (d. Morariu), and an upset of Kournikova at Philadelphia. On the $25,000 ITF circuit she won Reims. **2000:** A 2, F –, W 1, US 4. She reached qf Hobart, Palermo and Bratislava, upset Kournikova at US Open, where she was unseeded, extended Davenport to 3s at Montreal and won Liege on the $50,000 ITF circuit. An arm injury kept her out of French Open. **2000 HIGHLIGHTS – SINGLES: Australian Open 2r** (d. Guse 6–4 6–2, lost Hingis [seed 1] 6–3 6–3), **Wimbledon 1r** (lost Sanchez-Vicario [seed 9] 6–1 1–6 6–1), **US Open last 16** [unseeded] (d. Labat 6–2 6–4, Molik 6–2 6–2, Kournikova [seed 12] 6–4 7–6, lost Davenport [seed 2] 6–0 6–4); **won** Liege ITF (d. Rittner 6–0 3–1 ret).

KVETA HRDLICKOVA (CZE)

Born Bilovec, 9 July 1975, and lives there; RH; 2HB; 5ft 5in; 129lb; pro; career singles titles 1; final 2000 WTA ranking 47; 2000 prize money 176,701.

Named Kvetoslava but known as Kveta. Coached by Torsten Peschke. R/u European Jun 18s. **1992:** (325) Won ITF Lyss. **1993:** (232) Won ITF Vitkovice. **1994:** (241). **1995:** (185). **1996:** (312) On the ITF circuit she won Vitkovice and Prarov back-to-back. **1997:** (239). **1998:** (57) A –, F 2, W 1, US 2. Emerging from the satellite circuits, she broke into top 100 in April after winning her 1st career title at Makarska as a qualifier; it was her 1st career f and she was playing in her 1st WTA tourn for 4 years. She also reached qf Sopot, where she won the doubles with Vildova, and joined her country's Fed Cup squad. On the ITF circuit she won Rogaska and the $50,000 event at Cardiff. **1999:** (44) A 1, F 3, W 1, US 1. She was r/u Leipzig after qualifying (d.

Likhovtseva and Pierce), reached sf Bratislava (d. Nagyova and Habsudova) and on the ITF circuit won the $75,000 event at Poitiers. **2000:** A 3, F 3, W 1, US –. She upset Mauresmo and Tauziat on her way to sf Linz, reached qf Sopot (d. Chladkova), and surprised Van Roost at Montreal. **2000 HIGHLIGHTS – SINGLES: Australian Open 3r** (d. Ruano Pascual 6–2 6–1, Kuti Kis 7–6 6–7 6–3, lost Kournikova [seed 11] 2–6 6–3 6–4), **French Open 3r** (d. Yi 6–3 1–6 8–6, Dokic 6–3 6–1, lost Mauresmo [seed 13] 6–1 6–0), **Wimbledon 1r** (lost V. Williams [seed 5] 6–3 6–1), **Olympics 1r** (lost De Los Rios 6–3 6–0); **sf** Linz (d. Farina-Elia 6–3 7–6, Mauresmo 2–6 6–4 6–4, Tauziat 6–3 6–4, lost Davenport 6–1 6–1).

ANKE HUBER (GER)
Born Bruchsal, 4 December 1974; lives Salzburg, Austria; RH; 2HB; 5ft 8in; 128lb; turned pro 1989; career singles titles 12; final 2000 WTA ranking 19; 2000 prize money $447,441; career prize money $4,251,770.
Coached by Jens Wohrmann. **1986:** Won Nat 12s. **1987:** Won Nat 14s. **1988:** Won Nat 16s. **1989:** (203) Won European Jun Champs and played in winning FRG World Youth Cup team. **1990:** (34) A 3, F –, W 2, US 1. She showed great fighting spirit in extending Sabatini to 2s tb in their 2r encounter at Wimbledon. At end Aug. won her 1st tour title at Schenectady after qualifying and followed with r/u Bayonne, upsetting Garrison and breaking into top 100, then shooting up to top 50 by Oct. Voted WTA Most Impressive Newcomer. **1991:** (14) A qf, F 3, W 4, US 2. Upset Maleeva-Fragniere and Zvereva *en route* to qf Australian Open, unseeded, reached last 16 Wimbledon and ended Sabatini's winning run as she reached qf Berlin. The high spot of her year, though, came at Filderstadt in autumn, where she upset Garrison, Sukova and Navratilova in fs tb to take the title. It was the 1st time for 8 years that Navratilova had been beaten by an unseeded player. **1992:** (11) A qf, F2, W 3, US 1. Upset Novotna *en route* to qf Australian Open and appeared at same stage Olympics; reached sf Sydney, Hamburg, San Diego, Brighton and Oakland and was a member of winning German Fed Cup team. **1993:** (10) A 4, F sf, W 4, US 3. Won a 3rd career title at Kitzbuhel, was r/u Sydney (d. Sanchez-Vicario) and Brighton and reached sf VS Florida and VS Champs plus 4 more qf. **1994:** (12) A 3, F 4, W 2, US 2. Restricted early in year by injury, she did not pass qf until reaching sf Berlin in May. However, having split with coach Boris Breskvar after Wimbledon, she won Styria and Filderstadt (d. Navratilova and Pierce) before finishing the season with a flourish at Philadelphia, where she upset Sabatini and Pierce again to take the title. She also appeared in sf Leipzig and 4 more qf, but at VS Champs fell 1r to Davenport. **1995:** (10) A 4, F 4, W 4, US 4. Won Leipzig and reached sf Delray Beach, Hamburg, Filderstadt and Philadelphia (d. Sabatini), as well as qf Tokyo Pan Pacific, LIPC, Manhattan Beach and Toronto. However, she saved her best for the end, upsetting Pierce and Date on her way to f WTA Champs, where she extended Graf to 5s. **1996:** (6) A r/u, F 4, W 3, US 1. Her fine form continued into the new season, which she began on a high note by upsetting Martinez on the way to her 1st GS f at Australian Open, a performance that took her into top 5 1st time. Her 1st title on grass came at Rosmalen, followed by two indoors at Leipzig and Luxembourg. She also appeared in f Los Angeles and Filderstadt (d. Martinez again), sf Essen and Zurich, and qf Paris Open, LIPC, Berlin and Strasbourg. Her performance at Chase Champs was an anticlimax, though, as she lost 1r to Majoli. **1997:** (19) A 4, F 1, W 3, US 3. Although she won no title and was disappointing in the major tourns, she was r/u Paris Open (d. Novotna) and Toronto, reached sf Tokyo Pan Pacific, Rosmalen and Leipzig (d. Majoli), plus qf Auckland, FC Cup, Los Angeles and Philadelphia (d. Majoli). She twice extended Hingis to 3s during her unbeaten run at start of year, and qualified for Chase Champs, although she lost 1r to Majoli and finished the year outside the top 10. In doubles she won Hamburg with Pierce. **1998:** (21) A sf, F –, W –, US 1. Her best performance came at Australian Open, where she upset Coetzer and Sanchez-Vicario before extending Hingis to 3s. Her season was curtailed in March, when she underwent foot surgery for an achilles tendon injury, which kept her out until Aug. By then she had slipped far enough down the rankings to be unseeded at US Open, where Majoli beat her. Although she reached no f during the year, she was consistent in reaching sf Australian Open and Tokyo Toyota and qf Paris Open, Hannover, Boston, Montreal (d. Coetzer), New Haven (d. Schnyder), Luxembourg and Leipzig. **1999:** (16) A 2, F –, W 1, US qf. In another consistent year she reached sf Filderstadt (d. Halard-Decugis) and Leipzig, upset Novotna and Mauresmo to reach qf US Open, unseeded, and appeared in same stage Hope Island, Portschach, San Diego (d. Tauziat and Schett) and Moscow. After qualifying for Chase Champs she d. Halard-Decugis before falling to Davenport. She continued to suffer injury problems, withdrawing from Rome with a chronic toe injury and missing French Open with right foot injury. **2000:** A 1, F 4, W 4, US qf. She struggled at start of year, unable to pass 2r until Estoril in April when she took her 1st title since Luxembourg 1996. She followed in May with sf Hamburg (d. C. Martinez) and qf Berlin, before adding the title at Sopot in July. However, at US Open, she sprained her right wrist during qf and missed both Olympics and Chase Champs, for which she qualified. **2000 HIGHLIGHTS – SINGLES: Australian Open 1r** [seed 15] (lost Boogert 6–4 6–4), **French Open last 16** [seed 11] (d. Petrova 3–6 6–4 7–5, Morariu 7–6 6–1, Grzybowska 6–2 6–2, lost V. Williams [seed 4] 7–6 6–2), **Wimbledon last 16** [seed 11] (d. Ward 7–5 6–2, Latimer 5–7 6–3 6–3, Pisnik 6–2 6–3, lost Hingis [seed 1] 6–1 6–2), **US Open qf** [seed 10] (d. Tu 6–2 6–3, Panova 6–2 6–3, Likhovtseva 6–2 6–3, Pierce [seed 4] 6–4 ret, lost Dementieva 6–1 3–6 6–3); **won** Estoril (d. Krasnoroutskaia 6–1 6–7–6, Sanchez Lorenzo 6–2 6–1, Torrens-Valero 6–3 7–6, Garbin 6–2 1–6 7–5), Dechy 6–2 1–6 7–5), **won** Sopot (d. Garbin 6–3 6–3, Hrdlickova 6–7 6–1 6–1, Myskina 6–3 6–2, Leon Garcia 6–4 4–6 6–3); **sf** Hamburg (d. Chladkova 6–3 4–6 6–0, Appelmans 6–1 6–3, C. Martinez 6 / 7–6 6–2, lost Hingis 6–3 6–2). **CAREER HIGHLIGHTS – SINGLES: Australian Open – r/u 1996** (d. Kleinova 6–1 6–4, Carlsson 6–1 6–2, Richterova 6–2 6–1, Schett 6–3 6–2, Martinez 4–6 6–2 6–1, Coetzer 4–6 6–4 6–2, lost Seles 6–4 6–1), **sf 1998** (d. Pitkowski 5–7 6–0 6–0, A. Miller

6–4 6–0, Kruger 6–7 6–3 6–2, Coetzer 2–6 6–4 7–5, Sanchez-Vicario 7–6 7–5, lost Hingis 6–1 2–6 6–1); **qf 1991** (d. Richardson 6–4 6–1, Maleeva-Fragniere 6–4 6–4, Shriver 6–3 7–5, Zvereva 6–3 6–4, lost Seles 6–3 6–1), **qf 1992** (d. Zivec-Skulj 2–6 6–3 6–1, Jaggard-Lai 6–0 6–1, Fairbank-Nideffer 6–0 7–5, Novotna 5–7 7–6 6–4, lost Seles 7–5 6–3); **WTA Champs – r/u 1995** (d. Pierce 6–2 6–3, Date 3–6 6–2 6–1, Schultz-McCarthy 6–3 6–3, lost Graf 6–1 2–6 6–1 4–6 6–3), **sf 1993** (d. Mag. Maleeva 6–4 1–6 7–6, Martinez 6–3 6–3, lost Graf 6–2 3–6 6–3); **US Open – qf 1999** [unseeded] (d. Talaja 2–6 6–2 6–0, Kremer 6–1 7–6, Novotna [seed 8] 6–3 6–2, Mauresmo [seed 15] 6–4 6–4, lost Hingis [seed 1] 6–2 6–0), **qf 2000; Olympics – qf 1992** (d. Sawamatsu 6–0 4–6 6–2, Paulus 6–4 6–1, Muns-Jagerman 7–5 7–6, lost Capriati 6–3 7–6).

SONYA JEYASEELAN (CAN)
Born Newestminster, 24 April 1976; lives Toronto; RH; 2HF; 2HB; 5ft 2in; 120lb; pro; career singles titles 0; final 2000 WTA ranking 49; 2000 prize money $179,657.
Coached by Rene Simpson; formerly by her father, Reggie. **1992:** (779). **1993:** (223) R/u Orange Bowl 18s to Montolio. **1994:** (164) R/u French Open Jun to Hingis and in the senior game won her 1st pro title at Vancouver Futures. **1995:** (181) Won Fort Lauderdale Futures. **1996:** (179) A 1, F –, W –, US –. **1997:** (96) A –, F 1, W –, US –. Won Rochford Futures and joined her country's Fed Cup team. **1998:** (110) A 2, F 2, W 1, US –. Reached her 1st main tour f at Bogota and upset Halard-Decugis at Quebec City. **1999:** (149) A 2, F 2, W 1, US –. Upset V. Williams at Amelia Island, as a qualifier, and in doubles was r/u Palermo with Carlsson. **2000:** A 3, F 2, W 3, US 2. Although her only qf appearance was at Quebec City, she made her presence felt with upsets of Tauziat at Australian Open, Raymond at Amelia Island and C. Martinez at Wimbledon. In doubles she won Strasbourg with Labat. **2000 HIGHLIGHTS – SINGLES: Australian Open 3r** (d. Hopmans 6–2 3–6 6–1, Tauziat [seed 5] 7–6 6–4, lost Kandarr 6–2 0–6 6–3), **French Open 2r** (d. Cocheteux 6–7 6–2 6–4, lost Sanchez-Vicario [seed 8] 3–6 6–2 6–2), **Wimbledon 3r** (d. De Lone 6–4 6–4, C. Martinez 6–4 6–1, lost Raymond 6–2 6–1), **US Open 2r** (d. Cocheteux 6–2 7–5, lost Sanchez-Vicario [seed 9] 6–4 6–1) **Olympics 1r** (lost Appelmans 7–5 6–2). **2000 HIGHLIGHTS – DOUBLES:** (with Labat) **won** Strasbourg (d. Grant/Vento 6–4 6–3).

ANIKO KAPROS (HUN)
Born Budapest, 11 November 1983, and lives there; RH; 2HB; 5ft 7in; 132lb; career singles titles 0; final 2000 WTA ranking 582.
Grew up in the Bahamas, where her parents were acrobats. Coached by her father, Attila Kapros. **2000:** Won Australian Open Jun over M. J. Martinez and took the doubles there with Wheeler, with whom she was r/u US Open Jun.

ANNE KREMER (LUX)
Born Luxembourg, 17 October 1975; lives Hesperange; RH; 2HB; 5ft 5in; 121lb; turned pro 1998; career singles titles 2; final 2000 WTA ranking 35; 2000 prize money $207,639.
Coached by Laurent Marty. Her younger brother Gilles is top Jun in Luxembourg. Former r/u European Jun Champs. **1992:** (776). **1993:** (–). **1994:** (248) On the ITF circuit she won La Coruna, Koksijde and Varna. **1995:** (231). **1996:** (123) A –, F –, W 1, US –. Representing Luxembourg at Atlanta Olympics, she carried her country's flag at the opening ceremony. **1997:** (129) A 1, F –, W 1, US –. All-American for 2nd year, she helped Stanford to NCAA title and, encouraged by a good performance v Hingis 1r Wimbledon, she upset Pierce at the Stanford tour event. **1998:** (74) A –, F –, W –, US –. Won the $50,000 ITF tour at Albuquerque. **1999:** (31) A 2, F –, W 3, US 2. Interrupting her studies at Stanford to join the main tour, she reached her 1st qf at that level at Estoril, adding Eastbourne (d. Seles) and Stanford before finishing her year on a high note with r/u Pattaya. Other highlights included an upset of Sanchez-Vicario at LIPC and the title at Midland on the $75,000 ITF circuit. **2000:** A 1, F 2, W 1, US 2. She began the year by winning her 1st tour title at Auckland and closed the year with a second at Pattaya. In between she reached sf Eastbourne (d. Coetzer) and qf Hannover and Montreal. **2000 HIGHLIGHTS – SINGLES: Australian Open 1r** (lost Weingartner 6–2 2–6 6–4), **French Open 2r** (d. Kovalchuk 6–4 6–1, lost Sidot 6–4 4–6 6–1), **Wimbledon 1r** (lost C. Martinez [seed 4] 6–3 7–6), **US Open 2r** (d. Barabanschikova 6–2 6–4, lost Seles [seed 6] 6–3 6–4), **Olympics 2r** (d. Majoli 6–4 6–2, lost Coetzer [seed 7] 4–6 6–3 6–4); **won** Auckland (d. Baker 6–1 7–6, Diaz Oliva 7–6 6–1, Suarez 6–3 5–7 6–4, Shaughnessy 6–3 6–3, Black 6–4 6–4), **won** Pattaya (d. Yi 6–3 6–2, Kostanic 6–3 6–2, Kruger 6–4 6–1, Ostrovskaya 6–4 6–1, Panova 6–1 6–4); **sf** Eastbourne (d. Stevenson 6–7 6–1 6–4, Talaja 6–2 6–2, Coetzer 3–6 6–0 6–4, lost Van Roost 4–6 7–5 6–1).

GALA LEON GARCIA (ESP)
Born Madrid, 23 December 1973; lives Barcelona; LH; 5ft 4in; 124lb; pro; career singles titles 1; final 2000 WTA ranking 32; 2000 prize money $174,884.
Coached by Gabriel Urpi; trained by Jordi Llacer. **1991:** (694). **1992:** (481). **1993:** (289). **1994:** (329). **1995:** (134) On the Futures circuit she won 3 singles and 2 doubles titles. **1996:** (85) A –, F 4, W 1, US 3. Broke into top 100 after reaching last 16 French Open as a qualifier (d. Paulus). Played in ESP Fed Cup team r/u to USA. **1997:** (58) A 1, F 1, W 3, US 2. Reached her 1st qf on the main tour at Madrid, following with same stage Warsaw and Maria Lankowitz, and won Budapest Futures. **1998:** (53) A 1, F 3, W 1, US 3. She moved into

the top 50 after upsetting Basuki at French Open and surprising Paulus en route to her 1st career f at Maria Lankowitz, where she extended Schnyder to 3s. She also reached sf Makarska and Sopot, plus qf 's-Hertogenbosch. **1999:** (53) A 1, F 4, W 1, US 2. She reached sf Sao Paulo and qf Sopot, where she was r/u doubles. Elsewhere she upset Sanchez-Vicario at FC Cup and Tauziat at French Open, where she was unseeded. **2000:** A 1, F 2, W 2, US 1. Her best performance came at Madrid, where she won her 1st singles title and was r/u doubles with Sanchez Lorenzo. In other tourns she reached f Sopot, sf Bol (d. Halard-Decugis), qf Berlin (d. Kournikova and Rubin) and Klagenfurt and upset Mauresmo at Wimbledon. **2000 HIGHLIGHTS – SINGLES: Australian Open 1r** (lost Brandi 6–3 6–3), **French Open 2r** (d. Krasnoroutskaia 7–6 6–1, lost Coetzer [seed 9] 6–3 6–1), **Wimbledon 2r** (d. Mauresmo [seed 13] 4–6 6–3 7–5, lost Dokic 7–6 6–1), **US Open 1r** (lost Davenport [seed 2] 6–0 6–1); **won** Madrid (d. Shaughnessy 6–0 6–1, Grande 6–4 6–4, Montolio 6–4 6–3, Ruano Pascual 6–2 6–0, Zuluaga 4–6 6–2 6–2); **r/u** Sopot (d. Zarska 6–1 6–0, Grande 6–7 6–2 6–3, C. Martinez 5–2 ret, Suarez 6–4 4–6 6–3, lost Huber 7–6 6–3); **sf** Bol (d. Goni 6–3 6–3, Halard-Decugis 6–3 6–1, Suarez 6–7 7–5 7–6, lost Mauresmo 6–4 7–5). **2000 HIGHLIGHTS – DOUBLES:** (with Sanchez Lorenzo) **r/u** Madrid (lost Raymond/Stubbs 6–1 6–3).

ELENA LIKHOVTSEVA (KAZ)

Born Alma-Ata, 8 September 1975; lives Moscow, Russia; RH; 2HB; 5ft 8½in; 132lb; turned pro 1992; career singles titles 2; final 2000 WTA ranking 21 singles, 18 doubles; 2000 prize money $536,014; career prize money $2,209,665.

Coached by Charlton Eagle. Husband Michael Baranov (married 21 September 1999). **1991:** Won Orange Bowl 18s. **1992:** (353) Won Vilamoura Futures. **1993:** A –, F –, W –, US 1. Won her 1st tour title at Montpellier and reached qf San Diego (d. Medvedeva). **1994:** A 3, F –, W 1, US 4. After upsetting Sukova at Indian Wells and reaching qf Moscow, she reached last 16 US Open, unseeded. **1995:** (45) A 1, F 2, W 1, US 1. Upset Raymond and Frazier on her way to f Oklahoma and reached qf Hobart, Indian Wells (d. Frazier), Delray Beach, Moscow and Leipzig (d. Sukova). **1996:** (23) A 4, F 3, W 4, US 3. After removing defending champion Pierce at Australian Open, where she was unseeded, she went on to reach sf Oklahoma (d. Frazier), Berlin (d. Sanchez-Vicario) and Quebec City, plus qf Oakland (d. M. J. Fernandez). **1997:** (31) A 1, F 2, W 2, US 3. Her year began on a high note with the title at Gold Coast (d. Schultz-McCarthy) and a place in the top 20. Although she did not maintain that level, she reached qf Hannover and Stanford (d. Raymond), upset Basuki at Luxembourg and extended Novotna to 3s at Wimbledon. **1998:** (26) A 3, F 3, W 3, US 1. She continued to be a dangerous opponent, removing Basuki and Tauziat on her way to sf Strasbourg and upsetting Van Roost both at LIPC and to reach sf Birmingham (at which point tourn was cancelled). She reached the same stage at Luxembourg, and appeared in qf Stanford and Boston. In doubles she won 4 titles with Sugiyama to qualify for Chase Champs, where they did not pass 1r. **1999:** (18) A 3, F 3, W 3, US 4. It was a consistent year in which she was r/u Strasbourg and reached sf Hannover, qf Paris Open, FC Cup (d. Seles) and Eastbourne, as well as playing her part in the RUS team that reached f Fed Cup. These results took her to Chase Champs where she fell 1r to Van Roost. She was also a force in doubles, playing 7 f with 3 different partners, winning Sydney and Strasbourg with Sugiyama and FC Cup with Novotna. It was with Sugiyama that she qualified for Chase Champs, although they did not pass 1r. **2000:** A qf, F 1, W 2, US 3. She was r/u Leipzig (d. Dementieva and Tauziat) and reached sf Amelia Island (d. Schnyder and Pierce) and qf Australian Open, Auckland and Linz. She made her mark in GS: at Australian Open she upset S. Williams and extended C. Martinez to 9–7 fs; at Wimbledon she was 3–1 up in fs v Davenport before the American won next 5 games to take the match; and she was r/u US Open doubles with Black. At Chase Champs she was lucky to squeeze into both singles and doubles, taking the last singles place after Mauresmo withdrew, but then lost in 3s 1r to C. Martinez, and filling the last doubles spot with Black after Rubin/Testud withdrew. **2000 HIGHLIGHTS – SINGLES: Australian Open qf** [seed 16] (d. Nola 6–2 6–2, Shaughnessy 6–3 7–5, Callens 5–7 7–6 6–3, S. Williams [seed 3] 6–3 6–3, lost Martinez [seed 10] 6–3 4–6 9–7), **French Open 1r** (lost Grzybowska 6–0 2–6 7–5), **Wimbledon 2r** (d. Vavrinec 3–6 6–3 6–1, lost Davenport [seed 2] 3–6 6–3 6–3), **US Open 3r** (d. Schnitzer 7–6 6–4, Callens 7–6 4–6 6–1, lost Huber [seed 10] 6–2 6–3), **Olympics 1r** [seed 15] (lost Kandarr 6–4 6–4); **r/u** Leipzig (d. Husarova 4–6 6–3 6–0, Raymond 6–3 6–3, Dementieva 6–3 6–0, Tauziat 6–1 6–4, lost Clijsters 7–6 4–6 6–4); **sf** Amelia Island (d. Kruger 7–6 6–2, Nagyova 6–2 3–0 ret, Schnyder 6–3 7–6, Pierce 2–6 6–4 6–4, lost Martinez 6–3 6–2). **2000 HIGHLIGHTS – DOUBLES:** (with Black) **r/u US Open** (lost Halard-Decugis/Sugiyama 6–0 1–6 6–1). **CAREER HIGHLIGHTS – SINGLES: Australian Open – qf** 2000. **CAREER HIGHLIGHTS – DOUBLES:** (with Black) **US Open – r/u** 2000.

MAGDALENA MALEEVA (BUL)

Born Sofia, 1 April 1975, and lives there; RH; 2HB; 5ft 6in; 127lb; turned pro 1989; career singles titles 7; final 2000 WTA ranking 22; 2000 prize money $221,384; career prize money $2,111,543.

Coached by her brother-in-law François Fragniere, formerly by her mother, Yulia Berberian. Younger sister of Manuela and Katerina. **1988:** Won Orange Bowl 12s and became youngest Bulgarian nat champ at 13 yrs 4 mths. **1989:** (211) R/u Bari on Italian satellite circuit in first pro tourn. **1990:** (72) A –, F 3, W 2, US 1. In Jun singles won Australian Open (over Stacey), French Open (over Ignatieva) and US Open (over Van Lottum). On the senior tour reached qf Wellington and after upsetting Lindqvist at Wimbledon moved into the top 100. **1991:** (38) A 4, F 1, W 1, US 2. Upset Fairbank-Nideffer on her way to an unexpected appearance in last 16

Australian Open and in April upset Kelesi *en route* to her 1st tour f at Bol, where she also teamed with Golarsa to win the doubles. **1992:** (20) A 1, F 3, W 1, US qf. Won her 1st tour title at San Marino and, unseeded, upset Navratilova 2r US Open on her way to qf, where she retired against her sister, Manuela, with a thigh injury. Upset Capriati and Sukova back-to-back at Tokyo Pan Pacific, where she reached sf, as she did at Brisbane, and surprised Date *en route* to last 16 Olympics, unseeded. **1993:** (16) A 4, F 4, W 3, US 4. Voted WTA Most Improved Player of the Year, she continued to progress with r/u showing at Brisbane, sf Zurich and Hamburg, plus qf Osaka, Indian Wells, Barcelona, Berlin, San Diego, VS Los Angeles and Leipzig. Qualified for VS Champs but was eliminated 1r by Huber. She was playing Seles in qf Hamburg when the No. 1 was stabbed in the back at the changeover. **1994:** (11) A 4, F 1, W 2, US 4. Won Zurich (d. Sukova) and Moscow and upset Navratilova on her way to sf Chicago, reaching the same stage Brisbane and Barcelona. Although she was disappointing in GS, she appeared in 2 more qf and finished the year poised outside the top 10. Stress fracture of the ribs prevented her taking her place at VS Champs. **1995:** (6) A 1, F 2, W –, US 2. Upset Sabatini on her way to the title at Chicago, following with Moscow and Oakland. She surprised Pierce twice – on her way to f Berlin and sf Tokyo Pan Pacific – and was also r/u FC Cup and Leipzig and reached sf Amelia Island, Hamburg and Brighton. Although she took her place in the top 10, her year was not all plain sailing, for a back injury forced her to withdraw from Wimbledon and from San Diego in Aug. and in autumn flu caused her to withdraw from f Leipzig and to miss Zurich. She qualified for her 1st VS Champs, but that, too, ended in disappointment as she was beaten 1r by Schultz-McCarthy. **1996:** (18) A –, F 4, W 2, US 1. She was still affected by injury, being forced to withdraw from Linz with lower back strain. Although she won no title and slipped from the top 10, she was r/u Madrid (d. Sanchez Vicario) and reached sf Paris Open, plus qf Tokyo Toray, Italian Open, Montreal and Leipzig. **1997:** (36) A –, F 1, W 3, US 3. She tended to struggle again, with her best performance sf Hannover, and qf showings at Linz, Birmingham, Toronto and Filderstadt. **1998:** (115) A 1, F –, W –, US –. She reached qf Sydney and upset Huber at Tokyo Pan Pacific before undergoing shoulder surgery in June. **1999:** (89) A –, F 1, W –, US –. Returned to action in May after an absence of 11 months and upset Huber *en route* to her 1st sf for more than 2 years at 's-Hertogenbosch. A stress fracture of left forearm sidelined her again in summer, but she returned to upset Novotna at Luxembourg, where she had to qualify, and won the last tourn of year at Pattaya, again as a qualifier. **2000:** A 1, F 3, W 2, US 2. Although she had to qualify in Montreal, Tokyo and at Paris Open, she worked her way back into the top 25 with r/u Luxembourg (d. Kournikova) and qf Gold Coast, Klagenfurt, Montreal, Moscow (d. Sanchez-Vicario) and Leipzig. **2000 HIGHLIGHTS – SINGLES: Australian Open 1r** (lost Sugiyama 7–6 7–6), **French Open 3r** (d. Smashnova 6–3 6–4, Chladkova 7–6 2–6 6–2, lost Dragomir 7–6 6–1), **Wimbledon 2r** (d. Cocheteux 6–1 6–2, lost Oremans 1–6 7–5 6–3), **US Open 2r** (d. Yi 6–3 6–3, lost Pierce [seed 4] 7–5 2–6 6–1); **r/u** Luxembourg (d. Cristea 6–2 6–2, Sucha 6–3 6–4, Schnyder 6–3 5–7 7–6, Kournikova 6–2 6–4, lost Capriati 4–6 6–1 6–4). **CAREER HIGHLIGHTS – SINGLES: US Open – qf 1992** [unseeded] (d. Kroupova 6–2 6–1, Navratilova 6–4 0–6 6–3, Po 6–2 6–3, Rubin 7–5 5–7 6–1, lost Maleeva-Fragniere 6–2 5–3 ret'd).

MARTA MARRERO (ESP)
Born Las Palmas, 16 January 1983, and lives there; RH; 2HB; 5ft 7in; 133lb; career singles titles 0; final 2000 WTA ranking 70; 2000 prize money $114,054.
1998: (361) She won Orange Bowl 16s and in the women's game took her 1st pro title at Povoa ITF. **1999:** (147) She reached her 1st qf on the main tour at Knokke-Heist and on the ITF circuit she won Gexto, Otocec and Sofia. **2000:** A –, F qf, W –, US 1. In 2 of her only 3 tourns to end Aug. she removed Van Roost on her way to qf French Open after qualifying and upset Appelmans on her way to sf Knokke-Heist. On the $25,000 ITF circuit she won Taranto and both singles and doubles at Gelos. **2000 HIGHLIGHTS – SINGLES: French Open qf** [unseeded] (d. Spirlea 6–3 6–4, Van Roost 0–6 7–5 7–5, Sidot 7–6 6–2, De Los Rios 4–6 6–0 6–4, lost Martinez [seed 5] 7–6 6–1), **US Open 1r** (lost Clijsters 6–0 6–0); **sf** Knokke-Heist (d. Sucha 6–3 6–4, Courtois 3–6 7–6 6–1, Appelmans 6–3 5–7 6–3, lost Smashnova 6–3 6–1); **won** Taranto ITF (d. Pizzichini 6–4 6–4), **won** Gelos ITF (d. Medina Garrigues 2–6 7–5 7–5).

MARIA JOSE MARTINEZ (ESP)
Born Murcia, 12 August 1982; lives Barcelona; LH; 2HB; 5ft 9in; 152lb; career singles titles 0; final 2000 WTA ranking 153; 2000 prize money $27,429.
Coached by Miguel Sanchez. **1999:** Won Orange Bowl over Salerni. **2000:** R/u Australian Open Jun to Kapros and won French Open Jun doubles with Medina Garrigues. On the $25,000 ITF circuit she won Edinburgh, Gexto and then both singles and doubles at Valladolid the following week. **2000 HIGHLIGHTS – SINGLES: won** Edinburgh ITF (d. Gubacsi 6–2 6–3), **won** Gexto ITF (d. Vakulenko 6–4 6–0), **won** Valladolid ITF (d. Hermida 6–4 6–2).

AMELIE MAURESMO (FRA)
Born St Germain en Laye, 5 July 1979; lives Bornel; RH; 5ft 9in; 142lb; pro; career singles titles 1; final 2000 WTA ranking 16; 2000 prize money $365,074; career prize money $1,223,127.
Coached by Sophie Collardey. **1994:** (827). **1995:** (290) A –, F 1, W –, US –. Played in winning FRA World Youth Cup team, and in the women's game won her 1st satellite event at St Raphael. **1996:** (159) A –, F 2, W –, US –. Finished the year at No. 1 in ITF Jun singles rankings after winning French Open over Shaughnessy and Wimbledon over Serna, as well as taking the doubles there with Barabanschikova. **1997:** (109) A –, F 2,

W –, US –. Won Thessaloniki Futures and played in winning FRA team in HM Queen Sofia Cup. **1998:** (29) A 3, F 1, W 2, US 3. The highlight of her career to date came at Berlin, where she played through the qualifying then upset Van Roost, Davenport, Paulus and Novotna to reach her 1st career f, becoming the 1st qualifier ever to reach that stage in a Tier I tourn. Although she did not reach those heights again, she appeared in qf Prague and New Haven (d. Tauziat). Joining her country's Fed Cup team, she extended Hingis to 3s in that competition and again at US Open. **1999:** (10) A r/u, F 2, W –, US 4. She sprang to prominence in tremendous style at Australian Open where she was r/u, unseeded, upsetting Schnyder, Van Roost and Davenport on the way. She also made headlines there with an announcement regarding her sexuality and relationship with Sylvie Bourdon. At Paris Open she gained her revenge for Australian Open f defeat by upsetting Hingis, then Van Roost again, to reach f, where she submitted to S. Williams only 7–6 fs, and went on in Oct. to take her 1st title at Bratislava. She also reached sf Rome and Linz and qf Tokyo Toyota and New Haven, although a right ankle sprain suffered at French Open kept her out of Wimbledon. She qualified for GS Cup but lost 1r to Hingis and at Chase Champs lost to Davenport after taking 1s. **2000:** A 2, F 4, W 1, US –. Again she began the year in style in Australia, upsetting Pierce, Hingis and Davenport to take the title at Sydney. Acute sacroiliac pain kept her out for 6 weeks in spring, but she returned to reach f Bol and Rome (d. Pierce and Sanchez-Vicario) and also appeared in sf Hannover and Moscow. However, she withdrew Sopot with ongoing chronic back injury and did not play US Open. Then in Nov. she was troubled by a left thigh injury that kept her out of Chase Champs, for which she qualified. In doubles she won Linz with Rubin. **2000 HIGHLIGHTS – SINGLES: Australian Open 2r** [seed 7] (d. Torrens-Valero 6–1 6–2, lost Schnyder 6–4 6–4), **French Open last 16** [seed 13] (d. Osterloh 6–2 6–3, Montolio 6–3 6–4, Hrdlickova 6–1 6–0, lost Seles [seed 3] 7–5 6–3), **Wimbledon 1r** [seed 13] (lost Leon Garcia 4–6 6–3 7–5), **Olympics 1r** [seed 9] (lost Zuluaga 6–3 3–6 6–2); **won** Sydney (d. Sugiyama 6–7 6–0 7–6, Talaja w/o, Pierce 6–3 6–3, Hingis 7–6 6–3, Davenport 7–6 6–4); **r/u** Bol (d. Kuti Kis 7–5 6–7 6–2, Srebotnik 6–3 6–2, Morariu 4–6 7–5 6–3, Leon Garcia 6–4 7–5, lost Pisnik 7–6 7–6), **r/u** Rome (d. Leon Garcia 6–1 6–3, Hrdlickova 6–0 6–2, Pierce 6–3 6–4, Sanchez-Vicario 6–1 5–7 6–4, Zuluaga 6–1 6–2, lost Seles 6–2 7–6); **sf** Hannover (d. Pisnik def. Smashnova 6–2 6–1, lost S. Williams 6–2 6–7 7–6), **sf** Moscow (d. Dokic 6–1 6–4, Raymond 6–2 6–4, Maleeva 4–6 7–6, lost Hingis 7–5 6–3). **2000 HIGHLIGHTS – DOUBLES:** (with Rubin) **won** Linz (d. Sugiyama/Tauziat 6–4 6–4). **CAREER HIGHLIGHTS – SINGLES: Australian Open – r/u 1999** [unseeded] (d. Morariu 6–7 7–6 6–2, Schnyder 6–7 6–4 6–3, Pratt 6–3 6–3, Loit 6–0 7–5, Van Roost 6–3 7–6, Davenport 4–6 7–5 7–5, lost Hingis 6–2 6–3).

ANA ISABEL MEDINA GARRIGUES (ESP)

Born Valencia, 31 July 1982, and lives there; RH; 2HB; 5ft 6in; 130lb; career singles titles 0; final 2000 WTA ranking 114; 2000 prize money $30,853.
Known as Anabel. Coached by Gonzalo Lopez. **2000:** Won French Open Jun doubles with M. J. Martinez. In the women's game she won Denain on the $50,000 ITF circuit. **2000 HIGHLIGHTS – SINGLES: won** Denain ITF (d. M. J. Martinez 2–6 7–5 6–0).

HENRIETA NAGYOVA (SVK)

Born Nove Zamky, 15 December 1978, and lives there; RH; 2HB; 5ft 10in; 134lb; turned pro 1994; career singles titles 8; final 2000 WTA ranking 41; 2000 prize money $172,942.
Coached by Pavel Slozil. Has been hampered through her career by a string of injuries. **1994:** (379) Won French Open Jun doubles with Hingis and on the women's satellite circuit won Olsztyn and Porec back-to-back. **1995:** (137) Continuing to make her mark on the satellite circuit, she won Bordeaux and Athens, where she also took the doubles. **1996:** (42) A –, F 2, W 1, US 2. She broke into the top 100 in Feb., after winning Cali and later Bratislava on the Futures circuit. On the main tour, unseeded at Warsaw, she upset Paulus to take her 1st title in her 1st f at that level, upset Appelmans on her way to sf Cardiff, and reached same stage Pattaya, as well as qf Palermo, Karlovy Vary and Luxembourg (d. Coetzer). **1997:** (35) A 3, F 1, W 1, US 2. The highlight of her year came at Pattaya, in the last tourn, when she upset Dragomir and Van Roost to take the title. Earlier she had upset Dragomir on her way to f Warsaw, and reached the same stage Maria Lankowitz, plus sf Budapest and qf Luxembourg. She won Bol doubles with Montalvo and took both singles and doubles at Bratislava Futures. **1998:** (28) A 4, F 4, W 2, US 3. She upset Schultz-McCarthy at Australian Open, where she was unseeded, and broke into top 25 on 8 June after French Open (unseeded again). In Aug. she won Sopot and Istanbul back-to-back, and during the year appeared in sf Prague (extended Novotna to 3s) and Warsaw (extended Martinez to 3s), plus qf Hobart and Strasbourg. **1999:** (34) A 2, F 1, W 1, US 3. Before a recurring wrist injury interrupted her progress in autumn, she won Prostejov, and appeared in sf Portschach and qf Indian Wells (d. Farina and Seles), FC Cup and Warsaw, as well as upsetting Coetzer at Berlin and Tauziat at New Haven. **2000:** A 1, F 1, W 1, US 2. Injuries had seen her drop as low as 75 in the rankings before she won Warsaw, unseeded. Then in July she upset Grande and Farina-Elia on her way to a second title at Palermo, following in Nov. with a third at Kuala Lumpur, again unseeded, and also taking the doubles with Plischke. Elsewhere she reached sf Pattaya and qf Linz and Bratislava. **2000 HIGHLIGHTS – SINGLES: Australian Open 1r** (lost Tauziat [seed 5] 6–1 2–6 6–1), **French Open 1r** (lost Serna 6–2 6–4), **Wimbledon 1r** (lost Kandarr 6–4 6–2), **US Open 2r** (d. Vavrinec 6–4 6–2, lost Capriati [seed 15] 6–2 6–2), **Olympics 1r** (lost V. Williams [seed 2] 6–2 6–2); **won** Warsaw (d. Nacuk 7–5 6–2, Boogert 6–0 6–3, Garbin 6–3 7–6, Hopkins 6–0 6–4, Hopmans 2 6–4 7–5), **won** Palermo (d. Grande 6–2 6–4, Llagostera 6–3 4–6 6 4, Henin 7–5 6–4, Farina-Elia 6–2 6–4, Nola 6–3 7–5), **won** Kuala Lumpur (d. Basuki 7–5 6–0, Carlsson 6–4 6–2, Morariu 5–7 6–3 6–2, Tanasugarn 6–4 6–1, Majoli 6–4 6–2); **sf** Pattaya (d. Plischke 6–3 6–2, Wartusch 6–2

4–6 6–4, Farina-Elia 6–3 6–4, lost Panova w/o. **2000 HIGHLIGHTS – DOUBLES:** (with Plischke) **won** Kuala Lumpur (d. Horn/Webb 6–4 7–6).

LILIA OSTERLOH (USA)
Born Columbus, Ohio, 7 April 1978; lives Canal Winchester, Ohio; RH; 2HB; 5ft 7in; 132lb; turned pro 1997; career singles titles 0; final 2000 WTA ranking 44; 2000 prize money $226,653.
Coached by Al Matthews. **1996:** (188) A –, F –, W –, US 2. Won nat 18s singles and doubles. **1997:** (194) A –, F –, W –, US 3. In her freshman year at Stanford she won NCAA singles, helped Stanford to team title and was All-American in singles and doubles. **1998:** (111) A –, F –, W 1, US –. **1999:** (80) A 1, F 2, W 1, US 1. A qualifier at Oklahoma City, she upset Raymond *en route* to her 1st sf on the main tour, and removed Schett at Indian Wells. **2000:** A 1, F 1, W 4, US 4. She reached qf Tokyo Pan Pacific (d. Pierce) and Strasbourg (d. Likhovtseva) and upset Coetzer at Wimbledon, where she was unseeded. In doubles she won Shanghai with Tanasugarn. **2000 HIGHLIGHTS – SINGLES: Australian Open 1r** (lost Schnyder 6–3 6–4), **French Open 1r** (lost Mauresmo [seed 13] 6–2 6–3), **Wimbledon last 16** [unseeded] (d. Farina-Elia 6–3 5–7 6–3, Coetzer [seed 12] 7–6 6–2, Wartusch 4–6 6–2 8–6, lost Serna 7–6 6–3), **US Open last 16** [unseeded] (d. Torrens-Valero 6–0 3–6 6–3, Van Roost [seed 14] 7–6 4–6 ret, Asagoe 7–5 6–0, lost Dementieva 6–3 6–7 7–6). **2000 HIGHLIGHTS – DOUBLES:** (with Tanasugarn) **won** Shanghai (d. Grande/Shaughnessy 7–5 6–1).

TATIANA PANOVA (RUS)
Born Moscow, 13 August 1976, and lives there; RH; 2HB; 5ft 1in; 116lb; turned pro 1994; career singles titles 0; final 2000 WTA ranking 34; 2000 prize money $203,867.
Coached by David Anikine. **1992:** Won Siauliat Futures in only her 2nd pro event. **1993:** (814). **1994:** (141) Won 4 Futures titles. **1995:** (190) Upset McNeil 1r Berlin. **1996:** (151) Upset Coetzer at Moscow. **1997:** (97) A –, F 1, W 1, US 1. She broke into top 100 after taking a set off Pierce 1r French Open and winning Samara Futures. **1998:** (78) A 2, F 2, W 2, US 1. She upset Raymond at French Open and took a set off Novotna 2r Wimbledon. **1999:** (40) A 2, F 1, W 3, US 1. She upset Tauziat in Fed Cup as RUS moved to f 1st time. **2000:** A 1, F 1, W 1, US 2. She saved her best for season's end, appearing in her 1st sf on the main tour at Kuala Lumpur and following a week later with her 1st f at Pattaya. Until then her best performances had been qf Oklahoma City and Moscow (d. Halard-Decugis). **2000 HIGHLIGHTS – SINGLES: Australian Open 1r** (lost Coetzer [seed 8] 6–3 6–3), **French Open 1r** (lost Mandula 6–2 6–4), **Wimbledon 1r** (lost Pitkowski 6–3 7–6), **US Open 2r** (d. Sfar 6–3 6–1, lost Huber [seed 10] 6–2 6–3); **r/u** Pattaya (d. Nejedly 7–6 6–1, Kleinova 6–1 6–2, Webb 6–2 6–3, Nagyova w/o, lost Kremer 6–1 6–4); **sf** Kuala Lumpur (d. Srebotnik 6–2 7–5, Nejedly 6–4 6–4, Sucha 6–3 6–3, lost Majoli 1–6 6–4 6–2).

TATIANA PEREBIYNIS (UKR)
Born Ukraine, 15 December 1982; lives Khazkov; RH; 2HB; 5ft 8in; 132lb; career singles titles 0; final 2000 WTA ranking 188, junior ranking 5 singles and doubles; 2000 prize money $20,657.
Coached by Sergey Sitkovskiy. A member of the ITF Touring Team. **2000:** R/u Wimbledon Jun and US Open Jun to Salerni and won Wimbledon Jun doubles with Gaspar. On the $50,000 ITF circuit she won Istanbul. **2000 HIGHLIGHTS – SINGLES: won** Istanbul ITF (d. Vavrinec 6–4 6–3).

LISA RAYMOND (USA)
Born Norristown, Pa, 10 Aug 1973; lives Wayne, Pa; RH; 5ft 5in; 122lb; turned pro 1993; career singles titles 2; final 2000 WTA ranking 31 singles, 5 doubles; 2000 prize money $560,474; career prize money $2,797,956.
Coached by Jim Dempsey. Won 5 Nat Jun Champs. **1988:** R/u USTA 18s GC. **1989:** (438) A –, F –, W –, US 1. No. 2 in USTA 18s. **1990:** (327) A –, F –, W –, US 1. R/u US Open Jun doubles with De Lone and was ranked No. 1 in USTA 18s. **1991:** (251) A –, F –, W –, US –. Qf Westchester. **1992:** (76) A –, F –, W –, US 2. A freshman at Univ. of Florida, she won NCAA Champs over McCarthy. In the women's game she reached qf Puerto Rico and Philadelphia. **1993:** (54) A –, F –, W 4, US 2. Took Nat Collegiate title 2nd straight year, winning all 34 of her matches. Turned pro at end of college year and at Wimbledon, unseeded and in only her 2nd tourn as pro, she took Capriati to 8–6 3s in last 16, breaking into top 50. At end of year she reached sf Sapporo and won Tokyo Nicherei doubles with Rubin. **1994:** (44) A 2, F 1, W 1, US 3. In singles she reached f Lucerne, unseeded (d. Mag. Maleeva and Frazier), and appeared in qf Eastbourne. In doubles with Davenport was r/u French Open, won Indian Wells and qualified for VS Champs. **1995:** (20) A 3, F –, W 4, US 1. Upset Zvereva, Frazier and Garrison-Jackson on her way to f Chicago (unseeded) and reached same stage San Diego, plus qf Oklahoma. Played 2 doubles f, winning Indian Wells with Davenport. **1996:** (33) A 1, F 1, W 2, US 4. Having failed to pass qf in singles all year, she upset Schultz-McCarthy on the way to her 1st main tour title at Quebec City in Oct. She also reached qf Oklahoma, Eastbourne and Philadelphia (d. Martinez) and extended M. Maleeva to 12–10 fs 1r French Open. In doubles she won Chicago and Philadelphia with Stubbs, with whom she qualified for Chase Champs, and took a 1st GS title at US Open mixed with Galbraith. **1997:** (17) A 2, F 4, W 2, US 2. An impressive 10-day period in Oct., with 4 major upsets, saw her move into the top 15 1st time. She upset Novotna and Spirlea on her way to f Filderstadt, where she lost to Hingis, then at Zurich the

following week she removed Coetzer before becoming one of just 5 players all year to beat Hingis – only to lose sf to Tauziat. She was also r/u Oklahoma City, reached sf Quebec City and qf Chicago, and upset Dragomir at US Open. She played 5 women's doubles f, winning Luxembourg and Philadelphia with Stubbs, r/u Australian Open with Davenport and r/u French Open with M. J. Fernandez. In mixed she was r/u Australian Open with Galbraith. **1998:** (27) A 3, F 1, W 1, US 3. She was consistent, if less spectacular, reaching sf FC Cup and Boston, plus qf Auckland, Hannover, Linz, Amelia Island (d. Seles), Rome, Filderstadt and Philadelphia (d. Coetzer). In doubles with Stubbs she won Hannover and Boston from 5 f and qualified for Chase Champs, where they lost sf to Davenport/Zvereva. **1999:** (28) A 1, F 1, W 4, US 2. In singles she reached sf Moscow and qf Auckland and Leipzig, as well as upsetting Fernandez at Berlin and Sanchez-Vicario at Wimbledon, where she was unseeded. In doubles she won 5 of 7 f with Stubbs, with whom she qualified for Chase Champs, reaching sf. In mixed she won Wimbledon with Paes. **2000:** A 2, F 2, W qf, US 3. She upset Capriati and Tauziat to win the 2nd title of her career at Birmingham and appeared in qf Wimbledon (unseeded), Oklahoma City and Los Angeles. In doubles with Stubbs she won Australian Open and 3 other titles from a total of 6 f to qualify for Chase Champs, where they reached sf again. She crowned the year by winning doubles with Capriati in Fed Cup f as USA d. ESP 5–0. **2000 HIGHLIGHTS – SINGLES: Australian Open 2r** (d. Fusai 5–7 6–4 6–4, lost Sanchez-Vicario 6–1 3–6 6–3), **French Open 2r** (d. Bovina 6–4 6–, lost Garbin 6–1 3–6 6–4), **Wimbledon qf** [unseeded] (d. Nejedly 6–1 4–6 6–2, Kandarr 6–2 6–1, Jeyaseelan 6–2 6–1, Barabanschikova 6–4 6–2, lost S. Williams [seed 8] 6–2 6–0), **US Open 3r** (d. Grzybowska 6–1 6–0, Dragomir 6–4 6–2, lost Pierce [seed 4] 6–4 7–6); **won** Birmingham (d. Cross 6–0 6–3, Kremer 6–7 7–5 6–1, Capriati 6–2 4–6 7–5, Tauziat 6–4 6–2, Tanasugarn 6–2 6–7 6–4). **2000 HIGHLIGHTS – DOUBLES:** (with Stubbs) **won** Australian Open (d. Hingis/Pierce 5–0 ret) **won** Rome (d. Sanchez-Vicario/Serna 6–3 4–6 6–3), **won** Madrid (d. Leon Garcia/Sanchez Lorenzo 6–1 6–3), **won** San Diego (d. Davenport/Kournikova 4–6 6–3 7–6); **r/u** Eastbourne (lost Sugiyama/Tauziat 2–6 6–3 7–6), **r/u** Philadelphia (lost Hingis/Kournikova 6–2 7–5). **CAREER HIGHLIGHTS – DOUBLES:** (with Davenport unless stated) **Australian Open** – (with Stubbs) **won 2000**, **r/u 1997** (lost Hingis/Zvereva 6–2 6–2); **French Open** – **r/u 1994** (lost G. Fernandez/Zvereva 6–2 6–2), (with M. J. Fernandez) **r/u 1997** (lost G. Fernandez/Zvereva 6–2 6–3). **MIXED DOUBLES: Wimbledon** – (with Paes) **won 1999** (d. Bjorkman/Kournikova 6–4 3–6 6–3); **US Open** – (with Galbraith) **won 1996** (d. Leach/Bollegraf 7–6 7–6).

VIRGINIE RAZZANO (FRA)

Born Dijon, 12 May 1983; lives Nimes; RH; 2HB; 5ft 8in; 132lb; career singles titles 0; final 2000 WTA ranking 204; 2000 prize money $49,006.

Coached by Bruno Dadillon. **1999:** (371) A –, F 1, W –, US –. Won Australian Open Jun singles over Basternakova and took the doubles there with Danilidou, finishing No. 3 in singles and 2 in doubles in ITF Jun rankings. In the women's game she won the $10,000 ITF event at Deauville. **2000:** A 1, F 3, W –, US –. Won French Open Jun over Salerni. **2000 HIGHLIGHTS – SINGLES: Australian Open 1r** (lost Chladkova 7–6 6–2), **French Open 3r** (d. Bacheva 5–7 7–6 6–0, Dementieva w/o, lost Pierce [seed 6] 6–4 6–0).

CHANDA RUBIN (USA)

Born Lafayette, La, 18 February 1976, and lives there; RH; 2HB; 5ft 6in; 128lb; turned pro 1991; career singles titles 3; final 2000 WTA ranking 13 singles, 22 doubles; 2000 prize money $528,020; career prize money $2,488,798.

Coached by Benny Simms. Did not attend a tennis academy, as her parents put an academic background before tennis. **1988:** Won Nat 12s and Orange Bowl in same age group. **1989:** Won Nat 14s. **1990:** (522) A –, F –, W –, US 1. **1991:** (83) A –, F –, W –, US 2. She announced her presence on the senior tour by upsetting Bollegraf at LIPC in spring, and a year later broke into the top 100 after reaching her 1st tour f at Phoenix. **1992:** (68) A 1, F 1, W 1, US 4. Surprised K. Maleeva at US Open, where she was unseeded, and upset Zvereva VS Florida. In the Jun game won Wimbledon over Courtois. **1993:** (69) A 1, F –, W 2, US 3. Reached sf Birmingham (d. Coetzer) and qf FC Cup. In doubles won Tokyo Nicherei with Raymond. **1994:** (25) A 4, F 1, W 1, US 1. Broke into top 50 after a fine start to the year, in which she followed sf appearance at Hobart with upsets of K. Maleeva and Coetzer at Australian Open. She went on to reach f Chicago (d. Mag. Maleeva) and sf VS Florida (d. Coetzer), Lucerne (d. Sukova) and Quebec City. Played 2 doubles f with Harvey-Wild, winning Hobart. **1995:** (15) A 2, F qf, W 3, US 4. She broke into the top 20 after reaching f Eastbourne (d. Date), and surprised Sabatini and Sanchez-Vicario on her way to the same stage Manhattan Beach, where she took a set off Martinez. She also reached sf Zurich and Filderstadt (d. Davenport and Zvereva and extended Majoli to fs tb), plus 3 more qf, being voted WTA Most Improved Player. She made her mark in GS: unseeded at French Open, she upset Novotna – 0–5 0–40 down in fs, she was aiming simply to win just 1 game in the set, but Novotna let the game slip away as Rubin saved 9 mps. In 2r Wimbledon she beat Hy-Boulais 7–6 6–7 17–15, breaking the Championship records for the longest women's singles match (beating by 4 games the previous record of 54 by A. Weiwers and O. Anderson in 1948) and the longest set (their 32 games being 6 more than the previous record of 26, achieved 6 times since 1919). Then she upset Sukova at US Open, where she was unseeded, and beat Sanchez-Vicario in Fed Cup. She also won Midland Futures in both singles and doubles and from 2 doubles f on the main tour won Prague with Harvey-Wild. Qualified for her 1st WTA Champs, but lost 1r to M. J. Fernandez. **1996:** (12) A sf, F –, W –, US –. It was a frustrating year for her. She broke into top 10 1st time after reaching her 1st GS sf at Australian Open, with upsets of Sabatini and then Sanchez-Vicario 6–4 2–6 16–14 in qf. Continuing her record of lengthy matches, it was the longest women's match in the history of the tourn – lasting 3 hours 33 min, comprising the most games in a set (30) and most in a woman's match (48) – and being the 6th-longest on the WTA tour. In sf against Seles, she let slip a lead of 5–2 in 3s and at 5–3 30–15 served a double fault to let Seles back into the match, but was the only player to take a set off the eventual winner. She and Sanchez-Vicario were on court together again, upsetting G. Fernandez and Zvereva on their way to the doubles title. LIPC was her 1st major singles f, but it was at that tourn that she suffered a fracture of the hook of the hamate bone of her right hand. She missed Fed Cup and French Open with recurring tendinitis of the wrist, which caused her to retire during her 1st match at Eastbourne and withdraw from Wimbledon and then the Olympics and US Open. Underwent surgery in Sept. to remove hook of hamate bone in right wrist and was out until Nov., when she lost 1r Oakland to Wild, before upsetting Majoli on her way to qf Philadelphia. During the year she also reached sf Oklahoma, plus qf Sydney and Indian Wells. In doubles she teamed with Schultz-McCarthy to win Oklahoma and Indian Wells and with Sanchez-Vicario to add Amelia Island to their Australian title. **1997:** (30) A 4, F 2, W 1, US 1. She began the year by winning Hopman Cup with Gimelstob and made a stunning comeback at Linz, upsetting Novotna and Habsudova on the way to her 1st career title. Thereafter, though, she struggled to recapture her best form and reached no other qf until Quebec City, where she advanced to sf. **1998:** (34) A 1, F 4, W 3, US 2. She was still struggling for form and fitness in a difficult year. She upset Spirlea at Moscow, and at Quebec City she was r/u both singles (d. Van Roost) and doubles (with Testud), but her only other qf appearances were at Madrid and 's-Hertogenbosch. **1999:** (22) A 4, F 2, W 1, US 1. She began the year with the title at Hobart, then at Indian Wells upset Martinez, Coetzer and Hingis to reach her 1st Tier I sf since LIPC in 1996, extending Graf to 3s. She added r/u Quebec City in Nov. and appeared in sf Madrid and Quebec City, plus qf Auckland and Oklahoma City, as well as upsetting Zvereva at Australian Open, where she was unseeded. In doubles with Testud, she was r/u US Open and won Filderstadt from 2 other f. **2000:** A 2, F qf, W 1, US 3. She moved back towards her old place in the rankings with the title at Quebec City, r/u Hobart, sf Tokyo Pan Pacific (d. Coetzer), Eastbourne (d. Kournikova) and Linz, plus qf French Open (unseeded, d. Tauziat), Indian Wells (d. Testud), Stanford and Zurich. These results enabled her to qualify for Chase Champs 1st time since 1995, although she was hampered by tendinitis of the left knee and fell 1r to Coetzer. The same injury forced her to withdraw from doubles there with Testud, with whom she had won Stanford, before taking Linz with Mauresmo. **2000 HIGHLIGHTS – SINGLES: Australian Open 2r** (d. Smashnova 6–3 6–4, lost Appelmans 6–1 3–6 6–3), **French Open qf** [unseeded] (d. Nacuk 6–1 7–5, Oremans 1–6 7–6 6–3, Tauziat [seed 7] 6–4 7–6, Zvereva 6–4 7–5, lost Hingis [seed 1] 6–1 6–3), **Wimbledon 1r** (lost Dechy 6–3 6–1), **US Open 3r** (d. Carlsson 6–2 6–2, Schett 2–6 6–1 6–1, lost Seles [seed 6] 6–3 4–6 6–4); **won** Quebec City (d. Hopkins 6–2 7–5, Zuluaga 6–2 3–6 6–2, Tu 7–5 6–1, Capriati 6–4 6–2); **r/u** Hobart (d. Pratt 6–2 6–7 6–3, Black 3–6 7–5 6–3, Henin 7–5 0–6 6–2, Frazier 6–2 6–1, lost Clijsters 2–6 6–2 6–2); **sf** Tokyo Pan Pacific (d. Panova 6–0 ret, Stevenson 6–4 6–1, Coetzer 6–4 6–4, lost Hingis 7–6 6–4), **sf** Eastbourne (d. Pitkowski 7–5 6–3, Panova 6–1 7–5, Kournikova 7–5 0–6 6–3, lost Halard-Decugis 6–2 3–6 6–4), **sf** Linz (d. Appelmans 7–5 6–4, Nagyova 6–4 6–4, lost V. Williams 6 4 6–0). **2000 HIGHLIGHTS – DOUBLES:** (with Testud) **won** Stanford (d. Black/Frazier 6–4 6–4), (with Mauresmo) **won** Linz (d. Sugiyama/Tauziat 6–4 6–4). **CAREER HIGHLIGHTS – SINGLES: Australian Open** – sf 1996 (d. McQuillan 4–6 6–3 6–2, Krizan 6–7 6–2 6–3, Courtois 6–0 6–2, Sabatini 6–2 6–4, Sanchez-Vicario [seed 3] 6–4 2–6 16–14, lost Seles 6–7 6–1 7–5); **French Open** – qf 1995 [unseeded] (d. Makarova 7–6 6–3, Babel 6–3 6–2, Novotna 7–6 4–6 8–6, Sugiyama 6–2 1–6 6–2, lost Sanchez-Vicario 6–3 6–1), **qf 2000**. **CAREER HIGHLIGHTS – DOUBLES: Australian Open** – (with Sanchez-Vicario) **won 1996** (d. Davenport/ M. J. Fernandez 6–4 2–6 6–2); **US Open** – (with Testud) **r/u 1999** (lost S./V. Williams 4–6 6–1 6–4).

MARIA EMILIA SALERNI (ARG)

Born Rafaela, 14 May 1983, and lives there; RH; 2HB; 5ft 8in; 132lb; career singles titles 0; final 2000 WTA ranking 206, junior ranking 1 singles and doubles; 2000 prize money $18,090.
Coached by Sergio Ledesma and Leonardo Lerda. **1998:** Finished the year at No. 3 in ITF Jun doubles rankings. **1999:** (460) Won Wimbledon Jun doubles with Bedanova, was r/u Orange Bowl to M. J. Martinez and played in winning ARG World Youth Cup team. On the $10,000 ITF circuit she won Asuncion, Montevideo and Santiago back-to-back. **2000:** She won Wimbledon Jun and US Open Jun over Perebiynis and was r/u French Open Jun to Razzano; in Jun doubles she won US Open with Dulko and was r/u Wimbledon with Bedanova. In the women's game she joined the ARG Fed Cup team, while on the $10,000 ITF circuit she won San Severo and Caserta, followed by both singles and doubles at Horb, and then the $50,000 event at Ettenheim the following week. **2000 HIGHLIGHTS – SINGLES: Olympics 2r** (d. Zvereva 6–3 4–6 6–2, lost Schett [seed 12] 7–6 6–4); **won** San Severo ITF (d. Krauth 6–4 6–1), **won** Caserta ITF (d. Essaadi 6–4 6–1), **won** Horb ITF (d. Jerabek 7–6 6–4), **won** Ettenheim ITF (d. Sucha 6–4 6–2).

BARBARA SCHETT (AUT)

Born Innsbruck, 10 March 1976, and lives there; RH; 2HB; 5ft 9½in; 149lb; turned pro 1992; career singles titles 1; final 2000 WTA ranking 23 singles, 12 doubles; 2000 prize money $470,987; career prize money $1,891,782.
Coached by Thomas Prerovsky. **1991:** (753). **1992:** (299) Won Zaragoza Futures. **1993:** (136) Upset K. Maleeva after qualifying for her 1st event on the main tour at Kitzbuhel and reached same stage Montpel-

lier. **1994:** (100) A –, F 1, W 1, US 1. In jun tennis she was r/u Australian Open Jun to Musgrave. She made her mark in the senior game with another upset of K. Maleeva on her way to sf Linz, as well as reaching qf Tokyo Japan Open and Prague to move into the top 100. **1995:** (83) A 1, F 1, W –, US 1. Upset McNeil LIPC and Cecchini on her way to sf Palermo and appeared in qf Prague. **1996:** (38) A 4, F 1, W 2, US 2. The high point of her year came at Palermo, where she won her 1st main tour singles and doubles titles (with Husarova). She reached sf Moscow, upset Frazier at Australian Open, where she was unseeded, surprised M. Maleeva on her way to qf Amelia Island and held 5 mps v Seles at Madrid, although she could not close out the match. **1997:** (38) A 3, F 1, W 2, US 2. At Maria Lankowitz she upset Wiesner on the way to her 2nd career title and 1st in her own country. She also reached sf Palermo, where she took the doubles with Farina, and upset Huber *en route* to qf Hamburg. **1998:** (23) A 4, F 1, W 2, US 3. She upset Coetzer on her way to f Boston, where, serving for the title at 5–1 3s v De Swardt, she let the match slip away. She reached the same stage Palermo, sf Hamburg (d. Majoli) and Madrid, plus qf Hobart, Maria Lankowitz and Zurich (d. Schnyder). Played 3 doubles f with Schnyder, winning Hamburg. **1999:** (8) A 4, F 3, W 4, US qf. By mid-Jan. she had reached sf at both Auckland (where she won doubles with Farina), and Sydney, where she upset Martinez and Sanchez-Vicario and extended Hingis to fs t-b. She followed with another upset of Sanchez-Vicario at Australian Open, where she was unseeded. During the year she added r/u Moscow, her 3rd sf of year at Hamburg and qf Hannover, LIPC (d. Kournikova), Berlin, Manhattan Beach, Toronto (extended Seles to 3s), US Open, Filderstadt and Chase Champs. These consistent results took her quietly through the rankings and after her 1st GS qf at US Open, she slipped into the top 10, where she was well established by end of year. Qualifying 1st time for both GS Cup and VS Champs, she was beaten in both by V. Williams. **2000:** A 4, F 4, W 1, US 2. Although she could not maintain her top 10 ranking, she won Klagenfurt, where she was r/u doubles with Schnyder, upset Coetzer and Tauziat on her way to sf Zurich and reached qf Olympics, Amelia Island, Sopot, Linz, Moscow and Leipzig. **2000 HIGHLIGHTS – SINGLES: Australian Open last 16** [seed 6] (d. Tu 6–2 6–7 6–4, Vavrinec 6–4 6–4, Labat 6–1 6–3, lost Sanchez-Vicario [seed 13] 1–6 6–0 7–5), **French Open last 16** [seed 16] (d. Kleinova 6–3 6–4, Fusai 6–1 6–2, Casoni 6–2 6–1, lost Sanchez-Vicario [seed 8] 0–6 6–4 6–2), **Wimbledon 1r** [seed 15] (lost Barabanschikova 6–2 6–2), **US Open 2r** (d. Farina-Elia 6–4 3–6 7–6, lost Rubin 2–6 6–1 6–1), **Olympics qf** [seed 12] (d. Molik 7–6 6–2, Salerni 7–6 6–4, Halard-Decugis 2–6 6–2 6–1, lost Dementieva [seed 10] 2–6 6–2 6–1); **won** Klagenfurt (d. Kandarr 5–7 6–3 6–3, Kruger 6–3 6–1, Montolio 6–3 6–4, Schnyder 5–7 6–4 6–4; **sf** Zurich (d. Likhovtseva 6–0 6–1, Coetzer 7–6 3–6 6–4, Tauziat 3–6 6–3 6–3, lost Davenport 6–2 6–1). **2000 HIGHLIGHTS – DOUBLES:** (with Schnyder) **r/u** Klagenfurt (lost Montalvo/Suarez 7–6 6–1), (with Sanchez-Vicario) **r/u** Filderstadt (lost Hingis/Kournikova 6–4 6–2)

PATTY SCHNYDER (SUI)

Born Basel, 14 December 1978; lives Bottmingen; LH; 2HB; 5ft 6½in; 129lb; turned pro 1994; career singles titles 6; final 2000 WTA ranking 25; 2000 prize money $263,318; career prize money $1,852,192.

Coached by Vito Gugolz. **1994:** (786) Nat Jun champ for 2nd year. **1995:** (152) On the Futures circuit she won Nitra and Presov back-to-back, following with Cureglia, and on the main tour upset Spirlea 1r Zurich. **1996:** (58) A –, F 1, W 1, US –. She reached her 1st f on the main tour at Karlovy Vary, removing Paulus on the way, and joined the Swiss Fed Cup squad. **1997:** (26) A 4, F 3, W 1, US 3. She upset Majoli at Australian Open, where she was unseeded, surprised Raymond at Madrid, and extended Davenport to 9–7 fs at French Open, taking her to 3s again at US Open. Her best showing was sf Rome, and although she did not progress again beyond qf, she reached that stage at Maria Lankowitz and Filderstadt (d. Sukova and Majoli after qualifying). **1998:** (11) A 4, F qf, W 2, US 4. She began an impressive year by winning her 1st career title at Hobart and following with her 2nd at Hannover in Feb. (d. Majoli, Tauziat and Novotna). By end July, having added Madrid (d. Testud and Van Roost), Maria Lankowitz and Palermo, she had won more titles than anyone else all season to date, and by mid Aug. was a member of the top 10. After that, though, her best performance was r/u GS Cup (unseeded, d. Novotna) and she finished the season just outside the elite. She also reached sf Hamburg (d. Sanchez-Vicario), qf FC Cup and French Open (unseeded, d. Coetzer); upset Raymond at Australian Open (unseeded) and Graf at US Open. She qualified for her 1st Chase Champs, where she extended Hingis to 3s 1r, and was voted WTA Most Improved Player of the Year. In doubles she won Hamburg from 3 f with Schett. Helped take SUI to 1st ever f in Fed Cup, but there lost all her matches as SUI went down 3–2 to ESP. **1999:** (21) A 2, F 3, W 1, US 3. Her year began well with the title at Hope Island. However, she fired coach Van Harpen after 2r defeat by Mauresmo at Australian Open, employed old friend Vito Gugolz for just 4 practice sessions, and then her boyfriend/advisor Rainer Harnecker (whom she'd met in Dec.) took over her life. He put her on a vegan diet, as a result of which she lost a lot of weight, alienated her from family and friends and tried to sever all her ties with the past. Her form crashed and in April she was talking of giving up tennis, but instead she gave up Harnecker in spring and began to return to her old form. During the year she reached sf FC Cup (where she was r/u doubles with Schett) and qf Sydney, Amelia Island, Cairo and Berlin. **2000:** A 4, F 1, W 2, US 2. At Klagenfurt she reached her 1st f since early 1999, and was also r/u doubles there with Schett. Otherwise her best performances were qf Gold Coast, Hannover, 's-Hertogenbosch, Sopot and Luxembourg, plus upsets of Mauresmo at Australian Open, where she was unseeded, Testud at Amelia Island, and Halard-Decugis at New Haven. **2000 HIGHLIGHTS – SINGLES: Australian Open last 16** [unseeded] (d. Osterloh 6–3 6–4, Mauresmo [seed 7] 6–4 6–4, Petrova 7–6 4 6 6–2, lost Capriati 6–3 4–6 6–1), **French Open 1r** (lost Gayliardi 6–3 6–4), **Wimbledon 2r** (d. Garbin 6–3 6–2, lost Suarez 6–7 6–3 6–3),

US Open 2r (d. Craybas 5–7 6–1 6–3, lost Asagoe 7–5 6–4); **r/u** Klagenfurt (d. Glass 5–7 7- 5 6–4, Leon Garcia 2–6 7–5 6–4, Gersi 6–0 6–3, lost Schett 5–7 6–4 6–4). **2000 HIGHLIGHTS – DOUBLES:** (with Schett) **r/u** Klagenfurt (lost Montalvo/Suarez 7–6 6–1). **CAREER HIGHLIGHTS – SINGLES: French Open – qf 1998** [unseeded] (d. Coetzer 6–4 3–6 8–6, Halard-Decugis 6–3 3–6 6–1, Farina 6–2 6–1, Serna 6–1 6–3, lost Sanchez-Vicario 6–2 6–7 6–0).

MAGUI SERNA (ESP)
Born Las Palmas, 1 March 1979; lives Barcelona; LH; 5ft 6in; 142lb; turned pro 1993; career singles titles 0; final 2000 WTA ranking 38; 2000 prize money $311,384.
Coached by Lorenzo Fargas. Named Maria Luisa, she is known as Magui. Formerly nat champ in 12s and 14s. **1994:** (342) Won 2 Futures tourns back-to-back. **1995:** (357) Continued to make her mark on the satellite circuit with the title at Mallorca. **1996:** (138) R/u Wimbledon Jun to Mauresmo and in the senior game she won 3 Futures titles in the space of four weeks. **1997:** (41) A 3, F 3, W 3, US 4. Reached qf Gold Coast after qualifying (d. Dragomir) and upset Po at US Open, where she was unseeded. **1998:** (24) A 2, F 4, W 4, US 1. She was consistent through the year, reaching qf FC Cup (d. Huber and Novotna), Madrid, Birmingham, Eastbourne (d. Likhovtseva), Montreal (d. Graf) and Moscow (d. Schnyder). Other notable upsets included Pierce at French Open, where she was unseeded, and Schultz-McCarthy at Berlin, and she broke into top 25 1st time in July. **1999:** (39) A 2, F 1, W 1, US 3. She reached her 1st sf on the main tour at Birmingham, appeared in qf Hope Island, Madrid and New Haven, and upset Testud at US Open. **2000:** A 2, F 3, W qf, US 4. The highlight of her year came at Wimbledon, where she upset Pierce on her way to sf, unseeded. She reached same stage Knokke-Heist, upset Coetzer at US Open, where she was unseeded, and was r/u doubles in Rome with Sanchez-Vicario. **2000 HIGHLIGHTS – SINGLES: Australian Open 2r** (d. Drake 6–4 6–2, lost Labat 7–6 7–5), **French Open 3r** (d. Nagyova 6–2 6–4, Brandi 5–7 6–2 6–2, lost Sanchez-Vicario 7–5 6–4), **Wimbledon sf** [unseeded] (d. Cross 6–3 6–4, Pierce [seed 3] 7–6 7–6, Oremans 4–6 6–4 6–4, Osterloh 7–6 6–3, lost Dokic 6–3 6–2), **US Open last 16** [unseeded] (d. Wartusch 7–6 7–5, Grande 7–6 6–3, Coetzer [seed 13] 7–5 7–6, lost V. Williams [seed 3] 6–2 6–2), **Olympics 1r** (lost Dechy [seed 11] 6–1 6–2); **sf** Knokke-Heist (d. Loit 6–0 7–6, Henin 6–4 7–6, Wartusch 6–0 ret, lost Van Roost 6–3 6–0). **2000 HIGHLIGHTS – DOUBLES:** (with Sanchez-Vicario) **r/u** Rome (lost Raymond/Stubbs 6–3 4–6 6–3). **CAREER HIGHLIGHTS – SINGLES: Wimbledon – sf 2000.**

MEGHANN SHAUGHNESSY (USA)
Born Richmond, Va, 13 April 1979; lives Scottsdale, Ariz.; RH; 2HB; 5ft 11in; 140lb; turned pro 1996; career singles titles 1; final 2000 WTA ranking 39; 2000 prize money $238,659.
Coached by Rafael Font de Mora; trained by Tom Rogers. Won USTA 16s CC at age 14. **1994:** (705). **1995:** (425) Played 5 f on the satellite circuit, winning Morelia, Toluca and Sao Paulo. **1996:** (187) A –, F –, W –, US 1. R/u French Open Jun to Mauresmo. After qualifying for her 1st ever tourn on the main tour at Budapest, she progressed to qf. **1997:** (164) A –, F –, W –, US –. **1998:** (72) A 1, F –, W –, US 1. Qf finishes at Prague and Istanbul on the main tour and the title at Sochi ITF ($50,000) took her into the top 100. **1999:** (97) A 1, F 1, W 2, US 1. She reached her 1st sf on the main tour at Bogota and was r/u twice in doubles. **2000:** A 2, F 2, W 2, US 3. She moved into top 50 1st time after winning her 1st title from her 1st f at Shanghai, also appearing in sf Auckland, qf Bogota and Antwerp and upsetting Halard-Decugis at French Open. In doubles she played 2 f, winning Quebec City with Pratt. **2000 HIGHLIGHTS – SINGLES: Australian Open 2r** (d. Snyder 6–0 1–6 10–8, lost Likhovtseva [seed 16] 6–2 6–2), **French Open 2r** (d. Halard-Decugis [seed 12] 7–6 6–4, lost Dragomir 6–1 7–5), **Wimbledon 2r** (d. Sanchez Lorenzo 7–5 6–2, lost Capriati 7–6 6–2), **US Open 3r** (d. Habsudova 6–4 6–4, Nola 6–3 6–2, lost V. Williams [seed 3] 7–6 6–1); **won** Shanghai (d. Perebiynis 7–6 6–1, Irvin 6–4 1–6 7–5, Obata 6–3 6–2, Nola 7–5 6–2, Tulyaganova 7–6 7–5); **sf** Auckland (d. Labat 6–7 6–1 7–6, Webb 7–6 6–0, Smashnova 6–4 6–2, lost Kremer 6–3 6–3). **2000 HIGHLIGHTS – DOUBLES:** (with Pratt) **won** Quebec City (d. Callens/Po 6–3 6–4); (with Grande) **r/u** Shanghai (lost Osterloh/Tanasugarn 7–5 6–1)

ANNE-GAELLE SIDOT (FRA)
Born Enghien-les-Bains, 24 July 1979; lives Montlignon; LH; 5ft 8in; 124lb; turned pro 1994; career singles titles 0; final 2000 WTA ranking 36 singles, 24 doubles; 2000 prize money $312,537; career prize money $1,005,360.
Coached by Regis De Camaret. **1995:** (163) A –, F 1, W –, US –. Won Flensburg Futures. **1996:** (55) A –, F 1, W 2, US 3. After winning Wurzburg Futures, she extended Date to 3s 2r Wimbledon and upset Halard-Decugis *en route* to her 1st sf on the main tour at Luxembourg, before closing her season with the title at Cardiff Futures. **1997:** (33) A 2, F 1, W 1, US 1. She recorded some useful upsets on her way to sf Gold Coast, Hamburg (d. Schultz-McCarthy) and Luxembourg (d. Habsudova, whom she had earlier beaten at Zurich), qf Hobart (d. Hack) and Hannover (d. Appelmans). Made her Fed Cup debut as part of the FRA team that won 1st time. **1998:** (54) A 3, F 2, W 1, US 1. Although her year was restricted by a stress fracture of the foot, suffered in Feb., she reached qf Hobart, Stanford (d. Kruger) and Leipzig (d. Sanchez-Vicario), and on the ITF circuit won the $50,000 Southampton tourn. **1999:** (33) A 1, F 1, W 1, US 2. She had not passed 2r all year until Toronto in Aug., where she reached her 1st career sf (d. Halard-Decugis and Coetzer), followed in Nov. by qf Leipzig (d. Van Roost). **2000:** A 1, F 3, W 3, US 1. She reached sf Hannover, qf Paris Open, Birmingham,

Luxembourg, Filderstadt (d. Rubin) and Bratislava, as well as upsetting Kournikova at Wimbledon and Capriati at Rome. From 3 doubles f she won Leipzig with Sanchez-Vicario. **2000 HIGHLIGHTS – SINGLES: Australian Open 1r** (lost Petrova 6–4 6–2), **French Open 3r** (d. Bachmann 6–3 7–6, Kremer 6–4 4–6 6–1, lost Marrero 7–6 6–2), **Wimbledon 3r** (d. Bedanova 6–3 6–1, Kournikova 6–3 6–4, lost Tanasugarn 6–1 4–6 6–4), **US Open 1r** (lost V. Williams [seed 3] 6–3 6–4); **sf** Hannover (d. Cocheteux 6–2 6–3, Clijsters 6–7 6–4 6–4, Boogert 6–4 6–2, lost Chladkova 6–3 6–7 7–6). **2000 HIGHLIGHTS – DOUBLES:** (with Po unless stated) (with Sanchez-Vicario) **won** Leipzig (d. Clijsters/Courtois 6–7 7–5 6–3); **r/u** Los Angeles (lost Callens/Van Roost 6–2 7–5), **r/u** Zurich (lost Hingis/Kournikova 6–3 6–4).

ANNA SMASHNOVA (ISR)
Born Minsk, Russia, 16 July 1976; lives Herzelia; RH; 5ft 2in; 120lb; turned pro 1991; career singles titles 2; final 2000 WTA ranking 46; 2000 prize money $161,935.
Coached part-time by David Cody. Emigrated to Israel from USSR with her parents in 1990. Completed a mandatory year's service in Israeli army after graduating from High School in July 1995, although her basic 2-week training was delayed to allow her to compete in Wimbledon and US Open that year. **1990:** No. 1 Jun in USSR from age 11. **1991:** (347) Won French Open Jun over Gorrochategui. **1992:** (213) Joined the Israeli Fed Cup team. **1993:** (147) Won Erlangen Futures. **1994:** (48) A 2, F 2, W 2, US 3. Reached her 1st main tour qf at Auckland in Jan. and made her mark in GS with upsets of Novotna 1r French Open and McNeil 1r US Open. **1995:** (68) A 3, F 4, W 1, US 1. Upset Garrison-Jackson FC Cup and Frazier at French Open, where she was unseeded, but reached no qf all year. **1996:** (149) A 2, F 1, W 1, US –. Upset Zvereva 1r Australian Open. **1997:** (140) A –, F –, W –, US –. At Jaffa on the ITF circuit she won her 1st pro title for 4 years. **1998:** (50) A –, F 4, W 1, US 1. She moved back into the top 50 with sf finish at Sopot and qf Istanbul, as well as the titles at Oporto and Santa Clara at the $75,000 ITF circuit. **1999:** (49) A 2, F 3, W 1, US 1. The highlight of her year came at Tashkent, where she won her 1st title on the main tour. She also appeared in qf Madrid and on the ITF circuit won the $50,000 tourn at Largo. **2000:** A 1, F 1, W 3, US 1. She won Knokke-Heist over Van Roost and appeared in sf Strasbourg (d. Van Roost again) and Palermo, as well as qf Auckland, Hannover (d. Dragomir) and Shanghai. There were tears and tantrums at Wimbledon when she hit the ball into the crowd, aiming for her opponent Marosi-Aracama's husband, who she said was putting her off and behaving badly. **2000 HIGHLIGHTS – SINGLES: Australian Open 1r** (lost Rubin 6–3 6–4), **French Open 1r** (lost Maleeva 6–3 6–4), **Wimbledon 3r** (d. Mandula 6–2 7–6, Marosi-Aracama 6–2 5–7 6–2, lost Appelmans 6–3 6–4)), **US Open 1r** (lost Dokic 6–1 6–0); **won** Knokke-Heist (d. Pavlina 6–3 6–2, Gagliardi 6–2 6–2, Pitkowski 6–1 6–1, Marrero 6–3 6–1, Van Roost 6–2 7–5); **sf** Strasbourg (d. Van Roost 6–0 6–4, Tanasugarn 6–4 6–2, Osterloh 7–6 6–4, lost Kuti Kis 7–6 6–3), **sf** Palermo (d. Krizan 6–4 6–3, Medina Garrigues 4–6 6–3 6–0, Pizzichini 6–4 4–6 6–1, lost Nola 6–1 6–3).

RENNAE STUBBS (AUS)
Born Sydney, 26 March 1971; lives there and Orlando, Fla.; RH; 5ft 10in; 143lb; pro; career singles titles 0; final 2000 WTA ranking 683 singles, 6 doubles; 2000 prize money $340,407; career prize money $1,651,786.
Coached by Ray Ruffels. **1988:** (352) Won 6 doubles titles on the satellite circuits. **1989:** (225) A 2, F –, W –, US –. Continued to make her mark in doubles on the satellite circuits. **1990:** (232) A 1, F –, W 1, US –. Won her 1st pro singles title at Perth on the satellite circuit. **1991:** (239) A 1, F –, W 1, US –. Won Mildura on the Australian satellite circuit. **1992:** (85) A 2, F 1, W 2, US –. Burst on to the main tour with an upset of Zvereva at Tokyo Pan Pacific and qf appearance at Eastbourne. In doubles won 2 titles with McNeil and 1 each with Sukova and Graf, qualifying for VS Champs with McNeil. **1993:** (170) A 1, F – W 1, US –. Reached 5 doubles f with 4 different partners, winning Indian Wells with Sukova, Hamburg with Graf, and qualifying for VS Champs with McNeil. **1994:** A 1, F –, W –, US –. In a quieter year she won Osaka with Neiland and Strasbourg with McNeil. **1995:** (90) A –, F –, W 2, US 1. Upset Raymond on her way to sf Quebec City. Played 6 doubles f with 4 different partners, winning Birmingham with Bollegraf and reaching her 1st GS f at US Open with Schultz-McCarthy. **1996:** (106) A 2, F 1, W 1, US 1. In singles she reached qf Essen and upset Habsudova at Montreal. In doubles she won Chicago and Philadelphia with Raymond, with whom she qualified for Chase Champs, and was r/u Linz with Sukova. **1997:** (–) A –, F –, W –, US –. She was out for much of the season with tendinitis of the right wrist, returning in autumn to win Luxembourg and Philadelphia doubles with Raymond. **1998:** (231) A 1, F –, W 1, US –. Her doubles partnership with Raymond continued to flourish, bringing 2 titles from 5 f and a place at Chase Champs, where Davenport/Zvereva beat them in sf. **1999:** (254) A –, F –, W –, US –. From 7 doubles f with Raymond, she won 5 titles and qualified for Chase Champs, where they reached sf. **2000:** A –, F –, W –, US –. She was again a force in doubles with Raymond, winning Australian Open, Rome, Madrid and San Diego from 6 f to qualify for Chase Champs, where they reached sf again. In mixed she won Australian Open with Palmer and was r/u French Open with Woodbridge. **2000 HIGHLIGHTS – DOUBLES:** (with Raymond) **won Australian Open** (d. Hingis/Pierce 5–0 ret); **won** Rome (d. Sanchez-Vicario/Serna 6–3 4–6 6–3), **won** Madrid (d. Leon Garcia/Sanchez Lorenzo 6–1 6–3), **won** San Diego (d. Davenport/Kournikova 4–6 6–3 7–6); **r/u** Eastbourne (lost Sugiyama/Tauziat 2–6 6–3 7–6), **r/u** Philadelphia (lost Hingis/Kournikova 6–2 7–5). **MIXED DOUBLES:** (with Palmer) **won Australian Open** (d. Woodbridge/Sanchez-Vicario 7–5 7–6), (with Woodbridge) **r/u** French Open (lost Adams/De Swardt 6–3 3–6 6–3). **CAREER HIGHLIGHTS – DOUBLES: Australian Open** – (with Raymond) **won 2000; US Open** – (with

Schultz-McCarthy) **r/u 1995** (lost G. Fernandez/Zvereva 7–5 6–3). **MIXED DOUBLES:** (with Palmer) **Australian Open – won 2000.**

PAOLA SUAREZ (ARG)
Born Pergamino, 23 June 1976; lives Munro; RH; 2HB; 5ft 7in; 142lb; turned pro 1994; career singles titles 1; final 2000 WTA ranking 37 singles, 7 doubles; 2000 prize money $333,084.
Coached by Daniel Pereyra. **1991:** (580) Won Buenos Aires and Florianapolis Futures. **1992:** (241) R/u French Open Jun to De Los Rios and won 4 consec. titles on Spanish Futures circuit. **1993:** (269) Qf Curitiba and won La Plata Futures. **1994:** (110) A –, F 1, W 1, US 2. Upset Boogert *en route* to her 1st tour sf at Prague, after qualifying. **1995:** (130) A –, F 2, W –, US 1. A qualifier at French Open, she upset M. J. Fernandez 1r, and on the Futures circuit won Buenos Aires. **1996:** (59) A –, F 2, W 1, US 2. Her best performance came at Bol, where she reached sf singles and won the doubles with Montalvo. Joined her country's Fed Cup team. **1997:** (115) A 2, F 1, W 1, US 3. It was a quieter year in which she reached no qf. **1998:** (85) A 2, F 2, W 1, US 1. She returned to the top 100 after winning her 1st career singles title at Bogota, where she was unseeded and also took the doubles with Husarova. In all she played and won 6 doubles f with 3 different partners. On the $25,000 ITF circuit she won Santiago and Montevideo (both singles and doubles), and finished the year with Buenos Aires ($10,000). **1999:** (71) A 1, F 2, W 1, US 2. Her best performance came at Madrid, where she was r/u singles as LL (d. Schnyder, Serna and Rubin and extended Davenport to 3s) and won the doubles with Ruano Pascual. She also reached sf Bogota and won 2 more doubles titles with Montalvo. On the $25,000 ITF circuit she won Buenos Aires. **2000:** A 1, F 1, W 3, US 1. She was r/u Sao Paulo and reached sf Amelia Island (d. Kournikova) and Sopot (d. Schnyder), plus qf Auckland, Bogota and Bol, as well as upsetting Mauresmo at Berlin and Schnyder at Wimbledon and Linz. In doubles she played 8 f with 3 different partners, winning 3 with Montalvo and 2 with Ruano Pascual, with whom she was r/u French Open and qualified for Chase Champs. **2000 HIGHLIGHTS – SINGLES: Australian Open 1r** (lost Dementieva 6–0 3–6 8–6), **French Open 1r** (lost Dementieva 1–6 6–1 6–4), **Wimbledon 3r** (d. Gagliardi 6–4 6–3, Schnyder 6–7 6–3 6–3, lost Davenport [seed 2] 6–4 6–2), **US Open 1r** (lost Plischke 6–3 6–3), **Olympics 1r** (lost Davenport [seed 1] 6–2 6–2); **r/u** Sao Paulo (d. Mandula 6–6 ret, Nemeckova 2 6 6–0 6–1, Plischke 6–7 4–6 6–4, Kruger 6–2 6–3, lost Kuti Kis 4–6 6–4 7–5); **sf** Amelia Island (d. Obziler 6–1 6–1, S. Williams 6–3 4–6 5–2 ret, Jeyaseelan 6–2 6–3, Kournikova 2–6 6–2 6–4, lost Seles 6–3 6–2), **sf** Sopot (d. Nagyova 4–6 6–3 6–2, Carlsson 6–2 6–2, Schnyder 6–4 7–5, lost Leon Garcia 6–4 4–6 6–3). **2000 HIGHLIGHTS – DOUBLES:** (with Ruano Pascual unless stated) **r/u French Open** (lost Hingis/Pierce 6–2 6–4); (with Montalvo) **won** Bogota (d. Kuti Kis/Mandula 6–4 6–2), (with Montalvo) **won** Sao Paulo (d. Husarova/Labat 5–7 6–4 6–3), **won** FC Cup (d. Martinez/Tarabini 7–5 6–3), **won** Sopot (d. Carlsson/Grande 7–5 6–1), (with Montalvo) **won** Klagenfurt (d. Schett/Schnyder 6–2 7–5), **r/u** New Haven (lost Halard-Decugis/Sugiyama 6–4 5–7 6–2), (with Miyagi) **r/u** Tokyo Toyota (lost Halard-Decugis/Sugiyama 6–0 6–2). **CAREER HIGHLIGHTS – DOUBLES:** (with Ruano Pascual) **French Open – r/u 2000.**

AI SUGIYAMA (JPN)
Born Tokyo, 5 July 1975; lives Kanagawa; RH; 5ft 4in; 121lb; turned pro 1992; career singles titles 3; final 2000 WTA ranking 31 singles, 2 doubles; 2000 prize money $729,635; career prize money $2,264,798.
Coached by Junichi Maruyama. **1991:** (568) No. 2 in ITF Jun Rankings singles. **1992:** (180) Won Roanoke Futures. **1993:** (142) A –, F –, W 1, US –. **1994:** (72) A –, F –, W 1, US 1. Reached f both singles and doubles at Surabaya, but was forced to retire in singles and def doubles with heat exhaustion. She also reached sf Osaka and qf Tokyo Nicherei (d. Sawamatsu). **1995:** (46) A 1, F 4, W 1, US 2. R/u Oakland (d. Spirlea and Garrison-Jackson), upset Sukova at French Open, where she was unseeded, and surprised Coetzer at San Diego, as well as reaching qf Zagreb. Played 2 doubles f with Nagatsuka, winning Hobart. **1996:** (32) A 3, F 1, W 4, US 2. She reached sf Tokyo Japan Open and qf Hobart, as well as scoring some big upsets across the year. At Wimbledon, where she was unseeded, she removed Huber before extending M. J. Fernandez to 3s, upset Wiesner at Auckland, Novotna at LIPC and Hingis at Olympics. In doubles she won Tokyo Japan Open with Date and joined with Nagatsuka to beat Graf/Huber as JPN d. GER in qf Fed Cup. **1997:** (20) A 2, F 2, W 1, US 2. She won her 1st ever singles title on the main tour at Tokyo Japan Open and was r/u Gold Coast and Moscow (d. Schultz-McCarthy and Sanchez-Vicario), as well as reaching qf Eastbourne. Adapting to the pressures of her new role as Japanese No. 1 after Date's retirement, she broke into top 20 1st time in Nov. In doubles she won Tokyo Nicherei with Seles and r/u Strasbourg with Likhovtseva. **1998:** (18) A 4, F 2, W 1, US 2. She began the year in style by winning both singles and doubles at Gold Coast and followed in April with Tokyo Japan Open. At Sydney she upset Martinez *en route* to sf, and in other tourns reached qf Tokyo Pan Pacific, Berlin (d. Coetzer), Strasbourg, San Diego (d. Graf) and Luxembourg. She was restricted in autumn by an ankle injury, which forced her retirement at US Open. In doubles with Likhovtseva, she won all 4 f played and qualified for her 1st Chase Champs, although they did not pass 1r. **1999:** (24) A 1, F 2, W 2, US 3. She was r/u Tokyo Japan Open and reached sf Hope Island and Tokyo Toyota (d. Halard-Decugis), plus qf Strasbourg and Moscow (d. Pierce). Always a dangerous opponent, she extended Hingis to 3s at Tokyo Toray and other upsets included Coetzer at French Open, Pierce at San Diego and Novotna at Toronto. From 4 doubles f with Likhovtseva, she won Sydney and Strasbourg to qualify for Chase Champs, where they fell 1r. In mixed she won US Open with Bhupathi. **2000:** A qf, F 4, W 2, US 2. Her best singles performance came at

Australian Open, where she reached qf, unseeded and upsetting Pierce on the way, and was followed by same stage Scottsdale (d. Halard-Decugis). From 10 doubles f she won 1 with Tauziat and 6, including US Open, with Halard-Decugis, with whom she was also r/u Wimbledon and qualified for Chase Champs as 1st pairing, although they fell 1r to Callens/Van Roost. **2000 HIGHLIGHTS – SINGLES: Australian Open qf** [unseeded] (d. Maleeva 7–6 7–6, Gersi 6–1 6–4, Carlsson 6–4 4–6 6–3, Pierce [seed 4] 7–5 6–4, lost Capriati 6–0 6–2), **French Open last 16** [unseeded] (d. Clijsters 6–2 3–6 6–2, Gersi 6–3 7–6, Plischke 6–4 6–1, lost Martinez [seed 5] 5–7 6–3 6–4), **Wimbledon 2r** (d. Yoshida 6–1 6–3, lost V. Williams [seed 5] 6–1 6–4), **US Open 2r** (d. Nacuk 6–1 6–7 6–3, lost Boogert 6–3 6–4), **Olympics 1r** [seed 14] (lost Dokic 6–0 7–6). **2000 HIGHLIGHTS – DOUBLES:** (with Halard-Decugis unless stated) **r/u Wimbledon** (lost S./V. Williams 6–3 6–2), **won US Open** (d. Black/Likhovtseva 6–0 1–6 6–1); **won** Sydney (d. Hingis/Pierce 6–0 6–3), **won** Ericsson Open (d. Arendt/Bollegraf 4–6 7–5 6–4), (with Tauziat) **won** Eastbourne (d. Raymond/Stubbs 2–6 6–3 7–6), **won** New Haven (d. Ruano Pascual/Suarez 6–4 5–7 6–2), **won** Tokyo Toyota (d. Miyagi/Suarez 6–0 6–2), **won** Moscow (d. Hingis/Kournikova 4–6 6–4 7–6); **r/u Montreal** (lost Hingis/Tauziat 6–3 3–6 6–4), (with Tauziat) **r/u** Linz (lost Mauresmo/Rubin 6–4 6–4). **CAREER HIGHLIGHTS – DOUBLES:** (with Halard-Decugis) **US Open – won 2000; Wimbledon – r/u 2000. MIXED DOUBLES:** (with Bhupathi) **US Open – won 1999** (d. Johnson/Po 6–4 6–4).

SILVIJA TALAJA (CRO)
Born Imotski, 14 January 1978; lives Makarska; RH; 2HB; 5ft 8in; 126lb; turned pro 1992; career singles titles 2; final 2000 WTA ranking 30; 2000 prize money $224,103.
Coached by Mark Petchey. **1992:** (577). **1993:** (247). **1994:** (247). **1995:** (269). **1996:** (97) After winning Makarska on the ITF circuit, she received a wild-card for Bol on the senior tour, where she was the second-lowest ranked player in the main draw at 298. There she delighted home fans by reaching her 1st f at that level, and followed in her next 2 tourns with sf Maria Lankowitz and qf Karlovy Vary (d. Habsudova). **1997:** (195) A 1, F 2, W –, US –. A right shoulder injury suffered after US Open kept her out of action for rest of year. **1998:** (89) A –, F –, W 1, US –. She continued to excel at Bol, reaching sf there after qualifying, and finished the year with same stage Pattaya (d. Nagyova). **1999:** (29) A 1, F 3, W 1, US 1. She swept into the top 50 with r/u 's-Hertogenbosch and Portschach (d. Farina) either side of Wimbledon, plus sf Warsaw, Sopot, Knokke-Heist and Pattaya and qf Estoril. She upset S. Williams at Toronto, extended V. Williams to 9–7 fs 1r Australian Open and took Novotna to 3s at French Open. **2000:** A 1, F 1, W 3, US 1. She began the year in style, upsetting Kournikova, Sanchez-Vicario and C. Martinez back-to-back to win her 1st career title at Gold Coast, following in May with a 2nd at Strasbourg (d. Tauziat). Other upsets included Sugiyama at Eastbourne and Schett at Montreal. **2000 HIGHLIGHTS – SINGLES: Australian Open 1r** (lost Molik 6–1 5–7 7–5), **French Open 1r** (lost Seles [seed 3] 6–2 6–2), **Wimbledon 3r** (d. Spirlea 6–4 6–2, Lucic 6–2 6–2, lost Hingis [seed 1] 6–2 6–2), **US Open 1r** (lost Schiavone 6–3 6–3), **Olympics 2r** [seed 13] (d. Etienne 6–1 6–0, lost Farina-Elia 3–6 6–4 6–4); **won** Gold Coast (d. Arendt 6–3 6–1, Hrdlickova 7–6 7–5, Kournikova 4–6 6–4 6–2, Sanchez-Vicario 6–1 3–6 6–0, C. Martinez 6–0 0–6 6–4), **won** Strasbourg (d. Snyder 6–4 4–6 6–3, Nejedly 3–6 6–2 6–1, Tauziat 7–5 6–2, Dechy 6–1 1–6 6–3, Kuti Kis 7–5 4–6 6–3).

TAMARINE TANASUGARN (THA)
Born Los Angeles, USA, 24 May 1977; lives Bangkok; RH; 2HB; 5ft 5in; 140lb; turned pro 1994; career singles titles 0; final 2000 WTA ranking 29; 2000 prize money $232,786.
Coached by Panoomkom Pradchumir; formerly by her father, Virachai Tanasugarn. Ranked No. 1 in Thailand, and also holds US citizenship. **1992:** (654). **1993:** (494). **1994:** (249). **1995:** (209) R/u Wimbledon Jun to Olsza. **1996:** (79) Upset Wild on the way to her 1st main tour sf at Beijing, then crowned her year with r/u Pattaya. On the satellite circuits, she won 2 titles from 4 f in 4 weeks in Australia and singles and doubles at Saga. **1997:** (46) A 3, F 2, W 3, US 3. She reached sf Auckland, won Surbiton Futures and upset Dragomir at Toronto. **1998:** (37) A 4, F 1, W 4, US 1. Played sf Tokyo Toyota and qf Auckland (where she won the doubles with Miyagi), Stanford and Pattaya. At Australian Open (unseeded) she upset Majoli and took a set off Testud. **1999:** (72) A 1, F 1, W 4, US 2. Upset Testud at Wimbledon, where she was unseeded, reached qf Kuala Lumpur and on the $25,000 ITF circuit won Saga and Surbiton. **2000:** A 3, F 2, W 4, US 3. After beginning the year as r/u Hopman Cup with Srichaphan, she upset Halard-Decugis *en route* to her 2nd career f at Birmingham and reached sf Tokyo Japan Open, Shanghai (where she won the doubles with Osterloh) and Kuala Lumpur, plus qf Pattaya. On the $50,000 ITF circuit she won Gifu. **2000 HIGHLIGHTS – SINGLES: Australian Open 3r** (d. Grande 6–3 6–4, Nejedly 7–5 6–4, lost Testud [seed 12] 4–6 7–5 6–2), **French Open 2r** (d. Erre 7–6 7–6, lost V. Williams [seed 4] 6–2 6–2), **Wimbledon last 16** [unseeded] (d. De Los Rios 7–5 6–2, Zvereva 6–1 6–3, Sidot 6–1 4–6 6–4, lost S. Williams [seed 8] 6–1 6–1), **US Open 3r** (d. Montolio 6–1 6–1, Ruano Pascual 3–6 6–3 6–1, lost Davenport [seed 2] 6–2 6–1), **Olympics 2r** (d. Pisnik 6–4 6–3, lost V. Williams [seed 2] 6–2 6–3); **won** Gifu ITF (d. Asagoe 7–5 6–4) **r/u Birmingham** (d. Boogert 6–3 3–6 6–1, Latimer 7–6 6–3, Krasnoroutskaia 7–5 6–2, Halard-Decugis 6–4 6–4, Black 7–6 6–1, lost Raymond 6–2 6–7 6–4); **sf** Tokyo Japan Open (d. Tulyaganova 6–3 6–2, Osterloh 6–3 6–1, Snyder 6–4 6–1, lost Halard-Decugis 7–6 6–0), **sf** Shanghai (d. Fernandez 7–5 6–4, N. Li 7–5 6–1, Smashnova 6–3 6–2, lost Tulyaganova 6–1 6–4), **sf** Kuala Lumpur (d. Medina 6–3 6–1, Zaric 6–2 1–6 6–1, Kruger 6–3 5–7 6–3, lost Nagyova 6–4 6–1). **2000 HIGHLIGHTS – DOUBLES:** (with Osterloh) **won** Shanghai (d. Grande/Shaughnessy 7–5 6–1), (with Tatarkova) **r/u** Oklahoma City (lost Morariu/Po 6–4 4–6 6–2).

SANDRINE TESTUD (FRA)

Born Lyon, 3 April 1972, and lives there; RH; 5ft 9½in; 150lb; pro; career singles titles 2; final 2000 WTA ranking 17 singles, 23 doubles; 2000 prize money $547,384; career prize money $2,560,220.

Husband Vittorio Magnelli (married 13 June 1998). **1989:** (279) Won Nat Jun 18s and in the senior game won her 1st Futures title at Limoges. **1990:** (185) A –, F 1, W –, US –. Won Futures titles at Eastbourne, Caltagirone and Swindon. **1991:** (118) A –, F 1, W –, US –. Reached sf Bol, plus qf Albuquerque and St Petersburg. **1992:** (108) A 2, F 2, W 1, US 2. Qf Strasbourg. **1993:** (98) A 1, F 1, W 1, US 1. Upset McNeil on her way to sf Strasbourg and Strnadova to reach qf Pattaya City. **1994:** (81) A 4, F 1, W 1, US 2. Upset Sukova at Australian Open, where she was unseeded, but reached no qf on the main tour. **1995:** (41) A 3, F 2, W 2, US 3. Broke into the top 50 after appearances in sf Strasbourg (d. M. J. Fernandez) and San Diego (d. Zvereva), plus qf Puerto Rico (d. Halard) and Quebec City. **1996:** (39) A 1, F 3, W 2, US 4. Her best performances were sf Beijing and qf San Diego (d. Sugiyama). **1997:** (13) A 2, F 3, W 4, US qf. She won her 1st career singles title at Palermo and upset Habsudova and Majoli on her way to f Atlanta, unseeded. She played no other sf, but moved into top 15 with qf US Open (unseeded, d. Majoli), Hannover (d. Schultz-McCarthy), Indian Wells (d. Raymond), LIPC (d. Sanchez-Vicario), Strasbourg, San Diego (d. Sanchez-Vicario again) and Moscow, and removed Davenport at Berlin. Having upset Seles 3r Wimbledon, again unseeded, she suffered a cruel reverse v Tauziat in her next match: 5–4 and 40–15 up in 3s when rain interrupted play for 75 minutes, she dropped the next 10 points, going on to lose the set 10–12. Won her 2 crucial singles matches in Fed Cup f as FRA d. NED and qualified 1st time for Chase Champs, where she extended Spirlea to 3s 1r. **1998:** (14) A qf, F 4, W 4, US 3. At Filderstadt, where she was unseeded, she upset Van Roost and Davenport on the way to the title. She was consistent through the year in reaching f Prague, sf Auckland, Madrid, 's-Hertogenbosch and Moscow (d. Martinez), and qf Australian Open, Oklahoma City, Budapest, Rome (d. Seles), Montreal (d. Spirlea) and Quebec City, where she was r/u doubles with Rubin. She qualified for Chase Champs, where, despite a leg injury, she looked set to upset Davenport 1r before losing momentum. **1999:** (13) A 4, F 2, W 3, US 2. Her 1st f of the year came at Linz in Nov. with an upset of Tauziat. During another consistent year, she also appeared in sf Indian Wells (d. Tauziat), Sopot and Filderstadt (d. S Williams, recovering from 1–5 down fs, and extended Hingis to 3s), plus qf Hannover, Rome, Stanford, San Diego (d. Sanchez-Vicario), Toronto, New Haven and Philadelphia. She qualified for Chase Champs but there fell 1r to Hingis. In doubles with Rubin she was r/u US Open and won Filderstadt from 2 other f. **2000:** A 4, F 3, W 1, US 4. She broke into top 10 1st time in Feb. after r/u showing at Tokyo Pan Pacific (d. Tauziat), then at Ericsson Open she extended Davenport to fs tb in sf. She added qf appearances at Scottsdale, Bol, Berlin (extended Hingis to 3s), 's Hertogenbosch, Stanford, San Diego, Los Angeles and Montreal, but withdrew Olympics with stress fracture of rib. She was fit again for Chase Champs, but lost 1r to Seles. In doubles she won Paris Open with Halard-Decugis and Stanford with Rubin. **2000 HIGHLIGHTS – SINGLES: Australian Open last 16** [seed 10] (d. Mandula 6–3 4–6 6–3, Gavaldon 6–1 6–2, Tanasugarn 4–6 7–5 6–2, lost Hingis [seed 1] 6–1 7–6), **French Open 3r** [seed 10] (d. Noorlander 7–6 6–1, Grande 6–1 6–1, lost Carlsson 4–6 6–3 7–5), **Wimbledon 1r** [seed 10] (lost Kournikova 7–5 5–7 6–4), **US Open last 16** [seed 11] (d. Pratt 6–3 6–1, Tulyaganova 6–4 6–3, Boogert 6–0 6–1, lost Hingis [seed 1] 6–2 6–1); **r/u** Tokyo Pan Pacific (d. Habsudova 6–1 6–2, Morariu 6–1 4–6 6–1, Tauziat 7–6 6–0, Srebotnik 3–6 7–5 6–1, lost Hingis 6–3 7–5); **sf** Ericsson Open (d. Zuluaga 6–4 3–6 7–6, Plischke 6–0 6–0, Dementieva 6–2 6–2, Capriati 6–3 6–4, lost Davenport 6–1 6–7 7–6). **2000 HIGHLIGHTS – DOUBLES:** (with Halard-Decugis) **won** Paris Open (d. Carlsson/Loit 3–6 6–3 6–4), (with Rubin) **won** Stanford (d. Black/Frazier 6–4 6–4). **CAREER HIGHLIGHTS – SINGLES: Australian Open – qf 1998** (d. Leon Garcia 6–3 6–2, Kandarr 6–7 6–0 6–1, Gersi 6–4 6–2, Tanasugarn 3–6 6–1 6–2, lost Martinez 6–3 6–2); **US Open – qf 1997** (d. Sanchez Lorenzo 6–3 6–3, Majoli 6–4 2–6 6–1, Wagner 6–1 6–3, Habsudova 6–3 4–6 7–6, lost V. Williams 7–5 7–5). **CAREER HIGHLIGHTS – DOUBLES:** (with Rubin) **US Open – r/u 1999** (lost S./V. Williams 4–6 6–1 6–4).

DOMINIQUE VAN ROOST (BEL)

Born Verviers, 3 May 1973; lives Leuven; RH; 5ft 7in; 122lb; turned pro 1991; career singles titles 4; final 2000 WTA ranking 24; 2000 prize money $351,854; career prize money $2,013,032.

Coached by Alfonso Gonzalez. Husband Bart Van Roost (married 1995); maiden name Monami. **1989:** (695). **1990:** (272) Won 5 consec. Futures titles on the European circuit. **1991:** (129) A –, F –, W –, US 1. Upset Golarsa at Linz and made her Fed Cup debut. **1992:** (101) A 4, F 1, W 1, US 2. Surprised Sukova at Australian Open, where she was unseeded, and reached qf Linz and Bayonne. **1993:** (59) A 2, F 1, W 1, US 2. In singles she reached her 1st tour f at Montpellier and appeared in qf Palermo and Sapporo (d. Wang). From 3 doubles f she won Kitzbuhel with Li. **1994:** (133) A 1, F 1, W 3, US 1. In a quieter year she reached only qf Taipei and took a set off Novotna at Wimbledon. **1995:** (43) A –, F 2, W 2, US 2. Returned to the top 100 with r/u showing at Quebec City, where she upset Gorrochategui and Coetzer, and won both singles and doubles at Southampton Futures. **1996:** (46) A 1, F 1, W 3, US 1. Won her 1st singles title on the main tour at Cardiff and reached qf Rosmalen (d. Appelmans). On the Futures circuit, she won Limoges. **1997:** (18) A qf, F 3, W 1, US 1. Her best year yet saw her breaking into top 20 by end of year. She began it in style with an upset of Wild on her way to the title at Hobart, where she was r/u doubles with Rittner, and finished it with a flourish at Pattaya, where she was r/u both singles and doubles (with Labat). Unseeded at Australian Open, she upset

Sanchez-Vicario and Rubin, before being forced to retire qf with an abdominal injury. She added the title at Surabaya, r/u Quebec City (d. Raymond), sf Moscow (d. Huber and Spirlea) and reached qf Cardiff, Birmingham, Rosmalen and Atlanta (d. Dragomir). **1998:** (12) A 3, F 3, W 4, US 3. Improving still further, in Oct. she became the 1st Belgian to break into the top 10, although by end of year she had slipped just outside again. She began in Jan. with the title at Auckland, following the next week with r/u Hobart. By end May she had also reached the same stage Paris Open (d. Majoli and Tauziat), Linz and Madrid (where she won the doubles with Labat), but could not add further to her tally of singles titles. She upset V. Williams and Hingis back-to-back *en route* to sf Filderstadt, removed Majoli on her way to the same stage Leipzig and played qf Birmingham, Zurich and Quebec City. She qualified for her 1st Chase Champs, where she upset Martinez but fell qf to Spirlea. **1999:** (14) A qf, F 1, W 4, US 3. Despite being hampered by minor injuries, she maintained her top 20 ranking with r/u Auckland (d. Schett) and Luxembourg, sf Paris Open and Moscow (d. Halard-Decugis), and qf Australian Open, Sydney, Rome (d. Tauziat), 's-Hertogenbosch, San Diego and Zurich. At Chase Champs she d. Likhovtseva but lost to Tauziat. **2000:** A 2, F 2, W 1, US 2. She was r/u Eastbourne and Knokke-Heist and appeared in qf Olympics, Sydney and Filderstadt. Notable upsets included Davenport 1r French Open and at Eastbourne, and Coetzer at Sydney and Indian Wells. In doubles with Callens she won Los Angeles, took an Olympic bronze medal and upset Halard-Decugis/Sugiyama at Chase Champs. However, she was not enjoying her tennis as much as she had and decided to retire at season's end. **2000 HIGHLIGHTS – SINGLES: Australian Open 2r** (d. Clijsters 3–6 6–1 6–1, lost Capriati 6–1 4–6 8–6), **French Open 2r** (d. Davenport [seed 2] 6–7 6–4 6–3, lost Marrero 0–6 7–5 7–5), **Wimbledon 1r** [seed 16] (lost Capriati 6–2 6–4), **US Open 2r** [seed 14] (d. Bachmann 6–3 6–3, lost Osterloh 7–6 4–6 ret), **Olympics qf** [seed 8] (d. Gersi 6–1 6–1, Myskina 6–2 6–3, Farina-Elia 6–1 7–5, lost Seles [seed 3] 6–0 6–2); **r/u** Eastbourne (d. Pisnik 6–4 7–6, Likhovtseva 6–2 6–4, Davenport 4–6 6–3 6–4, Kremer 4–6 7–5 6–1, lost Halard-Decugis 7–6 6–4), **r/u** Knokke-Heist (d. Babel 6–3 6–1, Medina Garrigues 6–1 6–4, Randriantefy 6–1 6–2, Serna 6–3 6–0, lost Smashnova 6–2 7–5). **2000 HIGHLIGHTS – DOUBLES:** (with Callens) **Olympics bronze medal** (d. Barabanschikova/Zvereva 4–6 6–4 6–1); (with Callens) **won** Los Angeles (d. Po/Sidot 6–2 7–5). **CAREER HIGHLIGHTS – SINGLES: Australian Open – qf 1997** (d. Fulco-Villella 6–0 6–3, Yoshida 4–6 7–5 6–3, Sanchez-Vicario 1–6 6–4 8–6, Rubin 7–5 6–4, lost M. J. Fernandez 7–5 4–0 ret), **qf 1999** (d. Petrova 6–3 6–4, Noorlander 7–6 6–0, Nejedly 6–1 6–1, Sanchez-Lorenzo 6–2 6–3, lost Mauresmo 6–3 7–6)**.**

CHRISTINA WHEELER (AUS)
Born Ukraine, 15 April 1982; lives Melbourne; RH; 2HB; 5ft 3in; 112lb; career singles titles 0; final 2000 WTA ranking 333, junior ranking 3 doubles; 2000 prize money $11,489.
Coached by Craig Morris. **2000:** In Jun doubles with Kapros she won Australian Open and was r/u US Open. In the women's game she won Swansea on the $10,000 ITF circuit. **2000 HIGHLIGHTS – SINGLES: won** Swansea ITF (d. Zaric 6–4 7–6).

FABIOLA ZULUAGA (COL)
Born Cucuta, 7 January 1979; lives Bogota; RH; 2HB; 5ft 8in; 142lb; turned pro 1994; career singles titles 2; final 2000 WTA ranking 42; 2000 prize money $137,549.
Coached by Jorge Todero. Trained at Bollettieri Academy from age 13 and currently trains in Madrid when in Europe. **1994:** (398) Joined COL Fed cup squad. **1995:** (292) Won her 1st pro title at Cali Futures. **1996:** (124) Won Bogota and Bytom on the satellite circuit. **1997:** (208) Won Bogota ITF. **1998:** (95) Reached her 1st qf on the main tour at Bogota, and on the ITF circuit won Ortebello. **1999:** (48) A –, F 3, W 1, US 2. Won her 1st main-tour title at her 1st tourn of the year at Bogota in Feb. and continued her success in South America by taking Sao Paulo in Oct. She also reached qf Amelia Island (d. Raymond) and upset Majoli at LIPC. **2000:** A 2, F 3, W –, US –. At Rome she upset Talaja, Halard-Decugis and Tauziat on the way to her 1st Tier I sf, after qualifying, and followed with r/u Madrid (unseeded, d. Sugiyama). She also reached qf Quebec City and upset Capriati 1r French Open. She missed Wimbledon with a viral illness and withdrew US Open with right shoulder tendinitis, although she was able to play Olympics, where she upset Mauresmo. **2000 HIGHLIGHTS – SINGLES: Australian Open 2r** (d. Dechy 6–1 3–6 6–1, lost Halard-Decugis [seed 9] 6–3 6–3), **French Open 3r** (d. Capriati [seed 15] 6–3 7–5, Mandula 6–1 6–0, lost Zvereva 4–6 6–2 1–0 ret), **Olympics 3r** (d. Mauresmo 6–3 3–6 6–2, Callens 6–3 6–2, lost Sanchez-Vicario [seed 5] 6–2 6–0); **r/u** Madrid (d. Serna 4–6 6–4 6–3, Sugiyama 6–2 6–4, Carlsson 6–2 6–4, Majoli 6–3 6–4, lost Leon Garcia 4–6 6–2 6–2); **sf** Rome (d. Talaja 6–2 6–3, Martincova 6–0 6–7 6–3, Halard-Decugis 6–3 4–6 6–2, Tauziat 3–6 6–0 6–4, lost Mauresmo 6–1 6–2).

All-Time Greats

David Gray and John Barrett

DAPHNE JESSIE **AKHURST** (Australia)
Born 22/4/03. Died 10/1/33. Became Mrs.R.S.Cozens (1930). The first of Australia's great women champions, she won five Australian singles titles (**1925/26/28/29/30**), five doubles titles with three different partners – S.Lance (**1924**), R.Harper (nee Lance) (**1925**), Esna Boyd (**1928**) and L.M. Bickerton (**1929/31**), plus four mixed with three partners – J.Willard (**1924/25**), Jean Borotra (**1928**) and E.F. Moon (**1929**). She first travelled to Europe in **1925** and got to the quarter-finals at Wimbledon. Three years later she returned and reached the semi-finals after being a quarter-finalist at Paris, results which earned her an unofficial world ranking of No.3 that year. JB

WILMER LAWSON **ALLISON** (USA)
Born 8/12/04. Died 20/4/77. One of the greatest and most spectacular of American doubles specialists, he also gained some notable singles successes. Possessing a fierce smash, a serve with the 'kick of a Texas mustang', considerable power on the volley, and a fine backhand drive, he found an ideal doubles partner in John Van Ryn. They won at Wimbledon in **1929–30** and were runners-up in **1935**. They took the US title in **1931** and **1935** and reached the final in **1930/32/34/36**. His singles form was less consistent, but on his day could play brilliantly. He defeated Perry and Hood to win the US title in **1935**, and in **1930**, after beating Cochet, he was runner-up to Tilden at Wimbledon. Between **1929–35** he played in 45 D Cup rubbers, winning 18 out of 29 singles and 14 of his 16 doubles.

MALCOLM ('**MAL**') JAMES **ANDERSON** (Australia)
Born 5/3/35. A rangy right-handed serve-and-volley specialist from Queensland who excelled on grass, he caused a sensation by beating fellow Aussie and top seed, Ashley Cooper, to win the **1957** US Championships, unseeded. Copper had his revenge in the following year's final, but only by 8–6 in the fifth set. Twice a finalist at the Australian Championships (**1958**, **1972**) he won the mixed doubles there in **1957** (with Fay Muller) and the same year won the French doubles (with Cooper). Turning pro in **1959** he had to wait fourteen years before annexing another Grand Slam title, the Australian doubles of **1973** (with Newcombe). In his four years of Davis Cup tennis between **1957** and **1973** he won 20 of his 27 singles rubbers and eight of his nine doubles rubbers in 15 ties. JB

JOSEPH ASBOTH (Hungary)
Born 18/9/17. A stylish right-hander whose victory in the **1947** French singles, when he beat Petra, Tom Brown and Sturgess, was Hungary's most important tennis success before their victory in the Saab King's Cup in 1976; 7 times nat champ; 6 times winner of the Hungarian int title; he played 1st at Wimbledon in **1939** and impressed those who saw him against Austin in 1r. Lost to Bromwich in the **1948** sfs. From **1938–57** he played 41 D Cup rubbers in 16 ties, winning 18 of his 30 singles and 6 of 11 doubles.

ARTHUR ROBERT **ASHE** (USA)
Born 10/7/43. Died 13/2/93. A cool, thoughtful, dogged competitor, he was the first black American to win the Wimbledon men's singles title and, in **1968**, playing as an amateur, he became the first US Open champion. Always happier on fast courts, he tried hard to succeed on clay but endured regular disappointments in Paris and never progressed further than the semi-finals (**1971**) in Rome. He was a semi-finalist at Wimbledon **1968–69** before surprising Connors in the **1975** final. He defeated Okker to win the US title in **1968** but in **1972** lost to Nastase after leading by two sets to one and 4–2 in the final. He won Australian singles **1970** and the WCT title **1975**. Refused a visa to South Africa in **1970**, he broke through apartheid laws to play in Johannesburg **1973**, losing to Connors in the final and winning the doubles with Okker. After missing most of the **1977** season, he regained his place among the leaders of the circuit in **1978** and reached match-point against McEnroe in the Masters final. Between **1963–78**, he appeared in 18 D Cup ties, winning 27 out of 32 singles and one of two doubles. US D Cup captain **1980–85**, following his retirement from active play owing to a heart condition that had necessitated triple by-pass surgery. Started Arthur Ashe Foundation for the defeat of Aids, the sickness that claimed his life following a transfusion of contaminated blood during his heart operations.

CILLY AUSSEM (Germany)
Born 4/1/09. Died 22/3/63. Later the Contessa della Corta Brae (1936). The first German to win the women's singles at Wimbledon. Her strokes were not strong but she was a model of steadiness and persistence. 'Quite small and more of a girl in appearance with round brown eyes and a cherub face', wrote Helen Wills. 'Her agility on court and the distance that she covers in spite of her shortness are really astonishing.' **1931** – when the Californian did not compete – was her best year. She beat Betty Nuthall in the French f and then defeated Hilde

Krahwinkel in Wimbledon's only all-German final. That was a disappointing match, because both women were handicapped by blistered feet. Her victory compensated for an unlucky failure in **1930**. Then she slipped and sprained an ankle at 4–4 in the fs of her sf against Elizabeth Ryan and had to be carried from the court.

HENRY WILFRED ('**BUNNY**') **AUSTIN** (Great Britain)
Born 26/8/06. Died 26/8/2000. Bunny Austin's Wimbledon record was remarkable (and unlucky), but his most important contribution to British tennis was in the D Cup. The possessor of elegant groundstrokes, which compensated for a lack of power in his serving and smashing, he played many of the crucial singles, alongside Perry, in Britain's successful campaigns in the **1930s**. A former Cambridge Univ captain, he played in 24 ties between **1929–37**, winning 36 of his 48 rubbers, all singles. He won 8 rubbers out of 12 and 5 out of 8 'live' rubbers in his 6 Challenge Rounds. At Wimbledon he failed only once to reach the qf or go further between **1929–39**. R/u to Vines **1932** and Budge **1938**, in sf **1929** and **1936/37**, and r/u to Henkel in **1937** French singles.

TRACY ANN **AUSTIN** (USA)
Born 12/12/62. Now Mrs. Scott Holt (married on 17th April 1993). An infant prodigy with 25 national age group titles to her name from the 12s to 18s, her meteoric rise under the coaching of Robert Lansdorp inspired a whole generation of teenage wonders. The youngest member of a keen tennis playing family, whose sister Pam and three brothers, Jeff, John and Doug were all tournament players, Tracy defeated Chris Evert for the US Open title in **1979** to become, at 16 years 9 months, the youngest ever champion there. The following year her relentless baseline driving, single-handed on the forehand, two-handed on the backhand, plus her excellent court coverage, earned her the No.1 ranking on the WTA computer, ending the four year reign of Evert and Martina Navratilova. In **1981** she won a second US Open title at the expense of Navratilova and, with 29 titles to her name, seemed destined to rule the game. But a series of back and neck injuries curtailed her appearances in **1983** and she retired from the game in February **1984**, the victim of physical burnout. She returned to the Tour in doubles during **1988** and had just started to play singles again in **1989** when she broke a leg in a motor accident, an injury that required surgery. This delayed her return until **1993** when she competed in a few tournaments and played Team Tennis for Raleigh Edge. JB

WILFRED BADDELEY (Great Britain)
Born 11/1/1872. Died 24/1/1929. Youngest winner – at 19 years, 5 months and 23 days – of Wimbledon singles in **1891** until Becker in **1985**. Also won singles in **1892/95**, and doubles (with twin brother Herbert) **1891/94/95/96**.

BORIS FRANZ **BECKER** (Germany)
Born 22/11/67. Born in Leimen, South Germany, just a few kilometres from Steffi Graf, his rise through the ranks of German men's tennis mirrored Steffi's rise in the women's game. Together they became national heroes and raised the profile of tennis in Germany to unprecedented heights. Exploding onto the men's scene while still a teenager (and already three times the national junior champion), Boris had the first of his 49 career tournament wins at Queens Club in **1985** thanks to a devastating display of serving that earned him the nickname 'Boom-Boom'. Three weeks later at Wimbledon, aged just 17 years and 7 months, he served more of his thunderbolts and threw himself headlong making spectacular diving volleys to become the youngest-ever men's champion there, the first unseeded winner and the first from Germany. It was the start of a brilliant career, masterminded by his agent Ion Tiriac, that saw him reach five more Wimbledon finals in the next six years two of which he would win – in **1986** against Ivan Lendl and in **1989** against his great Swedish rival, Stefan Edberg. That same year he beat Lendl to win his only US Open and two years later (**1991**) he beat Lendl again to win the first of his two Australian Opens. The second of those came in **1996**, when Michael Chang was his victim, and Boris dedicated the win to his wife Barbara Feltus who he had married two years earlier. His Davis Cup record – 38 singles wins from 41 matches and 15 doubles wins from 24 matches, from 27 ties in 11 years – contributed to Germany's two Cup wins in **1988** and **1989**, both against Sweden. Despite never concentrating on doubles he did win an Olympic Gold medal in doubles (with Michael Stich) at Barcelona in **1992**. JB

MARCEL BERNARD (France)
Born 18/5/14. Died 28/4/94. Shrewd and stylish, a canny left-hander with considerable touch, he is one of only two French players to have won in Paris since the days of the 'Musketeers' (the other is Noah, **1983**); demonstrated his promise early, reaching the French singles sf and, with Boussus, the doubles in **1932**, still in sufficient form to be chosen for the French D Cup team in **1956**. In **1946** he won 5 set matches against Petra in the sf and Drobny in the final to take the French title; in sf on 3 other occasions; won the doubles with Borotra (**1936**) and with Petra (**1946**) and the mixed with Lollette Payot (**1935**) and Billie Yorke (**1936**). Between **1935–56** he played 42 D Cup rubbers in 25 ties (singles 13–8, doubles 16–5) and he also served as President of the French Tennis Federation.

PAULINE MAY **BETZ** (USA)
Born 6/8/19. Now Mrs Addie (1949). An agile, athletic competitor, who might have gained many more titles if the war had not interrupted international competition. She was ranked eighth in the US in **1939** and was the most successful player in wartime competitions there, winning the national title from **1942–44**. She won Wimbledon at a cost of only 20 games in **1946**, defeating Louise Brough 6–2 6–4 in the final. She and Miss

Hart were runners-up to Miss Brough and Miss Osborne in the doubles and, if she was disappointed in Paris, where Miss Osborne beat her 1–6 8–6 7–5 in the final, after saving two match-points with drop-shots at 5–6 in the second set, she asserted her supremacy again at Forest Hills by defeating Doris Hart 11–9 6–3 in the final. Soon afterwards she turned professional.

BLANCHE BINGLEY (Great Britain)

Born 3/11/1863. Died 6/8/1946. Became Mrs Hillyard (1887). One of the determined pioneers of women's tennis. She competed in the first women's tournament at Wimbledon in **1884** and lost to Maud Watson, the eventual champion, in sfs. The following year Miss Watson defeated her in f, but she avenged those failures by beating the champion in the Challenge Round in **1886**. That was the first of her six victories. Further successes followed in **1889/94/97/99** and **1900**. Only Lottie Dod, who retired in **1893**, troubled her until Mrs Sterry ended her supremacy in **1901**. Like many early players, her game was founded on a powerful forehand and strict command of length. A reluctant volleyer who invariably ran round her backhand, she was so quick and so fit that she was difficult to outmanoeuvre. She wore white gloves to give her a better grip and her follow-through on the forehand was said to have been 'so complete that her left shoulder was often a mass of bruises from the impact of the racket'. She married Commander G. W. Hillyard, secretary of the All England Club from **1907–24**; altogether she competed in the Championships 24 times.

ANNA MARGRETHE ('**MOLLA**') **BJURSTEDT** (USA)

Born 6/3/1884; died 22/11/59. Became Mrs.F.I. Mallory in 1919. Born in Oslo, the daughter of an army officer, she spent her youth in Norway and became the national champion at an early age, winning Olympic bronze at the Stockholm Games of **1912** with her forceful baseline game. In **1915**, at the age of 31, she emigrated to the United States and that year, unheralded, won the first of her record eight US National singles titles. Retaining her title for the next three years (**1916,'17,'18**) she married Franklin Mallory on 3rd September 1919 and immediately resumed her winning course in **1920**, retaining the title in **1921** and **1922**. Her opponent in the final round that year was 16-year-old Helen Wills who beat Mallory, as she now was, in the next two finals. Mallory's last win, a thrilling 4–6 6–4 9–7 success against Elizabeth Ryan, came in **1926** when she was 42. Perhaps her greatest moment had come in a first round match in **1921** when, having taken the opening set from Suzanne Lenglen, the Frenchwoman retired saying she felt ill. This was Lenglen's only appearance in the US Championships and she revenged herself at Wimbledon the following year by beating Mallory 6–2 6–0 in the final. Mallory reached the Wimbledon semi-final on two other occasions and played on five US Wightman Cup teams between **1923** and **1928**.

PENELOPE **DORA** HARVEY **BOOTHBY** (Great Britain)

Born 2/8/1881. Died 22/2/1970. Became Mrs Geen (1914). One of the group of players from the county of Middlesex who dominated the early years of women's tennis at Wimbledon. In **1909** she won one of the most exciting of the pre-**1914** f, defeating Miss A. M. Morton 6–4 4–6 8–6 'Few closer or more interesting struggles have ever been witnessed on the famous old court', wrote G. W. Hillyard. She lost the most dismal contest in the history of the Championships to Mrs Lambert Chambers, who beat her 6–0 6–0, in the **1911** Challenge Round. Mrs Lambert Chambers had beaten her by the same score at the Beckenham tournament two weeks earlier and had allowed her only four games in the Challenge Round in **1910**. Somewhat fortunately she and Mrs McNair became Wimbledon's first women's doubles champions in **1913**. They were down 4–6 2–4 to Mrs Lambert Chambers and Mrs Sterry in the final when Mrs Sterry fell and retired with a torn tendon. She and Mrs McNair were also semi-finalists in **1922**.

BJORN RUNE BORG (Sweden)

Born 6/6/56. One of the coolest match players the game has ever known, he matured early, winning his first important title, the **1974** Italian Open, shortly before his 18th birthday and the first of his six French Championships just after it. With fierce topspin on both his forehand and his double-handed backhand, a powerful serve and speedy court coverage plus an indomitable will to win, he was virtually invincible on European clay between **1974–81** adding the French Open in **1975/78/79/80/81** and a second Italian title in **1978** as well as the US Pro Champion-ship on US clay in **1974/75/76**. Never an instinctive volleyer, he confounded those observers who thought his game was unsuited to grass by setting a modern record at Wimbledon where he won five successive titles between **1976–80**. Only William Renshaw, in the days of the Challenge Round, won more (**1881–86**). He learned to win indoors, taking the WCT title in **1976** and the Masters twice (**1979/80**) and leading Sweden to their first D Cup success, a 3–2 victory over Czechoslovakia in Stockholm in **1975**. But he never solved the problems of the high, fast bounce and positive foothold of US hard courts. Four times he was beaten in the US Open final, twice by Connors (**1976/78**) and twice by McEnroe (**1980/81**), the last three being on asphalt at Flushing Meadows. By the autumn of **1981** he felt burnt out and virtually retired from the mainstream, playing only exhibitions and special events. Although he attempted two comebacks, in **1982/84** (coincidentally, he lost both times to Henri Leconte, in Monte Carlo and Stuttgart), he could no longer make the total commitment and turned to other interests. Seven years later he again attempted a return but fell in his first match to Jordi Arrese in Monte Carlo and competed no more in **1991**. His legacy to Swedish tennis is immeasurable for he sparked the flame that has burned so brightly ever since through Wilander, Sundstrom, Jarryd, Nystrom and Edberg. His style of errorless, counter-attacking topspin inspired a whole generation of players around the world. JB

JEAN ROBERT **BOROTRA** (France)

Born 13/8/1898. Died 17/7/94. A brilliantly agile volleyer and a shrewd player. One of the 'Four Musketeers' who won the D Cup for France from **1927–32**. Enthusiastic and popular, he continued to play competitive lawn tennis long past his 90th year. He represented France in every International Club match against Britain from the first in **1929** to his 116th and last in **1993**. Won Wimbledon singles **1924/26** and doubles (with R. Lacoste) **1925** and (with J. Brugnon) **1932/33**. French singles **1924/31**, and the doubles 6 times – (with Lacoste) **1924/25/29**, (with Brugnon) **1928/34**, (with Bernard) **1936**. Won Australian singles and doubles (with Brugnon) **1928**. Had long and spectacular covered court record, winning French singles title 12 times, British 11, and US 4. Played 54 D Cup rubbers **1922–47**, winning 19 of 31 singles and 17 of 23 doubles rubbers in 32 ties.

JOHN EDWARD **BROMWICH** (Australia)

Born 14/11/18. Died 21/10/99. A gracefully unorthodox player whose career might have been even more successful if it had not been interrupted by World War II. Ambidextrous but using both hands on the forehand, he used a very light, softly strung racket to control the ball with great subtlety. He won the Australian singles in **1939** and regained the title from Quist in **1946**. Those were his only major singles victories, although he won 18 State titles and was agonisingly close to success in f of **1948** Wimbledon when he lost to Falkenburg after leading 5–2 in the fs and holding three match-points. But it was in doubles, mostly with Quist or Sedgman, that he earned most honours. He won at Wimbledon in **1948** (with Sedgman) **1950** (with Quist), took the US title three times, and he and Quist ruled in Australia from **1938–40** and **1946–50**. Won the Wimbledon mixed with Louise Brough, **1947/48**, and played in 51 D Cup rubbers between **1937–50**, winning 19 of his 30 singles and 20 of his 21 doubles in 23 ties.

NORMAN EVERARD **BROOKES** (Australia)

Born 14/11/1877. Died 28/9/1968. The first overseas winner of men's singles at Wimbledon. Left-handed and a notable volleyer, he lost to H. L. Doherty in Challenge Round on first visit to Wimbledon **1905**. Won singles and doubles (with A. F. Wilding) **1907** and **1914** and Australian singles in **1911** and doubles in **1924** with J. O. Anderson. With Wilding won the D Cup for Australasia in **1907**. Between **1905–20** he played 39 rubbers and was 6 times a member of a side which won the Challenge Round. Returned to Wimbledon in **1924** at 46 and reached the 4r. Nicknamed 'The Wizard' he received the French Legion of Honour for his services as a captain in the British Army in World War One, and in **1939** he was knighted.

ALTHEA **LOUISE BROUGH** (USA)

Born 11/3/23. Now Mrs Clapp (1958). An aggressive server and volleyer, she played a major part in establishing American domination of women's tennis immediately after World War II. Won Wimbledon singles **1948/49/50** and again in **1955** after the retirement of Maureen Connolly (who beat her in **1952** and **1954** f), She also won US in **1947**, and Australian, **1950**. She and Margaret Osborne du Pont formed a redoubtable doubles partnership, winning 5 times at Wimbledon (**1946/48/49/50/54**) and 3 times in Paris, (**1946/47/49**) and holding the US title 12 times from **1942–50** and **1955–57**. She was mixed doubles champ at Wimbledon with Tom Brown (**1946**), Bromwich (**1947/48**) and Sturgess (**1950**) and took all 3 titles in **1948** and **1950**. She played 22 W Cup rubbers between **1946–57** and was never beaten.

JACQUES ('**TOTO**') **BRUGNON** (France)

Born 11/5/1895. Died 20/3/1978. The doubles specialist of the 'Four Musketeers', he gained most of his early success with Cochet and then formed a partnership with Borotra, which was still capable of reaching the **1939** French f, when he was 44 and Borotra 40, and coming three times within a point of the title. He and Borotra returned to Wimbledon and reached the 3r in **1948**. Won Wimbledon doubles with Cochet (**1926/28**) and Borotra (**1932/33**). Between **1927–34** won French doubles 3 times with Cochet (**1927/30/32**) and twice with Borotra (**1928/34**). Also Australian doubles with Borotra (**1928**). Reached singles sf at Wimbledon, **1926**. Played 31 D Cup doubles (winning 22) and 6 singles (winning 4) in 31 ties **1921–34**.

JOHN DONALD ('**DON**') **BUDGE** (USA)

Born 13/6/15. Died 28/1/2000. The first player to bring off the Grand Slam of the 4 historic singles titles in one year – **1938** – after which he immediately turned professional. A relentless competitor with a majestic backhand he won all 3 titles at Wimbledon in **1937** and **1938**, the doubles with G. Mako and mixed with Alice Marble. Won US singles **1937/38** and doubles with Mako **1936/38**. plus French and Australian singles **1938** and won 19 out of 21 singles and 6 out of 8 doubles rubbers in 11 D Cup ties from **1935** to **1938**.

MARIA ESTHER ANDION **BUENO** (Brazil)

Born 11/10/39. The most gracefully artistic of post-war women's champions. For nearly a decade her rivalry with Margaret Court provided the principal excitement of the women's game, but at the end she was plagued by injury. Won Wimbledon singles **1959/60/64**, and doubles (with Althea Gibson) **1958**, (with Darlene Hard) **1960/63**, (with Billie Jean King) **1965**, and (with Nancy Gunter) **1966**. US singles **1959/63/64/66** and doubles (with Darlene Hard) **1960/62**, (with Nancy Gunter) **1966**, and (with Margaret Court) **1968**. French doubles (with Darlene Hard) **1960**. Australian doubles (with Christine Truman) **1960**. Italian singles, **1958/61/65**.

DOROTHEA KATHERINE **CHAMBERS** (Great Britain)
Born 3/9/1878. Died 7/1/1960. Nee Douglass. Married Robert Lambert Chambers in 1907. The most successful British woman player before 1914, she won Wimbledon singles 7 times and lost dramatically to Suzanne Lenglen in 1919 Challenge Round after holding 2 match-points. Played in 1926 W Cup – 23 years after first success at Wimbledon. The daughter of an Ealing vicar, she became a coach in 1928. Won Wimbledon singles **1903/04/06/10/11/13/14**, the first mother to do so, and reached f of ladies' doubles in **1913**, its first year.

HENRI JEAN **COCHET** (France)
Born 14/12/01. Died 1/4/87. The great instinctive genius of lawn tennis, swift and imagin-ative, a master of the volley and half-volley, whose play could rise to dizzy heights and sometimes slip to unexpected disaster. Won Wimbledon singles **1927/29** and doubles (with J. Brugnon) **1926/28**. US singles **1928**. French singles **1922/26/28/30/32** and doubles (with Brugnon) **1927/30/32**. With the other 'Musketeers', he played successfully in 6 Challenge Rounds. Between **1922** and **1933**, when he turned professional, he won 34 of 42 D Cup singles rubbers and 10 out of 16 doubles from 26 ties. After the war reinstated as an amateur.

MAUREEN ('LITTLE MO') CATHERINE **CONNOLLY** (USA)
Born 17/9/34. Died 21/6/69. Became Mrs. Norman Brinker (1955). The most determined and concentrated of post-war women's champions she hit her groundstrokes with remorseless accuracy. Won US singles in **1951** at the age of 16 and thereafter lost only 4 matches – 2 to Doris Hart, one to Shirley Fry, and another to Beverley Fleitz – before she broke her leg in a riding accident in **1954** and retired. She was never beaten in singles at Wimbledon, winning **1952/53/54**. She won US singles **1951/52/53** French singles **1953/54** and (with Mrs H. C. Hopman) doubles **1954**. Australian singles and doubles (with Julie Sampson) **1953** Italian singles **1954**. She won all 9 of her W Cup rubbers and in **1953** she was the first woman to bring off the Grand Slam of the 4 major singles titles in the same year.

JAMES ('**JIMMY**') SCOTT **CONNORS** (USA)
Born 2/9/52. One of the most durable of champions and a natural entertainer, he grew up in Bellville, Illinois where his mother Gloria, herself a fine player, and his grandmother, instilled the never-say-die attitude that was to make him one of the most competitive players of all time. Moving to California as a teenager, he was guided by the two Pancho's – Gonzales and Segura – and in **1971** won the NCAA Championships as a freshman at UCLA. A year later in Jacksonville, shrewdly guided by his manager Bill Riordan, he won his first professional title. Seventeen years later, in Tel Aviv, he won his last. It was his 109th tournament success – a record for men. Altogether he had spent 268 weeks as the world's No.1 ranked player (second only to Lendl's 270). His 160 consecutive weeks at the top from 29/7/74 to 23/8/77 was a world record. An aggressive left-hander with a lethal double-handed backhand, he was a natural 'street fighter', whose early vulgarity (which diminished with age), was ignored by his fans and forgiven by those who recognised his extraordinary ability as a fearless match player. The first Grand Slam title he won was the **1973** Wimbledon doubles, with Ilie Nastase, who also partnered him to victory in the **1975** US Open doubles. His service returns and passing shots were among the greatest ever seen and brought him one Australian (**1974**), two Wimbledon (**1974,1982**) and five US Open (**1974,1976,1978,1982,1983**) singles titles. He is the only man to have won the US title on all three surfaces – grass, clay and hard courts. His failure to win a major international title on clay was the only blemish on an otherwise brilliant career. JB

ASHLEY JOHN **COOPER** (Australia)
Born 15/9/36. A strong and determined competitor who maintained Australia's command of the international game after Hoad and Rosewall turned professional. After being overwhelmed by Hoad in the **1957** f at Wimbledon, he returned to beat Fraser in a stern test of endurance in **1958**. He was US champion **1958** and won Australian **1957–58**. His doubles victories included Australia **1958**, France **1957–58** and US **1957**. He played singles when Australia successfully defended the D Cup in **1957** and in **1958** when Australia lost to the USA in Brisbane, winning one rubber in each match. He beat Seixas and lost to Mackay **1957** and beat Mackay and lost to Olmedo **1958**.

CHARLOTTE REINAGLE **COOPER** (Great Britain)
Born 22/9/1870. Died 10/10/1966. Became Mrs Sterry (1901). One of the first successful women volleyers, she won at Wimbledon **1895/96/98/1901/08**. Overshadowed at first by Mrs Hillyard – her first three victories were gained in years when the older player did not compete – she defeated her at last in **1901**, the year of her marriage, after losing to Mrs Hillyard in four previous matches at the Championships. In **1902** she lost in the famous re-played Challenge Round to Muriel Robb (they stopped at 4–6 13–11 on the first evening, then began again and Miss Robb won 7–5 6–1) and then regained the title in **1908** after beating Mrs Lambert Chambers in the quarter-finals. She reached the All-Comers' final in **1912** and took Mrs McNair to 9–7 in the third set of a qf in **1913**. Her attacking spirit delighted her contemporaries. 'Her smiling good temper and sportsmanship made her as popular a player as ever went on to the Centre Court', wrote Burrow. 'She had a constitution like the proverbial ostrich. She never knew what it was to be tired and was never sick or sorry', said Hillyard.

JAMES ('**JIM**') **COURIER** (USA)

Born 17/08/70. A ruggedly competitive performer who first came to prominence internationally as the **1989** Italian doubles champion with Pete Sampras. His two French Open victories over Andre Agassi (**1991**) and Petr Korda (**1992**) were earned on the qualities of supreme fitness and relentless aggression that set the fashion among young players everywhere. His legendary work rate surprised even his two coaches, Jose Higueras and Brad Stine, who had encouraged him to reduce his error percentage without losing the ability to hit the blazing forehand winners that made him famous. It was a tightrope he trod with great success during a golden spell that earned him back-to-back Australian titles (**1992, 1993**) and took him to the final of the US Open in **1991**, the French Open again in **1993**, and Wimbledon the same year. Following his first Australian victory he rose to No.1 in the world rankings in February 1992, a position he occupied for 55 weeks altogether. His seven year Davis Cup record for the United States was a distinguished one with 17 wins and 10 losses in 14 ties (16–10 singles, 1–0 doubles). Furthermore, his two five-set wins in the fifth and deciding rubbers of the ties against Russia (**1998**) and Great Britain (**1999**) are unique among American Davis Cup players. JB

THELMA DOROTHY **COYNE** (Australia)

Born 14/10/18. Became Mrs.M.N. Long (30/1/41). A great all-rounder whose career coincided with that of Nancy Bolton who became a great friend and rival. She first reached the Australian final in **1940** where Bolton beat her, as she did again in **1951**. The following year (**1952**) she won the first of two Australian titles (the other was in **1954**). Ten of her twelve Australian doubles titles were won with Bolton (**1936/37/38/ 39/40/47/48/49/51/52**) and the other two with Mary Hawton (**1956/58**). Her four mixed titles were won with George Worthington (**1951/52/55**) and Rex Hartwig (**1954**). Her lone success outside Australia came in **1956** when she combined with Chile's Luis Ayala to win the French mixed title. JB

JOHN ('**JACK**') HERBERT **CRAWFORD** (Australia)

Born 22/3/08. Died 10/9/91. Classic stylist, he beat H. E. Vines in **1933** in one of the greatest of all Wimbledon f. Won Wimbledon doubles (with A. K. Quist) **1935**. French singles **1933** and doubles (with Quist) **1935**,   Australian singles **1931, '32, '33, '35** and doubles (with H. C. Hopman) **1929/30**, (with E. F. Moon) **1932**, and (with V. B. McGrath) **1935**. Won 36 out of 58 D Cup rubbers (23–16 singles, 13–5 doubles) between **1928–37**.

DWIGHT FILLEY **DAVIS** (USA)

Born 5/7/1879. Died 28/11/1945. The donor of the D Cup, the trophy at stake in the International Team Championship. A Harvard undergraduate, he played against the British Isles in the first two matches of that competition, winning a single and partnering Holcombe Ward successfully in the doubles in **1900** and, with H. Ward again, losing to the Dohertys in the doubles in **1902**. A left-hander, he won the US doubles with H. Ward from **1899–1901**, retiring undefeated, and also the All-Comers' final at Wimbledon with Ward in **1901**, only to fall to the Dohertys in the Challenge Round. He was President of the US LTA in **1923**, US Secretary of War **1925–29** and later Governor-General of the Philippines.

MAXIME ('**MAX**') OMER **DECUGIS** (France)

Born 24/9/1882. Died 6/9/1978. The first great French player. He spent his schooldays in England and won his first tournaments there. Short, quick, and wiry, he was an aggressive competitor, whom Laurie Doherty described as 'the most promising young player in the world'. He dominated French tennis from **1903**, when he won in Paris for the first time, to the outbreak of World War I, winning the singles **1903/04/07/08/09/12/13/14**, and the doubles from **1902–9**, **1911–14** and again in **1920** when the Champs were resumed. He was still playing well enough to reach the singles final in **1923** when he was 41. By that time the age of the 'Musketeers' was dawning. Although he competed regularly at Wimbledon, he never progressed beyond the singles sf (**1911/12**) but, with Gobert, he gained France's first title by winning the doubles in **1911**.

CHARLOTTE ('**LOTTIE**') **DOD** (Great Britain)

Born 24/9/1871. Died 27/6/1960. The first lawn tennis prodigy. Won the first of 5 Wimbledon titles in **1887** from a field of 5 challengers at the age of 15 years and 10 months. When she retired, she became an international golfer and hockey player. Nicknamed the 'Little Wonder', she won Wimbledon singles **1887/88/91/92/93** in years when there were never more than 9 players in the All-Comers' draw.

HUGH **LAURENCE DOHERTY** (Great Britain)

Born London, 8/10/1875. Died 21/8/1919. Learnt game with elder brother, Reginald Frank ('Reggie'), at Westminster School. Played for Cambridge Univ against Oxford in **1896–98** and developed into one of the most spectacular, aggressive, stylish, and successful of British players. 'Laurie' Doherty was celebrated for smashing and volleying, and for speed about the court. With his brother, formed one of the greatest doubles partnerships in the history of the game. Won All-Comers' singles at Wimbledon, **1898**, and singles champ **1902–06**. Doubles champ (with R. F. Doherty) **1897–1901**, **1903–05**. First overseas player to win US singles, **1903**, and doubles, **1902/03**. In 5 D Cup Challenge Rounds, **1902–06**, he was never beaten, winning 7 singles rubbers and 5 doubles.

REGINALD FRANK **DOHERTY** (Great Britain)
Born London, 14/10/1872. Died 29/12/1910. The senior partner of the great Doherty combination and the most notable stylist of early lawn tennis. Contemporary observers called his backhand, produced with back swing, full follow-through and remarkable touch, 'a model of perfection'. Was Wimbledon singles champ **1897–1900** and doubles champ **1897–1901** and **1903–05**. Reached the doubles Challenge Round at Wimbledon for first time with H. A. Nisbet in **1896**. Thereafter he and his brother, H. L. Doherty, were beaten only by S. H. Smith and F. L. Riseley at Wimbledon. They lost to this pair in **1902**, then beat them in the next three Challenge Rounds before falling to them again in **1906**. The Dohertys won the US doubles in **1902/03**. Won South African singles and doubles **1909**.

JAROSLAV DROBNY (Great Britain)
Born 12/10/21. Exiled himself from Czechoslovakia in **1950**, became Egyptian subject in **1950** and a naturalised Briton in **1960**. One of the great post-war clay court competitors with tremendous left-hand serve and smash, and delicate touch, he played in some of Wimbledon's most dramatic and emotional matches and eventually won the singles in **1954** at the age of 32. In **1946** he beat Kramer, the favourite in 4 r and lost to Geoff Brown (AUS) in sf; he lost to Schroeder in the **1949** f; in **1950** he let a two-set lead slip against Sedgman; Mottram surprised him in **1951**; he fell to Sedgman again in the **1952** f; and in **1953** he never recovered from beating Patty 8–6 16–18 3–6 8–6 12–10 in Wimbledon's second longest singles. The following year, when his chance seemed to be slipping away, he beat Rosewall, then 19, in f. He won in Paris in **1951/52** (after another series of dramatic failures), Italy **1950/51/53** and Germany **1950**. Between **1946–49** he won 37 of his 43 D Cup rubbers in 15 ties, (24–4 singles, 13–2 doubles).

FRANCOISE DURR (France)
Born 25/12/42. Now Mrs Browning (1975). The outstanding French woman player of the 1960s and 1970s. Shrewd and unorthodox, particularly in her serve and on the backhand, she excelled in doubles. She gained her major singles successes in **1967** when she won the French and German titles and reached the US semifinals, but in doubles won a host of titles with a variety of partners, including five successive French victories – with Gail Sheriff (later Mrs Chanfreau and now Mrs Lovera) **1967** and **1970/71**, and with Ann Jones, **1968/69**. Won US doubles **1972** with Betty Stove, and Italian and South African titles **1969** with Jones. She failed, however, in six Wimbledon doubles finals between **1965–75**. Won Wimbledon mixed doubles with Tony Roche **1976** and the French with Jean-Claude Barclay in **1968/71/73**.

STEFAN EDBERG (Sweden)
Born 19/1/66 in Vastervik, Sweden. One of the greatest of modern serve-and-volley players, he broke the Swedish double-handed mould created by Bjorn Borg when his first coach, Percy Rosberg (who had also coached Borg) advised him to change to a single-handed stroke because of his natural volleying ability. It was sound advice. In **1983**, at the end of an outstanding junior career, he won the junior Grand Slam, the only time the feat has been achieved since the four major tournaments became Championship events in **1975**. (Butch Buchholz had won all four in **1958** when they were invitation tournaments). Major honours soon followed. Revelling in the fast conditions of Australian grass he won the last two Opens played at Kooyong in December **1985** and January **1987** (no Championship was held in 1986 to accommodate a return to the traditional January date). A year later (**1988**) he won the first of his two Wimbledon titles, beating his great rival Boris Becker in the final, a success he would repeat in **1990** after losing to the German in the **1989** final. On 13th August **1990** he became the No.1 player in the world, a position he would hold for a total of 66 weeks in three spells until finally displaced by Jim Courier on 5 October **1992**. In **1991** he won the first of two US Opens with a blistering display of attacking tennis against Courier that Edberg himself believed was his best ever performance. His second US win in **1992**, against Pete Sampras, was his last major success in a career that brought him 41 titles altogether from the 77 singles finals he contested and 18 doubles titles from 29 finals. His three Grand Slam doubles success came ten years apart – the first two (with Jarryd) were in **1987** at the Australian and US Opens, the last (with Korda) at the **1996** Australian Open in his farewell year. His only major disappointment was the loss to Chang in the French Open final of **1989**. In Davis Cup he was a member of Sweden's successful teams in **1984**, **1985** and **1994** winning 35 of his 50 singles rubbers and 12 of his 20 doubles rubbers in 35 ties between **1983** and **1996**. At the Olympic Games he won the **1984** demonstration event in Los Angeles and won bronze medals in singles and doubles at the Seoul Games in **1988**. In Barcelona(**1992**) he carried the Swedish flag in the opening ceremony. In a long and distinguished career that earned him prize money alone totalling $20.6 million, he was respected as much for his impeccable manners and his chivalry in victory and defeat as for his beautiful backhand, fluid court coverage and wonderfully quick reflexes. It was no surprise when his peers named the annual ATP Tour Sportsmanship Award after him. JB

MARK RONALD **EDMONDSON** (Australia)
Born 28/6/54. On two golden afternoons on the fast grass at Kooyong, this burly battler from Gosford, NSW. beat first Ken Rosewall, then defending champion John Newcombe, to capture the **1976** Australian Championships. Between **1980** and **1984** he won the Australian doubles title four times with three different partners (**1980**, **1981** with Warwick, **1983** with McNamee, **1984** with Stewart). Warwick was again his partner when he won the **1985** French doubles, his only other Grand Slam success. JB

ROY STANLEY EMERSON (Australia)

Born 3/11/36. A remarkable athlete, lean, keen, and 'trained to the last ounce', who led Australia's international challenge for five years after Laver turned professional in **1962**. A Queenslander, his 28 Grand Slam titles (12 singles, 16 doubles) are a record for men. The only man to win singles and doubles at all four major championships, he won Wimbledon singles **1964/65** but injury in **1966** spoilt his chance of equalling Perry's record of three successive titles. Won the doubles **1959/61** (with Fraser) and **1971** (with Laver), US singles **1961/64** and doubles **1959/60** (with Fraser) and **1965/66** (with Stolle), Australian singles **1961** and **1963/64/65/66/67** and doubles **1962** (with Fraser), **1966** (with Stolle) and **1969** (with Laver). On clay courts won the French singles **1963/67**, Italian doubles **1959/61/66** and German singles **1967**. His most interesting doubles achievement was to take the French title from **1960–65** with five different partners, Fraser **1960/62**, Laver **1961**, Santana **1963**, Fletcher **1964**, and Stolle **1965**. He won 34 of his 38 D Cup rubbers (21–2 singles, 13–2 doubles) in 18 ties and played in 9 successive Challenge Rounds between **1959–67**.

CHRISTINE ('CHRIS') MARIE EVERT (USA)

Born 21/12/54 in Fort Lauderdale, Fl. Now Mrs Andy Mill (married 30 July 1988). Coached by father Jimmy in Fort Lauderdale to become the most consistent back-court player of her generation: she won at least one Grand Slam singles title every year from **1974** to **1986** during which period her friendly rivalry with Martina Navratilova dominated the women's game. When she and Jimmy Connors (who were engaged at the time) won the two Wimbledon singles titles in **1974** with their double-handed backhands they legitimised the stroke and set a fashion that became a world trend. Her metronomic consistency, unshakeable concentration and fearless resolve to go for her shots were legendary and earned her more professional titles (157) than any other player, male or female, during the Open era until Martina Navratilova passed that total in **1992**, plus a fortune in prize money ($8,896,195). She competed for 19 consecutive years at the US Open and reached 9 finals, 8 semi-finals and was twice beaten in the quarter-finals, including her last year **1989** when she won her 101st match at these Championships, a record. As a sixteen-year-old, in **1971**, she reached the first of four consecutive semi-finals on grass at Forest Hills. In **1975/76/77** she won the title there on US clay and repeated that success on hard courts at Flushing Meadows in **1978/80/82**, by which time her first husband, John Lloyd (married 17 April 1979, divorced April 1987) had helped her to become a much better volleyer. In 13 challenges in Paris between **1973** and **1988** she won seven of the nine finals she contested (**1974/75/79/80/83/85/86**) and only in her last year failed to reach the semi-final, losing in the third round to Arantxa Sanchez Vicario. She competed at Wimbledon every year from **1972–89** and only in **1983** (when she was ill and lost to Kathy Jordan) did she fail to reach the semi-finals. She was the champion 3 times (**1974/76/81**), a finalist 7 times (**1973/78/79/80/82/84/85**) and a semi-finalist 7 times (**1972/75/77/86/87/88/89**). She competed in the Australian Open six times between **1974–88**, winning the title in **1982** and **1984** and reaching the final in **1974/81/85/88**. Her 18 Grand Slam singles titles place her equal fourth with Martina Navratilova behind Margaret Court (24), Steffi Graf (21) and Helen Wills Moody (19) on the list of great champions. Her streak of 125 consecutive wins on clay courts **August 1973–May 1979** is an all-time record and her prodigious achievement in reaching the semi-finals or better at 52 of her last 56 Grand Slams is unlikely ever to be equalled. She represented the United States eight times in the Fed Cup and won all but two of her 42 singles rubbers and 16 of 18 doubles rubbers in 42 ties between **1977–89**. She was unbeaten in 26 W Cup singles rubbers and won 8 of the 12 doubles rubbers she contested in 13 ties between **1971– 85**. JB

ROBERT ('BOB') FALKENBURG (USA)

Born 29/1/26. Won the US Junior Championship in **1943–44** and came to Europe in **1947** with the reputation of possessing the fastest service in the US. He won at Queen's Club, but lost to Pails in qf at Wimbledon and then won the doubles with Kramer, defeating Mottram and Sidwell in f. The following year **1948** he won one of Wimbledon's most dramatic f, defeating Bromwich 7–5 0–6 6–2 3–6 7–5 after saving three match-points as 3–5 in 5s. He was born in New York, learnt most of his tennis in Los Angeles and moved to Brazil, for whom he played in the D Cup on a residential qualification.

NEALE ANDREW FRASER (Australia)

Born 3/10/33. A consistently aggressive left-hander, with a plain, direct serve-and-volley game, he was trained by Harry Hopman, winning 18 of 21 D Cup rubbers (11–1 singles, 7–2 doubles) in 11 ties between **1958** and **1963**, and later captained the Australian team which recaptured the trophy at Cleveland in **1973** and at Sydney in **1977** and Melbourne in **1983** and **1986**. Fraser started his Wimbledon career in the qualifying competition and began by winning the singles in **1960** after a remarkable escape in the qf. when Butch Buchholz, who had held 5 match-points against him, retired with cramp. He won the doubles with   Emerson **1959/61** and mixed with du Pont in **1962** – the year in which he and his brother, John, a   Melbourne doctor, both reached the singles sf. Neither got through to the f. He won the US singles **1959/60** and doubles in **1957** (with Cooper) and **1959/60** (with Emerson), the French doubles in **1958** (with Cooper) and **1960/62** (with Emerson) and Australian doubles, in **1957** (with Hoad), **1958** (with Cooper) and **1962** (with Emerson).

SHIRLEY JUNE FRY (USA)

Born 30/6/27. Now Mrs Irvin (1957). A persistent competitor, whose most notable performances were in doubles. She was first ranked in the top ten in the US in **1944**, but she did not gain her two major singles successes until **1956** when she won both Wimbledon and Forest Hills. Until then she had always been thwarted by fellow-Americans. She won the Wimbledon doubles from **1951–53** with Doris Hart, losing only four games in capturing the title in **1953** and beat Helen Fletcher and Jean Quertier 6–0 6–0 in sf and Julie Sampson and Maureen Connolly by the same score in f. They won the US title **1951–54**. Her other successes included the Wimbledon mixed, with Seixas, **1956**, the Australian singles and doubles, with Althea Gibson, **1957**, and the French singles, **1951**, and doubles, with Hart, **1950–53**. She played in six W Cup contests, winning 10 rubbers and losing twice.

VITAS KEVIN **GERULAITIS** (USA)
Born 26/7/54. Died 18/9/94. Ranked among the world's top ten from **1977–1982** when he won 27 titles from 55 finals, this popular American, the son of Lithuanian immigrants, reached three Grand Slam finals on three different surfaces, thanks to a fine all-court game that lacked only a really decisive winning weapon. He won the Australian Open (**1977**), lost to John McEnroe in the US Open final (**1979**), and to his great friend Bjorn Borg in the French final (**1980**). Borg had also beaten him in the Wimbledon semi-final of **1977**. This five set match of brilliant rallies contained few losers and was one of the greatest Centre Court battles of modern times. Two years earlier he had won the doubles at Wimbledon (**1975**) with Sandy Mayer, unseeded. He also reached two Masters finals. In **1979** Borg was simply too good for him but in **1981** he won the first two sets against Ivan Lendl and held a match point in the third but lost in five. He first represented the United States in the Davis Cup in **1977** and won 11 of the 14 rubbers he played, all in singles, in 7 ties. After retiring from the mainstream at the end of **1985** he played a lot of golf, became an excellent colour commentator on television, and played the guitar alongside John McEnroe to raise funds to help underprivileged kids in the New York area. In **1994**, still a lively 40-year-old, he had started competing again on the seniors tour. Tragically, he died of carbon monoxide poisoning while watching TV at the poolside home of a friend in Southampton, Long Island, where the heater proved to be faulty. JB

ALTHEA GIBSON (USA)
Born 25/8/27. Became Mrs W A Darben (1965) and Mrs S Llewellyn (1983). The first black player to dominate international lawn tennis, relying on fierce serving and considerable strength and reach. Won Wimbledon singles **1957/58** and (doubles (with Angela Buxton) **1956**, (with Hard) **1957** and (with Maria Bueno) **/58**. US singles **1957/58**. French singles and doubles (with Angela Buxton) **1956**. Australian doubles (with Shirley Fry) **1957**. Italian singles **1956**. W Cup **1957/58**, turned professional **1958** and for a brief spell competed on the women's golf tour.

ANDRE HENRI **GOBERT** (France)
Born 30/9/1890. Died 6/12/1951. Wallis Myers described him as 'perhaps the greatest indoor player of all time'. With Decugis, he gained France's first Wimbledon title by defeating the holders, Ritchie and Wilding, in **1911**. Although they were beaten by Dixon and Roper Barrett the following year, the brilliant Gobert's compensation was a place in the All-Comers' singles f in which he lost to the experienced A. W. Gore. He won the French covered court title from **1911–13** and again in **1920** and the British covered court event in **1911–12** and again from **1920–22**. He first played in the D Cup in **1912** and won 2 of his 7 singles and one of his 3 doubles rubbers in 5 ties He also won two Olympic gold medals in **1912**.

RICHARD ALONZO ('**PANCHO**') **GONZALES** (USA)
Born 9/5/28. Died 3/7/95. A dramatic and spectacular competitor, who was undoubtedly the best player in the world for most of the 1950s. He turned pro in **1949** after winning the US singles in **1948/49**, taking the US Clay Court title **1948/49**, the US indoor title **1949**, and winning the doubles in Paris and at Wimbledon – in his only amateur appearances there – in **1949** with Parker. Thereafter he played his brilliant, angry tennis away from the main arenas of the game until, at last, open competition was allowed. By then he was 40, but he played one last great match for the Wimbledon crowd. In **1969** he beat Pasarell 22–24 1–6 16–14 6–3 11–9 in 5hr 12min – the longest singles seen at Wimbledon. His only D Cup appearance was in the **1949** Challenge Round v. Australia when he beat both Sedgman and Sidwell as the USA retained the trophy.

EVONNE FAY **GOOLAGONG** (Australia)
Born 31/7/51. Now Mrs Roger Cawley (married in 1975). One of the most naturally gifted of champions, she was the first of her Aborigine race to excel at the game. Suddenly in **1971** at the age of 19, 3 years before her coach Vic Edwards had forecast she would, she swept through both the French Championships and Wimbledon on a cloud of inspiration to win her first major titles. Although she reached the Wimbledon final again the following year and twice more, in **1975** and **1976**, it was not until **1980** that she won again – three years after the birth of her daughter, Kelly. This was the first win by a mother since Dorothea Lambert Chambers's success in **1914**. The nine-year gap between her championships was also the greatest since Bill Tilden's wins in **1921** and **1930**. She was always more at home on faster surfaces where her beautifully instinctive volleying paid handsome dividends and she won her native Australian Open on that surface four times – **1974/75/76/77**. She was always a competent player on clay but tended to be rather erratic as her famous 'walkabouts' led to extravagant errors. Nevertheless, besides the French Open in **1971** she also won the Italian title in **1973**. The other highlights of her singles career were the victories in the South African Championships (**1972**) and the Virginia Slims Champs (**1974/76**). She was a good doubles player and won once at Wimbledon (**1974**), four

times in Melbourne (**1971/74/75/ 76**) and twice in Johannesburg (**1971/72**). In seven years of Fed Cup duty for Australia from **1971–82** she won 33 of the 38 rubbers she contested in 24 ties. JB

ARTHUR WILLIAM CHARLES (WENTWORTH) **GORE** (Great Britain)

Born 2/1/1868. Died 1/12/1928. Wimbledon's oldest champ and probably the most persistent and industrious competitor in the history of the Champs. He played there for the first time in **1888** and although the Dohertys, Brookes, and Wilding were among his contemporaries, won the singles 3 times **1901** and **1908/09** and, at the age of 44 years and 6 months, won the right to challenge Wilding for the title in **1912**. That was his sixth appearance in the Challenge Round in 13 years and he was twice in the All-Comers final **1907–08**. He was almost entirely a forehand player, hitting the ball flat with the racket in a dead line with his outstretched arm. His lightness of foot enabled him to protect his backhand which was no more than a safe push. He competed at every Wimbledon between **1888–1927** and captained the first British D Cup team at Boston in **1900**, reaching sf at the US Champs on that trip.

STEFANIE (**'STEFFI'**) MARIA **GRAF** (Germany)

Born 14/6/69. Arguably the greatest of all female champions, she amassed 22 Grand Slam singles titles in her seventeen years as a professional, only two fewer than Margaret Court, who won 11 of her 24 titles in Australia when few overseas players ventured down under. A superb natural athlete, she was coached by her father Peter from an early age. He helped her to develop one of the game's great shots, a powerful forehand on which she swung very late but timed to perfection. She also used an accurate, sliced backhand and a powerful serve. She won an Olympic gold medal in **1988**, the year of her Golden Grand Slam – itself a unique achievement. That same year she beat Martina Navratilova for the first time at Wimbledon and supplanted the Czech-born left-hander as the great grass court expert, adding titles in **1989** (Navratilova), **1991** (Sabatini), **1992** (Seles), **1993** (Novotna), **1995** (Sanchez-Vicario) and **1996** (Sanchez-Vicario). Only twice did she lose in a Wimbledon final – in 1987 to Navratilova and in 1999 to Davenport. That last appearance followed her sensational sixth success at Roland Garros where, aged 17.11, she had started her run of Grand Slam wins in **1987** (Navratilova). The other winning years in Paris (from nine finals) were **1988** (Zvereva), **1993** (M-J Fernandez), **1995** (Sanchez-Vicario), **1996** (Sanchez-Vicario), **1999** (Hingis). Her four Australian wins from ten visits were scored in **1988** (Evert), **1989** (Sukova), **1990** (M-J Fernandez) and **1994** (Sanchez-Vicario). At the US Open she was successful five times, in **1988** (Sabatini), **1989** (Navratilova), **1993** (Sukova), **1995** (Seles) and **1996** (Seles). Her **1995** US win meant that, unique among men and women, she had now won all four of the world's major titles at least four times. In seven years of Fed Cup tennis she won 20 of her 22 singles and 8 of her 10 doubles in 20 ties. JB

KAREN JANICE **HANTZE** (USA)

Born 11/12/42. Now Mrs Susman (1961). One of the new generation of aggressive Californians who arrived on the international scene at the start of the 1960s, she won the doubles at Wimbledon with the 17-year-old Billie Jean Moffitt in **1961** and then defeated Vera Sukova in the **1962** singles final. Marriage and motherhood restricted her tennis, but she won US doubles (again with Moffitt) **1964**. She played W Cup **1960–62** and **1965**, winning six of her nine matches, and Fed Cup **1965**, when she played only in doubles and won all 4 rubbers.

DARLENE RUTH **HARD** (USA)

Born 6/1/36. An energetic volleyer, a shrewd tactician, and one of the best doubles players of her generation, she won the US singles in **1960/61** and the French singles **1960**, but she failed in both her Wimbledon finals, losing to Althea Gibson in **1957** and Maria Bueno **1959**. She won the Wimbledon doubles, with Gibson (**1957**), Jeanne Arth (**1959**), and twice with Bueno (**1960/63**) and the mixed in **1957** (with Rose), **1959–60** (with Laver). She won the US doubles six times – with Arth (**1958/59**), Bueno (**1960/62**), Turner (**1961**) and Durr (**1969**) and the French doubles three times – with Fleitz (**1955**), Bloomer (**1957**) and Buero (**1960**). Perhaps her most surprising American success came in **1969**, some years after she had retired from regular competition, when she and Francoise Durr defeated Margaret Court and Virginia Wade 0–6 6–3 6–4 in f.

DORIS JANE **HART** (USA)

Born 20/6/25. In spite of childhood illness which impeded her movement, she became one of the subtlest and most graceful of post-war competitors. Won Wimbledon singles **1951**, doubles (with Pat Todd) **1947** and (with Shirley Fry) **1951/52/53**. US singles **1954/55** and doubles (with Shirley Fry) **1951/52/53/54**. French singles **1950/52** and doubles (with Pat Todd) **1948** and (with Shirley Fry) **1950/51/52/53**. Australian singles **1949** and doubles (with Louise Brough) **1950**. Italian singles **1951/53** and South African singles **1952**. Also won many mixed titles, notably with E. V. Seixas at Wimbledon **1953/54/55**. Turned professional **1955**.

ADRIANNE ('**ANN**') SHIRLEY **HAYDON** (Great Britain)

Born 17/10/38. Married Philip (Pip) Jones in 1962. A shrewd, persistent left-hander, who reached sf at Wimbledon 8 times in 12 years, she captured the title at last in **1969** after beating Margaret Court in sf and Billie Jean King, to whom she had been r/u in **1967**, in f. She achieved international fame as a table tennis player, but decided to concentrate on lawn tennis after being r/u in three events in the **1957** World Table Tennis Champs. She won the French title in **1961/66**, Rome in **1966** and was twice r/u at Forest Hills

1961/67. She took the French doubles (with Renee Schuurman) in **1963** and (with Francoise Durr) in **1968/69** and won the Wimbledon mixed with Stolle in **1969**. Her W Cup record – 15 successful rubbers out of 32 in 12 matches – is another remarkable illustration of her tenacity and consistency.

ROBERT ('**BOB**') ANTHONY JOHN **HEWITT** (South Africa)

Born 12/1/40 in Sydney, Australia. He moved to South Africa in the early **1960s** and started to represent that country when his residential qualification matured in **1967**. A big brooding volcano of a man, he had a deceptively fine touch and became one of the greatest right-court returners of the serve of modern times. He enjoyed two careers – first with fellow-Australian Fred Stolle and then with South Africa's Frew McMillan. With Stolle he won Wimbledon twice (**1962/64**) the Australian Championship twice (**1963/64**) and the Italian twice (**1963/64**) and with McMillan he added three more Wimbledon crowns (**1967/72/78**), two German (**1967/70**), one French (**1972**), one US (**1977**), one Masters (**1977**) and one WCT (**1974**) title as well as the Italian in **1967** and six at home in South Africa (**1967/70/72/74/75/79**). He registered six major mixed doubles successes with four different partners, winning in Australia with Jan Lehane in **1961**, in Paris with Billie Jean King in **1970** and with Wendy Turnbull in **1979**, twice at Wimbledon with his pupil, Greer Stevens, in **1977/79** and once in New York with Stevens in **1979**. He represented South Africa in D Cup **1967–74** and was a member of the successful team of **1974** that won by default from India. JB

LEWIS ('**LEW**') ALAN **HOAD** (Australia)

Born 23/11/34. Died 3/7/94. Capable of generating fierce power with great ease, he was one of the 'boy wonders' Harry Hopman produced to beat the US in the **1953** D Cup final. The other was Rosewall, 21 days Hoad's senior, who was to thwart his attempt on the Grand Slam in **1956** by beating him at Forest Hills. That year Hoad had won the Australian and French titles, and had beaten Rosewall at Wimbledon. In **1957** he defeated Ashley Cooper in one of the most devastating Wimbledon f ever and then turned professional, but constant back trouble spoilt his pro career and also ended his attempt to return to the circuit when the game was opened to the pros. He won the Wimbledon doubles with Rosewall (**1953/56**) and Hartwig (**1955**), the US doubles (**1956**) and the French doubles (**1953**) both with Rosewall, and the Australian doubles with Rosewall (**1953/56**) and Fraser (**1957**). He won 17 rubbers out of 21 in 9 D. Cup duties between **1953–56** (10–2 singles, 7–2 doubles).

HENRY ('**HARRY**') CHRISTIAN **HOPMAN** (Australia)

Born 12/8/06. Died 27/12/85. Small in stature, he was a giant as Australia's Davis Cup captain, winning 16 Challenge Rounds between **1939** and **1967** and motivating some of the finest talent that has ever emerged from any country. The list of his teams reads like a who's who of post war tennis legends and includes Sedgman, McGregor, Hoad, Rosewall, Rose, Hartwig, Emerson, Stolle, Cooper, Anderson, Newcombe, Roche and Alexander. A fine player himself, especially in men's doubles and mixed, he reached three successive Australian singles finals (**1930/31/32**), losing the last two to Jack Crawford, his partner in winning the doubles in **1929/30**. His four mixed wins, all achieved with his wife Nell (nee Hall, they married in March 1934) came in **1930/36/37/39**. His own Davis Cup playing record was modest. He took part in 8 ties between **1928** and **1939**, winning 4 of his 9 singles and four of seven doubles. JB

HAZEL VIRGINIA **HOTCHKISS** (USA)

Born 20/12/1886. Died 5/12/1974. Became Mrs G. W. Wightman (1912). One of the most remarkable and enthusiastic competitors that the game has known. She was the donor of the W Cup and a considerable influence in American tennis for more than 60 years. She gained the first of her four US singles titles (**1909/10/11/19**) in **1909** and won the US indoor doubles for the 10th (**1919/21/24 /27/28/29/30/31/33/43**) and last time in **1943**. A remarkable volleyer with great speed about the court, she and Helen Wills were never beaten in doubles. They won the Wimbledon doubles in **1924** and the US doubles in **1924/28**. Her four other US doubles wins came with E. E. Rotch (**1909/10**) and E. Sears (**1911/15**). She captained the first US W Cup team in **1923** and between **1923–31** won 3 doubles rubbers in 5 matches.

HELEN HULL **JACOBS** (USA)

Born 6/8/08. Died 2/6/97. A tenacious competitor, notable for duels with fellow-Californian, Helen Wills Moody, 5 times a Wimbledon finalist between **1929–38** but won only in **1936**. Won US singles **1932/33/34/35** and doubles (with Sarah Palfrey Fabyan) **1932/34/35** and mixed with George Lott **1934**. Also won Italian singles **1934**.

WILLIAM M. **JOHNSTON** (USA)

Born 2/11/1894. Died 1/5/1946. 'Little Bill', a Californian, small in physique but a brilliant volleyer and the possessor of a formidable topspin forehand, was 'Big Bill' Tilden's principal rival at home in the first half of the **1920s**. He defeated McLoughlin to win the US singles in **1915**, the first year at Forest Hills, lost to Williams in the **1916** final and then regained the title by beating Tilden in straight sets in **1919**. Tilden gained his revenge the following year and, although Johnston reached the final five times between **1920** and **1925**, Tilden always frustrated him. He beat Hunter in the **1923** Wimbledon final, losing only one set in the tournament. He won the US doubles with Griffin **1915/16** and **1920** and played in eight D Cup challenge rounds, winning 18 of his 21 D Cup rubbers (14–3 singles, 4–0 doubles) in 10 ties from **1920–1927**.

BILLIE JEAN MOFFITT **KING** (USA)

Born 22/11/43. Perhaps the most important single figure in the history of women's tennis, as player, stateswoman, innovator and entrepreneur (usually with lawyer husband Larry King, whom she married in **1965**), she has worked tirelessly to gain recognition and respect for the women's game. One of the founders of the women's pro tour in **1970**, twice President of the Women's Tennis Association, and the prime mover behind Team Tennis, she has been involved in most aspects of the game. As a player her natural exuberance and bubbling personality suited her attacking serve-and-volley game and made her a fearsome opponent. She will best be remembered for her 'Battle of the Sexes' against Bobby Riggs at the Houston Astrodome on 20 September, **1973** where the world's largest-ever crowd of 30,492 and some 50 million more around the world on TV, saw her win 6–4 6–3 6–3. In **1979** she achieved her 20th Wimbledon title to pass the record she had shared with fellow-Californian Elizabeth Ryan who, ironically, had died on the eve of that unique achievement. Her unparalleled record comprises 6 singles – **1966/67/68/72/73/75**; 10 women's doubles between **1961** and **1979** – with Hantze-Susman (**1961/62**) Bueno (**1965**), Casals (**1967/68/70/71/73**), Stove (**1972**) and Navratilova (**1979**); 4 mixed doubles with Owen Davidson (**1967/ 71/ 73/74**). She first played at Wimbledon in **1961** and won the doubles with Karen Hantze. At her last appearance in **1983** she was competing for the 22nd year (she had not entered in **1981**) and reached the mixed doubles final with Steve Denton when she played her 265th and last match at Wimbledon. It was also her 28th final and, as they lost to John Lloyd and Wendy Turnbull 7–5 in the final set, she was losing at that stage for only the 8th time. She was almost as successful in her own US Championships where she won 13 titles, 4 in singles – **1967/71/72/74**, five in doubles – with Susman (**1964**), Casals (**1967/74**) and Navratilova (**1978/80**) and four in mixed – with Davidson (**1967/71/73**) and Phil Dent (**1976**) and, in addition she became the only woman to win US National titles on all four surfaces – grass, clay, hard and indoor – a feat she repeated in doubles – with Rosie Casals. She won the French Open singles and doubles with Stove in **1972** and the mixed – with Davidson (**1967**) and Hewitt (**1970**) and was successful in singles and mixed at the Australian Open in **1968** (with Crealy), the first year of open tennis. Her 39 Grand Slam titles put her third behind Margaret Court who won 62 and Navratilova who won 56. She was also the singles and doubles champion of Italy (**1970**) and of Germany (**1971**) and won the South African title 3 times **1966/67/69**). With 21 winning rubbers from 26 played in 9 W Cup matches between **1961–78**, plus 52 wins from 58 rubbers (26–3 singles, 26–1 doubles) in 6 years of Fed Cup play from **1963–79** she contributed hugely to American dominance in those team competitions. JB

JAN KODES (Czechoslovakia)

Born 1/3/46. A dogged, industrious player with great strength and determination. He won his first major victories on clay, winning the French singles **1970/71** and reaching the Italian final **1970/71/72**, but he won the Wimbledon singles in the boycott year of **1973** (when he won the first tie-break used in a Wimbledon final) and was runner-up in the US Champs **1971/73**. Having served his apprenticeship in European junior team competitions (he was on a winning Galea Cup team), he first represented Czechoslovakia in D Cup in **1966**, took them to the final in **1975** and was a member of their winning team in **1980**. Altogether, in 39 ties over 15 years he won 39 of his 59 singles and 21 of his 36 doubles rubbers. For six years (**1982–87**) he was Davis Cup captain and for 5 years (**1994–98**) President of the Czech Federation.

HILDE KRAHWINKEL (West Germany)

Born 26/3/08. Died 7/3/81. Became Mrs Sperling (1933). A tall German, later Danish by marriage, whose dogged ability to retrieve from the back of the court turned her matches into long tests of endurance. She won the German indoor title in **1929** and then, emerging rapidly as an international player, lost to Cilly Aussem in the only all-German women's f at Wimbledon in **1931**. She reached the final again in **1936**, losing 6–2 4–6 7–5 to Helen Jacobs, and altogether she was in qf (or better) 8 times. She won the French singles **1935–37**, defeating Mrs Mathieu in each of the three f, the Italian title **1935** and she was German singles champ **1933/34/35/37/38/39**. (There was no competition in 1936.) Her last important victory was in the Scandinavian indoor final in **1950**.

JOHN ('**JACK**') ALBERT **KRAMER** (USA)

Born 1/8/21. A methodical and powerful exponent of the serve-and-volley game. Played for the US in the last pre-war D Cup Challenge Round against Australia and returned to the competition in **1946** and **1947** as USA regained, then retained the trophy v Australia. His brief D Cup record produced 7 wins from 9 rubbers (6–0 singles 1–2 doubles) in 4 ties. Won Wimbledon singles title in **1947** after losing dramatically to the unknown Jaroslav Drobny in **1946**. Won doubles **1946** (with T. Brown) and **1947** (with Falkenburg). Won US singles **1946/47** and doubles **1940/41/47** (with Schroeder) and **1943** (with Parker). Turned pro **1947** and then controlled pro tennis for 15 years. He was the first executive director of ATP Sept. 1972–April 1975.

JOHAN KRIEK(USA)

Born 5/4/58. This speedy South African shot to prominence at the end of **1981** by winning the Australian Open. In April that year he had already given notice of his improvement by reaching the WCT final in Dallas where McEnroe had beaten him. In **1982**, now an American citizen, he retained his Australian title after saving a match point in his semi-final against McNamee by beating the same opponent as in the previous year's final, the tall American with the cannonball serve, Steve Denton. IB

JEAN **RENE LACOSTE** (France)

Born 2/7/04. Died 12/10/96. In spite of ill health, he became the best groundstroke player and most astute tactician of pre-war lawn tennis. Won Wimbledon singles **1925/28** and doubles (with J. Borotra) **1925**. Won US singles **1926/27**, French singles **1925/27/29** and French doubles (with Borotra) **1924/25/29**. Won 40 of his 51 D Cup rubbers in 26 ties between **1923–28** (32–8 singles, 8–3 doubles) and won the crucial rubbers of the **1927** challenge round which brought France the trophy for the first time, when he beat Tilden and Johnston in the singles. Retiring from the mainstream in **1929** he built up his Chemise Lacoste clothing business until it became one of the world's best known brands with its crocodile emblem.

WILLIAM ('**BILL**') AUGUSTUS **LARNED** (USA)

Born 30/12/1872. Committed suicide on 16/12/1926. Coming late to tennis, Larned won the first of his seven US Championships in **1901** at the age of 28 with his heavy groundstrokes, hit with considerable top-spin on the forehand. He added the titles of **1902/07/08/09/10/11** and was 38 when he won for the last time, making him the oldest male champion. Ranked in the US Top Ten 19 times, he was the US No.1 eight times, a total second only to Tilden's 10. He played in 8 D Cup ties from **1902**, winning 9 of his 14 singles. JB

ARTHUR ('**ART**') DAVID ('TAPPY') **LARSEN** (USA)

Born 6/4/25. A graceful, elegant left-hander with exquisite touch and some notable eccentricities, he was famous for his dressing-room superstitions, his physical twitches and his rituals on court. He was known as Tappy because he would have a lucky number for the day and would always tap the baseline, the umpire's chair – even his own toe – with his racket the required number of times before continuing. He won US singles **1950**, US Clay Courts **1952** and US Indoor **1953**. A motor scooter accident in which he suffered severe head injuries ended his career in **1957**.

RODNEY ('**ROD**') GEORGE **LAVER** (Australia)

Born 9/8/38. Arguably the greatest of all male champions, he became the first player to achieve the Grand Slam twice and the master of the old professional circuit, with Rosewall as his great rival, in its last days. A left-hander, red-haired like Budge, with a spectacularly aggressive style, he brought off the slam of the four major singles titles, as an amateur, in **1962** and then, as a professional, in **1969**. Disciplined, unassuming, quick and light in movement, he could produce sudden bombardments of shots, heavy with spin, which totally disconcerted his opponents. Born at Rockhampton, Queensland, 'Rocket' was a perfect nickname for the first tennis millionaire. If he had not turned professional in **1963**, he would have won many more of the traditional titles. As it was, he won the singles at Wimbledon **1961/62** and **1968/69**, the doubles with Emerson **1971** and the mixed, with Darlene Hard, **1959/60**. He took the US singles and French singles **1962** and **1969**, also winning the French doubles with Emerson and the mixed with Hard in **1961**. His Australian singles victories came in **1960/62/69**, with doubles **1959–61** (Mark) and **1969** (Emerson). He was Italian singles champion **1962** and **1971**, German champion **1961/62** and a member of the undefeated D Cup team from **1959–62**. He returned to D Cup in **1973**, collecting three more rubbers in Australia's 5–0 victory over the US in the final at Cleveland. Altogether, he won 20 of his 24 rubbers in 11 ties between **1959–73**, (16–4 singles, 4–0 doubles).

IVAN **LENDL** (USA)

Born 7/3/60. Grew up in Ostrava, Czechoslovakia, but went to live in Greenwich, Connecticut in **1984** and became an American citizen on 7th July **1992**. This 6'2" 175lb right-hander was blessed with a fine physique and abundant talent, based on a lethal match-winning forehand, a reliable backhand that he would develop into a second winning weapon, and a heavy serve – plus superb fitness and deep concentration. He was nurtured from an early age by his lawyer father Jiri, himself a ranked player, and by his mother Olga, a former Czech No.3. The Orange Bowl 18's champion in **1977**, Lendl became the first ITF World Junior Champion in **1978** after winning the Wimbledon, French and Italian junior titles. Turning pro the same year, he made rapid strides in the men's game and in **1980** won the first seven of the 94 singles titles he would amass before his retirement at the end of **1994**, successes that earned him $21,262,417 in prize money alone. (Only Jimmy Connors, with 109 titles, has won more tournaments in modern times though Tilden won 138 titles in the **1920's**.) During those 15 years he reached 19 Grand Slam singles finals, winning 8 of them. After failing once in Paris (**1981**), twice in New York (**1982/83**) and once in Melbourne (**1983**) some observers wrote him off, saying he did not have the belief of a true champion. Over the next seven years, guided by his Australian coach, Tony Roche, he proved his critics spectacularly wrong by claiming the French Open three times (**1984/86/87**), the US Open three times (**1985/86/87**), and the Australian Open twice (**1989/90**) as well as The Masters five times (**1981/82/85/86/87**) from a record nine consecutive appearances in the final between **1980** and **1988**. At Wimbledon he was unlucky to face inspired opponents in two consecutive finals; in **1986** 18-year-old Boris Becker successfully defended his title and in **1987** Pat Cash proved irresistible. Lendl first headed the world rankings on 28th February **1983** and altogether occupied the No.1 spot for a record 270 weeks, a span that inluded 157 consecutive weeks between **9/9/85** and **12/9/88**. In a relatively short Davis Cup career (**1978–1985**) Lendl won 22 of the 37 rubbers he contested, including 18 of his 29 singles matches. JB

SUZANNE RACHEL FLORE **LENGLEN** (France)
Born 24/5/1899. Died 4/7/1938. The most exciting, and successful of women players. She survived 2 match-points to win at Wimbledon in **1919** against Mrs Lambert Chambers and thereafter lost only in a controversial match to Molla Mallory (US) in **1921** US Champs until her retirement in **1926**. Quarrelled with the Wimbledon referee in **1926** and turned pro. Won Wimbledon singles and doubles (with Elizabeth Ryan) **1919/20/21/22/23/25**. French singles and doubles (with various partners) **1920/21/22/23**, while the Championships were closed to foreigners, and again in **1925** and **1926** (doubles with D. Vlasto) when they became international.

GEORGE MARTIN **LOTT** (USA)
Born 16/10/06. Died 2/12/91. A fine, natural doubles player, he was five times the US doubles champion – in **1928** (with John Hennessey), **1929** and **1930** (with John Doeg), **1933** and **1934** (with Lester Stoefen). Two Wimbledon titles – in **1931** (with John Van Ryn) and **1934** (with Stoefen), plus one French in **1931** (with Van Ryn). In six years of Davis Cup competition from **1928** he won 18 of his 22 rubbers (7–4 in singles, 11–0 in doubles) then, in **1934**, he turned professional. JB

JOHN PATRICK **McENROE** (USA)
Born 16/2/59. A left-hander with immense talent and exquisite touch, he caused a sensation at Wimbledon in **1977** by reaching the semi-final from the qualifying competition, thus winning a record eight matches. He was to be the centre of many other sensations throughout a turbulent career during which his perfectionist attitude made it impossible for him to accept the incompetence (as he saw it) of court officials, many of whom were subjected to a torrent of intimidating verbal abuse. Fined for his behaviour on several occasions, he was finally defaulted at the Australian Open in **1990** during his fourth round match against Michael Pernfors. In between these outbursts he could produce tennis of a sublime quality. His deceptive serve, delivered from a closed stance, was difficult to read and there has never been a better close volleyer. His ability to take his service returns and passing shots early and project them to unlikely angles made him a very difficult opponent. His singles successes included four US Open titles (**1979,1980,1981,1984**) and three at Wimbledon (**1981,1983,1984**) where his two heroic battles against Bjorn Borg in the **1980** and **1981** finals reached epic proportions. Among his 77 career titles the three Masters successes (**1978, 1983,1984**) and five WCT victories (**1979,1981,1983,1984,1989**) were outstanding. He was never successful in Paris, where Lendl beat him in the **1984** final, or in Australia, where he lost to Wilander in the **1983** semi-final. His lightning-fast reflexes and an instinctive positional sense made him an outstanding doubles player, arguably the best there has ever been. The **1977** French Open, won with Mary Carillo, his neighbour from Douglaston, N.Y., was his first Grand Slam success. At Wimbledon he won four times with Peter Fleming (**1979,1981,1983,1984**) and once with Michael Stich (**1992**). At the US Open Fleming helped him to three titles (**1979,1981,1983**) His seven consecutive Masters wins with Fleming (**1978–1984**) constitute a record that, surely, will never be broken. Always proud to represent his country, he had an outstanding D Cup record for the United States. In 12 years from **1978** he won 41 of his 49 singles rubbers and 18 of his 20 doubles rubbers in 30 ties. JB

KENNETH ('**KEN**') BRUCE **McGREGOR** (Australia)
Born 2/6/29. Tall, athletic and a natural competitor, this modest South Australian possessed one of the biggest serves in post war tennis. He at last became the Australian champion in **1952** by beating in the final his great friend and doubles partner, Frank Sedgman, who had thwarted him in the **1950** final. In between McGregor had lost the **1951** final to America's Dick Savitt who would also win their Wimbledon final six months later. With his height of 6'3", his long reach, his fast reactions and his fine touch on the volley, McGregor excelled in doubles. His short partnership with Sedgman was particularly fruitful. Together they became the Australian, French and Wimbledon champions in **1951** and **1952**, and the US champions in **1951**. Thus, in **1951** they became the first pair (and so far the only pair) to win the Grand Slam of men's doubles. With Margaret DuPont he also won the US mixed doubles of **1950** and in three years of Davis Cup play (**1950–1952**) he won four of his seven singles rubbers and both doubles rubbers in 5 ties, three of them Challenge Rounds. In **1953** he was lost to the amateur game when he and Sedgman signed professional forms for Jack Kramer. JB

KATHLEEN ('**KITTY**') **McKANE** (Great Britain)
Born 7/5/1896. Died 19/6/92. Became Mrs Godfree (**1926**). A fine match-player with a quick, aggressive game, she achieved the notable distinction of winning the Wimbledon singles twice – even though she was a contemporary of Suzanne Lenglen and Helen Wills. In Lenglen's absence, she beat the Californian (a feat which no other player achieved in the next 14 years at Wimbledon) in the **1924** final after trailing by a set and 1–4, and in **1926** she regained the title after being within a point of 1–4 in the third set against Lili d'Alvarez. She won the Wimbledon mixed (with Gilbert) in **1924** and in **1926** (with her husband, Leslie Godfree, the only married couple ever to do so). She was r/u to Miss Wills at Forest Hills in **1925** after beating Elizabeth Ryan and Molla Mallory, and she won the US doubles in **1923** (with Mrs Covell) **1927** (with Miss Harvey). She won 7 rubbers out of 17 in 7 W Cup matches between **1923–34**.

CHARLES ('**CHUCK**') ROBERT **McKINLEY** (USA)
Born 5/1/41. Died 11/8/86. An energetic and athletic match-player, who won the Wimbledon singles title in **1963** without meeting another seeded player in the course of the tournament. He was runner-up to Laver in

1961, a disappointing competitor in **1962** but in **1963** bounced back to take the title. In the US Championships he never progressed further than the semi-finals, failing three times at that stage, but, with Ralston, he won the doubles in **1961** and **1963–64**. Played in 16 D Cup ties between **1960–65** and won 29 of his 38 rubbers (16–6 singles, 13–3 doubles).

MAURICE EVANS McLOUGHLIN (USA)
Born 18/11/1890. Died 10/12/1957. 'The Californian Comet' was the first notable exponent of the cannon-ball service. Fiercely effective with volley and smash, he was US champ in **1912–13** and his appearance at Wimbledon was, as a contemporary remarked, a sign of the way the modern game was developing. His spectacular style had considerable appeal. When he met Wilding for the title in **1913**, there was such an indecent crush round the barriers of the Centre Court that, to avoid serious injury, several ladies had to be lifted over by policemen into the security of the arena. Wilding beat him 8–6 6–3 10–8, but McLoughlin had the consolation of winning 2 rubbers in the American capture of the D Cup from Britain at Wimbledon. In the **1914** D Cup Challenge Round at Forest Hills he beat both Brookes and Wilding, but Australasia took the trophy. He did not play after the war. His aggressive style was said to have burnt him out.

FREW DONALD McMILLAN (South Africa)
Born 20/5/42 in Springs, a small Transvaal town. A gifted and unusual doubles player who invariably wore a peaked white cloth cap and held the racket with two hands on both sides to produce just the right blend of disguise, finesse and power. His partnership with expatriate Australian Bob Hewitt was particularly fruitful and they became one of the three greatest pairs of the post-Second World War years. Together they won their native South African title six times (**1967/70/72/74/75/78**) and succeeded at Wimbledon three times (**1967/72/78**). They won once each the French (**1972**), the US (**1977**), the Masters (**1977**) played in Jan '78), the WCT (**1974**) and the Italian (**1967**) titles and won the German twice (**1967/70**). But it was in mixed doubles that he won his first and last major championships. In **1966** he partnered Annette Van Zyl to the French title and in **1981** he captured the Wimbledon mixed for the second time with Betty Stove, with whom he had been successful in **1978** – the same year they won a second US Open together (**1977/ 78**). He played D Cup from **1965–76** and was a member of the only team ever to win the famous trophy by default – from India in **1974**. In 28 ties he played 30 rubbers, winning both singles and 23 of his 28 doubles. JB

HANA MANDLIKOVA (Australia)
Born 19/2/62. Became Mrs J. Sadlek (1986). This Czech-born right-hander, who helped her country win the Federation Cup three years in a row **1983–85**, became an Australian citizen on 1 January **1988**. A talented athlete who won four Grand Slam singles titles and might have won more had her career not coincided with two truly outstanding champions – Evert and Navratilova. She first shot to prominence in Australia where, on the grass of Kooyong which ideally suited her natural serve-and-volley game, she won the **1980** title aged 18. When she took the **1981** French Open and 4 weeks later reached the Wimbledon final it seemed she might dislodge Evert and Navratilova from their dominant positions atop the world rankings. It was not to be. Two final round appearances, this time at the US Opens of **1980** and **'82**, flattered to deceive. But in **1985** she did annexe that title and the following year reached the Wimbledon final for the second time. Sadly this was not the breakthrough to the summit all her supporters had hoped for. Her fourth Grand Slam success came in Melbourne in **1987**, the last time the Australian Open was played on grass. Her lone Grand Slam doubles success came at the **1989** US Open in partnership with Navratilova. JB

ALICE MARBLE (USA)
Born 28/9/13. Died 13/12/90. The first brilliant server and volleyer in women's tennis whose career was interrupted by ill health and the war. Won Wimbledon singles **1939** and doubles (with Sarah Palfrey Fabyan) **1938/39**. Won US singles **1936/38/39/40** and doubles (with Sarah Palfrey Fabyan) **1937/38/39/40**. Turned pro **1941**.

SIMONE MATHIEU (France)
Born 31/1/08. Died 7/1/80. Née Passemard, had married Rene Mathieu in Oct. 1925, before her tennis career had begun. A formidable clay court player, she succeeded Lenglen as the leader of the women's game in France. She was junior champ – as a married woman – at 18, and 3 years later reached the French f, losing 6–3 6–4 to Wills. She was r/u again in **1932/33/35/36/37** before she won at last in **1938**, defeating Landry, and then retained her title **1939** against Jedrzejowska. She won the French doubles 6 times, twice with Ryan, (**1933/34**) three times with Yorke (**1936/37/38**) and once with Jedrzejowska (**1939**), and the Wimbledon doubles twice with Ryan (**1933/34**) and once with Yorke (**1937**.) Her soundness from the baseline carried her 6 times to the singles sf at Wimbledon (**1930/31/32/34/36/37**).

FLORENCE **ANGELA** MARGARET **MORTIMER** (Great Britain)
Born 21/4/32. Now Mrs Barrett (1967). Britain's first post-war Wimbledon singles champ. Coached by Arthur Roberts at Torquay, she used an armoury of firmly controlled ground-strokes most effectively and considerable determination enabled her to overcome a certain frailty of physique. Her first notable success was the capture of the French title in **1955** – the first British victory in Paris since Peggy Scriven won in **1934** – and in the same year she won the Wimbledon doubles (with Anne Shilcock). She won the Australian title in **1958**, after travelling there to recover from illness, and 6 months later was r/u to Althea Gibson at Wimbledon. She won the

title in **1961** by beating Christine Truman in the first all–British f of the modern Wimbledon. She won 5 rubbers out of 16 in 6 W Cup matches and became W Cup captain **1964–70** and Fed Cup captain **1967–70**.

THOMAS MUSTER

Born 2/10/67 in Leibnitz. A rugged, uncompromising left-hander, he turned himself into one of the greatest clay court players of his generation. With a phenomenal appetite for hard work on and off the court he shot to prominence in **1985** by reaching the final of the French Open junior event and the Orange Bowl, progress which led to his selection for the Austrian Davis Cup team the same year. The following year, in Hilversum, he won the first of the 44 singles titles he would accumulate during more than a decade of triumph and disaster on the Tour. In **1988** came his first triumph when he won three clay court titles in the space of five weeks. It was evidence of the will power and endurance he had already developed, qualities that would be necessary one year later when disaster struck. Three months after reaching his first Grand Slam semi-final at the **1989** Australian Open, Muster beat Yannick Noah to reach the Lipton final. That evening the car he was standing behind was hit by a drunken driver and he suffered torn ligaments and a torn cartilage in his left knee, a horrific accident which required immediate reconstructive surgery. During the months he spent in plaster, encouraged by his coach and manager Ronnie Leitgeb, he started to hit tennis balls again from a specially designed wheel chair. Astonishingly, after only four months of rehabilitation he was competing again on the circuit, in doubles at first. In January **1991** he won his first singles tournament since the injury. This was a triumph of the spirit. It was determination of this sort that helped him to his greatest triumph, the capture of the French Open in **1995**. In a spectacular year he won 12 titles altogether, more than anyone since John McEnroe had won 13 in **1984**. Altogether he had put together 86 wins, the most since Ivan Lendl's 106 in **1982**, and had an unbroken streak of 40 between October **1994** and July **1995**. For two brief spells in **1996**, one of only a single week, another for five weeks, Muster held the No.1 ranking position, the 13th man to do so. It was a pinnacle of achievement for this courageous battler whose career inevitably wound down as the strains on his knee, which had required several bouts of arthroscopic surgery since 1989, made it impossible for him to sustain long periods of competition. Particularly satisfying were the victories over Jim Courier and Sergi Bruguera in **1997** that earned him the Lipton title, almost eight years to the day since his accident there. Playing only a few tournaments in **1999**, he had slipped to 170 in the rankings by the year's end and decided to retire. During his distinguished career Muster earned prize money of more than $12.2 million. It was a fine example of what can be achieved through determination, self-belief and sheer hard work.

LLIE NASTASE (Romania)

Born 19/7/46. One of the most gifted shot-makers and fluid movers in the game's history, he was the first to be ranked No 1 on the ATP computer (**23/08/1973**) and was in top 10 **1973–77**, but despite his 57 singles and 51 doubles titles, he never quite fulfilled his enormous potential. His two Grand Slam titles were won on different surfaces – on grass in New York in **1972** and on clay in Paris the following year. He could also play beautifully indoors as his four Masters titles in **1971/72/73/75** testify. Sadly for his many admirers, a childlike and sometimes mischievous streak was his undoing on many occasions, particularly towards the end of his playing days when he fell foul of authority for his behaviour. Throughout his career the showman in him struggled constantly with the athlete so that there was often a lack of steel about his match play. This failing, and an inability to put the ball away with his somewhat lightweight volleys, cost him two chances to win the Wimbledon title – in **1972** when Smith beat him and in**1976** when Borg won the first of his five titles. His lightning reflexes made him an excellent doubles player and he won major titles in Paris (**1970**) and Rome (**1970/72**) with fellow Romanian, Ion Tiriac, at Wimbledon (**1973**) with Connors and in New York (**1975**) also with Connors. He also won two mixed titles at Wimbledon with Rosie Casals (**1970/72**). His biggest disappointment was his failure to lead Romania to victory in the **1972** D Cup final against the Americans on clay in Bucharest where his loss to Smith in the opening rubber proved decisive. JB

MARTINA NAVRATILOVA (USA)

Born 18/10/56. One of the greatest of all women players, this Czech-born left-hander grew up in Prague but defected to the USA in **1975** and became an American citizen on 21st July **1981**. With her defection she turned professional and embarked upon two decades of conquest that brought her a total of 56 Grand Slam titles (18 singles, 31 doubles, 7 mixed) between **1974** and **1995**. Navratilova's attacking serve-and-volley game was ideally suited to the fast grass of Wimbledon where she reached 12 singles finals and won a record 9 times (**1978/79/82/83/84/85/86/87/90**). She also won 7 of her 9 doubles finals there (**1976** with Chris Evert, **1979** with Billie Jean King, **1981/82/83/84/86** with Pam Shriver) and 3 of her 4 mixed finals (**1985** with Paul McNamee, **1993** with Mark Woodforde and **1995** with Jonathan Stark) giving her a total of 19 Wimbledon titles, one short of Mrs. King's record of 20 which she had helped the American achieve in **1979**. This glittering Grand Slam career included a victory over Chris Evert at the **1981** Australian Open where she won twice more in singles (**1983/85**) from 6 appearances in the final. She won eight Australian doubles titles (**1980** with Betsy Nagelsen, **1982/83/84/85/87/88/89** with Shriver), but none in mixed. Slow red clay was the most difficult surface for her and despite appearing in 6 finals at the French Open she was successful only twice (**1982/84**). However, she won all 7 of her French doubles finals (**1975** with Evert, **1982** with Ann Smith, **1984/85/87/88** with Shriver) and **1986** with Andrea Temesvari, and both mixed finals (**1974** with Ivan Molina, **1985** with Heinz Gunthardt). At the US Open she was in 8 singles finals, winning 4 (**1983/84/86/87**), in 11 doubles finals, winning 9 (**1977** with Betty Stove, **1978/80** with King, **1983/84/86/87** with Shriver, **1989** with Hana Mandlikova and **1990** with Gigi Fernandez), and in 4 mixed finals, winning 2 (**1985** with Gunthardt, **1987** with Emilio Sanchez). Despite this formidable record she never won a calendar-year Grand Slam, though her victory at the French Open in **1984** meant that she held all four major titles at the same time, a feat that earned her a \$1 million prize from the ITF. Her 167 singles and 165 doubles titles are a record for men and women as was her winning streak of 74 matches achieved in **1984** between January 16th and December 6th. For a total of 331 weeks she was ranked No.1 in the world and by training intensively and adopting the Haas diet she set new standards of strength and fitness which others have tried to follow. With career prize money of \$20,283,727 at the time of her retirement, Navrartilova had won more from her sport than any other female athlete and has been very generous in suporting charities and other deserving causes. Her endorsement income, though considerable, would undoubtedly have been higher had she not made public several lesbian relationships. JB

JOHN DAVID **NEWCOMBE** (Australia)
Born 23/5/44. The supreme exponent of the simple, rugged style in modern tennis. Splendidly confident and with great strength of personality, Newcombe relied upon a heavy service, forceful volleying and solid, powerful groundstrokes. His best singles successes were on grass – Wimbledon **1967/70/71**, US Championships **1967/73**, and Australia **1973/75** – but he also won, by doggedness and determination, the German (**1968**) and Italian (**1969**) titles. He and Roche formed one of the most successful of modern doubles partnerships, winning Wimbledon in **1965, 1968–70**, and **1974**. When Roche was injured in **1966**, Fletcher replaced him at short notice and he and Newcombe won the title. He won the US doubles with Roche **1967**, with Taylor **1971**, and with Davidson **1973**, the French twice with Roche (**1967/69**) and once with Okker (**1973**) and the Australian four times with Roche (**1965/67/71/76**) and once with Anderson (**1973**). In **1981**, aged 37, he and Stolle (42) took McEnroe/Fleming to 5s tie-break in US Open sf. He first played in the D Cup in **1963** when, aged 19, he became the youngest player to compete in a Challenge Round, and finally against Italy in Rome, **1976**. Perhaps his best performance was in **1973** when he and Laver inflicted a 5–0 defeat upon the United States at Cleveland. In 15 ties he won 25 of his 34 rubbers (16–7 singles, 9–2 doubles).

YANNICK NOAH (France)
Born 16/5/60. The son of an African father who had met Yannick's mother when playing soccer for Sedan, he was discovered as a ten-year-old by Arthur Ashe on a goodwill tour in the Cameroons. Sent to the French Federation's training school in Nice, he was coached by Patrice Beust and then sent on to the FFT's school in Paris. A tall athletic figure with a tremendous serve, he was at his best on clay and although he could volley well he preferred to play aggressively from the baseline. He won his first professional title in **1979** in Nancy and eventually fulfilled all expectations by winning the French Open in **1983**, the first Frenchman to do so since Marcel Bernard in **1946**. The fairy tale had come true. In **1984** he teamed with fellow Frenchman, Henri Leconte, to win the French Open doubles title. After leading France to the final of the Davis Cup in **1982**, when France had lost to the USA 4–1 in Grenoble, he became Davis Cup captain in **1991** and was the architect of a famous 3–1 revenge win against the Americans in Lyon, the first French success since **1932**. JB

JANA NOVOTNA (Czech Republic)
Born 2/10/68. With her gracefully aggressive game she became one of the great all-rounders, equally happy playing singles or doubles. After several near misses and playing in her 34th Grand Slam Championship at the age of 29, she at last captured the Wimbledon title in **1998** where, for good measure, she added the doubles as well – the first woman to win both since Steffi Graf in **1988**. This first Grand Slam singles win, the finest of her 24 career titles, came after two final round defeats at Wimbledon. During the first, in **1993**, she had led Steffi Graf by a set and 4–1 but had choked on her lead. In the **1997** final, hampered by a strained abdominal muscle, she had lost to Hingis in three sets. In **1991** at the Australian Open she reached her only other Grand Slam final and she won the Chase Championships in **1997**. In doubles she was highly successful, winning all four of the major titles at least twice: the Australian in **1990** (Sukova) and **1995** (Sanchez-Vicario); the French in **1990** (Sukova), **1991** (G.Fernandez) and **1998** (Hingis); Wimbledon in **1989,1990** (Sukova), **1995** (Sanchez-Vicario) and **1998** (Hingis); the US in **1994** (Sanchez-Vicario), **1997** (Davenport) and **1998** (Hingis). In mixed doubles she won four Grand Slam titles, all with America's Jim Pugh: the Australian Open in **1988** and **1989**; Wimbledon in **1989** and the US Open in **1988**. In 11 years of Fed Cup play, from **1987**, she won 22 of her 29 singles and 11 of her 16 doubles in 33 ties. JB

BETTY MAY **NUTHALL** (Great Britain)
Born 23/5/11. Died 8/11/83. Became Mrs Shoemaker. An aggressive and attractive competitor, with a remarkable record as a junior, she never progressed beyond qf at Wimbledon but gained her most impressive victories abroad. At 16, after beating Molla Mallory, No. 6 seed, at Wimbledon in **1927**, she astonished the tennis world by reaching f at F Hills, where Helen Wills beat her 6–1 6–4. In **1930** she became the first British player to win that title with 6–4 6–1 victory over Mrs Harper. She won the US doubles **1930/31/33** with three different partners – Palfrey, Whittingstall and James and mixed **1929/31** with Lott and the French doubles **1931** with Whittingstall and mixed **1931/32** with Spence and Perry. Her only British success in a nat singles event was the capture of the HC title in **1927**. She won the HC doubles **1926/28/31/32** and the mixed in **1927**. She played in 8 W Cup matches between **1927–39**, winning 6 rubbers and losing 7.

ALEJANDRO ('**ALEX**') RODRIGUEZ **OLMEDO** (USA)

Born 24/3/36. The son of a groundsman in Peru, this superb natural athlete rose like a comet in **1958** to win the D Cup for America in Brisbane almost single-handed. Selected by the captain, Perry T. Jones, Olmedo had rewarded him with two singles wins and a share with Ham Richardson in the doubles win that had sealed the victory. Success in the **1959** Australian Championships confirmed the quality of his play as he beat Neale Fraser in four sets. Six months later 'The Chief', as he was popularly known, won the **1959** Wimbledon from Rod Laver for the loss of only two sets, with one of the most competent displays of power tennis seen since the war. After taking part in the unsuccessful defence of the D Cup where he lost to Fraser but beat Laver again, he reached the final of the US Championships but failed once more against Fraser. Immediately he turned professional. JB

MANUEL ('**MANOLO**') **ORANTES** (Spain)

Born 6/2/49. A consumate artist on European clay with exquisite touch and gentle, generous manner, he quickly became an international favourite. A left-hander who, after leading Spain to two Galea Cup victories in **1968/69**, won his first two important titles in **1972** – the German and Italian Opens. His best year was **1975** for, besides winning a second German title, the Canadian Open and the second of his three US Clay Court crowns (he won the others in **1973** and **1977**), he was triumphant on the clay at Forest Hills to win the US Open. After recovering miraculously to defeat Vilas in a night-time semi-final, having trailed one set to two and 0–5 in the fourth, he was back on court 15 hours later to thrash Jimmy Connors 6–4 6–3 6–3 in a near-perfect display of the clay-court art. In **1976** he won the Spanish Open and at the year's end won the Masters in Houston against Fibak with another brave recovery, coming back from one set to two and 1–4. He played in the losing Spanish team in the D Cup challenge round of **1967** in Brisbane but led his country to victory in the World Team Cup in Dusseldorf 11 years later. JB

MARGARET EVELYN **OSBORNE** (USA)

Born 4/3/18. Now Mrs du Pont (1947). One of the finest of American doubles players and a formidably successful competitor in singles. With her splendidly consistent serving and her strength and skill at the net, she did much to set the pattern for the period of American supremacy in women's tennis, which began in 1946. Won Wimbledon singles in **1947** Forest Hills **1948/49/50** and Paris in **1946/49**. She and Louise Brough won the Wimbledon doubles in **1946/48/49/50/54**. They ruled the US doubles from **1942–50** and **1955–57**, and held the French title **1946/47/49**. She won the Wimbledon mixed with Neale Fraser in **1962** – 15 years after her first singles victory, at the age of 44 years 125 days, to become Wimbledon's oldest champion of either sex in any event.

SARAH HAMMOND **PALFREY** (USA)

Born 18/9/12. Died 27/2/96 became Mrs J. A. Danzig (1951) formerly Mrs M. Fabyan (1934), and Mrs E. T. Cooke (1940). A fine volleyor with a sweeping backhand and a notable doubles player, she partnered Alice Marble to victory at Wimbledon in **1938/39** and won the US doubles title 9 times with a variety of partners – Betty Nuthall (**1930**), Helen Jacobs (**1932/34/35**), Alice Marble (**1937/38/39/40**) and Margaret Osborne (**1941**). She won the US singles in **1941/45** and was r/u to Helen Jacobs in**1934/35**. She was the US mixed champion on 4 occasions with Perry (**1932**), Maier (**1935**), Budge (**1937**) and Kramer (**1941**). She played in 10 W Cup matches and won 14 rubbers out of 21.

ADRIANO **PANATTA** (Italy)

Born 9/7/50. Without doubt, **1976** was the *annus mirabilis* of Panatta's career. Until then he had always been dashing and stylish, but had never made full use of his talent. In **1976**, however, he lived dangerously and survived brilliantly. In Rome he became the first home player to win in Italy for 15 years after frustrating Warwick no fewer than 11 times at m-p in the first round. In Paris, against Hutka, he again faced a first-round m-p and again went on to take the championship. Four months later, when Italy won D Cup for the first time, Panatta played a major role in their victory. Paris, Rome and D Cup – this was Panatta's year! He was also the leading player in the Italian teams which reached the **1977/79/80** D Cup finals. He reached the French sf in **1973/75** and was runner-up in Rome **1978** and Hamburg **1972**.

FRANK ANDREW **PARKER** (USA)

Born 31/1/16. Died 24/7/97. Shrewd, persistent, and accurate in spite of a certain lightness of shot, he shared with Trabert the distinction, rare for an American, of winning the French title twice. At his best on slow courts, he was ranked in the first 10 in the US for 17 consecutive years between **1933**, the year of the first of his 5 US Clay Court victories, and **1949** when he turned pro. His victories in Paris were in **1948/49**, and in **1949** he won the doubles in Paris and Wimbledon with Gonzales. He won the US singles in **1944/45** as an Army sergeant and the doubles with Kramer in **1943**. He played in the D Cup challenge round against Britain in **1937** when the US regained the trophy after 10 years and in the **1939** and **1948** challenge rounds. In 7 ties between **1932** and **1948**, won 12 of 14 singles rubbers.

GERALD LEIGHTON **PATTERSON** (Australia)

Born 17/12/1895. Died 13/6/1967. Formidably aggressive with a cannonball service modelled on McLoughlin's, he was the dominating player when international competition was resumed in 1919. After being r/u to O'Hara Wood in the **1914** Australian singles, he became Wimbledon's first post-war champ by defeating Brookes in **1919**. He lost his Wimbledon title to Tilden in **1920** but regained it against Lycett in **1922**. R/u doubles in**1922** (O'Hara Wood) and **1928** (Hawkes) and won the mixed with Suzanne Lenglen in**1920**. He won the Australian singles in his fourth final in **1927**. Between **1919–28** he played 46 D Cup rubbers for Australia and Australasia, winning 21 out of his 31 singles and 11 of his 15 doubles in 16 ties. He was a nephew of Dame Nellie Melba and was the first man to win the Wimbledon singles by playing through when the Challenge Round was abolished there in **1922**.

JESSE EDWARD ('**BUDGE**') **PATTY** (USA)
Born 11/2/24. An American who lived in Paris and developed his game there, 'Budge' Patty, with his elegant, effective forehand volley, was one of the great post-war stylists.**1950** – when he won both the Wimbledon and French singles – was the peak of his career, but his rivalry with Drobny captured the public's imagination. The most notable of their long and dramatic matches was in the third round at Wimbledon in **1953**. After 4 hours 20 minutes Patty lost 8–6 16–18 3–6 8–6 12–10 after holding 6 m-ps. He had beaten the Czech at Wimbledon in **1947** and 3 years later by 6–1 6–2 3–6 5–7 7–5 in his French f. The last of their meetings was in **1954**. Drobny, on his way to the title, won a 4-set sf. Patty won his last title there in **1957** when he and Mulloy, then aged 43, beat Hoad and Fraser to take the men's doubles. He won the Italian singles **1954**, and the German singles **1953/54** and doubles **1953/54/55**.

FREDERICK ('**FRED**') JOHN **PERRY** (Great Britain)
Born 18/5/09. Died 2/2/95. A US citizen. The most successful modern British player, and the first man to win all four Grand Slam titles, a feat achieved only by four others – Budge, Emerson, Laver and Agassi. He was an aggressive competitor with boundless self-confidence and a remarkable running forehand. Won Wimbledon singles **1934/35/36** – the first player since A. F. Wilding (**1910–13**) to take the title 3 years in succession – and mixed (with Dorothy Round) **1935/36**. US singles **1933/34/36**. French singles **1935** and doubles (with G. P. Hughes) **1933**. Australian singles **1934** and doubles (with Hughes) **1934**. The world no 1 **1934–36**, he won 45 out of 52 D Cup rubbers, (34–4 singles, 11–3 doubles) between **1931–36** leading Britain to victory in **1933/34/35/36**. Turned pro in **1936** and toured with Vines and Tilden, winning US Pro Champ **1938/41**. Then founded a sports clothing business and became journalist and broadcaster for BBC Radio.

YVON FRANCOIS MARIE **PETRA** (France)
Born 8/3/16 in Indo–China. Died 12/9/84. Wimbledon's first post-war men's singles champion. Reached mixed f at Wimbledon **1937** with Simone Mathieu and won French doubles**1938** with Destremau, defeating Budge and Mako in f. Between **1942**, when he was released from a prisoner-of-war camp, and **1945**, he consolidated his reputation as France's most aggressive competitor in wartime domestic competitions. At Wimbledon,**1946**, his strength, flair and, notably, the consistency of his heavy serving gained this formidably built player an unexpected title. Drobny beat Kramer, the favourite, in 4r. Petra disposed of Pails, the other expected finalist, in qf and then won 5s matches against Tom Brown and Geoff Brown. That was the peak of his career. Marcel Bernard beat him in the French sf – played in July that year – and his consolation was a doubles victory, partnered by Bernard, over Morea and Segura in f. Patty beat him easily on the second day at Forest Hills and in **1947** he lost to Tom Brown in qf at Wimbledon.

NICOLA PIETRANGELI (Italy)
Born 11/9/33. A master of the European clay court style, he was born in Tunis (of a French father and Russian mother) and between **1954–72** played in 164 D Cup rubbers for Italy, more than anyone in history. Won most rubbers (120), played most singles (110) and won most (78), played most doubles (54) and won most (42), and played in most ties (66). Appeared in the **1960/61** Challenge Rounds against Australia, but won only one 'dead' singles. Won French singles **1959/60** and doubles (with Sirola), Italian singles **1957/61**, and German singles **1960**. Reached sf at Wimbledon, **1960**, and doubles final (with Sirola) **1956**.

DR JOSHUA PIM (Ireland)
Born 20/5/1869. Died 15/4/1942. A robust, adventurous competitor, regarded by contemporary critics as one of the great geniuses of early tennis. 'When Pim was at his best he was virtually unplayable,' wrote Wallis Myers. 'It is scarcely exaggerating to say that he could hit a coin placed anywhere on the court.' He reached sf at Wimbledon **1890**, losing to Hamilton, who became Wimbledon's first Irish champ, then lost in **1891** to Wilfred Baddeley in the All-Comers' f and again in **1892** Challenge Round. He gained his revenge, however, by beating Baddeley in the **1893/94** finals. Pim won the Irish title for the 3rd and last time in **1895** but then played little first-class tennis until he was controversially picked for the D Cup match against USA at New York in **1902**. He was preferred to Laurie Doherty, lost both his singles badly and the British Isles were beaten 3–2. 'Although still very good, Pim had no more than a shadow of his former skill, but alas a great deal more than the shadow of his former weight,' wrote Commander Hillyard.

ADRIAN KARL **QUIST** (Australia)
Born 23/1/13. Died 17/11/91. A shrewd, graceful doubles player, whose wins at Wimbledon were separated by a 15 year gap. Won with J. H. Crawford in **1935** and, when almost a veteran, with J. E. Bromwich **1950**. Held Australian title from **1936–50**, winning twice with D. P. Turnbull (**1936/37**) and 8 times with Bromwich (**1938/39/40/46/47/48/49/50**). Won US doubles (with Bromwich) **1939**, French doubles (with J. H. Crawford)

1935, and Australian singles **1936/40/48**. Won 42 out of 56 D Cup rubbers in 28 ties between **1933–48** (24–10 singles, 19–3 doubles)

WILLIAM CHARLES RENSHAW (Great Britain)

Born 3/1/1861. Died 12/8/1904. The first great champion. Learnt on asphalt at school at Cheltenham with twin brother, Ernest, a more graceful but less determined competitor. They were the first spectacular players and their skill – particularly in volleying and smashing – brought crowds to Wimbledon and contributed considerably to the development of lawn tennis as a spectator sport. 'Willie' Renshaw was singles champ at Wimbledon from **1881–86** and in **1889** and his seven titles remain a record for men. He held the doubles, with Ernest, in **1884/85/86/88/89**. Ernest won the singles title in **1888** and was beaten by William in the challenge rounds of **1882**, **1883** and **1889**.

NANCY ANN RICHEY (USA)

Born 23/8/42. Later Mrs Gunter (1970). A Texan, famous for her shorts and peaked cap, she was, like her brother, George Clifford Richey, a tenacious baseliner, impressive on clay. Her determination occasionally brought unexpected success on grass. She reached the **1969** US final, losing 6–2 6–2 to Margaret Court. She won in Australia **1967**, beating Lesley Turner, another clay-court specialist, in the final. At Wimbledon she reached qf seven times in nine years **1964–72** but was semi-finalist only in **1968**. She won Wimbledon doubles with Maria Bueno **1966**. On clay she won French singles **1968**, beating Ann Jones to avenge a defeat in the **1966** final, but the best evidence of her quality was her record in US Clay Courts. She won Indianapolis from **1963–68** and even as late as **1975** led Chris Evert 7–6 5–0 in the semi-finals there, twice reaching m-p before retiring with cramp at 2–4 in the final set. She played W Cup from **1962–68** and three years of Fed Cup between **1964–69** winning 15 of her 17 rubbers (10–1 singles, 5–1 doubles).

ROBERT ('BOBBY') LARIMORE RIGGS (USA)

Born 25/2/18. Died 25/10/95. A shrewd, confident match–player, with remarkable versatility of shot, he won all 3 titles on his first appearance at Wimbledon in **1939**. He also won Forest Hills in **1939**, but lost to McNeill in the French f. He turned pro in **1941** and later became a notable competitor in veterans' events, but his greatest fame came at the age of 55. Profiting from the Women's Lib controversy, he challenged and beat Margaret Court 6–2 6–1 in a singles match in Ramona, Cal, and then lost to Billie Jean King 6–4 6–3 6–3, before a record television audience of almost 50 million and 30,492 paying spectators at the Houston Astrodome in September **1973**.

ANTHONY ('TONY') DALTON ROCHE (Australia)

Born 17/5/45. Strong, rugged and a fine volleyer, he was the left-hander in one of Wimbledon's most successful doubles partnerships. He won the doubles with John Newcombe in **1965**, from **1968–70** (the first hat-trick of titles since the Dohertys **1903–5**) and in **1974**. Other doubles victories with Newcombe included US **1967**, French 1967/69, Australia 1965/67/71/76 (he also won in **1977** with Ashe) and Italy 1965/71. He also won Wimbledon mixed doubles with Francoise Durr **1976**. He did not achieve as much as expected in singles, partly because of injury. The extraordinary operation on his left elbow, performed without knife or anaesthetic in the Philippines by a faith healer, received worldwide publicity. He never reached an Australian final in spite of numerous attempts, but was runner-up to Laver at Wimbledon in **1968** and lost two US Open finals: **1969** when Laver beat him to complete the Grand Slam and **1970** to Rosewall. His most successful year was **1966** when he won French and Italian titles. Played Davis Cup **1964–78** but did not play singles in a final until he beat Panatta in the opening match **1977**. His record in 12 ties was 7–3 in singles and 7–2 in doubles.

KENNETH ('KEN') ROBERT ROSEWALL (Australia)

Born 2/11/34. For a quarter of a century Rosewall's grace and easy, economical style delighted the connoisseurs and the only regret about his long and distinguished career is that, in spite of four finals over a period of 20 years, he never won the Wimbledon singles title. He began in the 1950's as a Hopman prodigy and it was not until the end of **1979** that he retired from Grand Prix tennis. In **1953**, aged 18, he won the Australian and French singles and, with Hoad, the French and Wimbledon doubles. In **1954** he lost to Drobny in the Wimbledon final. Hoad beat him in the **1956** Wimbledon final, but Rosewall avenged that defeat in the US final, frustrating Hoad in the last leg of his attempt on the Grand Slam. Turning professional in **1957**, he took over the leadership of the professional circuit from Gonzales until Laver's arrival in **1963**. Rosewall's skills endured. In **1968** he won the first open tournament at Bournemouth and then recaptured some of his former titles. He regained the French singles and doubles (with Stolle) in **1968**. In **1970** – 14 years after his first success and aged 35 – he won the US title again and reached his fourth final at Forest Hills in **1974**. The gap between his Australian successes was even wider. After his victories in 1953/55, he won again in 1971/72. But Wimbledon always eluded him. Newcombe beat him in **1970**, his third final, and Connors overwhelmed him in the **1974** final. In the D Cup he won 19 of his 22 rubbers in 11 ties between **1953** and **1975** (17–2 singles, 2–1 doubles).

DOROTHY EDITH ROUND (Great Britain)

Born 13/7/09. Died 12/11/82. Became Mrs D. L. Little (1937). Determined and efficient, possessing a fine forehand drive and shrewd drop-shot, she was one of the two British women's singles champs at Wimbledon between the wars. She gained her first notable victory there against Lili d'Alvarez in **1931**, was r/u to Helen Wills Moody in **1933**, then beat Helen Jacobs to win the title in **1934** and regained it against

Jadwiga Jedrzejowska in **1937**. She won the Australian singles in **1935** and the Wimbledon mixed in **1934** (with Miki) and **1935/36** (with Perry). She won 4 of her 13 W Cup rubbers between **1931–36**.

ELIZABETH MONTAGUE **RYAN** (USA)

Born 5/2/1892. Died 6/7/1979. Suzanne Lenglen's doubles partner and the winner of 19 Wimbledon titles. A determined competitor with a cunningly chopped forehand and a great appetite for match-play, she was regarded by contemporaries as 'the best player never to win a great singles Championship'. With a variety of playing partners, she was victorious in the Wimbledon doubles 12 times – **1914** with Morton, **1919/20/21/ 22/23/25** with Lenghen, **1926** with Browne, **1927/30** with Wills Moody, **1933/34** with Matthieu. She won 7 mixed titles **1919/21/23** with Lycett, **1927** with Hunter, **1928** with Spence, **1930** with Crawford, **1932** with Maier. She also won US doubles in **1926** with Goss and the French doubles **1930/32** with Moody, **1933/34** with Matthieu.

GABRIELA **SABATINI** (Argentina)

Born on 16 May 1970 in Buenos Aires, Argentina. One of the most glamorous players ever to reach the heights 'Gaby' first appeared on the scene as an outstanding junior, inspired to take up the game by the example of Argentina's great men's champion Guillermo Vilas whose backhand she copied. Won the Orange Bowl 18s and ended the year as the No.1 junior on the ITF rankings in **1984** and No.1 in Argentina and South America from **1985–1989**. The youngest semi-finalist (at the time) in the **1985** French Open she never did better in Paris during the next 10 consecutive challenges. It was at the **1990** US Open that her considerable talent finally came to full flower when she upset the reigning champion and world No.1 Steffi Graf with a brilliant display of all-court tennis. She never reached those heights again and could look back on the **1988** US final and the **1991** Wimbledon final (when she twice served for the match against Graf) as the other highlights of her 43 Grand Slam appearances. Her **1988** doubles win at Wimbledon (with Graf) was her only major doubles title. Elsewhere her **1988** and **1994** Virginia Slims Championship wins were the best of her 27 career successes that earned her a total of $8.7 million. Her silver medal at the Seoul Olympics in **1988** brough her great personal satisfaction. In **1992** a rose was named after her and a Gaby Doll was marketed in her name. Towards the end of her career she developed her talent as a singer to make several recordings. JB

MANUEL ('**MANOLO**') **SANTANA** (Spain)

Born 10/5/38. Learnt the game as a ballboy in Madrid and, after a period in which he was the most admired clay court player in Europe, won US singles **1965**, and Wimbledon singles **1966**. Possesed a remarkable forehand and great delicacy of touch. Won French singles **1961/64**, defeating Pietrangeli in both finals, and doubles (with Emerson) **1963**, and South African singles **1967**. The most successful Spanish player in history, he won 92 D Cup rubbers out of 120 in 46 ties between **1958–73** (69–17 singles, 23–11 doubles).

RICHARD ('**DICK**') **SAVITT** (USA)

Born 4/3/27. His talent was discovered in the classic fashion by a complete stranger who saw him playing in a public park, and after a modest junior career he became a powerful exponent of the serve-and-volley game. Concentrating on tennis after a basketball injury in **1949**, he rose rapidly on the US ranking list, moving up from 16th to 6th after reaching sf at Forest Hills, **1950**, with victories over Seixas and Bromwich. His remarkable year was **1951**. He won both the Australian and Wimbledon titles, defeating McGregor in both finals. This was his first trip to Europe and he never achieved the same kind of success again, although he played some memorable matches, notably qf against Rosewall at Forest Hills, **1956**, and a vain defence of his US indoor title in a three-hour f in **1959**. He was a member of the US D Cup team in **1951**, but was not chosen to play in the Challenge Round against Australia.

FREDERICK ('**TED**') RUDOLPH **SCHROEDER** (USA)

Born 20/7/21. A powerful Californian whose aggressive serve-and-volley game brought him much success on fast surfaces. The US National Junior Champion in **1939**, he won the NCAA Championships from Stanford in **1942** and the same year won the US Championships, defeating Frank Parker in the final. In **1949** he reached the final again but lost in five sets to Pancho Gonzales. Earlier that same year, on his only visit to Wimbledon he had won the singles in heroic fashion after surviving four five-set matches. In the first round he had beaten his doubles partner, Gardnar Mulloy, 7–5 in the fifth (later they reached the doubles final and lost to Gonzales and Parker). In the quarter-finals he had been m-p down to Frank Sedgman and, despite being foot-faulted on his first serve, had followed in his second serve to hit a winning volley and finally won 9–7 in the final set. In all he played 291 games. Only two champions played more – Boris Becker (292) in **1985** and Ashley Cooper (322) in **1958**. In doubles he won the US Championships with Jack Kramer in **1940/41/47** and the mixed with Louise Brough in **1942**. A distinguished member of the US D Cup team between **1946–51**, he played in six Challenge Rounds, winning eight of his 11 singles and one of his four doubles. Played in 8 ties, winning 13 of 19 rubbers (11–3 singles, 2–3 doubles). JB

RICHARD ('**DICK**') DUDLEY **SEARS** (USA)

Born 16/10/1861 Died 8/4/1943. The first US Champion in **1881** while he was still a 19-year-old student at Harvard, this great Boston athlete was the youngest winner until the slightly younger Oliver Campbell won in **1890** aged 19 and a half. (They were both older than Pete Sampras who became the youngest ever winner in **1990** aged 19 years, 28 days). Sears retained his title for the next six years, playing through in **1882/83** and winning the newly introduced Challenge Round in **1884/85/86/87**. He also won six doubles titles, five with James Dwight (**1882/83/84/86/87**) and one with Joseph Clark (**1885**). JB

FRANCIS ('**FRANK**') ARTHUR **SEDGMAN** (Australia)

Born 29/10/27. A superb volleyer who seemed to glide about the court, he was Australia's first post-war Wimbledon singles champ and, with Ken McGregor, he achieved the Grand Slam of the 4 major doubles titles in **1951**. Won Wimbledon singles **1952** and doubles (with J. E. Bromwich) **1948** and (with McGregor) **1951/52**. US singles **1951/52** and doubles (with Bromwich) **1950** and (with McGregor) **1951**. French doubles (with McGregor) **1951/52**. Australian singles **1949/50** (with McGregor) doubles **1951/52**. Italian singles and doubles (with Drobny) **1952**. Won 25 D Cup rubbers out of 28 in 10 ties between **1949–52**(16–3 singles, 9–0 doubles). Turned pro in **1953**.

FRANCISCO ('**PANCHO**') **SEGURA** (Ecuador)

Born 20/6/21. An unorthodox showman who made his reputation in his pro years – he achieved little as an amateur. Won the NCAA singles **1943/44/45**, the only triple winner this century, plus the US Clay Court title in **1944** and the US Indoor in **1946**, but made little mark at Wimbledon, losing to Tom Brown and to Drobny in his two singles appearances. He turned pro in **1947** and immediately became one of the great entertainers of the pro game, winning the US Pro title **1950/51/52**. With his double-fisted forehand, his deadly lobs, his scuttling speed about the court, and his beaming smile, he was a most popular competitor for 20 years. If he did not win as many titles as he deserved, he was always capable of testing players of the quality of Kramer, Rosewall, and Gonzales.

ELIAS VICTOR ('**VIC**') **SEIXAS** (USA)

Born 30/8/23. A doggedly successful American competitor. Won Wimbledon singles **1953** and mixed 3 times with Doris Hart (**1953/54/55**) and once with Shirley Fry (**1956**). US singles **1954** and doubles (with M. G. Rose) **1952** and (with M. A. Trabert) **1954**. French doubles (with Trabert) **1954/55**. Played in 7 successive D Cup Challenge Rounds and won 38 out of 55 rubbers in 19 ties between **1951–57** (24–12 singles, 14–5 doubles).

MARGARET SMITH (Australia)

Born 16/7/42. Now Mrs Court (1967). In **1970** she became the second woman to achieve the Grand Slam of the major singles championships, having brought off a unique mixed doubles slam with Fletcher in **1963**. A powerful athlete, superbly fit, with a heavy service, great stamina and a formidable reach on the volley, she won a record number of 62 GS titles (24 singles, 19 doubles, 19 mixed) – and would have won more if she had not been afflicted by occasional and often inexplicable losses of confidence. Her major singles successes were Wimbledon **1963/65/70**, US Championships **1962/65/69/70/ 73**, French Championships **1962/64/69/70/73**, and Australian Championships **1960–66**, **1969–71** and **1973**. She was also three times the holder of the Italian (**1962/63/64**), German (**1964/65/66**) and South African (**1968/70/71**) titles. In addition, she won the doubles at Wimbledon twice, with Turner (**1964**) and Tegart (**1969**) and the mixed five times, with Fletcher (**1963/65/66/68**) and Riessen (**1975**). She took the US doubles five times – with Ebbern (**1963**), Bueno (**1968**) Dalton (**1970**) and Wade (**1973/75**), and the mixed on eight occasions with Mark (**1961**), Stolle (**1962/65**), Fletcher (**1963**), Newcombe (**1964**) and Riessen (**1969/70/ 72**). She won the French four times in doubles with Turner (**1964/65**), Tegart (**1966**) and Wade (**1973**) and mixed with Fletcher (**1963/64/65**) and Riessen (**1969**), and she held eight Australian doubles with Reitano (**1961**), Ebbern (**1962/63**), Turner (**1965**), Dalton (**1969/70**), Goolagong (**1971**) and Wade (**1973**) and two mixed titles with Fletcher (**1963/64**). She toured successfully, with the help of her husband, Barry, with two children, but retired in **1977** when she found that she was expecting a third baby.

STANLEY ('**STAN**') ROGER **SMITH** (USA)

Born 14/12/46. The very epitome of the All-American boy with his tall straight-backed figure, his fair hair and his clean-cut good looks, he became a national hero in **1972**, as well as the world's No.1 player, when he won a magnificent Wimbledon final against Nastase and then beat the Rumanian again in the opening rubber of the D Cup final on unfriendly clay in Bucharest to launch the United States towards an improbable victory against the odds. Earlier, in **1969**, he had won the US Nationals and the following year had beaten Laver and Rosewall to capture the first-ever Masters which, that year, was a round-robin competition. When he won the US Open in **1971** on the grass of Forest Hills he was perfecting the serve-and-volley technique that made him such an awkward opponent. Although his groundstrokes were never his strength, he used them intelligently to secure the few breaks of serve that were necessary as he blanketed the net to secure his own service games. His doubles partnership with Lutz was one of the best American pairings there has ever been. They are the only pair to have won US National titles on all four surfaces – grass, clay, hard and indoor. Four times they won the US Open – **1968/74/78/ 80** and in **1977** they were successful both in South Africa and the US Pro at Boston. In D Cup they are the only American pair to have won three Challenge Round rubbers and two in the Final Round. Overall his D Cup record is 35 wins and 7 losses in 24 ties between **1968–79** (15–4 singles, 20–3 doubles). JB

MICHAEL DETLEF STICH (Germany)

Born 18/10/68. Emerging from Boris Becker's shadow in **1991**, he beat his fellow German in the Wimbledon final with a brilliant display of grass court skill that stamped him as one of the game's great fast-court players. The following year, **1992**, he teamed with John McEnroe to win the doubles at Wimbledon and then joined Becker to win an Olympic gold medal in Barcelona. But it was not until **1993** that he was truly accepted as a great champion by his countrymen. In that *annus mirabilis* he led his country to the final of the World Team Cup, remained undefeated as he beat Sampras to win the ATP Tour World Championship, was a finalist in the Compaq Grand Slam Cup and, in Becker's absence, led Germany to a decisive Davis Cup final win over Australia in Dusseldorf. By winning six of his eight finals that year on four different surfaces he finished as the world's No.2, the highest ranking he ever achieved. In **1994** he reached the US Open final but lost to Agassi. In **1996** he surprised everyone by reaching the French Open final where Kafelnikov beat him. Tall, slim and wiry he always looked physically frail and it was injuries to his shoulder and ankle that eventually forced him to retire from the game in **1997** after reaching the sf at Wimbledon. Altogether he recorded 18 singles wins and nine in doubles and in seven years of Davis Cup play had a 35–11 win/loss record (21–9 in singles, 14–2 in doubles) from 17 ties. JB

FREDERICK ('FRED') SYDNEY STOLLE (Australia)

Born 8/10/38. Former Sydney bank clerk, regarded primarily as doubles specialist, who by diligence and determination became one of the most successful singles players of the 1960s. Powerful serving and volleying, added to dogged consistency in return of service on the backhand, compensated for his lack of mobility and flexibility. Shared with Von Cramm the unlucky distinction of losing in 3 successive Wimbledon singles f, falling to McKinley (**1963**) and Emerson (**1964/65**). Was also r/u to Lundquist in **1964** Italian f, but won French singles **1965** and US and German titles **1966**. Established himself first as a doubles player with Hewitt. They won Australia **1963/64**, Wimbledon **1962/64** and Italy **1963/64**. With Emerson, who had dominated him in singles, won French and US doubles **1965** and Australia, Italy and US **1966**. In **1981**, aged 42, he and Newcombe (37) took McEnroe/ Fleming to 5s tie-break in US Open sf. Became contract professional **1967** and reached Wimbledon doubles f with Rosewall **1968**, and won mixed doubles there with Ann Jones in **1969**. Between **1964–66** he won 13 out of his 16 D Cup rubbers in 6 ties (10–2 singles, 3–1 doubles). Coached NY Sets to victory in World Team Tennis competition **1976** and **1977** (now called NY Apples).

ERIC WILLIAM STURGESS (South Africa)

Born 10/5/20. South Africa's most successful singles competitor and their nat champ on no fewer than 11 occasions, beginning a sequence of victories in **1939/40** and continuing in **1946**, **1948–54**, and **1957**. Outside Johannesburg his major achievement was the capture of the German singles **1952; ** r/u in Paris **1947/51** and lost to Gonzales in **1948** US f. Twice he was in Wimbledon sf, but in spite of speed, steadiness, and elegance, he lacked the weight of shot to win in the highest class and his second service was vulnerable. He won the French doubles with Fannin **1947** and a number of mixed titles, notably Wimbledon **1949** (with Sheila Summers) and **1950** (with Louise Brough), and F Hills **1949** (with Brough).

MAY GODFREY SUTTON (USA)

Born 25/9/1886 in Plymouth, England. Died 4/10/1975. Became Mrs T.C. Bundy (1912). In **1905** the first overseas player to win a Wimbledon title. The seventh and youngest child of a British naval officer, Captain A. de G. Sutton, she learnt tennis on asphalt courts after her family moved to California in **1893**. She was forceful and vigorous with a disconcerting top-spin forehand. F. R. Burrow commented: 'She took a deep breath before every stroke and then hit the ball with all her force to the accompaniment of a very audible expiration.' After winning the US singles and doubles in **1904** she went, aged 18, to Wimbledon **1905** and defeated the holder, Miss Douglass, in the Challenge Round. Miss Douglass regained the title the following year, but then lost a third battle with the Californian in **1907**. After winning the US Clay Court singles **1912**, Miss Sutton married Thomas Bundy, 3 times a US doubles champ. She played doubles in the **1925** W Cup and in **1929** returned to Wimbledon at 42 to defeat Eileen Bennett, seeded 4, and reach the qf. She was still playing 44 years later. Her daughter Dorothy represented the US 3 times in the W Cup and won the Australian singles **1938**, and a nephew, John Doeg, was US champ in **1930**.

WILLIAM ('BILLY') FRANKLIN TALBERT (USA)

Born 4/9/18. Died 28/2/99. An expert in the practice, technique and strategy of doubles. The best right-court player of his generation, his most important victories were gained with Mulloy, with whom he won the US doubles **1942/45/46/48**, and a total of 84 out of 90 tournaments in ten years. With a variety of partners, he won US Clay Court doubles **1942/44/45/46** and the US Indoor Doubles **1949/50/51/52/54**. Abroad, with the young Trabert, also from Cincinnati, he won French and Italian doubles **1950**. He was runner-up to Parker in US singles **1944/45** and US Indoor champion **1948/51**. He won nine of his ten D Cup rubbers **1946–53**, in 8 ties, (2–0 singles, 7–1 doubles) and from **1953–57** he captained the US D Cup team. Later became Tournament Director of the US Open. All this was achieved despite the disability of diabetes.

WILLIAM ('BILL') TATEM TILDEN (USA)

Born 10/2/1893. Died 5/6/1953. For many critics the greatest player and student of match-strategy in the history of the game who was world No 1 **1920–25** and US No 1 ten years in a row **1920–29**, a record. Tall, with a long reach and a long stride, great strength and versatility of shot, and a powerful sense of drama, Tilden did not win a major title until he was 27. Then won Wimbledon singles **1920/21/30**, and doubles (with F. T. Hunter) **1927**, and US singles **1920/21/22/23/24/25/29**, and doubles (with Richards) **1918/21/22**, (with Norton) **1923**, (with Hunter) **1927**. Was imprisoned for homosexual activities in **1951**, and died in tragic circumstances two years later, penniless and with few remaining friends. Was first Italian champ in **1930** and played D Cup from **1920–30** winning 34 rubbers out of 41 and 21 out of 28 in Challenge Rounds. Between **1920–26** won 13 successive Challenge Round singles. His final record from 17 ties was 25–5 in singles and 9–2 in doubles. Turned pro in **1931** after winning 138 of the 192 tournaments he had contested as an amateur.

MARION ANTHONY ('**TONY**') **TRABERT** (USA)
Born 16/8/30. Won Wimbledon singles **1955** and US singles **1953/55** without losing a set. Won French singles **1954/55** and doubles victories included US in **1954** (with E. V. Seixas), French **1950** (with W. F. Talbert) and **1954/55** (with Seixas) and Italian **1950** (with Talbert). Won 27 out of 35 D Cup rubbers in 14 ties between **1951–55** (16–5 singles, 11–3 doubles). Served a term as US captain in the **1970s**. Turned pro in **1955**.

CHRISTINE CLARA **TRUMAN** (Great Britain)
Born 16/2/41. Now Mrs G. T. Janes (1967). Britain's most popular post-war player. She possessed a powerful forehand, a disconcerting ability to hit her way out of crises, a remarkable capacity for unorthodox volleying, and a temperament and court manners that made her a model for every schoolgirl in the country. She was always regarded as a potential Wimbledon champ and reached sf at the age of 16 in her first Wimbledon, where she lost to Althea Gibson, the eventual winner. Afterwards came a series of spectacular failures until she reached the **1961** f, only to fall to Angela Mortimer. Her best performances were a victory over Miss Gibson in the **1958** W Cup match, which helped to give Britain the trophy for the first time since the war, and the capture of the French and Italian singles titles in **1959**. Won **1960** Australian doubles with Maria Bueno. She and her sister, Nell, formed an aggressively effective – and sometimes erratic – doubles partnership. She won 10 rubbers out of 25 in 11 W Cup matches.

WENDY MAY **TURNBULL** (Australia)
Born 26/11/52. Known popularly as 'Rabbit' for her speed about the court, this Australian doubles expert was nevertheless a singles finalist at three of the four Grand Slams and was ranked among the world's top ten for eight years (**1977–1984**). Twice she lost to Chris Evert (US Open **1977**, French Open **1979**) and once to Hana Mandlikova (Australian Open **1980**). For someone whose doubles prowess made her a much sought after partner it is curious that she never won a doubles or mixed title at the Australian Open. Her four ladies doubles successes came in **1978** at Wimbledon (with Kerry Reid), in **1979** at the French and US Opens (both with Betty Stove), and in **1982** at the US Open (with Rosie Casals). In mixed doubles she won five Grand Slam titles – the French Open in **1979** (with Bob Hewitt) and **1982** (with John Lloyd), the US Open in **1980** (with Marty Riessen), and Wimbledon twice, in **1983** and **1984** (both with John Lloyd). Her last important success came at the Seoul Olympics in **1988** where she was a doubles bronze medallist with Liz Smyllie. She appeared in a record 45 Federation Cup ties from **1977** contributing 46 wins from her 62 rubbers (17–8 in singles 29–8 in doubles) and later served as Fed Cup captain. She was awarded the OBE in 1984 for services to tennis. JB

LESLEY ROSEMARY **TURNER** (Australia)
Born 16/8/42. Now Mrs W. W. Bowrey (1968). Clever, strong and persistent, she gained her principal successes on European clay courts. In **1961** on her first European tour she lost to Maria Bueno in the Italian final and was runner-up again **1963/64** before winning the title **1967/68**. She won the French singles **1963**, defeating Ann Jones, and **1965**, beating Margaret Court, and was runner-up **1962/67**. She reached the Australian final **1964/67**. In doubles, with Margaret Court, she won Wimbledon **1964**, Paris **1964/65** and Australia **1965**. Also took the Australian doubles title, with Judy Tegart, **1964/67** and the US doubles, with Darlene Hard, **1961**. Won Wimbledon mixed doubles with Fred Stolle **1961/64**.

JOHN ('**JOHNNY**') WILLIAM **VAN RYN** (USA)
Born 30/6/05. Died 7/8/99. Formed one of the most famous of all doubles partnerships with Wilmer Allison. Pat Hughes described their combination as 'a perfect blending of styles...Van Ryn dipped the ball over from the right court and his partner stepped in at the psychological moment for the final volley'. George Lott thought that their deep personal friendship and knowledge of each other's movements and reactions played an important part in their success. With Allison, Van Ryn succeeded at Wimbledon in **1929–30** and took the US title in **1931/35**. He won Paris and Wimbledon with Lott in **1931**. In the **1929** D Cup Challenge Round he and Allison beat Cochet and Borotra and in the **1932** match they defeated Cochet and Brugnon. He was a member of the US team from **1928–36** and won 32 of his 44 rubbers in 24 ties. (18–10 singles, 14–2 doubles).

GUILLERMO VILAS (Argentina)
Born 17/8/52. For a man who had learned his tennis on the slow red clay of Buenos Aires it is remarkable that his first major success should have been to win the **1974** Masters title on grass at Kooyong Stadium, Melbourne. This was the only time the tournament was played on grass and his wins over Newcombe, Borg and Nastase were as brilliant as they were unexpected. He proved that this had been no fluke by winning the Aus-

tralian Open twice, in **1978** and **1979**. A powerfully built left-hander with heavily topped groundstrokes, he specialised in wearing down the opposition, which he did successfully in **1977** both at the French Open and the US Open, which for the third and last time was being played on American clay courts. That year he claimed 15 titles altogether. Coached and managed shrewdly by Ion Tiriac, he won 61 of the 103 finals he contested in a long career and in the **1977** season he won 50 consecutive singles matches between July 12 in Kitsbuhel and his retirement while playing Nastase (who was using the spaghetti strung rackets) in the final of the Aiz-en-Provence on October 2. This is a record in the open era. JB

HENRY **ELLSWORTH VINES** (USA)
Born 28/9/11. Died 17/3/94. The possessor of a fine forehand and one of the fastest services of all time. Defeated Bunny Austin in **1932** 6–4 6–2 6–0 in one of the shortest Wimbledon f and lost title next year in a classic f against Jack Crawford. Won US singles **1931/32** and Australian doubles **1933** with Gledhill. Played D Cup **1932/33**, winning 13 rubbers out of 16, all singles, in 8 ties. Turned pro **1934**.

BARON **GOTTFRIED** ALEXANDER MAXIMILIAN WALTER KURT **VON CRAMM** (Germany)
Born 7/7/09. Died in car accident in Egypt 9/11/76. An elegant stylist and Germany's most successful pre-war player. Won French singles **1934/36** and doubles (with H. Henkel) **1937**, and German singles **1932/33/34/35/48/49** and doubles **1948/49/53/54/55**. Like F. S. Stolle, he was losing singles finalist at Wimbledon for 3 successive years – **1935–37**. Won Wimbledon mixed (with Hilda Krahwinkel) **1933** and US doubles (with Henkel) **1937**. Won 82 D Cup rubbers out of 102 (58–10 singles, 24–9 doubles) in 37 ties between **1932–53**.

SARAH **VIRGINIA WADE** (Great Britain)
Born 10/7/45. A spectacular and dramatic competitor, at her 16th attempt she finally achieved her ambition of winning the women's singles at Wimbledon in the Centenary year of **1977**. Until then her career had been an extravagant mixture of bitter disappointments, many of the worst endured at Wimbledon, and dazzling successes. Her first major success was gained at US Open **1968** when she defeated Billie Jean King 6–4 6–2 in the final. She won the Australian title, beating Evonne Goolagong in **1972** and gained her only major clay-court success in **1971**, when she defeated Helga Masthoff in the Italian final. Her best doubles victories – France **1973**, US **1973/75**, Australia **1973** and Italy **1968** – were won with Margaret Court, but she also succeeded in Rome **1971** with Mrs Masthoff and **1973** with Olga Morozova. She also holds the record for the most appearances of any player of any nation in both Fed Cup (100 rubbers in 57 ties) and the W Cup (56 rubbers in 20 ties).

MATS ARNE OLOF **WILANDER** (Sweden)
Born 22/8/64. When he won the French Open junior title in **1981**, little did anyone suspect that twelve months later, aged 17 years 9 months and 15 days, and unseeded, he would become the youngest ever French Open Champion (**1982**). (He would remain the youngest man to win a Grand Slam singles crown until Boris Becker won Wimbledon in 1985, aged 17 years 7 months. Then Michael Chang lowered the record to 17 years 3 months when he dramatically won the French Open in 1989). His relentless topspin driving, single-handed on the forehand, double-handed on the backhand, plus intense concentration and speedy court coverage (all so reminiscent of his great Swedish predecessor Bjorn Borg), brought him two more successes in Paris (**1985,1988**). It was a mark of his all-round ability that he should have been able to win the Australian Open on grass in **1983** with back-to-back wins against McEnroe and Lendl. The following year (**1984**) he won a second Australian title on grass and then won for a third time in **1988** when the Championship was played for the first time at the new National Tennis Centre at Flinders Park. When, later in **1988**, he ended Lendl's streak of 157 consecutive weeks at No.1 to win the US Open title, he became the first man since Connors in **1974** to hold three of the four Grand Slam titles in the same year. That win also lifted him to the No.1 world ranking, a position he would hold for 20 weeks. Already in **1985** his second French win had given him a fourth Grand Slam title before his 21st birthday – the only man ever to achieve that feat. Altogether he won 33 singles and 7 doubles titles and went on competing spasmodically up to the end of **1996**. A member of Sweden's successful Davis Cup teams in **1984** (d.USA 4–1), **1985** (d. W.Germany 3–2) and **1987** (d. India 5–0), he won 36 of his 50 singles rubbers and 7 of his 9 doubles rubbers in 26 ties spanning ten years from 1981. JB

ANTHONY FREDERICK **WILDING** (New Zealand)
Born 31/10/1883. Killed in action in Belgium 9/5/1915. Coached by his father, a notable cricketer, he won the champ of Canterbury, New Zealand, at the age of 17 and went to Cambridge Univ for which he played **1904–05**. The Aus singles champion **1906/09** and **1906** doubles winner (with Heath), he became one of the great heroes of Edwardian tennis, winning the singles champ at Wimbledon **1910/11/12/13**. Won doubles (with N. E. Brookes) in **1907/14** and (with M. J. G. Ritchie) **1908/10**. He won 21 of the 30 D Cup rubbers which he played in 11 ties for Australasia between **1905–14** (15–6 singles, 6–3 doubles).

HELEN NEWINGTON **WILLS** (USA)
Born 6/10/05. Died 1/1/98. Became Mrs F. S. Moody (1929), later Mrs A. Roark (1939). Lenglen's successor as ruler of Wimbledon. A relentless baseliner, she won the singles 8 times in 9 attempts, losing only to Kitty McKane in 1924. Between **1927–32** she won all the major singles champs, except Australia, without losing a set. Won Wimbledon singles **1927/28/29/30/32 /33/35/38** and doubles (with Hazel Wightman) **1924** and (with Elizabeth Ryan) **1927/30**. US singles **1923/24/25 /27/28/29/31**, and doubles (with Mrs J. B. Jessup)

1922, (with Hazel Wightman) **1924/28**, and (with Mary K. Browne) **1925**. French singles **1928/29/30/32** and doubles (with Elizabeth Ryan) **1930/32**.

SIDNEY BURR BEARDSLEE **WOOD** (USA)
Born 1/11/11. A nephew of the late Julian Myrick, a former President of the US LTA and the prime mover in **1913** in the development of Forest Hills as the national centre of tennis in the US, he made his first appearance at Wimbledon, aged 15, in **1927**, playing Lacoste on the Centre Court. In **1931**, aged 19 years and 243 days, he became Wimbledon's second youngest champion at the time. He won by default. Frank Shields fell in 4s of his sf against Borotra and damaged an ankle. Shields won, but was not fit enough to play in f. A shrewd strategist and a graceful stroke-maker, Wood was r/u to Allison at Forest Hills in **1935** but lost 6–2 6–2 6–3 in one of the tournament's most disappointing finals. He played in 7 Davis Cup ties, winning 8 out of his 14 rubbers (5–6 singles, 3–0 doubles) between **1931** and **1934**.

NANCYE MEREDITH **WYNNE** (Australia)
Born 10/6/17. Became Mrs.G.F. Bolton (1940). The most successful of Australian champions until the arrival of Margaret Court, Nancy Wynne Bolton's career spanned the years of the Second World War. She won the Australian singles six times (**1937/40/46/47/48/51**) and the doubles on ten occasions, all with her great friend, Thelma Coyne Long (**1936/37/38/39/40/ 47/48/49/ 51/52**), plus four mixed with Colin Long (**1940/46/47/48**). In 1938 she became the first Australian to reach the final of the US Championships, losing to Alice Marble. In **1947** she was a quarter-finalist at Wimbledon and a semi-finalist in New York, performances that earned her a world ranking of No.4. JB

Obituaries

BUNNY AUSTIN, who died on 26th August, his 94th birthday, was the last British player to reach the men's singles final at Wimbledon. He achieved the feat twice, in 1932 when Ellsworth Vines beat him and in 1938 when his opponent was the world No.1 Don Budge. Austin was unlucky to have faced the two greatest champions to have emerged in America since Bill Tilden's domination of the sport in the 1920s. Nevertheless, he did beat both men – Vines in the 1933 Inter-Zone final of the Davis Cup, Budge at the same stage two years later.

Austin was also the first man to wear shorts on Centre Court. It happened in 1933 nine months after he had done the same thing at Forest Hills. 'It was so hot in New York that my long white flannels became soaked with sweat and weighed a ton, so I decided to cut them off just above the knee' he said. Little did Austin know that he was setting a trend that would soon become universal.

It was as a member of Britain's successful Davis Cup team of that period alongside Fred Perry (Britain won the trophy in 1933 and retained it for three years), that Austin had already become a national hero. As a result of marrying the actress Phyllis Konstam in 1931 Austin had also become something of a matinee idol. The couple moved in exclusive circles. Among his friends and acquaintances Austin could number the actor Ronald Coleman, sportsmen like Jesse Owens and Babe Ruth as well as President Roosevelt and Mother Theresa.

Austin's decision to leave Britain for America shortly after the outbreak of World War II led to accusations of pacifism. Yet so important was religion in Austin's life that he saw his work with Moral Rearmament as equal in importance to contributing to the war effort more directly.

He was certainly not a conscientious objector. In fact he joined the American Army Air Corps in 1943 and served for three years.

Born in Norwood, Surrey, in 1906, Henry Wilfred Austin was the son of well-to-do parents who sent him to Repton where he became a fine all-round sportsman. Eventually tennis became his first love and his easy, rhythmical style, accurate and dependent from the baseline, helped him to dominate the British junior scene. Three times he was national junior champion before going up to Cambridge to read history at Pembroke College. For three years he represented the light blues against the old enemy in the annual varsity match.

On his return to Britain in 1962, Austin's attempt to rejoin the All England Club, where he had first been elected a member in 1924, was rebuffed. Some of the diehard committee members still clung to misconceptions about his wartime activities. Not until 1984 did attitudes soften. Typically, Austin never complained about the time it had taken to restore his membership. He had always loved his association with Wimbledon and was visibly moved during the

Bunny Austin, the last British man to play in a singles final at Wimbledon, made his last appearance on Centre Court during the Champions' Parade. (Stephen Wake)

Parade of Champions in 2000. Arriving on Centre Court in a wheelchair, the result of a fall at the retirement home in Surrey where he resided, he waved to the crowd as he was pushed forward to meet the Duchess of Gloucester. 'I think it was the happiest day of my life' he said afterwards. His wife had died in 1976. They had a son and a daughter.

DON BUDGE, who died on 28th January aged 84, was the last and greatest of the pre-Second World War champions whose capture of all four of the major titles in 1938 made him the first to win a Grand Slam. His immediate predecessor as the world No.1, Fred Perry, had been the first man ever to win the Australian, French, Wimbledon and US titles – but he had not won them in the same year. When Perry retired in 1936 after helping Britain to their fourth successive Davis Cup success, Budge, outstandingly the best player of the day, realised he could set a new record by winning the big four all in the same year. Accordingly he made his plans.

Travelling by sea to Australia with his doubles partner Gene Mako, Budge duly annexed the Australian title, beating the young John Bromwich in the final. In Paris he had to overcome the powerful Czech giant, Roderik Menzel which he did with ease. At Wimbledon it was Bunny Austin who opposed him but the British No.1 was swept aside with magisterial authority as the American again claimed all three titles, the only man to achieve the feat twice.

Arriving in the US final Budge was in the same position that the great Australian Jack Crawford had been in 1933 when he had faced Perry needing only the US Championship to complete his hand of the four majors. On that occasion the *New York Times* tennis correspondent, John Kieran, a regular bridge player, wrote 'If Crawford wins today it would be something like winning a grand slam on the courts, doubled and vulnerable'.

Thus the phrase was born. Crawford, in his 14th consecutive final (he had won the previous 13), lost that day after leading by two sets to one but five years later Budge made no mistake. His opponent in the final at Forest Hills was his friend Mako who did manage to take the second set before being overwhelmed.

So, at last, the game did have a Grand Slam champion, an achievement that remains the Everest of tennis. It is a measure of the difficulty surrounding this feat that only one other man – Rod Laver – and three women, Maureen Connolly, Margaret Court and Steffi Graf have scaled those heights – and the great Laver did it twice.

In that pre-war age the red-headed Budge totally dominated the men's game. Born in Oakland, California, in June 1915, he had learned his tennis on the cement courts that abounded on the West coast. He was a tall man with a wonderfully athletic physique, inherited from a Scottish father who had played football with Glasgow Rangers. Budge's powerful game was built on a backhand of immense power, thought by many to have been the best ever, plus a forehand that was equally powerful though less consistent, a devastating serve and great touch at the net. Furthermore, he had a great attitude. He was always relaxed on court and confident of his own superiority without giving way to arrogance.

Budge's contemporaries thought of him as invincible. He was the complete all-rounder and it was no surprise when in 1938, having turned down an offer the previous year, he joined the professional ranks after helping the USA to retain the Davis Cup.

Budge is survived by his second wife Lori who was his constant companion on frequent trips to the great tennis events in the latter years of his life.

PHILIPPE CHATRIER, who died on 23rd June aged 72, was the greatest tennis administrator of modern times. A former junior champion of France and later a Davis Cup captain, he became a journalist and founded *Tennis de France* which became respected as one of the world's leading sports magazines.

In 1972 he became President of the French Tennis Federation, a post he held for 20 years during which period he led a spectacular growth in tennis that turned it into the second most popular sport in France behind soccer. The French Championships, too, grew in stature and importance under his leadership as the facilities were upgraded and commercial sponsorship was extended.

In 1977 he also became President of the International Tennis Federation and filled the joint roles with great distinction until he resigned from the ITF in 1991 after witnessing his proudest moment, the recapture of the Davis Cup for France after a gap of 59 years. His other great achievement was to have tennis restored to the Olympic Games. After extensive lobbying of the International Olympic Committee – a process in which David Gray, the former British sports writer who had become the ITF's first General Secretary, played a major part – their efforts were rewarded. Tennis was restored to the Olympics, first as a demonstration event in Los Angeles and finally as a full medal sport at the Seoul Games in 1988.

He eventually became a member of the IOC but the onset of Alzheimer's disease forced him to give up all his sporting associations. By a curious coincidence, his former wife Susan, neé Partridge, a leading British tennis player made famous by her near defeat of the young American champion Maureen Connolly at Wimbledon in the fourth round in 1952 (she was beaten by 6–3 5–7 7–5), had died on 4th December 1999 of a similar debilitating disease of the central nervous system.

(Note: A feature on Philippe Chatrier by his friend Alain Deflassieux appears on p 165)

Maiden Names and Married Names

* = since divorced

MAIDEN NAME	MARRIED NAME(S)	MAIDEN NAME	MARRIED NAME(S)
Adamson, Nellie	Landry, Mme. P.H.	Bossi, Annelise	Bellani, Sra. G.
	Renault, Mme M.	Boucher, Edith M.	Hannam, Mrs. F.J.
Akhurst, Daphne S.	Cozens, Mrs. R.S.	Boulle, Michelle	Rodriguez, Mrs. P.H.
Albert, Jane	Freedman, Mrs. B.	Bowder, Irene E.	Peacock, Mrs. G.E.
Alvarez, Elia (Lili) M.	Valdene, Countess,	Bowes, Beverley	Hackney, Mrs. H.M.
	J. de G.	Boyd, Esna	Robertson, Mrs. A.
Andrus, Dorothy B.	Burke, Mrs. W.A.	Breit, Barbara	Gordon, Mrs. B.
Anthony, Julie	Butera, Mrs. R.	Bricka, Justina	Horwitz, Mrs. R.
Appel, Elly	Vessies, Mrs. J.	Bridger, Jean	Walker-Smith, Mrs. J. J.
Appelmans, Sabine	Haubourdin, Mrs. S.	Broquedis, M. Marguerite	Billout, Mme. J.
Arnold, Mimi	Wheeler, Mrs. J.H.		Bordes, Mme. P.R.M.
* Arraya, Laura	Gildermeister, Mrs. H.	Brough, A. Louise	Clapp, Mrs. A.T.
Aussem, Cilly	Brae, Countess F.M.	Brown, Nina B.	Hamilton, Mrs. E.R.
	Della Corte	Browne, Mary K.	Kenneth-Smith, Mrs. K.
Austin, Joan W.	Lycett, Mrs. R.	Buding, Edda	Duechting, Mrs. E.
	Chiesman, Mrs. F.R.	Buding, Ilse	Davies, Mrs. M. G.
	Jepson, Mrs. D.S.		Michael, Fra. I.
	Baker, Mrs. D.A.	Bundy, Dorothy(Dodo) M.	Cheney, Mrs. A.C.
Austin, Tracy A.	Holt, Mrs. S.	Burke, Judy	Jinnock, Mrs. W. J.
Austin, Edith L.	Greville, Mrs. T.G.P.	* Buxton, Angela	Silk, Mrs. D.W.
Baker, Beverley	Beckett, Mrs. S.	Bykova, Natalia	Egorova, Mrs. N.
	Fleitz, Mrs. J.G.	Caldwell, Carole A.	Graebner, Mrs. C.E.
Barclay, Joyce S.	Williams, Mrs. G.M.	Camp, Caroline	Battrick, Mrs. G.
	Hume, Mrs. I.	Canning, M. Patricia	Todd, Mrs. R.B.
	Engelfield, Mrs. J.S.	Carillo, Mary	Bowden, Mrs. B.
	Sacerdote, Mrs. J.	Carr, Bernice	Vukovich, Mrs. V.
	Bennett, Mrs. R.D.	Carter, Mary M.	Reitano, Mrs. S.J.
Barg, Penny	Mager, Mrs. L.	* Catt, Diedre	Keller, Mrs. J.
Barker, Sue	Tankard, Mrs. L. P.		McMahon, Mrs. N.
* Bartkowicz, Jane	Krot, Mrs. J.	Chabot, Kathy	Willette, Mrs. L.
(Peaches)	Schafer, Mrs. B.	Chaffee, Nancy	Kiner, Mrs. R.
Bartos, Csilla	Serepy, Mrs. D.		Whitaker, Mrs. N.
Bassett, Carling	Seguso, Mrs. R.A.	Cherneva, Svetlana	Parkhomenko, Mrs. A.
Basuki, Yayuk	Suharyadi, Mrs. H.	Clements, Betty	Hilton, Mrs. R.
Baudone, Nathalie	Furlan. Mrs. R.		Harrison, Mrs. A. J. C.
Baylon, Norma	Planas, Sra. B. P.		Smart, Mrs. L. R.
Bennett, Eileen V.	Fearnley Whittingstall,	Coghlan, Lorraine G.	Robinson, Mrs. J.D.G.
	Mrs. E.O.		Green, Mrs. G.S.
	Marsh, Mrs. M.M.	Coles, Glynis	Bond, Mrs. G.
	Akroyd, Mrs. G.	Colyer, Evelyn L.	Munro, Mrs. H.A.
	Forslind, Mrs. C.V.	Connolly, Maureen C.	Brinker, Mrs. N.
Berberian, Yulia	Maleeva, Mr. Y.	Connor, Judith N.	Chaloner Mrs. J.D.
Betz, Pauline M.	Addie, Mrs. R.R.	Cooper, Charlotte R.	Sterry, Mrs. A.
Bevis, Mary R.	Hawton, Mrs. K.E.	Coortzen, Valerie	Forbes, Mrs. G. L.
Bingley, Blanche	Hillyard, Mrs. G.W.	Cornell, Lorna	Cawthorn, Mrs. J. W.
Bjurstedt, A.	Mallory, Mrs. F.I.		Greville-Collins,
Margrethe (Molla)			Mrs. W. D.
Blake, Kathy	Thornbrough, Mrs. G.	Coronado, Carmen	Mandarino, Sra. J. E.
Blakelock, Robin	Lloyd, Mrs. J. A. G.	Cox, Marjorie	Crawford, Mrs. J. H.
	Primrose, Mrs. G. B.	Coyne, Thelma D.	Long, Mrs. M. N.
Bloomer, Shirley J.	Brasher, Mrs. C.W.	Croft, Annabel	Coleman, Mrs. M.
Bonder, Lisa	Kriess, Mrs. T.	Cross, Edith A.	Jensen, Mrs. C .J.
Bonicelli, Fiorella	Duxin, Mme. P.	Csurgo, Virag	Tamas, Mrs. N.
Boothby, P. Dora	Geen, Mrs. A.C.	Curry, Joan	Hughesman, Mrs. E.
Boshoff, Linky	Mortlock, Mrs. L.	Daniell, Agnes K.R.	Tuckey, Mrs. C.O.

MAIDEN NAME	MARRIED NAME(S)
Dearman, Evelyn	Cleverley, Mrs. E.
Dechaume, Alexia	Balleret, Mrs. B.
De Fina, Stefanie	Johnson, Mrs. S.
	Hagan, Mrs. J.
De La Courtie, Florence	Billat, Mrs. F.
De Los Rios, Rossana	Neffa, Sra. G.
Delhees, Petra	Jauch, Mrs. P.
Denning, Kaye	Bradshaw, Mrs. R.
Dias, Niege	Enck, Sra. L.
Dmitrieva, Anna	Tolstoy, Mrs. A.
	Chukovsky, Mrs. D.
Douglass, Dorothea K.	Chambers, Mrs.
	R. Lambert
Durr, Francoise	Browning, Mrs. B.J.
Eastlake-Smith, G.	Lamplough, Mrs. G.
Ebbern, Robin	Vincenzi, Mrs. E.J.
Eisel, Mary Ann	Curtis, Mrs. P.W.
	Beattie, Mrs. M.A.
Emmanuel, Esme	Faerber, Mrs. E.
Evers, Dianne	Brown, Mrs. D.
Evert, Chris M.	Lloyd, Mrs. J.M.
	Evert Lloyd, Mrs. C.
	Mill, Mrs. A.R.
Evert, Jeanne	Dubin, Mrs.B.
Fageros, Karol	Short, Mrs. E.
Fairbank, Rosalyn	Nideffer, Mrs. R.
Farina, Sylvia	Elia, Sra. F.
Fendick, Patty	McCain, Mrs. S. L.
Fernandez, Mary Jo	Godsick, Mrs. A.
Fitch, Joyce	Rymer, Mrs. J.
Fletcher, Helen	Barker, Mrs. M.
Floyd, Donna	Fales, Mrs. H.G.
Forbes, Jean R.	Drysdale, Mrs. E.C.
Frendelius, Katarina	Bartholdson, Mrs. K.
Fromholtz, Diane L.	Balestrat, Mrs. C.M.
Fry, Joan C.	Lakeman, Mrs. T.A.
Fry, Shirley J.	Irvin, Mrs. K.E.
Fulco, Bettina	Villela, Mrs. P.
Gannon, Joy	Mottram, Mrs. A.J.
* Garrison, Zina L.	Jackson, Mrs. W.
Gengler, Marjorie	Smith, Mrs. S. R.
Gerson, Marlene	Bethlehem, Mrs. B.
* Ghiradi, Lea	Rubbi, Mrs. L.
Gibb, Anthea	Warwick, Mrs. I. J.
Gibson, Althea	Darben, Mrs. W.A.
	Llewellyn, Mrs. S.
Gibson, Joan	Cottrill, Mrs. J. A.
Gillou, Kate	Fenwick, Mme. F.
Gladman, Marjorie	Van Ryn, Mrs. J. W.
	Buck, Mrs. R. A.
Godwin, Maryna	Procter, Mrs. M.J.
Goldsack, Elsie A.	Pitman, Mrs. J.B.
	Rowbottom, Mrs. G.F.
	Furlonge, Lady G.W.
Goolagong, Evonne F.	Cawley, Mrs. R.A.
Gourlay, Helen	Cawley, Mrs. R.L.
	Cape, Mrs. W.T.
Groenman, Trudy	Walhof, Mrs. C. G.
	Hoolboom, Mrs. M. A.
Grossman, Ann	Wunderlich, Mrs. E.
Grubb, Betty Ann	Stuart, Mrs. B.
	Hansen, Mrs. G.
*	Dent, P. C.
Halard, Julie	Decugis, Mrs. A.
Hall, Eleanor (Nell) M.	Hopman, Mrs. H.C.

MAIDEN NAME	MARRIED NAME(S)
Hanks, Carol	Aucamp, Mrs. D.C.
Hamill, Merrill	Mark, Mrs. R.
Hammond, Anne	Phillkips-Moore,
	Mrs. B. J.
Hantze, Karen J.	Susman, Mrs. J.R.
Hard, Darlene R.	Waggoner, Mrs. R.
Hardwick, Mary	Hare, Mrs. C. E.
Harford, Tanya	Gemmell Mrs. D.
Hart, Mary M.	McIlquham, Mrs. C.G.
Harter, Kathy	Marcus, Mrs. M. P.
	Shubin, Mrs. S. P.
Hartigan, Joan	Bathurst, Mrs. H. B.
Haydon, Adrianne (Ann) S.	Jones, Mrs. P.F.
Head, Dorothy	Knode, Mrs. D.P.
Heeley, G.Mary	Cartwright, Mrs. D.F.
	Bosomworth, Mrs. C.R.
Heine, E.A.L.(Bobbie)	Miller, Mrs. J.H.K.
	Davie, Mrs. W.R.
Heldman, Julie	Weiss, Mrs.B.
Helgeson, Ginger	Nielsen, Mrs. T.
Hellyer, Margaret	Burston. Mrs. K.J.
Herreman, Nathalie	Bagby, Mrs. D.
Hogan, Patti. St.A.	Fordyce, Mrs. I.M.
Holcroft, Phoebe C.	Watson, Mrs. M.R.
	Blakstad, Mrs. W.L.
Hood, Emily	Westacott, Mrs.V.
Hopps, Janet	Adkisson,
	Mrs. W. C. D.
Horckickova, jitka	Volavkova, Mrs. J.
Hotchkiss, Hazel V.	Wightman, Mrs. G.W.
Houlihan, Geraldine	Barniville, Mrs. H.
Housset, Nathalie	Gilbert, Mrs. R.
Howkins, Phyllis, L.	Covell, Mrs. B.C.
Hunt, Lesley	Hambeuchen, Mrs. J.
	Revdavy, Mrs. G.
Hunt, Margaret	Price, Mrs. M.
	Barnard, Mrs. A. J.
Hutchings, Lynette	Nette, Mrs. N.
Hy, Patricia	Boulais, Mrs. P.
Ibarra, Carmen	Fernandez, Mrs. J.
Jackson, Helen	Atkins, Mrs. H.
Jagerman, Nicole	Muns, Mrs. K .
Jaggard, Michelle	Lie, Mrs. G.
James, Winifred (Freda) A.	Hammersley, Mrs. S.H.
Jansen, Marijke	Schaar, Mrs. M.
Jarvis, Rita	Anderson, Mrs. O.
	Drobny, Mrs. J.
Jedrzejowska, Jadwiga	Gallert, Mrs. A.
Jolissaint, Christiane	Vaudroz, Mme. C.
Jones, Kimberley	Shaefer, Mrs. L.
Jung, Sylvia	Lafaurie, Mrs. R.
	Henrotin, Mrs. C.F.
	Welton, Mrs. S.
Kemmer, Kristien	Shaw, Mrs. R.
	Ziska, Mrs. F.
Kilian, Dora	Shaw, Mrs. K.
Kiyomura, Ann K.	Hayashi, Mrs. D.
Kodesova, Vlasta	Vopicova, Mrs. V.
Kormoczy, Zsuzsa (Suzy)	Branny, Mrs. S.
	Broz, Mrs. G.
Krahwinkel, Hilde	Sperling, Mrs. S.
Krocke, Elly	Blomberg, Mrs. S.
Lance, Sylvia	Harper, Mrs. R.
Lehane, Janice (Jan) P.	O'Neill, Mrs. J.J
Lewis, Valerie	Clark, Mrs. C. T.

MAIDEN NAME	MARRIED NAME(S)
Lidderdale, Kathleen E.	Bridge, Mrs. A.V.
Liem, Lita	Sigiarto, Mrs. R.
Likhovtseva, Elena	Baranov, Mrs. M.
Lincoln, Molly	Blair, Mrs. N. W.
Lindqvist, Caterina	Ryan, Mrs. J. W.
Lizana, Anita	Ellis, Mrs. R. A.
* Lofdahl, Ingrid A.R.F.	Bentzer, Mrs. J.A.
Loosemoore, Sarah	Lion-Cachet, Mrs. S.
Louie, Mareen	Harper, Mrs. T.
Lumb, Margot	Gordon, Mrs. W. H. L.
Luthy, Alice	Tym, Mrs. W. A.
Lyle, Nancy	Glover, Mrs. P.F.
MacLennan, Frances V.M.	Taylor, Mrs. R.
Madruga, Ivana	Ossies, Mrs. O.
Maleeva, Katerina	Stolmenor, Mrs. G.
Maleeva, Manuela	Fragniere, Mrs. F.
* Mandlikova, Hana	Sadlek, Mrs. J.
Marcinkowski, Rita	Baranski, Mrs. A.
Marosi, Katalin	Aracama, Mrs. A.
Mascarin, Susan	Keane, Mrs. P.
May, Kathryn(Kathy)	Teacher, Mrs. B.D.
	Paben, Mrs. D
McCorkindale, Peggy	Dawson-Scott,
	Mrs. E. W.
McCune, Anna V.	Harper, Mrs. L.A.
McInnes, Coral	Buttsworth, Mrs. C.
McKane, Margaret	Stocks, Mrs. A.D.
McKane, Kathleen (Kitty)	Godfree, Mrs. L.A.
McLenaughan, Patricia	Faulkener, Mrs. R. N.
Medalie, Gladys	Heldman, Mrs. J.
Melville, Kerry A.	Reid, Mrs. G.E.
Mercelis, Christiane	Spruyt, Mrs. C.
Meshki, Leila	Nadibaidze, Mrs. P.
Metaxa, Doris E.	Howard, Mrs. P.D.
Minter, Anne	Harris, Mrs. G.
Moffitt, Billie Jean	King, Mrs. L.W.
Monami, Dominique	van Roost, Mrs. B.
Montgomery, Marilyn	Rindfuss, Mrs. J.
Moran, Gertrude A.	Corbally, Mrs. T.J.
	Hand, Mrs. E.J.
	Simpson, Mrs. F.M.
Morariu, Corina	Turkinovic, Mrs. A.
Morozova, Olga V.	Rubanov, Mrs. V.B.
Morrison, Ruia	Davy, Mrs. R.
Mortimer, Angela	Barrett, Mrs. J.E.
Morton, Agnes M.	Stewart, Lady H.H.
Mudford, Phyllis E.	King, Mrs. M.R.
Muller, E.Fay	Robinson, Mrs. A.A.
	Colthorpe, Mrs. R.W.
Mundel, Jennifer	Reinbold, Mrs. D.
Mutch, Margaret (Mal)	Molesworth, Mrs. M.
Nagelsen, H. Elizabeth	McCormack, Mrs. M.H.
(Betsy)	
Nelson, Vicki L.	Dunbar, Mrs. K.
Neumannova, M.	Pinterova, Mrs. M.
Newberry, Janet S.	Wright Mrs. F.I.
Nicholas, Delaile	Hewitt, Mrs. R. A. J.
Nicholl, Jean	Bostock, Mrs. E.W.A.
Nicholls, Heather	Brewer, Mrs. W.
	Segal, Mrs. A. A.
Niessen, Helga	Masthoff, Fra. H.
Niox-Chateau, Sybil	Fleurian, Mme J. P.
Noel, Susan	Powell, Mrs. G. F.
Nuthall, Betty	Shoemaker, Mrs. F. C.

MAIDEN NAME	MARRIED NAME(S)
Osborne, Margaret E.	duPont, Mrs. W.
Osterman, Renate	Drisaldi, Sra. M.
Palfrey, Sarah H.	Fabyan, Mrs. M.
	Cooke, Mrs. E.T.
	Danzig, Mrs. J.A.
Pampoulova, Elena	Wagner, Mrs. A.
Paradis, Pascale	Mangon, Mrs. P.
Partridge, Susan	Chatrier, Mme. P.
	Crosnier, Mme. J. R.
Passemard, Simone	Mathieu, Mme. R.
Pedersen, helen	Rihbany, Mrs. E. H.
Peisachov, Paulina	Peled, Mrs. E.
Penrose, Beryl	Collier, Mrs. J. A. F.
Pericoli, Lea	Fontana, Sra. L.
Piatek, Mary Lou	Daniels, Mrs. P.
Piercey, Sheila A.	Summers, Mrs. R.A.
Pigeon, Kristy	Crawford, Mrs. R.
Polzl, Judith	Wiesner, Mrs. H.W.
Prosen, Carol A.	Kalogeropoulos,
	Mrs. N.
Provis, Nicole A.L.	Bradtke, Mrs. M.R.
Puzejova, Vera	Sukova, Mrs. C.
Quentrec, Karine	Eagle, Mrs. K.
* Quertier, Jean	Rinkel, Mrs. I. F.
Radford, Kristine	Kunce, Mrs. D.
Rajchrtova, Regina	Korda, Mrs. P.
Ramirez, Yolanda	Ochoa, Mrs. A.
Ramsey, Winifred G.	Beamish, Mrs. A.E.
Raponi, Emilse	Longo, Mrs. N.
Redondo, Marita	Stephens, Mrs. J.
Rees-Lewis, Jacqueline	Vives, Mme. J.
Reggi, Raffaela	Concato, Mrs. M.
Reinach, Elna	Carstens, Mrs. P. A.
Reinach, Monica	Van Rensburg, Mrs. C.
Reyes, Rosa (Rosie) M.	Darmon, Mrs. P.
Reynolds, Sandra	Price, Mrs. L.E.G.
Richey, Nancy A.	Gunter, Mrs. K.S.
Ridley, Joan C.	O'Meara, Mrs. D.J.P.
Riedl, Iris	Kuhn, Mrs. K.
Rigollet, Violet	Alvensleben,
	Mme. M. L.
Rinaldi, Kathy	Stunkel, Mrs. B.
Ritter, Petra	Schwartz, Mrs. P.
Rittner, Barbara	Diehl, Fra. D.
Rook, Jill	Mills, Mrs. A. R.
Rosenquest, Charlotte	Pratt, Mrs. E.C.S.
(Betty)	
Rosser, Carole	Matheson, Mrs. H. S.
Round, Dorothy E.	Little, Mrs. D.L.
Rush, Gretchen A.	Magers, Mrs. S.W.
Russell, JoAnne C.	Longdon, Mrs. G.
Salfati, Monique	Di Maso, Sra. M.
Sampson, Julia, A.	Haywood, Mrs. D.A.
Sanchez, Arantxa	Vehils, Sra. J.
Saunders, Margaret A.	Michell, Mrs. L.R.C.
Savchenko, Larisa I.	Neiland, Mrs. A.
Sawamatsu, Kazuko	Yoshida, Mrs. M.
Sayers, Elizabeth M.	Smylie, Mrs. P.D.
Schallau, Ramona	Guerrant, Mrs. T.
Schildknecht, Heide	Orth, Fra. L.
Schmidt, Suzanne	De Besnerais, Mme. S.
Schofield, Barbara	Davidson, Mrs. G.
Schultze, Helga	Hoesl, Mrs. H.
	Thaw, Mrs. D. M.
Schultze, Margot	Gisbert, Sra. J. M.

MAIDEN NAME	MARRIED NAME(S)	MAIDEN NAME	MARRIED NAME(S)
Schulz, Brenda	McCarthy, Mrs. S.	Testud, Sandrine	Magnelli, Mrs. V.
Schuurman, Renee	Haygarth, Mrs. P.	Thomson, Ethel W.	Larcombe, Mrs. D.T.R.
Scriven, Margaret (Reggy)	Vivian, Mrs. F. H.	Titchener, Pauline	Roberts, Mrs. V. A.
Seeney, Daphne G.	Fancutt, Mrs. T.T.		Cox, Mrs. P. M.
Seghers, Pierette	Tacchini, Mrs. S.	Toleafoa, Claudine	Limberger, Mrs. C.
Shaw, Winnie M.	Wooldridge, Mrs. K.	Tomanova, Renata	Roth, Mrs. W.R.
Shepherd, Dorothy C.	Barron, Mrs. W.P.	Tort, Maria	Ayala, Mrs. L. A.
Sheriff, Carol	Zeeman, Mrs. C.E.	Toyne, Fay	Moore, Mrs. J. L.
Sheriff, Gail V.	Chanfreau, Mrs. J.B.	Truman, Christine C.	Janes, Mrs. G.T.
*	Lovera, Mrs. J.J.	Truman, Frances (Nell)	Robinson, Mrs. C.
Shilcock, J. Anne	Spann, Mrs. J.K.	Tucker, Ginette	Bucaille, Mme. G.
Shriver, Pamena	Shapiro, Mrs. J.		Grandguillot, Mme. P.
Sieler, Cynthia	Doerner, Mrs. P. M.	Tuckey, Kay	Maule, Mrs. J.
Sigart, Josane	de Meulemeester,	Tuero, Linda	Blatty, Mrs. W. P.
	Mme. J.	Turner, Lesley R.	Bowrey, Mrs. W.W.
* Simionescu, Mariana	Borg, Mrs. B.	* Vail, Linda	Van Der Meer, Mrs. D.
	Marsan, Mme. J. P.	Van Deventer, Anita	Summers, Mrs. S.
Simpson, Alice M.	Pickering, Mrs. W.H.	Varner, Margaret	Bloss, Mrs. W.G.
* Simpson, Rene	Alter, Mrs. B.	Villagran, Adriana	Reami, Mrs. J.
Sloane, Susan	Lundy, Mrs. D.	Vlasto, Didi	Serpieri, Mrs. J.
Slocock, Winifred M.	McNair, Mrs. R.J.	Walkden, Pat M.	Pretorius, Mrs. Q.C.
Smith, Margaret	Court, Mrs. B.M.	Walsh, Rosemary	Deloford, Mrs. J. L.
Soisbault, Annie	De Montaign, Mch. P.	* Walsh, Sharon A .	Pete, Mrs. M.H.
Spain, Lisa	Short, Mrs. H.	Ward, Patricia E.	Hales, Mrs. R.
Spruyt, Elsie	Veentjer, Mrs. E	Watanabe, Tina B.	Mochizuki, Mrs. H.A.
Squire, Mabel B.	Parton, Mrs. E.G.	Watermeyer, Pamela	Diepraam, Mrs. K.
	Mavrogordato,	Watson, Elaine	Shenton, Mrs. B.
	Mrs. T.M.	Werdel, Marianne	Witmeyer, Mrs. R.
St.George, Floris	Conway, Mrs. J.R.	Wheeler, Patricia	Roberts, Mrs. D. H.
Staley, Jennifer	Hoad, Mrs. L.A.	White, Wendy	Prausa, Mrs. S.R.
Stafford, Shaun	Beekish, Mrs. M.	Whitlinger, Tami	Jones, Mrs. K.
Stammers, Katherine	Menzies, Mrs. M.	Whitmarsh, Mary	Halford, Mrs. W. C. J.
(Kay) E.	Bullitt, Mrs. T.W.	Wills, Helen N.	Moody, Mrs. F.S.
Starkie, Elizabeth	Wagstaff, Mrs. E.		Roark, Mrs. A.
Stevens, Greer R.	Leo-Smith, Mrs. K.	Woodgate, Georgie	Cox, Mrs. M. H.
Strnadova, Andrea	Stoltenberg, Mrs. J.	Wynne, Nancye M.	Bolton, Mrs. G.F.
Stroud, Alison	Cox, Mrs. M.	Yates-Bell, Caroline	Hamilton, Mrs. I.
Sutton, May G.	Bundy, Mrs. T.C.	Young, Janet	Langford, Mrs. J.
Tegart, Judy A.M.	Dalton, Mrs. D.E.	Ziegenfuss, Valerie	Bradshaw, Mrs. D.
* Temesvari, Andrea	Trunkos, Mrs. A.	Zrubakova, Radka	Karabin, Mrs. L.
Teran, Maria	Weiss, Sra. H.	Zyl, Annette, M. van	Plooy, Mrs. J. du
Ter Riet, Helas	Eltingh, Mrs. J. F.		

Championship Rolls

AUSTRALIAN CHAMPIONSHIPS

1. Title: Held as the Australasian Championships from 1905 to 1926. In 1927 became the Australian Championships to coincide with the opening of the Kooyong Stadium in Melbourne. **2. Status:** The Championships became open in 1969. **3. Venues:** Since 1905 there have been 87 Championships held in the following cities (there were two Championships in 1977 (Jan and Dec) and from then until 1985 the event was staged in December. In 1986 there was no Championship so that the Jan date could be resumed in 1987): **MELBOURNE (40):** 1905, '14, '24, '27, 30, '33, '35, '39, '48, '50, '53, '57, '61, '65, '68, 1972–present (1927–1987 at Kooyong; since 1988 at the National Tennis Centre, Flinders Park). **SYDNEY (17):** 1908, '19, '22, '25, '28, '31, '34, '37, '40, '47, '51, '54, '58, '62, '66, '70, '71. **ADELAIDE (14):** 1910, '20, '26, '29, '32, '36, '38, '46, '49, '52, '55, '59, '63, '67. **BRISBANE (8):** 1907, '11, '15, '23, '56, '60, '64, '69. **PERTH (3):** 1909, '13, '21. **CHRISTCHURCH, NZL (1):** 1906. **HASTINGS, NZL (1):** 1912. **4. Surface:** Grass 1905–87; Rebound Ace (hard) 1988–present. **5. Note:** The asterisk symbol * denotes best of three sets only.

MEN'S SINGLES

	CHAMPION	RUNNER-UP	SCORE				
1905	R. W. Heath	A. H. Curtis	4–6	6–3	6–4	6–4	
1906	A. F. Wilding	F. M. B. Fisher	6–0	6–4	6–4		
1907	H. M. Rice	H. A. Parker	6–3	6–4	6–4		
1908	F. B. Alexander	A. W. Dunlop	3–6	3–6	6–0	6–2	6–3
1909	A. F. Wilding	E. F. Parker	6–1	7–5	6–2		
1910	R. W. Heath	H. M. Rice	6–4	6–3	6–2		
1911	N. E. Brookes	H. M. Rice	6–1	6–2	6–3		
1912	J. C. Parke	A. E. Beamish	3–6	6–3	1–6	6–1	7–5
1913	E. F. Parker	H. A. Parker	2–6	6–1	6–3	6–2	
1914	A. O'Hara Wood	G. L. Patterson	6–4	6–3	5–7	6–1	
1915	F. G. Lowe	H. M. Rice	4–6	6–1	6–1	6–4	
1916–18	*Not held*						
1919	A. R. F. Kingscote	E. O. Pockley	6–4	6–0	6–3		
1920	P. O'Hara Wood	R. V. Thomas	6–3	4–6	6–8	6–1	6–3
1921	R. H. Gemmell	A. Hedeman	7–5	6–1	6–4		
1922	J. O. Anderson	G. L. Patterson	6–0	3–6	3–6	6–3	6–2
1923	P. O'Hara Wood	C. B. St John	6–1	6–1	6–3		
1924	J. O. Anderson	R. E. Schlesinger	6–3	6–4	3–6	5–7	6–3
1925	J. O. Anderson	G. L. Patterson	11–9	2–6	6–2	6–3	
1926	J. B. Hawkes	J. Willard	6–1	6–3	6–1		
1927	G. L. Patterson	J. B. Hawkes	3–6	6–4	3–6	18–16	6–3
1928	J. Borotra	R. O. Cummings	6–4	6–1	4–6	5–7	6–3
1929	J. C. Gregory	R. E. Schlesinger	6–2	6–2	5–7	7–5	
1930	E. F. Moon	H. C. Hopman	6–3	6–1	6–3		
1931	J. H. Crawford	H. C. Hopman	6–4	6–2	2–6	6–1	
1932	J. H. Crawford	H. C. Hopman	4–6	6–3	3–6	6–3	6–1
1933	J. H. Crawford	K. Gledhill	2–6	7–5	6–3	6–2	
1934	F. J. Perry	J. H. Crawford	6–3	7–5	6–1		
1935	J. H. Crawford	F. J. Perry	2–6	6–4	6–4	6–4	
1936	A. K. Quist	J. H. Crawford	6–2	6–3	4–6	3–6	9–7
1937	V. B. McGrath	J. E. Bromwich	6–3	1–6	6–0	2–6	6–1
1938	J. D. Budge	J. E. Bromwich	6–4	6–2	6–1		
1939	J. E. Bromwich	A. K. Quist	6–4	6–1	6–3		
1940	A. K. Quist	J. H. Crawford	6–3	6–1	6–2		
1941–45	*Not held*						
1946	J. E. Bromwich	D. Pails	5–7	6–3	7–5	3–6	6–2
1947	D. Pails	J. E. Bromwich	4–6	6–4	3–6	7–5	8–6
1948	A. K. Quist	J. E. Bromwich	6–4	3–6	6–3	2–6	6–3
1949	F. A. Sedgman	J. E. Bromwich	6–3	6–2	6–2		
1950	F. A. Sedgman	K. B. McGregor	6–3	6–4	4–6	6–1	

	CHAMPION	RUNNER-UP	SCORE					
1951	R. Savitt	K. B. McGregor	6–3	2–6	6–3	6–1		
1952	K. B. McGregor	F. A. Sedgman	7–5	12–10	2–6	6–2		
1953	K. R. Rosewall	M. G. Rose	6–0	6–3	6–4			
1954	M. G. Rose	R. N. Hartwig	6–2	0–6	6–4	6–2		
1955	K. R. Rosewall	L. A. Hoad	9–7	6–4	6–4			
1956	L. A. Hoad	K. R. Rosewall	6–4	3–6	6–4	7–5		
1957	A. J. Cooper	N. A. Fraser	6–3	9–11	6–4	6–2		
1958	A. J. Cooper	M. J. Anderson	7–5	6–3	6–4			
1959	A. Olmedo	N. A. Fraser	6–1	6–2	3–6	6–3		
1960	R. G. Laver	N. A. Fraser	5–7	3–6	6–3	8–6	8–6	
1961	R. S. Emerson	R. G. Laver	1–6	6–3	7–5	6–4		
1962	R. G. Laver	R. S. Emerson	8–6	0–6	6–4	6–4		
1963	R. S. Emerson	K. N. Fletcher	6–3	6–3	6–1			
1964	R. S. Emerson	F. S. Stolle	6–3	6–4	6–2			
1965	R. S. Emerson	F. S. Stolle	7–9	2–6	6–4	7–5	6–1	
1966	R. S. Emerson	A. R. Ashe	6–4	6–8	6–2	6–3		FIRST
1967	R. S. Emerson	A. R. Ashe	6–4	6–1	6–4			PRIZE
1968	W. W. Bowrey	J. M. Gisbert	7–5	2–6	9–7	6–4		(Aus $)
1969	R. G. Laver	A. Gimeno	6–3	6–4	7–5			5,000
1970	A. R. Ashe	R. D. Crealy	6–4	9–7	6–2			3,800
1971	K. R. Rosewall	A. R. Ashe	6–1	7–5	6–3			10,000
1972	K. R. Rosewall	M. J. Anderson	7–6	6–3	7–5			2,240
1973	J. D. Newcombe	O. Parun	6–3	6–7	7–5	6–1		8,750
1974	J. S. Connors	P. Dent	7–6	6–4	4–6	6–3		9,750
1975	J. D. Newcombe	J. S. Connors	7–5	3–6	6–4	7–6		12,489
1976	M. Edmondson	J. D. Newcombe	6–7	6–3	7–6	6–1		32,000
1977	(Jan) R. Tanner	G. Vilas	6–3	6–3	6–3			32,000
1977	(Dec) V. Gerulaitis	J. M. Lloyd	6–3	7–6	5–7	3–6	6–2	28,000
1978	(Dec) G. Vilas	J. Marks	6–4	6–4	3–6	6–3		41,000
1979	(Dec) G. Vilas	J. Sadri	7–6	6–3	6–2			50,000
1980	(Dec) B. Teacher	K. Warwick	7–5	7–6	6–3			65,000
1981	(Dec) J. Kriek	S. Denton	6–2	7–6	6–7	6–4		65,000
1982	(Dec) J. Kriek	S. Denton	6–3	6–3	6–2			70,000
1983	(Dec) M. Wilander	I. Lendl	6–1	6–4	6–4			77,500
1984	(Dec) M. Wilander	K. Curren	6–7	6–4	7–6	6–2		100,000
1985	(Dec) S. Edberg	M. Wilander	6–4	6–3	6–3			100,000
1986	Not held							
1987	(Jan) S. Edberg	P. Cash	6–3	6–4	3–6	5–7	6–3	103,875
1988	M. Wilander	P. Cash	6–3	6–7	3–6	6–1	8–6	104,997
1989	I. Lendl	M. Mecir	6–2	6–2	6–2			140,000
1990	I. Lendl	S. Edberg	4–6	7–6	5–2	ret		200,000
1991	B. Becker	I. Lendl	1–6	6–4	6–4	6–4		246,400
1992	J. Courier	S. Edberg	6–3	3–6	6–4	6–2		274,909
1993	J. Courier	S. Edberg	6–2	6–1	2–6	7–5		410,000
1994	P. Sampras	T. Martin	7–6	6–4	6–4			460,000
1995	A. Agassi	P. Sampras	4–6	6–1	7–6	6–4		480,000
1996	B. Becker	M. Chang	6–2	6–4	2–6	6–2		562,000
1997	P. Sampras	C. Moya	6–2	6–3	6–3			585,000
1998	P. Korda	M. Rios	6–2	6–2	6–2			615,000
1999	Y. Kafelnikov	T. Enqvist	4–6	6–0	6–3	7–6		722,000
2000	A. Agassi	Y. Kafelnikov	3–6	6–3	6–2	6–4		755,000

WOMEN'S SINGLES

	CHAMPION	RUNNER-UP	SCORE		
1922	Mrs M. Molesworth	Miss E. F. Boyd	6–3	10–8	
1923	Mrs M. Molesworth	Miss E. F. Boyd	6–1	7–5	
1924	Miss S. Lance	Miss E. F. Boyd	6–3	3–6	8–6
1925	Miss D. S. Akhurst	Miss E. F. Boyd	1–6	8–6	6–4
1926	Miss D. S. Akhurst	Miss E. F. Boyd	6–1	6–3	
1927	Miss E. F. Boyd	Mrs S. Harper	5–7	6–1	6–2
1928	Miss D. S. Akhurst	Miss E. F. Boyd	7–5	6–2	
1929	Miss D. S. Akhurst	Miss L. M. Bickerton	6–1	5–7	6–2
1930	Miss D. S. Akhurst	Mrs S. Harper	10–8	2–6	7–5
1931	Mrs C. Buttsworth	Mrs J. H. Crawford	1–6	6–3	6–4
1932	Mrs C. Buttsworth	Miss K. Le Mesurier	9–7	6–4	

	CHAMPION	RUNNER-UP	SCORE				FIRST PRIZE (Aus $)
1933	Miss J. Hartigan	Mrs C. Buttsworth	6–4	6–3			
1934	Miss J. Hartigan	Mrs M. Molesworth	6–1	6–4			
1935	Miss D. E. Round	Miss N. M. Lyle	1–6	6–1	6–3		
1936	Miss J. Hartigan	Miss N. M. Wynne	6–4	6–4			
1937	Miss N. M. Wynne	Mrs V. Westacott	6–3	5–7	6–4		
1938	Miss D. M. Bundy	Miss D. Stevenson	6–3	6–2			
1939	Mrs V. Westacott	Mrs H. C. Hopman	6–1	6–2			
1940	Mrs G. F. Bolton	Miss T. D. Coyne	5–7	6–4	6–0		
1941–45		Not held					
1946	Mrs G.F. Bolton	Miss J. Fitch	6–4	6–4			
1947	Mrs G.F. Bolton	Mrs H. C. Hopman	6–3	6–2			
1948	Mrs G.F. Bolton	Miss M. Toomey	6–3	6–1			
1949	Miss D. J. Hart	Mrs G.F. Bolton	6–3	6–4			
1950	Miss A. L. Brough	Miss D. J. Hart	6–4	3–6	6–4		
1951	Mrs G.F. Bolton	Mrs M. N. Long	6–1	7–5			
1952	Mrs M. N. Long	Miss H. Angwin	6–2	6–3			
1953	Miss M. Connolly	Miss J. Sampson	6–3	6–2			
1954	Mrs M. N. Long	Miss J. Staley	6–3	6–4			
1955	Miss B. Penrose	Mrs M. N. Long	6–4	6–3			
1956	Miss M. Carter	Mrs M. N. Long	3–6	6–2	9–7		
1957	Miss S. J. Fry	Miss A. Gibson	6–3	6–4			
1958	Miss A. Mortimer	Miss L. Coghlan	6–3	6–4			
1959	Mrs S. J. Reitano	Miss R. Schuurman	6–2	6–3			
1960	Miss M. Smith	Miss J. Lehane	7–5	6–2			
1961	Miss M. Smith	Miss J. Lehane	6–1	6–4			
1962	Miss M. Smith	Miss J. Lehane	6–0	6–2			
1963	Miss M. Smith	Miss J. Lehane	6–2	6–2			
1964	Miss M. Smith	Miss L. R. Turner	6–3	6–2			
1965	Miss M. Smith	Miss M. E. Bueno	5–7	6–4	5–2	ret	
1966	Miss M. Smith	Miss N. Richey	w.o.				
1967	Miss N. Richey	Miss L. R. Turner	6–1	6–4			
1968	Mrs L. W. King	Mrs B. M. Court	6–1	6–2			2,000
1969	Mrs B. M. Court	Mrs L. W. King	6–4	6–1			700
1970	Mrs B. M. Court	Miss K. Melville	6–1	6–3			1,800
1971	Mrs B. M. Court	Miss E. Goolagong	2–6	7–6	7–5		1,200
1972	Miss S. V. Wade	Miss E. Goolagong	6–4	6–4			5,700
1973	Mrs B. M. Court	Miss E. Goolagong	6–4	7–5			9,000
1974	Miss E. Goolagong	Miss C. M. Evert	7–6	4–6	6–0		8,115
1975	Miss E. Goolagong	Miss M. Navratilova	6–3	6–2			12,000
1976	Mrs R. A. Cawley	Miss R. Tomanova	6–2	6–2			12,000
1977	(Jan) Mrs G. Reid	Miss D. Fromholtz	7–5	6–2			9,000
1977	(Dec) Mrs R. A. Cawley	Mrs R. L. Cawley	6–3	6–0			6,000
1978	(Dec) Miss C. O'Neil	Miss B. Nagelsen	6–3	7–6			10,000
1979	(Dec) Miss B. Jordan	Miss S. Walsh	6–3	6–3			32,000
1980	(Dec) Miss H. Mandlikova	Miss W. M. Turnbull	6–0	7–5			34,000
1981	(Dec) Miss M. Navratilova	Mrs J. M. Lloyd	6–7	6–4	7–5		40,000
1982	(Dec) Mrs J. M. Lloyd	Miss M. Navratilova	6–3	2–6	6–3		75,000
1983	(Dec) Miss M. Navratilova	Miss K. Jordan	6–2	7–6			100,000
1984	(Dec) Mrs J. M. Lloyd	Miss H. Sukova	6–7	6–1	6–3		100,000
1985	(Dec) Miss M. Navratilova	Mrs J. M. Lloyd	6–2	4–6	6–2		
1986		Not held					
1987	(Jan) Miss H. Mandlikova	Miss M. Navratilova	7–5	7–6			115,000
1988	Miss S. Graf	Miss C. Evert	6–1	7–6			115,000
1989	Miss S. Graf	Miss H. Sukova	6–4	6–4			135,000
1990	Miss S. Graf	Miss M. J. Fernandez	6–3	6–4			190,000
1991	Miss M. Seles	Miss J. Novotna	5–7	6–3	6–1		246,400
1992	Miss M. Seles	Miss M. J. Fernandez	6–2	6–3			274,909
1993	Miss M. Seles	Miss S. Graf	4–6	6–3	6–2		410,000
1994	Miss S. Graf	Miss A. Sanchez-Vicario	6–0	6–2			460,000
1995	Miss M. Pierce	Miss A. Sanchez-Vicario	6–3	6–2			480,000
1996	Miss M. Seles	Miss A. Huber	6–4	6–1			510,000
1997	Miss M. Hingis	Miss M. Pierce	6–2	6–2			542,000
1998	Miss M. Hingis	Miss C. Martinez	6–3	6–3			572,000
1999	Miss M. Hingis	Miss A. Mauresmo	6–2	6–3			679,000
2000	Miss L. Davenport	Miss M. Hingis	6–1	7–5			717,000

MEN'S DOUBLES

	CHAMPIONS	RUNNERS-UP	SCORE				
1905	R. Lycett/T. Tachell	E. T. Barnard/B. Spence	11–9	8–6	1–6	4–6	6–1
1906	R. W. Heath/A. F. Wilding	C. C. Cox/H. A. Parker	6–2	6–4	6–2		
1907	W. A. Gregg/H. A. Parker	H. M. Rice/G. W. Wright	6–2	3–6	6 3	6 2	
1908	F. B. Alexander/A. W. Dunlop	G. G. Sharpe/A. F. Wilding	6–3	6–2	6–1		
1909	J. P. Keane/E. F. Parker	C. Crooks/A. F. Wilding	1–6	6–1	6–1	9–7	
1910	A. Campbell/H. M. Rice	R. W. Heath/J. L. O'Dea	6–3	6–3	6–2		
1911	H. W. Heath/R. Lycett	J. J. Addison/N. E. Brookes	6–2	7–5	6–0		
1912	C. P. Dixon/J. C. Parke	A. E. Beamish/F. G. Lowe	6–4	6–4	6–2		
1913	A. H. Hedemann/E. F. Parker	H. Parker/R. Taylor	8–6	4–6	6–4	6–4	
1914	A. Campbell/G. L. Patterson	R. W. Heath/A. O'Hara Wood	7–5	3–6	6–3	6–3	
1915	H. M. Rice/C. V. Todd	F. G. Lowe/C. St John	8–6	6–4	7–9	6–3	
1916–1918		Not held					
1919	P. O'Hara Wood/R. V. Thomas	J. O. Anderson/A. H. Lowe	7–5	6–1	7–9	3–6	6–3
1920	P. O'Hara Wood/R. V. Thomas	H. Rice/R. Taylor	6–1	6–0	7–5		
1921	S. H. Eaton/R. H. Gemmell	E. Stokes/N. Brearley	7–5	6–3	6–3		
1922	J. B. Hawkes/G. L. Patterson	J. O. Anderson/N. Peach	8–10	6–0	6–0	7–5	
1923	P. O'Hara Wood/C. B. St John	H. Rice/J. Bullough	6–4	6–3	3–6	6–0	
1924	J. O. Anderson/N. E. Brookes	P. O'Hara Wood/G. L. Patterson	6–2	6–4	6–3		
1925	P. O'Hara Wood/G. L. Patterson	J. O. Anderson/F. Kalms	6–4	8–6	7–5		
1926	J. B. Hawkes/G. L. Patterson	J. O. Anderson/P. O'Hara Wood	6–1	6–4	6–2		
1927	J. B. Hawkes/G. L. Patterson	I. McInnes/P. O'Hara Wood	8–6	6–2	6–1		
1928	J. Borotra/J. Brugnon	E. F. Moon/J. Willard	6–2	4–6	6–4	6–4	
1929	J. H. Crawford/H. C. Hopman	R. O. Cummings/E. F. Moon	6–1	6–8	4–6	6–1	6–3
1930	J. H. Crawford/H. C. Hopman	J. Fitchett/J. B. Hawkes	8–6	6–1	2–6	6–3	
1931	C. Donohoe/R. Dunlop	J. H. Crawford/H. O. Hopman	8–6	6–2	5–7	7–9	6–4
1932	J. H. Crawford/E. F. Moon	H. C. Hopman/G. L. Patterson	4–6	6–4	12–10	6–3	
1933	K. Gledhill/H. E. Vines	J. H. Crawford/E. F. Moon	6–4	10–8	6–2		
1934	G. P. Hughes/F. J. Perry	A. K. Quist/D. P. Turnbull	6–8	6–3	6–4	3–6	6–3
1935	J. H. Crawford/V. B. McGrath	G. P. Hughes/F. J. Perry	6–4	8–6	6–2		
1936	A. K. Quist/D. P. Turnbull	J. H. Crawford/V. B. McGrath	6–8	6–2	6–1	3–6	6–2
1937	A. K. Quist/D. P. Turnbull	J. E. Bromwich/J. E. Harper	6–2	9–7	1–6	6–8	6–4
1938	J. E. Bromwich/A. K. Quist	H. Henkel/G. Von Cramm	7–5	6–4	6–0		
1939	J. E. Bromwich/A. K. Quist	C. F. Long/D. P. Turnbull	6–4	7–5	6–2		
1940	J. E. Bromwich/A. K. Quist	J. H. Crawford/V. B. McGrath	6–3	7–5	6–1		
1941–1945		Not held					
1946	J. E. Bromwich/A. K. Quist	M. Newcombe/L. A. Schwartz	6–3	6–1	9–7		
1947	J. E. Bromwich/A. K. Quist	F. A. Sedgman/G. Worthington	6–1	6–3	6–1		
1948	J. E. Bromwich/A. K. Quist	C. Long/F. A. Sedgman	1–6	6–8	9–7	6–3	8–6
1949	J. E. Bromwich/A. K. Quist	G. Brown/O. W. Sidwell	1–6	7–5	6–2	6–3	
1950	J. E. Bromwich/A. K. Quist	J. Drobny/E. W. Sturgess	6–3	5–7	4–6	6–3	8–6
1951	K. B. McGregor/F. A. Sedgman	J. E. Bromwich/A. K. Quist	11–9	2–6	6–3	4–6	6–3
1952	K. B. McGregor/F. A. Sedgman	D. Candy/M. G. Rose	6–4	7–5	6–3		
1953	L. A. Hoad/K. R. Rosewall	D. Candy/M. G. Rose	9–11	6–4	10–8	6–4	
1954	R. N. Hartwig/M. G. Rose	N. A. Fraser/C. Wilderspin	6–3	6–4	6–2		
1955	E. V. Seixas/M. A. Trabert	L. A. Hoad/K. R. Rosewall	6–4	6–2	2–6	3–6	6–1
1956	L. A. Hoad/K. R. Rosewall	D. Candy/M. G. Rose	10–8	13–11	6–4		
1957	N. A. Fraser/L. A. Hoad	M. J. Anderson/A. J. Cooper	6–3	8–6	6–4		
1958	A. J. Cooper/N. A. Fraser	R. S. Emerson/R. Mark	7–5	6–8	3–6	6–3	7–5
1959	R. G. Laver/R. Mark	D. Candy/R. N. Howe	9–7	6–4	6–2		
1960	R. G. Laver/R. Mark	R. S. Emerson/N. A. Fraser	1–6	6–2	6–4	6–4	
1961	R. G. Laver/R. Mark	R. S. Emerson/M. F. Mulligan	6–3	7–5	3–6	9–11	6–2
1962	R. S. Emerson/N. A. Fraser	R. A. J. Hewitt/F. S. Stolle	4–6	4–6	6–1	6–4	11–9
1963	R. A. J. Hewitt/F. S. Stolle	K. N. Fletcher/J. D. Newcombe	6–2	3–6	6–3	3–6	6–3
1964	R. A. J. Hewitt/F. S. Stolle	R. S. Emerson/K. N. Fletcher	6–4	7–5	3–6	4–6	14–12
1965	J. D. Newcombe/A. D. Roche	R. S. Emerson/F. S. Stolle	3–6	4–6	13–11	6–3	6–4
1966	R. S. Emerson/F. S. Stolle	J. D. Newcombe/A. D. Roche	7–9	6–3	6–8	14–12	12–10
1967	J. D. Newcombe/A. D. Roche	W. W. Bowrey/O. K. Davidson	3–6	6–3	7–5	6–8	8–6
1968	R. D. Crealy/A. J. Stone	T. Addison/R. Keldie	10–8	6–4	6–3		PRIZE
1969	R. S. Emerson/R. G. Laver	K. R. Rosewall/F. S. Stolle	6–4	6–4	*		(Aus$)
1970	R. C. Lutz/S. R. Smith	J. G. Alexander/P. Dent	8–6	6–3	6–4		500
1971	J. D. Newcombe/A. D. Roche	T. S. Okker/M. C. Riessen	6–2	7–6	*		
1972	O. K. Davidson/K. R. Rosewall	R. Case/G. Masters	3–6	7–6	6–3*		600
1973	M. J. Anderson/J. D. Newcombe	J. G. Alexander/P. Dent	6–3	6 4	7 6		
1974	R. Case/G. Masters	S. Ball/R. Giltinan	6–7	6–3	6–4*		

	CHAMPIONS	RUNNERS-UP	SCORE					
1975	J. G. Alexander/P. Dent	R. Carmichael/A. J. Stone	6–3	7–6*				
1976	J. D. Newcombe/A. D. Roche	R. Case/G. Masters	7–6	6–4*				
1977	A. R. Ashe/A. D. Roche	C. Pasarell/E. Van Dillen	6–4	6–4*				
1977	(Dec) R. O. Ruffels/A. J. Stone	J. G. Alexander/P. Dent	7–6	7–6*				
1978	(Dec) W. Fibak/K. Warwick	P. Kronk/C. Letcher	7–6	7–5*				
1979	(Dec) P. McNamara/P. McNamee	P. Kronk/C. Letcher	7–6	6–2*				
1980	(Dec) M. R. Edmondson/ K. Warwick	P. McNamara/P. McNamee	7–5	6–4*				
1981	(Dec) M. R. Edmondson/ K. Warwick	H. Pfister/J. Sadri	6–3	6–7	6–3*			24,000
1982	(Dec) J. G. Alexander/J. Fitzgerald	A. Andrews/J. Sadri	6–4	7–6*				28,000
1983	(Dec) M. Edmondson/P. McNamee	S. Denton/S. E. Stewart	6–3	7–6*				30,000
1984	(Dec) M. Edmondson/ S. E. Stewart	J. Nystrom/M. Wilander	6–2	6–2	7–5			38,700
1985	(Dec) P. Annacone/ C. Van Rensburg	M. R. Edmondson/K. Warwick	3–6	7–6	6–4	6–4		34,193
1986		Not held						
1987	(Jan) S. Edberg/A. Jarryd	P. Doohan/L. Warder	6–4	6–4	7–6			35,518
1988	R. Leach/J. Pugh	M. J. Bates/P. Lundgren	6–3	6–2	6–3			36,400
1989	R. Leach/J. Pugh	D. Cahill/M. Kratzmann	6–4	6–4	6–4			48,533
1990	P. Aldrich/D. Visser	G. Connell/G. Michibata	6–4	4–6	6–1	6–4		125,000
1991	S. Davis/D. Pate	P. McEnroe/D. Wheaton	6–7	7–6	6–3	7–5		125,000
1992	T. Woodbridge/M. Woodforde	K. Jones/R. Leach	6–4	6–3	6–4			147,500
1993	D. Visser/L Warder	J. Fitzgerald/A. Jarryd	6–4	6–3	6–4			168,000
1994	J. Eltingh/P. Haarhuis	B. Black/J. Stark	6–7	6–3	6–4	6–3		190,000
1995	J. Palmer/R. Reneberg	M. Knowles/D. Nestor	6–3	3–6	6–3	6–2		200,000
1996	S. Edberg/P. Korda	S. Lareau/A. O'Brien	7–5	7–5	4–6	6–1		234,000
1997	T. Woodbridge/M. Woodforde	S. Lareau/A. O'Brien	4–6	7–5	7–5	6–3		244,000
1998	J. Bjorkman/J. Eltingh	T. Woodbridge/M. Woodforde	6–2	5–7	2–6	6–4	6–3	256,000
1999	J. Bjorkman/P. Rafter	M. Bhupathi/L. Paes	6–3	4–6	6–4	6–7	6–4	301,000
2000	E. Ferreira/R. Leach	W. Black/A. Kratzmann	6–4	3–6	6–3	3–6	18–16	314,000

WOMEN'S DOUBLES

	CHAMPIONS	RUNNERS-UP	SCORE		
1922	E. F. Boyd/M. Mountain	St George/H. S. Utz	3–6	6–4	7–5
1923	E. F. Boyd/S. Lance	M. Molesworth/H. Turner	6–1	6–4	
1924	D. S. Akhurst/S. Lance	K. Le Mesurier/M. O'Hara Wood	7–5	6–2	
1925	D. S. Akhurst/R. Harper	E. F. Boyd/K. Le Mesurier	6–4	6–3	
1926	E. F. Boyd/M. O'Hara Wood	D. S. Akhurst/M. Cox	6–3	6–8	8–6
1927	L. M. Bickerton/M. O'Hara Wood	E. F. Boyd/R. Harper	6–3	6–3	
1928	D. S. Akhurst/E. F. Boyd	K. Le Mesurier/D. Weston	6–3	6–1	
1929	D. S. Akhurst/L. M. Bickerton	R. Harper/M. O'Hara Wood	6–2	4–6	6–2
1930	E. Hood/M. Molesworth	M. Cox/R. Harper	6–3	0–6	7–5
1931	L. M. Bickerton/R. S. Cozens	A. Lloyd/H. S. Utz	6–2	6–4	
1932	C. Buttsworth/J. H. Crawford	K. Le Mesurier/D. Weston	6–2	6–2	
1933	M. Molesworth/V. Westacott	J. Hartigan/J. Van Ryn	6–3	6–3	
1934	M. Molesworth/V. Westacott	J. Hartigan/U. Valkenborg	6–8	6–4	6–4
1935	E. M. Dearman/N. M. Lyle	L. M. Bickerton/H. C. Hopman	6–3	6–4	
1936	T. D. Coyne/N. M. Wynne	M. Blick/K. Woodward	6–2	6–4	
1937	T. D. Coyne/N. M. Wynne	H. C. Hopman/V. Westacott	6–2	6–2	
1938	T. D. Coyne/N. M. Wynne	D. M. Bundy/D. E. Workman	9–7	6–4	
1939	T. D. Coyne/N. M. Wynne	M. Hardcastle/V. Westacott	7–5	6–4	
1940	T. D. Coyne/G.F. Bolton	J. Hartigan/E. Niemeyer	7–5	6–2	
1941–1945		Not held			
1946	M. Bevis/J. Fitch	G. F. Bolton/M. N. Long	9–7	6–4	
1947	G.F. Bolton/M. N. Long	M. Bevis/J. Fitch	6–3	6–3	
1948	G.F. Bolton/M. N. Long	M. Bevis/N. Jones	6–3	6–3	
1949	G.F. Bolton/M. N. Long	D. Hart/M. Toomey	6–0	6–1	
1950	L. Brough/D.J. Hart	G. F. Bolton/M. N. Long	6–3	2–6	6–3
1951	G.F. Bolton/M. N. Long	J. Fitch/M. Hawton	6–2	6–1	
1952	G.F. Bolton/M. N. Long	R. Baker/M. Hawton	6–1	6–1	
1953	M. Connolly/J. Sampson	M. Hawton/B. Penrose	6–4	6–2	
1954	M. Hawton/B. Penrose	H. Redick–Smith/J. Wipplinger	6–3	8–6	
1955	M. Hawton/B. Penrose	H. C. Hopman/A. Thiele	7–5	6–1	
1956	M. Hawton/M. N. Long	M. Carter/B. Penrose	6–3	5–7	9–7

	CHAMPIONS	RUNNERS-UP	SCORE			
1957	S. J. Fry/A. Gibson	M. Hawton/F. Muller	6–2	6–1		
1958	M. Hawton/M. N. Long	L. Coghlan/A. Mortimer	7–5	6–8	6–2	
1959	S. Reynolds/R. Schuurman	L. Coghlan/M. Reitano	7–5	6–4		
1960	M. E. Bueno/C. Truman	L. Robinson/M. Smith	6–2	5–7	6–2	
1961	M. Reitano/M. Smith	M. Hawton/J. Lehane	6–4	3–6	7–5	
1962	R. Ebbern/M. Smith	D. R. Hard/M. Reintano	6–4	6–4		
1963	R. Ebbern/M. Smith	J. Lehane/L. R. Turner	6–1	6–3		
1964	J. A. M. Tegart/L. R. Turner	R. Ebbern/M. Smith	6–4	6–4		
1965	M. Smith/L. R. Turner	R. Ebbern/B. J. Moffitt	1–6	6–2	6–3	
1966	C. Graebner/N. Richey	M. Smith/L. R. Turner	6–4	7–5		
1967	J. A. M. Tegart/L. R. Turner	L. Robinson/E. Terras	6–0	6–2		FIRST
1968	K. Krantzcke/K. Melville	J. A. M. Tegart/L. R. Turner	6–4	3–6	6–2	PRIZE
1969	B. M. Court/J. A. M. Tegart	R. Casals/L. W. King	6–4	6–4		(Aus $)
1970	B. M. Court/D. Dalton	K. Krantzcke/K. Melville	6–3	6–1		120
1971	B. M. Court/E. F. Goolagong	J. Emmerson/L. Hunt	6–0	6–0		
1972	H. Gourlay/K. Harris	P. Coleman/K. Krantzcke	6–0	6–4		500
1973	B. M. Court/S. V. Wade	K. Harris/K. Melville	6–4	6–4		
1974	E. F. Goolagong/M. Michel	K. Harris/K. Melville	7–5	6–3		
1975	E. F. Goolagong/M. Michel	B. M. Court/O. Morozova	7–6	7–6		
1976	R. A. Cawley/H. Gourlay	W. W. Bowrey/R. Tomanova	8–1	(one set)		
1977	D. Fromholtz/H. Gourlay	B. Nagelsen/G. E. Reid	5–7	6–1	7–5	
1977	(Dec) R. A. Cawley/R. L. Cawley div'd with M. Guerrant/G. E. Reid					
1978	(Dec) B. Nagelsen/R. Tomanova	N. Sato/P. Whytcross	7–5	6–2		
1979	(Dec) D. D. Chaloner/D. R. Evers	L. Harrison/M. Mesker	6–2	1–6	6–0	
1980	(Dec) B. Nagelsen/M. Navratilova	A. Kiyomura/C. Reynolds	6–4	6–4		
1981	(Dec) K. Jordan/A. E. Smith	M. Navratilova/P. H. Shriver	6–2	7–5		13,000
1982	(Dec) M. Navratilova/P. H. Shriver	C. Kohde/E. Pfaff	6–4	6–2		16,000
1983	(Dec) M. Navratilova/P. H. Shriver	A. E. Hobbs/W. M. Turnbull	6–4	6–7	6–2	30,000
1984	(Dec) M. Navratilova/P. H. Shriver	C. Kohde-Kilsch/H. Sukova	6–3	6–4		39,900
1985	(Dec) M. Navratilova/P. H. Shriver	C. Kohde-Kilsch/H. Sukova	6–3	6–4		40,000
1986		Not held				
1987	(Jan) M. Navratilova/P. H. Shriver	Z. Garrison/L. McNeil	6–1	6–0		40,000
1988	M. Navratilova/P. H. Shriver	C. Evert/W. M. Turnbull	6–0	7–5		35,000
1989	M. Navratilova/P. H. Shriver	P. Fendick/J. Hetherington	3–6	6–3	6–2	40,000
1990	J. Novotna/H. Sukova	P. Fendick/M. J. Fernandez	7–6	7–6		125,000
1991	P. Fendick/M. J. Fernandez	G. Fernandez/J. Novotna	7–6	6–1		125,000
1992	A. Sanchez-Vicario/H. Sukova	G. Fernandez/Z. Garrison	6–4	7–6		147,500
1993	G. Fernandez/N Zvereva	P. Shriver/E. Smylie	6–4	6–3		168,000
1994	G. Fernandez/N. Zvereva	P. Fendick/M. McGrath	6–3	4–6	6–4	190,000
1995	J. Novotna/A. Sanchez-Vicario	G. Fernandez/N. Zvereva	6–3	6–7	6–4	200,000
1996	S. Rubin/A. Sanchez-Vicario	L. Davenport/M. J. Fernandez	7–5	2–6	6–4	212,000
1997	M. Hingis/N. Zvereva	L. Davenport/L. Raymond	6–2	6–2		225,000
1998	M. Hingis/M. Lucic	L. Davenport/N. Zvereva	6–4	2–6	6–3	237,000
1999	M. Hingis/A. Kournikova	L. Davenport/N. Zvereva	7–5	6–3		283,000
2000	L. Raymond/R. Stubbs	M. Hingis/M. Pierce	6–4	5–7	6–4	298,500

MIXED DOUBLES

	CHAMPIONS	RUNNERS-UP	SCORE		
	CHAMPIONS	RUNNERS-UP	SCORE		
1922	J. B. Hawkes/Miss E. F. Boyd	H. S. Utz/Mrs Utz	6–1	6–1	
1923	H. M. Rice/Miss S. Lance	C. St John/Miss M. Molesworth	2–6	6–4	6–4
1924	J. Willard/Miss D. S. Akhurst	G. M. Hone/Miss E. F. Boyd	6–3	6–4	
1925	J. Willard/Miss D. S. Akhurst	R. E. Schlesinger/Mrs R. Harper	6–4	6–4	
1926	J. B. Hawkes/Miss E. F. Boyd	J. Willard/Miss D. S. Akhurst	6–2	6–4	
1927	J. B. Hawkes/Miss E. F. Boyd	J. Willard/Miss Y. Anthony	6–1	6–3	
1928	J. Borotra/Miss D. S. Akhurst	J. B. Hawkes/Miss E. F. Boyd	w.o		
1929	E. F. Moon/Miss D. S. Akhurst	J. H. Crawford/Miss M. Cox	6–0	7–5	
1930	H. C. Hopman/Miss N. Hall	J. H. Crawford/Miss M. Cox	11–9	3–6	6–3
1931	J. H. Crawford/Mrs Crawford	A. Willard/Mrs V. Westacott	7–5	6–4	
1932	J. H. Crawford/Mrs Crawford	J. Satoh/Mrs P. O'Hara Wood	6–8	8–6	6–3
1933	J. H. Crawford/Mrs Crawford	H. E. Vines/Mrs J. Van Ryn	3–6	7–5	13–11
1934	E. F. Moon/Miss J. Hartigan	R. Dunlop/Mrs V. Westacott	6–3	6–4	
1935	C. Boussus/Miss L. Bickerton	V. G. Kirby/Mrs Bond	1–6	6–3	6–3
1936	H. C. Hopman/Mrs Hopman	A. A. Kay/Miss M. Blick	6–2	6–0	
1937	H. C. Hopman/Mrs Hopman	D. P. Turnbull/Miss D. Stevenson	3–6	6–3	6–2
1938	J. E. Bromwich/Miss J. Wilson	C. Long/Miss N. Wynne	6–3	6–2	

	CHAMPIONS	RUNNERS-UP	SCORE			
1939	H. C. Hopman/Mrs Hopman	J. E. Bromwich/Miss J. Wilson	6–8	6–2	6–3	
1940	C. Long/Mrs G. F. Bolton	H. C. Hopman/Mrs Hopman	7–5	2–6	6–4	
1941–1945		*Not held*				
1946	C. Long/Mrs G. F. Bolton	J. Bromwich/Miss J. Fitch	6–0	6–4		
1947	C. Long/Mrs G. F. Bolton	J. E. Bromwich/Miss J. Fitch	6–3	6–3		
1948	C. Long/Mrs G. F. Bolton	O. W. Sidwell/Mrs M. N. Long	7–5	4–6	8–6	
1949	F. A. Sedgman/Miss D. J. Hart	J. E. Bromwich/Miss J. Fitch	6–1	5–7	12–10	
1950	F. A. Sedgman/Miss D. J. Hart	E. W. Sturgess/Miss J. Fitch	8–6	6–4		
1951	G. A. Worthington/ Mrs M. N. Long	J. May/Miss C. Proctor	6–4	3–6	6–2	
1952	G. A. Worthington/ Mrs M. N. Long	T. Warhurst/Mrs A. R. Thiele	9–7	7–5		
1953	R. N. Hartwig/Miss J. Sampson	H. Richardson/Miss M. Connolly	6–4	6–3		
1954	R. N. Hartwig/Mrs M. N. Long	J. E. Bromwich/Miss B. Penrose	4–6	6–1	6–2	
1955	G. A. Worthington/ Mrs M. N. Long	L. A. Hoad/Miss J. Staley	6–2	6–1		
1956	N. A. Fraser/Miss B. Penrose	R. S. Emerson/Mrs M. Hawton	6–2	6–4		
1957	M. J. Anderson/Miss F. Muller	W. A. Knight/Miss J. Langley	7–5	3–6	6–1	
1958	R. N. Howe/Mrs M. Hawton	A. Newman/Miss A. Mortimer	9–11	6–1	6–2	
1959	R. Mark/Miss S. Reynolds	R. G. Laver/Miss R. Schuurman	4–6	13–11	6–2	
1960	T. Fancutt/Miss J. Lehane	R. Mark/Mrs M. Reitano	6–2	7–5		
1961	R. A. J. Hewitt/Miss J. Lehane	J. Pearce/Mrs M. Reitano	9–7	6–2		
1962	F. S. Stolle/Miss L. R. Turner	R. Taylor/Miss D. R. Hard	6–3	9–7		
1963	K. N. Fletcher/Miss M. Smith	F. S. Stolle/Miss L. R. Turner	7–5	5–7	6–4	
1964	K. N. Fletcher/Miss M. Smith	M. J. Sangster/Miss J. Lehane	6–3	6–2		
1965	J. D. Newcombe/Miss M. Smith div'd with O. K. Davidson/Miss R. Ebbern					
1966	A. D. Roche/Miss J. A. Tegart	W. W. Bowrey/Miss R. Ebbern	6–1	6–3		
1967	O. K. Davidson/Miss L. R. Turner	A. D. Roche/Miss J. A. M. Tegart	9–7	6–4		
1968	R. D. Crealy/Mrs L. W. King	A. J. Stone/Mrs B. M. Court	w.o.			PRIZE
1969	M. C. Riessen/Mrs B. M. Court div'd with F. S. Stolle/Mrs P. F. Jones					MONEY
1969–1986		*Not held*				*(Aus$)*
1987	S. E. Stewart/Miss Z. Garrison	A. Castle/Miss A. E. Hobbs	3–6	7–6	6–3	13,954
1988	J. Pugh/Miss J. Novotna	Tim Gullikson/ Miss M. Navratilova	5–7	6–2	6–4	13,954
1989	J. Pugh/Miss J. Novotna	S. Stewart/Miss Z. Garrison	6–3	6–4		18,140
1990	J. Pugh/Miss N. Zvereva	R. Leach/Miss Z. Garrison	4–6	6–2	6–3	40,000
1991	J. Bates/Miss J. Durie	S. Davis/Miss R. White	2–6	6–4	6–4	40,000
1992	M. Woodforde/Miss N. Provis	T. Woodbridge/ Miss A. Sanchez-Vicario	6–3	4–6	11–9	62,600
1993	T. Woodbridge/ Miss A. Sanchez-Vicario	R. Leach/Miss Z. Garrison Jackson	7–5	6–4		71,400
1994	A. Olhovskiy/Mrs L. Neiland	T. Woodbridge/Miss H. Sukova	7–5	6–7	6–2	80,000
1995	R. Leach/Miss N. Zvereva	C. Suk/Miss G. Fernandez	7–6	6–7	6–4	83,000
1996	M. Woodforde/Mrs L. Neiland	L. Jensen/Miss N. Arendt	4–6	7–5	6–0	88,000
1997	R. Leach/Miss M. Bollegraf	J. De Jager/Mrs L. Neiland	6–3	6–7	7–5	92,000
1998	J. Gimelstob/Miss V. Williams	C. Suk/Miss H. Sukova	6–2	6–1		92,000
1999	D. Adams/Miss M. De Swardt	M. Mirnyi/Miss S. Williams	6–4	4–6	7–6	108,000
2000	J. Palmer/Miss R. Stubbs	T. Woodbridge/ Miss A. Sanchez-Vicario	7–5	7–6		112,800

FRENCH CHAMPIONSHIPS

1. Venue and conditions of entry: From 1891 to 1924 the Championships, restricted to members of French clubs, were played at the Stade Francais ground at the Faisanderie in St. Cloud Park. A separate event, the 'World Hard Court Championship' was held in Paris (except for one year when it was held in Brussels) between 1912 and 1923 when the title was abolished. International from 1925, the Championships were played for three years alternately at the Racing Club at Croix-Catelan in Paris and the Stade Francais at the Faisanderie. Since 1928 the Championships have been played continuously at the Stade Roland Garros, Porte D'Auteuil, Paris. **2. Status:** The Championships became 'Open' in 1968. Since 1990 the Men's Doubles has been reduced to the best of three sets. **3. Surface:** Red clay (Terre Battu).

MEN'S SINGLES

1891	H. Briggs	1903–04	M. Decugis	1920	A. H. Gobert
1892	J. Schopfer	1905–06	M. Germot	1921	J. Samazeuilh
1893	L. Riboulet	1907–09	M. Decugis	1922	H. Cochet
1894–96	A. Vacherot	1910	M. Germot	1923	P. Blanchy
1897–1900	P. Ayme	1911	A. H. Gobert	1924	J. Borotra
1901	A. Vacherot	1912–14	M. Decugis		
1902	M. Vacherot	1915–19	*Not held*		

	CHAMPION	RUNNER-UP	SCORE					
1925	R. Lacoste	J. Borotra	7–5	6–1	6–4			
1926	H. Cochet	R. Lacoste	6–2	6–4	6–3			
1927	R. Lacoste	W. T. Tilden	6–4	4–6	5–7	6–3	11–9	
1928	H. Cochet	R. Lacoste	5–7	6–3	6–1	6–3		
1929	R. Lacoste	J. Borotra	6–3	2–6	6–0	2–6	8–6	
1930	H. Cochet	W. T. Tilden	3–6	8–6	6–3	6–1		
1931	J. Borotra	C. Boussus	2–6	6–4	7–5	6–4		
1932	H. Cochet	G. De Stefani	6–0	6–4	4–6	6–3		
1933	J. H. Crawford	H. Cochet	8–6	6–1	6–3			
1934	G. von Cramm	J. H. Crawford	6–4	7–9	3–6	7–5	6–3	
1935	F. J. Perry	G. von Cramm	6–3	3–6	6–1	6–3		
1936	G. von Cramm	F. J. Perry	6–0	2–6	6–2	2–6	6–0	
1937	H. Henkel	H. W. Austin	6–1	6–4	6–3			
1938	J. D. Budge	R. Menzel	6–3	6–2	6–4			
1939	W. D. McNeill	R. L. Riggs	7–5	6–0	6–3			
1940–45		*Not held*						
1946	M. Bernard	J. Drobny	3–6	2–6	6–1	6–4	6–3	
1947	J. Asboth	E. W. Sturgess	8–6	7–5	6–4			
1948	F. A. Parker	J. Drobny	6–4	7–5	5–7	8–6		
1949	F. A. Parker	J. E. Patty	6–3	1–6	6–1	6–4		
1950	J. E. Patty	J. Drobny	6–1	6–2	3–6	5–7	7–5	
1951	J. Drobny	E. W. Sturgess	6–3	6–3	6–3			
1952	J. Drobny	F. A. Sedgman	6–2	6–0	3–6	6–4		
1953	K. R. Rosewall	E. V. Seixas	6–3	6–4	1–6	6–2		
1954	M. A. Trabert	A. Larsen	6–4	7–5	6–1			
1955	M. A. Trabert	S. Davidson	2–6	6–1	6–4	6–2		
1956	L. A. Hoad	S. Davidson	6–4	8–6	6–3			
1957	S. Davidson	H. Flam	6–3	6–4	6–4			
1958	M. G. Rose	L. Ayala	6–3	6–4	6–4			
1959	N. Pietrangeli	I. C. Vermaak	3–6	6–3	6–4	6–1		
1960	N. Pietrangeli	L. Ayala	3–6	6–3	6–4	4–6	6–3	
1961	M. Santana	N. Pietrangeli	4–6	6–1	3–6	6–0	6–2	
1962	R. G. Laver	R. S. Emerson	3–6	2–6	6–3	9–7	6–2	
1963	R. S. Emerson	P. Darmon	3–6	6–1	6–4	6–4		
1964	M. Santana	N. Pietrangeli	6–3	6–1	4–6	7–5		
1965	F. S. Stolle	A. D. Roche	3–6	6–0	6–2	6–3		FIRST
1966	A. D. Roche	I. Gulyas	6–1	6–4	7–5			PRIZE
1967	R. S. Emerson	A. D. Roche	6–1	6–4	2–6	6–2		*(in French francs)*
1968	K. R. Rosewall	R. G. Laver	6–3	6–1	2–6	6–2		15,000
1969	R. G. Laver	K. R. Rosewall	6–4	6–3	6–4			35,000
1970	J. Kodes	Z. Franulovic	6–2	6–4	6–0			56,000
1971	J. Kodes	I. Nastase	8–6	6–2	2–6	7–5		48,000
1972	A. Gimeno	P. Proisy	4–6	6–3	6–1	6–1		48,000
1973	I. Nastase	N. Pilic	6–3	6–3	6–0			70,000
1974	B. Borg	M. Orantes	2–6	6–7	6–0	6–1	6–1	120,000

	CHAMPION	RUNNER-UP	SCORE					
1975	B. Borg	G. Vilas	6–2	6–3	6–4			120,000
1976	A. Panatta	H. Solomon	6–1	6–4	4–6	7–6		130,000
1977	G. Vilas	B. E. Gottfried	6–0	6–3	6–0			190,000
1978	B. Borg	G. Vilas	6–1	6–1	6–3			210,000
1979	B. Borg	V. Pecci	6–3	6–1	6–7	6–4		208,200
1980	B. Borg	V. Gerulaitis	6–4	6–1	6–2			221,000
1981	B. Borg	I. Lendl	6–1	4–6	6–2	3–6	6–1	250,000
1982	M. Wilander	G. Vilas	1–6	7–6	6–0	6–4		400,000
1983	Y. Noah	M. Wilander	6–2	7–5	7–6			500,000
1984	I. Lendl	J. P. McEnroe	3–6	2–6	6–4	7–5	7–5	1,058,600
1985	M. Wilander	I. Lendl	3–6	6–4	6–2	6–2		1,338,200
1986	I. Lendl	M. Pernfors	6–3	6–2	6–4			1,397,250
1987	I. Lendl	M. Wilander	7–5	6–2	3–6	7–6		1,303,800
1988	M. Wilander	H. Leconte	7–5	6–2	6–1			1,500,240
1989	M. Chang	S. Edberg	6–1	3–6	4–6	6–4	6–2	1,791,390
1990	A. Gomez	A. Agassi	6–3	2–6	6–4	6–4		2,226,100
1991	J. Courier	A. Agassi	3–6	6–4	2–6	6–1	6–4	2,448,000
1992	J. Courier	P. Korda	7–5	6–2	6–1			2,680,000
1993	S. Bruguera	J. Courier	6–4	2–6	6–2	3–6	6–3	2,680,000
1994	S. Bruguera	A. Berasategui	6–3	7–5	2–6	6–1		3,160,000
1995	T. Muster	M. Chang	7–5	6–2	6–4			3,320,000
1996	Y. Kafelnikov	M. Stitch	7–6	7–5	7–6			3,542,000
1997	G. Kuerten	S. Bruguera	6–3	6–4	6–2			3,668,000
1998	C. Moya	A. Corretja	6–3	7–5	6–3			3,852,000
1999	A. Agassi	A. Medvedev	1–6	2–6	6–4	6–3	6–4	4,040,000
2000	G. Kuerten	M. Norman	6–2	6–3	2–6	7–6		4,240,000

WOMEN'S SINGLES

1897–99	Mlle F. Masson	1906	Mme F. Fenwick	1915–19	Not held
1900	Mlle Y. Prevost	1907	Mme De Kermel	1920–23	Mlle S. Lenglen
1901	Mme P. Girod	1908	Mme F. Fenwick	1924	Mlle D. Vlasto
1902–03	Mlle F. Masson	1909–12	Mlle J. Matthey		
1904–05	Mlle K. Gillou	1913–14	Mlle M. Broquedis		

	CHAMPION	RUNNER-UP	SCORE		
1925	Mlle S. Lenglen	Miss K. McKane	6–1	6–2	
1926	Mlle S. Lenglen	Miss M. K. Browne	6–1	6–0	
1927	Mlle K. Bouman	Mrs G. Peacock	6–2	6–4	
1928	Miss H. N. Wills	Miss E. Bennett	6–1	6–2	
1929	Miss H. N. Wills	Mme R. Mathieu	6–3	6–4	
1930	Mrs F. S. Moody	Miss H. H. Jacobs	6–2	6–1	
1931	Frl C. Aussem	Miss B. Nuthall	8–6	6–1	
1932	Mrs F. S. Moody	Mme R. Mathieu	7–5	6–1	
1933	Miss M. C. Scriven	Mme R. Mathieu	6–2	4–6	6–4
1934	Miss M. C. Scriven	Miss H. H. Jacobs	7–5	4–6	6–1
1935	Mrs H. Sperling	Mme R. Mathieu	6–2	6–1	
1936	Mrs H. Sperling	Mme R. Mathieu	6–3	6–4	
1937	Mrs H. Sperling	Mme R. Mathieu	6–2	6–4	
1938	Mme R. Mathieu	Mme N. Landry	6–0	6–3	
1939	Mme R. Mathieu	Miss J. Jedrzejowska	6–3	8–6	
1940–45		Not held			
1946	Miss M. E. Osborne	Miss P. M. Betz	1–6	8–6	7–5
1947	Mrs P. C. Todd	Miss D. J. Hart	6–3	3–6	6–4
1948	Mme N. Landry	Miss S. J. Fry	6–2	0–6	6–0
1949	Mrs W. du Pont	Mme N. Adamson	7–5	6–2	
1950	Miss D. J. Hart	Mrs P. C. Todd	6–4	4–6	6–2
1951	Miss S. J. Fry	Miss D. J. Hart	6–3	3–6	6–3
1952	Miss D. J. Hart	Miss S. J. Fry	6–4	6–4	
1953	Miss M. Connolly	Miss D. J. Hart	6–2	6–4	
1954	Miss M. Connolly	Mme G. Bucaille	6–4	6–1	
1955	Miss A. Mortimer	Mrs D. P. Knode	2–6	7–5	10–8
1956	Miss A. Gibson	Miss A. Mortimer	6–0	12–10	
1957	Miss S. J. Bloomer	Mrs D. P. Knode	6–1	6–3	
1958	Mrs Z. Kormoczy	Miss S. J. Bloomer	6–4	1–6	6–2
1959	Miss C. C. Truman	Mrs Z. Kormoczy	6–4	7–5	
1960	Miss D. R. Hard	Miss Y. Ramirez	6–3	6–4	

	CHAMPION	RUNNER-UP	SCORE				
1961	Miss A. S. Haydon	Miss Y. Ramirez	6–2	6–1			
1962	Miss M. Smith	Miss L. R. Turner	6–3	3–6	7–5		
1963	Miss L. R. Turner	Mrs P. F. Jones	2–6	6–3	7–5		
1964	Miss M. Smith	Miss M. E. Bueno	5–7	6–1	6–2		
1965	Miss L. R. Turner	Miss M. Smith	6–3	6–4			FIRST
1966	Mrs P. F. Jones	Miss N. Richey	6–3	6–1			PRIZE
1967	Mlle F. Durr	Miss L. R. Turner	4–6	6–3	6–4		(in French francs)
1968	Miss N. Richey	Mrs P. F. Jones	5–7	6–4	6–1		5,000
1969	Mrs B. M. Court	Mrs P. F. Jones	6–1	4–6	6–3		10,000
1970	Mrs B. M. Court	Miss H. Niessen	6–2	6–4			17,800
1971	Miss E. Goolagong	Miss H. Gourlay	6–3	7–5			13,500
1972	Mrs L. W. King	Miss E. Goolagong	6–3	6–3			13,500
1973	Mrs B. M. Court	Miss C. M. Evert	6–7	7–6	6–4		25,000
1974	Miss C. M. Evert	Mrs O. Morozova	6–1	6–2			40,000
1975	Miss C. M. Evert	Miss M. Navratilova	2–6	6–2	6–1		40,000
1976	Miss S. Barker	Miss R. Tomanova	6–2	0–6	6–2		30,000
1977	Miss M. Jausovec	Miss F. Mihai	6–2	6–7	6–1		35,000
1978	Miss V. Ruzici	Miss M. Jausovec	6–2	6–2			100,000
1979	Mrs J. M. Lloyd	Miss W. M. Turnbull	6–2	6–0			126,900
1980	Mrs J. M. Lloyd	Miss V. Ruzici	6–0	6–3			178,500
1981	Miss H. Mandlikova	Miss S. Hanika	6–2	6–4			200,000
1982	Miss M. Navratilova	Miss A. Jaeger	7–6	6–1			300,000
1983	Mrs J. M. Lloyd	Miss M. Jausovec	6–1	6–2			375,000
1984	Miss M. Navratilova	Mrs J. M. Lloyd	6–3	6–1			791,600
1985	Mrs J. M. Lloyd	Miss M. Navratilova	6–3	6–7	7–5		1,262,700
1986	Mrs J. M. Lloyd	Miss M. Navratilova	2–6	6–3	6–3		1,278,400
1987	Miss S. Graf	Miss M. Navratilova	6–4	4–6	8–6		1,178,840
1988	Miss S. Graf	Miss N. Zvereva	6–0	6–0			1,463,390
1989	Miss A. Sanchez	Miss S. Graf	7–6	3–6	7–5		1,593,175
1990	Miss M. Seles	Miss S. Graf	7–6	6–4			1,762,900
1991	Miss M. Seles	Miss A. Sanchez-Vicario	6–3	6–4			2,237,000
1992	Miss M. Seles	Miss S. Graff	6–2	3–6	10–8		2,470,000
1993	Miss S. Graf	Miss M. J. Fernandez	4–6	6–2	6–4		2,470,000
1994	Miss A. Sanchez-Vicario	Miss M. Pierce	6–4	6–4			2,930,000
1995	Miss S. Graf	Miss A. Sanchez-Vicario	7–5	4–6	6–0		3,100,000
1996	Miss S. Graf	Miss A. Sanchez-Vicario	6–3	6–7	10–8		3,224,000
1997	Miss I. Majoli	Miss M. Hingis	6–4	6–2			3,450,000
1998	Miss A. Sanchez-Vicario	Miss M. Seles	7–6	0–6	6–2		3,624,000
1999	Miss S. Graf	Miss M. Hingis	4–6	7–5	6–2		3,840,000
2000	Miss M. Pierce	Miss C. Martinez	6–2	7–5			4,028,000

MEN'S DOUBLES

	CHAMPIONS	RUNNERS-UP	SCORE				
1925	J. Borotra/R. Lacoste	J. Brugnon/H. Cochet	7–5	4–6	6–3	2–6	6–3
1926	H. O. Kinsey/V. Richards	J. Brugnon/H. Cochet	6–4	6–1	4–6	6–4	
1927	J. Brugnon/H. Cochet	J. Borotra/R. Lacoste	2–6	6–2	6–0	1–6	6–4
1928	J. Borotra/J. Brugnon	R. De Buzelet/H. Cochet	6–4	3–6	6–2	3–6	6–4
1929	J. Borotra/R. Lacoste	J. Brugnon/H. Cochet	6–3	3–6	6–3	3–6	8–6
1930	J. Brugnon/H. Cochet	H. C. Hopman/J. Willard	6–3	9–7	6–3		
1931	G. M. Lott/J. Van Ryn	N. G. Farquharson/V. G. Kirby	6–4	6–3	6–4		
1932	J. Brugnon/H. Cochet	M. Bernard/C. Boussus	6–4	3–6	7–5	6–3	
1933	G. P. Hughes/F. J. Perry	V. B. McGrath/A. K. Quist	6–2	6–4	2–6	7–5	
1934	J. Borotra/J. Brugnon	J. H. Crawford/V. B. McGrath	11–9	6–3	2–6	4–6	9–7
1935	J. H. Crawford/A. K. Quist	V. B. McGrath/D. P. Turnbull	6–1	6–4	6–2		
1936	M. Bernard/J. Borotra	G. P. Hughes/C. R. D. Tuckey	6–2	3–6	9–7	6–1	
1937	G. Von Cramm/H. Henkel	N. G. Farquharson/V. G. Kirby	6–4	7–5	3–6	6–1	
1938	B. Destremau/Y. Petra	J. D. Budge/G. Mako	3–6	6–3	9–7	6–1	
1939	C. Harris/W. D. McNeil	J. Borotra/J. Brugnon	4–6	6–4	6–0	2–6	10–8
1940–1945		Not held					
1946	M. Bernard/Y. Petra	E. Morea/F. Segura	7–5	6–3	0–6	1–6	10–8
1947	E. Fannin/E. W. Sturgess	T. P. Brown/O. W. Sidwell	6–4	4–6	6–4	6–3	
1948	L. Bergelin/J. Drobny	H. C. Hopman/F. A. Sedgman	8–6	6–1	12–10		
1949	R. A. Gonzales/F. Parker	E. Fannin/E. W. Sturgess	6–3	8–6	5–7	6–3	
1950	W. F. Talbert/M. A. Trabert	J. Drobny/E. W. Sturgess	6–2	1–6	10–8	6–2	
1951	K. B. McGregor/F. A. Sedgman	G. Mulloy/R. Savitt	6–2	2–6	9–7	7–5	
1952	K. B. McGregor/F. A. Sedgman	G. Mulloy/R. Savitt	6–3	6–4	6–4		

	CHAMPIONS	RUNNERS-UP	SCORE				
1953	L. A. Hoad/K. R. Rosewall	M. G. Rose/C. Wilderspin	6–2	6–1	6–1		
1954	E. V. Seixas/M. A. Trabert	L. A. Hoad/K. R. Rosewall	6–4	6–2	6–1		
1955	E. V. Seixas/M. A. Trabert	N. Pietrangeli/O. Sirola	6–1	4–6	6–2	6–4	
1956	D. W. Candy/R. M. Perry	A. J. Cooper/L. A. Hoad	7–5	6–3	6–3		
1957	M. J. Anderson/A. J. Cooper	D. W. Candy/M. G. Rose	6–3	6–0	6–3		
1958	A. J. Cooper/N. A. Fraser	R. N. Howe/A. Segal	3–6	8–6	6–3	7–5	
1959	N. Pietrangeli/O. Sirola	R. S. Emerson/N. A. Fraser	6–3	6–2	14–12		
1960	R. S. Emerson/N. A. Fraser	J. L. Arilla/A. Gimeno	6–2	8–10	7–5	6–4	
1961	R. S. Emerson/R. G. Laver	R. N. Howe/R. Mark	3–6	6–1	6–1	6–4	
1962	R. S. Emerson/N. A. Fraser	W. P. Bungert/C. Kuhnke	6–3	6–4	7–5		
1963	R. S. Emerson/M. Santana	G. L. Forbes/A. Segal	6–2	6–4	6–4		
1964	R. S. Emerson/K. N. Fletcher	J. D. Newcombe/A. D. Roche	7–5	6–3	3–6	7–5	
1965	R. S. Emerson/F. S. Stolle	K. N. Fletcher/R. A. J. Hewitt	6–8	6–3	8–6	6–2	
1966	C. E. Graebner/R. D. Ralston	I. Nastase/I. Tiriac	6–3	6–3	6–0		
1967	J. D. Newcombe/A. D. Roche	R. S. Emerson/K. N. Fletcher	6–3	9–7	12–10		
1968	K. R. Rosewall/F. S. Stolle	R. S. Emerson/R. G. Laver	6–3	6–4	6–3		
1969	J. D. Newcombe/A. D. Roche	R. S. Emerson/R. G. Laver	4–6	6–1	3–6	6–4	6–4
1970	I. Nastase/I. Tiriac	A. R. Ashe/C. Pasarell	6–2	6–4	6–3		FF8,000
1971	A. R. Ashe/M. C. Riessen	T. W. Gorman/S. R. Smith	6–8	4–6	6–3	6–4 11–9	6,000
1972	R. A. J. Hewitt/F. D. McMillan	P. Cornejo/J. Fillol	6–3	8–6	3–6	6–1	10,000
1973	J. D. Newcombe/T. S. Okker	J. S. Connors/I. Nastase	6–1	3–6	6–3	5–7 6–4	24,000
1974	R. D. Crealy/O. Parun	R. C. Lutz/S. R. Smith	6–3	6–2	3–6	5–7 6–1	30,000
1975	B. E. Gottfried/R. Ramirez	J. G. Alexander/P. Dent	6–2	2–6	6–2	6–4	30,000
1976	F. McNair/S. E. Stewart	B. E. Gottfried/R. Ramirez	7–6	6–3	6–1		47,000
1977	B. E. Gottfried/R. Ramirez	W. Fibak/J. Kodes	7–6	4–6	6–3	6–4	76,000
1978	G. Mayer/H. Pfister	J. Higueras/M. Orantes	6–3	6–2	6–2		84,000
1979	A. A./G. Mayer	R. Case/P. Dent	6–4	6–4	6–4		83,280
1980	V. Amaya/H. Pfister	B. E. Gottfried/R. Ramirez	1–6	6–4	6–4	6–3	89,250
1981	H. Gunthardt/B. Taroczy	T. Moor/E. Teltscher	6–2	7–6	6–3		108,400
1982	S. E. Stewart/F. Taygan	H. Gildemeister/B. Prajoux	7–5	6–3	1–1	ret	160,400
1983	A. Jarryd/H. Simonsson	M. R. Edmondson/S. E. Stewart	7–6	6–4	6–2		262,970
1984	H. Leconte/Y. Noah	P. Slozil/T. Smid	6–4	2–6	3–6	6–3 6–2	423,380
1985	M. R. Edmondson/K. Warwick	S. Glickstein/H. Simonsson	6–3	6–4	6–7	6–3	535,400
1986	J. Fitzgerald/T. Smid	S. Edberg/A. Jarryd	6–3	4–6	6–3	6–7 14–12	558,900
1987	A. Jarryd/R. Seguso	G. Forget/Y. Noah	6–7	6–7	6–3	6–4 6–2	451,000
1988	A. Gomez/E. Sanchez	J. Fitzgerald/A. Jarryd	6–3	6–7	6–4	6–3	520,080
1989	J. Grabb/P. McEnroe	M. Bahrami/E. Winogradsky	6–4	2–6	6–4	7–6	621,024
1990	S. Casal/E. Sanchez	G. Ivanisevic/P. Korda	7–5	6–3			US$151,000
1991	J. Fitzgerald/A. Jarryd	R. Leach/J. Pugh	6–0	7–6			FF1,000,000
1992	J. Hlasek/M. Rosset	C. Adams/A. Olhovskiy	7–6	6–7	7–5		1,100,000
1993	L. Jensen/M. Jensen	M. K. Goellner/D. Prinosil	6–4	6–7	6–4		1,100,000
1994	B. Black/J. Stark	J. Apell/J. Bjorkman	6–4	7–6			1,200,000
1995	J. Eltingh/P. Haarhuis	N. Kulti/M. Larsson	6–7	6–4	6–1		1,364,000
1996	Y. Kafelnikov/D. Vacek	G. Forget/J. Hlasek	6–2	6–3			1,420,000
1997	Y. Kafelnikov/D. Vacek	T. Woodbridge/M. Woodforde	7–6	4–6	6–3		1,508,000
1998	J. Eltingh/P.Haarhuis	M. Knowles/D. Nestor	6–3	3–6	6–3		1,584,000
1999	M. Bhupathi/L. Paes	G. Ivanisevic/J. Tarango	6–2	7–5			1,660,000
2000	T. Woodbridge/M. Woodforde	P. Haarhuis/S. Stolle	7–6	6–4			1,740,000

WOMEN'S DOUBLES

	CHAMPIONS	RUNNERS-UP	SCORE		
1925	S. Lenglen/D. Vlasto	E. Colyer/K. McKane	6–1	9–11	6–2
1926	S. Lenglen/D. Vlasto	E. Colyer/L. A. Godfree	6–1	6–1	
1927	E. L. Heine/G. Peacock	P. Saunders/P. H. Watson	6–2	6–1	
1928	E. Bennett/P. H. Watson	S. Deve/A. Lafaurie	6–0	6–2	
1929	L. De Alvarez/K. Bouman	E. L. Heine/A. Neave	7–5	6–3	
1930	F. S. Moody/E. Ryan	S. Barbier/S. Mathieu	6–3	6–1	
1931	B. Nuthall/E. F. Whittingstall	C. Aussem/E. Ryan	9–7	6–2	
1932	F. S. Moody/E. Ryan	B. Nuthall/E. F. Whittingstall	6–1	6–3	
1933	S. Mathieu/E. Ryan	S. Henrotin/C. Rosambert	6–1	6–3	
1934	S. Mathieu/E. Ryan	H. H. Jacobs/S. Palfrey	3–6	6–4	6–2
1935	M. C. Scriven/K. Stammers	N. Adamoff/H. Sperling	6–4	6–0	
1936	S. Mathieu/A. M. Yorke	S. Noel/J. Jedrzejowska	2–6	6–4	6–4
1937	S. Mathieu/A. M. Yorke	D. Andrus/S. Henrotin	3–6	6–2	6–2
1938	S. Mathieu/A. M. Yorke	A. Halff/N. Landry	6–3	6–3	

	CHAMPIONS	RUNNERS-UP	SCORE			
1939	J. Jedrzejowska/S. Mathieu	A. Florian/H. Kovac	7–5	7–5		
1940–1945		Not held				
1946	L. Brough/M. Osborne	P. Betz/D. Hart	6–4	0–6	6–1	
1947	L. Brough/M. Osborne	D. Hart/P. C. Todd	7–5	6–2		
1948	D. Hart/P. C. Todd	S. Fry/M. A. Prentiss	6–4	6–2		
1949	L. Brough/W. du Pont	J. Gannon/B. Hilton	7–5	6–1		
1950	S. Fry/D. Hart	L. Brough/W. du Pont	1–6	7–5	6–2	
1951	S. Fry/D. Hart	B. Bartlett/B. Scofield	10–8	6–3		
1952	S. Fry/D. Hart	H. Redick–Smith/J. Wipplinger	7–5	6–1		
1953	S. Fry/D. Hart	M. Connolly/J. Sampson	6–4	6–3		
1954	M. Connolly/N. Hopman	M. Galtier/S. Schmitt	7–5	4–6	6–0	
1955	B. Fleitz/D. R. Hard	S. J. Bloomer/P. Ward	7–5	6–8	13–11	
1956	A. Buxton/A. Gibson	D. R. Hard/D. Knode	6–8	8–6	6–1	
1957	S. J. Bloomer/D. R. Hard	Y. Ramirez/R. M. Reyes	7–5	4–6	7–5	
1958	Y. Ramirez/R. M. Reyes	M. K. Hawton/M. N. Long	6–4	7–5		
1959	S. Reynolds/R. Schuurman	Y. Ramirez/R. M. Reyes	2–6	6–0	6–1	
1960	M. E. Bueno/D. R. Hard	R. Hales/A. Haydon	6–2	7–5		
1961	S. Reynolds/R. Schuurman	M. E. Bueno/D. R. Hard	w.o.			
1962	S. Price/R. Schuurman	J. Bricka/M. Smith	6–4	6–4		
1963	P. F. Jones/R. Schuurman	R. A. Ebbern/M. Smith	7–5	6–4		
1964	M. Smith/L. R. Turner	N. Baylon/H. Schultze	6–3	6–1		
1965	M. Smith/L. R. Turner	F. Durr/J. Lieffrig	6–3	6–1		
1966	M. Smith/J. A. M. Tegart	J. Blackman/F. Toyne	4–6	6–1	6–1	
1967	F. Durr/G. Sheriff	A. M. Van Zyl/P. Walkden	6–2	6–2		
1968	F. Durr/P. F. Jones	R. Casals/L. W. King	7–5	4–6	6–4	
1969	F. Durr/P. F. Jones	M. Court/N. Richey	6–0	4–6	7–5	
1970	F. Durr/G. Chanfreau	R. Casals/L. W. King	6–1	3–6	6–3	FF6,000
1971	F. Durr/G. Chanfreau	H. Gourlay/K. Harris	6–4	6–1		4500
1972	L. W. King/B. Stove	W. Shaw/F. E. Truman	6–1	6–2		5,000
1973	M. Court/S. V. Wade	F. Durr/B. Stove	6–2	6–3		7,000
1974	C. Evert/O. Morozova	G. Chanfreau/K. Ebbinghaus	6–4	2–6	6–1	8,000
1975	C. Evert/M. Navratilova	J. Anthony/O. Morozova	6–3	6–2		8,000
1976	F. Bonicelli/G. Lovera	K. Harter/H. Masthoff	6–4	1–6	6–3	8,000
1977	R. Marsikova/P. Teeguarden	R. Fox/H. Gourlay	5–7	6–4	6–2	8,000
1978	M. Jausovec/V. Ruzici	N. Bowey/G. Lovera	5–7	6–4	8–6	20,000
1979	B. Stove/W. M. Turnbull	F. Durr/S. V. Wade	6–4	7–6		42,300
1980	K. Jordan/A. E. Smith	I. Madruga/I. Villagran	6–1	6–0		68,000
1981	R. Fairbank/T. Harford	C. Reynolds/P. Smith	6–1	6–3		80,000
1982	M. Navratilova/A. E. Smith	R. Casals/W. M. Turnbull	6–3	6–4		120,000
1983	R. Fairbank/C. Reynolds	K. Jordan/A. E. Smith	5–7	7–5	6–2	210,000
1984	M. Navratilova/P. H. Shriver	C. Kohde-Kilsch/H. Mandlikova	5–7	6–3	6–2	316,000
1985	M. Navratilova/P. H. Shriver	C. Kohde-Kilsch/H. Sukova	4–6	6–2	6–2	384,300
1986	M. Navratilova/A. Temesvari	S. Graf/G. Sabatini	6–1	6–2		398,200
1987	M. Navratilova/P. H. Shriver	S. Graf/G. Sabatini	6–2	6–1		365,300
1988	M. Navratilova/P. H. Shriver	C. Kohde-Kilsch/H. Sukova	6–2	7–5		453,230
1989	L. Savchenko/N. Zvereva	S. Graf/G. Sabatini	6–4	6–4		552,316
1990	J. Novotna/H. Sukova	L. Savchenko/N. Zvereva	6–4	7–5		US$103,080
1991	G. Fernandez/J. Novotna	L. Savchenko/N. Zvereva	6–4	6–0		FF786,500
1992	G. Fernandez/N. Zvereva	C. Martinez/A. Sanchez-Vicario.	6–3	6–2		865,000
1993	G. Fernandez/N. Zvereva	L. Neiland/J. Novotna	6–3	7–5		944,000
1994	G. Fernandez/N. Zvereva	L. Davenport/L. Raymond	6–2	6–2		1,020,000
1995	G. Fernandez/N. Zvereva	J. Novotna/A. Sanchez-Vicario	6–7	6–4	7–5	1,070,000
1996	L. Davenport/M. J. Fernandez	G. Fernandez/N. Zvereva	6–2	6–1		1,112,800
1997	G. Fernandez/N. Zvereva	M. J. Fernandez/L. Raymond	3–6	6–4	6–1	1,182,400
1998	M. Hingis/J. Novotna	L. Davenport/N. Zvereva	6–1	7–6		1,241,500
1999	S. Williams/V. Williams	M. Hingis/A. Kournikova	6–3	6–7	8–6	1,328,000
2000	M. Hingis/M. Pierce	V. Ruano Pascual/P. Suarez	6–2	6–4		1,392,000

MIXED DOUBLES

	CHAMPIONS	RUNNERS-UP	SCORE		
1925	J. Brugnon/Miss S. Lenglen	H. Cochet/Miss D. Vlasto	6–2	6–2	
1926	J. Brugnon/Miss S. Lenglen	J. Borotra/Mrs Le Besnerais	6–4	6–3	
1927	J. Borotra/Miss M. Broquedis	W. T. Tilden/Miss L. De Alvarez	6–4	2–6	6–2
1928	H. Cochet/Miss E. Bennett	F. T. Hunter/Miss H. Wills	3–6	6–3	6–3
1929	H. Cochet/Miss E. Bennett	F. T. Hunter/Miss H. Wills	6–3	6–2	
1930	W. T. Tilden/Miss C. Aussem	H. Cochet/Mrs F. Whittingstall	6–4	6–4	

	CHAMPIONS	RUNNERS-UP	SCORE			
1931	P. D. B. Spence/Miss B. Nuthall	H. W. Austin/Mrs D. C. Shepherd-Barron	6–3	5–7	6–3	
1932	F. J. Perry/Miss B. Nuthall	S. B. Wood/Mrs F. S. Moody	6–4	6–2		
1933	J. H. Crawford/Miss M. C. Scriven	F. J. Perry/Miss B. Nuthall	6–2	6–3		
1934	J. Borotra/Miss C. Rosambert	A. K. Quist/Miss E. Ryan	6–2	6–4		
1935	M. Bernard/Miss L. Payot	A. M. Legeay/Mrs S. Henrotin	4–6	6–2	6–4	
1936	M. Bernard/Miss A. M. Yorke	A. M. Legeay/Mrs S. Henrotin	7–5	6–8	6–3	
1937	Y. Petra/Mrs S. Mathieu	R. Journu/Miss M. Horne	7–5	7–5		
1938	D. Mitic/Mrs S. Mathieu	C. Boussus/Miss N. Wynne	2–6	6–3	6–4	
1939	E. T. Cooke/Mrs S. Fabyan	F. Kukuljevic/Mrs S. Mathieu	4–6	6–1	7–5	
1940–1945		*Not held*				
1946	J. E. Patty/Miss P. M. Betz	T. P. Brown/Miss D. Bundy	7–5	9–7		
1947	E. W. Sturgess/Mrs S. P. Summers	C. Caralulis/Miss J. Jedrzejowska	6–0	6–0		
1948	J. Drobny/Mrs P. C. Todd	F. A. Sedgman/Miss D. Hart	6–3	3–6	6–3	
1949	E. W. Sturgess/Mrs S. P. Summers	G. D. Oakley/Miss J. Quertier	6–1	6–1		
1950	E. Morea/Miss B. Scofield	W. F. Talbert/Mrs P. C. Todd	w.o.			
1951	F. A. Sedgman/Miss D. Hart	M. G. Rose/Mrs M. N. Long	7–5	6–2		
1952	F. A. Sedgman/Miss D. Hart	E. W. Sturgess/Miss S. Fry	6–8	6–3	6–3	
1953	E. V. Seixas/Miss D. Hart	M. G. Rose/Miss M. Connolly	4–6	6–4	6–0	
1954	L. A. Hoad/Miss M. Connolly	R. N. Hartwig/Mrs J. Patorni	6–4	6–3		
1955	G. L. Forbes/Miss D. R. Hard	L. Ayala/Miss J. Staley	5–7	6–1	6–2	
1956	L. Ayala/Mrs M. N. Long	R. N. Howe/Miss D. R. Hard	4–6	6–4	6–1	
1957	J. Javorsky/Miss V. Puzejova	L. Ayala/Miss E. Buding	6–3	6–4		
1958	N. Pietrangeli/Miss S. J. Bloomer	R. N. Howe/Miss L. Coghlan	9–7	6–8	6–2	
1959	W. A. Knight/Miss R. Ramirez	R. G. Laver/Miss R. Schuurman	6–4	6–4		
1960	R. N. Howe/Miss M. Bueno	R. S. Emerson/Miss A. Haydon	1–6	6–1	6–2	
1961	R. G. Laver/Miss D. R. Hard	J. Javorsky/Miss V. Puzejova	6–0	2–6	6–3	
1962	R. N. Howe/Miss R. Schuurman	F. S. Stolle/Miss L. R. Turner	3–6	6–4	6–4	
1963	K. N. Fletcher/Miss M. Smith	F. S. Stolle/Miss L. R. Turner	6–1	6–2		
1964	K. N. Fletcher/Miss M. Smith	F. S. Stolle/Miss L. R. Turner	6–3	6–4		
1965	K. N. Fletcher/Miss M. Smith	J. D. Newcombe/Miss M. Bueno	6–4	6–4		
1966	F. D. McMillan/Miss A. M. Van Zyl	C. Graebner/Mrs P. F. Jones	1–6	6–3	6–2	
1967	O. K. Davidson/Mrs L. W. King	I. Tiriac/Mrs P. F. Jones	6–3	6–1		
1968	J. C. Barclay/Miss F. Durr	O. K. Davidson/Mrs L. W. King	6–1	6–4		*Prize Money*
1969	M. C. Riessen/Mrs. B. M. Court	J. C. Barclay/Miss F. Durr	7–5	6–4		*(FF per team)*
1970	R. A. J. Hewitt/Mrs L. W. King	J. C. Barclay/Miss F. Durr	3–6	6–3	6–2	FF6,000
1971	J. C. Barclay/Miss F. Durr	T. Lejus/Miss W. Shaw	6–2	6–4		4,500
1972	K. Warwick/Miss E. F. Goolagong	J. C. Barclay/Miss F. Durr	6–2	6–4		5,000
1973	J. C. Barclay/Miss F. Durr	P. Dominguez/Miss B. Stove	6–1	6–4		6,000
1974	I. Molina/Miss M. Navratilova	M. Lara/Mrs R. M. Darmon	6–3	6–3		8,000
1975	T. Koch/Miss F. Bonicelli	J. Fillol/Miss P. Teeguarden	6–4	7–6		8,000
1976	K. Warwick/Miss I. Kloss	C. Dowdeswell/Miss L. Boshoff	5–7	7–6	6–2	8,000
1977	J. P. McEnroe/Miss M. Carillo	I. Molina/Miss F. Mihai	7–6	6–3		8,000
1978	P. Slozil/Miss R. Tomanova	P. Dominguez/Miss V. Ruzici	7–6	ret		10,000
1979	R. A. J. Hewitt/Miss W. M. Turnbull	I. Tiriac/Miss V. Ruzici	6–3	2–6	6–3	6,000
1980	W. Martin/Miss A. E. Smith	S. Birner/Miss R. Tomanova	2–6	6–4	8–6	11,000
1981	J. Arias/Miss A. Jaeger	F. D. McNair/Miss B. Stove	7–6	6–4		11,000
1982	J. M. Lloyd/Miss W. M. Turnbull	C. Motta/Miss C. Monteiro	6–2	7–6		13,200
1983	E. Teltscher/Miss B. Jordan	C. Strode/Miss L. Allen	6–2	6–3		20,000
1984	R. L. Stockton/Miss A. E. Smith	L. Warder/Miss A. Minter	6–2	6–4		32,000
1985	H. P. Gunthardt/Miss M. Navratilova	F. Gonzalez/Miss P. Smith	2–6	6–3	6–2	46,000
1986	K. Flach/Miss. K. Jordan	M. R. Edmondson/Miss. R. Fairbank	3–6	7–6	6–3	83,000
1987	E. Sanchez/Miss P. H. Shriver	S. E. Stewart/Miss L. McNeil	6–3	7–6		86,000
1988	J. Lozano/Miss L. McNeil	M. Schapers/Miss B. Schultz	7–5	6–2		120,000
1989	T. Nijssen/Miss M. Bollegraf	H. De la Pena/Miss A. Sanchez-Vicario	6–3	6–7	6–2	135,000
1990	J. Lozano/Miss A. Sanchez-Vicario	D. Visser/Miss N. Provis	7–6	7–6		US$30,000
1991	C. Suk/Miss H. Sukova	P. Haarhuis/Miss C. Vis	3–6	6–4	6–1	FF220,000
1992	T. Woodbridge/ Miss A. Sanchez-Vicario	B. Shelton/Miss L. McNeil	6–2	6–3		242,000
1993	A. Olhovskiy/Miss E. Maniokova	D. Visser/Miss E. Reinach	6–2	4–6	6–4	264,000
1994	M. Oosting/Miss K. Boogert	A. Olhovskiy/Mrs L. Neiland	7–5	3–6	7–5	285,000
1995	M. Woodforde/Mrs L. Neiland	J. De Jager/Miss J. Hetherington	7–6	7–6		300,000
1996	J. Frana/Miss P. Tarabini	L. Jensen/Miss N. Arendt	6–2	6–2		312,000
1997	M. Bhupathi/Miss R. Hiraki	P. Galbraith/Miss L. Raymond	6–4	6–1		330,000
1998	J. Gimelstob/Miss V. Williams	L. Lobo/Miss S. Williams	6–4	6–4		346,000
1999	P. Norval/Miss K. Srebotnik	K. Leach/Mrs L. Neiland	6–3	3–6	6–3	363,000
2000	D. Adams/Miss M. De Swardt	T. Woodbridge/Miss R. Stubbs	6–3	3–6	6–3	380,000

THE CHAMPIONSHIPS – WIMBLEDON

1. Venue: From 1877–1921 The Championships were played at the Worple Road ground. Since 1922 they have been played at the present ground in Church Road. **2. Title:** For the years 1913, 1914, and 1919–23 inclusive, these records include the 'World's Championship on Grass' granted to the LTA by the ILTF. This title was then abolished. **3. Challenge Round:** Prior to 1922 the holder did not compete in the Championship but met the winner of the All-Comers singles in the Challenge Round. The Challenge Round was abolished in 1922 and the holder subsequently played through. **4. Seeding:** 'Modified seeding' was introduced in 1924. 'Full seeding', as we know it today, was first practised in 1927. **5. Status:** The Championships became 'open' in 1968. (There was a tie-break at 8–all in all sets except the fifth in men's events and the third in women's events and mixed in the years 1971–78. Thereafter the tie-break was played at 6–all.) **6. Surface:** Alone of the four Grand Slams, The Championships have always been played on grass courts. **7.** In the years marked with an asterisk*, the holder(s) did not defend the title.

MEN'S SINGLES

	CHAMPIONS	RUNNER-UP	SCORE				
1877	S. W. Gore	W. C. Marshall	6–1	6–2	6–4		
1878	P. F. Hadow	S. W. Gore	7–5	6–1	9–7		
1879*	J. T. Hartley	V. St L. Goold	6–2	6–4	6–2		
1880	J. T. Hartley	H. F. Lawford	6–3	6–2	2–6	6–3	
1881	W. Renshaw	J. T. Hartley	6–0	6–1	6–1		
1882	W. Renshaw	E. Renshaw	6–1	2–6	4–6	6–2	6–2
1883	W. Renshaw	E. Renshaw	2–6	6–3	6–3	4–6	6–3
1884	W. Renshaw	H. F. Lawford	6–0	6–4	9–7		
1885	W. Renshaw	H. F. Lawford	7–5	6–2	4–6	7–5	
1886	W. Renshaw	H. F. Lawford	6–0	5–7	6–3	6–4	
1887*	H. F. Lawford	E. Renshaw	1–6	6–3	3–6	6–4	6–4
1888	E. Renshaw	H. F. Lawford	6–3	7–5	6–0		
1889	W. Renshaw	E. Renshaw	6–4	6–1	3–6	6–0	
1890	W. J. Hamilton	W. Renshaw	6–8	6–2	3–6	6–1	6–1
1891*	W. Baddeley	J. Pim	6–4	1–6	7–5	6–0	
1892	W. Baddeley	J. Pim	4–6	6–3	6–3	6–2	
1893	J. Pim	W. Baddeley	3–6	6–1	6–3	6–2	
1894	J. Pim	W. Baddeley	10–8	6–2	8–6		
1895*	W. Baddeley	W. V. Eaves	4–6	2–6	8–6	6–2	6–3
1896	H. S. Mahony	W. Baddeley	6–2	6–8	5–7	8–6	6–3
1897	R. F. Doherty	H. S. Mahony	6–4	6–4	6–3		
1898	R. F. Doherty	H. L. Doherty	6–3	6–3	2–6	5–7	6–1
1899	R. F. Doherty	A. W. Gore	1–6	4–6	6–3	6–3	6–3
1900	R. F. Doherty	S. H. Smith	6–8	6–3	6–1	6–2	
1901	A. W. Gore	R. F. Doherty	4–6	7–5	6–4	6–4	
1902	H. L. Doherty	A. W. Gore	6–4	6–3	3–6	6–0	
1903	H. L. Doherty	F. L. Riseley	7–5	6–3	6–0		
1904	H. L. Doherty	F. L. Riseley	6–1	7–5	8–6		
1905	H. L. Doherty	N. E. Brookes	8–6	6–2	6–4		
1906	H. L. Doherty	F. L. Riseley	6–4	4–6	6–2	6–3	
1907*	N. E. Brookes	A. W. Gore	6–4	6–2	6–2		
1908*	A. W. Gore	H. Roper Barrett	6–3	6–2	4–6	3–6	6–4
1909	A. W. Gore	M. J. G. Ritchie	6–8	1–6	6–2	6–2	6–2
1910	A. F. Wilding	A. W. Gore	6–4	7–5	4–6	6–2	
1911	A. F. Wilding	H. Roper Barrett	6–4	4–6	2–6	6–2	ret
1912	A. F. Wilding	A. W. Gore	6–4	6–4	4–6	6–4	
1913	A. F. Wilding	M. E. McLoughlin	8–6	6–3	10–8		
1914	N. E. Brookes	A. F. Wilding	6–4	6–4	7–5		
1915–18		*Not held*					
1919	G. L. Patterson	N. E. Brookes	6–3	7–5	6–2		
1920	W. T. Tilden	G. L. Patterson	2–6	6–2	6–3	6–4	
1921	W. T. Tilden	B. I. C. Norton	4–6	2–6	6–1	6–0	7–5
1922*	G. L. Patterson	R. Lycett	6–3	6–4	6–2		
1923*	W. M. Johnston	F. T. Hunter	6–0	6–3	6–1		
1924*	J. Borotra	R. Lacoste	6–1	3–6	6–1	3–6	6–4
1925	R. Lacoste	J. Borotra	6–3	6–3	4–6	8–6	
1926*	J. Borotra	H. Kinsey	8–6	6–1	6–3		
1927	H. Cochet	J. Borotra	4–6	4–6	6–3	6–4	7–5
1928	R. Lacoste	H. Cochet	6–1	4–6	6–4	6–2	

	CHAMPIONS	RUNNER-UP	SCORE					FIRST PRIZE (£)
1929*	H. Cochet	J. Borotra	6–4	6–3	6–4			
1930	W. T. Tilden	W. L. Allison	6–3	9–7	6–4			
1931*	S. B. Wood	F. X. Shields	w.o.					
1932	H. E. Vines	H. W. Austin	6–4	6–2	6–0			
1933	J. H. Crawford	H. E. Vines	4–6	11–9	6–2	2–6	6–4	
1934	F. J. Perry	J. H. Crawford	6–3	6–0	7–5			
1935	F. J. Perry	G. von Cramm	6–2	6–4	6–4			
1936	F. J. Perry	G. von Cramm	6–1	6–1	6–0			
1937*	J. D. Budge	G. von Cramm	6–3	6–4	6–2			
1938	J. D. Budge	H. W. Austin	6–1	6–0	6–3			
1939*	R. L. Riggs	E. T. Cooke	2–6	8–6	3–6	6–3	6–2	
1940–45		Not held						
1946*	Y. Petra	G.Brown	6–2	6–4	7–9	5–7	6–4	
1947	J. Kramer	T.Brown	6–1	6–3	6–2			
1948*	B. Falkenburg	J. Bromwich	7–5	0–6	6–2	3–6	7–5	
1949	T. Schroeder	J. Drobny	3–6	6–0	6–3	4–6	6–4	
1950*	B. Patty	F. A.Sedgman	6–1	8–10	6–2	6–3		
1951	D. Savitt	K. B. McGregor	6–4	6–4	6–4			
1952	F. A. Sedgman	J. Drobny	4–6	6–2	6–3	6–2		
1953*	V. Seixas	K. Nielsen	9–7	6–3	6–4			
1954	J. Drobny	K. Rosewall	13–11	4–6	6–2	9–7.		
1955	T. Trabert	K. Nielsen	6–3	7–5	6–1			
1956*	L. A. Hoad	K. R. Rosewall	6–2	4–6	7–5	6–4		
1957	L. A. Hoad	A. J. Cooper	6–2	6–1	6–2			
1958*	A. J. Cooper	N. A. Fraser	3–6	6–3	6–4	13–11		
1959*	A. Olmedo	R. G. Laver	6–4	6–3	6–4			
1960*	N. A. Fraser	R. G. Laver	6–4	3–6	9–7	7–5		
1961	R. G. Laver	C. R. McKinley	6–3	6–1	6–4			
1962	R. G. Laver	M. F. Mulligan	6–2	6–2	6–1			
1963*	C. R. McKinley	F. S. Stolle	9–7	6–1	6–4			
1964	R. S. Emerson	F. S. Stolle	6–1	12–10	4–6	6–3		
1965	R. S. Emerson	F. S. Stolle	6–2	6–4	6–4			
1966	M. Santana	R. D. Ralston	6–4	11–9		6–4		
1967	J. D. Newcombe	W. P. Bungert	6–3	6–1	6–1			2,000
1968	R. G. Laver	A. D. Roche	6–3	6–4	6–2			2,000
1969	R. G. Laver	J. D. Newcombe	6–4	5–7	6–4	6–4		3,000
1970	J. D. Newcombe	K. R. Rosewall	5–7	6–3	6–2	3–6	6–1	3,000
1971	J. D. Newcombe	S. R. Smith	6–3	5–7	2–6	6–4	6–4	3,750
1972*	S. R. Smith	I. Nastase	4–6	6–3	6–3	4–6	7–5	5,000
1973*	J. Kodes	A. Metreveli	6–1	9–8	6–3			5,000
1974	J. S. Connors	K. R. Rosewall	6–1	6–1	6–4			10,000
1975	A. R. Ashe	J. S. Connors	6–1	6–1	5–7	6–4		10,000
1976	B. Borg	I. Nastase	6–4	6–2	9–7			12,500
1977	B. Borg	J. S. Connors	3–6	6–2	6–1	5–7	6–4	15,000
1978	B. Borg	J. S. Connors	6–2	6–2	6–3			19,000
1979	B. Borg	R. Tanner	6–7	6–1	3–6	6–3	6–4	20,000
1980	B. Borg	J. P. McEnroe	1–6	7–5	6–3	6–7	8–6	20,000
1981	J. P. McEnroe	B. Borg	4–6	7–6	7–6	6–4		21,600
1982	J. S. Connors	J. P. McEnroe	3–6	6–3	6–7	7–6	6–4	41,667
1983	J. P. McEnroe	C. J. Lewis	6–2	6–2	6–2			66,600
1984	J. P. McEnroe	J. S. Connors	6–1	6–1	6–2			100,000
1985	B. Becker	K. Curren	6–3	6–7	7–6	6–4		130,000
1986	B. Becker	I. Lendl	6–4	6–3	7–5			140,000
1987	P. Cash	I. Lendl	7–6	6–2	7–5			155,000
1988	S. Edberg	B. Becker	4–6	7–6	6–4	6–2		165,000
1989	B. Becker	S. Edberg	6–0	7–6	6–4			190,000
1990	S. Edberg	B. Becker	6–2	6–2	3–6	3–6	6–4	230,000
1991	M. Stich	B. Becker	6–4	7–6	6–4			240,000
1992	A. Agassi	G. Ivanisevic	6–7	6–4	6–4	1–6	6–4	265,000
1993	P. Sampras	J. Courier	7–6	7–6	3–6	6–3		305,000
1994	P. Sampras	G. Ivanisevic	7–6	7–6	6–0			345,000
1995	P. Sampras	B. Becker	6–7	6–2	6–4	6–2		365,000
1996	R. Krajicek	M. Washington	6–3	6–4	6–3			392,500
1997	P. Sampras	C. Pioline	6–4	6–2	6–4			415,000
1998	P. Sampras	G. Ivanisevic	6–7	7–6	6–4	3–6	6–2	435,000
1999	P. Sampras	A. Agassi	6–3	6–4	7–5			455,000
2000	P. Sampras	P. Rafter	6–7	7–6	6–4	6–2		477,500

WOMEN'S SINGLES

	CHAMPION	RUNNER-UP	SCORE		
1884	Miss M. Watson	Miss L. Watson	6–8	6–3	6–3
1885	Miss M. Watson	Miss B. Bingley	6–1	7–5	
1886	Miss B. Bingley	Miss M. Watson	6–3	6–3	
1887	Miss C. Dod	Miss B. Bingley	6–2	6–0	
1888	Miss C. Dod	Mrs G. W. Hillyard	6–3	6–3	
1889*	Mrs G. W. Hillyard	Miss H. Rice	4–6	8–6	6–4
1890*	Miss H. Rice	Miss M. Jacks	6–4	6–1	
1891*	Miss C. Dod	Mrs G. W. Hillyard	6–2	6–1	
1892	Miss C. Dod	Mrs G. W. Hillyard	6–1	6–1	
1893	Miss C. Dod	Mrs G. W. Hillyard	6–8	6–1	6–4
1894*	Mrs G. W. Hillyard	Miss L. Austin	6–1	6–1	
1895*	Miss C. Cooper	Miss H. Jackson	7–5	8–6	
1896	Miss C. Cooper	Mrs W. H. Pickering	6–2	6–3	
1897	Mrs G. W. Hillyard	Miss C. Cooper	5–7	7–5	6–2
1898*	Miss C. Cooper	Miss L. Martin	6–4	6–4	
1899	Mrs G. W. Hillyard	Miss C. Cooper	6–2	6–3	
1900	Mrs G. W. Hillyard	Miss C. Cooper	4–6	6–4	6–4
1901	Mrs A. Sterry	Mrs G. W. Hillyard	6–2	6–2	
1902	Miss M. E. Robb	Mrs A. Sterry	7–5	6–1	
1903*	Miss D. K. Douglass	Miss E. W. Thomson	4–6	6–4	6–2
1904	Miss D. K. Douglass	Mrs A. Sterry	6–0	6–3	
1905	Miss M. Sutton	Miss D. K. Douglass	6–3	6–4	
1906	Miss D. K. Douglass	Miss M. Sutton	6–3	9–7	
1907	Miss M. Sutton	Mrs R. Lamb. Chambers	6–1	6–4	
1908*	Mrs A. Sterry	Miss A. M. Morton	6–4	6–4	
1909*	Miss D. P. Boothby	Miss A. M. Morton	6–4	4–6	8–6
1910	Mrs R. Lambert Chambers	Miss D. P. Boothby	6–2	6–2	
1911	Mrs R. Lambert Chambers	Miss D. P. Boothby	6–0	6–0	
1912*	Mrs D. R. Larcombe	Mrs A. Sterry	6–3	6–1	
1913*	Mrs R. Lambert Chambers	Mrs R. J. McNair	6–0	6–4	
1914	Mrs R. Lambert Chambers	Mrs D. R. Larcombe	7–5	6–4	
1915–18		Not held			
1919	Mlle S. Lenglen	Mrs R. Lamb. Chambers	10–8	4–6	9–7
1920	Mlle S. Lenglen	Mrs R. Lamb. Chambers	6–3	6–0	
1921	Mlle S. Lenglen	Miss E. Ryan	6–2	6–0	
1922	Mlle S. Lenglen	Mrs F. Mallory	6–2	6–0	
1923	Mlle S. Lenglen	Miss K. McKane	6–2	6–2	
1924	Miss K. McKane	Miss H. N. Wills	4–6	6–4	6–4
1925	Mlle S. Lenglen	Miss J. Fry	6–2	6–0	
1926	Mrs L. A. Godfree	Sta E. De Alvarez	6–2	4–6	6–3
1927	Miss H. N. Wills	Sta E. De Alvarez	6–2	6–4	
1928	Miss H. N. Wills	Sta E. De Alvarez	6–2	6–3	
1929	Miss H. N. Wills	Miss H. H. Jacobs	6–1	6–2	
1930	Mrs F. S. Moody	Miss E. Ryan	6–2	6–2	
1931*	Frl C. Aussem	Frl H. Krahwinkel	6–2	7–5	
1932*	Mrs F. S. Moody	Miss H. H. Jacobs	6–3	6–1	
1933	Mrs F. S. Moody	Miss D. E. Round	6–4	6–8	6–3
1934*	Miss D. E. Round	Miss H. H. Jacobs	6–2	5–7	6–3
1935	Mrs F. S. Moody	Miss H. H. Jacobs	6–3	3–6	7–5
1936*	Miss H. H. Jacobs	Mrs S. Sperling	6–2	4–6	7–5
1937	Miss D. E. Round	Miss J. Jedrzejowska	6–2	2–6	7–5
1938*	Mrs F. S. Moody	Miss H. H. Jacobs	6–4	6–0	
1939*	Miss A. Marble	Miss K. E. Stammers	6–2	6–0	
1940–45		Not held			
1946*	Miss P. M. Betz	Miss A. L. Brough	6–2	6–4	
1947*	Miss M. E. Osborne	Miss D. J. Hart	6–2	6–4	
1948	Miss A. L. Brough	Miss D. J. Hart	6–3	8–6	
1949	Miss A. L. Brough	Mrs W. du Pont	10–8	1–6	10–8
1950	Miss A. L. Brough	Mrs W. du Pont	6–1	3–6	6–1
1951	Miss D. J. Hart	Miss S. J. Fry	6–1	6–0	
1952	Miss M. Connolly	Miss A. L. Brough	6–4	6–3	
1953	Miss M. Connolly	Miss D. J. Hart	8–6	7–5	
1954	Miss M. Connolly	Miss A. L. Brough	6–2	7–5	
1955*	Miss A. L. Brough	Mrs J. G. Fleitz	7–5	8–6	

	CHAMPION	RUNNER-UP	SCORE			
1956	Miss S. J. Fry	Miss A. Buxton	6–3	6–1		
1957*	Miss A. Gibson	Miss D. R. Hard	6–3	6–2		
1958	Miss A. Gibson	Miss A. Mortimer	8–6	6–2		
1959*	Miss M. E. Bueno	Miss D. R. Hard	6–4	6–3		
1960	Miss M. E. Bueno	Miss S. Reynolds	8–6	6–0		
1961*	Miss A. Mortimer	Miss C. C. Truman	4–6	6–4	7–5	
1962	Mrs J. R. Susman	Mrs V. Sukova	6–4	6–4		
1963*	Miss M. Smith	Miss B. J. Moffitt	6–3	6–4		
1964	Miss M. E. Bueno	Miss M. Smith	6–4	7–9	6–3	
1965	Miss M. Smith	Miss M. E. Bueno	6–4	7–5		FIRST
1966	Mrs L. W. King	Miss M. E. Bueno	6–3	3–6	6–1	PRIZE
1967	Mrs L. W. King	Mrs P. F. Jones	6–3	6–4		(£)
1968	Mrs L. W. King	Miss J. A. M. Tegart	9–7	7–5		750
1969	Mrs P. F. Jones	Mrs L. W. King	3–6	6–3	6–2	1,500
1970*	Mrs B. M. Court	Mrs L. W. King	14–12	11–9		1,500
1971	Miss E. F. Goolagong	Mrs B. M. Court	6–4	6–1		1,800
1972	Mrs L. W. King	Miss E. Goolagong	6–3	6–3		2,400
1973	Mrs L. W. King	Miss C. M. Evert	6–0	7–5		3,000
1974	Miss C. M. Evert	Mrs O. Morozova	6–0	6–4		7,000
1975	Mrs L. W. King	Mrs R. A. Cawley	6–0	6–1		7,000
1976*	Miss C. M. Evert	Mrs R. A. Cawley	6–3	4–6	8–6	10,000
1977	Miss S. V. Wade	Miss B. F. Stove	4–6	6–3	6–1	13,500
1978	Miss M. Navratilova	Miss C. M. Evert	2–6	6–4	7–5	17,100
1979	Miss M. Navratilova	Mrs J. M. Lloyd	6–4	6–4		18,000
1980	Mrs R. A. Cawley	Mrs J. M. Lloyd	6–1	7–6		18,000
1981*	Mrs J. M. Lloyd	Miss H. Mandlikova	6–2	6–2		19,440
1982	Miss M. Navratilova	Mrs J. M. Lloyd	6–1	3–6	6–2	37,500
1983	Miss M. Navratilova	Miss A. Jaeger	6–0	6–3		60,000
1984	Miss M. Navratilova	Mrs J. M. Lloyd	7–6	6–2		90,000
1985	Miss M. Navratilova	Mrs J. M. Lloyd	4–6	6–3	6–2	117,000
1986	Miss M. Navratilova	Miss H. Mandlikova	7–6	6–3		126,000
1987	Miss M. Navratilova	Miss S. Graf	7–5	6–3		139,500
1988	Miss S. Graf	Miss M. Navratilova	5–7	6–2	6–1	148,500
1989	Miss S. Graf	Miss M. Navratilova	6–2	6–7	6–1	171,000
1990	Miss M. Navratilova	Miss Z. Garrison	6–4	6–1		207,000
1991	Miss S. Graf	Miss G. Sabatini	6–4	3–6	8–6	216,000
1992	Miss S. Graf	Miss M. Seles	6–2	6–1		240,000
1993	Miss S. Graf	Miss J. Novotna	7–6	1–6	6–4	275,000
1994	Miss C. Martinez	Miss M. Navratilova	6–4	3–6	6–3	310,000
1995	Miss S. Graf	Miss A. Sanchez-Vicario	4–6	6–1	7–5	328,000
1996	Miss S. Graf	Miss A. Sanchez-Vicario	6–3	7–5		353,000
1997*	Miss M. Hingis	Miss J. Novotna	2–6	6–3	6–3	373,000
1998	Miss J. Novotna	Miss N. Tauziat	6–4	7–6		391,500
1999	Miss L. Davenport	Miss S. Graf	6–4	7–5		409,500
2000	Miss V. Williams	Miss L. Davenport	6–3	7–6		430,000

MEN'S DOUBLES

	CHAMPIONS	RUNNERS-UP	SCORE				
1884	E./W. Renshaw	E. W. Lewis/E. L. Williams	6–3	6–1	1–6	6–4	
1885	E./W. Renshaw	C. E. Farrer/A. J. Stanley	6–3	6–3	10–8		
1886	E./W. Renshaw	C. E. Farrer/A. J. Stanley	6–3	6–3	4–6	7–5	
1887*	P. B-Lyon/W. W. Wilberforce	E. Barratt-Smith/J. H. Crispe	7–5	6–3	6–2		
1888	E./W. Renshaw	P. B-Lyon/W. W. Wilberforce	2–6	1–6	6–3	6–4	6–3
1889	E./W. Renshaw	G. W. Hillyard/E. W. Lewis	6–4	6–4	3–6	0–6	6–1
1890*	J. Pim/F. O. Stoker	G. W. Hillyard/E. W. Lewis	6–0	7–5	6–4		
1891	H./W. Baddeley	J. Pim/F. O. Stoker	6–1	6–3	1–6	6–2	
1892	H. S. Barlow/E. W. Lewis	H./W. Baddeley	4–6	6–2	8–6	6–4	
1893	J. Pim/F. O. Stoker	H. S. Barlow/E. W. Lewis	4–6	6–3	6–1	2–6	6–0
1894*	H./W. Baddeley	H. S. Barlow/C. II. Martin	5–7	7–5	4–6	6–3	8–6
1895	H./W. Baddeley	W. V. Eaves/E. W. Lewis	8–6	5–7	6–4	6–3	
1896	H./W. Baddeley	R. F. Doherty/H. A. Nisbet	1–6	3–6	6–4	6–2	6–1
1897	H. L./R. F. Doherty	H./W. Baddeley	6–4	4–6	8–6	6–4	
1898	H. L./R. F. Doherty	C. Hobart/H. A. Nisbet	6–4	6–4	6–2		
1899	H. L./R. F. Doherty	C. Hobart/H. A. Nisbet	7–5	6–0	6–2		
1900	H. L./R. F. Doherty	H. A. Nisbet/H. Roper Barrett	9–7	7–5	4–6	3–6	6–3

	CHAMPIONS	RUNNERS-UP	SCORE				
1901	H. L./R. F. Doherty	D. F. Davis/H. Ward	4–6	6–2	6–3	9–7	
1902	F. L. Riseley/S. H. Smith	H. L./R. F. Doherty	4–6	8–6	6–3	4–6	11–9
1903	H. L./R. F. Doherty	F. L. Riseley/S. H. Smith	6–4	6–4	6–4		
1904	H. L./R. F. Doherty	F. L. Riseley/S. H. Smith	6–3	6–4	6–3		
1905	H. L./R. F. Doherty	F. L. Riseley/S. H. Smith	6–2	6–4	6–8	6–3	
1906	F. L. Riseley/S. H. Smith	H. L./R. F. Doherty	6–8	6–4	5–7	6–3	6–3
1907*	N. E. Brookes/A. F. Wilding	K. Behr/B. C. Wright	6–4	6–4	6–2		
1908*	M. J. G. Ritchie/A. F. Wilding	A. W. Gore/H. Roper Barrett	6–1	6–2	1–6	1–6	9–7
1909*	A. W. Gore/H. Roper Barrett	S. N. Doust/H. A. Parker	6–2	6–1	6–4		
1910	M. J. G. Ritchie/A. F. Wilding	A. W. Gore/H. Roper Barrett	6–1	6–1	6–2		
1911	M. Decugis/A. H. Gobert	M. J. G. Ritchie/A. F. Wilding	9–7	5–7	6–3	2–6	6–2
1912	C. P. Dixon/H. Roper Barrett	M. Decugis/A. H. Gobert	3–6	6–3	6–4	7–5	
1913	C. P. Dixon/H. Roper Barrett	H. Kleinschroth/F. W. Rahe	6–2	6–4	4–6	6–2	
1914	N. E. Brookes/A. F. Wilding	C. P. Dixon/H. Roper Barrett	6–1	6–1	5–7	8–6	
1915–1918		Not held					
1919*	P. O'Hara Wood/R. V. Thomas	R. W. Heath/R. Lycett	6–4	6–2	4–6	6–2	
1920*	C. S. Garland/R. N. Williams	A. R. F. Kingscote/J. C. Parke	4–6	6–4	7–5	6–2	
1921*	R. Lycett/M. Woosnam	A. H./F. G. Lowe	6–3	6–0	7–5		
1922	J. O. Anderson/R. Lycett	P. O'Hara Wood/G. L. Patterson	3–6	7–9	6–4	6–3	11–9
1923	L. A. Godfree/R. Lycett	E. Flaquer/Count M. De Gomar	6–3	6–4	3–6	6–3	
1924	F. T. Hunter/V. Richards	W. M. Washburn/R. N. Williams	6–3	3–6	8–10	8–6	6–3
1925	J. Borotra/R. Lacoste	R. Casey/J. Hennessey	6–4	11–9	4–6	1–6	6–3
1926	J. Brugnon/H. Cochet	H. Kinsey/V. Richards	7–5	4–6	6–3	6–2	
1927	F. T. Hunter/W. T. Tilden	J. Brugnon/H. Cochet	1–6	4–6	8–6	6–3	6–4
1928	J. Brugnon/H. Cochet	J. B. Hawkes/G. L. Patterson	13–11	6–4	6–4		
1929	W. L. Allison/J. Van Ryn	I. G. Collins/J. C. Gregory	6–4	5–7	6–3	10–12	6–4
1930	W. L. Allison/J. Van Ryn	J. H. Doeg/G. M. Lott	6–3	6–3	6–2		
1931	G. M. Lott/J. Van Ryn	J. Brugnon/H. Cochet	6–2	10–8	9–11	3–6	6–3
1932	J. Borotra/J. Brugnon	G. P. Hughes/F. J. Perry	6–0	4–6	3–6	7–5	7–5
1933	J. Borotra/J. Brugnon	R. Nunoi/J. Satoh	4–6	6–3	6–3	7–5	
1934	G. M. Lott/L. R. Stoefen	J. Borotra/J. Brugnon	6–2	6–3	6–4		
1935	J. H. Crawford/A. K Quist	W. L. Allison/J. Van Ryn	6–3	5–7	6–2	5–7	7–5
1936	G. P. Hughes/C. R. D. Tuckey	C. E. Hare/F. H. D. Wilde	6–4	3–6	7–9	6–1	6–4
1937	J. D. Budge/G. Mako	G. P. Hughes/C. R. D. Tuckey	6–0	6–4	6–8	6–1	
1938	J. D. Budge/G. Mako	H. Henkel/G. von Metaxa	6–4	3–6	6–3	8–6	
1939	E. T. Cooke/R. L. Riggs	C. E. Hare/F. H. D. Wilde	6–3	3–6	6–3	9–7	
1940–1945		Not held					
1946	T. Brown/J. A. Kramer	G. E. Brown/D. Pails	6–4	6–4	6–2		
1947	R. Falkenburg/J. A. Kramer	A. J. Mottram/O. W. Sidwell	8–6	6–3	6–3		
1948	J. E. Bromwich/F. A. Sedgman	T. Brown/G. Mulloy	5–7	7–5	7–5	9–7	
1949	R. A. Gonzales/F. A. Parker	G. Mulloy/F. R. Schroeder	6–4	6–4	6–2		
1950	J. E. Bromwich/A. K. Quist	G. E. Brown/O. W. Sidwell	7–5	3–6	6–3	3–6	6–2
1951	K. B. McGregor/F. A. Sedgman	J. Drobny/E. W. Sturgess	3–6	6–2	6–3	3–6	6–3
1952	K. B. McGregor/F. A. Sedgman	E. V. Seixas/E. W. Sturgess	6–3	7–5	6–4		
1953	L. A. Hoad/K. R. Rosewall	R. N. Hartwig/M. G. Rose	6–4	7–5	4–6	7–5	
1954	R. N. Hartwig/M. G. Rose	E. V. Seixas/M. A. Trabert	6–4	6–4	3–6	6–4	
1955	R. N. Hartwig/L. A. Hoad	N. A. Fraser/K. R. Rosewall	7–5	6–4	6–3		
1956	L. A. Hoad/K. R. Rosewall	N. Pietrangeli/O. Sirola	7–5	6–2	6–1		
1957	G. Mulloy/J. E. Patty	N. A. Fraser/L. A. Hoad	8–10	6–4	6–4	6–4	
1958	S. Davidson/U. Schmidt	A. J. Cooper/N. A. Fraser	6–4	6–4	8–6		
1959	R. Emerson/N. A. Fraser	R. Laver/R. Mark	8–6	6–3	14–16	9–7	
1960	R. H. Osuna/R. D. Ralston	M. G. Davies/R. K. Wilson	7–5	6–3	10–8		
1961	R. Emerson/N. A. Fraser	R. A. J. Hewitt/F. S. Stolle	6–4	6–8	6–4	6–8	8–6
1962	R. A. J. Hewitt/F. S. Stolle	B. Jovanovic/N. Pilic	6–2	5–7	6–2	6–4	
1963	R. H. Osuna/A. Palafox	J. C. Barclay/P. Darmon	4–6	6–2	6–2	6–2	
1964	R. A. J. Hewitt/F. S. Stolle	R. Emerson/K. N. Fletcher	7–5	11–9	6–4		FIRST
1965	J. D. Newcombe/A. D. Roche	K. N. Fletcher/R. A. J. Hewitt	7–5	6–3	6–4		PRIZE
1966	K. N. Fletcher/J. D. Newcombe	W. W. Bowrey/O. K. Davidson	6–3	6–4	3–6	6–3	(£ per
1967	R. A. J. Hewitt/F. D. McMillan	R. Emerson/K. N. Fletcher	6–2	6–3	6–4		team)
1968	J. D. Newcombe/A. D. Roche	K. R. Rosewall/F. S. Stolle	3–6	8–6	5–7	14–12 6–3	800
1969	J. D. Newcombe/A. D. Roche	T. S. Okker/M. C. Riessen	7–5	11–9	6–4		1,000
1970	J. D. Newcombe/A. D. Roche	K. R. Rosewall/F. S. Stolle	10–8	6–3	6–1		1,000
1971	R. Emerson/R. Laver	A. R. Ashe/R. D. Ralston	4–6	9–7	6–8	6–4	6–4	750
1972	R. A. J. Hewitt/F. D. McMillan	S. R. Smith/E. Van Dillen	6–2	6–2	9–7		1,000
1973	J. S. Connors/I. Nastase	J. R. Cooper/N. A. Fraser	3–6	6–3	6–4	8–9	6–1	1,000
1974	J. D. Newcombe/A. D. Roche	R. C. Lutz/S. R. Smith	8–6	6–4	6–4		2,000

	CHAMPIONS	RUNNERS-UP	SCORE					
1975	V. Gerulaitis/A. Mayer	C. Dowdeswell/A. J. Stone	7–5	8–6	6–4			2,000
1976	B. E. Gottfried/R. Ramirez	R. L. Case/G. Masters	3–6	6–3	8–6	2–6	7–5	3,000
1977	R. L. Case/G. Masters	J. G. Alexander/P. C. Dent	6–3	6–4	3–6	8–9	6–4	6,000
1978	R. A. J. Hewitt/F. D. McMillan	P. Fleming/J. P. McEnroe	6–1	6–4	6–2			7,500
1979	P. Fleming/J. P. McEnroe	B. E. Gottfried/R. Ramirez	4–6	6–4	6–2	6–2		8,000
1980	P. McNamara/P. McNamee	R. C. Lutz/S. R. Smith	7–6	6–3	6–7	6–4		8,400
1981	P. Fleming/J. P. McEnroe	R. C. Lutz/S. R. Smith	6–4	6–4	6–4			9,070
1982	P. McNamara/P. McNamee	P. Fleming/J. P. McEnroe	6–3	6–2				16,666
1983	P. Fleming/J. P. McEnroe	T. E./T. R. Gullikson	6–4	6–3	6–4			26,628
1984	P. Fleming/J. P. McEnroe	P. Cash/P. McNamee	6–2	5–7	6–2	3–6	6–3	40,000
1985	H. P. Gunthardt/B. Taroczy	P. Cash/J. Fitzgerald	6–4	6–3	4–6	6–3		47,500
1986	J. Nystrom/M. Wilander	G. Donnelly/P. Fleming	7–6	6–3	6–3			48,500
1987	K. Flach/R. Seguso	S. Casal/E. Sanchez	3–6	6–7	7–6	6–1	6–4	53,730
1988	K. Flach/R. Seguso	J. Fitzgerald/A. Jarryd	6–4	2–6	6–4	7–6		57,200
1989	J. B. Fitzgerald/A. Jarryd	R. Leach/J. Pugh	3–6	7–6	6–4	7–6		65,870
1990	R. Leach/J. Pugh	P. Aldrich/D. Visser	7–6	7–6	7–6			94,230
1991	J. B. Fitzgerald/A. Jarryd	J. Franai/L. Lavalle	6–3	6–4	6–7	6–1		98,330
1992	J. P. McEnroe/M. Stich	J. Grabb/R. Reneberg	5–7	7–6	3–6	7–6	19–17	108,570
1993	T. Woodbridge/M. Woodforde	G. Connell/P. Galbraith	7–5	6–3	7–6			124,960
1994	T. Woodbridge/M. Woodforde	G. Connell/P. Galbraith	7–6	6–3	6–1			141,350
1995	T. Woodbridge/M. Woodforde	R. Leach/S. Melville	7–5	7–6	7–6			149,450
1996	T. Woodbridge/M. Woodforde	B. Black/G. Connell	4–6	6–1	6–3	6–2		160,810
1997	T. Woodbridge/M. Woodforde	J. Eltingh/P. Haarhuis	7–6	7–6	5–7	6–3		170,030
1998	J. Eltingh/P. Haarhuis	T. Woodbridge/M. Woodforde	2–6	6–4	7–6	5–7	10–8	178,220
1999	M. Bhupathi/L. Paes	P. Haarhuis/J. Palmer	6–7	6–3	6–4	7–6		186,420
2000	T. Woodbridge/M. Woodforde	P. Haaarhuis/S. Stolle	6–3	6–4	6–1			195,630

WOMEN'S DOUBLES

	CHAMPIONS	RUNNERS-UP	SCORE		
1913	R. J. McNair/P. D. H. Boothby	A. Sterry/R. Lambert Chambers	4–6	2–4	ret
1914	A. M. Morton/E. Ryan	F. J. Hannam/D. R. Larcombe	6–1	6–3	
1915–1918		Not held			
1919	S. Lenglen/E. Ryan	R. Lambert Chambers/D. R. Larcombe	4–6	7–5	6–3
1920	S. Lenglen/E. Ryan	R. Lambert Chambers/D. R. Larcombe	6–4	6–0	
1921	S. Lenglen/E. Ryan	A. E. Beamish/G. E. Peacock	6–1	6–2	
1922	S. Lenglen/E. Ryan	K. McKane/A. D. Stocks	6–0	6–4	
1923	S. Lenglen/E. Ryan	J. Austin/E. L. Colyer	6–3	6–1	
1924	G. Wightman/H. N. Wills	B. C. Covell/K. McKane	6–4	6–4	
1925	S. Lenglen/E. Ryan	A. V. Bridge/C. G. McIlquham	6–2	6–2	
1926	M. K. Browne/E. Ryan	L. A. Godfree/E. L. Colyer	6–1	6–1	
1927	H. N. Wills/E. Ryan	E. L. Heine/G. Peacock	6–3	6–2	
1928	P. Saunders/M. Watson	E. Bennett/E. H. Harvey	6–2	6–3	
1929	L. R. C. Michell/M. Watson	B. C. Covell/W. P. Shepherd-Barron	6–4	8–6	
1930	F. S. Moody/E. Ryan	E. Cross/S. Palfrey	6–2	9–7	
1931	W. P. Shepherd–Barron/P. E. Mudford	D. Metaxa/J. Sigart	3–6	6–3	6–4
1932	D. Metaxa/J. Sigart	H. H. Jacobs/E. Ryan	6–4	6–3	
1933	R. Mathieu/E. Ryan	W. A. James/A. M. Yorke	6–2	9–11	6–4
1934	R. Mathieu/E. Ryan	D. B. Andrus/S. Henrotin	6–3	6–3	
1935	F. James/K. E. Stammers	R. Mathieu/S. Sperling	6–1	6–4	
1936	F. James/K. E. Stammers	M. Fabyan/H. H. Jacobs	6–2	6–1	
1937	S. Mathieu/A. M. Yorke	M. R. King/J. B. Pittman	6–3	6–3	
1938	M. Fabyan/A. Marble	R. Mathieu/A. M. Yorke	6–2	6–3	
1939	M. Fabyan/A. Marble	H. H. Jacobs/A. M. Yorke	6–1	6–0	
1940–1945		Not held			
1946	A. L. Brough/M. E. Osborne	P. M. Betz/D. J. Hart	6–3	2–6	6–3
1947	D. J. Hart/R. B. Todd	A. L. Brough/M. E. Osborne	3–6	6–4	7–5
1948	A. L. Brough/W. du Pont	D. J. Hart/R. B. Todd	6–3	3–6	6–3
1949	A. L. Brough/W. du Pont	G. Moran/R. B. Todd	8–6	7–5	
1950	A. L. Brough/W. du Pont	S. J. Fry/D. J. Hart	6–4	5–7	6–1
1951	S. J. Fry/D. J. Hart	A. L. Brough/W. du Pont	6–3	13–11	
1952	S. J. Fry/D. J. Hart	A. L. Brough/M. Connolly	8–6	6–3	
1953	S. J. Fry/D. J. Hart	M. Connolly/J. Sampson	6–0	6–0	
1954	A. L. Brough/W. du Pont	S. J. Fry/D. J. Hart	4–6	9–7	6–3
1955	A. Mortimer/J. A. Shilcock	S. J. Bloomer/P. E. Ward	7–5	6–1	
1956	A. Buxton/A. Gibson	F. Muller/D. G. Seeney	6–1	8–6	
1957	A. Gibson/D. R. Hard	K. Hawton/M. N. Long	6–1	6–2	

	CHAMPIONS	RUNNERS-UP	SCORE			
1958	M. E. Bueno/A. Gibson	W. du Pont/M. Varner	6–3	7–5		
1959	J. Arth/D. R. Hard	J. G. Fleitz/C. C. Truman	2–6	6–2	6–3	
1960	M. E. Bueno/D. R. Hard	S. Reynolds/R. Schuurman	6–4	6–0		
1961	K. Hantz/B. J. Moffitt	J. Lehane/M. Smith	6–3	6–4		
1962	B. J. Moffitt/J. R. Susman	L. E. G. Price/R. Schuurman	5–7	6–3	7–5	
1963	M. E. Bueno/D. R. Hard	R. A. Ebbern/M. Smith	8–6	9–7		
1964	M. Smith/L. R. Turner	B. J. Moffitt/J. R. Susman	7–5	6–2		FIRST
1965	M. E. Bueno/B. J. Moffitt	F. Durr/J. Lieffrig	6–2	7–5		PRIZE
1966	M. E. Bueno/N. Richey	M. Smith/J. A. M. Tegart	6–3	4–6	6–4	(£ per
1967	R. Casals/L. W. King	M. E. Bueno/N. Richey	9–11	6–4	6–2	team)
1968	R. Casals/L. W. King	F. Durr/P. F. Jones	3–6	6–4	7–5	500
1969	B. M. Court/J. A. M. Tegart	P. S. A. Hogan/M. Michel	9–7	6–2		600
1970	R. Casals/L. W. King	F. Durr/S. V. Wade	6–2	6–3		600
1971	R. Casals/L. W. King	B. M. Court/E. Goolagong	6–3	6–2		450
1972	L. W. King/B. Stove .	D. E. Dalton/F. Durr	6–2	4–6	6–3	600
1973	R. Casals/L. W. King	F. Durr/B. Stove	6–1	4–6	7–5	600
1974	E. F. Goolagong/M. Michel	H. F. Gourlay/K. M. Krantzcke	2–6	6–4	6–3	1,200
1975	A. Kiyomura/K. Sawamatsu	F. Durr/B. Stove	7–5	1–6	7–5	1,200
1976	C. Evert/M. Navratilova	L. W. King/B. Stove	6–1	3–6	7–5	2,400
1977	R. L. Cawley/J. C. Russell	M. Navratilova/B. Stove	6–3	6–3		5,200
1978	G. E. Reid/W. Turnbull	M. Jausovec/V. Ruzici	4–6	9–8	6–3	6,500
1979	L. W. King/M. Navratilova	B. Stove/W. M. Turnbull	5–7	6–3	6–2	6,930
1980	K. Jordan/A. E. Smith	R. Casals/W. M. Turnbull	4–6	7–5	6–1	7,276
1981	M. Navratilova/P. H. Shriver	K. Jordan/A. E. Smith	6–3	7–6		7,854
1982	M. Navratilova/P. H. Shriver	K. Jordan/A. E. Smith	6–4	6–1		14,450
1983	M. Navratilova/P. H. Shriver	R. Casals/W. M. Turnbull	6–2	6–2		23,100
1984	M. Navratilova/P. H. Shriver	K. Jordan/A. E. Smith	6–3	6–4		34,700
1985	K. Jordan/P. D. Smylie	M. Navratilova/P. H. Shriver	5–7	6–3	6–4	41,100
1986	M. Navratilova/P. H. Shriver	H. Mandlikova/W. M. Turnbull	6–1	6–3		42,060
1987	C. Kohde-Kilsch/H. Sukova	B. Nagelsen/P. D. Smylie	7–5	7–5		46,500
1988	S. Graf/G. Sabatini	L. Savchenko/N. Zvereva	6–3	1–6	12–10	49,500
1989	J. Novotna/H. Sukova	L. Savchenko/N. Zvereva	6–1	6–2		56,970
1990	J. Novotna/H. Sukova	K. Jordan/P. D. Smylie	6–3	6–4		81,510
1991	L. Savchenko/N. Zvereva	G. Fernandez/J. Novotna	6–4	3–6	6–4	85,060
1992	G. Fernandez/N. Zvereva	J. Novotna/L. Savchenko-Neiland	6–4	6–1		93,920
1993	G. Fernandez/N. Zvereva	L. Neiland/J. Novotna	6–4	6–7	6–4	108,100
1994	G. Fernandez/N. Zvereva	J. Novotna/A. Sanchez-Vicario	6–4	6–1		122,200
1995	J. Novotna/A. Sanchez-Vicario	G. Fernandez/N. Zvereva	5–7	7–5	6–4	129,300
1996	M.Hingis/H. Sukova	M. J. McGrath/L. Neiland	5–7	7–5	6–1	139,040
1997	G. Fernandez/N. Zvereva	N. Arendt/M. Bollegraf	6–1	6–2		147,010
1998	M. Hingis/J. Novotna	L. Davenport/N. Zvereva	6–3	3–6	8–6	154,160
1999	L. Davenport/C. Morariu	M. De Swardt/E. Tatarkova	6–4	6–4		167,770
2000	S. Williams/V. Williams	J. Halard-Decugis/A. Sugiyama	6–3	6–2		176,070

MIXED DOUBLES

	CHAMPIONS	RUNNERS-UP	SCORE		
1913	H. Crisp/Mrs C. O. Tuckey	J. C. Parke/Mrs D. R. Larcombe	3–6	5–3	ret
1914	J. C. Parke/Mrs D. R. Larcombe	A. F. Wilding/Mlle M. Broquedis	4–6	6–4	6–2
1915–1918		Not held			
1919	R. Lycett/Miss E. Ryan	A. D. Prebble/Mrs R. Lamb. Chambers	6–0	6–0	
1920	G. L. Patterson/Mlle S. Lenglen	R. Lycett/Miss E. Ryan	7–5	6–3	
1921	R. Lycett/Miss E. Ryan	M. Woosnam/Miss P. L. Howkins	6–3	6–1	
1922	P. O'Hara Wood/Mlle S. Lenglen	R. Lycett/Miss E. Ryan	6–4	6–3	
1923	R. Lycett/Miss E. Ryan	L. S. Deane/Mrs W. P. Shep.–Barron	6–4	7–5	
1924	J. B. Gilbert/Miss K. McKane	L. A. Godfree/Mrs W. P. Shep.d–Barron	6–3	3–6	6–3
1925	J. Borotra/Mlle S. Lenglen	V. L. De Morpurgo/Miss E. Ryan	6–3	6–3	
1926	L. A./Mrs Godfree	H. Kinsey/Miss M. K. Browne	6–3	6–4	
1927	F. T. Hunter/Miss E. Ryan	L. A./Mrs Godfree	8–6	6–0	
1928	P. D. B. Spence/Miss E. Ryan	J. H. Crawford/Miss D. S. Akhurst	7–5	6–4	
1929	F. T. Hunter/Miss H. N. Wills	I. G. Collins/Miss J. Fry	6–1	6–4	
1930	J. H. Crawford/Miss E. Ryan	D. Prenn/Frl H. Krahwinkel	6–1	6–3	
1931	G. M. Lott/Mrs L. A. Harper	I. G. Collins/Miss J. C. Ridley	6–3	1–6	6–1
1932	E. Maier/Miss E. Ryan	H. C. Hopman/Mlle J. Sigart	7–5	6–2	
1933	G. von Cramm/Frl H. Krahwinkel	N. G. Farquharson/Miss M. Heeley	7–5	8–6	
1934	R. Miki/Miss D. E. Round	H. W. Austin/Mrs W. P. Shep.–Barron	3–6	6–4	6–0

	CHAMPIONS	RUNNERS-UP	SCORE		
1935	F. J. Perry/Miss D. E. Round	H. C./Mrs Hopman	7–5	4–6	6–2
1936	F. J. Perry/Miss D. E. Round	J. D. Budge/Mrs M. Fabyan	7–9	7–5	6–4
1937	J. D. Budge/Miss A. Marble	Y. Petra/Mme R. Mathieu	6–4	6–1	
1938	J. D. Budge/Miss A. Marble	H. Henkel/Mrs M. Fabyan	6–1	6–4	
1939	R. L. Riggs/Miss A. Marble	F. H. D. Wilde/Miss N. B. Brown	9–7	6–1	
1940–1945		*Not held*			
1946	T. Brown/Miss A. L. Brough	G. E. Brown/Miss D. Bundy	6–4	6–4	
1947	J. E. Bromwich/Miss A. L. Brough	C. F. Long/Mrs N. M. Bolton	1–6	6–4	6–2
1948	J. E. Bromwich/Miss A. L. Brough	F. A. Sedgman/Miss D. J. Hart	6–2	3–6	6–3
1949	E. W. Sturgess/Mrs R. A. Summers	J. E. Bromwich/Miss A. L. Brough	9–7	9–11	7–5
1950	E. W. Sturgess/Miss A. L. Brough	G. E. Brown/Mrs R.B. Todd	11–9	1–6	6–4
1951	F. A. Sedgman/Miss D. J. Hart	M. G. Rose/Mrs G. F. Bolton	7–5	6–2	
1952	F. A. Sedgman/Miss D. J. Hart	E. Morea/Mrs M. N. Long	4–6	6–3	6–4
1953	E. V. Seixas/Miss D. J. Hart	E. Morea/Miss S. J. Fry	9–7	7–5	
1954	E. V. Seixas/Miss D. J. Hart	K. R. Rosewall/Mrs W. du Pont	5–7	6–4	6–3
1955	E. V. Seixas/Miss D. J. Hart	E. Morea/Miss A. L. Brough	8–6	2–6	6–3
1956	E. V. Seixas/Miss S. J. Fry	G. Mulloy/Miss A. Gibson	2–6	6–2	7–5
1957	M. G. Rose/Miss D. R. Hard	N. A. Fraser/Miss A. Gibson	6–4	7–5	
1958	R. N. Howe/Miss L. Coghlan	K. Nielsen/Miss A. Gibson	6–3	13–11	
1959	R. Laver/Miss D. R. Hard	N. A. Fraser/Miss M. E. Bueno	6–4	6–3	
1960	R. Laver/Miss D. R. Hard	R. N. Howe/Miss M. E. Bueno	13–11	3–6	8–6
1961	F. S. Stolle/Miss L. R. Turner	R. N. Howe/Miss E. Buding	11–9	6–2	
1962	N. A. Fraser/Mrs W. du Pont	R. D. Ralston/Miss A. S. Haydon	2–6	6–3	13–11
1963	K. N. Fletcher/Miss M. Smith	R. A. J. Hewitt/Miss D. R. Hard	11–9	6–4	
1964	F. S. Stolle/Miss L. R. Turner	K. N. Fletcher/Miss M. Smith	6–4	6–4	FIRST
1965	K. N. Fletcher/Miss M. Smith	A. D. Roche/Miss J. A. M. Tegart	12–10	6–3	PRIZE
1966	K. N. Fletcher/Miss M. Smith	R. D. Ralston/Mrs L. W. King	4–6	6–3	6–3 (£ per
1967	O. K. Davidson/Mrs L. W. King	K. N. Fletcher/Miss M. E. Bueno	7–5	6–2	team)
1968	K. N. Fletcher/Mrs B. M. Court	A. Metreveli/Miss O. Morozova	6–1	14–12	450
1969	F. S. Stolle/Mrs P. F. Jones	A. D. Roche/Miss J. A. M. Tegart	6–2	6–3	500
1970	I. Nastase/Miss R. Casals	A. Metreveli/Miss O. Morozova	6–3	4–6	9–7 500
1971	O. K. Davidson/Mrs L. W. King	M. C. Rieseen/Mrs B. M. Court	3–6	6–2	15–13 375
1972	I. Nastase/Miss R. Casals	K. Warwick/Miss K. Goolagong	6–4	6–4	500
1973	O. K. Davidson/Mrs L. W. King	R. C. Ramirez/Miss J. Newberry	6–3	6–2	500
1974	O. K. Davidson/Mrs L. W. King	M. J. Farrell/Miss L. J. Charles	6–3	9–7	1,000
1975	M. C. Riessen/Mrs B. M. Court	A. J. Stone/Miss B. Stove	6–4	7–5	1,000
1976	A. D. Roche/Miss F. Durr	R. L. Stockton/Miss R. Casals	6–3	2–6	7–5 2,000
1977	R. A. J. Hewitt/Miss G. R. Stevens	F. D. McMillan/Miss B. Stove	3–6	7–5	6–4 3,000
1978	F. D. McMillan/Miss B. Stove	R. O. Ruffels/Mrs L. W. King	6–2	6–2	4,000
1979	R. A. J. Hewitt/Miss G. R. Stevens	F. D. McMillan/Miss B. Stove	7–5	7–6	4,200
1980	J. R. Austin/Miss T. Austin	M. R. Edmondson/Miss D. L. Fromholtz	4–6	7–6	6–3 4,420
1981	F. D. McMillan/Miss B. Stove	J. R. Austin/Miss T. Austin	4–6	7–6	6–3 4,770
1982	K. Curren/Miss A. E. Smith	J. M. Lloyd/Miss W. M. Turnbull	2–6	6–3	7–5 6,750
1983	J. M. Lloyd/Miss W. M. Turnbull	S. Denton/Mrs L. W. King	6–7	7–6	7–5 12,000
1984	J. M. Lloyd/Miss W. M. Turnbull	S. Denton/Miss K. Jordan	6–3	6–3	18,000
1985	P. McNamee/Miss M. Navratilova	J. Fitzgerald/Mrs P. D. Smylie	7–5	4–6	6–2 23,400
1986	K. Flach/Miss K. Jordan	H. P. Gunthardt/Miss M. Navratilova	6–3	7–6	25,200
1987	M. J. Bates/Miss J. M. Durie	D. Cahill/Miss N. Provis	7–6	6–3	27,900
1988	S. E. Stewart/Miss Z. Garrison	K. Jones/Mrs S. W. Magers	6–1	7–6	29,700
1989	J. Pugh/Miss J. Novotna	M. Kratzmann/Miss J. Byrne	6–4	5–7	6–4 34,200
1990	R. Leach/Miss Z. Garrison	J. Fitzgerald/Mrs P. D. Smylie	7–5	6–2	40,000
1991	J. B. Fitzgerald/Mrs P. D. Smylie	J. Pugh/Miss N. Zvereva	7–6	6–2	41,720
1992	C. Suk/Mrs L. Savchenko Neiland	J. Eltingh/Miss M. Oremans	7–6	6–2	46,070
1993	M. Woodforde/Miss M. Navratilova	T. Nijssen/Miss M. Bollegraf	6–3	6–4	53,020
1994	T. Woodbridge/Miss H. Sukova	T. Middleton/Miss L. McNeil	3–6	7–5	6–3 60,000
1995	J. Stark/Miss M. Navratilova	C. Suk/Miss G. Fernandez	6–4	6–4	63,500
1996	C. Suk/Miss H. Sukova	M. Woodforde/Miss L. Neiland	1–6	6–3	6–2 68,280
1997	C. Suk/Miss H. Sukova	A. Olhovskiy/Mrs L. Neiland	4–6	6–2	6–3 72,200
1998	M. Mirnyi/Miss S. Williams	M. Bhupathi/Miss M. Lucic	6–4	6–4	75,700
1999	L. Paes/Miss L. Raymond	J. Bjorkman/Miss A. Kournikova	6–4	3–6	6–3 79,180
2000	D. Johnson/Miss K. Po	L. Hewitt/Miss K. Clijsters	6–3	6–4	83,100

US CHAMPIONSHIPS

1. **Challenge Round:** A Challenge Round was introduced in the men's singles in 1884 and discontinued following the 1911 Championship. It was introduced in the women's singles in 1888 and discontinued following the 1918 Championship. In men's doubles it was instituted in 1891 and abolished in 1918, restored in 1919 and finally abolished in 1920. In the years marked with an asterisk (*) the holder did not defend his/her title so the winner of the All-Comers Singles became the champion. From 1891–1901 inclusive (but not in 1893) the women's singles final was contested over five sets. 2. **The War Years:** In 1917 a National Patriotic Tournament was held in all five events. The winners were not recognised as National Champions. During World War II (1942–45) all five National Championships were staged together at the West Side Tennis Club, Forest Hills, NY. 3. **Last Amateur Events:** During the first two years of Open Tennis (1968–69) a National Amateur Championship was held for all five events at the Longwood Cricket Club, Boston, as well as an Open Championship at Forest Hills, New York (although there was no open mixed in 1968). Thereafter the Amateur event was discontinued. 4. **Dress:** The 'predominantly white' clothing rule was last enforced at the 1971 Championships. 5. **Prize Money:** Equal prize money for men and women was introduced in 1973. 6. **Surfaces:** 1881–1974 Grass; 1975–77 American clay (Har-Tru); 1978–present Hard courts (DecoTurf II). 7. **Venues:** *Men's singles:*1881–1914 The Casino, Newport, RI. 1915–20 West Side Tennis Club, Forest Hills, NY. 1921–23 Germantown Cricket Club, Philadelphia, PA. 1924–77 West Side Tennis Club, Forest Hills, NY. 1978–present National Tennis Center, Flushing Meadows, NY. *Women's singles:* 1887–1920 Philadelphia Cricket Club, PA. 1921–77 West Side Tennis Club, Forest Hills, NY. 1978–present National Tennis Center, Flushing Meadows, NY. *Men's doubles:* 1881–1914 The Casino, Newport, RI. 1915–16 West Side Tennis Club, Forest Hills, NY. 1917–33 Longwood Cricket Club, Boston, MA. 1934 Germantown Cricket Club, Philadelphia, PA. 1935–41 Longwood Cricket Club, Boston, MA. 1942–45 West Side Tennis Club, Forest Hills, NY. 1946–69 Longwood Cricket Club, Boston, MA (1968–69 Amateur). 1968–77 West Side Tennis Club, Forest Hills, NY. 1978–present National Tennis Center, Flushing Meadows, NY. *Women's doubles:*1887–1920 Philadelphia Cricket Club, PA (1887,1888 non-Championship). 1921–34 West Side Tennis Club, Forest Hills, NY. 1935–41 Longwood Cricket Club, Boston, MA. 1942–45 West Side Tennis Club, Forest Hills, NY. 1946–69 Longwood Cricket Club, Boston, MA (1968–69 Amateur). 1968–77 West Side Tennis Club, Forest Hills, NY. 1978– present National Tennis Center, Flushing Meadows, NY. *Mixed doubles:* 1892–1920 Philadelphia Cricket Club, PA. 1921–34 Longwood Cricket Club, Boston, MA. 1935–66 West Side Tennis Club, Forest Hills, NY. 1967–69 Longwood Cricket Club, Boston, MA. 1969–77 West Side Tennis Club, Forest Hills, NY (not held 1968). 1978–present National Tennis Center, Flushing Meadows, NY. 8. **Status:** Since 1993 the men's doubles has been reduced to the best-of-three sets.

MEN'S SINGLES

	CHAMPION	RUNNER-UP	SCORE			
1881	R. D. Sears	W. E. Glyn	6–0	6–3	6–2	
1882	R. D. Sears	C. M. Clark	6–1	6–4	6–0	
1883	R. D. Sears	J. Dwight	6–2	6–0	9–7	
1884	R. D. Sears	H. A. Taylor	6–0	1–6	6–0	6–2
1885	R. D. Sears	G. M. Brinley	6–3	4–6	6–0	6–3
1886	R. D. Sears	R. L. Beeckman	4–6	6–1	6–3	6–4
1887	R. D. Sears	H. W. Slocum	6–1	6–3	6–2	
1888*	H. W. Slocum	H. A. Taylor	6–4	6–1	6–0	
1889	H. W. Slocum	Q. A. Shaw	6–3	6–1	4–6	6–2
1890	O. S. Campbell	H. W. Slocum	6–2	4–6	6–3	6–1
1891	O. S. Campbell	C. Hobart	2–6	7–5	7–9	6–1	6–2
1892	O. S. Campbell	F. H. Hovey	7–5	3–6	6–3	7–5
1893*	R. D. Wrenn	F. H. Hovey	6–4	3–6	6–4	6–4
1894	R. D. Wrenn	M. F. Goodbody	6–8	6–1	6–4	6–4
1895	F. H. Hovey	R. D. Wrenn	6–3	6–2	6–4	
1896	R. D. Wrenn	F. H. Hovey	7–5	3–6	6–0	1–6	6–1
1897	R. D. Wrenn	W. V. Eaves	4–6	8–6	6–3	2–6	6–2
1898*	M. D. Whitman	D. F. Davis	3–6	6–2	6–2	6–1
1899	M. D. Whitman	J. P. Paret	6–1	6–2	3–6	7–5
1900	M. D. Whitman	W. A. Larned	6–4	1–6	6–2	6–2
1901*	W. A. Larned	B. C. Wright	6–2	6–8	6–4	6–4
1902	W. A. Larned	R. F. Doherty	4–6	6–2	6–4	8–6
1903	H. L. Doherty	W. A. Larned	6–0	6–3	10–8	
1904*	H. Ward	W. J. Clothier	10–8	6–4	9–7	
1905	B. C. Wright	H. Ward	6–2	6–1	11–9	
1906	W. J. Clothier	B. C. Wright	6–3	6–0	6–4	
1907*	W. A. Larned	R. LeRoy	6–2	6–2	6–4	
1908	W. A. Larned	B. C. Wright	6–1	6–2	8–6	
1909	W. A. Larned	W. J. Clothier	6–1	6–2	5–7	1–6	6–1
1910	W. A. Larned	T. C. Bundy	6–1	5–7	6–0	6–8	6–1
1911	W. A. Larned	M. E. McLoughlin	6–4	6–4	6–2	
1912	M. E. McLoughlin	W. F. Johnson	3–6	2–6	6–2	6–4	6–2
1913	M. E. McLoughlin	R. N. Williams	6–4	5–7	6–3	6–1
1914	R. N. Williams	M. E. McLoughlin	6–3	8–6	10–8	
1915	W. M. Johnston	M. E. McLoughlin	1–6	6–0	7–5	10–8

	CHAMPION	RUNNER-UP	SCORE					
1916	R. N. Williams	W. M. Johnston	4–6	6–4	0–6	6–2	6–4	
1917	R. L. Murray	N. W. Niles	5–7	8–6	6–3	6–3		
1918	R. L. Murray	W. T. Tilden	6–3	6–1	7–5			
1919	W. M. Johnston	W. T. Tilden	6–4	6–4	6–3			
1920	W. T. Tilden	W. M. Johnston	6–1	1–6	7–5	5–7	6–3	
1921	W. T. Tilden	W. F. Johnson	6–1	6–3	6–1			
1922	W. T. Tilden	W. M. Johnston	4–6	3–6	6–2	6–3	6–4	
1923	W. T. Tilden	W. M. Johnston	6–4	6–1	6–4			
1924	W. T. Tilden	W. M. Johnston	6–1	9–7	6–2			
1925	W. T. Tilden	W. M. Johnston	4–6	11–9	6–3	4–6	6–3	
1926	R. Lacoste	J. Borotra	6–4	6–0	6–4			
1927	R. Lacoste	W. T. Tilden	11–9	6–3	11–9			
1928	H. Cochet	F. T. Hunter	4–6	6–4	3–6	7–5	6–3	
1929	W. T. Tilden	F. T. Hunter	3–6	6–3	4–6	6–2	6–4	
1930	J. H. Doeg	F. X. Shields	10–8	1–6	6–4	16–14		
1931	H. E. Vines	G. M. Lott	7–9	6–3	9–7	7–5		
1932	H. E. Vines	H. Cochet	6–4	6–4	6–4			
1933	F. J. Perry	J. H. Crawford	6–3	11–13	4–6	6–0	6–1	
1934	F. J. Perry	W. L. Allison	6–4	6–3	1–6	8–6		
1935	W. L. Allison	S. B. Wood	6–2	6–2	6–3			
1936	F. J. Perry	J. D. Budge	2–6	6–2	8–6	1–6	10–8	
1937	J. D. Budge	C. Von Cramm	6–1	7–9	6–1	3–6	6–1	
1938	J. D. Budge	G. Mako	6–3	6–8	6–2	6–1		
1939	R. L. Riggs	S. W. Van Horn	6–4	6–2	6–4			
1940	W. D. McNeill	R. L. Riggs	4–6	6–8	6–3	6–3	7–5	
1941	R. L. Riggs	F. Kovacs	5–7	6–1	6–3	6–3		
1942	F. R. Schroeder	F. A. Parker	8–6	7–5	3–6	4–6	6–2	
1943	J. R. Hunt	J. A. Kramer	6–3	6–8	10–8	6–0		
1944	F. A. Parker	W. F. Talbert	6–4	3–6	6–3	6–3		
1945	F. A. Parker	W. F. Talbert	14–12	6–1	6–2			
1946	J. A. Kramer	T. P. Brown	9–7	6–3	6–0			
1947	J. A. Kramer	F. A. Parker	4–6	2–6	6–1	6–0	6–3	
1948	R. A. Gonzales	E. W. Sturgess	6–2	6–3	14–12			
1949	R. A. Gonzales	F. R. Schroeder	16–18	2–6	6–1	6–2	6–4	
1950	A. Larsen	H. Flam	6–3	4–6	5–7	6–4	6–3	
1951	F. A. Sedgman	E. V. Seixas	6–4	6–1	6–1			
1952	F. A. Sedgman	G. Mulloy	6–1	6–2	6–3			
1953	M. A. Trabert	E. V. Seixas	6–3	6–2	6–3			
1954	E. V. Seixas	R. N. Hartwig	3–6	6–2	6–4	6–4		
1955	M. A. Trabert	K. R. Rosewall	9–7	6–3	6–3			
1956	K. R. Rosewall	L. A. Hoad	4–6	6–2	6–3	6–3		
1957	M. J. Anderson	A. J. Cooper	10–8	7–5	6–4			
1958	A. J. Cooper	M. J. Anderson	6–2	3–6	4–6	10–8	8–6	
1959	N. A. Fraser	A. Olmedo	6–3	5–7	6–2	6–4		
1960	N. A. Fraser	R. G. Laver	6–4	6–4	9–7			
1961	R. S. Emerson	R. G. Laver	7–5	6–3	6–2			
1962	R. G. Laver	R. S. Emerson	6–2	6–4	5–7	6–4		
1963	R. H. Osuna	F. Froehling	7–5	6–4	6–2			
1964	R. S. Emerson	F. S. Stolle	6–4	6–2	6–4			
1965	M. Santana	E. C. Drysdale	6–2	7–9	7–5	6–1		
1966	F. S. Stolle	J. D. Newcombe	4–6	12–10	6–3	6–4		
1967	J. D. Newcombe	C. Graebner	6–4	6–4	8–6			PRIZE
1968#	A. R. Ashe	R. C. Lutz	4–6	6–3	8–10	6–0	6–4	MONEY
1969#	S. R. Smith	R. C. Lutz	9–7	6–3	6–1			(US$)
1968	A. R. Ashe	T. S. Okker	14–12	5–7	6–3	3–6	6–3	14,000
1969	R. G. Laver	A. D. Roche	7–9	6–1	6–2	6–2		16,000
1970	K. R. Rosewall	A. D. Roche	2–6	6–4	7–6	6–3		20,000
1971	S. R. Smith	J. Kodes	3–6	6–3	6–2	7–6		15,000
1972	I. Nastase	A. R. Ashe	3–6	6–3	6–7	6–4	6–3	25,000
1973	J. D. Newcombe	J. Kodes	6–4	1–6	4–6	6–2	6–2	25,000
1974	J. S. Connors	K. R. Rosewall	6–1	6–0	6–1			22,500
1975	M. Orantes	J. S. Connors	6–4	6–3	6–3			25,000
1976	J. S. Connors	B. Borg	6–4	3–6	7–6	6–4		30,000
1977	G. Vilas	J. S. Connors	2–6	6–3	7–6	6–0		33,000

#US Amateur Championships

	CHAMPION	RUNNER-UP	SCORE					
1978	J. S. Connors	B. Borg	6–4	6–2	6–2			38,000
1979	J. P. McEnroe	V. Gerulaitis	7–5	6–3	6–3			39,000
1980	J. P. McEnroe	B. Borg	7–6	6–1	6–7	5–7	6–4	46,000
1981	J. P. McEnroe	B. Borg	4–6	6–2	6–4	6–3		60,000
1982	J. S. Connors	I. Lendl	6–3	6–2	4–6	6–4		90,000
1983	J. S. Connors	I. Lendl	6–3	6–7	7–5	6–0		120,000
1984	J. P. McEnroe	I. Lendl	6–3	6–4	6–1			160,000
1985	I. Lendl	J. P. McEnroe	7–6	6–3	6–4			187,500
1986	I. Lendl	M. Mecir	6–4	6–2	6–0			210,000
1987	I. Lendl	M. Wilander	6–7	6–0	7–6	6–4		250,000
1988	M. Wilander	I. Lendl	6–4	4–6	6–3	5–7	6–4	275,000
1989	B. Becker	I. Lendl	7–6	1–6	6–3	7–6		300,000
1990	P. Sampras	A. Agassi	6–4	6–3	6–2			350,000
1991	S. Edberg	J. Courier	6–2	6–4	6–0			400,000
1992	S. Edberg	P. Sampras	3–6	6–4	7–6	6–2		500,000
1993	P. Sampras	C. Pioline	6–4	6–4	6–3			535,000
1994	A. Agassi	M. Stich	6–1	7–6	7–5			550,000
1995	P. Sampras	A. Agassi	6–4	6–3	4–6	7–5		575,000
1996	P. Sampras	M. Chang	6–1	6–4	7–6			600,000
1997	P. Rafter	G. Rusedski	6–3	6–2	4–6	7–5		650,000
1998	P. Rafter	M. Philippoussis	6–3	3–6	6–2	6–0		700,000
1999	A. Agassi	T. Martin	6–4	6–7	6–7	6–3	6–2	750,000
2000	M. Safin	P. Sampras	6–4	6–3	6–3			800,000

WOMEN'S SINGLES

	CHAMPION	RUNNER-UP	SCORE				
1887	Miss E. Hansell	Miss L. Knight	6–1	6–0			
1888	Miss B. L. Townsend	Miss E. Hansell	6–3	6–5			
1889	Miss B. L. Townsend	Miss L. D. Voorhees	7–5	6–2			
1890	Miss E. C. Roosevelt	Miss B. L. Townsend	6–2	6–2			
1891	Miss M. E. Cahill	Miss E. C. Roosevelt	6–4	6–1	4–6	6–3	
1892	Miss M. E. Cahill	Miss E. H. Moore	5–7	6–3	6–4	4–6	6–2
1893*	Miss A. Terry	Miss A. L. Schultz	6–1	6–3			
1894	Miss H. Hellwig	Miss A. Terry	7–5	3–6	6–0	3–6	6–3
1895	Miss J. Atkinson	Miss H. Hellwig	6–4	6–2	6–1		
1896	Miss E. H. Moore	Miss J. Atkinson	6–4	4–6	6–2	6–2	
1897	Miss J. Atkinson	Miss E. H. Moore	6–3	6–3	4–6	3–6	6–3
1898	Miss J. Atkinson	Miss M. Jones	6–3	5–7	6–4	2–6	7–5
1899*	Miss M. Jones	Miss M. Banks	6–1	6–1	7–5		
1900*	Miss M. McAteer	Miss E. Parker	6–2	6–2	6–0		
1901	Miss E. H. Moore	Miss M. McAteer	6–4	3–6	7–5	2–6	6–2
1902	Miss M. Jones	Miss E. H. Moore	6–1	1–0	ret		
1903	Miss E. H. Moore	Miss M. Jones	7–5	8–6			
1904	Miss M. G. Sutton	Miss E. H. Moore	6–1	6–2			
1905*	Miss E. H. Moore	Miss H. Homans	6–4	5–7	6–1		
1906*	Miss H. Homans	Mrs M. Barger-Wallach	6–4	6–3			
1907*	Miss Evelyn Sears	Miss C. Neely	6–3	6–2			
1908	Mrs M. Barger-Wallach	Miss Evelyn Sears	6–3	1–6	6–3		
1909	Miss H. Hotchkiss	Mrs M. Barger-Wallach	6–0	6–1			
1910	Miss H. Hotchkiss	Miss L. Hammond	6–4	6–2			
1911	Miss H. Hotchkiss	Miss F. Sutton	8–10	6–1	9–7		
1912*	Miss M. K. Browne	Miss Eleanora Sears	6–4	6–2			
1913	Miss M. K. Browne	Miss D. Green	6–2	7–5			
1914	Miss M. K. Browne	Miss M. Wagner	6–2	1–6	6–1		
1915*	Miss M. Bjurstedt	Mrs G. W. Wightman	4–6	6–2	6–0		
1916	Miss M. Bjurstedt	Mrs L. H. Raymond	6–0	6–1			
1917	Miss M. Bjurstedt	Miss M. Vanderhoef	4–6	6–0	6–2		
1918	Miss M. Bjurstedt	Miss E. E. Goss	6–4	6–3			
1919	Mrs G. W. Wightman	Miss M. Zinderstein	6–1	6–2			
1920	Mrs F. Mallory	Miss M. Zinderstein	6–3	6–1			
1921	Mrs F. Mallory	Miss M. K. Browne	4–6	6–4	6–2		
1922	Mrs F. Mallory	Miss H. N. Wills	6–3	6–1			
1923	Miss H. N. Wills	Mrs F. Mallory	6–2	6–1			
1924	Miss H. N. Wills	Mrs F. Mallory	6–1	6–3			
1925	Miss H. N. Wills	Miss K. McKane	3–6	6–0	6–2		

	CHAMPION	RUNNER-UP	SCORE			
1926	Mrs F. Mallory	Miss E. Ryan	4–6	6–4	9–7	
1927	Miss H. N. Wills	Miss B. Nuthall	6–1	6–4		
1928	Miss H. N. Wills	Miss H. H. Jacobs	6–2	6–1		
1929	Miss H. N. Wills	Mrs P. H. Watson	6–4	6–2		
1930	Miss B. Nuthall	Mrs L. A. Harper	6–4	6–1		
1931	Mrs F. S. Moody	Mrs F. Whittingstall	6–4	6–1		
1932	Miss H. H. Jacobs	Miss C. A. Babcock	6–2	6–2		
1933	Miss H. H. Jacobs	Mrs F. S. Moody	8–6	3–6	3–0	ret
1934	Miss H. H. Jacobs	Miss S. Palfrey	6–1	6–4		
1935	Miss H. H. Jacobs	Mrs S. P. Fabyan	6–2	6–4		
1936	Miss A. Marble	Miss H. H. Jacobs	4–6	6–3	6–2	
1937	Miss A. Lizana	Miss J. Jedrzejowksa	6–4	6–2		
1938	Miss A. Marble	Miss N. Wynne	6–0	6–3		
1939	Miss A. Marble	Miss H. H. Jacobs	6–0	8–10	6–4	
1940	Miss A. Marble	Miss H. H. Jacobs	6–2	6–3		
1941	Mrs E. T. Cooke	Miss P. M. Betz	7–5	6–2		
1942	Miss P. M. Betz	Miss A. L. Brough	4–6	6–1	6–4	
1943	Miss P. M. Betz	Miss A. L. Brough	6–3	5–7	6–3	
1944	Miss P. M. Betz	Miss M. E. Osborne	6–3	8–6		
1945	Mrs E. T. Cooke	Miss P. M. Betz	3–6	8–6	6–4	
1946	Miss P. M. Betz	Miss D. J. Hart	11–9	6–3		
1947	Miss A. L. Brough	Miss M. E. Osborne	8–6	4–6	6–1	
1948	Mrs W. D. du Pont	Miss A. L. Brough	4–6	6–4	15–13	
1949	Mrs W. D. du Pont	Miss D. J. Hart	6–3	6–1		
1950	Mrs W. D. du Pont	Miss D. J. Hart	6–4	6–3		
1951	Miss M. Connolly	Miss S. J. Fry	6–3	1–6	6–4	
1952	Miss M. Connolly	Miss D. J. Hart	6–3	7–5		
1953	Miss M. Connolly	Miss D. J. Hart	6–2	6–4		
1954	Miss D. J. Hart	Miss A. L. Brough	6–8	6–1	8–6	
1955	Miss D. J. Hart	Miss P. E. Ward	6–4	6–2		
1956	Miss S. J. Fry	Miss A. Gibson	6–3	6–4		
1957	Miss A. Gibson	Miss A. L. Brough	6–3	6–2		
1958	Miss A. Gibson	Miss D. R. Hard	3–6	6–1	6–2	
1959	Miss M. E. Bueno	Miss C. C. Truman	6–1	6–4		
1960	Miss D. R. Hard	Miss M. E. Bueno	6–4	10–12	6–4	
1961	Miss D. R. Hard	Miss A. S. Haydon	6–3	6–4		
1962	Miss M. Smith	Miss D. R. Hard	9–7	6–4		
1963	Miss M. E. Bueno	Miss M. Smith	7–5	6–4		
1964	Miss M. E. Bueno	Mrs C. Graebner	6–1	6–0		
1965	Miss M. Smith	Miss B. J. Moffitt	8–6	7–5		
1966	Miss M. E. Bueno	Miss N. Richey	6–3	6–1		
1967	Mrs L. W. King	Mrs P. F. Jones	11–9	6–4		

							FIRST PRIZE
1968#	Mrs B. M. Court	Miss M. E. Bueno	6–2	6–2			(US$)
1969#	Mrs B. M. Court	Miss S. V. Wade	4–6	6–3	6–0		6,000
1968	Miss S. V. Wade	Mrs L. W. King	6–4	6–2			6,000
1969	Mrs B. M. Court	Miss N. Richey	6–2	6–2			7,500
1970	Mrs B. M. Court	Miss R. Casals	6–2	2–6	6–1		5,000
1971	Mrs L. W. King	Miss R. Casals	6–4	7–6			10,000
1972	Mrs L. W. King	Miss K. Melville	6–3	7–5			25,000
1973	Mrs B. M. Court	Miss E. Goolagong	7–6	5–7	6–2		22,500
1974	Mrs L. W. King	Miss E. Goolagong	3–6	6–3	7–5		25,000
1975	Miss C. M. Evert	Mrs R. A. Cawley	5–7	6–4	6–2		30,000
1976	Miss C. M. Evert	Mrs R. A. Cawley	6–3	6–0			33,000
1977	Miss C. M. Evert	Miss W. Turnbull	7–6	6–2			38,000
1978	Miss C. M. Evert	Miss P. Shriver	7–5	6–4			39,000
1979	Miss T. A. Austin	Miss C. M. Evert	6–4	6–3			46,000
1980	Mrs J. M. Lloyd	Miss H. Mandlikova	5–7	6–1	6–1		60,000
1981	Miss T. A. Austin	Miss M. Navratilova	1–6	7–6	7–6		90,000
1982	Mrs J. M. Lloyd	Miss M. Mandlikova	6–3	6–1			120,000
1983	Miss M. Navratilova	Mrs J. M. Lloyd	6–1	6 3			160,000
1984	Miss M. Navratilova	Mrs J. M. Lloyd	4–6	6–4	6–4		187,500
1985	Miss H. Mandlikova	Miss M. Navratilova	7–6	1–6	7–6		210,000
1986	Miss M. Navratilova	Miss H. Sukova	6–3	6–2			250,000
1987	Miss M. Navratilova	Miss S. Graf	7–6	6–1			

#US Amateur Championships

	CHAMPION	RUNNER UP	SCORE			
1988	Miss S. Graf	Miss G. Sabatini	6–3	3–6	6–1	275,000
1989	Miss S. Graf	Miss M. Navratilova	3–6	7–5	6–1	300,000
1990	Miss G. Sabatini	Miss S. Graf	6–2	7–6		350,000
1991	Miss M. Seles	Miss M. Navratilova	7–6	6–1		400,000
1992	Miss M. Seles	Miss A. Sanchez-Vicario	6–3	6–3		500,000
1993	Miss S. Graf	Miss H. Sukova	6–3	6–3		535,000
1994	Miss A. Sanchez-Vicario	Miss S. Graf	1–6	7–6	6–4	550,000
1995	Miss S. Graf	Miss M. Seles	7–6	0–6	6–3	575,000
1996	Miss S. Graf	Miss M. Seles	7–5	6–4		600,000
1997	Miss M. Hingis	Miss V. Williams	6–0	6–4		650,000
1998	Miss L. Davenport	Miss M. Hingis	6–3	7–5		700,000
1999	Miss S. Williams	Miss M. Hingis	6–3	7–6		750,000
2000	Miss V. Williams	Miss L. Davenport	6–4	7–5		800,000

MEN'S DOUBLES

	CHAMPIONS	RUNNERS-UP	SCORE				
1881	C. M. Clark/F. W. Taylor	A. Van Rensselaer/A. E. Newbold	6–5	6–4	6–5		
1882	J. Dwight/R. D. Sears	W. Nightingale/G. M. Smith	6–2	6–4	6–4		
1883	J. Dwight/R. D. Sears	A. Van Rensselaer/A. E. Newbold	6–0	6–2	6–2		
1884	J. Dwight/R. D. Sears	A. Van Rensselaer/W. V. R. Berry	6–4	6–1	8–10	6–4	
1885	J. S. Clark/R. D. Sears	W. P. Knapp/H. W. Slocum	6–3	6–0	6–2		
1886	J. Dwight/R. D. Sears	G. M. Brinley/H. A. Taylor	7–5	5–7	7–5	6–4	
1887	J. Dwight/R. D. Sears	H. W. Slocum/H. A. Taylor	6–4	3–6	2–6	6–3	6–3
1888	O. S. Campbell/V. G. Hall	C. Hobart/E. P. MacMullen		6–4	6–2	6–4	
1889	H. W. Slocum/H. A. Taylor	O. S. Campbell/V. G. Hall	6–1	6–3	6–2		
1890	V. G. Hall/C. Hobart	C. W. Carver/J. A. Ryerson	6–3	4–6	6–2	2–6	6–3
1891	O. S. Campbell/R. P. Huntington	V. G. Hall/C. Hobart	6–3	6–4	8–6		
1892	O. S. Campbell/R. P. Huntington	V. G. Hall/E. L. Hall	6–4	6–2	4–6	6–3	
1893	C. Hobart/F. H. Hovey	O. S. Campbell/R. P. Huntington	6–3	6–4	4–6	6–2	
1894	C. Hobart/F. H. Hovey	C. B. Neel/S. R. Neel	6–3	8–6	6–1		
1895	M. G. Chace/R. D. Wrenn	C. Hobart/F. H. Hovey	7–5	6–1	8–6		
1896	C. B./S. R. Neel	M. G. Chace/R. D. Wrenn	6–3	1–6	6–1	3–6	6–1
1897*	L. E. Ware/G. P. Sheldon	H. S. Mahony/H. A. Nisbet	11–13	6–2	9–7	1–6	6–1
1898	L. E. Ware/G. P. Sheldon	D. F. Davis/H. Ward	1–6	7–5	6–4	4–6	7–5
1899	D. F. Davis/H. Ward	L. E. Ware/G. P. Sheldon	6–4	6–4	6–3		
1900	D. F. Davis/H. Ward	F. B. Alexander/R. D. Little	6–4	9–7	12–10		
1901	D. F. Davis/H. Ward	L. E. Ware/B. C. Wright	6–3	9–7	6–1		
1902	H. L./R. F. Doherty	D. F. Davis/H. Ward	11–9	12–10	6–4		
1903	H. L./R. F. Doherty	L. Collins/L. H. Waldner	7–5	6–3	6–3		
1904*	H. Ward/B. C. Wright	K. Collins/R. D. Little	1–6	6–2	3–6	6–4	6–1
1905	H. Ward/B. C. Wright	F. B. Alexander/H. H. Hackett	6–3	6–1	6–2		
1906	H. Ward/B. C. Wright	F. B. Alexander/H. H. Hackett	6–3	3–6	6–3	6–3	
1907*	F. B. Alexander/B. C. Wright	W. J. Clothier/W. A. Larned	6–3	6–1	6–4		
1908*	F. B. Alexander/H. H. Hackett	R. D. Little/B. C. Wright	6–1	7–5	6–2		
1909	F. B. Alexander/H. H. Hackett	G. J. Janes/M. E. McLoughlin	6–4	6–1	6–0		
1910	F. B. Alexander/H. H. Hackett	T. C. Bundy/T. W. Hendrick	6–1	8–6	6–3		
1911	R. D. Little/G. F. Touchard	F. B. Alexander/H. H. Hackett	7–5	13–15	6–2	6–4	
1912	T. C. Bundy/M. E. McLoughlin	R. D. Little/G. F. Touchard	3–6	6–2	6–1	7–5	
1913	T. C. Bundy/M. E. McLoughlin	C. J. Griffin/J. R. Strachan	6–4	7–5	6–1		
1914	T. C. Bundy/M. E. McLoughlin	G. M. Church/D. Mathey	6–4	6–2	6–4		
1915	C. J. Griffin/W. M. Johnston	T. C. Bundy/M. E. McLoughlin	6–2	3–6	4–6	6–3	6–3
1916	C. J. Griffin/W. M. Johnston	W. Dawson/M. E. McLoughlin	6–4	6–3	5–7	6–3	
1917	F. B. Alexander/ H. A. Throckmorton	H. C. Johnson/I. C. Wright	11–9	6–4	6–4		
1918	V. Richards/W. T. Tilden	F. B. Alexander/B. C. Wright	6–3	6–4	3–6	2–6	6–2
1919	N. E. Brookes/G. L. Patterson	V. Richards/W. T. Tilden	8–6	6–3	4–6	6–2	
1920	C. J. Griffin/W. M. Johnston	W. F. Davis/R. Roberts	6–2	6–2	6–3		
1921	V. Richards/W. T. Tilden	W. M. Washburn/R. N. Williams	13–11	12–10	6–1		
1922	V. Richards/W. T. Tilden	P. O'Hara Wood/G. L. Patterson	4–6	6–1	6–3	6–4	
1923	B. I. C. Norton/W. T. Tilden	W. M. Washburn/R. N. Williams	3–6	6–2	6–3	5–7	6–2
1924	H. O./R. G. Kinsey	P. O'Hara Wood/G. L. Patterson	7–5	5–7	7–9	6–3	6–4
1925	V. Richards/R. N. Williams	J. B. Hawkes/G. L. Patterson	6–2	8–10	6–4	11–9	
1926	V. Richards/R. N. Williams	A. H. Chapin/W. T. Tilden	6–4	6–8	11–9	6–3	
1927	F. T. Hunter/W. T. Tilden	W. M. Washburn/R. N. Williams	10–8	6–3	6–3		
1928	J. F. Hennessey/G. M. Lott	J. B. Hawkes/G. L. Patterson	6–2	6–1	6–2		

	CHAMPIONS	RUNNERS-UP	SCORE				
1929	J. H. Doeg/G. M. Lott	R. B. Bell/L. N. White	10–8	16–14	6–1		
1930	J. H. Doeg/G. M. Lott	W. L. Allison/J. Van Ryn	8–6	6–3	3–6	13–15	6–4
1931	W. L. Allison/J. Van Ryn	R. B. Bell/G. S. Mangin	6–4	6–3	6–2		
1932	K. Gledhill/H. E. Vines	W. L. Allison/J. Van Ryn	6–4	6–3	6–2		
1933	G. M. Lott/L. R. Stoefen	F. A. Parker/F. X. Shields	11–13	9–7	9–7	6–3	
1934	G. M. Lott/L. R. Stoefen	W. L. Allison/J. Van Ryn	6–4	9–7	3–6	6–4	
1935	W. L. Allison/J. Van Ryn	J. D. Budge/G. Mako	6–2	6–3	2–6	3–6	6–1
1936	J. D. Budge/G. Mako	W. L. Allison/J. Van Ryn	6–4	6–2	6–4		
1937	G. Von Cramm/H. Henkel	J. D. Budge/G. Mako	6–4	7–5	6–4		
1938	J. D. Budge/G. Mako	J. E. Bromwich/A. K. Quist	6–3	6–2	6–1		
1939	J. E. Bromwich/A. K. Quist	J. H. Crawford/H. C. Hopman	8–6	6–1	6–4		
1940	J. A. Kramer/F. R. Schroeder	G. Mulloy/H. J. Prussoff	6–4	8–6	9–7		
1941	J. A. Kramer/F. R. Schroeder	G. Mulloy/W. Sabin	9–7	6–4	6–2		
1942	G. Mulloy/W. F. Talbert	F. R. Schroeder/S. B. Wood	9–7	7–5	6–1		
1943	J. A. Kramer/F. A. Parker	D. Freeman/W. F. Talbert	6–2	6–4	6–4		
1944	R. Falkenburg/W. D. McNeill	F. Segura/W. F. Talbert	7–5	6–4	3–6	6–1	
1945	G. Mulloy/W. F. Talbert	R. Falkenburg/J. Tuero	12–10	8–10	12–10	6–2	
1946	G. Mulloy/W. F. Talbert	G. Guernsey/W. D. McNeill	3–6	6–4	2–6	6–3	20–18
1947	J. A. Kramer/F. R. Schroeder	W. F. Talbert/O. W. Sidwell	6–4	7–5	6–3		
1948	G. Mulloy/W. F. Talbert	F. A. Parker/F. R. Schroeder	1–6	9–7	6–3	3–6	9–7
1949	J. Bromwich/O. W. Sidwell	F. A. Sedgman/G. Worthington	6–4	6–0	6–1		
1950	J. Bromwich/F. A. Sedgman	G. Mulloy/W. F. Talbert	7–5	8–6	3–6	6–1	
1951	K. B. McGregor/F. A. Sedgman	D. Candy/M. G. Rose	10–8	6–4	4–6	7–5	
1952	M. G. Rose/E. V. Seixas	K. B. McGregor/F. A. Sedgman	3–6	10–8	10–8	6–8	8–6
1953	R. N. Hartwig/M. G. Rose	G. Mulloy/W. F. Talbert	6–4	4–6	6–2	6–4	
1954	E. V. Seixas/M. A. Trabert	L. A. Hoad/K. R. Rosewall	3–6	6–4	8–6	6–3	
1955	K. Kamo/A. Miyagi	G. Moss/W. Quillian	6–3	6–3	3–6	1–6	6–4
1956	L. A. Hoad/K. R. Rosewall	H. Richardson/E. V. Seixas	6–2	6–2	3–6	6–4	
1957	A. J. Cooper/N. A. Fraser	G. Mulloy/J. E. Patty	4–6	6–3	9–7	6–3	
1958	A. Olmedo/H. Richardson	S. Giammalva/B. McKay	3–6	6–3	6–4	6–4	
1959	R. S. Emerson/N. A. Fraser	E. Buchholz/A. Olmedo	3–6	6–3	5–7	6–4	7–5
1960	R. S. Emerson/N. A. Fraser	R. G. Laver/R. Mark	9–7	6–2	6–4		
1961	C. McKinley/R. D. Ralston	A. Palafox/R. H. Osuna	6–3	6–4	2–6	13–11	
1962	A. Palafox/R. H. Osuna	C. McKinley/R. D. Ralston	6–4	10–12	1–6	9–7	6–3
1963	C. McKinley/R. D. Ralston	A. Palafox/R. H. Osuna	9–7	4–6	5–7	6–3	11–9
1964	C. McKinley/R. D. Ralston	G. Stilwell/M. Sangster	6–3	6–2	6–4		
1965	R. S. Emerson/F. S. Stolle	F. Froehling/C. Pasarell	6–4	10–12	7–5	6–3	
1966	R. S. Emerson/F. S. Stolle	C. Graebner/R. D. Ralston	6–4	6–4	6–4		
1967	J. D. Newcombe/A. D. Roche	O. K. Davidson/W. W. Bowrey	6–8	9–7	6–3	6–3	
1968#	R. C. Lutz/S. R. Smith	R. A. J. Hewitt/R. J. Moore	6–4	6–4	9–7		
1969#	R. D. Crealy/A. Stone	W. W. Bowrey/C. Pasarell	9–11	6–3	7–5		
1968	R. C. Lutz/S. R. Smith	A. R. Ashe/A. Gimeno	11–9	6–1	7–5		FIRST
1969	K. R. Rosewall/F. S. Stolle	C. Pasarell/R. D. Ralston	2–6	7–5	13–11	6–3	PRIZE
1970	P. Barthes/N. Pilic	R. S. Emerson/R. G. Laver	6–3	7–6	4–6	7–6	(US$)
1971	J. D. Newcombe/R. Taylor	S. R. Smith/E. Van Dillen	6–7	6–3	7–6	4–6	7–6	2,000
1972	E. C. Drysdale/R. Taylor	O. K. Davidson/J. D. Newcombe	6–4	7–6	6–3		
1973	O. K. Davidson/J. D. Newcombe	R. G. Laver/K. R. Rosewall	7–5	2–6	7–5	7–5	4,000
1974	R. C. Lutz/S. R. Smith	P. Cornejo/J. Fillol	6–3	6–3			4,500
1975	J. S. Connors/I. Nastase	T. S. Okker/M. C. Riessen	6–4	7–6			4,500
1976	T. S. Okker/M. C. Riessen	P. Kronk/J. Letcher	6–4	6–4			10,000
1977	R. A. J. Hewitt/F. D. McMillan	B. E. Gottfried/R. Ramirez	6–4	6–0			13,125
1978	R. C. Lutz/S. R. Smith	M. C. Riessen/S. E. Stewart	1–6	7–5	6–3		15,500
1979	P. Fleming/J. P. McEnroe	R. C. Lutz/S. R. Smith	6–2	6–4			15,750
1980	R. C. Lutz/S. R. Smith	P. Fleming/J. P. McEnroe	7–6	3–6	6–1	3–6	6–3	18,500
1981	P. Fleming/J. P. McEnroe	H. Gunthardt/P. McNamara	w.o.				26,400
1982	K. Curren/S. Denton	V. Amaya/H. Pfister	6–2	6–7	5–7	6–2	6–4	36,000
1983	P. Fleming/J. P. McEnroe	F. Buehning/V. Winitsky	6–3	6–4	6–2		48,000
1984	J. Fitzgerald/T. Smid	S. Edberg/A. Jarryd	7–6	6–3	6–3		64,000
1985	K. Flach/R. Seguso	H. Leconte/Y. Noah	6–7	7–6	7–6	6–0	65,000
1986	A. Gomez/S. Zivojinovic	J. Nystrom/M. Wilander	4–6	6–3	6–3	4–6	6–3	72,800
1987	S. Edberg/A. Jarryd	K. Flach/R. Seguso	7–6	6–2	4–6	5–7	7–6	87,000
1988	S. Casal/E. Sanchez	R. Leach/J. Pugh	w.o.				95,000
1989	J. P. McEnroe/M. Woodforde	K. Flach/R. Seguso	6–4	4–6	6–3	6–3	104,000
1990	P. Aldrich/D. Visser	P. Annacone/D. Wheaton	6–2	7–6	6–2		142,800

#US Amateur Championships

	CHAMPIONS	RUNNERS-UP	SCORE					
1991	J. B. Fitzgerald/A. Jarryd	S. Davis/D. Pate	6–3	3–6	6–3	6–3		163,500
1992	J. Grabb/R. Reneberg	K. Jones/R. Leach	3–6	7–6	6–3	6–3		184,000
1993	K. Flach/R. Leach	M. Damm/K. Novacek	6–7	6–4	6–2			200,000
1994	J. Eltingh/P. Haarhuis	T. Woodbridge/M. Woodforde	6–3	7–6				200,000
1995	T. Woodbridge/M. Woodforde	A. O'Brien/S. Stolle	6–3	6–3				210,000
1996	T. Woodbridge/M. Woodforde	J. Eltingh/P. Haarhuis	4–6	7–6	7–6			240,000
1997	Y. Kafelnikov/D. Vacek	J. Bjorkman/N. Kulti	7–6	6–3				300,000
1998	S. Stolle/C. Suk	M. Knowles/D. Nestor	4–6	7–6	6–2			320,000
1999	S. Lareau/A. O'Brien	M. Bhupathi/L. Paes	7–6	6–4				330,000
2000	L. Hewitt/M. Mirnyi	E. Ferreira/R. Leach	6–4	5–7	7–6			340,000

WOMEN'S DOUBLES

	CHAMPIONS	RUNNERS-UP	SCORE				
1887†	E. F. Hansell/L. Knight	L. Allderdice/Church	6–0	6–4			
1888†	E. C. Roosevelt/G. W. Roosevelt	A. K. Robinson/V. Ward	3–6	6–3	6–4		
1889	M. Ballard/B. L. Townsend	M. Wright/L. Knight	6–0	6–2			
1890	E. C. Roosevelt/G. W. Roosevelt	B. L. Townsend/M. Ballard	6–1	6–2			
1891	M. E. Cahill/Mrs W. F. Morgan	E. C. Roosevelt/G. W. Roosevelt	2–6	8–6	6–4		
1892	M. E. Cahill/A. M. McKinlay	Mrs A. H. Harris/A. R. Williams	6–1	6–3			
1893	H. Butler/A. M. Terry	A. L. Schultz/Stone	6–3	6–3			
1894	J. P. Atkinson/H. R. Hellwig	A. R. Williams/A. C. Wistar	6–4	8–6	6–2		
1895	J. P. Atkinson/H. R. Hellwig	E. H. Moore/A. R. Williams	6–2	6–2	12–10		
1896	J. P. Atkinson/E. H. Moore	A. R. Williams/A. C. Wistar	6–4	7–5			
1897	J. P. Atkinson/K. Atkinson	F. Edwards/E. J. Rastall	6–2	6–1	6–1		
1898	J. P. Atkinson/K. Atkinson	C. B. Neely/M. Wimer	6–1	2–6	4–6	6–1	6–2
1899	J. W. Craven/M. McAteer	M. Banks/E. J. Rastall		6–1	6–1	7–5	
1900	H. Champlin/E. Parker	M. McAteer/M. Wimer		9–7	6–2	6–2	
1901	J. P. Atkinson/M. McAteer	M. Jones/E. H. Moore		w.o.			
1902	J. P. Atkinson/M. Jones	M. Banks/N. Closterman		6–2	7–5		
1903	E. H. Moore/C. B. Neely	M. Jones/M. Hall		6–4	6–1	6–1	
1904	M. Hall/M. G. Sutton	E. H. Moore/C. B. Neely		3–6	6–3	6–3	
1905	H. Homans/C. B. Neely	V. Maule/M. F. Oberteuffer		6–0	6–1		
1906	Mrs L. S. Coe/Mrs D. S. Platt	C. Boldt/H. Homans		6–4	6–4		
1907	C. B. Neely/M. Wimer	E. Wildey/N. Wildey		6–1	2–6	6–4	
1908	M. Curtis/Evelyn Sears	C. B. Neely/M. Steever		6–3	5–7	9–7	
1909	H. V. Hotchkiss/E. E. Rotch	D. Green/L. Moyes		6–1	6–1		
1910	H. V. Hotchkiss/E. E. Rotch	A. Browning/E. Wildey		6–4	6–4		
1911	H. V. Hotchkiss/Eleanora Sears	D. Green/F. Sutton		6–4	4–6	6–2	
1912	M. K. Browne/D. Green	Mrs M. Barger-Wallach/Mrs F. Schmitz		6–2	5–7	6–0	
1913	M. K. Browne/ Mrs R. H. Williams	D. Green/E. Wildey		12–10	2–6	6–3	
1914	M. K. Browne/ Mrs R. H. Williams	Mrs E. Raymond/E. Wildey		8–6	6–2		
1915	Eleanora Sears/ Mrs G. W. Wightman	Mrs G. L. Chapman/Mrs M. McLean		10–8	6–2		
1916	M. Bjurstedt/Eleanora Sears	Mrs E. Raymond/E. Wildey		4–6	6–2	10–8	
1917	M. Bjurstedt/Eleanora Sears	Mrs R. LeRoy/P. Walsh		6–2	6–4		
1918	E. E. Goss/M. Zinderstein	M. Bjurstedt/Mrs J. Rogge		7–5	8–6		
1919	E. E. Goss/M. Zinderstein	E. Sears/Mrs G. W. Wightman		10–8	9–7		
1920	E. E. Goss/M. Zinderstein	H. Baker/E. Tennant		13–11	4–6	6–3	
1921	M. K. Browne/ Mrs R. H. Williams	H. Gilleaudeau/Mrs L. G. Morris		6–3	6–2		
1922	Mrs J. B. Jessup/H. N. Wills	Mrs F. I. Mallory/E. Sigourney		6–4	7–9	6–3	
1923	Mrs B. C. Covell/K. McKane	E. E. Goss/Mrs G. W. Wightman		2–6	6–2	6–1	
1924	Mrs G. W. Wightman/ H. N. Wills	E. E. Goss/Mrs J. B. Jessup		6–4	6–3		
1925	M. K. Browne/H. N. Wills	Mrs T. C. Bundy/E. Ryan		6–4	6–3		
1926	E. E. Goss/E. Ryan	M. K. Browne/Mrs A. H. Chapin		3–6	6–4	12–10	
1927	Mrs L. A. Godfree/E. H. Harvey	J. Fry/B. Nuthall		6–1	4–6	6–4	
1928	Mrs G. W. Wightman/H. N. Wills	E. Cross/Mrs L. A. Harper		6–2	6–2		
1929	Mrs L. R. C. Michell/ Mrs P. H.Watson	Mrs B. C. Covell/ Mrs D. C. Shepherd-Barron		2–6	6–3	6–4	
1930	B. Nuthall/S. Palfrey	E. Cross/Mrs L. A. Harper		3–6	6–3	7–5	
1931	B. Nuthall/ Mrs E. F. Whittingstall	H. H. Jacobs/D. E. Round		6–2	6–4		

†Not recognised as an official championship

	CHAMPIONS	RUNNERS-UP	SCORE		
1932	H. H. Jacobs/S. Palfrey	A. Marble/Mrs M. Painter	8–6	6–1	
1933	F. James/B. Nuthall	Mrs F. S. Moody/E. Ryan	w.o.		
1934	H. H. Jacobs/S. Palfrey	Mrs D. B. Andrus/C. A. Babcock	4–6	6–3	6–4
1935	H. H. Jacobs/Mrs M. Fabyan	Mrs D. B. Andrus/C. A. Babcock	6–4	6–2	
1936	C. A. Babcock/Mrs J. Van Ryn	H. H. Jacobs/Mrs M. Fabyan	9–7	2–6	6–4
1937	Mrs M. Fabyan/A. Marble	C. A. Babcock/Mrs J. Van Ryn	7–5	6–4	
1938	Mrs M. Fabyan/A. Marble	J. Jedrzejowska/Mrs R. Mathieu	6–8	6–4	6–3
1939	Mrs M. Fabyan/A. Marble	Mrs S. H. Hammersley/K. E. Stammers	7–5	8–6	
1940	Mrs M. Fabyan/A. Marble	D. M. Bundy/Mrs J. Van Ryn	6–4	6–3	
1941	Mrs E. T. Cooke/M. E. Osborne	D. M. Bundy/D. J. Hart	3–6	6–1	6–4
1942	A. L. Brough/M. E. Osborne	P. M. Betz/D. J. Hart	6–7	7–5	6–0
1943	A. L. Brough/M. E. Osborne	P. M. Betz/D. J. Hart	6–1	6–3	
1944	A. L. Brough/M. E. Osborne	P. M. Betz/D. J. Hart	4–6	6–4	6–3
1945	A. L. Brough/M. E. Osborne	P. M. Betz/D. J. Hart	6–4	6–4	
1946	A. L. Brough/M. E. Osborne	Mrs P. C. Todd/Mrs M. A. Prentiss	6–1	6–3	
1947	A. L. Brough/M. E. Osborne	Mrs P. C. Todd/D. J. Hart	5–7	6–3	7–5
1948	A. L. Brough/Mrs W. D. du Pont	Mrs P. C. Todd/D. J. Hart	6–4	8–10	6–1
1949	A. L. Brough/Mrs W. D. du Pont	S. J. Fry/D. J. Hart	6–4	10–8	
1950	A. L. Brough/Mrs W. D. du Pont	S. J. Fry/D. J. Hart	6–2	6–3	
1951	S. J. Fry/D. J. Hart	N. Chaffee/Mrs P. C. Todd	6–4	6–2	
1952	S. J. Fry/D. J. Hart	A. L. Brough/M. Connolly	10–8	6–4	
1953	S. J. Fry/D. J. Hart	A. L. Brough/Mrs W. D. du Pont	6–2	7–9	9–7
1954	S. J. Fry/D. J. Hart	A. L. Brough/Mrs W. D. du Pont	6–4	6–4	
1955	A. L. Brough/Mrs W. D. du Pont	S. J. Fry/D. J. Hart	6–3	1–6	6–3
1956	A. L. Brough/Mrs W. D. du Pont	Mrs B. R. Pratt/S. J. Fry	6–3	6–0	
1957	A. L. Brough/Mrs W. D. du Pont	A. Gibson/D. R. Hard	6–2	7–5	
1958	J. M. Arth/D. R. Hard	A. Gibson/M. E. Bueno	2–6	6–3	6–4
1959	J. M. Arth/D. R. Hard	S. Moore/M. E. Bueno	6–2	6–3	
1960	M. E. Bueno/D. R. Hard	D. M. Catt/A. A. Haydon	6–1	6–1	
1961	D. R. Hard/L. Turner	E. Buding/Y. Ramirez	6–4	5–7	6–0
1962	M. E. Bueno/D. R. Hard	Mrs R. Susman/B. J. Moffitt	4–6	6–3	6–2
1963	R. Ebbern/M. Smith	M. E. Bueno/D. R. Hard	4–6	10–8	6–3
1964	Mrs R. Susman/B. J. Moffitt	M. Smith/L. Turner	3–6	6–2	6–4
1965	N. Richey/Mrs C. Graebner	Mrs R. Susman/B. J. Moffitt	6–4	6–4	
1966	M. E. Bueno/N. Richey	R. Casals/Mrs L. W. King	6–3	6–4	
1967	R. Casals/Mrs L. W. King	M. A. Eisel/Mrs D. Fales	4–6	6–3	6–4
1968#	M. E. Bueno/M. Smith	S. V. Wade/Mrs G. M. Williams	6–3	7–5	
1969#	Mrs B. M. Court/S. V. Wade	Mrs P. W. Curtis/V. Ziegenfuss	6–1	6–3	
1968	M. E. Bueno/Mrs B. M. Court	R. Casals/Mrs L. W. King	4–6	9–7	8–6
1969	F. Durr/D. R. Hard	Mrs B. M. Court/S. V. Wade	0–6	6–3	6–4
1970	Mrs B. M. Court/Mrs D. Dalton	R. Casals/S. V. Wade	6–3	6–4	
1971	R. Casals/Mrs D. Dalton	Mrs J. B. Chanfreau/F. Durr	6–3	6–3	
1972	F. Durr/B. Stove	Mrs B. M. Court/S. V. Wade	6–3	1–6	6–3
1973	Mrs B. M. Court/S. V. Wade	R. Casals/Mrs L. W. King	3–6	6–3	7–5
1974	R. Casals/Mrs L. W. King	F. Durr/B. Stove	7–6	6–7	6–4
1975	Mrs B. M. Court/S. V. Wade	R. Casals/Mrs L. W. King	7–5	2–6	7–5
1976	L. Boshoff/I. Kloss	O. Morozova/S. V. Wade	6–1	6–4	
1977	M. Navratilova/B. Stove	R. Richards/B. Stuart	6–1	7–6	
1978	Mrs L. W. King/Mrs M. Navratilova	Mrs G. E. Reid/W. M. Turnbull	7–6	6–4	
1979	B. Stove/W. M. Turnbull	Mrs L. W. King/M. Navratilova	7–5	6–3	
1980	Mrs L. W. King/M. Navratilova	P. H. Shriver/B. Stove	7–6	7–5	
1981	K. Jordan/A. E. Smith	R. Casals/W. M. Turnbull	6–3	6–3	
1982	R. Casals/W. M. Turnbull	B. Potter/S. A. Walsh	6–4	6–4	
1983	M. Navratilova/P. H. Shriver	R. Fairbank/C. Reynolds	6–7	6–1	6–3
1984	M. Navratilova/P. H. Shriver	A. E. Hobbs/W. M. Turnbull	6–2	6–4	
1985	C. Kohde-Kilsch/H. Sukova	M. Navratilova/P. H. Shriver	6–7	6–2	6–3
1986	M. Navratilova/P. H. Shriver	H. Mandlikova/W. M. Turnbull	6–4	3–6	6–3
1987	M. Navratilova/P. H. Shriver	K. Jordan/Mrs P. Smylie	5–7	6–4	6–2
1988	G. Fernandez/R. White	J. Hetherington/P. Fendick	6–4	6–1	
1989	H. Mandlikova/M. Navratilova	M. J. Fernandez/P. H. Shriver	5–7	6–4	6–4
1990	G. Fernandez/M. Navratilova	J. Novotna/H. Sukova	6–2	6–4	
1991	P. H. Shriver/N. Zvereva	J. Novotna/L. Savchenko	6–4	4–6	7–6
1992	G. Fernandez/N. Zvereva	J. Novotna/L. Savchenko Neiland	7–6	6–1	
1993	A. Sanchez-Vicario/H. Sukova	A. Coetzer/I. Gorrochategui	6–4	6–2	

#US Amateur Championships

	CHAMPIONS	RUNNERS-UP	SCORE			
1994	J. Novotna/A. Sanchez-Vicario	K. Maleeva/R. White	6–3	6–3		
1995	G. Fernandez/N. Zvereva	B. Schultz-McCarthy/R. Stubbs	7–5	6–3		*FIRST*
1996	G. Fernandez/N. Zvereva	J. Novotna/A. Sanchez-Vicario	1–6	6–1	6–4	*PRIZE*
1997	L. Davenport/J. Novotna	G Fernandez/N. Zvereva	3–6	7–6	6–2	*(US$)*
1998	M. Hingis/J. Novotna	L. Davenport/N. Zvereva	6–3	6–3		320,000
1999	S. Williams/V. Williams	C. Rubin/S. Testud	4–6	6–1	6–4	330,000
2000	J. Halard-Decugis/A. Sugiyama	C. Black/E. Likhovtseva	6–0	1–6	6–1	340,000

MIXED DOUBLES

	CHAMPIONS	RUNNERS-UP	SCORE			
1887†	J. S. Clark/Miss L. Stokes	E. D. Faries/Miss L. Knight	7–5	6–4		
1888†	J. S. Clark/Miss M. Wright	P. Johnson/Miss A. Robinson	1–6	6–5	6–4	6–3
1889†	A. E. Wright/Miss G. W. Roosevelt	C. T. Lee/Miss B. L. Townsend	6–1	6–3	3–6	6–3
1890†	R. Beach/Miss M. E. Cahill	C. T. Lee/Miss B. L. Townsend	6–2	3–6	6–2	
1891†	M. R. Wright/Miss M. E. Cahill	C. T. Lee/Miss G. W. Roosevelt	6–4	6–0	6–5	
1892	C. Hobart/Miss M. E. Cahill	R. Beach/Miss E. H. Moore	6–1	6–3		
1893	C. Hobart/Miss E. C. Roosevelt	R. N. Willson/Miss E. Bankson	6–1	4–6	10–8	6–1
1894	E. P. Fischer/Miss J. P. Atkinson	G. Remak/Mrs McFadden	8–6	6–2	6–1	
1895	E. P. Fischer/Miss J. P. Atkinson	M. Fielding/Miss A. R. Williams	4–6	6–3	6–2	
1896	E. P. Fischer/Miss J. P. Atkinson	M. Fielding/Miss A. R. Williams	6–2	6–3	6–3	
1897	D. L. Magruder/Miss L. Henson	R. A. Griffin/Miss M. Banks	6–4	6–3	7–5	
1898	E. P. Fischer/Miss C. B. Neely	J. A. Hill/Miss H. Chapman	6–2	6–4	8–6	
1899	A. L. Hoskins/Miss E. J. Rastall	J. P. Gardner/Miss J. W. Craven	6–4	6–0	ret	
1900	A. Codman/Miss M. J. Hunnewell	G. Atkinson/Miss T. Shaw	11–9	6–3	6–1	
1901	R. D. Little/Miss M. Jones	C. Stevens/Miss M. McAteer	6–4	6–4	7–5	
1902	W. C. Grant/Miss E. H. Moore	A. L. Hoskins/Miss E. J. Rastall	6–2	6–1		
1903	H. F. Allen/Miss H. Chapman	W. H. Rowland/Miss C. B. Neely	6–4	7–5		
1904	W. C. Grant/Miss E. H. Moore	F. B. Dallas/Miss M. Sutton	6–2	6–1		
1905	C. Hobart/Mrs Hobart	E. B. Dewhurst/Miss E. H. Moore	6–2	6–4		
1906	E. B. Dewhurst/Miss S. Coffin	J. B. Johnson/Miss M. Johnson	6–3	7–5		
1907	W. F. Johnson/Miss M. Sayres	H. M. Tilden/Miss N. Wildey	6–1	7–5		
1908	N. W. Niles/Miss E. E. Rotch	R. D. Little/Miss L. Hammond	6–4	4–6	6–4	
1909	W. F. Johnson/Miss H. V. Hotchkiss	R. D. Little/Miss L. Hammond	6–2	6–0		
1910	J. R. Carpenter/Miss H. V. Hotchkiss	H. M. Tilden/Miss E. Wildey	6–2	6–2		
1911	W. F. Johnson/Miss H. V. Hotchkiss	H. M. Tilden/Miss E. Wildey	6–4	6–4		
1912	R. N. Williams/Miss M. K. Browne	W. J. Clothier/Miss Evelyn Sears	6–4	2–6	11–9	
1913	W. T. Tilden/Miss M. K. Browne	C. S. Rogers/Miss D. Green	7–5	7–5		
1914	W. T. Tilden/Miss M. K. Browne	J. R. Rowland/Miss M. Myers	6–1	6–4		
1915	H. C. Johnson/Mrs G. W. Wightman	I. C. Wright/Miss M. Bjurstedt	6–0	6–1		
1916	W. E. Davis/Miss Evelyn Sears	W. T. Tilden/Miss F. A. Ballin	6–4	7–5		
1917	I. C. Wright/Miss M. Bjurstedt	W. T. Tilden/Miss F. A. Ballin	10–12	6–1	6–3	
1918	I. C. Wright/Mrs G. W. Wightman	F. B. Alexander/Miss M. Bjurstedt	6–2	6–4		
1919	V. Richards/Miss M. Zinderstein	W. T. Tilden/Miss F. A. Ballin	2–6	11–9	6–2	
1920	W. F. Johnson/Mrs G. W. Wightman	C. Biddle/Mrs F. I. Mallory	6–4	6–3		
1921	W. M. Johnston/Miss M. K. Browne	W. T. Tilden/Miss F. I. Mallory	3–6	6–4	6–3	
1922	W. T. Tilden/Mrs F. I. Mallory	H. Kinsey/Miss H. N. Wills	6–4	6–3		
1923	W. T. Tilden/Mrs F. I. Mallory	J. B. Hawkes/Miss K. McKane	6–3	2–6	10–8	
1924	V. Richards/Miss H. N. Wills	W. T. Tilden/Mrs F. I. Mallory	6–8	7–5	6–0	
1925	J. B. Hawkes/Miss K. McKane	V. Richards/Miss E. H. Harvey	6–2	6–4		
1926	J. Borotra/Miss E. Ryan	R. Lacoste/Mrs G. W. Wightman	6–4	7–5		
1927	H. Cochet/Miss E. Bennett	R. Lacoste/Mrs G. W. Wightman	2–6	6–0	6–2	
1928	J. B. Hawkes/Miss H. N. Wills	G. Moon/Miss E. Cross	6–3	6–3		
1929	G. M. Lott/Miss B. Nuthall	H. W. Austin/Mrs B. C. Lovell	6–3	6–3		
1930	W. L. Allison/Miss E. Cross	F. X. Shields/Miss M. Morrill	6–4	6–4		
1931	G. M. Lott/Miss B. Nuthall	W. L. Allison/Mrs L. A. Harper	6–3	6–3		
1932	F. J. Perry/Miss S. Palfrey	H. E. Vines/Miss H. H. Jacobs	6–3	7–5		
1933	H. E. Vines/Miss E. Ryan	G. M. Lott/Miss S. Palfrey	11–9	6–1		
1934	G. M. Lott/Miss H. H. Jacobs	L. R. Stoefen/Miss E. Ryan	4–6	13–11	6–2	
1935	E. Maier/Mrs M. Fabyan	R. Menzel/Miss K. E. Stammers	6–3	3–6	6–4	
1936	G. Mako/Miss A. Marble	J. D. Budge/Mrs M. Fabyan	6–3	6–2		
1937	J. D. Budge/Mrs M. Fabyan	Y. Petra/Mme S. Henrotin	6–2	8–10	6–0	
1938	J. D. Budge/Miss A. Marble	J. E. Bromwich/Miss T. D. Coyne	6–1	6–2		
1939	H. C. Hopman/Miss A. Marble	E. T. Cooke/Mrs M. Fabyan	9–7	6–1		
1940	R. L. Riggs/Miss A. Marble	J. A. Kramer/Miss D. M. Bundy	9–7	6–1		

†Not recognised as an official championship

	CHAMPIONS	RUNNERS-UP	SCORE		
1941	J. A. Kramer/Mrs E. T. Cooke	R. L. Riggs/Miss P. M. Betz	4–6	6–4	6–4
1942	F. R. Schroeder/Miss A. L. Brough	A. D. Russell/Mrs P. C. Todd	3–6	6–1	6–4
1943	W. F. Talbert/Miss M. E. Osborne	F. Segura/Miss P. M. Betz	10–8	6–4	
1944	W. F. Talbert/Miss M. E. Osborne	W. D. McNeill/Miss D. M. Bundy	6–2	6–3	
1945	W. F. Talbert/Miss M. E. Osborne	R. Falkenburg/Miss D. J. Hart	6–4	6–4	
1946	W. F. Talbert/Miss M. E. Osborne	R. Kimbrell/Miss A. L. Brough	6–3	6–4	
1947	J. Bromwich/Miss A. L. Brough	F. Segura/Miss G. Morgan	6–3	6–1	
1948	T. P. Brown/Miss A. L. Brough	W. F. Talbert/Mrs W. D. du Pont	6–4	6–4	
1949	E. W. Sturgess/Miss A. L. Brough	W. F. Talbert/Mrs W. D. du Pont	4–6	6–3	7–5
1950	K. B. McGregor/Mrs W. D. du Pont	F. A. Sedgman/Miss D. J. Hart	6–4	3–6	6–3
1951	F. A. Sedgman/Miss D. J. Hart	M. G. Rose/Miss S. J. Fry	6–3	6–2	
1952	F. A. Sedgman/Miss D. J. Hart	L. A. Hoad/Mrs T. C. Long	6–3	7–5	
1953	E. V. Seixas/Miss D. J. Hart	R. N. Hartwig/Miss J. A. Sampson	6–2	4–6	6–4
1954	E. V. Seixas/Miss D. J. Hart	K. R. Rosewall/Mrs W. D. du Pont	4–6	6–1	6–1
1955	E. V. Seixas/Miss D. J. Hart	G. Mulloy/Miss S. J. Fry	7–5	5–7	6–2
1956	K. R. Rosewall/Mrs W. D. du Pont	L. A. Hoad/Miss D. R. Hard	9–7	6–1	
1957	K. Nielsen/Miss A. Gibson	R. N. Howe/Miss D. R. Hard	6–3	9–7	
1958	N. A. Fraser/Mrs W. D. du Pont	A. Olmedo/Miss M. E. Bueno	6–3	3–6	9–7
1959	N. A. Fraser/Mrs W. D. du Pont	R. Mark/Miss J. Hopps	7–5	13–15	6–2
1960	N. A. Fraser/Mrs W. D. du Pont	A. Palafox/Miss M. E. Bueno	6–3	6–2	
1961	R. Mark/Miss M. Smith	R. D. Ralston/Miss D. R. Hard	w.o.		
1962	F. S. Stolle/Miss M. Smith	F. Froehling/Miss L. Turner	7–5	6–2	
1963	K. Fletcher/Miss M. Smith	E. Rubinoff/Miss J. Tegart	3–6	8–6	6–2
1964	J. D. Newcombe/Miss M. Smith	E. Rubinoff/Miss J. Tegart	10–8	4–6	6–3
1965	F. S. Stolle/Miss M. Smith	F. Froehling/Miss J. Tegart	6–2	6–2	
1966	O. K. Davidson/Mrs D. Fales	E. Rubinoff/Miss C. A. Aucamp	6–1	6–3	
1967	O. K. Davidson/Mrs L. W. King	S. R. Smith/Miss R. Casals	6–3	6–2	
1968#	P. W. Curtis/Miss M. A. Eisel	R. N. Perry/Miss T. A. Fretz	6–4	7–5	
1969#	P. Sullivan/Miss P. S. A. Hogan	T. Addison/Miss K. Pigeon	6–4	2–6	12–10
1968		Not held			
1969	M. C. Riessen/Mrs B. M. Court	R. D. Ralston/Miss F. Durr	7–5	6–3	
1970	M. C. Riessen/Mrs B. M. Court	F. D. McMillan/Mrs D. Dalton	6–4	6–4	
1971	O. K. Davidson/Mrs L. W. King	R. R. Maud/Miss B. Stove	6–3	7–5	
1972	M. C. Riessen/Mrs B. M. Court	I. Nastase/Miss R. Casals	6–3	7–5	
1973	O. K. Davidson/Mrs L. W. King	M. C. Riessen/Miss B. M. Court	6–3	3–6	7–6
1974	G. Masters/Miss P. Teeguarden	J. S. Connors/Miss C. M. Evert	6–1	7–6	
1975	R. L. Stockton/Miss R. Casals	F. S. Stolle/Mrs L. W. King	6–3	7–6	
1976	P. Dent/Mrs L. W. King	F. D. McMillan/Miss B. Stove	3–6	6–2	7–5
1977	F. D. McMillan/Miss B. Stove	V. Gerulaitis/Mrs L. W. King	6–2	3–6	6–3
1978	F. D. McMillan/Miss B. Stove	R. O. Ruffels/Mrs L. W. King	6–3	7–6	
1979	R. A. J. Hewitt/Miss G. Stevens	F. D. McMillan/Miss B. Stove	6–3	7–5	
1980	M. C. Riessen/Miss W. M. Turnbull	F. D. McMillan/Miss B. Stove	7–5	6–2	
1981	K. Curren/Miss A. E. Smith	S. Denton/Miss J. Russell	6–4	7–6	
1982	K. Curren/Miss A. E. Smith	F. Taygan/Miss B. Potter	6–7	7–6	7–6
1983	J. Fitzgerald/Miss E. Sayers	F. Taygan/Miss B. Potter	3–6	6–3	6–4
1984	Tom Gullikson/Miss M. Maleeva	J. Fitzgerald/Miss E. Sayers	2–6	7–5	6–4
1985	H. Gunthardt/Miss M. Navratilova	J. Fitzgerald/Mrs P. Smylie	6–3	6–4	
1986	S. Casal/Miss R. Reggi	P. Fleming/Miss M. Navratilova	6–4	6–4	
1987	E. Sanchez/Miss M. Navratilova	P. Annacone/Miss B. Nagelsen	6–4	6–7	7–6
1988	J. Pugh/Miss J. Novotna	P. McEnroe/Mrs P. Smylie	7–5	6–3	
1989	S. Cannon/Miss R. White	R. Leach/Miss M. McGrath	3–6	6–2	7–5
1990	T. Woodbridge/Mrs P. Smylie	J. Pugh/Miss N. Zvereva	6–4	6–2	
1991	T. Nijssen/Miss M. Bollegraf	E. Sanchez/Miss A. Sanchez-Vicario	6–2	7–6	
1992	M. Woodforde/Miss N. Provis	T. Nijssen/Miss H. Sukova	4–6	6–3	6–3
1993	T. Woodbridge/Miss H. Sukova	M. Woodforde/Miss M. Navratilova	6–3	7–6	

					FIRST
					PRIZE
					(US$)
1994	P. Galbraith/Miss E. Reinach	T. Woodbridge/Miss J. Novotna	6–2	6–4	
1995	M. Lucena/Miss M. McGrath	C. Suk/Miss G. Fernandez	6–4	6–4	
1996	P. Galbraith/Miss L. Raymond	R. Leach/Miss M. Bollegraf	7–6	7–6	
1997	R. Leach/Miss M. Bollegraf	P. Albano/Miss M. Paz	3–6	7–5	7–6	100,000
1998	M. Mirnyi/Miss S. Williams	P. Galbraith/Miss L. Raymond	6–2	6–2	120,000
1999	M. Bhupathi/Miss A. Sugiyama	D. Johnson/Miss K. Po	6–4	6–4	124,000
2000	J. Palmer/Miss A. Sanchez-Vicario	M. Mirnyi/Miss A. Kournikova	6–4	6–3	126,000

#US Amateur Championships

GRAND SLAMS

The Grand Slam denotes holding the four championship titles of Australia, France, Wimbledon and the United States in the same year (shown in bold below). The list also includes consecutive wins, not in the same year.

MEN'S SINGLES
J. D. Budge: Wimbledon, US 1937, **Australia, France, Wimbledon, US 1938**
R. G. Laver: **Australia, France, Wimbledon, US 1962**
R. G. Laver: **Australia, France, Wimbledon, US 1969**

WOMEN'S SINGLES
Miss M. Connolly: Wimbledon, US 1952, **Australia, France, Wimbledon, US 1953**
Mrs B. M. Court: US 1969, **Australia, France, Wimbledon, US 1970,** Australia 1971
Miss M. Navratilova: Wimbledon, US, Australia 1983, France, Wimbledon, US 1984
Miss S. Graf: **Australia, France, Wimbledon, US 1988,** Australia 1989, France, Wimbledon, US 1993, Australia 1994

MEN'S DOUBLES
F. A. Sedgman: (With J. E. Bromwich) US 1950, **(with K. McGregor) Australia, France, Wimbledon, US 1951,** Australia, France, Wimbledon 1952
K. McGregor: **(With F. A. Sedgman) Australia, France, Wimbledon, US 1951,** Australia, France, Wimbledon 1952

WOMEN'S DOUBLES
Miss A. L. Brough: (with Mrs W. du Pont) France, Wimbledon, US 1949, (with Miss D. J. Hart) Australia 1950
Miss M. E. Bueno: **(with Miss C. C. Truman) Australia 1960, (with Miss D. R. Hard) France, Wimbledon, US 1960**
Miss M. Navratilova/Miss P. H. Shriver: Wimbledon, US, Australia 1983, **France, Wimbledon, US, Australia 1984,** France 1985; *Wimbledon, US 1986, Australia, France 1987
Miss G. Fernandez/Miss N. Zvereva: France, Wimbledon, US 1992, Australia, France, Wimbledon 1993
Miss M. Hingis: **(with Miss M. Lucic) Australia 1998, (with Miss J. Novotna) France, Wimbledon, US 1998**
* Miss Navratilova also won France 1986 with Miss A. Temesvari.

MIXED DOUBLES
Miss M. Smith: (With F. S. Stolle) US 1962, **(with K. N. Fletcher) Australia, France, Wimbledon, US 1963,** Australia, France 1964
K. N. Fletcher: **(With Miss M. Smith) Australia, France, Wimbledon, US 1963,** Australia, France 1964
O. K. Davidson: (With Mrs D. Fales) US 1966, **(with Miss L. R. Turner) Australia 1967, (with Mrs L. W. King) France, Wimbledon, US 1967**
Mrs L. W. King: (With O. K. Davidson) France, Wimbledon, US 1967, (with R. D. Crealy) Australia 1968

JUNIOR SINGLES
E. H. Buchholz: **Australia, France, Wimbledon, US 1958** (Note: The US event was not then conducted as an international event and entries at all four were by nomination of National Associations.)
S. Edberg: **France, Wimbledon, US, Australia 1983** (Note: All Championship events.)

DAVIS CUP

The International Men's Team Championship of the World was initiated in 1900 when the British Isles, then comprising Great Britain and Ireland, challenged the United States for the trophy presented by Dwight F. Davis. The competition was enlarged in 1904 when Belgium and France took part. Each tie has comprised two players engaged in reverse singles plus a doubles match with the best of five sets throughout. In 1989 the tie-break was introduced for all sets except the fifth, in all matches.

From 1900 to 1971 the Champion Nation stood out until challenged by the winner of a knock-out competition between the challenging nations and had the choice of venue. Thereafter the Champion Nation played through. The format was changed in 1981, when the competition became sponsored by NEC and prize money was introduced. The winner of the World Group of the 16 strongest nations became the Champion Nation. Other nations competed in zonal groups, with eight earning the right to play against the eight first round losers in the World Group for places alongside the first round winners of the World Group in the following year's competition. A Zonal Group Three, in which nations from each geographic region play one another on a round-robin basis during one week at one venue to decide promotion to Zonal Group Two, was introduced in 1992. Entries passed the 100 mark for the 1993 competition when 101 nations entered. By 2000 the total had risen to 136.

CHALLENGE ROUNDS (in playing order)

1900 USA (Capt. Dwight Davis) **d.** British Isles (Capt. Arthur Gore) **3–0**, *Boston:* M. D. Whitman d. A. W. Gore 6–1 6–3 6–2; D. F. Davis d. E. D. Black 4–6 6–2 6–4 6–4; Davis/H. Ward d. Black/H. Roper Barrett 6–4 6–4 6–4; Davis div'd with Gore 9–7 9–9.

1901 Not held

1902 USA (Capt: Malcolm Whitman) **d.** British Isles (Capt: William Collins) **3–2**, *Brooklyn, New York:* W. A. Larned lost to R. F. Doherty 6–2 6–3 3–6 4–6 4–6; M. D. Whitman d. J. Pim 6–1 6–1 1–6 6–0; Larned d. Pim 6–3 6–2 6–3; Whitman d. R. F. Doherty 6–1 7–5 6–4; D. F. Davis/H. Ward lost to R. F./H. L. Doherty 6–3 8–10 3–6 4–6.

1903 British Isles (Capt: William Collins) **d. USA** (Capt: William Larned) **4–1**, *Boston:* H. L. Doherty d. R. D. Wrenn 6–0 6–3 6–4; R. F. Doherty lost to W. A. Larnedret'd; R. F./H. L. Doherty d. R. D./G. L. Wrenn 7–5 9–7 2–6 6–3; H. L. Doherty d. Larned 6–3 6–8 6–0 2–6 7–5; R. F. Doherty d. R. D. Wrenn 6–4 3–6 6–3 6–8 6–4.

1904 British Isles (Capt: William Collins) **d. Belgium** (Capt: Paul De Borman) **5–0**, *Wimbledon:* H. L. Doherty d. P. De Borman 6–4 6–1 6–1; F. L. Riseley d. W.Lemaire 6–1 6–4 6–2; R. F./H. L. Doherty d. De Borman/Lemaire 6–0 6–1 6–3; H. L. Doherty w.o. Lemaire; Riseley d. De Borman 4–6 6–2 8–6 7–5.

1905 British Isles (Capt: William Collins) **d. USA** (Capt: Paul Dashiel) **5–0**, *Wimbledon:* H. L. Doherty d. H. Ward 7–9 4–6 6–1 6–2 6–0; S. H. Smith d. W. A. Larned 6–4 6–4 5–7 6–4; R. F./H. L. Doherty d. Ward/B. Wright 8–10 6–2 6–2 4–6 8–6; Smith d. W. J. Clothier 4–6 6–1 6–4 6–3; H. L. Doherty d. Larned 6–4 2–6 6–8 6–4 6–2.

1906 British Isles (Capt: William Collins) **d. USA** (Capt: Beals Wright) **5–0**, *Wimbledon:* S. H. Smith d. R. D. Little 6–4 6–4 6–1; H. L. Doherty d. H. Ward 6–2 8–6 6–3; R. F./H. L. Doherty d. Little/Ward 3–6 11–9 9–7 6–1; Smith d. Ward 6–1 6–0 6–4; H. L. Doherty d. Little 3–6 6–3 6–8 6–1 6–3.

1907 Australasia (Capt: Norman Brookes) **d.** British Isles (Capt: Alfred Hickson) **3–2**, *Wimbledon:* N. E. Brookes d. A. W. Gore 7–5 6–1 7–5; A. F. Wilding d. H. Roper Barrett 1–6 6–4 6–3 7–5; Brookes/Wilding lost to Gore/Roper Barrett 6–3 6–4 5–7 2–6 11–13; Wilding lost to Gore 6–3 3–6 5–7 2–6; Brookes d. Roper Barrett 6–2 6–0 6–3.

1908 Australasia (Capt: Norman Brookes) **d. USA** (Capt: Beals Wright) **3–2**, *Melbourne:* N. E. Brookes d. F. B. Alexander 5–7 9–7 6–2 4–6 6–3; A. F. Wilding lost to B. Wright 6–3 5–7 3–6 1–6; Brookes/Wilding d. Alexander/Wright 6–4 6–2 5–7 1–6 6–4; Brookes lost to Wright 6–0 6–3 5–7 2–6 10–12; Wilding d. Alexander 6–3 6–4 6–1.

1909 Australasia (Capt: Norman Brookes) **d. USA** (Capt: Maurice McLoughlin) **5–0**, *Sydney:* N. E. Brookes d. M. E. McLoughlin 6–2 6–2 6–4; A. F. Wilding d. M. H. Long 6–2 7–5 6–1; Brookes/Wilding d. Long/McLoughlin 12–10 9–7 6–3; Brookes d. Long 6–4 7–5 8–6; Wilding d. McLoughlin 3–6 8–6 6–2 6–3.

1910 Not held

1911 Australasia (Capt: Norman Brookes) **d. USA** (Capt: William Larned) **5–0**, *Christchurch, NZ:* N. E. Brookes d. B. Wright 6–4 2–6 6–3 6–3; R. W. Heath d. W. A. Larned 2–6 6–1 7–5 6–2; Brookes/A. W. Dunlop d. Wright/M. E. McLoughlin 6–4 5–7 7–5 6–4; Brookes d. McLoughlin 6–4 3–6 4–6 6–3 6–4; Heath w.o. Wright.

1912 British Isles (Capt: Charles Dixon) **d. Australasia** (Capt: Norman Brookes) **3–2**, *Melbourne:* J. C. Parke d. N. E. Brookes 8–6 6–3 5–7 6–2; C. P. Dixon d. R. W. Heath 5–7 6–4 6–4 6–4; A. E. Beamish/Parke lost Brookes/A. W. Dunlop 4–6 1–6 5–7; Dixon lost to Brookes 2–6 4–6 4–6; Parke d. Heath 6–2 6–4 6–4.

1913 USA (Capt: Harold Hackett) **d.** British Isles (Capt: Roger McNair) **3–2**, *Wimbledon:* M. E. McLoughlin lost to J. C. Parke 10–8 5–7 4–6 6–1 5–7; R. N. Williams d. C. P. Dixon 8–6 3–6 6–2 1–6 7–5; H. Hackett/McLoughlin d. Dixon/H. Roper Barrett 5–7 6–1 2–6 7–5 6–4; McLoughlin d. Dixon 8–6 6–3 6–2; Williams lost to Parke 2–6 7–5 7–5 4–6 2–6.

1914 Australasia (Capt: Norman Brookes) **d. USA** (Capt: Maurice McLoughlin) **3–2**, *Forest Hills, NY:* A. F. Wilding d. R. N. Williams 7–5 6–2 6–3; N. E. Brookes lost to M. E. McLoughlin 15–17 3–6 3–6; Brookes/Wilding d. T. C. Bundy/McLoughlin 6–3 8–6 9–7; Brookes d. Williams 6–1 6–2 8–10 6–3; Wilding lost to McLoughlin 2–6 3–6 6–2 2–6.

1915–18 Not held

1919 Australasia (Capt: Norman Brookes) **d.** British Isles (Capt: Algernon Kingscote) **4–1**, *Sydney:* G. L. Patterson d. A. H. Lowe 6–4 6–3 2–6 6–3; J. O. Anderson lost to A. R. F. Kingscote 5–7 2–6 4–6; N. E. Brookes/Patterson d. A. E. Beamish/Kingscote 6–0 6–0 6–2; Patterson d. Kingscote 6–4 6–4 8–6; Anderson d. Lowe 6–4 5–7 6–3 4–6 12–10.

1920 USA (Capt: Sam Hardy) **d. Australasia** (Capt: Norman Brookes) **5–0**, *Auckland:* W. T. Tilden d. N. E. Brookes 10–8 6–4 1–6 6–4; W. M. Johnston d. G. L. Patterson 3–6 1–6 6–1; Johnston/Tilden d. Brookes/Patterson 4–6 6–4 6–0 6–4; Johnston d. Brookes 5–7 7–5 6–3 6–3; Tilden d. Patterson 5–7 6–2 6–3 6–3.

1921 USA (Capt: Norris Williams) **d. Japan** (Capt: Ichiya Kumagae) **5–0**, *Forest Hills, NY:* W. M. Johnston d. I. Kumagae 6–2 6–4 6–2; W. T. Tilden d. Z. Schimidzu 5–7 4–6 7–5 6–2 6–1; W. Washburn/R. N. Williams d. Kumagae/Shimizdu 6–2 7–5 4–6 7–5; Tilden d. Kumagae; 9–7 6–4 6–1; Johnston d. Shimizdu 6–3 5–7 6–2 6–4.

1922 USA (Capt: Norris Williams) **d. Australasia** (Capt: James Anderson) **4–1**, *Forest Hills, NY:* W. T. Tilden d. G. L. Patterson 7–5 10–8 6–0; W. M. Johnston d. J. O. Anderson 6–1 6–2 6–3; V. Richards/Tilden lost to P. O'Hara Wood/Patterson 4–6 0–6 3–6; Johnston d. Patterson 6–2 6–2 6–1; Tilden d. Anderson 6–4 5–7 3–6 6–4 6–2.

1923 USA (Capt: Norris Williams) **d. Australia** (Capt: Garald Patterson) **4–1**, *Forest Hills, NY:* W. M. Johnston lost to J. O. Anderson 6–4 2–6 6–2 5–7 2–6; W. T. Tilden d. J. B. Hawkes 6–4 6–2 6–1; Tilden/R. N. Williams d. Anderson/Hawkes 17–15 11–13 2–6 6–3 6–2; Johnston d. Hawkes 6–0 6–2 6–1; Tilden d. Anderson 6–2 6–3 1–6 7–5.

1924 USA (Capt: Norris Williams) **d. Australia** (Capt: Gerald Patterson) **5–0**, *Philadelphia:* W. T. Tilden d. G. L. Patterson 6–4 6–2 6–3; V. Richards d. P. O'Hara Wood 6–3 6–2 6–4; W. M. Johnston/Tilden d. O'Hara Wood/Patterson 5 7 6 3 6 4 6 1; Tilden d. O'Hara Wood 6–2 6–1 6–1; Richards d. Patterson 6–3 7–5 6–4.

1925 USA (Capt: Norris Williams) **d. France** (Capt: Max Decugis) **5–0**, *Philadelphia:* W. T. Tilden d. J. Borotra 4–6 6–0 2–6 9–7 6–4; W. M. Johnston d. R. Lacoste 6–1 6–1 6–8 6–3; V. Richards/R. N. Williams d. Borotra/Lacoste 6–4 6–4 6–3; Tilden d. Lacoste 3–6 10–12 8–6 7–5 6–2; Johnston d. Borotra 6–1 6–4 6–0.

1926 USA (Capt: Norris Williams) **d. France** (Capt: Pierre Gillou) **4–1**, *Philadelphia:* W. M. Johnston d. R. Lacoste 6–0 6–4 0–6 6–0; W. T. Tilden d. J. Borotra 6–2 6–3 6–3; V. Richards/R. N. Williams d. J. Brugnon/H. Cochet 6–4 6–4 6–2; Johnston d. Borotra 8–6 6–4 9–7; Tilden lost to Lacoste 6–4 4–6 6–8 6–8.

1927 France (Capt: Pierre Gillou) **d. USA** (Capt: Charles Garland) **3–2**, *Philadelphia:* R. Lacoste d. W. M. Johnston 6–3 6–2 6–2; H. Cochet lost to W. T. Tilden 4–6 6–2 2–6 6–8; J. Borotra/J. Brugnon lost to F. Hunter/Tilden 6–3 3–6 3–6 6–4 0–6; Lacoste d. Tilden 6–4 4–6 6–3 6–3; Cochet d. Johnston 6–4 4–6 6–2 6–4.

1928 France (Capt: Pierre Gillou) **d. USA** (Capt: Joseph Wear) **4–1**, *Paris:* R. Lacoste lost to W. T. Tilden 6–1 4–6 4–6 6–2 3–6; H. Cochet d. J. Hennessey 5–7 9–7 6–3 6–0; J. Borotra/Cochet d. F. Hunter/Tilden 6–4 6–8 7–5 4–6 6–2; Lacoste d. Hennessey 4–6 6–1 7–5 6–3; Cochet d. Tilden 9–7 8–6 6–4.

1929 France (Capt: Pierre Gillou) **d. USA** (Capt: Fitz-Eugene Dixon) **3–2**, *Paris:* H. Cochet d. W. T. Tilden 6–3 6–1 6–2; J. Borotra d. G. M. Lott 6–1 3–6 6–4 7–5; Borotra/Cochet lost to W. Allison/J. Van Ryn 1–6 6–8 4–6; Cochet d. Lott 6–1 3–6 6–0 6–3; Borotra lost to Tilden 6–4 1–6 4–6 5–7.

1930 France (Capt: Pierre Gillou) **d. USA** (Capt: Fitz-Eugene Dixon) **4–1**, *Paris:* J. Borotra lost to W. T. Tilden 6–2 5–7 4–6 5–7; H. Cochet d. G. M. Lott 6–4 6–2 6–2; J. Brugnon/Cochet d. W. Allison/J. Van Ryn 6–3 7–5 1–6 6–2; Borotra d. Lott 5–7 6–3 2–6 6–2 8–6; Cochet d. Tilden 4–6 6–3 6–1 7–5.

1931 France (Capt: Rene Lacoste) **d. Great Britain** (Capt: Herbert Barrett) **3–2**, *Paris:* H. Cochet d. H. W. Austin 3–6 11–9 6–2 6–4; J. Borotra lost to F. J. Perry 6–4 8–10 0–6 6–4 4–6; J. Brugnon/Cochet d. G. P Hughes/C. H. Kingsley 6–1 5–7 6–3 8–6; Cochet d. Perry 6–4 1–6 9–7 6–3; Borotra lost to Austin 5–7 3–6 6–3 5–7.

1932 France (Capt: Rene Lacoste) **d. USA** (Capt: Bernon Prentice) **3–2**, *Paris:* H. Cochet d. W. Allison 5–7 7–5 3–6 7–5 6–2; J. Borotra d. H. E. Vines 6–4 6–2 2–6 6–4; J. Brugnon/Cochet lost to Allison/J. Van Ryn 3–6 13–11 5–7 6–4 4–6; Borotra d. Allison 1–6 3–6 6–4 6–2 7–5; Cochet lost to Vines 6–4 6–0 5–7 6–8 2–6.

1933 Great Britain (Capt: Herbert Barrett) **d. France** (Capt: Rere Lacoste) **3–2**, *Paris:* H. W. Austin d. A. Merlin 6–3 6–4 6–0; F. J. Perry d. H. Cochet 8–10 6–4 8–6 3–6 6–1; G. P. Hughes/H. G. N. Lee lost to J. Borotra/J. Brugnon 3–6 6–8 2–6; Austin lost to Cochet 7–5 4–6 6–4 4–6 4–6; Perry d. Merlin 4–6 8–6 6–2 7–5.

1934 Great Britain (Capt: Herbert Barrett) **d. USA** (Capt: Norris Williams) **4–1**, *Wimbledon:* F. J. Perry d. S. B. Wood 6–1 4–6 5–7 6–0 6–3; H. W. Austin d. F. X. Shields 6–4 6–4 6–1; G. P. Hughes/H. G. N. Lee lost to G. M. Lott/L. Stoefen 5–7 0–6 6–4 7–9; Perry d. Shields 6–4 4–6 6–2 15–13; Austin d. Wood 6–4 6–0 6–8 6–3.

1935 Great Britain (Capt: Herbert Barrett) **d. USA** (Capt: Joseph Wear) **5–0**, *Wimbledon:* F. J. Perry d. J. D. Budge 6–0 6–8 6–3 6–4; H. W. Austin d. W. Allison 6–2 2–6 4–6 6–3 7–5; G. P. Hughes/C. R. D. Tuckey d. Allison/J. Van Ryn 6–2 1–6 6–8 6–3 6–3; Perry d. Allison 4–6 6–4 7–5 6–3; Austin d. Budge 6–2 6–4 6–8 7–5.

1936 Great Britain (Capt: Herbert Barrett) **d. Australia** (Capt: Cliff Sproule) **3–2**, *Wimbledon:* H. W. Austin d. J. H. Crawford 4–6 6–3 6–1 6–1; F. J. Perry d. A. K. Quist 6–1 4–6 7–5 6–2; G. P. Hughes/C. R. D. Tuckey lost to Crawford/Quist 4–6 6–2 5–7 8–10; Austin lost to Quist 4–6 6–3 7–5 6–2; Perry d. Crawford 6–2 3–6 6–3.

1937 USA (Capt: Walter Pate) **d. Great Britain** (Capt: Herbert Barrett) **4–1**, *Wimbledon:* F. A. Parker lost to H. W. Austin 3–6 2–6 5–7; J. D. Budge d. C. E. Hare 15–13 6–1 6–2; Budge/G. Mako d. C. R. D. Tuckey/F. H. D. Wilde 6–3 7–5 7–9 12–10; Parker d. Hare 6–2 6–4 6–2; Budge d. Austin 8–6 3–6 6–4 6–3.

1938 USA (Capt: Walter Pate) **d. Australia** (Capt: Harry Hopman) **3–2**, *Philadelphia:* R. L. Riggs d. A. K. Quist 4–6 6–0 8–6 6–1; J. D. Budge d. J. E. Bromwich 6–2 6–3 4–6 7–5; Budge/G. Mako lost to Bromwich/Quist 6–0 3–6 4–6 2–6; Budge d. Quist 8–6 6–1 6–2; Riggs lost to Bromwich 4–6 6–4 0–6 2–6.

1939 Australia (Capt: Harry Hopman) **d. USA** (Capt: Walter Pate) **3–2**, *Philadelphia:* J. E. Bromwich lost to R. L. Riggs 4–6 0–6 5–7; A. K. Quist lost to F. A. Parker 3–6 6–2 4–6 6–1 5–7; Bromwich/Quist d. J. R. Hunt/J. Kramer 5–7 6–2 7–5 6–2; Quist d. Riggs 6–1 6–4 3–6 3–6 6–4; Bromwich d. Parker 6–0 6–3 6–1.

1940–45 Not held

1946 USA (Capt: Walter Pate) **d. Australia** (Capt: Gerald Patterson) **5–0**, *Melbourne:* F. R. Schroeder d. J. E. Bromwich 3–6 6–1 6–2 0–6 6–3; J. Kramer d. D. Pails 8–6 6–2 9–7; Kramer/Schroeder d. Bromwich/A. K. Quist 6–2 7–5 6–4; Kramer d. Bromwich 8–6 6–4 6–4; G Mulloy d. Pails 6–3 6–3 6–4.

1947 USA (Capt: Alrick Man) **d. Australia** (Capt: Roy Cowling) **4–1**, *Forest Hills, NY:* J. Kramer d. D. Pails 6–2 6–1 6–2; F. R. Schroeder d. J. E. Bromwich 6–4 5–7 6–3 6–3; Kramer/Schroeder lost to Bromwich/C. F. Long 4–6 6–2 2–6 4–6; Schroeder d. Pails 6–3 8–6 4–6 9–11 10–8; Kramer d. Bromwich 6–3 6–2 6–2.

1948 USA (Capt: Alrick Man) **d. Australia** (Capt: Adrian Quist) **5–0**, *Forest Hills, NY:* F. A. Parker d. O. W. Sidwell 6–4 6–4 6–4; F. R. Schroeder d. A. K. Quist 6–3 4–6 6–0 6–0; G. Mulloy/W. F. Talbert d. C. F. Long/Sidwell 8–6 9–7 2–6 7–5; Parker d. Quist 6–2 6–2 6–3; Schroeder d. Sidwell 6–2 6–1 6–1.

1949 USA (Capt: Alrick Man) **d. Australia** (Capt: John Bromwich) **4–1**, *Forest Hills, NY:* F. R. Schroeder d. O. W. Sidwell 6–1 5–7 4–6 6–2 6–3; R. A. Gonzales d. F. A. Sedgman 8–6 6–4 9–7; G. Mulloy/W. F. Talbert lost to J. E. Bromwich/Sidwell 6–3 6–4 8–10 7–9 7–9; Schroeder d. Sedgman 6–4 6–3 6–3; Gonzales d. Sidwell 6–1 6–3 6–3.

1950 Australia (Capt: Harry Hopman) **d. USA** (Capt: Alrick Man) **4–1**, *Forest Hills, NY:* F. A. Sedgman d. T. Brown 6–0 8–6 9–7; K. McGregor d. F. R. Schroeder 13–11 6–3 6–4; J. E. Bromwich/Sedgman d. G. Mulloy/Schroeder 4–6 6–4 6–2 4–6; Sedgman d. Schroeder 6–2 6–2 6–2; McGregor lost to Brown 11–9 10–8 9–11 1–6 4–6.

1951 Australia (Capt: Harry Hopman) **d. USA** (Capt: Frank Shields) **3–2**, *Sydney:* M. G. Rose lost to E. V. Seixas 3–6 4–6 7–9; F. A. Sedgman d. F. R. Schroeder 6–4 6–3 4–6 6–4; K. McGregor/Sedgman d. Schroeder/M. A. Trabert 6–2 9–7 6–3; Rose lost to Schroeder 4–6 11–13 5–7; Sedgman d. Seixas 6–4 6–2.

1952 Australia (Capt: Harry Hopman) **d. USA** (Capt: Vic Seixas) **4–1**, *Adelaide:* F. A. Sedgman d. E. V. Seixas 6–3 6–4 6–3; K. McGregor d. M. A. Trabert 11–9 6–4 6–1; McGregor/Sedgman d. Seixas/Trabert 6–3 6–4 1–6 6–3; Sedgman d. Trabert 7–5 6–4 10–8; McGregor lost to Seixas 3–6 6–8 8–6 3–6.

1953 Australia (Capt: Harry Hopman) **d. USA** (Capt: Bill Talbert) **3–2**, *Melbourne:* L. A. Hoad d. E. V. Seixas 6–4 6–2 6–3; K. R. Rosewall lost to M. A. Trabert 3–6 4–6 4–6; R. Hartwig/Hoad lost to Seixas/Trabert 2–6 4–6 4–6; Hoad d. Trabert 13–11 6–3 2–6 3–6 7–5; Rosewall d. Seixas 6–2 2–6 6–3 6–4.

1954 USA (Capt: Bill Talbert) **d. Australia** (Capt: Harry Hopman) **3–2**, *Sydney:* M. A. Trabert d. L. A. Hoad 6–4 2–6 12–10 6–3; E. V. Seixas d. K. R. Rosewall 8–6 6–8 6–4 6–3; Seixas/Trabert d. Hoad/Rosewall 6–2 4–6 6–2 10–8; Trabert lost to Rosewall 7–9 5–7 3–6; Seixas lost to R. Hartwig 6–4 3–6 2–6 3–6.

1955 Australia (Capt: Harry Hopman) **d. USA** (Capt: Bill Talbert) **5–0**, *Forest Hills, NY:* K. R. Rosewall d. E. V. Seixas 6–3 10–8 4–6 6–2; L. A. Hoad d. M. A. Trabert 4–6 6–3 6–3 8–6; R. Hartwig/Hoad d. Seixas/Trabert 12–14 6–4 6–3 3–6 7–5; Rosewall d. H. Richardson 6–4 3–6 6–1 6–4; Hoad d. Seixas 7–9 6–1 6–4 6–4.

1956 Australia (Capt: Harry Hopman) **d. USA** (Capt: Bill Talbert) **5–0**, *Adelaide:* L. A. Hoad d. H. Flam 6–2 6–3 6–3; K. R. Rosewall d. E. V. Seixas 6–2 7–5 6–3; Hoad/Rosewall d. S. Giammalva/Seixas 1–6 6–1 7–5 6–4; Hoad d. Seixas 6–2 7–5 6–3; Rosewall d. Giammalva 4–6 6–1 8–6 7–5.

1957 Australia (Capt: Harry Hopman) **d. USA** (Capt: Bill Talbert) **3–2**, *Melbourne:* A. J. Cooper d. E. V. Seixas 3–6 7–5 6–1 1–6 6–3; M. J. Anderson d. B. MacKay 6–3 7–5 3–6 7–9 6–3; Anderson/M. G. Rose d. MacKay/Seixas 6–4 6–4 8–6; Cooper lost to MacKay 4–6 6–1 6–4 4–6 3–6; Anderson lost to Seixas 3–6 6–4 3–6 6–0 11–13.

1958 USA (Capt: Perry Jones) **d. Australia** (Capt: Harry Hopman) **3–2**, *Brisbane:* A. Olmedo d. M. J. Anderson 8–6 2–6 9–7 8–6; B. MacKay lost to A. J. Cooper 6–4 3–6 2–6 4–6; Olmedo/H. Richardson d. Anderson/N. A. Fraser 10–12 3–6 16–14 6–3 7–5; Olmedo d. Cooper 6–3 4–6 6–4 8–6; MacKay lost to Anderson 5–7 11–13 9–11.

1959 Australia (Capt: Harry Hopman) **d. USA** (Capt: Perry Jones) **3–2**, *Forest Hills, NY:* N. A. Fraser d. A. Olmedo 8–6 6–8 6–4 8–6; R. G. Laver lost to B. MacKay 5–7 4–6 1–6; R. S. Emerson/Fraser d. E. Buchholz/Olmedo 7–5 7–5 6–4; Laver lost to Olmedo 7–9 6–4 8–10 10–12; Fraser d. MacKay 8–6 3–6 6–2 6–4.

1960 Australia (Capt: Harry Hopman) **d. Italy** (Capt: Vanni Canapele) **4–1**, *Sydney:* N. A. Fraser d. O. Sirola 4–6 6–3 6–3 6–3; R. G. Laver d. N. Pietrangeli 8–6 6–4 6–3; R. S. Emerson/Fraser d. Pietrangeli/Sirola 10–8 5–7 6–3 6–4; Laver d. Sirola 9–7 6–2 6–3; Fraser lost to Pietrangeli 9–11 3–6 6–1 2–6.

1961 Australia (Capt: Harry Hopman) **d. Italy** (Capt: Vanni Canapele) **5–0**, *Melbourne:* R. S. Emerson d. N. Pietrangeli 8–6 6–4 6–0; R. G. Laver d. O. Sirola 6–1 6–4 6–3; Emerson/N. A. Fraser d. Pietrangeli/Sirola 6–2 6–3 6–4; Emerson d. Sirola 6–2 6–3 4–6 6–2; Laver d. Pietrangeli 6–3 3–6 4–6 6–3 8–6.

1962 Australia (Capt: Harry Hopman) **d. Mexico** (Capt: Franciso Contreras) **5–0**, *Brisbane:* N. A. Fraser d. A. Palafox 7–9 6–3 6–4 11–9; R. G. Laver d. R. H. Osuna 6–2 6–1 7–5; R. S. Emerson/Laver d. Osuna/Palafox 7–5 6–2 6–4; Fraser d. Osuna 3–6 11–9 6–1 3–6 6–4; Laver d. Palafox 6–1 4–6 6–4 8–6.

1963 USA (Capt: Robert Kelleher) **d. Australia** (Capt: Harry Hopman) **3–2**, *Adelaide:* R. D. Ralston d. J. D. Newcombe 6–4 6–1 3–6 4–6 7–5; C. R. McKinley lost to R. S. Emerson 3–6 6–3 5–7 5–7; McKinley/Ralston d. Emerson/N. A. Fraser 6–3 4–6 11–9 11–9; Ralston lost to Emerson 2–6 3–6 6–3 2–6; McKinley d. Newcombe 10–12 6–2 9–7 6–2.

1964 Australia (Capt: Harry Hopman) **d. USA** (Capt: Vic Seixas) **3–2**, *Cleveland, Ohio:* F. S. Stolle lost to C. R. McKinley 1–6 7–9 6–4 2–6; R. S. Emerson d. R. D. Ralston 6–3 6–1 6–3; Emerson/Stolle lost to McKinley/Ralston 4–6 6–4 6–4 3–6 4–6; Stolle d. Ralston 7–5 6–3 3–6 9–11 6–4; Emerson d. McKinley 3–6 6–2 6–4 6–4.

1965 Australia (Capt: Harry Hopman) **d. Spain** (Capt: Jaime Bartroli) **4–1**, *Sydney:* F. S. Stolle d. M. Santana 10–12 3–6 6–1 6–4 7–5; R. S. Emerson d. J. Gisbert 6–3 6–2 6–2; J. D. Newcombe/A. D. Roche d. J. L. Arilla/Santana 6–3 4–6 7–5 6–2; Emerson lost to Santana 6–2 3–6 4–6 13–15; Stolle d. Gisbert 6–2 6–4 8–6.

1966 Australia (Capt: Harry Hopman) **d. India** (Capt: Raj Khanna) **4–1**, *Melbourne:* F. S. Stolle d. R. Krishnan 6–3 6–2 6–4; R. S. Emerson d. J. Mukerjea 7–5 6–4 6–2; J. D. Newcombe/A. D. Roche lost to Krishnan/Mukerjea 6–4 5–7 4–6 4–6; Emerson d. Krishnan 6–0 6–2 10–8; Stolle d. Mukerjea 7–5 6–8 6–3 5–7 6–3.

1967 Australia (Capt: Harry Hopman) **d. Spain** (Capt: Jaime Bartroli) **4–1**, *Brisbane:* R. S. Emerson d. M. Santana 6–4 6–1 6–1; J. D. Newcombe d. M. Orantes 6–3 6–3 6–2; Newcombe/A. D. Roche d. Orantes/Santana 6–4 6–4 6–4; Newcombe lost to Santana 5–7 4–6 2–6; Emerson d. Orantes 6–1 6–1 2–6 6–4.

1968 USA (Capt: Donald Dell) **d. Australia** (Capt: Harry Hopman) **4–1**, *Adelaide:* C. Graebner d. W. W. Bowrey 8–10 6–4 8–6 3–6 6–1; A. R. Ashe d. R. O. Ruffels 6–8 7–5 6–3 6–3; R. C. Lutz/S. R. Smith d. J. G. Alexander/Ruffels 6–4 6–4 6–2; Graebner d. Ruffels 3–6 8–6 2–6 6–3 6–1; Ashe lost to Bowrey 6–2 3–6 9–11 6–8.

1969 USA (Capt: Donald Dell) **d. Romania** (Capt: Georgy Cobzucs) **5–0**, *Cleveland, Ohio:* A. R. Ashe d. I. Nastase 6–2 15–13 7–5; S. R. Smith d. I. Tiriac 6–8 6–3 5–7 6–4 6–4; R. C. Lutz/Smith d. Nastase/Tiriac 8–6 6–1 11–9; Smith d. Nastase 4–6 4–6 6–4 6–1 11–9; Ashe d. Tiriac 6–3 8–6 3–6 4–0 ret.

1970 USA (Capt: Edward Turville) **d. West Germany** (Capt: Ferdinand Henkel) **5–0**, *Cleveland, Ohio:* A. R. Ashe d. W. Bungert 6–2 10–8 6–2; C. Richey d. C. Kuhnke 6–3 8–6 6–2; R. C. Lutz/S. R. Smith d. Bungert/Kuhnke 6–3 7–5 6–4; Richey d. Bungert 6–4 6–4 7–5; Ashe d. Kuhnke 6–8 10–12 9–7 13–11 6–4.

1971 USA (Capt: Edward Turville) **d. Romania** (Capt: Stefan Georgescu) **3–2**, *Charlotte, NC:* S. R. Smith d. I. Nastase 7–5 6–3 6–1; F. A. Froehling d. I. Tiriac 3–6 1–6 6–1 6–3 8–6; Smith/E. Van Dillen lost to Nastase/Tiriac 5–7 4–6 6–8; Smith d. Tiriac 8–6 6–3 6–0; Froehling lost to Nastase 3–6 1–6 6–1 4–6.
Challenge Round abolished

FINAL ROUND SCORES

1972 USA (Capt: Dennis Ralston) **d. Romania** (Capt: Stefan Georgescu) **3–2**, *Bucharest:* S. R. Smith d. I. Nastase 11–9 6–2 6–3; T. Gorman lost to I. Tiriac 6–4 6–2 4–6 3–6 2–6; Smith/E. Van Dillen d. Nastase/Tiriac 6–2 6–0 6–3; Smith d. Tiriac 4–6 6–2 6–4 2–6 6–0; Gorman lost to Nastase 1–6 2–6 7–5 8–10.

1973 Australia (Capt: Neale Fraser) **d. USA** (Capt: Dennis Ralston) **5–0**, *Cleveland, Ohio (indoors):* J. D. Newcombe d. S. R. Smith 6–1 3–6 6–3 3–6 6–4; R. G. Laver d. T. Gorman 8–10 8–6 6–8 6–3 6–1; Laver/Newcombe d. Smith/E. Van Dillen 6–1 6–2 6–4; Newcombe d. Gorman 6–2 6–1 6–3; Laver d. Smith 6–3 6–4 3–6 6–2.

1974 South Africa w.o. India

1975 Sweden (Capt: Lennart Bergelin) **d. Czechoslovakia** (Capt: Antonin Bolardt) **3–2**, *Stockholm (indoors):* O. Bengtson lost to J. Kodes 4–6 6–2 5–7 4–6; B. Borg d. J. Hrebec 6–1 6–3 6–0; Bengtson/Borg d. Kodes/V. Zednik 6–4 6–4 6–4; Borg d. Kodes 6–4 6–2 6–2; Bengtson lost to Hrebec 6–1 3–6 1–6 4–6.

1976 Italy (Capt: Nicola Pietrangeli) **d. Chile** (Capt: Luis Ayala) **4–1**, *Santiago:* C. Barazzutti d. J. Fillol 7–5 4–6 7–5 6–1; A. Panatta d. P. Cornejo 6–3 6–1 6–3; P. Bertolucci/Panatta d. Cornejo/Fillol 3–6 6–2 9–7 6–3; Panatta d. Fillol 8–6 6–4 3–6 10–8; A. Zugarelli lost to B. Prajoux 4–6 4–6 2–6.

1977 Australia (Capt: Neale Fraser) **d. Italy** (Capt: Nicola Pietrangeli) **3–1**, *Sydney:* A. D. Roche d. A. Panatta 6–3 6–4 6–4; J. G. Alexander d. C. Barazzutti 6–2 8–6 4–6 6–2; Alexander/P. Dent lost to P. Bertolucci/Panatta 4–6 4–6 5–7; Alexander d. Panatta 6–4 4–6 2–6 8–6 11–9; Roche div'd with Barazzutti 12–12.

1978 USA (Capt: Tony Trabert) **d. Great Britain** (Capt: Paul Hutchins) **4–1**, *Palm Springs, California:* J. P. McEnroe d. J. M. Lloyd 6–1 6–2 6–2; B. E. Gottfried lost to C. J. Mottram 6–4 6–2 8–10 4–6 3–6; R. C. Lutz/S. R. Smith d. M. Cox/D. A. Lloyd 6–2 6–2 6–3; McEnroe d. Mottram 6–2 6–2 6–1; Gottfried d. J. M. Lloyd 6–1 6–2 6–4.

1979 USA (Capt: Tony Trabert) **d. Italy** (Capt: Vittorio Crotta) **5–0**, *San Francisco (indoors):* V. Gerulaitis d. C. Barazzutti 6–3 3–2 ret; J. P. McEnroe d. A. Panatta 6–2 6–3 6–4; R. C. Lutz/S. R. Smith d. P. Bertolucci/Panatta 6–4 12–10 6–2; McEnroe d. A. Zugarelli 6–4 6–3 6–1; Gerulaitis d. Panatta 6–1 6–3 6–3.

1980 Czechoslovakia (Capt: Antonin Bolardt) **d. Italy** (Capt: Vittorio Crotta) **4–1**, *Prague (indoors):* T. Smid d. A. Panatta 3–6 3–6 6–3 6–4 6–4; I. Lendl d. C. Barazzutti 4–6 6–1 6–1 6–2; Lendl/Smid d. P. Bertolucci/Panatta 3–6 6–3 3–6 6–3 6–4; Smid lost to Barazzutti 6–3 3–6 2–6; Lendl d. G. Ocleppo 6–3 6–3.

1981 USA (Capt: Arthur Ashe) **d. Argentina** (Capt: Carlos Junquet) **3–1**, *Cincinnati (indoors):* J. P. McEnroe d. G. Vilas 6–3 6–2 6–2; R. Tanner lost to J. L. Clerc 5–7 3–6 6–8; P. Fleming/McEnroe d. Clerc/Vilas 6–3 4–6 6–4 4–6 11–9; McEnroe d. Clerc 7–5 5–7 6–3 3–6 6–3; Tanner div'd with Vilas 11–10.

1982 USA (Capt: Arthur Ashe) **d. France** (Capt: Jean-Paul Loth) **4–1**, *Grenoble (indoors):* J. P. McEnroe d. Y. Noah 12–10 1–6 3–6 6–2 6–3; G. Mayer d. H. Leconte 6–2 6–2 7–9 6–4; P. Fleming/McEnroe d. Leconte/Noah 6–3 6–4 9–7; Mayer lost to Noah 1–6 0–6; McEnroe d. Leconte 6–2 6–3.

1983 Australia (Capt: Neale Fraser) **d. Sweden** (Capt: Hans Olsson) **3–2**, *Melbourne:* P. Cash lost to M. Wilander 3–6 6–4 7–9 3–6; J. Fitzgerald d. J. Nystrom 6–4 6–2 4–6 6–4; M. R. Edmondson/P. McNamee d. A. Jarryd/H. Simonsson 6–4 6–4 6–2; Cash d. Nystrom 6–4 6–1 6–1; Fitzgerald lost to Wilander 8–6 0–6 1–6.

1984 Sweden (Capt: Hans Olsson) **d. USA** (Capt: Arthur Ashe) **4–1**, *Gothenburg:* M. Wilander d. J. S. Connors 6–1 6–3 6–3; H. Sundstrom d. J. P. McEnroe 13–11 6–4 6–3; S. Edberg/A. Jarryd d. P. Fleming/McEnroe 7–5 5–7 6–2 7–5; Wilander lost to McEnroe 3–6 7–6 3–6; Sundstrom d. J. Arias 3–6 8–6 6–3.

1985 Sweden (Capt: Hans Olsson) **d. West Germany** (Capt: Wilhelm Bungert) **3–2**, *Munich:* M. Wilander d. M. Westphal 6–3 6–4 10–8; S. Edberg lost to B. Becker 3–6 5–7 6–8; Wilander/J. Nystrom d. Becker/A. Maurer 6–4 6–2 6–1; Wilander lost to Becker 3–6 6–2 3–6 3–6; Edberg d. Westphal 3–6 7–5 6–4 6–3.

1986 Australia (Capt: Neale Fraser) **d. Sweden** (Capt: Hans Olsson) **3–2**, *Melbourne:* P. Cash d. S. Edberg 13–11 13–11 6–4; P. McNamee lost to M. Pernfors 3–6 1–6 3–6; Cash/J. Fitzgerald d. Edberg/A. Jarryd 6–3 6–4 4–6 6–1; Cash d. Pernfors 2–6 4–6 6–3 6–4 6–3; McNamee lost to Edberg 8–10 4–6.

1987 Sweden (Capt: Hans Olsson) **d. India** (Capt: Vijay Amritraj) **5–0**, *Gothenburg:* M. Wilander d. R. Krishnan 6–4 6–1 6–3; A. Jarryd d. V. Amritraj 6–3 6–1 6–1; Wilander/J. Nystrom d. An./V. Amritraj 6–3 3–6 6–1 6–2; Jarryd d. Krishnan 6–4 6–3; Wilander d. V. Amritraj 6–2 6–0.

1988 West Germany (Capt: Niki Pilic) **d. Sweden** (Capt: Hans Olsson) **4–1**, *Gothenburg:* C.–U. Steeb d. M. Wilander 8–10 1–6 6–2 6–4 8–6; B. Becker d. S. Edberg 6–3 6–1 6–4; Becker/E. Jelen d. Edberg/A. Jarryd 3–6 2–6 7–5 6–3 6–2; Steeb lost to Edberg 4–6 6–8; P. Kuhnen w.o. K. Carlsson.

1989 West Germany (Capt: Niki Pilic) **d. Sweden** (Capt: John Anders Sjogren) **3–2**, *Stuttgart:* C.–U. Steeb lost to M. Wilander 7–5 6–7 7–6 2–6 3–6; B. Becker d. S. Edberg 6–2 6–2 6–4; Becker/E. Jelen d. A. Jarryd/J. Gunnarsson 7–6 6–4 3–6 6–7 6–4; Becker d. Wilander 6–2 6–0 6–2; Steeb lost to Edberg 2–6 4–6.

1990 USA (Capt: Tom Gorman) **d. Australia** (Capt: Neale Fraser) **3–2**, *St Petersburg:* A. Agassi d. R. Fromberg 4–6 6–4 4–6 6–2 6–4; M. Chang d. D. Cahill 6–2 7–6 6–0; R. Leach/J. Pugh d. P. Cash/J. Fitzgerald 6–4 6–2 3–6 7–6; Agassi lost to Cahill 4–6 6–4 ret.; Chang lost to Fromberg 5–7 6–2 3–6.

1991 France (Capt: Yannick Noah) **d. USA** (Capt: Tom Gorman) **3–1**, *Lyon:* G. Forget lost to A. Agassi 7–6 2–6 1–6 2–6; H. Leconte d. P. Sampras 6–4 7–5 6–4; Forget/Leconte d. K. Flach/R. Seguso 6–1 6–4 4–6 6–2; Forget d. Sampras 7–6 3–6 6–4; Leconte v Agassi not played.

1992 USA (Capt: Tom Gorman) **d. Switzerland** (Capt: Dmitri Sturdza) **3–1**, *Fort Worth:* A. Agassi d. J. Hlasek 6–1 6–2 6–2; J. Courier lost to M. Rosset 3–6 7–6 6–3 4–6 4–6; J. McEnroe/P. Sampras d. Rosset/Hlasek 6–7 6–7 7–5 6–1 6–2; Courier d. Hlasek 6–3 3–6 6–3 4–6; Agassi v Rossi not played.

1993 Germany (Capt: Niki Pilic) **d. Australia** (Capt: Neale Fraser) **4–1**, *Dusseldorf:* M. Stich d. J. Stoltenberg 6–7 6–3 6–1 4–6 6–3; R. Fromberg d. M.-K. Goellner 3–6 5–7 7–6 6–2 9–7; P. Kuhnen/Stich d. T. Woodbridge/M. Woodforde 7–6 4–6 6–3 7–6; Stich d. Fromberg 6–4 6–3 6–2; Goellner d. Stoltenberg 6–1 7–6 3–6.

1994 Sweden (Capt: John Anders Sjogren) **d. Russia** (Capt: Vadim Borisov) **4–1**, *Moscow:* S. Edberg d. A. Volkov 6–4 6–2 6–7 0–6 8–6; M. Larsson d. Y. Kafelnikov 6–0 6–2 3–6 2–6 6–3; J. Apell/J. Bjorkman d. Y. Kafelnikov/A. Olhovskiy 6–7 6–2 6–3 1–6 8–6; Edberg lost to Kafelnikov 6–4 4–6 0–6; Larsson d. Volkov 7–6 6–4.

1995 USA (Capt: Tom Gullikson) **d. Russia** (Capt: Anatoli Lepeshin) **3–2**, *Moscow:* P. Sampras d. A. Chesnokov 3–6 6–4 6–3 6–7 6–4; Y. Kafelnikov d. J. Courier 7–6 7–5 6–3 7–5; T. Martin/P. Sampras d. Y. Kafelnikov/A. Olhovskiy 7–5 6–4 6–3; P. Sampras d. Y. Kafelnikov 6–2 6–4 7–6; A. Chesnokov d. J. Courier 6–7 7–5 6–0.

1996 France (Capt: Yannick Noah) **d. Sweden** (Capt: Carl Axel-Hageskog) **3–2**, *Malmo SWE:* C. Pioline d. S. Edberg 6–3 6–4 6–3; T. Enqvist d. A. Boetsch 6–4 6–3 7–6(2); G. Forget/G. Raoux d. J. Bjorkman/N. Kulti 3–6 1–6 6–3 6–3; T. Enqvist d. C. Pioline 3–6 6–7(8) 6–4 6–4 9–7; A. Boetsch d. N. Kulti 7–6(2) 2–6 4–6 7–6(5) 10–8.

1997 Sweden (Capt: Carl-Axel Hageskog) **d. USA** (Capt: Tom Gullikson) **5–0**, *Gothenburg:* J. Bjorkman (SWE) d. M. Chang (USA) 7–5 1–6 6–3 6–3; M. Larsson (SWE) d. P. Sampras (USA) 3–6 7–6(1) 2–1 ret; J. Bjorkman/N. Kulti (SWE) d. T. Martin/J. Stark (USA) 6–4 6–4 6–4; J. Bjorkman (SWE) d. J. Stark (USA) 6–1 6–1 6–4; M. Larsson (SWE) d. M. Chang (USA) 7–6(4) 6–7(6) 6–4.

1998 Sweden (Capt: Carl-Axel Hageskog) **d. Italy** (Capt: Paolo Bertolucci) **4–1**, *Milan:* M. Norman (SWE) d. A. Gaudenzi (ITA) 6 7(9) 7 6(0) 4 6 3 6 6 ret; M. Gustafsson (SWE) d. D. Sanquinetti (ITA) 6 1 6 4 6 0; J. Bjorkman/N. Kulti (SWE) d. D. Nargiso/D. Sanguinelli (ITA) 7–6(1) 6–1 6–3; M. Gustafsson (SWE) d. G. Pozzi (ITA) 6–4 6–2; D. Nargiso (ITA) d. M. Norman (SWE) 6–3 6–2.

1999 Australia (Capt: John Newcombe) **d. France** (Capt: Guy Forget) **3–2**, *Nice:* M. Philippoussis (AUS) d. S. Grosjean (FRA) 6–4 6–2 6–4; C. Pioline (FRA) d. L. Hewitt (AUS) 7–6(7) 7–6(6) 7–5; T. Woodbridge/M. Woodforde (AUS) d. O. Delaitre/F. Santoro (FRA) 2–6 7–5 6–2 6–2; M. Philippoussis (AUS) d. C. Pioline (FRA) 6–3 5–7 6–1 6–2; S. Grosjean (FRA) d. L. Hewitt (AUS) 6–4 6–3.
2000 Spain (Capt: Javier Duarte) **d. Australia** (Capt. John Newcombe) 3–1, *Barcelona:* L. Hewitt (AUS) d. A. Costa (ESP) 3–6 6–1 2–6 6–4 6–4;   J-C. Ferrero (ESP)d. P. Rafter (AUS) 6–7(4) 7–6(2) 6–2 3–1 ret. (cramp); J. Balcells/ A. Corretja (ESP) d. S. Stolle/M. Woodforde (AUS) 6–4 6–4 6–4; J-C. Ferrero (ESP) d. L. Hewitt (AUS) 6–2 7–6(5) 4–6 6–4; A. Corretja (ESP) v P. Rafter (AUS) not played.

QUALIFIERS FOR WORLD GROUP 2001

Belgium	France	Netherlands	Sweden
Ecuador	Morocco	Romania	Switzerland

FED CUP

Launched in 1963 to celebrate the 50th anniversary of the International Tennis Federation, the Federation Cup (as it was known until 1994) was played annually at one site as a week-long knock-out competition. Each tie comprised two singles rubbers and one doubles. A qualifying competition was introduced in 1992 to accommodate growing numbers. By 1994 there were 73 entries and it was decided to relaunch the competition in 1995 as the Fed Cup, to be played as a season-long home and away zonal competition with the eight top teams contesting the World Group. The final is played in the country of one of the finalists, towards the end of the year. Ties consist of five rubbers, two reverse singles and the doubles. Sponsored first by Colgate (1976–80), then by NEC (1981–94) it has been supported since 1996 by KB (Komereni Banka), one of the largest banks in the Czech Republic.

FINAL ROUNDS

1963 USA (Capt: William Kellog) **d. Australia** (Capt: Nell Hopman) **2–1**, *Queen's Club, London, 18–21 June:* D. R. Hard lost to M. Smith 3–6 0–6; B. J. Moffitt d. L. R. Turner 5–7 6–0 6–3; Hard/Moffitt d. Smith/Turner 3–6 13–11 6–3.
1964 Australia (Capt: Brian Tobin) **d. USA** (Capt: Madge Vosters) **2–1**, *Germanstown Cricket Club, Philadelphia, 2–5 September:* M. Smith d. B. J. Moffitt 6–2 6–3; L. R. Turner d. N. Richey 7–5 6–1; Smith/Turner lost to Moffitt/Mrs J. R. Susman 6–4 5–7 1–6.
1965 Australia (Capt: Margaret Smith) **d. USA** (Capt: Billie Jean Moffitt) **2–1**, *Kooyong Stadium, Melbourne, 12–18 January:* L. R. Turner d. Mrs C. Graebner 6–3 2–6 6–3; M. Smith d. B. J. Moffitt 6–4 8–6; Smith/J. M. Tegart lost to Graebner/Moffitt 5–7 6–4 4–6.
1966 USA (Capt: Ros Greenwood) **d. West Germany** (Capt: Edda Buding) **3–0**, *Turin, 11–15 May:* J. M. Heldman d. H. Niessen 4–6 7–5 6–1; Mrs L. W. King d. E. Buding 6–3 3–6 6–1; Mrs C. Graebner/Mrs King d. Buding/H. Schultse 6–4 6–2.
1967 USA (Capt: Donna Fales) **d. Great Britain** (Capt: Angela Mortimer Barrett) **2–0**, *Rot-Weiss Club, Berlin, 7–11 June:* R. Casals d. S. V. Wade 9–7 8–6; Mrs L. W. King d. Mrs P. F. Jones 6–3 6–4; Casals/Mrs King div'd with Mrs Jones/Wade 6–8 9–7.
1968 Australia (Capt: Margaret Court) **d. Netherlands** (Capt: Jenny Ridderhof) **3–0**, *Stade Roland Garros, Paris, 23–26 May:* K. A. Melville d. M. Jansen 4–6 7–5 6–3; Mrs B. M. Court d. A. Suurbeck 6–1 6–3; Court/Melville d. Suurbeck/L. Venneboer 6–3 6–8 7–5.
1969 Australia (Capt: Donna Fales) **d. Australia** (Capt: Wayne Reid) **2–1**, *Athens, 19–25 May:* N. Richey d. K. A. Melville 6–4 6–3; J. M. Heldman lost to Mrs B. M. Court 1–6 6–8; J. Bartkowicz/Richey d. Court/J. M. Tegart 6–4 6–4.
1970 Australia (Capt: Alf Chave) **d. West Germany** (Capt: Edward Dorrenberg) **3–0**, *Freiburg, Germany, 19–24 May:* K. M. Krantzcke d. Mrs H. Hoesl 6–2 6–3; Mrs D. E. Dalton d. H. Niessen 4–6 6–3 6–3; Dalton/Krantzcke d. Hoesl/Niessen 6–2 7–5.
1971 Australia (Capt: Margaret Court) **d. Great Britain** (Capt: Ann Haydon Jones) **3–0**, *Perth, Australia, 26–29 December 1970:* Mrs B. M. Court d. Mrs P. F. Jones 6–8 6–3 6–2; E. F. Goolagong d. S. V. Wade 6–4 6–1; Court/L. Hunt d. W. M. Shaw/Wade 6–4 6–4.
1972 South Africa (Capt: Dr. Jackie Du Toit) **d. Great Britain** (Capt: Virginia Wade) **2–1**, *Ellis Park, Johannesburg, 19–26 March:* Mrs Q. C. Pretorius lost to S. V. Wade 3–6 2–6; B. Kirk d. W. M. Shaw 4–6 7–5 6–0; Kirk/Pretorius d. Wade/G. M. Williams 6–1 7–5.
1973 Australia (Capt: Vic Edwards) **d. South Africa** (Capt: Dr. Jackie Du Toit) **3–0**, *Bad Homburg, Germany, 30 April–6 May:* E. F. Goolagong d. Mrs Q. C. Pretorius 6–0 6–2; P. Coleman d. B. Kirk 10–8 6–0; Goolagong/J. Young d. Kirk/Pretorius 6–1 6–2.
1974 Australia (Capt: Vic Edwards) **d. USA** (Capt: Donna Fales) **2–1**, *Naples, 13–19 May:* E. F. Goolagong d. J. M. Heldman 6–1 7–5; D. L. Fromholtz lost to J. Evert 6–2 5–7 3–6; Goolagong/J. Young d. Heldman/S. A. Walsh 7–5 8–6.
1975 Czechoslovakia (Capt: Vera Sukova) **d. Australia** (Capt: Vic Edwards) **3–0**, *Aix-en-Provence, 6–11 May:* M. Navratilova* d. E. F. Goolagong 6–3 6–4; R. Tomanova d. H Gourlay 6–4 6–2; Navratilova/Tomanova d. D. L. Fromholtz/Gourlay 6–3 6–1.
1976 USA (Capt: Billie Jean King) **d. Australia** (Capt: Neale Fraser) **2–1**, *Spectrum Stadium, Philadelphia, 22–29 August:* R. Casals lost to Mrs G. Reid 6–1 3–6 5–7; Mrs L. W. King d. Mrs E. Cawley 7–6 6–4; Casals/King d. Cawley/Reid 7–5 6–3.

1977 USA (Capt: Vicky Berner) **d. Australia** (Capt: Neale Fraser) **2–1**, *Devonshire Park, Eastbourne, 13–18 June:* Mrs L. W. King d. D. L. Fromholtz 6–1 2–6 6–2; C. M. Evert d. Mrs G. Reid 7–5 6–3; Casals/Evert lost to Reid/W. M. Turnbull 3–6 3–6.

1978 USA (Capt: Vicky Berner) **d. Australia** (Capt: Neale Fraser) **2–1**, *Kooyong Stadium, Melbourne, 27 November–3 December:* T. A. Austin lost to Mrs G. Reid 3–6 3–6; C. M. Evert d. W. M. Turnbull 3–6 6–1 6–1; Evert/Mrs L. W. King d. Reid/Turnbull 4–6 6–1 6–4.

1979 USA (Capt: Vicky Berner) **d. Australia** (Capt: Neale Fraser) **3–0**, *Madrid, 30 April–6 May:* T. A. Austin d. Mrs G. Reid 6–3 6–0; Mrs J. M. Lloyd d. D. L. Fromholtz 2–6 6–3 8–6; R. Casals/Mrs L. W. King d. Reid/W. M. Turnbull 3–6 6–3 8–6.

1980 USA (Capt: Vicky Berner) **d. Australia** (Capt: Mary Hawton) **3–0**, *Rot–Weiss Club, Berlin, 19–25 May:* Mrs J. M. Lloyd d. D. L. Fromholtz 4–6 6–1 6–1; T. A. Austin d. W. M. Turnbull 6–2 6–3; R. Casals/K. Jordan d. Fromholtz/S. Leo 2–6 6–4 6–4.

1981 USA (Capt: Mrs J. M. Lloyd) **d. Great Britain** (Capt: Sue Mappin) **3–0**, *Tokyo, 9–15 November:* A. Jaeger d. S. V. Wade 6–3 6–1; Mrs J. M. Lloyd d. S. Barker 6–2 6–1; R. Casals/K. Jordan d. J. M. Durie/Wade 6–4 7–5.

1982 USA (Capt: Mrs J. M. Lloyd) **d. West Germany** (Capt: Klaus Hofsass) **3–0**, *Santa Clara, California, 19–25 July:* Mrs J. M. Lloyd d. C. Kohde 2–6 6–1 6–3; M. Navratilova d. B. Bunge 6–4 6–4; Lloyd/Navratilova d. Bunge/Kohde 3–6 6–1 6–2.

1983 Czechoslovakia (Capt: Jan Kukal) **d. West Germany** (Capt: Klaus Hofsass) **2–1**, *Zurich, 18–24 July:* H. Sukova d. C. Kohde 6–4 2–6 6–2; H. Mandlikova d. B. Bunge 6–2 3–0 ret; I. Budarova/M. Skuherska lost to E. Pfaff/Kohde 6–3 2–6 1–6.

1984 Czechoslovakia (Capt: Jan Kukal) **d. Australia** (Capt: Judy Dalton) **2–1**, *Sao Paulo, 15–22 July:* H. Sukova lost to A. Minter 5–7 5–7; H. Mandlikova d. E. Sayers 6–1 6–0; Mandlikova/Sukova d. W. Turnbull/Sayers 6–2 6–2.

1985 Czechoslovakia (Capt: Jiri Medonos) **d. USA** (Capt: Tom Gorman) **2–1**, *Nagoya, 7–13 October:* H. Sukova d. E. Burgin 6–3 6–7 6–4; H. Mandlikova d. K. Jordan 7–5 6–1; A. Holikova/R. Marsikova lost to Burgin/Jordan 2–6 3–6.

1986 USA (Capt: Marty Riessen) **d. Czechoslovakia** (Capt: Jiri Medonos) **3–0**, *Prague, 21–27 July:* Mrs J. M. Lloyd d. H. Sukova 7–5 7–6; M. Navratilova d. H. Mandlikova 7–5 6–1; Navratilova/P. H. Shriver d. Mandlikova/Sukova 6–4 6–2.

1987 West Germany (Capt: Klaus Hofsass) **d. USA** (Capt: Marty Riessen) **2–1**, *Vancouver, 27 July–2 August:* C. Kohde-Kilsch lost to P. H. Shriver 0–6 6–7; S. Graf d. C. M. Evert 6–2 6–1; Kohde-Kilsch/Graf d. Evert/Shriver 1–6 7–5 6–4.

1988 Czechoslovakia (Capt: Jiri Medonos) **d. USSR** (Capt: Olga Morozova) **2–1**, *Melbourne, 7–11 December:* R. Zrubakova d. L. Savchenko 6–1 7–6; H. Sukova d. Zvereva 6–3 6–4; J. Novotna/J. Pospisilova lost to Savchenko/Zvereva 6–7 5–7.

1989 USA (Capt: Marty Riessen) **d. Spain** (Capt: Juan Alvarino) **3–0**, *Tokyo, 1–8 October:* C. Evert d. C. Martinez 6–3 6–2; M. Navratilova d. A. Sanchez 0–6 6–3 6–4; Z. Garrison/P. H. Shriver d. Martinez/Sanchez 7–5 6–1.

1990 USA (Capt: Marty Riessen) **d. USSR** (Capt: Olga Morozova) **2–1**, *Atlanta, 22–29 July:* J. Capriati d. L. Meskhi 7–6 6–2; Z. Garrison lost to N. Zvereva 6–4 3–6 3–6; Z. Garrison/G. Fernandez d. N. Zvereva/L. Savchenko 6–4 6–3.

1991 Spain (Capt: Juan Alvarino) **d. USA** (Capt: Marty Riessen) **2–1**, *Nottingham, 22–28 July:* C. Martinez lost to J. Capriati 6–4 6–7 1–6; A. Sanchez d. M. J. Fernandez 6–3 6–4; Martinez/Sanchez d. G. Fernandez/Z. Garrison 3–6 6–1 6–1.

1992 Germany (Capt: Klaus Hofsass) **d. Spain** (Capt: Juan Alvarino) **2–1**, *Frankfurt, 13–19 July:* A. Huber d. C. Martinez 6–3 6–7 6–1; S. Graff d. A. Sanchez-Vic. 6–4 6–2; A. Huber/B. Rittner lost to A. Sanchez-Vicario/C. Martinez 1–6 2–6.

1993 Spain (Capt: Miguel Margets) **d. Austrialia** (Capt: Wendy Turnbull) **3–0**, *Frankfurt, 19–25 July:* C. Martinez d. M. Jaggard-Lai 6–0 6–2; A. Sanchez-Vicario d. N. Provis 6–2 6–3; Martinez/Sanchez-Vicario d. E.. Smylie/R. Stubbs 3–6 6–1 6–3.

1994 Spain (Capt: Miguel Margets) **d. USA** (Capt: Marty Riessen) **3–0**, *Frankfurt, 18–25 July:* C. Martinez d. M. J. Fernandez 6–2 6–2; A. Sanchez-Vicario d. L. Davenport 6–2 6–1; Martinez/Sanchez-Vicario d. G. Fernandez/M. J. Fernandez 6–3 6–4.

1995 Spain (Capt: Miguel Margets) **d. USA** (Capt: Billie Jean King) **3–2**, *Valencia, 25–26 November:* C. Martinez d. C. Rubin 7–5 6–3; A. Sanchez-Vicario d. M. J. Fernandez 6–3 6–2; C. Martinez d. M. J. Fernandez 6–3 6–4; A. Sanchez-Vicario lost to C. Rubin 6–1 4–6 4–6; V. Ruano/M. A. Sanchez Lorenzo lost to L. Davenport/G. Fernandez 3–6 6–7.

1996 USA (Capt: Billie Jean King) **d. Spain** (Capt: Miguel Margets) **5–0**, *Atlantic City, 28–29 September:* M. Seles d. C. Martinez 6–2 6–4; L. Davenport d. A. Sanchez-Vicario 7–5 6–1; M. Seles d. A. Sanchez-Vicario 3–6 6–3 6–1; L. Davenport d. G. Leon Garcia 7–5 6–2; M. J. Fernandez/L. Wild d. G. Leon Garcia/V. Ruano-Pascual 6–1 6–4.

1997 France (Capt: Yannick Noah) **d. Netherlands** (Capt: Fred Hemmes) **4–1**, *Den Bosch, 4–5 October:* S. Testud d. B. Schultz-McCarthy 6–4 4–6 6–3; M. Pierce d. M. Oremans 6–4 6–1; B. Schultz-McCarthy d. M. Pierce 4–6 6–3 6–4; S. Testud d. M. Oremans 0–6 6–3 6–3; A. Fusai/N. Tauziat d. M. Bollegraf/C. Vis 6–3 6–4.

1998 Spain (Capt: Miguel Margets) **d. Switzerland** (Capt: Melanie Molitor) **3–2**, *Geneva, 19–20 September:* A. Sanchez-Vicario d. P. Schnyder 6–2 3–6 6–2; M. Hingis d. C. Martinez 6–4 6–4; M. Hingis d. A. Sanchez-Vicario 7–6 6–3; C. Martinez d. P. Schnyder 6–3 2–6 9–7; C. Martinez/A. Sanchez-Vicario d. M. Hingis/P. Schnyder 6–0 6–2.

* *M. Navratilova became a US citizen in 1981.*

1999 USA (Capt: Billie Jean King) **d. Russia** (Capt: Konstantin Bogordetskiy) **4–1**, *Stanford, CA, 18–19 September:* V. Williams d. E. Likhovtseva 6–3 6–4; L. Davenport d. E. Dementieva 6–4 6–0; L. Davenport d. E. Likhovtseva 6–4 6–4; E. Dementieva d. V. Williams 1–6 6–3 7–6; V. Williams/S. Williams d. Dementieva/E. Makarova 6–2 6–1.

2000 USA (Capt: Billie Jean King) **d. Spain** (Capt: Miguel Margets) **5–0**, *Las Vegas 24–25 November:* M. Seles d. C. Martinez 6–2 6–3; L. Davenport d. A. Sanchez-Vicario 6–2 1–6 6–3; L. Davenport d. C. Martinez 6–1 6–2; J. Capriati d. A. Sanchez-Vicario 6–1 1–0 ret.; J. Capriati/L. Raymond d. V. Ruano-Pascual/ M. Serna 4–6 6–4 6–2.

OLYMPIC MEDAL WINNERS

1896 Athens
Men's singles: Gold – J Boland (IRL), Silver – D Kasdaglis (GRE). Men's Doubles: Gold – J Boland(IRL) and F Traun (AUT); Silver – D Kasdaglis and D Petrokokkinos (GRE).

1900 Paris
Men's singles: Gold – L Doherty (GBR), Silver – H Mahony (IRL), Bronze – R Doherty (GBR) and A Norris (GBR). Men's doubles: Gold – L and R Doherty (GBR), Silver – M Decugis (FRA) and S De Garmendia (USA), Bronze – A Prevost and G De la Chapelle (FRA); H Mahony (IRL) and A Norris (GBR). Women's singles: Gold – C Cooper (GBR), Silver – H Prevost (FRA), Bronze – M Jones (USA) and H Rosenbaumova (TCH). Mixed doubles: Gold – R Doherty and C Cooper (GBR), Silver – H Mahony (IRL) and H Prevost (FRA), Bronze – A Warden (GBR) and H Rosenbaumova (TCH); L Doherty (GBR) and M Jones (USA).

1904 St Louis
Men's singles: Gold – B Wright (USA), Silver – L LeRoy (USA). Men's doubles: Gold – E Leonard and B Wright (USA), Silver – A Bell and R LeRoy (USA).

1908 London
(Indoors at Queen's Club) Men's singles: Gold – A Gore (GBR), Silver – G Caridia (GBR), Bronze -M Ritchie (GBR). Men's doubles: Gold – A Gore and H Roper Barrett (GBR) Sllver – G Caridia and G Simond (GBR), Bronze – W Bostrom and G Setterwall (SWE). Women's singles: Gold – G Eastlake Smith (GBR), Silver – A Greene (GBR), Bronze Mrs M Adlerstrahle (SWE). (Outdoors at Wimbledon) Men's singles: Gold – M Ritchie (GBR), Silver – O Froitzheim (GER), Bronze – W Eaves (GBR). Men's doubles: Gold – R Doherty and G Hillyard (GBR), Silver – M Ritchie and J Parke (GBR), Bronze – C Cazalet and C Dixon (GBR). Women's singles: Gold – Mrs R Lambert Chambers (GBR), Silver – D Boothby (GBR), Bronze – Mrs R Winch (GBR).

1912 Stockholm
(Indoors) Men's singles: Gold – A Gobert (FRA), Silver – C Dixon (GBR), Bronze -A Wilding (NZL). Men's Doubles: Gold – M Germot and A Gobert (FRA), Silver – C Kempe and G Setterwall (SWE), Bronze – A Beamish and C Dixon (GBR). Women's singles: Gold – Mrs F Hannam (GBR), Silver – S Castenschoild (DEN), Bronze – Mrs E Parton (GBR). Mixed Doubles; Gold – C Dixon and Mrs Hannam (GBR), Silver – H Roper Barrett and F Aitchison (GBR), Bronze – G Setterwall and Mrs H Fick (SWE). (Outdoors). Men's singles: Gold – C Winslow (RSA), Silver – H Kitson (RSA), Bronze – O Kreuzer (GER). Men's doubles: Gold – H Kitson and C Winslow (RSA), Silver – F Pipes and A Zborzil (AUT), Bronze – A Canet and M Meny (FRA). Women's singles: Gold – M Broquedis (FRA), Silver – D Koring (GER), Bronze – M Bjorstedt (NOR). Mixed doubles: Gold – H Schomburgk and D Koring (GER), Silver – G Setterwall and Mrs H Fick (SWE), Bronze – A Canet and M Broquedis (FRA).

1920 Antwerp
Men's singles: Gold – L Raymond (RSA), Silver – I Kumagae (JPN), Bronze – C Winslow (RSA). Men's Doubles: Gold – O Turnbull and M Woosnam (GBR), Silver – S Kashio and Kumagae (JPN), Bronze – P Albarran and M Decugis (FRA). Women's singles: Gold – S Lenglen (FRA) , Silver – E Holman (GBR), Bronze – K McKane (GBR). Women's doubles: Gold – Mrs R McNAir and K McKane (GBR), Silver -MRs A Beamish and E Holman (GBR), Bronze – S Lenglen and E D'Ayen (FRA). Mixed doubles; Gold – M Decugis and S Lenglen (FRA), M Woosnam and K McKane (GBR), Bronze – M Zemla and M Skrobkova (TCH).

1924 Paris
Men's singles: Gold – V Richards (USA), Silver – H Cochet (FRA), Bronze – H De Morpurgo (ITA). Men's doubles: Gold – F Hunter and V Richards (USA), Silver – J Brugnon and H Cochet (FRA), Bronze – J Borotra and H Lacoste (FRA). Women's singles: Gold – H Wills (USA), Silver – J Vlasto (FRA), Bronze -K McKane (GBR). Women's doubles: Gold – Mrs H Wightman and H Wills (USA), Silver – Mrs E Covell and K McKane (GBR), Bronze – Mrs D Shepherd-Barron and E Colyer (GBR). Mixed doubles: Gold – R Williams and Mrs H Wightman (USA), Silver -V Richards and Mrs M Jessup (USA), Bronze – H Timmer and C Bouman (HOL).

1968 Mexico City (Demonstration Sport)
Men's singles: Gold – M Santana(ESP), Silver – M Orantes (ESP), Bronze – H Fitzgibbon (USA). Men's doubles: Gold – R Osuna and V Zarazua (MEX), Silver – J Gisbert and M Santana (ESP), Bronze – P Darmon(FRA) and J Loyo-Mayo (MEX). Women's singles: Gold – H Neissen (GER), Silver – J Bartkowicz (USA), Bronze – J Heldman (USA). Women's doubles: E Buding and H Neissen (GER), Silver – Mrs R Darmon (FRA) and J Heldman (USA), Bronze – J Bartkowicz and V Ziegenfuss (USA). Mixed doubles: Gold – H Fitzgibbon and J Heldman (USA), Silver – J Fassbender and H Neissen (GER), Bronze – J Osborne and J Bartkowicz (USA).

1984 Los Angeles (Demonstration Sport) 6–11 August. Held at the Los Angeles Tennis Center, UCLA, on hard courts.
Men's singles: Gold – S Edberg (SWE), Silver – F Maciel (MEX), Bronze – P Cane (ITA) and J Arias (USA). Women's singles: Gold – S Graf (GER), Silver – S Goles (YUG), Bronze -C Tanvier (FRA) and R Reggi (ITA).

1988 Seoul 20 September–1 October. Held at Olympic Park Tennis Centre on hard courts.
Men's singles: Gold – M Mecir (TCH), Silver – T Mayotte (USA), Bronze – S Edberg (SWE) and B Gilbert (USA). Men's doubles: Gold – K Flach and R Seguso (USA), Silver – S Casal and E Sanchez (ESP), Bronze – S Edberg and A Jarryd (SWE) and M Mecir and M Srejber (TCH). Women's singles: Gold – S Graf (GER), Silver – G Sabatini (ARG), Bronze – Z Garrison (USA) and M Maleeva (BUL). Women's doubles: Gold – P Shriver and Z Garrison (USA), Silver – J Novotna and H Sukova (TCH), Bronze – W Turnbull and E Smylie (AUS) and S Graf and C Kohde-Kilsch (GER).

1992 Barcelona *28 July–8 August*. Held at Vall D'Hebron Tennis Centre on red clay.
Men's singles: Gold – M Rosset (SUI), Silver – J Arrese (ESP), Bronze – G Ivanisevic (CRO) and A Cherkasov (CIS). Men's doubles: Gold – B Becker and M Stich (GER), Silver – W Ferreira and P Norval (RSA), Bronze – G Ivanisevic and G Prpic (CRO) and J Frana and C Miniussi (ARG). Women's singles: Gold – J Capriati (USA), Silver – S Graf (GER), Bronze – M J Fernandez (USA) and A Sanchez-Vicario (ESP). Women's doubles: Gold – M J Fernandez and G Fernandez (USA), Silver – C Martinez and A Sanchez-Vicario (ESP), Bronze – R McQuillan and N Provis (AUS) and L Meskhi and N Zvereva (CIS).

1996 Atlanta *23 July–3 August*. Held at Stone Mountain Park Tennis Center on hard courts.
Men's singles: Gold – A. Agassi (USA), Silver – S. Bruguera (ESP), Bronze – L. Paes (IND). Men's doubles: Gold – T. Woodbridge and M. Woodforde (AUS), Silver – N. Broad and T. Henman (GBR), Bronze – M. Goellner and D. Prinosil (GER). Women's singles: Gold – L. Davenport (USA), Silver – A. Sanchez-Vicario (ESP), Bronze – J. Novotna (CZE). Women's doubles: Gold – G. Fernandez and M. J. Fernandez (USA), Silver – J. Novotna and H. Sukova (CZE), Bronze – C. Martinez and A. Sanchez-Vicario (ESP).

2000 Sydney *19–28 September*. Held at New South Wales Tennis Centre on hard courts.
Men's singles: Gold – Y. Kafelnikov (RUS), Silver – T. Haas (GER), Bronze – A. Di Pasquale (FRA). Men's doubles: Gold – S. Lareau and D. Nestor (CAN), Silver – T. Woodbridge and Mark Woodforde (AUS), Bronze – A. Corretja and A. Costa (ESP). Women's singles: Gold – V. Williams (USA), Silver – E. Dementieva (RUS), Bronze – Monica Seles (USA). Women's doubles: Gold – S. Williams and V. Williams (USA), Silver – K. Boogert and M. Oremans (NED), Bronze – E. Callens and D. Van Roost (BEL).

WIGHTMAN CUP

Women's annual team contest between USA and Great Britain, for a silver trophy presented by Mrs Hazel Hotchkiss Wightman in 1923, each match comprising five singles and two doubles, with reverse singles played between the two top players. Discontinued in 1989.
Summary: USA 51 wins; Great Britain 10 wins. (Note: Full match results can be found in previous issues of *World of Tennis* up to 1996.)

EUROPEAN CUP – MEN

Formerly King's Cup. International men's team championship on indoor courts. It was staged on a knock-out basis 1936–38, on a league basis, 1952–74, with ties home and away 1976–83. From 1984 the ties in each division were held concurrently at one venue. The Challenge Round system was used in the two opening years, with 1937 the only Challenge Round.

FINALS
1936 France d. Sweden 4–1, Stockholm: J. Borotra d. K. Schroder 2–6 6–2 6–1 6–3, d. C. Ostberg 6–1 6–3 7–5; B. Destremau d. Schroder 3–6 7–5 6–2 6–4, d. Ostberg 6–2 6–2 6–4; C. Boussus/J. Brugnon lost to Ostberg/ Schroder 2–6 6–3 3–4 6 6–3 4–6.
1937 France d. Sweden 5–0, *Paris*: B. Destremau d. K. Schroder 8–6 1–6 2–6 11–9 8–6, d. N. Rohlsson 1–6 1–6 6–3 6–1 6–0; Y. Petra d. Rohlsson 6–1 6–4 6–2, d. Schroder 6–3 3–6 6–3 6–4; H. Bolelli/J. Lesueur d. Schroder/H. Wallen 10–8 6–4 6–4.
1938 Germany d. Denmark 5–0, *Hamburg*: R. Menzel d. H. Plougmann 6–3 6–2 8–6; H. Henkel d. I. Gerdes 6–4 6–0 6–3, d. Plougmann 6–2 6–1 6–3; R. Redl d. Gerdes 6–3 6–3 6–2; Henkel/Menzel d. Gerdes/Plougmann 6–0 6–4 6–2.
1939–51 Not held
1952 Denmark d. Sweden 3–2, *Stockholm*: K. Nielsen lost to S. Davidson 3–6 7–9 4–6; T. Ulrich d. T. Johansson 7–5 0–6 6–4 6–2; Nielsen/Ulrich d. Davidson/Johansson 6–2 2–6 4–6 8–6 7–5; Nielsen d. Johansson 6–3 6–4 6–1; Ulrich lost to Davidson 6–4 4–6 1–6 6–1 2–6.
1953 Denmark d. Sweden 3–2, *Copenhagen*: T. Ulrich d. S. Davidson 14–12 11–9 1–6 11–9; J. Ulrich lost to T. Johansson 0–6 2–6 7–9; J. Ulrich/T. Ulrich d. Davidson/N. Rohlsson 6–4 6–4 4–6 3–6 6–3; J. Ulrich lost to Davidson 3–6 4–6 0–6; T. Ulrich d. Johansson 6–3 2–6 6–4 5–7 6–3.
1954 Denmark d. Italy 3–2, *Milan*: T. Ulrich d. G. Merlo 7–5 2–6 9–7 9–7; K. Nielsen lost to O. Sirola 5–7 6–8 8–6 6–2 3–6; Nielsen/Ulrich d. N. Pietrangeli/Sirola 2–6 2–6 11–9 6–1 12–10; Nielsen lost to Pietrangeli 5–7 6–3 9–7 3–6 5–7; Ulrich d. Sirola 7–5 10–8 6–4.
1955 Sweden d. Denmark 4–1, *Copenhagen*: S. Davidson d. J. Ulrich 7–5 12–10 6–1; U. Schmidt lost to K. Nielsen 3–6 2–6 6–4 4–6; Davidson/T. Johansson d. Nielsen/J. Ulrich 11–9 6–3 14–12; Davidson d. Nielsen 8–10 6–2 7–9 12–10 7–5; Schmidt d. J. Ulrich 7–9 6–4 6–0 8–6 6–3.
1956 Sweden d. France 4–1, *Paris*: S. Davidson lost to P. Darmon 7–9 6–2 5–7 6–8; U. Schmidt d. R. Haillet 6–1 /6–2 6–4; Davidson/Schmidt d. Darmon/P. Remy 8–6 3–6 6–1 6–4; Davidson d. Haillet 6–2 2–6 6–4 6–1; Schmidt d. Darmon 6–1 10–8 6–3.
1957 Sweden d. Denmark 3–2, *Copenhagen*: J. E. Lundqvist d. K. Nielsen 4–6 6–3 10–8 6–4; U. Schmidt lost to T. Ulrich 4–6 7–9 2–6; Lundqvist/Schmidt d. J. Ulrich/T. Ulrich 6–3 5–7 6–0 6–3; Lundqvist d. T. Ulrich 7 5 6 1 6 2, Schmidt lost to Nielsen 6–4 4–6 2–6 5–7.

1958 Sweden d. Denmark 3–2, *Stockholm:* B. Folke lost to J. Ulrich 11–13 3–6 4–6; S. Davidson d. K. Nielsen 6–0 6–1 6–4; Davidson/T. Johansson d. Nielsen/J. Ulrich 10–8 1–6 6–3 6–8 6–3; Folke lost to Nielsen 4–6 3–6 3–6; Davidson d. J. Ulrich 6–4 6–3 1–6 6–1.

1959 Denmark won, *Stockholm:* Denmark d. Italy 2–1, lost to Sweden 2–1, d. France 2–1 (12–11 sets); Sweden lost to France 2–1, d. Denmark 2–1, d. Italy 2–1 (10–10 sets); Italy lost to Denmark 2–1, d. France 2–1, lost to Sweden 2–1 (11–11 sets); France d. Sweden 2–1, lost to Italy 2–1, lost to Denmark 2–1 (10–11 sets). Danish team: K. Nielsen and J. Ulrich.

1960 Denmark d. West Germany 3–0, *Paris:* J. Leschly d. B. Nitsche 6–4 8–6; J. Ulrich d. P. Scholl 6–2 6–3; Leschly/J. Ulrich d. Nitsche/Scholl 6–8 6–2 6–0.

1961 Sweden d. Denmark 2–1, *Cologne:* U. Schmidt d. J. Leschly 6–4 6–2; J. E. Lundqvist d. J. Ulrich 6–3 6–1; Lundqvist/Schmidt lost to Leschly/J. Ulrich 5–7 6–4 5–7.

1962 Denmark d. Italy 3–0, *Copenhagen:* J. Leschly d. G. Merlo 6–3 8–6; J. Ulrich d. N. Pietrangeli 6–4 6–2; Leschly/J. Ulrich d. Pietrangeli/O. Sirola 9–7 7–5.

1963 Yugoslavia d. Denmark 3–0, *Belgrade:* Yugoslav team: B. Jovanovic and N. Pilic.

1964 Great Britain d. Sweden 3–0, *Stockholm:* M. J. Sangster d. J. E. Lundquist 13–15 10–8 12–10; R. Taylor d. B. Holmstrom 6–3 9–7; Sangster/R. K. Wilson d. Holmstrom/L. Olander 4–6 12–10 6–4.

1965 Great Britain d. Denmark 2–1, *Torquay:* R. K. Wilson lost to J. Leschly 1–6 4–6; M. Cox d. C. Hedelund 6–4 6–3; A. R. Mills/Wilson d. Leschly/Hedelund 3–6 6–2 6–4 12–10.

1966 Great Britain d. Italy 3–0, *Milan:* R. Taylor d. N. Pietrangeli 6–4 6–4; M. J. Sangster d. G. Maioli 7–9 6–4 11–9; Sangster/R. K. Wilson d. D. Di Maso/Maioli 6–4 6–1.

1967 Great Britain d. Sweden 2–1, *Stockholm:* R. Taylor d. O. Bengtson 2–6 6–3 9–7; R. K. Wilson d. M. Carlstein 8–6 6–2; M. Cox/Taylor lost to Bengtson/B. Homstrom 4–6 7–9.

1968 Sweden d. Netherlands 2–1, *Bratislava:* O. Bengtson lost to T. S. Okker 12–14 4–6; M. Carlstein d. J. Hordjik 6–4 6–3; Bengtson/Carlstein d. N. Fleury/Okker 1–6 4–6 7–5 6–3 6–4.

1969 Czechoslovakia d. Sweden 2–1, *Cologne:* V. Zednik d. H. Zahr 6–4, 7–5; J. Kukal d. O. Bengtson 6–1 5–7 11–9; Kukal/Zednik lost to Bengtson/H. Nerell 4–6 4–6.

1970 France d. Denmark 2–1, *Copenhagen:* J. B. Chanfreau d. J. Ulrich 6–3 8–6; G. Goven lost to J. Leschly 1–6 3–6; Chanfreau/Goven d. Ulrich/Leschly 2–6 6–4 7–5.

1971 Italy d. Spain 2–1, *Ancona:* A. Panatta lost to M. Orantes 2–6 3–6; N. Pietrangeli d. J. Gisbert 7–9 8–6 6–4; Panatta/Pietrangeli d. Gisbert/Orantes 4–6 8–6 6–3 6–4.

1972 Spain d. Hungary 3–0, *Madrid:* A. Gimeno d. S. Baranyi 10–8 6–2; J. Gisbert d. B. Taroczy 6–1 7–9 6–3; J. Herrera/A. Munoz d. R. Machan/Taroczy 6–4 3–6 7–5.

1973 Sweden d. Italy 2–1, *Hannover:* L. Johansson d. A. Zugarelli 6–4 6–3; B. Borg d. A. Panatta 4–6 6–2 8–6; Borg/Johansson lost to P. Bertolucci/Zugarelli 6–3 5–7 4–6.

1974 Italy d. Sweden 3–0, *Ancona:* A. Panatta d. R. Norberg 6–3 6–4; A. Zugarelli d. T. Svensson 6–3 6–4; P. Bertolucci/A. Panatta d. B. Andersson/Norberg 6–2 6–4.

1975 Not held

1976 Hungary 11 wins, Great Britain 10 wins (played entirely as round robin, each tie home and away). Hungarian team: P. Szoke, B. Taroczy. British team: M. Cox, J. M. Lloyd, C. J. Mottram, R. Taylor.

1977 Sweden d. West Germany 5–1, *Berlin:* R. Norberg d. U. Marten 6–2 4–6 6–4; K. Johansson d. K. Meiler 6–4 6–4; O. Bengtson/Norberg d. P. Elter/Meiler 6–2 6–2; *Linkoping:* Norberg d. U. Pinner 7–6 6–2; Johansson d. Meiler 6–7 6–2 6–3; Bengtson/Norberg lost to Elter/Marten 6–3 4–6 4–6.

1978 Sweden d. Hungary 3–3 (9–7 sets), *Uppsala:* T. Svensson d. P. Szoke 6–2 6–4; O. Bengtson lost to B. Taroczy 6–7 6–7; Bengtson/Svensson lost to Szoke/Taroczy 6–7 4–6; *Debrecen:* Svensson d. Szoke 6–2 6–2; Bengtson d. Taroczy 6–4 7–6; Bengtson/Svensson lost to Szoke/Taroczy 3–6 6–3 3–6.

1979 Czechoslovakia d. Hungary 4–2, *Pecs:* I. Lendl lost to J. Benyik 6–7 7–5 6–7; T. Smid d. B. Taroczy 5–7 6–3 6–4; P. Slozil/T. Smid d. P. Szoke/Taroczy 6–4 6–4; *Chrudin:* Lendl lost to Benyik 6–4 2–6 0–6; Smid d. Szoke 6–3 3–6 6–2; Slozil/Smid d. Benyik/Szoke 6–4 6–2.

1980 Czechoslovakia d. Hungary 5–1, *Chrudin:* T. Smid d. R. Machan 6–4 6–2; I. Lendl d. B. Taroczy 6–2 6–1; Smid/P. Slozil d. P. Szoke/Machan 6–4 7–5; *Debreden:* Smid d. J. Benyik 6–2 3–6 6–2; Lendl d. Machan 6–0 6–2; Smid/Slozil lost to Machan/Szoke 6–3 3–6 2–6.

1981 West Germany d. USSR 3–3 (9–7 sets), *Moscow,* **2–1**, and Hamburg, **1–2.**

1982 West Germany d. Czechoslovakia 2–1, *Dortmund:* K. Eberhard lost to J. Navratil 4–6 1–6; U. Pinnder d. P. Slozilp 6–4 6–4; C. Zipf/H. D. Beutel d. Navratil/Slozil 6–3 6–4.

1983 West Germany d. Czechoslovakia 2–1, *Uppsala:* H. J. Schwaier lost to L. Pimek 6–4 2–6 3–6; M. Westphal d. J. Navratil 3–6 6–2 6–3; E. Jelen/W. Popp d. Navratil/Piimek 6–1 1–6 7–6.

1984 Czechoslovakia d. Sweden 2–1, *Essen:* M. Mecir d. J. Gunnarsson 7–6 6–4; L. Pimek lost to J. Nystrom 3–6 5–7; Pimek/J. Navratil d. Gunnarsson/Nystrom 3–6 6–2 6–4.

1985 Sweden d. Switzerland 3–0, *Essen:* T. Hogstedt d. R. Stadler 6–3 6–2; J. Gunnarsson d. J. Hlasek 7–5 4–6 6–2; S. Simonsson/H. Simonsson d. Hlasek/Stadler 6–3 3–6 6–3.

1986 Switzerland d. Czechoslovakia 2–1, *Queen's Club, London:* R. Stadler d. M. Vajda 6–4 7–5; J. Hlasek lost L. Pimek 7–5 3–6 5–7; Hlasek/Stadler d. Pimek/P. Korda 6–2 6–3.

1987 Switzerland d. Great Britain 2–1, *Hannover:* R. Stadler lost to M. J. Bates 6–7 2–6; J. Hlasek d. A. Castle 6–3 6–7 6–2; Hlasek/Stadler d. Bates/Castle 3–6 7–5 6–0.

1988 Czechoslovakia d. Netherlands 2–0, *Zurich:* P. Korda d. M. Oosting 6–3 7–6; M. Srejber d. M. Schapers 7–5 7–6; doubles not played.

1989 Czechoslovakia d. West Germany 2–1, *Ostrava:* P. Korda lost to C.–U. Steeb 3–6 3–6; M. Srejber d. E. Jelen 7–5 6–3; Srejber/Korda d. P. Kuhnen/Jelen 7–6 7–6.

1990 Germany d. USSR 2–1, *Metz:* U. Riglewski lost to D. Poliakov 7–5 3–6 2–6; M. Stich d. A. Cherkasov 6–3 7–6; Stich/Riglewski d. A. Olhovskiy/V. Gabrichidze 6–3 7–6.
1991 Czechoslovakia d. Netherlands 2–1, *Lengnau:* D. Rikl lost to T. Kempers 6–3 5–7 1–6; M. Damm d. F. Wibier 6–4 6–1; Damm/T. Zdrazila d. Kempers/Wibier 6–3 6–3.
1992 Italy d. Germany 2–1, *Trieste:* N. Kulti d. M. Goellner 6–4 7–6; T. Enqvist lost to M. Naewie 3–6 4–6; M. Tillstrom/N. Kulti d. M. Naewie/M. Goellner 4–6 6–3 7–6
1993 Sweden d. Germany 2–0, *Trieste:* J. Bjorkman d. J. Renzenbrink 6–1 6–3; N. Kulti d. D. Prinosil 6–4 6–4 (doubles not played).
1994 Italy d. Sweden 2–1, *Trieste:* O. Camporese d. M. Norman 6–2 6–4; C. Caratti lost to T. Johansson 4–6 1–6; Camporese/C. Brandi d. Flyght/Johansson 6–4 6–2.
1995 Italy d. Czech Republic 2–0, *Reggio Calabria:* O. Camporese d. D. Miketa 6–2 6–4; C. Caratti d. Novak 6–7(5–7) 6–4 6–0. Doubles not played.
1996 Sweden d. Italy 2–1, *Reggio Calabria:* G. Galimberti d. T. Johansson 2–6 6–3 6–3; N. Timfjord d. M. Navarra 6–2 6–4; M. Rentröm/N. Timfjord d. M. Navarra/M. Martelli 6–7 6–4 6–1.
1997 Great Britain d. Netherlands 2–1, *Reggio Calabria:* M. Verkerk (NED) d. M. Lee (GBR) 4–6 7–6 6–2; D. Sapsford (GBR) d. P. Wessels (NED) 7–6 6–4; D. Sapsford/M. Lee (GBR) d. T. Kempes/P. Wessels (NED) 6–3 7–5.
1998 Italy d. Bulgaria 2–0, *Montecatini:* G. Galimberti (ITA) d. I. Traykov (BUL) 7–6 6–3; M. Martelli (ITA) d. M. Velev (BUL) 6–2 6–2; doubles not played.
1999 Sweden d. Italy 2–1, *Montecatini:* G. Giorgio (ITA) d. R. Lindsted (SWE) 6–4 3–6 6–3; A. Vinceguerra (SWE) d. I. Gaudi (ITA) 6–2 6–3; R. Lindsted/A. Vinciguerra (SWE) d. D. Bracciali/ G. Galimberti (ITA) 6–0 6–2.
2000 Czech Republic d. Slovenia 2–0, *Montecatini, Italy:* O. Fukarek (CZE) d. A. Kracman (SLO) 6–4 6–1; J. Vacek (CZE) d. M. Tkalec (SLO) 6–2 6–2.

EUROPEAN CUP – WOMEN

A team competition for women launched in 1986 to commemorate the 50th anniversary of the European Cup for men (which had originally been the King's Cup). Ties consist of two singles rubbers and one doubles rubber.

FINALS

1986 Sweden d. W. Germany 2–0 *Eindhoven 27–30 November:* C. Carlsson(SWE) d. A. Betzner (GER) 6–0 6–3; C. Lindqvist (SWE) d. S. Meier (GER) 6–2 7–6. Doubles not played.
1987 France d. Netherlands 2–0 *Lomma-Bjarred 26–29 November:* P. Paradis (FRA) d. M. Mesker (NED) 3–6 7–5 6–2; J. Halard (FRA) d. M. Bollegraf (NED) 6–2 6–4. Doubles not played.
1988 France d. Netherlands 2–1 *Nantes 7–13 November:* K. Quentrec (FRA) d. M. Bollegraf (NED) 6–3 6–4; C. Suire (FRA) d. H. Schultz (NED) 6–2 6–1; Bollegraf/C. Vis (NED) d. Suire/C. Tanvier (FRA) 6–4 4 6–7–6.
1989 USSR d. Great Britain 2–1 *Nantes 23–26 November:* J. Durie (GBR) d. N. Zvereva (URS) 7–6 6–4; L. Meskhi d. C. Wood 6–3 6–1; L. Savchenko/Zvereva (URS) d. Durie/A. Hobbs (GBR) 6–2 6–2.
1990 USSR d. Great Britain 2–1 *Nantes 29 November – 2 December:* Brioukhovets (URS) d. M. Javer (GBR) 7–5 6–3; N. Medvedeva (URS) d. J. Durie 6–3 6–3; Durie/C. Wood (GBR) d. Brioukhovets/ Medvedeva (URS) 7–6 ret.
1991 Netherlands d. Italy 2–0 *Nantes 28 November – 1 December:* M. Oremans d. K. Piccolini 6–4 6–2; S. Rottier (NED) d. L. Ferrando (ITA) 6–1 3–6 7–5. Doubles not played.
1992 Great Britain d. Netherlands 2–1 *Prague, 26–29 November:* C. Wood (GBR) lost to M. Kiene 2–6 3–6; J. Durie (GBR) d. N. Muns Jagerman 7–6 6–4; Durie/Wood d. Kiene/M. Oremans 6–3 6–2.
1993 Germany d. Netherlands 2–0 *Sheffield, 24–28 November:* C. Porwick (GER) d. K. Boogert (NED) 7–5 6–3; B. Rittner (GER) d. S. Rottier (NED) 7–5 6–2. Doubles not played.
1994 Italy d. Germany 2–1 *Aachen, 23–27 November:* M. Babel (GER) d. L. Golarsa (ITA) 6–4 6–2; S. Cecchini (ITA) d. B. Rittner (GER) 6–2 6–4; Cecchini/Golarsa (ITA) d. Rittner/C. Singer (GER) 7–6 6–4.
1995 Netherlands d. Belgium 2–1 *Aachen, 29 November–1 December:* M. Oremans (NED) d. D. Monami (BEL) 6–2 5–7 6–4; S. Appelmans (BEL) d. K. Boogert (NED) 5–7 6–1 6–1; Oremans/C. Vis (NED) d. Appelmans/ L.Courtois (BEL) 6–2 6–4.
1996 Germany d. Netherlands 2–0, *Aachen:* M. Weingartner d. C. Vis 6–0 3–6 6–1; B. Rittner d. M. Oremans 7–5 6–7 6–2; Doubles not played.
1997 Spain d. Italy 2–1, *Barcelona:* G. Leon (ESP) d. F. Perfetti (ITA) 6–4 7–6(3); F. Lubiani (ITA) d. V. Ruano-Pascual (ESP) 4–6 6–4 7–6(6); G. Leon/V. Ruano-Pascual (ESP) d. G. Casoni/F. Perfetti (ITA) 6–2 6–2.
1998 Italy d. Czech Republic 3–0, *Frydlant Nad Ostravici:* G. Pizzichini (ITA) d. M. Pastikova (CZE) 6–3 7–6; F Perfetti (ITA) d. K. Hrdlickova (CZE) 6–1 6–3; G. Casoni/P. Zavagli (ITA) d. D. Bedanova/M. Pastikova (CZE) 6–3 5–7 7–5.
1999 Spain d. Czech Republic 3–0, *Frydlant Nad Ostravici:* A Medina (ESP) d. M. Pastikova (CZE) 6–7 6–2 6–3; M. Marrero (ESP) d. L. Nemeckova (CZE) 7–5 6–2; M. Martinez/A. Medina (ESP) d. M. Pastikova/H. Vildova (CZE) 6–1 6–3.
2000 Italy d. Great Britain 2–1, *Cesky Krumlov, Czech Republic:* E. Baltacha (GBR) d. G. Casoni (ITA) 3–6 6–3 7–5; F. Schiavone (ITA) d. L. Latimer (GBR) 6–3 6–2; G. Casoni/F. Schiavone (ITA) d. E. Baltache/J. Pullin (GBR) 6–1 6–2.

WORLD TEAM CUP

Eight-nation men's team event, qualification by individual ATP rating. Formerly Nations Cup.

FINALS
Played at Kingston, Jamaica
1975 USA d. Great Britain 2–1: R. Tanner (USA) d. R. Taylor (GBR) 6–3 2–6 6–4; A. R. Ashe (USA) lost to C. J. Mottram (GBR) 5–7 7–5 1–6; Ashe/Tanner d. Mottram/Taylor 6–1 1–6 6–4.
1976–77 Not held
Played at Dusseldorf
1978 Spain d. Australia 2–1: J. Higueras (ESP) d. J. D. Newcombe (AUS) 6–2 6–3; M. Orantes (ESP) d. P. Dent (AUS) 6–3 6–4; Higueras/ Orantes lost to Dent/Newcombe 6–7 4–6.
1979 Australia d. Italy 2–1: J. G. Alexander (AUS) d. C. Barazzutti (ITA) 6–2 6–0; P. Dent (AUS) lost to A. Panatta (ITA) 3–6 3–6; Alexander/Dent d. P. Bertolucci/Panatta 6–3 7–6.
1980 Argentina d. Italy 3–0: G. Vilas (ARG) d. C. Barazzutti (ITA) 6–3 6–2; J. L. Clerc (ARG) d. A. Panatta (ITA) 7–6 6–3; Clerc/Vilas d. P. A Bertolucci/Panatta 6–2 6–3.
1981 Czechoslovakia d. Australia 2–1: I. Lendl (TCH) lost to P. McNamara (AUS) 3–6 4–6; T. Smid (TCH) d. P. McNamee (AUS) 6–4 7–6; Lendl/Smid d. McNamara/McNamee 6–4 6–3.
1982 USA d. Australia 2–1: G. Mayer (USA) d. K. Warwick (AUS) 7–6 6–2; E. Teltscher (USA) d. P. McNamara (AUS) 6–4 7–6; Mayer/S. E. Stewart lost to M. R. Edmondson/McNamara 1–6 1–6.
1983 Spain d. Australia 2–1: J. Higueras (ESP) d. M. R. Edmondson (AUS) 6–2 6–4; M. Orantes (ESP) d. P. Cash (AUS) 6–3 6–2; A. Gimenez/Higueras lost to Cash/Edmondson 5–7 6–4 1–6.
1984 USA d. Czechoslovakia 2–1: J. P. McEnroe (USA) d. I. Lendl (TCH) 6–3 6–2; J. Arias (USA) lost to T. Smid (TCH) 6–4 6–7 4–6; P. Fleming/McEnroe d. Lendl/Smid 6–1 6–2.
1985 USA d. Czechoslovakia 2–1: J. P. McEnroe (USA) lost to I. Lendl (TCH) 7–6 6–7 3–6; J. S. Connors (USA) d. M. Mecir (TCH) 6–3 3–6 7–5; K. Flach/R. Seguso (USA) d. Lendl/T. Smid 6–3 7–6
1986 France d. Sweden 2–1: H. Leconte (FRA) d. A. Jarryd (SWE) 6–3 3–6 6–1; T. Tulasne (FRA) lost to M. Wilander (SWE) 1–6 4–6; G. Forget/Leconte d. Jarryd/Wilander 6–3 2–6 6–2.
1987 Czechoslovakia d. USA 2–1: M. Mecir (TCH) d. J. P. McEnroe (USA) 7–5 2–6 2–1 disqual.; M. Srejber (TCH) lost to B. Gilbert (USA) 4–6 7–5 4–6; Mecir/T. Smid d. Gilbert/R. Seguso 6–3 6–1.
1988 Sweden d. USA 2–1: S. Edberg (SWE) d. T. Mayotte (USA) 6–4 6–2; K. Carlsson (SWE) d. A. Krickstein (USA) 6–4 6–3; Edberg/A. Jarryd lost to K. Flach/R. Seguso (USA) 7–6 3–6 6–7.
1989 West Germany d. Argentina 2–1: B. Becker (GER) d. G. Perez Roldan (ARG) 6–0 2–6 6–2; C.–U. Steeb (GER) lost to M. Jaite (ARG) 4–6 3–6; Becker/E. Jelen d. J. Frana/G. Luna 6–4 7–5.
1990 Yugoslavia d. USA 2–1: G. Prpic (YUG) d. B. Gilbert (USA) 6–4 6–4; G. Ivanisevic (YUG) d. J. Courier (USA) 3–6 7–5 6–1; Prpic/S. Zivojinovic lost to K. Flach/R. Seguso (USA) 5–7 6–7.
1991 Sweden d. Yugoslavia 2–1: M. Gustafsson (SWE) d. G. Prpic (YUG) 6–2 3–6 6–4; S. Edberg (SWE) d G. Ivanisevic (YUG) 6–4 7–5; Edberg/Gustafsson lost to Prpic/S. Zivojinovic 6–3 3–6 4–6.
1992 Spain d. Czechoslovakia 3–0: E. Sanchez (ESP) d. P. Korda (TCH) 3–6 6–2 7–6; S. Brugera (ESP) d. K. Novacek (TCH) 6–2 6–4; S. Casal/E. Sanchez d. K. Novacek/C. Suk 1–6 6–4 6–3.
1993 USA d. Germany 3–0: P. Sampras (USA) d. M. Stich (GER) 6–4 6–2; M. Chang (USA) d. C.-U. Steeb (GER) 6–3 7–6; P. McEnroe/R. Reneberg (USA) d. P. Kuhnen/M. Stich 6–4 6–3.
1994 Germany d. Spain 2–1: M. Stich (GER) d. S. Bruguera (ESP) 2–6 6–4 6–3; C. Costa (ESP) d. B. Karbacher (GER) 6–2 4–6 6–0; P. Kuhnen/Stich (GER) d. T. Carbonnel/Costa (ESP) 7–5 4–6 6–4.
1995 Sweden d. Croatia 2–1: M. Larsson (SWE) lost to G. Ivanisevic (CRO) 4–6 4–6; S. Edberg (SWE) d. S. Hirszon (CRO) 6–1 6–4; J. Bjorkman/S. Edberg (SWE) d. S. Hirszon/S. Ivanisevic (CRO) 4–6 6–3 6–3.
1996 Switzerland d. Czech Republic 2–1: J. Hlasek (SUI) lost to P. Korda (CZE) 3–6 4–6; M. Rosset (SUI) d. B. Ulihrach (CZE) 7–6 6–2; Hlasek/Rosset (SUI) d. Korda/D. Vacek (CZE) 6–3 6–4.
1997 Spain d. Australia 3–0: F. Mantilla (ESP) d. M. Woodforde (AUS) 7–5 6–2; A. Costa (ESP) d. M. Philippoussis (AUS) 3–6 7–6(3) 7–6(7); T. Carbonell/F.Roig (ESP) d. T. Woodbridge/M. Woodforde (AUS) 6–3 7–5.
1998 Germany d. Czech Republic 3–0: T. Haas (GER) d. S. Dosedel (CZE) 6–1 6–4; N. Kiefer (GER) d. P. Korda (CZE) 7–5 6–3; B. Becker/D. Prinosil (GER) d. C. Suk/D. Vacek (CZE) 6–4 4–6 6–2.
1999 Australia d. Sweden 2–1: J. Bjorkman (SWE) d. M. Philippoussis (AUS) 6–4 7–6; P. Rafter (AUS) d. T. Enqvist (SWE) 5–7 6–3 6–3; P. Rafter/S. Stolle (AUS) d. J. Bjorkman/N. Kulti (SWE) 7–6 6–4.
2000 Slovak Republic d. Russia 3–0: D. Hrbaty (SVK) d. Y Kafelnikov (RUS) 6–4 7–6; K. Kucera (SVK) d. M. Safin (RUS) 6–3 6–2; D. Hrbaty/J. Kroslak (SVK) d. Y. Kafelnikov/M. Safin (RUS) 6–4 6–2.

MEN'S GRAND PRIX (1970–1989)

A points-linked circuit of men's tournaments with a bonus pool distributed to the points leaders at the end of the year and a Masters tournament where field varied in size. Full details available in *World of Tennis 1996*, and previous issues.

GRAND SLAM CUP

Discontinued in 2000 when it was merged with the ATP Tour World Championship to become the Tennis Masters Cup. (see p 468)

A knockout competition launched in 1990 and held in Munich in December until 1997 when it moved to September, for the 16 men who had amassed the most points in the four Grand Slam Championships of Australia, France, Great Britain and the USA. In 1998 a women's event was introduced for eight players and the men's field was reduced from 16 to 12. The competition, administered by the Grand Slam Committee (the four Chairmen) and an Administrator, was promoted by an independent German company and offered prize money of $6 million. A further $2 million went annually to the Grand Slam Development Fund, administered by the ITF.

MEN'S COMPETITION

	WINNER	RUNNER-UP	SCORE					FIRST PRIZE (US$)
1990	P. Sampras	B. Gilbert	6–3	6–4	6–2			2,000,000
1991	D. Wheaton	M. Chang	7–5	6–2	6–4			2,000,000
1992	M. Stich	M. Chang	6–2	6–3	6–2			2,000,000
1993	P. Korda	M. Stich	2–6	6–4	7–6	2–6	11–9	1,625,000
1994	M. Larsson	P. Sampras	7–6	4–6	7–6	6–4		1,625,000
1995	G. Ivanisevic	T. Martin	7–6	6–3	6–4			1,625,000
1996	B. Becker	G. Ivanisevic	6–3	6–4	6–4			1,875,000
	WINNER	RUNNER-UP	SCORE					FIRST PRIZE (US$)
1997	P. Sampras	P. Rafter	6–2	6–4	7–5			2,000,000
1998	M. Rios	A. Agassi	6–4	2–6	7–6	5–7	6–3	1,300,000
1999	G. Rusedski	T. Haas	6–3	6–4	6–7	7–6		1,300,000

WOMEN'S COMPETITION

	WINNER	RUNNER-UP	SCORE			FIRST PRIZE (US$)
1998	V. Williams	P. Schnyder	6–2	3–6	6–2	800,000
1999	S. Williams	V. Williams	6–1	3–6	6–3	800,000

ATP TOUR WORLD CHAMPIONSHIP

Discontinued in 2000 when it was merged with the Grand Slam Cup to become the Tennis Masters Cup. (see p 468)

A season-ending tournament for the top eight men on the ATP Tour ranking list, played in two round-robin groups of four players each and knock-out semi-finals and final.

SINGLES

	VENUE	WINNER	RUNNER-UP	SCORE						FIRST PRIZE
1990	Frankfurt	A. Agassi	S. Edberg	5–7	7–6	7–5	6–2			$950,000
1991	Frankfurt	P. Sampras	J. Courier	3–6	7–6	6–3	6–4			$1,020,000
1992	Frankfurt	B. Becker	J. Courier	6–4	6–3	7–5				$1,020,000
1993	Frankfurt	M. Stich	P. Sampras	7–6	2–6	7–6	6–2			$1,240,000
1994	Frankfurt	P. Sampras	B. Becker	4–6	6–3	7–5	6–4			$1,235,000
1995	Frankfurt	B. Becker	M. Chang	7–6	6–0	7–6				$1,225,000
1996	Hannover	P. Sampras	B. Becker	3–6	7–6	7–6	6–7	6–4		$1,340,000
1997	Hannover	P. Sampras	Y. Kafelnikov	6–3	6–2	6–2				$1,340,000
1998	Hannover	A. Corretja	C. Moya	3–6	3–6	7–5	6–3	7–5		$1,360,000
1999	Hannover	P. Sampras	A. Agassi	6–1	7–5	6–4				$1,385,000

DOUBLES

	VENUE	WINNER	RUNNER-UP	SCORE						FIRST PRIZE
1990	Sanctuary Cove	G. Forget/J. Hlasek	S. Casal/E. Sanchez	6–4	7–6	5–7	6–4			$225,000
1991	Johannesburg	J. Fitzgerald/A. Jarryd	K. Flach/R. Seguso	6–4	6–4	2–6	6–4			$325,000
1992	Johannesburg	T. Woodbridge/M. Woodforde	J. Fitzgerald/A. Jarryd	6–2	7–6	5–7	3–6	6–3		$325,000
1993	Johannesburg	J. Eltingh/P. Haarhuis	T. Woodbridge/ M. Woodforde	7–6	7–6	6–4				$365,000
1994	Jakarta	J. Apell/J. Bjorkman	T. Woodbridge/ M. Woodforde	6–4	4–6	4–6	7–6	7–6		$275,000
1995	Eindhoven	G. Connell/P.Galbraith	J. Eltingh/P. Haarhuis	7–6	7–6	3–6	7–6			$225,000
1996	Hartford	T. Woodbridge/M. Woodforde	S. Lareau/A. O'Brien	6–4	5–7	6–2	7–6			$165,000
1997	Hartford	R. Leach/J. Stark	M. Bhupathi/L. Paes	6–3	6–4	7–6				$145,000
1998	Hartford	J. Eltingh/P. Haarhuis	M. Knowles/D. Nestor	6–4	6–2	7–5				$258,500
1999	Hartford	S. Lareau/A. O'Brien	M Bhupathi/L.Paes	6–3	6–2	6–2				$250,000

TENNIS MASTERS CUP

A new event, jointly owned by The ATP Tour, the Grand Slams and the ITF, replacing the ATP Tour World Championship and the Grand Slam Cup. Played in Lisbon in 2000, it is intended to change the venue each year to a different country, making it a truly global competition.

	WINNER	RUNNER-UP	SCORE			FIRST PRIZE (US$)
2000	G. Kuerten	A. Agassi	6–4	6–4	6–4	1,400,000

WOMEN'S INTERNATIONAL SERIES CHAMPIONSHIPS

(1977–80 Colgate, 1981–82 Toyota, 1983–94 Virginia Slims, 1995 Corel, 1996 to present Chase). Best of 3 sets 1977–1982, best of 5 sets 1983–1998, best of 3 sets 1999 to present.

SINGLES

	VENUE	WINNER	RUNNER-UP	SCORE				FIRST PRIZE
1977	Palm Springs	Miss C. M. Evert	Mrs L. W. King	6–2	6–2			$75,000
1978	Palm Springs	Miss C. M. Evert	Miss M. Navratilova	6–3	6–3			$75,000
1979*	Landover, Maryland	Miss M. Navratilova	Miss T. A. Austin	6–2	6–1			$75,000
1980*	Palm Springs	Miss T. A. Austin	Miss A. Jaeger	6–2	6–2			$75,000
1981	East Rutherford, NJ	Miss T. A. Austin	Miss M. Navratilova	2–6	6–4	6–2		$75,000
1982	East Rutherford, NJ	Miss M. Navratilova	Mrs J. M. Lloyd	4–6	6–1	6–2		$75,000
1983*	Madison Sq. Gdn, NY	Miss M. Navratilova	Mrs J. M. Lloyd	6–3	7–5	6–1		$125,000
1984*	Madison Sq. Gdn, NY	Miss M. Navratilova	Miss H. Sukova	6–3	7–5	6–4		$125,000
1985*	Madison Sq. Gdn, NY	Miss M. Navratilova	Miss H. Mandlikova	6–2	6–0	3–6	6–1	$125,000
1986	Madison Sq. Gdn, NY	Miss M. Navratilova	Miss S. Graf	7–6	6–3	6–2		$125,000
1987	Madison Sq. Gdn, NY	Miss S. Graf	Miss G. Sabatini	4–6	6–4	6–0	6–4	$125,000
1988	Madison Sq. Gdn, NY	Miss G. Sabatini	Miss P. H. Shriver	7–5	6–2	6–2		$125,000
1989	Madison Sq. Gdn, NY	Miss S. Graf	Miss M. Navratilova	6–4	7–5	2–6	6–2	$125,000
1990	Madison Sq. Gdn, NY	Miss M. Seles	Miss G. Sabatini	6–4	5–7	3–6	6–4	6–2 $250,000
1991	Madison Sq. Gdn, NY	Miss M. Seles	Miss M. Navratilova	6–4	3–6	7–5	6–0	$250,000
1992	Madison Sq. Gdn, NY	Miss M. Seles	Miss M. Navratilova	7–5	6–3	6–1		$250,000
1993	Madison Sq. Gdn, NY	Miss S. Graf	Miss A. Sanchez-Vic.	6–1	6–4	3–6	6–1	$250,000
1994	Madison Sq. Gdn, NY	Miss G. Sabatini	Miss L. Davenport	6–3	6–2	6–4		$250,000
1995	Madison Sq. Gdn, NY	Miss S. Graf	Miss A. Huber	6–1	2–6	6–1	4–6	6–3 $500,000
1996	Madison Sq. Gdn, NY	Miss S. Graf	Miss M. Hingis	6–3	4–6	6–0	4–6	6–0 $500,000
1997	Madison Sq. Gdn, NY	Miss J. Novotna	Miss M. Pierce	7–6	6–2	6–3		$500,000
1998	Madison Sq. Gdn, NY	Miss M. Hingis	Miss L. Davenport	7–5	6–4	4–6	6–2	$500,000
1999	Madison Sq. Gdn, NY	Miss L. Davenport	Miss M. Hingis	6–4	6–2			$500,000
2000	Madison Sq. Gdn, NY	Miss M. Hingis	Miss M. Seles	6–7	6–4	6–4		$500,000

DOUBLES

	WINNERS	RUNNERS-UP	SCORE		
1977	Miss F. Durr/Miss S. V. Wade	Mrs H. Gourlay Cawley/Miss J. Russell	6–1	4–6	6–4
1978	Mrs L. W. King/Miss M. Navratilova	Mrs G. E. Reid/Miss W. M. Turnbull	6–3	6–4	
1979*	Mrs L. W. King/Miss M. Navratilova	Miss R. Casals/Mrs J. M. Lloyd	6–4	6–3	
1980*	Miss R. Casals/Miss W. M. Turnbull	Miss C. Reynolds/Miss P. Smith	6–3	4–6	7–6
1991	Miss M. Navratilova/Miss P. H. Shriver	Miss R. Casals/Miss W. M. Turnbull	6–3	6–4	
1982	Miss M. Navratilova/Miss P. H. Shriver	Miss C. Reynolds/Miss P. Smith	6–4	7–5	
1983*	Miss M. Navratilova/Miss P. H. Shriver	Miss J. M. Durie/Miss A. Kiyomura	6–3	6–1	
1984*	Miss M. Navratilova/Miss P. H. Shriver	Miss C. Kohde-Kilsch/Miss H. Sukova	6–7	6–4	7–6
1985*	Miss H. Mandlikova/Miss W. M. Turnbull	Miss C. Kohde-Kilsch/Miss H. Sukova	6–4	6–7	6–3
1986	Miss M. Navratilova/Miss P. H. Shriver	Miss C. Kohde-Kilsch/Miss H. Sukova	7–6	6–3	
1987	Miss M. Navratilova/Miss P. H. Shriver	Miss C. Kohde-Kilsch/Miss H. Sukova	6–1	6–1	
1988	Miss M. Navratilova/Miss P. H. Shriver	Miss L. Savchenko/Miss N. Zvereva	6–3	6–4	
1989	Miss M. Navratilova/Miss P. H. Shriver	Miss L. Savchenko/Miss N. Zvereva	6–3	6–2	
1990	Miss K. Jordan/Mrs P. Smylie	Miss M. Paz/Miss A. Sanchez-Vicario	7–6	6–4	
1991	Miss M. Navratilova/Miss P. H. Shriver	Miss G. Fernandez/Miss J. Novotna	4–6	7–5	6–4
1992	Miss A. Sanchez-Vicario./Miss H. Sukova	Miss J. Novotna/Mrs L. Savchenko-Neil.	7–6	6–1	
1993	Miss G. Fernandez/Miss N. Zvereva	Miss L. Neiland/J. Novotna	6–3	7–6	
1994	Miss G. Fernandez/Miss N. Zvereva	Miss J. Novotna/Miss A. Sanchez-Vicario	6–3	6–7	6–3
1995	Miss J, Novotna/Miss A. Sanchez-Vicario	Miss G. Fernandez/Miss N. Zvereva	6–2	6–1	
1996	Miss L. Davenport/Miss M. J. Fernandez	Miss J. Novotna/Miss A. Sanchez-Vicario	6–2	6–3	
1997	Miss L. Davenport/Miss J. Novotna	Miss A. Fusai/Miss N. Tauziat	6–7	6–3	6–2
1998	Miss L. Davenport/Miss N. Zvereva	Miss A. Fusai/Miss N. Tauziat	6–7	7–5	6–3
1999	Miss M. Hingis/Miss A. Kournikova	Mrs L. Neiland/Miss A. Sanchez-Vicario	6–4	6–4	
2000	Miss M. Hingis/Miss A. Kournikova	Miss N. Arendt/Miss M. Bollegraf	6–2	6–3	

* Played in the following year.

WORLD CHAMPIONSHIP TENNIS

An independent circuit organised by Lamar Hunt's Dallas-based World Championship Tennis Inc which pre-dated the Grand Prix. The eight-man playoff staged annually in Dallas for the points leaders on the circuit set the standard for professionally promoted tennis tournaments. Begun in 1971, the circuit ended with the 1989 World Championship of Tennis. A doubles event was added in 1973 and continued until 1985. From 1986 the doubles event was incorporated into the Masters Doubles. Final round results and prize money can be found in *World of Tennis 1996* and previous issues.

HOPMAN CUP

A mixed team event which takes place annually at the Burswood Resort, Perth, Western Australia. Each tie consists of a men's singles, a ladies' singles and a mixed doubles. Held annually in January. In 1997 became the ITF's official Mixed Teams Championship.

1989 Czechoslovakia d. Australia 2–0: H.Sukova (TCH) d H.Mandlikova (AUS) 6–4 6–3; M.Mecir/Sukova (TCH) d P.Cash/Mandlikova (AUS) 6–2 6–4

1990 Spain d. USA 2–1: A.Sanchez-Vicario (ESP) d P.Shriver (USA) 6–3 6–3; E.Sanchez (ESP) d P.McEnroe (USA) 5–7 7–5 7–5; McEnroe/Shriver (USA) d Sanchez/Sanchez-Vicario (ESP) 6–3 6–2

1991 Yugoslavia d. USA 3–0: M.Seles (YUG) d Z.Garrison (USA) 6–1 6–1; G.Prpic (YUG) d D.Wheaton (USA) 4–6 6–3 7–5; Prpic/Seles (YUG) d Wheaton/Garrison 8–3 (pro set)

1992 Switzerland d. Czechoslovakia 2–1: M.Maleeva-Fragniere (SUI) d H.Sukova (TCH) 6–2 6–4; J.Hlasek (SUI) d K.Novacek (TCH) 6–4 6–4; Novacek/Sukova (TCH) d Hlasek/Maleeva-Fragniere (SUI) 8–4 (pro set)

1993 Germany d. Spain 3–0: S.Graf (GER) d A.Sanchez-Vicario (ESP) 6–4 6–3; M.Stich (GER) d E.Sanchez (ESP) 7–5 6–4; Doubles conceded

1994 Czech Republic d. Germany 2–1: J.Novotna (CZE) d A.Huber (GER) 1–6 6–4 6–3; P.Korda (CZE) d B.Karbacher (GER) 6–3 6–3; Karbacher/Huber (GER) d Korda/Novotna (CZE) 8–3 (pro set)

1995 Germany d. Ukraine 3–0: A.Huber (GER) d N.Medvedeva (UKR) 6–4 3–6 6–4; B.Becker (GER) d A.Medvedev (UKR) 6–3 6–7 6–3; Becker/Huber (GER) wo Medvedev/Medvedeva (UKR) (Medvedev injured)

1996 Croatia d Switzerland 2–1: M.Hingis (SUI) d I.Majoli (CRO) 6–3 6–0; G.Ivanisevic (CRO) d M.Rosset (SUI) 7–6 7–5 ; Ivanisevic/Majoli d Rosset/Hingis (SUI) 3–6 7–6 5–5 ret (Rosset injured)

1997 USA d. South Africa 2–1: C. Rubin (USA) d. A. Coetzer (RSA) 7–5 6–2; W. Ferreira (RSA) d. J. Gimelstob (USA) 6–4 7–6; Gimelstob/Rubin (USA) d. Ferreira/Coetzer (RSA) 3–6 6–2 7–5.

1998 Slovak Republic d. France 2–1: M. Pierce (FRA) d. K. Habsudova (SVK) 6–4 7–5; K. Kucera (SVK) d. C. Pioline (FRA) 7–6 6–4; Kucera/Habsudova (SVK) d. Pioline/Pierce (FRA) 6–3 6–4.

1999 Australia d. Sweden 2–1: J. Dokic (AUS) d. A. Carlsson (SWE) 6–2 7–6; M. Philippoussis (AUS) d. J. Bjorkman (SWE) 6–3 7–6; Bjorkman/Carlsson (SWE) d. Philippoussis/Dokic (AUS) 8–6 (pro set).

2000 South Africa d. Thailand 3–0: A. Coetzer (RSA) d. T. Tanasugarn (THA) 3–6 6–4 6–4; W. Ferreira (RSA) d. P. Srichaphan (THA) 7–6 6–3; W. Ferreira/A. Coetzer (RSA) d. Srichaphan/Tanasugarn 8–1 (pro. set).

ITF VETERAN WORLD CHAMPIONSHIPS

Records from 1981–1989 can be found in previous editions of *World of Tennis*.

1990 Umag, Yugoslavia, 26 May–3 June

MEN			WOMEN		
35 Singles	Robert Machan	(HUN)	40 Singles	Marie Pinterova	(HUN)
35 Doubles	Robert Machan	(HUN)	40 Doubles	Barbara Mueller	(USA)
	Lajos Levai	(GER)		Louise Cash	(USA)
45 Singles	Harald Elschenbroich	(GER)	50 Singles	Margit Schultze	(ESP)
45 Doubles	Dick Johnson	(USA)	50 Doubles	Kay Schiavinato	(AUS)
	Jiim Parker	(USA)		Jan Blackshaw	(AUS)
55 Singles	Istvan Gulyas	(HUN)	60 Singles	Louise Owen	(USA)
55 Doubles	Ken Sinclair	(CAN)	60 Doubles	Lurline Stock	(AUS)
	Lorne Main	(CAN)		Dulcie Young	(AUS)
60 Singles	Sven Davidson	(SWE)			
60 Doubles	Sven Davidson	(SWE)			
	Hugh Stewart	(USA)			
65 Singles	Robert McCarthy	(AUS)			
65 Doubles	Oskar Jirkovsky	(AUT)			
	Josef Karlhofer	(AUT)			
70 Singles	William Parsons	(USA)			
70 Doubles	Alex Swetka	(USA)			
	Albert Ritzenberg	(USA)			

1991 Perth, Australia, 17–23 May

MEN			WOMEN		
35 Singles	Paul Torre	(FRA)	40 Singles	Carol Bailey	(USA)
35 Doubles	Yustedjo Traik	(INA)	40 Doubles	Carol Bailey	(USA)
	Atet Wijono	(INA)		Barbara Mueller	(USA)
45 Singles	Don McCormick	(CAN)	50 Singles	Charleen Hillebrand	(USA)
45 Doubles	Bruce Burns	(AUS)	50 Doubles	Betty Whitelaw	(AUS)
	John Weaver	(AUS)		Jan Blackshaw	(AUS)
55 Singles	Peter Froelich	(AUS)	55 Singles	Carol Wood	(USA)
55 Doubles	Gordon Davis	(USA)	55 Doubles	Carol Wood	(USA)
	Herman Ahlers	(USA)		Margaret Kohler	(USA)
60 Singles	Lorne Main	(CAN)	60 Singles	Betty Pratt	(USA)
60 Doubles	Frank Sedgman	(AUS)	60 Doubles	Ruth Illingworth	(GBR)
	Clive Wilderspin	(AUS)		Ann Williams	(GBR)
65 Singles	Robert McCarthy	(AUS)			
65 Doubles	Robert McCarthy	(AUS)			
	Bob Howe	(AUS)			
70 Singles	Robert Sherman	(USA)			
70 Doubles	Verne Hughes	(USA)			
	Merwin Miller	(USA)			

1992 Palermo, Sicily, 17–23 May

35 Singles	Ferrante Rocchi-Landir	(ITA)	35 Singles	Sally Freeman	(GBR)
35 Doubles	Paul French	(GBR)	35 Doubles	Luisa Figueroa	(ARG)
	Stanislav Birner	(CZE)		Oliveira Villani	(BRA)
45 Singles	Rolf Staguhn	(GER)	40 Singles	Marilyn Rasmussen	(AUS)
45 Doubles	Gary Penberthy	(AUS)	40 Doubles	Marilyn Rasmussen	(AUS)
	Bens De Jell	(NED)		Lesley Charles	(GBR)
50 Singles	Jorge Lemann	(BRA)	45 Singles	Marie Pinterova	(HUN)
50 Doubles	Gerhard Schelch	(AUT)	45 Doubles	Marie Pinterova	(HUN)
	Peter Fuchs	(AUT)		Shirley Brasher	(GBR)
55 Singles	Klaus Fuhrmann	(GER)	50 Singles	Charleen Hillebrand	(USA)
55 Doubles	Hugh Stewart	(USA)	50 Doubles	Charleen Hillebrand	(USA)
	Les Dodson	(USA)		Jacqueline Boothman	(GBR)
60 Singles	Werner Mertins	(GER)	55 Singles	Nancy Reed	(USA)
60 Doubles	Ken Sinclair	(CAN)	55 Doubles	Nancy Reed	(USA)
	Lorne Main	(CAN)		Belmar Gunderson	(USA)
65 Singles	Robert McCarthy	(AUS)	60 Singles	Beverley Rae	(AUS)

1992 Palermo, Sicily, 17–23 May (continued)

65 Doubles	Robert McCarthy	(AUS)	60 Doubles	Beverley Rae	(AUS)
	Bob Howe	(AUS)		Astri Hobson	(AUS)
70 Singles	Robert Sherman	(USA)			
70 Doubles	Robert Sherman	(USA)			
	Mario Isidori	(ITA)			
75 Singles	Gaetano Longo	(ITA)			
75 Doubles	Tiverio De Grad	(ROM)			
	Georg Hunger	(GER)			

1993 Barcelona, Spain, 4–11 April

35 Singles	Fernando Luna	(ESP)	35 Singles	Jutta Fahlbusch	(GER)
35 Doubles	Steven Packham	(AUS)	35 Doubles	Jutta Fahlbusch	(GER)
	Tony Luttrell	(AUS)		Dagmar Anwar	(GER)
45 Singles	Robert Machan	(HUN)	40 Singles	Maria Geyer	(AUT)
45 Doubles	Robert Machan	(HUN)	40 Doubles	Elizabeth Craig	(AUS)
	Miodrag Mijuca	(GER)		Carol Campling	(AUS)
50 Singles	Jorge Lemann	(BRA)	45 Singles	Marie Pinterova	(HUN)
50 Doubles	James Parker	(USA)	45 Doubles	Marie Pinterova	(HUN)
	Ken Robinson	(USA)		Tuija Hannuakainen	(FIN)
55 Singles	King Van Nostrand	(USA)	50 Singles	Cathie Anderson	(USA)
55 Doubles	King Van Nostrand	(USA)	50 Doubles	Brigitte Hoffman	(GER)
	Juan Manuel Couder	(ESP)		Siegrun Fuhrmann	(GER)
60 Singles	Lorne Main	(CAN)	55 Singles	Roberta Beltrame	(ITA)
60 Doubles	Lorne Main	(CAN)	55 Doubles	Belmar Gunderson	(USA)
	Ken Sinclair	(CAN)		Nancy Reed	(USA)
65 Singles	Jason Morton	(USA)	60 Singles	Nancy Reed	(USA)

MEN

65 Doubles	Laci Legenstein	(AUT)
	Hugh Stewart	(USA)
70 Singles	Tom Brown	(USA)
70 Doubles	Tom Brown	(USA)
	Buck Archer	(USA)
75 Singles	Gordon Henley	(AUS)
75 Doubles	Albert Ritzenberg	(USA)
	Mirek Kizlink	(GBR)

1994 (Group A) Buenos Aires, Argentina, 30 October–6 November

35 Singles	Jose Luis Clerc	(ARG)
35 Doubles	Jose Luis Clerc	(ARG)
	Victor Pecci	(PAR)
45 Singles	Jairo Velasco	(ESP)
45 Doubles	Jairo Velasco	(ESP)
	Thomaz Koch	(BRA)
50 Singles	James Parker	(USA)
50 Doubles	James Parker	(USA)
	Ken Robinson	(USA)

1994 (Group B) Los Gatos, California, USA 22–29 May

55 Singles	Gil Howard	(USA)
55 Doubles	Klaus Fuhrmann	(GER)
	Leslie Dodson	(USA)
60 Singles	King Van Nostrand	(USA)
60 Doubles	Russell Seymour	(USA)
	Whitney Reed	(USA)
65 Singles	Jason Morton	(USA)
65 Doubles	Jason Morton	(USA)
	William Davis	(USA)
70 Singles	Oskar Jirkovsky	(AUT)
70 Doubles	Francis Bushmann	(USA)
	Vincent Fotre	(USA)
75 Singles	Alex Swetka	(USA)
75 Doubles	Dan Walker	(USA)
	Verne Hughes	(USA)

1995 (Group A), Bad Neuenahr, Germany, 6–13 August

35 Singles	Thibaut Kuentz	(FRA)
35 Doubles	Thibaut Kuentz	(FRA)
	Stephan Medem	(GER)
45 Singles	Robert Machan	(HUN)
45 Doubles	Armistead Neely	(USA)
	Larry Turville	(USA)
50 Singles	Giorgio Rohrich	(ITA)
50 Doubles	Jody Rush	(USA)
	Richard Johnson	(USA)

1995 (Group B), Nottingham, England, 21–28 May

55 Singles	Len Saputo	(USA)
55 Doubles	Leslie Dodson	(USA)
	Klaus Fuhrmann	(GER)
60 Singles	James Nelson	(USA)
60 Doubles	James Nelson	(USA)
	Leonard Lindborg	(USA)
65 Singles	Lorne Main	(CAN)
65 Doubles	Lorne Main	(CAN)
	Ken Sinclair	(CAN)
70 Singles	Oskar Jirkovsky	(AUT)
70 Doubles	Brian Hurley	(AUS)
	Neale Hook	(AUS)
75 Singles	Robert Sherman	(USA)
75 Doubles	Mirek Kizlink	(GBR)
	Antony Starling	(GBR)

WOMEN

60 Doubles	Marta Pombo	(ESP)
	Ana Maria Estalella	(ESP)
65 Singles	Betty Pratt	(USA)
65 Doubles	Betty Pratt	(USA)
	Betty Cookson	(USA)

1994 (Group A) Buenos Aires, Argentina, 30 October–6 November

35 Singles	Jutta Fahlbusch	(GER)
35 Doubles	Marcela De Gregorio	(ARG)
	Beatriz Villaverde	(ARG)
45 Singles	Renata Vojtischek	(GER)
45 Doubles	Tina Karwasky	(USA)
	Susan Stone	(CAN)
50 Singles	Louise Cash	(USA)
50 Doubles	Carol Campling	(AUS)
	Elizabeth Craig	(AUS)

1994 (Group B) Los Gatos, California, USA 22–29 May

50 Singles	Petro Kruger	(RSA)
50 Doubles	Ellen Bryant	(USA)
	Barbara Mueller	(USA)
55 Singles	Rosie Darmon	(FRA)
55 Doubles	Dorothy Matthiessen	(USA)
	Lynn Little	(USA)
60 Singles	Ilse Michael	(GER)
60 Doubles	Nancy Reed	(USA)
	Belmar Gunderson	(USA)
65 Singles	Louise Owen	(USA)
65 Doubles	Louise Owen	(USA)
	Liz Harper	(USA)

1995 (Group A), Bad Neuenahr, Germany, 6–13 August

35 Singles	Regina Marsikova	(CZE)
40 Singles	Renata Vojtishek	(GER)
40 Doubles	Renata Vojtishek	(GER)
	Tina Karwasky	(USA)
45 Singles	Marie Pinterova	(HUN)
45 Doubles	Elizabeth Craig-Allan	(AUS)
	Carol Campling	(AUS)

1995 (Group B), Nottingham, England, 21–28 May

50 Singles	Charleen Hillebrand	(USA)
50 Doubles	Elly Keocke	(NED)
	Jacqueline Boothman	(GBR)
55 Singles	Renate Mayer-Zdralek	(GER)
55 Doubles	Carol Wood	(USA)
	Sinclair Bill	(USA)
60 Singles	Jennifer Hoad	(ESP)
60 Doubles	Rita Lauder	(GBR)
	Ruth Illingworth	(GBR)
65 Singles	Betty Pratt	(USA)
65 Doubles	Louise Owen	(USA)
	Elaine Mason	(USA)

1996 (Group A) Velden, Austria 15–22 September 1996

MEN			WOMEN		
35 Singles	Greg Neuhart	(USA)	35 Singles	Regina Marsikova	(CZE)
35 Doubles	Greg Neuhart	(USA)	35 Doubles	Regina Marsikova	(CZE)
	Mike Fedderly	(USA)		Jutta Fahlbusch	(GER)
40 Singles	Julio Goes	(BRA)	40 Singles	Renata Vojtischek	(GER)
40 Doubles	Julio Goes	(BRA)	40 Doubles	Renata Vojtischek	(GER)
	Harry Ufer	(BRA)		Tina Karwasky	(USA)
45 Singles	Jairo Velasco	(ESP)	45 Singles	Marie Pinterova	(HUN)
45 Doubles	Jairo Velasco	(ESP)	45 Doubles	Marie Pinterova	(HUN)
	Robert Machan	(HUN)		Heide Orth	(GER)
50 Singles	Peter Pokorny	(AUT)	50 Singles	Eva Szabo	(HUN)
50 Doubles	Ted Hoehn	(USA)	50 Doubles	Carol Campling	(AUS)
	Richard Johnson	(USA)		Elizabeth Craig-Allan	(AUS)

1996 (Group B), Vienna, Austria 26 May–2 June 1996

55 Singles	Giorgio Rohrich	(ITA)	55 Singles	Charleen Hillebrand	(USA)
55 Doubles	Peter Pokorny	(AUT)	55 Doubles	Dorothy Matthiessen	(USA)
	Hans Gradischnig	(AUT)		Sinclair Bill	(USA)
60 Singles	King Van Nostrand	(USA)	60 Singles	Ilse Michael	(GER)
60 Doubles	Jim Nelson	(USA)	60 Doubles	Inge Weber	(CAN)
	Bob Duesler	(USA)		Nancy Reed	(USA)
65 Singles	Lorne Main	(CAN)	65 Singles	Ines De Pla	(ARG)
65 Doubles	Lorne Main	(CAN)	65 Doubles	Ruth Illingworth	(GBR)
	Ken Sinclair	(CAN)		Rita Lauder	(GBR)
70 Singles	Fred Kovaleski	(USA)	70 Singles	Betty Pratt	(USA)
70 Doubles	Fred Kovaleski	(USA)	70 Doubles	Betty Pratt	(USA)
	Bob Howe	(AUS)		Elaine Mason	(USA)
75 Singles	Robert Sherman	(USA)			
75 Doubles	Merwin Miller	(USA)			
	Verne Hughes	(USA)			
80 Singles	Dan Miller	(USA)			
80 Doubles	Dan Miller	(USA)			
	Irving Converse	(USA)			

1997 (Group A) Johannesburg, South Africa 21–28 September 1997

35 Singles	Greg Neuhart	(USA)	35 Singles	Tracy Houk	(USA)
35 Doubles	Chris Loock	(RSA)	35 Doubles	Alexi Beggs	(USA)
	Kobus Visagie	(RSA)		Vikki Beggs	(USA)
40 Singles	Pierre Godfroid	(BEL)	40 Singles	Renata Vojtischek	(GER)
40 Doubles	Pierre Godfroid	(BEL)	40 Doubles	Sherri Bronson	(USA)
	Bruce Osborne	(AUS)		Helle Viragh	(USA)
45 Singles	Frank Puncec	(RSA)	45 Singles	Rita Theron	(RSA)
45 Doubles	Max Bates	(AUS)	45 Doubles	Kerry Ballard	(AUS)
	Andrew Rae	(AUS)		Wendy Gilchrist	(AUS)
50 Singles	Jairo Velasco	(ESP)	50 Singles	Marie Pinterova	(HUN)
50 Doubles	Jairo Velasco	(ESP)	50 Doubles	Elizabeth Craig-Allan	(AUS)
	Luis Flor	(ESP)		Carol Campling	(AUS)

1997 (Group B) Newcastle, New South Wales 14–20 April 1997

55 Singles	Bob Howes	(AUS)	55 Singles	Heide Orth	(GER)
55 Doubles	Maurice Broom	(AUS)	55 Doubles	Lyn Wayte	(AUS)
	Max Senior	(AUS)		Margaret Wayte	(AUS)
60 Singles	Klaus Fuhrmann	(GER)	60 Singles	Judith Dalton	(AUS)
60 Doubles	Robert Duesler	(USA)	60 Doubles	Lorice Forbes	(AUS)
	Jim Nelson	(USA)		Peg Hoysted	(AUS)
65 Singles	Russell Seymour	(USA)	65 Singles	Beverley Rae	(AUS)
65 Doubles	William Davis	(USA)	65 Doubles	Ruth Illingworth	(GBR)
	Chuck De Voe	(USA)		Rita Lauder	(GBR)
70 Singles	Laci Legenstein	(AUT)	70 Singles	Twinx Rogers	(RSA)
70 Doubles	Laci Legenstein	(AUT)	70 Doubles	Deedy Krebs	(USA)
	Fred Kovaleski	(USA)		Elaine Mason	(USA)
75 Singles	Robert Sherman	(USA)			
75 Doubles	Robert Sherman	(USA)			
	Ellis Williamson	(USA)			
80 Singles	Alex Swetka	(USA)			
80 Doubles	Alex Swetka	(USA)			
	Gordon Henley	(AUS)			

1998 (Group A) Nottingham, England 27 September–4 October 1998

MEN			WOMEN		
35 Singles	Nick Fulwood	(GBR)	35 Singles	Tracy Houk	(USA)
35 Doubles	Nick Fulwood	(GBR)	35 Doubles	Susanne Turi	(HUN)
	Brad Properjohn	(AUS)		Kathy Vick	(USA)
40 Singles	Pierre Godfroid	(BEL)	40 Singles	Ros Balodis	(AUS)
40 Doubles	Pierre Godfroid	(BEL)	40 Doubles	Ros Balodis	(AUS)
	Bruce Osbourne	(AUS)		Kaye Nealon	(AUS)
45 Singles	Wayne Cowley	(AUS)	45 Singles	Marlie Buehler	(USA)
45 Doubles	Benson Greatrex	(GBR)	45 Doubles	Elizabeth Boyle	(GBR)
	Philip Siviter	(GBR)		Pauline Fisher	(GBR)
50 Singles	Frank Briscoe	(RSA)	50 Singles	Marie Pinterova	(HUN)
50 Doubles	Keith Bland	(GBR)	50 Doubles	Carol Campling	(AUS)
	Richard Tutt	(GBR)		Elizabeth Craig-Allan	(AUS)

1998 (Group B) Palm Beach Gardens, FL, USA 3–10 May 1998

55 Singles	Bob Howes	(AUS)	55 Singles	Heide Orth	(GER)
55 Doubles	Stasys Labanauskas	(LIT)	55 Doubles	Heide Orth	(GER)
	Peter Pokorny	(AUT)		Rosy Darmon	(FRA)
60 Singles	Bodo Nitsche	(GER)	60 Singles	Judith Dalton	(AUS)
60 Doubles	Henry Leichtfried	(USA)	60 Doubles	Belmar Gunderson	(USA)
	Leonard Lindborg	(USA)		Katie Koontz	(USA)
65 Singles	Jim Perley	(USA)	65 Singles	Clelia Mazzoleni	(ITA)
65 Doubles	Lorne Main	(CAN)	65 Doubles	Astri Hobson	(AUS)
	Kenneth Sinclair	(CAN)		Margaret Robinson	(AUS)
70 Singles	Jason Morton	(USA)	70 Singles	Betty Eisenstein	(USA)
70 Doubles	Jason Morton	(USA)	70 Doubles	Phyllis Adler	(USA)
	Fred Kovaleski	(USA)		Elaine Mason	(USA)
75 Singles	Robert Sherman	(USA)	80 Singles	Alex Swetka	(USA)
75 Doubles	Fran Bushmann	(USA)	80 Doubles	Irving Converse	(USA)
	George Druliner	(USA)		Dan Miller	(USA)

1999 (Group A) Amsterdam, The Netherlands, 15–22 August 1999

35 Singles	Ned Caswell (USA)		35 Singles	Klaartje Van Baarle (BEL)
35 Doubles	Ned Caswell (USA)		35 Doubles	Jackie Reardon (GBR)
	Mike Fedderly (USA)			Jackie Van Wijk (NED)
40 Singles	Maris Rozentals (LAT)		40 Singles	Anna Iuale (ITA)
40 Doubles	Pierre Godfroid (BEL)		40 Doubles	Gerda Preissing (GER)
	Maris Rozentals (LAT)			Beatriz Villaverde (ARG)
45 Singles	Andrew Rae (AUS)		45 Singles	Renata Vojtischek (GER)
45 Doubles	Rob Prouse (AUS)		45 Doubles	Mary Ginnard (USA)
	Andrew Rae (AUS)			Lilian Peltz-Petow (USA)
50 Singles	Lito Alvarez (AUS)		50 Singles	Marie Pinterova (HUN)
50 Doubles	Lito Alvarez (AUS)		50 Doubles	Elizabeth Allan (AUS)
	Peter Rigg (AUS)			Carol Campling (AUS)

1999 (Group B) Barcelona, Spain, 28 March–4 April 1999

55 Singles	Giorgio Rohrich (ITA)		55 Singles	Heide Orth (GER)
55 Doubles	Giorgio Rohrich (ITA)		55 Doubles	Petro Kuger (RSA)
	Bepi Zambon (ITA)			Marietjie Viljoen (RSA)
60 Singles	Roberto Aubone (ARG)		60 Singles	Jan Blackshaw (AUS)
60 Doubles	Bob Duesler (USA)		60 Doubles	Jan Blackshaw (AUS)
	Henry Leichtfried (USA)			Mary Gordon (AUS)
65 Singles	Jim Perley (USA)		65 Singles	Nancy Reed (USA)
65 Doubles	Lorne Main (CAN)		65 Doubles	Belmar Gunderson (USA)
	Kenneth Sinclair (CAN)			Nancy Reed (USA)
70 Singles	William Davis (USA)		70 Singles	Ines Pla (ARG)
70 Doubles	Kingman Lambert (USA)		70 Doubles	Amelia Cury (BRA)
	Jason Morton (USA)			Ines Pla (ARG)
75 Singles	Oskar Jirkovsky (AUT)		75 Singles	Dorothy Cheney (USA)
75 Doubles	Francis Bushman (USA)		75 Doubles	Julia Borzone (ARG)
	Newton Meade (USA)			Carmen Fernandez (MEX)
80 Singles	Alex Swetka (USA)			
80 Doubles	Nehemiah Atkinson (USA)			
	Gardnar Mulloy (USA)			
85 Singles	Gardnar Mulloy (USA)			
85 Doubles	Edward Baumer (USA)			
	David Carey (USA)			

2000 (Group A) Buenos Aires, Argentina, 29 October – 5 November 2000

MEN			WOMEN		
35 Singles	Jaroslav Bulant	(CZE)	35 Singles	Raquel Contreras	(MEX)
35 Doubles	Ricardo Rivera	(ARG)	35 Doubles	Beatrix Mezger-Reboul	(GER)
	Gustavo Tiberti	(ARG)		Cora Salimei	(ARG)
40 Singles	Patrick Serrett	(AUS)	40 Singles	Gabriela Groell-Dinu	(GER)
40 Doubles	Mike Fedderly	(USA)	40 Doubles	Ros Balodis	(AUS)
	Paul Smith	(USA)		Kaye Nealon	(AUS)
45 Singles	Victor Pecci	(PAR)	45 Singles	Elly Appel	(NED)
45 Doubles	Michael Collins	(AUS)	45 Doubles	Ann Brown	(GBR)
	Wayne Pascoe	(AUS)		Pauline Fisher	(GBR)
50 Singles	Bruno Renoult	(FRA)	50 Singles	Heidi Eisterlehner	(GER)
50 Doubles	Max Bates	(AUS)	50 Doubles	Elizabeth Allan	(AUS)
	Xavier Lemoine	(FRA)		Carol Campling	(AUS)

2000 (Group B) Cape Town, South Africa, 26 March-2 April 2000

55 Singles	Hugh Thomson	(USA)	55 Singles	Ellie Krocke	(NED)
55 Doubles	Ben de Jel	(NED)	55 Doubles	Charleen Hillebrand	(USA)
	Hans-Joa Ploetz	(GER)		Suella Steel	(USA)
60 Singles	Robert Howes	(AUS)	60 Singles	Rosy Darmon	(FRA)
60 Doubles	Bodo Nitsche	(GER)	60 Doubles	Sinclair Bill	(USA)
	Peter Pokorny	(AUT)		Rosy Darmon	(FRA)
65 Singles	Joseph Mateo	(FRA)	65 Singles	Lee Burling	(USA)
65 Doubles	Abie Nothnagel	(RSA)	65 Doubles	Patricia Bruorton	(RSA)
	Neville Whitfield	(RSA)		Jackie Zylstra	(RSA)
70 Singles	Lorne Main	(CAN)	70 Singles	Louise Owen	(USA)
70 Doubles	Lorne Main	(CAN)	70 Doubles	Louise Owen	(USA)
	Kenneth Sinclair	(CAN)		Louise Russ	(USA)
75 Singles	Vincent Fotre	(USA)	75 Singles	Elaine Mason	(USA)
75 Doubles	Neale Hooke	(AUS)	75 Doubles	Twinx Rogers	(RSA)
	Brian Hurley	(AUS)		Amy Wilmot	(RSA)
80 Singles	Robert Sherman	(USA)			
80 Doubles	Nehemiah Atkinson	(USA)			
	Alex Swetka	(USA)			
85 Singles	David Carey	(CAN)			
85 Doubles	David Carey	(CAN)			
	Edward Baumer	(USA)			

ITALIA CUP

International Men's Team Competition for 35 year age group.

Records for before 1990 can be found in previous editions of *World of Tennis*.

	VENUE	WINNERS	RUNNERS-UP	FINAL SCORE
1990	Glasgow (GBR)	Spain	Australia	2–1
1991	Melbourne (AUS)	Australia	Spain	3–0
1992	Ancona, (ITA)	Italy	France	2–1
1993	Barcelona (ESP)	Spain	France	3–0
1994	Rosario, Argentina (ARG)	Germany	USA	2–1
1995	Dormagen (GER)	Germany	USA	2–1
1996	Rome (ITA)	USA	Italy	2–1
1997	Johannesburg (RSA)	USA	Great Britain	2–1
1998	Winchester (GBR)	Great Britain	Italy	2–1
1999	Velbert (GER)	Great Britain	Germany	2–1
2000	Buenos Aires (ARG)	Germany	USA	3–0

TONY TRABERT CUP

International Men's Team Competition for 40 year age group.

	VENUE	WINNERS	RUNNERS-UP	FINAL SCORE
2000	Santa Cruz (BOL)	USA	Germany	3–0

DUBLER CUP

International Men's Team Competition for 45 year age group.
Records for before 1990 can be found in previous editions of *World of Tennis*.

FINALS

	VENUE	WINNERS	RUNNERS-UP	FINAL SCORE
1990	Bol (YUG)	Germany	USA	2–1
1991	Sydney (AUS)	USA	Germany	3–0
1992	Portschach (AUT)	Germany	Spain	2–1
1993	Barcelona (ESP)	Spain	France	2–1
	VENUE	WINNERS	RUNNERS-UP	FINAL SCORE
1994	Santiago (CHI)	USA	Chile	2–1
1995	Saarbrucken (GER)	USA	Germany	2–1
1996	Velden (AUT)	USA	Australia	3–0
1997	Pretoria (RSA)	Austria	South Africa	2–1
1998	Dublin (IRL)	USA	Spain	2–1
1999	Luxembourg (LUX)	Brazil	Spain	2–1
2000	Asuncion (PAR)	USA	France	2–1

FRED PERRY CUP

International Men's Team Competition for 50 year age group.

	VENUE	WINNERS	RUNNERS-UP	FINAL SCORE
1991	Bournemouth (GBR)	Germany	Great Britain	3–0
1992	Berlin (GER)	Germany	USA	3–0
1993	Royan (FRA)	Germany	USA	2–1
1994	Buenos Aires (ARG)	France	USA	2–1
1995	Luchow (GER)	France	Germany	2–1
1996	Pörtschach (AUT)	Germany	Austria	2–1
1997	Sun City (RSA)	Spain	Germany	2–1
1998	Glasgow (GBR)	USA	Spain	2–1
1999	Amstelveen (NED)	USA	Spain	3–0
2000	Santiago (CHI)	USA	Chile	2–1

AUSTRIA CUP

International Men's Team Competition for 55 year age group.
Records for before 1990 can be found in previous editions of *World of Tennis*.

	VENUE	WINNERS	RUNNERS-UP	FINAL SCORE
1990	Pörtschach (AUT)	Canada	USA	3–0
1991	Sydney (AUS)	USA	Australia	3–0
1992	Monte Carlo (FRA)	Germany	USA	3–0
1993	Murcia (ESP)	USA	Australia	3–0
1994	Carmel Valley (USA)	Australia	USA	2–1
1995	Dublin (IRL)	Germany	Austria	2–1
1996	Pörtschach (AUT)	Austria	USA	2–1
1997	Canberra (AUS)	Austria	Germany	2–1
1998	Naples (USA)	USA	Netherlands	3–0
1999	Teia (ESP)	France	Germany	2–0
2000	Pietermaritzburg (RSA)	USA	France	2–1

VON CRAMM CUP

International Men's Team Competition for 60 year age group.
Records for before 1990 can be found in previous editions of *World of Tennis*.

	VENUE	WINNERS	RUNNERS-UP	FINAL SCORE
1990	Ontario (CAN)	USA	Austria	2–1
1991	Adelaide (AUS)	USA	New Zealand	2–1
1992	Bournemouth (GBR)	Canada	USA	2–1
1993	Aix les Bains (FRA)	USA	France	3–0
1994	Burlingame (USA)	USA	Germany	3–0
1995	Pörtschach (AUT)	USA	Germany	3–0
1996	Velden (AUT)	USA	France	3–0

VENUE/WINNERS		RUNNERS-UP	FINAL SCORE
1997	Hamilton (NZL)	USA	Australia	3–0
1998	Fort Lauderdale (USA)	Germany	USA	2–1
1999	Tarragona (ESP)	Germany	Argentina	2–1
2000	Cape Town (RSA)	Austria	Australia	2–1

BRITANNIA CUP

International Men's Team Competition for 65 year age group.
Records for before 1990 can be found in previous editions of *World of Tennis*.

	VENUE	WINNERS	RUNNERS-UP	FINAL SCORE
1990	Bournemouth (GBR)	USA	Australia	2–1
1991	Canberra (AUS)	Austria	Australia	2–1
1992	Seefeld (AUT)	Australia	Austria	2–1
1993	Le Touquet (FRA)	USA	Italy	2–1
1994	Portola Valley (USA)	USA	Austria	2–1
1995	Glasgow (GBR)	USA	Canada	2–1
1996	Villach (AUT)	USA	Canada	2–1
1997	Hamilton (NZL)	USA	Canada	2–1
1998	Palm Beach Gardens (USA)	Canada	USA	3–0
1999	Girona (ESP)	USA	Canada	2–1
2000	Cape Town (RSA)	Australia	USA	2–1

CRAWFORD CUP

International Men's Team Competition for 70 year age group.
Records for before 1990 can be found in previous editions of *World of Tennis*.

	VENUE	WINNERS	RUNNERS-UP	FINAL SCORE
1990	Brand (AUT)	USA	Brazil	3–0
1991	Canberra (AUS)	Germany	USA	2–1
1992	Le Touquet (FRA)	USA	Germany	3–0
1993	Menorca (ESP)	USA	France	3–0
1994	Oakland (USA)	Australia	France	2–1
1995	Aix-les-Bains (FRA)	USA	Australia	2–1
1996	Seeboden (AUT)	Austria	USA	2–1
1997	Adelaide (AUS)	Austria	USA	2–1
1998	Pompano Beach (USA)	USA	Austria	2–1
1999	Barcelona (ESP)	USA	Australia	3–0
2000	Cape Town (RSA)	Canada	USA	2–1

BITSY GRANT CUP

International Men's Team Competition for 75 year age group.

	VENUE	WINNERS	RUNNERS-UP	FINAL SCORE
1994	Mill Valley (USA)	USA	Mexico	3–0
1995	Bournemouth (GBR)	USA	Sweeden	3–0
1996	Bad Waltersdorf (AUT)	USA	Germany	3–0
1997	Hobart, Tasmania (AUS)	USA	Australia	3–0
1998	Boca Raton (USA)	USA	Australia	3–0
1999	Barcelona (ESP)	USA	Mexico	3–0
2000	Cape Town (RSA)	USA	Great Britain	3–0

GARDNAR MULLOY CUP

International Men's Team Competition for 80 year age group.

	VENUE	WINNERS	RUNNERS-UP	FINAL SCORE
1996	Seefeld (AUT)	USA	Mexico	Round Robin
1997	Melbourne (AUS)	USA	Australia	Round Robin
1998	Naples (USA)	USA	Australia	Round Robin
1999	Murcia (ESP)	USA	Australia	3–0
2000	Cape Town (RSA)	USA	Australia	2–1

YOUNG CUP

International Women's Team Competition for 40 year age group.

Records for before 1990 can be found in previous editions of *World of Tennis*.

	VENUE	WINNERS	RUNNERS-UP	FINAL SCORE
1990	Keszthely (HUN)	France	USA	3–0
1991	Brisbane (AUS)	Australia	Germany	2–1
1992	Macahide (IRE)	Great Britain	Australia	2–1
1993	Bournemouth (GBR)	USA	Great Britain	2–1
1994	Montivideo (URU)	USA	Germany	2–1
1995	Dortmund (GER)	USA	Germany	2–1
1996	Bad Hofgastein (AUT)	USA	Germany	2–1
1997	Pretoria (RSA)	USA	Germany	3–0
1998	Halton (GBR)	USA	South Africa	3–0
1999	Gladbeck (GER)	USA	Argentina	3–0
2000	Mar del Plata (ARG)	Germany	Argentina	2–0

MARGARET COURT CUP

International Women's Team Competition for 45 year age group.

	VENUE	WINNERS	RUNNERS-UP	FINAL SCORE
1994	Perth (AUS)	France	USA	2–1
1995	Gladbeck (GER)	USA	Australia	3–0
1996	Seeboden (AUT)	USA	South Africa	2–1
1997	Pretoria (RSA)	USA	France	3–0
1998	Warwick (GBR)	USA	South Africa	2–1
1999	Hoofddorp (NED)	Germany	Austria	3–0
2000	Montevideo (URU)	USA	Netherlands	3–0

MARIA ESTHER BUENO CUP

International Women's Team Competition for 50 year age group.

Records for before 1990 can be found in previous editions of *World of Tennis*.

	VENUE	WINNERS	RUNNERS-UP	FINAL SCORE
1990	Barcelona (ESP)	Australia	Spain	2–1
1991	Perth (AUS)	USA	France	3–0
1992	Bagnoles De L'Orne (FRA)	USA	France	2–1
1993	Barcelona (ESP)	USA	Germany	2–1
1994	San Francisco (USA)	USA	Germany	3–0
1995	Velden (AUT)	Netherlands	USA	2–1
1996	St. Kanzian (AUT)	Australia	Germany	2–1
1997	Pretoria (RSA)	Australia	Germany	2–1
1998	Dublin (IRL)	USA	Australia	2–1
1999	Hoofddorp (NED)	USA	Germany	3–0
2000	Sao Paolo (BRA)	France	USA	2–1

MAUREEN CONNOLLY CUP

International Women's Team Competition for 55 year age group.

	VENUE	WINNERS	RUNNERS-UP	FINAL SCORE
1992	Tyler (USA)	Australia	Great Britain	2–1
1993	Corsica (FRA)	USA	France	3–0
1994	Carmel (USA)	USA	France	2–1
1995	Le Touquet (FRA)	France	South Africa	2–1
1996	Eugendorf (AUT)	France	USA	2–1
1997	Canberra (AUS)	USA	France	3–0
1998	Pompano Beach (USA)	Germany	Great Britain	3–0
1999	Murcia (ESP)	USA	Netherlands	3–0
2000	Durban (RSA)	South Africa	USA	2–1

ALICE MARBLE CUP

International Women's Team Competition for 60 year age group.
Records for before 1990 can be found in previous editions of *World of Tennis.*

	VENUE	WINNERS	RUNNERS-UP	FINAL SCORE
1990	Paderborn (GER)	USA	Germany	2–1
1991	Perth (AUS)	USA	Great Britain	3–0
1992	Keszthely (HUN)	Great Britain	USA	2–1
1993	Pörtschach (AUT)	USA	Great Britain	2–1
1994	Carmel Valley (USA)	USA	Great Britain	2–1
1995	Worthing (GBR)	USA	Spain	2–1
1996	Bad Hofgastein (AUT)	USA	Spain	3–0
1997	Adelaide (AUS)	USA	Canada	3–0
1998	Boca Raton (USA)	Australia	USA	2–1
1999	Sabadell (ESP)	France	South Africa	2–0
2000	Sun City (RSA)	Australia	South Africa	2–1

KITTY GODFREE CUP

International Women's Team Competition for 65 year age group.

	VENUE	WINNERS	RUNNERS-UP	FINAL SCORE
1995	Bournemouth (GBR)	USA	Canada	2–1
1996	Brand (AUT)	Great Britain	USA	2–1
1997	Melbourne (AUS)	Great Britain	USA	2–1
1998	Fort Lauderdale (USA)	Great Britain	USA	2–1
1999	Girona (ESP)	USA	Great Britain	2–0
2000	Cape Town (RSA)	USA	South Africa	2–1

ALTHEA GIBSON CUP

International Women's Team Competition for 70 year age group.

	VENUE	WINNERS	RUNNERS-UP	FINAL SCORE
1998	Palm Beach Gardens (USA)	USA	Germany	Round Robin
1999	Barcelona (ESP)	Great Britain	USA	2–1
2000	Cape Town (RSA)	USA	South Africa	2–1

AUSTRALIAN INTERNATIONAL JUNIOR CHAMPIONSHIPS

BOYS' SINGLES

1946	F. A. Sedgman	1956	R. Mark	1965	G. Goven (FRA)
1947	D. Candy	1957	R. G. Laver	1966	K. Coombes
1948	K. B. McGregor	1958	M. Mulligan	1967	B. Fairlie (NZL)
1949	C. Wilderspin	1959	E. Buchholz (USA)	1968	P. Dent
1950	K. R. Rosewall	1960	W. Coghlan	1969	A. McDonald
1951	L. Hoad	1961	J. D. Newcombe	1970	J. Alexander
1952	K. Rosewall	1962	J. D. Newcombe	1971	C. Letcher
1953	W. Gilmour	1963	J. D. Newcombe	1972	P. Kronk
1954	W. A. Knight (GBR)	1964	A. Roche	1973	P. McNamee
1955	G. Moss				

	WINNER	RUNNER-UP	SCORE		
1974	H. Brittain (AUS)				
1975	B. Drewett (AUS)				
1976	R. Kelly (AUS)	J. Dilouie (USA)	6–2	6–4	
1977	(Jan.) B. Drewett (AUS)	T. Wilkison (USA)	6–4	7–6	
1977	(Dec.) R. Kelly (AUS)				
1978	P. Serrett (AUS)	C. Johnstone (AUS)	6–4	6–3	
1979	G. Whitecross (AUS)	C. Miller (AUS)	6–4	6–3	
1980	C. Miller (AUS)	W. Masur (AUS)	7–6	6–2	
1981	J. Windahl (SWE)	P. Cash (AUS)	6–4	6–4	
1982	M. Kratzmann (AUS)	S. Youl (AUS)	6–3	7–5	
1983	S. Edberg (SWE)	S. Youl (AUS)	6–4	6–4	
1984	M. Kratzmann (AUS)	P. Flyn (AUS)	6–4	6–1	
1985	S. Barr (AUS)	S. Furlong (AUS)	7–6	6–7	6–3

	WINNER	RUNNER-UP	SCORE		
1986	*Not held*				
1987	J. Stoltenberg (AUS)	T. Woodbridge (AUS)	6–2	7–6	
1988	J. Anderson (AUS)	A. Florent (AUS)	7–5	7–6	
1989	N. Kulti (SWE)	T. Woodbridge (AUS)	6–2	6–0	
1990	D. Dier (GER)	L. Paes (IND)	6–4	7–6	
1991	T. Enqvist (SWE)	S. Gleeson (AUS)	7–6	6–7	6–1
1992	G. Doyle (AUS)	B. Dunn (USA)	6–2	6–0	
1993	J. Baily (GBR)	S. Downs (NZL)	6–3	6–2	
1994	B. Ellwood (AUS)	A. Illie (AUS)	5–7	6–3	6–3
1995	N. Kiefer (GER)	J-M Lee (KOR)	6–4	6–4	
1996	B. Rehnqvist (SWE)	M. Hellstrom (SWE)	2–6	6–2	7–5
1997	D. Elsner (GER)	W. Whitehouse (RSA)	7–6	6–2	
1998	J. Jeanpierre (FRA)	A. Vinciguerra (SWE)	4–6	6–4	6–3
1999	K. Pless (DEN)	M. Youzhny (RUS)	6–4	6–3	
2000	A. Roddick (USA)	M. Ancic (CRO)	7–6	6–3	

GIRLS' SINGLES

1946	S. Grant	1956	L. Coghlan	1965	K. Melville
1947	J. Tuckfield	1957	M. Rayson	1966	K. Krantzcke
1948	B. Penrose	1958	J. Lehane	1967	A. Kenny
1949	J. Warnock	1959	J. Lehane	1968	L. Hunt
1950	B. McIntyre	1960	L. Turner	1969	L. Hunt
1951	M. Carter	1961	R. Ebbern	1970	E. Goolagong
1952	M. Carter	1962	R. Ebbern	1971	P. Coleman
1953	J. Staley	1963	R. Ebbern	1972	P. Coleman
1954	E. Orton	1964	K. Dening	1973	C. O'Neill
1955	E. Orton				

	WINNER	RUNNER-UP	SCORE		
1974	J. Walker (AUS)				
1975	S. Barker (GBR)	C. O'Neill (AUS)	6–2	7–6	
1976	S. Saliba (AUS)	J. Fenwick (AUS)	2–6	6–3	6–4
1977	(Jan.) P. Bailey (AUS)	A. Tobin (AUS)	6–2	6–3	
1977	(Dec.) A. Tobin (AUS)	L. Harrison (AUS)	6–1	6–2	
1978	E. Little (AUS)	S. Leo (AUS)	6–1	6–2	
1979	A. Minter (AUS)	S. Leo (AUS)	6–4	6–3	
1980	A. Minter (AUS)	E. Sayers (AUS)	6–4	6–2	
1981	A. Minter (AUS)	C. Vanier (FRA)	6–4	6–2	
1982	A. Brown (GBR)	P. Paradis (FRA)	6–3	6–4	
1983	A. Brown (GBR)	B. Randall (AUS)	7–6	6–3	
1984	A. Croft (GBR)	H. Dahlstrom (SWE)	6–0	6–1	
1985	J. Byrne (AUS)	L. Field (AUS)	6–1	6–3	
1986	*Not held*				
1987	M. Jaggard (AUS)	N. Provis (AUS)	6–2	6–4	
1988	J. Faull (AUS)	E. Derly (FRA)	6–4	6–4	
1989	K. Kessaris (USA)	A. Farley (USA)	6–1	6–2	
1990	M. Maleeva (BUL)	L. Stacey (AUS)	7–5	6–7	6–1
1991	N. Pratt (AUS)	K. Godridge (AUS)	6–4	6–3	
1992	J. Limmer (AUS)	L. Davenport (USA)	7–5	6–2	
1993	H. Rusch (GER)	A. Glass (GER)	6–1	6–2	
1994	T. Musgrave (AUS)	B. Schett (AUT)	4–6	6–4	6–2
1995	S. Drake-Brockman (AUS)	A. Elwood (AUS)	6–3	4–6	7–5
1996	M. Grzybowska (POL)	N. Dechy (FRA)	6–1	4–6	6–1
1997	M. Lucic (CRO)	M.Weingartner (GER)	6–2	6–2	
1998	J. Kostanic (CRO)	W. Prakusya (INA)	6–0	7–5	
1999	V. Razzano (FRA)	K. Basternakova (SVK)	6–1	6–1	
2000	A. Kapros (HUN)	M. Martinez (ESP)	6–2	3–6	6–2

BOYS' DOUBLES

	WINNERS	RUNNERS-UP	SCORE		
1983	J. Harty (AUS)/D. Tyson (AUS)	A. Lane (AUS)/D. Cahill (AUS)	3–6	6–4	6–3
1984	M. Kratzman (AUS)/M. Baroch (AUS)	B. Custer (AUS)/D. Macpherson (AUS)	6–2	5–7	7–5
1985	B. Custer (AUS)/D. Macpherson (AUS)	C. Suk (TCH)/P. Korda (TCH)	7–5	6–2	
1986	*Not held*				
1987	J. Stoltenberg (AUS)/T. Woodbridge (AUS)	S. Barr (AUS)/D. Roe (AUS)	6–2	6–4	

	WINNERS	RUNNERS-UP	SCORE		
1988	J. Stoltenberg (AUS)/T. Woodbridge (AUS)	J. Anderson (AUS)/R. Fromberg (AUS)	6–3	6–2	
1989	J. Anderson (AUS)/T. Woodbridge (AUS)	J. Morgan (AUS)/A. Kratzmann (AUS)	6–4	6–2	
1990	R. Petterson (SWE)/M. Renstroem (SWE)	R.Janecek (CAN)/E.Munoz De Cote (MEX)	4–6	7–6	6–1
1991	G. Doyle (AUS)/J. Eagle (AUS)	J. Holmes (AUS)/P. Kilderry (AUS)	7–6	6–4	
1992	G. Doyle (AUS)/B. Sceney (AUS)	L. Carrington (USA)/J. Thompson (USA)	6–4	6–4	
1993	L. Rehmann (GER)/C. Tambue (GER)	S. Humphries (USA)/J. Jackson (USA)	6–7	7–5	6–2
1994	B. Ellwood (AUS)/M. Philippoussis (AUS)	J. Delgado (GBR)/R. Kukal (SVK)	4–6	6–2	6–1
1995	L. Borgeois (AUS)/J.-M. Lee (KOR)	N. Kiefer (GER)/U. Seetzen (GER)	6–2	6–1	
1996	D. Bracciali (ITA)/J.-Robichaud (CAN)	M. Lee (GBR)/ J. Trotman (GBR)	6–2	6–4	
1997	D. Sherwood (GBR)/J. Trotman (GBR)	J. Van Der Westhuizen (RSA)/ W. Whitehouse (RSA)	7–6	6–3	
1998	J. Haehnel (FRA)/J. Jeanpierre (FRA)	M. Pehar (CRO)/L. Zovko (CRO)	6–3	6–3	
1999	J. Melzer (AUT)/K.Pless (DEN)	L. Chramosta (CZE)/M. Navratil (CZE)	6–7	6–3	6–0
2000	N. Mahut (FRA)/T. Robredo (ESP)	T. Davis (USA)/A. Roddick (USA)	6–2	5–7	11–9

GIRLS' DOUBLES

	WINNERS	RUNNERS-UP	SCORE		
1983	B. Randall (AUS)/K. Staunton (AUS)	J. Byrne (AUS)/J. Thompson (AUS)	3–6	6–3	6–3
1984	L. Field (AUS)/L. Savchenko (URS)	M. Parun (NZL)/J. Masters (AUS)	7–6	6–2	
1985	J. Byrne (AUS)/J. Thompson (AUS)	A. Scott (AUS)/S. McCann (AUS)	6–0	6–3	
1986	*Not held*				
1987	N. Provis (AUS)/A. Devries (BEL)	D. Jones (AUS)/G. Dwyer (AUS)	6–3	6–1	
1988	R. McQuillan (AUS)/J. Faull (AUS)	R. Stubbs (AUS)/K. McDonald (AUS)	6–1	7–5	
1989	A. Strnadova (TCH)/E. Sviglerova (TCH)	N. Pratt (AUS)/A. Woolcock (AUS)	6–2	6–0	
1990	L. Zaltz (ISR)/R. Mayer (ISR)	J. Hodder (AUS)/N. Pratt (AUS)	6–4	6–4	
1991	K. Habsudova (TCH/B. Rittner (GER)	J. Limmer (AUS)/A. Woolcock (AUS)	6–2	6–0	
1992	L. Davenport (USA)/N. London (USA)	M. Avotins (AUS)/J. Limmer (AUS)	6–2	7–5	
1993	J. Manta (SUI)/L. Richterova (TCH)	A. Carlsson (SWE)/C. Cristea (ROM)	6–3	6–2	
1994	C. Morariu (USA)/L. Varmuzov (CZE)	Y. Basting(NED)/A. Scheider(GER)	7–5	2–6	7–5
1995	C. Morariu (USA)/L. Varmuzov (CZE)	S. Obata(JPN)/N. Urabe (JPN)	6–1	6–2	
1996	M. Pastikova (CZE)/J. Schonfeldova (CZE)	O. Barabanschikova (BLR)/M. Lucic (CRO)	6–1	6–3	
1997	M. Lucic (CRO)/J. Wohr (GER)	Y-J. Cho (KOR)/S. Hisamatsu (JPN)	6–2	6–2	
1998	E. Dominikovic (AUS)/A. Molik (AUS)	L. Baker (NZL)/R. Hudson (NZL)	6–3	3–6	6–2
1999	E. Danilidou (GRE)/V. Razzano (FRA)	N. Rencken (RSA)/N. Grandin (RSA)	6–1	6–1	
2000	A. Kapros (HUN)/C. Wheeler (AUS)	L. Barnikow (USA)/E. Burdette (USA)	6–3	6–4	

FRENCH INTERNATIONAL JUNIOR CHAMPIONSHIPS

BOYS' SINGLES

	WINNER	RUNNER-UP	SCORE		
1974	C. Casa (FRA)	U. Marten (GER)	2–6	6–1	6–4
1975	C. Roger–Vasselin (FRA)	P. Elter (GER)	6–1	6–2	
1976	H. Gunthardt (SUI)	J. L. Clerc (ARG)	4–6	7–6	6–4
1977	J. P. McEnroe (USA)	R. Kelly (AUS)	6–1	6–1	
1978	I. Lendl (TCH)	P. Hjertquist (SWE)	7–6	6–4	
1979	R. Krishnan (IND)	B. Testerman (USA)	2–6	6–1	6–0
1980	H. Leconte (FRA)	A. Tous (ESP)	7–6	6–3	
1981	M. Wilander (SWE)	J. Brown (USA)	7–5	6–1	
1982	T. Benhabiles (FRA)	L. Courteau (FRA)	7–6	6–2	
1983	S. Edberg (SWE)	F. Fevrier (FRA)	6–4	7–6	
1984	K. Carlsson (SWE)	M. Kratzman (AUS)	6–3	6–3	
1985	J. Yzaga (PER)	T. Muster (AUT)	2–6	6–3	6–0
1986	G. Perez Roldan (ARG)	S. Grenier (FRA)	4–6	6–3	6–2
1987	G. Perez Roldan (ARG)	J. Stoltenberg (AUS)	6–3	3–6	6–1
1988	N. Pereira (VEN)	M. Larsson (SWE)	7–6	6–3	
1989	F. Santoro (FRA)	J. Palmer (USA)	6–3	3–6	9–7
1990	A. Gaudenzi (ITA)	T. Enqvist (SWE)	2–6	7–6	6–4
1991	A. Medvedev (URS)	T. Enqvist (SWE)	6–4	7–6	
1992	A. Pavel (ROM)	M. Navarra (ITA)	7–6	6–3	
1993	R. Carretero (ESP)	A. Costa (ESP)	6–0	7–6	
1994	J. Diaz (ESP)	G. Galimberti (ITA)	6–3	7–6	
1995	M. Zabaleta (ARG)	M. Puerta (ARG)	6–2	6–3	
1996	A. Martin (ESP)	B. Rehnqvist (SWE)	6–3	7–6	
1997	D. Elsner (GER)	L. Horna (PER)	6–4	6–4	
1998	F. Gonzalez (CHI)	J. Ferrero (ESP)	4–6	6–4	6–3

	WINNER	RUNNER-UP	SCORE		
1999	G. Coria (ARG)	D. Nalbandian (ARG)	6–4	6–3	
2000	P. Mathieu (FRA)	T. Robredo (ESP)	3–6	7–6	6–2

GIRLS' SINGLES

	WINNER	RUNNER-UP	SCORE		
1974	M. Simionescu (ROM)	S. Barker (GBR)	6–3	6–3	
1975	R. Marsikova (TCH)	L. Mottram (GBR)	6–3	5–7	6–2
1976	M. Tyler (GBR)	M. Zoni (ITA)	6–1	6–3	
1977	A. E. Smith (USA)	H. Strachanova (TCH)	6–3	7–6	
1978	H. Mandlikova (TCH)	M. Rothschild (FRG)	6–1	6–1	
1979	L. Sandin (SWE)	M. L. Piatek (USA)	6–3	6–1	
1980	K. Horvath (USA)	K. Henry (USA)	6–2	6–2	
1981	B. Gadusek (USA)	H. Sukova (TCH)	6–7	6–1	6–4
1982	M. Maleeva (BUL)	P. Barg (USA)	7–5	6–2	
1983	P. Paradis (FRA)	D. Spence (USA)	7–6	6–3	
1984	G. Sabatini (ARG)	K. Maleeva (BUL)	6–3	5–7	6–3
1985	L. Garrone (ITA)	D. Van Rensburg (RSA)	6–1	6–3	
1986	P. Tarabini (ARG)	N. Provis (AUS)	6–3	6–3	
1987	N. Zvereva (URS)	J. Pospisilova(TCH)	6–1	6–0	
1988	J. Halard (FRA)	A. Farley (USA)	6–2	4–6	7–5
1989	J. Capriati (USA)	E. Sviglerova (TCH)	6–4	6–0	
1990	M. Maleeva (BUL)	T. Ignatieva (URS)	6–2	6–3	
1991	A. Smashnova (ISR)	I. Gorrochategui (ARG)	2–6	7–5	6–1
1992	R. De Los Rios (PAR)	P. Suarez (ARG)	6–4	6–0	
1993	M. Hingis(SUI)	L. Courtois (BEL)	7–5	7–5	
1994	M. Hingis (SUI)	S. Jeyaseelan (CAN)	6–3	6–1	
1995	A. Cocheteux (FRA)	M. Weingartner (GER)	7–5	6–4	
1996	A. Mauresmo (FRA)	M. Shaughnessy (USA)	6–0	6–4	
1997	J. Henin (BER)	C. Black (ZIM)	4–6	6–4	6–4
1998	N. Petrova (RUS)	J. Dokic (AUS)	6–3	6–3	
1999	L. Dominguez Lino (ESP)	S. Foretz (FRA)	6–4	6–4	
2000	V. Razzano (FRA)	M. Salerni (ARG)	5–7	6–4	8–6

BOYS' DOUBLES

	WINNERS	RUNNERS-UP	SCORE		
1983	M. Kratzman (AUS)/S. Youl (AUS)	A. Chesnokov (URS)/A. Olhovskiy (URS)	6–2	6–3	
1985	P. Korda (TCH)/C. Suk (TCH)	V. Godrichidze (URS)/V. Volkov (URS)	4–6	6–0	7–5
1986	F. Davin (ARG)/G. Perez-Roldan (ARG)	T. Carbonell (ESP)/J. Sanchez (ESP)	7–5	5–7	6–3
1987	J. Courier (USA)/J. Stark (USA)	F. Davin (ARG)/G. Perez-Roldan (ARG)	6–7	6–4	6–3
1988	J. Stoltenberg (AUS)/T. Woodbridge (AUS)	C. Caratti (ITA)/G. Ivanisevic (YUG)	7–6	7–5	
1989	J. Anderson (AUS)/T. Woodbridge (AUS)	L. Herrera (MEX)/M. Knowles (BAH)	6–3	4–6	6–2
1990	S. La Reau (CAN)/P. Le Blanc (CAN)	C. Marsh (RSA)/M. Ondruska (RSA)	7–6	6–7	9–7
1991	T. Enqvist (SWE)/M. Martinelle (SWE)	J. Knowle (AUT)/J. Unterberger (AUT)	6–1	6–3	
1992	E. Abaroa (MEX)/G. Doyle (AUS)	Y. Kafelnikov (CIS)/A. Radulescu (ROM)	7–6	6–3	
1993	S. Downs (NZL)/J. Greenhalgh (NZL)	N. Godwin (RSA)/G. Williams (RSA)	6–1	6–1	
1994	G. Kuerten (BRA)/N. Lapentti (ECU)	M. Boye (FRA)/N. Escude (FRA)	6–2	6–4	
1995	R. Sluiter (NED)/P. Wessels (NED)	J. Gimelstob (USA)/R. Wolters (USA)	7–6	7–5	
1996	S. Grosjean (FRA)/O. Mutis (FRA)	J. Brandt (GER)/D. Elsner (GER)	6–2	6–3	
1997	J. De Armas (VEN)/M. Horna (PER)	A. Di Pasquale (FRA)/J. Jeanpierre (FRA)	6–4	2–6	7–5
1998	J. De Armas (VEN)/F. Gonzalez (CHI)	J. Ferrero (ESP)/F. Lopez (ESP)	6–7	7–5	6–3
1999	I. Labadze (GEO)/L. Zovko (CRO)	K. Pless (DEN)/O. Rochus (BEL)	6–1	7–6	
2000	M. Lopez (ESP)/T. Robredo (ESP)	J Johansson (SWE)/A. Roddick (USA)	7–6	6–0	

GIRLS' DOUBLES

	WINNERS	RUNNERS-UP	SCORE		
1983	C. Anderholm (SWE)/H. Olsson (SWE)	K./M. Maleeva (BUL)	6–4	6–1	
1985	M Perez-Roldan (ARG)/P. Tarabini (ARG)	A. Holikova (TCH)/R. Zrubakova (TCH)	6–3	5–7	6–4
1986	L. Meskhi (URS)/N. Zvereva (URS)	J. Novotna (TCH)/R. Rajchrtova (TCH)	1–6	6–3	6–0
1987	N. Medvedeva (URS)/N. Zvereva (URS)	M. Jaggard (AUS)/N. Provis (AUS)	6–3	6–3	
1988	A. Dechaume (FRA)/E. Derly (FRA)	J. Halard (FRA)/M. Laval (FRA)	6–4	3–6	6–3
1989	N. Pratt (AUS)/S.–T. Wang (TPE)	C. Caverzasio (ITA)/S. Farina (ITA)	7–5	3–6	8–6
1990	R. Dragomir (ROM)/I. Spirlea (ROM)	T. Ignatieva (URS)/I. Soukhova (URS)	6–3	6–1	
1991	E. Bes (ESP)/I. Gorrochategui (ARG)	Z. Malkova (TCH)/E. Martincova (TCH)	6–1	6–3	
1992	L. Courtois (BEL)/N. Feber (BEL)	L. Davenport (USA)/C. Rubin (USA)	6–1	5–7	6–4
1993	L. Courtois (BEL)/N. Feber (BEL)	L. Bitter (NED)/M. Koulstaal (NED)	6–4	7–6	
1994	M. Hingis (SUI)/M. Nedelkova (SVK)	L. Cenkova (CZE)/L. Richterova (CZE)	6–3	6–2	

WINNERS		RUNNERS-UP	SCORE		
1995	C. Morariu (USA)/L. Varmuzova (CZE)	A. Canepa (ITA)/G. Casoni (ITA)	7–6	7–5	
1996	A. Canepa (ITA)/G. Casoni (ITA)	A. Kournikova (RUS)/L. Varmuzova (SMR)	6–2	5–7	7–5
1997	C. Black (ZIM)/I. Selyutina (KAZ)	M. Matevzic (SLO)/K. Srebotnik (SLO)	6–0	5–7	7–5
1998	K. Clijsters (BEL)/J. Dokic (AUS)	E. Dementieva (RUS)/N. Petrova (RUS)	6–4	7–6	
1999	F. Pennetta (ITA)/R.Vinci (ITA)	M. Buric (GER)/K. Clijsters (BEL)	7–5	5–7	6–4
2000	M. Martinez (ESP)/A. Medina (ESP)	M. Mezak (CRO)/D. Safina (RUS)	6–0	6–1	

WIMBLEDON INTERNATIONAL JUNIOR CHAMPIONSHIPS

The event originated as an invitation tournament, boys' singles in 1947 and girls' singles in 1948. It became a Championship event in 1975.

BOYS' SINGLES

1947	K. Nielsen (DEN)				
1948	S. Stockenberg (SWE)	1957	J. I. Tattersall (GBR)	1966	V. Korotkov (URS)
1949	S. Stockenberg (SWE)	1958	E. Buchholz (USA)	1967	M. Orantes (ESP)
1950	J. A. T. Horn (GBR)	1959	T. Lejus (URS)	1968	J. G. Alexander (AUS)
1951	J. Kupferburger (RSA)	1960	A. R. Mandelstam (RSA)	1969	B. Bertram (RSA)
1952	R. K. Wilson (GBR)	1961	C. E. Graebner (USA)	1970	B. Bertram (RSA)
1953	W. A. Knight (GBR)	1962	S. Matthews (GBR)	1971	R. Kreiss (USA)
1954	R. Krishnan (IND)	1963	N. Kalogeropoulous (GRE)	1972	B. Borg (SWE)
1955	M. P. Hann (GBR)	1964	I. El Shafei (EGY)	1973	W. Martin (USA)
1956	R. Holmberg (USA)	1965	V. Korotkov (URS)	1974	W. Martin (USA)

	WINNER	RUNNER-UP	SCORE		
1975	C. J. Lewis (NZL)	R. Ycaza (ECU)	6–1	6–4	
1976	H. Gunthardt (SUI)	P. Elter (FRG)	6–4	7–5	
1977	V. Winitsky (USA)	E. Teltscher (USA)	6–1	1–6	8–6
1978	I. Lendl (TCH)	J. Turpin (USA)	6–3	6–4	
1979	R. Krishnan (IND)	D. Siegler (USA)	6–3	6–4	
1980	T. Tulasne (FRA)	H. D. Beutel (FRG)	6–4	3–6	6–4
1981	M. Anger (USA)	P. Cash (AUS)	7–6	7–5	
1982	P. Cash (AUS)	H. Sundstrom (SWE)	6–4	6–7	6–3
1983	S. Edberg (SWE)	J. Frawley (AUS)	6–3	7–6	
1984	M. Kratzman (AUS)	S. Kruger (RSA)	6–4	4–6	6–3
1985	L. Lavalle (MEX)	E. Velez (MEX)	6–4	6–4	
1986	E. Velez (MEX)	J. Sanchez (ESP)	6–3	7–5	
1987	D. Nargiso (ITA)	J. Stoltenberg (AUS)	7–6	6–4	
1988	N. Pereira (VEN)	G. Raoux (FRA)	7–6	6–2	
1989	N. Kulti (SWE)	T. Woodbridge (AUS)	6–4	6–3	
1990	L. Paes (IND)	M. Ondruska (RSA)	7–6	6–2	
1991	T. Enqvist (SWE)	M. Joyce (USA)	6–4	6–3	
1992	D. Skoch (TCH)	B. Dunn (USA)	6–4	6–3	
1993	R. Sabau (ROM)	J. Szymanski (VEN)	6–1	6–3	
1994	S. Humphries (USA)	M. Philippoussis (AUS)	7–6	3–6	6–4
1995	O. Mutis (FRA)	N. Kiefer (GER)	6–2	6–2	
1996	V. Voltchkov (BLR)	I. Ljubicic (CRO)	3–6	6–2	6–3
1997	W. Whitehouse (RSA)	D. Elsner (GER)	6–3	7–6	
1998	R. Federer (SUI)	I. Labadze (GEO)	6–4	6–4	
1999	J. Melzer (AUT)	K. Pless (DEN)	7–6	6–3	
2000	N. Mahut (FRA)	M. Ancic (CRO)	3–6	6–3	7–5

GIRLS' SINGLES

1948	O. Miskova (TCH)	1957	M. Arnold (USA)	1966	B. Lindstrom (FIN)
1949	C. Mercelis (BEL)	1958	S. M. Moore (USA)	1967	J. Salome (HOL)
1950	L. Cornell (GBR)	1959	J. Cross (RSA)	1968	K. Pigeon (USA)
1951	L. Cornell (GBR)	1960	K. Hantze (USA)	1969	K. Sawamatsu (JPN)
1952	ten Bosch (HOL)	1961	G. Baksheeva (URS)	1970	S. Walsh (USA)
1953	D. Kilian (RSA)	1962	G. Baksheeva (URS)	1971	M. Kroschina (URS)
1954	V. A. Pitt (GBR)	1963	D. M. Salfati (RSA)	1972	I. Kloss (RSA)
1955	S. M. Armstrong (GBR)	1964	P. Barkowicz (USA)	1973	A. Kiyomura (USA)
1956	A. S. Haydon (GBR)	1965	O. Morozova (URS)	1974	M. Jausovec (YUG)

	WINNER	RUNNER-UP	SCORE		
1975	N. Y. Chmyreva (URS)	R. Marsikova (TCH)	6–4	6–3	
1976	N. Y. Chmyreva (URS)	M. Kruger (RSA)	6–3	2–6	6–1

	WINNER	RUNNER-UP	SCORE		
1977	L. Antonoplis (USA)	Mareen Louie (USA)	6–5	6–1	
1978	T. A. Austin (USA)	H. Mandlikova (TCH)	6–0	3–6	6–4
1979	M. L. Piatek (USA)	A. Moulton (USA)	6–1	6–3	
1980	D. Freeman (AUS)	S. Leo (AUS)	7–6	7–5	
1981	Z. Garrison (USA)	R. Uys (RSA)	6–4	3–6	6–0
1982	C. Tanvier (FRA)	H. Sukova (TCH)	6–2	7–5	
1983	P. Paradis (FRA)	P. Hy (HKG)	6–2	6–1	
1984	A. N. Croft (GBR)	E. Reinach (RSA)	3–6	6–3	6–2
1985	A. Holikova (TCH)	J. Byrne (AUS)	7–5	6–1	
1986	N. Zvereva (URS)	L. Meskhi (URS)	2–6	6–2	9–7
1987	N. Zvereva (URS)	J. Halard (FRA)	6–4	6–4	
1988	B. Schultz (HOL)	E. Derly (FRA)	7–6	6–1	
1989	A. Strnadova (TCH)	M. McGrath (USA)	6–2	6–3	
1990	A. Strnadova (TCH)	K. Sharpe (AUS)	6–2	6–4	
1991	B. Rittner (GER)	E. Makarova (URS)	6–7	6–2	6–3
1992	C. Rubin (USA)	L. Courtois (BEL)	6–2	7–5	
1993	N. Feber (BEL)	R. Grande (ITA)	7–6	1–6	6–2
1994	M. Hingis (SUI)	M-R. Jeon (KOR)	7–5	6–4	
1995	A. Olsza (POL)	T. Tanasugarn (THA)	7–5	7–6	
1996	A. Mauresmo (FRA)	M. Serna (ESP)	4–6	6–3	6–4
1997	C. Black (ZIM)	A. Rippner (USA)	6–3	7–5	
1998	K. Srebotnik (SLO)	K. Clijsters (BEL)	7–6	6–3	
1999	I. Tulyaganova (UZB)	L. Krasnoroutskaia (RUS)	7–6	6–4	
2000	M. Salerni (ARG)	T. Perebiynis (UKR)	6–4	7–5	

BOYS' DOUBLES

	WINNERS	RUNNERS-UP	SCORE		
1982	P. Cash (AUS)/J. Frawley (AUS)	R. Leach (USA)/J. Ross (USA)	6–3	6–2	
1983	M. Kratzman (AUS)/S. Youl (AUS)	M. Nastase (ROM)/O. Rahnasto (FIN)	6–4	6–4	
1984	R. Brown (USA)/R. Weiss (USA)	M. Kratzman (AUS)/J. Svensson (SWE)	1–6	6–4	11–9
1985	A. Moreno (MEX)/J. Yzaga (PER)	P. Korda (TCH)/C. Suk (TCH)	7–6	6–4	
1986	T. Carbonell (ESP)/P. Korda (TCH)	S. Barr (AUS)/H. Karrasch (CAN)	6–1	6–1	
1987	J. Stoltenberg (AUS)/T. Woodbridge (AUS)	D. Nargiso (ITA)/E. Rossi (ITA)	6–3	7–6	
1988	J. Stoltenberg (AUS)/T. Woodbridge (AUS)	D. Rikl (TCH)/T. Zdrazila (TCH)	6–4	1–6	7–6
1989	J. Palmer (USA)/J. Stark (USA)	J.-L. De Jager (RSA)/W. Ferreira (RSA)	7–6	7–6	
1990	S. Lareau (CAN)/S. LeBlanc (CAN)	C. Marsh (RSA)/M. Ondruska (RSA)	7–6	4–6	6–3
1991	K. Alami (MAR)/G. Rusedski (CAN)	J-L. De Jager (RSA)/A. Medvedev (URS)	1–6	7–6	6–4
1992	S. Baldas (AUS)/S. Draper (AUS)	M. Bhupathi (IND)/N. Kirtane (IND)	6–1	4–6	9–7
1993	S. Downs (NZL)/J. Greenhalgh (NZL)	N. Godwin (RSA)/G. Williams (RSA)	6–7	7–6	
1994	B. Ellwood (AUS)/M. Philippoussis (AUS)	V. Platenik(SVK)/R. Schlachter (BRA)	6–2	6–4	
1995	M. Lee (GBR)/G. Trotman (GBR)	A. Hernandez (MEX)/M. Puerta (ARG)	7–6	6–4	
1996	D. Bracciali (ITA)/J. Robichaud (CAN)	D. Roberts (RSA)/W. Whitehouse (RSA)	6–2	6–4	
1997	L. Horna (PER)/N. Massu (CHI)	J. Van Der Westhuizen (RSA)/ W. Whitehouse (RSA)	6–4	6–2	
1998	R. Federer (SUI)/O. Rochus (BEL)	M. Llodra (FRA)/A. Ram (ISR)	6–4	6–4	
1999	G. Coria (ARG)/D. Nalbandian (ARG)	T. Enev (BUL)/J. Nieminen (FIN)	7–5	6–4	
2000	D. Coene (BEL)/K. Vliegen (BEL)	A. Banks (GBR)/B. Riby (GBR)	6–3	1–6	6–3

GIRLS' DOUBLES

	WINNERS	RUNNERS-UP	SCORE		
1982	B. Herr (USA)/P. Barg (USA)	B. S. Gerken (USA)/G. Rush (USA)	6–1	6–4	
1983	P. Fendick (USA)/P. Hy (HKG)	C. Anderholm (SWE)/H. Olsson (SWE)	6–1	7–5	
1984	C. Kuhlman (USA)/S. Rehe (USA)	V. Milvidskaya (URS)/L. Savchenko (URS)	6–3	5–7	6–4
1985	L. Field (AUS)/J. Thompson (AUS)	E. Reinach (SAF)/J. Richardson (NZL)	6–1	6–2	
1986	M. Jaggard (AUS)/L. O'Neill (AUS)	L. Meskhi (URS)/N. Zvereva (URS)	7–6	6–4	
1987	N. Medvedeva (URS)/N. Zvereva (URS)	I. S. Kim (KOR)/P. M. Modena (HKG)	2–6	7–5	6–0
1988	J. Faull (AUS)/R. McQuillan (AUS)	A. Dechaume (FRA)/E. Derly (FRA)	4–6	6–2	6–3
1989	J. Capriati (USA)/M. McGrath (USA)	A. Strnadova (TCH)/E. Sviglerova (TCH)	6–4	6–2	
1990	K. Habsudova (TCH)/A. Strnadova (TCH)	N. Pratt (AUS)/K. Sharpe (AUS)	6–2	6–4	
1991	C. Barclay (AUS)/L. Zaltz (ISR)	J. Limmer (AUS)/A. Woolcock (AUS)	6–4	6–4	
1992	P. Nelson (USA)/J. Steven (USA)	M. Avotins (AUS)/L. McShea (AUS)	2–6	6–4	6–3
1993	L. Courtois (BEL)/N. Feber (BEL)	H. Mochizuki (JPN)/Y. Yoshida (JPN)	6–3	6–4	
1994	E. De Villiers (RSA)/F. Jelfs (GBR)	C. Morariu (USA)/L. Varmuzova (SMR)	6–3	6–4	
1995	C. Black (ZIM)/A. Olsza (POL)	I. Musgrave (AUS)/J. Richardson (AUS)	6–0	7–6	
1996	O. Barabanschikova (BLR)/A. Mauresmo (FRA)	L. Osterloh (USA)/S. Reeves (USA)	5–7	6–3	6–1

WINNERS	RUNNERS-UP	SCORE		
1997 C. Black (ZIM)/I. Selyutina (KAZ)	M. Matevzic (SLO)/K. Srebotnik (SLO)	3–6	7–5	6–3
1998 E. Dyrberg (DEN)/J. Kostanic (CRO)	P. Rampre (SLO)/I. Tulyaganova (UZB)	6–2	7–6	
1999 D. Bedanova (CZE)/M. Salerni (ARG)	T. Perebiynis (UKR)/I. Tulyaganova (UZB)	6–1	2–6	6–2
2000 I. Gaspar (ROM)/T. Perebiynis (UKR)	D. Bedanova (CZE)/M. Salerni (ARG)	7–6	6–3	

US INTERNATIONAL JUNIOR CHAMPIONSHIPS

BOYS' SINGLES

WINNER	RUNNER-UP	SCORE		
1974 W. Martin (USA)	F. Taygan (USA)	6–4	6–2	
1975 H. Schonfield (USA)	C. J. Lewis (NZL)	6–4	6–3	
1976 Y. Ycaza (ECU)	J. L. Clerc (ARG)	6–4	5–7	6–0
1977 V. Winitsky (USA)	E. Teltscher (USA)	6–4	6–4	
1978 P. Hjertquist (SWE)	S. Simonsson (SWE)	7–6	1–6	7–6
1979 S. Davis (USA)	J. Gunnarsson (SWE)	6–3	6–1	
1980 M. Falberg (USA)	E. Korita (USA)	6–0	6–2	
1981 T. Hogstedt (SWE)	H. Schwaier (FRG)	7–5	6–3	
1982 P. Cash (AUS)	G. Forget (FRA)	6–3	6–3	
1983 S. Edberg (SWE)	S. Youl (AUS)	6–2	6–4	
1984 M. Kratzman (AUS)	B. Becker (FRG)	6–3	7–6	
1985 T. Trigueiro (USA)	J. Blake (USA)	6–2	6–3	
1986 J. Sanchez (ESP)	F. Davin (ARG)	6–2	6–2	
1987 D. Wheaton (USA)	A. Cherkasov (URS)	7–5	6–0	
1988 N. Pereira (VEN)	N. Kulti (SWE)	6–1	6–2	
1989 J. Stark (USA)	N. Kulti (SWE)	6–4	6–1	
1990 A. Gaudenzi (ITA)	M. Tillstroem (SWE)	6–2	4–6	7–6
1991 L. Paes (IND)	K. Alami (MAR)	6–4	6–4	
1992 B. Dunn (USA)	N. Behr (ISR)	7–5	6–2	
1993 M. Rios (CHI)	S. Downs (NZL)	7–6	6–3	
1994 S. Schalken (NED)	M. Tahiri (MAR)	6–2	7–6	
1995 N. Kiefer (GER)	U. Seetzen (GER)	6–3	6–4	
1996 D. Elsner (GER)	M. Hipfl (AUT)	6–3	6–2	
1997 A. Di Pasquale (FRA)	W. Whitehouse (RSA)	6–7	6–4	6–1
1998 D. Nalbandian (ARG)	R. Federer (SUI)	6–3	7–5	
1999 J. Nieminen (FIN)	K. Pless (DEN)	6–7	6–3	6–4
2000 A. Roddick (USA)	R. Ginepri (USA)	6–1	6–3	

GIRLS' SINGLES

WINNER	RUNNER-UP	SCORE		
1974 I. Kloss (RSA)	M. Jausovec (YUG)	6–4	6–3	
1975 N. T. Chmyreva (URS)	G. Stevens (RSA)	6–7	6–2	6–2
1976 M. Kruger (RSA)	L. Romanov (ROM)	6–3	7–5	
1977 C. Casabianca (ARG)	L. Antonoplis (USA)	6–3	2–6	6–2
1978 L. Siegel (USA)	I. Madruga (ARG)	6–4	6–4	
1979 A. Moulton (USA)	M. L. Piatek (USA)	7–6	7–6	
1980 S. Mascarin (USA)	K. Keil (USA)	6–3	6–4	
1981 Z. Garrison (USA)	K. Gompert (USA)	6–0	6–3	
1982 B. Herr (USA)	G. Rush (USA)	6–3	6–1	
1983 E. Minter (AUS)	M. Werdel (USA)	6–3	7–5	
1984 K. Maleeva (BUL)	N. Sodupe (USA)	6–1	6–2	
1985 L. Garrone (ITA)	A. Holikova (TCH)	6–2	7–6	
1986 E. Hakami (USA)	S. Stafford (USA)	6–2	6–1	
1987 N. Zvereva (URS)	S. Birch (USA)	6–0	6–3	
1988 C. Cunningham (USA)	R. McQuillan (AUS)	6–3	6–1	
1989 J. Capriati (USA)	R. McQuillan (AUS)	6–2	6–3	
1990 M. Maleeva (BUL)	N. Van Lottum (FRA)	7–5	6–2	
1991 K. Habsudova (TCH)	A. Mall (USA)	6–1	6–3	
1992 L. Davenport (USA)	J. Steven (USA)	6–2	6–2	
1993 M. F. Bentivoglio (ITA)	Y. Yoshida (JPN)	7–6	6–4	
1994 M. Tu (USA)	M. Hingis (SUI)	6–2	6–4	
1995 T. Snyder (USA)	A. Ellwood (AUS)	6–4	4–6	6–2
1996 M. Lucic (CRO)	M. Weingartner (GER)	6–2	6–1	
1997 C. Black (ZIM)	K. Chevalier (FRA)	6–7	6–1	6–3
1998 J. Dokic (AUS)	K. Srebotnik (SLO)	6–4	6–2	
1999 L. Krasnoroutskala (RUS)	N. Petrova (RUS)	6–3	6–2	
2000 M. Salerni (ARG)	T. Perebiynis (UKR)	6–3	6–4	

BOYS' DOUBLES

	WINNERS	RUNNERS-UP	SCORE		
1982	J. Canter (USA)/M. Kures (USA)	P. Cash (AUS)/J. Frawley (AUS)	7–6	6–3	
1983	M. Kratzman (AUS)/S. Youl (AUS)	P. McEnroe (USA)/B. Pearce (USA)	6–1	7–6	
1984	L. Lavelle (MEX)/M. Nastase (ROM)	J. Ycaza (PER)/A. Moreno (MEX)	7–6	1–6	6–1
1985	J. Blake (USA)/D. Yates (USA)	P. Flynn (USA)/D. McPherson (USA)	3–6	6–3	6–4
1986	T. Carbonell (ESP)/J. Sanchez (ESP)	J. Tarango (USA)/D. Wheaton (USA)	6–4	1–6	6–1
1987	G. Ivanisevic (YUG)/D. Nargiso (ITA)	Z. Ali (IND)/B. Steven (NZL)	3–6	6–4	6–3
1988	J. Stark (USA)/J. Yoncey (USA)	M. Boscatta (ITA)/S. Pescosolido (ITA)	7–6	7–5	
1989	W. Ferreira (RSA)/G. Stafford (RSA)	M. Damm (TCH)/J. Kodes (TCH)	6–3	6–4	
1990	M. Renstroem (SWE)/M. Tillstroem (SWE)	S. LeBlanc (CAN)/G. Rusedski (CAN)	6–7	6–3	6–4
1991	K. Alami (MAR)/J–L. De Jager (RSA)	M. Joyce (USA)/V. Spadea (USA)	6–4	6–7	6–1
1992	J. Jackson (USA)/E. Taino (USA)	M. Rios (CHI)/G. Silberstein (CHI)	6–3	6–7	6–4
1993	N. Godwin (RSA)/G. Williams (RSA)	B. Ellwood (AUS)/J. Sekulov (AUS)	6–3	6–3	
1994	B. Ellwood (AUS)/N. Lapentti (ECU)	P. Goldstein (USA)/S. Humphries (USA)	6–2	6–0	
1995	J-M. Lee (KOR)/J. Robichaud (CAN)	R. Sluiter (NED)/P. Wessels (NED)	7–6	6–2	
1996	B. Bryan (USA)/M. Bryan (USA)	D. Bracciali (ITA)/J. Robichaud (CAN)	5–7	6–3	6–4
1997	F. Gonzalez (CHI)/N. Massu (CHI)	J-R. Lisnard (FRA)/M. Llodra (FRA)	6–4	6–4	
1998	K. Hippensteel (USA)/D. Martin (USA)	A. Ram (ISR)/L. Zovko (CRO)	6–7	7–6	6–2
1999	J. Benneteau (FRA)/N. Mahut (FRA)	T. Davis (USA)/A. Francis (USA)	6–4	3–6	6–1
2000	L. Childs (GBR)/J. Nelson (GBR)	T. Davis (USA)/R. Ginepri (USA)	6–2	6–4	

GIRLS' DOUBLES

	WINNERS	RUNNERS-UP	SCORE		
1982	P. Barg (USA)/B. Herr (USA)	A. Hulbert (AUS)/B. Randall (AUS)	1–6	7–5	7–6
1983	A. Hulbert (AUS)/B. Randall (AUS)	N. Riva (URS)/L. Savchenko (URS)	6–4	6–2	
1984	G. Sabatini (ARG)/M. Paz (ARG)	S. MacGregor (USA)/S. London (USA)	6–4	3–6	6–2
1985	R. Zrubakova (TCH)/A. Holikova (TCH)	P. Tarabini (ARG)/M. Perez Roldan (ARG)	6–4	2–6	7–5
1986	R. Zrubakova (TCH)/J. Novotna (TCH)	E. Brioukhovets (URS)/L. Meskhi (URS)	6–4	6–2	
1987	M. McGrath (USA)/K. Po (USA)	Il-Soon Kim (KOR)/Shi-Ting Wang (TPE)	6–4	7–5	
1988	M. McGrath (USA)/K. Po (USA)	K. Caverzasio (ITA)/L. Lapi (ITA)	6–3	6–1	
1989	J. Capriati (USA)/M. McGrath (USA)	J. Faull (AUS)/R. McQuillan (AUS)	6–0	6–3	
1990	K. Godridge (AUS)/K. Sharpe (AUS)	E. deLone (USA)/L. Raymond (USA)	4–6	7–5	6–2
1991	K. Godridge (AUS)/N. Pratt (AUS)	A. Carlsson (SWE)/C. Cristea (ROM)	7–6	7–5	
1992	L. Davenport (USA)/N. London (USA)	K. Schlukebit (USA)/J. Steven (USA)	7–5	6–7	6–4
1993	N. London (USA)/J. Steven (USA)	H. Mochizuki (JPN)/Y. Yoshida (JPN)	6–3	6–4	
1994	S. De Beer (RSA)/C. Reuter (NED)	N. De Villiers (RSA) /E. Jelfs (GBR)	4–6	6–4	6–2
1995	C. Morariu (USA)/L. Varmuzova (SMR)	A. Kournikova (RUS)/A. Olsza (POL)	6–3	6–3	
1996	S. De Beer (RSA)/J. Steck (RSA)	P. Rampre (SLO)/K. Srebotnik (SLO)	6–4	6–3	
1997	M. Irvin (USA)/A. Stevenson (USA)	C. Black (ZIM)/I. Selyutina (KAZ)	6–2	7–6	
1998	K. Clijsters (BEL)/E. Dyrberg (DEN)	J. Dokic (AUS)/E. Dominikovic (AUS)	7–6	6–4	
1999	D. Bedanova (CZE)/I. Tulyaganova (UZB)	G. Fokina (RUS)/L. Krasnoroutskaia (RUS)	6–3	6–4	
2000	G. Dulko (ARG)/M. Salerni (ARG)	A. Kapros (HUN)/C. Wheeler (AUS)	3–6	6–2	6–2

ITALIAN INTERNATIONAL JUNIOR CHAMPIONSHIPS

The event originated as an Under-21 Invitational tournament for boys and girls singles in 1959. It became a Championship event in 1976.

BOYS' SINGLES

	WINNER	RUNNER–UP	SCORE		
1976	H. Gunthardt (SUI)	F. Luna (ESP)	6–4	6–1	
1977	Y. Noah (FRA)	R. Venter (ESP)	6–4	6–2	
1978	I. Lendl (TCH)	P. Hjertquist (SWE)	2–6	6–2	6–0
1979	H. Simonsson (SWE)	B. Testerman (USA)	6–0	6–3	
1980	T. Tulasne (FRA)	H. Leconte (FRA)	6–2	6–3	
1981	B. Zivojinovic (YUG)	L. Bottazzi (ITA)	7–6	2–6	6–3
1982	G. Forget (FRA)	M. Zampieri (ITA)	6–3	6–4	
	WINNER	RUNNER–UP	SCORE		
1983	M. Fioroni (ITA)	K. Novacek (TCH)	5–7	6–1	6–3
1984	L. Jensen (USA)	B. Oresar (YUG)	6–4	6–4	
1985	A. Padovani (ITA)	C. Pistolesi (ITA)	6–2	6–1	
1986	F. Davin (ARG)	G. Perez-Roldan (ARG)	6–4	4–6	6–0
1987	J. Courier (USA)	A. Aramburu (PER)	7–6	1–6	6–3
1988	G. Ivanisevic (YUG)	F. Fontang (FRA)	6–3	6–2	
1989	S. Pescosolido (ITA)	F. Santoro (FRA)	6–1	6–0	
1990	I. Baron (USA)	O. Fernandez (MEX)	7–5	6–1	

	WINNER	RUNNER–UP	SCORE		
1991	G. Doyle (AUS)	K. Carlsen (DEN)	1–6	6–3	9–7
1992	Y. Kafelnikov (CIS)	D. Skoch (TCH)	7–6	6–4	
1993	J. Szymanski (VEN)	R. Sabau (ROM)	6–3	6–4	
1994	F. Browne (ARG)	G. Galimberti (ITA)	6–3	6–2	
1995	M. Zabaleta (ARG)	M. Lee (GBR)	6–4	6–2	
1996	O. Mutis (FRA)	D. Sciortino (ITA)	6–1	6–3	
1997	F. Allgauer (ITA)	L. Horna (PER)	6–3	6–4	
1998	G. Coria (ARG)	J. Jeanpierre (FRA)	7–6	6–3	
1999	K. Pless (DEN)	G. Coria (ARG)	6–0	7–6	
2000	T. Enev (BUL)	A. Dernovskyy (UKR)	6–3	6–3	

GIRLS' SINGLES

	WINNER	RUNNER–UP	SCORE		
1977	H. Strachanova (CZE)	C. Casabianca (ARG)	7–6	6–0	
1978	H. Mandlikova (TCH)	I. Madruga (ARG)	7–6	6–3	
1979	M. L. Piatek (USA)	L. Sandin (SWE)	6–3	3–6	6–3
1980	S. Mascarin (USA)	K. Horvath (USA)	6–4	6–3	
1981	A. Minter (USA)	E. Sayers (AUS)	1–6	6–2	6–3
1982	G. Rush (USA)	B. Herr (USA)	6–7	7–6	6–4
1983	S. Goles (YUG)	A.M. Cecchini (ITA)	6–3	6–4	
1984	G. Sabatini (ARG)	S. Schilder (HOL)	7–6	6–1	
1985	P. Tarabini (ARG)	L. Golarsa (ITA)	6–0	6–1	
1986	B. Fulco (ARG)	P. Tarabini (ARG)	7–6	6–2	
1987	N. Zvereva (URS)	C. Martinez (ESP)	6–3	6–2	
1988	C. Tessi (ARG)	F. Labat (ARG)	3–6	7–6	6–3
1989	F. Labat (ARG)	M. Anderson (RSA)	6–2	6–2	
1990	S. Farina (ITA)	N. Baudone (ITA)	6–1	6–2	
1991	Z. Malkova (TCH)	E. Makarova (URS)	6–2	6–1	
1992	R. De Los Rios (PAR)	N. Feber (BEL)	6–1	7–5	
1993	N. Louarssabichvili (GEO)	J. Lee (USA)	6–4	6–7	7–5
1994	T. Panova (RUS)	S. Ventura (ITA)	1–6	6–3	6–0
1995	A. Kournikova (RUS)	C. Reuter (NED)	6–2	6–0	
1996	O. Barabanschikova (BLR)	S. Drake-Brockman (AUS)	2–6	7–5	6–2
1997	K. Srebotnik (SLO)	T. Pisnik (SLO)	6–1	6–2	
1998	A. Serra-Zanetti (ITA)	A. Vedy (FRA)	6–3	5–7	6–4
1999	L. Krasnoroutskaia (RUS)	S. Kotschwara (GER)	6–3	6–1	
2000	I. Gaspar (ROM)	M. Salerni (ARG)	6–7	6–3	8–6

BOYS' DOUBLES

	WINNER	RUNNER–UP	SCORE		
1993	N. London (USA)/J. Steven (USA)	H. Mochizuki (JPN)/Y. Yoshida (JPN)	6–3	6–4	
1976	F. Van Oertzen (BRA)/C.Sacomandi (BRA)	C. Motta (BRA)/H. Roverano (BRA)	6–3	6–2	
1980	S. Giammalva (USA)/M. Anger (USA)	W. Masur (AUS)/C. Miller (AUS)	7–6	6–0	
1981	E. Korita (USA)/J.Brown (USA)	R. Bengston (CAN)/M. Perkins (CAN)	6–2	6–4	
1982	F. Maciel (MEX)/F.Perez (MEX)	M. Kures (USA)/R. Leach (USA)	6–3	7–5	
1983	S. Edberg (SWE)/J.Svensson (SWE)	F. Garcia (ESP)/E. Sanchez (ESP)	6–2	6–3	
1984	A. Moreno (MEX)/J.Yzaga (PER)	A. Antonitsch (AUT)/H. Skoff (AUT)	6–7	7–6	6–3
1985	F. Errard (FRA)/P. Lacombrade (FRA)	G. Saacks (RSA)/D. Shapiro (RSA)	7–6	4–6	6–4
1986	F. Davin (ARG)/G. Perez-Roldan (ARG)	A. Mancini (ARG)/N. Pereira (URU)	6–2	6–2	
1987	G. Carbonari (ARG)/J.L. Noriega (PER)	L. Bale (RSA)/D. Naikin (RSA)	2–6	6–3	6–4
1988	S. Hirszon (YUG)/G. Ivanisevic (YUG)	M. Boscatto (ITA)/F. Pisilli (ITA)	6–3	6–4	
1989	M. Bascatto (ITA)/ S. Pescosolido (ITA)	W. Ferreira (RSA)/ G. Stafford (RSA)	7–5	6–4	
1990	W. Bulls (USA)/ B. MacPhie (USA)	J. De Jager (RSA)/ J. De Beer (RSA)	7–6	5–7	6–4
1991	G. Doyle (AUS)/ J. Eagle (AUS)	S. Sargsian (URS)/D. Tomachevitch (URS)	6–1	6–1	
1992	M. Bertolini (ITA)/ M. Navarra (ITA)	Y. Kafelnikov (CIS)/ A. Radulescu (ROM)	6–4	4–6	6–4
1993	T. Johansson (SWE)/M. Norman (SWE)	B. Ellwood (AUS)/ J. Sekulov (AUS)	7–6	6–3	
1994	B. Ellwood (AUS)/M. Philippoussis (AUS)	A. Hernandez (MEX)/ G. Venegas MEX)	6–2	6–3	
1995	G. Canas (ARG)/ M. Garcia (ARG)	S. Grosjean (FRA)/Y. Romero (VEN)	6–2	7–6	
1996	M. Lee (GBR)/J. Trotman (GBR)	A. Krasevec (SLO)/G. Krusic (SLO)	7–6	2–6	6–1
1997	J. Van Der Westhuizen (RSA)/ W. Whitehouse (RSA)	F. Gonzalez (CHI)/N. Massu (CHI)	2–0	ret	
1998	J. De Armas (VEN)/F. Gonzalez (CHI)	N. Healey (AUS)/A. Kracman (SLO)	2–6	7–5	6–4
1999	G. Coria (ARG)/D. Nalbandian (ARG)	S. Dickson (GBR)/K. Pless (DEN)	7–5	6–2	
2000	J. Cassaigne (FRA)/A. Roddick (USA)	B. Soares (BRA)/S. Wiespeiner (AUT)	4–6	6–3	6–2

GIRLS' DOUBLES

	WINNER	RUNNER–UP	SCORE		
1980	B. Mould (RSA)/ R. Uys (RSA)	K. Horvath (USA)/ P. Murgo (ITA)	4–6	6–2	6–4
1981	H. Sukova (TCH)/ M. Maleeva (BUL)	M. Linstrom (SWE)/ C. Lindquist (SWE)	3–6	6–4	6–4
1982	B. Gerken (USA)/ B. Herr (USA)	B. Randall (AUS)/ E. Minter (AUS)	6–3	6–4	
1983	P. Fendick (USA)/ J. Fuchs (USA)	B. Bowes (USA)/ A. Hubert (USA)	6–4	6–4	
1984	D. Ketelaar (HOL)/ S. Schilder (HOL)	M. Paz (ARG)/ G. Sabatini (ARG)	5–7	6–4	6–2
1985	P. Tarabini (ARG)/M. Perez-Roldan (ARG)	J. Novotna (TCH)/ R. Rajchrtova (TCH)	6–4	6–4	
1986	A. Dechaurne (FRA)/S. Niox Chateau (FRA)	E. Derly (FRA)/ F. Martin (FRA)	6–2	6–4	
1987	N. Medvedeva (URS)/ N. Zvereva (URS)	P. Miller (URU)/ C. Tessi (ARG)	7–5	6–1	
1988	D. Graham (USA)/ A. Grossman (USA)	C. Cunningham (USA)/ A. Farley (USA)	6–2	7–5	
1989	R. Bobkova (TCH)/ A. Strnadova (TCH)	N. Baudone (ITA)/ S. Farina (ITA)	5–7	6–4	6–4
1990	T. Ignatieva (URS)/ I. Sukhova (URS)	C. Barclay (AUS)/ J. Stacey (AUS)	5–7	6–2	9–7
1991	B. Martincova (TCH)/ I. Horvat (YUG)	I. Gorrochategui (ARG)/ R. Grande (ITA)	6–3	6–4	
1992	N. Feber (BEL)/ L. Courtois (BEL)	M. Avotins (AUS)/ L. McShea (AUS)	6–4	5–7	6–3
1993	C. Moros (USA)/ S. Nickitas (USA)	M. D. Campana (CHI)/ B. Castro (CHI)	7–5	7–5	
1994	M. Nedelkova (SVK)/ M. Hasanova (SVK)	K. Mesa (COL)/ C. Giraldo (COL)	1–6	6–3	6–4
1995	A. Canepa (ITA)/ G. Casoni (ITA)	O. Barabanschikova (BLR)/L. Varmuzova (SMR)	6–4	5–7	6–3
1996	A. Canepa (ITA)/G. Casoni (ITA)	S. Drake-Brockman (AUS)/A. Kournikova (RUS)	5–7	6–4	6–3
1997	T. Hergold (SLO)/T. Pisnik (SLO)	S. Bajin (CAN)/I. Visic (CRO)	6–1	6–2	
1998	Finalists: E. Dyrberg (DEN)/A Vedy (FRA) and M. E. Salemi (ARG)/C. Fernandez (ARG) Final not played due to rain.				
1999	F. Pennetta (ITA)/R. Vinci (ITA)	G. Dulko (ARG)/M. Salerni (ARG)	6–2	7–5	
2000	I. Gaspar (ROM)/T. Perebiynis (UKR)	M. Babakova (SVK)/S. Stasur (AUS)	6–3	7–5	

NEC WORLD YOUTH CUP

International Team Championship for boys and girls aged 16 and under. Early rounds played zonally.

BOYS' FINALS

1985 Australia d. USA 2–1, *Kobe Japan:* R. Fromberg lost to F. Montana 2–6 2–6, S. Barr d. J. A. Falbo 6–4 6–4; Barr/J. Stoltenberg d. Montana/Falbo 4–6 6–7 7–5.

1986 Australia d. USA 2–1, *Tokyo, Japan:* J. Stoltenberg d. J. Courier 6–2 6–4; R. Fromberg lost to M. Chang 4–6 4–6; Stoltenberg/T. Woodbridge d. Courier/Kass 7–6 6–2.

1987 Australia d. Netherlands 3–0, *Freiburg, West Germany:* T. Woodbridge d. P. Dogger 7–5 3–6 6–2; J. Anderson d. F. Wibier 6–0 6–1; J. Morgan/Woodbridge d. Dogger/Wibier 6–3 6–2.

1988 Czechoslovakia d. USA 2–1, *Perth, Australia:* J. Kodes d. J. Leach 7–6 6–2; M. Damm d. B. MacPhie 6–2 6–7 6–4; Damm/L. Hovorka lost to W. Bull/Leach 4–6 4–6.

1989 West Germany d. Czechoslovakia 2–1, *Asuncion, Paraguay:* S. Gessner lost to L. Thomas 5–7 5–7; G. Paul d. P. Gazda 6–4 6–4; Paul/D. Prinosil d. Gazda/Thomas 7–5 6–1.

1990 USSR d. Australia 2–1, *Rotterdam, Netherlands:* D. Thomashevitch d. T. Vasiliadis 6–3 6–2; A. Medvedev lost to G. Doyle 6–2 4–6 5–7; E. Kafelnikov/Medvedev d. Doyle/B. Sceney 7–6 6–3.

1991 Spain d. Czechoslovakia 2–1, *Barcelona, Spain:* G. Corrales d. D. Skock 7–5 7–5; A. Costa lost to F. Kascak 4–6 5–7; Corrales /Costa d. Kascak/Skock 6–4 6–2.

1992 France d. Germany 2–1, *Barcelona, Spain:* M. Boye d. A. Nickel 7–5 0–6 6–3; N. Escude lost to R. Nicklish 2–6, 6–3, 3–6; Boye/Escude d. Nickel/Nicklish 6–7 6–0 6–3.

1993 France d. New Zealand 2–1, *Wellington, New Zealand:* O. Mutis lost to T. Susnjak 1–6 6–1 3–6; J-F Bachelot d. S. Clark 4–6 6–4 6–4; Mutis/J. Potron d. Clark/N. Nielsen 6–3 6–4.

1994 Netherlands d. Austria 2–1, *Tucson, Arizona:* P. Wessels lost to C. Trimmel 6–4 3–6 5–7; R. Sluiter d. M. Hipfl 7–6 6–1; Sluiter/Wessels d. Hipfl/Trimmel 6–3 6–4.

1995 Germany d. Czech Republic 3–0, *Essen, Germany:* T. Messmer d. P. Kralert 6–3 7–5; D. Elsner d. M. Tabara 6–3 6–4; D. Elsner/T. Zivnicek d. P. Kralert/P. Riha 6–7 6–4 6–4.

1996 France d. Australia 2–1, *Zurich, Switzerland:* J. Haehnel d. N. Healey 6–4 6–2; J. Jeanpierre d. L. Hewitt 6–3 7–5; J. Haehnel/O. Patience lost to N. Healey/L. Hewitt 5–7 6–4 6–7.

1997 Czech Republic d. Venezuela 2–0, *Vancouver, Canada:* J. Levinsky d. E. Nastari 6–0 6–2; L. Chramosta d. J. De Armas 7–6 6–2.

1998 Spain d. Croatia 2–1, *Cuneo, Italy:* M. Lopez lost to R. Karanusic 6–3 3–6 3–6; T. Robredo d. M. Radic 6–3 6–4; M. Lopez/T. Robredo d. R. Karanusic/M. Radic 6–4 6–2.

1999 USA d. Croatia 3–0, *Perth, Australia:* R. Redondo d. I. Stelko 7–6 6–4; A. Bogomolov d. M. Ancic 7–6 6–3; R. Redondo/T. Rettenmaier d. M. Ancic/T. Peric 7–6 7–6.

2000 Australia d. Austria 2–0, *Hiroshima, Japan:* R. Henry d. S. Wiespeiner 5–7 6–4 8–6; T. Reid d. J. Ager 6–4 7–5.

GIRLS' FINALS

1985 Czechoslovakia d. Australia 3–0, *Kobe, Japan:* J. Pospisilova d. S. McCann 6–4 6–4; R. Zrubakova d. N. Provis 7–6 7–5; Pospisilova/Zrubakova d. Provis/W. Frazer 7–5 6–4.

1986 Belgium d. Czechoslovakia 2–1, *Tokyo, Japan:* A. Devries d. R. Zrubakova 6–3 6–4; S. Wasserman d. P. Langrova 6–4 7–5; Devries/C. Neuprez lost to Langrova/Zrubakova 4–6 2–6.
1987 Australia d. USSR 2–1, *Freiburg, West Germany:* J. Faull lost to N. Medvedeva 6–4 2–6 2–6; R. McQuillan d. E. Brioukhovets 3–6 6–2 6–3; Faull/McQuillan d. Brioukhovets/Medvedeva 6–3 6–1.
1988 Australia d. Argentina 2–1, *Perth, Australia:* K. A. Guse d. F. Haumuller 7–6 6–4; L. Guse d. C. Tessi 7–6 1–6 6–2; K. A. Guse/K. Sharpe d. I. Gorrachategui/Tessi 6–0 6–2.
1989 West Germany d. Czechoslovakia 2–1, *Asuncion, Paraguay:* M. Skulj–Zivec d. K. Matouskova 6–0 7–5; A. Huber d. K. Habsudova 6–0 6–3; K. Duell/Skulj–Zivec lost to Habsudova/P. Kucova 3–6 0–6.
1990 Netherlands d. USSR 2–1, *Rotterdam, Netherlands:* P. Kamstra d. I. Soukhova 6–1 7–6; L. Niemansverdriet lost to T. Ignatieva 0–6 6–1 4–6; Kamstra/Niemansverdriet d. Ignatieva/Soukhova 6–3 4–6 6–1.
1991 Germany d. Paraguay 2–1, *Barcelona, Spain:* H. Rusch lost to L. Schaerer 6–7 3–6; M. Kochta d. R De los Rios 6–3 6–1; K. Freye/Kochta d. De los Rios/Schaerer 5–7 6–3 6–3.
1992 Belgium d. Argentina 3–0, *Barcelona, Spain:* L. Courtois d. L. Montalvo 6–1 6–3; N. Feber d. L. Reynares 1–6 6–4 6–1; Courtois/S. Deville d. M. Oliva/Montalvo 1–6 7–5 6–4.
1993 Australia d. USA 2–1, *Wellington, New Zealand:* S. Drake-Brockman d. S. Nickitas 6–2 5–7 6–2; A. Ellwood d. A. Basica 6–2 6–1; Ellwood/J. Richardson lost to C. Maros/Nickitas 6–2 5–7 0–6.
1994 South Africa d. France 3–0, *Tucson, Arizona:* J. Steck d. A. Cocheteux 7–5 6–3; S. De Beer d. A. Castera 6–4 6–3; doubles not played.
1995 France d. Germany 2–1, *Essen, Germany:* K. Jagieniak lost to S. Kovacic 4–6 3–6; A. Mauresmo d. S. Klosel 6–0 6–3; K. Chevalier/A. Mauresmo d. C. Christian/S.-Kovacic 6–3 7–5.
1996 Slovenia d. Germany 2–1, *Zurich, Switzerland:* K. Srebotnik d. S. Kovacic 6–1 6–3; P. Rampre lost to J. Wohr 2–6 1–6; P. Rampre/K. Srebotnik d. S. Kovacic/J. Wohr 6–1 6–4.
1997 Russia d. France 2–0, *Vancouver, Canada:* A. Myskina d. S. Schoeffel 6–3 2–6 8–6; E. Dementieva d. S. Rizzi 6–2 4–6 6–4.
1998 Italy d. Slovak Republic 2–1, *Cuneo, Italy:* R. Vinci lost to S. Hrozenska 6–2 2–6 6–8; M. E. Camerin d. D. Hantuchova 6–4 6–2; F. Pennetta/R. Vinci d. D. Hantuchova/S. Hrozenska 6–4 6–1.
1999 Argentina d. Slovak Republic 2–1, *Perth, Australia:* G. Dulko lost to L. Dlhopolcova 3–6 3–6; M. Salerni d. L. Kurhajcova 6–3 6–4; E. Chialvo/M. Salerni d. L Dlhopolcova/L. Kurhajcova 6–3 6–2.
2000 Czech Republic d. Hungary 2–1, *Hiroshima, Japan:* E. Birnerova d. D. Magas 7–6(5) 6–3; P. Cetkovska lost to V. Nemeth 5–7 6–4 6–8; P. Cetkovska/E. Janaskova d. D. Magas/ V. Nemeth 7–5 5–7 6–1.

WORLD JUNIOR TENNIS COMPETITION

International Team Championship for boys and girls aged 14 and under, known as NTT World Junior Tennis 1991–96; Cesky Telecom World Junior Tennis from 2000.

BOYS' FINALS
1991 Spain d. Italy 2–1, *Yamanakako, Japan:* A. Martin d. C. Zoppi 6–2 7–6; J-A. Saiz d. P. Tabini 6–2 6–1; Martin/J-M. Vincente lost to A. Ciceroni/Tabini 7–5 4–6 6–8.
1992 Austria d. USA 2–1, *Yamanakako, Japan:* K. Trimmel d. C. Brill 4–6 6–2 6–2; M. Hipfl d. G. Adams 6–4 6–0; Trimmel/Hipfl lost to Abrams/R. Bryan 6–1 6–2.
1993 France d. Slovenia 2–1, *Yamanakako, Japan:* J-R. Lisnard d. A. Krasevec 7–6 6–3; A. Di Pasquale d. M. Gregoric 6–1 6–1; A. Di Pasquale/V. Lavergne lost to P. Kralert/J. Krejci 2–6 6–2 6–7.
1994 Italy d. Belgium 2–1, *Yamanakako, Japan:* N. Frocassi lost to O. Rochus 6–7 6–3 3–6; F. Luzzi d. X. Malisse 6–3 7–6; Frocassi/Luzzi d. Malisse/Rochus 6–4 1–6 6–3.
1995 Great Britain d. Germany 3–0, *Yamanakako, Japan:* M. Hilton d. P. Hammer 6–3 4–6 6–4; S. Dickson d. B. Bachert 7–5 6–2; S. Dickson/A. Mackin d. B. Bachert/R. Neurohr 7–5 6–1.
1996 Argentina d. Sweden 3–0, *Nagoya, Japan:* G. Coria d. F. Prpic 6–1 6–1; D. Nalbandian d. J. Johansson 6–3 6–3; G. Coria/A. Pastorino d. J. Johansson/F. Prpic 6–1 6–3.
1997 South Africa d. Czech Republic 2–1, *Nagoya, Japan:* A. Anderson d. M. Kokta 7–5 6–4; D. Stegmann d. J. Masik 6–3 6–0; A. Anderson/R. Blair lost to D. Karol/J. Masik 1–6 0–6.
1998 Austria d. Argentina 3–0, *Nagoya, Japan:* J. Ager d. J. Monaco 6–4 6–4; S. Wiespeiner d. B. Dabul 4–6 6–4 6–1; J. Ager/C. Polessnig d. B. Dabul/J. Ottaviani 6–4 7–5.
1999 France d. Chile 2–1, *Prostejov, Czech Republic:* J. Tsonga d. G. Hormazabal 6–4 6–3; R. Gasquet d. J. Aguilar 7–6 3–6 6–4; J. Robin/J. Tsonga lost to J. Aguilar/G. Hormazabal 5–7 3–6.
2000 Spain d. Russia 3–0, *Prostejov, Czech Republic:* B. Salva d. A. Sitak 6–3 6–3; R. Nadal d. N. Soloviev 6–3 6–2; M. Granollers/R. Nadal d. D. Matsoukevitch/A. Sitak 4–6 6–1 6–4.

GIRLS' FINALS
1991 Czechoslovakia d. Australia 3–0, *Yamanakako, Japan:* L. Cenkova d. A. Ellwood 7–5 6–2; A. Havrlkova d. A. Venkatesan 6–1 6–2; Cenkova/Havrlkova d. Ellwood/E. Knox 6–2 7–6.
1992 USA d. Australia 3–0, *Yamanakako, Japan:* M. Tu d. A. Ellwood 6–4 6–4; A. Basica d. R. Reid 6–3 6–7 6–4; Basica/A. Augustus d. Reid/S. Drake-Brockman 6–2 7–5.
1993 Germany d. USA 2–1, *Yamanakako, Japan:* C. Christian lost to S. Halsell 0–6 3–6; S. Klosel d. K. Gates 6–4 7–6; C. Christian/S. Klosel d. K. Gates/S. Halsell 3–6 6–3 7–5.
1994 Germany d. Czech Republic 2–1, *Yamanakako, Japan:* J. Wohr d. J. Schonfeldova 7–5 6–0; S. Kovacic d. M. Pastikova 6–2 7–5; S. Lozel/Wohr lost to Pastikova/Schonfeldova 4–6 1–6.

1995 Slovenia d. Hungary 2–1, *Yamanakako, Japan:* T. Pisnik d. S. Szegedi 7–6 6–3; K. Srebotnik lost to Z. Gubacsi 6–4 3–6 4–6; T. Pisnik/K. Srebotnik d. Z. Gubacsi/I. Szalai 6–3 6–3.
1996 Slovak Republic d. Great Britain 3–0, Nagoya, Japan: S. Hrozenska d. S. Gregg 6–1 6–2; K. Basternakova d. H. Collin 6–3 6–1; S. Hrozenska/Z. Kucova d. H. Collin/H. Reesby 6–4 6–2.
1997 Russia d. Slovak Republic 2–1, *Nagoya, Japan:* L. Krasnoroutskaia d. D. Hantuchova 6–2 6–4; E. Bovina d. M. Babakova 6–4 6–1; G. Fokina/L. Krasnoroutskaia lost to D. Hantuchova/L. Kurhajcova 2–6 6–2 2–6.
1998 Czech Republic d. Russia 2–1, *Nagoya, Japan:* E. Birnerova d. V. Zvonareva 6–3 6–4; P. Cetkovska lost to G. Fokina 2-6 6–2 4–6; E. Birnerova/P. Cetkovska d. G. Fokina/R. Gourevitch 7–5 1–6 6–3.
1999 Russia d. Slovak Republic 2–1, *Prostejov, Czech Republic:* D. Safina d. M. Zivcicova 6–3 6–1; A. Bastrikova d. K. Kachlikova 6–3 6–2; A. Bastrikova/N. Brattchikova lost to L. Smolenakova/M. Zivcicova 3–6 4–6.
2000 Russia d. Czech Republic 3–0, *Prostejov, Czech Republic:* D. Tchemarda d. L. Safarova 7–6(3) 6–2; V. Douchevina d. B. Strycova 4–6 6–1 6–2; I. Kotkina/D. Tchemarda d. N. Freislerova/L. Safarova 6–4 6–0.

ORANGE BOWL

International 18 and Under Championship played in Miami each December. There are also events for players aged 16 and under, and 14 and under.

BOYS' SINGLES

	WINNER	RUNNER-UP	SCORE				
1974	W. Martin (USA)	T. Smid (TCH)	6–7	4–6	6–2	6–1	7–6
1975	F. Luna (ESP)	B. E. Gottfried (USA)	6–4	6–4			
1976	J. P. McEnroe (USA)	E. Teltscher (USA)	7–5	6–1			
1977	I. Lendl (TCH)	Y. Noah (FRA)	4–6	7–6	6–3		
1978	G. Urpi (ESP)	S. Van der Merwe (SAF)	6–3	6–1			
1979	R. Viver (ECU)	P. Arraya (PER)	7–6	6–4			
1980	J. Nystrom (SWE)	C. Castqtellan (ARG)	7–5	7–6			
1981	R. Arguello (ARG)	R. Joaquim (BRA)	6–2	6–1			
1982	G. Forget (FRA)	J. Bardou (ESP)	7–5	2–6	6–1		
1983	K. Carlsson (SWE)	E. Sanchez (ESP)	6–2	6–4			
1984	R. Brown (USA)	J. Berger (USA)	6–3	6–3			
1985	C. Pistolesi (ITA)	B. Oresar (YUG)	6–2	6–0			
1986	J. Sanchez (ESP)	A. Parker (USA)	6–3	6–4			
1987	J. Courier (USA)	A. Cherkasov (URS)	6–3	6–2			
1988	M. Rosset (SUI)	S. Pescosolido (ITA)	7–6	3–6	6–1		
1989	F. Meligeni (ARG)	G. Lopez (ESP)	7–6	7–6			
1990	A. Medvedev (URS)	O. Fernandez (MEX)	6–4	2–6	6–2		
1991	M. Charpentier (ARG)	K. Alami (MAR)	6–4	6–3			
1992	V. Spadea (USA)	G. Etlis(ARG)	7–6	6–3			
1993	A. Costa (ESP)	R. Carretero (ESP)	6–3	6–4			
1994	N. Lapentti (ECU)	G. Kuerten (BRA)	6–3	7–6			
1995	M. Zabaleta (ARG)	T. Haas (GER)	6–2	3–6	6–1		
1996	A. Martin (ESP)	A. Di Pasquale (FRA)	6–0	6–1			
1997	N. Massu (CHI)	R. Rake (USA)	6–1	6–7	6–3		
1998	R. Federer (SUI)	G. Coria (ARG)	7–5	6–3			
1999	A. Roddick (USA)	M. Abel (GER)	6–1	6–7	6–4		
2000	T. Enev (BUL)	B. Soares (BRA)	7–5	6–2			

GIRLS' SINGLES

	WINNER	RUNNER-UP	SCORE		
1974	L. Epstein (USA)	C. Penn (USA)	6–1	6–2	
1975	L. Epstein (USA)	S. McInerny (USA)	6–2	6–1	
1976	M. Kruger (SAF)	A. .E. Smith (USA)	2–6	6–3	6–4
1977	A. E. Smith (USA)	H. Strachonova (TCH)	7–6	7–5	
1978	A. Jaeger (USA)	R. Fairbank (SAF)	6–1	6–3	
1979	K. Horvath (USA)	P. Murgo (ITA)	7–5	6–0	
1980	S. Mascarin (USA)	R. Sasak (YUG)	6–3	3–6	6–4
1981	P. Barg (USA)	H. Fukarkova (TCH)	6–2	6–3	
1982	C. Bassett (CAN)	M. Maleeva (BUL)	6–4	ret	
1983	D. Spence (USA)	A. Cecchini (ITA)	2–6	7–5	6–4
1984	G. Sabatini (ARG)	K. Maleeva (BUL)	6–1	6–3	
1985	M. J. Fernandez (USA)	P. Tarabini (ARG)	7–5	6–1	
1986	P. Tarabini (ARG)	B. Fulco (ARG)	6–2	6–2	
1987	N. Zvereva (URS)	L. Lapi (ITA)	6–2	6–0	
1988	C. Cunningham (USA)	L. Lapi (ITA)	6–0	6–1	
1989	L. Spadea (USA)	S. Albinus (DEN)	6–0	6–3	
1990	P. Perez (ESP)	S. Ramon (ESP)	6–1	7–6	

WINNER	RUNNER-UP	SCORE		
1991 E. Likhovtseva (URS)	M-J. Gaidono (ARG)	7–6	6–1	
1992 B. Mulej (SLO)	R. De Los Rios (PAR)	7–5	7–5	
1993 A. Montolio (ESP)	S. Jeyaseelan (CAN)	6–7	6–1	6–1
1994 M. Ramon (ESP)	A. Kournikova (RUS)	7–5	6–4	
1995 A. Kournikova (RUS)	S. Nacuk (YUG)	6–3	6–2	
1996 A. Alcazar (ESP)	K. Srebotnik (SLO)	6–3	6–0	
1997 T. Pisnik (SLO)	G. Volekova (SVK)	6–2	6–0	
1998 E. Dementieva (RUS)	N. Petrova (RUS)	3–6	6–4	6–0
1999 M. Martinez (ESP)	M. Salerni (ARG)	6–4	6–1	
2000 V. Zvonareva (RUS)	E. Gallovits (ROM)	7–6(4) 6–4		

GALEA CUP AND ANNIE SOISBAULT CUP (Discontinued in 1990)

International Team Championship for men and women respectively aged 20 and under. Full results of final rounds can be found in *World of Tennis 1996* and earlier editions.

VALERIO/GALEA CUP

International Team Championship for boys aged 18 and under. Played zonally with the final stages in Lesa, Italy. Administered by the European Tennis Association.

FINALS

1970 Sweden d. France 4–1: L. Johansson d. F. Caujolle 10–8 6–3; T. Svensson d. E. Naegelen 6–4 6–0; R. Norbeg lost to E. Deblicker 4–6 0–6; M. Stig d. A. Collinot 6–3 6–1; Johansson/Stig d. Deblicker/Naegelen 6–3 6–3.

1971 Italy d. West Germany 4–0: M. Consolini d. U. Pinner 6–2 1–0 ret; N. Gasparini d. R. Gehring 6–1 3–6 6–0; C. Borea d. A. Hongsag 3–6 6–4 6–3; C. Barazzutti v L. Jelitto 5–1 abandoned; Barazzutti/Gasparini d. Gehring/Jelitto 6–4 6–4.

1972 Czechoslovakia d. USSR 3–2: I. Hora lost to V. Borisov 6–4 7–9 5–7; P. Slozil d. A. Machavez 6–2 2–6 6–4; Slozil/J. Granat d. A. Bogomolov/Borisov 6–3 7–5; T. Smid lost to K. Pugaev 3–6 8–6 4–6; Granat d. Bogomolov 6–3 6–4.

1973 Czechoslovakia d. USSR 4–1: A. Jankowski lost to V. Borisov 6–4 2–3 ret; P. Slozil d. A. Machavez 6–3 5–7 6–4: J. Granat d. K. Pugaev 3–6 6–4 6–3; T. Smid d. V. Katsnelson 6–4 6–4; Jankowski/Slozil d. Borisov/Pugaev 6–8 10–8 6–3.

1974 Spain d. Italy 3–2: L. Fargas d. A. Meneschincheri 6–1 6–1; A. Capitan /M. Mir lost to A. Marchetti/A. Vattuone 6–3 4–6 3–6; M. Mir lost to G. Ocleppo 4–6 2–6; A. Torralbo d. Vattuone 9–11 6–4 6–3; Capitan d. G. Marchetti 8–6 3–6 6–3.

1975 Italy d. USSR 3–2: G. Ocleppo d. S. Baranov 7–5 6–5 ret; A. Spiga d. S. Molodoikov 6–4 6–8 6–0; A. Merlone d. V. Gruzman 6–2 0–6 6–3; A. Meneschincheri lost to S. Elerdashvili 9–11 4–6; Ocleppo/Merlone lost to Baranov/Gruzman 5–7 4–6.

1976 West Germany d. France 4–1: P. Elter d. P. Portes 6–3 6–2; W. Popp lost to Y. Noah 3–6 0–6; J. Henn d. J. Kuentz 6–2 6–2; A. Maurer d. G. Geniau 6–4 6–3; Elter/Popp d. G. Moretton/Noah 6–3 3–6 6–3.

1977 Italy d. Rumania 5–0: G. Rinaldini d. E. Pana 6–1 6–1; M. Rivaroli d. L. Mancas 6–2 6–4; N. Canessa d. A. Dirzu 6–3 2–6 6–4; P. Parrini d. F. Segarceanu 6–1 6–0; Canessa/Parrini d. Dirzu/Segarceanu 7–5 6–2.

1978 Sweden d. Italy 3–2: M. Wennberg d. F. Moscino 6–2 6–2; P. Hjertquist/S. Simonsson d. M. Alciati/C. Panatta 6–1 6–3; Hjertquist d. M. Ferrari 6–1 6–3; Simonsson lost to Alciati 4–6 1–6; A. Jarryd lost to Panatta 0–6 1–6.

1979 Sweden d. West Germany 4–1: S. Simonsson d. H. D. Beutel 6–4 6–0; T. Svensson d. C. Zipf 2–6 6–4 6–4; A. Jarryd d. K. Vogel 6–2 7–5; J. Gunnarsson d. A. Schulz 7–5 6–4; Simonsson/Svensson lost to Beutel/Zipf 3–6 6–2 6–8.

1980 Spain d. France 4–1: J. Aguilera d. T. Pham 6–4 1–6 6–3; A. Tous/S. Casal d. J. Potier/J. M. Piacentile 6–2 3–6 6–4; Tous lost to Potier 1–6 6–7; R. Mensua d. P. Kuchna 6–4 6–1; Casal d. Miacentile 6–1 6–1.

1981 Sweden d. Italy 3–2: H. Sundstrom d. S. Ercoli 6–4 6–2; J. Nystrom/M. Tideman lost to L. Botazzi/F. Cancellotti 6–1 3–6 4–6; Nystrom d. Botazzi 6–3 6–2; T. Hogstedt lost to Cancellotti 4–6 1–6; Tideman d. S. Colombo 6–2 7–6.

1982 Italy d. Spain 3–2: S. Ercoli lost to M. Jaite 2–6 6–7; M. Fiorini d. D. De Miguel 6–2 7–5; P. Cane d. E. Sanchez 6–1 3–6 6–4; M. Zampieri lost to J. Bardou 4–6 4–6; Cane/Fioroni d. Bardou/Jaite 4–6 6–3 8–6.

1983 Sweden d. Spain 4–1: J. Svensson d. G. R. Fernando 4–6 6–4 7–5; J./K. Carlsson d. D. De Miguel/J. Bardou 6–2 1–6 6–2; J. Carlsson lost to Bardou 4–6 2–6; K. Carlsson d. E. Sanchez 3–6 6–0 6–1; P. Lundgren d. L. F. Garcia 6–3 6–4.

1984 Italy d. France 3–1: F. Ricci d. G. Tournant 6–4 3–6 7–5; N. Devide d. P. Gardarein 6–3 6–4; I. Cappelloni d. O. Cayla 7–5 7–6; Gardarein/Winogradski d. Devide/Pistolesi 5–7 6–4 6–4.

1985 Italy d. Sweden 3–2: A. Baldoni lost to D. Engel 2–6 1–6; C. Pistolesi/S. Mezzadri d. C. Allgaardh/T. Nydahll 6–4 6–4; Pistolesi d. Allgaardh 6–3 6–4; U. Colombini d. C. Bergstrom 7–6 6–2; O. Camporese lost to U. Stenlund 0–6 3–6.

1986 Italy d. Spain 3–2: E. Rossi lost to J. Sanchez 6–7 4–6; O. Camporese lost to T. Carbonell 3–6 4–6; U. Pigato d. F. Anda 6–1 6–3; A. Baldoni d. F. Roig 7–5 6–4; Camporese/Rossi d. Carbonell/Sanchez 3–6 6–3 6–4.

1987 Czechoslovakia d. West Germany 2–0: D. Rikl d. C. Arriens 6–1 6–1; T. Zdrazila d. S. Nensel 6–1 4–6 6–2.

1988 Sweden d. Israel 3–0: N. Kulti d. R. Weidenfeld 7–6 6–2; L. Jonsson d. B. Merenstein 6–2 6–1; Kulti/M. Larsson d. Merenstein/O. Weinberg 6–3 3–6 6–4.

1989 Sweden d. West Germany 3–0: O. Kristiansson d. A. Kloodt 6–2 6–3; R. PettersAoson d. R. Leissler 6–2 6–1; D. Geivald/Kristiansson d. Kloodt/Leissler 6–7 6–1 6–2.

1990 Sweden d. USSR 2–1: M. Renstroem d. A. Rybalko 6–3 7–6; O. Ogorodov lost to R. Petterson 6–3 6–7 0–6; Renstroem/M. Tillstroem d. Ogordov/Rybalko 6–2 6–1.

1991 Spain d. Germany 2–0: A. Berasategui d. S. Gessner 6–4 6–2; A. Corretja d. G. Paul 6–2 3–6 6–0.

1992 Spain d. Italy 2–0: A. Corretja d. M. Navarra 6–3 6–1; J. Gisbert d. M. Bertolini 6–1 7–6 (doubles not played).
1993 Spain d. Germany 3–0: R. Carretero d. C. Vinck 6–4 6–4; A. Costa d. L. Rehmann 6–3 6–3; G. Corrales/Costa d. Rehmann/Tambue 7–6 7–5.
1994 Spain d. France 2–1: C. Moya d. M. Huard 6–1 6–0; J. Diaz lost to N. Escude 6–3 6–7 2–6; C. Moya/F. Vicente d. J. F. Bachelot/N. Escude 7–5 6–2.
1995 Czech Republic d. Sweden 2–1: J. Vanek d. N. Timfjord 6–4 6–3; M. Tabara d. F. Jonsson 7–5 6–4; O. Fukarek/J. Vanek lost to F. Jonsson/N. Timfjord 6–7 6–3 3–6.
1996 France d. Czech Republic 2–1: S. Grosjean lost to J. Vanek 5–7 4–6; O. Mutis d. M. Tabara 7–6(6) 6–2; S. Grosjean/O. Mutis d. R. Stepanek/J. Vanek 6–0 6–4.
1997 France d. Czech Republic 3–0: J. Jeanpierre d. P. Kralert 6–3 6–2; A. Di Pasquale d. M. Tabara 6–2 6–0; A. Di Pasquale/J. Jeanpierre d. P. Kralert/M. Stepanek 6–3 7–6.
1998 Spain d. France 2–1: F. Lopez lost to J. Haehnel 6–4 1–6 1–6; J. C. Ferrero d. J. Jeanpierre 3–6 6–1 6–4; J. C. Ferrero/F. Lopez d. J. Jeanpierre/M. Llodra 6–2 7–5.
1999 France d. Czech Republic 3–0: N. Mahut d. L. Chramosta 5–7 6–0 6–4; E. Prodon d. J. Levinsky 6–2 6–3; J. Benneteau/N. Mahut d. T. Cakl/J. Levinsky 6–3 6–0.
2000 Spain d. France 2–0: M. Fornells d. J. Cassaigne 6–1 6–4; T. Robredo d. N. Mahut 7–6 6–4; doubles not played.

JEAN BOROTRA CUP

International Team Championship for boys aged 16 and under; originally the Jean Becker Cup. Finals played in Le Touquet. Administered by the European Tennis Association.

FINALS

1972 Spain d. France 4–1: M. Mir d. Ph. Gruthchet 6–3 6–2; F. Riba d. C. Freyss 6–2 1–6 6–4; A. Capitan d. R. Brunet 6–3 7–5; Masana/Mir lost to Frantz/Grutchet 6–4 6–7 3–6; Capitan/Riba d. Brunet/Freyss 7–5 3–6 9–7.
1973 Italy d. West Germany 3–2: M. Attolini lost to K. Eberhardt 1–6 1–6; G. Sileo d. P. Elter 7–5 6–4; M. Spiga d. U. Wellerdieck 6–2 7–5; Attolini/Sileo lost to Eberhardt/Elter 0–6 5–7; Mazzocchi/Spiga d. Liebthal/WellerAdieck 6–3 6–2.
1974 West Germany d. Italy 4–1: Buchbinder d. G. Rinaldi 6–2 6–2; P. Elter d. Risi 6–0 6–1; A. Maurer d. Gardi 6–7 7–5 6–1; Buchbinder/W. Popp lost to Gardi/Rinaldi 6–2 6–7 8–10; Elter/Maurer d. Risi/M. Rivarolli 6–0 6–3.
1975 Czechoslovakia d. Italy 3–2: M. Lacek d. G. Rinaldini 7–5 6–1; I. Lendl d. A. Ciardi 6–1 6–3; J. Kucera d. P. Parreni 6–4 6–4; Lacek/Kucera lost to Parreni/A. Rivaroli 4–6 4–6; Lendl/A. Vantuch lost to Ciardi/Rinaldini 6–1 4–6 3–6.
1976 Sweden d. Czechoslovakia 3–2: P. Hjertquist lost to I. Lendl 6–0 3–6 4–6; S. Simonsson d. A. Vikopa 6–3 6–0; H. Johansson d. T. Pitra 6–3 6–2; Simonsson/A. Fritzner lost to Lendl/J. Kerezek 6–4 3–6 1–6; Hjertquist/Johansson d. Pitra/J. Vikopal 6–3 6–2.
1977 Italy d. Sweden 3–2: A. Costa d. A. Jarryd 7–5 6–2; A. Giacomini lost to S. Simonsson 1–6 1–6; A. Moscino d. S. Svensson 6–4 6–4; Giacomini/A. Odling lost to Simonsson/Jarryd 3–6 4–6; Costa/Moscino d. Svensson/M. Wennberg 6–2 6–4.
1978 Sweden d. France 3–2: S. Svensson d. T. Tulasne 6–4 6–2; H. Simonsson lost to J. Potier 6–3 2–6 7–9 disqualified; J. Gunnarsson d. T. Pham 6–2 5–7 6–2; M. Wilander lost to J. L. Cotard 2–6 7–5 4–6; Svensson/ Simonsson d. Cotard/J. M. Piacentile 6–3 6–1.
1979 Sweden d. France 4–1: J. Windahll lost to T. Tulasne 2–6 1–6; M. Wilander d. H. Leconte 6–2 1–6 6–3; T. Hogstedt d. P. Kuchna 6–2 6–1; J. Sjogren d. J. M. Piacentile 6–1 6–1; Hogstedt/Wilander d. Leconte/Piacentile 3–6 6–3 6–4.
1980 Sweden d. Czechoslovakia 3–0: M. Wilander d. M. Mecir 3–6 6–1 6–1; A. Mansson d. K. Novacek 6–3 6–3; H. Sundstrom/Wilander d. Mecir/B. Stankovic 6–3 3–0 ret.
1981 France d. Sweden 3–2: T. Benhabiles d. S. Edberg 6–4 6–4; F. Hamonet d. J. B. Svensson 6–0 6–2; T. Chamsion lost to P. Svensson 3–6 6–2 0–6; O. Cayla lost to A. Henricsson 6–1 4–6 3–6; Hamonet/G. Forget d. Edberg/P. Svensson 6–4 1–6 6–2.
1982 Sweden d. Spain 4–1: J. Svensson d. J. Maso 6–2 6–2; S. Edberg d. F. Garcia 6–4 6–4; P. Svensson d. J. Oltra 6–2 6–1; J. Carlsson lost to S. Castello 5–7 1–6; Edberg/P. Svensson d. Garcia/Oltra 6–2 6–1.
1983 Sweden d. USSR 3–2: D. Engel d. V. Gabritchidze 7–5 6–1; K. Carlsson d. A. Volkov 6–2 6–4; C. Allgaardh d. A. Tchernetsky 7–5 6–3; C. Bergstrom lost to I. Metreveli 6–0 6–7 3–6; Carlsson/Allgaardh d. Volkov/Metreveli 6–3 6–7 6–3.
1984 Italy d. Sweden 4–1: P. Chinellato lost to T. Nydhal 4–6 6–4 3–6; O. Camporese d. H. Holm 6–4 6–0; A. Baldoni d. A. Rosen 6–4 6–0; S. Sorensen d. N. Utgren 6–2 6–4; Baldoni/E. Rossi d. T. Nydal/P. Henricsson 7–6 1–6 6–3.
1985 Sweden d. France 3–2: P. Henricsson lost to A. Boetsch 3–6 2–6; P. Wennberg d. V. Ventura 6–2 6–2; N. Utgren d. S. Blanquie 6–1 6–2; M. Zeile d. C. Sebastiani 6–1 6–3; Henricsson/Utgren lost to Boetsch/R. Pedros 2–6 6–3 4–6.
1986 Italy d. Netherlands 3–2: F. Mordegan lost to P. Dogger 5–7 6–3 1–6; D. Nargiso lost to J. Eltingh 5–7 2–6; C. Caratti d. J. Siemerink 7–5 6–0; R. Furlan d. R. Heethius 7–5 5–7 7–5; Caratti/Nargiso d. Eltingh/Siemerink 4–6 7–5 6–3.
1987 Austria d. Italy 3–2: T. Buchmayer d. F. Pisilli 6–3 6–1; O. Fuchs lost to S. Pescosolido 4–6 1–6; H. Priller d. M. Ardinghi 6–3 6–4; G. Bohm lost to M. Boscatto 6–2 1–6 6–8; Buchmayer/Priller d. Boscatto/Pescosolido 1–6 6–4 6–4.
1988 Sweden d. Czechoslovakia 3–2: J. Alven d. M. Damm 6–1 6–4; R. Pettersson d. P. Gazda 6–1 2–6 6–2; Sunnemark lost to L. Hovorka 6–3 0–6 3–6; M. Renstroem d. P. Gazda 6–1 2–6 6–2; Alven/Pettersson lost to Damm/Horkova 0–6 6–3 6–7.
1989 Czechoslovakia d. West Germany 4–1: P. Gazda d. A. Kriebel 7–5 6–3; R. Hanak d. D. Prinosil 6–0 6–4; L. Thomas d. J. Weinzierl 6–2 6–4; B. Galik d. M. Kohlmann 6–4 6–2; Gazda/Thomas lost to M. Kuckenbecker/ Prinosll 6–4 3–6 4–6.

1990 France d. Spain 3–2: N. Kischkewitz d. J. Gisbert 6–4 6–2; P. Lasserre d. A. Corretja 6–4 6–3; J. Hanquez lost to J. Martinez 7–6 5–7 2–6; O. Tauma d. G. Corrales 3–6 6–4 6–0; Kischkewitz/Tauma lost to Corretja/Gisbert 3–6 2–6.
1991 Spain d. Czechoslovakia 4–1: A. Costa d. F. Kascak 6–4 6–2; G. Corrales d. P. Pala 6–7 6–1 6–3; R. Carretero d. D. Skoch 5–7 7–6 7–5; J. Balcells lost to D. Miketa 5–7 6–1 1–6; Corrales/Costa d. Kascak/Pala 6–1 6–4.
1992 France d. Sweden 2–1: N. Escude d. M. Norman 2–6 6–4 6–4; M. Huard lost to A. Stenman 5–7 5–7; Esude/Huard d. Norman/M. Sjoquist 6–2 6–2.
1993 France d. Sweden 2–1: J-F Bachelot lost to F. Jonsson 1–6 6–3 12–14; J. Potron d. N. Timfjord 6–2 6–2; O. Mutis/Potron d. Jonsson/Timfjord 4–6 6–1 6–0.
1994 Spain d. Netherlands 3–0: O. Serrano d. P. Wessels 6–4 1–6 6–3; A. Martin d. R. Sluiter 6–3 6–3; A. Gordon/O. Serrano d. R. Sluiter/P. Wessels 3–6 6–4 14–13.
1995 Germany d. France 2–1: T. Zivnicek d. N. Tourte 6–2 6–2; D. Elsner d. A. Di Pasquale 6–2 0–6 6–2; D. Elsner/T. Messmer lost to A. Di Pasquale/N. Tourte 2–6 2–6.
1996 Belgium d. Russia 2–1: O. Rochus lost to A. Derepasko 6–2 3–6 4–6; X. Malisse d. M. Safin 6–4 6–1; X. Malisse/O. Rochus d. A. Derepasko/K. Ivanov-Smolenski 7–5 6–1.
1997 Spain d. Italy 2–1: T. Robredo lost to F. Volandri 3–6 3–6; F. Lopez d. U. Vico 6–3 4–6 7–5; F. Lopez/T. Robredo d. U. Vico/F. Volandri 4–6 6–1 6–1.
1998 Spain d. France 2–1: D. Ferrer d. N. Mahut 7–6 1–6 8–6; T. Robredo d. P-H. Mathieu 6–3 3–6 6–2; G. Grias/T. Robredo lost to N. Mahut/J. Maigret 4–6 6–3 2–6.
1999 Czech Republic d. Russia 2–1: J. Hajek lost to D. Sitak 6–2 4–6 3–6; M. Kokta d. P. Mukhometov 7–5 3–6 6–3; J. Hajek/M. Kokta d. P. Ivanov/D. Sitak 4–6 6–3 6–4.
2000 France d. Austria 2–1: R. Gasquet d. C. Kern 6–3 6–4; J. Tsonga lost to J. Ager 6–2 7–6; R. Gasquet/J. Tsonga d. J. Ager/C. Kern 6–2 7–6.

DEL SOL CUP

International Team Championship for boys aged 14 and under. Played in zones with finals in Barcelona. Administered by the European Tennis Association.

FINALS
1979 Italy d. France 3–2: M. Fioroni d. M. Cartier 6–0 6–2; G. Possani d. G. Forget 6–7 7–5 6–3; A. Paris lost to T. Benhabiles 0–6 5–7; L. Baglioni lost to F. Hamonet 0–6 0–6; Possani/Paris d. Benhabiles/Hamonet 6–1 6–4.
1980 Sweden d. Italy 4–1: P. Svensson d. R. Salemme 6–4 7–6; S. Edberg d. F. Ricci 7–5 6–3; R. Lofquist d. F. Filippi 6–3 6–4; J. Svensson lost to P. Poggioli 4–6 2–6; Edberg/P. Svensson d. Filippi/A. Vacca 6–4 6–1.
1981 Sweden d. Israel 3–2: T. Johansson lost to A. Naor 2–6 6–7; C. Allgaardh lost to G. Blom 4–6 6–2 4–6; K. Carlsson d. R. Weinberg 6–0 6–0; C. Bergstrom d. M. Osherov 2–6 7–5 7–5; Allgaardh/Carlsson d. Blom/ Osherov 6–2 6–1.
1982 Sweden d. West Germany 4–1: H. Kolm d. U. Kraft 6–1 6–0; K. Carlsson d. O. Sachau 6–0 6–0; P. Ekstrand lost to I. Kroll 0–6 2–6; T. Nydahl d. C. Guhl 6–0 1–6 6–1; Carlsson/Nydahl d. Guhl/Kraft 6–1 6–4.
1983 Sweden d. West Germany 3–2: U. Persson d. H. Stang 6–2 6–2; P. Henricsson d. P. Pfleger 6–4 6–1; U. Eriksson lost to U. Kraft 7–6 3–6 2–6; P. Wennberg lost to L. Orzessek 2–6 3–6; Henricsson/M. Urgren d. Kraft/Orzessek 6–2 6–3.
1984 West Germany d. Spain 4–1: S. Scheider d. F. Alfonso 6–3 4–6 7–5; F. Loddenkemper/A. Thoms d. J. Olivert/S. Bruguera 6–3 6–2; Loddenkemper d. Olivert 7–6 7–6; D. Richter d. A. Martinez 6–1 7–5; A. Thoms lost to Bruguera 3–6 6–2 4–6.
1985 Austria d. Italy 5–0: G. Bohm d. F. Casa 6–4 6–2; T. Buchmayer/O. Fuchs d. S. Pescosolido/F. Pisilli 6–2 6–3; Buchmayer d. Pescosolido 6–3 4–6 6–4; Fuchs d. Pisilli 6–3 7–6; H. Prilled d. M. Ardinghi 6–2 6–1.
1986 Sweden d. Yugoslavia 4–1: J. Alven d. S. Hirszon 6–3 6–4; R. Pettersson lost to B. Trupy 2–6 3–6; M. Ekstrand d. A. Tonejc 3–6 6–4 6–3; J. Henriksson d. S. Ban 6–4 7–6; Alven/Pettersson d. Hirszon/Trupej 6–2 6–4.
1987 West Germany d. Austria 4–1: J. Weinzierl lost to R. Wawra 3–6 2–6; G. Paul d. N. Patzak 6–0 6–1; S. Petraschek d. J. Knowle 3–6 6–2 6–2; A. Kriebel d. H. Kugler 6–2 6–3; Paul/Petraschek d. Knowle/Wawra 4–6 6–2 6–2.
1988 West Germany d. Spain 3–2: M. Kohlman d. A. Corretja 6–2 6–1; T. Ruhle lost to A. Bragado 0–6 3–6; J. Schors d. J. Martinez 6–2 6–4; G. Hecht lost to J. Velasco 6–0 5–7 1–6; Kohlman/M. Nacke d. Bragado/Corretja 7–6 7–6.
1989 France d. Sweden 4–1: N. Bertsch d. T.A Johansson 7–5 7–6; A. De Cret d. K. Bergh 6–4 6–2; S. Martinez d. P. Salasca 6–2 6–3; M. Dallay d. D. Winberg 7–5 6–4; Bertsch/De Cret lost to Johansson/Salasca 6–4 3–6 1–6 7–6 7–6.
1990 France d. Spain 5–0: M. Boye d. A. Pastor 7–6 3–6 6–4; N. Maurier d. J. Diaz 7–6 6–4; J. Van Lottum d. A. Gandarias 1–6 6–2 6–2; K. Dous d. E. Xapelli 6–4 6–1; Boye/Maurier d. Diaz/Pastor 6–2 6–2.
1991 Spain d. USSR 5–0: J–A. Saiz d. I. Pridankine 7–6 6–1; F. Vincente d. J. Michejev 7–6 6–7 6–4; J. Vincente d. A. Gonopolskij 6–0 6–4; A. Martin d. A. Stoljarov 6–7 6–3 8–6; Martin/J. Vincente d. Pridankine/Stoljarov 7–6 6–3.
1992 Germany d. France 3–1: T. Haas lost to O. Mutis 4–6 4–6; J.-R. Brandt d. J.-R. Lisnard 7–5 6–1; J.-P. Wenner d. J. Barras 6–3 7–6; Brandt/Haas d. M.-O. Baron/Mutis 6–4 6–3.
1993 France d. Italy 4–1: K. Fernandez d. D. Bramanti 7–6 7–5; A Di Pasquale d. F. Allgauer 7–5 6–3; V. Lavergne lost to A. Capodimonte 6–4 3–6 2–6; J-R Lisnard d. D. Sciortino 6–3 6–1; Di Pasquale/Lisnard d. Capodimonte/ Sciortino 6–3 4–6 7–5.
1994 France d. Italy 3–2: N. Senelle d. M. Aprile 6–4 6–3; J. Haenelt d. N. Frocassi 6–4 6–3; A. Rafidison lost to F. Luzzi 3–6 1–6; J. Jeanpierre d. M. Armadroy 6–1 6–1; N. Devilder/J. Jeanpierre lost to N. Frocassi/Luzzi 5–7 2–6.
1995 Great Britain d. Spain 3–2: A. Mackin d. I. Navarro 6–3 6–7 7–5; N. Greenhouse lost to M. Marco w/o; M. Hilton d. F. Lopez 2–6 6–4 6–1; S. Dickson d. T. Robredo 6–1 6–0; S. Dickson/M. Hilton lost to F. Lopez/T. Robredo 5–7 6–4 5–7.
1996 France d. Croatia 4–1: D. Voravoncsa d. V. Sirola 6–0 6–1; P. Capdeville d. M. Ancic 2–6 6–0 6–2; N. Mahut lost

to M. Radic 2–6 7–5 3–6; P-H. Mathieu d. R. Karanusic 6–2 6–0; P. Capdeville/P-H. Mathieu d. R. Karanusic/M. Radic 6–3 6–0.

1997 France d. Czech Republic 5–0: N. Beuque d. D. Novak 6–0 7–5; C. Roche d. D. Karol 6–3 6–1; J-M. Ali-Cayol d. M. Kokta 6–2 6–1; J. Maigret d. J. Masik 7–5 6–0; J-M. Ali-Cayol/C. Roche d. D. Karol/J. Masik 7–5 7–6.

1998 Germany d. France 3–2: M. Bayer d. M. Auradou 5–7 6–4 6–4; D. Schubert lost to T. Cazes Carrere 1–6 5–7; N. Muschiol lost to R. Gasquet 2–6 6–7; P. Petzschner d. E. Petit 7–5 6–2; P. Petzschner/D. Schubert d. T. Cazes Carrere/C. Morel 7–5 7–5.

1999 France d. Russia 3–2: C. Mokaiesh d. A. Pavlioutchenkov 6–3 6–1; J. Robin lost to A. Sitak 2–6 5–7; J. Tsonga lost to N. Soloviev 4–6 2–6; R. Gasquet d. T. Gabachvili 6–1 6–1; R. Gasquet/J. Tsonga d. T. Gabachvili/A. Pavlioutchenkov 6–3 6–4.

2000 Russia d. Germany 3–2: A. Krasnoroutski lost to A. Weber 6–4 6–1; A. Sitak/D. Matsoukevitch lost to D. Muller/S. Rieschick 6–2 7–6; N. Soloviev d. D. Muller 3–6 6–1 6–0; A. Sitak d. C. Blocker 6–2 6–3; D. Matsoukevitch d. S. Rieschick 4–6 6–2 6–2.

SOISBAULT/REINA CUP

International Team Championship for girls aged 18 and under. Played zonally with the final stages in Spain. Administered by the European Tennis Association.

FINALS
1972 Rumania d. West Germany 3–2: F. Mihai d. A. Spiedel 6–4 7–5; V. Ruzici/M. Simionescu d. B. Portcheller/B. Kasler 8–6 6–1; Ruzici d. Portcheller 2–6 6–0 6–1; Simionescu lost to Kasler 4–6 3–6; M. Neuweiller lost to K. Pohmann 4–6 3–6.

1973 Great Britain d. Spain 4–1: B. L. Thompson d. G. Nogues 6–4 6–4; L. J. Mottram d. J. Mateo 6–3 12–10; S. Barker d. J. Alvarez 7–5 6–0; Barker/Mottram d. Mateo/C. Chillida 6–2 6–2; J. Potterton lost to Chillida 3–6 0–6.

1974 Czechoslovakia d. France 4–1: L. Plchova d. M. Cozaux 6–4 6–1; Y. Brzakova lost to B. Simon 6–8 6–2 4–6; H. Strachonova d. C. Gimmig 6–3 6–0; R. Marsikova d. F. Thibault 8–4 6–4; Brzakova/A. Kulankova d. Thibault/A. Duguy 9–7 4–6 6–4.

1975 Great Britain d. Czechoslovakia 4–1: M. Tyler d. A. Kulhankova 6–1 3–6 6–3; C. Harrison d. J. Kopekova 6–3 6–3; L. J. Mottram d. H. Strachonova 2–6 11–9 6–3; J. Cottrell lost to K. Skronska 1–6 1–6; A. Cooper/Cottrell d. Skronska/Kulhankova 1–6 6–4 6–4.

1976 Great Britain d. Switzerland 3–1: J. M. Durie d. C. Jolissaint 4–6 6–3 6–4; A. Cooper lost to M. Simmen 6–4 0–6 4–6; C. Harrison d. A. Ruegg 6–4 6–7 6–2; M. Tyler d. P. Delhees 6–2 6–2.

1977 Czechoslovakia d. Sweden 5–0: H. Mandlikova d. M. Wiedel 6–2 6–2; I. Budarova d. H. Brywe 6–1 6–1; Mandlikova/Budarova d. A. C. Mansson/A. Nilsson 6–1 6–3; M. Skuherska d. Nilsson 6–0 6–4; H. Strachonova d. Mansson 6–3 7–5.

1978 Czechoslovakia d. Sweden 5–0: M. Skuherska d. L. Jacobson 6–3 6–2; H. Mandlikova d. H. Brywe 6–1 6–1; I. Budarova/Mandlikova d. Jacobson/L. Sandin 6–3 6–1; I. Petru d. A. Nilsson 6–1 6–2; Budarova d. Sandin 6–3 5–7 7–5.

1979 Czechoslovakia d. Switzerland 3–1: I. Bendlova d. P. Frey 6–1 6–1; M. Skuherska/I. Petru lost to C. Jolissaint/I. Villiger 3–6 4–6; Skuherska d. Villiger 3–6 6–1 6–1; I. Novakova d. Jolissaint 6–7 6–3 6–3; Petru v C. Pasquale 5–7 4 abandoned.

1980 Switzerland d. USSR 3–2: K. Stampfli d. J. Kashevarova 6–3 6–3; I. Villiger/L. Drescher lost to O. Zaitseva/S. Cherneva 4–6 5–7; Villiger d. Zaitseva 6–2 7–5; C. Pasquale lost to Cherneva 4–6 7–5 7–9; Drescher d. J. Salnikova 7–6 6–4.

1981 Sweden d. Czechoslovakia 3–2: B. Bjort d. P. Dutkova 6–2 6–3; M. Lindstrom/C. Lindqvist d. H. Sukova/M. Pazderova 6–3 6–3; C. Jexell lost to Pazderova 6–3 2–6 0–6; Lindqvist d. N. Piskackova 6–2 6–2; Lindstrom lost to Sukova 6–7 3–6.

1982 Italy d. Czechoslovakia 4–1: R. Reggi d. I. Petru 6–3 6–4; N. Virgintino lost to H. Fukarkova 7–5 2–6 3–6; A. Cecchini d. P. Dutkova 7–6 7–6; F. Bonsignori d. A. Souckova 6–3 6–0; Reggi/Virgintino d. Petru/Fukarkova 7–5 4–6 6–2.

1983 Italy d. Czechoslovakia 4–1: L. Ferrando d. A. Souckova 6–0 6–3; B. Romano/N. Virgintino d. A. Holikova/Souckova 6–3 6–7 6–3; A. M. Cecchini d. O. Votavova 6–7 6–3 6–1; Virgintino d. P. Tesarova 6–3 6–1; S. Dalla Valle lost to Holikova 5–7 3–6.

1984 Sweden d. Czechoslovakia 3–2: H. Dahlstrom d. O. Votavova 6–3 6–3; A. Karlsson d. A. Holikova 6–3 6–0; A. Souckova d. M. Lundquist 7–5 7–5; K. Karlsson d. P. Tesarova 6–1 6–2; Votavova/Holikova d. Lundquist/Olsson 6–4 6–2.

1985 Italy d. Sweden 4–1: L. Lapi lost to C. Dahlman 0–6 1–6; L. Garrone/L. Golarsa d. A. K. Ollson/M. Lundquist 6–1 6–3; Garrone d. H. Dahlstrom 6–2 6–7 6–2; C. Nozzoli d. Ollson 6–4 6–4; Golarsa d. Lundquist 6–2 6–0.

1986 Czechoslovakia d. Sweden 5–0: R. Rajchrtova d. C. Dahlstrom 6–4 6–0; R. Zbrubakova d. J. Jonerup 6–3 6–3; J. Novotna d. M. Stradlund 6–4 6–2; D. Krajcovicova d. M. Ekstrand 6–3 7–5; Novotna/Rajchrtova d. M. Nilsson/Stradlund 6–0 6–1.

1987 France d. Czechoslovakia 3–0: A. Dechaume d. R. Zrubakova 6–4 6–3; E. Derly d. P. Langrova 7–5 6–1; Dechaume/S. Niox–Chateau d. Langrova/Zrubakova 6–7 6–4 6–3.

1988 Spain d. USSR 2–1: A. Sanchez d. N. Medvedeva 3–6 6–2 6–3; C. Martinez d. E. Brioukhovets 6–2 6–2; Martinez/Sanchez lost to Brioukhovets/Medvedeva 6–7 0–4 ret.

1989 Spain d. Czechoslovakia 3–0: A. Sanchez d. A. Strnadova 6–1 6–3; N. Avila d. J. Dubcova 6–3 6–0; S. Ramon/Sanchez d. K. Balnova/Strnadova 6–4 7–5.

1990 Spain d. France 2–1: P. Perez d. A. Zugasti 6–4 6–0; S. Ramon lost to A. Fusai 6–3 4–6 1–6; Perez/Ramon d.

Fusai/Zugasti 7–5 6–2.
1991 Spain d. Sweden 3–0: E. Botini d. A. Carlsson 5–7 6–2 6–4; E. Bes d. M. Vallin 6–2 6–1; Botini/C. Torrens d. Vallin/Carlsson 4–6 7–6 6–2.
1992 Germany d. Spain 2–1: P. Begerow d. E. Bottini 6–2 7–5; K. Freye lost to C. Torrens 2–6 3–6; Freye/S. Wachtershauser d. Bottini/E.Jimenez 2–6 7–5 6–2.
1993 France d. Italy 3–0: S. Pitkowski d. P. Tampieri 6–0 6–0; A. Olivier d. A. Serra-Zanetti 0–6 6–2 6–1; Olivier/C. Toyre d. Serra-Zanetti/Tampieri 8–3.
1994 Italy d. Spain 2–1: F. Lubiani d. M. Ramon 6–4 6–3; A. Serrazanetti lost to M. A. Sanchez 5–7 6–4 1–6; F. Lubiani/A. Serezzanetti d. M. Ramon/M .A. Sanchez 6–0 6–4.
1995 Italy d. Czech Republic 2–1: G. Casoni lost to P. Plackova 3–6 6–4 4–6; A. Canepa d. S. Kleinova 6–2 7–6; A. Canepa/G. Casoni d. S. Kleinova/J. Ondrouchova 6–0 6–2.
1996 Slovak Republic d. Spain 2–1: L. Cervanova d. A. Alcazar 7–5 6–4; Z. Valekova lost to M-L. Serna 0–6 1–6; L. Cervanova/Z. Valekova d. A. Alcazar/M-L. Serna 1–6 6–3 10–8.
1997 France d. Czech Republic 2–1: A. Mauresmo d. M. Pastikova 6–3 6–3; N. Dechy d. J. Schonfeldova 6–3 6–4; France defaulted in doubles.
1998 Croatia d. Italy 2–1: D. Krstulovic d. L. Dell'Angelo 6–4 6–4; J. Kostanic lost to A. Serra-Zanetti 1–6 4–6; J. Kostanic/D. Krstulovic d. L. Dell'Angelo/F. Schiavone 6–4 6–7 6–4.
1999 Spain d. Slovak Republic 3–0: A. Medina d. S. Hrosenska 7–6 6–2; L. Dominguez d. D. Hantuchova 7–6 6–4; L. Dominguez/M. Martinez d. D. Hantuchova/S. Hrosenska 6–0 6–4.
2000 Spain d. France 3–0: A. Medina d. S. Cohen-Aloro 6–1 6–2; M. Martinez d. O. Sanchez 6–1 4–6 6–1; M. Martinez/A. Medina d. V. Razzano/O. Sanchez 6–2 6–2.

HELVETIE CUP

International Team Championship for girls aged 16 and under. Played zonally with final stages at Leysin, Switzerland.

FINALS
1977 Italy d. Switzerland 3–2: P. Cigognani lost to C. Jolissaint 0–6 3–6; B. Rossi d. I. Villiger 6–3 6–7 8–6; M. Calabria d. K. Stampfli 6–1 6–2; P. Murgo d. C. Pasquale 6–3 6–3; Rossi/Murgo lost to Jolissaint/Villiger 4–6 3–6.
1978 Bulgaria d. West Germany 5–0: M. Condova d. C. Kohde 1–6 6–3 6–1; A. Veltcheva d. Haas 6–3 5–7 6–4; I. Chichkova d. Hammig 6–3 6–0; I. Christova d. Wilmsmeyer 3–6 7–6 6–3; Condova/Veltcheva d. Kohde/Haas 3–6 6–2 6–2.
1979 Sweden d. France 5–0: C. Lindqvist d. I. Vernhes 6–7 6–3 6–0; B. Bjork d. C. Vanier 4–6 6–3 6–3; A. Flodin d. S. Gardette 6–0 6–1; H. Olsson/K. Marivall d. M. Callejo/Vanier 6–3 6–3; Olsson d. Calleja 6–2 6–1.
1980 Sweden d. West Germany 3–2: C. Anderholm d. M. Schropp 6–1 6–2; H. Olsson lost to K. Reuter 5–7 4–6; M. Schultz d. P. Keppeler 6–4 6–4; N. Nielson d. M. Reinhard 6–7 6–3 6–2; Olsson/Schultz lost to Reuter/Reinhard 6–1 4–6 5–7.
1981 Sweden d. Italy 3–2: A. Bjork lost to F. Sollenti 2–6 6–7; H. Olsson/C. Anderholm d. R. Reggi/F. Virgintino 0–6 6–2 6–1; Olsson d. A. M. Cecchini 6–4 7–5; Anderholm d. Reggi 6–3 3–6 6–4; I. Sjogreen lost to Virgintino 0–6 0–6.
1982 USSR d. France 3–2: I. Fishkina d. I. Demongeot 6–1 6–2; L. Savchenko/V. Milvidskaya lost to P. Paradis/N. Phan-Thanh 4–6 7–5 4–6; N. Bykova lost to Paradis 1–6 2–6; Savchenko d. Phan-Thanh 6–2 6–3; Mildvidskaya d. N. Herreman 6–1 6–4.
1983 USSR d. Sweden 3–2: A. Kuzmina d. A. K. Olsson 6–3 1–6 6–3; V. Milvidskaya d. H. Dahlmstrom 3–6 6–2 6–4; I. Fischkina lost to M. Lundquist 4–6 4–6; I. Fateeva lost to E. Helmersson 2–6 3–6; Fishkina/Mildvidskaya d. Dahlstrom/Lundquist 6–4 7–5.
1984 Czechoslovakia d. West Germany 4–1: R. Wlona lost to M. Gartner 7–6 3–6 4–6; J. Novotna/R. Rajchrotova d. S. Meier/R. Weiser 6–0 7–6; Novotna d. Meier 7–5 6–2; Rajchrotova d. Weiser 6–3 4–6 6–1; P. Sedkackova d. S. Hack 6–4 4–6 6–2.
1985 West Germany d. Sweden 4–1: M. Schurhoff d. M. Ekstrand 6–2 4–6 6–4; M. Gartner/S. Hack lost to M. Strandlund/M. Nilsson 3–6 3–6; Gartner/J. Jonerup 7–6 6–2; Hack d. Strandlund 6–1 6–1; W. Probst d. M. Nilsson 6–1 6–1.
1986 Switzerland d. Czechoslovakia 3–1 (one rubber not played)**:** E. Zardo d. M. Frimmelova 6–4 6–2; M. Strebel d. L. Laskova 7–5 6–1; S. Jaquet v. P. Langrova not played; M. Plocher d. E. Sviglerova 6–4 6–2; Jacquet/Plocher lost to Frimmelova/Langrova 6–0 1–6 5–7.
1987 Netherlands d. Switzerland 3–2: N. Van Dierendonck lost to S. Jacquet 6–7 3–6; B. Sonneveld lost to M. Plocher 6–2 3–6 4–6; Y. Grubben d. G. Villiger 7–5 7–6; E. Haslinghuis d. S. Bregnard 6–1 6–0; Sonneveld/Van Dierendonck d. Jacquet/Plocher 7–5 6–3..
1988 West Germany d. Czechoslovakia 3–2: V. Martinek d. K. Balnova 6–3 6–0; K. Duell lost to A. Strnadova 2–6 3–6; M. Skulj-Zivec d. H. Vildova 7–5 6–1; A. Popp lost to R. Bobkova 4–6 1–5 5–7; C. Hofmann/Martinek d. Balnova/Strnadova 7–5 7–5.
1989 Czechoslovakia d. USSR 3–2: R. Bobkova d. S. Komleva 6 2 6 1; K. Habsudova d. E. Makarova 7–6 6–0; K. Matouskova lost to M. Chirikova 3–6 6–3 5–7; K. Kroupova lost to T. Ignatieva 2–6 2–6; Bobkova/Matouskova d. Chirikova/Komleva 4–6 6–0 8–6.
1990 USSR d. West Germany 3–2: T. Ignatieva d. K. Freye 6–4 4–6 6–3; I. Soukhova d. S. Wachterhauser 7–5 6–2; V. Vitels lost to M. Babel 4–6 0–3 ret.; G. Beleni lost to P. Begerow 3–6 3–6; Ignatieva/Soukhova d. Babel/J. Dobberstein 6–4 6–4.
1991 Czechoslovakia d. Spain 4–1: Z. Malkova d. E. Jiminez 6–4 6–0; E. Martincova lost to M. Cruells 3–6 6–7; E.

Hostacova d. A. Ortuno 6–3 7–5; M. Hautova d. A. Montolio 4–6 6–3 6–1; Malkova/Martincova d. Cruells/ Jiminez 6–3 6–1.

1992 Belgium d. Germany 2–1: N. Feber d. A. Glass 6–3 6–2; L. Courtois lost to H. Rusch 6–3 6–7 3–6; Courtoios/Feber d. Glass/C. Muller 6–7 6–3 6–0.

1993 Czech/Slovak Republic d. Netherlands 2–1: L. Cenkova d. C. Reimering 6–3 6–3; A. Havrlikova lost to Y. Basting 3–6 6–1 2–6; Cenkova/L. Richterova d. Basting/D. Haak 6–3 7–5.

1994 France d. Czech Republic 2–1: A. Cocheteaux d. D. Chadkova 6–2 6–3; A. Castera d. S. Kleinova 7–5 1–6 6–0; A. Cocheteaux/I. Taesch lost to D. Chadkova/S. Kleinova 1–6 6–0 2–6.

1995 Czech Republic d. Germany 2–1: J. Lubasova lost to M. Frohlich 6–7 3–6; D. Chladkova d. C. Christian 6–2 7–6; D. Chladkova/J. Lubasova d. C. Christian/M. Frohlich 6–2 6–4.

1996 Slovenia d. France 2–1: K. Srebotnik d. K. Chevalier 2–6 7–5 6–2; P. Rampre d. E. le Bescond 6–4 4–6 6–0; M. Matevzic/P. Rampre lost to K. Chevalier/E. le Bescond 6–4 1–6 4–6.

1997 Slovenia d. Spain 2–1: T. Hojnik lost to M. Marrero 3–6 7–6 4–6; T. Pisnik d. L. Dominguez 6–2 6–0; T. Hergold/T. Pisnik d. L. Dominguez/M. Marrero 7–6 6–3.

1998 Slovak Republic d. Italy 3–0: S. Hrozenska d. R. Vinci 6–3 6–4; D. Hantuchova d. F. Pennetta 7–5 3–6 6–2; K. Basternakova/S. Hrozenska d. M. E. Camerin/F. Pennetta 6–4 7–5.

1999 Slovak Republic d. Czech Republic 2–1: L. Dlhopolcova d. E. Birnerova 6–4 7–5; L. Kurhajcova lost to D. Bedanova 3–6 2–6; L. Dlhopolcova/L. Kurhajcova d. D. Bedanova/E. Birnerova 6–2 6–2.

2000 Slovak Republic d. Hungary 2–1: D. Nociarova d. D. Magas 6–3 6–2; L. Dlhopolcova lost to V. Nemeth 6–2 6–4; D. Nociarova/Z. Zemenova d. D. Magas/V. Nemeth 3–6 6–2 6–3.

EUROPA CUP

International Team Championship for girls aged 14 and under. Administered by the European Tennis Association.

FINALS

1981 West Germany d. France 3–2, *Winterslag, Belgium:* I. Cueto d. J. Clerin 6–3 2–6 6–1; R. Wieser lost to E. Folcher 1–6 6–3 1–6; S. Graf d. M. Phan-Thanh 7–5 6–3; S. Luidinant d. E. Grousseau 6–2 6–2; Graf/Wieser lost to Folcher/Grousseau 6–4 2–6 1–6.

1982 Sweden d. West Germany 3–2, *Mons, Belgium:* C. Dahlman d. S. Meier 7–5 7–5; H. Dahlstrom d. B. Herget 6–0 6–4; E. Helmersson lost to I. Cueto 3–6 7–6 0–6; I. Mattiasson lost to E. Walliser 5–7 2–6; Dahlstrom/Helmersson d. Cueto/Walliser 6–2 6–2.

1983 West Germany d. France 3–2, *Lee-on-Solent, Hampshire:* N. Vassen d. S. N. Chateau 4–6 6–3 6–2; W. Probst d. M. C. Rolet 7–5 5–7 ret; S. Hack lost to C. Bourdais 6–3 2–6 0–6; M. Gartner d. A. Dechaume 6–4 4–6 7–5; Gartner/Vassen lost to Bourdais/Dechaume 3–6 1–6.

1984 France d. Sweden 4–1: S. Dussault lost to R. Narbe 0–6 6–4 3–6; A. Dechaume/E. Derly d. M. Ekstrand/H. Johnsson 6–3 6–3; Dechaume d. Ekstrand 7–5 6–2; Derly d. Salsgard 6–4 3–6 6–1; M. Laval d. Johnsson 6–4 6–4.

1985 USSR d. Italy 3–2: N. Zvereva d. A. Dell'Orso 6–2 4–6 6–4; T. Tchernysova lost to F. Romano 3–6 2–6; E. Brihovec lost to S. Favini w.o.; A. Blumberga d. G. Boscheiro 6–3 4–6 6–4; Zvereva/Tchernysova d. Boscheiro/Dell'Orso 6–4 6–3.

1986 Netherlands d. Italy 3–2: Y. Grubben lost to Boscheiro 5–7 4–6; N. Van Lottum d. Favini 6–2 6–1; E. Markestein d. Migliori 6–4 6–4; E. Haslinghuis lost to Bertelloni 2–6 2–6; Grubben/Van Lottum d. Boscheiro/Migliori 6–2 6–2.

1987 Czechoslovakia d. Austria 3–2: P. Kucova lost to U. Priller 3–6 0–6; R. Bobkova d. D. Bidmon 6–2 6–4; P. Markova lost to N. Dobrovits 4–6 1–6; K. Matouskova d. S. Suchan 1–6 6–0 10–8; Bobkova/Kucova d. Dobrovits/Priller 6–4 4–6 7–5.

1988 Hungary d. West Germany 3–2: A. Foeldenyi d. A. Huber 6–0 3–6 8–6; B. Bathory lost to K. Denn–Samuel 0–6 3–6; M. Zsoldos d. P. Kemper 6–1 4–6 6–4; K. Kocsis lost to M. Kochta 6–4 1–6 1–6; Foeldenyi/Zsoldos d. Denn–Samuel/Huber 4–6 7–6 6–3.

1989 Czechoslovakia d. Italy 5–0: E. Martiucova d. R. Grande 7–6 6–3; I. Malkova d. G. Pizzichini 6–2 7–5; O. Hostakova d. S. Pifferi 5–7 6–1 7–5; M. Hautova d. A. Serra-Zanetti 6–0 6–2; Malkova/Martiucova d. Grande/Pifferi 6–1 6–4.

1990 Czechoslovakia d. Yugoslavia 3–2: S. Radevicova lost to I. Majoli 2–6 6–4 1–6; Z. Rebekova lost to T. Doric 5–7 4–6; A. Havrlikova d. S. Milas 6–1 6–2; A. Gersi d. D. Karadz 7–6 6–0; Havrlikova/Redevicova d. Doric/Majoli 6–3 7–5.

1991 Germany d. Czechoslovakia 5–0: M. Vladulescu d. A. Havrlikova 6–0 6–3; N. Raidt d. R. Surova 7–6 6–2; S. Schmidle d. K. Bakalarova 6–0 6–4; A. Barna d. R. Pelikanova 6–2 6–4; Barna/T. Karsten d. L. Cenkova/Havrlikova 6–2 6–1.

1992 Czechoslovakia d. France 3–2: L. Varmuzova d. I. Taesch 4–6 6–43 6–4; H. Nagyova lost to A. Castera 3–6 2–6; S. Kleinova lost to E. Curutchet 3–6 6–3 2–6; J. Ondrouchova d. G. Goultefard 6–2 6–2; Kleinova/Ondrouchova d. Castera/Curutchet 3–6 7–5 6–4.

1993 Czech/Slovak Republic d. Germany 3–2: J. Lubasova lost to S. Kovacic 3–6 3–6; D. Chladkova d. M. Weingartner 6–4 6–3; L. Faltynkova lost to M. Frohlich 5–7 3–6; L. Varmuzova d. S. Klosel 6–1 4–6 6–2; Chladkova/Faltynkova d. E. Brunn/Klosel 5–7 6–2 8–6.

1994 Germany d. Czech Republic 3–2: D. Wallenhorst d. D. Luzarova 6–4 6 0; I. Wohr lost to B. Stejsjkalova w/o; S. Losel lost to J. Schonfeldova 7–6 1–6 2–6; S. Kovacic d. M. Pastikova 6–2 6–2; L. Fritz/S. Kovacic d. M. Pastikova/J. Schonfeldova 3–6 6–1 6–1.

1995 Slovenia d. Slovak Republic 4–1: T. Hojnik lost to E. Fislova 2–6 2–6; T. Hergold d. K. Basternakova 1–0 ret; T. Pisnik d. V. Stoklasova 5–7 6–0 10–8; K. Srebotnik d. G. Volekova 6–3 6–1; T. Pisnik/K. Srebotnik d. V. Stoklasova/ G. Volekova 2–6 6–1 6–3.

1996 Belgium d. Slovak Republic 3–1: E. Clijsters lost to D. Hantuchova 7–5 1–6 2–6; K. Clijsters d. Z. Kucova; J. Henin d. K. Basternakova 6–3 6–2; K. Clijsters/J. Henin d. S. Hrozenska/K. Basternakova 1–6 7–5 7–5.

1997 Slovak Republic d. Russia 4–1: M. Kunova d. G. Fokina 7–5 6–3; L. Kurhajcova d. I. Murashkintceva 6–1 7–6(4); D. Hantuchova d. L. Krasnoroutskaia 6–3 6–1; M. Babakova lost to E. Bovina 2–6 6–4 4–6; M. Babakova/ D. Hantuchova d. E. Bovina/L. Krasnoroutskaia 7–6(3) 6–4.

1998 Russia d. Czech Republic 3–2: R. Gourevitch lost to B. Strucovad 6–4 5–7 1–6; V. Zvonareva lost to P. Ticha 6–4 1–6 2–6; G. Fokina d. E. Birnerova 7–6 2–6 6–3; L. Krasnoroutskaia d. P. Cetkovska 6–2 5–7 6–3; G. Fokina/R. Gourevitch d. P. Cetkovska/P. Ticha 3–6 6–1 6–3.

1999 Czech Republic d. Russia 3–2: J. Rybova lost to N. Bratchikova 2–6 3–6; K. Kocibova d. E. Linetskaya 3–6 6–4 6–2; P. Cetkovska d. D. Safina 6–4 6–2; B. Strycova lost to A. Bastrikova 3–6 3–6; P. Cetkovska/B. Strycova d. A. Bastrikova/D. Safina 7–6 7–5.

2000 Russia d. Czech Republic 4–1: I. Kotkina d. N. Freislerova 6–1 7–6; V. Douchevina/D. Tchemarda d. B. Strycova/V. Prokopova 6–3 7–5; E. Linetskaia d. B. Strycova 7–5 6–4; V. Douchevina d. J. Rybova 6–3 6–4; D. Tchemarda lost to L. Safarova 3–6 6–4 6–3.

The International Tennis Federation

Regional Reports • ITF Development Programme
Wheelchair Tennis • ITF Junior Tennis
ITF Vets Tennis • National Association Addresses

Not only did Argentina's Maria Emilia Salerni win the Wimbledon and US Open junior titles to finish the year as the world's best junior, she also competed in the Olympic Games and beat Natasha Zvereva in the first round. (Stephen Wake)

The International Tennis Federation

Bank Lane, Roehampton, London SW15 5XZ
Telephone: 44 208 878 6464 Fax: 44 208 878 7799
Web site http://www.itftennis.com

President: Francesco Ricci Bitti.

Honorary Life Presidents: Philippe Chatrier, Brian Tobin.

Vice Presidents: Christian Bimes, Judy Levering, Juan Margets, Geoff Pollard.

Honorary Life Vice-President: Pablo Llorens.

Honorary Life Counsellors: Paolo Angeli, Jim Cochrane, Robert A Cookson, Jean Claude Delafosse, Hunter L Delatour, J Howard Frazer, J Randolph Gregson, Gordon Jorgensen, R K Khanna, Stan Malless, David Markin, Enrique Morea, Geoff Paish, Alvaro Peña, Francesco Ricci Bitti, William H Woods.

Trustees: Hunter L Delatour, David Jude, Pablo Llorens.

Board of Directors: Christian Bimes, Ruurd de Boer, Ismail El Shafei, Jan Francke, Heinz Grimm, Eiichi Kawatei, Ian King, Judy Levering, Juan Margets (Executive Vice President), Harry Marmion, Eduardo Moline O'Connor, Geoff Pollard, Francesco Ricci Bitti (President).

Honorary Treasurer: David Jude.

Auditors: Messrs Ernst & Young, London.

Legal Counsel: UK – Townleys, Wedlake Bell.

Committees: Davis Cup, Fed Cup, Finance, ITF Women's Circuit, Junior Competitions, Olympic, Constitutional, Rules of Tennis, Vets, Wheelchair Tennis.

Commissions: Athletes, Coaches, Media, Medical, Technical, Development Advisers Group.

GRAND SLAM COMMITTEE

Australian Open: Geoff Pollard; *French Open:* Christian Bimes;
Wimbledon: Tim Phillips; *US Open:* Mervin Heller;
ITF President: Francesco Ricci Bitti; *Administrator:* William Babcock.

WTA TOUR BOARD OF DIRECTORS

ITF Representative: Deborah Jevans; Alternate: Francesco Ricci Bitti.

ITF MEN'S CIRCUIT COMMITTEE

ITF Representatives: Chairman: Juan Margets; Members: Brian Earley, Eiichi Kawatei, Balazs Taroczy.

CHALLENGERS JOINT COMMITTEE

ITF Representatives: Eiichi Kawatei, Juan Margets, Balazs Taroczy.

SECRETARIAT

President: Francesco Ricci Bitti.
Executive Vice President: Juan Margets.

Executive Directors: William Babcock, Davis Cup & Men's Tennis/Grand Slam Administrator/Officials • John Garnham, Finance & Administration • Deborah Jevans, Fed Cup & Women's Tennis/Medical & Olympic Games Administrator • Jan Menneken, Commercial • Dave Miley, Tennis Development.

Managers: Frances Cason, Finance • Andrew Coe, Head of Product Development & Technical • Ellen de Lange, Wheelchair Tennis • Paul Hurst, Information Technology • Jackie Nesbitt, Junior Competitions and Vets Tennis • Clive Painter, Human Resources & Administration • Paul Smith, Operations • Barbara Travers, Communications.

Administrators: Tori Billington & Frank Couraud, Development • Clare Collinson, Executive Assistant to the President/AGM • Stefan Fransson, Officiating • Rosie Hyde, Junior Competitions and Vets Tennis • James Mercer, Guy Winter & Rik van Vliet, Sponsorship Sales • Carole Munn, Women's Tennis • Sarah Orr, Men's Tennis • Fiona Rumsby, TV • Alison Sowersby, Fed Cup • John Treleven, Rankings • Jo Turner, Event Operations.

Regional Reports

ASIAN TENNIS FEDERATION (ATF)

The Asian Tennis Federation continues to focus its attention on the development aspects of the game in the region. Asia has made some significant progress in the various development activities carried out by the National Associations.

Much effort has been put into the area of coaches' education. With this in mind a number of Level 1 and Level 2 coaches courses have been in held in several countries in the region. With the hope of making National Associations self sufficient, appropriate tutors' courses have also been organized. Much credit has to be given to the ITF Development Department for their continued support and the work of Suresh Menon, our Development Officer for the region.

Placing emphasis on youth, junior development circuits, particularly in the 14 & Under category have been organized in West, Central, South and East Asian regions. Similar development tournaments have also been held in China as part of a special project. Based on results of these development circuits, ITF Asian Travelling teams have been selected to play in several European age group tournaments in the July-August period.

In excess of 150 coaches from several Asian countries participated in the 10th Asian Coaches Workshop that was held from 16–21 October. Several top ITF experts lectured at the workshop. The ATF is pleased to note that Bangkok, Thailand has been chosen to be the host city for the 2001 ITF Worldwide Coaches Workshop. This will be the first time that a workshop of this magnitude has been held in Asia.

We have seen some qualitative and quantitative improvements in tournaments in Asia. This is especially so with the increase in the number of junior as well as women's events. India, in particular, has added several more new events to its ever-growing tournament calendar. The Asian player now has some 140 international events (covering all junior and professional tournaments) to participate in.

The ATF organized its first ever Tournament Workshop in Bangkok from 2–3 November, with the main aim of coordinating the Tournament Calendar. The workshop also discussed issues on tournament organization, officiating and marketing and sponsorship matters. The workshop also enabled participants to discuss and exchange ideas that will be mutually beneficial to them. Non professional events like Vets tennis and wheelchair tennis have grown dramatically in the region and the ATF will continue to promote such events among National Associations.

The awareness of officiating has never been higher in the region than it is now. The Officiating Committee has been tireless in upgrading its officials by conducting more Level I and refresher schools within the region. Nitkin Kanmawar has been placed on the ITF Star Trek programme. Asian officials were also assigned to work at the Sydney 2000 Olympics as well as Grand Slam Championships.

As of mid-July 2000, the bulk of the Federations' administration has been shifted to Singapore. Ms Vijayal is now employed in the Singapore office as a coordinator. The Hong Kong office continues to exist, managing aspects of finance and officiating.

The ATF marketing programme made strong progress in 2000. Sponsorship was enhanced with all Official Sponsors being retained and working more closely with the Federation. The Asian Tennis Partnership program was launched to provide an avenue for corporations and individuals to participate in the development of Asian tennis. The ATF's quarterly magazine, *Tennis Asia*, has improved and its circulation expanded. This year also saw the launch of the ATF's website at *www.AsianTennis.com*

Officers: *President*: Eiichi Kawatei; *Vice President, Chairman of Development*: Sheikh Ahmad Al-Jaber Al-Sabah; *Vice President, Chairman Events and Officiating*: Salvador H. Andrada; *Vice President, Chairman Finance and Administration*: Herman Hu; *Vice President, Chairman Men's Events*: Anil Kumar Khanna; *Chairman Marketing*: Abdulaziz S. Kridis; *Chairman Veterans*: Gen Wichar Siritham; *Chairman Women's Events*: Masaru Uchiyama; *Chairman Junior Development*: Zhang Xaio-Ning; *Member*: Rustam Shoabdurahmanov; *Executive Director*: S. Uthrapathy.

EUROPEAN TENNIS ASSOCIATION (ETA)

The first year of the new millennium has been very special for the ETA. In March, there was a celebration of the Association's 25-year history at the AGM in Barcelona, where all past-Presidents received gifts thanking them for their commitment to European Tennis over the past 25 years. The AGM was also concerned with the election of a new ETA President after the appointment of Francesco Ricci Bitti as President of the ITF in July 1999. Two candidates (P.P. de Keghel, Belgium and A. Pujol, Spain) contested the position and A. Pujol was duly elected President for the next two years.

The Olympic games featured prominently in the international tennis calendar this year and for European Tennis, these games were arguably the best ever. In all events, European tennis players came home with medals; gold, silver and bronze! Yevgeny Kafelnikov, Russia, Tommy Haas, Germany, and Arnaud di Pasquale, France, took gold, silver and bronze in the men's singles event and Elena Dementieva had an outstanding event, taking the silver medal in the women's singles.

ETA events this year were extremely successful and some great tennis was played. The European Club Championships for women was held at TC Bonnevoie in Luxembourg and the host club were the eventual winners, defeating the Italian TC Napoli in the final. The European Club Championships for Men was held at the Real Club Tennis Barcelona 1899 in Spain and, in an exciting final, the host club was defeated by CT Barcino (ESP).

The 2000 ITF Men's Circuit in Europe consisted of 100 weeks of Satellite Circuits and 128 weeks of Futures Events with total prize money of $2,245,000. The Women's circuit in Europe consisted of 161 weeks with a total prize money of $2,940,000.

The 2000 ETA Tour had another successful year with a total of 58 14 & Under tournaments, 52 16 & Under tournaments while the new 12 & Under Tour comprised 36 tournaments.

The ITF/ETA Development programme has continued to do important work for the promotion of tennis throughout Europe and this year's total budget of $767,500 was distributed across the continent in the form of travel grants, grants for professional and junior tournaments, coaches' and administrators' education and equipment.

There was another well-attended series of ETA conferences throughout the year. The AGM in Barcelona, Spain, the Regional Meeting in Antayla, the Coaches' Symposium in Otocec, Slovenia, the Top Executives' Meeting in Maribor, Slovenia, the European Tournament Conference in Barcelona, Spain and lastly the Junior General Meeting in Monaco.

In addition to all the above, the ETA has concentrated a lot of time and effort on the launch of the ETA homepage (www.etatennis.com) which went live in January. Other communications developments have included the replacement of ETA Flash by the Internet Newsletter, ETA News. There has also been a unique development in the women's department where all women's tournaments acceptance lists are available on the internet and are updated automatically every two hours. Last, but by no means least, the ETA is producing an official Jubilee publication, which will be a permanent, commemorative record of the Association's history, influential figures and players. It will contain comprehensive details of all ETA events winners and runners-up and information about the Association's member nations.

CONFEDERATION OF SOUTH AMERICAN TENNIS (COSAT)

There has been another year of hard work from all those who are part of the South American Confederation of Tennis (COSAT). These past months have seen many improvements in our work and much effort and optimism has been put into the task.

South American youth tennis activities got underway with the COSAT 2000 Circuit, in which Venezuela was taking part for the first time. Overall 74.8% of the youngsters who took part in these tournaments were local, and 25.2% were foreign players. In the girls' events, an average of 104.3 players took part in each circuit while in the boys', there were an average of 137.2 competitors. A total of 2415 players were involved, an increase in participation of 8.64% on 1999.

Within the same youth category, we mention, as we do every year, the European tour for 14 & 16 year olds. South American players have always performed well in these tournaments, and outstanding performances came from Carlos Zarhi of Chile in the 14-year-old event and Brian Dabul of Argentina in the 16-year-old category. The South American events for 14 &16 year-olds had Brazilian and Argentinian champions in girls' and boys' respectively.

On the men's and women's professional circuits, there was a total of 35 tournaments. These consisted of 25 tournaments with prize money of $10,000, six with prize money of $15,000 and four with prize money of $25,000 for the champions. Thirteen tournaments were played with a purse of $10,000 for the runners-up.

South American players who have performed outstandingly at the highest level include:

- Maria Emilia Salerni of Argentina who won the junior girls' events at Wimbledon and the US Open. She was also girls' runner-up at Roland Garros and the champion at the Santa Croce juniors event.
- Gisela Dulko of Argentina, semi-finalist at Santa Croce and Bonfiglio, quarter-finalist at the Astrid Bowl tournament.
- Gustavo Kuerten of Brazil, who won the men's title at Roland Garros for the second time.
- Nicolas and Giovanni Lapentti, Luis Morejon and Andres Intriago who took Ecuador into the World Group of the Davis Cup for 2001, defeating Great Britain 3-2 at home at Wimbledon.
- The Brazilian Davis Cup team, which was outstanding in reaching the semi-finals of the 2000 competition with the help of Gustavo Kuerten, Fernando Meligeni, Jaime Oncins and Andre Sa. Brazil will play in the World Group again next year alongside Ecuador.

Also, we cannot forget the contributions of Marcelo Rios of Chile, Daniel Orsanic Mariano Zabaleta, Mariano Puerta, Franco Squillari, all from Argentina, and Ramon Delgado of Paraguay together with others who have benefited from their experience on COSAT circuits. This 'Cradle of Champions' has produced all our promising South American players.

In the area of tennis development, six courses for coaches and teachers at level 5 (Level II) have been run in different countries in South America. There were seminars and work shops in Venezuela (North Zone) and Brazil (South Zone).

A seminar called 'Principles of Coaching & Paralympic tennis' was organised by COSAT in conjunction with Paralympics Latin America and had 19 participants. These seminars were chaired by the Regional General Manager, Juan Pablo Delano, and Miguel Miranda, Development Officer of COSAT.

The Vets tournament calendar included 14 international tournaments. The South American tournament was held in Santiago, Chile and the ITF Vets Team Competitions were held in six South American countries, these being: Argentina (Men +35, Women +40), Bolivia (Men +40), Paraguay (+45), Chile (+50), Uruguay (Women +45) and Brazil (Women +50). The ITF Vets World Championships for the younger age categories was held in Buenos Aires, Argentina.

Lastly, there were two congresses in May and September with the COSAT Managing Committee being re-elected until 2004 in the second one. Mr V. Calderon (Bolivia) remains President, M. Carrizosa (Paraguay) and N. Nastas (Brazil) remain Vice Presidents, and the directors are Carmen Elisa de Carvajal (Colombia), Sergio Elias (Chile) and Dr E. Moline O'Connor ITF Board of Directors member. They resumed their responsibilities, looking to building on what has already been achieved and with a firm commitment to reach new goals in association with COSAT's affiliated nations.

THE CONFEDERATION OF AFRICAN TENNIS (CAT)

The Confederation of African Tennis (CAT) relaunched its administration in June 1999, two months after a new Executive Committee took over. This elected Committee is composed of a President, Mamadou Diagna Ndiaye (Senegal) and four (4) Zonal Presidents who are: Tarak Chérif (Tunisia), Zone I (North Africa); Luc Kouassi Dofontien (Togo), Zone II & III (West and Central Africa); Gideon Karyoko (Uganda), Zone IV (East Africa); Mohamed Sheik (South Africa), Zone V (Southern Africa)

The CAT Headquarters has moved from Johannesburg to Dakar, Senegal where it has become an ITF/CAT Office. The new committee started working immediately towards consolidating ties with the ITF and the member nations, improving communication with its affiliated members, and running its administration and projects as well as ITF delegated ones. An African five-year plan (1999-2003) is in place, and takes into account all these projects.

The administration is managed by Nicolas Ayeboua, Secretary General of CAT, who is assisted in this task by Merry Loum and Aminata Mané.

This year started with the West Africa ITF 18 & Under circuit in Nigeria, Togo and Ghana. Some eighty players attended, Indians, Austrians and Britons. In April came the ITF/CAT 23rd African Junior Championships in South Africa with the participation of thirty-five nations.

The CAT AGM was held during this event, and was attended by ITF President, Francesco Ricci-Bitti. Some of the best performances at the African Junior Championships were attained by players currently based at the ITF Training Centre in Pretoria under full-time scholarships.

CAT organised and supervised four (4) ITF/CAT 14 & Under circuits and training camps in its zones in July and August. October saw the 5th African Nations Cup (CAN 2000) held in Algiers. The Algerian Tennis Federation put in a tremendous effort to make this one of the best events held, in this way demonstrating their strong support of CAT and its activities.

CAT's first medical forum took place during CAN 2000 with speakers of world-wide renown.

It is important to note the performances of some African nations in Davis Cup, such as Morocco which is now in the World Group of this competition.

At the last ITF AGM in Turkey, six African nations were accepted as ITF full members. They joined the twenty-two African nations that were already in the class B group, and will all play the Davis Cup and Fed Cup competitions in 2001.

Many satellites circuits and futures tournaments were organised in North, West and Southern Africa, and prize money tournaments were also staged in the East, West and Southern Zones in order to provide competitive opportunities to the top African players.

There is also a revival in the organisation of Open tournaments. The Lagos Governor's Cup and the Heineken Open in Nigeria respectively attained a record of US$45,000 and US$25,000 prize money with accommodation, while Rwanda had its first International Open since its genocide in 1994 with US$10,000 prize money.

A Level II Officiating course also took place in South Africa in October and provided the continent with fourteen (14) new white badge officials.

The ITF organised an administration course in South Africa, as well as many coaches' courses, including a Level II in Nigeria in September, the African Regional Coaches Workshop in November and another Level II in Madagascar planned for December 2000.

Among other CAT programmes, is the School Tennis Initiative (STI) in which thirty-one (31) countries are currently participating.

While many of the targets outlined in the African Five Year Plan have been attained, there are still areas to be worked on over the coming months.

OCEANIA TENNIS FEDERATION (OTF)

Creating opportunities for young players from the Pacific Island nations continues to be the primary focus of Oceania Tennis Federation (OTF). The ITF Pacific Oceania junior and OTF Pacific Oceania senior teams saw in the new year in New Zealand, the first nation in the world to see the light of the new millennium, before heading off on their tournament circuits, the juniors in Australia and the seniors around New Zealand. The junior teams' results were outstanding and demonstrated the success of the development programmes in the Pacific Islands recently.

In late January the teams met up in Fiji for the Pacific Oceania Closed Championships, which were held for the first time at the new regional tennis centre in Lautoka. Lency Tenai (Solomon Islands) defended his men's singles title beating Brett Baudinet (Cook Islands) in the final.

Meanwhile the women players were taking part in a training camp under the tutelage of new Fed Cup captain Jeff Race whose team won promotion to group one for next year beating a number of more highly rated teams in the Asia/Oceania qualifying competition in Osaka.

Unfortunately the Pacific Oceania Davis Cup team were relegated to group four but the whole region celebrated Australia making the final for the second year in a row.

After a wonderful start many of the activities were disrupted mid-year due to the political unrest in Fiji which is the hub of OTF development programmes. The tennis and academic programmes of many of the scholarship players at the regional training centre were disrupted, the first ITF world junior circuit tournament planned for Lautoka was postponed to 2001 and the ITF Pacific Oceania junior circuit was reduced to two legs. All is back on track for 2001.

For the first time the Olympic tennis event was held in the Oceania region at the New South Wales tennis centre. Mike Daws, former Joint-Secretary General of the OTF was the venue and competition manager for the tennis event which drew sellout crowds every day.

Close cooperation has continued with ITF development officer Dan O'Connell and ONOC to enhance all programmes, including coach education. In October five Pacific Oceania coaches attended the Asian coaches workshop. During the year Australia and New Zealand coaches visited the regional training centre in Lautoka to assist the coaches there as well as the players.

The OTF continues to expand its Tennis in Schools programme with support from the ITF and our sponsors ANZ Bank. We now have an enthusiastic group of school teachers throughout the Pacific who have learnt their skills from OTF development officers Lency Tenai and Francis Ali. With this rapidly expanding programme we are confident that tennis will boom amongst youngsters right across the Pacific in the next few years.

ITF Development Programme

Rachel Woodward

ITF Tennis Participation Coaches' Workshop

This year saw the launch of one of the ITF's most significant development initiatives; marking not only the beginning of a new millennium but also a new era in tennis development. The ITF designated the year 2000 as its year for growth and introduced the 'Marketing the Game – the Drive for Growth' programme with the primary objective of attracting more people into all levels of the game.

This initiative is the second phase of a long-term marketing programme that began in 1997 with an international research project to ascertain participation trends and attitudes to the game of tennis. This initiative will involve a number of key partners, in particular the ITF's more mature and developed member nations who can influence and contribute to the growth of the game.

One highlight of this initiative in 2000 and a new venture in the Development Programme was the ITF Tennis Participation Coaches' Workshop which was held in June at the University of Bath. Organised in conjunction with the Lawn Tennis Association of Great Britain, the week-long conference was primarily aimed at educating coaches involved in grass roots tennis programmes worldwide, with the theme 'More Tennis.... More Often.....More Fun.....'

This was the first time that the ITF had conducted such a workshop and the event attracted 280 delegates from over 80 countries. Experts in attendance included, Louis Cayer, Canadian Davis Cup captain and Olympic coach, Dennis Van der Meer, Jean-Claude Marchon whose success with the French Tennis Federation's mini-tennis programme is well documented and Ron Woods, Director of the USA Tennis Plan for Growth, to name but a few. Feedback from both developing and mature tennis nations was very positive, highlighting a need to focus on this area of coaches' education more in the future. We hope to continue with the Participation Workshop every two years.

'More Tennis, More Often, More Fun'

African Junior Championships

Pretoria, South Africa played host to the 23rd African Junior Championships for a second successive year in May of this year. Seventeen-year-old Arnaud Segodo from Benin held off stiff competition to take the 18 & Under boys' singles title by defeating Raven Klaasen from Cape Town. Segodo, a product of the ITF/SATA Training Centre in Pretoria, follows in the footsteps of some great African Champions including Byron Black, Karim Alami and Yaya Doumbia. 170 players from 26 countries competed in the event, which held singles and doubles events in three age groups, 18 & Under, 16 & Under and 14 & Under. A feed-in consolation system was operated so that every player played a singles match every day, resulting in a ranking of all the players in each category.

Of the six singles titles, four went to the home nation, with Segodo and the boys' 16 & Under champion Lamine Ouhab of Algeria taking the other two. South Africa clearly won the overall trophy as best junior tennis nation in Africa, but there were encouraging results for other nations.

The regional qualifying events for the ITF Junior Team events were also held in conjunction with the African Junior Championships, and the following countries qualified for the world finals later in 2000:

Sunshine Cup (Boys 18 & Under): South Africa
Connolly Continental Cup (Girls 18 & Under): South Africa
World Youth Cup (16 & Under) Boys: South Africa
World Youth Cup (16 & Under) Girls: South Africa
World Junior Tennis (14 & Under) Boys: South Africa/Morocco
World Junior Tennis (14 & Under) Girls: South Africa/Egypt

China Project

Tennis development in China received a further boost in May of this year, when ITF Development Projects Administrator, Frank Couraud and ITF Research Officer, Miguel Crespo travelled to China to conduct a Level II Coaches' Course. The course was part of a five-year co-operation project established between the ITF and the Chinese Tennis Association (CTA) to foster the growth of tennis through training coaches and provide greater competitive opportunities at the junior level.

Following its inception in 1998, the ITF has continued to organise courses designed to instruct Chinese coaches in modern training methods using the ITF's recommended Level I and Level II coaching syllabus. By 2002 – year four of the five-year Coach Education programme, it is expected that the CTA will be self-sufficient and that Level I and Level II courses will be conducted solely by Chinese coaches.

While the education of Chinese coaches is ongoing, the game is also becoming more popular at grass roots level. Over 40,000 children play mini-tennis with 435 coaches receiving training in mini-tennis during the last year.

In 1998, there were only four national tournaments for players aged 14 & under, so to counteract this, last year the ITF inaugurated a new event – the ITF/China 14 & Under Development Championships. The tournament is open to the best 32 boys and 32 girls in China. The eight most talented girls and boys are selected to travel to Europe as part of the ITF Chinese 14 & Under team, gaining valuable experience of international competition outside China alongside some of the top juniors in their age group. In May of this year, Peng Shuai joined her teammates Du Rui and Qing Yue to become the first Chinese girls' team to win the Asian qualifying 14 & Under World Junior Tennis Finals.

Training Centres

The ITF continues to operate three successful Training Centres throughout the world.

At the ITF/OTF Regional Training Centre in Lautoka, Fiji, there were 11 full-time resident players throughout 2000. Many of them have shown marked improvement over the year, as seen in the results of the region's principal junior event – the Pacific Oceania Junior Circuit/Championships – held in August/September. Almost all the 2000 scholarship players will return to the RTC for the 2001 academic year commencing in January.

During the past year, 183 players from 18 countries attended the ITF African Training Centre in Pretoria, South Africa, while the Performance Tennis Academy in Florida now boasts 18 resident players. Most of the resident players at the Academy are from the Central American and Caribbean region, but some of the visiting players who attend for shorter periods are from countries as far afield as Kazakhstan and American Samoa.

School Tennis Initiative

There are currently 80 countries taking part in the ITF School Tennis Initiative and an estimated 3 million children have been introduced to tennis through the programme since its inception in 1996. The main objective of the STI programme is to introduce mini-tennis to school children aged 6–12 by working together with the National Association to ensure the inclusion of mini-tennis in the school curriculum. The ITF will be looking to build on the success of the STI programme next year by targeting successful STI programmes for involvement in the follow-up programme – the Performance Tennis Initiative.

Equipment Distribution Programme

Eligible developing nations continued to receive ITF-branded equipment via the ITF Equipment Distribution Programme. A credit system is now in place, whereby eligible nations can specify, on the basis of a submitted development plan, what equipment they wish to receive up to the value of their credit. Many nations were also able to purchase ITF-branded equipment at low prices for their federations through the Equipment Purchase Programme.

Coaches' Education

In the past year, the ITF has organised 52 coaches' courses throughout the world to help member nations who currently do not have a system of certifying their own coaches. Countries as widespread as Laos, Surinam, Zimbabwe, Ecuador, Malta and Venezuela have benefited from such an initiative during the year.

Furthermore, it is encouraging to see some of the more established tennis nations such as Australia, Brazil, Czech Republic and Italy, incorporating the ITF coaching syllabus into their own existing coaches education programme.

Every two years, the ITF Development Department organises regional coaches' workshops. The workshops take place over a week and cover a wide-range of topics presented by some of the world's leading experts in coaches' education. This year saw five regional events taking place:

- Central America and Caribbean: Fort Lauderdale, USA (120 coaches/20countries).
- Europe: The European Tennis Association organised, in conjunction with the Slovenian Tennis Association, one of its most successful ETA Coaches Symposium's with 90 high-level European coaches representing 33 countries attending this event.
- Asia: Kuala Lumpar, Malaysia hosted by the Lawn Tennis Association of Malaysia (110 coaches/26 countries).
- South America: Two events hosted by the Venezuelan and Brazilian Tennis Federations respectively (250 coaches/10 countries).
- Africa: Johannesburg, South Africa hosted by the South African Tennis Association (90 coaches/23 countries).

ITF Teams

Every year the ITF invites talented juniors at the 14, 16 and 18 & Under level, from less developed tennis nations to join ITF teams to participate in tournaments outside their region under the supervision of an ITF coach. In 2000 there were 20 teams, involving 227 players from 76 countries. Notable highlights at the 18 & Under level included:

- Todor Enev (Bulgaria), a member of the ITF International 'A' Team was a semi-finalist at both Roland Garros and Wimbledon.
- Tatiana Perebiynis (Ukraine), a member of the ITF International 'A' Team was a finalist at Wimbledon and the US Open.
- Yeu Tzuoo Wang (Chinese Taipei), a member of the ITF International Team to North America won the Canadian Junior Championships.
- Peng Shuai (China), as a member of the ITF International 16 & Under Team in June/July went on to win the girls' singles event at the Prince Cup 18 & Under in December 2000, as a member of the ITF International Team to the Orange Bowl.

All of the above programmes are only possible because of the generous donation of US$ 1.5 million each year by the Grand Slam Nations. This contribution combined with the ITF's own investment, means that over US$ 4 million is available each year for Development Projects worldwide.

Peng Shuai (China) (right) and Su Wei Hsieh (Chinese Taipei) (left) during their European tour as part of the ITF Int. 16 & Under Team 2000. (ITF)

Review of Wheelchair Tennis

Ellen de Lange

Just as President Samaranch had of the Olympic Games, Mr Robert Steadward, President of the International Paralympic Committee, declared the Sydney Paralympic Games the best Games ever. The final days of the Paralympic Tennis Event ended on a high note for the host nation. Australia claimed its first gold medal in tennis when David Hall outlasted Stephen Welch of the United States 6–7 6–4 6–2 in one of the most riveting duels of the entire competition. The men's final involved two of the most gifted players in the men's draw. Add to this that it would be performed before Hall's sports-loving home crowd, and the contest was already charged with emotion, passion, courage and national pride.

It is a tribute to both players that the occasion actually lived up to such high expectations – with sport being the ultimate winner. Dutch women captured all three singles medals in a repeat of their feat at Atlanta. In all, the Netherlands has won eight medals in the women singles event at the Paralympics since the first medal competition in 1992. The youngest Paralympic gold tennis medallist, Esther Vergeer, beat Sharon Walraven 6–0 6–4. Maaike Smit took the bronze medal after beating Kimberly Dell of Great Britain. In the men's doubles event, the Aussie pairing of David Hall and David Johnson narrowly missed out on a gold to Robin Ammerlaan and Ricky Molier, with the Dutch squeezing through 7–5 1–6 6–3. Entertaining a packed Centre Court, the match unfolded into an epic contest fusing skill and courage to produce just over two hours of nail-biting tennis. The Netherlands earned its third gold medal in the tennis event when Esther Vergeer and Maaike Smit vindicated their top seeding to defeat Aussies Daniela Di Toro and Branka Pupovac 7–6 6–2 in the women's doubles, the match being a tense tussle for gold between the No. 1 and No. 2 seeds. The Dutch victory represents their third consecutive gold in women's doubles since the first Paralympic tennis medal event at the 1992 Barcelona Games.

In July, 32 men's, 16 women's and 8 quad teams participated in the 2000 Invacare World Team Cup, organised at Cercle du Bois de Boulogne, Paris, France. A junior event for 4 teams was organised alongside the main event. This inaugural competition was won in a very exciting final by the strong USA team. After a one-year hiatus as World Team champions the Dutch women returned the cup to the Dutch Tennis Federation in a rematch of last year's final in New York. Bringing the world's No. 2, 3, 4, and 5 players together in one team there was little question as to who was the heavy favourite at the start of the week and this was confirmed. The Australian men celebrated victory in the men's event: spearheaded by the former ITF Wheelchair World Champion David Hall, they upset the top-seeded Dutch team 2–1 to win their third World Team Cup. Australia's Hall and Johnson clinched a third-set in the crucial doubles match. The Quad event was won for a second consecutive time by the strong Israeli team which defeated the USA in the final.

The continued support of NEC enabled the ITF Wheelchair Tennis department to provide a full programme of activities including the NEC Wheelchair Tennis Tour and the NEC Wheelchair Tennis Masters. Invacare Corporation provided a substantial backing for the Invacare World Team Cup while also continuing to support a number of camps for juniors and novice players around the world.

An increase in number and quality of tournaments on the NEC Tour provided wheelchair tennis players with a variety of opportunities at all levels. From the start of the season, the competition was fierce, with the challenge for ranking points to determine the World Champions at the end of the year. At the ITF World Champions Dinner in Paris held during Roland Garros, the 1999 World Champions Stephen Welch (USA) and Daniela Di Toro (AUS) were presented with their awards alongside their able-bodied peers.

In conjunction with the Dutch Open, the ITF once again organised an international junior camp, which attracted players and coaches from various countries. The camp provided an excellent opportunity for some of the most promising athletes to be taught by top coaches.

Development continued to be an important part of the ITF Wheelchair Tennis department and through the wheelchair tennis development officer many new and existing wheelchair

The Netherlands won the women's World Team Cup in 2000; their 13th success in the event's 16-year history. (Gordon Gillespie)

Left: David Hall, Australia's Paralympic gold medal winner in Sydney. (Gordon Gillespie)

tennis countries were visited. Some of these countries now have strong wheelchair tennis programmes in place and are planning to organise an NEC Wheelchair Tennis Tour event within the near future. More programmes for quads were introduced this year to provide a stimulus for growth in this section of wheelchair tennis.

The year concluded with the NEC Wheelchair Tennis Masters held in Amersfoort, the Netherlands, for the world's top eight men and women players. For the first time a doubles event was organised alongside the singles event in a tournament that is fast becoming the most prestigious in the game. Four exciting finals brought the season to a fitting end, with the host country winning both singles titles. No. 5 seed Robin Ammerlaan successfully defended his 1999 Masters title by defeating countryman and No. 2 seed Ricky Molier 7–6 6–1. There was another victory for the defending champion in the women's event, with Esther Vergeer crowning a perfect season to become the first ever three-time Masters Champion, adding the title to her wins at the Paralympics and the US Open. Vergeer defeated the Dutch No. 6 seed Djoke Van Marum 6–1 6–3 in the final. In the inaugural doubles, Molier found success with Stephen Welch in the men's event, while Daniela Di Toro partnered Maaike Smit to victory in the women's event.

The year 2001 will celebrate the 25th anniversary of wheelchair tennis. The sport has many challenges ahead, and the dedicated support from grass roots to international level will be essential to ensure that this part of the game continues to go from strength to strength.

NEC Wheelchair Tennis Ranking (Top 20 as of 20.11.00)

Men's Singles

1	HALL, David	AUS	4881
2	MOLIER, Ricky	NED	4659
3	WELCH, Stephen	USA	3879
4	SCHRAMEYER, Kai	GER	3432
5	AMMERLAAN, Robin	NED	3137
6	LEGNER, Martin	AUT	2651
7	JOHNSON, David	AUS	2573
8	MISTRY, Jayant	GBR	1966
9	SAIDA, Satoshi	JPN	1892
10	GIAMMARTINI, Laurent	FRA	1819
11	KRUSZELNICKI, Tadeusz	POL	1774
12	STUURMAN, Eric	NED	1637
13	JOHNSON, Paul	CAN	1470
14	BONNET, Philippe	FRA	1463
15	NIJHOFF, Taco	NED	1354
16	BRYCHTA, Miroslav	CZE	1259
17	SNOW, Randy	USA	1223
18	WEISANG, Ralph	GER	1104
19	PURSCHKE, Torsten	GER	1099
20	DOCKERILL, Bob	GBR	1069

Women's Singles

1	VERGEER, Esther	NED	3595
2	DI TORO, Daniela	AUS	3234
3	PETERS, Sonja	NED	2848
4	SMIT, Maaike	NED	2577
5	WALRAVEN, Sharon	NED	2234
6	MAAS, Angela	NED	1939
7	VAN MARUM, Djoke	NED	1887
8	AMERYCKX, Brigitte	BEL	1735
9	MCMORRAN, Janet	GBR	1481
10	DELL, Kimberly	GBR	1391
11	OHMAE, Chiyoko	JPN	1351
12	PUPOVAC, Branka	AUS	1165
13	KORB, Karin	USA	1057
14	RACINEUX, Arlette	FRA	1045
15	CHOKYU, Yuka	CAN	860
16	LEWELLEN, Hope	USA	857
17	KHANTHASIT, Sakhorn	THA	811
18	OTTERBACH, Christine	GER	788
19	ROLLINSON, Patricia	USA	768
20	ARNOLT, Beth	USA	743

Quad Singles

1	DRANEY, Rick	USA	2788
2	STUDWELL, Chris	USA	2657
3	ECCLESTON, Mark	GBR	2451
4	TAYLOR, Nicholas	USA	2263
5	TACHIBANA, Nobuhiro	JPN	1714
6	ROUSSET, Andre	FRA	1688
7	SANDERS, Robert	USA	1584
8	HUMPHREYS, Roy	GBR	1419
9	BARTEN, Bryan	USA	1344
10	WHALEN, Kevin	USA	1207
11	TAKASHIMA, Masao	JPN	888
12	OHASHI, Kazumi	JPN	874
13	KIMURA, Sadahiro	JPN	725
14	JORDAN, David	USA	715
15	LEV, Chaim	ISR	688
16	VAN DEN HEUVEL, Michel	NED	625
17	POLIDORI, Guiseppe	ITA	604
18	WEINBERG, Shraga	ISR	570
19	JOHNSON, Chris	GBR	538
20	WEINBERG, Avi	ISR	450

WHEELCHAIR TENNIS CONTACTS
ITF Wheelchair Tennis Department
Bank Lane, Roehampton, London SW15 5XZ,
Great Britain
Tel: (44) 0208 878 6464
Fax: (44) 0208 392 4741
Email:wheelchairtennis@itftennis.com
Wheelchair Tennis Manager: Miss Ellen de Lange

ITF WHEELCHAIR TENNIS WORLD CHAMPIONS

Men

1991	Randy Snow	USA
1992	Laurent Giammartini	FRA
1993	Kai Schrameyer	GER
1994	Laurent Giammartini	FRA
1995	David Hall	AUS
1996	Ricky Molier	NED
1997	Ricky Molier	NED
1998	David Hall	AUS
1999	Stephen Wlech	USA
2000	David Hall	AUS

Women

1991	Chantal Vandierendonck	NED
1992	Monique Kalkman	NED
1993	Monique Kalkman	NED
1994	Monique Kalkman	NED
1995	Monique Kalkman	NED
1996	Chantal Vandierendonck	NED
1997	Chantal Vandierendonck	NED
1998	Daniela Di Toro	AUS
1999	Daniela Di Toro	AUS
2000	Esther Vergeer	NED

NEC Wheelchair Tennis Tour 2000

Dates	Tournament	Grade	Singles	Doubles
20–23 Jan	Queensland Open	CS4	D Hall d. D Johnson 6-2 6-2 B Pupovac d. Chiyoko Ohmae 6-4 4-6 6-4	D Johnson/D Hall d. T Nijhoff/P Bonnet 7-6 6-3 K Dell/B Pupovac d. Chiyojo Ohmae/Yuka Chokyu 6-4 6-1
26–30 Jan	Sydney International	CS1	R Molier d. D Hall 6-1 7-6 E Vergeer d. D van Marum 6-2 2-6 6-0 G Baker d. C Johnson 6-3 6-4	D Hall/D Johnson d. R Molier/E Stuurman 5-7 6-4 6-3 E Vergeer/S Peters d. D Di Toro/M Smit 6-4 6-3
2–6 Feb	Australian Open	CS1	R Molier d. D Hall 6-3 2-6 6-1 D Di Toro d. A Maas 6-1 6-3	D Hall/D Johnson d. R Molier/E Stuurman 6-2 6-2
8–11 Feb	New Zealand Open	CS4	J Mistry d. P Bonnet 7-5 4-6 6-0 J McMorran d. B Pupovac 7-5 6-3	E Vergeer/S Peters d. S Walraven/D van Marum 6-2 6-3 J Mistry/P Bonnet d. J Greer/P Johnson 5-7 7-6 6-2
14–17 Feb	Malaysian Open	CS4	F Mazzei d. I Yoshida 7-6 6-7 6-2 B Pupovac d. R Arnolt 6-2 6-0	A Bonaccurso/I Yoshida d. N Sugamura/M Taga 3-6 6-3 6-2 J Lauman de Velk/R Techamaneewat d. B Arnolt/B Pupovac 6-3 7-5
16–20 Feb	Comfort Lines Open	CS4	R Molier d. K Schrameyer 6-2 4-6 6-3 S Walraven d. B Ameryckx 4-6 7-5 6-4	R Ammerlaan/R Molier d. M Legner/K Schrameyer 6-4 6-2
29 Feb–4 Mar	Hungarian Open	CS4	J Mistry d. T Kruszelnicki 6-3 6-1	T Kruszelnicki/J Mistry d. L Farkas/T Nijhoff 6-0 6-0
17–19 Mar	Kolibri Lyss Indoor	CS4	T Purschke d. M Brychta 4-6 7-6 6-4 C Seyen d. M Fink 6-3 7-5	T Nijhoff/M Brychta d. L Majdi/L Fischer 6-2 6-2 K Erath/S Kalt d. C Seyen/M Fink 3-2 w/o
29 Mar–1 Apr	Ericsson Champs	CS2	R Molier d. K Schrameyer 6-2 6-4 E Vergeer d. D Di Toro 6-1 6-4	D Hall/D Johnson d. M Legner/K Schrameyer 1-6 6-3 7-6 D Di Toro/M Smit d. S Walraven/D van Marum 6-3 6-3
5–9 Apr	Florida Open	CS1	D Hall d. K Schrameyer 6-3 6-3 D Di Toro d. M Smit 6-7 6-2 7-5 N Taylor d. C Studwell 6-4 6-7 6-2	S Douglas/M Legner d. D Hall/D Johnson 5-7 6-3 6-2 E Vergeer/S Peters d. D Di Toro/M Smit 6-1 1-6 7-6 B Barten/D Jordan d. S Everett/N Taylor 6-3 7-5
11–16 Apr	Croatia Open	CS4	R Ammerlaan d. M Legner 6-2 6-4	M Legner/M Brychta d. R Ammerlaan/T Nijhoff 6-3 7-6
11–15 Apr	Chilean Open	CS4	R Molier d. L Majdi 6-3 6-3	R Molier/P Bonnet d. S Hatt/B Dockerill 6-4 6-3
17–20 Apr	Argentinian Open	CS4	R Molier d. P Bonnet 6-4 6-2	R Molier/P Bonnet d. S Hatt/S Wood 6-3 6-4
21–24 Apr	Uruguay Open	CS3	R Molier d. B Dockerill 6-1 6-0	R Molier/P Bonnet d. B Dockerill/S Hatt 6-4 6-1
26–30 Apr	Brasilia Open	CS4	R Molier d. O Diaz 6-1 6-1	
27–30 Apr	Kobe Open	CS2	R Ammerlaan d. E Stuurman 6-2 6-2 S Walraven d. D van Marum 6-1 7-6	R Ammerlaan/E Stuurman d. S Saida/A Yamakura 6-0 6-0 S Walraven/D van Marum d. Y Chokyu/R Techamaneewat 6-2 6-1
27–30 Apr	Cajun Classic	CS2	S Welch d. D Johnson 6-3 6-3 S Peters d. B Ameryckx 7-5 5-7 6-4 C Studwell d. R Sanders 5-7 6-0 6-2	D Johnson/R Snow d. D Bolton/M Foulks 6-0 6-1 K Korb/P Rollinson d. B Ameryckx/P Rollinson 6-7 6-3 6-3
3–7 May	Polish Open	CS3	K Schrameyer d. M Legner 6-4 6-2 J McMorran d. B Ameryckx 6-4 6-3	K Schrameyer/T Kruszelnicki d. M Legner/P Jaroszewski 6-3 6-2 J McMorran/C Otterbach d. B Ameryckx/C Seyen 6-2 6-7 6-3
10–14 May	Slovakia Open	CS3	T Kruszelnicki d. M Legner 1-6 6-3 6-1	R Ammerlaan/M Legner d. L Shevchick/T Kruszelnicki 6-2 6-4
11–14 May	USTA National Outdoor Champs	CS2	S Welch d. D Johnson 6-3 6-2 S Peters d. B Ameryckx 7-6 6-1	S Welch/S Douglas d. D Johnson/J Mistry 6-2 6-7 6-4 S Walraven/D van Marum d. Y Chokyu/H Simard 7-6 6-3

Dates	Tournament	Grade	Singles C Studwell d. R Sanders 6-1 3-6 6-4	Doubles
17-21 May	Czech Open	CS2	R Ammerlaan d. R Molier 7-5 4-6 6-3 S Walraven d. P Sax-Scharf 6-1 6-2	M Brychta/T Kruszelnicki d. R Ammerlaan/E Stuurman 7-6 6-1
18-21 May	Gateway Classic	CS2	S Welch d. D Johnson 6-3 6-0 S Peters d. D van Marum 7-6 6-1	S Douglas/S Welch d. D Johnson/D Lachman 7-5 6-2 S Peters/D van Marum d. B Ameryckx/C Seyen 6-3 6-1
18-21 May	Thailand Open	CS4	C Studwell d. N Taylor 6-7 6-4 7-5 D Hall d. S Hatt 6-2 6-3	R Sanders/C Studwell d. S Everett/N Taylor 6-1 6-1 P Bonnet/S Hatt d. D Hall/J Yodyangdeang 6-3 6-1
24-28 May	Japan Open	CS1	S Khunthasit d. B Pupovac 6-3 6-1 D Hall d. L Giammartini 6-3 6-4 D Di Toro d. M Smit 6-3 7-6 M Eccleston d. N Tachibana 6-2 6-3	S Khunthasit/R Nongnuch d. Y Hong/M Hwang 6-3 6-4 D Hall/L Giammartini d. S Saida/A Yamakura 6-1 6-2 D Di Toro/M Smit d. K Kitamoto/C Ohmae 6-2 6-1 M Eccleston/R Humphreys d. N Tachibana/M Takashima 6-4 6-2
30 May-4 Jun	Lakeshore Foundation World Challenge	CS2	S Welch d. D Johnson 6-4 6-4 E Vergeer d. S Peters 4-6 6-1 6-1 R Draney d. C Studwell 6-4 6-0	D Hall/D Johnson d. S Welch/S Douglas 6-0 4-6 6-3 E Vergeer/S Peters d. M Smit/S Walraven 6-4 3-6 7-6 R Sanders/C Studwell d. D Jordan/N Taylor 6-3 6-2
31 May-3 Jun	Taegu Open	CS3	I Yoshida d. R Weisang 7-5 4-6 6-3 C Ohame d. M Hwang 6-3 6-7 7-5	S Saida/I Yoshida d. S Hatt/S Wood 6-2 6-4
1-4 Jun	Sardinia Open	CS4	M Legner d. K Schrameyer 7-5 ret	G Vos/M Brychta d. K Schrameyer/A Corradi 7-5 6-4
5-9 Jun	Korea Open	CS4	S Saida d. S Hatt 6-2 6-3	S Saida/I Yoshida d. S Hatt/S Wood 6-0 6-1
6-9 June	Israel Open	CS3	S Khunthasit d. M Hwang 6-1 6-2 J Mistry d. S Biron 6-4 6-7 6-3 K Dell d. A Racineux 6-2 6-2	N Naor/E Sartov d. S Biron/P Bonnet 6-2 5-7 6-2 K Dell/J McMorran d. F Birra/A Racineux 1-6 6-4 6-2
8-11 Jun	Eastern Regional Champs	CS3	A Weinberg d. S Weinberg 7-5 7-6 D Johnson d. R Snow 7-6 6-2 K Korb d. B Arnolt 6-1 6-2 M Dispaltro d. P Herath 6-2 7-6	D Johnson/J Johnston d. T Nijhoff/B Dockerill 7-5 4-6 6-0
8-11 Jun	Carinthian Open	CS4	M Legner d. M Brychta 6-1 6-2	M Legner/M Brychta d. H Pfunder/T Mossier 6-1 6-0
9-12 Jun	Hamburg Open	CS4	T Purschke d. E Ruitenberg 1-6 6-2 6-3	P Jaroszewski/G Vos d. E Ruitenberg/C Desgroux 6-1 6-3
14-18 Jun	Catalonia Open	CS4	C Otterbach d. B Siegers 6-2 6-1 S Welch d. S Biron 6-1 6-0	S Welch/C Gross d. P Bonnet/L Majdi 6-2 3-6 6-2
15-18 Jun	Far-west Regional Champs	CS2	A Racineux d. B Klave 2-6 7-6 6-1 T Nijhoff d. P Johnson 6-3 6-4 S Walraven d. D van Marum 7-6 4-6 7-5 B Barten d. R Humphreys 6-4 6-3	P Johnson/D Lachman 6-4 7-5 6-3 S Walraven/D van Marum d. Y Chokyu/S Peters 6-4 6-3 R Draney/R Humphreys d. S Everett/B Barten 6-3 6-4
15-18 Jun	Birrhard Open	CS4	M Legner d. T Purschke 6-1 6-2 K Dell d. C Otterbach 6-4 6-3	M Legner/T Purschke d. G Nespethal/M Gatelli 6-1 6-2
19-15 Jun	Spanish Open	CS3	L Farkas d. P Bonnet 7-6 5-7 6-3 A Racineux d. L Ochoa 6-4 6-1 A Rousset d. P Sappino 6-2 6-1	L Farkas/C Tresch d. P Bonnet/L Madji 6-2 3-6 6-2 F Birra/A Racineux d. B Klave/M van Dongen 6-7 6-0 6-2

Dates	Tournament	Grade	Singles	Doubles
21–25 Jun	Dornbirn Cup	CS2	R Molier d. R Ammerlaan 6-2 6-1	G Vos/R Molier d. M Legner/T Kruszelnicki 4-6 6-1 6-3
21–25 Jun	Canadian Open	CS3	S Peters d S Walraven 6-2 6-7 6-3 D Johnson d. P Johnson 6-0 6-1 H Simard d. Y Chokyu 6-4 6-2 K Whalen d. S Hunter 6-4 6-2	S Peters/S Walraven d. C Seyen/B Ameryckx 6-3 6-3 M Pruitt/T Nijhoff d. D Johnson/A Bonaccurso 6-3 7-6
27 Jun–2 Jul	Belgian Open	CS1	K Schrameyer d. R Molier 6-4 7-6 E Vergeer d. S Walraven 6-4 6-1 G Polidori d. R Humphreys 6-4 6-0	D Hall/D Johnson d. T Kruszelnicki/M Legner 7-6 6-4 S Peters/E Vergeer d. M Smit/S Walraven 6-4 4-6 6-3 R Ammerlaan/P Hermans d. I Yoshida/S Saida 6-1 7-5
29 Jun–2 Jul	Kiwanis Amsterdam Open	CS4	R Ammerlaan d. S Saida 7-5 6-3	R Draney/B van Erp d. M Eccelston/R Humphreys 6-1 6-4
30 Jun–3 Jul	Capital City Classic	CS4	P Johnson d. B Dockerill 6-4 6-4	B Dockerill/K Plowman d. B Butler/M Larose 6-0 6-0
4–9 Jul	Dutch Open	CS1	S Welch d. R Molier 6-3 4-6 6-2 E Vergeer d. D Di Toro 6-4 6-4	J Mistry/M Legner d. R Molier/T Nijhoff 6-2 6-4 D Di Toro/M Smit d. S Peters/E Vergeer 6-3 6-0 M Eccelston/R Humphreys d. B van Erp/M Van Den Heuvel 6-2 6-3
12–16 Jul	French Open	CS1	M Eccelston d. N Tachibana 1-6 6-3 6-2 R Molier d. K Schrameyer 6-1 6-4 D Di Toro d. E Vergeer 6-4 3-6 7-6 C Studwell d. A Rousset 6-1 6-7 6-3	D Hall/D Johnson d. M Legner/K Schrameyer 7-5 6-1 D Di Toro/M Smit d. S Vergeer/S Peters 2-6 6-4 6-3 R Sanders/C Studwell d. A Blanchard/N Taylor 6-1 6-1
25–30 Jul	British Open	SS	R Molier d. D Hall 6-3 1-6 7-6 S Peters d. E Vergeer 5-7 6-1 6-0 R Draney d. C Studwell 6-2 6-4	D Hall/D Johnson d. R Ammerlaan/J Mistry 6-4 6-2 D Di Toro/M Smit d. S Peters/E Vergeer 6-3 6-1 N Taylor/K Whalen d. B van Erp/P Norfolk 5-7 6-3 6-0
2–6 Aug	Austrian Open	CS1	D Hall d. S Welch 3-6 6-3 6-2 M Smit d. S Walraven 6-3 5-7 7-6	D Hall/D Johnson d. L Giammartini/R Molier 6-3 6-4 M Smit/S Walraven d. B Ameryckx/B Arnolt 6-4 6-1
4–7 Aug	Japan Cup	CS3	S Saida d. N Sugamura 6-2 6-2 S Khanthasit d. C Ohmae 6-3 7-6	S Saida/A Yamakura d. N Sugamura/I Yoshida 6-4 6-1 S Khunthasit/N Chinpraus 6-4 6-2 N Tachibana/M Takashima d. R Kakinokihara/H Ohashi 6-4 6-4
8–13 Aug	Swiss Open	CS1	N Tachibana d. M Takashima 6-3 6-2 D Hall d. S Welch 6-2 3-6 6-4 M Smit d. S Walraven 6-1 6-0	L Giammartini/R Molier d. J Mistry/S Welch 6-2 1-6 6-4 M Smit/S Walraven d. K Dell/A Maas 6-3 7-5 R Humphreys/M Eccleston 3-2 w/o
11–3 Aug	Midwest Regional Champs	CS4	A Rousset d. M Eccleston 7-6 6-2 E Ruitenberg d. D Lachman 6-4 6-3 S Clark d. P Rollinson 6-3 6-1	D Lachman/M Weise d. F Peter/E Ruitenberg 6-3 6-4
10–13 Aug	Antwerp Open	CS4	C Studwell d. B Barten 6-0 6-1 R Ammerlaan d. E Stuurman 6-2 6-1	R Ammerlaan/P Hermans d. P Jaroszewski/R Weisang 6-3 7-5 H Lewellen/D van Marum d. B Ameryckx/C Seyen 6-1 7-5
17–20 Aug	Sunrise Medical Open	CS4	B Ameryckx d. B Klave 6-3 1-6 6-1 S Welch d. K Schrameyer 7-6 6-4	K Schrameyer/M Legner d. S Welch/R Snow w/o B Ameryckx/H Lewellen d. K Erath/I Mueller 6-3 3-6 6-0
23–27 Aug	German Open	CS2	B Ameryckx d. H Lewellen 4-6 6-3 7-5 K Schrameyer d. M Legner 6-4 4-6 6-4	M Legner/K Schrameyer d. M Brychta/P Jaroszewski 7-5 6-2 B Klave/H Lewellen d. A Maas/A Racineux 5-7 7-5 7-5
29 Aug–3 Sep	Citta di Livorno	CS2	A Maas d. B Ameryckx 7-6 6-2 M Legner d. K Schrameyer 3-6 7-6 7-6 S Walraven d. K Dell 6-2 6-3	M Legner/K Schrameyer d. J Mistry/P Wikstrom 6-2 6-1 S Walraven/K Dell d. A Racineux/F Birra 6-3 7-6

Dates	Tournament	Grade	C Lev d. G Polidori 7-5 6-4 Singles	Doubles
4–9 Sep	Italian Open	CS3	K Schrameyer d. M Legner 6-3 6-1	M Legner/K Schrameyer d. L Giammartini/E Stuurman 2-6 6-1 6-0
7–10 Sep	Southwest Regional Champs	CS2	S Walraven d. K Dell 4-6 6-1 6-1 S Welch d. D Johnson 6-1 3-6 6-2	S Walraven/K Dell d. F Birra/A Racineux 2-6 6-0 6-2 S Welch/S Douglas d. D Johnson/R Snow 6-4 7-5
12–16 Sep	Jesolo Euro Beach Cup	CS4	B Pupovac d. Y Chokyu 6-1 6-3 K Schrameyer d. L Giammartini 5-7 6-2 6-2 L Giammartini/P Jaroszewski 6-4 6-2	Y Chokyu/P Rollinson d. B Pupovac/B Arnolt 6-2 6-2
14–17 Sep	Salzburg Open	CS4	M Legner d. M Brychta 6-0 6-3	M Legner/M Brychta d. R Weisang/T Purschke 6-0 6-2
17–19 Sep	ROHO/USPTR Champs	CS3	S Welch d. D Johnson 6-4 6-1 J McMorran d. K Korb 6-4 6-2	S Douglas/S Welch d. D Johnson/R Snow 7-6 3-6 6-3
15–17 Sep	Tahoe Donner Intl Champs	CS3	D Lachman d. M Pruit 6-4 4-6 6-2 P Rollinson d. D Esrey 6-1 6-1 B Barten d. S Hunter 6-4 6-3	D Johnson/D Lachman d. D Weise/M Baldwin 6-4 6-3 S Hunter/B McPhate 4-6 7-5 7-6
19–24 Sep	Austrian Indoors	CS3	M Legner d. K Schrameyer 4-6 6-3 6-2	M Legner/K Schrameyer d. L Giammartini/R Weisang 6-1 6-3
25 Sep–1 Oct	US Open	SS	D Hall d. R Molier 7-6 6-2 E Vergeer d. D Di Toro 6-1 6-2 N Taylor d. C Studwell 6-0 4-6 7-6	R Ammerlaan/R Molier d. D Hall/D Johnson 6-3 6-2 M Smit/E Vergeer d. N Kawashima/C Ohmae 6-1 6-3 R Draney/B Poppen d. N Tachibana/M Takashima 6-3 6-2
20–28 Oct	Paralympic Games	CS2	D Hall d. S Welch 6-7 6-4 6-2 E Vergeer d. S Walraven 6-0 6-4	R Ammerlaan/R Molier d. D Hall/D Johnson 6-3 5-7 6-1 E Vergeer/S Walraven d. D Di Toro/B Pupovac 7-6 6-2
8–12 Nov	Nottingham Indoor	CS4	J Mistry d. P Hermans 6-2 6-3 J McMorran d. B Klave 6-0 6-2	J Mistry/P Hermans d. B Dockerill/S Hatt 6-4 6-3 B Klave/J McMorran d. C. Blackmore/K van Boven 6-0 6-1
9–12 Nov	Prague Cup Czech Indoor	CS3	M Legner d. L Giammartini 6-4 3-6 6-4	M Legner/L Giammartini d. T Nijhoff/M Brychta 6-4 7-5
9–12 Nov	Peace Cup	CS4	S Saida d. H Nakano 6-3 6-1 Y Chokyu d. K Kitamoto 6-3 6-3	Y Watanbe/I Yoshida d. K Katou/K Takeuchi 6-2 1-6 6-4 Y Chokyu/C Ohmae d. M Yakushi/M Yaosa 6-1 6-0
14–19 Nov	NEC Wheelchair Tennis Masters	CS1	R Ammerlaan d. R Molier 7-6 6-1 E Vergeer d. D van Marum 6-1 6-3	R Molier/S Welch d. R Ammerlaan/E Stuurman 6-3 6-1 D Di Toro/M Smit d. S Peters/E Vergeer 6-4 6-4
14–19 Nov	Doubles Masters	CS2		

Double Tops in ITF Junior World Champion Race

Jackie Nesbitt

A great year for South American tennis ended when Argentina's Maria Emilia Salerni became the first girl, for a decade, to claim both singles and doubles crowns. There was another double achieved by Lee Childs and James Nelson, who jointly claimed the boys doubles crown, when USA's Andy Roddick, the only player with a possibility of catching the Britons at the year end, declared himself satisfied with succeeding Denmark's Kristian Pless as boys singles' champion.

As a double champion, Salerni deserves top billing. Indeed 2000 proved to be a special year for the 17-year-old, who had led her country to victory in the prestigious NEC World Youth Cup in 1999. Not only did she claim two world junior titles, but as the junior ranking leader she received a wild card from the ITF to compete in the Sydney Olympic Games.

The early year tournaments proved something of a slow start for Maria Emilia as she reached the final in Argentina, but surprisingly lost to compatriot Gisela Dulko. Another final in Paraguay brought another disappointment, this time at the hands of title contender Renata Voracova, who herself was to finish the year in 4th spot overall.

A first Group A title finally came her way, however, in Brazil, where Maria Emilia defeated both Voracova and Lenka Dlhopolcova to claim the Banana Bowl title. The next Group A title proved frustratingly elusive as the Argentine reached the finals of both the Italian and French Opens, only to suffer narrow defeats at the hands of Ioana Gaspar and Virginie Razzano respectively.

The wait was worth it though, as the all-court adaptability of the Argentine gave her another chance at Wimbledon, where she defeated her biggest rival, Aniko Kapros, Gaspar and Tatiana Perebiynis, to win the girls' singles event. Although Kapros was to keep the title chase alive with a win over Salerni in the Canadian Open Final, the Argentine was relentless in her pursuit of the crown. She bounced back in some style at the US Open, where her win not only gave her three Group A titles, but also an unassailable lead at the top of the girls' singles ranking list.

Kapros, the Australian and Canadian Open champion, had to settle for 2nd place overall, but looks to be an outstanding prospect for 2001. Another player, who looks to have a bright future is Kaia Kanepi – third in the overall rankings. The Estonian had no fewer than six tournament wins in Europe, but did not manage to show her best in the majors. Glimpses of her potential, however, were clear to see by the year-end as she helped her country to the final of the ITF Connolly Continental Cup and reached the semi-finals of the Orange Bowl.

Just behind Kanepi in the rankings lies Voracova. The Czech also appeared to be coming into her best form in time for the new season, with wins at the Group A Super Junior Championships in Japan and the Group 1 Eddie Herr Tournament securing her a top five finish. Despite reaching the finals of both Wimbledon and the US Open, a Group A title eluded fifth placed Tatiana Perebiynis.

The boys' singles race was also packed with quality players and earned the eventual champion, Andy Roddick, a call-up to the US Davis Cup squad. The USTA reaped the benefits when Andy, already confirmed as world singles champion, led his team to the ITF Sunshine Cup title in December.

The year got off to the best possible start for Andy, when he defeated great rivals, Todor Enev, Joachim Johansson and Mario Ancic to clinch the Australian Open title. A second Group A title quickly followed at the Banana Bowl and although the summer was disappointing – defeat at the French Open by eventual champion Paul-Henri Mathieu and an injury hit Wimbledon – Andy gained his greatest wish when he won his home title – the US Open.

Bulgaria's Todor Enev, a member of the ITF Touring Team, repaid his selectors with a second place showing in the ranking lists. Indeed his exploits might on another occasion have had him striving for top spot, with wins at the Japan and Italian Opens and the Orange Bowl. Third placed Johansson will enjoy his Group A win in Japan, but was unable to produce his best at the other majors.

After a spectacular year, Andy Roddick of the United States became the undisputed World No. 1 junior. (Paul Zimmer)

Victory at the Australian Open was the prelude to a great year for Hungary's Aniko Kapros, who ended the year ranked No. 2 in singles and doubles. (Stephen Wake)

Mario Ancic, the runner-up in Australia, took the prestigious pre-Wimbledon title at Roehampton and looked to be on course for the title at the main event. Unfortunately for the young Croatian, the big summer titles belonged to the French, as Nicolas Mahut followed up compatriot Mathieu's win in Paris with a stunning performance at the All England Club to dash Ancic's title aspirations and clinch a deserving top finish for himself.

In doubles, Salerni, dominated the South American circuit, collecting titles in Argentina, Paraguay and Brazil. Although somewhat unexpectedly defeated in the Wimbledon final, where she and reigning world girls' doubles champion, Daniela Bedanova, lost to Gaspar and Perebiynis, Salerni, partnered by Gisela Dulko, bounced back to win again at the US Open.

Kapros also had a stunning doubles campaign, winning at the Australian Open, the Canadian Open and the Orange Bowl. Her loss to Salerni in the US Open final, however, proved costly in more ways than one.

Despite losing with Kapros in the final of the US Open, Australia's Christina Wheeler, had an otherwise terrific year in doubles, winning the Canadian Open, Astrid Bowl and Sugar Bowl titles. The highlight will no doubt remain the early year win, again in tandem with Kapros, at the Australian Open. Wimbledon and Italian Open champions, Gaspar and Perebiynis, deservingly finished respectively 4th and 5th.

Roddick had a mathematical chance to overhaul Childs and Nelson in the doubles rankings going into the year-end US circuit, but would readily acknowledge that the joint Banana Bowl, European Closed and US Open champions were the more appropriate winners.

Congratulations, too, to the Mexican pairing of Bruno Echagaray and Santiago Gonzalez who combined to win eight titles during the year, the most satisfying of which came at the last – their win at the Orange Bowl giving them a major title to finish the year.

ITF JUNIOR WORLD RANKINGS 2000 – POINTS EXPLANATION

The ITF Junior Circuit is a worldwide points-linked circuit of 195 tournaments, including six regional championships and four team competitions in 95 countries, under the management of the International Tennis Federation. There are eleven separate points categories covering the three types of events. There is no limit to the number of tournaments in which a player may compete each year. The best six results from tournaments (Groups A and 1–5), regional championships (Groups B1–B3) and team competitions (Group C) count towards a player's ranking. To qualify for a final year-end ranking a player must have competed in at least six events, including at least three Group A tournaments and at least three outside his or her own country.

TOURNAMENTS & REGIONAL CHAMPIONSHIPS

Singles

	A	1	2	3	4	5	B1	B2	B3
Winner	250	150	100	60	40	30	180	120	80
Runner-up	180	100	75	45	30	20	120	80	50
Semi-Finalist	120	80	50	30	20	15	80	60	30
Quarter-Finalists	80	60	30	20	15	10	60	40	15
Losers in last 16	50	30	20	15	10	5	30	25	5
Losers in last 32	30	20	–	–	–	–	20	10	–

Doubles

	A	1	2	3	4	5	B1	B2	B3
Winners	180	100	75	50	30	20	120	80	50
Runners-up	120	75	50	30	20	15	80	60	30
Semi-Finalists	80	50	30	20	15	10	60	40	15
Quarter-Finalists	50	30	20	15	10	5	30	25	5
Losers in last 16	30	20	–	–	–	–	20	10	–

Group A Super Series bonus points

	Singles	Doubles
Winner of three or more Group A events	200	180

Group C – Team Competitions – Regional Qualifying

	No. 1 Singles Player Win	No. 2 Singles Player Win	Doubles Win Each Player
Final	80	60	60
Semi-Final	60	40	40
Quarter-Final	40	20	20

Group C – Team Competitions – Final

	No. 1 Singles Player Win	No. 2 Singles Player Win	Doubles Win Each Player
Final	180	120	120
Semi-Final	120	80	80
Quarter-Final	80	60	60

ITF JUNIOR WORLD RANKINGS 2000

Only those players who qualified for a year-end ranking are listed. The minimum requirements for this were having played six events, three of which were outside the player's own country and three of which were group A status.

Boys' Singles

1	Andrew Roddick	USA
2	Todor Enev	BUL
3	Joachim Johansson	SWE
4	Mario Ancic	CRO
5	Nicolas Mahut	FRA
6	Ytai Abougzir	USA
7	Roman Valent	SUI
8	Yen-Hsun Lu	TPE
9	Adrian Cruciat	ROM
10	Bruno Soares	BRA
11	Janko Tipsarevic	YUG
12	Andriy Dernovskyy	UKR
13	Alejandro Falla Ramirez	COL
14	Robby Ginepri	USA
15	Michael Lammer	SUI
16	Simon Stadler	GER
17	Michal Kokta	CZE
18	Cristian Villagran	ARG
19	Yeu-Tzuoo Wang	TPE
20	Stefan Weispeiner	AUT

Girls' Singles

1	Maria Emilia Salerni	ARG
2	Aniko Kapros	HUN
3	Kaia Kanepi	EST
4	Renata Voracova	CZE
5	Tatiana Perebiynis	UKR
6	Ioana Gaspar	ROM
7	Edina Gallovits	ROM
8	Vera Zvonareva	RUS
9	Lenka Dlhopolcova	SVK
10	Eva Birnerova	CZE
11	Jelena Jankovic	YUG
12	Gisela Dulko	ARG
13	Ashley Harkleroad	USA
14	Matea Mezak	CRO
15	Claudine Schaul	LUX
16	Yuliya Beygelzimer	UKR
17	Marie-Eve Pelletier	CAN
18	Alyssa Cohan	USA
19	Sunitha Rao	USA
20	Melissa Dowse	AUS

Boys' Doubles

1=	Lee Childs	GBR
1=	James Nelson	GBR
3	Andrew Roddick	USA
4	Bruno Echagaray	MEX
5	Santiago Gonzalez	MEX
6	Tres Davis	USA
7	Darko Madarovski	YUG
8	Janko Tipsarevic	YUG
9	Michal Kokta	CZE
10	Adam Kennedy	AUS
11	Todor Enev	BUL
12	Todd Reid	AUS
13	Raven Klaasen	RSA
14	Bruno Soares	BRA
15	Hiroki Kondo	JPN
16	Yen-Hsun Lu	TPE
17	Karol Beck	SVK
18	Philip Gubenco	CAN
19	Yeu-Tzuoo Wang	TPE
20	Julien Cassaigne	FRA

Girls' Doubles

1	Maria Emilia Salerni	ARG
2	Aniko Kapros	HUN
3	Christina Wheeler	AUS
4	Ioana Gaspar	ROM
5	Tatiana Perebiynis	UKR
6	Gisela Dulko	ARG
7	Renata Voracova	CZE
8	Melissa Torres	MEX
9	Dinara Safina	RUS
10	Kumiko Iijima	JPN
11	Bethanie Mattek	USA
12	Yuki Arai	JPN
13	Petra Cetkovska	CZE
14	Samantha Stosur	AUS
15	Neyssa Etienne	HAI
16	Maria Jose Lopez	MEX
17	Galina Voskoboeva	RUS
18	Su-Wei Hsieh	TPE
19	Angelique Widjaja	INA
20	Eva Birnerova	CZE

2000 ITF JUNIOR WORLD RANKING RESULTS

Date	Tournament	Grade	Boys' singles final	Girls' singles final
27 Dec–2 Jan	Mexico	1	A. Cruciat (ROM) d. D. Madarovski (YUG) 7-6(4) 6-4	A. Cargill (USA) d. M. Mezak (CRO) 6-2 6-4
3–8 Jan	Costa Rica	1	J. Maigret (FRA) d. J. Tipsarevic (YUG) 6-3 3-6 7-5	M. Mezak (CRO) d. G. Mortello (ITA) 6-3 7-6
4–8 Jan	Nigeria	5	K. Loglo (TOG) d. D. Khumalo (ZIM) 6-3 6-1	K. Berthe (SEN) d. A. Mohammed (GHA) 6-2 6-4
5–9 Jan	Sweden	4	R. Soderling (SWE) d. P. Lobanov (RUS) 6-2 6-4	K. Kanepi (EST) d. K. Petersson (SWE) 6-1 6-0
7–12 Jan	Australia	2	J. Johansson (SWE) d. T. Enev (BUL) 6-2 7-5	J. Hewitt (AUS) d. M-E. Pelletier (CAN) 6-4 3-6 6-4
10–14 Jan	Togo	5	K. Loglo (TOG) d. A. Segodo (BEN) 1-6 7-5 6-3	K. Berthe (SEN) d. A. Mohammed (GHA) 6-3 6-3
10–16 Jan	Sweden	4	R. Soderling (SWE) d. M. Smith (GBR) 6-0 3-6 6-3	S. Arvidsson (SWE) d. K. Kanepi (EST) 6-3 6-1
10–16 Jan	Colombia	1	Y. Abougzir (USA) d. A. Matijevic (CRO) 6-1 6-1	E. Birnerova (CZE) d. R. Jukovkan (YUG) 6-1 1-6 6-4
16–20 Jan	Ghana	4	A. Segodo (BEN) d. K. Loglo (TOG) 6-3 6-2	A. Mohammed (GHA) d. S. Panford (GHA) 6-1 6-4
16–22 Jan	Australia	4	T. Robredo (ESP) d. A. Roddick (USA) 6-3 7-6(1)	M. Martinez (ESP) d. B. Mattek (SVK) 6-0 6-1
17–22 Jan	Austria	5	M. Mirnegg (AUT) d. A. Dernovsky (UKR) 3-6 7-5 6-4	D. Casanova (SUI) d. S. Klemenschits (AUT) 6-1 6-1
17–23 Jan	Ecuador	2	A. Falla (COL) d. H. Kondo (JPN) 3-6 6-2 6-3	E. Birnerova (CZE) d. M. Cueva (ECU) 6-3 2-6 6-4
17–23 Jan	Sri Lanka	4	S. Kumar (IND) d. A. Singh (IND) 7-5 6-2	N. Chandrasekar (IND) d. S. Mirza (IND) 6-1 6-4
24–30 Jan	**Australian Open**	**A**	**A. Roddick (USA) d. M. Ancic (CRO) 7-6(2) 6-3**	**A. Kapros (HUN) d. M.J. Martinez (ESP) 6-2 3-6 6-2**
24–30 Jan	Slovakia	2	A. Cruciat (ROM) d. R. Valent (SUI) 7-6(0) 7-5	D. Nociarova (SVK) d. P. Slitrova (CZE) 3-6 7-5 6-3
24–30 Jan	Peru	2	A. Falla (COL) d. P. Rusevski (MKD) 6-3 6-1	M. Schneider (POL) d. R. Ljukovcan (YUG) 2-6 6-4 6-4
24–29 Jan	India	4	S. Kumar (IND) d. P. Chaturvedi (IND) 7-5 6-1	S. Peng (CHN) d. Y.Z. Xie (CHN) 6-1 6-4
29 Jan–6 Feb	Czech Republic	4	R. Valent (SUI) d. D. Coene (BEL) 6-2 2-0 ret	E. Janaskova (CZE) d. P. Slitrova (CZE) 6-2 6-4
29 Jan–6 Feb	India	4	H. Sofyan (ARM) d. R. Luchici (ROM) 6-2 6-3	S. Peng (CHN) d. R. Tulpule (IND) 6-1 4-6 6-2
29 Jan–6 Feb	Bolivia	3	J. Silva (POR) d. K. Mitrovski (MKD) 3-6 6-3 3-2 ret	M. Schneider (POL) d. I. Collischonn (GER) 6-4 6-0
5–12 Feb	India	5	A. Sofian (ARM) d. V. Sewa (IND) 6-1 6-1	S. Peng (CHN) d. R. Tulpule (IND) 7-5 6-3
7–13 Feb	Chile	5	M. A. Lopez (BRA) d. S. Weispeiner (AUT) 5-7 6-4 6-3	Z. Reyes (MEX) d. G. Dulko (ARG) 3-6 7-5 7-6(5)
7–13 Feb	New Zealand	5	S. Rea (NZL) d. D. Mulhane (NZL) 2-6 6-0 6-3	T. O'Connor (NZL) d. A. Burns (AUS) 6-0 6-3
9–13 Feb	Great Britain	2	K. Vliegen (BEL) d. R. Thys (BEL) 6-4 4-6 6-4	T. Perebiynis (UKR) d. C. Maes (BEL) 6-4 6-1
14–19 Feb	Bangladesh	4	S. Kumar (IND) d. H. Sofian (ARM) 6-3 6-4	E. Janaskova (CZE) d. Z. Zemenova (SVK) 6-4 6-1
14–20 Feb	Czech Republic	5	D. Karol (CZE) d. M. Otava (CZE) 6-2 6-3	G. Dulko (ARG) d. M.E. Salerni (ARG) 3-6 6-2 6-4
14–20 Feb	Argentina	2	C. Villagran (ARG) d. R. Lukaev (BUL) 6-7(3) 6-3 6-2	K. Coetzee (RSA) d. R. Tulpule (IND) 6-3 6-2
20–26 Feb	Bangladesh	3	S. Timu (CAN) d. S. Mishra (IND) 7-6(4) 7-5	C. Scheepers (RSA) d. S-W. Hsieh (TPE) 6-4 6-1
20–26 Feb	Finland	4	J. Holmia (FIN) d. M. Axen (SWE) 6-0 6-3	H. Norfeldt (SWE) d. O. Karyshakova (RUS) 7-5 4-6 7-6(10)
20–28 Feb	Uruguay	2	B. Soares (BRA) d. A. Falla (COL) 7-6(5) 6-3	M. Schneider (POL) d. J. Sakowicz (POL) 5-7 6-0 6-1
22–27 Feb	Germany	2	D. Vlassov (RUS) d. M. Kokta (CZE) 7-6 1-6 6-3	K. Kanepi (EST) d. C. Schaul (LUX) 6-4 6-3
28 Feb–3 Mar	Brunei	4	C. Kwon (USA) d. D. Doskarayev (KAZ) 6-3 6-4	S-W. Hsieh (TPE) d. C. Scheepers (RSA) 6-3 6-4
28 Feb–3 Mar	Norway	5	F. Mayer (GER) d. S. Linda (GER) 6-3 4-6 6-3	S. Arvidsson (SWE) d. R. Gourevitch (RUS) 6-4 6-4
28 Feb–5 Mar	Paraguay	1	T. Alves (BRA) d. J. Hernandez (MEX) 6-4 6-2	R. Voracova (CZE) d. M.E. Salerni (ARG) 1-6 6-2 6-1
4–10 Mar	Sweden	5	R. Soderling (SWE) d. J. Berg (SWE) 7-6 ret	S. Arvidsson (SWE) d. H. Norfeldt (SWE) 6-1 6-4
4–11 Mar	El Salvador	5	D. Hoskins (USA) d. E. Martinez (MEX) 4-6 6-4 6-2	B. Ko (CAN) d. G. Charron (CAN) 7-5 6-1

Date	Tournament	Grade	Boys' singles final	Girls' singles final
4-12 Mar	Banana Bowl, Brazil	A	A. Roddick (USA) d. J. Johansson (SWE) 6-2 3-6 7-6(3)	M.E. Salerni (ARG) d. L. Dlhopolcova (SVK) 6-0 6-7(2) 6-1
5-12 Mar	Indonesia	3	Y-T. Wang (TPE) d. L. Kubot (POL) 6-4 4-6 6-2	A. Widjaja (INA) d. D. Sumantri (INA) 4-6 6-4 6-2
11-17 Mar	Algeria	5	L. Ouahab (ALG) d. R. Chaki (MAR) 7-5 6-0	M. Bartoli (FRA) d. F. Esseghir (ALG) 6-2 2-1
11-19 Mar	Russia	5	D. Sitak (RUS) d. A. Pavlioutchenkov (RUS) 2-6 6-3 6-3	A. Bastrikova (RUS) d. A. Kostikova (RUS) 6-4 4-6 7-5
11-19 Mar	Brazil	3	C. Villagran (ARG) d. T. Alves (BRA) 6-1 6-4	T. Nemeth (HUN) d. G. Dulko (ARG) 6-1 6-1
13-18 Mar	Costa Rica	5	M. Tutter (CZE) d. J. Stokke (USA) 6-2 6-3	A. Wei (USA) d. M. Arroyo (MEX) 6-1 1-6 6-0
13-19 Mar	Malaysia	5	Y-T. Wang (TPE) d. C. Jacobs (RSA) 6-4 6-1	D. Sumantri (INA) d. A. Takeuchi (JPN) 6-1 2-6 6-2
18-26 Mar	Venezuela	1	D. Munoz (ESP) d. A. Falla (COL) 6-7(1) 6-3 7-6(4)	A. Cohen (USA) d. L. Dlhopolcova (SVK) 6-4 1-6 6-3
18-26 Mar	Panama	4	M. Tutter (CZE) d. M. Santoso (INA) 6-4 6-2	A. Wei (USA) d. A. Espinosa (PAN) 6-3 6-1
19-26 Mar	Singapore	2	Y-H. Lu (TPE) d. O. Alver (NOR) 6-0 6-3	D. Magas (HUN) d. D. Sumantri (INA) 6-2 7-5
25 Mar-1 Apr	Martinique	2	M. Tutter (CZE) d. B. Aneiros (PAN) 6-2 6-4	B. Burlet (FRA) d. C. Treber (FRA) 6-3 6-1
25 Mar-1 Apr	Uzbekistan	4	P. Ivanov (RUS) d. F. Doudtchik (BLR) 6-4 7-5	A. Bastrikova (RUS) d. R. Gourevitch (RUS) 6-2 6-1
25 Mar-2 Apr	Thailand	2	Y-H. Lu (TPE) d. M. Mirnegg (AUT) 7-6(7) 3-6 6-1	C. Tidemand (NOR) d. R. Tarjan (GER) 6-1 6-7(7) 6-2
27 Mar-2 Apr	Argentina	5	F. Uelstchi (ARG) d. A. Torchia (ARG) 7-5 6-4	M. Tissera (ARG) d. S. Lizana (CHI) 6-4 6-0
1-8 Apr	Uzbekistan	4	P. Ivanov (RUS) d. V. Zhyshkevicz (BLR) 6-3 6-1	A. Bastrikova (RUS) d. L. Biktyakova (UZB) 7-5 6-2
1-9 Apr	France	4	C. Roche (FRA) d. B. Balleret (FRA) 6-2 6-3	C. Schaul (LUX) d. G. Voskoboeva (RUS) 7-5 6-1
2-9 Apr	Ph lippines	2	S. Stadler (GER) d. M. Emery (USA) 6-2 6-0	A. Widjaja (INA) d. N. Kriz (AUS) 6-4 6-4
5-10 Apr	Guadeloupe	5	R. Russell (JAM) v. M. Riddell (USA) not played	B. Burlet (FRA) d. C. Treber (FRA) 6-1 6-4
8-16 Apr	France	3	C. Roche (FRA) d. M. Ali-Cayol (FRA) 6-0 6-1	C. Schaul (LUX) d. S. Kuznetsova (RUS) 7-5 6-3
8-15 Apr	Barbados	5	R. Russell (JAM) d. T. Mayers (TRI) 6-4 5-2	B. Burlet (FRA) d. R. Le Saldo (BAR) 2-6 6-4 6-3
11-15 Apr	South Africa	3	A. Segodo (BEN) d. R. Klaasen (RSA) 7-6(4) 6-3	C. Scheepers (RSA) d. A. Mojzis (RSA) 6-3 3-6 6-4
10-16 Apr	Croatia	3	V. Ionita (ROM) d. A. Cruciat (ROM) 2-6 6-3 7-6(10)	I. Gaspar (ROM) d. C. Maes (BEL) 6-7(4) 7-5 6-1
10-16 Apr	Japan	1	T. Enev (BUL) d. J. Johansson (SWE) 6-4 6-3	J. O'Donoghue (GBR) d. T. O'Connor (NZL) 3-6 6-0 7-5
17-22 Apr	African Closed	B2	A. Segodo (BEN) d. R. Klaasen (RSA) 4-6 6-3 6-4	A. Mojzis (RSA) d. F. Esseghir (ALG) 2-6 6-3 6-4
17-22 Apr	Israel	4	T. Suissa (ISR) d. R. Bloomfield (GBR) 6-0 6-1	C. Bargil (ISR) d. Y. Savransky (ISR) 7-6(5) 6-2
17-23 Apr	Canada	5	A. Korch (CAN) d. B. Kolvek (CAN) 6-2 6-2	D. Srebrovic (CAN) d. D. Bechliwanis (CAN) 7-6(5) 4-6 6-2
17-23 Apr	France	3	C. Roche (FRA) d. A. Pinet (FRA) 6-1 6-1	G. Voskoboeva (RUS) d. M. Bartoli (FRA) 6-2 6-4
18-23 Apr	Paraguay	4	H. Pinto E Silva (BRA) d. H. Mello (BRA) 6-4 6-3	L. Migliarini (URU) d. P. Guerrero (ECU) 7-6(5) 6-4
18-23 Apr	Asian Open	2	S. Stadler (GER) d. B. Gronefeld (GER) 3-6 6-3 6-2	K. Ijima (JPN) d. S. Stosur (AUS) 2-6 6-4 6-4
19-23 Apr	Slovakia	2	K. Beck (SVK) d. S. Wiespeiner (AUT) 6-1 6-3	V. Zvonareva (RUS) d. J. Lindstrom (SWE) 6-2 6-0
19-24 Apr	Italy	4	S. Linda (GER) d. D. Madarovski (YUG) 4-6 6-3 6-4	K. Kanepi (EST) d. R. Vinci (ITA) 7-5 6-0
24-29 Apr	Israel	4	M. Smith (GBR) d. P. Petschner (GER) 6-1 1-6 6-4	C. Bargil (ISR) d. T. Luzhanska (ISR) 6-4 6-3
24-30 Apr	Italy	2	S. Bohli (SUI) d. R. Valent (SUI) 3-6 4-6 4	K. Kanepi (EST) d. V. Nemeth (HUN) 6-3 6-3
25-30 Apr	Chinese Taipei	3	Y-T. Wang (TPE) d. Y-H. Lu (TPE) 6-4 6-2	S-W. Hsieh (TPE) d. K. Iijima (JPN) 6-4 7-5
8-13 May	Italy	2	M. Lammer (SUI) d. R. Valent (SUI) 6-7(3) 6-1 6-3	V. Zvonareva (RUS) d. E. Gallovits (ROM) 6-3 7-6(4)
15-21 May	Italy	1	R. Valent (SUI) d. M. Lammer (SUI) 5-7 6-4 6-2	M-E. Salerni (ARG) d. T. Perebiynis (UKR) 7-5 3-6 6-2
16-21 May	Russia	4	A. Pavlioutchenkov (RUS) d. E. Koleganov (RUS) 4-6 6-3 6-2	O. Lyubtsova (UKR) d. I. Mourachkintseva (RUS) 6-4 5-7 6-2
17-21 May	Austria	2	L. Kubot (POL) d. G. Novak (AUT) 6-4 6-1	J. Lindstrom (SWE) d. C. Schiechtl (AUT) 7-6 6-3

Date	Location		Boys' Singles	Girls' Singles
20–28 May	Italy	A	T. Enev (BUL) d. A. Dernovskyy (UKR) 6-3 6-3	I. Gaspar (ROM) d. M.E. Salerni (ARG) 6-7(4) 6-3 8-6
21–28 May	Russia	5	E. Koleganov (RUS) d. M. Kartachov (RUS) 6-4 6-2	V. Doushevina (RUS) d. M. Yuferova (RUS) 6-0 6-1
29 May–3 Jun	Belgium	1	S. Wauters (BEL) d. K. Vliegen (BEL) 3-6 6-3 6-3	E. Gallovits (ROM) d. I. Gaspar (ROM) 3-6 6-0 3-1 ret
29 May–3 Jun	Estonia	5	V. Zetterholm (SWE) d. A. Tuomi (FIN) 6-4 7-6(6)	M. Ruutel (EST) d. K. Bengtsson (SWE) 6-2 6-4
30 May–3 Jun	Austria	3	M. Zgaga (SLO) d. J. Masik (CZE) 3-6 6-2 6-4	P. Cetkovska (CZE) d. C. Schiechtl (AUT) 6-4 6-3
4–11 Jun	**France**	**A**	**P-H. Mathieu (FRA) d. T. Robredo (ESP) 3-6 7-6(3) 6-2**	**V. Razzano (FRA) d. M.E. Salerni (ARG) 5-7 6-4 8-6**
7–11 Jun	Hungary	3	I. Cerovic (CRO) d. S. Sipaeva (IND) 6-7(6) 6-1 6-3	V. Nemeth (HUN) d. B. Berecz (HUN) 6-2 7-5
7–13 Jun	Kyrghyzstan	5	I. Sazonov (KGZ) d. I. Kovalev (KAZ) 6-4 6-1	I. Israilova (UZB) d. S. Zaharenko (RUS) 6-1 6-1
11–18 Jun	Russia	5	P. Ivanov (RUS) d. V. Davletshine (RUS) 6-7(3) 7-6(1) 6-2	G. Fokina (RUS) d. A. Bastrikova (RUS) 6-1 7-6(7)
12–17 Jun	Germany	2	M. Abel (GER) d. L. Vitullo (ARG) 6-4 6-4	S. Arvidsson (SWE) d. M. Torres (MEX) 4-6 6-1
12–18 Jun	Poland	5	J. Kmita (POL) d. M. Przysiezny (POL) 6-2 6-0	C. Kuleszka (GER) d. Y. Fedak (UKR) 6-4 6-4
12–18 Jun	Great Britain	5	Y-H. Lu (TPE) d. A. Kennedy (AUS) 6-2 6-3	C. Wheeler (AUS) d. S. Stosur (AUS) 7-5 7-5
17–23 Jun	Denmark	4	P. Petschner (GER) d. B. Boutry (FRA) 3-6 6-4 6-4	M. Casanova (SUI) d. M. Rasic (CRO) 4-6 6-4 6-4
17–24 Jun	Morocco	4	C. Jacobs (RSA) d. M. Baghdatis (CYP) 6-3 6-1	S. Babos (HUN) d. J. Jankovic (YUG) 6-1 7-6(2)
17–25 Jun	Ukraine	5	H. Sofyan (ARM) d. P. Kuduma (UKR) 4-6 6-3 6-2	Y. Fedak (UKR) d. E. Ostapenko (RUS) 6-0 6-3
19–25 Jun	Great Britain	1	M. Ancic (CRO) d. S. Stadler (GER) 7-6(5) 6-1	A. Kapros (HUN) d. T. Perebiynis (UKR) 6-3 1-6 6-4
23–30 Jun	Bahamas	5	R. Gubser (USA) d. D. Mortimer (BAH) 6-2 2-6 6-3	M. Applebaum (USA) d. D. Alvarez (BOL) 6-1 6-1
24 Jun–1 Jul	Morocco	3	I. Cerovic (CRO) d. M. Baghdatis (CYP) 6-2 6-1	J. Jankovic (YUG) d. L. Smolenakova (SVK) 6-2 6-0
24 Jun–2 Jul	Ukraine	5	M. Filima (UKR) d. P. Kuduma (UKR) 6-0 3-6 6-3	Y. Fedak (UKR) d. M. Yuferova (RUS) 6-4 4-6 6-0
26 Jun–2 Jul	Australia	5	R. Henry (AUS) d. M. Khvorostin (AUS) 2-6 6-4 6-4	L. Breadmore (AUS) d. I. Jovanovich (NZL) 6-4 6-2
28 Jun–2 Jul				
1–9 Jul	**Wimbledon**	**A**	**N. Mahut (FRA) d. M. Ancic (CRO) 3-6 6-3 7-5**	**M. E. Salerni (ARG) d. T. Perebiynis (UKR) 6-4 7-5**
3–8 Jul	Curacao	5	R. Gubser (USA) d. W.Mau Asam (AHO) 6-1 6-2	R. Dandeniya (GBR) d. C Shelton (USA) 6-7(5) 6-4 7-6(3)
4–8 Jul	Australia	5	R. Durek (AUS) d. R. Henry (AUS) 6-2 6-1	B. Acquist (AUS) d. K. Browne (AUS) 6-2 6-3
4–9 Jul	Netherlands	2	K. Schweizer (GER) d. D. Kollerer (AUT) 6-1 6-0	K. Kanepi (EST) d. S. Arvidsson (SWE) 6-3 6-1
5–9 Jul	Tunisia	4	H. Suppan (AUT) d. F. Nielsen (DEN) 7-5 6-4	D. Van Boekel (NED) d. B. Ko (CAN) 6-3 6-3
10–16 Jul	Malta	5	M. Egger (AUT) d. G. Austerhuber (AUT) 5-7 7-6 0-6 6-4	A. Milenkovic (FRA) d. L. Ekner (DEN) 3-6 6-3 6-2
10–16 Jul	New Zealand	5	M. Henderson (AUS) d. J. Olsen (NZL) 6-1 6-4	I. Jovanovich (NZL) d. L. Breadmore (AUS) 6-4 6-4
11–15 Jul	Aruba	4	P. Amritraj (USA) d. H. Mirzadeh (USA) 2-6 6-2 6-1	M. E. Brito (MEX) d. M. Applebaum (USA) 6-3 6-4
11–16 Jul	Germany	1	A. Dernovskyy (UKR) d. S. Linda (GER) 7-5 6-4	K. Kanepi (EST) d. E. Birnerova (CZE) 6-0 6-2
12–16 Jul	Slovakia	4	B. De Gier (NED) d. M. Miklo (SVK) 7-6(6) 6-4	K. Kachlikova (SVK) d. D. Kix (AUT) 6-3 2-6 6-3
17–22 Jul	Dominican Republic	4	P. Amritraj (USA) d. J. Hazley (CAN) 6-1 7-5	M. Marois (CAN) d. N. Etienne (HAI) 6-2 7-5
17–22 Jul	Great Britain	5	I. Flanagan (GBR) d. A. Banks (GBR) 6-1 7-6(5)	Y. Arai (JPN) d. A. Takeuchi (JPN) 6-7 6-1 6-2
18–23 Jul	Switzerland	1	F. Prpic (SWE) d. R. Valent (SUI) 6-4 7-6(5)	C. Schaul (LUX) d. R. Voracova (CZE) 6-2 4-6 6-4
19–23 Jul	Czech Republic	3	I. Minar (CZE) d. T. Berdych (CZE) 3-6 6-3 6-3	D. Magas (HUN) d. S. Montero (FRA) 7-5 6-1
19–23 Jul	South Africa	3	R. Blair (RSA) d. J. Pieters (RSA) 6-1 3-6 7-6(7)	C. Scheepers (RSA) d. K. Coetzee (RSA) 6-1 6-1
24–28 Jul	Canada	5	J. Zimmermann (USA) d. R. Kuruppu (CAN) 6-4 6-4	L. Rutherford (CAN) d. S. Spence (CAN) 6-1 7-5
24–30 Jul	Portugal	5	A. Brizzi (ITA) d. J. Dionision Moreno (ESP) 6-4 6-1	M. Yuferova (RUS) d. A. Kostikova (RUS) 6-1 6-0
24–30 Jul	European Closed	B1	L. Childs (GBR) d. K. Beck (SVK) 3-6 6-1 6-4	Y. Beygelzimer (UKR) d. M. Mikaelian (ARM) 2-6 6-3 6-4
24–30 Jul	Mexico	4	B. Echagaray (MEX) d. S. Gonzalez (MEX) 6-4 6-4	M. Arroyo Vergara (MEX) d. M. E. Brito (MEX) 6-4 7-5
25–29 Jul	South Africa	3	R. Klaasen (RSA) d. A. Anderson (RSA) 6-3 7-6(2)	C. Scheepers (RSA) d. K. Coetzee (RSA) 6-3 6-1

Date	Tournament	Grade	Boys' singles final	Girls' singles final
31 Ju–5 Aug	Namibia	4	H. Heyl (RSA) d. R. Blair (RSA) 1–6 6–4 6–4	M. Van Niekerk (RSA) d. N. Waseem (PAK) 6–2 6–1
31 Ju–5 Aug	JITICC, Mexico	B3	B Echagaray (MEX) d. S. Gonzalez (MEX) 6–7(4) 7–6(6) 6–3	M. E. Brito (MEX) d. M. Torres (MEX) 6–1 1–6 6–3
31 Ju–6 Aug	Luxembourg	3	J. Masik (CZE) d. G. Posch (AUT) 6–4 6–2	K. Sprem (CRO) d. E. Bahn (AUT) 6–1 6–0
1–5 Aug	Portugal	3	A. Brizzi (ITA) d. J. Dionisio Moreno (ESP) 6–1 6–1	D-J. Hong (KOR) d. D. Van Boekel (NED) 3–6 6–1 6–1
6–8 Aug	European Team	C	Spain d. France 2–0	Spain d. France 3–0
7–12 Aug	Botswana	3	K. Loglo (TOG) d. H. Heyl (RSA) 7–6 4–6 6–4	M. Van Niekerk (RSA) d. C. Vermeulen (RSA) 6–3 6–2
7–13 Aug	Egypt	3	R. Chaki (MAR) d. I. Rosenberg (ISR) 3–6 6–1 6–4	Y. Farid (EGY) d. N. Mohsen (EGY) 6–4 6–4
7–13 Aug	Portugal	3	A. Brizzi (ITA) d. R. Bloomfield (GBR) 6–2 6–2	L. Kurhajcova (SVK) d. M. Yuferova (RUS) 7–6(5) 6–2
8–11 Aug	Canada	5	V. Sewa (IND) d. K. Sherry (USA) 4–1 ret	C. Goulet (CAN) d. J. McKeown (CAN) 6–2 6–0
8–12 Aug	Jamaica	4	R. Russell (JAM) d. R. Abreu (VEN) 6–0 6–2	N. Etienne (HAI) d. R. Dandeniya (GBR) 2–6 6–0 6–0
8–12 Aug	El Salvador	4	F. Barton (MEX) d. R. Gabriel (GUA) 7–6(3) 6–4	M. Serra (ARG) d. M. Blanco (MEX) 6–1 6–2
9–13 Aug	Slovenia	4	S. Tuksar (CRO) d. A. Kapun (SLO) 6–1 6–3	K. Sprem (CRO) d. D. Kix (AUT) 6–4 3–6 7–5
9–13 Aug	Poland	5	L. Wodnicki (POL) d. L. Pelowski (POL) 5–7 7–5 6–3	S. Kuznetsova (RUS) d. M. Zivcicova (SVK) 6–0 4–6 6–3
13–19 Aug	USA	3	A. Seri (USA) d. K. Capalik (YUG) 6–3 7–6	M. Irvin (USA) d. C. Grey (USA) 6–1 6–4
14–18 Aug	Egypt	3	R. Chaki (MAR) d. C. Chao (FRA) 6–4 6–4	D. Van Boekel (NED) d. N. Mohsen (EGY) 7–5 6–3
14–19 Aug	St Lucia	5	J. Zimmermann (USA) d. K. Sherry (USA) 6–4 6–4	R. Le Saldo (BAR) d. M. E. Lopez (VEN) 6–1 6–4
14–19 Aug	Mozambique	4	K. Loglo (TOG) d. F. Kobena (CIV) 6–2 6–3	M. Van Niekerk (RSA) d. C. Vermeulen (RSA) 6–2 6–3
14–20 Aug	Guatemala	5	A. Carrascosa (MEX) d. F. Montenegro (CRC) 2–6 6–0 6–2	C. Martinez (MEX) d. M. Serra (ARG) 6–2 6–2
15–19 Aug	Belgium	5	G. Maquet (BEL) d. O. Grignard (BEL) 7–6 6–1	D. Bercek (YUG) d. K. Kues (BEL) 6–4 6–3
16–20 Aug	Austria	2	S. Tuksar (CRO) d. F. Lemke (GER) 7–6(4) 6–3	J. Jankovic (YUG) d. D. Safina (RUS) 6–0 6–0
16–20 Aug	Poland	5	D. Olejniczak (POL) d. L. Pelowski (POL) 6–1 ret	S. Kuznetsova (RUS) d. T. Uvarova (RUS) 5–3 ret
16–20 Aug	Netherlands	5	B. Van Der Valk (NED) d. B. Beck (GER) 6–3 7–6	S. Bauer (NED) d. F. Van Haasteren (NED) 4–6 6–4 6–2
16–20 Aug	Kyrghyzstan	5	D. Doskaraev (KAZ) d. I. Kovalev (KAZ) 6–4 7–6	A. Amanmuradova (UZB) d. A. Shchupak (UZB) 6–4 6–4
16–20 Aug	Guatemala	4	A. Carrascosa (MEX) d. F. Montenegro (CRC) 2–6 6–0 6–2	C. Martinez (MEX) d. M. Serra (ARG) 6–2 6–2
21–26 Aug	Belgium	4	I. Rosenberg (ISR) d. G. Maquet (BEL) 4–6 7–5 6–2	D. Bercek (YUG) d. Y. Savransky (ISR) 0–6 6–4 6–3
21–26 Aug	Moldova	5	A. Gorban (VEN) d. J. Zimmerman (USA) 6–2 6–3	T. Bula (UKR) d. O. Lyubtsova (UKR) 6–3 6–1
21–26 Aug	Trinidad	5	R. Abreu (VEN) d. J. Zimmerman (USA) 7–6(5) 6–0	E. Villalobos (CRC) d. D. Cherkasova (RUS) 6–2 6–3
21–26 Aug	Syria	5	R. Chaki (MAR) d. K. Al Nabhani (OMA) 7–6(4) 6–3	Y. Farid (EGY) d. A. Khalifa (EGY) 3–6 6–4 6–1
21–27 Aug	USA	4	B. Baker (USA) d. A. Kennedy (AUS) 6–4 6–2	E. Burdette (USA) d. T. Cochran (USA) 4–6 7–5 6–1
23–27 Aug	Croatia	5	S. Tuksar (CRO) d. A. Brizzi (ITA) 6–3 6–4	I. Gerlova (CZE) d. J. Gajdosova (SVK) 6–4 6–4
24–28 Aug	Kazakhstan	5	D. Doskaraev (KAZ) d. I. Kovalev (KAZ) 0–6 7–6(6) 6–2	A. Kalsariyeva (KGZ) d. O. Dzyuba (KAZ) 6–3 6–2
28 Aug–2 Sep	France	1	L. Walter (FRA) d. C. Morel (FRA) 6–2 3–6 6–4	E. Laine (FIN) d. D. Feys (BEL) 6–1 6–3
28 Aug–3 Sep	Canada	5	Y-T. Wang (TPE) d. R. Valent (SUI) 6–3 7–5	A. Kapros (HUN) d. M. E. Salerni (ARG) 6–4 6–1
28 Aug–3 Sep	Lebanon	5	H. Balbaa (EGY) d. V. Zetterholm (SWE) 6–2 7–5	Y. Farid (EGY) d. A. Basha (EGY) 6–1 6–3
29 Aug–2 Sep	Hungary	3	M. Miklo (CZE) d. J. Kmita (POL) 6–7(8) 6–3 6–1	S. Kuznetsova (RUS) d. B. Berecz (HUN) 6–0 6–2
29 Aug–3 Sep	Corfu	5	M. Dickhardt (GER) d. D. Sela (ISR) 7–5 6–0	L. Smolenakova (SVK) d. A. Brumen (SLO) 5–7 6–0 6–1
30 Aug–3 Sep	Romania	4	E. Corduneanu (MDV) d. A. Barbu (ROM) 6–2 6–3	A. Orasanu (ROM) d. R. But (ROM) 4–6 7–5 7–5
2–7 Sep	Samoa	B3	M. Godinet (ASA) d. R. Penn (SAM) 6–1 6–1	D. Godinet (ASA) d. N. Angat (PNG) 6–1 7–6

Date	Location	Code
3-10 Sep	**US Open**	**A**
5-10 Sep	Greece	5
11-16 Sep	Cyprus	4
12-17 Sep	USA	1
18-22 Sep	Egypt	3
18-22 Sep	Yugoslavia	5
18-23 Sep	India	5
18-24 Sep	USA	3
20-24 Sep	Bulgaria	5
20-24 Sep	Czech Republic	3
26 Sep-1 Oct	Chile	5
25-29 Sep	Yugoslavia	4
25-30 Sep	India	4
2-8 Oct	Saudi Arabia	5
2-8 Oct	Pakistan	5
3-8 Oct	USA	B1
9-15 Oct	Pakistan	5
9-15 Oct	**Japan**	**A**
10-15 Oct	USA	5
9-15 Oct	USA	4
10-15 Oct	Saudi Arabia	4
16-22 Oct	Hong Kong	2
16-22 Oct	Brazil	5
23-29 Oct	Thailand	5
1-5 Nov	Malaysia	4
7-11 Nov	Luxembourg	3
8-12 Nov	Brunei	4
8-12 Nov	China	4
9-12 Nov	USA	4
13-19 Nov	Malaysia	5
14-18 Nov	Finland	5
14-19 Nov	USA	5
20-25 Nov	Thailand	5
21-26 Nov	Indonesia	4
27 Nov-3 Dec	USA	1
27 Nov-3 Dec	Vietnam	4
4-9 Dec	USA	3
11-17 Dec	**USA**	**A**
11-17 Dec	Kenya	4
18-23 Dec	Mexico	1

A.Roddick (USA) d. R.Ginepri (USA) 6-1 6-3
M.Dickhardt (GER) d. F.Poth (GER) 6-1 6-1
M.Baghdatis (CYP) d. S.Demekhin (RUS) 6-2 6-4
A.Roddick (USA) d. R.Valent (SUI) 6-4 6-3
P.Leao (POR) d. M.Baghdatis (CYP) 7-6(4) 6-3
I.Racic (BIH) d. S.Radman (CRO) 6-3 6-3
B.Xavier (IND) d. A.Sitaram (IND) 7-6(4) 6-2
J.Cohen (USA) d. J.Chu (USA) 6-4 6-3
E.Kuniawan (INA) d. T.Bolanu (ROM) 6-3 6-7(4) 6-4
M.Bayer (GER) d. F.Lemke (GER) 6-7 6-3 7-5
L.Noviski (ARG) d. P.Capdeville (CHI) 6-4 6-2
D.Mihailovic (YUG) d. A.Gavrila (ROM) 6-4 6-2
R.Gajjar (IND) d. V.Sewa (IND) 6-3 6-4
M.Al Jazzaf (KUW) d. A.Barbu (ROM) 6-4 7-6(3)
O.Mostyuk (UKR) d. A.Bykov (UKR) 7-5 7-6(5)
Y.Abougzir (USA) d. F.Dancevic (CAN) 6-4 7-6(4)
O.Mostyuk (UKR) d. B.Hung (HKG) 7-6(4) 6-3
J.Johansson (SWE) d. Y-H.Lu (TPE) 6-7(0) 7-6(3) 6-3
L.Cook (USA) d. D.Bauer (USA) 7-6(5) 5-7 6-0
M.Melo (BRA) d. F.Lemos (BRA) 4-6 7-6(2) 6-2
A.Barbu (ROM) d. A.Nour (KSA) 6-4 6-3
R.Soderling (SWE) d. J.Masik (CZE) 5-7 6-1 6-2
L.Noviski (ARG) d. F.Lemos (BRA) 6-2 6-4
C.Kwon (USA) d. R.Henry (AUS) 6-4 2-6 7-6
G.Austerhuber (AUT) d. R.Durek (AUS) 6-3 6-0
G.Muller (LUX) d. R.Karanusic (CRO) 7-5 3-6 7-6(6)
V.Sewa (IND) d. S.Spacya (IND) 6-3 6-3
L.Zhang (CHN) d. L.Kim (KOR) 3-6 6-4 7-5
J.Witten (USA) d. R.Rajeev (USA) 7-6(5) 6-0
B.Hunter (AUS) d. J.Kim (KOR) 2-6 6-3 7-6(3)
T.Virdhage (SWE) d. C.Johansson (SWE) 6-7(6) 6-2 7-5
R.Ram (USA) d. S.Brown (USA) 6-4 6-0
P.Malasitt (THA) d. P.Niroj (THA) 6-0 6-0
C.Letcher (AUS) d. A.Imron (INA) 6-1 6-1
L.Vitullo (AUS) d. R.Valent (SUI) 6-4 6-2
P.Malasitt (THA) d. J.Victorino (PHI) 6-4 6-2
J.Tipsarevic (YUG) d. B.Dabul (ARG) 6-1 6-2
T.Enev (BUL) d. B.Soares (BRA) 7-5 6-2
J.Stancik (SLO) d. C.Irie (CIV) 6-1 6-2
J.Tipsarevic (YUG) d. M.Baghdatis (CYP) 6-1 3-6 6-4

M.E.Salerni (ARG) d. T.Perebiynis (UKR) 6-3 6-4
L.Smolenakova (SVK) d. I.Boulykina (RUS) 4-6 6-3 6-0
B.Majstorovic (YUG) d. A.Milenkovic (FRA) 4-6 6-2 7-5
T.Perebiynis (UKR) d. J.Jankovic (YUG) 2-6 6-3 7-5
Y.Farid (EGY) d. A.Kostikova (RUS) 6-4 6-3
B.Majstorovic (YUG) d. D.Bercek (YUG) 6-3 6-3
M.Kharia (IND) d. P.Laosirichon (THA) 6-2 6-2
M.Gerards (NED) d. S.Peng (CHN) 7-6(12) 6-3
N.Vassileva (BUL) d. E.Gantcheva (BUL) 6-1 1-0 ret
S.Kuznetsova (RUS) d. K.Kachlikova (SVK) 6-0 6-1
J.Arguello (BRA) d. V.Garcia-Sokol (ARG) 6-4 6-4
D.Bercek (YUG) d. B.Majstorovic (YUG) 4-6 6-2 6-2
S.Mirza (IND) d. M.Vakaria (IND) 7-5 6-4

S.Mirza (IND) d. B.Ajam (PAK) 6-0 6-0
S.Rao (USA) d. J.Jackson (USA) 6-4 6-1

R.Voracova (CZE) d. J.Jankovic (YUG) 3-6 6-4 6-2
A.Podkolzina (USA) d. M.Karnaukhova (RUS) 6-4 6-4
I.Azzi (BRA) d. A.Sanches (BRA) 7-6(2) 6-1

P.Cetkovska (CZE) d. B.Strycova (CZE) 3-6 6-2 6-2
Y.Sokol (ARG) d. J.Arguello (BRA) 6-1 6-2
S.Hsieh (TPE) d. Lekner (DEN) 6-2 6-0
S.Hsieh (TPE) d. C.Chuang (TPE) 6-2 6-1
V.Razzano (FRA) d. M.Gerards (NED) 6-4 6-2
S.Hsieh (TPE) d. C.Arevalo (PHI) 6-2 6-4
Z.Yan (CHN) d. X.Sheng (CHN) 6-4 6-3
E.Subbotina (BLR) d. T.Zawacki (USA) 6-3 6-4
S.Hsieh (TPE) d. M.Ivanov (AUS) 7-5 7-6(5)
E.Laine (FIN) d. I.Csordas (HUN) 6-4 6-4
K.Schilkebir (USA) d. H.Fritche (USA) 7-5 6-0
M.Vakharia (IND) d. D.Hollands (NZL) 6-1 6-4
S.Hsieh (TPE) d. T.Welford (AUS) 2-6 6-1 6-2
E.Gallovits (ROM) d. R.Voracova (CZE) 6-0 6-4
R.Du (CHN) d. C.Arevalo (PHI) 6-1 7-6(0)
S.Peng (CHN) d. Y.Beygelzimer (UKR) 7-6 3-6 7-5
V.Zvonareva (RUS) d. E.Gallovits (ROM) 7-6(4) 6-4
K.Berthe (SEN) d. T.Masviba (ZIM) 6-1 6-2
M.Bartoli (FRA) d. R.Voracova (CZE) 5-7 6-0 6-1

ITF Vets Tennis

Jackie Nesbitt

Vets entertain South American crowds

The youngsters of Vets Tennis gathered in South America for the 35–50 age category world team and individual championships. No less than six different nations in the region played host to the various prestigious Cup competitions and the competitors were full of praise for the hospitable welcome extended by all the organising hosts.

The USA exceeded their own expectations by claiming four of the seven team titles on offer and finishing second in two other Cups. Their victory at the Tony Trabert Cup (Men's 40) was not at all unexpected – as top seeds and fielding former tour player Tim Wilkison at number one they defeated second seeded Germany in the Final. Top seeded again in the Fred Perry Cup (Men's 50), they had their work cut out to defeat a Chile side consisting of Jaime Fillol and Patricio Cornejo, but managed to ease through in the deciding doubles to claim the title.

Host nation, Paraguay, had high hopes in the Dubler Cup (Men's 45) with Victor Pecci captaining their side; however, it was to be another US victory with the team of Bob Wright, Claude England, Sal Castillo and John Peckshamp defeating France in a tight tussle.

The final US title came in the Women's 45 age category – the Margaret Court Cup. Ann Etheridge, Tina Karwasky, Karen Gallagher and Sherri Bronson did well to upset the Netherlands represented by Elly Appel, Nora Blom and Yvonne Van der Eeckhout.

Elsewhere, Europe claimed the honours. The German team of Patrick Baur, Stefan Eiksson, Stefan Fasthoff and Stefan Hackmanns held off the USA in the Italia Cup (Men's 35). A Women's 35 event, due to be introduced in 2001, will no doubt prove to be equally popular.

The Young Cup (Women's 40) saw a second German victory thanks to formidable performances from Gerda Preissing and Gabriela Groell-Dinu who found themselves severely tested by host nation Argentina. The competition had also attracted talented players such as Catherine Suire representing France and Patricia Medrado of Brazil.

The final event – the Maria Esther Bueno Cup was fittingly played in Brazil, but sadly for the hosts there was to be no home victory. Instead the runners-up from 1999 – France – led by Nicole Hesse-Cazaux, Gail Lovera and Martine Monlibert, toppled the top seeded US team in another close encounter.

For week two, from 29 October–5 November, the players gathered in Buenos Aires, Argentina, for the chance of individual glory. The World Championships attracted 417 entrants and the competition was such that the top seeds triumphed in only three events. In the Men's 35, a terrific line-up saw Peru's former Davis Cup star Pablo Arraya challenging for the title. However Czech Republic's Jaroslav Bulant justified his top seed status by overcoming Arraya's semi-final conqueror, Adrian Graimprey, in a closely contested final, 5–7 6–4 6–4.

In the Women's 35 age category the top seeded Beatrix Mezger-Reboul was surprisingly upset in the semi-final by Mexico's Raquel Contreras, but at least the favourite could take consolation from losing to the eventual winner. Contreras claimed the title with a fine 7–5 6–2 win over Chile's Monica Fuentealba.

The surprise of the Championships was Australia's Patrick Serett, who engineered a series of unexpected wins en route to the Men's 40 title. Despite being unseeded, Serett outplayed the sixth seed Frederic Dewaegeneire of France in the final, winning the trophy 7–6 7–5.

A number of former Fed Cup stars graced the ladies 40s draw, with Brazil's Patricio Medrado an overwhelming favourite. However Medrado's abrupt departure in the second round at the hands of Marcela Auroux, left the way open for the second seed Ros Balodis. In the final, the Australian found herself well beaten by the impressive Gabriela Groell-Dinu of Germany, who had earlier accounted for French star, Catherine Suire.

Paraguay's Victor Pecci's presence in the Men's 45 draw certainly pulled the crowds and the former French Open finalist did not disappoint, taking the title from local favourite Richard Cano 6–2 6–4. Not to be outdone, the top seeded Elly Appel was equally impressive in the Women's 45 draw. In the final, the Dutchwoman faced Italy's Eugenia Birukova: a match that was marred by Birukova having to retire at 5–7 3–2 because of injury.

Gabriela Groell-Dinu of Germany winner of the Women's 40 event. (Sergio Llamera)

Below: Victor Pecci of Paraguay, the Men's 45 champion. (Sergio Llamera)

Women's 45 medallists (left to right) Nora Blom (3rd), Elly Appel (1st) and Eugenia Birukova (2nd). (Sergio Llamera)

However, it was the oldest competitors who produced some of the finest play of the Championships. In the Men's 50, Brazil's Jose Rodrigues posted a notable victory over top seeded Lito Alvarez to reach the final in a run which included a win over former Bolivian Davis Cupper Ramiro Benavides. Waiting for him in the final was Frenchman Bruno Renoult. Spurred on by superb victories over third seeded Max Bates and second seeded Xavier Lemoine, Renoult, maintained the pressure and duly recorded a 6–3 6–2 win. The last chance for the host nation to clinch a title slipped away when Germany's Heidi Eisterlehner overcame Argentina's Ines Roget in the Women's 50 final.

20th ITF VETS WORLD CHAMPIONSHIPS (GROUP A)
29 October–5 November 2000
Tenis Club Argentino, Buenos Aires, Argentina

MEN
35 Singles
Semi-finals: Jaroslav Bulant (CZE) d. Ricardo Rivera (ARG) 6–3 6–2; Adrian Graimprey (ARG) d. Franck Fevrier (FRA) 0–6 7–6 6–4. *Final*: Bulant d. Graimprey 5–7 6–4 6–4.
35 Doubles
Semi-finals: Stefan Fasthoff (GER)/Stefan Heckmanns (GER) d. Paul Hand (GBR)/Orlando Lourenco (USA) 6–3 4–6 6–2; Ricardo Rivera (ARG)/Gustavo Tiberti (ARG) d. Martin Bidinost (ARG)/Alesandro Fernandez (ARG) 6–4 3–6 6–4. *Final*: Rivera/Tiberti d. Fasthoff/Heckmanns 0–6 7–5 6–0.
40 Singles
Semi-finals: Patrick Serrett (AUS) d. Alejandro Cerundolo (ARG) 6–4 6–0; Frederic Dewaegeneire (FRA) d. Eduardo Bengoechea (ARG) 6–3 1–6 6–4. *Final*: Serrett d. Dewaegeneire 7–6 7–5.
40 Doubles
Semi-finals: Brett Edwards (AUS)/Pierre Godfroid (BEL) d. John Chatlak (USA)/Clifford Skakle (USA) 6–4 6–2; Mike Fedderly (USA)/Paul Smith (USA) d. Luis Lobao (BRA)/Carlos Soares (BRA) 6–4 6–2. *Final*: Fedderly/Smith d. Edwards/Godfroid 6–3 6–3.
45 Singles
Semi-finals: Victor Pecci (PAR) d. Sal Castillo (USA) 6–4 3–6 6–1; Ricardo Cano (ARG) d. Eduaard Wretschitsch (AUT) 6–2 6–0. *Final*: Pecci d. Cano 6–2 6–4.
45 Doubles
Semi-finals: Alan Rasmussen (DEN)/Rafael Ruiz (ESP) d. Bruno Renoult (FRA)/Marc Renoult (FRA) 5–7 7–6 6–4; Michael Collins (AUS)/Wayne Pascoe (AUS) d. Sal Castillo (USA)/Claude England (USA) 7–5 6–3. *Final*: Collins/Pascoe d. Rasmussen/Ruiz 6–1 6–3.
50 Singles
Semi-finals: Jose Rodrigues (BRA) d. Lito Alvarez (AUS) 7–6 6–3; Bruno Renoult (FRA) d. Xavier Lemoine (FRA) 6–4 6–4. *Final*: Renoult d. Rodrigues 6–3 6–2
50 Doubles
Semi-finals: Paulo Lopes (BRA)/Jose Rodrigues (BRA) d. Aldo Bruzoni (ARG)/Alfredo Morelli (ARG) 6–2 6–3; Max Bates (AUS)/Xavier Lemoine (FRA) d. Julio Lavagno (ARG)/Alberto Romero (ARG) 6–2 6–2. *Final*: Bates/Lemoine d. Lopes/Rodrigues 6–0 6–3.

WOMEN
35 Singles
Semi-finals: Raquel Contreras (MEX) d. Beatrix Mezger-Reboul (GER) 6–3 6–3; Monica Fuentealba (CHI) d. Alexandra Beggs (USA) 6–3 6–4. *Final*: Contreras d. Fuentealba 7–5 6–2.
35 Doubles
Semi-finals: Mary Mottola (USA)/Karen O'Sullivan (USA) d. Bibiana Alvarez (ARG)/Laura Fernandez (ARG) 6–0 6–0; Beatrix Mezger-Reboul (GER)/Cora Salimei (ARG) d. Jane Langstaff (GBR)/Julie Willson (GBR) 6–1 6–7 6–2. *Final*: Mezger-Reboul/Salimei d. Mottola/O'Sullivan 7–6 7–6.
40 Singles
Semi-finals: Gabriela Groell-Dinu (GER) d. Catherine Suire (FRA) 1–6 6–1 6–4; Ros Balodis (AUS) d. Viktoria Beggs (USA) 6–2 6–1. *Final*: Groell-Dinu d. Balodis 6–4 6–0.
40 Doubles
Semi-finals: Tina Karwasky (USA)/Catherine Suire (FRA) d. Alexandra Beggs (USA)/Viktoria Beggs (USA) 6–4 1–6 6–4; Ros Balodis (AUS)/Kaye Nealon (AUS) d. Gabriela Groell-Dinu (GER)/Patricia Medrado (BRA) 1–6 6–2 6–4. *Final*: Balodis/Nealon d. Karwasky/Suire 7–5 2–6 6–4.
45 Singles
Semi-finals: Elly Appel (NED) d. Luisa Figueroa (ARG) 6–4 6–3; Eugenia Birukova (ITA) d. Nora Blom (NED) 6–1 2–6 6–4. *Final*: Appel d. Birukova 7–5 2–3 ret.
45 Doubles
Semi-finals: Ann Brown (GBR)/Pauline Fisher (GBR) d. Luisa Figueroa (ARG)/Denise Gwatkin (GBR) 6–3 6–1; Helen Holcombe (AUS)/Suzie Kelly (AUS) d. Katalin Fagyas (HUN)/Claudia Solari (ARG) 1–6 6–2 6–3. *Final*: Brown/Fisher d. Holcombe/Kelly 6–1 6–2.

50 Singles
Semi-finals: Ines Roget (ARG) d. Leyla Musalem (CHI) 6–3 3–6 6–3; Heidi Eisterlehner (GER) d. Elizabeth Allan (AUS) 6–2 4–6 7–6. *Final*: Eisterlehner d. Roget 6–4 6–2.
50 Doubles
Semi-finals: Elizabeth Allan (AUS)/Carol Campling (AUS) d. Margarit Karas (AUT)/Ines Roget (ARG) w/o; Adrienne Avis (AUS)/Helen Worland (AUS) d. Heidi Eisterlehner (GER)/Heide Orth (GER) 4–6 6–2 7–6. *Final*: Allan/Campling d. Avis/Worland 6–3 6–1.

20th ITF VETS WORLD CHAMPIONSHIPS (GROUP B)
26 March–2 April 2000
Kelvin Grove Sports Club, Cape Town, South Africa

MEN
55 Singles
Semi-finals: Hugh Thomson (USA) d. Ben De Jel (NED) 3–6 6–1 6–2; Denley Richards (RSA) d. Peter Adrigan (GER) 6–2 1–6 6–3. *Final*: Thomson d. Richards 7–5 6–3.
55 Doubles
Semi-finals: Ben de Jel (NED)/Hans-Joa Ploetz (GER) d. Michael Francis (GBR)/Michael Hayes (GBR) 6–1 6–1; Richard Landenberger (USA)/Hugh Thomson (USA) d. Hiralal Soma (GBR)/Jasmat Soma (GBR) 6–2 7–6. *Final*: De Jel/Ploetz d. Landenberger/Thomson 6–4 4–6 7–6 (3).
60 Singles
Semi-finals: Robert Howes (AUS) d. Eberhard Madelsberger (AUT) 6–4 3–6 6–1; Giorgio Rohrich (ITA) d. Peter Pokorny (AUT) 6–3 6–4. *Final*: Howes d. Rohrich 6–2 6–4.
60 Doubles
Semi-finals: Bodo Nitsche (GER)/Peter Pokorny (AUT) d. Peter Froelich (AUS)/Robert Howes (AUS) 5–7 6–4 6–4; Robert Duesler (USA)/James Nelson (USA) d. Friedhelm Krauss (GER)/Klaus Fuhrmann (GER) 6–3 7–6. *Final*: Nitsche/Pokorny d. Duesler/Nelson 6–4 6–0.
65 Singles
Semi-finals: Joseph Mateo (FRA) d. James Perley (USA) 6–2 6–3; Henri Crutchet (FRA) d. James Nelson (USA) 6–3 6–4. *Final*: Mateo d. Crutchet 7–6 (2) 6–2.
65 Doubles
Semi-finals: James Perley (USA)/John Powless (USA) d. Hector Arellano (MEX)/Joseph Mateo (FRA) 6–4 6–3; Abie Nothnagel (RSA)/Neville Whitfield (RSA) d. David Garman (GBR)/Anthony Klima (GBR) 6–7 6–1 6–3. *Final*: Nothnagel/Whitfield d. Perley/Powless 4–6 6–1 6–4.
70 Singles
Semi-finals: Lorne Main (CAN) d. Russell Seymour (USA) 6–1 6–0; Kenneth Sinclair (CAN) d. William Davis (USA) 6–4 6–2. *Final*: Main d. Sinclair 6–4 6–4.
70 Doubles
Semi-finals: Lorne Main (CAN)/Kenneth Sinclair (CAN) d. William Davis (USA)/Charles Devoe (USA) 6–3 6–4; Jason Morton (USA)/Russell Seymour (USA) d. Adalbert Huessmuller (GER)/Peter Schoenboerner (GER) 6–1 6–2. *Final*: Main/Sinclair d. Morton/Seymour 6–2 6–3.
75 Singles
Semi-finals: Oskar Jirkovsky (AUT) d. Eugenio Ibanez (VEN) 6–4 6–1; Vincent Fotre (USA) d. Newton Meade (USA) 6–2 6–1. *Final*: Fotre d. Jirkovsky 6–3 6–1.
75 Doubles
Semi-finals: Neale Hook (AUS)/Brian Hurley (AUS) d. Francis Bushman (USA)/Vincent Fotre (USA) 7–6 (5) 6–4; Neville Halligan (AUS)/Newton Meade (USA) d. Eugenio Ibanez (VEN)/Miguel Siliano (ARG) 5–7 6–2 6–2. *Final*: Hook/Hurley d. Halligan/Meade 6–4 6–1.
80 Singles
Semi-finals: Nehemiah Atkinson (USA) d. Alex Swetka (USA) 4–6 6–1 6–4; Robert Sherman (USA) d. Franz Kornfeld (AUS) 6–0 6–0. *Final*: Sherman d. Atkinson 6–1 6–1.
80 Doubles
Semi-finals: Federico Barboza (ARG)/Carlos Urien (ARG) d. Charles Roe (AUS)/Trevor Wigmore (AUS) 6–4 6–2; Nehemiah Atkinson (USA)/Alex Swetka (USA) d. Gardnar Mulloy (USA)/Robert Sherman (USA) 6–4 6–1. *Final*: Atkinson/Swetka d. Barboza/Urien 6–4 2–6 6–3.
85 Singles
Semi-finals: Garnar Mulloy (USA) d. Edward Baumer (USA) 6–0 6–2; David Carey (CAN) d. Georg Hunger (GER) 6–0 6–1. *Final*: Carey d. Mulloy 6–3 7–6 (6).
85 Doubles
Final: David Carey (CAN)/Edward Baumer (USA) d. Georg Hunger (GER)/William Lurie (USA) 7–6(1) 6–1.

WOMEN
55 Singles
Semi-finals: Ellie Krocke (NED) d. Heide Orth (GER) 7–6 5–7 7–5; Suella Steel (USA) d. Renate Schroeder (GER) 7–6 6–7 4–2 ret. *Final*: Krocke d. Steel 6–2 6–2.

55 Doubles
Semi-finals: Petro Kruger (RSA)/Marietjie Viljoen (RSA) d. Catherine Anderson (USA)/Frances Taylor (GBR) 7–6 6–4; Charleen Hillebrand (USA)/Suella Steel (USA) d. Marie Blignaut (RSA)/Margaret Bornman (RSA) 6–1 5–7 7–5. *Final*: Hillebrand/Steel d. Kruger/Viljoen 4–6 6–3 6–4.

60 Singles
Semi-finals: Jeannine Lieffrig (RSA) d. Siegrun Fuhrmann (GER) 6–1 6–0; Rosy Darmon (FRA) d. Jan Blackshaw (AUS) 6–3 6–2. *Final*: Darmon d. Lieffrig 6–4 6–1.

60 Doubles
Semi-finals: Jan Blackshaw (AUS)/Mary Gordon (AUS) d. Dori De Vries (USA)/Katie Koontz (USA) 7–5 6–3; Sinclair Bill (USA)/Rosy Darmon (FRA) d. Judith Dalton (AUS)/Ann Fotheringham (AUS) 6–4 6–3. *Final*: Bill/Darmon d. Blackshaw/Gordon 3–6 6–3 6–3.

65 Singles
Semi-finals: Mary Blair (USA) d. Jackie Zylstra (RSA) 7–6 6–4; Lee Burling (USA) d. Rita Lauder (GBR) w/o. *Final*: Burling d. Blair 7–5 6–4.

65 Doubles
Semi-finals: Mary Blair (USA)/Lee Burling (USA) d. Alina Pinedo (MEX)/Yola Ramirez (MEX) 6–4 6–2; Patricia Bruorton (RSA)/Jackie Zylstra (RSA) d. Lorice Forbes (AUS)/Peg Hoysted (AUS) 1–6 6–4 7–6. *Final*: Bruorton/Zylstra d. Blair/Burling 6–3 6–2.

70 Singles
Semi-finals: Louise Owen (USA) d. Ines Pla (ARG) 6–4 6–4; Louise Russ (USA) d. Rosemarie Asch (CAN) 7–6 7–5. *Final*: Owen d. Russ 6–4 6–4.

70 Doubles
Semi-finals: Amelia Cury (BRA)/Ines Pla (ARG) d. Marjorie Niccol (AUS)/Lurline Stock (AUS) 6–2 6–2; Louise Owen (USA)/Louise Russ (USA) d. Rosemarie Asch (CAN)/Joyce Jones (CAN) 6–1 6–2. *Final*: Owen/Russ d. Cury/Pla 6–1 6–4.

75 Singles
Semi-finals: Elaine Mason (USA) d. Mary Marsh (GBR) 6–4 6–1; Twinx Rogers (RSA) d. Amy Wilmot (RSA) 6–4 2–6 7–6 (6). *Final*: Mason d. Rogers 6–3 6–2.

75 Doubles
Semi-finals: Elaine Mason (USA)/Irmgard Stronk (GER) d. Julia Borzone (ARG)/Gladys Weiss (ARG) 6–3 6–2; Twinx Rogers (RSA)/Amy Wilmot (RSA) d. Liselotte Carstens (GER)/Annemarie Deinert (GER) 6–0 6–0. *Final*: Rogers/Wilmot d. Mason/Stronk 6–2 6–3.

ITF VETS TEAM COMPETITIONS 2000

MEN'S 35
Italia Cup, Asociacion Deportes Racionales, Buenos Aires, Argentina
Semi-finals: USA d. Great Britain 3–0; Germany d. Italy 3–0. *Final*: Germany d. USA 3–0.

MEN'S 40
Tony Trabert Cup, Club de Tenis Santa Cruz, Santa Cruz, Bolivia
Semi-finals: Germany d. Great Britain 2–0; USA d. Australia 2–0. *Final*: USA d. Germany 3–0.

MEN'S 45
Dubler Cup, Yacht y Golf Club Paraguayo, Asuncion, Paraguay
Semi-finals: France d. Brazil 2–1; USA d. Paraguay 2–1. *Final*: USA d. France 2–1.

MEN'S 50
Fred Perry Cup, Estadio Manquehue, Santiago, Chile
Semi-finals: USA d. South Africa 3–0; Chile d. Australia 2–1. *Final*: USA d. Chile 2–1.

MEN'S 55
Austria Cup, Kershaw Park, Pietermaritzburg, South Africa
Semi-finals: France d. Germany 2–1; USA d. Netherlands 3–0. *Final*: USA d. France 2–1.

MEN'S 60
Von Cramm Cup, Kelvin Grove, Cape Town, South Africa
Semi-finals: Australia d. France 2–1; Austria d. Germany 2–1. *Final*: Austria d. Australia 2–1.

MEN'S 65
Britannia Cup, University of Cape Town, Cape Town, South Africa
Semi-finals: USA d. France 3–0; Australia d. Great Britain 2–1. *Final*: Australia d. USA 2–1.

MEN'S 70
Jack Crawford Cup, Ronderbosch Tennis HQ, Cape Town, South Africa
Semi-finals: USA d. France 3–0; Canada d. Austria 2–1. *Final*: Canada d. USA 2–1.

MEN'S 75
Bitsy Grant Cup, Kelvin Grove, Cape Town, South Africa
3rd/4th place playoff: Australia d. Sweden 3–0. ***Final***: USA d. Great Britain 3–0.

MEN'S 80
Gardnar Mulloy Cup, Constantia Tennis Club, Cape Town, South Africa
Semi-finals: USA d. Great Britain 3–0; Australia d. Argentina 2–1. ***Final***: USA d. Australia 2–1.

WOMEN'S 40
Young Cup, Nautico Mar del Plata, Mar del Plata, Argentina
Semi-finals: Germany d. USA 2–1; Argentina d. Brazil 2–1. ***Final***: Germany d. Argentina 3–0.

WOMEN'S 45
Margaret Court Cup, Carrasco Lawn Tennis Club, Montevideo, Uruguay
Semi-finals: USA d. Germany 3–0; Netherlands d. France 3–0. ***Final***: USA d. Netherlands 3–0.

WOMEN'S 50
Maria Esther Bueno Cup, Esporte Clube Sirio, Sao Paulo, Brazil
Semi-finals: USA d. Australia 3–0; France d. Great Britain 2–1. ***Final***: France d. USA 2–1.

WOMEN'S 55
Maureen Connolly Cup, Durban Country Club, Durban, South Africa
3rd/4th place playoff: Great Britain d. Netherlands 3–0; ***Final***: South Africa d. USA 2–1.

WOMEN'S 60
Alice Marble Cup, Sun City, South Africa
Semi-finals: Australia d. France 3–0; South Africa d. USA 2–1. ***Final***: Australia d. South Africa 2–1.

WOMEN'S 65
Kitty Godfree Cup, Pinelands, Cape Town, South Africa
Semi-finals: USA d. Australia 2–1; South Africa d. Mexico 3–0. ***Final***: USA d. South Africa 2–1.

WOMEN'S 70
Althea Gibson Cup, Constantia Tennis Club, Cape Town, South Africa
Semi-finals: South Africa d. Australia 2–1; USA d. Argentina 2–1. ***Final***: USA d. South Africa 2–1.

National Associations and Voting Rights

Correct at 1 January 2001

The date given in parenthesis denotes the foundation date of the National Tennis Association where known.

Class B (Full) Members with voting rights (141)

ALGERIA – ALG (1962) (Votes 1)

Federation Algerienne de Tennis
Centre des Federations Sportives
Cite Olympique B.P. 88 El Biar Algers 16030
T 213 21922 970 **FAX** 213 21924 613
E-mail: fat.tennis@caramailcom
Pres: Dr Mohamed Bouabdallah
Sec: Mr Sellami Mebarek

ANDORRA – AND (1986) (Votes 1)

Federacion Andorrana de Tenis Sant Antoni
C/ Verge del Pilar 5 3er Desp. no 10
Andorra la Vella
T 376 861 381 **FAX** 376 868 381
Pres: Mr Antoni Ricart **Sec:** Mr Joan Grau

ANGOLA – ANG (1983) (Votes 1)

Federacao Angolana de Tenis
Cidadeia Desportive PO Box 3677 Luanda
T/FAX 244 2 399 650
E-mail: luisrosa.lopes@snet.co.ao
Pres: Mr Luis Rosa Lopes
Sec: Mr Francisco Barros

ANTIGUA & BARBUDA – ANT (1982) (Votes 1)

Antigua & Barbuda Tennis Association
PO Box 2758 St John's
T 1 268 461 3708 **FAX** 1 268 462 4811
E-mail: elijah@candw.ag
Pres: Mr. Cordell Williams
Sec: Mr Dereld Williams

ARGENTINA – ARG (1921) (Votes 7)

Asociacion Argentina de Tenis
Avda San Juan 1307 1148 Buenos Aires
T 54 114 304 2256 **FAX** 54 114 305 0296
E-mail: info@aat.com.ar
Website: www.tenisargentina.com
Pres: Mr Enrique Morea
Sec: Mr Roberto Fernandaz

ARMENIA – ARM (1940) (Votes 1)

Armenian Tennis Association
Tennis School of Armenia Yerevan 375082
T 3741 576 036
FAX 3742 151 069
E-mail: atf@acc.am
Pres: Mr Harutyun Pambukian
Sec: Mr Hajk Kirakossian

AUSTRALIA – AUS (1904) (Votes 12)

Tennis Australia
Private Bag 6060 Richmond South
Victoria 3121
T 61 392 861 177 **FAX** 61 396 502 743
Website: www.tennisaustralia.com.au
Pres: Mr Geoff Pollard
Sec: Mr Fenton Coull

AUSTRIA – AUT (1902) (Votes 5)

Osterreichischer Tennisverband
Haeckelstrasse 33 1235 Vienna
T 43 1 865 4506 **FAX** 43 1 865 9806
E-mail: oetv@asn.or.at
Pres: Dr Ernst Wolner
Sec: Mr Martin Reiter

AZERBAIJAN – AZE (1956) (Votes 1)

Azerbaijan Tennis Federation
Flat 46 44-46 B Madjedov Str Baku 370002
T 994 12 395 172 **FAX** 994 12 394 023
Pres: Mr Nazim Ibraqimov
Sec: Mr Djavanshir Ibragimov

BAHAMAS – BAH (1961) (Votes 1)

The Bahamas Lawn Tennis Association
PO Box N-10169 Nassau
T 1 242 328 7238 **FAX** 1 242 322 8000
E-mail: bltatennis@batelnet.bs
Pres: Mr George Baxter
Sec: Mr R E Barnes

BAHRAIN – BRN (1981) (Votes 1)

Bahrain Tennis Federation
PO Box 26985
T 973 687 236 **FAX** 973 781 533
Pres: Mr Ahmed Al Kalifa
Sec: Mr Mohammad Saleh Abdul Latif

BANGLADESH – BAN (1972) (Votes 1)

Bangladesh Tennis Federation
Tennis Complex Ramna Green Dhaka 1000
T 880 2 862 6287 **FAX** 880 2 966 2711
Pres: Mr Syed Chowdhury
Sec: Mr Sanaul Haque

BARBADOS – BAR (1948) (Votes 1)

Barbados Lawn Tennis Association
PO Box 615c Bridgetown
T 1 246 426 6453 **FAX** 1 246 427 8317
Pres: Dr Raymond Forde **Sec:** Mrs Jean Date

BELARUS – BLR (1990) (Votes 1)

Tennis Association of the Republic of Belarus
Masherov Avenue 63 Minsk 220035
T 375 172 271 735 **FAX** 375 172 269 823
Pres: Mr Simon Kagan
Sec: Mr Georgy Matsuk

BELGIUM – BEL (1990) (Votes 1)

Federation Royale Belge de Tennis
Galerie de la Porte Louise 203
(8eme Etage) 1050 Brussels
E-mail: aft@pophost.eunet.be
T 32 2 513 2927 **FAX** 32 2 513 7950
Pres: Mr Yves Freson
Sec: Mr Walter Goethals

BENIN – BEN (1963) (Votes 1)

Federation Beninoise de Lawn Tennis
BP 2709 Cotonou I
T 229 315 153 **FAX** 229 311 252
Pres: Mr Edgar-Yves Monnou
Sec: Mr Ladami Gafari

BERMUDA – BER (1994) (Votes 1)

Bermuda Lawn Tennis Association
PO Box HM 341
Hamilton HM BX
T 1 441 296 0834 **FAX** 1 441 295 3056
Pres: Mr David Lambert
Sec: Ms Airlie Arton

BOLIVIA – BOL (1937) (Votes 1)

Federacion Boliviana de Tennis
Calle Rene Moreno 685 Casilla Postal No. 1041
Santa Cruz
T 591 911 2976 **FAX** 591 336 8625
E-mail: fbtenis@bibosi.scz.entelnet.bo
Pres: Mr Edmundo Rodriguez
Sec: Mr Jaime Guillen

BOSNIA/HERZOGOVINA – BIH (1950) (Votes 1)

Tennis Association of Bosnia and Herzogovina
72000 Zenica Obalni Bulevar 30
T/FAX 387 32 411 077 Extra T. 387 32 286 610
E-mail: tsbih@mail.miz.ba
Pres: Mr Neven Tomic
Sec: Mr Haris Barucija

BOTSWANA – BOT (1964) (Votes 1)

Botswana Tennis Association
PO Box 1174 Gaborone
T/FAX 267 373 193
E-mail: bta@ib.bw
Pres: Captain Botsang Tshenyego
Sec: Mr Charles Bewlay

BRAZIL – BRA (1956) (Votes 7)

Confederacao Brasileira de Tenis
Av Paulista Nr. 326 – 2° Cj 26/27
01310-902 Sao Paulo
T 55 11 283 1788 **FAX** 55 11 283 0768
E-mail: cbt@cbtenis.com.br
Website: www.cbtenis.com.br
Pres: Mr Nelson Nastas
Sec: Mr Carlos Alberto Martolette

BRUNEI – BRU (1967) (Votes 1)

Brunei Darussalam Tennis Association
PO Box 859 Pejabat Pos Gadong
Bandar Seri Bagawan BE 3978
T 673 2 381 205 **FAX** 673 2 381 205
E-mail: Bdta@brunet.bn
Pres: Mr Abdu Bakar Abdul Rahman
Sec: Mr Hj Zuraimi Hj Abd Sani

BULGARIA – BUL (1930) (Votes 1)

Bulgarian Tennis Federation
Bul. Vasil Levski 75 Sofia 1040
T 359 2 963 1310 **FAX** 359 2 981 5728
E-mail: btf@mail.techno-link.com
Pres: Mr Krassimir Angarski
Sec: Mr Chavdar Ganev

BURKINA FASO – BUR (1970) (Votes 1)

Federation Burkinabe de Tennis
01 BP 45 Ouagadougou 1
T 226 312 733 **FAX** 223 304 031
Pres: Mr Zambo Martin Zongo
Sec: Mr Andre Batiana

CAMEROON – CMR (1966) (Votes 1)

Federation Camerounaise de Tennis
BP 13 001 Douala
T 237 370 790 **FAX** 237 372 302
Pres: Mr Gilbert Kadji
Sec: Mr Victor Momha

CANADA – CAN (1920) (Votes 9)

Tennis Canada
3111 Steeles Avenue West Downsview
Ontario M3J 3H2
T 1 416 665 9777 **FAX** 1 416 665 9017
E-mail: commnctn@tenniscanada.com
Pres: Mr Robert H Moffatt
Sec: tba

CHILE – CHI (1920) (Votes 5)

Federacion de Tenis de Chile
Jose Joaquin Prieto No. 4040, Paradero 7
Gran Avenida Santiago
T 56 25 540 068 **FAX** 56 25 541 078
E-mail: stellapn@tennishle.org
Website: www.fedtenis.cl
Pres: Mr Jose Ramon de Camino
Sec: Mr Guillermo Toral Bustamante

CHINA HONG KONG – HKG (1909) (Votes 1)

Hong Kong Tennis Association Ltd
Room 1021, Sports House
1 Stadium Path So Kon Po Causeway Bay
T 852 289 48704 **FAX** 852 250 48266
E-mail: hktf@tennishk.org
Pres: Dr Philip Kwok **Sec:** tba

**CHINA, PEOPLE'S REPUBLIC OF
– CHN (1953)** (Votes 3)

Tennis Association of the People's Republic of China
9 Tiyuguan Road Beijing 100763
T 86 10 6715 8622
FAX 86 10 6711 4096
Pres: Mr Lu Zhenchao
Sec: Mr Zhang Xiaoning

CHINESE TAIPEI – TPE (1973) (Votes 3)

Chinese Taipei Tennis Association
Room 1108, 11th Floor 20 Chu Lun Street
T 886 2 2772 0298 **FAX** 886 2 2771 1696
E-mail: ctta@gcn.net.tw
Pres: Mr F T Hsieh
Sec: Mr Samuel Mu

COLOMBIA – COL (1932) (Votes 5)

Federacion Colombiana de Tenis
Carrera de alto Rendimiento Calle 63 No 47 –06
Santa Fe de Bogota DC
T 571 314 3885 **FAX** 571 660 4234
E-mail: fedtenis@multi.net.co
Pres: Dr Ricardo Mejia Pelaez
Sec: tba

CONGO – CGO (1962) (Votes 1)

Federation Congolaise de Lawn Tennis
BP 550 Brazzaville
T 242 411 222 **FAX** 242 810 330
E-mail: fecoten@hotmail.com
Pres: Mr Germain Ickonga Akindou
Sec: Mr Antoine Ouabonzi

COSTA RICA – CRC (1960) (Votes 1)

Federacion Costarricense de Tenis
Apartado 1815-1250 Escazu
T 506 289 3909 **FAX** 506 289 3908
E-mail: fedcrtenis@hotmail.com
Pres: Mr Xavier Roca
Sec: Mr Jurgen G Nanne-Koberg

COTE D'IVOIRE – CIV (1969) (Votes 1)

Federation Ivoirienne de Tennis
01 BPV 273 Abidjan 01
T/FAX 225 22 441 354
225 22 447 434
Pres: Mr Jean-Claude Delafosse
Sec: Mr Gadjiro

CROATIA – CRO (1922) (Votes 5)

Croatian Tennis Association
HR-10 000 Zagreb Gundulieeva 3
T 385 148 30 747 **FAX** 385 148 30 720
E-mail: cro-tennis.zg.tel.hr
Pres: Mr Slaven Ledica
Sec: Mr Dubravko Lipnjak

CUBA – CUB (1925) (Votes 1)

Federacion Cubana de Tenis de Campo
Calle 13 NR 601 Esq AC Vedado Habana 4
T 53 7 972 121 **FAX** 53 7 972 121
E-mail: fctennis@inder.co.cu
Pres: Mr Rolando Martinez Perez
Sec: Mr Juan Baez

CYPRUS – CYP (1951) (Votes 1)

Cyprus Tennis Federation
Ionos Str. 20 PO Box 3931 Nicosia 1687
T 357 2 666 822 **FAX** 357 2 668 016
E-mail: cytennis@spidernet.com.cy
Pres: Mr Philios Christodoulou
Sec: Mr Stavros Ioannou

CZECH REPUBLIC – CZE (1906) (Votes 9)

Czech Tenisova Asociace
Ostrov Stvanice 38 170 00 Prague 7
T 420 2 24 810 238 **FAX** 420 2 24 810 301
E-mail: ctatennis@gts.cz
Website: www.ctatennis.cz
Pres: Mr Ivo Kaderka
Sec: Mr Karel Papousek

DENMARK – DEN (1920) (Votes 5)

Dansk Tennis Forbund
Idraettens Hus Broendby Stadion 20
DK-2605 Broendby
T 45 43 262 660 **FAX** 45 43 262 670
E-mail: dtf@dtftennis.dk
Website: www.dtftennis.dk
Pres: Mr Peter Schak Larsen
Sec: Mr Niels Persson

DJIBOUTI – DJI (1978) (Votes 1)

Federation Djiboutienne de Tennis
BP 3592 Djibouti
T/FAX 253 352 536
E-mail: oned@intnet.dj
Pres: Mr Houmed Houssein
Sec: tba

DOMINICAN REPUBLIC – DOM (1929) (Votes 1)

Federacion Dominicana de Tennis
Club Deportivo Naco Calle Central
Ens Naco Santo Domingo
T 1 809 549 5031 **FAX** 1 809 565 0835
E-mail: fedotenis@hotmail.com
Pres: Mr Gonzalo Mejia **Sec:** Mr J Ravelo

ECUADOR – ECU (1967) (Votes 3)

Federacion Ecuatoriana de Tenis
Edificio de la Federacion Ecuatoriana de Tenis
Tres Cerritos
Lomas de Urdesa Guayaquil
T 593 4 610 467 **FAX** 593 4 610 466
E-mail: fetenis@gye.satnet.net
Pres: Mr Jaime Guzman Maspons
Sec: Mrs Nuria Guzman De Ferretti

EGYPT – EGY (1920) (Votes 5)

Egyptian Tennis Federation
13 Kasr El Nile Street Cairo
T 20 2 574 7697 **FAX** 20 2 575 3235
E-mail: etf@urgentmail.com
Pres: Mr Mohamed Halawa
Sec: Miss May Elwany

EL SALVADOR – ESA (1949) Votes 1)

Federacion Salvadorena de Tenis
Apartado Postal (01) 110 San Salvador
T 503 278 8087 **FAX** 503 221 0564/503 271 5681
Pres: Mr Enrique Molins Rubio
Sec: Mr Jose Martinez

ESTONIA – EST (1932) (Votes 1)

Estonian Tennis Association 1-5P Regati Avenue
11911 Tallinn ESTONIA
T/FAX 372 6 398 635
E-mail: estonian.tennis@tennis.ee
Pres: Mr Endel Siff **Sec:** Mr Mati Kuum

ETHIOPIA – ETH (1972) (Votes 1)

Ethiopian Tennis Federation
PO Box 3241 Addis Ababa
T 251 1 152 028 **FAX** 251 1 513 345
Pres: Colonel Mohammed Abduslam
Sec: Mr Seifu W/yohannes

FIJI – FIJ (1934) (Votes 1)

Fiji Tennis Association
c/o Mr Paras Naidu PO Box 3664 Lautoka
T 679 315 988 **FAX** 669 667 082
E-mail: parasfta@is.com.fj
Pres: Mr Cliff Benson
Sec: Mr Paras Naidu

FINLAND – FIN (1911) (Votes 3)

Suomen Tennisliitto
Varikkotie 4 SF – 00900 Helsinki
T 358 9 3417 1533 **FAX** 358 9 323 1105
E-mail: jukka.roiha@lindstrom.fi
Pres: Mr Mauri K Elovainio
Sec: Mr Mika Bono

FRANCE – FRA (1920) (Votes 12)

Federation Francaise de Tennis
Stade Roland Garros 2 Avenue Gordon Bennett
75016 Paris
T 33 1 4743 4800 **FAX** 33 1 4743 0494
Website: www.fft.fr
Pres: Mr Christian Bimes
Sec: tba

GABON – GAB (1988) (Votes 1)

Federation Gabonaise de Tennis
PO Box 4241 Libreville
T 241 778 971 **FAX** 241 703 190
E-mail: fegabten@hotmail.com
Website: raa.rdd-gabon.gouv.ga.fegaten
Pres: Mr Samuel Minko Mindong
Sec: Mr Marcel Desire Mebale

GEORGIA – GEO (1992) (Votes 1)

Georgian Tennis Federation
K Marjanishvili St 29 Tbilisi
T 995 32 952 781 **FAX** 995 32 953 829
E-mail: geonoc@access.sanet.ge
Pres: Ms Leila Meskhi
Sec: Mr Zurab Katsarava

GERMANY – GER (1902) (Votes 12)

Deutscher Tennis Bund eV
Hallerstrasse 89 20149 Hamburg
T 49 40 411 780 **FAX** 49 40 411 782 22
E-mail: dtbpress@aol.com
Website: www.dtb-tennis.de
Pres: Dr Georg Von Waldenfels
Sec: Mr Reimund Schneider

GHANA – GHA (1909) (Votes1)

Ghana Tennis Association
PO Box T-95 Sports Stadium Post Office Accra
T 233 21 667 267 **FAX** 233 2166 2281
E-mail: gtennis@africaonline.com.gh
Pres: Mr Edmund Annan
Sec: Mr Charles James Aryeh

GREAT BRITAIN – GBR (1888) (Votes 12)

The Lawn Tennis Association
The Queen's Club West Kensington
London W14 9EG
T 44 171 381 7000 **FAX** 44 171 381 5965
E-mail: info@lta.org.uk
Website: www.lta.org.uk
Pres: Mr Malcolm Gracie
Sec: Mr John James

GREECE – GRE (1938) (Votes 3)

Hellenic Tennis Federation
267 Imitou Street
11631 Pagrati Athens
T 30 1 756 3170 **FAX** 30 1 756 3173
E-mail: efoa@otenet.gr
Pres: Mr Spyros Zannias
Sec: Mr Ntinos Nikolaidis

GUATEMALA – GUA (1948) (Votes 1)

Federacion Nacionale de Tenis de Guatemala
Section 1551 PO Box 02-5339
Miami, FL 33102-5339, USA
T 502 331 0261 **FAX** 502 331 0261
E-mail: fedtenis@infovia.com.gt
Pres: Mr Carlos Saravia **Sec:** Mr Francis Bruderer

HAITI – HAI (1950) (Votes 1)

Federation Haitienne de Tennis
PO Box 1442 Port Au Prince
T 509 246 2798 **FAX** 509 249 1233
E-mail: tennis_haiti@abhardware.com
Pres: Mr Maxime Sada
Sec: Mr Benjie Theard Russo

HONDURAS – HON (1989) (Votes 1)

Federacion Hondurena de Tenis
PO Box 30152 Toncontin Comayaguela MDC
T 504 2 396 890 **FAX** 504 239 6887
Pres: Mr Humberto Rodriguez
Sec: Mr Rodulio Perdomo

HUNGARY – HUN (1907) (Votes 5)

Magyar Tenisz Szovetseg
Dozsa Gyorgy ut 1-3 H-1143 Budapest
T 36 1 252 6687 **FAX** 36 1 251 0107
E-mail: tennis@mail.matav.hu
Pres: Dr Janos Berenyi
Sec: Mr Attila Deak

ICELAND – ISL (1987) (Votes 1)

Icelandic Tennis Association
Ithrotamidstoedinni I Laugardal 104 Reykjavik
T 354 5 813 377 **FAX** 354 5 888 848
E-mail: jongg@islandia.is
Pres: Mr Skjoldur Vatnar Bjornsson
Sec: tba

INDIA – IND (1920) (Votes 9)

All India Tennis Association
R K Khanna Tennis Stadium
Africa Avenue New Delhi 110 029
T 91 11 617 9062 **FAX** 91 11 617 3159
E-mail: aitaten@del3.vsnl.net.in
Pres: Mr Yashwant Sinha
Sec: Mr Anil Khanna.

INDONESIA – INA (1935)   (Votes 5)

Indonesian Tennis Association
Gelora Senayan Tennis Stadium Jakarta 10270
T 62 21 571 0298 **FAX** 62 21 570 0157
E-mail: pelti@vision.net.id
Pres: Mr Tanri Abeng
Sec: Mr Soegeng Sarjadi

IRAN, ISLAMIC REPUBLIC OF
– IRI (1937)   (Votes 3)

Tennis Federation of Islamic Republic of Iran
PO Box 15815 – 1881 Tehran
T 98 21 884 4731 **FAX** 98 21 884 4731
Pres: Mr Seyed Lankarani
Sec: Mr Hamid R Shayesteh Zad

IRAQ – IRQ (1959)   (Votes 1)

Iraqi Tennis Federation
PO Box 440 Baghdad
T 964 17 748 261 **FAX** 964 1 885 4321
E-mail: inoc@uruklink.net
Pres: Mr Harith Ahmed Al-Ayash
Sec: Mr Manhal Kuba

IRELAND – IRL (1895)   (Votes 3)

Tennis Ireland
Argyle Square Donnybrook Dublin 4
T 353 16 681 841 **FAX** 353 16 683 411
E-mail: tennis@iol.ie
Pres: Dr T Walter Hall
Sec: Mr Ciaran O'Donavan

ISRAEL – ISR (1946)   (Votes 3)

Israel Tennis Association
2 Shitrit Street Tel Aviv 69482
T 972 36 499 440 **FAX** 972 36 499 144
E-mail: igutenis@netvision.net.il
Pres: Mr David Harnik **Sec:** Mr Yoram Baron

ITALY – ITA (1910)   (Votes 9)

Federazione Italiana Tennis
Viale Tiziano 74 00196 Rome
T 390 636 858 406 **FAX** 390 363 868 606
E-mail: fit_segr@gisa.net
Pres: tba
Sec: Mr Gianfranco Carabelli

JAMAICA – JAM   (Votes 1)

(Tennis Jamaica Limited)
Tennis Jamaica 68 Lady Musgrave Road
Kingston 10 JAMAICA W.1.
PO Box 175 2a Piccadilly Road Kingston 5
T 1 876 927 9466 **FAX** 1 876 927 9436
E-mail: tennisjam@cwjamaica.com
Pres: Mr Ken Morgan
Sec: Mrs Jocelin Morgan

JAPAN – JPN (1922)   (Votes 9)

Japan Tennis Association
c/o Kishi Memorial Hall 1-1-1 Jinnan
Shibuya-Ku Tokyo 8050
T 81 33 481 2321 **FAX** 81 33 467 5192
E-mail: info@jta-tennis.or.jp
Website: www.tennis.or.jp
Pres: Mr Masaaki Morita
Sec: Mr Shin-ichi Shimizu

JORDAN – JOR (1980)   (Votes 1)

Jordan Tennis Federation
PO Box 961046 Amman
T/FAX 962 65 682 796
E-mail: tennisfed@tennisfed.com.jo
Pres: Mr Saad Hijjawi **Sec:** Ms Tamara Qunash

KAZAKHSTAN – KAZ (1991)   (Votes 1)

Kazakhstan Tennis Federation
Central Sports Club of the Army 480051 Almaty
T 7 3272 641 759 **FAX** 7 3272 640 469
Pres: Mr Pavel Novikov **Sec:** Mr Valery Kovalev

KENYA – KEN (1922)   (Votes 1)

Kenya Lawn Tennis Asssociation
PO Box 43184 Nairobi
T 254 2 725 672 **FAX** 254 2 725 672
E-mail: jkenani@kcb.co.ke
Pres: Mr James Kenani **Sec:** Mr Baldev Aggarwal

KOREA, REPUBLIC OF – KOR (1945)   (Votes 5)

Korean Tennis Association
Room 108, Olympic Gym No. 2
88-2 Oryun-Dong, Songpa-Gu Seoul 138-151
T 82 2 420 4285 **FAX** 82 2 420 4284
E-mail: tennis@sports.or.kr
Pres: Mr Doo Hwan Kim
Sec: Mr Yeong-Moo Huh

KUWAIT – KUW (1967)   (Votes 1)

Kuwait Tennis Federation
PO Box 1462 Hawalli 32015
T 965 539 7261 **FAX** 965 539 0617
Pres: Sheik Ahmed Al-Sabah
Sec: Mr Abdul-Ridha Ghareeb

LATVIA – LAT (1928)   (Votes 1)

Latvian Tennis Union
Oskara Kalpaka Pr.16 LV 2010 Jurmala
T 371 775 2121 **FAX** 371 775 5021
E-mail: teniss@parks.lv
Pres: Mr Juris Savickis **Sec:** Mr Janis Pliens

LEBANON – LIB (1945)   (Votes 1)

Federation Libanaise de Tennis
1st Floor Beirut-Lebanon & Kuwait Bk Building
Dora Main Street Beirut
T 961 1 879 288 **FAX** 961 1 879 277
E-mail: nvs@leb-online.com
Pres: Mr Riad Haddad
Sec: Mr Nohad V Schoucair

LESOTHO – LES (1920)   (Votes 1)

Lesotho Lawn Tennis Association
PO Box 156 Maseru 100
T 266 317 340 **FAX** 266 321 543
Pres: Mr Makase Nyaphisi
Sec: Mr Clement M Nots'l

LIBYA – LBA (1996)   (Votes 1)

Libyan Arab Tennis & Squash Federation
PO Box 879 – 2729 Tripoli
T 218 21 333 9150 **FAX** 218 21 333 9150
E-mail: liyan_tennis_fed@hotmail.com
Pres: Mr Abdul-Hamid M Shamash
Sec: Mr Abdulssalam A Bellel

LIECHTENSTEIN – LIE (1968) (Votes 1)

Liechtensteiner Tennisverband
Heiligkreuz 28 9490 Vaduz
T 423 235 8181 **FAX** 423 392 4418
Pres: Mr Daniel Kieber
Sec: Mr Werner Schachle

LITHUANIA – LTU (1992) (Votes 1)

Lithuanian Tennis Union
Zemaites 6
2675 Vilnius
T/FAX 3702 333 898
Pres: Mr Vytautas Lapinskas
Sec: Mr Mindaugas Dagys

LUXEMBOURG – LUX (1946) (Votes 1)

Federation Luxembourgeoise de Tennis
Boite Postale 134 L-4002 Esch-Sur-Alzette
T 352 574 470 **FAX** 352 574 473
E-mail: fltennis@pt.lu
Pres: Mr Paul Helminger **Sec:** Mr Erny Betzen

MACEDONIA, FORMER YUGOSLAV REPUBLIC OF – MKD (1993) (Votes 1)

FYR Macedonian Tennis Association
91000 Skopje Gradski Park 88 Skopje
T 389 91 129 200 **FAX** 389 91 116 146
Pres: Mr George Gurkovic
Sec: Miss Marija Gavrilovska

MADAGASCAR – MAD (1979) (Votes 1)

Federation Malgache de Tennis
Siege du Comite Olympique Malgache
Mahamasina – 101 Antananarivo
T 261 202 263 198 **FAX** 261 202 263 199
E-mail: jserger@simicro.mg
Pres: Mr Serge Ramiandrasoa
Sec: Dr Serge Amdriamampandry

MALAYSIA – MAS (1921) (Votes 1)

Lawn Tennis Association of Malaysia
c/o Employees Provident Fund
26th Floor, KWSP Building
Jalan Raja Laut 50350 Kuala Lumpur
T 603 620 161 73 **FAX** 603 620 161 67
E-mail: ltam@first.net.my
Pres: Mr Tan Sri Sallehuddin Mohamed
Sec: Mr Musaladin Dahalan

MALI – MLI (1963) (Votes 1)

Federation Malienne de Tennis
IFA-BACO 425 Avenue de L'Yser
Bamako Quartier du Fleuve
T 223 232 326 **FAX** 223 232 324
E-mail: ifabaco@cefib.com
Pres: Mr Mohamed Traore
Sec: tba

MALTA – MLT (1966) (Votes 1)

Malta Tennis Federation
PO Box 50 Sliema Post Office Sliema
T 356 330 363 **FAX** 356 345 330
E-mail: burgcardona@kemmunet.net.mt
Pres: Dr Peter Zammit
T 356 330 757 **FAX** 356 331 259
Sec: Miss Tanya Gravina

MAURITIUS – MRI (1910) (Votes 1)

Mauritius Lawn Tennis Association
La Croix Street Curepipe
T 230 670 2603 **FAX** 230 370 2539
Pres: Mrs Francoise Desvaux de Marigny
Sec: Mr Akhtar Toorawa

MEXICO – MEX (1952) (Votes 7)

Federacion Mexicana de Tenis
Miguel Angel de Quevedo 953
Mexico City 04330 DF
T 52 5 689 9733 **FAX** 52 5 689 6307
E-mail: federacion@fmttenis.com
Pres: Mr Francisco Maciel
Sec: tba

MOLDOVA – MDA (1953) (Votes 1)

59 Coca Street Chisinau 2039
T/FAX 3732 744 725 (Addit Fax) 3732 223 536
Pres: Mr Grigorii Kushnir
Sec: Ms Larisa Mitrofanova

MONACO – MON (1927) (Votes 1)

Federation Monegasque de Lawn Tennis
BP No 253 MC 98005 Monaco Cedex
T 377 93 255 574 **FAX** 377 93 305 482
E-mail: fedemt@club-internet.fr
Pres: Mrs Elisabeth de Massy
Sec: Mr Alain Manigley

MOROCCO – MAR (1957) (Votes 3)

Federation Royale Marocaine de Tennis
Parc de la Ligue Arabe BP 15794 Casablanca
T 212 22981 266 **FAX** 212 24422 921
Pres: Mr Mohamed M'Jid
Sec: Mr Hachem Kacimimy

NAMIBIA – NAM (1930) (Votes 1)

Namibia Tennis Association
PO Box 479 Windhoek 9000
T 212 2 981 266/212 2 981 262
FAX 264 61 251 718
E-mail: cariena@iafrica.com.na
Pres: Dr Pietie Loubser
Sec: Mrs Carien du Plessis

NETHERLANDS – NED (1899) (Votes 9)

Koninklijke Nederlandse Lawn Tennis Bond
PO Box 1617 3800 BP Amersfoot
T 31 33 454 2600 **FAX** 31 33 454 2645
E-mail: knltb@knltb.nl
Pres: Mr Randall Rojer
Sec: Mr Evert-Jan Hulshof

NETHERLANDS ANTILLES – AHO (1941) (Votes 1)

Netherlands Antilles Tennis Association
c/o Herman J Behr New Haven Office Centre
Emancipatie Boulevard 31 PO Box 6122
Curacao
T 599 9 734 1000 **FAX** 599 9 734 1200
E-mail: info@natf.an
Pres: Mr Herman Behr
Sec: Mr Norman Macares

NEW ZEALAND – NZL (1886)   (Votes 7)

PO Box 11-541 Level 7 Compudigm House
49 Boulcott Street Wellington
T 64 4 476 1115 **FAX** 64 4 473 5267
E-mail: info@tennis.org.nz
Pres: Mr David Howman
Sec: Mrs Christine Burr

NIGERIA – NGR (1927)   (Votes 3)

Nigeria Tennis Association
National Stadium Surulere PO Box 145 Lagos
T 234 1 264 6444 **FAX** 234 1 545 4471
E-mail: nigertennis@hotmail.com
Pres: Mr Chuka Momah
Sec: Mrs Funmi Koya-Adaku

NORWAY – NOR (1909)   (Votes 3)

Norges Tennisforbund
Haslevangen 33 PO Box 287 – Okern Oslo 0511
T 47 2 265 7550 **FAX** 47 2 264 6409
E-mail: tennis@nif.idrett.no
Pres: Mr Jarl Whist **Sec:** Mr Jarle Aambo

OMAN – OMA (1986)   (Votes 1)

Oman Tennis Association
PO Box 2226 Ruwi Postal Code 112
T 968 751 402 **FAX** 968 751 394
E-mail: tennis@gto.net.om
Pres: Mr Rashad Mohammed Al Zubair
Sec: Mr Mohamad Salim Khawwar

PAKISTAN – PAK (1947)   (Votes 3)

Pakistan Tennis Federation
39-A Jinnah Stadium Pakistan Sports Complex
Kashmir Highway Islamabad
T 92 519 212 846 **FAX** 92 519 212 846
E-mail: pktenfed@isb.comsats.net.pk
Pres: Mr Anwar Saifullah Khan
Sec: Mr Mohammad Ali Akbar

PANAMA – PAN (1986)   (Votes 1)

Federacion Panamena de Tenis
Apartado 6-4965 El Dorado
T 507 232 5196 **FAX** 507 232 6841
Pres: Mrs Norma Maduro
Sec: Mr Juan B Quintero

PARAGUAY – PAR (1920)   (Votes 3)

Asociacion Paraguaya de Tenis
Centro Nacional de Tenis
Av Eusebio Ayala Km. 41/2 y RI.6
Boqueron Consejo Nacional de Deportes
T/FAX 595 21 520 674
E-mail: apt@supernet.com.py
Pres: Mr Miguel Carrizosa
Sec: Mrs Esther Tami

PERU – PER (1930)   (Votes 3)

Federacion de Tenis del Peru
Cercado Campo de Marte S/N
Casilla Nro 11-0488 Lima 11
T 511 424 9979 **FAX** 511 431 0533
E-mail: tenisperu@.com.pe
Pres: Ing Alfredo Acuna
Sec: Mr Julio Chang

PHILIPPINES – PHI (1946)   (Votes 3)

Philippine Tennis Association
Rizal Memorial Sports Complex
Pablo Ocampo Sr. Street Manila
T 63 2 525 6434 **FAX** 63 2 525 2016
Pres: Colonel Salvador H Andrada
Sec: Mr Romeo Magat

POLAND – POL (1921)   (Votes 3)

Polski Zwiazek Tenisowy
Ul. Marszalkowska 2 3rd Floor 00-581 Warsaw
T 48 22 629 2621 **FAX** 48 22 621 8001
E-mail: pzt@pzt.top.pl
Pres: Mr Jacek Durski
Sec: Ms Regina Sokolowska

PORTUGAL – POR (1925)   (Votes 3)

Federacao Portuguesa de Tenis
Rua Actor Chaby Pinheiro, 7-A
2795 Linda-A-Velha
T 351 21 415 1356 **FAX** 351 21 414 1520
E-mail: fptenis@mail.telepac.pt
Pres: Dr Paulo Andrade
Sec: Mr Jose Carlos Machado Costa

PUERTO RICO – PUR (1959)   (Votes 1)

Associacion de Tenis de Puerto Rico
1611 Fernandez Juncos Avenue
Santurce PR 00909
T 1 787 928 7782 **FAX** 1 787 982 7783
Pres: Mr Pedro Beauchamp
Sec: Dr Carlos Rivera

QATAR – QAT (1984)   (Votes 1)

Qatar Tennis and Squash Federation
PO Box 4959 Doha
T 974 409 666 **FAX** 974 832 990
Pres: Mr Ali Hussein Al Fardan
Sec: Mr Mohammad Ismail Moh'd Noor

ROMANIA – ROM (1929)   (Votes 1)

Federatia Romana de Tennis
Str Vasile Conta 16 Sector 2 70139 Bucharest
T 401 324 5330 **FAX** 401 324 5329
E-mail: frtenis@mts-gw.pub.ro
Pres: tba
Sec: Prof Lucian Vasiliu

RUSSIA – RUS (1975)   (Votes 5)

All Russia Tennis Association
Lutzhnetskaya Nab 8 119871 Moscow
T 7 095 725 4695 **FAX** 7 095 201 0362
Pres: Mr Shamil Tarpirschev
Sec: Mr Alexander Kalivod

RWANDA – RWA (1984)   (Votes 1)

Federation Rwandaise de Tennis
BP 1974 Kigali
T 250 74521 **FAX** 250 74074
E-mail: thierryn@usa.net
Pres: Dr Charles Ruadkubana
Sec: Mr Freddy Somayire Rubona

SAINT LUCIA – LCA (1997)　　　(Votes 1)

St Lucia Lawn Tennis Association
PO Box 126 Castries West Indies
T 1 758 450 0106 **FAX** 1 758 450 9277
E-mail: huntet@candw.lc
Pres: Mr Stephen McNamara
Sec: Mrs Pauline Erlinger-Ford

SAN MARINO – SMR (1956)　　　(Votes 1)

Federazione Sammarinese Tennis
Casella Postal No 2 Dogana 47031
T 378 990 578 **FAX** 378 990 584
Pres: Mr Remo Raimondi
Sec: Mr Christian Forcellini

ARABIA, KINGDOM OF – KSA (1956)　　(Votes 1)

Saudi Arabian Tennis Federation
PO Box 29454 Riyadh 11457
T 966 1 482 0188 **FAX** 966 1 482 2829
E-mail: sf@sauditenfed.gov.sa
Pres: Mr Abdulaziz S Kridis
Sec: Mr Rasheed Abu Rasheed

SENEGAL – SEN (1960)　　　(Votes 1)

BP 1712 Dakar
T 221 822 4411 **FAX** 221 823 1222
E-mail: catennis@telecomplus
Pres: Mr Amadou Ndiaye
Sec: Mr Layti Ndiaye

SINGAPORE – SIN (1928)　　　(Votes 1)

Singapore Lawn Tennis Association
Unit 10 National Stadium
15 Stadium Road 397718
T 65 348 0124 **FAX** 65 348 2414
E-mail: slta@pacific.net.sg
Pres: Mr Edwin Lee
Sec: Dr Tan Hai Chuang

SLOVAK REPUBLIC – SVK (1968)　　(Votes 5)

Slovak Tennis Association
Junacka 6 832 80 Bratislava
T 421 7 49249 134 **FAX** 421 7 49249 561
E-mail: stz@mbox.bts.sk
Pres: Mr Tibor Macko
Sec: Mr Igor Moska

SLOVENIA – SLO (1946)　　　(Votes 1)

Slovene Tennis Association
Vurnikova 2/Vi1000 Ljubljana
T 386 611 337 170 **FAX** 386 611 334 281
E-mail: teniska.zveza@sting.si
Pres: Dr Drasko Veselinovic
Sec: Mr Tone Preseren

SOUTH AFRICA, REPUBLIC OF – RSA (1991)　　　(Votes 9)

South African Tennis Association
PO Box 15978 Doornfontein Johannesburg 2028
T 27 11 402 3616 **FAX** 27 11 402 0242
E-mail: satennis@icon.co.za
Website: www.tennisnet.co.za
Pres: Mr Gordon Forbes
Sec: Mr Mohamed Sheik

SPAIN – ESP (1901)　　　(Votes 9)

Real Federacion Espanola de Tenis
Avda Diagonal 618 3 D 08021 Barcelona
T 34 93 200 5355 **FAX** 34 93 202 1279
E-mail: rfet@fedetenis.es
Pres: Mr Agustin Pujol Niubo
Sec: Mr Thomas Garcia Balmaseda

SRI LANKA – SRI (1915)　　　(Votes 1)

Sri Lanka Tennis Association
45 Sir Marcus Fernando Mawatha Colombo 7
T 94 1 686 174 **FAX** 94 1 686 174
Pres: Mr Lalith Withana
Sec: Mr Maxwell de Silva

SUDAN – SUD (1956)　　　(Votes 1)

Sudan Lawn Tennis Association
PO Box 3792 Africa House Khartoum
T 249 11 770 246 **FAX** 246 11 781 818
Pres: Mr Hassab Elrasoul Mohamed Eltayeb
Sec: Mr Nour Eldine Elsadig

SWEDEN – SWE (1906)　　　(Votes 9)

The Swedish Tennis Association
Box 27915 S-115 94 Stockholm
T 46 86 679 770 **FAX** 48 86 646 606
E-mail: info@tennis.se
Website: www.tennis.se
Pres: Mr Jan Carlzon
Sec: Mr Anders Wetterberg

SWITZERLAND – SUI (1896)　　　(Votes 7)

Swiss Tennis Association
Solothurnstrasse 112 2501 Biel
T 41 32 344 0707 **FAX** 41 32 344 0700
Pres: Mrs Christine Ungricht
Sec: Mr Pierre-Alain Morard

SYRIA – SYR (1953)　　　(Votes 1)

Syrian Arab Tennis Federation
PO Box 967 421 Baramke Damascus
T 963 11 212 5026 **FAX** 963 11 212 3346
Pres: Mr Samer Mourad
Sec: Mr Fakhr Al Deen Moukahel

TAJIKISTAN – TJK (1992)　　　(Votes 1)

National Tennis Federation of
the Republic of Tajikistan
Tennis Palace A/B 308 Dushanbe 734001
T/FAX 992 377 2361 206
E-mail: info@ft.tajik.net
Pres: Mr Amircul Azimov
Sec: Mr Vazirbek Nazirov

THAILAND – THA (1927)　　　(Votes 3)

The Lawn Tennis Association of Thailand
Tennis Complex
Muang Thong Thani Sports Complex
Chaengwattana Pakkred
Nonthaburi 11120
T 66 2 504 0382/83 **FAX** 66 2 504 0381
E-mail: thtennis@ksc.th.com (temp)
Pres: General Akaradej Sasiprapha
Sec: Gen Wichar Siritham

TOGO – TOG (1955)   (Votes 1)
Federation Togolaise de Tennis
BP 12720 Lome
T 228 215 181 **FAX** 228 222 397
E-mail: fttennis@togo-imet.com
Pres: Mr Kouassi Luc Dofontien
Sec: Mr Koffi Galokpo

TRINIDAD AND TOBAGO – TRI (1951) (Votes 1)
The Tennis Association of Trinidad and Tobago
21 Taylor Street Woodbrook Port of Spain
Trinidad West Indies
T 1 868 625 3939 **FAX** 1 686 625 3939
Pres: Ms Sadie Robarts **Sec:** Ms Maureen Lalman

TUNISIA – TUN (1954)   (Votes 1)
Federation Tunisienne de Tennis
BP 350 El Menzah 1004 Tunis
T 216 1 844 144 **FAX** 216 1 798 844
Pres: Mr Tarak Cherif **Sec:** Mr Zohra Bouhafa & Mr
Mustapha Zouabi

TURKEY – TUR (1923)   (Votes 3)
Turkiye Tenis Federasyonu
Ulus Is Hani Ankara
T 90 312 310 7345 **FAX** 90 312 311 254
Pres: Mr Sadi Toker **Sec:** Mr Yener Dogru

UGANDA – UGA (1948)   (Votes 1)
Uganda Tennis Association
PO Box 9825 Kampala
T 256 41 236 688/257 327 **FAX** 256 41 236 333
Pres: Mr Peter Ntaki **Sec:** Mr Gideon M Karyoko

UKRAINE – UKR (1946)   (Votes 1)
Ukrainian Tennis Federation
A/C B-2 PO 252001 Kiev
T 38 044 224 8782 **FAX** 38 044 290 4062
Pres: Mr German Benyaminov
Sec: Mr Volodimir Gerashchenko

UNITED ARAB EMIRATES – UAE (1982)(Votes 1)
United Arab Emirates Tennis Association
PO Box 22466 Dubai
T 971 4 669 0390 **FAX** 971 4 666 9390
E-mail: khafief@emirates.net.ae
Pres: Sheikh Hasher Al-Maktoum
Sec: Mohammed Al-Merry

UNITED STATES OF AMERICA –
USA (1881)   (Votes 12)
United States Tennis Association
70 West Red Oak Lane White Plains
New York NY 10604
T 1 914 696 7000 **FAX** 1 914 696 7167
Website: www.usta.com
Pres: Ms Julia A Levering
Sec: Mr Michael Kohlhoff

UNITED STATES VIRGIN ISLANDS
– ISV (1973)   (Votes 1)
Virgin Islands Tennis Association
PO Box 306715 St Thomas Usvi 00803-6715
T 1 340 776 1010 **FAX** 1 340 776 2185
Pres: Mr Wilbur Callender
Sec: Ms Delores Stephen Rivas

URUGUAY – URU (1915)   (Votes 3)
Asociacion Uruguaya de Tenis
Galicia 1392 CP 11.200 Montevideo
T 598 2 901 5020 **FAX** 598 2 902 1809
E-mail: aut@montevideo.com.uy
Pres: Sr Gilberto Saenz **Sec:** Sr Elbio Arias

UZBEKISTAN – UZB (1992)   (Votes 3)
Uzbekistan Tennis Federation
1 Uljanovskij Pereulok House 14
Tashkent 700035
T 99 87 11 37 255 **FAX** 99 87 12 30 2272
E-mail: shepelev@uzbektennis.uz
Pres: Mr R Inoyatov **Sec:** Mr I Shepelev

VENEZUELA – VEN (1927)   (Votes 5)
Federacion Venezolana de Tenis
Calle Apartado 70539 Caracas 1070-A
T 58 29 797 095 **FAX** 58 29 792 694
E-mail: fevtnis@ibm.net
Pres: Mr Jose Amador Diaz
Sec: Ms Rebeca Torrealba

YUGOSLAVIA – YUG (1922)   (Votes 3)
Tenis Savez Yugoslavije
Aleksandra Stamboliskog 26
11000 Beograd
T 381 116 675 40 **FAX** 381 116 616 35
E-mail: yugtenis@verat.net.
Pres: Mr Radoman Bozovic **Sec:** Mr Dejan Simic

ZAMBIA – ZAM (1975)   (Votes 1)
Zambia Lawn Tennis Association
c/o Ndola Tennis Club
PO Box 70436 Ndola
T 260 2 441 832 **FAX** 260 2 412 651
E-mail: zimbam@mcm.com.zm
Pres: Mr Henry Musenge **Sec:** Mr M Zimba

ZIMBABWE – ZIM (1904)   (Votes 3)
Tennis Zimbabwe
PO Box A575 Avondale Harare
T 263 4 229 939 **FAX** 263 4 224 079
E-mail: teniszim@africaonline.co.zw
Pres: Mr Paul Chingoka
Sec: Ms Gladys Mutyiri

Class C (Associate) Members without voting rights (57)

AFGHANISTAN – AFG (1963)

Afghan Lawn Tennis Association
House No. 400 Street No. 89
Sector G-9/4 Islamabad
T 92 51 260 987 **FAX** 92 51 299 756
E-mail: k_chughtai@usa.net
Pres: Mr Homayun Paravanta
Sec: Mr Muhammad Khalil

ALBANIA – ALB (1996)

Rruga Siri Kodra Shtypshkronja PSH 2015
Blloku Magazinave Tirana
T 355 422 5925 **FAX** 335 423 0895
E-mail: att@abissnet.com.al
Pres: Mr Perlat Voshtina
Sec: Mr Arben Alushi

AMERICAN SAMOA – ASA (1985)

American Samoa Tennis Association
PO Box 3501 Pago Pago AS 96799
T 684 699 2100 **FAX** 684 699 2105
E-mail: tigi@samoatelco.com
Pres: Miss Fiaapia Devoe
Sec: Dr Jerome Amoa

ARUBA – ARU (1954)

Aruba Lawn Tennis Bond
Fergusonstraat Nr 40-A PO Box 1151 Oranjestad
T 297 827 578 **FAX** 297 831 643
E-mail: aruba_lawntennis@hotmail.com
Pres: Mr Lucas Rasmijn
Sec: Mr Peter Mohamed

BELIZE – BIZ (1910)

Belize Tennis Association
PO Box 365 Belize City
T 501 277 070 **FAX** 501 275 593
Pres: Mr Edward Nabil Musr Sr
Sec: Mr Clement Usher

BHUTAN – BHU (1976)

Bhutan Tennis Federation
PO Box 103 Thimphu
T 975 232 2138 **FAX** 975 232 3937
E-mail: bhusport@druknet.net.bt
Pres: Mr Dasho Passang Dorji
Sec: Mr Tshering Namgay

BRITISH VIRGIN ISLANDS – IVB (1983)

British Virgin Islands Lawn Tennis Association
PO Box 948 Road Town Tortola
T 1 284 494 3650 **FAX** 1 284 494 5671
Pres: Mr Lloyd Black
Sec: Mr Clive Gumbs

BURUNDI – BDI (1993)

Federation de Tennis du Burundi
BP 2221 Bujumbura
T 257 242 443**FAX** (257) 222 247
(Addit Fax) 257 242 445
E-mail: ftb@cbinf.com
Pres: Mr Edouard Hicintuka
Sec: Mrs Dominique Niyonizigiye

CAPE VERDE ISLANDS – CPV (1986)

Federacao Cabo-Verdiana de Tenis
Ministerio da Informacao Cultura E Desportos
Rua 5 de Julho Praia
T 238 613 309 **FAX** 238 621 312
E-mail: fedcabtenis@cvtelecom.cv
Pres: Mr Hugo Almeida
Sec: Mr Antonio Ferreira

CAYMAN ISLANDS – CAY (1973)

Tennis Federation of the Cayman Islands
PO Box 219 GT Grand Cayman
British West Indies
T 1 345 949 7000 **FAX** 1 345 949 8154
Pres: Mr Chris Johnson
Sec: Mr John Smith

CENTRAL AFRICAN REPUBLIC – CAF (1990)

Federation Centrafricaine de Tennis
BP 804 Bangui R C A
T 236 611 805 **FAX** 236 615 660
Pres: Mr I Kamach
Sec: Mr Jean Om

CONGO, DEMOCRATIC REPUBLIC OF – COD (1984)

Federation Congolaise Democratique
de Lawn Tennis
BP 20750 Kin 15 Kinshasa
T 243 881 0013 **FAX** 243 881 0034
Pres: Mr Kanyama Mishindu
Sec: Mr Eleko Botuna Bo'Osisa

COOK ISLANDS – COK (1947)

Tennis Cook Islands
PO Box 780 Rarotonga
T 682 22 327 **FAX** 682 23 602
T/FAX: 682 27 113
E-mail: raina@gatepoly.co.ck
Pres: Mr Chris McKinley
Sec: Mr Brendan Stone

DOMINICA – DMA (1960)

Dominica Lawn Tennis Association
PO Box 1593 Roseau
T 1 767 448 2681 **FAX** 1 767 448 7010
Pres: Mr Kenny Alleyne
Sec: Mr Thomas Dorsett

EQUATORIAL GUINEA – GEQ (1992)

Equatorial Guinea Tennis Federation
PO Box 980 B.N Malabo
T 240 9 2866 **FAX** 240 9 3313
Pres: Mr Enrique Mercader Costa
Sec: Mr Francisco Sibita

ERITREA – ERI (1998)

Eritrean Tennis Federation
PO Box 4115 Asmara
T 291 1 121 284 **FAX** 291 1 127 255
Pres: Mr Tewoldeberhan Mehari
Sec: Dr Fesseha Haile

GAMBIA – GAM (1938)

Gambia Lawn Tennis Association
PMB 664 Serekunda
T 220 495 834 **FAX** 220 496 270
E-mail: gnosc@commit.gm
Pres: Mr Charles Thomas
Sec: Mr Geoffrey Renner

GRENADA – GRN (1973)

Grenada Tennis Association
PO Box 1202 St George's
T 1 473 440 3343 **FAX** 1 473 440 1977
Pres: Mr Ken Aberdeen
Sec: Ms Salesha Patrick

GUAM – GUM (1973)

Guam National Tennis Federation
PO Box 4379 Agana GUAM 96932
T 1 671 472 6270 **FAX** 1 671 472 8719
E-mail: yasnit@hotmail.com
Website: www.tennis.guam.org
Pres: Mr Rick Ninete
Sec: Ms Analiza Tubal

GUINEE-CONAKRY – GUI (1980)

Federation Guineenne de Tennis
BP 4897
T 224 444 019 **FAX** 224 411 926
Pres: Mme Magass-Malado Diallo
Sec: Mr Baba Bayo

GUYANA – GUY (1933)

Guyana Lawn Tennis Association
PO Box 10205 Georgetown
T 592 265 251 **FAX** 592 267 559
Pres: Mr William Skeete
Sec: Ms Georgia Inniss

KIRIBATI – KIR (1979)

Kiribati Tennis Association
PO Box 80 Antebuka Tarawa
T 686 28075 **FAX** 686 28384
Pres: Mr Peter Birati **Sec:** Eritibete Tomizuka

KYRGHYZSTAN – KGZ (1992)

Kyrghyzstan Tennis Federation Kyrghyzstan
Moskovskey Str 121/58 Bishkek 720000
T/FAX 996 312 214 756
E-mail: tfkr@imfiko.bishkek.su
Pres: Mr Nikolai Tanaev
Sec: Mr Valentin Akinshin

LAO, DEMOCRATIC PEOPLE'S REPUBLIC – LAO (1998)

Lao Tennis Federation
PO Box 6280 Vientiane
T 856 212 956 **FAX** 856 21 215 274
Pres: Mr Kikham Vongsay
Sec: Mr Khounno Phonesomdeth

LIBERIA – LBR (1987)

PO BOX 10-1742 Buchannan Street Monrovia
LIBERIA
T/FAX 231 227 124 & (addit fax) 231 227 044
Pres: Mr Siake Toure
Sec: Mr Edmund Dassin

MALAWI – MAW (1966)

Lawn Tennis Association of Malawi
PO Box 1417 Blantyre
T 265 672 298 & 265 672 196 **FAX** 265 672 417
Pres: Mr Ronnie Pitcher **Sec:** Ms Barbara Halse

MALDIVES – MDV (1983)

Tennis Association of the Maldives
PO Box 20175 Male
T 960 317 018 **FAX** 960 310 325
E-mail: info@tennismaldives.com.mv
Website: www.tennismaldives.com.mv
Pres: Mr Ahmed Aslam
Sec: tba

MARSHALL ISLANDS – MSH (1996)

Marshall Island Tennis Federation
PO Box 197 Marjuro MH96960
T 692 625 5275 **FAX** 692 625 5277
E-mail: troyb@ntamar.com
Pres: Mr Oscar Debrum
Sec: Ms Netty Nathan

MAURITANIA – MTN (1989)

Federation Mauritanienne de Tennis
BP 654 Nouakchott
FAX only 222 25 69 37
Pres: Mr Isaac Ould Rajel
Sec: Mr Cheickh Ould Horomtala

MICRONESIA, FEDERATED STATES OF – FSM (1985)

Federated States of Micronesia
Lawn Tennis Association
PO Box PS319 Paliker Pohnpei FM 96941
T 691 320 619 **FAX** 691 320 8915
E-mail: fsmnoc@mail.fm
Pres: Mr Richard Alex
Sec: Mr James Tobin

MONGOLIA – MGL (1990)

Mongolian Tennis Association
PO Box 522 Ulaanbaatar 44
T 976 1 372 980
FAX 976 1 343 611 & 976 1 343 033
E-mail: mta@magicnet.mn
Pres: Mr A Ganbaatar
Sec: Janchiv Batjargal

MOZAMBIQUE – MOZ (1979)

Federacao Mocambicana de Tenis
Caixa Postal 4351 Maputo
T 258 1 42 7027 **FAX** 258 1 303 665
E-mail: FMTenis@hotmail.com
Pres: Mr Arao Nhancale
Sec: Mr Albino Nguenha

MYANMAR – MYA (1949)

Myanmar Tennis Federation
627-635 Merchant Street
PO Box No 204 Yangon
T 951 71 731 **FAX** 951 571 061
Pres: Mr U Chit Swe
Sec: Dr Myint Soe

NAURU – NRU (1992)

Nauru Tennis Association
PO Box 274
T 674 444 3118 **FAX** 674 444 3179
E-mail: naurutennis@yahoo.com
Pres: Chief Paul Aingimea
Sec: Mr Preston Itaia

NEPAL – NEP (1968)

All Nepal Tennis Association
PO Box 3943 Kathmandu
T 977 1 426 002 **FAX** 977 1 416 427
E-mail: anlta@mos.com.np
Pres: Mr Siddheshwar K Singh
Sec: Mr Ramji Thapa

NICARAGUA – NCA (1994)

Federacion Nicaraguense de Tenis
PO Box 2878 Sucursal Jorge Navarro Managua
T 505 265 1572 **FAX** 505 278 7039
E-mail: donar@ibw.com.ni
Pres: Mr Jose Antonio Arguello
Sec: tba

NIGER – NIG (1988)

Federation Nigerienne de Tennis
Stade du 29 Juillet 1991 Avenue du Zarmaganda
BP 10 788 Niamey
T 227 735 893 **FAX** 227 732 876
E-mail: bdaniger@intnet.ne
Pres: Mr Ahmed Ousman Diallo
Sec: Mr Boubacar Djibo

NORFOLK ISLANDS – NFK (1998)

Norfolk Islands Tennis Association
Queen Elizabeth Avenue Norfolk Island
South Pacific Ocean
T (6723) 229 66 **FAX** (6723) 236 03
E-mail: emaisey@ni.net.nf
Pres: Mr Thomas Greening
Sec: Emma Maisey

NORTHERN MARIANA ISLANDS – NMI

Northern Mariana Islands Tennis Association
PO Box 10,000 Saipan MP 96950-9504
T 670 234 8438 **FAX** 670 234 5545
E-mail: race@saipan.com
Pres: Mr Mike Walsh **Sec:** Mr Ed Johnson

PALAU, DEMOCRATIC REPUBLIC OF – PAL (1998)

Palau Amateur Tennis Association
PO Box 9 Koror 96940
T (608) 488 2690 **FAX** (680) 488 1310
E-mail: ekrengiil@palaunet.com
Pres: Ms Christina Michelsen
Sec: Mr Jay Olegerill

PALESTINE – PLE (1998)

Palestinian Tennis Association
Beit Sahour PO Box 131
T 972 2 277 5244
FAX 972 2 277 5245
E-mail: medrish@p-ol.com
Pres: Mr Issa Rishmawi
Sec: Mrs Samar Mousa Araj

PAPUA NEW GUINEA – PNG (1963)

Papua New Guinea Lawn Tennis Association
PO Box 5656 Boroko
T 675 321 1533 **FAX** 675 321 3001
E-mail: raisi@online.net.pg
Pres: Mr Robert Aisi **Sec:** tba

SAINT KITTS – SKN (1962)

Mr Raphael Jenkins President St Kitts Tennis
Association
Cayon Street Basseterre
T 869 465 6809 **FAX** 869 465 1190
Pres: Mr Raphael Jenkins
Sec: Ms Connie Marsham

SAINT VINCENT & THE GRENADINES – VIN (1972)

St Vincent & the Grenadines
Lawn Tennis Association PO Box 1487 Kingstown
T 1 784 457 4229 **FAX** 1 784 457 2901
E-mail: islandsports@caribsurf.com
Pres: Mr Michael Nanton **Sec:** Mr Peter Nanton

SAMOA – SAM (1955)

Tennis Samoa Inc.
PO Box 1297 Apia
T/FAX 685 21145
Pres: Mr Waikaremoaana Soonalole
Sec: Mr Lolane Auala

SEYCHELLES – SEY (1955)

Seychelles Tennis Association
PO Box 602 Victoria Mahe
T 248 323 908 **FAX** 248 324 066
E-mail: tennisey@seychelles.net
Pres: Mr Giancarlo Lauro **Sec:** Mr John Adam

SIERRA LEONE – SLE (1965)

Sierra Leone Lawn Tennis Association
National Sports Council PO Box 1181 Freetown
T 232 22 226 525 **FAX** 232 22 229 083
Pres: Mr Henry Moore
Sec: Mr E T Ngandi

SOLOMON ISLANDS – SOL (1993)

Solomon Islands Tennis Association
PO Box 111 Honiara
T 677 21 616 **FAX** 677 25 498
Pres: Mr Ranjit Hewagama
Sec: Mr Selwyn Miduku

SOMALIA – SOM

The Somali Tennis Association
c/o 5 Gabalaya Street 11567 El Borg Cairo
T 252 1 280 042 **FAX** 252 1 216 516
E-mail: yugtenis@verat.net
Pres: Mr Osman Mohiadin Moallim
Sec: Mr Abdurahman Warsame Abdulle

SURINAME – SUR (1936)

Surinaamse Tennisbond
PO Box 2087 Paramaribo-Zuid
T 597 476 703 **FAX** 597 471 047
E-mail: hindori@cq-link.sr
Pres: Mr Manodj Hindori
Sec: Ms Ann Meyer

SWAZILAND – SWZ (1968)

Swaziland National Tennis Union
PO Box 2397 Manzini
T 268 54564 **FAX** 268 40063
Pres: Mr Derick. Jele **Sec:** Mr Bosco Dludlu

TANZANIA – TAN

Tanzania Lawn Tennis Association
PO Box 965 Dar Es Salaam
T 255 222 120 519 **FAX** 255 222 116 566
E-mail: rugimbana@ud.co.tz
Pres: Mr Richard Rugimbana **Sec:** Mr Godfrey
Zimba

TONGA – TGA (1959)

Tonga Tennis Association
PO Box 816 Nuku'alofa
T 676 23933 **FAX** 676 24127
Pres: Mr Fuka Kitekeiaho **Sec:** Ms Kiu Tatafu

TURKMENISTAN – TKM (1992)

Turkmenistan Tennis Association
30 Mkrn Pr 2 Bulvarny 744020 Ashgabat
T 993 12 247 825 **FAX** 99 312 352 728
& 99 312 393 187
Pres: Mr Berdimurad Redjepov
Sec: Mr Bjashimov Serdar

VANUATU – VAN (1990)

Federation de Tennis de Vanuatu
BP 563 Port Vila
T 678 22087 **FAX** 678 22698 (& Tel)
E-mail: jacobe@tvl.net.vu
Pres: Mme Evelyne Jacobe
Sec: Mr Michel Mainguy

VIETNAM – VIE (1989)

175 Nguyen Thai Hoc Hanoi
T/FAX 844 733 0036
Pres: Mr Dang Huu Hai
Sec: Mr Nguyen Van Manh

YEMEN – YEM (1902)

Yemen Tennis Federation
PO Box 19816 Sanaa
T 967 1 217 780 **FAX** 967 1 268 456
Pres: Mr Abdul Wali Nasher
Sec: Mr Osama Ahmed Al Haithami

Affiliated Regional Associations

ASIAN TENNIS FEDERATION (ATF)

131 Tanglin Road
Tudor Court Unit F
247924 Singapore
T 65 738 3258 **FAX** 65 738 9278
E-mail: ATF@asiantennis.com
website: asiantennis.com
Pres: Mr Eiichi Kawatei
Sec: Mr Herman Hu

**CONFEDERACION DE TENIS DE
CENTROAMERICA CARIBE (COTECC)**

c/o Federacion Salvadorena
Apartado Postal (01) 110
San Salvador
El Salvador
T 503 278 8087 **FAX** 503 221 0564
E-mail: chilancalmo@aol.com
Pres: Mr Molins
Sec: Mr Frank Liautaud

**CONFEDERACION SUDAMERICANA DE TENIS
(COSAT)**

Casa de Federaciones
Calle Mexico No 1638
La Paz 14752 Bolivia
T 591 2 313 334 **FAX** 591 2 313 323
F-mail: seccosat@ceibo.entelnet.bo
Pres: Mr Vincente Calderon Zeballos
Sec: Mrs Janett La Fuente

CONFEDERATION OF AFRICAN TENNIS (CAT)

BP 1712 Dakar Senegal
T 221 822 5855 **FAX** 221 823 1222
E-mail: catennis @telecomplus
Website: www.cat.sn
Pres: Mr Diagna N'Diaye
Sec: Mr Nicolas Ayebona

EUROPEAN TENNIS ASSOCIATION (ETA)

Seltisbergerstrasse 6
4059 Basle Switzerland
T 41 61 331 76 75
FAX 41 61 331 72 53
E-mail: etatennis.com
website: www.etatennis.com
Pres: Mr Augustin Pujol Niubo
Sec: Mrs Charlotte Ferrari

OCEANIA TENNIS FEDERATION (OTF)

Private Bay 6060 Richmond South 3121
Victoria Australia
T 61 3 9286 1177
FAX 61 3 9650 2743
Pres: Mr Geoff Pollard
Sec: Mr Patrick O'Rourke

Country abbreviations used in this book

AFG	Afghanistan	GAB	Gabon	NFK	Norfolk Islands
AHO	Netherlands Antilles	GAM	Gambia	NGR	Nigeria
ALB	Albania	GBR	Great Britain	NIG	Niger
ALG	Algeria	GEO	Georgia	NMI	Northern Mariana Islands
AND	Andorra	GER	Germany	NOR	Norway
ANG	Angola	GEQ	Equatorial Guinea	NRU	Nauru
ANT	Antigua and Barbuda	GHA	Ghana	NZL	New Zealand
ARG	Argentina	GRE	Greece	OMA	Oman
ARM	Armenia	GRN	Grenada	POC	Pacific Oceania
ARU	Aruba	GUA	Guatemala	PAK	Pakistan
ASA	American Samoa	GUI	Guinee Conakry	PAN	Panama
AUS	Australia	GUM	Guam	PAR	Paraguay
AUT	Austria	GUY	Guyana	PER	Peru
AZE	Azerbaijan	HAI	Haiti	PHI	Philippines
BAH	Bahamas	HKG	Hong Kong	PLE	Palestine
BAN	Bangladesh	HON	Honduras	PLW	Palau
BAR	Barbados	HUN	Hungary	PNG	Papua New Guinea
BDI	Burundi	INA	Indonesia	POL	Poland
BEL	Belgium	IND	India	POR	Portugal
BEN	Benin	IRI	Iran	PUR	Puerto Rico
BER	Bermuda	IRL	Ireland	QAT	Qatar
BHU	Bhutan	IRQ	Iraq	ROM	Romania
BIH	Bosnia/Herzegovina	ISL	Iceland	RSA	South Africa
BIZ	Belize	ISR	Israel	RUS	Russia
BLR	Belarus	ISV	US Virgin Islands	RWU	Rwanda
BOL	Bolivia	ITA	Italy	SAM	Samoa
BOT	Botswana	IVB	British Virgin Islands	SEN	Senegal
BRA	Brazil	JAM	Jamaica	SEY	Seychelles
BRN	Bahrain	JOR	Jordan	SIN	Singapore
BRU	Brunei	JPN	Japan	SKN	Saint Kitts & Nevis
BUL	Bulgaria	KAZ	Kazakhstan	SLE	Sierra Leone
BUR	Burkina Faso	KEN	Kenya	SLO	Slovenia
CAF	Central African Republic	KGZ	Kyrgyzstan	SMR	San Marino
CAM	Cambodia	KIR	Kiribati	SOL	Soloman Islands
CAN	Canada	KOR	Korea, Republic	SOM	Somalia
CAY	Cayman Islands	KSA	Saudi Arabia	SRI	Sri Lanka
CGO	Congo	KUW	Kuwait	SUD	Sudan
CHI	Chile	LAO	Laos	SUI	Switzerland
CHN	People's Rep. of China	LAT	Latvia	SUR	Surinam
CIV	Cote d'Ivoire	LBA	Libya	SVK	Slovak Republic
CMR	Cameroon	LBR	Liberia	SWE	Sweden
COD	Democratic Rep. of	LCA	St Lucia	SWZ	Swaziland
	Congo (Zaire)	LES	Lesotho	SYR	Syria
COK	Cook Islands	LIB	Lebanon	TAN	Tanzania
COL	Colombia	LIE	Liechtenstein	TGA	Tonga
COM	Comoros	LTU	Lithuania	THA	Thailand
CPV	Cape Verde Islands	LUX	Luxembourg	TJK	Tajikstan
CRC	Costa Rica	MAD	Madagascar	TKM	Turkmenistan
CRO	Croatia	MAR	Morocco	TOG	Togo
CUB	Cuba	MAS	Malaysia	TPE	Chinese Taipei
CYP	Cyprus	MAW	Malawi	TRI	Trinidad & Tobago
CZE	Czech Republic	MDA	Moldova, Republic	TUN	Tunisia
DEN	Denmark	MDV	Maldives	TUR	Turkey
DJI	Dijbouti	MEX	Mexico	UAE	United Arab Emirates
DMA	Dominica	MGL	Mongolia	UGA	Uganda
DOM	Dominican Republic	MKD	Macedonia	UKR	Ukraine
ECA	East Caribbean States	MLI	Mali	URU	Uruguay
ECU	Ecuador	MLT	Malta	USA	United States
EGY	Egypt	MON	Monaco	UZB	Uzbekistan
ERI	Eritrea	MOZ	Mozambique	VAN	Vanuatu
ESA	El Salvador	MRI	Mauritius	VEN	Venezuela
ESP	Spain	MSH	Marshall Islands	VIE	Vietnam
EST	Estonia	MTN	Mauritania	VIN	Saint Vincent &
ETH	Ethiopia	MYA	Myanmar (Burma)		Grenadines
FIJ	Fiji	NAM	Namibia	YEM	Yemen
FIN	Finland	NCA	Nicaragua	YUG	Yugoslavia
FRA	France	NED	Netherlands	ZAM	Zambia
FSM	Micronesia	NEP	Nepal	ZIM	Zimbabwe

Index